Praise for *The Callan File: The Definitive Guide*

'With an efficiency even Hunter would grudgingly approve of, the authors not only treat the reader to a wealth of detail about the screen and literary appearances of Callan, but also map out the show's place in the wider realm of TV production and espionage fiction.'

DARREN SCHROEDER, *It's So Last Century*

'A comprehensive background check on one of British TV's most enigmatic anti-heroes.'

DICK FIDDY, Consultant to the British Film Institute

'Originally created for a one-off television drama in 1967, the character of David Callan – the surly but vulnerable and ferociously downbeat hitman, working for a very dirty section of British intelligence – struck an instant chord with the viewing public.'

BARRY FORSHAW, *Crime Time*

'Excellent. Thorough and full of insight. A first class piece of documentary work.'

PETER MITCHELL, son of *Callan*'s creator

'A wonderfully researched book. You can sense the labour of love it was for the authors on every page.'

BHARAT NALLURI, director of *Spooks: The Greater Good*

'An exhaustive piece of research into an iconic fictional character and all those involved in bringing him to life on the page and on screen. The authors have proved themselves so good at undercover work, they probably need to be in a Red File themselves.'

MIKE RIPLEY, *Shots*

Published by Quoit Media Limited,
Brynmawr, Llanfair Caereinion, Powys, SY21 0DG

For more copies of this book, please email quoit@quoitmedia.co.uk

ISBN: 978-1-911537-01-4

First published 2016
This first reprint published March 2019

A CIP catalogue record for this book is available from the British Library.

Book designed by Robert Fairclough

Printed and bound in Great Britain by Clays Ltd, Elcograf S.p.A.

THE CALLAN FILE

ROBERT FAIRCLOUGH
MIKE KENWOOD

THE DEFINITIVE GUIDE

QUOIT

R.F.
*For Peter, Charlotte, Anthony, Matthew, Mr. Boor
and Mrs. Godsmark, without whom... and Martin Wiggins and
George Williams, who first introduced me to the Section.*

M.K.
*For my late fianceé and soul mate, the lovely Zoe Anne Ride, née
Bates (1968-2015) and her family. This book is also dedicated
to my own family, in particular my father, Hedley Michael
Kenwood, who amongst much other wise counsel in life, advised
me one Saturday night in 1984 to stay in with him and
check out the repeat of a certain old spy show, that
he remembered being 'rather good'.*

CONTENTS

Acknowledgements

FIRST AND FOREMOST, SPECIAL THANKS to Peter, Charlotte and the rest of the Mitchell family for their blessing and encouragement.

Special thanks also to Zoe Bates, Ricard Berry, David Bickerstaff, Ted Childs, Rick Davy, Dawn Fairclough, Dick Fiddy, Sarah Guiver, Alan and Alys Hayes, Derek Horne, Peter le Page, Bharat Nalluri, Mike Ripley, Darren Schroeder and Mike Vardy.

We are particularly grateful to Anthony Goodman and Matthew Morgenstern, for access to their 'archives' and permission to use their interviews, recorded between 1984 and 1987, with Derek Bond, Reg Collin, Bill Craig, Peter Duguid, Terence Feely, Jim Goddard, Russell Hunter, Ray Jenkins, John Kershaw, George Markstein and Lloyd Shirley, James Mitchell, Shaun O'Riordan, Trevor Preston, Clifford Rose, William Squire, Anthony Valentine, Voytek and Edward Woodward. Thirty years ago Anthony and Matthew had their own book planned; hopefully their work lives on in our version, which was greatly enriched by their 'act of kindness'.

We're similarly indebted to Grant Taylor for permission to quote extensively from the Edward Woodward audio commentaries we researched for 'If He Can So Could I' and 'Call Me Enemy', on the Umbrella DVD box set of *Callan* Series Four. These were invaluable sources of information and anecdotes.

Thanks also to all our other interviewees, including the various *Callan* casts, crews, writers and associates, for sharing their reminiscences: Adrian Bean, Philip Bird, Robert Banks Stewart, Peter Bowles, Belinda Carroll, Geoff Case, Brian Croucher, Paul Darrow, Mark Duguid, Lee Dunne, Peter Egan, Moris Farhi, Michael Ferguson, John Flanagan, Kenneth Gilbert, Julian Glover, Roger Goodman, Joanna Green, Neville Green, Lewis Greifer, Kenneth Griffith, Piers Haggard, Gill Hewlett-Case, Alfred and Leila Hoffman, George Innes, Michael Jayston, Chris Jones, Stefan Kalipha, John Keeling, Troy Kennedy Martin, Burt Kwouk, David Marshall, Roger Marshall, Garfield Morgan, Patrick Mower, Brian Murphy, Phil Newman, Christopher Owen, Roger Parkes, Trevor Preston, Anthony Read, Catherine Schell, Frances Tomelty, Susan Valentine, Hugh Walters, Tessa Wyatt, David Wickes and Paul Williamson.

The Research Section: The British and Westminster Central Libraries, Anthony Brown, Simon Coward, Michael Cragie, Allen Dace, Andy Davidson, Dobs Evans, Sally Geeson, Toby Hadoke, Tim Harris, Marcus Hearn, Richard Higgins, Nick Lambert, Mo Mcfarland at Associated Newspapers, Ian McLachlan, Garron Martin, Owain Mattocks, Fiona Moore and Alan Stevens at Magic Bullet Productions, Frank Almiles Mole, Sophie Mortimer, Christopher Perry, Steve Roberts, Werner Schmidt, Michael Seely, Ed Stradling, Alwyn W. Turner, Andrew Webb, John Williams (London) and John Williams (Whitley Bay). Plus the helpful team at the BFI Reuben Library: Victoria Crabbe, Sarah Currant, Jonny Davis, Ayesha Khan and Liz Parkinson.

The Publishing Section: everyone at Quoit Media Ltd. and our readthrough crew: Stuart Burroughs, Darren Giddings, Matthew Lee and Liz Turner. Any remaining errors are naturally our responsibility, not theirs.

The Audio Section: BBC 6 Music, Ash, The Beatles, Blur, Boomtown Rats, David Bowie (missed always), Big Audio Dynamite, The Clash (forever), The Doors, Fingerprintz

('Wet Job'), The Jam ('What chance have you got against a tie and a crest?'), Manic Street Preachers, The Pogues, The Teardrop Explodes, Simple Minds, The Skids (next), The Smiths, Sparks, The Stranglers and lots of other bands beginning with 'S'.

Heartfelt thanks also to the following: Dan Albert at Dalzell and Beresford Ltd., Susan Angel at Angel & Francis, all at Blackfen library, Carole Blake at Blake Friedmann, David Barrie, Rachel Busch and Howard Heather, Luc Chaudhary at International Artists Management, Steve Chibnall at Leicester De Montfort University, Brian Clemens, Alan Coles, Gavin Collinson, Megan Cooper at Diamond Management, John Cox, Jeff Cummins, Chris and John Dixon, Michele Dotrice, Fiona Duffin, James Farr and Kate Smurthwaite, Rachael Fischer, Sayer Galib, James Gent, Sally Geeson, Derek Webster, Stephen Gittins and Nicola Mansfield at Associated International Management, Iris Godding at the Directors' Guild of Great Britain, Ali Gowans, Ian Greaves, Penny Harrison at Harrison BSA Ltd., Jo Haseltine, Charlie and Yvonne Henderson, Andy Herrity and Nicky James at Gardner Herrity, Henry ('brining the old girl into land') Holland, Nancy Husdon at Nancy Hudson Associates, Jennifer and Saeed Jaffrey, Chris Johnson, Rachael Jones, Mandy Knight-on-Clark, Tim Lambert, all at Memorabilia, Patricia Merrrick, Susan and Sylvester Morand, Alexandra Moreau at Equity, I.S. Mowis, Network Entertainment Ltd., Julian Owen, Lucia Pallaris atUnited Agents, Becky and Marcus Payne, the Performing Rights Society, Allison Piggott at *Emmerdale* ITV Leeds, Andrew Pixley, Dave Prowse, Lynda Ronan at Lynda Ronan Personal Management, Nadim Sawalha, Nick Setchfield at *SFX*, Jane Shepperd at Shepperd-Fox, Jeff Smart, Peter Ware and *Doctor Who Magazine*, Cary Woodward, our families and the Websdale massive: Pam, Colin, Sian and Harry Quirk. Apologies if we've missed anyone out.

Sadly several of the people acknowledged here are no longer with us, but they all played their part in making this book happen.

FOREWORD
by Peter Mitchell

A SMALL ROOM IN A TINY FLAT in London's Knightsbridge. Inside the room a desk and a chair – a chair that creaked. On the desk a lined pad and a royal blue Parker pen that would write a million words. On the creaking chair a writer who would craft them.

Without James Mitchell and his Parker pen, this book would not exist, if for no other reason than there would be no David Callan.

Callan was Mitchell's creation and he had a lot riding on a man who had never breathed air. As the young writer scribbled away in the rented one-bed Kinnerton Street apartment, he no doubt considered what a risk he'd taken.

An ambitious Geordie with a handful of published novels and a couple of jobbing screenplays to his credit, he turned his back on his native Tyneside and set out for the bright lights of the capital. He had a new wife in tow – a surprise addition to the wife and two children he'd decided to leave behind.

At that point in 1966, there was no television contract, no series, no movie, no money – nothing except the Parker pen and a blank writing pad. Back home, there had been security, a semi-detached, a car in the garage and a teacher's pay cheque in the bank. This was, by reasonable standards, a high-risk strategy but a strategy that was underpinned by a self-belief that was regularly re-fuelled by his new partner, Delia.

Come to think of it, they must have made quite the Bohemian couple. James was the son of a shipyard fitter who rose through the ranks of the Northern Regional Labour Party to become councillor, Alderman and mayor. A disappointing young Jimmy failed his 11-plus but redeemed himself by getting into Grammar School two years later and graduating from St. Edmund Hall, Oxford (albeit with a third class degree).

The rather gawky, myopic English graduate returned to his home-town of South Shields where he met and married a local girl, Norma, also a teacher. In his spare time he scribbled, endlessly. Poems, short stories, scripts and novels all spouted from his pen. When he wasn't writing, he was reading and top of the list were Dickens and Chandler (with P.G. Wodehouse for light relief). Somewhere along the line he landed a publishing deal and a London agent followed shortly thereafter. What followed were regular meetings in The Smoke, pitching sessions, TV work, story conferences and drinks parties. And after all that, there was Delia.

Born in Darjeeling of Anglo-Indian parents, Ethel Delia McCoy was educated at a convent school. Father Ken had been a Major in the Indian Army and a veteran of the Burma Campaign. After 1945 he stayed on to set up the BBC – the Burmese Broadcasting Com-pany. He was managing director, chief engineer, programme controller and senior announcer – all at the same time. And it was there that young Delia first had a taste of show business when she regularly sang live on the radio as a teenager. After a long spell in Rangoon, Ken was transferred to Karachi but his now grown-up daughter headed straight to England, unceremoniously dumped the name Ethel along with the stern warnings of Mother Superior and donned a new personality. Delia had arrived in town.

She was quite the head-turner, and the life and soul of every party. And the 'drinks do' where she met my father was no exception. He was as smitten as she was determined. In the flash of an eyelash they jettisoned their respective emotional attachments and set off to make their fortune.

By this time Delia had quit the singing career and was working for an artistes' agency in the West End. She understood networking, she understood the business and she understood money. In fact she was the perfect partner for the clearly talented but floundering Mitchell. So they found themselves in that pokey little flat in Kinnerton Street. And he found himself in that room, at that desk, on that chair. Eventually, once the Parker pen had flicked and twitched and done its damnedest, their First Born emerged out of the white. Enter David Callan.

OF COURSE, 'MR. CALLAN' was not the first government agent to emerge from Mitchell's Parker Pen. Four years earlier he'd created John Craig – a slightly more glamorous but nonetheless ruthless undercover foot soldier. But at this point, Craig existed in novel form only – penned under Mitchell's pseudonym of James Munro. David Callan was designed and engineered specifically for the small screen.

This is how Mr. Mitchell's Parker scratched out Callan's world in an early pitching document:

> 'Espionage is about people. Essentially, it is about one man, and the effect he has on others. He is a man alone: the nature of his trade isolates him from his kind. He can never hope for lasting human contacts: abiding love, enduring friendship. His weapons are treachery, corruption, betrayal, and yet he himself must be immune from these.
>
> In the world of the spy, it is not only necessary, it is good, to corrupt, to betray. So much is at stake that the spy can never hesitate. His enemy must be destroyed.
>
> By any means.
>
> Inevitably, then, the innocent are involved, manipulated. Inevitably they are hurt: sometimes they are destroyed. They confront one man, and he defeats them, because there is no weapon he will not use for their defeat, and yet he himself is a good man. He destroys one to save thousands, perhaps millions. He plays God because he must. There is no other way.
>
> This attitude of mind is true of every spy: and yet all spies are different, each an expert in his own field. The decoder, the chemist, the gambler, the soldier, the economist, the whore.
>
> Behind them all, is the most terrible, the most dangerous: the ultimate spy.
>
> His weapons are theft, blackmail, murder. The tools of his trade are the knife, the gun, and an icy courage no other kind of man possesses. He is the destroyer.
>
> Callan is such a man.
>
> He has never been seen on television before.'

AND IT TURNED OUT JUST LIKE THAT. The series remained true to the pitch and the result was iconic. Perhaps surprising, then, that so chilling a character became so intriguing to the television audience. But that audience was becoming increasingly sophisticated. The 'Swinging' 1960s were passing the baton to the more sceptical

1970s. The Cold War was at its height and the working man, the ordinary bloke in the street, was ever more questioning of established forms of authority. This was a time of transition: the old guard was in retreat and the new computer age was in its infancy. The sun was setting on the Empire and rising on globalisation and amidst this international chaos, Western governments directed their paranoia at the Enemy Within. It was there in that fluid space between what was and what appeared to be, in that gloomy under-world of double-dealing and deceit, that David Callan Esq. lived and worked. And it was a pretty sordid and grimy existence: no friends apart from a ridiculous and smelly petty-thief, no family, no social whirl, no partner, no comforting embrace, no escape.

What a contrast then to the spoils of Cold War that the newly married Mr. and Mrs. Mitchell enjoyed as a result of Callan's wretched labours. The rented Kinnerton Street flat gave way to a much plusher apartment in W8. The Philimore Court abode boasted extra rooms, a carpeted foyer, a concierge service and a spacious elevator. Their social *milieu* became elevated too, to include a liberal sprinkling of actors, directors, producers, agents and publishers as well as journalists and politicians, the odd Peer of the Realm and associated hangers-on. The red wine at dinner became chateau-bottled and the ubiquitous cigarettes swapped their golden jackets for the snowy white sleeves of Piccadilly Kingsize. All this for a lad who failed his 11 Plus and his immigrant partner.

THE SUCCESS OF THE TV SERIES continued to build to the end of the decade. Prime Minister Harold Wilson revealed it was his favourite programme and Thames Television performed the usual broadcaster's trick of killing off the protagonist before changing their minds and commissioning a new series ('Oh, my Gawd!')

By the mid-1970s the final target in Callan's sights was the feature movie and that was produced by a good friend of the Mitchells, one Derek Horne Esq. I first met Derek when my father moved to London years earlier. I would have been seven or eight years old. He was a regular visitor and I remember him as an intel-lectual and a gentleman – a kindly soul who, with hindsight, did not appear to be cut out for a career among the liars, cheats and thieves who made up much of the entertainment industry workforce. Nevertheless he must have had a spine of steel, despite the stomach ulcer, because there was a battle with Thames Television over rights before the film could be made and that must have tested his mettle. Eventually the movie was produced and Derek hired the Australian Don Sharp to direct. I remember having to suffer the ignominy of wearing a pink shirt (with French cuffs... 'Where's the buttons?') and a claret bow tie for the premiere and waiting hours for dinner. Film premieres are all very well but it was 11.30 at night and growing boys need their grub. The supper was at *Le Caprice*. Obviously.

And that was my introduction to *Callan* – something so far removed from the essence of the character himself that it makes me smile in retrospect. But somewhere in amongst the alcoholic frivolity and the expensive cigarettes, the starched linen table-cloths and the smell of London taxis, James Mitchell created and – even more tricky – sustained a small screen legend. The name David, means 'beloved' (which he became); 'Callan', rather circuitously, means 'brave in battle' (which the character undoubtedly proved himself to be).

The key to his popularity was his vulnerability – his conscience. He continually sought moral justification for the brutal things he was often ordered to do. And that was the point of identification with the viewing public – an ordinary man plunged into extraordinary situations against extraordinary odds. This was the crux of the narrative line that, for a while, captivated a nation.

I'll share one more memory of that time. We had travelled to Cyprus on holiday to stay with the Woodwards at their beautiful villa in the hills above Kyrenia. Mitchells and Woodwards were dining outside in the garden of a restaurant in the Greek quarter. The food had been cleared away and my Dad was holding court. Brandy swirling in the palm of one hand and an inch-and-a-half of ash hanging precariously from a cigarette poised between the fingers of the other. His long, dramatically drawn out tale had reached its crescendo and the laughter was beginning to subside. Teddy Woodward shook his head and smiled.

'Jim,' he said. 'You're a born storyteller.'

ALL THAT IS SO LONG AGO NOW that it seems as if it was almost another life. Sadly, most of the main players in *Callan* are no longer with us which is a shame because, no doubt, their memories would be so much better than my own childish recollections. But still these creations live on in the hearts and minds of other, younger enthusiasts and in their passion for quality screen drama from whatever era. And it is for this reason that I offer both praise and admiration to Rob and Mike for their unstinting efforts in putting this impressive tome together. It is THE definitive companion and they have gone to such impressive lengths in an effort to ensure its accuracy. They tell me it's been a labour of love. Perhaps, but in no way does that devalue their sheer hard graft. I wish you well with it boys, and, on behalf of Big Jim Mitchell, I offer a humble and posthumous 'thank you'.

Peter Mitchell
May 2016

INTRODUCTION:
'I've got a job for you...'

'The place hadn't changed. There was no reason to
suppose it ever would. Once it had been a school, and
the playground made a useful enough car-park.
The building itself had the special kind of nastiness –
red brick, green paint, mud-coloured corridors that
never got enough light – that Callan remembered from
his boyhood... There were the closed-circuit television
cameras as well, but you couldn't see them. You weren't
supposed to. They saw you.'

A Magnum for Schneider, James Mitchell, 1969

'For five years we bugged and burgled our
way across London at the State's behest, while
pompous bowler-hatted civil servants in Whitehall
pretended to look the other way.'

Spycatcher, Peter Wright, 1987

L ATE 1960S BRITAIN: Secret agent James Bond's assignments took him to the
Bahamas, Istanbul, Kentucky and Japan, while debonair John Steed often investigated
strange cases in quaint country villages. By contrast, David Callan's world was one
of greasy cafés, smoky pubs, cramped offices and wet pavements – usually in the less
salubrious parts of London. This was the same fatigued, post-World War 2 urban environment millions of Britons lived and worked in every day, and it formed part of this spy's
singular appeal: despite his brutal, clandestine profession, David Callan was one of us.

He was also one of British spy fiction's first popular anti-heroes. His government
employers, the mysterious 'Section', carried out what would now be called 'Black Ops'.
Involved whenever extermination or coercion were required, their tasks included blackmail, break-ins, frame-ups, torture and assassinations. Callan went along with this, often
finding the ends did not justify the means. Despising his job yet addicted to its risks, he was
courageous but also sardonic, bitter and unpredictable – 'a very lethal man in very short
moments'[1]. His opponents included not just enemy agents, but the callous paymasters and
colleagues on his own 'side', reflecting the anti-establishment spirit of the times.

Perhaps the most fascinating aspect of Callan's conflicted nature was his friendship
with a used and abused petty thief, Lonely. Made orphans in the London Blitz, both men
were outsiders and losers. They depended on each other, but Callan's attitude to his only

friend was complex. At times he was dutiful and protective; at others, bullying and cruel.

These key characters and situations, conceived by James Mitchell, started life in a single television play, but the concepts rapidly broadened into a full series. Mitchell's compact, bold scripts were snapped up by the independent broadcasting company ABC, a hothouse of original televised British drama. This proved to be a perfect storm of writing, acting and production, that ultimately went on to achieve critical acclaim and top ten UK TV ratings. At the height of its popularity, the series became front page news, and telephone switchboards were inundated with viewers' phone calls when Callan was apparently killed off in 1969.

Opening with memorable images of a swinging, exploding light bulb, *Callan* ran on ITV for four series, between 1967 and 1972. Casting clearly contributed to its success, as up and coming star Edward Woodward humanised the agent; in the hands of a less skilled actor, the part could have become repellent, a caricature, or both. Woodward went on to achieve further cult and mainstream success, in productions such as *The Wicker Man* (1973) and *The Equalizer* (1985-89). His co-stars Anthony Valentine and Patrick Mower also became household names, along with Russell Hunter, who brought a unique, seedy pathos to the part of Lonely. Callan and Lonely became one of television's great double acts, as popular in their day as Morecambe and Wise and *The Sweeney*'s Regan and Carter. Many other excellent character actors appeared in the programme, while behind the cameras, more first-rate writers joined Mitchell in providing scripts, and some of the industry's most distinguished directors and production teams worked hard to turn their narratives into reality.

Like *The Sweeney* and the BBC's *Doomwatch*, the series was one of the few UK TV dramas to make the transition into a feature film, at a time when the British cinema industry was on its knees. The resulting film only had a modest reception when released in 1974, but it has since acquired an honourable, ever-increasinng reputation. James Mitchell also wrote numerous additional short stories and novels featuring his creation. There's just as much fiction about Callan in print as there is on screen.

This book celebrates Callan in all these different forms. In recent years the character has deservedly undergone a revival, with DVDs, reprints of the novels, other books and radio adaptations. We hope we have added further value by providing the first critical examination of the Callan phenomenon, analysing and reviewing all the stories in detail, looking at their roots and the legacy they leave behind. In doing so, it's been our privilege to include first-hand reminiscences from people who took part. In addition to detailed biographies of all the key players, we have also covered the careers of the many other professionals involved in making the programme as our way of celebrating their lives, and thanking them for their contribution to what we sincerely believe was a golden age of British television.

Nearly 50 years on from Callan's grimy debut, the human dilemmas of his twilight world continue to be as disconcerting and vivid as ever.

Robert Fairclough and Mike Kenwood
July 2016

'He's alone, a man apart.
Bitter hurt, deep in his heart.
Does he have a heart of stone?
This man, this man alone.'

'This Man Alone', Edward Woodward, 1970

1: SECTION PERSONNEL

James Mitchell
Creator and Writer (1926-2002)

'I was born in South Shields. It's a very
masculine type of town.'

James Mitchell, *The Sunday Express*, 1974

I N THE 1960S AND 1970S, only a few television channels existed in Britain, each out-
putting their own diverse, extensive range of drama programmes. Some were literary
adaptations, others written specifically for the small screen; some historical, some
modern; some lavish, some modest; some realist and others more fanciful. Then as
now, many dramas were based around people's professions; they featured businessmen,
doctors, lawyers, teachers, journalists, and, as crime was a perennially popular genre, police
and private investigators. With the added backdrop of the Cold War, espionage stories
were also prominent in the schedules.

A survey of the credits for these popular dramas, particularly focussing on crime
and espionage series, shows the same fifty or so writers' names regularly cropping up: all
experienced, busy authors, who could be relied on by television producers to offer
entertaining, gripping stories. It's not too much of an exaggeration to suggest these
writers shaped much of British television drama as it still exists today. Listing them all
would be contentious, but James Mitchell's name would certainly feature, as one of the
most prolific and financially successful.

Like many of these contemporaries, Mitchell's formative years occurred amid the
horror and hardship of the Second World War (WW2). His origins were fairly humble; he
grew up in the South Shields region of the North East. Mitchell's father was a shipyard
fitter, shop steward and organiser for the Amalgamated Engineering Union. A committed
left-winger, Mitchell senior went on to become a Labour Councillor and in 1947 became
the Mayor of South Shields. Even though he rose high in local society, he never forgot his
roots, refusing to wear a dinner jacket to the annual civic dinner. '[Dad] was born in the
year of the General Strike, 1926, and was ten when the Jarrow March took place,'[1] said
James's son, Peter. 'All of that period was really rough around [Tyneside]. People's memory
of it now is rose tinted.'

Coming from a family background in which his father had broken class barriers clearly inspired Mitchell, as his education showed: he was taught at South Shields Grammar School and St Edmund Hall in Oxford, and received a Diploma in Education from King's College in Newcastle. Looking back on his early years, Mitchell would romanticise them, perhaps because he felt uncomfortable with his upbringing, perhaps because telling stories amused him, or both: 'He didn't fit in, my Dad,' Peter suggested. 'His sister, Wilhelmina, whom he adored, was fifteen years older than him. His mother had a veteran pregnancy, so it was 'Mina who really brought him up.

'He built this great myth about his academic and intellectual achievement, but in fact he failed his 11+, he passed the 13+ and got into grammar school at the second attempt. He went to Oxford, he had an M.A., but you could buy that for ten guineas. If you got your degree at Oxford in the 1950s, you could just upgrade it – it was like paying extra for Business Class. A degree from Oxford was worth more than anybody else's anyway, but his degree was third class. I suspect what he did with his undergraduate years is what he did with the rest of his life: he drank a lot and told lots of stories. There's nothing he liked better than to hold an audience, in a bar, with a drink, and tell a story.'

Mitchell would prove to be an accomplished raconteur, particularly when there was a journalist within earshot. Resembling 'a chubby cross between Eric Morecambe and Ernie Wise'[2], in 1970 he told the *News of the World:* 'I remember just before the war when Oswald Mosley, the fascist leader, came to speak in South Shields. His Blackshirts thought they could handle the miners the way they sorted out people in the East End of London – until they discovered the Geordies had pick-axe handles up the sleeves of their coats.'[3]

Two years later, Mitchell was citing his colourful and volatile grandfather to the *TV Times* as a major influence, rather than his father. 'I feared him almost as much as I longed for his company, and my fear of him was the most terrible fear I have ever known... A tall man, handsome and immensely strong.' A publican who drank most of his profits, Mitchell's grandfather once, apparently, beat up three rowdy Scandinavian sailors all by himself. 'In a world of work, he alone was idle, and living well on it,' Mitchell continued. 'But it was also because of his charm. Careless, selfish, drunken, cruel: every sin was forgiven him, because of that charm. It gave him more protection than a suit of armour... He was a terrible man, I know, violent in his rages, oblivious to family obligation; but he was feared and he was admired, and his charm always worked... My grandfather taught me a lot about conflict and I'm grateful. It's come in very useful.'[4]

Strikingly, Mitchell's description of his grandfather reveals characteristics common to all his best-known characters, from his spy anti-heroes John Craig and David Callan to the opportunist Jack Ford from his BBC series *When the Boat Comes In* (1976-77, 1981), set in the North East of England between the two World Wars. Whether the writer was remoulding his family history to fit his career path or not, the eloquence within these anecdotes demonstrates what a convincing, natural born storyteller Mitchell was.

IT SEEMS SELF-MYTHOLOGISING took hold when Mitchell began writing mini-biographies for his novels. The truth was subtly different, as Peter Mitchell explained: 'He had a very colourful description of his [early] life on the back of his book jackets: travel writer, journalist, courier... He was a school teacher when he came back from Oxford and that's what he did. He did a bit of theatre crit work, which is why it says "journalist", but he wasn't – I would say that, because I *am* a journalist! He did love to travel and he wrote when he travelled, which is why he called himself a travel writer.'[5]

Settled back in South Shields in the 1950s, Mitchell was attracted to the local theatre. He was self-deprecating about this experience: 'After my father died I became an actor in small local reps up North, but I gave it up on account of starvation. Oh yes: I was also no good at it.'[6] There was a major compensation, though: 'My father and my mother, Norma Haliday, met doing amateur dramatics,'[7] said Peter. 'They both adored acting. My mother was really good at it and she very nearly became professional – she nearly joined the People's Theatre in Newcastle.'

Not long before the birth of his first son Simon in 1956, Mitchell, now teaching English at a night school class in Sunderland College of Art, began developing a career as a writer. His first novel, *A Time for Murder*, was published in 1955. 'I just did it,'[8] Mitchell frankly recalled. 'When most people get into writing as a profession, they do it via short stories. I'd done an occasional piece of journalism for *New Statesman*, and I woke up one morning and decided I was going to write a novel. I looked for a publisher and went round in ever diminishing circles. Eventually it was taken by a firm called Peter Davies Ltd., which was nice, then they sold it to the States, which was much nicer.'

Peter was born in 1959, and some of his earliest memories are of books 'everywhere. Books are littered throughout my childhood because my mother and father were both avid readers... Charles Dickens was one of his favourite novelists. You can see the influence of Dickens in his descriptions: my father was very much a man of detail. He would use material things to enhance atmospheres... The pictorial image of Dad in my head is of him silhouetted against the window in the dining room, sitting at the dining room table writing, with the garden in the background: I remember that quite clearly.'[9]

Mitchell was extremely disciplined in his approach to the task, as Peter related. 'He used to get up in the morning, go in the shower, have his breakfast – he always had very, very shaky hands because he always drank too much – but he would sit at his desk at nine o'clock and write until twelve o'clock. He would come out at twelve o'clock, have a drink (only the one), go for a walk, and start again at two thirty and write till five o'clock, Monday to Friday. And he always had a pad and a pen with him. Everything was in long-hand: he wrote everything in longhand, right until he died. Never used a typewriter at all. And for many, many years he used the same pen. It was a blue Parker pen. I've looked for it but I've never been able to find it.'

The turning point for Mitchell came with his third book, *The Way Back* (1959); Sydney Newman, Head of Drama at the ITV network ABC, bought the rights for this story for the anthology *Armchair Mystery Theatre* (1960-65). '[Newman] said he had just finished the book and wanted it adapting for television. I asked if it was April the first!'[10] Mitchell later recollected, adding that in just one weekend Newman gave him a crash course in television production.

Transmitted on July 10 1960, the TV adaptation of *The Way Back*, re-titled *Flight from Treason*, was significant for several reasons. It presented Mitchell's work to a larger audience, and contained locations, themes and character types that would recur in his later work. Set in the industrial North East, Harry Walker (played by Ian Hendry) is a foundry worker blackmailed into theft by Communist spies, who know about a bomb he planted in South America that accidentally killed several children. Notably, Walker is a man who doesn't fit: too educated to be comfortable with his working-class work-mates and too experienced – and cynical – to engage with the left-wing intellectuals attracted to him. Mitchell also created two spy catchers, the enigmatic and brusque Butler (John Gregson) and the diffident Robinson (Donald Churchill). Six months before the similar pairing of crime-fighters John Steed (Patrick Macnee) and David Keel (Ian Hendry again) in the stylish new drama

The Avengers (1961-69), Butler and Robinson proved sufficiently popular to be revived in the *Armchair Theatre* production 'The Omega Mystery', investigating sabotage at an atomic research station. Hinting at where his writing interests were going, Mitchell remarked, 'What interested me particularly and made me want to write about a counter intelligence character, was how little we hear of these men.'[11]

As well as working on novels (roughly one every two years), Mitchell's time was increasingly taken up by television scriptwriting. He proved himself suited to popular series of the day such as the police drama *Z Cars* (in 1962) and the adventure series *Crane* (1963-64). He also continued developing his interest in spies and spying, contributing four scripts to *The Avengers* (from 1961-63); in 'Death on the Slipway', not for the last time, Mitchell brought his first-hand knowledge of a shipyard to a TV script. His *ITV Play of the Week*, 'Soldier in the Snow' (1961), set during the Napoleonic wars, brought him to the attention of Anthony Read, script editor on the BBC's oil industry drama *Mogul*, subsequently renamed *The Troubleshooters* (1965-1972). Read needed a Geordie writer to provide a story set in a North East shipyard and Mitchell duly delivered the 'cracking script'[12] 'A Job for Willy'. The collaboration with Read was a fruitful and happy one, producing five scripts over three years. Reviewing Mitchell's episode 'Four Cheers for Geoffrey', *The Times* commented, 'If the programme had to end, which is a pity, there have been fewer better constructed or acted pieces [than this story] by James Mitchell, depicting the inhuman lengths to which some men go to achieve success.'[13]

By the mid-1960s Mitchell's TV writing career was going well, but the same could not be said of his marriage, which may have been affected by his frequent absences in London. 'I remember coming downstairs one day and my mother was sat with my father by the fire, early in the morning, which was unusual: they'd clearly been up all night,'[14] Peter Mitchell recalled. 'He'd told her that he wanted to leave. I went with Dad to Gran's house. No big deal but at least he guts to face Mum's mother (although he had me for protection). Dad left home in January 1966, when I was six.'

IN 1963, MITCHELL BEGAN WORKING on a new literary character. 'What [Dad] probably thought was, "If there was a James Bond, he wouldn't be like that,"' Peter said. 'If you look at the timing of all that – *Dr. No* [1962] and *Goldfinger* [1964] were incredibly popular, there was le Carré, a bit of Philby, Burgess and Maclean kicking around – I think he just hitched his bandwagon up to the right vehicle.' Introduced in the 1964 novel *The Man Who Sold Death*, John Craig is an interesting character study. Independent, physically fit and resourceful, of a similar age to Mitchell, he fought in WW2 on the Greek islands. As with Mitchell, Craig has a yearning to escape the past, as after the war he turned away from his humble roots and reinvented himself as an upwardly mobile businessman. However, his marriage stagnates and Craig is left unfulfilled by his business success, turning to gunrunning and, eventually, to work as an agent for the ruthless Department K.

The tough, terse nature of Mitchell's prose caught the contemporary flavour of spy fiction by Ian Fleming, Len Deighton and John le Carré and the four Craig novels became global bestsellers, putting the writer from Tyneside on a new level of financial security and success. Published by Corgi Books in the UK, *The Man Who Sold Death* sold a quarter of a million paperbacks while in America, sales were an even more impressive million copies. Both publishers hoped for similar sales with the second Craig novel, *Die Rich, Die Happy* (published in paperback in 1967). 'The big money started coming in with *Die Rich*,

Die Happy,' recalled Peter. 'That was the big shift.'

Reflecting on the popularity of the Craig books in 1972, James Mitchell explained why he used a pen name for them. 'My earlier novels were alleged to have some literary qual-ity – which meant they were well received but nobody bought them – and I didn't want the John Craig things, classed as mere thrillers, to ruin my reputation, so I borrowed my grandfather's name for them.'[15] Peter remembered things differently: 'Using the name "James Munro" was a huge mistake. Dad did it under advice from his agent, Roger Hancock. It was a fashion at the time that if an author wanted to develop a new character, he did it under a different name.'[16] Whatever Mitchell's motivation for using a pseudonym, his reputation as a popular writer was established in the USA by the Craig novels: 'It was the James Munro books that out-sold everything else in the States,' Peter said. 'They were very pop-ular in America and they really made [my father] over there. When he died, the American obits in the *New York Times* and the *New York Post* were what they majored on. It was "John Craig writer dies" as opposed to "*Callan* writer" or "*When the Boat Comes In* writer dies."'

At the same time as Mitchell's career was on the rise, a further big change was imminent in his personal life. Good friends with the actor Burt Kwouk, Mitchell was at a drinks party when he met the vivacious socialite Ethel Delia McCoy, who would become his second wife. As Mitchell romantically described this meeting to his granddaughter Charlotte, 'Grandpa said something to Delia like "Come on, you've got to keep a friend entertained" – because Burt was on a hot date – and she slipped, he caught her, and just knew that he was in love with her.'[17] From then on, the couple were inseparable until Delia's early death in 1990. Paying tribute to his 'wife, PA, lover, gofer and best friend'[18] in 1995 when promoting the novel *So Far from Home*, whose protagonist Natalya Krilova was largely based on Delia, Mitchell movingly reflected, 'She was an extraordinary mixture – Irish-English-Portuguese-Hindi. Not the sort of person with whom one gets bored... Writing's lonely, there can be insecurity, and she was terrific at massaging my ego when necessary. She was my wife and it was wonderful.'[19]

'When he met Delia, [Dad] was doing half and half [in London and Newcastle] and had just about packed in any teaching he was doing,'[20] Peter Mitchell recalled. 'We'd lived in this little house in Cleadon and had moved to the much posher Marsden Road in Harton. My father had bought this Mark III Jaguar – he was a terrible driver; his eyesight was so bad – and being in the car was one of my earliest memories of him. Another early memory of a fall out with my father was of him driving the Jag onto the path and crushing my tricycle. He was angry because the Jag had got scratched, but my trike was completely written off!'

As well as introducing Mitchell to his second wife, Burt Kwouk also made a signifi-cant contribution to Mitchell's thriller writing. 'Burt used to have these fantastic books on martial arts: reference books,' Peter said. 'They were bound in hessian material and were obviously really expensive, with fantastic photographs inside of karate and judo moves. He gave them to Dad and he used a lot of those specific moves in his books. He had them for years and years and years.'

IN THE CANON OF MITCHELL'S WRITING, the most notable beneficiary of Kwouk's martial arts manuals remains John Craig's successor, David Callan. This new agent shared a little of Craig's persona in that he reinvents himself and doesn't quite fit in with either his upper-class, ruthless employers in British intelligence, or with the blue-collar London underworld, but a defiantly working-class side was added to the character, capturing the anti-establishment spirit of the times. Starting in 1967, Mitchell's *Callan* series completed the process the John Craig books had begun, making him wealthy by becoming a television fixture for over four years and spinning off into five novels, a movie and numerous short stories.

'I suppose like most things a writer produces there are bits and pieces of everybody. It's like playing at "heads, bodies and legs" until they come together. The only real spy I ever met was this Spaniard, who was not very Callan-like,'[21] James Mitchell said in 1985, reflecting on Callan himself and the other three key characters that would all go on to define the programme, revealing that even the character names were intentional. 'All the names had a kind of picture quality, they were allusive or alliterative. Hunter [is] self-explanatory. Meres – a mere is a deep dark very dangerous pool, you plunge into it at your peril, it's also very cold. Lonely was self-explanatory. Callan, somebody suggested – and it may be true – is the nearest one can get to "killing".'

Mitchell knew that he owed a lot of his success to Edward Woodward, the classical actor chosen to play Callan, and was more than happy to share the credit: 'When I met [him], I experienced a genuine shock of recognition: he simply *was* the actual man. We were lucky to get him. When the first script was submitted to him, he'd just returned from America and wanted a holiday... He changed his plans, bless him, and accepted the part.'[22] Woodward was equally complimentary about the writer who helped establish him as a major British star: 'It was one of those few scripts that I'd come across where the man was *there*. James Mitchell had written this man so precisely, and so extremely well, [he] just literally came off the page.'[23] Director Piers Haggard, who oversaw three of Mitchell's *Callan* scripts, praises both the characters and 'that gritty, sweaty fear in the way the establishment pick up and drop and use these petty criminals. Mitchell definitely had something, in that.'[24]

As *The Guardian* put it, 'with the massive assistance of Edward Woodward in the part, Mitchell made Callan a bleak outsider and professional killer... a potent bit of myth making.'[25] Showing just how much of a modern myth Callan would become, in 2013, Ostara began republishing Mitchell's Callan novels. 'James Mitchell showed us the chinks in Callan's psychological armour, chinks brilliantly exposed by the outstanding central performance of Edward Woodward,'[26] said Ostara editor Mike Ripley. 'With superb irony, Callan's only friend is called "Lonely" yet surely it was Callan who was the loneliest one of all and in the books Mitchell points this up by showing us Lonely's extended (and highly dodgy) family of aunties and assorted relatives. Callan not only has no family, he is also fighting a sort of personal class war, hating but having to rely on a cold-hearted commanding officer in the shape of the various Hunter figures, and his upper-class nemesis Meres. Mitchell's Callan novels all continue these themes and do so with terrific pace and economy of style.'

Woodward and Mitchell became close. In 1970, the actor accompanied the writer on a promotional tour of *Red File for Callan*, the paperback edition of the first Callan novel *A Magnum for Schneider*, and he was also enthusiastic about Mitchell's culinary tastes. '[Teddy] was dedicated to my step-mother's cookery,'[27] said Peter. 'When we went to his holiday home in Kyrenia in Cyprus – I was just a little kid, my brother was a bit older – we had to take a dekshi, which is a big Indian pot, full of frozen beef curry, through customs, and the customs officers weren't sure what to make of it. When they took the lid off and prodded it, of course it was solid, and they only let us through because this guy pulled this enormous great bayonet out of his belt, and stabbed the dekshi many times to make sure we weren't smuggling anything in there!'

When, nine years after *Callan* finished on Thames Television in 1972, the ATV network agreed to make the revival special *Wet Job* in 1981, Mitchell insisted that it should be produced exactly as he wrote it, without a word or scene being changed. It's notable that for the last Thames series – possibly because, as fellow writer Bill Craig recalled, he was 'not in the best of health' for some of that year[28] – Mitchell only wrote three of the thirteen episodes.[29] Significantly, none of Mitchell's scripts for *Callan* in 1972 involve that year's continuing story of Callan being promoted to Hunter, confirming that the series' creator didn't like the production team's plan (as, indeed, Woodward didn't).

Mitchell may sometimes have felt frustrated at Thames: he had created an incredibly popular set of characters to which he had the book, short story and – after a court case – film rights but didn't have overall artistic control of the TV series. Perhaps that's why Peter Mitchell recalled that '[Dad] hated script editors with a passion and he hated producers with a passion,'[30] while Mitchell himself once wryly remarked to a journalist, 'I'm only violent on the floor of a TV studio at rehearsals.'[31] On *Callan* this creative friction was a mixture of the personal and the political. After an initially harmonious working relationship with the series' first associate producer, Terence Feely – to the extent that he invited him to be Best Man at his wedding to Delia – Mitchell hardly saw him after Feely left to work for the film company Paramount Pictures. 'I don't think James ever really forgave me for kind of deserting [the series],'[32] Feely reflected in 1985. During Series Two, Mitchell clashed with the new production team of John Kershaw and Reg Collin over plans to kill Callan off. In this respect the television industry has changed; nowadays Mitchell would be an executive producer and/or show runner, pre-empting any such arguments arising.

A SOUGHT AFTER SCREENWRITER BY 1969, Mitchell's stock had risen to the point where he was courted by the film industry. It was a busy year, writing four episodes of *Callan*'s third series, five short stories featuring the agent, the fourth John Craig spy story *The Innocent Bystanders* and the historical novel *The Winners* set on Tyneside; he also worked on the movie adaptation of John Sherlock's novel *The Ordeal of Major Grigsby*, about a mercenary (Stanley Baker) caught in a final battle with an ex-friend turned traitor, Alex Cord (Kip Thompson). He shared credit for the film, retitled *The Last Grenade*, with Sherlock himself and Kenneth Ware; it seems Mitchell was brought in as a fashionable newcomer to try and salvage a troubled script. The critical response was mixed: 'The cryptic *Z Cars*-style dialogue goes well with the action stuff,'[33] applauded the *Daily Mail*, while the *Evening Standard* reported, 'I had trouble hearing parts of the script, on which three people worked, since dialogue like: "I know that the sensible and honourable thing is to go back to my husband," was punctuated by bursts of laughter. It took three people to write *that?*'[34]

If *The Last Grenade* wasn't a critical or commercial success, it did deliver a major asset for Mitchell's next film project, released in 1972. Although he wasn't involved in the casting of John Craig for a film adaptation of *The Innocent Bystanders* (as he hadn't been with *Callan*), the writer was delighted when Stanley Baker was offered and accepted the part, as 'long before I considered a film, I deliberately created Craig as a self-made man in every way. Stanley knows all about that because he is self-made too.'[35] Promoting the film, Mitchell took the time to highlight the differences between his two fictional spies: 'They are very different people who happen to operate in the same general area. I always see Craig as much richer than Callan. He uses expensive restaurants, Callan has a sandwich. Craig has the flat in Regent's park, Callan the pad in Notting Hill. Craig buys an expensive car because he saw it in a colour magazine, Callan takes the nearest one from the Ministry pool.'[36] Despite Mitchell's hopes that 'John Craig [would] be as big a success, off the printed page, as Callan,' John Craig's film debut didn't perform well at the box office. Perhaps Mitchell had unwittingly pinpointed why: shorn of the writer's tense, brutal prose, on film Craig didn't seem that different to James Bond or his many imitators.

Suggesting Mitchell was aware of being too closely identified with the spy genre, in the year's break between the third and fourth series of *Callan* he contributed five scripts to ITV's legal drama series *Justice* (1971-72), starring the 1940s film star Margaret Lockwood as 'a divorced and somewhat hard-bitten woman barrister'[37]. Mitchell's change of pace found favour with the critics, including the *Daily Telegraph* reviewer Richard Last: 'The casting is admirable, the writing tight and under-emphasised, very much in *Callan* and not all in *Perry Mason* [1957-1966] vein. Which is not wholly surprising, since the author of the first episode was James Mitchell, creator of *Callan*... [Mitchell] had no difficulty whatever in making me believe that the backstage fiddling by which a trial was switched from a tough judge to the lenient *could* just have happened.'[38]

BY 1974 MITCHELL'S THIRD TRY at a film career was imminent, thanks to his friend Derek Horne, who produced the movie version of *Callan*. 'Jimmy and I became very good friends,'[39] said the urbane Irishman who, like Woodward, shared Mitchell's enthusiasm for good food. 'His wife Delia used to go and visit her father on Wednesdays – in [Enfield] – so Jimmy was on his own, and he offered to teach me to cook. The first lesson I had was lamb chops. The next Wednesday I went along and he said "How did you get on?" "Get on with what?" "The lamb chops! If you're not going to practise, I'm not going to teach you!"' We were very, very, very close friends for many years, then all of a sudden we weren't. [Jimmy and Delia] moved from Marloes Road and I didn't see them after that.'

Even though the lack of success of the *Callan* film was to prove another frustrating brush with the film industry for Mitchell, particularly because he and Horne had seen it as the launch of a sure-fire film franchise, the author was in a contented and reflective mood when the *Sunday Express* interviewed him in December 1974. 'I'm modestly affluent,'[40] he professed, speaking in the 'huge luxury flat' he shared with Delia in Kensington. 'Okay, I'm rich. Yeah, I adore travelling to exotic places like Mexico, but then I don't even have a car. I don't like driving. I don't own boats or anything like that but I do squander money on books and records. And I love good wines. One of the greatest pleasures in life is a really excellent wine.

'The one thing I haven't got is time,'[41] he went on candidly. 'I didn't start writing 'til I was 30 and I've got to catch up on all those years. But it's great. I don't have a job. I have a damn well-paid hobby. But even if my Littlewoods Pools came up next week I'd still be at my desk on Monday, because this is what I want to do. I love writing. You're talking to a very happy man.' As his scripts for *Justice* in 1972 had suggested, part of Mitchell's catching up was the ambition to step out of the shadow of his famous Section agent. 'Look, I don't want to be only called The Man Who Created *Callan*. I've written four *Callan* novels and seven non-*Callan*s and I'm doing another non-*Callan* next year. I've done about 150 TV pieces – *Armchair Theatre* and so on – and only 30 or so were *Callan*s.'[42]

In the middle of the 1970s, Mitchell was tempted to Hollywood, the world capital of film-making, although, as with his previous involvement with the movie industry, it would be a bitter-sweet experience. 'Before *Smear Job* [the fourth Callan novel] came out, he was hired by a film studio,'[43] Peter Mitchell revealed. 'He'd be picked up from a five-star hotel in a big Cadillac, driven to a studio, which he described as "extraordinarily plush", to write all day. He spent months over there – and his time was paid for – to write films that never got made. But he always said to me that was the most [money] that he ever got.'

In January 1976, BBC television began transmitting the series that granted Mitchell's wish to achieve distance from *Callan* and further enhanced his reputation as a significant TV dramatist. *When the Boat Comes In* was a return to the writer's roots, set on Tyneside just after World War One (WW1), and based around the anti-heroic figure of Jack Ford (played by Geordie actor James Bolam, the original choice for the lead in 'A Job for Willy'). Over four series between 1976 and 1981, part of *When the Boat Comes In*'s appeal was that it was an unvarnished, at times unflinchingly brutal historical drama series, different to many seen before on British television, although arguably the BBC's *The Onedin Line* (1971–1980) had come close. This authenticity was largely due to Mitchell's drawing on his childhood experience of the depressed North-East, which informed his astonishing tally of 39 scripts for the series. 'When I started writing I could suddenly taste the flavour of those years,'[44] Mitchell recalled. 'You took poverty for granted. If there was a car in your street, someone had the doctor visiting. Where I came from was a very, very poverty-stricken area with houses to match. There was damn all to be nostalgic about but one rare treat was a Sunday school outing to the sea. We'd be given a bag of buns and sandwiches and a bottle of lemonade. The sea was beautiful. Just watching it and the big ships coming and going made life that much more tolerable.'

'Naturally the background of wheeling and dealing in union politics in which my father was involved was a great help,'[45] Mitchell elaborated. 'But he was a man of rectitude. I don't think he would have approved of Jack Ford at all, though I find him fascinating to write for... Ford is a rogue. But you go out of your way to forgive him. He is a kind of serious Bilko. [The comic character Ernie Bilko was a US army sergeant constantly out to make money, played by Phil Silvers.] He always has his eye on the main chance. He wants to get out of the shipyard and not be fitting bits to ships but owning the yard itself. Callan accepted his lot but for Ford there are no limitations and nothing but new horizons. Callan has his limitations, not the least of which is his conscience. Ford is not very strong on conscience.'[46] Like *Callan*, *When the Boat Comes In* also reflected Mitchell's idealistic regard for the working man. '[Dad] had a big respect for people who worked with their hands, tradesmen, and that, I think, is a slightly romantic view of his own father and what he did,'[47] Peter Mitchell believed.

When the Boat Comes In was a huge success (and like *Callan* before it, inspired a series of bestselling novels). Unfortunately, the same wasn't true of Mitchell's next television venture, and perhaps illustrated the danger of an author stepping too far outside his area of experience. The BBC2 series *Goodbye Darling...*, beginning in June 1981, may have been conceived as a response to ITV's highly-charged suburban dramas *Bouquet of Barbed Wire* (1976) and *Another Bouquet* (1977). Where the *Bouquet*s drew large audiences and media approval, *Goodbye Darling...*, centring on a different character every week, was dismissed by critics, drawing the worst reviews of Mitchell's career. 'The characters are awesomely wooden and uninspired, and in the first episode there wasn't a spark of originality or freshness that would warrant following the further programmes,'[48] complained the *New States-*

man, while Clive James in the *Observer* demolished the series with his customary wit: 'Awful dialogue unfolded... Lines the actors could do nothing with accumulated in heaps. The only way to play it would have been to get everyone into scuba gear and do the whole thing underwater.'[49] The *Daily Mail* felt it was 'written by someone who knows little about the leisured rich, or how they live... A case of slumming in reverse.'[50]

Mitchell felt the hostility exhibited by the press damaged the chances of *Callan* returning again, as Shaun O'Riordan, producer and director of the revival play *Wet Job*, which was shown four months after *Goodbye Darling...*, recalled: 'Just before, he'd written a series of plays for the BBC about suburbia which were slaughtered by the critics. He felt that the critics would never have another good word to say for him after that series, and he did feel that [*Wet Job*] was attacked because of that.'[51] Even though the play made the TV national top ten, it was to prove the final TV bow for David Callan.

Mitchell was back on surer ground with his next series for the BBC, *Spyship* (1983). Journalists Brian Haynes and John Keene had written a novel based on the mysterious disappearance in 1974 of the trawler *Gaul* with its 36-man crew, a disappearance that has still never been satisfactorily explained. The conspiracy that Haynes and Keene weaved around their fictional vanishing trawler *Caistor*, involving the KGB and British intelligence in cover-up investigated by the likeable, everyman journalist Martin Taylor (Tom Wilkinson), was ideal material for Mitchell to develop and this time both the reviewers and audience were won over. 'The series... goes... for a depth of characterisation unusual in what is basically a sleuth drama,'[52] approved Herbert Kretzmer, one of the principal detractors of *Goodbye Darling...* 'Care has been taken to place the story in a real and recognisable world with special attention, for example, paid to the wives left behind by the ill-fated trawlermen.' Perhaps the biggest compliment to Mitchell's screenplay was paid in the *Guardian*, as the paper considered *Spyship* had been made 'with more love and money than thrillers usually get unless they are produced by John le Carré.'[53]

The last TV work Mitchell did in England was with thriller writer Harry Patterson (a.k.a Jack Higgins), adapting the latter's novel *Confessional* into a serialised TV movie screened in 1989. A topical thriller about a terrorist attempting to disrupt peace talks concerning Northern Ireland, the production reunited the author with the director Gordon Flemyng, who, in a curious piece of artistic symmetry, had overseen *The Last Grenade*, Mitchell's first venture into film.

Because *When the Boat Comes In* had been hugely popular in Australia, Mitchell was arguably happier with the opportunities that Australian television offered him in his last ever TV and film work. He had the chance to write about military history, one of his favourite subjects, even though, as in Britain and America, he would again encounter the frustrations of working in the film industry. 'He got commissioned to write a couple of things,'[54] revealed Peter Mitchell. 'He wrote a film script about John Simpson Kirkpatrick. In the Anzac campaign against the Turks in the First World War, Kirkpatrick was the guy who rescued all the Anzac soldiers who were shot by sniper fire, putting them on the back of a donkey and leading them through Dead Man's Gulch. He became a famous figure in Australian history, and where we have the Cenotaph [monument], they have The Man with the Donkey, and he was born in South Shields.'

MITCHELL MAY HAVE DECIDED to turn his back on the film and TV industry after the mid-1980s because he was, by his own admission, financially secure; or it may have been disillusionment with getting any more film projects made, or the prospect of continuing battles with TV producers – perhaps both. Whatever the case, Mitchell was content to concentrate on his first love, writing novels. Of note to *Callan* enthusiasts were his new fictional duo, the private detective Tommaso Ronald Hogget and his ex-soldier minder, known only as 'Dave', who featured in three books between 1985 and 1988. By the 1990s, he had begun corresponding with the aspiring writer and *Callan* enthusiast Sarah Guiver, and his tone was bravely upbeat: 'I've been visiting Andalusia quite a lot as I'm on my own now and find it's a good idea to get away from time to time. My wife died, quite suddenly, two and a half years ago, and I still miss her dreadfully. Going away helps a little.'[55]

During the 1990s, Mitchell moved back to his native North East, which helped strengthen ties with his family. In particular, the relationship between the author and his son Peter hadn't always been easy, due largely to Mitchell's – perhaps surprising – right-wing politics. 'There were big periods in my adolescence and my 20s where we used to row a lot,'[56] Peter said honestly. 'In fact, Charlotte and my son, Jamie, being born ended a long period of no communication whatsoever between us. The miners' strike in 1984 did for us in a big way. We used to have many a row, and when it came to that strike, *he's very* successful, *he's* living in Marloes Road in W8 and I'm covering the miners' strike and seeing a *completely* different world: when these worlds collided, there were sparks. I'm seeing really starving people in the 1980s, and he's telling me that their children should be taken away from them at birth because they're not fit to be parents. I was straight off the picket line and witnessed all these coppers from London, like the [Special Patrol Group] coming up to County Durham, waving their pay slips at the miners. It was really nasty, it was all controlled and it was really political. It was an English Civil War and typically English because it was shrouded. As a result of all that, there were four years where I didn't speak to my father at all. Nothing.'

With the Mitchells reconciled, the family could see the funny side of James's confrontational and slightly pompous streak. 'He went into a jewellers in the 1990s,'[57] recalled Charlotte, 'and the assistant said "Hello, sir, can I help you?" and he said, "Don't you know who I am?" This is a canny little high street jewellers! He was a great character. When we went to restaurants, he'd click his fingers and say "Boy!" to the waiter. It was, "This is where I am, this is where you are." That's what he was like.' 'He *was* like that,'[58] Peter agreed, 'But somehow, he didn't mean to be offensive, he just expected to be looked up to for some reason.'

When Mitchell celebrated his 70th birthday in 1996 a reporter from the North East paper *Gazette* was on hand to record an interview. As well as looking back over his career, Mitchell explained what motivated him to write every day – 'the reason's simple – what the heck would I do with my life?'[59] – and amusingly he revealed why he lost his North East accent at Oxford: 'I had to, no-one could understand me: I used to say I was bilingual in English and Geordie.' However, the interview also revealed that Mitchell had been suffering from arthritis, and writing to Sarah Guiver, the author admitted to having been 'really very ill – hospitals and things, but now I'm getting better, looked after by my son and daughter-in-law, whom I love dearly. And their children, Charlotte and Jamie.'[60]

Three years later, Mitchell was on form enough to offer Guiver some valuable and heartening advice about writing: 'What works for me is to plan it all. I hate the planning, so I do it first – or most of it. In the head, over and over (a good walk helps) then on paper and then the sweetie after the medicine: "Chapter one, page one." Not that the planning's finished. Not till the end. But you'll have done the pick and shovel work. No sudden realisation that by page 103 the heroic Nicholas talks more and more like the delectable Nicola. Anyway it works for me. And don't be ashamed to think of money from time to time. Remember Dr. Johnson: "A man is a fool that ever wrote for anything but money." And he wrote some of the best prose in the language. Time for you to do the same.'[61]

Although he could be positive, Mitchell's final years were blighted by illness, and Peter encouraged him to write the last Callan novel *Bonfire Night* partly as a remedy for ill health. 'He suffered terribly from depression, he had a liver complaint and he had to stop drinking and that made him worse: absolutely worse. I said to him, "Why don't you go back to something that you created that was really tremendous?" He wrote *Bonfire Night* and he wrote another *When the Boat Comes In* book and he never finished; about three quarters of it's there. Unfortunately, like *Bonfire Night*, it's awful. In a way, I wish he'd written [*Bonfire Night*] and never got it published, but he did, and publishing the book, the hard copies arriving – having the result of his work with a nice glossy cover and his name there – that meant a lot to him.'[62]

After publication of the last novel to feature his most famous character, James Mitchell died on 15 September 2002, in the Freeman hospital, Newcastle. A private cremation was followed by a public service of commemoration at St. George's Church in Jesmond. In the press, significant figures in the author's life paid tribute to a writer who, as well as being a successful novelist for over 45 years, created two enduring television success stories – no small achievement. Christopher Sinclair-Stevenson, Mitchell's last publisher, said, 'He was a very fluent writer. He told a story, which was a good old-fashioned virtue. He was one of those authors who didn't really need much editing. His great strength was dialogue. His novels concentrated on that.'[63] Mitchell's two most well-known leading men were equally full of praise. 'He was a wonderfully devious writer,'[64] offered James Bolam. 'The character of Jack Ford was a marvellous character to play because he was all things to all men.' Edward Woodward's tribute was also heartfelt: 'During the time of *Callan* we were very close. As a television writer he was the best of the best of the best. He really created two classic characters in Callan and Lonely who are timeless. Good writing and good characters never die.'[65]

'He was a fantastic Dad, in a rather peculiar way,'[66] Peter Mitchell sad candidly. 'He was knowledgeable, well read, civilised and above all else he was a complete gentleman. He was never around when I needed him, never on the touchline when I played football, totally self-centred and utterly simplistic. But he loved flirting with women and was tremendous company. Women loved him right back – even the nurses in the Freeman Hospital when he was ill. In a bizarre way he was also utterly loyal to the family he decided to leave – most peculiar. I miss him. He will be a very tough act to follow.'

You get the feeling that John Craig, David Callan, Jack Ford and Tommaso Ronald Hogget would have all approved.

Edward Woodward
David Callan (1967-1972, 1974, 1981)

'Callan has been my passport to wider things, but I don't want
him to dominate me forever. When I put away my gun for the last
time, it will be with more than a twinge of nostalgia and regret.'

Edward Woodward, *TV Times,* January 1972

L IKE JAMES MITCHELL, the actor who breathed such memorable life into a professional killer also came from a working-class background, although his upbringing was
nowhere near as impoverished as *Callan*'s creator. Edward Albert Arthur Woodward
was born on 1 June 1930 and began his life on Broadway Avenue in a suburb of Croydon;
his father worked as the delivery man for a poultry farmer. An only child (like Callan), the
young Woodward recalled an idyllic childhood, listening to the radio, always playing with
other children and a family where there was an 'overall feeling of warmth and care and
cosiness.'[67] Rather shy, and by his own admission not a tough youngster, Woodward was
given an early feeling of maturity through being taught to box by his grandfather, 'almost
from the time I could toddle.'

When Woodward was nine, WW2 broke out and this made an impression on him. (Like
his Callan alter ego, as an adult he became fascinated by military history, collecting weapons
such as guns and swords and participating in war games using model soldiers.) In 1944, the
Woodwards' home was destroyed by a V1 flying bomb. Edward considered himself 'lucky.
I had caught my face on the side of the [air raid] shelter and my arm was lacerated... We all
escaped, but my father was pretty badly injured and he spent weeks in hospital.'[68] An almost
identical scenario was written into the first *Callan* episode, 'The Good Ones Are All Dead',
to explain the deaths of the agent's parents.

Aside from his parents, the most significant early influences on Woodward were two of
his teachers. At school, Grace King taught Woodward English, Music and Drama, subjects
that helped give him confidence. There was empathy between the pair, and their teach-
er-pupil relationship would continue as a friendship in later years. During his schooldays,
Woodward had a formative experience: 'I was eight years old and one day I saw [a film] with
Spencer Tracy. And something went *click* inside my head and I thought to myself: "That's
who I want to be when I grow up." And by the time I was sixteen, there was no question
of my being anything else.'[69] Joining Kingston Commercial College at fourteen, his talent
for acting was spotted by Marion Renner, 'who had gained practical experience as an actress
[and] was the first to actively suggest that I become an actor.'[70] Deciding against a career in
journalism, Woodward applied to London's Royal Academy of Dramatic Art (RADA) in

1946 and, while he waited to hear if he'd been awarded a fee-paid scholarship, worked as a junior clerk for a sanitary engineer, 'the only work I've ever done outside the theatre.' The Academy accepted him and he subsequently learned that he was the youngest student to have enrolled there, a great achievement for a formerly timid boy from Croydon.

FOLLOWING HIS TIME AT RADA, Woodward spent eight consecutive years gaining valuable experience in repertory theatres, regional acting companies that would produce a succession of plays with a speedy turn-over; this acting apprenticeship took him all over England and Europe. At the beginning of the 1950s, Woodward joined a London company about to undertake a Shakespeare tour of India at the invitation of his friend Alan Wilson. It would prove a dramatic revival in his romantic fortunes, as 'in the cast was this gorgeous girl called Venetia [Barrett] and instantly I fell heavily in love with her... She was pretty and blonde and very confident.'

Despite an initial coolness, Venetia responded to Woodward's feelings for her. During their Indian tour, which lasted over a year, he contracted paratyphoid fever and the actress alternated between her acting commitments and nursing him. Venetia eventually collapsed with a mild fever and exhaustion herself and both of them were sent home to England. Convalescing in his parents' garden in the summer of 1952, Woodward asked Venetia to marry him for a second time, she agreed, and, full of optimism, they moved into a rented flat in Notting Hill Gate in London. Initially, the couple both took acting jobs, but when their first child, Tim, was born in 1953, Venetia decided to leave the profession. (A second son, Peter, would follow in 1956, and a daughter, Sarah, in 1963).

With Edward now the sole provider for his family, times could be hard when he experienced spells of unemployment: 'Each week, I used to go... with Frank Finlay, who was also out of work, to pick up the [dole] cheques. Then we'd slink off to the nearest "caff" and drown our sorrow in a cup of black coffee. That was about the extent of our social life.'[71]

Woodward continued his acting apprenticeship working for repertory – "rep" – companies in Croydon, Perth and Oxford, and was eventually offered work in central London, a positive sign his career was moving in the right direction. However, he felt that he was being offered too much singing work in then fashionable revues, as well as musicals: 'I wasn't keen on doing [them] at the expense of acting. So I made up my mind deliberately to put myself out of work and refuse to do any more revues. I would wait until I could break into the West End; as an actor.'[72]

Venetia agreed with her husband's plan, despite the financial hardship. In 1957, two years after Woodward's first film role in *Where There's a Will* (1955), the biggest indication that his instincts were right was the success of the play *The Queen and the Welshman* by Rosemary Ann Sisson, which opened at the Guildford Theatre and was transferred to that year's Edinburgh Fringe festival. The play became a critical hit, ensuring it a place at the Lyric in Hammersmith in London and then, fulfilling Woodward's ambition, the Criterion in the West End. A two-month tour of Russia with the prestigious Shakespeare Memorial Theatre Company (renamed the Royal Shakespeare Company in 1961) followed, after which the actor was awarded his first television role in ITV's popular medical drama *Emergency Ward – 10* (1957). Like many actors of his generation, including Sean Connery, Kenneth Cope and Anthony Valentine, Woodward began wearing a toupée, a habit that lasted for most of his career; in acting circles at that time, baldness was seen as a serious career handicap.

Emboldened by his initial success, the Woodwards moved to a flat in Chiswick, which was precisely the point at which the momentum of Edward's career stalled. Despite gaining more television guest roles and continuing to appear in the theatre, Edward suffered a crisis of confidence in his chosen vocation, falling into a deep depression. The condition became so bad that, reflecting on this stage of his life later on in the 1970s, he confessed to the *TV Times* that 'If ever I had been near to suicide it was during that period.'[73] However, bolstered by Venetia's support, Woodward continued working until he was offered the lead role in the play *Rattle of a Simple Man* (1959) by Charles Dyer, about a Mancunian football fan who comes to London for the Cup Final and spends time with a prostitute.

Woodward's involvement with this production was a turning point: he considered the opening night at Richmond Theatre 'one of the best nights of my career'. He directed and starred in a South African version of the play, before returning to England to positive reviews when it reopened at London's Garrick Theatre in 1962. From there, Woodward and the play moved to the celebrated theatre district of Broadway in New York. Despite this wave of success, the actor was unhappy at leaving his family behind for six months and with his stature in the acting profession increasing, he decided that next time they would accompany him.

By now, Woodward's television credits were also increasing in prominence, with major guest roles in *Mogul*[74], *Armchair Mystery Theatre*, *The Saint* – 'The Persistent Patriots' (1967) and *The Baron* – 'Countdown' (1967). A major breakthrough for him was the 1967 BBC2 production of Evelyn Waugh's WW2 satire *Sword of Honour* – one of the first BBC television productions made in colour – in which Woodward took the lead role. One critic noted, 'Edward Woodward gave the character of Guy Crouchback the right blend of well-meaningness... sympathy and innocent egotism, often offending where no offence was meant.'[75]

Now established as a serious actor, Woodward had no hesitation in appearing in a musical by one of English theatre's most respected talents when the director and writer Noel Coward offered him a part in his Broadway version of *High Spirits*. This time his family did go with him. When the Woodwards returned to England, looking forward to a holiday, a script arrived from ABC for their anthology series *Armchair Theatre*. Rehearsals were beginning the following week, meaning Woodward couldn't join his family in having time off: 'Three times that evening I read a play, called "A Magnum for Schneider", by James Mitchell,'[76] he recalled in a 1972 interview. 'I woke Venetia and said, "I'm sorry, love. I can't make the holiday."' David Callan had arrived – and from now on, the actor's life would never be the same.

'I THINK THAT TELEVISION and film is writer driven,'[77] Woodward mused. 'If the writing is bad, then it's going to be bad anyway, and you can struggle as an actor. But actors spend their whole time, sometimes, building bricks without straw: some of the scripts aren't up to par, and you have to make it as good as you can. With *Callan,* you went into it and you were *privileged* to do it – I'm serious about that. You were actually *privileged,* because you knew that there wasn't one single line that was wrong: everything about it was right, everything tasted right, smelt right, sounded right. [James Mitchell] led you along – he presented an actor with a character, so I have to say that for the first time, and probably the last, it wasn't a question of the actor trying to fiddle around and find a character... Jim wrote him as a not particularly nice character... He was acerbic, he was tough, he was a one-liner... he wasn't a pleasant person to have around. I wouldn't have liked being in his company much, which is probably why he was attractive, I suppose, in a strange sort of way.'

Enjoying the scripts which established his first starring role on television, Woodward was partnered with a gifted ensemble cast, all of whom became friends: Anthony Valentine,

Russell Hunter, Ronald Radd, and later, Derek Bond, William Squire and Patrick Mower. 'The thing about this series was that from the very first day I did it, to the day I finished it, it was a joy,' Edward said. 'It was an absolute *joy* to work with these guys, and also to see friends and new actors coming in to it. And the scripts were *so* good, just were so good – [we] very rarely had a duff one. And so it was a joy to go to work, it really was.' In turn, he was equally highly regarded by the cast and crew.

Interviewed in the 1980s, the director Voytek (real name Wojciech Szendzikowski) clearly recalled the atmosphere on the programme being 'good'[78], attributing this partly to Woodward. 'He was very courteous and punctual. He knew his words before anyone else, he was always running through his business... He was very well prepared, which makes things easier.' 'Without Ted there would have been no *Callan*,'[79] producer Reg Collin stated. 'It was inspired casting.' An opinion shared by James Mitchell: 'If ever there was dream casting, that was it. He couldn't go wrong... It's very difficult imagining any-one else playing Callan.'[80] 'Edward... used [a] particular kind of emotional quality,'[81] said co-star Valentine, 'which was so important to the character, because it was the *volatility* of the character that made it compelling.' 'Teddy was very good at that confrontational element,'[82] Patrick Mower agreed. 'In every episode, he liked to explode.' Director Piers Haggard recalled Woodward as being 'very tight, very bound, very self-controlled; that nervy self-controlled quality captures really well [on camera].'[83]

Terence Feely noted, 'As an actor, he would reign himself in for so long and then he'd erupt spectacularly. He was so good at it that we deliberately wrote in a scene every week where he could do it. Seeing Eddie going up in flames was a great sight.'[84] Peter Duguid, the series' most prolific director, concurred. 'Teddy was a very magnetic draw: the women loved him, the more vicious he was... The most unlikely people, well-heeled, low-heeled alike, were just captivated by him.'[85] 'He was a very bright man,'[86] scriptwriter Trevor Preston said. 'He used to come up with some lovely ideas about the personality of Callan, which of course he'd explored more than anyone.'

ALTHOUGH IT TOOK A WHILE to achieve the massive audiences of its heyday, viewers were immediately struck by the originality of *Callan*'s concept and, particular-ly, Woodward's intense performance as the troubled secret service executioner. The ac-tor gave one of his earliest press interviews as a new television leading man to the *Daily Express* in September 1967, shortly after the first series finished. Things were really chang-ing for Woodward: he spoke of receiving 'up to 150 letters a week, many of them from young girls, and for the first time in his career... is being recognised in the street'[87]. He was estimated to be earning £10,000 a year in 1967, a generous salary that covered the upkeep of the family home in Twickenham and paid for his sons to attend public school.

Candidly, Woodward told the paper about his tendency towards a depressive world view: 'A friend told me... "You've always been a pessimist, but if you go around letting everyone know you are, you will never get anywhere." Until recently I was petrified by the thought of failure. I'm now getting the feeling that one has the right to fail – because there is something wrong with the person who is successful all the time.' With his new-found popularity, and remembering the hardship of his and Venetia's start as a married couple, Woodward was happy to take on promotional work for charities, including the housing trust Shelter. As for Callan, the actor enthused, 'His whole character is enigmatic – and that fascinates me... I haven't finished with him yet. There is still more I want to do with him.'

Woodward's wish was granted when the series returned to TV in 1969 and from there into the early 1970s, the success of *Callan* enabled the actor to promote himself independently from the series. He was always insistent on signing autographs 'Edward Woodward' rather than 'Callan', aware that newspaper story headlines tended to refer to him by the name of his character. In a move that couldn't have been more different from his tough screen alter ego, the actor began appearing on variety shows as a singer, and released the LP *Grains of Sand* in 1969.

There was clearly a keen mind at work behind the choice of songs on Woodward's next LP, *This Man Alone,* released at the start of *Callan*'s third series in 1970. 'Today I Killed a Man I Didn't Know', an American Civil War standard that questions the validity of killing an enemy, fits in with the melancholy mood conjured up by the title song. 'This Man Alone', a grander vocal version of the *Callan* theme, is a meditation on similar ethical themes. At the end of the album, The Beatles' 'Eleanor Rigby' segues into a reprise of the title track, showing that Woodward recognised the common theme of loneliness shared by the two songs.

Woodward made two appearances on the BBC's prestigious *Morecambe and Wise Show* in 1969 and 1970 – significantly, as at that time ITV's star actors rarely appeared on their rival broadcaster's variety shows – and hosted two entertainment ITV specials of his own in 1971. In 1973, he presented the first series of the crime panel game *Whodunnit?* (after being a guest on the pilot show). Every week, guests had to identify a murderer or murderers by questioning the characters that took part in a short mystery.

Woodward wasn't really comfortable as a panel presenter and in hindsight, charming as it is, this show was one of the few missteps in his career: '[He] was a total failure,'[88] *TV Times* columnist Alix Coleman assessed bluntly. 'His father, his greatest fan, used to say, "I saw you tonight." "Yes, yes?" his son would respond eagerly. "What," asked his father, "are you going to do next?"' In the actor's defence, Coleman went on, 'It was just part of... Woodward's determination to be a first-rate all-rounder.'

Throughout his appearances as himself in the 1970s, Woodward's Callan character was never far away. He responded to Eric Morecambe's comment that 'he can't act' by grabbing the comedian's lapels with a very Callanesque 'Watch it!', and when his *Callan* co-star Russell Hunter appeared as a guest panellist on *Whodunnit?*, the two friends delighted the studio audience by slipping back into their *Callan* personas. 'The last member of our panel... it was a shock to me when I knew he was going to be on... I've been trying to avoid him one way and another for many, many years,' Woodward began, before using his Callan voice: 'Just tell me something, mate, where've you been for the last year?' Playing along, Hunter as Lonely replied, 'I have been employed in the service of Her Majesty [i.e. prison].' 'What would you expect?' Woodward asked rhetorically; 'Fancy having him on a panel to investigate a crime!' At the end of the show, the quizmaster delighted in telling the TV and studio audience, 'Russell Hunter got every clue, but all the wrong people!'

On the first edition of his own variety show *The Edward Woodward Hour* in 1971, Woodward performed in a sketch fusing *Callan* with the popular ITV comedy *Father, Dear Father* (1968-1973). This unusual production found Callan and Lonely in sitcom land as they inveigled themselves into the house of writer Patrick Glover (played by Patrick Cargill) and blew up his television. Watching the sketch is disorientating: it's a TV sitcom with stripes of *Callan* running through it every time Woodward and Russell Hunter are on screen alone. The sketch is mainly notable for the transformation in Woodward as, moving away from his amiable light entertainment persona, he puts on his Callan costume, picks up a gun and prepares for the skit. Woodward's whole demeanour visibly – and strikingly – changes to that of the tense killer who had made him famous. That a government executioner could be one of the entertainments on offer on a Thames revue show demonstrated just how much of a 'cause celebre' *Callan* had become: 'I have a little job to do,' Woodward as Callan growls at the audience. 'While I'm gone – *behave yourselves*.' Maybe by that point the actor was open to his famous character appearing in a comedy as he felt audiences could distinguish between him and the part. 'I noticed suddenly, about twelve months ago [May 1971] that the public had sorted out the difference between me and the character I play. They call me Mr. Woodward now – not Callan.'[89]

Undoubtedly, *Callan* opened many doors for Woodward. Apart from his extra-curricular television work, in 1969 he starred in the West End musical *Two Cities*, based on the novel by Charles Dickens (although the production closed early). In 1970 Sir Laurence Olivier, artistic director of London's National Theatre, a *Callan* fan and one of Woodward's acting heroes – who in turn regarded Edward as 'one of the best actors in England'[90] – granted him lead roles in *The White Devil* and *Cyrano de Bergerac* on the strength of his performance in *Two Cities*. By this time, his face was well known. 'I remember once he told me he was working on *The White Devil* at the Old Vic,'[91] director Jim Goddard laughed. 'He was in the traffic and the cab in front of him put the brakes on and he went into the back of him. They both got out of their cars, and the cabbie said, "Oh, it would be you, guv!"'

Woodward also toured England with a cabaret act, at a time then this wasn't an easy thing to do: 'Try a Friday night in a Midlands club when the heavy drunks come in,'[92] Woodward related ruefully of an incident summing up the contradictions of being a popular entertainer: 'I was sitting on a stool on stage, starting "When I Fall in Love". A massive white blob appeared on the periphery of the light. A very big lady, naked from the waist up, came slowly and inexorably towards me... I thought, two months ago, I was standing on the stage of the National Theatre of Great Britain. What am I doing in this family venue in the Midlands, being engulfed by this vast, naked woman?' There was some consolation for Woodward as, in a sign that his popularity was peaking, in 1971 he was the subject of *This Is Your Life*, ITV's biographical series. (He was one of the few celebrities to feature for a second time, 26 years later in 1995).

With a love of theatre instilled in him at the age of five by pantomime, Wood-ward was happy to appear as Robin Hood in *Babes in the Wood* at the London Palladium at the end of 1972, even though some commentators considered the role a comedown for him. 'I can't understand why people should think this,'[93] he said at the time, reveal-ing himself to be refreshingly unpretentious. 'I try to do as many varied things as I can because I get very easily bored. But this results in my being offered many different kinds of work.' This was certainly true of the supporting film roles he took on, from the fashionably lurid *Incense of the Damned* (1970), to a law enforcer, Inspector Milton, in the thriller *Sitting Target*, to an army captain opposite Simon West's *Young Winston* (both 1972). In the same year, after *Callan*'s fourth series Woodward achieved another career goal. Following a false start in the film *A Fine and Private Place* (1970, which was never completed), he was cast in one of the lead parts in a movie – Anthony Shaffer's *The Wicker Man* (1973).

Released in London in December of 1973, the film, directed by Robin Hardy, is now recognised as a remarkable piece of work: part mystery, part musical, part fan-tasy, part philosophical battle between two belief systems. Woodward is electrifying as Sergeant Howie, a devoutly Christian policeman searching for a missing girl on a pagan Scottish island presided over by Lord Summerisle (a dignified – and all the more sinis-ter for it – Christopher Lee). It was a sign of how far Woodward had come that only seven years after *Callan* began, he was starring opposite one of British cinema's most famous actors on the big screen. However, *The Wicker Man* didn't turn out to be the distinguished launch of a movie career that Woodward might have hoped for. The film's distribution company, British Lion, didn't understand its eclectic content, cut it down to 102 minutes and initially allocated the film as the supporting feature to Nicolas Roeg's *Don't Look Now* (1973), with no advance publicity. It wasn't even shown nationally. 'Never mind something rotten in the state of Denmark; you need only to look at the story of *The Wicker Man* to realise there has always been a fair amount of rottenness spreading from Wardour Street outwards,'[94] Woodward later wrote concerning this, describing it as a 'superb' film, 'blighted by corporate stupidity.' The film has now rightly been reappraised, to the point it is viewed as presenting 'career-defining performances from Christopher Lee and Edward Woodward,'[95] with the latter 'fantastically uptight.'[96]

Edward's fortunes in cinema improved in 1974 when the *Callan* movie – which he had wanted to make since the first series – was released in England to generally favourable reviews. Far less favourable was the fate of his family's holiday home in Cyprus, lost to Turkish armed forces when they invaded in the summer. The attack was so sudden that Woodward, Venetia and Sarah (then ten) had to abandon everything they had and, with 30 other British tourists, walk 78 miles to the British army base at Dhekelia, hiding from attacking Turkish aircraft on the way. With the *Callan* film having opened in British cinemas in May, headlines about the incident were inevitable, among them 'Callan's Glad to Be Back'[97] and 'Callan in the Stew Queue'.[98]

THROUGH THE RISE of *Callan* and beyond, Woodward had been presented in interviews as a dedicated family man, particularly in the *TV Times*, which often reported on his home life. At a time when infidelity among celebrities was rare (or rarely reported), it was understandable that there was an unprecedented level of tabloid interest in Woodward's life when news of his affair with the actress Michele Dotrice broke. An attempted reconciliation with Venetia didn't work out, and Woodward and Michele subsequently became united until the end of Edward's life. By the time the otherwise engaging ITV comedy drama *The Bass Player and the Blonde* (1977-78) aired, starring Woodward as hard-up musician Mangham, the series had ironically become a case of art imitating life, as the character's romance with a young blonde woman (Jane Wymark) is central. Having committed to each other, from the late 1970s onwards Edward and Michele would rarely discuss their personal lives in the media. The most that Woodward could say was that 'things are going marvellously with me and Michele,'[99] and that he had no regrets about leaving Venetia: 'You can quote me as saying no. I regret sometimes the circumstances, of course, and all the publicity there was at the time. But I'm a very happy man.'

One respite from the press intrusion may have been the success of the BBC thriller series *1990*[100], which ran for two series over 1977 and 1978. Created by Wilfred Greatorex, who had previously written dramas *The Power Game* (1965-9) and *Hine* (1971) for ITV, it was set in an impoverished 'future' Britain led by a dictatorship; the rule of law is enforced by the Public Control Department, a paranoid vision of the civil service developed into a secret police force. At a time when the Labour government and the British economy were struggling, the series attracted mixed critical comment over its controversial subject matter. The *Evening News* believed that *1990* was 'an alarming glimpse of what life could be like in this country if we are not careful'[101], while *The Daily Telegraph* bemoaned an 'opportunity missed.'[102] Woodward though, starring as investigative reporter and resistance ringleader

Jim Kyle, was hailed as 'the indisputable master of this kind of role in television thrillers.'[103] Nowhere was this more apparent than in 'Non-Citizen', the last episode of the first series, in which Kyle's privileges are revoked and he is made homeless. The scenes of the desperate journalist struggling to deal with life on the streets are as powerful as anything in *Callan*.

The success of *Callan* in Australia, where imported British TV series have always been popular, led to more opportunities for Woodward. As well as a concert tour and starring with Michele in a stage production of Alun Owen's trilogy *Male of the Species*, he was awarded a second chance at headlining a movie in *Breaker Morant* (1980), a film that, like *Callan* and *The Wicker Man*, the actor was 'extremely proud of and enormously enjoyed doing.'[104] Like *1990*, the movie covered controversial political ground. It was based on a real case during the Boer War. Three lieutenants of the British-led Bushveldt Commandos, led by Harry 'Breaker' Morant (Woodward), were brought to trial for executing Boer prisoners. Even though they were following standard orders, their prosecution became political due to improving relations between the Boer and English governments. Woodward's Morant is in many ways the archetypal example of the tough but vulnerable characters he was known for up to this point. A universal chorus of critical praise variously commended the 'mixture of sensitivity and hot-headed ruthlessness of a complex personality,'[105] 'minute changes of expression, faint variations of tone... [conveying] the split man'[106] and the 'clenched face and abrupt gestures signalling the pent-up passions within.'[107] Sentenced to death with his fellow officers, Morant is given much of the defining dialogue of this powerful anti-war drama: 'This is what comes of empire building... Shoot straight, you bastards!'

In the early 1980s, Woodward continued to play a variety of strong guest and leading roles in Britain, such as in the SAS thriller *Who Dares Wins* (1982) and superior TV series like *Nice Work* (1980) and *Winston Churchill: The Wilderness Years* (1981). Even though his return to the Callan role in the same year's one-off TV play *Wet Job* may have been another rare career misstep, it would be James Mitchell's secret agent that again opened doors for Woodward, this time to the most lucrative phase of his career in which he finally became an international name through a popular American TV series. 'The background to *The Equalizer* [1985-88] was interesting,'[108] Edward recalled. 'There was a young guy [Michael J. Sloan] and his parents were Americans, running a lot of London shows. One day, I'm minding my own business walking through a little part of London, Soho, and there was a shout from the steps of an old gun shop, and [he] came up to me with a script, shoved it into my hand, and he said "Would you read that, Mr Woodward?" I said, "Fine, fine, OK," and took it back, and it was a thin, thin script for a short movie. I read it and thought, "My God, this is so good," so I contacted my agent, said "Yes," and I remember I was going to get £1,200 for it, and I did it – it was just a two-hander [*Hunted*, ITV, 1974]. And I never got paid! The money never came.

'Roll the moviola – I think it was ten years later – I get a phone call... "Look, um, remember me? I did the film." I said, "You owe me money, mate!" "Yes, but I've just written a script, which I've written for you, and I have to say it's based on *Callan*, because I was a *Callan* fanatic." So I went in front of a camera, which I hated, and did a so-called interview [and] a couple of scenes for the American producers. I thought "This is the end of it," and blow me down they said they wanted to do [a pilot]. Then I got the script and it was terrible; it was a *diabolical* script and I had to write back... It was rewritten, and it got about half as good as it should have been. Anyway, we did it, and it got picked up.'

BY THE 1970s, THANKS TO the success of the movies *Bullitt* (1968), *Dirty Harry* and *The French Connection* (both 1971), US TV executives were exploiting the format of the rebel cop, whether bald, a Texan cowboy, wheelchair-bound, based in Hawaii, or hiding a sharp mind beneath a shabby raincoat. In 1985, the loner detective archetype was given a gloss of serious espionage as *The Equalizer* arrived. Once the writers concentrated on Woodward's strengths as an actor, the show became notable as an exciting American crime and spy drama. (Producer Joel Surnow would go on to work on the counter-terrorist drama *24* in the 2000s). The series also tapped in to the American archetype of a maverick lawgiver who'll always do what's 'right'. Casting an English classical actor as the 'Equalizer', Robert McCall, an ex-secret agent for 'the Company', gave a character that was basically a vigilante some dignity, sophistication and moral depth. Tough, decent and charming, McCall was a guardian angel for the 1980s, armed with an Uzi.

Watching *The Equalizer*, it's easy to believe that, in Michael Sloan's mind, after *Callan*'s final episode, the character emigrated to the USA and manufactured a new identity for himself within American intelligence. After all, Callan had used several identities before and 'McCall' is only two letters short of being an anagram. The similarities weren't lost on Woodward: 'There was obviously a certain amount of *Callan*-like stuff in it; [although] McCall was highly educated and came from a much more sophisticated [intelligence] group...' Add McCall's disillusion with his job, his tendency to be exploited by his ex-colleagues and his old chief 'Control' (Robert Lansing), together with his emotional isolation, and it's understandable that James Mitchell apparently briefly considered suing.[109]

The British press weren't kind to *The Equalizer* when it was shown on ITV. It was greeted with a superior attitude, bemusement and the implication that a talented, respected actor had sold out for big bucks, which Woodward refuted. While *The Sunday Times* conceded that 'Edward Woodward plays [McCall] with the same impassive presence he brought to *Callan*,'[110] the reviewer in *Today* confessed, 'I can't imagine what Edward Woodward thinks he's doing in these gratuitous-violence slots.'[111] *The Sunday Telegraph* deplored 'the worst dress sense and the biggest paunch of any private investigator since Frank Cannon'[112] and dismissed the programme's content as 'a simplicity guaranteed not to tax the intellect of someone reared entirely on watching American wrestling.' In New York, however – where the series was shot on the graffitied, rubbish-strewn city streets – the *New York Times* TV critic understood the appeal of a spy seeking redemption by doing good in a violent urban landscape: '[Woodward's] eyes are sad and cold. He looks a little like Richard Burton, and a little like Michael Caine: there are bags under those eyes to contain all the sadness. He moves around like Orson Welles, hauling the luggage of himself... as if sleepwalking into heroism, as tired as John le Carré, a box-like Smiley. He is plausible and maybe necessary.'[113]

Despite the dismissive attitude in some quarters of the British press, Woodward didn't complain, maybe because *The Equalizer*, running to four seasons, made him a bankable star in America. Peter Egan, an actor with whom Edward worked on the 1974 *Callan* movie, observed, 'It's not often you get English actors cracking that mould - he had a really positive presence.'[114] Edward was initially amused by the attention McCall brought him: 'It's damned funny really. I'm nearly 56, yet people keep telling me that my television image is sexy[115]... I'm getting more letters in a week than I've had in a whole career to date. It's a great feeling.'[116] There was a downside, however, the actor admitting that 'making *The Equalizer* is the hardest work I've ever done.'[117] This plus a junk food diet due to long filming hours, plus 'a hundred cigarettes a day'[118], plus previous coronary trouble, unfortunately led to Woodward suffering a heart attack while making the spy drama *Codename: Kyril* (1988).[119]

With *The Equalizer* being a hit, CBS were sympathetic and the production team adapted to events. They contrived a plot in which McCall was kidnapped and an old colleague – played by none other than film star Robert Mitchum – led the search for him, in a storyline that gave a two-part episode extra suspense. Quickly restored to health, Edward was disappointed that he never met the Hollywood legend. He recovered, stopped smoking and completed a staggering total of 88 episodes overall, but *The Equalizer* proved to be a double-edged sword for the actor. Winning a prestigious Golden Globe award in 1988, Woodward was arguably the first British actor to become a major solo star in a hit US TV series; previously, only David McCallum had achieved this kind of international success as part of a double act in *The Man From UNCLE* (1964-68). *The Equalizer* also made Edward and Michele very wealthy, as he was paid a 'hundred per cent more than in Britain'[120] but, even more than *Callan*, he believed the series 'inevitably'[121] typecast him. By now, nearly 60 and putting on weight, there was a certain irony that in the spy roles he was offered after *The Equalizer*, Woodward was being contracted to play the commander figures who would originally have given Callan or McCall their orders.

Notable among the several espionage characters he took on was 'Mr Jones', head of the familiar-sounding Section One in the Canadian/US series *La Femme Nikita* (in 2001), bringing English gravitas and a cultured manner to that series' rock video ambience. As CI5 chief Harry Malone, Woodward lent his commanding presence to the reboot of the late 1970s and early 1980s action series created by Brian Clemens, 1999's *CI5: The New Professionals* (1999). Made for an international market by David Wickes Television and less successful than *The Professionals*, running for only a year, the unapologetically comic strip series about an anti-terrorist organisation has its moments. 'Choice Cuts' is a clever, unpredictable story about illegal organ-trafficking, in which Malone poses as the irritable millionaire Sir John Grover. 'Samurai Wind' is an accomplished mini-action movie set in the Pacific, while 'Hostage', featuring the televised trial in the UK of Eliz Risha, an Albanian minister who may or may not be a war criminal, is genuinely tense and includes a believably cynical attitude to the hostage by the British government. Woodward dominates effortlessly, asserting his authority over terrorists, Charlotte Cornwell's government minister, the Metropolitan Police and Risha, memorably snarling at the latter, 'Get out of my sight before you have a very nasty accident!' *CI5: The New Professionals* was also a stroll down memory lane for Woodward, as the interiors were filmed at Teddington studios (by 1999 available for hire to external television companies) where *Callan* had been made in the 1960s and 1970s.

'Edward was a lovely man,'[122] producer David Wickes reminisced. 'I can't remember anyone ever having a bad word to say about him. For someone who became famous for playing a hard-nosed killer, he came from that generation of actors who could sing and dance as well as act. When you gave one of them a job, they'd sometimes do you a little dance before they went off... We went to America to film some episodes and getting through [US] immigration was a *nightmare*. The customs officer I was dealing with really didn't want to let me into the country, even more so when she found out I was supposed to be working there. I'd been to America hundreds of times – as my passport showed – but overweight, and with a sense of humour bypass, she behaved like I'd been a stowaway on the plane. In the end, she asked me what I was there to make: "*The New Professionals* with Edward Woodward." "Edward *Woodward!*" Her attitude changed immediately and she was suddenly smiling from ear to ear: "I *love* him! He's *wonderful!*" She didn't even look at my passport as she stamped it, handed it back to me and waved me through.

'One day I had a call from Edward and he said he was concerned about the script. "It's a question of formality," he said rather obliquely and was adamant about talking to me about it on the set. Just as I was about to leave, the phone went and it was Edward's agent. "Do you know what's going on?" he said, a bit tersely. "Apparently it's a question of formality," I said. "It's more than that," the agent replied. "It's about Edward leaving the series." To say I was rather tense by the time I got to the set was a bit of an understatement! Edward was in his trailer and the crux of the problem for him was that in the script his character called Tina Bacchus, one of the regulars, by the nickname "Backup" that the two boys used. "Malone just wouldn't do it," he insisted. "He's the Commander." This grievance had developed into complete dissatisfaction with the whole script and production! I had to get Brian Clemens down to rewrite it. We moved lines around, cut dialogue, shortened scenes, changed some of the story and, in the end, Edward was happy. That was the only time that I ever saw him throw his weight around, but to be fair he had a point.'

In the 1990s, Woodward was into his fifth decade as a successful actor and, as well as taking on reliable employment as senior intelligence figures, he didn't lose his enthusiasm for diverse and challenging work. To follow up *The Equalizer, Over My Dead Body* (1990-91) was conceived as another star vehicle for him on US television, with Edward starring as the mystery author Maxwell Beckett, investigating real crimes. (The series was effectively a male version of the Angela Lansbury vehicle *Murder, She Wrote* (1984-96); Woodward's show had the same producer, William Link). Only eight episodes were made before the series was prematurely cancelled, but Woodward was still in demand as a quality guest star, with his most bizarre ever role being the voice of a chimpanzee in *The Lone Gunmen* (2001), the spin-off from the sci-fi conspiracy drama *The X-Files* (1993-2002, 2016); he's even referred to in the episode, 'Planet of the Frohikes', as 'Edward Woodward, the Equalizer.'

In 1992, Woodward brought over 40 years as a distinguished stage actor to a close in *The Dead Secret*, a theatrical version of Wilkie Collins' fourth novel. Other later career highlights included the TV film *Night Flight* (2002), in which Woodward gave a moving performance as Vic Green, a RAF crewman haunted by his cowardice, and *The Bill's* two-part story 'Sins of the Father' (2008), where Edward, his son Tim and grandson Sam appeared as three generations of the same criminal family. Like Anthony Valentine and Patrick Mower, in his later years Woodward also took a role in a soap opera; he played Tommy Clifford, an old man with a dark incident in his past, in BBC1's *EastEnders* (1985-). Simon Pegg, Nick Frost and Edgar Wright introduced him to a new, younger audience in their hilarious police/horror/action film *Hot Fuzz* (2007), partly inspired by *The Wicker Man*. 'It's one thing to meet your heroes, it's another to find them the person you hoped they would be,'[123] Simon Pegg later reflected. 'Edward was definitely one such hero.'

In a career that, in the public mind, would generally be associated with spies and spying, it must have been gratifying for Woodward that the last critically-applauded regular role of his TV career had nothing to do with espionage. After returning to England with Michele (whom he had married in 1987) and their daughter, Emily, Woodward took on the role of Nev Smith, the unassuming foreman of a council rubbish collection department in the comedy drama *Common as Muck* (1994-97). Written by William Ivory, who had left his college course in Mansfield to work as a dustbin man, the series' strength was its authenticity, as Nev and his colleagues dealt with the spectre of privatisation. Woodward still knew a hit script when one came through his letter box: '[Ivory's] characters are all heroes in a way, and all bastards; there's astonishing range in every one. [They] leapt straight off the page. It was a question of "Can we start tomorrow?"'[124]

His enthusiasm was rewarded with nine million viewers for the first series, a Royal Television Society Award, a BAFTA nomination and, in *The Times*, one of the most complimentary reviews he ever received: 'The death of [Irene, played by] June Whitfield – corny, or not – provided Edward Woodward with a great acting moment which clinched one's suspicions that Nev is the performance of his career.'[12]

EDWARD WOODWARD died from pneumonia on 16 November 2009 in Cornwall, where he had spent much of his life with Michele. In a sign of his enduring popularity, his life was commemorated on the following evening's *News at Ten*. Appropriately, one of the first to pay tribute was Anthony Valentine, who had witnessed his friend's career blossom in the 1960s and move on to ever more impressive heights in the following years. 'He was always marvellous to work with,'[126] Valentine recalled with obvious affection. 'Not only was he a fine actor, he had this quality that made him – special. There are quite a few fine actors around, but anything that Ted did, he did it in such a way that nobody else would have done it the same way. He had this wonderful air of *danger* about him as a performer, and he could also do anything; he had a very broad spectrum. He could play a cheeky chappie and he could play a professional assassin, and everything was always utterly, totally believable. He was a great guy as well as a great actor. The profession will miss all those qualities that he had.'

It still does.

Russell Hunter
Lonely (1967-1972, 1974, 1981)

**'In many ways Russell was the most consistent actor
of the series. He was always very strong.'**

Peter Duguid, interview 31 July 1985

'**L**ONELY, I THINK, WAS PROBABLY *THE* CLASSIC CHARACTER,
almost certainly, in the twentieth century of television,'[127] Edward Woodward
boldly claims of Callan's body odour-suffering, petty thief associate, so memorably
played by Russell Hunter. 'He was a nasty little man with a sort of heart of gold, in a way,
but he was very vulnerable. He was an outcast – he smelt. There's something curious about
a person who smells; they really are outcasts, and [a TV character] had never been written
in that way before. It was a character you felt sorry for, but at the same time felt annoyed
about, so the audience kind of understood Callan's attitude to Lonely. Every week they
waited to see what was coming up, how Callan was going to berate him: was he going to
physically abuse him, what kind of job was he going to set him, how was Lonely going
to mess up... It was a beautifully written character, a beautifully understood character, but
above all, it was the most beautifully *played* character... The actor's job is to basically recreate
the author's intentions, and this was a recreation of Russell's that was absolutely superb.'

Born Adam Russell Ellis on 18 February 1925 in Glasgow, Hunter spent his childhood
with maternal grandparents before returning to his mother and father – respectively a cleaner and a dockyard worker – when he was twelve. Leaving school, he took an apprenticeship
in a Clydebank shipyard and began acting in an amateur capacity for the Young Communist
League, turning professional in 1946; one of his earliest stage appearances was at the very
first Edinburgh Festival Fringe in Sean O'Casey's play *The Plough and the Stars* (1947).

Russell worked in repertory theatre and summer variety shows for several years
before making his first forays into film in *Lilli Marlene* (1950), *The Gorbals Story* (1950,
reprising his part from Robert McLeish's stage play) and as a pilot in the Battle of Britain
drama *Angels One Five* (1952). British television also saw potential in the young actor, and
he performed in popular series of the time like *Dixon of Dock Green* (1955), *Dr. Finlay's
Casebook* (1965) and *Redcap* – 'An Ambush Among Friends '(1966), as well as the first ever
television adaptation of Robert Louis Stevenson's story *Kidnapped* (1952), and the Francis
Durbridge thriller *The Broken Horseshoe* (1952).

Hunter was industrious on stage during this period too, notably for Peter Hall's
Royal Shakespeare Company; he also helped bring the Bard's work to the small screen in

BBC productions of *As You Like It* (1963) and *Love's Labour's Lost* (1965). It was through his Shakespearean performances that he came to be recruited for *Callan* by ABC casting director Dodo Watts: 'When I asked her afterwards why she'd cast me, she said, "Because I saw you playing in *A Midsummer Night's Dream*, in Regent's Park, in the open air theatre." She saw me play Bottom in an outrageous performance and thought, "If he can play that, he can play anything!" and gave me the part of Lonely.'[128]

'HE MADE THAT PART HIS OWN,'[129] Terence Feely said of Russell. 'I mean it's an actor's dream, isn't it, to have one absolutely outstanding character – that stinks to high heaven! It gets worse when you're frightened. Jimmy [Mitchell] and I discussed that: the smell of fear was very real, it's what would make a dog or a tiger go for you because, apparently, it infuriates them. It's not because they know you're frightened, they just can't stand it so they go for you, and we worked on this. Russell got hold of it – "I can't 'elp it, Mr Callan!" – and I can't think of any other actor who could have made Lonely so sympathetic... That was all part of his vulnerability.'

'I had no idea it would become a series,'[130] Hunter admits. 'We recorded ['A Magnum for Schneider'], I remember, in September [1966] and it wasn't shown until the following February. I was on holiday in Israel and came back through London Airport, and the man who looked at my passport as I came through looked very hard at me, smiled and said, "There's a dreadful smell here." I said, "Pardon?!" and he said, "Oh, didn't you see the television last night?" I said, "No". "You were very good," he said. And I did not know what he was talking about. In a way, it was the beginning of all the "smelly" jokes and it came from the very first one-off programme.' The joke became a running gag in subsequent episodes. 'He is so touching in it – you just feel for him,'[131] Piers Haggard said. 'A theatrical performance, but very, very touching. It doesn't date.'

Feely recalled that as further recording progressed, the crew and cast, Hunter included, would socialise in the pub next door to Teddington Studios. 'I didn't know for a long time – until I realised in the pub – that Russell was speaking like a Scotsman. I was still hearing him talk cockney. I'd say, "You're a bloody fraud, Russell, you're not a cockney at all!" And he'd say, "Aye, I'm bloody Glaswegian!"'[132] Trevor Preston, who joined the writing team in the second series, recalled Hunter being keen to cultivate his accent further. 'He found it difficult at first; he said, "There's a lot of actors who come down to do London accents and they can't – it's a weird mix of broken Australian and Irish!" But I know London perfectly, every area, and as you know there's a difference in tone from East London, South London, even South East London... So I knew what to write for him and he loved it: he absolutely loved it.'[133] Referring to real-life inspirations for Lonely's character, Preston adds, 'There was a sort of guy who used to pick up dog-ends from ashtrays and then open up a tin and make roll-ups, and throw the old tobacco in. On the street they were called "swoopers", because they'd nick anything in sight!'

Later in life, Russell became friends with a real life counterpart for his character: 'A small "recidivist", shall we call him, who *is* Lonely, no question about it. I recognise the eyes. It's been pointed out to me that when people in one of the local pubs have seen the pair of us sitting in a corner, arguing, it's hysterical. And, would you believe, we never argue about anything else but politics. We argue very quietly, but all my friends seem to think I'm doing very questionable deals with this man! Just to see him when he's very well dressed – by his standards – he looks awful. There's always something wrong; he tries very hard, but although he's convinced he's all right, he just does not fit in. He doesn't come out of the machine; he doesn't look like everybody else. Which in a way is nice: I like individuals like that, very much.'[134]

As his performance developed, Hunter embellished his character's personal life. 'After a few episodes, I decided I had to have some sort of character history which I could relate to without imposing it on somebody's script. So I just dreamed up an address, which was 4½A, Baths Approach, Fulham, because there is a little backstreet in Fulham called Baths Approach, and I discovered there was a 4A. And next door didn't have a number, it was just a basement, so I called it 4½A. I decided that was where I lived, in Fulham, just round the corner from where I actually lived. Then, after I met the author who wrote the original *Callan* stories, James Mitchell, who had the most charming, delightful, and truly beautiful Indian wife, I decided that she was not his wife at all, she was actually Lonely's wife! And that was the great secret, that's what kept Lonely going: he might be fiddling here, there and everywhere, but he's got a dolly bird hidden away!'[135] Intriguingly, James Mitchell adopted a very similar idea when writing Lonely's final TV appearance in *Wet Job* (1981).

The writers were keen to exploit the small thief's dramatic and comic potential. '"This character is wonderful – we've got to give him more to do",'[136] Terence Feely recalled telling James Mitchell. 'The idea of this smelly guy who was terrified of Callan, but admired him... "Let's build him up."' You get the humour when Lonely's put in a situation he can't deal with.'[137] Writer Ray Jenkins said: 'Lonely changes, he evolves, and the reason for that is because Russell Hunter was so brilliant.' 'I'd do naughty things with Lonely,'[138] Trevor Preston admits. 'I remember once I suggested a scene of Lonely waking up in bed, half drugged, in a seedy hotel. The telephone woke him up, he picked it up and his one line of dialogue was "No, I didn't order the *Jewish Chronicle*!" That went, swiftly!' Peter Mitchell suggested, 'As a writer you're a bit of a fool if you don't go, "Wow, there's mileage in that [character], I'm going to write to that."'[139]

'In my view – and it is only my personal view – the thing that actually brought *Callan* from ratings obscurity to being very popular was Russell Hunter,'[140] director Mike Vardy asserted. 'They developed his role, some of his scenes were really hysterical, and he did the part extremely well. Whenever I mention *Callan* to somebody now, the first word they say is "Lonely". That's not to detract from Edward or Tony [Valentine] or any of the Hunters, they were all very good, but what attracted the audience was Russell. I was very fond of him. He never put less than 150% into it, ever. He and Teddy worked wonderfully well together.'

'Quite often, you're only supposed to follow the leading character, and if another character gets too big or too popular, that character is pushed aside,'[141] Edward Woodward noted, regarding Lonely's increasing prominence. 'The opposite happened, because, quite rightly, Lonely became so popular and so marvellous that what James Mitchell then had to do – and make sure that other authors did – was treat that character extremely carefully. Callan and Lonely worked best of all when they were together, particularly on a job, with Lonely helping Callan in his own fumbling way.' 'The Lonely/Callan relationship was the first time anybody had used smell on television,' Jim Goddard added. 'It was quite funny. Russell and Teddy were a great double act.'[142] TV historian Dick Fiddy believed the character's 'lack of hygiene means he has difficulty making other friends and acquaintances,'[143] while Mike Vardy felt 'Lonely's relationship with Callan was probably something you'd find in a Shakespearean play... it was a double parasitical relationship.'[144]

The production team had to be careful to keep the comedy under control, as Woodward observed. '[The audience] waited for Callan's reaction to his smell – "Phew, mate, you pong, you really pong!" – so we had to [watch] how often we did [that].'[145] As some viewers realised in the 'Letters Page' of the *TV Times*, there are similarities between Callan's double-act with Lonely, and the love-hate relationship between Harold and his father in the sitcom *Steptoe and Son* (1962-74).[146] 'I think [the humour] made the third series a ratings success because it gave the whole thing more balance,'[147] Mike Vardy observed. '[*Callan*] was very intense a lot of the time, so the [lighter] scenes – particularly with Russell – gave it a whole extra dimension, which to me was what it needed.'

As well as providing some essential differentiation in tone, the lighter moments may have bled through naturally from the amiable working atmosphere on set. Hunter was known to lighten the mood during recordings with practical jokes. When Trevor Preston was the unwilling recipient of advances from a gay actor, he mentioned it to Hunter, who agreed to diffuse the tension. 'In the break, I went up to have a drink in the green room,'[148] Preston recalled. 'Russell appeared in a pair of white ballet leggings with hearts on them, and one of those flouncy princess wigs. And he did an *entrechat* across the room and gave me a great big kiss!... I used to run into him and we'd usually both be in a rush, but he'd always have a gag.' John Flanagan, in the late 1960s a novice actor, also recalled Hunter's strong sense of humour during the making of 'Death of a Hunter'. 'Russell, finding my character dead in some dark set, had a torch to shine on my face. He whispered to me on the camera rehearsal, "You better be nice to me, pal, 'cos I'm the fucking lighting man in this scene!"... In the end he managed to give my face plenty of well-lit exposure to the viewing nation.'[149]

The fourth and final series of *Callan* saw further developments for Lonely's character as he was given the regular profession of a cab driver. ('Russell couldn't drive, so we had to use low loaders for his taxi scenes,'[150] film cameraman John Keeling remembered.) The vocation stuck sufficiently to elicit jokes on the crime quiz show *Whodunnit?* (in 1973) when Hunter appeared in the first series, compèred by Edward Woodward. Watching Russell's edition is instructive because of the contrast it offers between the actor's own relaxed personality and his anxious characterisation of Lonely. 'People called him "smelly" but he was the sweetest smelling person in real life,'[151] Patrick Mower, who also appeared on the quiz, recalled. 'A lovely, very refined, comedic, well-educated Scottish actor, who played Lonely's character, and played it so well, that people thought he was really like that.' Actor, event organiser and interviewer David Bickerstaff, who got to know Russell later in his life, recalled when he met him for the first time, 'He was dressed immaculately in a suit, perfectly groomed and shaven.'[152]

Hunter was quite willing to reprise the part of Lonely and did so on two further occasions. 'I was astonished, when I first met him, at how *tall* Russell Hunter was,'[153] Derek Horne remarked, having first encountered him while making the *Callan* feature film. 'It's the cheating of film: the camera lies through its lens! I remember him as quite a lanky chap.' Hunter's movie co-star Peter Egan said, 'Lonely was a very sad character but Russell was a very extrovert, positive character. We also did *Travesties* together, a Tom Stoppard play. Terrific fun.'[154]

Hunter's Lonely was British television drama's first regular likeable minor criminal. Others followed, such as Sammy Carson in *Paul Temple* (1969-71), Ronald Bird, a.k.a. *Budgie* (1971–72), and Turtle in *Turtle's Progress* (1979–1980): they were slightly higher up the underworld hierarchy than Lonely, but still negotiated the same fine line between other, more dangerous villains and the police. Budgie, played by Adam Faith, was charismatic but an inept schemer who frequently displeased the local gangland boss Charlie Endell (Iain Cuthbertson). Endell was later revived in his own series, *Charles Endell, Esquire* (1979), which was developed by another *Callan* writer, Robert Banks Stewart; almost inevitably, Russell took a guest role, in an episode written by Terence Feely, 'The Moon Shines Bright on Charlie Endell'. The gangster attempts to set up an illegal distillery and the story culminates in a suitably big explosion, preceded by Hunter's character, Leakey, predicting Endell will end up 'in bits' all over Glasgow.

Minder (1979-1994), made by Euston Films, includes arguably the most well-known example of Lonely's TV successors. It features its own famous double act, the dodgy entrepreneur and 'fence' Arthur Daley (George Cole) and his hard-man bodyguard Terry McCann (Dennis Waterman), the 'minder' of the title. Russell was cast in a brief role in the episode 'In' (1982)[155]. Arthur is wrongfully arrested and Terry has to clear his name, which leads to a punch-up on top of a double-decker bus. Hunter's character, 'Billy the Ferret', is an informer very much in the style of Lonely, put into the same cell as Daley to listen out for evidence of his guilt. The scheme fails because Arthur already knows him.

HORROR AND TELEFANTASY were other genres where Russell made notable appearances. *Callan* director Peter Sasdy cast him in a brief part as Felix, a camp club owner in Hammer's *Taste the Blood of Dracula* (1970). ABC/Thames TV's *Mystery and Imagination* (1966-1970), worked on by several *Callan* directors and writers as well as Edward Woodward and Patrick Mower, featured Russell in multiple roles in 'Sweeney Todd' (1970). Associated TeleVision's popular anthology *Thriller* (1973-76) cast him as the shabby local Old Fred, swilling pints and keeping a pet rat in his anorak in 'Kiss Me and Die' (1974), an instalment was written by Terence Feely from a story by series creator Brian Clemens.

Ace of Wands (1970-72), a crime drama created by Trevor Preston for older children, contained supernatural elements, too. (Pamela Lonsdale, who gave Preston some of his first breaks in writing for children, produced the series.) The protagonist Tarot, played by Michael Mackenzie, was a magician/detective and he and his friends faced a gallery of grotesque villains in a similarly entertaining style to that of later episodes of *The Avengers*. Hunter was cast as the most prominent, the sorcerer Mr Stabs, who appeared in 'Seven Serpents, Sulphur and Salt'. This was another of Russell's most memorable TV roles, and the character's popularity was such that Hunter reprised the part in 1975, as part of the anthology series *Shadows*, in the tongue-twistingly entitled tale of 'Dutch Schlitz's Shoes'. Hunter would have returned in the role for a third time had Preston had his way, but a different producer took over at Thames, and by the time the third Stabs story was eventually made the part was recast. 'Russell was dead keen on making it,'[156] Preston said ruefully.

In 'Dutch Schlitz's Shoes', Stabs arrives at a manor house. Turning its occupant, who collects dangerous magical artefacts, into a toad, Stabs plans to secure the powerful Black Glove of Mendoza. Instead, he is possessed by the footwear and spirit of an American gangster. Slapstick ensues in the style of both old James Cagney gangster films and the ITC adventure series *Randall and Hopkirk (Deceased)* (1969-70) before Stabs gets out of trouble and departs for a career in the Stock Market, in a plot twist well ahead of its time. With his cadaverous looks, slicked back hair and pin-striped suit, Hunter revels in his dialogue as 'a malignant malcontent' and a 'grand purveyor of evil.' (His look is strikingly similar to that of Dave Vanian, the gothic singer of the punk band The Damned; the group made their debut the year after 'Dutch Schlitz's Shoes' was shown).

Stabs fans remember Hunter's signature phrase, 'Hand of Stabs,' being chanted in the school playground in much the same way as children cried 'Exterminate!' as they impersonated the Daleks from *Doctor Who*, and two years after *Shadows*, Hunter appeared in the BBC adventure series, in 'The Robots of Death' (1977). Set on a huge craft mining a desert for minerals and featuring Tom Baker as the iconic fourth Doctor, the story was voted by fans as one of the top ten best in the history of the programme.[157] When three of the miner's crew are strangled, the other humans cannot countenance the idea that their deferential robot servants might have been reprogrammed to kill. Hunter's performance as Uvanov, the vituperative, insecure Commander of the ship, gives an already admirable story a great boost. As with *Callan*, Hunter's co-stars remember the good-humoured atmosphere he generated in rehearsal and on set. 'He was irresistibly impish, and full of energy, and full of stories. Fantastic stories, none of which, of course, are repeatable!'[158] Tom Baker recalled. 'When he went into a bar he was never lonely – although he was always Lonely – because everybody bought him drinks and everything.'

A talented comic performer, Russell excelled in the sitcom genre. In 1960, he appeared in *Para Handy – Master Mariner*, a comic period piece set on Scotland's waterways. Based on a series of books by Neil Munro, the series was remade in colour with the same cast in 1974, then reinterpreted by comedian Gregor Fisher in 1995; Hunter had made several comic cameos in Fisher's sitcom about a string-vested Glaswegian alcoholic, *Rab C. Nesbitt* (1988-). Russell also collaborated with Tommy Cooper in the comedian's self-titled 1975 show, with Jasper Carrott and Robert Powell on *The Detectives* (1996) and with Frankie Howerd on the film version of *Up Pompeii* (1971).

Having had a regular part in *Rule Britannia!* (1975) and a guest appearance as a barely comprehensible, whisky-swilling chauffeur who disrupts the class in *Mind Your Language* (1979), Hunter gained more household recognition from his part as Harry, a tough talking, by-the-book shop steward, often at loggerheads with the corner-cutting figure of *The Gaffer* (1981-83).It was Bill Maynard's turn to play the scruffy chancer in this labour relations comedy, as his character Fred Moffatt runs a chaotic engineering business. Playing the left-wing Harry, Hunter clearly relished channelling his formative years in the dockyard into his performance, at one point prevaricating that his union members will be 'working normally – but hating every minute of it.' 'Russell was wonderful, and became a very good friend,'[159] Bill Maynard recalled in an interview with Jonathan Melville. 'He had the greatest collection of whiskies of any man I know.' For a while, Hunter was a director of the Scottish Malt Whisky Society.

RUSSELL WAS HIRED for a number of other engaging, off-kilter parts in drama series, such as Archie McNeil, a polygamist who was a defendant In *Crown Court* – 'A View to Matrimony' (1973). He would often play Scottish characters, like the querulous artist and murder suspect Matthew Gowan – barely recognisable under weighty and, unfortunately, obviously false facial hair and beard – in the Lord Peter Wimsey mystery *Five Red Herrings* (1975). In *The Sweeney* – 'I Want the Man' (1975), he played Popeye, an informant of Jack Regan's, who has incredibly close similarities with Lonely, an understated gay relationship with another 'snout', Jimmy Dancer (Henry Woolf) notwithstanding. In this downbeat episode, Popeye falls foul of Maynard (Michael Coles), a villain planning to steal a lorry full of old banknotes. Ray Jenkins was specifically commissioned to create a Lonely-like character because of his experience writing *Callan*; it seems the original intention had been to use Lonely himself – explaining why the two charcaters are so similar – but because Thames Television didn't own the rights to the character, Lonely became Popeye.

In *The Return of Sherlock Holmes* – 'Silver Blaze' (1988), Hunter was perfect casting as the Victorian rogue Silas Brown, who has hidden a prize racehorse in his stables; Russell had previously appeared in *Sherlock Holmes and the Masks of Death* (1984), a TV movie starring Peter Cushing as the great detective. In *Taggart* – 'Death Comes Softly' (1990), an instalment of the long-running Glasgow police series, Hunter played a cantankerous pensioner accusing his family of neglecting him; the OAP is then murdered while they're on holiday. In a scene of gallows humour typical of the show's superior early years, the police are all seen desperately trying not to vomit due to the smell at the crime scene. In *A Touch of Frost* – 'Fun Times for Swingers' (1996) Russell featured as Prentice, the puritanical sidekick of DI Frost (David Jason), who helps with two cases: an apparent suicide and a robbery at the local cricket club. His twitchy sexual prudery soon annoys Frost, and Hunter is wonderfully dour in the scene where Prentice reveals that his wife has left him for a professional darts player. Ultimately, to Frost's disbelief, Prentice takes early retirement citing 'stress', playing the police system to his advantage. Russell's other contributions to popular drama include *Dickens of London* (1976), *The Standard* (1978), *Ruth Rendell Mysteries* – 'Wolf to the Slaughter' (1987), *King & Castle* (1988), *Casualty* (1989), Trevor Preston's thriller pilot *The Negotiator* (1994), and *Lovejoy* – 'Angel Trousers' (1992), as hard-drinking submariner Harry Mackie.

Hunter also contributed to public education programmes and history documentaries, including *Scotland's Story* (1984, with Derek Bond and Billy Connolly) and worked on a number of single plays, including the innovative TV film *Suspect* (1969), one of two written and directed by Mike Hodges just prior to overseeing the gangster film *Get Carter* (1971). Russell clearly had an interest in political work; *Play for Tomorrow* – 'Nuclear Family' (1982), written by Glaswegian writer and CND sympathiser Thomas McGrath, reveals a dismal, computerised future in which the population are all unemployed and living underground. One family try to escape this situation by opting for a working holiday, a 'luxury' that turns out to consist of chopping wood and polishing nuclear missiles in a defence base. They are overseen by Hunter's character, Smellie (very firmly pronounced 'Smiley' by Hunter).

As well as achievements in film and television, Russell was as an exemplary theatre performer. Fellow actor Kenneth Gilbert recalled, 'He came to see a couple of things I did in Scotland, like *Anthony and Cleopatra*. He was quite outspoken and quite a fiery character: strongly supportive of the Scottish theatres, very active and very much a live wire. Every time I went to Scotland, we used to hear of Russell doing something.'[160] As a student actor, David Bickerstaff witnessed first-hand how forthright Hunter could be. 'My first job at drama school was a dreadful play called *The Hibbs Story* at the King's Theatre, and Russell played the lead. That's when I heard him shout at a director in rehearsal the famous words, "Actors are people, not automatons!"... The play had two directors, and everyone in the cast was pissed off because they kept contradicting each other.'[161] Bickerstaff also angrily recalled how the row was misreported in the local press. 'It was the first time I'd ever experienced the lies of the media. I remember being shocked by the atmosphere in rehearsals the day when this article came out. Russell left the play, so although I was in rehearsals with him, I never got to act with him on stage.'

Russell performed in two one-man plays, *Cocky* (1969) – as Lord Cockburn, the barrister who defended Burke's wife in the Burke and Hare grave robbing case – and *Jock* (1972 onwards). '[It] was a solo show about being Scottish,'[162] Trevor Preston laughed. 'He asked me if I enjoyed it and I said I could only understand half of it; could he translate the rest?'

Russell called on Jim Goddard to help with realising W. Gordon Smith's script for this second solo production. 'Jim was a godsend,'[163] Hunter said. 'When I was doing [*Jock*] at the Edinburgh Festival, which was a kind of history of the Scottish soldier, and I realised I was tackling something close to impossible, he came. He read it, and said "I don't understand a bloody word of it, but I think I know what it's about." We worked together for about three or four weeks, and out of that came not only a very good relationship, [but] a production of a play for the theatre which stood up for the next eight years, because there was no frippery, there was no phoney. It was all absolutely for real thanks to Jim Goddard.'

RUSSELL'S CAREER WAS NOT WITHOUT ITS SETBACKS. Even as far back as the early 1970s, some television production teams were unimaginative in their outlook towards casting him. In 1971 he told *The Sun*, 'I was offered a couple of TV series where I would simply have been Lonely under another name. I turned them all down.'[164] Actor Clifford Rose was similarly over-identified with his character Kessler, on *Secret Army* (1977-79): 'I was recognised all over the place. On *Callan* it didn't happen, because I was so occasional a character. Russell... got a lot of recognition and became very, very well known.'[165] Fellow actor Michael Jayston also recalled Hunter regularly being sent deodorants and other products: 'He got sent so many because he was supposed to be smelly – he got sent loads of lotions and things from fans: he got hundreds of pounds worth.'[166] 'He never got over [Lonely], like me and *Doctor Who*,'[167] Tom Baker suggested. Russell's part in that series had largely come about through director Michael E. Briant's insistence that the part of the Commander should 'not be a *Space: 1999*-type figure'[168], casting Russell strikingly against type. Briant recalled the series producer Philip Hinchcliffe being less sure, but ultimately trusting his director's judgement that Hunter would have the authority to be credible as Uvanov.

The press also predictably focused on Hunter when he divorced his second wife, the statuesque actress Caroline Blakiston, although the split was by all accounts cordial. He was married three times, to Marjorie Thomson (in 1949), Blakiston (from 1970 to 1979) and latterly to Una McLean (in 1991), having first met her when they worked on the pantomime *Babes in the Wood* (1989). Perhaps due to his typecasting, Russell suffered a few lean years, and once, down on his luck, was reportedly loaned a considerable amount of money by Billy Connolly. Once back on his feet again financially, Hunter tried to repay him, but the comedian wouldn't accept the money.

David Bickerstaff recalled that Russell delighted in meeting the public and talking about his work: 'I organised my first *Doctor Who* convention in Glasgow, and I invited Russell. He loved an audience, and the best guest panel I've ever been involved in was him, [and actors] Nick Courtney and Julian Glover, talking about the state of TV and how rubbish it was.'[169] Speaking about Hunter's acting technique, he adds, 'Russell had his little tricks. Every actor's got tricks, something that they always use, and with Russell you notice this when he plays Lonely: he always uses his hands, and he did that a lot in other things. One of the other things he could do instantly was cry, like in 'If He Can, So Could I'.'

In 2000, a series of audio plays by Magic Bullet Productions commenced release under the overall title *Kaldor City*. These developed Uvanov's story a few years on from 'The Robots of Death', and transferred the action to the city where his mining crew lived. Despite returning to the character over 20 years on, Hunter seamlessly reprised his role as the sharp-tongued Uvanov, clearly relishing the series' double-edged, caustic dialogue. 'Robots' scriptwriter Chris Boucher and producer Alan Stevens, Fiona Moore, Jim

Smith and Daniel O'Mahony all provided scripts. Also in the cast were Paul Darrow and Brian Croucher. 'They were good [stories], fun to do,'[170] Darrow said, while Croucher said, 'When Russell spoke to you he spoke to you as an actor. I love him in the best sense of the word, because nowadays people don't come into [acting] through drama school and local workshops. It's a different profession.'[171]

Bickerstaff performed in several of these productions and Hunter stayed at his London home during recording. The experience soon became a nostalgic one for Russell, revisiting one old role during the day and then happily viewing performances of another vintage part in the evenings. 'We watched every black and white episode of *Callan*,'[172] Bickerstaff recalled fondly. 'It was like having a live commentary. There was one episode he wasn't in [and] he turned round to me at the end and said, "Dear boy, can we just watch the ones with me in?", which I always thought was funny.'

Russell fell ill around this time but kept working. His acting deservedly received mainstream praise when the film *American Cousins* (2003), in which he appeared as a Glasgow chip shop owner suddenly having to accommodate Mafia relatives, won BAFTA and international awards. His final role on stage was in *Twelve Angry Men* in 2003, bringing his career full circle to the Edinburgh Festival Fringe. The following year, he passed away at Edinburgh Western General Hospital, on Thursday 26 February. 'During recording breaks, Russell used to keep all the actors entertained with his outrageous stories and wicked sense of humour,'[173] Alan Stevens paid tribute on the *Kaldor City* website. 'His ventriloquist act, performed without a dummy, had to be seen to be believed! He was a smashing actor and finally a very courageous human being.'

The press paid their respects, the *Scottish Herald* noting: 'He was a veteran Scottish stage star with the acting versatility to turn his hand to everything from Shakespeare to television and pantomime.'[174] David Bickerstaff recalled the funeral being very moving. 'I sat between Maurice Roëves and Graham Crowden. I remember being really upset, and Crowden, with his hand on my knee, saying, "Don't worry, laddie, don't worry." At the wake, they were serving shortbread and whisky, and it was a *Who's Who* of great actors, not just great Scottish actors – they were *all* there, to pay their respects to one of Scotland's finest.'[175]

Russell may never have quite achieved the levels of success that Edward Woodward did, but his always interesting choice of roles – realistic, whimsical, comedic, grotesque – and his consummate, diverse track record as a character actor have given him an abiding legacy. Of the character that remains the most enduring part of this history, Hunter simply said 'I think one of the best things Jimmy Mitchell ever wrote was "Lonely is Lonely is Lonely": he's just there and that's it. I believed in him totally. In the novels and in the very early scripts [he was] totally believable, because of the language he was given and his reaction to situations. I enjoyed him very much.'[176]

Edinburgh resident Garron Martin reported a story that, perhaps more than any other, summed up Hunter's distinctive personality. 'He bought the old CoOp store in Junction Street, and I remember he took the actor Tony Roper there. Tony asked [Russell], as he had a camp bed in one corner and all of this vast space of three floors, *what* was he going to do with it? Russell replied, "I'm gonna open a restaurant – but we are gonna be different – we're gonna sell nothin' but *pies!*" Tony asked, "Pies? What kind of pies?" "Well", Russell replied, "on the first floor, we're gonna sell steak pies, on the second floor we're gonna sell *fish* pies and on the third floor we're gonna sell *fruit* pies." Tony asked, "What about that wee bit up there on the roof at the top of the building?" "Ahh", said Russell, "That's special. That's where the bar is gonna be – that's where yeh go tae get PIE EYED!"'[177]

Anthony Valentine
Toby Meres (1967-69, 1972)

'I get blokes coming up to me, like this chap in Glasgow, who said, "I know you. You are not Callan, but I can sort you out." Even the car park attendant at Waterloo has looked me up and down and said he [doesn't] like my sort.'

Daily Mail, 14 January 1974

BORN ON 17 AUGUST 1939, Anthony Valentine had an unusual childhood, far removed from the glamour and sophistication of the acting roles he was best known for. He grew up in Blackburn, Lancashire, the son of parents who worked in a cotton mill, who were nonetheless open minded and keen for their son to improve his prospects in life. At the end of WW2, Valentine moved to London to train as an actor and by the remarkably young age of ten, he had already turned professional. 'My mother was always crazy about the pictures and she'd take me three times a week to see Gene Kelly and Fred Astaire,'[177] he remembered fondly. 'I wanted to be a dancer and I used to jump about the place, and this drove my dad mad, so he said, "If lad's going to jump around like that all the time, then get him bloody well trained." So I was sent to dancing lessons and used to perform at the local town hall sometimes. And it was while I was doing this [in a production of *Robin Hood* at Ealing Town Hall] that one of those peculiar creatures who I've never met since, spotted me – he was a talent scout.'

His theatre work led to a small part in the film *No Way Back* (1949, as 'Tony Valentine'), after which he 'just carried on' earning a living as a child actor by appearing in productions during British television's early years, 'playing a lot of boy-next-door, anyone-for-tennis sort of characters[178]... At first I used to sing on a children's programme called *Whirligig* [1950-56] while Steve Race played the piano, and then I moved on to roles [like] Harry Wharton in *Billy Bunter of Greyfriars School* [1955-57]. It was there that I had to say the classic line, "Roll along old fat man" every week.'[179] Anthony initially appeared in Frank Richards' famous sitcom as another character, Bob Cherry, until John Charlesworth, the actor who had originally played Wharton, left the cast.

Valentine alternated his early TV appearances with work on the stage. At thirteen, he joined Sadlers Wells as the lead singer in the children's chorus in a season of Italian and German operas. He also featured in the original stage productions of *Half a Sixpence*. 'It was a paralysing moment,'[180] he recalled of a bout of stage fright, 'standing there all alone on the Palladium stage with two thousand people in the house and thinking "My God, I've got to sing."' (While working on *Half a Sixpence*, he began a life-long friendship with the actor Tommy Steele, who would one day be his Best Man.) Anthony's charmed early life continued as the amount of acting work he was getting enabled him to drop out of Acton Courts Grammar School and be educated by a private tutor, an arrangement that continued until he was sixteen. At the same time, he made his West End debut as an adult actor opposite Bernard Braden in *Anniversary Waltz* (1955). When Valentine was between acting jobs, he made ends meet by playing guitar and singing in London's fashionable coffee bars or, by complete contrast, sometimes driving a bus.

At the same time, by his own admission the actor's relationship with alcohol brought out an aggressive, darker side to his personality. 'I started to drink when I was eighteen, just like the other boys. Beer I never did like, but I could drink whisky like there was no tomorrow. And straight away I began to do myself a bit of damage by picking on the wrong people to fight. And as I got older it got worse. I'd done some boxing at school, but that didn't prepare me for always going around being aggressive. I was stupid with it, too. The last time it happened really badly was when I was in my early 20s. I was with a bird in a pub in Westerham, one Sunday morning, giving her a lot of chat, and really fancying myself for the day.[181]

'Then when I went to get some drinks at the bar a couple of soldiers sat on either side of her. So when I got back and without even thinking I said "Right, no messing about, outside." One of them leant over to the other and said "I think he's talking to you, Charlie." And the other one said: "No, I think he means you." So I said, "Come on stop fooling around, *the pair of you* outside." That's just about all I remember, apart from the fact that they took their belts off first and there was a gravel forecourt to the pub. They really took me apart. I was in hospital for the next three days. A couple of times since then I've had a drink but it always ends up with me getting into trouble.' Valentine would sometimes be confronted by a belligerent member of the public, full of Dutch courage, keen to take him on in a fist fight but by 1972, he had learnt to walk away from trouble and he'd become teetotal.

'THERE WAS A LOT OF IRONY IN MY CAREER, actually,' Valentine observed in 1972. 'When I was little I had a very strong Lancashire accent and the very first thing I had to do was learn to lose it, because at that time you couldn't get work at the BBC unless you spoke nicely. It was virtually a collar and tie for rehearsals. And just about by the time I'd lost it the kitchen-sink, Northern drama thing began, and no one would believe that I could do it because they'd got used to seeing me in a blazer and flannels at Greyfriars. I think during that whole period of theatre – which must have lasted for about six years – I only got one of those parts.'

Despite his frustrations with the limited imagination of casting directors, Anthony continued to progress in his career in the late 1950s. Against the odds, in 1958 he appeared at London's Royal Court Theatre – often a forum for new, experimental dramatists – in Arnold Wesker's *Chicken Soup with Barley* as Ronnie, an idealistic Jewish Communist. In the same year, he won the role of Erhart in a prestigious *ITV Play of the Week* production of Henrik Ibsen's 'John Gabriel Borkman', with Laurence Oliver in the title role. From there, Valentine stayed with classical drama when he featured with the most promising talents of his acting generation in the BBC's landmark series of Shakespeare plays, *Age of Kings* (1960), as the Marques of Dorset and Sir John Mortimer. Also among the seminal cast were Sean Connery, Paul Daneman, Judi Dench, Julian Glover, Robert Hardy, Mary Morris, William Squire and Jerome Willis. After starring opposite veteran actor Trevor

Howard in John Mortimer's play *Two Stars for Comfort* in 1962, the following year Anthony returned to the cinema screen in an uncredited, adult role as a Teddy Boy in Joseph Losey's cult curio *The Damned*. By 1966, as an up-and-coming young actor, Valentine was offered a role opposite Caroline Mortimer in Hugo Charteris's 'The Wager', another of ABC's *Armchair Theatre* plays.

Because Anthony didn't fit with the fashionable clique of actors like Tom Courtenay and Michael Caine, whose careers benefited from a regional accent, the maturing actor went against current trends by cultivating an image of suave, well-spoken sophistication. This benefited the crime series *Riviera Police* (1965), as well as *Intrigue* (1966), the industrial espionage TV thriller created by Tony Williamson (one of the script writers on *The Avengers*.) It was this show, in the episode 'The Computer Didn't Confirm It', 'as a gentleman who tried to rape Caroline Mortimer', that led to arguably Valentine's most famous role: 'It was because of that I got the part of Toby Meres in *Callan*.'[182] In all, Valentine would co-star in 30 of the series' 43 episodes as the ex-Brigade of Guards officer, the third longest serving cast member after Edward Woodward and Russell Hunter.

Around the same time, Anthony featured in the second and third filmed series of *The Avengers*, firstly in 'The Bird Who Knew Too Much' (1967) as George Cunliffe, villain of the week 'the Commander', very obviously enjoying himself threatening Patrick Macnee with a fire axe. The following year he returned, this time as Calvin, an ill-fated colleague of John Steed's in 'Killer' (1968), fitting this into his by-now busy schedule during production of *Callan*'s second series. In the latter story, it's striking that he's dressed in a regimental blazer and tie, the favoured attire of Toby Meres.

The part of the Section agent put Valentine, at the age of 28, on the TV map. The popularity of his character, an ex-public school bully turned sadistic secret agent, led to the actor suddenly receiving both press coverage and public attention. Between 1967 and 1970, Valentine was living as a bachelor; at 24, he'd been in a relationship, but 'couldn't afford to keep myself, let alone keep the girl I was in love with.'[183] Consequently, his single status in the late 1960s attracted a lot of interest from the opposite sex, to the point where he was 'plagued by dozens of phone calls from twittering young girls, who giggle and hang up.'[184] Valentine regularly received a 'considerable' amount of provocative fan mail.

'The letters are what surprise me most of all,' the slightly bemused actor told the *Evening Standard*. 'Some are totally incredible. They range from the type that said "How about coming round to my place on Friday night, tying me up and whipping me!" to those who explain how they feel that what they need is a firm hand, that they like the way I treat women, that their husbands don't understand them, and that he's away at such and such a time... curiously, too, a favourite word among letter writers at the moment appears to be *spanking*. An awful lot of them want to be spanked.'

WHILE WORKING on *Callan*, Valentine forged a life-long friendship with his leading man Edward Woodward. Both came from humble origins, loved music and were accomplished singers, not to mention keen scuba divers and toupeé wearers. Valentine would often be invited to Woodward's holiday home in Northern Cyprus, where they'd go swimming and looking for exotic shells, one of Woodward's hobbies. 'Tony told me a story about when he went to stay in Teddy's [holiday] house,'[185] said scriptwriter Robert Banks Stewart. 'They went out on a boat and Teddy was always wearing a [hat] because he was bald. And then they went swimming, and he went over the side in the hat! He knew that Tony would be waiting for him to come up, so he came up on the other side of the boat, still wearing his hat and said, "Yeah, yeah, you almost caught me.'"

Being in the cast of *Callan* was an idyllic time for Valentine: 'I think that what we all felt about [the series] at the time we were doing it is that we were always – "desperate" is perhaps a slightly exaggerated word – always *deeply concerned*, in the best possible way, that it should be should be as *good* as it could possibly be because we all felt, without exception, that what we had on paper, in the scripts that came to us, were some of the best television writing that we'd ever personally known. I think that as an actor, when you're dealing with that, it's a bit like handling an important piece of china – you're not too careful, perhaps, about what you do with a cheap mug from a chain store, but if somebody hands you something and says "This is Ming" then you tend to treat it rather seriously, and we always wanted [*Callan*] to be absolutely superb, because we believed that the product was marvellous. And I suppose it's a hang-up that all actors have, that if you're handed something that you believe is worthy, there's a *tremendous passion,* a *tremendous* responsibility to give it its full worth and be as good as you should be, because the product deserves it.'[186]

What Banks Stewart calls Anthony's 'nasty little Etonian', like Russell Hunter's Lonely, was considered an essential part of the *Callan* ensemble. 'There was quite a good conflict relationship between [Anthony and Edward], on and off screen,'[187] Jim Goddard said. 'They were sort of vying for being in the piece, anyway: Teddy played it like a criminal, whereas Tony was a public schoolboy who'd naturally gone into this job. There was always conflict as [Meres] was slightly supercilious in his attitude to Callan, but maybe not such a high achiever in the job.' Trevor Preston was equally impressed: 'Valentine was a good guy – he was [playing] a nasty, seedy, real bastard. I think he [came across as] quite dangerous.'[188] Valentine himself summed up Meres' appeal by saying, 'The really frightening thing is that you just don't know which way he's going to jump. He can be a good chap in the bar having a drink one minute, and the next he's jamming a broken glass in your face.'[189]

Despite his good relationship with *Callan*'s actors and production team, when Valentine – by now 30 years old – was offered the opportunity to play the lead, Philip West, in the new colour BBC2 spy series, *Codename*, he took it; this precluded him appearing in the third series of *Callan*, which at that point had not been confirmed. Produced by Gerard Glaister and partly filmed on location in Portugal, *Codename* would prove to be a misstep in Anthony's career. On the whole, the critics weren't impressed with the show and the actor himself later considered it 'totally forgettable'[190], complaining in the press that he'd 'be playing spies or baddies all my life at the present rate.'[191] Valentine's unhappiness with the series was compounded by his ending of his romance with his co-star Alexandra Bastedo (who played the glamorous Diana Dalzell). At one point the couple had considered marriage, but, as Valentine later philosophically put it, 'everything went wrong between us.'[192]

There was some compensation when, in early 1971, Anthony's first major film role in *Performance* was released after a three-year delay. It was doubly rewarding because, for a fan of the Rolling Stones, it had meant working on the same project as the band's singer Mick Jagger, even if the two didn't share a scene. Donald Cammell and Nicolas Roeg's film was a fashionable mixture of London gangland and rock star decadence, personified respectively by the characters Chas (James Fox) and Turner (Jagger); it was hailed as 'a brilliant, ludicrous piece of work'[193] that was 'a fascinating hybrid of a film, often slipshod, occasionally grotesque and revolting.'[194] Among the psychedelic visuals and controversial sex, Anthony's performance as Joey Maddocks, the villain Chas murders, stands out, and is all the more notable because of his convincing cockney accent. Valentine was back on less contentious ground in Thames' legal drama *Justice* (1971-72), playing support to Margaret Lockwood's barrister Harriet Peterson; the pair also appeared together on the panel game *Whodunnit?* in 1974.

Valentine's fortunes continued to improve in the first few years of the 1970s after the false start of *Codename*. He began writing plays for television under an alias: 'At first I submitted [scripts] under my own name, and they were instantly turned down, because no one thinks actors can write... Now I use a pseudonym and I've had quite a lot of success.'[195] At the same time, always considered 'very much part of the production,'[196] Valentine returned to *Callan* to make several of the strongest stories in the series' run. Resuming his old partnership with Woodward was a delight for both actors and viewers, beginning with an electrifying scene in the episode 'First Refusal' as Meres and Callan are reunited for the first time since 'Death of a Hunter'. When *Callan* finished production in April 1972, Valentine went on to make a guest appearance in the BBC's rival espionage thriller *Spy Trap* (like Hunter actor William Squire), featuring as Edward Chance in the 1973 episode 'A Hero's Return'. By now, Anthony had earned enough to buy a cottage and live comfortably in picturesque Mortlake: 'When I think how my dad worked all his life, I can't believe my luck.'[197]

IN 1973 THE MAKERS OF *COLDITZ*, the WW2 drama series about the Germans' notorious prison[198], were looking for a new regular villain for its second season. With no fifth series of *Callan* forthcoming, Valentine was signed to play Major Horst Mohn, a Luftwaffe officer wounded in battle and transferred to Colditz as the new head of security. Like Meres before him, Mohn was a perfect fit for Valentine. His cruelty was mainly psychological instead of physical: Mohn broke wartime protocol by searching Red Cross parcels and by reading the letters sent to and received by the prisoners in his care, coolly, and memorably, insulting Flight Officer Simon Carter (David McCallum) with the remark, 'You write like a girl.' The TV reviewer in the *Daily Mail* was delighted, considering Valentine 'an actor for whom Nazi fanatics might have been invented... Major Mohn... could be a cliché, but too many people have taken the time to ensure he is not. There's a promising duel building up between him and David McCallum... full of class-war and emotional tension as well as the straight escape-or-die element.'[199] With the addition of, as Anthony put it, 'a highly decorated man who has been badly wounded and cannot fight any more,'[200] *Colditz*'s audience rose to eleven million. He, and the show, were a massive hit.

Mohn's story concluded with the remarkable episode 'Chameleon', written by Robert Muller. As the allied armies advance and the Third Reich begins to disintegrate, Mohn's beliefs are shaken and the indignities he inflicted on Colditz's inmates return to haunt him. The transformation from arrogant Nazi to a desperate, abandoned fugitive is one of Valentine's subtlest and most compelling performances, climaxing in the scene where Carter tells him that all the allied officers have signed a statement detailing his crimes. In the ultimate indignity, dressed in an anonymous suit, he is last seen clinging to the underside of a horse-drawn cart to escape his own prison.

'The thing about all these characters that fascinates me is not so much what you do as an actor, but what the audience reads into it,'[201] he said. 'In *Colditz* you would find less than half a dozen occasions when Mohn actually did something unpleasant. He never hit anyone, struck anyone in solitary confinement or threatened people. I've often thought it would be pertinent to ask the people who cast me in these parts why they see me as a nasty. It's whatever they feel as human beings that puts me in such roles.' Valentine felt his current, popular career path could be traced back to when he was a child actor. 'I remember when I did a telly show as a kid mother usually said: "I thought you were very good, but you don't smile enough. It changes your whole face when you smile." I used to try to explain: "But mum, I don't play smiling parts." You see, if I'd taken my mother's advice I would never have ended up playing nasty parts. I'd be known as Smiler Valentine.'

By the mid-1970s, the 'non-drinker who shuns film premieres, trendy clothes and fashionable venues' was rarely out of work – even finding time to provide the voiceover for a Fry's Turkish Delight advert – and was so busy that he couldn't return as Meres in the 1974 *Callan* movie. (The role was, ironically, taken by Anthony's long-time friend, Peter Egan.) 1975 was a good year: *Colditz* was repeated, and Valentine moved centre stage in 'The Crazy Kill', one of the productions in Brian Clemens' popular anthology series *Thriller*, as Garard, an escaped convict. Towards the end of the year, like Edward Woodward and Patrick Mower, Anthony starred in an *Armchair Cinema* (1973-75) TV film. 'Tully', centring on a stylish insurance investigator, was produced by Euston Films, Thames Television's newly created film-making venture. Euston's productions were an innovation for British TV; shot on 16mm film almost entirely on location and fast moving, they were an important step towards British TV competing with imported, slick, American shows such as *Columbo* (1968-2003) and *Kojak* (1973-78).

'Tully' looks a bit dubious today, as the middle-class English hero outsmarts his blue-collar Australian counterparts and their police force, beds an attractive Aussie girl and outwits the criminals. The plot is predictable by modern standards too, but overall the production shows how shrewd Euston Films were: the company arranged a co-production deal with the Australian Broadcasting Corporation that allowed for location shooting in Sydney, authentic overseas filming being a relative novelty for British television series in the mid-1970s. In a part perfectly tailored to his personality, Valentine carries the whole thing by being effortlessly charming, amusing, confident and by performing his own fight scenes. However, like all the 'pilots' made for *Armchair Cinema* apart from 'Regan' (1974), 'Tully' didn't become a series.

After providing a strong second lead to Hollywood actor Richard Widmark in Hammer Films' disturbing horror movie *To The Devil, A Daughter* (1976, as the boyfriend of Honor Blackman's Anna Foutain), Valentine was offered a starring role that could have been written for him. E.W. Hornung's stories about Arthur J. Raffles, an elegant 1900s gentleman about town who played cricket for England but was secretly an expert thief, was the flipside to Sherlock Holmes; with his friend Harry 'Bunny' Manders, the burglar delighted in stealing from the upper class social circle who feted him at their country estates and town houses. The mixture of aristocratic style and attractive villainy proved irresistible for Valentine, and following a pilot play, *Raffles* went into production as a thirteen part ITV series, written by Philip Mackie and screened in 1977. The channel clearly had high hopes for the series, granting it a *TV Times* cover and, every week in the listings magazine, a major publicity push.

Valentine was excellent: by turns amiable, witty, cunning and suave, his performance is a delight to watch as, like a dinner-suited Robin Hood, he regularly draws the wide-eyed Bunny (Christopher Strauli) into his criminal escapades. Unfortunately, the uneven tone of the the pilot – an uncertainty of dramatic and comic tone, thin plotting and leaden direction – persisted into the series, making it appear old-fashioned and static. Valentine found himself in the curious position of once again receiving flattering reviews but, ironically, for a series that was deeply flawed. The review in the *Daily Mail* was typical, praising him for '[epitomising] all those qualities easier to imagine than achieve, being genuinely debonair, disclosing devilment with the lift of an eyebrow,'[202] but condemning 'the launching story [for being] as weak as water.' Considering the series was a star vehicle for Anthony, it's notable that he didn't give interviews about *Raffles* in either the *TV Times* or national press, perhaps suggesting that he was as unhappy with the finished series as the critics were.

1979 WAS ANOTHER TURNING POINT for Valentine professionally. His decision to star in ATV's version of Ivor Novello's romantic musical *The Dancing Years*, about a penniless composer, Rudi, who falls in love with famous opera star when he's already promised himself to schoolgirl called Greta, was a deliberate break with the type of parts he had played in the past. 'I play the [non-singing] Novello part,'[203] Anthony said at the time. 'You can't ask for more variety of roles than that... [I've] done the hard gritty stuff.' Revealingly, he confessed to being a 'complete romantic and sentimentalist' and hoped 'people will have a good cry when they see it. I love a good weepie. I used to cry even at Lassie films, and I think most people are more romantic at heart than they are prepared to admit.'[204] *The Dancing Years* was a significant point in Valentine's personal life too, as he got married to one of the cast, Susan Skipper, on 7 July 1982. He remarked with typical charm, 'When you find someone you want to share things with, marriage seems eminently reasonable.'[205]

Into the 1980s and beyond, on television Valentine carved out an enviable niche for himself as a sought after guest star. His urbane, often steely charisma graced series like the comedy drama *Minder*, in which he made two appearances in 1979 and 1980 as Maurice Michaelson, a suave gambler who dropped his 'aitches. Other popular shows featuring him included the mystery anthology *Tales of the Unexpected* (in 1980 and 1982), detective drama *Bergerac* (1983), adventure series *Robin of Sherwood* (1984-85) as the sorcerer Simon De Belleme, *The Case-Book of Sherlock Holmes* - 'The Illustrious Client' (1991) as Baron Gruner, and BBC1's cold case drama *New Tricks* (2002). There were also recurring parts in the crime series *The Knock* (1994-96) as the criminal George Webster, the police series *The Commander* (2006-08) as the authoritarian Commissioner Sumpter and, his last TV role, George Wilson in *Coronation Street* (2009-10).

Like Edward Woodward he maintained his links with the theatre, with a diverse range, taking in Shakespeare – *Romeo and Juliet*, *Henry V* and *Macbeth* – modern comedy – *No Sex Please, We're British* and *Art*, with Peter Egan – and Jacobean tragedy, as a mesmerising, ruthless Monticelso in The Lyric Hammersith's 2000 production of *The White Devil* by John Webster (a play which Woodward had coincidentally starred in 30 years before). In the 2000s, Valentine became involved with The Mill Theatre at Sonning, as director and writer of *The Waiting Game*.[206] Among other productions, he staged Michael Frayn's provincial newspaper comedy *Alphabetical Order* (2007), concluding with Terence Rattigan's drama about loneliness *Separate Tables* (2012), the last stage role in which he featured as an actor. On 12 November 2005 there was a satisfying moment of career closure for Anthony, when he was honoured by being made patron of the Thwaites Empire Theatre in his home town of Blackburn.

Anthony Valentine died on 2 December 2015, after being diagnosed with Parkinson's disease in 2012. Like Edward Woodward, he was so highly regarded that his passing was reported by the UK's national news programmes, with *Callan* prominent in the obituaries which appeared in papers such as *The Guardian*, *The Stage* and *The Daily*

Telegraph, the latter noting the importance of Meres to the actor's career, as 'the role... established Valentine as television producers' baddie of choice.'[207] The *Telegraph* also reported that, like Woodward, Valentine could have had a career in Hollywood. In 1992 he made the pilot for the NBC thriller *The Fifth Corner*, featuring as a gangster called 'The Hat'. Unlike Woodward, however, Valentine chose to remain living in England, as making a full series 'would have meant complete upheaval of my life.' By the 1990s he clearly felt he didn't need to prove himself; having survived a near fatal attack of meningitis when he was 26, and the Turkish invasion of Cyprus in 1974, he believed 'everything since [had] been an incredible bonus.' Commenting on her husband's love of the written word, Suasan Valentine said, 'Anthony's writing was unique: a distinctive, economic style which was just brilliant.'[208]

Amongst his many, versatile appearances, for a certain generation and enthusiasts ofarchive television, Valentine will always be the definitive interpretation of the sinister Toby Meres. During the run of Channel 4 *Callan* repeats in 1984, the actor amusingly recalled chatting to a taxi driver, and the cabbie relating how he and his wife were avid viewers. 'I'll never forget it as long as I live, it's one of the funniest things I've ever heard,'[209] he said. 'It was done at the top of his voice, through the window, as we're driving down Regent Street. He said to me, " 'Ere, Mr Valentine, 'ave you bin watchin' that *Callan*? 'Ave you bin watchin' it? Well, what d'you think?" I said, "I don't know. I think it's alright."

"'Alright?!" he said. "Listen. I was sittin' there watchin' it with my wife and I said to 'er, 'What d'you think of that, then?' and she said to me, 'I love it, dun' I?' an' I said 'Well, I *know* you love it', I said, 'I love it too, but do you know *why* you love it?' and she said 'Well, I dunno what you mean' and I said, 'Well, what is it about it that you love?' and she said, 'Well, I mean I just love it,' and I said, 'Well, you've gotta be more analytical than that. *What is it that you love?'* 'I don't know.' I said, 'I'll tell you what you love,' I said, 'That programme is *fucking class*, that's what you love. FUCKING CLASS!'" I said, "I know what you mean," and he said, "That's the test of time, innit? You can look at stuff, very old stuff, and it's a load of fucking cobblers, but you get a bit of fucking class and it's *always* fucking class, innit?" And I said: "I think you're right."'

Part of that timeless quality is due to the contribution of the classy, witty and always very watchable Anthony Valentine.

Patrick Mower
James Cross (1970-72)

'In real life I'm a little boy, a joker. I get younger every year.
It's only acting, this tough guy image.'

'Mower the Merrier', Linda Hawkins,
TV Times, 15-24 September 1984.

P ATRICK ARCHIBALD MOWER was born on 12 September 1938 in the Rhondda Valley in Wales. That there's no official record of his birth is entirely due to his turbulent family background. His father, another Patrick, was a collier and self-confessed rogue, while his mother Peggy became amorously involved with various US airmen in WW2 when her husband was away in the army. The actor recalled there was little stability, either emotional or financial, as he was growing up.

The family, including young Patrick's brothers, Donald and Derek, moved to 86 Ridgefield Road in Cowley, Oxford, where their poverty was thrown into sharp relief against the more affluent areas within one of Britain's elite university towns. Two particularly humiliating memories for young Patrick during his attendance at St Mary and St John's infant schools were of him wearing clogs and of his mother's inventive attitude towards saving money on clothes: 'As there never seemed to be a penny in the house, our mother knitted trousers for Don and I to wear at school.'[210]

The return of his father on VE Day, 8 May 1945, did little to help the family's circumstances. Perhaps brutalised by his experiences in the war, Patrick's father became an angry, embittered man who started taking his frustrations out violently on his wife and children. However, the young Patrick was enterprising enough to escape from this domestic nightmare in two ways: he passed the Eleven Plus exam so he could attend Southfield Grammar School (even if he had to endure wearing a second hand uniform) and he became a member of St Mary and St John's Boys' Club, where he discovered the two passions that were to define his adult life: sport and acting. Like Edward Woodward, Mower forged an enduring friendship with a mentor figure outside the family home, in his case Father John Hemming.

While Patrick delighted in the camaraderie of football, cricket, basketball, bicycle speedway and rugby, he was also drawn to the team spirit of amateur plays. Owing to his ability to accurately imitate an American accent, he was asked to appear in a theatrical production directed by his friend Roy Copeman, an invitation Mower eagerly accepted. After speaking his first line of stage dialogue in the play at the age of 11 – 'Silas B Fortescue of the Baltimore Small Arms Company'[211] – he knew what he wanted to do with the rest of his life: '"Acting", it has famously been stated, "is the art of putting ourselves in a parallel universe,"' Mower said. 'At the tender age of eleven, I discovered that I could do precisely that.'[212]

By the time he was fifteen, Patrick was enrolled in three different drama groups in Oxford. There were acclaimed roles in an adaptation of Charles Dickens' *The Signalman* and an open-air production of *Much Ado About Nothing,* in which he was the youngest cast member. Despite clearly having the talent and ability to take A-levels and apply to RADA, his father's dislike of Mower's favoured profession forced his son into taking a local job, and he became a mechanical engineering draughtsman at the Pressed Steel Company in Cowley. Chris Jones, a work colleague, fondly remembered 'Archie' – as he was then known – appearing in local amateur dramatics productions in the evenings, and trying out different accents at work, at one point even pretending to be Irish at a meeting with one of the plant bosses, a gathering the workers usually referred to as the 'Monday morning bollocking'[213]. Mower kept his interests alive by running the St. Mary's and St. John's youth club in the evenings, directing the younger children in plays.

There was also romantic compensation for Mower in meeting the dark-haired and statuesque Audrey Giles. He was so enamoured that he joined the local Brett's Dance Academy just to get to know her. After a series of false starts, they began dating and, very much committed to each other, became engaged at seventeen. When they were married on 4 July 1957, Mower had a good job – perhaps for life – in the engineering industry. However, his desire for an acting career was still strong and, having already deferred a place at RADA to finish his apprenticeship, he reapplied and was awarded a scholarship on 1 October 1957.

Mower's time at RADA was a heady one. With more money than the other students, he and Audrey rented a two-roomed flat and would frequently entertain fellow ingénues and future acting luminaries such as John Hurt, Ian McShane, David Warner, Gemma Jones and Hywel Bennett. Patrick also made one of his best friends at the Academy in Michael Latimer, who shared Mower's first paid theatrical assignment when they were awarded £100 each for performing a song and dance routine. Older than the other students, Patrick was impatient to further his career and applied to the Shakespeare Memorial Theatre Company – like Edward Woodward before him – in 1961. Even though Mower was accepted, with the offer of a possible role in *Julius Caesar,* he ultimately turned it down and his first professional engagement on stage became the musical *House of Cards* at London's Phoenix Theatre. In quick succession, Mower featured in the original West End production of *Alfie,* as well as Henrik Ibsen's *John Gabriel Borkman* with Donald Wolfit and Flora Robson (coincidentally, Anthony Valentine had been in the 1958 TV version). At home, things were going equally well with the birth of two children, Simon in 1964 and Claudia in 1966.

MOWER'S ACTING was part of the new style of naturalistic performance typified by emerging stars like Tom Courtenay, Susannah York and Albert Finney in the late 1950s and early 1960s. It wasn't long before TV casting directors were asking to see the actor with the lean, slightly cruel Celtic looks; his first major role was as Kenneth Wiley in the BBC's twice-weekly satirical soap opera *Swizzlewick* (1964). Among other guest spots in *Z Cars, Riviera Police* and *The Wednesday Thriller* – 'The Lift', all in 1965, was a significant supporting role in *The Avengers* (1961-69). Mower was suave and menacing as the university bully Eric Duboys in the episode 'A Sense of History'. Despite his aspirations to become a respected stage actor – at the time, TV was still felt by many in the acting profession to be the poor relation to the theatre – he was enticed back to ABC. 'Dodo Watts, who was the head casting lady at the time, had seen me in a production of *Edward II*, playing Young Mortimer,'[214] Mower recalled. 'She told Michael Chapman, who eventually became the producer of *The Bill* [1984-2010], to come and see me with a view to playing this character called Michael West in a TV series called *Haunted*. He saw me, and liked me, so I played the part. This was when I first met Lloyd Shirley, who was Head of Drama at the time: a lovely character.

'We did [eight] episodes of *Haunted* where I played a university lecturer investigating "things that went bump in the night",' Mower explained. 'The problem was it went out on Saturday night, just when the BBC [started showing] football matches! So we were up against sport, but [the series] was still [relatively] successful. Lloyd Shirley invited me and my agent at the time, Philip Peerman, in, to say they were doing a new series called *Frontier* [1968] set in India and there was a marvellous part in it that they wanted me to play, and also that they wanted to do another series of *Haunted*. What they didn't know at the time was that the BBC were talking to me as well! In the end, my agent said "What do you really want to do?" I said, "I quite like the character in *Haunted*", and so we chose that over *Frontier*. Then ABC [became] Thames, and they decided, in their wisdom, that they weren't going to do any more *Haunted*. They'd started *Frontier*, so we couldn't do that. Thames then offered me another series, playing a magician[215]... We thought about that, but without sounding conceited, at the time I was being offered a lot of work.'

One of these offers was an invitation to a meeting in 1968 to discuss a fourth film about the spy Harry Palmer, based on Len Deighton's 1963 novel *Horse Under Water*.[216] The interview would take an unexpected turn for the aspiring young actor. 'They saw me for it, and I said, "I don't want to play Michael Caine with the glasses",' Mower said, understandably. 'They said "No, no, we're not doing that – the Michael Caine Harry Palmer is dead but they bring in a new spy with the same name." I said, "Oh, that sounds quite good". Dyson Lovell was the casting director and downstairs were people like Ian Holm. They had the top eight [actors] down in this waiting room, and there was a knock on the door as we were talking about *Horse Under Water*, and it was [James Bond film producers] Harry Saltzman and Cubby Broccoli. Dyson Lovell said, "Is everything OK?" and Harry Saltzman said, "Yes, don't worry." What I didn't realise was, all these other actors were waiting while Harry was talking to me, then Cubby's wife came in to check me out, and they kept me in that office for over half an hour.' A puzzled Mower handed his home number to Saltzman, who rang him on a Saturday night and arranged a meeting for the following morning. 'I went into the office and Harry and Cubby were both there, and they said "Patrick, do you know the Bond films?" "Yes." Then they said, "This is strictly between us." I was the first person to know about Sean Connery leaving. At the time, the films were incredible and he was a superstar, and they were saying, "Sean doesn't want to do any more Bonds," and I said "What?!" [then] "Who are you going to get as a replacement?" They were both looking at me and then the penny dropped.

'It's the gospel truth,' he insisted. 'I was sworn to secrecy. They'd seen me for this other film and suddenly thought of me from the way I looked.' Despite being offered the most famous role in British cinema, Mower felt his insecurity about accepting James Bond subsequently let him down. 'At the time – I think I was 28 – I thought of myself as a boy. Sean Connery was a *man*, a big man who played Bond. At the time, I thought it was silly and I talked myself out of it, but looking back at things like *Callan* and *Special Branch*,

I can now see what they saw in me. I couldn't see it at the time.' Ironically, the lead role in the next Bond film, 1969's *On Her Majesty's Secret Service*, went to 29 year-old George Lazenby.

Mower's secret association with Bond would continue throughout the tenure of Lazenby's eventual replacement Roger Moore. 'I saw [the Bond producers] before Roger was cast and I saw them again when he wouldn't sign [a new] contract,' Mower revealed. 'They had a picture of Roger at Cannes without his face because he wouldn't sign! That time I saw Cubby and Michael G. Wilson and Barbara Broccoli; I think Harry had [gone] by then. Roger wanted a contract for three films and they said, "We think he's too old and only got one more film in him. He won't do this next film unless we give him a contract for three", but then Roger did sign the contract. So I was *nearly* Bond. Every actor you speak to of that era says they were up for Bond, but I was that man. I knew what was going on. I was first reserve for about four years.'

Away from this frustrating brush with film superstardom, at the end of the 1960s Mower continued to add to his CV with guest roles in TV series like *Mystery and Imagination* (in 1970), *Paul Temple* (1971) and *UFO* (1970). He also provided solid performances in films such as *The Devil Rides Out* (1968), *The Smashing Bird I Used to Know* (1969), *Cry of the Banshee* (1970) and *Incense for the Damned* (1972) which latter also featuring Edward Woodward.

At the turn of the decade, he became associated with the espionage genre again, both in the superior caper movie *To Catch a Spy* (1971), recommended for 'an ingenious plot, full of nice little comic flashes, with double-agents everywhere'[216], and as a new foil replacing Anthony Valentine's character in *Callan*. (In 1970, both actors had featured in the same *Department S* episode, 'The Soup of the Day', although they didn't share a scene).

IT'S APPROPRIATE that the *Callan* episodes Mower appeared in began transmission in early 1970, as the decade would prove to be one of the actor's most successful periods as an actor. Firstly, he became nationally popular because of his portrayal of the Section agent James Cross, christened 'The Man We Love to Hate' by the popular press. The character triggered the formation of the Patrick Mower Fan Club, members of whom – almost exclusively female – were sent a photograph of a smiling Mower dressed in a style that would have seen him fit easily into the shaggy haired, wide lapel-flapping pop groups of the time like Slade or Roxy Music. Somehow, Mower's face fitted the 1970s, and by the time of *Special Branch* in 1973, his fan club had grown to 15,000 members, while he had changed his phone number to avoid being contacted by female admirers.

Aware of his good luck in landing a prestigious series with a highly respected cast, Mower recalled that '*Callan* [was] a show that transformed Britain's viewing habits. The streets emptied as everyone went home to watch [it].'[217] The working environment on the series was also to the actor's liking, as it was similar to his first love, the theatre. '*Callan* was very much done as a stage production which was why it was so good.'[219]

After Cross was killed off in the episode 'If He Can, So Could I', the reaction, at a time when Britain only had three terrestrial TV channels, was highly newsworthy. Mower had moved on to more work, and recalled, 'At the time, I was playing my favourite role, Jack Tanner, in *Man and Superman* by George Bernard Shaw, and I'd grown a full beard for it. We'd opened a new Birmingham rep theatre, it was a very big production, and when the episode went out, this chap in the wings was calling and saying "The papers are on the phone for you, Patrick." They were all ringing up! Eamonn Andrews used to have a chat show and they flew me back from Birmingham [to London] to do it to prove that I was still alive, because some people actually thought that Patrick Mower was dead! I went to the studio and I saw Eamonn and he came over to me and said "Patrick, would you mind shaving the beard off?" just before we did the interview. I asked why, and he said "On the show last night you didn't have a beard, and now you've got a beard, so it's going to confuse the viewers". I said "No, I can't shave it off, because I'm in the George Bernard Shaw play!"' During the furore over Cross's demise, someone even scrawled 'Cross Lives' (imitating the famous 'Callan Lives' graffiti of 1969) in the dirt on Mower's 2.4-litre Jaguar, scratching the paint with the same words. When the actor sold the car to a dealer for £350, Mower was later told by the very happy salesman that because of the ingrained slogan, he'd sold it on for £1,000; it was a sign of how popular he'd become.

If sustained success eluded Mower in the cinema in the 1970s, on television he was now a household name, making the cover of ITV's *TV Times* to publicise his next starring role. Lloyd Shirley cast Patrick opposite George Sewell in the revamped *Special Branch*; featuring the arm of the police that deals with political crime, this show had previously been a videotaped Thames production starring Derren Nesbitt, but was now becoming an all-film show, the first to be made by Euston Films.

'I was brought into *Special Branch* to do a similar thing to *Callan*,' Mower said. 'Lloyd Shirley took me out to dinner [after] they'd shot three. [The producer] Geoffrey Gilbert was there as well.' The meeting began formally until Lloyd interrupted proceedings with his characteristic bluntness: '"Cut the crap. Listen, Pat, we've got this guy we thought was going to be a star, but we don't think he's heavy enough to carry the series. We want you to come in, grab the show by the balls, and give it a kick up the ass!" I was brought into that series to do exactly the same thing as James Cross was brought in to do, to be a catalyst, to shake it up, to be the one who was treading on people's toes. People thought there might have been friction between me and George Sewell, but off-screen there wasn't.' Mower was also assigned the writers Tom Brennan and Roy Bottomley to specifically develop Patrick's character, DCI Tom Haggerty.

Special Branch was a success, running to two series in 1973 and 1974 (even though incoming producer Ted Childs and others felt it wasn't an accurate representation of policing.) For Mower, being a nationally-recognised face was by now becoming problematic. By his own admission, he was frequently unfaithful to Audrey and on occasions, like Anthony Valentine, he was confronted by members of the public wanting to take on a TV hard man; one such incident ended in him being stabbed outside Tokyo Joe's, a night club in Kensington. At the same time, fame brought him more work, such as being a regular panellist on the crime panel game *Whodunnit?* (1972-78) and lucrative adverts for Dunhill cigarettes and Top Shop. In common with other TV cop (and TV spy) actors of the period, Mower released the seemingly obligatory pop single, 'My Imagination', although with only 30,000 copies pressed, it was 10,000 under the amount needed to enter the UK Top 40.

In 1975, the actor was still well known at Euston Films and under the former *Callan* team of story editor John Kershaw and producer Reg Collin, he played Ian Bell, an idealistic doctor working in London, in the feature-length drama 'In Sickness and in Health' for the *Armchair Cinema* anthology series. The part was intended to initiate another star vehicle for Mower, but at the time he felt he had become a victim of his own success: 'That was going to be a series; we had lunches and dinners and talked about it.

We did the pilot, and everybody said, "This is good, it's going to be a goer," but there was so many things going on at the time. I was offered a contract by Michael Carreras at Hammer Films. I've always done a lot of theatre. I didn't know which direction to go... It's like having balls in the air: you have to catch the right one and that's always been tricky.'

While Mower made a conscious decision to seek other, less commercial work, taking roles in television productions of *King Lear* (1974) and *Peer Gynt* (1976), *Special Branch* was replaced by *The Sweeney*, a series about the Metropolitan Police's elite Flying Squad that fights violent crime. This time, cinematic production values, fast editing and action scenes were combined with muscular scripts that caught the authentic feel of life in London's underworld, and the show was a critical and ratings success. Familiar with Euston's fast production style, Mower was invited to play Colin McGruder along-side George Layton as Ray Stagpole. Introduced in 'Golden Fleece' and played in an enjoyably tongue-in-cheek manner, this pair of wise-cracking, gun-toting Australian criminals were the first villains in *The Sweeney* to face a rematch with DI Regan (John Thaw) and DS Carter (Dennis Waterman), in the story 'Trojan Bus'.

For the third series, it was even proposed that the pair would be sprung from prison by Colin's sister, played by Patrick's friend Anouska Hempel. However, the popularity of the Aussie duo wasn't universally appreciated by the regular cast. 'A directive came down from Thaw and Waterman that if we did [a third story], they weren't coming in!'[220] Col and Ray's creator, the writer Roger Marshall, recalled. 'They said, quite rightly, "Come on, it's *our* show!"' Even so, the potential of Mower and Layton's partnership was apparent to other people in the television industry. 'Somebody rang from the BBC who'd worked at Thames,' Marshall elaborated, 'and said, "There's a helluva good idea for a series there, have you thought about it? Would you be interested if I punted it around?" I said yes and of course never heard another thing.' It seems that the anonymous BBC executive's enthusiasm was well placed, as 'Golden Fleece' director David Wickes recalled that 'Pat said to me, only a few years ago, that people still come up to him and say, "Why wasn't that a series?"'[221]

In 1976, while filming *Carry On England*, a late entry in the bawdy comedy film series being made at Pinewood Studios, Mower met actress and model Suzanne Danielle. He left Audrey and began a relationship with Suzanne, despite initially negative tabloid coverage. A new phase of his life had begun; he started turning down most celebrity guest appearances and advertisements although he would model Burton suits in 1979. The first outcome of this new direction was one of the leading roles in Tom Stoppard's *Night and Day* at his old stamping ground the Phoenix Theatre, where he starred for nine months.

As part of Mower's resolve to take on more challenging work, he couldn't resist the leading role in *Target*, the BBC's own take on *The Sweeney*, stepping in at short notice after the lead actor originally cast dropped out.[222] Unfortunately, the culture of the BBC wasn't quite ready for a fast-moving film series. Mower noted the camera operator Ken Westbury had been filming tennis a week before he found himself on a dynamic drama and wasn't quick enough to cover the action scenes; equally, the make-up artist would have preferred to be working on the children's sho w *Jackanory* [1965-96, 2006]. Used to Euston's 'kick bollock and scramble' approach, Mower recalled being 'horrified as I watched [David] Wickes going hoarse, screaming at these amateurs as he battled to shoot the first episode in ten days.'[223]

As Superintendent Steve Hackett, Mower's assignments were generally even more aggressive than those pursued by *The Sweeney*. One episode has a pan of boiling water being thrown over a naked woman (mercifully, the action cuts away) while others feature a young woman vomiting from heroin withdrawal and another being violently machine-gunned. In trying to out-do *The Sweeney*, it was felt that without that series' authentic storytelling and sharply humorous dialogue, *Target* was beyond the pale. Criticism came from a police officer castigating the first episode 'Shipment' in the letters pages of the *Radio Times* – 'The whole programme was full of technical errors, and the scene in the restaurant [in which Hackett smears meat on a villain's face] was the final insult to all serving and ex-policemen'[224] and even David Wickes, poached from Euston Films, felt 'we never got the right characterisation and we never got the right stories.'[225]

The most influential voice of criticism, however, came from the National Viewers and Listeners Association (NVLA), a Christian pressure group run by the 'clean up TV' campaigner Mary Whitehouse. The BBC, a public service broadcaster, had to be seen to respond to criticism. The NVLA petitioned its members to write to the BBC's Director General Alasdair Milne demanding that *Target* should be cancelled. With 5,000 letters apparently received and with the BBC having already given in to complaints from Whitehouse about the level of violence in *Doctor Who*, *Target* was axed. This was despite Mower's claim that the BBC and his agent had received 'hundreds'[226] of other letters in support, together with an improvement in the standard of scripts for the second series in 1979. The last television series to feature Mower as a leading man, *Target* was a controversial end to his populist career in the 1970s.

AS MOWER WAS BLESSED with an optimistic and robust nature, the failure of *Target* didn't demoralise him for long. As the 1970s gave way to 1980s, he and Suzanne mixed with the likes of Elton John, George Best and Hurricane Higgins in nightclubs such as Tramp in Jermyn Street. The couple also toured New Zealand together in *Monkey Walk*, a two-handed stage comedy, and while there Patrick turned down a part in the Australian soap opera *Skyways* (1979-1981) despite the producers agreeing to pay him $200,000 dollars for six months' work. Back in England, in 1982 Mower repeated his double-act act with Suzanne in the final episode of the off-beat police series *Strangers*, demonstrating his flair for accents as the roguish Irish criminal Brendan O'Halloran.

Mower was recalled in 1984 by his old employers Euston Films to guest star in 'A Number of Old Wives' Tales', an episode of *Minder*. 'Confident', Patrick's character, wasn't a million miles away from the personality of the actor playing him. 'Confident's a real Jack-the-Lad, but lovable with it,'[226] Mower said at the time. 'He can't have an affair. He falls in love with a girl and marries her and afterwards he thinks, "Oh God, I've done it again!"'

Throughout the 1980s, Mower looked to Europe and America to expand his acting horizons, with mixed success. He was Father Damian in a seventeen-part Italian TV series of *Marco Polo* (1982-3); then he lost out to Gabriel Byrne in playing Christopher Columbus in the series of the same name in 1985. Work on the BBC supernatural thriller *The Dark Side of The Sun* (1983) took him to Rhodes, and he enjoyed himself as Montalvo, the heartless governor of a Mexican prison in the film *Escape from El Diablo* (1983), even though it made little impression internationally. At the same time, he was philosophical when a visit to Los Angeles to kick start his film career came to nothing (at the time, his old *Callan* partner Edward Woodward was becoming a major Stateside success in *The Equalizer*).

After seven years, his relationship with Suzanne ended and he returned to the single life.

Away from television and film, Mower delighted in his love of stage acting, a career path that would have far-reaching effects on his life. Apart from demonstrating his range in plays as varied as *Wife Begins at Forty*, *Verdict*, *Crazy for You*, *The Seven Year Itch*, *Don Juan*, *Lady Chatterley's Lover* (featuring controversial naked love scenes with Irina Brook), he met his second wife Anya Pope, an art student working on a production of *Death by Misadventure*, at the Liverpool Playhouse. Patrick candidly admitted 'It was love at first sight, a life-transforming experience which has brought me the deepest joy ever since.'[229] The 30 years-plus age gap bothered neither of them; a son, Maxim, followed after their marriage in 1997.

At the same time that he found domestic contentment with Anya, Mower's TV career began a renaissance, when his friend David Wickes cast him in a guest role in *CI5: The New Professionals*. For long-term followers of the actor, it was pleasing to see the old Callan/Cross rivalry revisited in the feud between Edward Woodward's Commander Malone and his ex-colleague, Mower's Jason Dane, now a revenge-hungry terrorist, in the episode 'Samurai Wind'. Mower is convincing, assured, cultured, polite and in control right from the start, a mastermind skilfully manipulating events; like Woodward, he rises above the clichés in the dialogue. The final confrontation between the pair alludes to the old rivalry between Callan and Cross – another younger man jealous of the top agent in his intelligence organisation – and the feud ends with satisfying amount of gore, as Dane is decapitated by the spinning rotor blades of a helicopter. In the same year that *CI5: The New Professionals* was in production, Mower finally got his long-cherished wish to star in a movie, in director Tinto Brass's erotic drama *Monella* (1998), about a French chef and his complicated love life.

Not long afterwards, like many of his generation of actors Patrick was courted by three UK soap operas – *EastEnders* (1985-), the revived *Crossroads* (2001-3) and his mother's favourite TV series, *Emmerdale* (1972-). Mower wryly acknowledged that the part on offer in the latter, millionaire rogue and womaniser Rodney Blackstock 'could be autobiographical'[228], and after a screen test the role was his. Since 2005, he has been delighting a new audience with a variety of romantic liaisons with the women of *Emmerdale*, one as young as 26.[230]

'I've enjoyed most of the things I've done,'[231] Mower amiably reflected. 'I did like [one of the] first things I did, *Haunted*. I've always liked that character: I was a university lecturer investigating the paranormal, whether it was telekinesis or the mind. Somebody was working on a script similar to that, a bit like a time traveller – not *Doctor Who* – but someone who was living forever as his body rate had slowed down. It had some really good ideas, but it didn't really come off [and] sadly it never got made.'

Despite any disappointments over his working life, Patrick Mower has proved himself to be an eclectic actor. Lazy journalism might still cast him as a 1970s playboy, but a closer look at his career reveals a man as at home in classical drama, comedy and musicals as he is in a car chase or a fist-fight. In particular, his performance as Cross reveals an actor of considerable intelligence and understatement, a quality sometimes obscured by his tabloid image. At the same time, Mower's renaissance as 'Rodders' Blackstock shows there will always be a place on British television for a lovable rogue. There's certainly no veteran actor better qualified to play one.

2: COLD WARRIORS

'Munro is writing of the end of innocence, of the
new era in which CIAs, Special Services and SMERSH
live by their own laws so that others may live or die.
But Munro has installed a giant brain in the smooth James
Bond machine, and added a half heart and semi-soul
to John le Carré's burned-out Leamas.'

Playboy review of *The Man Who Sold Death,* 1965

THERE'S A MOMENT IN THE BEATLES' cartoon feature film *Yellow Submarine* (1968) when Old Fred is fleeing from Pepperland because of an invasion by marauding Blue Meanies. He joins Beatles drummer Ringo to look for help from a room full of iconic figures, amongst them The Phantom, General Custer and Fred Astaire. Standing with these assorted heroes is a dapper gentleman in a tailored three-piece suit, complemented by a bowler hat and furled umbrella – cool, suave secret agent John Steed, accompanied by his assistant Tara King, from the Associated British Corporation's TV series *The Avengers*, which by the late 1960s had been successfully sold to America and was being shot on vibrant, 35mm colour film. This chapter explores the way in which the shadowy profession of espionage came to captivate the public imagination of '60s Britain through literature, cinema and television, setting the scene for the arrival of *Callan*.

ESPIONAGE FICTION HAS ALWAYS BEEN a genre intimately connected to the political and social mood of the time. Rudyard Kipling and Joseph Conrad, two novelists working at the beginning of the 20th century, understood this very well when they helped shape the character of the modern spy. Published in serialised instalments over 1900 and 1901, Kipling's *Kim* tells the story of an orphaned boy called Kimball O'Hara, recruited as an undercover agent during the British Empire's colonial occupation of India. Kim has one of the essential skills of espionage: the ability to infiltrate the opposition under a false identity. Significantly, he also comes from a vaguely scandalous, humble background (half Irish, half Indian).

He shares these characteristics with Verloc and Razumov, the protagonists of Conrad's stories *The Secret Agent* (adapted for television by ITV in 2016) and *Under Western Eyes*, which again originally appeared in serialised form, between 1906 and 1911. The two

East Europeans are involved in domestic terrorism, although for different reasons. Vladimir, a diplomat working for a deliberately unspecified foreign Embassy in London, employs Verloc. On Vladimir's orders, Verloc infiltrates anarchist groups in London with the aim of creating a srevolutionary outrage – a bomb attack on Greenwich Observatory, which kills his wife's brother.[2] Razumov, a student, shields Victor Haldin, a political assassin on the run from the Russian authorities, later betraying him. Razumov's life becomes emotionally complicated when he falls in love with Natalia, Haldin's sister.

Kipling and Conrad paint vivid portraits of the contemporary worlds in which their spies operate, from villages in rural India to the London slums. Conrad's stories, however, have a different feel to Kipling's: Kim approaches his espionage work with an uncomplicated eagerness, while Conrad's characters incur psychological and physical damage because of their occupation. The contrast between the two writers' styles – escapist and realist – laid down foundations for the genre, that were successfully built on as spy fiction developed over the coming century.

Kipling and Conrad's underprivileged characters weren't typical of their colleagues. In the early years of English espionage storytelling the profession was viewed as an unsavoury, un-gentlemanly occupation that, ironically, could only be dealt with by gentlemen. By contrast with Kim and Verloc, other fictional protagonists came from the privileged classes and were often moneyed, talented amateurs or ex-servicemen. The enigmatic private detective Sherlock Holmes, created by Arthur Conan Doyle, was a template for the form: intelligent, adaptable, sporting, physically fit and courageous. These qualities appeared in a variety of subsequent characters: Carruthers and Davies in *The Riddle of the Sands* (1903) by Erskine Childers; Denis Nayland Smith in the Fu Manchu stories by Sax Rohmer, and Richard Hannay, created by John Buchan for 1915's *The Thirty-Nine Steps*. The literary merit of Buchan's novel ensured that it stood out from the rest of the genre, attracting positive and serious critical appraisal. Rohmer's stories exaggerated the supposed threat against the British Empire from Far East through the creation of a Chinese master criminal, while Buchan pitched his gentleman adventurer against German spies attempting to steal British military secrets before the outbreak of hostilities (WW1 had been raging for a year when his book was published).

IN REALITY, THE PROTECTION OF THE CROWN'S security could not be entrusted to amateur adventurers, however resourceful or patriotic. In 1909, the Secret Service Bureau (SSB) was established under the command of the Admiralty and the War Office, formalising the gathering of intelligence from foreign dominions as well as dealing with counter-espionage within the British Isles. Its creation was primarily instigated by the threat posed by Germany, who declared war on the British Empire and its allies in August 1914. In 1916, the overseas division of the SSB became the 'Directorate of Military Intelligence 6' – MI6 – while the domestic office became the 'Directorate of Military Intelligence 5', MI5. This latter organisation, in collaboration with Special Branch (the division of the Metropolitan Police that deals with political crime), was initially responsible for the identification of foreign spies. After the war, MI5's duties became more wide-ranging and controversial: they kept trade unions and political groups under surveillance (such as pacifist organisations) and acted against Communist agents and the Irish Republican Army (IRA). MI6's activities were lower key; they collected intelligence from occupied and neutral countries and kept a watchful eye on Russia, which – worryingly as far as British, European and American governments were concerned – had become the world's first Communist state after the 'October Revolution' of 1917.

After WW1, fictional spy heroes were initially as foursquare as before but change was in the air, thanks largely to writers who had first-hand experience of intelligence work. The upright Roland Standish, devised by Herman Cyril ('Sapper') McNeile, first appeared in 1920; Captain Hugh 'Bulldog' Drummond, an ex-infantryman and amateur boxer who became the hero of his own series of popular novels, started life by assisting his friend Standish in his books. By contrast with escapist heroes like McNeile's, W. Somerset Maugham drew on his personal experience of working for British intelligence during WW1, which he described as 'on the whole monotonous... Fact is a poor storyteller.'[3] Maugham presented a detailed, matter-of-fact look at the covert world through *Ashenden* (1928), or its alternative title *The British Agent*. Innovatively, the spymaster was portrayed as a dedicated professional operating in a world where much is routine apart from the occasional dramatic incident. Eric Ambler developed this approach further; his stories *The Dark Frontier* (1936) and *Journey into Fear* (1940) used the premise of an amateur Englishman drawn into international intrigue on the eve of WW2. Like Buchan, Maugham and Ambler assisted in developing the critical respectability of spy fiction, and Graham Greene, one of the most widely-read authors of the twentieth century, helped that appreciation to grow even more. Greene had worked in intelligence when attached to the British Foreign Office, and wrote about moral issues in political settings. In *The Confidential Agent* (1939), a middle-aged professor known as 'D' is sent on a mission to England at the time Communists and Fascists were slaughtering each other in the Spanish Civil War; in Greene's later *Our Man in Havana* (1958), he examined the political tensions in Cuba before the rise of the Castro administration.

Greene also wrote for the cinema, which had been adapting espionage novels since its early days. Sax Rohmer's stories of conflicts between Nayland Smith and Fu Manchu were the subject of over twenty films from 1922 onwards; Sapper's creation, Bulldog Drummond, was similarly adapted and premiered in the cinema that year, initially with Carlyle Blackwell in the (silent) part. Arguably, however, auteur director Alfred Hitchcock did the most to popularise the genre in the cinema, bringing the works of Buchan, Maugham and Conrad to the screen in addition to original screenplays such as *The Man Who Knew Too Much* (1934), *The Lady Vanishes* (1938) and *Foreign Correspondent* (1940), the latter featuring a young American reporter in conflict with Nazi agents in London.

DURING WW2, INTELLIGENCE OPERATIONS were a cornerstone of the fight against Nazi Germany. MI6's Section D, which dealt with the application of sabotage, propaganda and other covert techniques during wartime, was merged with the GS(R) (later renamed MI(R)), which researched guerrilla warfare. The resulting Special Operations Executive (SOE) was formally created on 22 July 1940 to, in British Prime Minister Winston Churchill's words, 'set Europe ablaze'[4]. The SOE's agents were a curious mixture. In wartime, it seemed, no political or social groups were off-limits for recruitment and the organisation employed Communists, anti-British nationals, criminals, soldiers with bad service records and homosexuals (while homosexual acts were still illegal in British law) among its ranks. SOE personnel were regularly sent into occupied Europe to commit sabotage or liaise with resistance groups.

After the defeat of Nazi Germany and Imperial Japan in 1945, relations between the Union of Soviet Socialist Republics (USSR) – Russia and its satellite states – and the Western Allies quickly deteriorated. In February 1946, the Russian premier Joseph Stalin made a provocative statement about his former Western partners: 'The development of world capitalism proceeds not in the path of smooth and even progress but through crisis and catastrophes of war.'[5] This antagonistic relationship polarised further when, after the USA, Russia became the world's second nuclear power in 1949, using classified information supplied by the physicist Klaus Fuchs. The international climate then became even more complex as Russia began to 'de-Stalinise' in 1956 following its leader's death, causing a rift with Communist China, which was still committed to the personality cult of their Communist party chairman, Mao Tse-Tung; in 1964, China also became a nuclear power.

With the very real possibility of nuclear annihilation in a Third World War, the struggle between Communism and capitalism shifted towards conflicts by proxy in which espionage could provide advantages for either side. This shift in focus coincided with the creation of a new character that changed forever the perception of the secret agent in popular culture. Inspired by the charismatic operatives of the SOE, ex-Naval Intelligence officer Ian Fleming's first novel *Casino Royale*, published in 1953, introduced the fantasy figure of former Royal Navy Commander James Bond to the world; agent 007[6] was a far cry from the gentlemanly spies of Buchan and McNeile, being officer class (rather than 'other ranks'[7] like Ashenden) and licensed to kill by Her Majesty's Secret Service. Fleming capitalised on the public interest aroused by MI5 and MI6's place in the 'Cold War' opposing Communist infiltration and revolution, and he fostered the idea that such a shadowy world was glamorous and exciting as well as dangerous. Over the course of the 1950s, the popularity of Bond, and spy fiction generally, was enhanced by the public interest in the escape of the Soviet agents Guy Burgess and Donald Maclean.

In contrast with these and other real spy scandals, the Bond books were an intoxicating mixture of patriotism, sex and violence that, for many readers, made a welcome escape from post-war austerity in the UK. Bond's adventures took place in exotic locales such as the Bahamas, Istanbul and on the French Riviera. One perceptive critic astutely defined the author's appeal: 'by reason of his cool and analytical intelligence, his informed use of technical facts, his plausibility, sense of pace, brilliant descriptive powers and superb imagination, [Fleming] provides sheer entertainment.'[8]

SHORN OF THEIR MORE SALACIOUS ASPECTS for a family television audience, Fleming's books were an obvious source of inspiration for one of Britain's first TV spy series, the Independent Television Company (ITC) production *Danger Man* (1960-62,1964-66). One source suggests Fleming was involved in the project early on, in an attempt to launch a TV version of James Bond[9]. In the first series, which began transmission in 1960, Fleming's concept of a globetrotting[10] secret agent was now symbolised by the figure of John Drake, played with a trans-Atlantic, Irish-American accent by the enigmatic Patrick McGoohan; the series mixed this approach with the mature, downbeat style of Maugham, Ambler and Greene.

A real-life Dutch counterintelligence officer, Lieutenant-Colonel Oreste Pinto, inspired another early television spy drama, this time made by the BBC. Pinto's wartime work for MI5 uncovered several spies entering Britain posing as refugees, and he wrote three autobiographical books about his experiences. These were used by Robert Barr to form the basis of *Spycatcher* (1959-1961), a studio-bound TV series overseen by Terence Cook in a director-producer role, and featuring actor Bernard Archard. *Spycatcher* was low-budget, tending to favour one interrogation room set and small casts, but it made for highly rated drama, ran for 24 episodes and was re-made for BBC radio.

Premiering on the UK ABC network, *The Avengers* (1961-69) combined the old and the new in fictional spying. It was a hybrid programme in which the protagonists solved both conventional crimes and cases related to espionage. By pairing a talented, moral amateur, Dr. David Keel (Ian Hendry) with an experienced, amoral agent called John Steed (Patrick Macnee), the show's writers drew on the whole tradition of 20th century espionage fiction so far, including Fleming's cold-blooded professional. In August 1961, Associated Rediffusion's spy series *Top Secret* (1961-2) was launched; it stole a march on *Danger Man* by including authentic overseas filming, for 'good adventure stories set in places not used for television before.'[11]

OVERLAPPING WITH THE TRANSMISSION of these TV series, in 1961 the first James Bond feature film *Dr. No* went into production, made by the partnership of Albert R. Broccoli and Harry Saltzman. The little-known Glaswegian character actor Sean Connery was perfectly cast in the role of Bond, interpreting the sometimes intro-spective operative from the books as a flippant (but ruthless) playboy very much in tune with the optimistic mood of early 1960s Britain. However, *Dr. No* did not shy away from the unpleasant aspects of Bond's character, and one scene in particular indicated that a sea change inpopular culture was taking place. He shoots a defenceless opponent twice – once in the back – and shows no regret; it's all in a day's work for a professional executioner. The sequence was of great concern to the film's production team during script conferences, as screenwriter Joanna Harwood remembered. 'There was a lot of talk for and against. And they shot it both ways in case the censor objected. I thought, "Bond's going to lose the audience's sympathy."' I argued very, very firmly he shouldn't do it. I thought it was a very bad mistake.'[12] Moral concerns aside, the popularity of the 007 movies was largely responsible for *Danger Man*'s reboot as an hour long show – now with an Anglicised John Drake – in 1964. By then a new generation of spy writers had emerged who would initiate another significant change of emphasis in the genre.

ONE OF THE NEW BREED WAS JOHN LE CARRÉ (a *nom de plume* for David John Moore Cornwell), another intelligence officer-turned-author. Beginning with *Call for the Dead* (1961), he developed a coolly intellectual take on literary espionage, with Western intelligence services as ruthless as 'the opposition', exploiting and cheating people on their own side for the (apparent) greater good. Le Carré created two com-pelling anti-heroes: the ageing, gently-spoken spycatcher George Smiley and Alec Leamas, a kicked-around, cynical, middle-aged borderline alcoholic, the central character in *The Spy Who Came in from the Cold* (1963). Published not long after the partition of Germany's capital city Berlin, the book was a fatalistic novel in which Leamas pretends to defect as part of a plan to discredit Mundt, a vicious ex-Nazi working for East Germa-ny, by smearing him as a British agent. Leamas isn't told that the plan has been designed to fail; Mundt *is* a British agent and the real intent is to exonerate him and remove a rival officer, Fiedler, who suspects the truth. The book ends bleakly when the expendable Leamas, attempting to escape back to the West with his lover Liz through the Berlin Wall, allows himself to be shot dead by border guards after she is shot and killed.

The novel's whole ethos is a carefully considered answer to the flamboyance of the 007 books, partly driven by le Carré's discontent with the intelligence work he'd been engaged in himself: 'I know I was deeply unhappy in my professional and personal life, and I was enduring the extremes of loneliness and personal confusion. Perhaps some of that bitterness and solitude found its way into Alec Leamas.'[13] As *Time* magazine noted, le Carré's novel was 'a portrait of a man who has lived by lies and subterfuge for so long, he's forgotten how to tell the truth.'[14]

The IPCRESS File (1962), written by graphic designer and illustrator Leonard (Len) Deighton in a laconic, first-person idiom, introduced readers to a smart and sardonic anti-establishment loner who worked in a distinctly le Carré-style milieu. A member of the civilian intelligence organisation WOOC(P), based in 'one of those sleazy long streets in the district that would be Soho, if Soho had the strength to cross Oxford Street'[15], the nameless narrator has an engaging turn of phrase:

'It was the morning of my hundredth birthday. I shaved the final mirror-disc of old tired face under the merciless glare of the bathroom lighting. It was all very well telling oneself that Humphrey Bogart had that sort of face; but he also had a hairpiece, half a million dollars a year and a stand-in for the rough bits. I dabbed a soda-stick at the rough bits. In the magnifying mirror it looked like a white rocket landing on the uncharted side of the moon.'[16]

Deighton's central character, who went on to appear in several subsequent books, is made all the more intriguing because he remains anonymous. The only clue to his identity comes when a colleague calls him 'Harry'. At home, he has a collection of books on military history and occasionally employs a cockney burglar called Austin Butterworth, prone to saying 'luvaduck', to help him on his assignments. At a time when John Osborne's play Look Back in Anger (1956) had made a breakthrough in its vivid potrayal of the working-class malcontent Jimmy Porter, Deighton's character is defiantly blue-collar, enjoying a fractious relationship with his establishment bosses Dalby and George Dawlish. New social dramas like Room at the Top (1959), Saturday Night and Sunday Morning (1960) and A Taste of Honey (1961) were emerging in British cinemas, and the 'IPCRESS man' similarly brought a fashionable awareness of class politics to the spy genre. This attitude carried on into the films based on the books when the cockney Michael Caine, the son of a London fish porter, was cast as the central character, now christened Harry Palmer.

Deighton and le Carré's novels were a huge success. Deighton's second book Horse Under Water sold 60,000 copies of its Penguin edition in 48 hours and Deighton was proclaimed the greatest spy writer 'since Ambler and Graham Greene.'[17] Reviewing Funeral in Berlin (1964), the third IPCRESS novel, The Times Literary Supplement applauded the fact that 'the swinging style narrator (lacking a classical education but worldly omniscient all the same) has read his Dashiell Hammett carefully, as proved not only by his expert notation of transatlantic types and their habits of speech but also by the superficially [nit picking] method in which he has chosen to tell his story.'[18]

1963 WAS A SIGNIFICANT YEAR for both real and fictional spying. After the Cold War had become dangerously hot the year before, when Russian missiles were stationed on Cuba within striking range of the American mainland, the world saw a seamier side to the international power games conducted between East and West. John Profumo, the British Secretary of State for War, was revealed to be having an affair with Christine Keeler, a call girl – allegedly – romantically involved with Captain Eugene Ivanov, a Naval attaché at the Russian embassy in London. The ensuing scandal contributed to the downfall of the incumbent Conservative government, as did the escape to Russia of Kim Philby, an associate of Burgess and Maclean. Both events were so sensational they could have come straight from the typewriters of Fleming, Deighton or le Carré; Philby was even notoriously termed the 'Third Man', echoing the title of the famous 1949 *film noir* scripted by Graham Greene. In this excitable atmosphere, it wasn't surprising that the second James Bond film *From Russia with Love* became an international hit after its release in October. Containing a homage to the crop-duster scene from Hitchcock's spy thriller *North By Northwest*, as well as a vicious fight scene on a speeding train that was fully in character with the authentic violence in Fleming's source novels, the film became an instant box office hit, grossing an impressive $78.9 million worldwide.

The ITC's anthology film series *Espionage* (1963-64) looked at spying from the Restoration up to the early 1960s over 24 different fictional stories. By contrast with le Carré and Deighton's contemporary stories, characters in *Espionage* do questionable things in the name of security, but feel guilty about their actions. The notable exception is the first episode 'The Incurable One', in which the trainer and ex-lover of the WW2 assassin Celeste (Ingrid Thulin) has to kill her as, after the war, she begins to murder indiscriminately. The scene where 'Mr Smith' (Martin Miller), a German Jew, dies in her poison gas spray as he desperately reveals to her the concentration camp number tattooed on his arm, is still incredibly shocking today and must have come very close to being censored 50 years ago.

'The Whistling Shrimp' (1962) is uncharacteristic in showing a ruthless intelligence service. Screened a year after the unsuccessful invasion of Cuba by Central Intelligence Agency-backed exiles, the CIA is openly shown to engineer the removal of a pro-Marxist African leader, without the knowledge of America's representative to the United Nations. It was a bold political statement for a series shown on US network television to make.

Two other *Espionage* stories exemplify moves towards a more pessimistic interpretation of the spy on television. 'Never Turn Your Back on a Friend', overseen by the film director Michael Powell, features the allegorical trio of a close-knit unit of English, American and Russian WW2 saboteurs. When a German scientist working on a prototype atom bomb becomes their prisoner, their formerly strong alliance quickly disintegrates as each of them realises the advantage an atomic weapon will give his country. The story ends with Tovaritch (literally the Russian word for 'friend', played by Julian Glover) shooting dead his US and English comrades and taking the scientist's research.

'Once a Spy...' is practically a TV rewrite of *The Spy Who Came in from the Cold*, as the middle-aged, alcoholic Phil Mason (William Lucas) is expelled from intelligence work. Appealing to the better nature of his lover Susan (Millicent Martin), herself an agent, Mason talks himself on to her mission to rescue an imprisoned African political ally of Great Britain. The twist is that Mason's controller Waring (Peter Vaughn) correctly predicts his agent's behaviour and warns the African authorities of the rogue operator's arrival: when Mason is shot and killed, British security deny any involvement - the official statement is that he acted alone. Notably, Waring's strategy is still presented as action taken alone by one employee, rather than department policy.

The influence of Deighton, le Carré and *Espionage* inspired some of the most successful episodes of the revived *Danger Man*; there was also some continuity on the production side, as writers Raymond Bowers and Donald Jonson and casting director Rose Tobias Shaw had worked on the anthology series. The rebooted show's moral dilemmas and pessimism, particularly in relation to the United Kingdom's overseas colonies becoming independent, gave the series a depth and maturity lacking in some other contemporary thriller series. The origins of *Callan* can be seen in this credible spy series, lit in tough *film noir* monochrome and boasting a charismatic, professional hero who is sometimes troubled by the morally dubious missions he is assigned.

In 'That's Two of Us Sorry', Drake has to arrest a reformed Soviet agent who's not guilty of a contemporary crime but found guilty of an old one, while in 'Judgement Day' he has to defend a Nazi scientist (whom the British government wants for his scientific research) against an Israeli execution squad. Paradoxically, Drake also exhibits ruthless qualities. He blackmails Major Barrington (Nigel Stock) in the cynically titled 'Loyalty Always Pays' and threatens a reluctant double agent with exposure to the Communist authorities in 'The Man Who Wouldn't Talk': 'If I'm caught, I'll talk. And that'll be goodbye for you.'

Drake is also seen to be at odds with his own department. In 'It's Up to The Lady', he is deceived by his controller Hobbs (Peter Madden), as the M9 chief's promise not to prosecute a defector is a deliberate lie. Significantly, murder is practised by M9 assassins on two occasions: in 'Yesterday's Enemies' the fraudulent agent Archer (Howard Marion-Crawford) is disposed of in a staged car crash and in 'To Our Best Friend', Drake's married friends the Vincents (Donald Houston and Ann Bell) are nearly killed in another contrived car accident (clearly regarded as a standard intelligence assassination technique by television producers.)

BACK IN THE BOOK WORLD, a certain James Mitchell was contributing to the spy genre under his pen name, James Munro. Largely forgotten today, his 1960s 'Munro' stories about John Craig, a reluctant agent working for Department K under the control of the obese, callous Loomis (the commander's first name is never given) were as prominent as those by Fleming, le Carré and Deighton; Corgi Books in Britain sold approximately 250,000 paperback copies of the first book in the series[19] and it also became popular in America. Craig's debut, *The Man Who Sold Death*, was published in 1964, just as the 1960s global interest in spies was increasing. (The third Bond film, *Goldfinger*, was released at the end of that year). Appropriately, the first book stands at the crossroads of 1960s espionage fiction, mixing a Fleming-style global trek with the topical international conspiracies of le Carré, as one perceptive critic noted: 'If you are an admirer of 007, Ian Fleming's flamboyant James Bond, if you held your breath as John le Carré's Alec Leamas came in from the cold, if you are a member in good standing of the Eric Ambler cult, then, by all means do not miss James Munro's *The Man Who Sold Death*.'[20]

To stave off boredom both professionally and in his personal life, John Craig uses his shipping company to smuggle weapons to the rebels fighting against France for the independence of its African colony Algeria. His contribution is decisive – sovereign status was awarded by the French President Charles De Gaulle in 1961 – but Craig's actions put him and some of his colleagues on the death list of a cabal of right-wing French military officers, who believe Algeria should remain French. Craig goes on the run and is eventually offered protection by Department K if he'll become an agent for them. His first mission is to find and execute the French neo-Fascists.

Craig's second adventure, *Die Rich, Die Happy* (1965), saw the Department K agent assigned to a luxury yacht to protect the drug-addicted starlet wife of the Greek millionaire Naxos (an obvious fictionalisation of the Greek businessman Aristotle Onassis, who married President Kennedy's widow, Jackie). Set in Greece, at sea and in a glamorous Venice, Craig's eventful globetrotting would have been familiar to the readers of the 007 books. Things take a darker turn, however, when Philip Grierson, a likeable colleague of Craig's in the first two novels, suffers a mental breakdown because of the violent events at the climax of *Die Rich, Die Happy* and is invalided out of Department K. Grierson's fate prefigures Craig's in the third book, *The Money That Money Can't Buy* (1967). By this point work had begun on *Callan* and it is likely Mitchell was writing stories for both this new character and John Craig concurrently, because the tone of the third book is notably bleaker. At the same time, Mitchell's prose style has acquired an engaging sardonic touch: 'They flew to Tangier in a Comet 4B, and Boris took advantage of the quaint local custom that allowed him to drink cheap liquor because he was in a plane.'[21]

Craig is captured by the Fascistic Simmons and is nearly crippled by having his genitals repeatedly electrocuted.[22] Only the ministrations of Loomis's medical consultant Dr. Matthew Chinn restore the agent psychologically and physically enough for him to complete his mission. By *The Innocent Bystanders* (1969) Craig is disillusioned, seen as a burnt-out liability and actively looking to escape Department K before they dispose of him. This book was variously described by the US press as 'fast paced'[23], with 'fine action in this exceptionally well-written novel'[24]. The most positive recommendation came from the *Dallas Times-Herald*, complementing the fact that 'Munro creates imaginative plots into which he places his hero and writes with considerable skill... The women are luscious, beautiful and inviting; the plotting is clever, the men tough and violent. All are overshadowed by John Craig, the bold, resilient operator.'[25]

IN 1965, THE FOURTH BOND FILM *Thunderball* grossed an astonishing $142 million, making it in real terms, globally, one of the most profitable films of all time; its predecessor *Goldfinger* had made $125 million. Increasingly far-fetched elements were infiltrating the 007 films, such as lasers, jetpacks and cars with ejector seats. On television *The Avengers* was evolving along similar lines, and significantly two of its female leads, Honor Blackman and Diana Rigg, migrated between the two productions. The *New Statesman* TV critic recognised that both Steed and Bond had common ground: 'The giggly, pleasure-giving slickness which *The Avengers* shares with *From Russia with Love* doesn't come from black leather alone. Patrick Macnee, bouncing through his lines with umbrella, bowler hat and after-shave lotion smugness from ear to ear, is a true musical-comedy mixture of caricature and fantasy: his absurdity saves us from too close an identification with his exploits.'[26]

With secret agents such a proven money-spinner, by the mid-1960s they were everywhere. Bulldog Drummond and Nayland Smith were both revived for new runs of films. Even the *Carry On* team got in on the act with *Carry On Spying* (1964), with special agents Kenneth Williams, Charles Hawtrey, Bernard Cribbins and Barbara Windsor taking on a secret organisation with the mischievous acronym STENCH.

As well as being a parody of SMERSH and SPECTRE, the enemy organisations in the Bond novels and films, STENCH evokes *The Man from UNCLE* (1964-68), a popular American super spy series, which Fleming had been initially involved in. UNCLE – The United Network Command for Law and Enforcement – battled the world-dominating ambitions of THRUSH (the meaning of whose acronym was never revealed on screen). The series was a fashionable television import in the UK, not least because of the lucrative amount of spin-off merchandise it generated aimed at children. When its stars Robert Vaughn (Napoleon Solo) and David McCallum (Ilya Kuryakin) arrived on a promotional visit, Vaughn was mobbed as if he was a rock star – an alarming experience that also befell Sean Connery – while McCallum was christened 'the blonde Beatle'.[27]

By February 1966, the 'spy craze' was at its height in Britain. On ITV, there were four early evening 'secret agent' shows running: *The Avengers, Danger Man*[28], Associated Rediffusion's new drama *The Rat Catchers* and the imported American series *Amos Burke, Secret Agent* (a reboot of a police series starring Gene Barry), while on BBC1, *The Man from UNCLE* was being regularly shown in a primetime slot along with home-grown fare such as *The Mask of Janus* and its sequel, *The Spies*. ITC's *The Saint*, featuring Roger Moore's interpretation of suave Simon Templar, had now become another hybrid series, mixing espionage cases in with its usual crime and damsel-in-distress stories. On 6 February, Bond-mania arguably reached a 1960s peak with the screeniing of a documentary, *The Incredible World of James Bond*, on ITV.

The Rat Catchers continued in the vein of the film versions of *The IPCRESS File* and *Funeral in Berlin* by making its fictional protagonist fallible, and not a pin-up action hero. This series had overseas filming in Lisbon, Stockholm and Vienna[29], and featured an un-named department with no official status, making it 'easier for the government to disown if it was blown'[30]. (Another American import to Britain, *Mission: Impossible* (1966-1973) carried a similar caveat, stating that if any of the spies are captured, 'the Secretary will disavow any knowledge.') At the same time, ex-Superintendent Richard Hurst (Glyn Owen), seconded to the Rat Catchers, 'distrusts and dislikes his colleagues due to different social background... [and] dislikes obeying orders blindly without knowing reasons.'[31]

The film version of *The Quiller Memorandum*, also from 1966 and adapted from Adam Hall's international bestseller by the *avant garde* playwright Harold Pinter, deals with the contemporary subject of neo-Nazis undermining West Germany by '[infiltrating] themselves into the mind of the country over a period of years.' In an understated and dryly humorous performance, the American actor George Segal portrays Quiller as neither particularly heroic nor anti-heroic. Like McGoohan's Drake, Caine's Palmer or Owen's Hurst, Quiller is a tough man doing a potentially lethal job.[32]

IN 1967'S *Billion Dollar Brain,* the third cinema outing for Caine's Palmer, he has resigned from MI5 and is struggling to make ends meet as a private detective, before being black-mailed back into intelligence work by his old boss Colonel Ross (Guy Doleman).

Elsewhere, in a remarkable production run of 30 50-minute episodes made over two years, ITC's *Man in a Suitcase* also resigned, this time from 'American intelligence', falsely accused of treachery. Instalments of this crime/espionage series would often end on a downbeat note. In the Method-acting, bullish Texan form of Richard Bradford, McGill tried to make a living in Europe as an unlicensed inquiry agent, battling with his tattered conscience as much as the opposition. McGill could be self-centred, drank and smoked heavily, and was belligerent when provoked. Interviewed about the character, Bradford noted, 'If you are going to show a man as he really is, you have to show his bad traits as well as the good ones... There may be aspects of his character that you don't like – he can be aggressive and unnecessarily rude and he resents having been treated in such a cavalier fashion.'[33]

In the frenetic opening sequence of *The Prisoner* (1967-68), Patrick McGoohan's nameless character angrily quits intelligence work (becoming one of at least three fictional agents in 1967 to do so and then openly criticise their employers), only to be rendered unconscious by gas and shipped to a bizarre interrogation centre called the Village. (This was as much a resignation for the actor as the character; a line being drawn explicitly under *Danger Man* when, in *The Prisoner* title sequence, the actor's publicity photograph from the former series is crossed through and consigned to a filing cabinet drawer marked 'resigned'.) At its heart, *The Prisoner* had a grounding in spying's tradecraft of false identities, double agents and cover stories, which, together with an inherent paranoia, is developed into a dreamlike allegory of a consumer paradise gone mad. The Village may be run by the East, the West, both sides, or the Prisoner's subconscious mind. With its flamboyant visuals, *Billion Dollar Brain* also exemplified this tendency towards surrealism: Palmer (a clearly bored Caine) is treated almost as an extra in his own movie, in a wild, international travelogue, that looks as if producer Harry Saltzman and director Ken Russell were deliberately making an arty send up of the James Bond films.

GENERAL SCIENTIFIC ADVANCES, and the National Aeronautics and Space Administration's (NASA) race with the USSR to put a man on the moon by the end of the 1960s, inspired a further dimension to fictional espionage: Spy-fi. In *The Avengers*, John Steed and Emma Peel (Diana Rigg) fought off increasingly bizarre threats, including killer robots, mind-controlling alien plants, a shrinking machine and an electrified man, while in the fifth James Bond blockbuster, *You Only Live Twice* (1967), 007 prepared to conquer the final frontier – outer space. The same year saw the release of the first Bond adventure, *Casino Royale*, not made by the Saltzman/Broccoli partnership. This went beyond Spy-fi and surrealism into an outright, nonsensical spoof, with everyone from Jean Paul Belmondo to Orson Welles hitching themselves to the Bondwagon.[34]

The equally cartoon-like Flint and Helm movies continued the celebration and mockery of the genre. ZOWIE agent Flint (James Coburn) and his wolfish grin cohabit in a luxurious New York apartment with two Irish wolfhounds, an Alsatian called Caesar and four devoted young women; while the 1960s 007's dancing was strictly cheek to cheek, Flint (or Coburn) was cool enough to get down to the popular beat groups of the day. As Helm (agent for ICE, played by Dean Martin), the secret agent is remodelled as a polo-neck-wearing, crooning sex maniac with an army of willing women – the ICE man has a gun in one hand and an alcoholic drink semi-permanently in the other. The trailer for 1967's *The Wrecking Crew* hilariously proclaims, 'Just think! You'll actually see Dean Martin save the world!'[35] Joseph Losey's *Modesty Blaise* (1966) was based on an *actual* comic strip written by Peter O'Donnell, and for all its mad Mod stylings, this clever and witty film retains his cynical sense of *realpolitik*, with a moribund Britain financially dependent on a deal with an oil-rich Arab country. As one critic perceptively noted, the movie directed 'a bitter edge of malice... against a society that trusts its politicians and its generals.'[36]

AGAINST THE VOLATILE 1960s BACKGROUND of anti-establishment radicalism and social change, spy fiction continued to develop along the twin paths of realism and escapism. Irrespective of their origins, James Bond, Steed, Mrs Peel, Modesty Blaise and, in America, the men from UNCLE, Flint and Helm, all ended up sitting comfortably on film in the escapist camp (often with the emphasis on 'camp'.)

It was perhaps inevitable that videotaped, low-budget black and white television would produce another variation on the realist approach – a reluctant but ruthless agent from humble origins, working for a callous controller, who revealed that the methods the so-called free world's intelligence agencies used were just as ruthless as those of their opposition: 'Eliminating people. Framing. Extortion. Death. The jobs that are too dirty for Her Majesty's other security forces to touch.'[37] All the idea needed was a suitable environment for the character to develop in. The ideal place was the UK's ABC Television network.

3: ABC PRESENTS...

**'And now for your Sunday night dramatic entertainment,
we bring you *Armchair Theatre*.'**

Introductory voiceover from 1960 onwards.

I N 1974, THE FILM VERSION of *Callan* was shown nationwide by the ABC cinema chain. This was rather ironic because in the 1950s, the Associated-British Picture Corporation (ABPC) had vigorously campaigned against the introduction of advertising-supported Independent TeleVision – ITV – which subsequently ended the BBC's monopoly on small screen broadcasting in Great Britain. In a change of heart, ABPC's management decided the best way to deal with the threat of television was to become involved in it. The resulting ABC Television network within ITV would launch *Callan*, first as a single play, then as a series in its own right.

When ITV started, it was divided into several regional networks. The driving force behind ABC Television was its forward-thinking Managing Director, Howard Thomas, who had run ABPC's sister distribution company British Pathé, which produced its famous newsreels for the cinema until 1970. After the collapse of the bid put forward by Kelmsley Newspapers and Winnick Entertainment, one of the other groups bidding for a network licence, the Independent Television Authority – ITA – which had been set up to allocate the ITV franchises – offered ABC the contract to produce television for the Midlands and the North at weekends. The deal was facilitated by ABC being allocated a percentage of the £75,000 government grant designed to protect the new TV companies if ITV failed commercially.

The contract between the ITA and ABC was signed on 21 September 1955, the day before commercial television was officially launched; transmission of ABC programming would begin only five months later, on 18 February 1956. The nascent company had three main production centres, with studios in Aston (near Birmingham) and Didsbury (near Manchester), rather symbolically converted from two ABC cinemas, the Astoria and the Capitol. The third production base was at a refurbished film studio at Broom Road in Teddington, Middlesex, and it was here that *Callan* – amongst many other landmark television productions – would be made.

Part of ITV's remit had been to offer an alternative to the BBC, which was seen at the time as paternalistic and often (upper) middle-class in its programming. Associated Tele-Vision (ATV), the network run by the entrepreneur Lew Grade, offered variety and game shows such as *Beat the Clock* and *Sunday Night at the London Palladium*, as well as escapist fare such as *The Adventures of Robin Hood* (1955-1960), an American-style film series made with one canny eye on international sales. ABC's main contribution to ITV would be giving a voice to new writers.

Armchair Theatre – termed 'Britain's national theatre of the air' and initially produced by Dennis Vance – began transmission on July 8 1956. It ran until 1974. Although its first production, 'The Outsider', was an hour-long medical drama adapted for television by George Kerr, the following week's double bill of two half-hour plays, 'The Handshake' by Peter Key and 'Bid for Fame' by Duncan Greenwood, inaugurated the policy of commissioning original drama scripts. On its first night, *Armchair Theatre* had been confirmed as a major television event, being seen in '51% of homes equipped to receive ITV at that time'[1].

Almost from the beginning, *Armchair Theatre* had links with the ground-breaking Canadian Broadcasting Corporation (CBC). Leonard White, who produced the series in the late 1950s and between 1963 and 1969, had worked at the company with Sydney Newman (1917-97), one of the CBC's most innovative producers. One day, White observed the Canadian director Silvio Narizzano, who he had shared a house with in Canada, watching camera rehearsals for the sixth *Armchair Theatre* play, 'The Hollow Crown'. Narrizano had left the CBC to join Granada Television in Manchester and was assessing ABC's facilities. By *Armchair Theatre*'s second series in 1957, firm links between the CBC and ABC were established with the appointment to the anthology series of another Canadian émigré, director Ted Kotcheff.

In Canadian TV productions such as *General Motors Theatre*, the CBC directors were quietly but significantly revolutionising the way television drama was made, as White recalled: '[the CBC people] regarded television as a completely new medium, special and unlike any other. Whereas in the UK the general influence on television drama in the early years was from theatre, and in the USA from cinema, in Canada there was no such strong pre-conditioning. There, the small band of television directors at the heart of CBC's operation used the television camera uniquely... They used the [camera fixed to a pedestal] as a hand-held, entirely mobile unit. It rarely stood still for long... This change in the use of a basic tool changed the style of television drama in the UK. No longer the stand-off and photograph, theatre-wise [approach], but... get in close and move with the action.'[2] Once Teddington studios were equipped with similar pedestal-mounted cameras, this new, fluid style of directing introduced a sea change in British television drama.

In April 1956, the *General Motors Theatre* play 'Flight to Danger' by Arthur Hailey had been shown by the BBC. The story involved an outbreak of food poisoning on an airliner, necessitating a passenger with limited flying experience having to take over the controls. In the original, 'there was none of the treatment Hollywood would have given the story. There were no film stars, nor even any film inserts. It was produced very simply with two or three studio sets. But the action was intimate and utterly convincing. The producer's credit read "Sydney Newman".'[3] The play was so well received that another 34, all produced by Newman, began transmission at the end of 1956 under the umbrella title *Canadian Television Theatre*. These screenings would be the final link in fusing Canadian innovation with the *Armchair Theatre* team's progressive artistic ambitions.

'My name got known here a bit,'[4] Newman recalled with typical modesty. 'Then cross-cut to ABC Television and Howard Thomas wanted to promote Dennis Vance – who was the Head of Drama – and asked Dennis, could he find a replacement for himself? And that's how I was found and interviewed, flown to England, wined and dined, and accepted the job as Head of Drama for ABC Television.' The Canadian began work in April 1958 and, as White observed, 'British television was in for some shock treatment with Newman, the non-conformist outsider.'[5] Since its inception, *Armchair Theatre* had attracted a large working-class audience – a viewing constituency not typically catered for by the BBC – and Newman built on this area of the audience with plays that dealt with social and political issues. 'I am proud that I played some part in the recognition that the working man was a fit subject for drama, and not just a comic foil in a play on middle-class manners,'[6] Newman later reflected. 'To me, everything I did had to have some kind of meaning for the audience, some relevance. I think one reason that *Armchair Theatre* was a success was because that was my basic principle. I wanted to give the audiences something of value they couldn't get anywhere else.' As a result, in addition to book adaptations the anthology featured original work by such notable writers as Len Deighton, John le Carré, Wolf Mankowitz, David Mercer, John Mortimer, Robert Muller, David Nobbs, Harold Pinter, Alan Plater, Jack Rosenthal and Angus Wilson. The series was able to attract strong acting talent on the basis of these scripts; Mike Vardy recalled, 'You only had to say "*Armchair Theatre*" and actors would come quite willingly.'[7]

The earliest surviving play 'Now Let Him Go', transmitted on 15 September 1957, was written by the established and respected playwright J.B. Priestley. In its story of the dying artist Simon Kendall (Hugh Griffith), dealing with family, journalists and establishment figures pursuing his expensive paintings, the hesitant beginnings of *Armchair Theatre*'s interest in generational and class tensions can be seen, even if the direction is rather static. By the time Newman took over as producer, the camera had become more noticeably mobile, moving nimbly between performers and through scenes as the viewer is taken into the heart of the action.

As the 1960s progressed, so did *Armchair Theatre*'s ground-breaking agenda. In drama, comedy, thrillers and 'Musical Satire'[8], the anthology series tackled such important contemporary subjects as the Cold War, space exploration, the new, university-educated working class and their accompanying frustration, the sexual revolution, the emptyglamour of celebrity lifestyles and urban redevelopment. Consequently, *Armchair Theatre* was a frequent visitor to the 'Top Ten' of the most-watched programmes in the country, with Harold Pinter's 'A Night Out',s directed by Philip Saville, number one in the national ratings for its week of transmission; additionally on 13 December 1964, Donald Churchill's 'The Hothouse', starring Harry H. Corbett and Diana Rigg, drew the series' largest-ever audience, over 20 million viewers, still a record for an ITV play. With ratings like these, Newman's impact on Britain's cultural landscape was undeniable, as the *Sunday Times* TV critic observed: 'I recognise in him a man with a strong, almost righteous sense of the social possibilities, not to say responsibilities, of television drama.'[9]

'I think a lot of early TV dramas in those early days, not just plays but series as well, were ground-breaking,'[10] Robert Banks Stewart reflected. 'Most of the people involved creatively were people who were ex-stage writers, theatre directors and producers involved in "showbiz" – if I can use that term – who took a literary approach to what they were doing. I became great friends with Donald Churchill, a regular writer on *Armchair Theatre*; we used to share an office at one time. The point is, in the last 25 years, television has become a place for people who've only done media studies at university.'

In December 1962 Newman changed channels, perhaps surprisingly, taking his populist touch to the BBC. 'Nobody talks about ABC, but it was very exciting,'[11] remembered Trevor Preston, who began his television career with the company. 'Every actor wanted to work on *Armchair Theatre* because they were good scripts with good writers, very well made. The BBC said "Hang on a minute, they're beating us by a mile!" They knew [ABC] was making much better drama.' 'I joined the year after [Sydney Newman] left,'[12] Terence Feely recalled, 'but the legend was still strong and there was evidence of his work everywhere.'

Newman's replacement as Head of Drama was another Canadian, who had worked in various capacities at Station CFPL in Ontario, the red-haired and sometimes volatile Lloyd George Shirley. In 1957, aged only 27, Shirley joined ABC to become the Head of Light Entertainment; when Newman left for the BBC, Lloyd stepped up as Head of Drama.

'Lloyd probably got me involved in ABC, and I did a *Public Eye* first ['Twenty Pounds of Heart and Muscle'] in 1966,'[13] said Piers Haggard, referring to his work on the natural-istic detective series that ran between 1965 and 1975, starring Alfred Burke as the decent but solitary 'inquiry agent' Frank Marker. 'I liked *Public Eye*, because it was downbeat and realistic. It had a slightly lugubrious quality. I had been working with [Michelangelo] Antonioni on *Blow-Up* [1966] and I was still slightly under his spell.'

Like Sydney Newman before him, Lloyd Shirley proved to be shrewd in his com-missioning of original drama and many of his other ABC series are still well regarded. He believed strong characterisation was of paramount importance: 'Every human being is the hero of their own story; each human being surprises themselves and disappoints themselves. Each human being tends to measure the world in terms of their own per-sonality and finds it difficult to imagine their own non-existence. Your job is to suspend disbelief, to use the essayists' term.'[14] *Armchair Theatre* had its offshoots, such as *Armchair Mystery Theatre* (1960), hosted by Donald Pleasence, which specialised in crime and mystery stories. John Wyndham's short story 'Dumb Martian', adapted by Clive Exton, similarly signposted the advent of the spin-off science fiction anthology *Out of This World* (1962) which featured stories by genre authors such as Clifford D. Simak and Philip K. Dick. In addition to *The Avengers* and *Public Eye*, the ABC network produced the ghostly *Haunted* (1967-68), psychological drama *The Human Jungle* (1963-64), industrial spy series *Intrigue* (1966), military police drama *Redcap* (1964-66), sci-fi serial *Undermind* (1965), and many further plays and anthologies, such as *Mystery and Imagination* (1966-1970).

CAST, CREW AND WRITERS all remembered that the way videotaped dramas like ABC's were made in the 1960s and 1970s, used a production process a world away from the way equivalent programmes are made in the 21st century. 'If you look at the camera scripts, they're incredibly detailed,'[15] Piers Haggard noted. 'Typically if, for instance, you went to [Teddington] Studio One, you'd have two weeks to do a 50-minute drama. Firstly rehearsal, which could be starting on a Sunday or a Monday, then at some point – say the following Wednesday – [the producers] would come and look at it. By this time you would have had to have done your camera scripts – they'd have to be ready by Monday night so the Production Assistant could type them up on the Tuesday, sometimes later than that if you were really chasing your tail, so you had to work out what the shots were going to be.'

'You rehearsed, you read through the whole thing and discussed the script, and you had two weeks to work out your character, what he's going to do, and where you are going to go...'[16] Patrick Mower recalled, 'then you went in and shot it in one go.'[17] Actor Peter Bowles said. 'It was very nerve-wracking for the cameramen, who were always stripped down to their vests, because they were sweating so much.'

'A lot of things were done on television, in that particular way, largely because of time,'[18] Anthony Valentine recalled. 'Sometimes you would have two hours to record 50 minutes, [but] by the time you'd done the scene changes, and by the time you had done the first five scenes five times, someone suddenly realised that you only had three minutes to record Scene 27 which was in fact two minutes and 57 seconds long!'

'We recorded more or less in scene order, rather than completing scenes on one set then moving to the next one,'[19] director Jim Goddard said. 'People used to run from one set to the other, changing, and pretending they weren't out of breath.' Actor Kenneth Gilbert agreed recording was 'pretty tight at times – an hour and a half, two hours to do in almost continuous takes. Certainly the scenes were much longer.'[20] There was little time for joking on the set, but there was one big difference: 'People had a sense of humour about things, but in those days if you acted after a certain time of night all the crew got drinks!' Michael Jayston revealed. 'It wouldn't happen now.'[21]

'You didn't overrun,'[22] Peter Duguid stated emphatically. 'You played safe with the shots. You made it possible to do in the time and the dress rehearsal was a big [contribution]. But then you would get notes [feedback from the producers] a quarter of an hour before you had to record the bloody thing!' Mike Vardy explained, 'The unions had a strangle-grip on these schedules, and if you worked five hours, you would have to have a meal break of an hour and with all the problems lining up, it just dug into the whole time you were allowed, really. The company would only allow you certain overall hours, and out of that came meal breaks, line up times, so on and so forth.'[23]

'The technical line up would take hours,' he added. 'It did get better as people and engineers got more used to it, but it went on for *hours*... The sound guys worked from these huge giraffe things with microphones at the end, and the lighting rig would try to do their best to get effective lighting, and suddenly a great boom shadow would come across the actors. I'm not minimising the difficulty. You had to plan where the cabling went into the studio wall, otherwise you would get all your cables tangled up in a heap in the middle of the room and no one would be able to move.'

Shooting would be relentless, with cameras being released towards the end of scenes to go straight to another set so the next scene could begin recording right away. 'All the camera and sound men would have a copy of the ground plan that I'd drawn on with a protractor, with the camera positioning and cabling,' Vardy explained. 'I had to work all that out, and then that was copied, printed and each cameraman had one, gaffer-taped on his camera so he'd know where to go.'

The camera directions also allowed the crew to look ahead, Piers Haggard noted, 'so when you get to them when you're blocking [planning] it, they more or less know what you are asking for, and they can offer you [a shot], and hopefully they'll have a reasonable idea and then you can polish it. Everything was designed to save that precious studio time.'[24] A minimal number of breaks in taping would be incorporated, but only out of necessity. 'The number of breaks was typically only four or five, in order to move the camera, un-knit all the cables, let an actor do a costume change, change the set or set a clock and so on,' Haggard said. 'There were any number of reasons for a break but you had to ration them, because you had to fit recording into the time.'

'The planning was very clever, because these cameras were like dinosaurs. Some of those cameramen were fucking brilliant. It was like pushing a taxi around the place!'[25] Trevor Preston laughed, adding that the directors 'used to think of all sorts of crazy things to do to keep [shooting] going. They also allowed, in most programmes, two to three minutes of film outside, so you could get screaming ambulances coming in, and that sort of stuff.'

'The exterior sequences were very limited and there were no major scenes played outside,[26] 'Jim Goddard observed. 'The writing was essentially about interior space. It was slightly more theatrical; if you look at it now, it is slightly surreal, because it's all happening inside rooms.' To reduce costs, writer Bill Craig recalled that at the time, 'there was a general injunction that [any outside filming] should not be more than six or seven miles from the studio.'[27]

Freelance film cameraman John Keeling was often involved in these exterior film shoots, although his work went uncredited. 'As a film cameraman, I never worked in the live studio shooting onto tape; that was a completely different department. The commercial companies never gave credit for film cameramen – the BBC did, but ITV didn't,'[28] he explained ruefully. 'On location, I would do a walk-through with the director first, and we might have the camera on a dolly [a low truck]. Once we'd got the camera set we would do another walk through, probably with the director or me, for the camera crew, and we'd fine-tune it. Then it would be a rehearsal with the actors – then we'd shoot. The number of takes would depend on the shot. Normally I would say it was an average of about three takes. Unless it was something really tricky; often it wasn't tricky from the actor's point of view but there would be a tricky bit for the camera. If there was a lot of action, sometimes timing would go wrong, you'd rehearse it and it would be fine, but then on the take somebody's a second behind, or there'd be a car driving in [to shot] or something like that.'

These brief local forays outside would have been a welcome break from the studio, where every inch of space had to be cleverly utilised, with the claustrophobic look of the sets not simply being an artistic choice. 'Cost wise, because there wasn't any real accounting, most of the costs were below the line [i.e. variable],'[29] designer Peter le Page revealed. 'What we had to control were set cost and prop costs; *our* costs. Studio costs, camera time, stuff like that, weren't costed to programmes,'[30] his colleague David Marshall elaborated. 'There was a great deal going on around the actors from lighting, cameras, sound, tech ops, vision mixers, costume, make-up, prop buyers, prop men, scene men, electricians, stage managers, floor managers, all of whom, in some way, were connected to and bound by, the design of the sets. The money was tight; hard decisions needed to be made over what to cut, grand ideas compromised, reality faced. The sets were built round shots... Lighting was enormously important, the relationship between a lighting director and designer was crucial – just as it was in feature films. Everything was worked out in detail, before having the ground plans marked up with tape on the rehearsal room floor for the actors and director to *thoroughly* learn their moves, before a busy two days in the studio.' In this working situation, the designers would cooperate closely with their respective directors, again following practices established in the theatre.

All writers needed to work within these constraints too; Terence Feely recalled an average 50-minute drama with a few minutes of filming would cost approximately £20,000 to make at that time. Generally, writers would soon get used to adapting their ideas to fit the recording procedures in the studio. If a character needed to change their costume, then rather than stopping the tape, it was better to write a 'bridging scene', then cut back to them. 'That sounds weird, now, but in fact it produced some very good scenes,'[31] Feely reflected. 'I mean, when you're up against it and you know you've got to write a bridging scene, it can't be just a bridging scene: it's got to fit in with the story, it's got to contribute to the story and it's got to be damn good viewing. It's amazing what desperation like that can produce. And some of the best-written scenes were bridging scenes, and were simply there to allow an actor to get from one part of the studio to another. It was a great art.'

Scripts tended to be at an advanced stage by the time actors came in to rehearse. 'I don't think there was any rewriting in rehearsal, not that I was aware of: we rehearsed it as it was written,'[32] actor Clifford Rose said, noting that over time actors also became used to taping scenes out of sequence. The only difficulty, Rose found, was maintaining continuity with the pre-shot film sequences. 'If you come from film to studio and you have to pick up an emotional kind of state which you've done on film – coming through a door into a studio, and picking it up exactly as it was, is a very tricky thing to do.'

Problem-solving could not be deferred to the editing stage either. Much of the editing from shot to shot was done by selecting the picture from one camera at a time for recording onto the master tape; joining the recordings together to remove any breaks was then done by physically splicing this tape. 'The tapes were two inches wide and they were very heavy in their spools, and they were joined with silver foil and oscilloscopes and God knows what,'[33] Mike Vardy said. 'It was quite a process, and the editors wore white cotton gloves so they didn't get any marks on [the tapes].' 'Sometimes you could see an awful jump if they hadn't done it well,'[34] Trevor Preston pointed out. 'There were a couple of guys there who were geniuses, but you couldn't always get them, because everyone wanted them.' 'Tape used to be treated as deferred transmission,'[35] Lloyd Shirley explained. 'You edited it as little as possible... [and] shot it as close to live as possible.'

Despite the stress of the final performance in the studio, several actors interviewed for this book expressed their preference for this method of working, possibly, as Shirley acknowledged, because the process, including the pressure on the operational staff, was similar to a live show in the theatre, with all the associated preparation beforehand. 'Nowadays if you're in [a soap], you don't get *any* time,' Michael Jayston said. 'It's terrifying,'[36] fellow actor Alfred Hoffman, agreed. 'You [go] there, rehearse the scene – take. Rehearse the scene – take. Boom-boom-boom.'[37] 'I think most actors would prefer to have more rehearsal,'[38] Patrick Mower firmly believed. 'If you've got a jewel, and two weeks to [improve] it, it's much better.'

'You had to build everything up, '[39] said Piers Haggard. 'The one huge advantage to the technique was... the actors were doing it more like they do in the theatre, which is to say, line-testing, preparing, rehearsing, working up to a performance. It was depressing sometimes, because you couldn't go back and polish it. It wasn't for single camera – like in film – so the lighting was never that good. It was mass-produced lighting and you had slightly mass-produced shots too; you couldn't polish them. But as you learnt the techniques, you got good at inventing shots that would be good, so what you did do would look [refined].''

'[Videotape drama is] full of soft focuses and camera judder, stuff that you hadn't time to do a retake on,'[40] Peter Duguid acknowledged. 'But the sweep of it, actors performing a piece with very few stops, was very strong. It's shattering to see these things that you've recorded. If the actor's been doing his job he's *knackered* at the end of it. You have to use that adrenaline very carefully... It's the sustained tension. I really doubt very much if that sort of thing could be achieved in the circumstances of recording it today... the feeling of performance, the continuity, was something unique to that period of television in the studio. I think we have lost something.'

SADLY, MANY OF THE PROGRAMMES produced during this era, including multiple instalments of *The Avengers*, *Public Eye* and *Callan*, were purged from the archives in the 1960s and 1970s. The reasons are no less depressing for being understandable: videotapes took up space, were costly and could be re-used, black and white shows were giving way to colour, and some TV staff felt the programmes themselves were ephemeral, only meant to be watched once on transmission. 'It was very sad that the black and white episodes got wiped,'[41] John Keeling said, mourning the loss in particular of the LWT children's series, *The Growing Summer* (1968). 'Some of the best things I have ever done have been wiped, at the BBC as well,'[42] Peter Duguid added. Piers Haggard was dismayed to hear his *Public Eye* debut was another casualty: 'I had put my heart and soul into that. It was a good episode, shot on the canals around Wolverhampton. It had a pretty authentic working-class feeling.'[43] 'They lost an awful lot of things, some of which I wanted,'[44] Alfred Hoffman recalled. [The British Film Institute's 'Missing Believed Wiped' initiative and the Kaleidoscope organisation both work to recover lost programmes. If any reader finds what they genuinely believe to be a missing production, we recommend they contact one of these organisations.[45]]

On the management side, a shake-up of the ITV franchises in 1968 led to ABC merging with Associated Rediffusion to become Thames Television, while on the technical side, colour recording and broadcasting was brought in. (See Chapter 7.) However, the process of drama production, multi-camera, studio-based with pre-filmed inserts, remained essentially unchanged for another decade. 'I don't think there was a great deal of difference, from what I remember – not from the actor's point of view,'[46] Clifford Rose noted. Gradually practices did begin altering for most dramas, excluding soaps, in a move largely pioneered by the Thames subsidiary, Euston Films, which specialised in TV drama made entirely on 16mm film, such as *The Sweeney* (1975-78). In addition to its film and video drama, Thames was also well known for its current affairs coverage and comedies, successfully tempting Morecambe and Wise from the BBC in 1978 to join its ranks. Unhappily, Thames finally lost its week-day London ITV franchise in 1992, after the controversial 1990 Broadcasting Act 'deregulated' independent broadcasting. Teddington Studios have now ironically suffered the same fate as the BBC TV Centre, and are awaiting redevelopment into flats; even the blue plaques commemorating the site's significance have been stolen. 'It's *terribly* sad they're pulling the studios down,'[47] actress Tessa Wyatt said. 'That's where I had most of my work, with Eric and Ernie. It was a nice place to go to.'

'IN MY OPINION, BACK THEN, ABC was the best broadcasting company in the world,'[48] Trevor Preston believed, reflecting on the original company's contribution to British television culture. 'It had very important people: Sydney Newman was a genius. I suppose it was a bit like football – they wanted to transfer the best players in. A lot of people came over after him [from Canada]; there were a couple of very good directors who [came over]. Lloyd used to hire people – Mike Hodges, Dick Fontaine: the cream... I get sick to death of the way people talk about *The Wednesday Play* – they should look at *Armchair Theatre*.'

Peter le Page felt the company's success was due to its readiness to take risks. 'The BBC had the monopoly, so ITV had to prove something. [At ABC] the accountants weren't in charge, because they didn't know how to cost anything anyway, and the guys who were running it at the time had a pretty open view of things... we were always encouraged to experiment. And there was this peer-pressure thing between the directors: most of them had come from university and art school, and been through theatre to some extent – it would depend on their age – and they were all vying against each other. And we were all pushing our luck as designers, because we'd all been brought up, not with television, but with going to the cinema two or three times a week as teenagers. The whole Hollywood thing was what we looked to and wanted to emulate... There was a striving, that although we were a small company, we were going to do as well as the BBC, or better, and that ran all the way through until we finished, quite frankly.' Many of the company's designers went on to further career success: Assheton Gorton and Voytek both won BAFTAs, while Robert Fuest, Jim Goddard, Terry Green and Piers Haggard moved into feature films.

One attribute that makes the company stand out in television history is the sheer diversity and quantity of productions, as Peter Duguid recalled. 'In those days Lloyd Shirley gave a five-play contract. The five-play contract was meant to be used up over a year, which meant you could organise your career over that year as you wished, as a freelance. But in fact what happened was, as you got known, they used up their five plays in five or six months so you got much more work after that. I did all sorts – we were doing 80 hours a year, which was a large output for a smallish drama department.'[49] The staff eagerly accepted this workload, being 'keen to get on in television,'[50] as designer Neville Green put it.

'ABC/Thames was a powerhouse in the making of high standard productions and we shall not see the like again,'[51] Mike Vardy agreed. 'ABC were good to work for.'[52] John Keeling said. 'They had a good reputation. I worked on a few *Armchair Theatres*; they had great writing.'

'I suppose it's the 1960s really – the advent of working-class heroes,' Piers Haggard reflected, considering the company's most popular series. 'It's interesting from that point of view; not so much the angry young man, but that regional and working class voice. That was an absolutely key part of what ABC did.'[53]

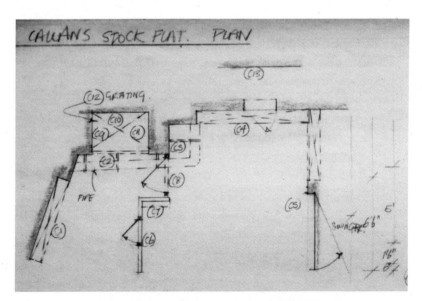

Designer Peter le Page's floor plan for Callan's flat, built in April 1967 for 'Goodness Burns Too Bright', the first episode of the series to be made. The letters and numbers indicate camera positions. *Peter le Page Collection*

4: A MAGNUM FOR SCHNEIDER, A RED FILE FOR CALLAN

'Down these mean streets a man must go who is not
himself mean, who is neither tarnished nor afraid...
He is a common man or he could not go among common
people. He has a sense of character, or he would not know his
job. He will take no man's money dishonestly and no man's
insolence without a due and dispassionate revenge. He is
a lonely man and his pride is that you will treat him as a
proud man or be very sorry you ever saw him.'

Essay by Raymond Chandler, *The Simple Art of Murder* (1950)

'There's only one rule: expediency... What the hell do you
think spies are? Moral philosophers measuring everything
they do against the word of God or Karl Marx? They're not.
They're just a bunch of seedy, squalid bastards like me.
Little men, drunkards, queers, hen-pecked husbands, civil
servants playing Cowboys and Indians to brighten their
rotten little lives... How big does the cause
have to be before you kill your friends?'

Alec Leamas, *The Spy Who Came in from the Cold* (1965)

Palmer: You used me as a decoy. I might have been
killed or driven stark raving mad.
Colonel Ross: That's what you're paid for.

Closing dialogue, *The IPCRESS File* (1965)

AMES MITCHELL'S LITERARY VISION of hard-edged espionage was about to collide with ABC's white-knuckled, socially aware, televised theatre to explosive effect – but it happened via a curiously roundabout route which took in the independent channel's opposition: the British Broadcasting Corporation.

Writer Anthony Read recollected, 'Back in 1963-64 I story-edited an anthology series at the BBC called *Detective*, which consisted of dramatisations of classic detective novels. It was essentially a series of pilots, and we got three or four good series out of it – Sherlock Holmes, Clough, Thorndyke, etc.'[1] The career of Read (1935-2015) is worthy of a volume in its own right, as he was a prolific television script writer, editor and producer from the 1960s through to the 1990s, as well as a historian and novelist. At the time he had only recently switched careers from journalism, and was fast becoming an experienced script editor, progressing to work on both *The Indian Tales of Rudyard Kipling* (1963), and *Sherlock Holmes* (1964-65,1968, first starring Douglas Wilmer, then more famously Peter Cushing, in the title role). BBC1's Chief of Programmes, Donald Baverstock, asked Read to set up a further series of *Detective*. 'I said we had done all the best available classic stories, and I would prefer to do a series of original stories, preferably as thrillers rather than simply detective stories,' Read elaborated. 'Baverstock agreed and I started to commission a run of eighteen scripts... One of the scripts was "A Magnum for Schneider".'

At this time, a political battle for resources, money and programme contracts was going on between Baverstock and Michael Peacock, the Chief of Programmes for the fledgling BBC2. Ultimately Baverstock quit and Peacock replaced him. During this conflict, Read recalled, *Detective* was firstly cut down to just half a dozen stories – then axed. (The BBC later decided this decision was a mistake, and the format was revived in 1968.) Read was therefore left with the 'unenviable task' of breaking the bad news to the writers, including James Mitchell; they would get their fees, but their work would remain unmade.

Read continued, 'I tried to place [Mitchell's] script elsewhere in the BBC – who had, after all, paid for it – but couldn't find it a home. There was no place in the schedules for a one-off thriller. It would have had to be done by the "Plays" department, who were only interested in high brow stuff at that time, and certainly didn't want anything to do with something from "Series". I thought the script was far too good to let it go to waste, so I talked to the Copyright Department and asked if they would let Jim buy it back. They said yes... I told Jim to go ahead and offer it to [ABC] with whom he already had a relationship. If they wanted it and were prepared to pay for it, he could use the money to buy it back from the BBC. In fact, they almost bit his hand off. He sold it to them... and the rest, as they say, is history.' Read concluded, '*Callan* was definitely Jim's baby – but I am very proud to have been the midwife who brought it into this world.'

Terence Feely, then *Armchair Theatre* story editor, recalled meeting Mitchell and reading his script, which he noted 'had been around; they get that dog-eared look.'[2] Unsolicited submissions, Lloyd Shirley recalled, were 'a little unusual. A more common occurrence on *Armchair Theatre* was that scripts would be commissioned. Television writers would come up with a story premise or intention, that would be discussed, and the writer would then be commissioned to take their idea into the form of the teleplay.'[3] Nevertheless, he, Feely and Leonard White were all keen to proceed, Shirley remembering, 'from there on it went through the usual process the *Armchair Theatre*s went through, nominating a director... and preparing the show for production.' Mitchell recalled it only taking two weeks, via his agent, for the commissioning decision to be made.[4]

By this time, ABC had a tradition of creating popular series in addition to its showcase one-off plays. Its regular private detective serial, *Public Eye*, for example, drew heavily on the social realist tradition adopted in several notable *Armchair Theatre* productions. *The Avengers*, now largely perceived by the public as a landmark series of stylish, quirky film adventures, originally started life as a predominantly video, performance-centred production. First transmitted on 7 January 1961, recorded by multiple video cameras with a handful of film inserts, the series was heavy on claustrophobia, shadows and moody close-ups. *Armchair Theatre*'s Leonard White was *The Avengers*' first producer, while Mitchelland Feely were among those engaged to write scripts. In contrast to later, more surreal, fare, the early adventures were hard-edged, featuring radiation poisoning, domestic violence, assassinations and protection rackets. In the opening two-parter, Dr David Keel (Ian Hendry) seeks to 'avenge' the death of his fiancé, Peggy (Catherine Woodville), by teaming up with an amoral 'civil servant', John Steed (Patrick Macnee) to bring a gang of herin smugglers 'to book'.[5] Over time, the series' hybrid mix of criminal intrigue and fashionable espionage became a hit with viewers nationally and internationally, offering, as second producer John Bryce put it, 'an hour's entertainment that is different from the show the audience has just seen and different from the one they are about to see.'[6] In 1964 the series was moved to 35mm film for sale to the American Broadcasting Company, and production transferred to the ABPC Studios at Elstree under a restructured management team.

At this point, Anthony Read felt that the new filmed episodes of *The Avengers* began to be 'camped-up'[7]. Not all the original crew at ABC were impressed by the transition to film either, although they acknowledged the reformatted show's commercial success. Jim Goddard believed the film series became a generic 'sausage machine'[8] and Peter le Page remembered feeling 'fed up with it'[9]. David Marshall concurred: 'It did become much more sophisticated, but they lost "it" somehow.'[10] Voytek observed, 'I thought the studio episodes were better, more inventive... [but] when it got passed to the film world they didn't understand the style. It was *all right*, but it lost its artistic qualities. A lot of the designers who worked on [the early episodes] were from the Royal College of Art and discovered Pop Art on those sets.'[11] With Leonard White at the helm, the urge to reclaim the adventure spy series back into television studios, and return the storytelling to a weightier, tougher style, was clearly a consideration at ABC.

ANOTHER FACTOR IN THE EVOLUTION of 'A Magnum for Schneider' was the emergence of the downbeat espionage saga in novels and the cinema, with the film adaptation of *The IPCRESS File* starring Michael Caine a particular influence. 'I like to think of myself as the spy next door,'[12] Caine had said when interviewed by the *London Evening Standard*. 'The wardrobe department have ordered that my clothes mustn't be pressed.' The *Standard* article described the film, then a work in progress, as 'Bond meets The Kitchen Sink,' which could practically be the mission statement for 'A Magnum for Schneider'. When *The IPCRESS File* was released, the *Standard*'s critic Alexander Walker enthused over its 'ruthlessly deglamourised... world of double-think and treble-cross, where the only loyalty is to money and the worst trap you can fall into is thinking you can trust someone... the film's great achievement is to suggest all of this going on beneath the humdrum surface of London life.'[13] Kenneth Tynan felt 'Harry Palmer [is]... not the star but the understudy, not the spy we'd like to be, but the spy we probably would be.'[14] *The Times* praised

Caine's performance[15] while *The Spectator*'s Isabel Quigley observed the film was set in 'a recognisable London where espionage is a seedy business conducted, not by impregnable Bonds, but by men as scared and venal as anyone else.'[16]

Marshall was open about the influence of both this film and the stark cinema adaptation of le Carré's *The Spy That Came in from the Cold* (featuring Richard Burton as Leamas) on the production team. 'It was a move to a more realistic, slightly seedy [style] that was what we were following, without anything like the resources.'[17]

While there are qualities similar to characters in these other productions – the proletarian insubordination, the ruthlessness, troubled consciences and emotional vulnerability – in 'A Magnum for Schneider', the first presentation of David Callan, the craftsmanship of Mitchell, Woodward *et al*, the attention to grim detail, as well as the emphatic social realist surroundings, establish the Section killer as a truly unique creation in his own right.

ARMCHAIR THEATRE: 'A MAGNUM FOR SCHNEIDER'

Writer: James Mitchell
Director: Bill Bain
Designer: David Marshall

FIRST UK TRANSMISSION

Sunday 4 Feb 1967, 10.05-11.05 pm: ABC, Anglia, Border, Southern,
Tyne Tees, Ulster :
Sunday 4 Feb 1967, 10.30-11.30 pm: ATV (London), Channel, Grampian, Scottish,
TWW/Teledu Cymru, Westward[18]

CAST: Ronald Radd (Colonel Hunter), Peter Bowles (Meres), Edward Woodward (Callan), Joseph Fürst (Rudolph Schneider), Ivor Dean (Waterman), Martin Wyldeck (Det.-Insp. Pollock), John Scarborough (Det.-Sgt. Jones), Helen Ford (Miss Brewis), Francesca Tu (Jenny), Judy Champ (Secretary)

PRODUCTION TEAM

Story Editor Terence Feely, *Producer* Leonard White
Uncredited on screen: *Floor Manager* (John Wayne), *Production Assistant* (Anne Summerton), *Stage Manager* (Mary Lewis), *Make Up Supervisor* (Launa Bradish), *Wardrobe Supervisor* (Frances Hancock)

PRODUCTION

Read Through: Thursday 25 August 1966, Steadfast Hall, Kingston.
Rehearsals: From Thursday 25 August 1966
Camera Rehearsals/Recording: Teddington Studio One, Wednesday 7 - Thursday 8 September 1966[19]

TV TIMES: 'Can a spy retire? Not if Control says "No".
"That's what security is for – protecting innocent people."' But can Security be both judge and jury – and the executioner?'
4 -10 February 1967, London edition

MISSION PROFILE: David Callan, an outcast secret agent, revisits his former department for talks. The 'Section' exists to deal with undesirables – people in 'Red Files'. Its supervisor, Hunter, offers to reinstate Callan but first he must carry out a killing. He must do this within one week, without help and without asking why. His target is Rudolf Schneider, a German businessman with whom he's already acquainted; Hunter has engineered Callan's placement in a company in the same office building.

Callan suspects Hunter's offer isn't genuine and takes a liking to the extrovert German, as they share an interest in war gaming. Nevertheless, he orders an illicit gun from Lonely, an old criminal associate. Meres, a Section operative, keeps watch on Callan.

Needing to know why Hunter wants Schneider killed, Callan searches the entrepreneur's office and home, finding he's been selling armaments made by a Japanese firm, Noguchi, to Indonesia, where they are being used to kill British troops. He specifically asks Lonely to get him a Noguchi Magnum .38 calibre revolver for the forthcoming execution.

Callan drinks as the job draws near, receiving an invitation from Schneider to come to dinner and play a war game. Distrusting Hunter, the ex-agent records a confession, but Meres knocks him out and destroys the tape. Viewing Callan as unreliable, Hunter ensures the police will visit Schneider's home just after Callan is scheduled to kill the German. Meres is sent to ensure the frame-up goes according to plan.

The police and Meres both converge on Schneider's home, where Callan and the German play war games. Meres breaks in, but Schneider catches him. Realising Callan's complicity, he prepares to kill both men, but Callan shoots the German dead. He then knocks Meres out and frames him for the killing.

Hunter assigns Callan to a Red File – marking him for death.

A MAN LIKE ME: Capable of bouts of insubordination, vindictiveness, depression, self-loathing and bullying, David Callan is the audience identification figure in this twilight world. In this first encounter, he is an introverted figure making do on a meagre income as a grocer's bookkeeper. His address is Flat 3, Stanmore House, Duke William Street, Bayswater.

Accustomed to working in a clandestine manner, Callan dresses as a window cleaner to search Schneider's home. He is very proficient, overcoming several deceptively arranged levels of security, including two burglar alarms and a safe (which he cracks by listening to the tumblers with a stethoscope). Callan watchfully covers his tracks afterwards, despite a near miss when Schneider returns home. He whistles a variation of 'The British Grenadiers', a traditional British and Canadian marching song, alluding to his military past.

A skilled liar, Callan has a finely tuned sense of self-preservation, suspecting a Section frame-up early on when police arrive to question Schneider. Anticipating being searched, he hides a gun by strapping it to his ankle and he kills Schneider pre-emptively when in danger. He also has a fallible side, nearly giving himself away by not asking for Schneider's address (in a possible piece of subconscious self-sabotage). His plan to take Hunter down with him if he is arrested is also unrealistic.

Callan's tactical abilities in the war games show he could have been officer material in the army but for his problems with authority. He wishes Waterman, the mean cockney grocer who currently employs him, were his target instead of Schneider.

Section Kills: Discounting his National Service, according to Hunter, Callan killed two people when he worked in the Section. Schneider's death takes makes three.

LONELY: Callan's criminal acquaintance. A nondescript individual, he gained the nickname 'Lonely' because, when frightened, he lets off appalling body odour and has halitosis (bad breath) that makes Callan flinch. Having not seen the ex-agent for several months, he is very wary of associating with Callan again, claiming to have other 'jobs' piling up, but, unfortunately for him, Lonely's network of underworld contacts includes gun dealers. (Callan has anticipated the £100 price; in today's money, this would equate to over twelve times that amount.) Lonely says he doesn't know how to write, but can memorise Callan's address quickly enough. He looks sufficiently seedy to attract the attention of Miss Brewis, Callan's suspicious neighbour.

Callan clearly sees Lonely as a liability at this point in their relationship. On two occasions he aggressively warns him to keep his mouth shut about their transactions.

A TIE AND A CREST: This section is about the Section: upper-class and ruthlessly authoritarian, it's the British Establishment in microcosm. The organisation has no official existence, and expects its operatives to follow orders without any explanation. In addition to Red Files, the department uses Yellow ones for people under surveillance and Blue ones for people who join the 'wrong' political party.

Its Commander, Hunter – codenamed 'Charlie' – is playing Meres and Callan off against each other, and seems to be contemplating Callan's imprisonment from the outset. He haltingly tells Meres that he didn't want Callan to become too 'close' to Schneider, but must have suspected this would happen. Hunter's rationale for wanting Schneider dead is that just imprisoning him would not be enough to deter other gun-runners. He is seen drawing a bullet hole on a photograph of Schneider. The Section chief also knows about Lonely and which pubs he uses.

In contrast to Callan, Meres (no first name) is upper-class and obeys orders without question; he favours a fashionable Italian-cut suit, black polo neck and white jeans. Meres puts his feet up on Hunter's desk when unobserved, a hint he might be coveting the top job. He and Callan are not acquainted, but he's eager to prove himself at the other's expense, suggesting he 'takes over' the task of execution. Hunter rebukes Meres for exhibiting complacency about the police, and later seems to acknowledge he has overestimated him. Meres is brutal in his attack on Schneider's girlfriend, Jenny, indicating a possible misogynistic, sadistic streak. Overall, he is presented as a less competent figure than Callan; and he is easily caught and disarmed by Schneider, at which point his self-assurance evaporates.

Having attended military college, Schneider is from the officer class, but although he likes the fine things in life he is not a snob, as his friendship with Callan testifies. Jenny is besotted with him and fearful for his safety.

ALCOHOL, TOBACCO AND FIREARMS: Despite menacing Lonely, Callan *does* buy him a drink – but not the one he wants. As a rule when the pair drink together, Callan has Scotch, while Lonely, a subordinate, is only ever allowed bitter. Lonely heads straight back to the bar to buy whisky with his commission as soon as Callan has departed.

Callan keeps more Scotch at home and drinks under stress. He doesn't smoke (although the rehearsal script envisaged he would.)

Before ordering a Noguchi, Callan asks for 'any .38' handgun'. Magnum revolver cartridges were originally created by Smith & Wesson and Winchester. Callan twice refers to the Magnum's stopping power. (It's worth noting, while it's probably a coincidence, that a few years later a similarly named maverick American detective, Callahan, tasked with doing 'every dirty job', would also wax lyrical about 'the most powerful handgun in the world' in *Dirty Harry* (1971)).

Callan is a 'very good shot': at the Section's firing range he first tries a Smith & Wesson, then switches to a Noguchi Magnum, his score improving from three bullseyes and a miss to four bulls. Callan's decision to use another Noguchi gun to do the job is a subtle hint to Hunter that he has defied his orders not to investigate why Schneider is in a Red File, as well as being poetic justice for the arms dealer. (However, Hunter may have planted this gun for this very reason, anticipating the forthcoming murder trial in which Callan's uncertain criminal background, military service in a country Schneider is selling armaments to, and very deliberate choice of firearm, could all be factors in securing a conviction.)

The firing range has a doorway opening outwards straight on to the line of fire. Even allowing for 'Health and Safety' not being high on the Section's priorities, this is still an insanely dangerous arrangement which the designers addressed in later stories.

SPY-SPEAK: Callan impresses throughout this play, with plenty of one-liners. Told he doesn't look like a burglar, he replies, having just completed a break-in, 'Good burglars never do.' Later, Callan reveals the chip on his shoulder to Schneider: 'I was a Corporal – twice... I didn't get on with officers.' He then quickly, wittily reassures the German ex-officer, 'You weren't on our side.' By contrast he loathes Waterman, addressing him as '*Obergruppenführer*' to his face.

Opening a safe with a stethoscope, Callan tells it to 'cough' in the manner of an army medical examination and baits Lonely several times, telling him he stinks, 'like a one-man sewage farm.' He warns him he could shoot him in the dark with his new Magnum (just by aiming in the direction of the smell). Callan has a sore head after being attacked by Meres but says sarcastically, 'He didn't hit me in a vital spot.'

Schneider mirrors Callan but exposes his own hidden nature by admitting, 'I do not care for blood, not any more.'

Jenny asks Callan to lose the second war game, as winning is important to Schneider. 'It's important to both of us,' he replies, having earlier noted, war is 'better with models; they don't bleed.' There is more smart subtext in Schneider's observations about the war games, when the German admits he has failed 'to see the obvious'.

PAWNS AND PLAYERS: Here we cover – and celebrate the lives of – the cast, crew and writers, especially those who made a key contribution to the series.

RONALD 'RONNIE' RADD (1929-1976) was born a few miles down the road from James Mitchell, in Sunderland, Durham. Following a period in 'rep' theatre in 1950s Birmingham, he made the transition to London's West End in 1956, appearing with Kenneth Williams in *The Buccaneer* and *The Boy Friend* at the Apollo, then in *Hotel Paradiso* at the Winter Garden Theatre. Radd would return to the theatre again several times – later with Claire Bloom and John Gielgud in *Ivanov* (1965) at the Theatre Royal, Brighton – but was keen to break further into television. He achieved this in a BBC adaptation of *A Tale of Two Cities* (1957) starring Peter Wyngarde as Sydney Carton, while Radd played the grave robbing Jerry Cruncher.

A similar classic adaptation of *Treasure Island* (1957) followed in which Radd was cast as Billy Bones, the violent, terrified drunk; a further notable BBC appearance was

Ordeal by Fire (1957), a play about Joan of Arc. Radd found time to travel to New York and appear on Broadway in a run of *My Fair Lady*, which enabled him to make contacts in the American TV industry. He would go on to appear in *The Shari Lewis Show* and 'You Can't Have Everything', a play for the anthology series *The United States Steel Hour* (both 1960). This latter series was the live American equivalent of *Armchair Theatre* in which Radd also appeared, in 'Night Conspirators' (1962) and 'The Cruel Kind' (1963). He was cast as three different characters in a year in instalments of Associated-Rediffusion's police show *No Hiding Place* (1962), and made appearances in the boardroom drama *The Plane Makers* (1963) and the popular medical soap *Emergency Ward 10* (1964).

Lew Grade's ITC, known for making populist, filmed adventure shows, recognised Radd's talent. He made appearances in *The Saint* – 'Starring the Saint' (1963) and *Danger Man* – 'A Date with Doris' (1964) and 'Sting in the Tail' (1965). Directed by Peter Yates, this latter episode features Radd as Alexandros, a café owner who helps John Drake take down Derren Nesbitt's villain. Radd also played the vulnerable Rook who wrecks Number 6's escape plan in *The Prisoner* – 'Checkmate' (1967), and made three appearances in *The Avengers*, in 'Bullseye' (1962), 'The Outside-In Man' (1964) and 'Mission... Highly Improbable' (1967).

Short but imposing, capable of humorous, villainous and sympathetic roles, he was an ideal fit for the Hunter character and briefly revisited the role a few times after his six-episode run in *Callan*'s first series (see Chapters 6 and 8). His reappearances are a clue to how highly regarded he was. 'I think the best Hunter by a long chalk was Ronald Radd, because he's such a subtle actor – you never quite know he's acting,'[20] director Piers Haggard believed. 'The others were actually soft, pretending to be hard. Ronald is really intelligent, a quick mind, so he's much more dangerous.'

'He was a lovely, funny man to work with,'[21] Russell Hunter said. 'There was a reality about his performance which I don't think anybody else quite got, simply because they altered the character a little bit when he left.' 'You just knew that [Radd's] Hunter would use anybody to get what he wanted,'[22] Terence Feely said. Anthony Valentine agreed: 'He had the most extraordinary, implicit, subjective strength.'[23]

'He was the most brutal and the most effective of the Hunters,'[24] James Mitchell noted. 'He was so wrong that he was right – because he didn't look like an establishment figure at all: he looked like a very angry bullfrog!'

Mitchell envisaged the Section being hidden in a disused school with Hunter ensconced in the Headmaster's office, making it ironic that one of Radd's subsequent parts was Wackford Squeers, the monstrous head of Dotheboys Hall in a BBC version of *Nicholas Nickleby* (1968); a future Hunter, Hugh Walters, was also in the cast. Radd featured in more ITC roles, in *The Saint* – 'The Ex-King of Diamonds' (1969), *Randall and Hopkirk (Deceased)* – 'Just for the Record' (1969), *Department S* – 'The Perfect Operation' (1969), *Jason King* – 'The Company I Keep' (1972) and as a suitably Napoleonic Latin American dictator in *The Champions* – 'Get Me Out of Here!' (1969).

One area of Radd's career where he was less successful was in feature films. Lurid publicity for Val Guest's *The Camp On Blood Island* (1958), in which Radd played Commander Yamamitsu, included the strap line 'The Brutal Truth About Japanese War Crimes!' (His casting was an unfortunate example of the then contemporary practice of casting Caucasian actors in ethnic parts).[25] More notable cinema roles included *The Double Man* (1967), *The Kremlin Letter* (1969) and *The Offence* (1973).

Brian Clemens' anthology *Thriller* cast him as another Hunter-esque figure, the no-nonsense Superintendent Terson in 'Murder in Mind' (1973). *Special Branch* – 'Stand and Deliver' (1974) saw Radd's cockney Len Gosling trying to talk sense into his son, a wayward squaddie (Dennis Waterman), who has stolen secret military equipment.

Afflicted with high blood pressure, Radd died in Toronto, Canada, on 23 April 1976 after coming off stage during a tour of the musical version of *Great Expectations*, with John Mills. His final TV appearances were in a Welsh period drama, *The Stars Look Down* (1975), the Jack Rosenthal comedy *Red Letter Day* (1976) and, coming full circle, as King Henry VIII in *The Prince and the Pauper* (1976), another BBC classic adaptation like the one that helped launch his TV career two decades earlier.

PETER BOWLES (born in 1936) made his first stage appearance in *Julius Caesar* in 1956 at the Nottingham Playhouse Theatre. Performances in *Romeo and Juliet* at the London Old Vic soon followed, with later theatre roles in plays as diverse as *Pygmalion* (1994), *Sleuth* (1999) and *The Rivals* (2010). His film credits include *Blow-Up* (1966), *The Offence* (1973), *The Legend of Hell House* (1973), *The Bank Job* (2008) and *Gangster Number One* (2000), on which he was also an executive producer. His first television appearance was in the *Armchair Theatre* play 'Underground' (1958) in which one of the cast, Gareth Jones, was taken ill during live transmission, leaving the other actors to improvise; the cast learned after transmission that Jones had sadly died. A regular in adventure shows, Bowles featured in *Danger Man* – 'Fish on the Hook' (1964), *The Saint* – 'Lida' (1964), 'The Art Collectors' (1967), *The Avengers* – 'Second Sight' (1963), 'Dial a Deadly Number' (1965), 'Escape in Time' (1967), 'Get-A-Way!' (1968) and played the suave defector 'A' in *The Prisoner* – 'A. B. and C' (1967). Married with three children by 1966, Bowles recalled being eager for work and believed he was cast as Meres because he had 'specialised in villains for years... I liked those sorts of parts. I gave up playing them after I played the most evil man in the universe in *Space: 1999*! [1975-77]. After that I switched to comedy.'[26] He became a household name when he appeared with Penelope Keith in the popular BBC romantic comedy *To the Manor Born* (1979-81, 2007).

Accounts concerning the continued casting of Bowles as Meres vary at this point[27]; the actor himself recalled being offered a regular part. 'They wanted to do a series, so I signed to do a series – seven episodes – and then I got offered [the film] *The Charge of the Light Brigade* [1968], so I had to disentangle myself.' Bowles had no regrets, as it gave him the opportunity to work with John Gielgud, David Hemmings, Vanessa Redgrave, Trevor Howard and director Tony Richardson, several of whom became close friends. As for ABC, he remembered that initially 'they said "You'll never work for us again!" or something like that!' Matters were later resolved, with Bowles returning once the company had been restructured as part of Thames Television.

By the 1970s, Bowles was well-known for his skill at carrying off urbane, sophisticated characters, with roles that included Major Todd Milligan in the Lord Peter Wimsey mystery *Murder Must Advertise* (1974), Abby Grant's ill-fated husband in the opening episode of *Survivors*, 'The Fourth Horseman' (1975), a police superintendent in *Thriller* – 'The Double Kill' (1975) and the prosecuting counsel in *Pennies From Heaven* (1978). Other celebrated performances include hypochondriac Archie Glover in the sitcom *Only When I Laugh* (1979-1982), the self-important Guthrie Featherstone in *Rumpole of the Bailey* (1978-1992), journalist Neville Lytton in *Lytton's Diary* (1984-86) and the debonair con man Guy Buchanan in *Perfect Scoundrels* (1989-1992).

AUSTRIAN JOSEPH FÜRST (1916–2005) originally studied Law in Vienna before becoming interested in acting. An unwillingly conscripted war hero in the German Army, Fürst was also secretly helping the Austrian Resistance Movement; after the war, the Allies released him from prison once they learned what his real sympathies were. Having assisted the occupying forces in their de-Nazification program, Fürst left Austria for Canada and a fresh start, finding emigration 'a challenge. I wanted to try my luck in a country where I knew no one and where I couldn't speak the language. At first I was an unskilled labourer – I washed cars, mended roads. I had more jobs in a year than other people have in a lifetime – and I was fired from every one. At one point I was ready to jump into Lake Ontario as a failure.'[28]

His luck changed once he had learned enough English to return to the acting profession. 'I became a film extra by day and a truck loader at night. And then I went back to acting full-time and life was wonderful.' Fürst's career prospered to the point where he started appearing in television productions for the Canadian Broadcasting Company, some of which were produced by Sydney Newman. Marrying a Canadian woman, Fürst moved to England when he was 43. He played scientists co-opted into working for the wrong side in *The Brides of Fu Manchu* (1966) and *Diamonds Are Forever* (1971) and as Major Heinrich Wolf he occupied the Channel Islands in the Sydney Newman ABC wartime children's serial *Counter-Attack!* (1960). Often playing authoritarian roles, he appeared in the nuclear themed *ITV Play of the Week* – 'The Poisoned Earth' (1961), *The Saint* three times (1963-66), *The Champions* – 'The Beginning' (1968), 'The Search' (1969) and *Doomwatch* – 'Re-Entry Forbidden' (1970). For some viewers, he will always be affectionately remembered as the lunatic scientist Professor Zaroff in *Doctor Who* – 'The Underwater Menace' (1967), screaming 'Nothing in ze world can stop me now!' at the end of an episode. Fürst returned to *Callan*, playing a different character, in the third series (see Chapter 7).

MARTIN WYLDECK (1914-1988) also reappeared in *Callan* (see Chapter 8). Wyldeck portrayed the first Commisaris Samson in *Van der Valk* (1972), was robbed by Australians in *The Sweeney* – 'Golden Fleece' (1975) and, as Sir Richard Morris, is seen beating a hasty retreat from *Fawlty Towers* in 'A Touch of Class' (1975).

IVOR DONALD DEAN (1917–1974) was in the horror film *The Oblong Box* (1969) with Martin Wyldeck. Dean also featured in *The Sorcerers* (1967) and as body snatcher Burke in *Dr Jekyll & Sister Hyde* (1971). Like Radd and Fürst, Dean would have been well-known to contemporary viewers, featuring as the mint chewing, lugubrious Chief Inspector Teal opposite Roger Moore in *The Saint* (1963-69). He subsequently played a similar character in *Randall and Hopkirk (Deceased)* (1968-69).

FRANCESCA TU featured as Lotus, Nayland Smith's Chinese housekeeper in *The Face of Fu Manchu* (1965), *The Brides of Fu Manchu* (1966) and *The Blood of Fu Manchu* (1968). Notable ITC appearances include *Danger Man* – 'A Very Dangerous Game' (1965), *Department S* – 'The Perfect Operation' (1969) and *Jason King* – 'A Thin Band of Air' (1972). She has a small, uncredited part as Osato's Secretary in *You Only Live Twice* (1967).

LEONARD WHITE (1916-2016) was an actor and theatre director in Britain, America and Canada. In the latter country, he learned the art of TV directing at the

Canadian Broadcasting Corporation, where he became friends with the actor Patrick Macnee, another Englishman working abroad. Returning to England, White joined ABC and worked with Sydney Newman on producing *Armchair Theatre*, chalking up a staggering 128 plays for the anthology series between 1963 and 1969. His first producing job was on *Inside Story* in 1960, a series set in the same block of flats that each week presented a play with different characters; Edward Woodward featured in one production. In the same year, White helped devise the thriller series *Police Surgeon* as a starring vehicle for Ian Hendry. When the show was cancelled, White, together with Newman, created another series for Hendry, partnering him with Macnee as agent John Steed in *The Avengers*.

After producing the first series, White moved on to indulge another of his interests, science fiction, working with story editor Irene Shubik on the anthology *Out of this World* (1962). At HTV, he oversaw two fantasy serials for children: *Sky* (1975), and *King of the Castle* (1977). His last producing work for television was the BBC family drama *Strathblair* (1992-93), starring Ian Carmichael.

BILL BAIN (1929-1982) handled UK historic dramas *Enemy at the Door* (1978-1980) and *The Duchess of Duke Street* (1976-77). The Australian won an 'Outstanding Directing in a Drama Series' Emmy Award for his work on *Upstairs, Downstairs* – 'The Sudden Storm' (1974), the episode in which WW1 breaks out. His other credits include *Redcap* (1965), *Undermind* (1965), *Haunted* (1967), *Man at the Top* (1971), *Public Eye*, *Within These Walls* (1974-75) and the nuclear drama *The Brack Report* (1982). 'He was new to English television and I worked with him quite a lot,'[29] David Marshall recalled of Bain's early career. 'I became his favourite designer, in a sense, because we hit it off well and he trusted me.'

DAVID MARSHALL himself studied Theatre Design at the Central School of Art. He moved into designing sets for commercials at Shaw Films after a summer season in repertory theatre with the White Rose Players in Redcar, putting on *Gigi*, *All for Mary* and *Look Back in Anger*. A friend from the Central School suggested he looked into a television career as the money was relatively good: 'About £2,000 a year, which included large amounts of overtime – far more than I was making – and a good amount for the time, 1961,' Marshall said. 'I rather looked down on TV. I didn't even have a TV set, but thought "Why not?" I got an interview with Tim O'Brien, the Head of Design at ABC Teddington. He seemed to like my theatre designs – he was very much a theatre designer himself – and gave me a job, starting as an assistant. He and I got on well in a "no-nonsense, get-on-with-it" way.' As well as continuing to work on *Armchair Theatre* and *Callan*, Marshall designed *The Rivals of Sherlock Holmes* (1971-73), the prestigious dramas *Love in a Cold Climate* (1980) and John Mortimer's *A Voyage Round My Father* (1984) and two *Morecambe & Wise Show* specials (1978), together with numerous instalments of *The Bill* (1990-93).

JAN STOECKART, under the pseudonym 'Jack Trombey', composed the *Callan* theme a.k.a 'Girl In The Dark' (Cat. Number: DW/LP 2969) for the production company De Wolfe Music, who became the first of Britain's music libraries. Other Stoeckart compositions have been used in *Monty Python's Flying Circus* ('Blackmail', 1970) and in the horror movie *Dawn of the Dead* (1978). His most famous signature tune was 'Eye Level', used as the theme for *Van der Valk*. Released with 'Distant Hills', his theme for *Crown Court*, on the B-side, it became a hit single in 1973. A version of the *Callan* theme features on an Ike Isaacs compilation[30]; it was also covered, as 'At The Sign of the Swinging

Lightbulb', by the 1980s experimental post-punk band Tools You Can Trust in a Radio 1 John Peel show session.[31] Elvis Costello referenced the theme in the guitar melody of 'Watching the Detectives', his seminal single with the Attractions.[32]

INFORMATION: The arrival of Mitchell's script in the ABC office caused an instant reaction, according to Terence Feely. 'Leonard White read "A Magnum for Schneider", which wasn't typical *Armchair Theatre* material and he said immediately, "This is absolutely wonderful, let's do it."'[33] By August 1966, the team producing the first *Callan* play, including director Bill Bain, was in place. According to Feely, White made the casting decisions for 'everyone in "A Magnum for Schneider" – he cast Ronald Radd, he cast Peter Bowles and he cast that silver-voiced actor who played Schneider, Joseph Fürst. He also cast Russell... Leonard made a great contribution.' Feely concluded, 'If we hadn't had Eddie, I can't think of anyone who could have played Callan so well. And again, that helped to get us a series, because the character was instantly there.'

Edward Woodward famously recalled casting director Dodo Watts resorting to unorthodox methods to ensure he would consider the part, aware the actor was intent on a holiday. 'She deliberately put it through my letterbox, knowing I would have to read it!'[34] Mitchell reflected that the two-year delay between first writing the script and seeing it on screen was in hindsight a 'good thing – otherwise I wouldn't have got Teddy. If it had been done when the BBC had it, he was in America doing a musical, *High Spirits* [1964].'[35]

'It was a very exciting time in television,'[36] the actor recalled of his casting as Callan. 'It really was the first of the anti-heroes, non-heroes, whatever you want to call it, and it really kind of led the way, as *Armchair Theatre* did many times. The thing that appealed to me about the character was that he had a chip on his shoulder, he was a hero with feet of clay and he was a prickly kind of person. I was very much looking for that kind of character to play: this man went right down the middle, you couldn't make up your mind what he was... It was quite a big chance to take for the television company at the time.'

'Class came into it a great deal, it was still very alive and kicking in those days... I suppose it still is a bit,'[37] Mike Vardy observed generally of the conflict between Callan and his employers. 'Take MI5, for instance, all their top brass were right out of what we would call the top drawer – Eton, Guards Officers and all the rest of it... Callan's background was that he'd been in prison, and he was somewhat downmarket, although sharp as a button, so there was a lot of antagonism.' This mutual antipathy would continue to be an essential part of the series that followed.

A sheet of descriptions was attached at the front of the rehearsal script, summarising some of the principal characters:

> <u>David Callan:</u> Former operative in Security, now a clerk.
> A basically kindly man but with a high degree of skill and
> security. Good pistol shot and a cunning thief. The clash
> of the two interests has left him bewildered as a human
> being. Lower Middle Class background. Age 35.
>
> <u>Hunter:</u> Head of Security section. Regular army in manner.
> Ruthless and well mannered. Makes plans like a first rate
> staff officer, which in fact he is. Age 50.

Meres: Ex public school, Etonian manner. Fascist in outlook. An executioner who loves his job. Mid twenties.

Schneider: Ex-regular German Army officer, now a gun runner to the Indonesians in Malaysia. Big, bluff, charming, immensely competent. Fond of the good things in life. Age 50.

Lonely is some way down this list, indicating he is a more minor character in this story, only featuring in a few scenes. He is described as a 'small, nervous crook who suffers badly from B.O. and specialises in obtaining firearms.' (A minor character with the same name and hygiene problem appears in Mitchell's first John Craig novel, *The Man Who Sold Death*.)

Short scenes trimmed from the rehearsal script included Hunter meeting Callan in the pub and insisting on knowing when he will do the job, and Callan ordering a distraught Jenny to take Schneider's money and run.

James Mitchell deliberately chose 'Hunter' as 'the name that goes with the job'[38] of the department's commander. 'I intended that from the beginning. I think in hindsight the [rank of] Colonel was a mistake: he should have just been Hunter.' Concerning the Section itself, he added, 'I knew, by reading, what the KGB "wet job" characters [executioners] were like, I had some idea of what CIA characters were like also by reading, and I'd heard gossip about French characters. Therefore, it seemed to me to be logical that if that's what they were like in Russia, America or France, then that's what they'd be like in England.'

Considering the organisation generally, Mike Vardy believed that the fictional Section would have been 'well outside the aegis of MI5... MI5 were not, and still are not, allowed to arrest people – they have to pass over their evidence to Special Branch who then arrest them, and that still exists today as far as I know... [but] what goes on in basements of course is another matter.'[39] 'If there is such a thing as a dirty tricks division then by definition it would have to be very low profile, and probably as few people as possible would know about it,'[40] Lloyd Shirley reasoned. 'Most people would not wish to know.' Trevor Preston recalled, 'I once asked a very senior policeman I was talking to about some work – he'd been in Special Branch and he quite liked *Callan* – if there was an [assassination department]. He said, "Let's put it this way, Mr. Preston. There are a lot of people that fly into Heathrow that don't fly out again!"'[41]

The lengthy sequence when Callan burgles Schneider's flat gave David Marshall plenty of authentic detail to add to his sets. 'I remember having problems with security devices, alarms, safes, etc. in Schneider's flat, in the sense of getting it right. I was never very happy about the result, but in the process of watching the drama unfold and being held by Edward Woodward's performance, these things seem a minor quibble. We didn't think we were producing art, but we recognised an original and topical script... and we saw that there was potential for a gritty, realistic, non-glossy but compelling way of putting it on screen. I don't mean that we were the originators of [this approach] – obviously the writer and producer had envisaged it in this way [too].'[42] 'The way we designed *Callan* was fairly gritty, fairly downplayed: social realism, if you like,'[43] Peter le Page noted, cautioning that, 'doing "grubby" was quite difficult for television in those days, because you had to put so much light on the [set].'

The *TV Times* publicised the play in most regions with photographs of Woodward, Fürst and Tu (whose christian name was incorrectly spelt 'Francisca' on the end titles) and a short feature, informing readers, 'A new secret agent makes his debut... His name: David Callan. His profession; licensed executioner for a security organisation.'[44]

The article made clear that this was only the first appearance of a character that would return later. Press reaction was positive, with reviewer Kenneth Easthaugh praising Mitchell's script. 'I spy a first-rate spy... His name is "Callan" and his portrayal by Edward Woodward in the *Armchair Theatre* play was the event of the weekend.'[45]

Reflecting on the episode in hindsight, future producer Reg Collin believed there were two key reasons for the play's success. 'The characters as drawn in "A Magnum for Schneider" were very good. Ted Woodward was brilliant casting as was Russell Hunter.'[46] Peter Egan was in the audience when the play was transmitted, unaware he would one day participate in its remake as a film. 'I remember seeing that – it was terrific. I thought, "What a great idea!" And two years later it was a smash series.'[47]

There was a clear sense amongst many of the cast and crew that the play was likely to be more than a one-off, several months before formal offers were made. 'More than anything I'd done before, I was certain that this *Armchair Theatre* play would spin-off into a series and if it did, it would be successful,'[48] Edward Woodward said. 'It was one of the first scripts I'd read where I had that feeling. There's a strange thing when you start something and it's turned into a series – you want it to succeed, but on the other hand you don't want to get trapped in a character. [But]... it was such a very good script.' Even before 'A Magnum for Schneider' was commissioned, Feely told Mitchell, "There's more than just an *Armchair Theatre* here, there's a series. Would you be prepared to let me write a presentation, as I promise you I'll sell it to [Head of ABC] Brian Tesler and Lloyd Shirley?" So that's what I did.'[49]

'I assumed the men upstairs were thinking about it because it was the great spy time,'[50] Mitchell recalled of the period after recording. 'I didn't know until I was told that there had been a mass of phone calls. That was the first information I had that a series was in the offing.' ABC held a special screening of 'A Magnum for Schneider' while looking around for directors to work on the projected series. Peter Duguid recalled attending the screening and being impressed enough to put his name forward.[51]

Callan's jocular comment about 'robbing mail trains' hints that he has a criminal background, as it's a clear reference to the meticulously planned heist in 1963 that became known as the Great Train Robbery. He also refers to Meres as a 'public school Capone'.

Mitchell may have mischievously named the fictional Magnum manufacturers in this story after Isamu Noguchi (1904-1988), a Japanese-American artist and architect known for his mass-produced furniture and lamps.

Callan and Schneider reprise two historic battles, Talavera and Gettysburg. Part of the Peninsular War, Talavera (1809) took place when an Anglo-Spanish army under Lieutenant General Sir Arthur Wellesley – later ennobled as Viscount Wellington – successfully repelled French forces led by King Joseph Bonaparte and his Chief-of-Staff Marshal Jourdan (rather than Marmont as shown in the war game).[52] Gettysburg (1863) was fought between opposing (loosely northern) Union and (southern) Confederate forces during the American Civil War. Major General George Meade's Army defeated attacks by Confederate General Robert E. Lee's forces and, as shown in the play, devastating artillery fire was used against the Southern division led by Major General George Pickett.[53]

At 35, Callan would have been born in 1932 and too young to serve in WW2, so it can be inferred that his military service probably took place during the long-running Malayan Emergency (1948-1960) which Mitchell's novels (considered separately in Chapter 9) confirm. Like the Cold War itself, the 'Emergency' had its roots in the conclusion of WW2, as several former British territories were consolidated. The pro-Chinese Communist Party of Malaya opposed the move and an insurgency resulted. Throughout the 1950s, many British soldiers, conscripted through National Service, were given jungle warfare training and sent to the country to fight, alongside troops from other Commonwealth countries such as Australia.

Villagers were interned, curfews were imposed on anyone thought to be assisting the rebels, and Agent Orange and other defoliants were used to destroy bushes, food crops, and trees, starving the insurgents out and depriving them of cover. Concessions were given to those who co-operated with the British: the conflict partly concerned autonomy and ended three years after the UK Parliament passed the Federation of Malaya Independence Act in 1957. Subsequently, in 1963, the British government's attempts to create an even larger Federation – Malaysia – combining the country with other colonies and ex-colonies – led to a confrontation ('Konfrontasi') with neighbouring Indonesia over control of Borneo. The Malaysian Ambassador was expelled from Indonesia, the British embassy was burnt down and Indonesian forces began attacking the Malaysian Peninsula in August 1964. The conflict ended in 1966 following an attempted coup in Indonesia, resulting in President Sukarno becoming side-lined.

MISSION ANALYSIS: *'I wonder what the hell he's done.'* Other contemporary spies like Bond, Drake, Steed and Palmer followed orders, although they were sometimes distasteful; even le Carré's Alec Leamas acquiesced, despite being manipulated and expressing disgust with the mission he completed. By contrast, 'A Magnum for Schneider' arguably takes John le Carré's scenario one step further, showing a disillusioned, expelled agent's relations with a callously pragmatic, inhuman organisation.

In any other equivalent TV espionage thriller of the time, the stylishly dressed, cultured agent would be the central character and the working class one would be the villain. James Mitchell iconoclastically inverts this formula, helped immeasurably – as the *Daily Mirror* TV critic noted – by a stunning performance from Edward Woodward.

The reaction against the norm continues in the decision to locate the characters in dingy office block, bedsit and pub sets, turning budgetary constraints into an asset; even Schneider's relatively luxurious apartment has a cramped, temporary feel, with Jenny talking about moving on. The humour is earthy, the swearing risqué (for 1967), there is Scotch and beer rather than champagne or cocktails, and the seamy tone is high-lighted by Lonely's rancid personal hygiene. The resulting production is both hard-bitten *and* high brow; the model soldiers Callan and Schneider collect and play war games with are an ironic metaphor for the larger three-way conflict taking place between them and Hunter. Additionally, Woodward's Raymond Chandler-style voiceovers of Callan's internal dialogue make the viewer complicit with his flawed character.

This is a dangerous, original, cold and compelling world in which the motives of every character are ambiguous. Accordingly, the actors' performances transcend the technical limitations of videotaped drama: Callan is by turns commanding, introspective, pressurised and fallible; Radd's Hunter is gregarious but chillingly dispassionate; Russell Hunter's Lonely is almost Dickensian in his subservient demeanour towards Callan, while Fürst's 'lovable rogue' veneer belies his macabre collection of press cuttings reporting on the consequences of his arms sales.

If there is a single flaw in this array of characters, it's Meres. He is underwritten, mostly functioning as Hunter's proxy, a stock 'Swinging London' heavy, and perhaps because of this, Peter Bowles's brand of smooth, accomplished villainy, previously seen to greatb effect in *The Avengers* and the ITC canon, doesn't quite fit with the rest of the downbeat, deliberately grubby ambience. Doubtless had he stayed on in the role, more thought would have gone into making this dynamic (and the fact that he's noticeably taller than Woodward) work.

The killing of Schneider is the emotional as well as the narrative conclusion of the story. After the body falls, Callan looks visibly drained, as if he's lost another shred of what remains of his humanity. The importance of this sequence and the intricate shifts in motivation leading up to it again separate 'A Magnum for Schneider' from other 1960s TV thrillers, in which the disposal of villains is generally achieved with a shoot-out or a set-piece action sequence. Every character in the story receives an appropriate pay-off; Hunter thwarted, Meres framed, Schneider shot and Callan now a target, having completed his mission, while hating himself for doing so and hating Hunter even more.

Overall, 'A Magnum for Schneider' is a taut, stripped-down story about loyalty, indecision and betrayal which works as both a gripping statement of intent for a full series and as the self-contained play it was initially intended to be. Callan's debut story has now been recognised as an iconic espionage drama, and it's not surprising that Mitchell would return to refine it twice more.

END TITLES: Under the play's credits for the actors and production team, Hunter's secretary transfers Callan's details from a Yellow File to a Red File.

5: SERIES ONE
Nobody Loves a
Freelance

'Callan and I seem to have arrived at a very good working
arrangement. What you might call a balance of terror.'

Hunter, 'The Good Ones are All Dead' (1967)

T HE EARLY DAYS OF ANY DRAMA series can be challenging, as Edward Woodward observed: 'You are struggling to establish exactly where you're going with the
character, and the writer's struggling to establish exactly where he's going.'[1]

With recording on 'A Magnum for Schneider' completed, a full series – simply titled
Callan – was under consideration. 'We could see the potential,'[2] Lloyd Shirley reflected.
'Edward Woodward was very happy, and Russell, and the characters seemed to be very
interesting. That tends to be – putting it in a sentence – the major criteria for a series. The
human beings tend to be rather more important than the story area. Somebody might
come along and say, "Wouldn't it be interesting to do a series about veterinary surgeons?"
The answer is it might be, and it might not be. If you've got a given story and the surgeon
is interesting, then the answer is probably "yes". The man, or woman, or individuals [and]
the middle-specific human beings are the most telling, necessary thing about all series.
They're the hardest to do, too, as that's where a writer requires art.' Shirley himself took
on the role of the putative *Callan* series' overall Executive Producer.

'He was so successful, the most successful executive [ABC and Thames] ever had,'[3]
David Wickes recalled of Lloyd George Shirley (1931-2003). 'He was the goose that laid
the golden egg.' After the first series of *Callan*, Shirley acted as executive producer
on *The Mind of Mr. J.G. Reeder* (1969-1971), the anthology series *The Rivals of Sherlock
Holmes* (1971-73) and John Braine's revival of Joe Lampton, *Man at the Top* (1970-72),
before setting up the TV film-making subsidiary of Thames Television, Euston Films, with
George Taylor in 1973. Euston was phenomenally successful under Shirley and George
Taylor's directorship, producing *The Sweeney* (1975-78), together with its two spin-off
feature films. Shirley remained involved after stepping down as a company director, achieving further success with *Minder* (1979-1989). At Thames, he continued commissioning
and overseeing popular dramas, including *Rumpole of the Bailey* (from 1987-1992), *Paradise*

Postponed (1986), *Mr. Palfrey of Westminster* (1984-85), *Hannay* (1988-89), and the first 35 episodes of *The Bill* (from 1984-87). He retired in 1992 when Thames lost its franchise to broadcast.

'Lloyd Shirley's record stands for itself,'[4] David Marshall believed. 'He was responsible for a vast number of productions and for introducing new writers and directors. Like Sydney Newman, a fellow Canadian, he kept a sharp eye on what was going on, at all levels in a production. He had certain impatience with some designers who he felt were inclined to be precious and arty and who he thought were losing sight of the overall objective. I remember a fractious meeting when he summoned the entire Design Department and accused us of being "bleeding hearts". The ensuing "discussion" was lively and at times acrimonious but he had, at least, noticed us as people who helped shape things. I personally liked Lloyd and he gave me many opportunities to design important shows for Thames TV.' Wickes famously recalled the Head of Drama once becoming so incensed, he threw a typewriter through an office window. 'It landed on [Programme Controller] Brian Tesler's car. They didn't fire him – they wouldn't dare! You don't fire Lloyd Shirley, because you know that the BBC would pick him up like *that*. The top brass were terrified of him, because he could do anything he wanted, virtually.'[5]

Many of the other ABC and Thames staff also remembered him with enormous affection and respect, and for his assistance to others in developing their careers. 'He hid his light under a bushel really – he had a good mind,'[6] Trevor Preston said, having first broken into television under Shirley's guidance. Voytek was one of several designers whom Shirley encouraged to move into directing: 'There was no real training program in those days; you followed your connections.'[7] Piers Haggard recalled, 'I was very fond of Lloyd and I owe a lot to him – after the *Callan*s, I did quite a few Dominic Behan plays. Also *The Folk Singer* [1972], a satire on Northern Ireland... Lloyd was always prepared to go out on a limb, that was the wonderful thing about him. He wouldn't have survived a minute today!'[8]

While Shirley had overall artistic and financial control of ABC and Thames' drama output, he knew when to delegate, describing his role as staying 'in immediate day-to-day touch with everybody you're working with... You try to be an effective sounding board for all your colleagues. As part and parcel of that you try and get as much [as you can] from them, rather than imposing your own ideas.'[9]

AN ASSOCIATE PRODUCER was appointed to oversee *Callan*'s day-to-day running and, as he had already built up an effective working relationship with James Mitchell on 'A Magnum for Schneider', Terence Feely was given the job. A Liverpudlian, Terence John Feely (1928–2000) studied English and Psychology and began his career as a journalist on a local paper in Middlesbrough. Moving to Fleet Street in London, he began submitting ideas for films, leading to a successful pitch to Alfred Hitchcock for a script entitled *Heartbeat*. After a brief period writing for the theatre, Feely broke into television, adapting the short story 'The Unconquered' for *The Somerset Maugham Hour* (1960), about a rape in occupied France during WW2.

Feely also worked on several episodes of the Associated-Redifussion police series *No Hiding Place* (between 1959 and 1961) and early instalments of *The Avengers* – 'Nightmare' and 'Dragonsfield' (both 1961). Featuring skulduggery in a hospital and a nuclear research centre, outlines of these episodes (the recordings are now sadly lost) show Feely rapidly grasping the series' early, idiosyncratic espionage and crime-fighting format.[10] 'It was more fun writing the black and white ones because there was so much improvisation,'[11] Feely recalled. 'In fact, the flip style of *The Avengers* arose purely from the fact that the scenery kept threatening to fall down in the early black and white ones, and Pat Macnee developed these very quick responses to cover it.'

Before story-editing *Armchair Theatre*, Feely contributed an episode to *The Saint* titled 'The Convenient Monster' (1966), about suspicious deaths at Loch Ness attributed to its legendary creature. He went on to write on several other series on which one or more fellow *The Avengers* writers Brian Clemens, Terry Nation and Dennis Spooner were involved, providing scripts for *The Persuaders!* (1971-72), *The Protectors* (1972-74), and *The New Avengers* (1976-77). He wrote seven instalments of *Thriller* (1973-75) from Brian Clemens' outlines, and contributed one story outline himself, 'Only a Scream Away' (1974); he also collaborated with Clemens on a stage version of *The Avengers*, which ran briefly in Birmingham and London in 1971.

After his work on *Callan*, Feely left ABC to join the British arm of Paramount Pictures, and was partly responsible for ensuring that production of the movie *If...* (1968) went ahead. Lindsay Anderson's metaphorical tale of revolution in a public school went on to gain critical success, but overall he found the experience at Paramount frustrating and left, pleased just to get this one film made. Approached by Patrick McGoohan, Feely had provided a script for *The Prisoner* – 'The Schizoid Man' (1967). 'It was all about surrealism,' he enthused. 'Television is made for surrealism: it's what the medium was invented for. That's what [co-creator] Patrick McGoohan wanted, that's what we tried to do... It was twenty years ahead of its time. Nobody's ever allowed us to do anything like it since.'

Contributing a second episode, 'The Girl Who Was Death' (1968), he subsequently joined McGoohan's company Everyman Films, becoming one of three directors (with the impulsive actor and the director David Tomblin). The trio had hoped to produce a film of Henrik Ibsen's *Brand*, which McGoohan had starred in on stage in London, but sadly funding fell through. 'I subsequently heard what happened,' Feely recalled. 'Lew Grade, quite naturally, said to him, "Look, £950,000 is more than enough, you're not getting [an] extra £50,000" at which point Pat, like Douglas Fairbanks Senior, in one bound leaped on to Lew's desk – it was about the size of Heathrow Airport – and kicked everything on it into the four corners of the room, with the result that when he came in the next morning, not only didn't we have the £50,000, we didn't have the £950,000 either. And that was it! That's when I said "Bye bye."'

The association with Tomblin led to Feely writing two instalments for Gerry and Sylvia Anderson's live-action science fiction series *UFO*, which Tomblin worked on as a director: 'The Man Who Came Back' and 'Timelash' (both 1971). The latter is arguably one of the best stories in the series, featuring a duel between Commander Ed Straker (Ed Bishop) and Turner (Patrick Allen), a traitor who, thanks to the alien invaders, can immobilise time. Finding himself affected, Straker injects himself with amphetamines to speed up his metabolism – a plot point that caused some controversy – so he can stop an imminent UFO attack.

Feely returned to the concepts of a duel and countdown in two of his contributions to *Return of the Saint* (1978), 'Duel in Venice' (involving a kidnapping) and 'The Armageddon Alternative' (featuring a nuclear bomb hidden in London). When his *Callan* and *Armchair Theatre* colleague and close friend Robert Banks Stewart asked him for a script for his 'private ear' series *Shoestring* (1979-1980), Feely contributed the gripping 'Listen to Me', in which detective Shoestring (Trevor Eve) has to prove a jailed man's innocence before his distraught wife carries out her threat to commit suicide. Feely worked with Banks Stewart on *Charles Endell, Esquire* (1979) and was entrusted with providing the finale of the first series of *Bergerac* (1981), 'The Hood and the Harlequin', which climaxed with a fight on a speeding boat.

He demonstrated his adaptability by writing for the children's historical adventure *Arthur of the Britons* (1972-73), the women's prison drama *Within These Walls* (1974-76), sitcom *Robin's Nest* (in 1978) and *The Dick Francis Thriller: The Racing Game* (1979), before creating the memorable ITV police drama *The Gentle Touch* (1980-84). A ratings hit, it was also the first British police TV drama with a female lead character (Maggie Forbes, played by Jill Gascoine). A successful three-series sequel, *CATS Eyes*, followed over 1985-87.[12]

Feely's obituary in *The Times* listed his other achievements as 'Novels – *Rich Little Poor Girl* (1981), *Limelight* (1984), which won the Book of the Year prize in New York; member of the Garrick Club; wrote to *The Times* letters page on subjects dear to his heart such as the use and abuse of the English language and what he believed to be the destructive auction of independent television franchises.'[13] Among his final works were various Barbara Cartland TV movie adaptations. While these might seem an unlikely choice of work to enthusiasts of *Callan* and his other TV thrillers, it demonstrates the versatility of which Feely and other popular television writers of his generation were capable.

FEELY PERFORMED A DUAL FUNCTION on *Callan*. As a producer he had to hire, fire, control budgets and manage schedules, and as the story editor he had, as he puts it, 'keep control of the [scenes], at the read-through, at the rehearsal... [and] be the author's proxy and stop other people changing things.'[14] Mitchell and Feely decided the series would continue from where 'A Magnum for Schneider' left off. 'It sort of became obvious that the Section and Lonely were what was needed,'[15] James Mitchell said of the series format. 'Because the Section was part of the machine, and you could use as much or little of it as you wanted, and Lonely because you needed the other half of Callan's life; also that Don Quixote/Sancho Panza kind of [double act] always works anyway.' Mitchell was clearly pleased with how the character of the thief had come to life. '[The potential] was always latent in the knowledge that they shared a prison cell. The dependency was always there, also Callan's ability to frighten him. Turner said painting was a rum business. That's a bit like writing – it's full of unconscious promptings.'

'There's your series: a man who is totally ruthless on behalf of his country,'[16] Feely elaborated. 'And if he's got a heart, he certainly doesn't show it, as the sort of people who are going to be agents are bastards. The job would appeal to people like Meres as he's sadistic and off-balance. These people have never grown up; they like living in a fantasy world, they love doing something that nobody knows about.' He qualified, 'There are [agents] that are totally, utterly sane and tough cookies: they're like the marines and they don't crack. The majority of them, I suppose, are like that – but they're not particularly interesting, dramatic characters.'

'Having established your central character, you have to make sure that your other running characters follow the main lines that you want them to,'[17] Edward Woodward said. 'They've got to follow Callan's thoughts and story, but at the same time, you have to make sure that the other leading characters are not merely cardboard cut-outs [and] have lives of their own. I thought James Mitchell, out of all the writers I've ever worked with, did that marvellously. He knew about Meres; Meres had a background. He knew about Lonely's life. You couldn't know much about the Hunter character's life, but again, [James would] brush things in there that were a surprise [for the audience, that] surprised Callan and the other characters.'

Mitchell and Feely's collaboration resulted in a document entitled *Callan Series Origins*. It contained a proposal for a run of episodes, appending three James Mitchell story outlines that ABC had purchased options for, and pitched the series to the ABC management: 'The reality [of spying] doesn't come from atomic fountain pens or poisoned wallpaper; it comes from people. And many of them are very ordinary people, caught up in extraordinary situations.'[18]

Sections in the document cited James Mitchell's track record as a writer of best-selling thrillers, and summarised the plots for three stories: 'The Death of Robert E. Lee', 'Goodness Burns Too Bright' and 'But He's a Lord, Mr Callan'. Character descriptions for Callan, Lonely and Hunter were also provided, the latter stating, 'Colonel Hunter is a very cold fish indeed. If he weren't, he couldn't do his job, which is to plan the destruction of people dangerous to the state... he is a brilliant organiser of murder, and sleeps every night without pills.' The proposal concluded: 'Callan worries too much about people: even the enemy whom he must destroy. Throughout the series there is a fierce antagonism between Hunter and Callan. Each unconsciously is striving to make the other man more like himself. Sometimes the antagonism is comic, sometimes it is deadly. It is always there.' According to TV researchers Anthony Goodman and Matthew Morgenstern, Brian Tesler was shown 'A Magnum For Schneider', accepted that there was potential in it and approved the proposal for a series: 'On December 1, 1966, Lloyd Shirley sent Terence Feely a memo: "Full steam ahead on *Callan*. If James Mitchell is able to underwrite the three story outlines he has submitted and the opening show, we would be delighted. If possible, he should write all six."'[19]

Feely supervised the day-to-day work, selecting directors, designers, actors and scripts. 'I ran the show and Lloyd Shirley was there as "executive clout" if I needed it,'[20] Feely explained. 'Lloyd really did very little on the series except to back me up when I was in trouble – which he did.' 'He used to give you a series and you got on with it,'[21] Feely's successor Reg Collin agreed. 'He would see the episodes as they were recorded and give his comments but there was no interference of any sort.' ABC wanted production to start in April 1967, with episodes ready for transmission by July. In January, Feely was given precise recording dates, and realised that as Mitchell already had three outlines to develop into scripts, plus a fourth opening episode to write, it would be sensible to call in Robert Banks Stewart, then a fellow *Armchair Theatre* story editor, to help. 'I went out for lunch with Terence and James Mitchell at some top London restaurant, we had lunch and talked about the series,'[22] Banks Stewart recalled. 'The transmission date was too soon for them to believe that James could write all six, so I was commissioned to write two for the first series, which is how I came to do "Goodbye, Nobby Clarke" and "Nice People Die at Home".'

At this point, while no one suggests any open dispute, a minor fault line seems to have opened up in relations between James Mitchell and ABC. 'It's never a perfect relationship, but you've got to live with it,'[23] Mitchell reflected on the prospect of a writer sharing his creations with other professionals and, possibly influenced by Shirley's suggestion that he should provide all six episodes for the series, *Callan*'s creator did submit six screenplays, a prodigious feat of authorship under such time constraints; Banks Stewart did as he had been asked too, resulting in eight complete scripts. Given this surplus to the six transmission slots available, it was inevitable that at least one of the writers would be disappointed.

Lloyd Shirley was seemingly impressed with 'Goodbye, Nobby Clarke', wanting it to be screened as the second episode. 'I think James got a bit twitchy,'[24] Banks Stewart reflected, aware of the potential importance episode transmission order can have in establishing a series, 'feeling that I might have been sharing some of the credit, which I wasn't at all.

I was just a humble foot-soldier, signed up to do a job.' He stressed, 'I'm not taking anything away from James, that would be totally unfair; he was the one who had the idea of Callan and Lonely – a huge creation. But somehow or other I'd written something that established the character [of the series], and I didn't realise I'd done that.' ('Goodbye, Nobby Clarke' features a colleague from Callan's military past; perhaps Mitchell was also aggrieved because, unknown to Banks Stewart, he was privately cultivating his own similar idea that eventually became 'The Worst Soldier I Ever Saw' in Series Two.)

Ultimately, the decision was made to produce, but defer transmission of, Banks Stewart's second script 'Nice People Die at Home', while Mitchell's 'Goodbye Mary Lee' would remain unmade, the net result being that Mitchell's episodes comprised five-sixths of the first series, including the opening instalment and the conclusion. As 'Nice People Die at Home' was made, a seventh transmission slot must have been originally scheduled, and Peter Bowles recalled that number of episodes was offered him as part of his contract for playing Meres.[25] However, at some point after recording the situation clearly changed, as Shirley remembered there only being 'slots for six transmissions.'[26]

Several artistic decisions were taken at this time, including incorporating the famous swinging light bulb title sequence. Musically, this would be accompanied by 'Girl In The Dark', (see 'A Magnum For Schneider', Chapter 4) and the composition's publisher, De Wolfe, was asked to reserve it for exclusive use on the series; this was arranged, despite a licencing dispute. The light bulb and brick wall titles were designed by Patrick Downing and filmed by Jim Gask with Edward Woodward in March 1967, prior to recording the episodes themselves (see 'The Good Ones Are All Dead'). Feely and Shirley opted to superimpose the end credits over dialogue-free concluding scenes, and to employ brief pre-credit 'teaser' sequences, emulating the approach used by contemporary ITC film series to draw in an audience. In contrast to ITC, the use of film was kept to a bare minimum and generally only carried out on location within the vicinity of Teddington. As with 'A Magnum for Schneider', the majority of the series would be a videotaped production at ABC's Teddington studios, following rehearsals in the Steadfast Sea Scout Hall in nearby Kingston-upon-Thames.

Feely needed to confirm the series cast and, in most cases, this simply meant re-contracting actors from the *Armchair Theatre* pilot. Francesca Tu (Jenny) was engaged for one story only, 'The Death of Robert E. Lee' because, as the producer admitted, 'There was no way we could think of developing her [character] advantageously.'[27] Lisa Langdon, a young Swedish actress, was cast as the Section's regular secretary, replacing Judy Champ. 'She was brought in, quite honestly, to add a bit of glamour,' Feely admits. 'We didn't actually need her to be there, but we did need someone pretty to look at; I mean, Lonely wasn't very pretty to look at! Teddy was all right for the girls, but we needed something for the guys. It was as simple and calculated as that.' Ironically, though, Hunter's secretary would remain off-screen for most of the first series.

One major challenge was to recast the part of Meres. '[Dodo Watts] was the Casting Director of ABC and she was a damn good one,' Feely said. 'So you simply said, "Look, this is the character, who can you suggest? Let's have a look at a few." And the Casting Director then goes through her mental notebook and comes up with a few choices, out of which you select who you want. Jeremy Lloyd was my conception of Meres as he had that aristocratic, laid back, smooth school-bully quality, which [Anthony] Valentine also had... I thought, "This is brilliant." [Jeremy] could be very sinister.' Feely recalled that Howard Thomas and Lloyd Shirley were involved with the final decision, with input from Leonard

White, and that Valentine was awarded the part. Jeremy Lloyd instead played the one-off role of Maitland, a character very similar to Meres, in 'Goodness Burns Too Bright'.

This story was the first to be recorded, in April 1967. Over the next fifteen weeks, six more stories were made in the following order: 'The Death of Robert E. Lee', 'But He's a Lord, Mr Callan', 'The Good Ones Are All Dead', 'Goodbye, Nobby Clarke', 'You Should Have Got Here Sooner' and 'Nice People Die at Home'. Production was completed in early July just as the series was beginning transmission, with an average of ten days devoted to making each episode.

THE FIRST SERIES takes Callan's relationships with Hunter, Meres and Lonely as seen in 'A Magnum for Schneider' and develops them a lot further. Callan's association with Hunter exemplifies his generally antagonistic relationship with authority, and in 'Goodbye, Nobby Clarke' he has to deal not only with his former Section boss but also his old army instructor. In this story, and 'But He's a Lord, Mr Callan', Hunter again attempts to get Callan imprisoned, viewing him as an unpredictable loose end. In 'Goodness Burns Too Bright', the Section are again seen to be no more moral than their Communist rivals: needing a decoy spy to be captured by East German intelligence, but reluctant to use a present operative, partly in case the plan leaks and impacts on morale, Hunter has no hesitation in selling Callan out and actively facilitates an attempt to abduct him. Class division continues to be part of the pair's ongoing feud: 'Goodbye, Nobby Clarke ' clarifies that Hunter was originally from a similar class to Callan, but he is a social climber, sending his children to a public school, even though he dislikes Meres' hereditary wealth just as much as Callan does. The caustic Colonel admires Callan's abilities and is always mindful not to let him find out too much about what he's planning, aware his former top operative is quite capable of killing him. Interviewed for the *Callan: This Man Alone* documentary, Dick Fiddy said of the conflict with Hunter, 'I can't think of any other series that took such a cynical view of the employer' while, in the same programme, Jim Goddard felt 'Callan did what he did because he had no choice – other than suicide, and he wasn't that sort of person.'[28]

Further complications arise in that Meres – now given a first name, Toby – resents Callan and the standing in which he is still held in by Hunter. In 'The Death of Robert E. Lee', he threatens to beat Callan up, and in 'But He's a Lord, Mr Callan' he sets the unstable Lord Lindale onto him. Sometimes the pair simply aggravate each other, at other times the gloves are off. In 'Goodbye, Nobby Clarke', Meres is ordered to escalate a conflict between Callan and his former tutor but is told not to let Callan get hurt; he interprets this rather liberally in helping two thugs set up an ambush for the ex-agent. Callan retaliates by knocking Meres out, just as he did in 'A Magnum for Schneider', describing this incident to Hunter as an 'accident'. Jeremy Lloyd's character, Maitland, is equally spiteful in 'Goodness Burns Too Bright', exceeding his brief by allowing the opposition to know that an injured Callan will be looking for medical help in Berlin.

All the stories expand on the character of Lonely, the novelty of a shabby, vulnerable petty criminal involved on the fringes of espionage adding a huge amount to the downbeat quality of the series. As well as being Callan's ammunition supplier, he's assigned to investigate and follow people and track down addresses, like a private detective. Lonely also acts as a chauffeur, burgles premises and, with his knowledge and contacts, performs much the same function as an informant in a police series. Thanks to Russell Hunter's exceptional skills as an actor, the character has a fragile humanity and humour that helped enormously in setting *Callan* apart from other contemporary thriller series.

Although Series One also features staple mid-1960s Cold War subjects such as Nazi war criminals, mercenaries, African wars of independence, Communist agents, black-mailers and traitorous scientists, they were dirtied down by the production's earthy style and made credible through the performances of the actors, led by Woodward, rather than action scenes. Mitchell's third *Callan* script, 'The Death of Robert E. Lee', showed how daring the series could be as it was possibly the first TV thriller to engage with the highly contentious Vietnam conflict, then raging in South East Asia.

The final story in the first series, 'You Should Have Got Here Sooner', weaves the key characters' interactions together even further. By putting Lonely in hospital after a vicious beating from Meres, Mitchell shrewdly raises the stakes into a showdown between Callan and his Section rival, which results in him reaching an accommodation with Hunter. Although this climactic tale serves as neat closure to the earliest, rawest series of *Callan*, Feely maintained this congruence happened purely by chance: 'There was no element of a serial to the series at all. The episodes stood by themselves: they didn't carry on.' Perhaps the consistency was achieved because only two writers and one story editor were involved, and – aside from slightly more humour in Banks Stewart's script – he and Mitchell had similar, matter-of-fact styles of storytelling.

'I possibly decided that there ought to be humorous [dialogue],'[29] Banks Stewart recollected. 'I might have thought, "This is so grim it needs lightening up a bit". Terence Feely may well have advised me to [do that].' 'A villain who can laugh is much more real, to me, than one who is a mono-track rogue,'[30] Feely believed. 'If he can make jokes, and they're good jokes, if he can laugh about something absolutely beastly, then immediately he becomes more human. But James could never see that – he wanted the villains to be villains and the heroes to be heroes.'

The first series launched on television in the summer of 1967, heralded by publicity in the *TV Times*. During the run-up to the first episode, ABC issued several press releases to promote their new 'Saturday thriller', citing the cast and crew's careers, including the 'attractive' Lisa Langdon. Part of the first, issued in May 1967 by ABC Press Officer Marie Donaldson, wove in an inevitable comparison to James Bond: 'This series was inspired by James Mitchell's *Armchair Theatre* play "A Magnum for Schneider" transmitted last February. That centred around a fictitious government department which exists to watch people who are so potentially dangerous to the security of Britain that they may need to be eliminated. In other words, the members of this department are the men who are licensed to kill.'[31] A second press release summed Callan himself up as being 'solitary and disenchanted, hating the ruthless world from which he can't escape, hating Hunter and the men who hold him in it – but bored and restless with his legal work in book-keeping, and unable quite to shake off the sensation of excitement which accompanies each job for the Section.' The publicity blurb emphasised, '*Callan*... is above all about Callan the man.'[32]

Although billed in most regions as a 'Saturday' event, *Callan* was also shown on Tuesdays on the Westward and Channel networks and on Thursdays on Border and Southern. For political and logistical reasons the other disparate ITV regions also transmitted the series in different time slots, with some screening the show at 9 pm, and others at the later, post-*News at Ten* (or post-pub) 10.30 time. Press reaction was minimal, but when it did appear was extremely positive: '[Callan] breaks the mould, because he has no loyalty except to his own fierce code of survival,'[33] Mary Malone wrote in the *Daily Mirror*. 'The opposition is quite as likely to be Callan's boss in Whitehall, or a mate in MI6, as an enemy agent... He knocks MI6 for six.' 'Since it began three months ago, the series has captured the interest of millions,'[34] Peter Dacre enthused in the *Daily Express*. In the same article, Woodward noted '*Callan* is becoming a cult,' an opinion borne out by the audience ratings[35] (viewing figures in millions):

'The Good Ones Are All Dead'	4.5
'Goodbye, Nobby Clarke'	4.4
'The Death of Robert E Lee'	3.8
'Goodness Burns Too Bright'	5.4
'But He's a Lord, Mr Callan'	4.7
'You Should Have Got Here Sooner'	6.2

For the first five episodes the viewing figures average out at the 4.6 million mark, with 'Goodness Burns Too Bright' possibly receiving a boost due to the *TV Times*' coverage of Gladys Cooper's guest appearance; the final episode's figure is notably higher, more on a par with the 6.8 million achieved for 'A Magnum for Schneider'. Maybe Woodward was right and word was beginning to spread about the innovation of the series' morally ambiguous characters and its cynical view of human nature, but in contemporary terms it was still what would be called a 'slow build'. Lloyd Shirley explained: 'Simple audience counting is very important, but it has to be [considered with] where [the series is] placed in the schedule. Almost no programme can be judged to be operating in a vacuum – it depends on what audience you have identified, what's against you, what show follows you.'[36] Overall, Shirley felt in hindsight that 'against strong opposition [*Callan*] had done quite well. Well enough to justify itself.' The series had accurately predicted a change in viewers' tastes in the spy genre, as television caught up with tougher, more pessimistic espionage stories in literature and the cinema.

Although four of the six episodes from *Callan*'s first series no longer exist, the surviving two are a tantalising, grimy window onto the programme's earliest days, clearly showing the conflict between the ex-agent and his former employers and highlighting the appeal of such anti-heroic characters. The next series of *Callan*, which started pre-production late in 1967, would be markedly different. 'Aside from *The Prisoner*, I thought *Callan* was the best series I ever worked on,'[37] Feely stated, although he had mixed feelings on how the programme later developed. 'I didn't approve of a lot of things that happened after I left. I thought they got sloppy; I thought they started letting shouting take the place of real emotion. In the first series, we tried to have people talking in a controlled way and let the power of the language do the work. After that, everybody seemed to be shouting. And the violence, again, I didn't really approve of... I suppose you're bound to feel [protective] when you [help] create something.'

SERIES 1 REGULAR CAST

Edward Woodward (David Callan)
Anthony Valentine (Toby Meres) 1-3, 5, 6
Russell Hunter (Lonely)
Ronald Radd (Hunter)
Lisa Langdon (Secretary) 1, 3, 6

PRODUCTION TEAM

Associate Producer: Terence Feely, *Executive Producer:* Lloyd Shirley

(Uncredited on screen) Floor Manager: Pat Kennedy (2), Bill Lawford (6), Denver Thornton (1, 4, 5), *Production Assistant:* Mary Ellis (2), Betty Kenworthy (1), Marian Lloyd (5), Dottie Rice (4, 6), *Stage Manager:* Shirley Cleghorn (6), Mary Lewis (4, 5), Stuart Orme (2), Dorothy Pope (1), *P.A. Timer:* Jacqueline Davis (5), *Make Up Supervisor:* Launa Bradish (1, 2, 4), Joan Watson (5, 6), *Wardrobe Supervisor:* Ambren Garland (1, 6), Frances Hancock (4), Jill Silverside (2, 5), *Technical (Operational) Supervisor:* Peter Cazalat [Cazaly] (1, 5), Mike Roberts (4), Peter Wayne (6), *Lighting:* Louis Bottone (4, 6), Peter Kew (5), 'Ritchie' (1), *Cameras:* Michael Baldock (1, 5), Dickie Jackman (4, 6), *Sound:* Mike Pontin[g], (4, 6) Peter Sampson (1, 5), *Racks:* Bill Marley (5), Bert White (4, 6), *Vision Mixer:* Nigel Evans (4, 6) Del Randall (1, 5), *Call Boy:* Peter Grove (4), Richard Mervin (6), *Grams:* Tony Dawe (1), Mike Fairburn (4), Vic Finch (6)[38]

S1.1 THE GOOD ONES ARE ALL DEAD

Writer: James Mitchell
Director: Toby Robertson
Designer: Malcolm Goulding

FIRST UK TRANSMISSION
Border, Southern: Thursday 6 July 1967, 10.30 pm
Westward, Channel: Tuesday 29 August 1967, 10.30 pm
All other regions: Saturday 8 July 1967, 9.00 pm

CAST: Powys Thomas (Stavros), Linda Marlowe (Jeanne), Tom Kempinski (Avram), David Lander (Berg)

EXTRAS/WALK-ONS: (*Uncredited on screen*) Contraced through John Dennison and Eric Blythe agency: Philip Becher, Harry Mitchell (Old Men), Eleanor Darling, May Warden (Old Ladies),Kevin Rowland, Daniel Sinclair (Lorry Drivers), Blair Stuart (Counterhand)[1100]

TV TIMES: 'You do this for me, Callan – or I'll have you destroyed. I mean it'
July 8-14 1967, Southern edition

PRODUCTION
Rehearsals: From Monday 22 May 1967
Location Filming: Manchester Square, Westminster (Friday 19 May)
Camera Rehearsals/Recording: Teddington Studio One, Wednesday 31 May and Thursday 1 June 1967.[39]

PRE-TITLES: Hunter threatens Callan with execution – he's now in a Red File – unless he helps arrest the Nazi war criminal *Obersturmbannführer* Strauss, 'a mass production killer' responsible for 3,000 known deaths. Callan warns him that if he tries to have him killed, he'll kill Hunter first. After all, the Section commander trained him...

MISSION PROFILE: Callan wants nothing to do with the assignment until Hunter tells him that Strauss worked on the Nazis' V2 missile program during WW2 – Callan's parents were killed by one of the weapons in an attack on London. Strauss, now calling himself Stavros and working as a cotton importer, needs a book-keeper. Callan goes to work for him at his flat in an operation to determine the man's identity for Israeli intelligence, who want Strauss to stand trial for war crimes. Avram, an Israeli intelligence agent, tells Callan that if he confirms the fugitive Nazi's identity, the Israelis will pay Callan for delivering him.

While Strauss does business on the phone, Callan takes an impression of one of his sets of keys. In a hidden safe, he discovers incriminating evidence – German army uniforms, Strauss's Nazi party membership card and, disturbingly, a bag of gold tooth-fillings and ledgers bound in what looks like human skin. Berg, a survivor of the V2 slave labour force that Strauss organised, confirms the war criminal's identity at a performance of the opera *Die Gotterdammerüng.* Jeanne, the businessman's young French lover, reveals to Callan that it was she who alerted the Western authorities after she discovered who Stavros really was. As she tries to leave, Jeanne is intercepted by Meres and he takes her in.

Learning of Jeanne's betrayal and Callan's mission, Strauss dresses in his army great-coat and pulls a Luger pistol on the freelance agent, but Callan took the precaution of unloading it. Initially unsympathetic, Callan allows Strauss to take his own life with a cyanide pill. Finding the Nazi dead, Avram angrily tells Callan he won't get paid.

A MAN LIKE ME: Callan hates being coerced into working for Hunter again and threatens the Section chief with execution. The ex-agent leaves his previous employment at Waterman's and the wholesale grocer is never seen again.

Throughout, Callan is in denial about the past, wanting to forget the 1939-1945 war – because of the death of his parents? – and remarking that Stavros' liking for Wagner 'doesn't make him a stormtrooper'. When confronted by the truth, on the phone to Hunter Callan spits out his list of incriminating Nazi evidence in disgust.

Under his aggressive exterior he is prone to sentimentality, genuinely believing Hunter could be wrong about Strauss due to the generosity he exhibits towards his girlfriend, Jeanne. He's also fallible, leaving behind one of his safe-breaking tools – from his bespoke burglary kit – which she discovers. Callan is revolted by Jeanne's greed and the drunken pass she makes at him, calling her 'a mess' and 'a whore'.

Callan's professional and entrepreneurial streaks show as he asks for a £200 advance from the Israelis so Lonely can buy him a new Noguchi Magnum. He wants to know all the angles on his assignment; his conflicted feelings about the war result in the suicide of Strauss and the loss of the rest of his fee.

LONELY: Subject to mixed feelings because of the ambivalent way Callan treats him. Lonely is invaluable in helping Callan open the safe concealed behind Strauss's wardrobe, identifying it as a Wallstein, Frankfurt and Main which has a 'simple action lock'. Callan knows exactly how much Lonely is going to charge for getting him a gun and has the money ready, unkindly taunting the petty thief about his BO by concealing the cash in a soap dish.

From somewhere the little man has acquired a shabby raincoat and a flat cap, which he habitually wears from now on. Lonely is not above morbid curiosity, nervously asking Callan what it feels like to kill. Callan coldly threatens to kill *him* if he tells anyone about their dealings, holding a knife to the thief's face in a 'greasy spoon' café.

A TIE AND A CREST: The key to the Section's exploitation of Callan is deniability: as in the Schneider affair, if an agent outside the intelligence service is caught by the civil authorities, the Section can say Callan was working directly for the Israelis. This is the first of Hunter's shady deals that we see with foreign intelligence services, as he offers to detain Strauss in return for information about Egypt.

Perhaps because of Hunter's influence with the Home Office, Meres has escaped the prison sentence Callan engineered for him, when he left the upper-class agent unconscious to be found by the police in Schneider's house. That incident has started a feud between the pair, but even though Meres detests his rival, he is objective enough to recognise Callan's professionalism and tells Avram that the ex-agent is 'a damn good operator.' Callan delights in provoking Meres when the rival operative visits Callan's flat, putting on a posh voice and asking, 'Hello, come slumming, have you?'

ALCOHOL, TOBACCO AND FIREARMS: Callan is a crack shot on both the Section firing range and a fairground stall, where he meets Avram. The short-barrelled .38 Noguchi Magnum has become his hand gun of choice, as he instructs Lonely to buy him another, together with fifty rounds of ammunition. Stavros keeps a Luger pistol from his Wehrmacht days under lock and key.

Meres, Stavros/Strauss and Jeanne all smoke, the latter hitting the bottle heavily in an attempt to anaesthetise her guilt over betraying Strauss. Callan appears equally alcohol-dependent, his hands shaking as he gulps down whisky after Strauss has killed himself.

SPY-SPEAK: Callan tells Hunter that Avram doesn't like him. The Section chief's priceless reply: 'I find that absolutely incredible.'

Meres makes a wry observation about Hunter's weight: 'You'll get fat, sir.' 'I am fat,' he tersely replies.

Callan's chillingly down-to-earth description of killing to Lonely: 'It's like eating your lunch: if you've got the stomach for it, it's easy.'

Callan enjoys a mock dirty phone call to Hunter's secretary: 'I love you with a sordid and overwhelming passion.'

PAWNS AND PLAYERS: LISA LANGDON, who played the Section's loyal secretary features for the first time. Born in Sweden and moving to Britain in 1959, Langdon's other television appearances include roles in *Mr. Aitch* (1967, Harry H. Corbett's attempt to break away from Harold Steptoe), the *Dixon of Dock Green* episode 'The Team' (1967) and a storyteller on the popular children's series *Jackanory* (1968); she read four stories, 'The Island of Sand Fleas', 'The Magic Scythe', 'The Little Pony' and 'East of the Sun and North of the Earth'. The first three were written by Susan Ball and the latter was her adaptation of a Norwegian folk tale, which Langdon translated.[40] She retired from acting in the early 1970s.

'She was very important in the series because she was basically the only running woman,'[41] Edward Woodward recalled, 'so young men like [Patrick Mower's character Cross] fell for her or flirted with her.' 'She was a one-parent family, which was unusual in those days,'[42] director Mike Vardy noted. 'I'm not sure if she'd recently been divorced... but I know she had a child. [Lisa] didn't give me the impression she was an ambitious career actress. I think she signed to an extras agency, came for an interview, she was liked and was taken on.'

SHOLTO DAVID MAURICE 'TOBY' ROBERTSON (1928 -2012) was better known in recent years as a leading theatre director, touring classic plays around the country as head of Prospect Productions. Earlier in his career, he worked on *Richard II* (1968) with Ian McKellen, *Saint Joan* (1977) with Eileen Atkins and, in 1979, took *Hamlet* around the world with Derek Jacobi, making a landmark visit to China with the first-ever Western theatre tour there.[19] Robertson began his career as an actor in the 1950s, sharing the stage with Clifford Rose on another production of *Richard II* (1954), before making the transition to directing and handling increasingly prestigious plays in Brighton, Nottingham and the West End of London. He became artistic director at the Theatre Clwyd in Mold and persuaded many leading actors to appear on stage in the North Wales town. Robertson was assistant director to Peter Brook on the harrowing film version of William Golding's *Lord of the Flies* (1963) and made several forays into television directing, on *ITV Television Playhouse* (between 1959-1960), *ITV Play of the Week* (1960-64), *Armchair Theatre* (1964-68) and *Mystery and Imagination* (1966-68).

POWYS THOMAS (1926-1977) was born in Wales and worked frequently in Canada. His memorable television productions there include *Macbeth* (1961), starring Sean Connery, and the TV movie of *The Three Musketeers* (1969); a young Christopher Walken was also in the cast. In England, the Welsh actor guested in Ian Hendry's crime series *The Informer* (1966-67).

LINDA MARLOWE was born in 1940 in Australia. She has worked with Steven Berkoff many times, including Franz Kafka's *Metamorphosis* (1986), later realised for television by Jim Goddard. She kept her acting surname from her marriage to fellow actor William Marlowe. For her first solo show, *Berkoff's Women*, Marlowe won the *What's On Stage People's Choice Theatre Award* for Best Actress, in 2001. On television, she has had roles in *The Green Man* (1990), the *Widows* sequel *She's Out* (1995), Steven Moffat's *Jekyll* (2007) and *EastEnders* (2014-). In 2011, Marlowe appeared in the film adaptation of John le Carre's *Tinker Tailor Soldier Spy*.

DAVID LANDER had roles in various comedies such as *Sykes* (1972-79), *Bless This House* (1971-76) and *Father Dear Father* (1972-73). Prior to 'The Good Ones Are All Dead', he featured in the BBC's espionage series *The Spies* (1966), starring Dinsdale Landen and Simon Oates. A prolific TV actor in the 1960s, Lander made two appearances in *Danger Man*, in the episodes 'A Date with Doris' (1964), which also featured Ronald Radd, and 'The Mercenaries' (1965). Switching channels, he featured in the BBC's *Adam Adamant Lives!* series in the episode 'The Sweet Smell of Disaster' (1966) about artificial killer flowers. In 1973 Lander worked with Woodward again, appearing in one of the *Whodunnit?* playlets.

TOM KEMPINSKI also worked with Woodward later in his career, in the *Root of All Evil?* anthology play 'A Bit of a Holiday' (1969). He went on to play Dr Stephen Partness in *Moonbase 3* (1973), the BBC's short-lived adult science fiction series. In 1972, Kempinski featured in *Spy Trap* (see Chapter 13).

INFORMATION: 'The Good Ones Are All Dead ' saw the debut of *Callan's* iconic and atmospheric title sequence: a naked light bulb swinging slowly past a grimy brick wall with the name of the series stencilled on it, inter-cut with Edward Woodward's face moving in and out of shadow. As the light moves slowly back and forth, the names of the main cast appear and the sequence ends with the bulb shattered by a gunshot; the episode's title, followed by the name of the writer, become visible over a photograph of Woodward's face fractured by a bullet-hole. The leading man made more of a contribution to this piece of TV history than simply appearing in a close-up. 'We shot it in a little studio in Staines, a tiny suburb of outer London,'[43] Woodward revealed. 'We had a shooter, who came along with an air pistol and an air gun, and we got to – I think it was Take 22 – and he hadn't shot [the bulb] out! I thought, "I can't go on like this," so I picked the gun up, shot it, and it went out first time. That's my great claim to fame about this series, I think!'

In addition to being used as used as the series' opening and closing theme, 'Girl In The Dark' extracts were also employed as incidental music. Other background music for this story consisted of a 'Traditional German Marching Song', 'Hurdy Gurdy Music' and an extract from the opera *Die Gotterdammerüng* by the German composer Wilhelm Richard Wagner (1813-1888), which Callan listens to on the radio.[44]

The Nazi dictator Adolf Hitler (1889-1945) felt Wagner's music symbolised his own aspirations for Germany; in a 1922 speech he claimed Wagner glorified 'the heroic Teutonic nature'[45] of the Aryan ideal; in reality, the Nazis used the parts of Wagner's oeuvre that suited them and ignored what didn't. Wagner has been referenced several times by popular culture, most famously in Francis Ford Coppola's feature film *Apocalypse Now* (1979), when 'Ride of the Valkyries' from *Die Gotterdammerüng* is played over a sequence in which Colonel Kilgore (Robert Duvall) attacks a Vietnam village with helicopter gunships so his troops can go surfing; the same piece became staple incidental music in the police series *Strangers* (1978-1983).

James Mitchell was pleased with how the episode turned out, having previously worked with Toby Robertson on the (intriguingly titled) *Armchair Mystery Theatre* – 'The Lonely Crime'. 'The pace is very slow. The creeping up of tension can only go at that speed, you can't intercut that with machine guns and car crashes or helicopters or whatever. What happens is, you put a tremendous weight on the actor. Here, it was very much Powys Thomas and Linda Marlowe who had a lot of work to do, and did extremely well.'[46] Mitchell had 'always been fascinated by Mossad anyway because it's so bloody good... [WW2] had only been over for 20 years then and the "SS man on the loose" was still very much a possibility, and you could still have him as a comparatively young man with all the vigour and danger that implies. He's guilty and so he must die, but whether he's now the man who committed those crimes sufficiently to hand him over and have him killed in that way is another matter...'

A black-and-white photograph of Woodward with Ronald Radd accompanied 'The Good Ones Are All Dead 'programme details in some editions of the *TV Times*. A brief accompanying article by Stewart Knowles brought new viewers up to speed: 'Callan is a disenchanted and reluctant executioner.'[47]

Always keeping a watchful eye on new British TV shows, the American entertainment magazine *Variety* reviewed the episode in its 2 August edition: 'The spy with cold feet and a butterfly stomach is no novelty, but this new TV format adds an agreeable irony of its own and the opener, after a slightly uncertain start, developed a dashing sense of seedy intrigue. The skein has been developed by James Mitchell and Terence Feely and centres around the character of Callan, played with appealing nervous anguish by Edward Woodward. He is used by an unscrupulous boss for further assignments, with threats of death and disaster over his luckless head if he fails. So he's a perpetual fall guy, and his own fate gives an extra tense dimension to the plotting,'[48] the reviewer 'Otta' enthused. 'The initialler [sic] had him on the trail of a wanted ex-Nazi, also on the black list of an Israeli group, and Callan was installed as clerk in the office of the suspected guy, finally identifying him by a bag of gold fillings taken from teeth and hidden in a locker. The plot gathered a nice momentum, and was salted with incisive character cameos, especially from Ronald Radd, as Callan's chilly chief, and Anthony Valentine as a supercilious sidekick. Toby Robertson's direction grew in assurance and flair as it progressed, and the skein shapes as one of the best of its kind in the current schedules and should compete with ABC's earlier *Public Eye* in holding power.'

Over 35 years later, this landmark production was screened as part of the National Film Theatre's celebratory *ITV at 50* season; in tandem with the *Danger Man* episode 'Say It with Flowers', it was shown on 19 and 28 November 2005. (The episode was incorrectly advertsised as 'The Good Guys Are All Dead' in the accompanying NFT booklet).

The Israelis want Strauss to stand trial for war crimes in the Israeli capital Tel Aviv. The precedent for this is the prosecution of Otto Adolf Eichmann (1906-1962), a German Nazi SS *Obersturmbannführer* (Lieutenant Colonel) who was one of the major architects of the Final Solution. In WW2, Eichmann was ordered by SS *Obergruppenführer* Reinhard Heydrich (1904-1942) to facilitate and manage the logistics of mass deportation of Jews to ghettos and extermination camps in German-occupied Eastern Europe. In 1960, he was captured in Argentina by Mossad, Israel's intelligence service. Following a widely publicised trial in Israel, Eichmann was found guilty of war crimes. He was also found guilty of membership of three organisations condemned as criminal at the Nuremberg trials: the Gestapo, the SD and the SS. When considering the sentence, the judges concluded that the Nazi had not merely been following orders, but believed wholeheartedly in Hitler and had been a key perpetrator of genocide. Eichmann was sentenced to death on 15 December 1961 and hanged in 1962.

The German V-weapons (V1 and V2) cost $3 billion (in wartime dollars) and were more costly than the Manhattan Project that produced the Allies' atomic bomb (at $1.9 billion). 6,048 V2s were built, at a cost of approximately 100,000 Reichsmarks (£2,370,000) each; 3,225 were launched. SS General Hans Kammler (1901; date of death unknown), may have been another inspiration behind Strauss. Kammler was an engineer who had constructed several concentration camps including the notorious Auschwitz, had a reputation for brutality and originated the idea of using concentration camp inmates as slave labour in Germany's rocket program; the V2 is perhaps the only weapons system to have caused more deaths by its production than its deployment. An estimated 2,754 civilians were killed in London by V2 attacks and another 6,523 were injured. One of the most notable figures in the Nazi missile program was Wernher von Braun (1912-1970), who developed the V2 rocket. Controversially, he was protected from prosecution for war crimes by the Americans, designing the Saturn 5 space rocket for NASA in the 1960s.

The Egyptian President, Gamal Abdel Nasser (1918-1970), refused to recognise the new state of Israel in 1948 and called for its destruction. Nasser also accepted financial aid from the Soviet Union to build the Aswan Dam, which would have put him near the top of Hunter's watch-list. (Construction began in 1960 and wasn't completed until ten years later).

In 1950, Egypt closed the Suez Canal to Israeli shipping and tensions mounted as armed clashes took place along the Israeli border. In 1956, Israel joined a secret alliance with Great Britain and France aimed at regaining control of the Canal, which the Egyptians had nationalised. The alliance launched an invasion to reclaim the waterway, but condemnation and lack of support from America led to the humiliating withdrawal of British forces.

MISSION ANALYSIS: *'The war is over and I've left the Section.'* With the benefit of hindsight, you have to wonder why ABC didn't bracket 'A Magnum for Schneider' with *Callan*'s new opening and closing titles and repeat that play as the series' first episode. 'The Good Ones Are All Dead' is very similar, even paraphrasing some of the original play's dialogue (Hunter wanting Callan for one more job, the exposition about the Section's function) and plot beats (Callan detailing Lonely to get him a Noguchi Magnum, the burgling of a suspect's safe and the infatuation of an old German soldier with his young lover.)

In all other respects, and even more than 'A Magnum for Schneider', 'The Good Ones Are All Dead' is overtly political and overwhelmingly serious, a far cry from the escapism of *The Man from UNCLE* and *The Avengers*. The character of Callan continues breaking the mould of fictional spies; he's seen here as a self-interested, sometimes bullying and violent man, hanging on to his tattered conscience by a thread and almost as ruthless as his former employer. He is completely in tune with the anti-establishment mood of the late 1960s, rejecting, questioning and double-crossing the organisation that trained him, an anarchic force to be reckoned with. Excusing the recycling of some elements of the plot is the recasting of Toby Meres, and Anthony Valentine impresses from the first moment he appears on screen. Now given a back story as an ex-officer in the Coldstream Guards, the slightly remodelled character is proud of his army career, wearing a smart regimental blazer and tie, while, in a clever visual contrast, Callan shuns his military heritage by dressing in an untidy and anonymous way. The cool Meres is now an ideal contrast with the volatile Callan, the defining characteristic of Valentine's performance being a superior, dry sarcasm which is always watchable.

Director Toby Robertson emphasises the claustrophobia of the sets and his novel, sophisticated approach enriches the serious content of the script. Tom Kempinski resembles Valentine, a clever piece of casting that reinforces Callan's remark that the Israelis are becoming indistinguishable from the Nazis they are fighting (an accusation that, rightly or wrongly, still echoes down the years). David Lander's portrayal of the fragile concentration camp survivor Berg is raw and poignant; his descriptions of Strauss breaking his ribs because he accidentally broke a plate in the SS man's quarters, and of nearly vomiting when Strauss brushed against him at the opera, reinforce the point that for popular TV thrillers, play time is over.

Powys Thomas's Stavros/Strauss is, like Callan, a man who can't escape his past. He has almost become a different person in two decades of commerce and philanthropy, but still hoards the grisly evidence of his previous life. Both he and Callan are trying to embrace the present but Strauss's history ultimately destroys him, something that would become a recurring theme in *Callan*. The Nazi's feeble excuses for his crimes and the climactic scene, where expressionistic lighting and Nazi chanting on the soundtrack highlight his disintegrating state of mind, is exceptionally disturbing. The ending is a shock: after executing a man he liked in 'A Magnum for Schneider', the audience would have expected Callan to hand over the clearly guilty Strauss to Israel – but he doesn't. Callan's erratic sense of humanity, in allowing Strauss to commit suicide, abandons the viewer in a world that is a moral vacuum, with no easy answers even from its key character.

In a story dealing with WW2 legacies that in 1967 were still raw for TV drama, the powerful ending is daring and emotionally exhausting. However, for Callan – and the audience – the war is just beginning...

END TITLES: Callan walks into Strauss's front room and shakily has a stiff drink of whisky.

S1.2 GOODBYE, NOBBY CLARKE

Writer: Robert Banks Stewart
Director: Peter Duguid
Designer: Bryan Graves

FIRST UK TRANSMISSION

Border, Southern: Thursday 13 July 1967, 10.30 pm
Westward, Channel: Tuesday 5 September 1967, 10.30 pm
All other regions: Saturday 15 July 1967, 9.00 pm

CAST: Michael Robbins (Nobby Clarke), Helen Ford (Miss Brewis), Fionnaula Flanagan (Rena), Dennis Alaba Peters (Kanaro), Alfred Hoffman (Stan Sheppick), Sally Travers (Launderette Attendant), Bruce Purchase (Blair), John Dunn-Hill (Fenton)

EXTRAS/WALK-ONS: (*Uncredited on screen*) Listed as being required for the launderette, the pub garden, the docks sequence, and in the hospital scenes.[49]

PRODUCTION

Rehearsals: From Friday 2 June 1967
Location Filming: Victoria Station, London (Friday 2 June 1967)
Camera Rehearsals/Recording: Teddington Studio Two, Tuesday 13 June and Wednesday 14 June 1967[50]

TV TIMES: 'You shouldn't have come here, Callan. I was always too good for you. I taught you, remember'
15 – 21 July 1967, Anglia edition

MISSING FILE: The master tapes of this story do not exist in the Studio Canal archive.

PRE-TITLES: Mercenary Ronald Clarke arrives in London and Meres tries to run him over.

MISSION PROFILE: Callan learns 'Nobby' Clarke, his old Army trainer, is hospitalised. Visiting him, he suspects that the Section tried to kill him. Hunter confirms Callan's suspicions – Clarke is now a mercenary, training forces in Africa who oppose British interests in the country. So he's a target – unless Callan can provide an alternative solution.

Outwardly, it appears that Clarke and his colleague, Kanaro, are recruiting a sales team trading in African novelties, but Callan learns he's really signing up more mercenaries.

Callan frames Clarke by staging a robbery at the launderette where his wife Rena works. Meanwhile, Meres has joined up with Clarke's outfit and informed him that Callan is a spy, aiming to provoke a fight. Meres is sent with two of Clarke's men, Fenton and Blair, to grab Callan in his flat, but, alerted by Lonely, Callan knocks all three unconscious. He then confronts his former mentor and knocks him out too, leaving him to be arrested.

A MAN LIKE ME: Callan still says he makes his living from doing the accounts for 'wholesale groceries'; on hearing this, Clarke says he's gone soft. The pair jokingly square up and Callan later throws a cigarette lighter at him as if it were a grenade. This anticipates their final fight, which is cathartic for Callan: he has always suspected that Clarke used him as a human shield when he carried him away from a fire fight in Malaya, which Clarke confirms. The mercenary seems to harbour a subconscious dislike for 'Dave' but also respects his abilities, believing Callan can 'track down anyone' if he wants to.

LONELY: Acts like a private detective, investigating Clarke's recruitment drive and procurement of false passports. He complains that Callan is 'always' riling him about his body odour when he's made to sit outdoors. Lonely helps Callan survey the launderette but doesn't like the idea of Callan having to knock out the owner, Sheppick. He is forced into the centre of the action when held hostage in Callan's flat, and has the presence of mind to kick an envelope surreptitiously under the door, alerting Callan to the intended ambush.

A TIE AND A CREST: The running joke concerning Hunter's corpulence continues as he eats hummus in his office. Clearly, he is a *bon viveur*, as this Middle Eastern dish would have been harder to obtain in 1960s Britain. Hunter finds Meres' aversion to garlic amusing.

Clarke has promoted himself to Major and (as scripted) grown a moustache, although he plays both these affectations of military seniority down while he's in Callan's company. His educated African contact Kanaro went to Sandhurst.

ALCOHOL, TOBACCO AND FIREARMS: Clarke drinks Pernod in the morning. (He calls it 'milk of amnesia.') This behaviour echoes Callan's own sporadic alcoholism – he's had a late night when his censorious neighbour, Miss Brewis, wakes him.

The Callan/Lonely, Scotch/beer demarcation continues.

SPY-SPEAK: Callan's wry comment on launderettes: 'I like watching other people's dirty washing for entertainment.'

His observation on Hunter's culinary skills: 'I might have known you'd be a cook. You're so bloody good at stirring things.' Callan later rages at the Section chief: 'What did your wife buy you for Christmas, a butcher's apron?'

He delivers a wonderful quip on seeing Lonely in the launderette: 'It's like Toulouse-Lautrec playing football.'

Hunter's perceptive assessment of Meres' character: 'You've got as much feeling as the bumper on your car.'

PAWNS AND PLAYERS: ROBERT BANKS STEWART (1931-2016) 'was an ordinary young reporter, then a feature writer'[51] in Scotland, on *Illustrated* magazine. 'That and *Picture Post* were the two [photo reportage] magazines. I spent three years travelling around the world doing feature articles. It was an extraordinary thing, to have that kind of luck at 24-25.' Observing legal trials had already fuelled his interest in writing fiction, and when *Illustrated* folded, Banks Stewart transferred into television journalism while contemplating a bigger career shift. 'My contemporaries at the time were people like James Cameron, Robert Key, Trevor Philpot, who later became giants of *Panorama* [the BBC current affairs series]... but I had the yearning to write – either for the stage, or film, or television.'

He joined the story department at the Rank Organisation, performing un-credited 'doctoring' on film scripts. One of his fellow 'rewrite men' was actor, novelist and future film director Bryan Forbes. When Rank diversified into making TV series, Banks Stewart story edited *Interpol Calling* (1959). 'I wrote a lot of the early ones... having been a magazine writer and gone to a lot of places, I gave them stories which just came tumbling out.'

Later work on *Danger Man* (1960-62) led to him being hired by Twentieth Century Fox to adapt Ian Fleming's novel *Casino Royale*, intended as the first in a James Bond film series. 'I was sticking to the book,' Banks Stewart said, remembering how he travelled Europe while working on the screenplay. The project was cancelled when the producer Gregory Ratoff suddenly died. 'Saltzman and Broccoli bought the rights to *Dr. No* and made the film with Sean Connery', Banks Stewart continued. 'And here's an irony: he and I were teenage buddies in Edinburgh. It was the most extraordinary sensation, going to see *Dr. No*, and there was my old mate – I hadn't seen him for years – using a macho voice that we used to adopt as teenagers to attract girls!'

Undermind (1965) was the first series Banks Stewart created in his own right, a science fiction conspiracy thriller about an alien 'fifth column' sabotaging Britain's institutions. Several times trusted characters were revealed as 'the opposition', a twist familiar in spy and science fiction. This fusion of two genres was innovative for its time and, in hindsight, the series has several parallels with *The X-Files* (1993-2002, 2016-), including unresolved sexual tension between the lead characters Drew Heriot (Jeremy Wilkin) and his sister-in-law, Anne Heriot (Rosemary Nicols).

Banks Stewart had worked on *The Avengers* and story edited many instalments of *Armchair Theatre*, making him an obvious choice to contribute to *Callan*. Afterwards, he went to Australia to work on *Riptide* (1969), an adventure series featuring an American widower. Returning to England, he edited the first series of the unsettling *Armchair Thriller* (1978-1980), oversaw *Charles Endell, Esquire* (1979-1980), and contributed to *New Scotland Yard* (in 1972), *Jason King* (1972), *The Protectors* (1974), *The Sweeney* (1975) and *Doctor Who*. This latter commission from script editor Robert Holmes resulted in two memorable stories, 'Terror of the Zygons' (1975) and 'The Seeds of Doom' (1976).

During this period, Banks Stewart was also trying to create his own series formats, one example being *Owner Occupied* (1977), a comedy about a Channel Islands hotel inhabited by Germans during WW2. The Controller of Thames Television was reluctant to take the idea further than the pilot, thinking viewers would think it was in bad taste. Perhaps this was a programme ahead of its time, as it predated the similar BBC sitcom *'Allo 'Allo!* (1982-1992) by several years.

In the late 1970s, the BBC were looking to revamp or replace their version of *The Sweeney*, the Patrick Mower vehicle *Target* (1977-78). Together with Richard Harris, Banks Stewart came up with the format for a film drama based in Bristol called *Shoestring* (1979-1980), featuring Trevor Eve's memorable 'private ear' who worked for a local radio station. 'Shoestring was an utter joy,' the writer said. 'I wanted Trevor Eve. I'd seen him in *Laurence Olivier Presents* [1976-78]; he was the lead [in 'Hindle Wakes'].' Banks Stewart recalled an executive at the BBC thinking the series might make a good vehicle for Michael Crawford, and having to fight hard to retain his own casting choice.

When Eve moved on, the writer was asked to come up with another series, which led to the idea of using Jersey as a location, and to a further clash over his casting of John Nettles as the leading man in *Bergerac* (1981-1991). 'He was the top actor at Stratford, and he'd done various things, and I thought, "This is the guy!" I went through this terrific struggle... I got my way, and that Christmas, Bill Cotton came over to me and admitted he'd been wrong.'

Bergerac became another memorable Sunday night hit, and Banks Stewart continued as a successful TV writer-producer, overseeing series such as *Lovejoy* (1986-1994), *Hannay* (1988-89), *Call Me Mister* (1986), *Moon and Son* (1992), *Frank Stubbs Promotes* (1993) and adaptations of *The Darling Buds of May* (1991) and *My Uncle Silas* (2003).

In his final years he wrote his first novel, *The Hurricane's Tail*[52], and his career memoir, *To Put You in the Picture*[53]. Having found modern TV commissioning processes frustrating, he fondly reflected on the industry in the 1960s. 'Whenever there was a big series around, like a new version of *The Avengers* on film, or whatever else, either you got a call from your agent or someone you knew saying, "How about coming in?" It may sound terrible to say this, but I belonged to an age of television writers.'

GEORGE 'PETER' DUGUID (1923–2009) was born on Tyneside and won a scholarship to Jarrow Grammar School, afterwards training as an engineering draughtsman. He began acting in amateur productions, winning a place at the Old Vic School and making his professional debut at the Theatre Royal Norwich with the Young Vic company. Duguid later appeared in *A Midsummer Night's Dream* (1954) with a cast including Ian Bannen, Zena Walker and Leo McKern before joining the English Stage Company at the Royal Court. He acted in several films, including *This Sporting Life* (1963), and on television he had character roles in *Z Cars* (1962-63) and *The Saint* – 'Marcia' (1963). Duguid was also appointed artistic director of the Glasgow Citizen's Theatre (where Russell Hunter had appeared on stage).

While there, he directed *The Crucible, A View from the Bridge* and *The Caine Mutiny*. Returning to London, he 'finally went into the BBC on the recruitment wave for BBC2 when it was being set up, in 1963. 'The Beeb had a very good training [system], a six-month contract with three months training in their school, and then [practical work]. I stayed at the BBC for four years but there were colossal changes over that time, and I wasn't very happy there towards the end and so I came to [ABC].'[54] While at the BBC, he worked alongside Ken Loach on Troy Kennedy Martin and John McGrath's ground breaking *Diary of a Young Man* (1964), and with the influential James MacTaggart on several editions of *The Wednesday Play* (1964-1970). He later directed the stand-out ITV series *Van der Valk* (1972), *The Rivals of Sherlock Holmes* (in 1973) and *Hazell* (1978), eight instalments of *Armchair Theatre* and eleven of *Callan*, making him the series' most prolific director. Duguid's other TV credits include the BBC Sunday Classic *Hound of the Baskervilles* (1982), the thirteen-part trial drama *Jury* (1983) and the children's series *Danger – Marmalade at Work* (1984).

MICHAEL ROBBINS (1930–1992) is best known for his regular role as Arthur in *On the Buses* (1969-1972). His many other deadpan comic turns take in appearances in *The New Statesman* (1991, as 'Mad Eddie'), *In Sickness and in Health* (1992), *One Foot in the Grave* (1990-91), and regular roles in *Thick as Thieves* (1974), *The Fuzz* (1977), *Devenish* (1977-78) and *Fairly Secret Army* (1986, as Sergeant-Major Throttle). One of his earliest stage performances was in *Caesar and Cleopatra* at the Birmingham Repertory Theatre with Albert Finney and Bernard Hepton, so Robbins was no stranger to more serious work, appearing variously in *Z Cars* (1962-1978), *The Sweeney* (1975), *The Main Chance* (1975), *Brendon Chase* (1981), *The Chinese Detective* and *Doctor Who* (both 1982). On the big screen, Robbins played a seedy lorry driver in *The Looking Glass War* (1969) and a casino manager fending off the police as they investigate Richard Burton's adenoidal *Villain* (1971).

ALFRED HOFFMAN. It's ironic that in a story featuring Africa and contentious attitudes to race, the cast included a white South African actor. One of Hoffman's most rewarding experiences was portraying a barrister in the BBC dramatic reconstruction series *Prisoners of Conscience* (1981), as he had initially studied law: 'Nelson Mandela was a mature student in my class.'[55] He began acting for radio when he was eight, moving to Britain in the 1950s and later appearing in *The Visit*, the 1956 play by Friedrich Durrenmatt (1921-1990). Hoffman transferred to Peter Brook's Broadway production of the play with Alfred Lunt, his wife Lynn Fontaine and Eric Porter. 'The Lunts were the King and Queen of Broadway,' he said happily. 'I was one of seven out of 34 [actors] who they kept when they recast it.'

His TV career began in the 1960s, playing two characters called 'Tubby' in two unrelated parts in *Operation Fantail* (1961, with a young Michele Dotrice) and *No Hiding Place* (1962). Often cast in quiet, subservient roles, he made memorable appearances in *Secret Army* – 'A Safe Place' (1979), the Wilkie Collins mystery story *The Woman in White* (1982, adapted by Ray Jenkins), and the comic family series *The Latchkey Children* (1980, overseen by Pamela Lonsdale): 'a lovely serial, with a lovely cast.' One of his best-known appearances was as Speyer in the BBC's ambitious, curtailed adaptation of *The Tripods* (1985-86) 'The Tripods were taking over the world, and I was underground – I was the head of the whole caboodle. I enjoyed doing that. I never understood why there wasn't a third series. We thought we were better than *Doctor Who*!'

FIONNGHUALA 'FIONNULA' FLANAGAN moved to Beverly Hills in 1968 and began a successful career in American television, guest-starring in many series such as *The Bionic Woman, Kojak* (both in 1976), *Columbo* (1989), and *Murder, She Wrote* (between 1987 and 1995). Flanagan was acclaimed for her work in *James Joyce's Women* (1985). More recently, she played the unsettling housekeeper Mrs Mills in the award-winning psychological horror film *The Others* (2001) and Eloise Hawking in the fantasy thriller *Lost* (2007-10).

DENNIS ALABA PETERS (died 1996). Two years after 'Goodbye Nobby Clarke', Peters became well known as the urbane Sir Curtis Seretse, Head of *Department S* (1969-1970), a rather more positive role model of an educated African man in a position of authority.

WILLIAM REGINALD BRUCE PURCHASE (1938-2008), born in New Zealand, was a founder member of the National Theatre Company. Along with many other actors well-versed in the Bard, he appeared in the BBC's seminal adaptation of Rupert Graves's novel, *I Claudius* (1976). Fans of telefantasy will vividly remember Purchase's portrayals of the very loud Captain in *Doctor Who*'s 'The Pirate Planet' (1978), as well as the equally thunderous warrior chief Gola in the *Blake's 7* story 'The Keeper' (1979). In a lower key, he was the troubled scientist Tommy Roach in the concluding chapter in the life of *Quatermass* (1979). Purchase returned in *Callan*'s second series, playing a different character, in 'Land of Light and Peace'.

INFORMATION: The script was originally given the title 'People Discolour with Time'[56], a remark Hunter makes about a yellowing photo of Clarke. This early draft version has Miss Brewis entering Callan's flat using a spare key hidden in a fuse box, an unlikely arrangement removed in later versions. Also excised was a reference to Callan knifing a waiter in Singapore, an incident which would have been an unpleasant addition to the character's back story. At one point Hunter and Callan meet in a supermarket, in a scene similar to one in *The IPCRESS File* where Harry Palmer meets his boss Colonel Ross; Callan and Hunter's argument was subsequently relocated to the latter's office. A photograph of Clarke involved in an atrocity was originally seen being clearly faked by Hunter; in the later script, its veracity is more ambiguous and Callan's reaction to it, a 'gasp of horror', was changed to angry disbelief.

Music used in the episode consisted of two classical pieces, 'La Montana' and 'Romances at Malarsee'.[57] Miss Brewis previously featured in 'A Magnum for Schneider'.

In the Anglia and Southern ITV regions, the episode was promoted with a *TV Times* cover showing Woodward thoughtfully studying a model soldier.

'My memory is that Terence wanted [the action] to be fairly hard,'[58] Peter Duguid recalled of the fight in the Afro Craft warehouse, which was staged in the studio. 'Mike Robbins had to throw a bottle, which was an insert.'

'I remember they came and visited my character in hospital, and brought me fruit and things,' Alfred Hoffman recalled of his role as the mild-mannered Stan Sheppick. 'In the first scene, he'd just bought the launderette and was taking it over.'[59] Hoffman was cast by Peter Duguid and fondly recalled the director giving him other work. Recording went well, apart from when an extra failed to hit his 'marks' and Hoffman even managed an ad-lib. 'There was a scene where he's looking at all these clothes, and there were a couple of lines that I put in, making derogatory remarks about them!'

'We always insisted on very strongly drawn characters,'[60] Terence Feely said. 'In "Nobby Clarke", we brought in [Michael Robbins] who has a great sense of humour. We even thought about incorporating him into the running cast because of that.'

The Section chief's remark that the Mau-Mau's actions in Kenya were 'child's play' compared with Clarke's plans elicited a complaint to the *TV Times*[61].

The premise of this episode had its roots in Robert Banks Stewart's days as a magazine writer. 'I went to lots of places like Nigeria and the Yemen and I was often in trouble spots.'[62] Of the title character, he recalled, 'At the age of eighteen I was conscripted for National Service and anybody called Clarke was always called "Nobby". I don't know what I was called – I hope I wasn't called a "Rupert"! Michael Robbins, who played Clarke, was one of those very good actors who moved from one supporting part to another.'

Post-Imperial Africa was a lucrative trouble spot for mercenaries. Generally their involvement worsened conflicts, with atrocities occurring in Biafra and the Congo. In 1960, the Congo natives voted for autonomy from Belgium. Facing reform, the army, which was exclusively formed of a white officer corps, started a mutiny; many Belgians fled to the Katanga region, which was rich in uranium and other precious metals. Intent on breaking away from the new independent republic, the mining companies in Katanga raised an army to protect their interests, hiring several hundred European mercenaries. The crisis mounted when the Congolese Prime Minister Lumumba was ousted in a CIA-sponsored coup and later killed by the Katangans, while the Soviets gave backing to other breakaway regions. The UN brokered peace talks between the factions and moved forces into the region to engage with the mercenaries, now led by Colonel 'Mad' Mike Hoare. Hoare, one potential inspiration behind Nobby Clarke, was Irish, serving with the British Army in WW2 and making a living organising mercenary groups afterwards.

Notably, the notorious Greek mercenary Kostas Giorgio (1952-1976) was christened 'Colonel Callan' by the British press in the 1970s. Giorgio had lived in England and served in the First Battalion of the Parachute Regiment in Northern Ireland. He was a crack shot, but was dishonorably discharged from the army after he was arrested for the failed armed robbery of a post office. After a five year prison term, Giorgio, now using the alias 'Colonel Tony Cullen' – after the surname of an old army friend – was made head (unpaid) of Angola's resistance army by Holden Roberto (1923-2007), founder of the National Liberation Front of Angola. Cullen's ill disciplined troops were no match for the People's Movement for the Liberation of Angola (the MPLA), which had Soviet backing and heavy weapons. When the MPLA won the war, Cullen stood trial for illegally entering Angola, the massacre of fourteen deserting mercenaries and the torture of enemy soldiers and civilians. He was executed on 10 July 1976.

'Goodbye, Nobby Clarke' clearly made an impression on one of the writers of the cartoon strip *Dredger*, which ran in the British comic *Action* (1976-78). The tough cockney character was partly inspired by *Callan*; an ex-Royal Marine, Dredger was licenced to carry a Magnum revolver and worked for 'DI6'. In a comic strip in the *Action Annual 1978*, Dredger goes undercover in the Marxist-funded mercenary army of 'Kompala'. While there, he faces his old enemy Sergeant Scanlon, who he served with in the Marines.

MISSION ANALYSIS: *'After all, Nobby* was *a mate of mine'* Like 'The Good Ones Are All Dead' this episode contains several allusions to 'A Magnum for Schneider'. These include an opponent for Callan whose likeably roguish exterior conceals more dangerous characteristics, the Section engineering a meeting between the pair, Meres attempting to frame Callan and the agent's own ambivalence and indecision about his initially unwitting target. However, there the similarities end: this story, the first *Callan* script to be written by someone other than James Mitchell, is a striking contrast to its predecessor, introducing a British antagonist, African culture and politics, and settings that would not seem out of place in a play from the social realist (or 'kitchen sink') tradition: dockyards, terraced houses, launderettes, pubs and warehouses all feature, as do broken relationships, austerity, love triangles and angry, disaffected males, all familiar features of the genre.

Clarke is an intriguing, flawed adversary, an overgrown playground bully and sadist despite his bonhomie. He once 'accidentally' broke Callan's arm in training and delays signing him up as a mercenary, despite saying he is 'exactly the sort' for his new platoon. Like Callan, he is a hired killer, clearly dissatisfied with domestic life and craving the excitement and wealth generated by his chosen career. He is one of several mirror-image opponents that Callan faces, and the first of two former mentors to go 'rogue'.[63]

As an Army instructor, Clarke, like 'Colonel Hunter', is also a recognisable, potentially disagreeable authority figure whom adult viewers would have recognised from their National Service days when the story was first shown. Working for a black African government, he is openly racist, making disparaging comments on several occasions. Callan spraying Clarke's face with black paint to disable him is therefore a fitting comeuppance as well as a stylish piece of earthy symbolism. The denouement as a whole is another touchstone of familiarity for the audience, being scripted as a grittier variation on the climactic fights seen in many contemporary thriller series, including *The Saint, The Avengers* and *Danger Man*.[64]

Callan's framing of Clarke would be unlikely to result in a conviction in a modern courtroom, but as a solution it demonstrates his innate, if often buried, humanity. Rather than killing his old friend he imprisons him, saving his life and potentially helping the suppressed romantic relationship blossom between Rena and Sheppick. She is Irish and he is Jewish, emphasising the story's anti-racist theme even further.

Overall, this is a cleverly paced story with an exciting opening and an action-packed third act. Slightly more conventional and certainly more optimistic than Mitchell's scripts, 'Goodbye Nobby Clarke' reveals that other writers could work, and work well, within the framework he had created for *Callan*.

END TITLES: Over scenes of Callan visiting Sheppick in hospital.[65]

S1.3 THE DEATH OF ROBERT E. LEE

Writer: James Mitchell
Director: Robert Tronson
Designer: David Marshall

FIRST UK TRANSMISSION

Border, Southern: Thursday 20 July 1967, 10.30 pm
Westward, Channel: Tuesday 12 September 1967, 10.30 pm
All other regions: Saturday 22 July 1967, 9.00 pm

CAST: George Roubicek (Curtis Dale), Francesca Tu (Jenny), Keith James (Waiter), Thick Wilson (Joe Limberg), Brian Harrison (Watcher), Basil Tang (Chinese gentleman), Burt Kwouk (Robert E. Lee)

PRODUCTION

Rehearsals: From Friday 21 April 1967
Location Filming: Hilton Hotel, London; Waterloo Station, London (Tuesday 25 April 1967)
Camera Rehearsals/Recording: Teddington Studio One, Wednesday 3 and
Thursday 4 May 1967 [66]

TV TIMES: 'Lee's going to come looking for Callan. And between him and Hunter, one way or another, Callan's going to end up dead.'
19 – 24 July 1967, Southern edition

MISSING FILE: The master tapes of this story do not exist in the Studio Canal archive.

PRE-TITLES: Hunter and Meres discuss the arrival of the CIA agent, Curtis Dale. US intelligence are offering the Section a deal – U-2 spy plane photographs of the Chinese H-Bomb tests in return for the killing of a Chinese operative.

MISSION PROFILE: Through Dale, the CIA ask Hunter about Li Pa Chao (now going by the name of Robert E. Lee), a Chinese assassin working against US forces in Vietnam – they want him terminated or captured. As a lure, the Section let Lee know through Schneider's mistress, Jenny, that two years ago Callan found his father in Hong Kong. Knowing of Lee's dedication to his father, Hunter reasons that he'll come to Britain looking for Callan, becoming an open target for the Section.

Threatening Callan with extradition to the States for a killing in Puerto Rico, Dale and his colleague Joe Limberg double-cross Hunter by contracting Callan to find and kill Lee. Callan goes to Jenny, under house arrest by the Section, and persuades her to mislead Hunter and direct Lee to him; in turn, Callan convinces Dale and Limberg to spring Jenny. Disguised as a nun, Lee eludes the Section and joins Callan and Jenny in hiding. Holding them at gunpoint, Lee reveals he was a double agent who worked within the CIA – betraying Dale – and that he's also in the UK to kill Hunter.

He forces Callan to phone the Section chief to lure him into an ambush, but alerted by Callan using the wrong code word 'Charles', Hunter arranges for Dale to find Lee and the CIA agent shoots the Chinese killer dead. Discovering the U-2 film is hidden in microdots in Dale's diary, Callan sells them to Hunter for an exorbitant fee.

A MAN LIKE ME: When he was working for the Section in 1961, Callan killed an opposition agent called Miguel Barragas in Puerto Rico. In 1965, he was sent to Hong Kong to find Li Pa Chao and discovered that his father was buried in the cemetery on Orchard Road, Kowloon.

Callan keeps himself in shape, judging by the fight he puts up against two trained CIA men when Dale and Limberg break into his flat. He proves to be a quick-thinking opportunist as he agrees to take Dale's money at 'the usual rate' to kill Li Pa Chao, then offers Jenny £750 to arrange a meeting with him, offering as bait the opportunity to find his father. His ruthless, manipulative side is revealed: he knows that Jenny could be killed when he arranges for the two CIA agents to rescue her from Section minders, and he's indirectly responsible for the serious injury to Limberg's arm in the ensuing gun battle. Significantly, despite the chance to have Hunter killed by Chao, he instead decides to warn the Section (possibly because he knows that Hunter would be replaced and his successor would take reprisals.)

In the manner of Sherlock Holmes, Callan improvises a dummy to fool the Section agent watching his flat. He uses equipment in a 'place in Soho' to enlarge microdots, using a microscope and camera.

LONELY: Enlisted by Callan as an errand boy, he takes a message to Curtis and Limberg and escorts Jenny to his cousin Arthur's. He does well – Dale gives him £5 and Callan pays him £25. This is the first time Lonely uses his dubious extended family to help Callan, hiding Jenny and Lee in his cousin Arthur's lock up among a lorry load of stolen tinned fruit that Lonely's cousin believed was whisky. Revealing another family trait – dislike of foreigners – Lonely makes a disparaging comment about 'Fu Manchu' and says that Arthur doesn't 'like Chinkies – not even dead ones.' Lonely's racism doesn't extend to attractive young women, however. His lecherous tendencies are seen for the first time as he likens Jenny to a parcel, sleazily commenting that it's a 'pity it had so much wrapping on it.'

A TIE AND A CREST: Hunter once visited the Far East. Meres appears on edge, rebuked by Hunter for drinking 'during his meeting with Jenny and, later, openly threatening her with violence; overhearing his threats, Callan says Meres needs a rest. His mood isn't helped by Curtis and Dale rescuing Jenny from his custody in a firefight. Searching Callan's flat for the U-2 pictures, Meres sadistically tells Callan that he'd like to beat the information about their whereabouts out of him.

ALCOHOL, TOBACCO AND FIREARMS: Meres uncharacteristically indulges in three large whiskies. Hunter takes a large Scotch and water in his meeting with Jenny. Eavesdropping on the Section men's conversation with the Chinese woman, Limberg has a beer. A nervous Lonely wants one when he's holed up with Callan and Lee, but Lee won't let him drink as he's worried about him talking. Callan warns Lonely not to get drunk.

Chao's gun is a copy of a copy of a German weapon.

SPY-SPEAK: Meres is unambiguously psychopathic and misogynistic in his treatment of Jenny: 'You scared of me? You should be. I wouldn't make love to you. I would hurt you.' Callan has a low opinion of Lonely: 'Lecherous, greedy, evil-minded... 'It's in the family, guv,' the thief confesses.

Chao/Lee is amusingly cynical about the provenance of his hand gun: 'This is a Chinese remake of a Japanese copy of a German automatic.' The Communist agent has utter contempt for the USA, and Dale in particular: 'He told them all how I loved America – all that crap. He believed it too. Jerk. Bourgeois, sentimental jerk. We share a room at college and I can't be a traitor.'

Callan reassures Lonely: 'Take it easy. I'm not going to wash you.'

PAWNS AND PLAYERS: ROBERT DU COUDRÉ TRONSON (1924-2008) joined the BBC after wartime naval service on Atlantic convoys. He wanted to be a writer, authoring some scripts for the comedy *At Your Service, Ltd.* (1951) before switching to directing. He was an experienced film director by the time he took on the challenge of working on a videotaped series like *Callan*. Tronson was well acquainted with the espionage genre having directed the feature film *Ring of Spies* (1964), based on the 1961 Portland spy scandal (see Chapter 7). He was an experienced hand on ITC adventure series, overseeing numerous episodes of *The Saint* (in 1967), *The Baron* (1967) and *Man in a Suitcase* (1967-68). In later years, he worked for Robert Banks Stewart on *The Darling Buds of May* (1991-93)

BURT KWOUK (1930-2016) was born in Manchester but raised in Shanghai. He was a friend of James Mitchell and appeared in *Callan* twice, the second time as Tao Tsung, the Chinese Chargé d'Affaire in 1969's 'The Running Dog'. Kwouk played a variety of oriental characters in *The Saint* and *Danger Man*, featuring in the Patrick McGoohan series five times between 1961 and 1966.[67]

Kwouk remains best known for his portrayal of the manservant Kato, opposite Peter Sellers' accident-prone Inspector Clouseau, beginning with *The Pink Panther* (1963). Kwouk was also one of the ensemble cast of the psychedelic spy romp *Casino Royale* (1967), as an overexcited Chinese army officer. In later years, he gave a distinguished performance as Captain – later Major – Yamauchi, the Japanese commander of the women's prison camp in the WW2 drama *Tenko* (1981-84). Between 2002 and 2010, Kwouk starred as Entwistle in the BBC's pensioner comedy *Last of the Summer Wine*. In 2011, he was awarded an OBE.

GEORGE ROUBICEK appeared in the 1967 spy movies *You Only Live Twice* and *Billion Dollar Brain*. Later in his career, he became a dialogue director and English language adaptor of foreign films and TV shows, including *Monkey* (1978-1980) and *The Water Margin* (1973-74), for which Burt Kwouk provided the narration.

THICK WILSON, often cast as overweight authority figures, played Captain Haskell in *The Dirty Dozen* (1967). He can be seen as an American tourist in *Return of the Saint* – 'Tower Bridge Is Falling Down' (1978) and later became known for his voiceovers on the fantasy film *The Dark Crystal* (1982).

BASIL TANG played assorted oriental roles, featuring in the adventure series *Adam Adamant Lives!* in 1966 and the film *Stand Up, Virgin Soldiers*, which featured Edward Woodward as the ironically named Sergeant Wellbeloved.

INFORMATION: In Mitchell's original story outline,[68] the American agent who contacts Hunter was called Peters and offered the Section chief information about 'Russian Security techniques' rather than aerial photographs of the Chinese H-Bomb tests. In a final struggle with Lee, Callan helps Peters kill the Communist agent; the American then honours his deal with the ex-agent and pays him.

'Burt as a nun, that's one of my favourite memories!'[69] James Mitchell laughed. 'That was a nice, wild Gothic story. It got as close to fantasy as you could go. with *Callan*' Of Francesca Tu's role, reprised from 'A Magnum for Schneider', he added. 'Jenny being Chinese came out in the casting, and because of [her] almost childlike look, given the character she had to play it worked extremely well.'

Li Pa Chao names himself after General Robert E. Lee (1807-1870), who commanded the Confederate Army of North Virginia in the American Civil War (1862-1865). A favourite of Callan's in his wargaming, Lee took major offensives against the North but, due to his aggressive tactics, casualties among his forces were high. He surrendered to the Union commander General Grant at Appomattox Court House on 9 April 1865. Lee rejected the move for guerrilla resistance against the North and promoted reconciliation between both sides. He has subsequently become a revered, heroic figure of the Civil War.

The United States' Central Intelligence Agency (CIA) was formed in 1947 to replace the Office of Strategic Services (OSS), which had been America's intelligence-gathering organisation during WW2. Dale would have worked for National Clandestine Services, the branch of the CIA responsible for collecting foreign intelligence. By 1967, the CIA had been behind covert actions against several left-wing governments; most notoriously, they had been behind attempts to assassinate the Cuban president Fidel Castro – all of which failed – and the aborted 'Bay of Pigs' invasion by Cuban exiles.

Lee has killed 300 Americans in the war in Vietnam. After the defeat of French armed forces at the battle of Dien Bien Phu in on May 7 1954, the protection of democratic South Vietnam, part of a former French dominion, passed to the United States (American advisers had been on the ground since 1950). By 1965, regular army units were being deployed; by 1967, General William Westmoreland (1914-2005), commander of US forces, instituted a three-point plan that went on the offensive against the Communist North's forces, predicting victory by the end of the year. It didn't happen: despite spending billions of dollars on South Vietnamese assets, analysts, computers and spy satellites, CIA intelligence-gathering in Vietnam was a failure. The Agency never developed crucial sources in North Vietnam, underestimated the tenacity of Viet Cong resistance and was taken by surprise in major attacks. On 30 April 1975, the USA withdrew and the South fell to the North.

From the late 1950s, the USA had the advantage over the USSR in the struggle for intelligence on each other's military capabilities. From July 1956 onwards, the primary aircraft used in aerial spying missions over Russia was the Lockheed U-2, a high-altitude reconnaissance jet with a range of 2,600 miles. They were fitted with cameras, equipment able to detect radar and radio transmissions and, at 75,000 feet, were out of the range of Soviet aircraft and anti-aircraft missiles. Controlled by the CIA, in 1960 the secret flights became a major embarrassment for President Eisenhower when a U-2 was shot down. Its pilot, Gary Powers, was the subject of a show trial in the USSR, although he was eventually exchanged for the Russian spy Rudolf Abel in 1962.[70]

A major cause of the rift between China and Russia in the 1950s was the latter's refusal to share atomic weapons technology with its neighbour. Undeterred, China accelerated its weapons development program, exploding its first atom bomb on 16 October 1964.

'The Death of Robert E. Lee' correctly predicts the detonation of China's first H-bomb – on 17 June 1967 – even though when the story was written, the testing of the weapon hadn't taken place. It remains *Callan*'s most up-to-the-minute piece of *realpolitik*.

Microdots – in which secret information is reduced to a microscopic level inside small black dots which can be easily hidden – were the most common form of trafficking stolen intelligence before the rise of computer technology.

Lonely's reference to Fu Manchu was likely to have been prompted by the 1960s film revival of the oriental master criminal, which had done well at the box office in British cinemas. The early films were directed by Don Sharp, who went on to make the *Callan* feature film in late 1973 and early 1974.

Fu Manchu is an obvious source of inspiration for Ian Fleming's *Dr. No* and the film of the same name in 1962 tapped into contemporary Western fears about Red China. This anxiety also inspired the plots of *Goldfinger* – the millionaire plans to explode a Chinese nuclear device in Fort Knox (supplied by Burt Kwouk's Mr Ling) – to contaminate America's gold supply, and *You Only Live Twice*, in which SPECTRE use China's rocket technology to hijack US and Soviet space capsules in a Chinese bid to cause WW3.

MISSION ANALYSIS: *'Look at me, Callan, I'm unique. The only Commie in the CIA.'* With the real-world background of hostilities in Vietnam at their height, 'The Death of Robert E. Lee' is raw stuff indeed. Lonely's sexism and casual racism is deeply unpleasant, Meres' sadism is almost out of control and in Lee, Callan faces an opponent whose hatred of the West is overpowering: even when he's facing death, the man who's killed 300 Americans taunts Dale by sarcastically singing the United States' national anthem 'The Star Spangled Banner'. The febrile atmosphere is heightened further by Mitchell's unflattering view of the CIA as better-resourced than the British security services, as Hunter points out, but lacking initiative, two-faced, gullible and vindictive. Dale wants Lee dealt with for revenge as much as he does to protect the lives of American servicemen.

Three stories in, the writers are still finding convincing ways to involve Callan with the Section, and reintroducing Jenny from 'A Magnum for Schneider' creates extra tension. Those members of the audience familiar with the *Armchair Theatre* play are given an extra thrill, as they're unsure whether or not Jenny will try and use Lee for retribution against the ex-agent.

If the story has a fault, it's that Callan is so skilled at manipulating everyone that he comes rather close to being the super-spy that the series was created as an antidote to. The only time Callan is on the back foot is when Chao reveals himself as a double agent, and even then the former Section man quickly turns it to his advantage by saving Hunter's life.

Mitchell's intelligent allusions continue to mark *Callan* out as something different. Chao, a Communist agent, taking as his US name that of a famous American Civil War hero, is a lacerating piece of satire, even more so in 1967. Lee (a male assassin) coming through customs dressed as a nun (a female religious figure) shows that for all its much-praised realism, *Callan* isn't afraid to embrace the bizarre. The ex-agent disguising Dale's microdots as Jenny's beauty spots is a highly original twist and the same is true of the implied, unexpected attraction between Callan and the young Chinese woman.

With the intriguing development that the Section operates abroad, the grim but unsurprising revelation that Western intelligence agencies don't trust – and even actively undermine – each other, together with the other unusual, exotic touches, 'The Death of Robert E. Lee' sees *Callan* continuing to break new ground.

END TITLES: Callan, Jenny and Hunter in the Section office.[71]

S1.4. GOODNESS BURNS TOO BRIGHT

Writer: James Mitchell
Director: Bill Bain
Designer: Peter Le Page

FIRST UK TRANSMISSION

Westward, Channel: Tuesday 19 September 1967, 10.30 pm
Border, Southern: Thursday 27 July 1967, 10.30 pm
All other regions: Saturday 29 July 1967, 9.00 pm

CAST: Robert Lang (Bauer), Jeremy Lloyd (Maitland), Rosemary Frankau (Eva), Les White (Franz), Dame Gladys Cooper (Dr Schultz)[72]

PRODUCTION

Rehearsals: From 6 April 1967
Camera Rehearsals/Recording: Teddington Studio Two, Tuesday 18 and Wednesday 19 April 1967[73]

TV TIMES: 'No, love. They never taught me how to wound, only how to kill.'
29 July – 4 August 1967, North edition

MISSING FILE: The master tapes of this story do not exist in the Studio Canal archive.

PRE-TITLES: Hunter and Maitland, a Section agent normally stationed in East Germany, meet Bauer, a freelance German spy. Callan is referred to as 'a lamb to the slaughter... top quality meat.'

MISSION PROFILE: Bauer has devised a scheme for planting an agent in a top-security East German ministry. To bring this plan off a decoy is needed; when the lure is caught, the authorities will relax and the real spy can be infiltrated. Callan is the perfect scapegoat: the East Germans have heard of him, he's a trained spy, under interrogation he will reveal himself to be one but, crucially, has no recent dangerous knowledge.

In West Berlin, Callan is kidnapped by Bauer. The ex-Section man escapes but breaks two ribs in the process. Alone and knowing that Bauer's agents are hunting him, Callan bursts into the flat of Doctor Schultz, an elderly woman. They speak German at first, than she realises that, like her, he is English. The doctor's husband was a liberal like she is, always concerned with treating people honestly and decently.

Doctor Schultz treats Callan for his injury, growing to like him. He is young enough to be her son... Callan searches the flat and finds her husband's old army Luger pistol, together with two rounds of ammunition. The doctor learns a little of his story, but feels the police should be told. Bauer traces him to Schultz's flat but Callan shoots him dead. [74]

A MAN LIKE ME: Callan is on edge from the outset, getting plenty of shooting practice in. When he sees Eva, an old flame who's a freelance Hungarian spy, he tells her he lives in his current flat because it 'suits him'. She cooks him goulash like 'in the old days', stays for several hours (so might have slept with him) and gives him a model soldier – a Hungarian Hussar. Eva has just finished a mission in Britain that may have antagonised Hunter, so

Callan is concerned for her welfare. Hunter plays on this belief, confirming she is *persona non grata* so Callan will go to Berlin to rescue her after she is temporarily kidnapped (by Bauer, rather than the Section).

Callan once gave Bauer a beating that hospitalised him for a month, after a previous unsuccessful double-cross. In return, Bauer enjoys taunting Callan about his fate – interrogation in the East. Callan provokes him into a fight and gets the better of him, despite the German having a gun (a scene recalling Sean Connery's James Bond tricking the similarly resentful Red Grant, played by Robert Shaw, in *From Russia with Love*).

Callan is convinced Dr Schmidt will call the police and the pair are initially suspicious of each other. As she gets to know him, she admits her own late husband killed a Russian soldier to protect her from being raped. Realising Schultz's husband would have had a WW2 Luger pistol, Callan exhibits his deductive skills by finding the weapon and two bullets. 'Maybe I won't use them,' he says to reassure her. She replies: 'I think you want to.'

Callan displays some multilingual skill as well as brutal humour, informing Franz how he shot Bauer – 'One in the heart. One in the head' – in both English and German; earlier, he had promised the thug a language lesson. Callan again reveals his vicious side, provoking Bauer by saying he 'screamed like a girl' when the ex-agent beat him.

Section Kills: 4

LONELY: Callan tells Lonely to change ammunition supplier as they are asking awkward questions. Lonely complains that he doesn't know what Callan's business is. 'Just as well, you'd only worry, and you know what that does to your halitosis,' Callan tells him. The thief acts as a lookout at the airport.

A TIE AND A CREST: Maitland is another 'public school' spy like Meres, 'brought over' as he's worked with Bauer before. 'Take care of yourself, old boy,' he advises the German. This isn't just Etonian bonhomie, but a repeated coded warning not to underestimate Callan.

It's implied that the Section regularly search Callan's flat and do a stock-take of his belongings, including his model soldiers.

ALCOHOL, TOBACCO AND FIREARMS: Refusing an injection while being operated on, Callan takes a swig of Schnapps instead.

SPY-SPEAK: Hunter reflects 'an agent's entire life is betrayal' and advises Bauer, 'in our business revenge is a very dangerous luxury.'

When Hunter visits Callan's flat, he is treated as a door-to-door salesman: 'Sorry mate, I've got too much insurance already.' When Hunter remarks about the smell of Eva's perfume, Callan dryly retorts, 'Since I left the firm I've changed in lots of ways.'

The verbal cat-and-mouse continues when Hunter spots that Callan's collection has a new soldier 'from 1860'. Callan: 'I keep forgetting how old you are, you carry it so well.'

Hunter surveys Callan's war game, which again becomes subtext. He enquires, 'Casualties?' Callan replies, 'Sometimes I get carried away.'

With some insight, Dr Schultz compares Callan to an animal: 'The way you watch and listen. Your body's always ready to fight for you.'

PAWNS AND PLAYERS: GLADYS CONSTANCE COOPER (1888–1971) first appeared on stage at the age of seventeen and worked on the early British silent film *The*

Eleventh Commandment (1913). By the end of WW1, she had become involved with managing London's Playhouse Theatre as well as acting. In the 1930s, Cooper made her Broadway debut, and in 1940 worked with Laurence Olivier and Alfred Hitchcock on the feature film *Rebecca*. She later became known for playing elderly, well-to-do women, such as the mother of Rex Harrison's patronising elocution professor in *My Fair Lady* (1964). She continued working right up to the end of her life, moving between theatre and film work across continents.

In the UK, she guested in the hospital drama *Emergency Ward 10* (1965) and the BBC's 'Swinging Sixties' adventure *Adam Adamant Lives!* – 'Black Echo' (1967) as Grand Duchess Vorokhov. One of Cooper's last roles was as another Grand Duchess, Ozerov, in the Tony Curtis and Roger Moore romp *The Persuaders!* – 'The Ozerov Inheritance' (1972). She was also cast in several anthology series, working with Hitchcock again on *The Alfred Hitchcock Hour* and in three instalments of *The Twilight Zone*; the first, 'Nothing in the Dark' (1962), parallels her *Callan* story as it features an old woman being visited by a wounded man.

ROBERT LANG (1934–2004) put in a memorable turn as the murderer silently stalking the heroine in the gripping Brian Clemens' *Thriller* – 'I'm the Girl He Wants to Kill' (1974), directed by Shaun O'Riordan (see Chapter 12), and took the part of Felix Kane, the half-robot villain in *The New Avengers* – 'The Last of the Cybernauts...?' (1976). In 1977 and 1978, Lang appeared opposite Edward Woodward again as Public Control Department Chief Skardon in the futuristic thriller *1990*, his character sharing a surname with the real-life MI5 officer who questioned Kim Philby. His cinema roles include *The House That Dripped Blood* (1971), *The First Great Train Robbery* and *The Medusa Touch* (both 1978).

JOHN JEREMY LLOYD (1930-2014) was a contender to play Toby Meres (see overview); Lloyd's role in the *Armchair Theatre* play 'Afternoon of a Nymph' (1962), as sleazy Lord Tony Bright, shows how he might have been in the part. He is best-known for his work with David Croft, co-creating the popular sitcoms *Are You Being Served?* (1972-1985), *Grace & Favour* (1992, in which he made cameo appearances) and *'Allo 'Allo* (1982-1992). Lloyd had roles in several prominent films in 1965, including *The Liquidator*, *A Study in Terror* and *Those Magnificent Men in Their Flying Machines*. In *A Hard Day's Night* (1964), the first feature film starring The Beatles, he can be seen dancing energetically with Ringo Starr. Spy fiction featured on Lloyd's resume again in three episodes of *The Avengers* – 'From Venus with Love' (1967), 'Super Secret Cypher Snatch' (1968) and 'Thingumajig' (1969). He also portrayed 'M15 Agent Carruthers' in Terence Feely and Brian Clemens' stage adaptation of the series. With Lance Percival, Lloyd co-created and wrote all of *Whodunnit?*.

ROSEMARY FRANKAU played Beattie Harris in the long running BBC sitcom *Terry and June* (1979-1987).

LES WHITE performed stunts in *The Persuaders!*, *The Sweeney* and the second series of the BBC sci-fi series *Blake's 7* (1979).

PETER LE PAGE debuted on *Callan* as production designer with this episode. 'I was at the Royal College of Art doing the graphics course, and in the final year of that course you could take film and television, which I did. In 1963, the tutor was George Haslam, who was a freelance designer at ABC Television... quite a lot of the designers from the Royal College at that time went to ABC, so it was a fairly natural progression for me.'[75]

Just before graduating, he took a temporary job at the company in his Easter holiday. 'It wasn't a very big department. There were about a dozen designers who did graphics and we were all at one end of the production building on the top floor. Tim [O'Brien] paid me to come in as a freelance over the Easter holidays, when I designed one of those [advertising magazine programmes]. Even though I was dropped in at the deep end, it went down all right, and he offered me a job.'

Initially working with David Marshall, and sometimes commuting between London and Manchester, le Page also designed for *Man at the Top* (1971-72), *The Rivals of Sherlock Holmes* (1971-73), *Public Eye* (1969-1975) and Thames Television's version of *The Morecambe & Wise Show* (1979-1981).

INFORMATION: Mitchell's original pitch saw Callan breaking his wrist rather than his ribs, and passing out in the surgery, only to be woken by Bauer's search. (Taping up broken ribs would not happen today, due to the risk of chest infection.) Hunter was to leak the 'decoy' story to Callan, casting Eva as the victim, luring him to Berlin. The final scenes were to include Hunter appearing in Berlin and informing Callan the infiltration scheme had been cancelled. Intriguingly, 'superiors' of Hunter were meant to be seen approving the plan. The final camera script makes no mention of employing any establishing stock footage of Berlin, distancing *Callan* from the visual short-hand for 'abroad' employed in contemporary thriller film series.

'Characters turning up from Callan's past was an incredibly useful device, soldiers, people he'd met in prison, and the fact that he'd been in the Section and out again... it meant he had a wide range of acquaintances,'[76] James Mitchell believed. 'In a way I broke "the rule" by sending him abroad: the point was I never said whether Hunter's Section was MI5 or MI6 or the Home Office or the Foreign Office, and therefore you weren't tied down by actual facts: you had the leeway of fiction. One didn't have to go through the farce of saying [Callan] was being seconded to do a special job, he just went. If you've only got 50 minutes in which to tell the story that's very important. I think "Goodness Burns Too Bright" was quite a nice one. East Berlin was very much a flashpoint at that time and so it was a good place to tell a tale.'

Concerning Hunter's plan, Mitchell added, 'People always think of Hunter as a human being which is a mistake: he's weighing the odds. Usually he wants Callan to stay alive because that's the best thing, but in this case he's after a bargain and he got it, and if the price is Callan's body then he delivers; it all has to be worked out dispassionately. That's why people loved Hunter and hated him as well.'

'Quite often we never got a finished script, particularly with things like *Callan* and *Public Eye*, because there were so many of them,'[77] Peter le Page revealed. 'You can imagine the problems for the producers and the script editors with getting the scripts through in time. From my point of view and the director's point of view, we were doing these things on a six-weekly turnaround from start to finish, and quite often we'd get a [script] outline, a set list and that would be it. We wouldn't get a full script until [the actors] went into rehearsal, which would be a fortnight before recording. I would always visit to see what props, particularly action props, were needed. I basically had a week, or a week and a half, to work with the director, design the thing, make a model, then another week or so to do the ground plans. They went out to the contractor, and in the last fortnight the sets were being built either in [London] or in Manchester at Watts and Currys: they started off as being theatre scenery makers and used to hire out sets to amateur theatre companies. They had that as a background, and they'd got some very good carpenters, and some very good painters. It was the sort of set-up that wasn't particularly union-bound, so I could go there and pick up a paint brush and show them what I wanted.' Le Page kept photographs of his sets, examples of which are included in the photograph section.

At the end of WW2, Germany was divided into four occupation zones, each controlled by an Allied power: France, Soviet Russia, the United States and Great Britain. The capital of Berlin was similarly subdivided, although the city was fully within the Russian zone.

The Western allies were not permitted to enter the city until two months after Germany's surrender, and during this time the Soviets administered punishment beatings and shootings to the local population. (Eva says her Hungarian grandfather was shot by the Russians and her father by the Nazis, an ironic inversion of the situation.) Emigration to the West became a significant economic problem for the Communists, as many emigrants were well educated. The government tried to stop people leaving by fortifying the Inner German Border, previously established in 1945 as the boundary between the Western and Soviet zones (see also 'Heir Apparent' in Chapter 6). East Germans could still cross from East to West Berlin after overcoming bureaucratic restrictions, but this loophole was closed when the Berlin Wall was constructed in 1961.

During the 1960s, informants for West German intelligence (the BND, which superseded the Gehlen organisation) were notoriously unreliable. Several worked as double agents for the East German security service, later known as the Stasi, making Callan's belief that he will not be completely safe until he's on a British European Airways flight out of the city understandable.

Most editions of the *TV Times* printed an interview with guest star Dame Gladys Cooper, then 77, about her career to promote the episode. Her character's line, 'First the Jews, then the socialists...' echoes the famous poem 'First They Came...' about Nazism, attributed to pastor Martin Niemàller (1892-1984).

MISSION ANALYSIS: *'Callan? No such person, love. He doesn't exist.'* The feud between the Section and Callan intensifies as he is lured abroad and betrayed. With cruel irony, at one point the script cuts from him admiring a model soldier to Hunter plotting his fate. The plot is reminiscent of *Funeral in Berlin* and *The Quiller Memorandum*; both 1966 films are set in Berlin and feature the abduction of the central character, as well as an ambivalent romantic interest.

Callan's kidnapping serves as a prelude to the second half of the episode, which favours a two-handed confrontation in the style of *Armchair Theatre* between Callan and the pacifist Doctor Schultz. Mitchell's writing covers a lot of ground: the pair's dialogue mentions the brutality of WW2 – the Luftwaffe's bombing of Coventry, the battle for the Russian city of Stalingrad, the Gestapo, the shame and horror of concentration camps – contextualising the developing mother/son subtext between the ex-agent and Dr Schultz, as Mitchell's outline notes: '[She] has begun to need Callan as a son is needed.' The doctor lost her boys to the war and Callan's parents were killed in the Blitz. Notably, although WW2 casts a long shadow over the story, Mitchell also reveals a Germany rarely seen in TV thrillers up to 1967, of educated liberals who actively resisted the Nazis.

On another level, the pacifism-versus-violence debate common to the mid-1960s *zeitgeist* is economically and effectively played out between Callan and Schultz. She throws his gun down a drain, maintaining 'I can't let you kill. Killing never helps.' 'If I fight fair I always lose,' Callan responds, begging and brow-beating her into helping him. He later regrets his harshness: 'I forgot there was something better... You'll always be right, I'll always be wrong and I can't change.' The couple seem to have reached an understanding, but then Bauer arrives. After Schultz has witnessed Bauer's death – perpetrated by Callan in her own surgery – she likens his detachment to working in a slaughterhouse. He agrees.

The conclusion of 'Goodness Burns Too Bright' is the series at the bleakest it's been – so far – as Callan's relationship with Eva is ended by distrust, and Doctor Schultz is left feeling violated and disillusioned. David Callan's world continues to be long way from the comforting moral certainties other contemporary TV secret agents.

END TITLES: Projected over the closed door of Dr Schultz's surgery.

S1.5 BUT HE'S A LORD, MR CALLAN

Writer: James Mitchell
Director: Guy Verney
Designer: Darrell Lass

FIRST UK TRANSMISSION

Border, Southern: Thursday 3 August 1967, 10.30pm
Westward, Channel: Thursday 28 September 1967, 10.30 pm
All other regions: Saturday 5 August 1967, 9.00 pm

CAST: Donald Hewlett (Lord Lindale), Ann Bell (Caroline Fielding), Dene Cooper (Croupier), Gerald Flood (Miller), Martha Gibson (Parlour Maid), Kenneth Campbell (Police Sergeant)

EXTRAS/WALK-ONS: *(Uncredited on screen)* Gerry Jardine (Barman) John Moore (Croupier) Wendy Davis, Avril Ellis, Carla Stevens (35 year old ladies), Doris Littlewood, Jean Gay, Dorothy Robson (50 year-old ladies), Leslie Weekes (35 yea-old man), Ernest Jennings, Vernon Drake (50 year old men), Terry Lee, Leonard Kingston (Policemen), Carol Rochelle, Sandra Gosling, Carol Craig, Penny Mackenzie, Anya Mason, Zoe Houssain, Stuart Bevan, Peter Winter (Unknown).

PRODUCTION

Rehearsals: From Friday 5 May
Camera Rehearsals/Recording: Teddington Studio Two, Tuesday 16 and
Wednesday 17 May 1967[78]

TV TIMES: 'This your gun? Beautiful. You could get yourself a lord with a gun like this.'
2-7 August 1969, Southern edition

MISSING FILE: The master tapes of this story do not exist in the Studio Canal archive.

PRE-TITLES: Hunter decides with Meres that it's time Lord Lindale was in a Red File.

MISSION PROFILE: Miller is an expert on every form of gambling – and cheating – who works in the Section. He approaches Callan and asks for his help in fleecing someone at cards, using a technique they both practised. Callan suspects another Hunter plot.

Having met him in a club, Barlows, Miller and Callan play cards with Lord Lindale, who loses heavily. He invites the pair to his house in the Border Country, where he is holding a shooting party. There he can 'have his revenge' by winning his money back.

Hunter has Lindale in a Red File as he is a collector of dangerous secrets, which, if the price is right, he will sell. His hold on Fielding – a 'close friend' of the American President's son – could damage the UK's trade interests with America if the affair is brought to the attention of the 'puritanical' President. Lindale is about to sell compromising photographs of Fielding to the Russians and, as a further hold over him, he keeps the diplomat's beautiful young wife Caroline with him.

Lindale plays cards with Miller and Callan – and faces ruin. Miller does the card cheating, but Callan is by far the bigger winner, with a pile of IOUs from the Lord.

Lindale locks Callan in his gun-room, searching him for the IOUs. He denies knowing where they are. Callan throws the IOUs to Miller from a window and the vindictive agent gives Callan a single bullet in return. Hiding from Lindale, he shoots him dead and retrieves the negatives for Caroline, which she burns. Withholding the surviving set of photographs from Hunter, Callan makes the Section chief agree to have Miller framed for Lindale's murder in exchange for the prints.[79]

A MAN LIKE ME: Once again, Hunter is using Callan as a deniable executioner. Once the freelancer cleans Lindale out, the Lord will be informed he's been cheated and Callan will have to kill him in self defence.

Callan distrusts Miller but has a 'bad case of conscience' about his former colleague: on Hunter's orders, Callan once betrayed his fellow agent, which resulted in a prison sentence. Miller harbours a grudge and later extracts his revenge, refusing to help when Callan suffers the ironic fate of being locked in a room full of guns with no accessible ammunition. After throwing down one cartridge for Callan, Miller runs off when he realises his former colleague has survived.

Callan likes Caroline, the episode's feminine interest, but he is not prepared to stick his neck out for her: 'You've got wrong ideas about me. I'm not going to do time to save your husband.'

Section Kills: 5

LONELY: Still procuring ammunition for Callan. He uses a breath-freshener spray before meeting him. Lonely lied to Callan 'once' and knows never to do it again. He helps Callan search Lindale's London home, but worries that 'Lindale's bird' will interrupt them. Callan assures Lonely she's away having a sauna bath, adding, 'I wish you would!'

Lonely later poses as a chauffeur, complaining he feels like a 'right nana' in the uniform; he is billeted at the Bootwood Arms, off the grounds of Lindale's estate. Callan entrusts Lonely with posting the blackmail photographs to safe keeping with 'a friend'.

A TIE AND A CREST: Lindale is in debt, clinging on to his stately home. He habitually entertains house guests during the grouse season and is a Peer of the Realm, as Meres deferentially reminds Hunter. Lindale knows nothing of the occupation of 'Colonel Hunter', dismissing him as 'a bore'. The Lord seems unbalanced when he tries to recover his IOUs, insisting 'I must have them. It's a matter of honour.'

The Section are surprisingly non-homophobic (or biphobic) when looking through Lindale's compromising photo collection, which features Caroline's husband. Even Toby simply opines the photos are 'very naughty' and denies knowing the man 'intimately'. Callan's running feud with Meres continues as the rival agent is tasked (off-screen) with telling Lindale that Callan cheated at cards.

ALCOHOL, TOBACCO AND FIREARMS: Callan mingles with the champagne set in Barlows club and offers whisky to Miller at home. Lindale and Caroline later try to spike his drink to make him lose the card game, but he holds it together. Callan refuses Caroline's offer of a cigarette: 'only one vice at a time at my age.'

'I'll be back!' threatens Lindale, brandishing an eight-shot Luger Automatic. Callan retaliates with a 12-bore shotgun.

SPY-SPEAK: 'Anyone would think I was blackmailing you,' Lindale says, leeching money off Caroline in a way that would make Conan Doyle's extortioner Charles Augustus Milverton proud.

Lindale is also cheating in the card games, just 'not terribly well.' 'That's why he took up blackmail, to pay his debts,' Hunter says. 'After all, he is a gentleman.'

Callan cannot resist making Hunter uncomfortable by flaunting his proletarian credentials inside the snobbish gambling club Barlows, claiming 'there's a better class of bird here.' Meres is wickedly disparaging of Callan's shabby suit: 'I didn't know they cater to coach parties.'

Amid much other dialogue about the upper-classes, Callan opines that Miller will be 'horsewhipped' if he is caught cheating at cards (a curiously popular aristocratic punishment later brought to public notice by the late Alan Clark MP (1928-1999)).

Lindale's ancestors included a Foreign Secretary and a King's mistress. 'The rest of us just lived gracefully.' 'I just live,' Callan replies.

Hunter advises him, 'Ignorance is a virtue.'

PAWNS AND PLAYERS: GUY VERNEY (1915-1970) began his career as an actor, appearing uncredited in Hitchcock's *The Man Who Knew Too Much* (1956) and ITC's first film series *The Adventures of Robin Hood* (1957), before moving behind the camera and working as a director on *Public Eye* (from 1965-69), *Redcap* (1965-66), *Special Branch* (in 1970) and *Armchair Theatre* (1957-1970). Verney helmed an impressive 28 productions, including prestigious adaptations of Noel Coward's *Star Quality* and *Bon Voyage* (both 1968). He shared directing duties with Reg Collin on *Pathfinders to Venus* (1961) and oversaw all episodes of the sequels *Pathfinders in Space* (1960) and *Pathfinders to Mars* (1960-61). Verney's other contributions to the fantasy genre included *Plateau of Fear* (1961), *Out of This World* – 'Little Lost Robot' (1962), *City Beneath the Sea* (1962) and *Secret Beneath the Sea* (1963).

DONALD MARLAND HEWLETT (1920-2011) started out in rep with Ronnie Barker and was best known for comical upper-class figures, one of the earliest being Captain 'Snooty' Pilkington in *The Adventures of Brigadier Wellington-Bull* (BBC, 1959). He played similar characters in *Bachelor Father* (1971), *Now Look Here* (1971-73), *Come Back Mrs Noah* (1978) and *You Rang, M'Lord?* (1988–1993). Hewlett is arguably best remembered as the avuncular, pipe-smoking Colonel Reynolds in *It Ain't Half Hot Mum* (1974-1981), Jimmy Perry and David Croft's WW2 Burma comedy. In a more serious vein, he played the ill-fated Sir George Hardiman in *Doctor Who* – 'The Claws of Axos' (1971), a ministry bureaucrat in *The New Avengers* – 'Faces '(1976) and an admiral in *Goldeneye* (1989), a documentary-drama about the life of Ian Fleming.

GERALD FLOOD (1927-1989) was frequently cast as the leading man in Verney's productions, initially becoming popular as journalist Conway Henderson in the *Pathfinders* science fiction franchise. He featured as the robophobic technician Black in 'Little Lost Robot', and near the end of his career provided the voice of the shape-shifting android Kamelion in *Doctor Who* – 'The King's Demons' (1983), also portraying its impersonation of King John 'in the flesh'. Flood had regular roles in the smuggling series *Crane* (1963-65) and *The Rat Catchers*, and featured in *Man in a Suitcase*, *Randall and Hopkirk (Deceased)* and the horror film *Frightmare* (1974).

ANN BELL (born 1940) played several notable early roles that are now 'missing believed wiped', including *The Avengers* – 'The Deadly Air' (1961) and Nigel Kneale's classic play *The Road* (1963). She made guest appearances in *The Saint, Danger Man* and *Department S*, performed with Peter Cushing's Sherlock Holmes in 'The Sign of Four' (1968) and gained further recognition as Marion Jefferson in the prisoner of war drama *Tenko*, which also starred Burt Kwouk. She married Robert Lang and he appeared with her in the sequel *Tenko Reunion* (1985). On the big screen, Bell can be seen in the 'creeping vine' segment of *Dr. Terror's House of Horrors* (1965) and in Francois Truffaut's film adaptation of Ray Bradbury's dystopian novel, *Fahrenheit 451* (1966).

INFORMATION: As the script progressed from the original story outline proposed by Mitchell, characters were renamed. Lord Lindale was initially the more Dickensian-sounding 'Borrowdale' and Miller was 'Beverly'. Miller's gambling addiction was transferred to Lindale, giving the Lord a clearer motive. Callan was 'publicly insulted' by the Lord before a more plausible rationale for him entering the story was decided on, while Lonely's appalled reaction, 'But he's a Lord, Mr Callan', originally came on being informed that Lindale was a blackmailer.

'As I remember, Lonely couldn't believe it because he's obsessed with Lords and the Queen and the Royal family,'[80] James Mitchell said. 'On one occasion he told Callan he didn't hold with Communists because they were against the Queen! Like an awful lot of crooks he's a staunch Conservative.'

The British public wouldn't have been that surprised by the existence of a suspicious member of the gentry, as in July 1964 the *Sunday Mirror* had printed the headline 'The Pictures We Dare Not Print', alluding to the existence of an incriminating photograph of a prominent House of Lords politician and a major London criminal. The newspaper further implied a homosexual relationship between the pair (at a time when gay intercourse was illegal). The duo were later named by German magazine *Stern* as Life Peer Baron Robert John Graham 'Lord' Boothby (1900-1986) and gangster Ronald 'Ronnie' Kray (1933-1993), twin of 'Reggie' (1933-2000). Boothby immediately issued denials, suing the *Sunday Mirror* for libel; the paper publicly apologised and paid £40,000 to Boothby in damages. Suspicions remained that the story was true, although the newspaper was only officially vindicated years later when related MI5 files were declassified. The Kray twins were convicted of murder in 1969.

The camera script has an unfortunate typo, as Callan asks Miller if he has 'turd honest'. There is a further mistake, when the Jacks and Kings in Callan's hand are not revealed in the right order for him to win the crucial hand in the poker game.

'Dad wasn't a gambler, but he liked the mechanics of how card games worked,'[81] Peter Mitchell recmembered. 'He always adored that scene in *The Sting* [1973] when Paul Newman plays the Irish gangster at poker... Cards were a definite fascination for him.'

Significantly, Callan hints for the first time that 'Hunter' is a codename.

MISSION ANALYSIS: *'A Lord cheating at cards. Positively eighteenth century.'* This is an enjoyably iconoclastic story where almost everyone has an ulterior motive and strength of character is shown as an important trait. Significantly, Lindale is a 'bounder and a cad' in the vein of *The Avengers*' early stories (and one of its later ones – the 1968 episode 'False Witness' features Barry Warren as Lord Melville, another blackmailer from the aristocracy). Mitchell was clearly impressed with Ronald Radd's portrayal of Hunter, as the character gets more to do both here and in the next story; Hunter acquaints himself with Lindale and travels to his stately home to pressurise Miller and Callan in person. While this risks him being caught up in a police investigation, in the pre-mobile phone era the situation is plausible.

Budgetary limitations would have dictated a studio-bound ending rather than a film climax involving the 'shooting party' (as in the 1966 *Danger Man* story of the same name) in the estate grounds, but this is offset by the scenes where Callan arranges the evidence to frame Miller for killing Lindale. 'It's amazing, the things a man will do when he is driven to it,' Callan remarks to Hunter as they both casually lie to the police. Caroline might think of Callan as heroic but as this story harshly shows, when it comes to self-preservation he can be just as ruthless as his opponents.

END TITLES: Projected over Lindale's gun room.[82]

S1.6 YOU SHOULD HAVE GOT HERE SOONER

Writer: James Mitchell
Director: Piers Haggard
Designer: Darrell Lass

FIRST UK TRANSMISSION

Border, Southern: Thursday 10 August 1967, 10:30 pm
Westward, Channel: Thursday 5 October 1967, 10:30 pm
All other regions: Saturday 12 August 1967, 9:00 pm

CAST: Derek Newark (Loder), Jon Laurimore (Pollock), Bernard Stone (Flat Porter), Pinkie Johnstone (Sue Lyall), Anne Blake (Mrs Lyall), Philip Ryan, Stanley Stewart (Police Sergeants)

EXTRAS/WALK-ONS: (*Uncredited on screen*) Tony Leary, David James (Ambulance Men), Paul Leeson-Cole (member of Hunter's staff)

PRODUCTION

Rehearsals: From Friday 16 June
Location Filming: Flat A, Palmerston Court, Holland Park, London; Derby Gardens, Sunbury-on-Thames (Monday 19 June 1967)
Camera Rehearsals/Recording: Teddington Studio One, Wednesday 28 and Thursday 29 June 1967[83]

TV TIMES: 'It's no use, Mr Callan. I can't tell you anything. It was all a dream. You should have got here sooner.'
12-18 August 1967, London edition

PRE-TITLES: Someone is searching Lonely's room in the middle of a thunderstorm. He surprises the intruder, who demands 'Where is it?' as he viciously beats the petty thief.

MISSION PROFILE: Calling round to buy more ammunition, Callan finds Lonely badly beaten. The culprit is a Section man, Loder, who with Meres is guarding Dan Pollock, a biochemist and Soviet spy. Pretending to be KGB agents, Loder and Meres have sprung Pollock from prison to secure his formula for a new nerve gas. When Lonely burgled Flat 3, Palmerston Court, a Holland Park residence that the Section is using as a safe house, he stole the scientist's wallet.

Callan discovers that it conceals the address of the house 'Little Orchard' in Crayhorpe, Sussex, where Sue Lyall, Pollock's girlfriend, lives with her mother. Pollock once hid the gas formula in a ruby engagement ring he gave Sue, so Callan and Meres converge on the Lyalls' house; Meres is hospitalised by Pollock when Callan reveals in a phone call that the scientist has been tricked by British intelligence. Sue's ring is a glass fake – Mrs Lyall confesses she sold the ruby ring to fund her purchase of the house. Callan agrees with Hunter to retrieve it, as long as he's paid 'top rate' and the cheque is made out to Lonely.

A MAN LIKE ME: Although Callan cares for Lonely after Loder's assault and makes sure he gets hospital treatment after the thief gets a second beating from Meres, Hunter asserts that the freelancer's motivation is selfish and controlling. Callan suggests to Lonely that if anyone's going to beat him up, it will be him, and he doesn't seem to be joking. Callan also views Meres' attack on the thief as an assault against him by proxy. In short, Lonely seems to be Callan's property to use and abuse as he – and only he – wants; disturbing behaviour.

In 1964, Callan was instrumental in arresting Pollock and it was apparently Callan's third assignment for the Section. The spy was sentenced to eighteen years imprisonment and Callan posed as a Special Branch officer in his dealings with the Lyalls.

Callan twice demonstrates his role-playing skills, firstly by adopting the guise of the officious 'J.A. Pomfret' from the Inland Revenue (complete with bowler hat) to investigate the flat at Palmerston Court. Assuming cover identities is so effortless for him that when he meets Sue Lyall three years later, he automatically updates the rank of 'Sergeant Callan' to Inspector (he may have taken inspiration from the long-running ITV series *No Hiding Place* (1959-1967), as DI Harry Baxter (Eric Lander) wore a homburg similar to the one Callan uses). He borrows a flat cap from Lonely, later acquiring another one to go with his final disguise of tradesman's overalls to gain access to the Lyalls' house.

Callan shows his inventive and manipulative side by using a stethoscope to eavesdrop on Meres and the Lyalls, and then provokes Pollock into knocking Meres out, although he wishes he could have done it himself. Notably, Callan's motivation for interfering in the Pollock operation is solely to make trouble for Meres. While visiting the Section, he easily floors Loder with two severe blows. Callan also acquires a car.

He was on a previous assignment which involved the Section's van.

LONELY: The thief lives in a ground-floor bedsit at 19 Old Market, a run down area of Shepherds Bush (inviting comparisons with the sitcom *Steptoe and Son*.) When he discovers Loder searching his home, he automatically assumes he's a policeman. Lonely has been on the receiving end of violent treatment from the Met in the past, as after being assaulted by Loder he tells Callan 'bogeys don't hit like that.' His luck doesn't improve as an explicit beating from Meres is so bad it puts him in hospital.

Lonely's extended family is mentioned again: he has an auntie who hides and sells on stolen goods for him – including Pollock's wallet – although she's been semi-retired from 'fencing' since 'uncle died'. He proudly considers stealing to be his 'living' and, as a professional criminal, can tell if paper money is 'snide' (counterfeit). Crucially, Lonely alerts Callan to Pollock's escape from prison by pointing out his photograph in a newspaper; at the same time, he's clearly frightened of Callan too.

This is the only time in the entire series that Lonely takes a bath.

A TIE AND A CREST: In addition to Meres, three other agents, including Loder, are on the Section's strength, and Hunter is confident that – en masse – they can take Callan. The organisation's men are fluent in Russian (even if Meres isn't convincing enough as a Soviet agent to fool Sue Lyall) and the operation to trick Pollock is typically devious. It's the most flagrant breach yet by the Section of the laws of the land, as they break a Russian spy out of prison.

In the absence of Callan, Meres maintains the Special Branch cover story, posing as 'Sergeant Turner' to visit the Lyalls. The Section operative is at his nastiest, viciously attacking Lonely and threatening Sue Lyall with violence. By contrast, Hunter knows that on his own, Loder isn't up to Callan's standard and has a lot to learn.

ALCOHOL, TOBACCO AND FIREARMS: Lonely always drinks beer before a burglary as thieving makes him nervous. Hiding out in the Holland Park flat, Pollock drinks vodka (predictably), while Meres takes Scotch.

Nervous because of Pollock's escape, Sue Lyall begins smoking, although she claims she hasn't 'really' started again.

SPY-SPEAK: Callan's ironic reaction to finding Lonely in a state of undress: 'You look a little lovelier every day.' Privately, he's less dismissive of the formidable Mrs Lyall: 'You must meet Hunter, lady. He's just about your mark.'

Meres' threat to Lonely before the agent beats the terrified thief is the public school bully personified: 'It's no good, old stinker. I'm going to have to teach you.'

Hunter's memorable proletarian threat to Callan: 'There are three blokes here who'd just about murder you, chum.' He's equally acerbic dealing with Mrs Lyall when she warns him, 'This is my house.' 'Hardly', he replies.

PAWNS AND PLAYERS: PIERS INIGO HAGGARD (born 1939) is the great, great nephew of fantasy writer H. Rider Haggard. He began his career directing for the anthology *Thirty-Minute Theatre* (1965-1971) before moving on to *Public Eye* (in 1966). Haggard's most distinguished work is *Pennies from Heaven* (1978), Dennis Potter's musical drama starring Bob Hoskins and Cheryl Campbell. '[It's] very dear to my heart,'[84] he said. 'Really ambitious, with brilliant pieces of music, but a very dark central theme – I really did like that material.' The following year, he directed the apocalyptic film serial *Quatermass* (1979).

His contributions to cinema include the horror film *The Blood on Satan's Claw* (1971), which features Patrick Wymark and Michele Dotrice, and has parallels with *The Wicker Man*. '[It's] not quite my first movie, but the first one I was pleased with. It really is quite strong, and it was made with real passion. It's about country life and I grew up in the country.' Another film worthy of note is *Venom* (1981), an Oliver Reed horror thriller about a Black Mamba snake on the loose in the middle of a siege. Intriguingly, Haggard said of working with Reed, 'There are some pretty ghastly stories!'

'Going forward into the 1990s, I enjoyed two Jack Rosenthal films, *Eskimo Day* [1996] and *Cold Enough for Snow* [1997] with Maureen Lipman. They were Jacobean bitter-sweet comedies, and again very particularly near to my heart.' His latest work was the TV movie *Shell Seekers* (2006), starring Vanessa Redkgrave.

DEREK NEWARK (1933-1998) was often cast as a copper or hard man, appearing in *The Avengers* (between 1964-68), *Man in a Suitcase* (1967-68), *Budgie* (1971-72), six episodes of *Z Cars* (1969-1972), and *Barlow at Large* (1974-75, as DI Eddie Tucker). He played the same character on *The Two Ronnies* (1975) and continued in a comic vein as an angry wrestler who breaks his leg after falling over Rigsby's cat in *Rising Damp* (1974-75), and as a motorcycle courier boss who employs Frank Spencer in *Some Mothers Do 'Ave 'Em* (1978). Newark played a caveman in the first-ever *Doctor Who* story '100,000 BC' (1963), and returned to portray a cocky engineer opposite Jon Pertwee's Doctor in 'Inferno' (1970; this could have been the last-ever *Doctor Who* story). Newark's stage work included Harold Pinter's *The Hothouse* and Alan Ayckbourn's *Bedroom Farce*, which was later televised and had runs in the West End and on Broadway. Newark's films include a forceful performance as Sean Connery's assistant in Sidney Lumet's *The Offence* (1972).

JON ('JOHN') LAURIMORE played the regular character Duffer in the children's series *Orlando* (1965-68). He had roles in *The Avengers* (1966-67) and played Ernst, a violent gunrunner in *The Prisoner* – 'Many Happy Returns' (1967). His portrayal of Jacobean villain Count Federico in *Doctor Who*'s 'The Masque of Mandragora' (1976) – 'You can no more tell my future than you can tell my chamber pot!' – may have led to him being cast opposite Patrick Mower in 'Shipment', the opening instalment of the violent police series *Target* (1978), as Philip Hinchcliffe produced both series. Laurimore played the sycophantic Lentulus in *I, Claudius* (1976) and featured in the concluding instalment of *Reilly – Ace of Spies* (1983).

ANNE BLAKE (1908–2000) was a character actress who worked on *Armchair Theatre*, *ITV Play of the Week* (1960-67), *Theatre 625* (1964-68) and *Emergency Ward 10* (1964, as Dr. Tabitha Chalmers). Her cinema appearances include the iconic horror films *Taste of Fear* (1961) and *The Curse of the Werewolf* (1961), the Northern drama *Saturday Night and Sunday Morning* (1960) and a snobbish librarian in *The Spy Who Came in from the Cold* (1965). Blake's other TV credits include *Department S, The Saint, Danger Man, Ivanhoe* (1970), *War and Peace* (1972-73) and Dennis Potter's adaptation of Angus Wilson's novel *Late Call* (1975).

PINKIE JOHNSTONE had previously appeared in the *Blackmail* anthology series in the play 'Please Do Not Disturb' (1966).

INFORMATION: There is more incidental music than normal: in addition to 'Girl In The Dark' and 'Mystery Project', two further Jack Trombey compositions, 'The Killer' and 'Darkness'[85], were used. Lisa Langdon appears on screen in the series for the first time, on a TV monitor in the Section HQ.

Directing his first *Callan* episode, Piers Haggard had no doubt what a major part of the series' appeal was: 'The great, great thing about *Callan* was the relationship with Lonely – the affection for this stinking, lying character. You get really involved, you feel for him. It's unashamed affection: [Callan] disguises it, he's clipped, but that love, people remember that: the human quality. It was bang on in the central relationship.'[86] The first story to feature Lonely prominently reflected Edward Woodward's views on the importance of the character: 'One of the things that Callan despised in Lonely, and one of the things I always worked on, was "There but for the grace of God go I. Here's this man and he's my only friend. Fancy having that as a friend!" They were both extremely loyal to each other, for their own ends, possibly, but nevertheless there was a tremendous friendship, which worked extremely well, and most of the letters [we got] were about that.'[87] 'Callan was the physical thing of his life,'[88] Haggard noted, 'in that Callan had actually stood up for him in prison, when he was going to be battered by one party or the other. For that he owed him. He'd never be able to repay it, but he'd try to.'

For Russell Hunter, 'You Should Have Got Here Sooner' featured one of his best scenes in the role. 'I remember the enjoyment of acting certain things. It probably says something very weird about me as a private person – I hope not! I enjoyed the little scenes with Teddy, and I think I only had about two in the whole series with Tony Valentine, when real threat was in the air, [there was] physical violence between two sets of eyes on the television screen, when you knew that this man... would kill Lonely and not even blink. Those, to me, are the moments – and I don't mean to be melodramatic about it – when it was a matter of life, or death, and one was able to do that in quite small terms, in [an] intelligent expression of acting: you're either terrified or you're not. I remember in those scenes, that one got a sense of life or death on to a television screen. I think that's very satisfying.'[89]

By now, Valentine himself had firm views about Meres: 'A pretty unpleasant human being, actually, not the sort of man that you'd want to spend any of your spare time with. You wouldn't go to a rugby match with someone like Toby Meres. You certainly wouldn't go fishing with him.'[90]

Hunter agreeing to Meres being placed in the adjacent bed to Lonely was 'a punishment for Meres'[91] on the Section chief's behalf, James Mitchell said. 'Can you imagine anything worse than being in bed next to Lonely? He'd failed, and you're not allowed to fail.'

'I only did three Callans,'[92] Haggard reflected, 'and left with the sense that it wasn't my thing because I was more interested in the relationships than the violence – and looking at it, it's laughable really, a chop to the back of the neck, people drop to the floor and you never hear a screech. Doing it in studio, we didn't have stunt arrangers, we just figured it out. That's the weakest part; we failed to deliver convincing violence in my Callans. I was interested to see the stories again, and it's slightly altered my perception, as actually the relationships – the human values – still resonate through.

'I've always been very particular about lighting and even in those early days, I was increasingly impatient with a lot of TV lighting. Gradually, in my work over the next ten years, we used filters and lights on the floor and various other ways and means of making it more convincing.' Remarking on the stylistic device of Callan's internal dialogues, Haggard said, 'I don't mind voiceover myself particularly, but you have to be very careful when you use it, as it [can be] slightly self-conscious. I didn't think any of [my stories] needed it.'

The inspiration for Pollock is most likely to have been Emil Julius Klaus Fuchs (1911-1988). A theoretical physicist rather than a chemist, and German rather than British, Fuchs was one of the most notorious scientific traitors in history. In 1950, he was convicted of supplying atomic bomb-building information from the American, British and Canadian Manhattan Project to Soviet Russia, during and shortly after WW2; his espionage effectively started the nuclear arms race with the USSR. Fuchs was stripped of his British citizenship and sentenced14 years in prison. Released in 1959 after serving nine years, Fuchs emigrated to the German Democratic Republic of East Germany.

The prison break mirrors that of notorious double agent George Blake né Behar. In 1961, after an in camera trial at the Old Bailey, Blake was sentenced to the maximum term of fourteen years consecutively on each of three counts of spying, adding up to 42 years in total. Five years later, he escaped from Wormwood Scrubs with the assistance of three men whom he had previously met in jail: Irish Republican Sean Bourke and (as was later discovered) two anti-nuclear campaigners, Michael Randle and Pat Pottle. The escape involved Blake climbing through a window and then scaling the perimeter wall using a rope ladder.

Callan mentions Diana Dors (1931-1984), a British film star who would undoubtedly have made an impression on the ex-agent during his formative years. By contrast, Meres and Pollock discuss Scottish poet Robert Burns (1759-1796).

TV Times promoted the series again, as journalist Ann Morrow gave her impressions of the male cast in the listings magazine.[93]

After the series' concluded, G. Seery of Bradford wrote to the magazine to express his appreciation, saying 'Callan made 'the rest of the "cloak and dagger" boys pale by comparison.' In a postscript, the magazine announced that a second, thirteen part series was 'planned' for 1968.[94]

MISSION ANALYSIS: *'Master Spy Escapes. Warder Unconscious.'* The last episode of the first series is striking for several reasons. Reflecting the popularity of the character with both the production team and the viewers, Lonely is put centre stage, drawing the sympathy of even the most hardened of viewers to have seen or experienced bullying. For the first time, the series references a specific espionage incident – the recent escape from prison of the Soviet spy George Blake in 1966, an event so compelling *Callan* would return to it for inspiration twice more. The twist is that the Section is behind the breakout and Meres and Loder are posing as KGB agents, a striking example of the devious complexity in James Mitchell's fictional universe.

Watching well over 40 later, it's striking how fast Piers Haggard makes the story move, using an innovative vocabulary of film sequences – shooting up and down a stairwell in a block of flats, inside Callan's moving car – and heightens the threatening atmosphere by inventive use of sound and lighting; a thunder storm rages when Callan finds the injured Lonely and, later, a neon light blinks on and off hypnotically as Meres prepares to beat the small thief. Haggard's handling of the actors is no less impressive. He brings Callan and Meres' year-long feud to an unexpected conclusion and, in the supporting characters, creates a believably dysfunctional relationship between the Lyalls. The story isn't perfect; of all the first series scripts it's the most contrived, with the enormous coincidence of Lonely burgling a flat the Section happen to have commandeered as a safe house (haven't they got one of their own?), and Pollock, an experienced chemist, would surely be able to recall or recalculate the nerve gas formula from memory. Contrivances would occur more in Mitchell's later work, but here Haggard's confident direction effectively glosses over them.

After seven TV plays, the audience was coming to terms with a character very different from his contemporaries. The other TV spies of the period all support and protect the establishment or moral status quo (even the Prisoner); by contrast, Callan is an anarchist, as opposed to his nominal employers as much as he is to war criminals, mercenaries and Communist agents. He is a transgressor, defiantly working-class in an upper-class system and he does things other British thriller heroes of the mid-1960s never would – physically abuse his only friend and ex-colleagues, drink heavily and exist on the edge of poverty, while harbouring a cynical moral sense compromised by a love of money. At the same time, he can be humane and witty and, uniquely for the time, the audience is invited inside Callan's mind-set with his conspiratorial voiceovers. No wonder he captured the public's imagination.

At the end of the story Callan leaves, having hospitalised Meres, outwitted Hunter again and left a mother and daughter reflecting on the causes of their ruined relationship. It's a brilliant end to the first series.

END TITLES: A triumphant Callan drives away.

S1.0 GOODBYE MARY LEE

Writer: James Mitchell

CHARACTERS: Callan, Lonely, Hunter, Hunter's Secretary, Charlotte Rigby, Mary Lee Townsend, Robert Hacker, Detective Inspector, Barman, Cyprian, Poet

EXTRAS: Guests at party; People in Cocktail Bar; Police

TEASER SEQUENCE: Hunter and Section agent Charlotte Rigby observe Mary Lee's arrival at London Airport.

MISSION PROFILE: Mary Lee is the estranged daughter of US Senator Townsend. He finds her an embarrassment as she is involved in the American civil rights movement and has protested in favour of nuclear disarmament. More seriously, Mary Lee's job as an American Airlines air hostess between Panama and the West Indies means she is an ideal courier for Cuban intelligence. Townsend fears that his daughter will be deliberately exposed by the Communists and the resulting trial and publicity will wreck his career. Through the CIA man Robert Hacker, and in return for shared information, Townsend wants Hunter to have Mary Lee gaoled in England. When she's in the UK, she stays with her boyfriend – David Callan.

When Mary Lee discovers that papers she was carrying for the Cubans have been removed, Callan becomes involved and realises that the Western security services are on to her. He turns the tables on Rigby, who has been ordered by Hunter to deal with Mary Lee, incriminating her and Hacker with planted drugs intended for his girlfriend. Coming to the grim realisation that the Section will continue to persecute Mary Lee because of pressure from Senator Townsend and the CIA, Callan drugs her so she's arrested for causing an affray and deported to America, where she'll be safe.

A MAN LIKE ME: Callan met Mary Lee on a holiday flight to Jamaica and can pull off a Deep South American accent as he once 'did a job' in Richmond, Virginia (where he also learned to mix a good mint julep).

When he learns that the secret papers Mary Lee was carrying have been stolen, Callan deduces how the envelope they were in was opened so quickly and how they were replaced with cut-down pages of the *New York Times*. He despairs of her idealism, knowing she is being used by the Eastern Bloc, but agrees to help her. Callan cleverly reverses the Section's plan to have her imprisoned for five years for possession of heroin, hiding the drugs on their operatives.

Although Callan genuinely loves Mary Lee, he knows that Hunter won't stop until she has been dealt with; he also considers himself unworthy of her and knows she won't leave Britain voluntarily. He takes the drastic action of spiking Mary Lee's whisky so she's arrested for drunk and disorderly behaviour. The plan works but destroys their relationship; when she ignores him at London Airport, it's clear that Callan regrets the loss.

LONELY: In luck because Callan has 'two birds for [him] to follow.' He recognises there is something not right about Charlotte but would rather tail Mary Lee. After Lonely has left the upmarket bar where he meets Callan, the barman removes his stool as he's left some of his rank aroma behind on it. Lonely minds Callan's flat for him, passing the time drinking beer and cheating at patience. Following young women is, apparently, 'just a hobby'.

A TIE AND A CREST: Meres is in Geneva. Charlotte Rigby, the Section's senior female operative, has a flat in fashionable Chelsea and has been posing as an air hostess to befriend Mary Lee. Addicted to the covert lifestyle – 'I couldn't give this up' – she knows people in London's hippy set, including Cyprian, who hosts psychedelic parties. Charlotte's career in the Section is short lived, as Callan hides drugs in her coat, she's arrested and faces a five year prison sentence.

Like Lonely, Hunter cheats at cards.

ALCOHOL, TOBACCO AND FIREARMS: In an expensive bar, Lonely has a lager and buys Callan a Scotch. He tips the barman, who says 'Thank you sir, it'll come in useful if I want to make a phone call'; Lonely calls him a 'sarcastic git.'

After Lonely's gone, Mary Lee joins Callan for a whisky 'sour'. Staying away from the drugs at a hippy party, she and Callan take Scotch instead. Hunter drinks whisky when he calls at Callan's flat, where beer is kept in the cupboard. In a West End bar, Callan has a double whisky and orders Mary Lee another whisky sour.

Hacker pretends to be drunk in Charlotte's flat so she'll let her guard down (she doesn't). Mary Lee's bout of loud drunkenness is brought on by Callan deliberately drugging her whisky.

SPY-SPEAK: Callan has some firm advice for Mary Lee: 'Rule Number One is "Doubt everybody". You'd better start remembering that.'

Mary Lee has no illusions about Callan: 'He's the kind of man – if you got him mad, really mad – he wouldn't stop 'til he'd killed you.'

Hunter asks Charlotte if she ever finds her profession 'disgusting'. 'No, sir,' she replies. 'Just necessary.'

Callan's internal dialogue is heard as he thinks about Mary Lee: 'She deserves the best that one. The very best. And that isn't you, mate.'

PAWNS AND PLAYERS: If the episode had been made, the American actress LEILA GOLDINI, who worked with the independent film maker John Cassavetes in New York and featured in the *Danger Man* stories 'Fair Exchange' (1964) and 'Two Birds with One Bullet' (1966), would have been ideal casting as Mary Lee. The calculating Charlotte Rigby would have been a joy to watch in the hands of RACHEL HERBERT, a stylish actress who could also be very sinister and appeared in both *Danger Man* and *The Prisoner*. In 1970 she would guest star in a *Callan* story, the third series episode 'God Help Your Friends'.

ED BISHOP, British television's resident American, would have fitted the role of Robert Hacker perfectly. He'd been in a host of UK drama series, including *The Saint* (1962-69) – in four different roles – *The Troubleshooters* (1965-1972) and *Court Martial* (1965-66). In 1967, he was busy on the fifth James Bond film *You Only Live Twice*, playing a NASA technician ('Hawaii CapCom'). Bishop's most famous role was Commander Ed Straker, head of the secret Supreme Headqaurters Alien Defence Organisation – SHADO – in Gerry and Sylvia Anderson's live action sceience fiction series *UFO* (1970-73).

INFORMATION: Under the working title 'The Senator's Daughter' the script was commissioned for *Callan*'s first series but was never made. Location filming was planned for the then

London Airport (now Heathrow) and a short scene of Mary Lee leaving a phone box after she's called Callan.

The Second Battle of Bull Run that Callan is recreating when Mary Lee calls was part of the American Civil War, and took place between 28-30 August 1862. Fought between General Robert E. Lee for the Confederates and Major General John Pope's Army of Northern Virginia, it was a decisive victory by Lee against the Union forces.

Mary Lee's role as a courier for the Cuban Intelligence Directorate – DI – is highly topical. Cuba was a Cold War flashpoint in the early 1960s. A socialist revolution led by the Castro brothers Fidel a (1926-) and Raul (1931-) in 1959 had installed a Communist government only a few hundred miles from the American mainland. Castro's forces defeated an invasion by CIA-backed Cuban exiles in 1961 and, in 1963, Soviet missile bases were installed on the island, bringing the antagonism between the USA and Cuba to a head; when US warships blockaded the island against the delivery of more rockets, the USSR backed down and the missiles were withdrawn. The Russians trained 1,500 DI agents – including Cartro's right-hand man Ernesto 'Che' Guevara (1928-1967) – in intelligence techniques and Cuban forces were subsequently active in revolutionary conflicts in North Africa and the Congo.

Mary Lee's interest in nuclear disarmament would have waned after 1963, as in that year the major powers signed the atomic Test Ban Treaty. Causes she took up after that as an American student are protests at the ongoing war in Vietnam – which her Senator father champions – and, as she mentions to Callan, the black American Civil Rights Movement. It began in Montgomery, Alabama in 1955, when Rosa Parks was arrested for refusing to give up her seat on a bus to a white man, the catalyst which eventually led to all of the city's buses being racially integrated. Civil Rights protests reached a peak over 1963-65, with violent confrontations in Selma and Birmingham; after the last disturbance, the American Congress passed the 1964 Civil Rights Act, banning racial segregation throughout the USA.

LSD, which Cyprian offers the poet at his party, was the emerging 1960s' counter culture's drug of choice. Lysergic acid diethylamide, often known as 'acid', alters psychological perception and causes hallucinations. The drug was popularised by the psychologist Timothy Leary (1920-96), who with likeminded friends like the poet Allen Ginsberg (1926-97), began a campaign of introducing LSD and other psychedelic drugs to artists and intellectuals, which reached the mainstream through rock groups like The Beatles, Pink Floyd and The Doors. Mitchell's take on drug culture is very authentic: 'blocked' is a slang term for being high, LSD is ingested on a sugar lump and users of the drug can often experience 'a bad trip.'

Lonely thinks that Charlotte might be 'on the batter' – another slang term, for a drinking binge.

MISSION ANALYSIS: *'You're like my father, d'you know that, Callan? You get me and use me – then you betray me.'* Despite some inventive dialogue and situations, the grim theme that no-one trusts anyone and the novelty of seeing Callan in a romantic relationship, it's clear why 'Goodbye Mary Lee' didn't make it into production in *Callan*'s first year (or any time after that). The coincidence of the ex-agent dating someone Hunter has been asked to target stretches dramatic credibility to breaking point, exposing the inherent weakness of the initial set-up: finding a believable reason to involve Callan in Section intrigue. The plot beat of Callan's girlfriend being involved with Hunter is identical to the situation in 'Goodness Burns too Bright', another possible reason why 'Goodbye Mary Lee' was spiked.

On the plus side, there is a female Section member equally as ruthless as Meres, the only time a senior female SIS field agent appears in a Callan script. Dispassionate and attractive, she follows in the tradition of femme fatales like *Thunderball*'s SPECTRE executioner Fiona Volpe (Luciana Paluzzi) and Elke Sommer and Sylva Koscina's assassins in *Deadlier than the Male* (both 1965). With the benefit of hindsight, making Charlotte Rigby a recurring or regular character would have given the Section an interesting dynamic. It's slightly disappointing that this progressive idea wasn't developed further.

'Goodbye Mary Lee' is Callan is at its most anti-establishment. As well as the generation gap between the radical Mary Lee and her conservative father, and the counter cultural detail, Callan's sole opposition is Western intelligence: he has a Section agent imprisoned and a CIA man deported. There's also a disturbing Oedipal element, which Mary Lee acknowledges, that in Callan she's chosen a father substitute who eventually betrays her. Perhaps that's another reason why the story was never made.

END TITLES: A forlorn Callan at London Airport.

6: SERIES TWO
Hunter/Hunted

'These days, especially in America, you'd do a television series
and if it's successful, you do 22 in one year, then 22 the next
and you can go on for 11 years by which time the actors
become multimillionaires. It still doesn't work that way in
England – but it didn't work that way *at all* in those days.
It was very much on an "Old Boys" network system, really.'[1]

Edward Woodward, 2000

AROUND THE TIME THE FIRST SERIES of *Callan* was concluding transmission, ABC management were debating whether to go ahead with more episodes. As Mike Vardy recmembered, 'The first series did not go that well in terms of audience ratings.'[2] One cause for this may have been the series' fragmented scheduling across different times and days in different parts of the country. The company commissioned a survey to gauge audience feeling about the programme; 1,552 ITV-viewing adults were interviewed and the results were reported back to Brian Tesler, Director of Programmes. The report's author, R.T. Edwards, summarised the results: 'This programme is seen as a man's programme, more gripping, exciting and violent than most spy stories. Also it is thought to be better acted and more true to life. In terms of pace it is thought to be on a par with other spy stories and it is also considered less humorous.'[3]

'They actively used tape recorders for interviews and the production team actually heard what people were saying,'[4] Terence Feely recalled. 'It was really interesting: there were women saying, "Well, I don't really like the violence." We absolutely know that [real agents used] violence, but it was controlled.' Regarding the characters, the survey reported viewers seeing Lonely as 'an important character... likeable and amusing, although the women questioned were not quite so sure what to make of him... he is more popular with regular viewers.'[5] Meres was viewed as 'the villain of the piece... genuinely disliked' while Callan himself was considered to be a 'likeable character, human, competent and with a sense of humour. He seems equally acceptable to men and women... as viewers become more familiar with him, his image is developed and is found to be favourable.'

This encouraging feedback may have influenced the ABC management and Feely also recalled vigorously fighting *Callan*'s corner and having 'tremendous faith in it.'[6] Before long, confirmation was given that a second series would be made.

With Mitchell scripts in the pipeline, Feely wanted to broaden the series' range by bringing in more writers, including *Z Cars* author Ray Jenkins. 'Most of the outside writers simply got the format [to work from],' Feely said. 'It served as a very good guide to any new writer who came up, because it told them exactly where we are. And also we did not use any writers who had not seen the previous *Callan* episodes... We always insisted that writers should know what *Callan* [was about].'

'Halfway' into commissioning scripts for the second series – according to Feely's recollection – he received his career-changing job offer at Paramount. 'I think he wanted to write,'[7] James Mitchell considered. 'Being a story editor is a bit of a pest, constantly juggling other people's words instead of your own.' His subsequent acceptance and departure from ABC left a vacancy, and as Feely had been performing a dual function, it was decided he needed replacing by two people, a story editor/associate producer, as well as a producer. John Kershaw and Reg Collin respectively took on these two roles, while Lloyd Shirley remained as *Callan*'s executive producer.

REGINALD 'REG' THOMAS COLLIN (1927-2011) began acting in amateur dramatics while doing his National Service at RAF Bomber Command Headquarters in High Wycombe. After being demobbed, he won a scholarship to the newly opened Old Vic Theatre School in London before directing pantomimes and summer shows. He moved into television as a director with ABC in 1959, directing two episodes of the children's serial *Pathfinders to Venus* (1961) before beginning work on *Tempo* (1962-67). This fortnightly magazine programme was ITV's answer to *Monitor*, the BBC arts review, and covered everything from music, film and literature to the performing arts and architecture. By 1963, Collin was producer of the programme; he also oversaw *Sat'day While Sunday* (1967), a fourteen-part drama serial about the lives of teenagers in the north of England. 'Believe it or not we had the guy who did *A Clockwork Orange* – Malcolm McDowell – and Tim Dalton, all in this cast and fresh out of drama school, I would think! And a lovely girl called Sarah-Jane Gwillim,'[7] Mike Vardy recalled of directing this series. 'It was pretty tough, it was all up in Manchester. Some scripts were written by Roger McGough, a well-known poet. He was part of The Scaffold during the Beatles' time.'

In addition to taking on responsibility for *Callan*, Collin oversaw the first nine episodes of *Special Branch* (1969); another *Armchair Theatre* story editor, George Markstein, took on script supervision duties for this series, while Wensley Pithey and a fashionably dressed Derren Nesbitt led the cast. Further Collin-produced series included *Six Days of Justice* (1972), set in a magistrates' court, in 1973 seven episodes of *The Rivals of Sherlock Holmes*, which adapted lesser known detective stories by writers who were contemporaries of Sir Arthur Conan Doyle. '[Collin] was a good working producer,'[8] Lloyd Shirley observed. Neville Green added, 'The relationship we had was always very good. There was an immense amount of trust between us. He used to let you get on with it; he trusted you. He had very tight budgets and often complained about that.'[9]

In 1975, Collin left television to work with the British Academy of Film and Television Arts (BAFTA), where he was given credit for establishing the organisation's regional branches, devising the 'jury system' for voting for awards, and organising gala events such as the tribute to Sean Connery in 1990. Collin was married to Pamela Lonsdale, another successful ITV producer; in 1987 he was awarded a fellowship by the Royal Television Society in recognition of 'an outstanding contribution to the furtherance of television'. His final work before leaving ITV involved teaming up with some former *Callan* colleagues to work on two instalments of Euston Films' *Armchair Cinema* (1975). 'When Day is Done' and 'In Sickness and in Health' starred Edward Woodward and Patrick Mower respectively and both films were scripted by John Kershaw

'I WAS BORN IN 1931 and brought up by an aunt and uncle who'd had a very rough time in the Depression,'[9] John Kershaw remembered. 'They were obsessed with security and the idea that I should have a good, safe life, so I left school at 16 and went to work in a bank. I failed the medical for military service – in those days there was still conscription – so the bank wouldn't put me on its permanent staff, and anyway I wasn't happy with the work. I went into local government for a while. But my father was an actor. And I wanted to get back to London, and the sort of life I had remembered as a small child with him. I got a job at a bank in London – the only reason my aunt and uncle would let me come back – and then I gave everything up in order to write. I spent some years doing odd bits of journalism, wrote a novel, got on the teaching staff at London University, then got asked to do a piece for a magazine called *New Society* about television and the arts. So I met Huw Wheldon at *Monitor* and Reg Collin at ABC on *Tempo*. He had an editor who was leaving and he recommended me to Lloyd to replace [him].'

By the mid-1960s John Hugh D'Allenger Kershaw (christened with his French mother's maiden name) was well-accustomed to working with Collin after the pair collaborated on *Sat'day While Sunday*. 'In those days, John Kershaw almost went with me as a package; his function was the same as any other story editor,'[11] Collin explained. 'We would discuss authors and agree who to go to. He would then approach the authors who would come in and have a talk. The author would then go away and devise a story line... John as story editor would keep his eye on that episode and the other episodes as well, until we were in "go" condition for the studio. John was exceptional and I cannot praise him too much.'

After his year-long stint on *Callan*, Kershaw took over producing duties from Leonard White on *Armchair Theatre*, while George Markstein switched over to the story editor's chair on *Callan*. 'Lloyd Shirley was manoeuvring me towards being a producer... he wanted me to have a little more to do with production than a story editor normally has,' Kershaw recalled. 'I sat in with Reggie in his office so I knew what was going on.'[12] In the gaps between *Armchair Theatre* plays, Kershaw also produced the suspense anthology *Shadows of Fear* (1971), writing one play himself, 'Sugar and Spice', about a murderous child. Another contributor to this anthology was Roger Marshall and over the next few years Kershaw wrote several episodes for Marshall's *Public Eye*, including 'Who Wants to Be Told Bad News?' (1971) about a racism accusation. (This programme was repeated in 1989 along with *Callan* – 'That'll be the Day' as part of Thames Television's 21st anniversary.) Kershaw also had connections with Euston Films, contributing to the revamped *Special Branch* in addition to *Armchair Cinema*. During this period, he also wrote for *Spy Trap* (1975), *Z Cars* (1978) and Guernsey wartime drama *Enemy at the Door* (1978-1980).

Another aspect of his career was his work for children, including TV productions made in collaboration with Collin's wife Pamela Lonsdale. She had been Kershaw's producer on *The Present Stage* (1966), an adaptation of his book about contemporary drama, and she moved on to supervise many series for older children, including Trevor Preston's *Ace of Wands* (1970, see 'Jack On Top'); she also created the acclaimed *Rainbow* (1972-1992), which won the Society of Film and Television Arts Award for Best Children's Programme during its run. In a total contrast to *Callan*, Kershaw devised several editions of *Rainbow* and also contributed to *The Squad* (1980), Lonsdale's series about young police trainees.

1981 saw Kershaw reunited with Robert Banks Stewart and assigned the task of editing the first series of Jersey-set drama *Bergerac*. 'John Kershaw was a very good, very clever guy,'[13] Banks Stewart recalled. 'A funny thing happened to him; at the end of the first season of *Bergerac*, he was hired to be the screenwriter on one of the Harold Robbins novels [*The Lonely Lady*, 1983] about a mad millionaire. It was quite funny! I met him `afterwards, we all had lunch, and he told me this wonderful story about going to Heathrow, getting on this private jet of this millionaire who was trying to make his wife an international star. John was sitting in an armchair on a private jet with someone opening the fridge and serving a bottle of champagne. That kind of thing was unimaginable at that point for a British TV writer!'

Kershaw's last major work with Thames involved sharing story editing and writing duties on *The Bill* through its formative years (in 1984-1990), as it assembled a likeable ensemble cast fronted by its first two irascible CID chiefs, Galloway (John Salthouse) and later Burnside (Christopher Ellison). Kershaw's contribution helped the show through its transition from hour-long dramas to a twice-weekly half-hour show. After his departure it went through various other transformations, but ran for another two decades.

BY OCTOBER 1967 both Collin and Kershaw had cleared other commitments and fully taken on Feely's mantle. Having watched the first series to get up to speed, they were given a relatively free hand by Lloyd Shirley to develop the programme; immediately, they felt one shortfall in the preceding episodes was Callan's split with the Section, which necessitated constantly finding new, plausible reasons for drawing him into the stories. They decided the easiest way to address this was for Callan to be reinstated.

'I think it was inevitable,'[14] Edward Woodward remarked. 'If you're going to do a series for X number of episodes, you're put in a straitjacket if you're going to have a character who's a loner outside the pale of society: you'll soon run out of ideas. If you take him into the Section, it's a very wise move. The "outside the Section" was one kind of *Callan* and the "inside the Section" was another kind of *Callan*.'

Collin remembered wanting to inject 'a harsher attitude of reality'[15] and insisting on the series being 'done differently.' Kershaw agreed: 'We made a totally clean start. We didn't like coincidences. We didn't like the fiction – although the whole thing was of course fiction.'

Research by Anthony Goodman and Matthew Morgenstern shows that by the middle of November, Collin and Kershaw had settled on their own 'blueprint'[15] for the direction of the series, envisaging Callan's reinstatement and calling for increased authenticity and realism in the characterisation of the title character, Lonely, Meres, and a new dynamic with the head of the Section, a role that needed recasting due to the unavailability of Ronald Radd. This unavailability may have been due to other commitments, or on medical advice, or for both reasons. Robert Banks Stewart recalled, 'When Ronald Radd did the first series of *Callan* I think he'd already had some heart problems.'[16] 'We would certainly have had Ronnie, he just wasn't available,'[17] Collin said. A few days after their blueprint document, the production team circulated a memo about Hunter's successor – who would go under the same name. 'It can be a disaster but you have to think on your feet,'[18] James Mitchell admitted. 'It's an interesting, rather bizarre situation, where you're producing a different character that's got the same name.'

'HUNTER is the code name of the head of the Section which employs Callan,'[21] the memo explained. 'When one man called Hunter is "no longer attached to this service" (an official euphemism that covers anything from violent death to promotion) another man called Hunter replaces him.' The note went on to outline the background of the second Hunter, from his family background ('second son of the Bishop of Worcester') to his academic qualifications (a Cambridge Double First), and intelligence career. 'Hunter is an academic civil servant in looks and manner with a donnish acid wit... His strength is a planner. He has a brilliant mind, admirably adapted to creative action. Though he can and must gamble, he uses his intelligence as far as possible to reduce the element of risk. Moreover his superiors discovered, quite early in his career, he is immune from worry about the fate of the men and women who must act out his schemes with their lives. His objectivity is absolute. On the debit side, Hunter has never been an agent in the field.' The memo adds that the new Hunter dislikes Callan because he is 'a fighter' and for his deliberately 'prole approach' – 'his accent, his slang, his humour', before ominously concluding 'The KGB do not yet know the identity of the new Hunter... [but] in any case they want him destroyed. The KGB wants every Hunter destroyed.'

'Two of us, Michael Goodliffe and I, were up for the part.'[19] Derek Bond reflected on the casting of the role. 'I went along to see Reg Collin. He described the character as James Mitchell had written him as a dry, donnish sort of character. I was far too honest as I said, "If it was for a one-off play I could do that, but I couldn't sustain that for a series," as it was too far from my own character. I said, "I see him as a sort of ex-Guards officer who's sort of drifted into intelligence, who's got all the privileges and background which is the barrier between him and Callan. Callan hates him because of the smoothness, he's languid and always tucking into a good meal in the office.'

'We talked about this for a long time, Reggie and I, and Derek Bond was the person we thought about,'[20] John Kershaw said. 'Then we thought perhaps he [had] the wrong image.' They therefore opted to cast Michael Goodliffe as the new chief, his approach on screen showing exactly the contrast to Radd they were looking for. 'Michael, for the short period he was with us, I thought, showed what the part called for. He was very real,'[21] Mike Vardy noted, joining the directing team to handle the third story, 'You're Under Starter's Orders'. Two other stories, 'The Most Promising Girl of Her Year' and 'The Little Bits and Pieces of Love,' were both completed prior to recording Stewart's episode, with minor revisions accommodating the new character and format. James Mitchell provided the fourth story into production, 'Red Knight, White Knight' as the series opening episode, showing Callan's return to the Section.

Ray Jenkins recalled asking about handling the change of Hunter. 'The assumption [was] we were to deal with it as a part, not as a new person with new idiosyncrasies. The idea was that it was [007's commander] "M" – he can be "Myrtle" or "Michael", it doesn't matter: it's "M".'[22] Essentially, Jenkins believed all the Hunter actors played a similar kind of 'straight, abrasive role.'

Unfortunately, behind the scenes it appears Goodliffe was unhappy and suffering from ill health. He opted to leave, necessitating the quick casting of a third Hunter. 'To cut a long story short we realised he had to go, so we had him shot – which he was quite happy about,'[23] John Kershaw explained. The fifth story, Ray Jenkins' 'Let's Kill Everybody,' was therefore amended to write Goodliffe's Hunter out, and work started on a follow-up script, 'Heir Apparent', to introduce a successor. This was undertaken at short notice by John Kershaw, allowing recording on other episodes with the third Hunter, 'The Running Dog' and 'Death of a Friend', to progress in the meantime; this time, Derek Bond *was* given the part. Bond was having cartilage taken out of his knee in hospital when he heard from the production team. 'They said, "When can you work?" I said, "For money? Tomorrow!" I was out of hospital the following morning and Reg Collin cane to see me. He said, "Having had the Goodliffe Hunter we've got to get away from that character so what I would suggest is a rather smooth Army officer...!"'[24]

AS WELL AS THESE ALTERATIONS, the writing team needed to cater for Russell Hunter's temporary absence. Hunter recalled, 'I was doing a telly [programme] in Germany, and I said, "Could I please be out of the episode after next?" and they replied, "No problem, no problem, what we'll do is put you in prison"... they let me go to Germany on the condition I brought back five or six big cigars each for the producer and the director, but I just sent them all postcards – that was it!'[25] Lonely's imprisonment was incorporated into both 'Heir Apparent' and a further James Mitchell script, 'Land of Light and Peace'.

Mitchell's extensive contributions – six scripts in the second series, including rewrites to meet the revised blueprint – elaborated on Callan's past history and he was able to tie these into his concurrently published novelisation of *A Magnum for Schneider*. (See Chapter 10). However, it seems there was some creative tension between Mitchell and the production team during this series; according to *Action TV*[26], the Executive Producer was outspoken in giving feedback on Mitchell's 'The Little Bits and Pieces of Love': 'In a memo dated 31 October, 1967, Lloyd Shirley was not impressed. "Ouch, I'm afraid this contains a great many of James Mitchell's faults as an author, and precious few of his virtues. The Cold War element's very nasty and the situation between Lonely and Callan is repetitive to the point of tedium. We will have to grasp the nettle on this one."' Even relayed in more diplomatic phraseology, if it reached him such feedback could still have offended Mitchell's sensibilities.

Additionally, the departure of Terence Feely, the obligation to work with a new production team requesting rewrites (albeit paid ones), the abandonment of one of his scripts ('Goodbye Mary Lee') and an influx of more new writers may well have led Mitchell to think he was losing control of his own series. 'All those disagreements go back to [when I] started [and] said I was doing the series my way. It didn't always meet with approval outside Thames,'[27] Reg Collin said with cautious diplomacy. 'But there were never any problems – just different ideas.' Matters were evidently smoothed over, as Mitchell continued to contribute scripts and said himself, 'In general terms I was allowed to do what I wanted,'[28] but relations do appear to have cooled a little between him and ABC during production of Series Two, and this could have had consequences later. (See Chapters 10-12.)

The additional writers commissioned by Kershaw included Trevor Preston, who he knew from *Tempo*, William Emms and Lee Dunne. 'James Mitchell was bound to get the bulk of the commissions,'[29] Kershaw said. 'I think he would have liked to have done *all* of them but a) I think it is not a good thing to ask one man to do everything, it's not good for him and b) even if he's capable he's going to dry up, so we limited the number of scripts that he had to do, for his sake and because he couldn't have physically delivered in time. So for our own sake we needed a few scripts from other people to make sure we had [enough] scripts there.' Reg Collin meanwhile took Peter Sasdy, Mike Vardy and Jim Goddard onto his team of directors. '[On] *Sat'day While Sunday* I used young directors. When I took *Callan* over, I brought a load of those with me because they were exciting directors prepared to go the way I wanted them to go, to try things, to try new technology and along with more experienced people like Peter Duguid, we had a terrific output [on *Callan*.]'[30] Stylistic touches from the first series – Callan's internal monologues and the use of incidental music and pre-title sequences – were both phased out. 'I never used incidental music [aside from] a sting at the closing caption for each part. I disapprove of incidental music full stop,' Collin said. 'If you go home tonight and switch on [a drama] there's music splashed all over it. It's because the film industry hasn't realised that talkies have arrived! I'm serious – the film industry thinks unless you've got music something isn't right. I believe quite the opposite.'

OVERALL, BETWEEN APRIL AND JULY 1968 a further six episodes were completed in the following order – 'Jack-on-Top', 'Land of Light and Peace', 'Heir Apparent', 'Once a Big Man, Always a Big Man', 'Blackmailers Should Be Discouraged' and 'The Worst Soldier I Ever Saw', prior to the planned concluding episode of the series. This did leave a further question for Collin and Kershaw to resolve, which was how best to make use of the remaining, held-over Series One episode 'Nice People Die at Home'. Their solution was to remount a handful of scenes and edit them together with the previously completed story, as outlined on a further memo from Collin: 'The idea is that in the second half of the season, Bond will take some time off and Radd will return from unknown places to stand in... It will, however, be necessary to re-shoot the office scenes in the recorded programme for continuity.'[31] Shirley approved of the plan, and the remounted scenes were accommodated towards the end of the series' recording schedule. The remounts for 'Nice People Die at Home,' plus one introducing Derek Bond's Hunter, took the total number of episodes to fifteen, but this was not an issue. 'There's a central network planning committee composed as a rule of all the managing directors and the directors of programs,'[32] Lloyd Shirley explained. 'They discuss the network schedule... If a company is doing very well in trading terms, the provision of programmes is greater.'

IN TERMS OF STORY CONTENT and themes, the second series marks a watershed in the programme's development. In addition to Callan's reinstatement, in this series the other characters within the ensemble, especially Lonely, begin to rise to prominence. 'I think everybody was sorry for him, and everybody felt sympathetic because they were terrified there was a tiny bit of Lonely in their own character,'[33] Russell Hunter noted regarding the thief's increasing importance. 'Blackmailers Should Be Discouraged' contains a subplot devoted to Lonely's troubles, while in 'Once a Big Man, Always a Big Man' and 'Jack-on-Top' he is (although unofficially and quite unwittingly) an integral part of the Section team, questioning people and ferreting out information for Callan.

In *Callan*'s second series, as Anthony Valentine put it, 'Meres became a lot cooler, a lot calmer, and developed some aspects of self-control, and then... a kind of intimacy in his relationship with Callan. His attitude towards Callan at the beginning was very much "Gentlemen and Players". Meres was a "Gentleman", upper-class, and Callan was a "Player", working-class, not [seen by Meres as] appetising on any level, and Meres took the piss out of him and constantly patronised him. Gradually, throughout the series, there was a kind of respect that was developed by both of them, because I think Callan detested all those public school characters, particularly the nasty ones, and Meres' attitude changed: although he always considered [Callan] to be working-class, at least he was a man who could do the job.'[34]

'Red Knight, White Knight' emphasises Meres's professional capability: he is the only agent other than Callan trusted enough to act as a bodyguard for the new Hunter. In 'You're Under Starter's Orders', he does not believe Callan can be a traitor, while Callan has to admit that he's worried by the news that Meres is pursuing him, telling Hunter that his fellow operative is 'too bloody good'. Robert Banks Stewart reflected on the changes in Meres' charcater: 'If you make characters in a TV series too vivid, you come unstuck. They've got to develop. I'll give you an example: in *Bergerac*, Barney Crozier, the boss, is always snapping at Bergerac. But then there came an episode where Bergerac went to his house and discovered that he liked hanging model aeroplanes from the ceiling. If you don't fall into the trap of making characters totally one thing or the other, you have room for a bit of development, which is important in a long running series.'[35]

'The thing with Lonely and with Meres had to develop,'[36] John Kershaw insisted. 'You can't just have them saying, "My God, you stink" every week. Things can't stand still if you're going on for thirteen weeks and the same with Meres… Characters aren't just there to speak words.'

'The Running Dog' shows Meres engaging in political discourse, 'Jack-on-Top' and 'Once a Big Man, Always a Big Man' have him and Callan working together as a team, and the story of his uneasy reconciliation with Callan occurs across 'Let's Kill Everybody' and 'Heir Apparent'. This repositioning still has its limits: Callan is furious with Meres after he accidentally kills a man in 'Land of Light and Peace', and in 'The Worst Soldier I Ever Saw', he angrily has to remind him he knows how to do his job.

'In America it's not so important; they tend to like a character being the same every week,'[37] Edward Woodward observed. 'Here, that has never really been so. People like to identify, but they do like to see a life take a different direction, and also, if you are working with somebody week after week over a period of time, relationships do change. [Callan] never grew to love Meres; he never grew to care, but they had a rapprochement. Callan always had the feeling, I think, that Meres could take over, and also he'd begun to realise that one thing he worshipped was professionalism. It might have been his own kind of professionalism that he also saw in Meres. [But] it was a very prickly rapprochement – it wasn't buddy-buddy.'

Callan's relationship with his supervisors also evolves over this series. As the third Hunter, Derek Bond's interpretation differs from both Goodliffe's theoretician and Radd's stony autocrat. 'Bond's Hunter is a public school boy who has been in the forces and likes life with the lads, he enjoys the camaraderie [even if he sees] Callan as an inferior or subordinate,'[38] Kershaw said of the contrast. 'Goodliffe's Hunter would say, "You do this," and Bond's would say, "What should we do?"' The Bond Hunter defends his team to a senior Home Office official in 'Land of Light and Peace', takes active part in the investigation in 'Jack-on-Top', and pragmatically tells Callan to take a holiday, circumventing officialdom, in 'The Running Dog'. 'Land of Light and Peace' shows he can still be just as hard-nosed as his predecessors, however, as he tastelessly says it's a 'pity' that a spy-ring member has died, provoking sarcasm from Callan.

The Section's secretary similarly receives some welcome development and a name, Liz March, in 'Heir Apparent'. (The camera script for 'You're Under Starter's Orders' also names her, as 'Miss Evans'; this contradicts later episodes, but still indicates the production team were thinking about expanding her character.) The Section staff are seen interacting more with other departments too, such as the Regular Army and the Foreign Office in 'Heir Apparent', and MI5 in 'Jack-on-Top'. It is worth noting throughout these associations, however, that the Section is still generally disapproved of by these other, more respectable organisations.

Another trait within the second series is that, having emphasised the key characters, it then places them in increasingly dangerous situations. In 'Red Knight, White Knight', the Goodliffe Hunter is targeted for assassination; in 'Let's Kill Everybody' he dies, as foreshadowed in 'You're Under Starter's Orders'. Several other Section agents perish during this series and Lonely only just misses being caught by a gunman in 'The Running Dog'. In 'Death of a Friend', Meres is caught up in an explosion, while in 'Once a Big Man,

Always a Big Man', he is shot and wounded. It seems everyone in, or associated with, the department is living on borrowed time – all the time.

The evolving affinities between Callan, Lonely, Meres, the Bond Hunter, other Security departments and the increasing sense of vulnerability all converge in the final story, 'Death of a Hunter'. This denouement was screened in April 1969, approximately nine months after production had concluded. The series was left 'sat on a shelf'[39], as Reg Collin put it. Mike Vardy believed the delay in transmission was due to 'horse trading for network time'[40] between the different regional ITV structures; co-ordinating screenings, and the corporate changes within ABC as it completed its amalgamation into Thames Television, were clearly also factors.

'Death of a Hunter' was eagerly awaited both by the press, who had treated the second series in an increasingly positive light throughout its second run, and by the viewing public, who gravitated to the remodelled programme. Speculation went on prior to transmission of the final episode that the programme was ending, and Callan would be killed off. Reg Collin cannily exploited this via the *TV Times*, in a manner anticipating the publicity and 'hype' on many modern TV productions. Had this series been judged to have under performed, it clearly would have been the last; ultimately, however, the ratings[41] proved otherwise (viewing figures in millions):

'Red Knight, White Knight'	6.3
'The Most Promising Girl of Her Year'	7.1
'You're Under Starter's Orders'	7.6
'The Little Bits and Pieces of Love'	7.9
'Let's Kill Everybody'	7.9
'Heir Apparent'	7.2
'Land of Light and Peace'	9.3
'Blackmailers Should Be Discouraged'	8.9
'Death of a Friend'	9
'Jack-on-Top'	10.4
'Once a Big Man, Always a Big Man'	9.1
'The Running Dog'	10.6
'The Worst Soldier I Ever Saw'	10.5
'Nice People Die at Home'	10.8
'Death of a Hunter'	13

These figures show that, having started out from a modest position near to where the first series ended, *Callan* gained at least a million extra regular viewers for its early episodes; the instalments after the Bond Hunter settled in saw this figure climbing to over nine million, and then to over ten-and-a-half million once the schedulers began screening episodes nationally at 9 pm. 'Death of a Hunter' achieved another leap as viewers tuned in to learn the agent's fate; it came first in that week's Joint Industry Committee for Television Advertising Research (JICTAR) poll. Collin recollected that from the moment this change happened, 'I don't think we were ever out of the top ten. It was a total cult and everybody rushed home.'[42] He recalled even BBC executives being envious of the programme's position, as it had dented the ratings for *The Wednesday Play*, which was shown in a rival slot.

The increased viewing figures ensured that *Callan* would be working for the Section for some time to come, as the series capitalised on the public's taste for a bleaker take on spy fiction – which *Callan* had helped initiate – evident in the 1969 feature film adaptations of the novels *The Kremlin Letter*, about a Section-style organisation, and *The Looking Glass War*, in which an expendable amateur is recruited to spy for British intelligence. In December, the James Bond movies also caught this new mood in *On Her Majesty's Secret Service*, as the formerly unassailable 007 has to deal with the traumatic murder of his new wife, Tracy (Diana Rigg).

Cleverly turning production setbacks to their advantage, largely by making the loss of two lead actors/characters pivotal moments in the series' ongoing narrative, the new production team, writers, cast and crew had put *Callan* firmly on the television map.

SERIES 2 REGULAR CAST

Edward Woodward (David Callan)
Russell Hunter (Lonely) 1-5, 8-15
Anthony Valentine (Toby Meres) 1-7, 9-15
Michael Goodliffe (Hunter) 1-5
Lisa Langdon (Secretary) 1, 3-9, 13-16
Derek Bond (Hunter) 6-13, 15

SERIES 2 RECURRING CAST

John Wentworth (Sir Michael Harvey) 6, 13, 15
Ronald Radd (Colonel Leslie/Hunter I) 13, 14

PRODUCTION TEAM

Producer Reginald Collin, *Associate Producer* John Kershaw

Uncredited on screen:[42] *Floor Manager:* John Wayne (1, 2, 3, 8, 10,12), Denver Thornton (4, 6,14), Harry Lock(e) (7,13, 14 [R], 15)) Patrick Kennedy (11), *Stage Manager:* Mari Markus (1, 4), Mary Lewis (2), Dorothy Pope (3), Daphne Lucas (6,10,12,13,14), Shirley Cleghorn (7, 11), Stuart Orme (8), Billy Jay (14 [R]), *Production Assistant:* Paddy Dewey (1, 2, 6, 14 [R]), Dottie Rice (3,10,11) Marion Lloyd (4,8,12) Anne Summerton (7) Rosalind Houchen (13) Mary Ellis (14) Mary Morgan (15) *P.A. Timer:* Marian Lloyd (1), Jacqueline Davis (2), Mickey Fisher (3,4) Paddy Dewy (11), Betty Kenworthy (12), Dottie Rice (13), *Make Up Supervisor:* Jean Macken- zie (1, 4) Carole Bright (2, 6, 7,10,13), Launa Bradish (3,11,14 [R]), Mini Kimmins (8, 12,15), Joan Watson (14), *Wardrobe Supervisor:* Ambren Garland (1, 2), Jill Silverside (3, 10, 13, 14, (14 [R]), Gillian Grimes (4, 6, 7, 8, 11), Jane Robinson (15), *Technical (Operational) Supervisor:* Peter Kew (1, 3, 7), Del Randall (2, 4,10, 11, 12, 13, 14 [R]), Campbell Keenan (8), *Lighting Super- visor:* Brian Turner (1, 3, 11), Harry Richards (2, 13,14 [R]), Louis Bottone (4, 12), Ken Brown (7, 10), *Senior Cameraman:* Roy Easton (1, 3) David Hughes (2, 4, 10, 14 [R]), Dick(ie) Jackman (7, 11, 12, 13), Mike Baldock (8), *Lighting Film Cameraman:* John Keeling, *Sound Supervisor:* Mike Westlake (1, 3, 4, 8), Mike Pontin (2, 7, 11, 12), Peter Sampson (10, 13, 14 [R]), *Racks:* John Turner (1, 8), Alan Fowler (2), Jim Fergus Smith (3, 7, 11, 12, 13), Will Marley (4, 10, 14 [R]), *Vision Mixer:* John White-Jones (1, 4, 10,12), Nigel Evans (2, 7, 11), Peter Howell (3,13,14 [R]), *Call Boy:* Peter Groome (1, 2, 12), Richard Mervyn (3, 7, 8, 10, 11, 14 [R]), *Grams:* Bill Rawcliffe (1), Vic Finch (2, 10), Bob Davies (3, 8), Mike Fairburn (7, 11, 13), Tony Morley (10, 14 [R]), *Graphic Artist:* Ian Kestle (4, 6, 7, 15), *Series Developer:* Terence Feely (14)

S2.1 RED KNIGHT, WHITE KNIGHT

Writer: James Mitchell
Director: Peter Duguid
Designer: Neville Green

FIRST UK TRANSMISSION

Scottish: Wednesday 8 January 1969 8.00 pm
Grampian: Saturday 11 January 1969 8.30 pm
All other regions: Wednesday 8 January 1969 9.00 pm[43]

CAST: Douglas Fielding (Truman), Jon Croft (Customs Officer), Duncan Lamont (Bunin), George Ghent (Goncharov)[44], John Savident (Henson)

EXTRAS/WALK-ONS: (*Uncredited on screen*) Bruce Wells, Daryl Richards, Bernard Egan, George Day, Eric Kent, Charles Bird, William Castleman, Harry Tierney, Fred Davies, Gregory Scott, Doreen Ubels, Dorothy Watson, Robert Case, Alan Harris, John Caesar, Roland Porrott, Charles Hands, William Curran (as Chauffeur, Russian Trade delegates, postman, member of country house staff, customs officer, two ambulance men, airport policeman, two airport porters).

TV TIMES: '... in this game most of us are pawns. You and I, who have learned a little more, we are the Knights.'
4-10 January 1969, Southern edition

PRODUCTION

Rehearsals: From Thursday 22 February
Location Filming: Caherine Road, Surbiton, Sunbury Court, Sunbury-on-Thames (Friday 16 February); Teddington Studios, Sunbury Court (Monday 19 February)
Camera Rehearsals/Recording: Teddington Studio One, Wednesday 28th and Thursday 29 February 1968[45]

MISSION PROFILE: The Colonel has been replaced by a new Hunter, who insists that Callan rejoins the Section. The alternative is prison, so Callan agrees.

A KGB executioner named Bunin apparently defects to the Section and says he is an envoy from Mirsky, assistant to the Ministry of Defence in Russia, who also wants to come over to the West. The condition is that Mirsky will only defect to the West's top agent in the USSR. Callan is suspicious, as he's met Bunin before and believes he is loyal to the KGB. He instructs Lonely to follow another Soviet agent, Goncharov, who arrived on the plane from Russia with Bunin.

Out of date information offered by Bunin and the interrogation of Goncharov, who proves to be another KGB spy, confirm that Bunin's defection was a trap: the aim being both to expose a senior Western agent in Russia *and* eliminate the new Hunter, which Bunin, having escaped, still intends to do. Overnight, Meres and Callan guard Hunter in a safe house in the country. The following morning, Callan spots Bunin masquerading as Hunter's chauffeur and shoots him dead, saving Hunter's life.

A MAN LIKE ME: Callan's Section file says that he's 'emotionally unstable, a one-time crook...

has a dubious circle of acquaintances and he tends to take the law into his own hands.' The new Hunter also accuses him of being short of money, although he angrily denies it. Predictably, Callan's relationship with him is immediately fractious, particularly as he's black-mailed into rejoining the Section full-time. However, once on active duty again he kicks into 'professional' mode as if he has never been away, even showing the new recruit Truman how to handle a gun. This suggests that the Section is really where he wants, or needs, to be.

Callan was sent to the 1963 Trade Fair in Leipzig with orders to kill Bunin, but the agents were 'too good for each other'; significantly, Meres comments that they're 'two of a kind'. Each killed the other's colleague, although Callan points out his 'colleague' was also 'a friend', Bob Purdie. Callan's instinct that Bunin wouldn't turn traitor is crucial to the Section uncovering the KGB deception. Callan's file is correct in predicting he'll act independently, as he details Lonely to look out for anyone arriving with Bunin, and Callan is infuriated when Hunter later asks him to bring the thief in for debriefing. The agent later admits he doesn't understand the new Section commander's motives.

Even out of the Section, Callan has clearly stayed in shape, as he has no trouble over-powering Goncharov and reacts with lightning speed in shooting down Bunin.

Curiously, Callan doesn't play chess, and Bunin has to explain the game to him. Callan has visited this Section safe house before. He's fond of cats.

Section Kills: 6 (assuming Bunin's 'colleague' was on the previous Hunter's orders, prior to 'A Magnum for Schneider'.)

LONELY: Sent to London (now Heathrow) Airport by Callan to tail anyone who arrives from Moscow with Bunin. He spots and follows Goncharov to a guest room and Bunin's press conference, later watching the Russian's accommodation until Callan arrives.

Lonely is again a comic foil, sagely discerning that because Bunin comes from Moscow he must be Russian. Callan continues to be appalled by the thief's body odour and tells him to take a bath. With some understatement, Meres describes Lonely as being 'rather fragrant'.

A TIE AND A CREST: Without explanation, 'Colonel Hunter' has disappeared and been superseded by an official from the Foreign Office, who was a 'Balkan specialist' during WW2. His name remains unknown but his continued use of the title 'Hunter' confirms that the designation is a codename. An authoritarian, the new Hunter insists that the Section will be run 'my way' and gives Callan no option other than rejoining. He's confident about venturing from HQ, debriefing Bunin at the Section safe house and later staying there to try and deliberately draw the KGB man's fire. Callan earns Hunter's respect when his suspicions about the would-be defector are confirmed. In turn – correctly and ominously – Callan concludes that the newcomer has no experience of working as an agent and because of this his days could be numbered. The replacement commander seems naive, at one point standing dangerously near the safe house window, and has a tactless streak, telling his staff that it doesn't matter if one of them is shot as the other could still deal with Bunin.

The antagonism between Callan and the Section has clearly mellowed since 'You Should Have Got Here Sooner'. Even though Meres has wickedly placed Callan's photograph in the firing range as a target, relations between the two men are guardedly respectful; Meres says he 'detests' his counterpart but believes he 'knows the job'. The Section staff are now relaxed enough to allow Callan to come in and use their firing range for target practice.

For the first time, the Section's position in the intelligence hierarchy comes into focus through the figure of Hanson, another Foreign Office official who has the authority to authorise defections. The Section also has access to a country house (complete with a gardener) where it can debrief apparent defectors from the East. The West's top agent in Russia will, in a few years, be a member of the Politburo, the highest decision-making authority within the USSR – a considerable achievement. The Section are also keen to obtain the details of a secret project named 'Seahorse'.

Farmer, unseen, is another Section operative who spent two years in Washington as CIA liaison. There's no sign of Loder: perhaps he proved not to be up to scratch and was replaced by Truman, who is being trained by Meres. Unfortunately, the novice agent is killed by Bunin while escorting the Russian to the Section's safe house. The Section entrusting a high level defector to such an inexperienced operative says a lot about both this Hunter's judgement and the department's meagre resources.

Meres punches Goncharov in retaliation for Truman's death, adding an unexpected dimension to his character: he's genuinely angry that the opposition have killed one of the men he's respinsible for.

This is the first time the Section's secretary is fully seen. Young, blonde, and wearing a fashionable mini dress, she's anxious to make a good impression on the new Hunter. Significantly, she accepts Callan's return to the Section before her new boss does.

The Section has a scheduled time for morning coffee to be delivered, reflecting working practices in the Civil Service.

ALCOHOL, TOBACCO AND FIREARMS: Hunter offers Callan a cigarette from his personal supply but he refuses; the Section commander later has a Scotch at the safe house but Meres and Callan decline as they're on duty.

Hunter's two 'best men' use .38 Magnums, while Truman is seen practising with an army issue Webley revolver. Bunin presumably steals the trainee's gun.

SPY SPEAK: Hunter believes that his predecessor's regime was 'all together too free and easy.' 'I wouldn't say that, sir,' Meres replies, revealing a knack for ironic understatement. Getting into his sardonic stride, the upper-class agent believes that Callan would adapt to the new Hunter's appointment with his 'gift for diplomacy' and 'handle it in [his] own charming, characteristic way.' (Hunter and Callan immediately have a blazing row.)

There's a classic exchange about the merits of education between Callan and Lonely: 'You'll be up to your O-Levels soon.'[46] 'O-what, Mr Callan?' 'Oh, Gawd!'

After he's saved Hunter from execution, Callan confides in a white cat: 'I think he must have nine lives, mate. He's going to need 'em all.' (A line that could be seen as setting up events later in the series but was, according to James Mitchell, was just 'serendipity.'[47])

PAWNS AND PLAYERS: LAWRENCE MICHAEL ANDREW GOODLIFFE (1914-76) was born in Cheshire and studied at Keble College, Oxford. He began his acting career in repertory theatre in Liverpool before moving on to the Shakespeare Memorial Theatre at Stratford, appearing in *The Comedy of Errors*, *Much Ado about Nothing* and *Twelfth Night*. When WW2 broke out, Goodliffe enlisted with the Royal Warwickshire Regiment as a Second Lieutenant; four months later, he was wounded in the leg and captured at the battle of Dunkirk, incorrectly listed as killed in action and spent the rest of his war years in German prison camps. While incarcerated, Goodliffe produced and acted in many plays and sketches to entertain fellow prisoners, including two productions of *Hamlet*.

He recalled later, 'We had space for a theatre and unlimited time for rehearsal, but no stage, no lighting, no plays, no musical instruments, no make-up or costumes, very little money... we had all been shaved completely bald by our captors.'[48]

Despite being transferred between various prisons, by the end of the war Goodliffe had managed to establish an organised theatre with a regular cast and crew, putting on plays by Terence Rattigan, George Bernard Shaw and a production of Noel Coward's anti-war polemic *Post Mortem*, in which Goodliffe played a dying soldier. There were several fellow actors among the inmates, including Desmond Llewellyn, later to play Q in the James Bond films.

Post-WW2, Goodliffe initially focussed on the theatre. He developed his career as a classical actor in productions of *Anthony and Cleopatra*, *Much Ado about Nothing* with John Gielgud, *Dr Faustus*, Oscar Wilde's *An Ideal Husband* (with Margaret Lockwood) and *The Chalk Garden* (with Gladys Cooper) in the West End and on Broadway. Additionally, Goodliffe appeared in several war films, possibly to try and exorcise demons from the time he spent incarcerated: *The Wooden Horse* (1950), based on the real-life escape attempt from Stalag Luft III using a tunnel under a vaulting horse; *The One That Got Away* (1957), *Sink the Bismarck!* (1960), *633 Squadron* (1964) and *Von Ryan's Express* (1965).

Goodliffe's other cinematic roles include *Night to Remember* (1958), arguably his best-known film, in which he played the designer of the RMS *Titanic*; the Ralph Thomas remake of *The 39 Steps* (1959), the unsettling serial-killer movie *Peeping Tom* (1960) and the science fiction thriller *The Day the Earth Caught Fire* (1961). Also of interest are his falling victim to *The Gorgon* (1964) and his uncredited cameo as M's Chief of Staff Bill Tanner in *The Man with the Golden Gun* (1974). Goodliffe's final film role was in *To the Devil a Daughter* (1976), alongside Anthony Valentine, playing a member of the cult following Christopher Lee's satanic priest.

His television guest appearances include *The Saint* – 'The Invisible Millionaire' (1963), *Man in a Suitcase* – 'All That Glitters' (1967), *Redcap* – 'Information Received' (1966), *Special Branch* – 'Inside' (1970) and, memorably, the deranged scientist Professor Keller with a grudge against Emma Peel, in *The Avengers'* disturbing 'The House That Jack Built '(1966): 'At the end of the experiment... you, Mrs. Peel, will be quite, quite mad.' In the early 1970s, Goodliffe regularly played the company chairman of Pendles, an arms manufacturer that were the competition of international dealer Joe *Hine* (1971).

Historical drama was a genre Goodliffe favoured. He starred in *Inheritance* (1967), an ITV series about successive generations of a Yorkshire mill-owning family from the Industrial Revolution to the 1950s, and *Judge Dee* (1969), in which he and the rest of the English cast portrayed oriental characters: fellow actor Garfield Morgan recalled this series was made in black and white just as colour serials were starting to be transmitted, and that 'it may have suffered as a result'.[49] Goodliffe later featured as a miner in the coming-of-age drama *Sam* (1973-75), worked with Patrick Mower in Euston Films' *Armchair Cinema* production 'In Sickness and in Health' (1975) and made his final TV appearance in *The Madness* (1976), a BBC play set during the Spanish Civil War, which also starred Zena Walker and Patrick Stewart.

DUNCAN LAMONT (1918-1978) appeared in the films *The Man in the White Suit* (1951), *I Was Monty's Double* (1958), *The 39 Steps* (1959) and *Evil of Frankenstein* (1964). In the BBC TV serial *Quatermass and the Pit* (1967), he played the disturbed drill operator, Sladden; Lamont had previously starred as Victor Carroon, the first man-into-monster the scientist fought, in *The Quatermass Experiment* (1953). He had the regular role of Station Sergeant Cooper in *Dixon of Dock Green* (1965-68) and guest-starred in *Danger Man* – 'The Relaxed Informer' (1961) and 'That's Two of Us Sorry' (1965), *Man in a Suitcase* – 'All That Glitters' (1967) and 'Why They Killed Nolan' (1968), as well as *The Avengers* – 'Stay Tuned' (1969). Lamont put in an enjoyably dour performance in *Doctor Who* – 'Death to the Daleks' (1974), as anti-heroic suicide bomber Dan Galloway. His last TV appearance was as Victor Hervé, a member of the Lifeline escape route in *Secret Army* – 'A Matter of Life and Death' (1978).

JOHN SAVIDENT (1939), a Guernsey born ex-policeman, is now best known as the vain Fred Elliot in *Coronation Street* (1994-2006). Familiar for his distinctive balding appearance, he featured in children's spy serial *Tightrope* (1972), *The Saint* – 'Where the Money Is' (1968), *Department S* – 'The Double Death of Charlie Crippen' (1969), *The Avengers* – 'My Wildest Dream' (1968) and *Man in a Suitcase* – 'Web with Four Spiders' (1967). In the science fiction series *Blake's 7*, Savident played a stern courtroom arbiter and a barking mad scientist in the episodes 'Trial' (1979) and 'Orbit' (1981) respectively, giving rather more restrained portrayals of authority in *Doomwatch* – 'Burial at Sea' (1970) and 'The Web of Fear' (1971), *The Professionals* – 'Servant of Two Masters' (1979) and *1990* (1977). Savident again showed his comical side as the bumptious Sir Frederick 'Jumbo' Stewart in *Yes, Minister* (in 1980).

JON CROFT was in the *Special Branch* episode 'A Date with Leonidas' (1969) and was a disciple of the Master in *Doctor Who* – 'The Daemons' (1971). A decade later, he played coastguard Joe McGrath, a victim of *The Nightmare Man* (1981).

DOUGLAS FIELDING played PC Quilley in *Z Cars* (1969-78) and Detective Sergeant Quick in *EastEnders* (1985-86).

NEVILLE GREEN joined *Callan* as production designer on 'Red Knight, White Knight'. 'I went to the Royal College of Art and studied Film and Television Design under George Haslam,'[50] he recalled, 'then I went into British Lion films until they collapsed. After that I moved on to ABC. It was very experimental and quite good fun. The one thing you wanted to work on was *Armchair Theatre*, because [they were] single plays... Lloyd [Shirley] was very enthusiastic.' Later in his career, Green switched to directing. 'It was at Thames. It was sort of mixed in with the theatre, because Thames Television had a deal with the National Theatre and brought along theatre directors [to tutor]. I wanted to be a film director originally, but films had disappeared: the British film industry had virtually collapsed.' A new challenge for Green was dealing with actors' egos, as had to do on 'Dr Ziegler's Casebook', an episode of the ITV detective series *Jemima Shore Investigates* (1983): '[Tom Baker and Patricia Hodge] refused to come out of their caravans because Tom thought he was a star, and Pat wouldn't come out of her caravan until *he* came out!'

INFORMATION: 'We were turning around so many dramas in a week, and *Callan* was one of the run-of-the-mill things that you got put on to,'[51] Neville Green said frankly of his time on the programme. 'I enjoyed it. We were always trying to come up with locations that were different from the other things we did... They were a good team of people. All the actors were very good, fitted in and went along with it really well.' Green also clearly remembered location filming at Sunbury Court, then a Salvation Army hostel.

'Eddie... had to break the window with the butt of his gun. The glass was so thick that the gun just bounced off; he dropped the gun, and shook his hand, going *"Fucking hell!"* We had to get some prop men, or carpenters, to [remove] the window [and put in sugar glass].' Green thinks that the accident was symptomatic of the way the actors handled firearms: 'When I first started, Eddie didn't seem to know how to hold a revolver. Reg [Collin] sent him off to see *The IPCRESS File* and said, "Note how *they* hold guns, Eddie."' Peter Duguid also remembered the location as 'a nice house with a very good facade and a good entrance, just along the river past Hampton Court. It was hideous inside but we only used [the exterior] for arrivals.'[52]

Bunin explicitly identifies the characters in the story with chess pieces, a common theme in the spy fiction of the time. The idea was popularised in Len Deighton's novel *Funeral in Berlin*, in which each chapter was introduced by a chess move. In *The Prisoner*, the analogy was taken to its symbolic extreme in the episode 'Checkmate' when, as well as playing a human chess game, the characters were identified with the pieces they represented. Ronald Radd played 'the Rook'.

In the early 1960s, there were several defections from the KGB to the CIA including Michael Goleniewski, the deputy head of Polish military counter-intelligence and Anatoliy Golitsyn, a Major in the KGB. Golitsyn's brief visit to Britain in 1963 attracted press coverage and speculation that espionage-related revelations would be forthcoming. The Soviet Trade Delegation often provided cover for KGB and GRU operatives and was kept under MI5 surveillance.

Callan was part of the New Year season on ITV which also included new series for *The Power Game* (1965-69) and *Armchair Theatre*. In several regions, the *TV Times* marked the occasion of *Callan*'s revival with a photograph of Woodward, and a longer than usual episode write-up concluding with a quote from Reg Collin: 'The Secret Service is a real organisation, and we hope to show it realistically, as a job of work much like any other. The only difference is – you might be killed at any moment!'[53]

MISSION ANALYSIS: *'One has to risk a great deal, Callan, to take a queen.'* From the initial scenes onwards, this story shows a more informal relationship between Callan and the Section, in contrast to the direct conflict that went on in the first series. However, the switch to Collin and Kershaw's new format is implemented with such confidence by Peter Duguid that the audience is swept along with Callan's re-engagement as a Section operative, straight into the Bunin storyline. Whether out in the cold or not, Callan is still the top man: although he is blackmailed into rejoining the Section, his instincts about Bunin, honed by operational experience, are proved right, while the new Hunter's wish for a prestigious intelligence coup very nearly end in disaster.

James Mitchell takes to the new format immediately. Moving Callan from being the troubled, compromised conscience of spying outside the Section back into the fold feels like a natural development, allowing more room for more subtle but equally memorable sparring with both Hunter and Meres. For the first time, Mitchell uses the idea of Callan and a KGB agent being the mirror image of each other (as Meres observes), and the fashionable likening of espionage to chess adds a satisfying layer of symbolism, over and above Callan's wargaming, that *Callan* would frequently return to.

Another welcome development is the full appearance of Lisa Langdon in the opening scene. Unseen for most of the first series, she immediately impresses as Hunter's (still unnamed) dutiful secretary, helping to reinforce the production team's view of the Section as a goverment department that just happens to deal with life and death; as the major new addition to the cast, Michael Goodliffe could be the immaculately-dressed, disciplined director of a successful British company. An effective contrast with Ronald Radd's jovial bully, he enquires about coffee as easily as he threatens Callan with jail. Sharing more scenes together, Hunter's two top employees Callan and Meres are re-orientated as a potential double act, and it's obvious that Woodward and Valentine relish their scenes together. Amid all the reformatting, Duncan Lamont impresses as a lethally plausible infiltrator.

The increase in exterior filming is another welcome development: scenes such as Meres finding Truman's body by a road, Lonely staking out Goncharov's room at night, and a climax in a country house that includes a shoot-out, are all ambitiously staged, increasing the scale of the drama. They help to confirm that Collin and Kershaw's accomplished reboot would be as much of a compulsive viewing experience as the first series – if not more so.

S2.2 THE MOST PROMISING GIRL OF HER YEAR

Writer: James Mitchell
Director: Peter Duguid
Designer: Peter le Page

FIRST UK TRANSMISSION

Thames/LWT, Southern:* Wednesday 15 January 1969, 10.30 pm
ATV, Anglia, Border, Channel, Granada, Harlech, Westward, Yorkshire: 9.00 pm Scottish:
Wednesday 15 January 1969, 8.00 pm
Grampian: Saturday 18 January 1969, 8.30 pm[54]

CAST: Elizabeth Bell (Joan Mather), Raymond Young (Dr Bradford), Clifford Rose (Snell),
Joan Crane (Sonia Prescott), Peter Blythe (Horst), David Hargreaves (Karl Donner)

EXTRAS/WALK-ONS: *(Uncredited on screen)* Bruce Wells (male nurse) Trevor Lawrence
(Hunter's office boy) John Hunt (Barman) Paul Bond, Jackie Lawrence, Max Hartnell,
Betty Goulding, Lawrence Farrer, Anna Hilton (three young couples), Peter Blair-Stuart
(man), Mary Lyons, Sheila Parr, Jan Blair-Stuart (girls).

PRODUCTION

Rehearsals: From Thursday 4 January 1968
Location Filming: Whitehead's Grove, London (Tuesday 2 January 1968); National Car
Park, National Film Theatre, London (Wednesday 3 January 1968)
Camera Rehearsals/Recording: Teddington Studio One, Tuesday 16 and Wednesday
17 January 1968[55]

TV TIMES: 'Love among scientists is always suspect – especially when the girl is English and
the boy is German.'
January 11-17 1969, Southern edition

MISSION PROFILE: Joan Mather, a biochemist, wants to leave her job at the Biological
Research Centre. Suspecting there is more behind this decision than pacifism, and
aware she's been working on a potentially lethal new microbe, Hunter orders her to be
investigated by Callan. Snell, a psychiatrist the Section consults, hypnotises her and
confirms she has a photographic memory.

Callan and Meres become friendly with Joan and her flatmate Sonia. Lonely burgles
the girls' home and discovers letters from Joan's boyfriend, Karl Donner, a German. Joan
plans to join him in Europe, but Donner is in fact an MFS agent for East Germany's Section 5, who wants her knowledge for the Soviet bloc.

Horst, another MFS operative who delivered the letters for Donner, is captured by the
Section and interrogated by Snell. Horst reveals Donner's real identity and motives to Joan,
but she refuses to assist in capturing him. Pressurised by Callan, she agrees to help, but the
plan goes wrong. Donner is caught, but not before Joan is accidentally shot dead by Callan.

A MAN LIKE ME: Callan says he doesn't like investigating women, particularly ones 'with
brains'; conversely, Hunter knows that women respond to Callan because they 'trust him,
poor devil.' Callan adopts an effective cover persona when he meets Joan at a Vivaldi

concert, pretending to be a bashful music novice who was in the army, like her father. Taken by surprise by Donner arriving at Joan's flat, he's skilled enough to quickly adopt another alias, the flustered 'Doctor Bennett'.

Having gained Joan's confidence and despite his reservations about the assignment, Callan is professionally remorseless and matter-of-fact in trying to destroy her faith in Donner, revealing that the German has exploited women like Joan before. Callan's reserve only cracks when she accuses him of being in love with killing, his angry reaction showing that she's touched a nerve. His comment to Joan afterwards reveals that Callan sees soldiering as noble and honourable – the exact opposite of what he's doing in the Section. He's equally thin-skinned when Donner goads him, saying Callan's accidental shooting of Joan is convenient as she's been silenced for good. Knowing he's exploited, bullied and helped destroy a young woman, Callan turns his anger on Donner, ruthlessly clubbing him to the floor.

His antagonism towards Meres hasn't totally evaporated. Finding himself on an impromptu double-date with the agent, Callan 'accidentally' spills hot coffee on him. (It's implied he believes Meres is a sadist who will subject Joan to rough handling if given the opportunity, and he's only continuing the assignment to keep the rival agent away from her.)

Notably, he uses one of his few covert gadgets: an earpiece to eavesdrop on phone calls.
Section Kills: 7 (Joan Mather – an accident)

LONELY: Does very well out of Callan: paid £50 to burgle Joan and Sonia's flat, £25 to watch who visits, and another £25 to steal the letter Horst delivers. He shows his sleazy side again, as he gets excited by Sonia's racy underwear, which is all 'transparent with bows on', to the point that he can't resist pausing for another look when he returns to steal Donner's letter. Callan trusts Lonely enough to telephone Joan's flat, making three rings to warn when Donner's arrival is imminent.

Although Lonely said in 'A Magnum For Schneider' that he couldn't write, he *can* read here. (This is not necessarily a continuity error as there are people who have this problem; in Lonely's case this would seem to stem from poor education rather than a neurological condition like dysgraphia.) He is discerning enough to be offended by Joan's taste in literature – James Joyce, D.H. Lawrence and Dostoyevsky.

A TIE AND A CREST: The Section have Joan Mather in a Yellow File (surveillance only) and have access to the CCTV footage in the Biological Research Centre.

Hunter employs 'a fellow we know in Harley Street', a doctor called Snell who is proficient in hypnotism – which he applies to Joan – and the use of drugs in interrogations. He uses tranquilisers, 'Baxter's derivative of LSD' and pentathol[56] (a truth drug) on Horst, a service he chillingly regards as 'a pleasure.' Even Meres looks queasy. Detached and clinical, Snell admires Joan's gift for total recall, at the same time recognising it as 'lethal.'

Meres enjoys his liaison with the lubricious Sonia, at the same time securing a key to her flat, and he also takes sadistic pleasure in disabling Horst.

ALCOHOL, TOBACCO AND FIREARMS: There's no alcohol on display, and Callan and Lonely confer in a coffee bar. Understandably, Joan smokes nervously.

The shoot-out between Donner, with a revolver, and Callan, with a .38 Magnum, ends tragically with Joan's death.

SPY-SPEAK: Callan attempts to explain Lonely's excitement over Sonia's underwear: 'You been eating raw meat again?' In turn, Lonely tries to account for Donner's ardour: 'They're very passionate some of these foreigners. I reckon it must be the grub.'

Hunter unwittingly defines part of the appeal of the series: 'You're the lovable agent, Callan – Meres is the nasty one.'

Sardonically, Donner asks Callan: 'Tell me, doctor, does your Health Service issue you with Magnum revolvers?'

PAWNS AND PLAYERS: JOHN CLIFFORD ROSE (born in Hertfordshire in 1929) was educated at Kings School in Worcester, where class visits to Stratford-on-Avon inspired an interest in acting. He studied English in London, but had already decided to follow in the footsteps of his brother David and become an actor. 'I started off in repertory, like a lot of actors did, in 1953, and did about seven years of that,'[57] Rose said. 'After that, I went to Stratford to join the RSC under Peter Hall, and I remained there for a long time, in fact ten years, playing all sorts of parts, both there and in London. I left in 1970 and then I went into television, and really since then 'til now [1985] I've done almost entirely television. I was involved in the early episodes of several series, things like *The Troubleshooters* [1965-1972] – *Callan*, of course – *Roads to Freedom* [1970], *Elizabeth R* [1971], various plays of the month and classic plays for the BBC.' One of his earliest television roles was Adam in an adaptation of *As You Like It* (1963) with Vanessa Redgrave and Ian Richardson. Rose's subsequent theatre work included many supporting parts in Shakespeare, as well as in Peter Brook's film version of his play *Marat/Sade* (1967), with Glenda Jackson and Patrick Magee.

Director Peter Duguid cast him in a TV version of *The Comedy of Errors* (1964), and after his *Callan* appearances, Rose went on to the Lord Peter Wimsey mystery *The Unpleasantness at the Bellona Club*, and featured as a fraudster in *Special Branch* – 'Inquisition' (both 1973).

Rose made inroads into fantasy fiction in the 1976 BBC2 anthology series *The Mind Beyond* – 'Double Echo' (1976) and gained recognition for his portrayal of the muck-raking journalist Quintus Slide in historical drama *The Pallisers* (1974). In 1977 Rose landed the role that came to define his career, *Sturmbannführer/Standartenführer* Ludwig Kessler in the gripping BBC wartime drama *Secret Army* (1977-79). Over three series, aided by strong writing and Rose's portrayal, the character of Kessler, an acerbic, ruthless, totally dedicated Nazi, was, through his actions, his relationships with his fellow officers and his ongoing romance with a lonely Belgian woman, consistently fleshed out and developed in a way that never failed to convince, carefully avoiding all the clichés of other WW2 German villains. The character was allowed to escape to fight another day and the same production team brought the character back two years later in the sequel, *Kessler* (1981). The fugitive Nazi linked up with neo-Nazi movements in South America, while being hunted by a German agent and an avenging Israeli woman. The series had a memorable final scene – Kessler wrapped himself in the Swastika flag and shot himself. 'That was my idea, because I didn't want to do any more,' Rose admitted. 'They were talking about carrying on. I thought it was a mistake setting it 40 years later. The original idea was to carry it on straight after the war, and follow the story through how [Kessler] escaped and set up his new life and his new identity. But they then decided it was going to cost too much because of the period [setting], and said "We've got to save money by making it modern."'

Two other memorable roles from this period are tycoon Charles Burton in the Sunday night airline drama *Buccaneer* (1980) and the slave trader Captain Rorvik, who becomes increasingly frustrated and unbalanced in *Doctor Who* – 'Warriors' Gate' (1981). Casting directors evidently remembered Rose's early powerful TV roles and he subsequently appeared in popular television dramas including *Foyle's War* (2008) and *Midsomer Murders* (2010), as well as the Margaret Thatcher movie *The Iron Lady* (2011) starring Meryl Streep.

ELIZABETH BELL (1941-2012) was mainly a stage actress, appearing at the Royal Court, National Theatre and New Vic at Newcastle-under-Lyme. Peter Duguid taught her as a drama student. On television, she was Julia Mangini in the children's adventure series *Sexton Blake*, in the story 'The Organisation' (1968), and was a feature of anthology series, starring in *Out of the Unknown* – 'The Man in My Head' (1971) and five instalments of *Play for Today* (1973-1984). Her final TV role was Sister Agnes, in the *Midsomer Murders* thriller 'Master Class' (2010).

PETER BLYTHE (1934-2004) worked on Troy Kennedy Martin's ground-breaking TV drama *Diary of a Young Man* (1964) with Peter Duguid. He appeared as Anton in the horror film *Frankenstein Created Woman* (1967) and in the *Man in a Suitcase* episode 'Sweet Sue' (1967). In *The Avengers*, Blythe featured in 'The Positive Negative Man' (1967) and 'A Sense of History' (1966) with Patrick Mower; he would share air-time with Mower again in *Special Branch* – 'Downwind of Angels' (1974). In 1969, Blythe starred in the *Armchair Theatre* play 'The Mandarins'; David Garfield was also in the cast and Bill Bain directed. Blythe took over Peter Bowles' job as Head of Chambers as 'Soapy' Sam ('Bollard') Ballard, in *Rumpole of the Bailey* (1983-1992). He became known for upper-class characters, such as the dubious Commander Sparrow in *Between the Lines* – 'The Great Detective' (1993) and the real-life figure of Tom King in *The Alan Clark Diaries* (2004-06). Duguid cast Blythe again in *Callan* again in 'If He Can, So Could I' (1972).

DAVID HARGREAVES (born in 1940) portrayed DS Jellineck, an underling of T.P. McKenna's Superintendent Grant, in *The Sweeney* – 'Night Out' (1975), another off-hand police officer in *Armchair Thriller* – 'A Dog's Ransom' (1978) and Detective Chief Inspector Rainbow in *Strangers* (1978-79). As an earnest social worker, he regularly got under his Police Inspector wife Jean's feet in *Juliet Bravo* (1980-82).

INFORMATION: The opening scene featured a virus being tested on a laboratory rat, apparently killing the rodent in five seconds. This was meant to be simulated for the programme by stunning a rat with gas but the animal sadly couldn't be revived. 'It was supposed to have been knocked out temporarily according to the vet we used in the studio,'[58] John Kershaw explained ruefully. 'The vet told us privately after he'd done it there was no way it could be revived at all. That was one of the first little chinks in Michael Goodliffe's armour. He didn't like that. He very much liked the story and the concerns, but he didn't like being party to that. After the first episode, he began to have reservations, and after the second episode, very serious reservations. He'd got himself into something he didn't think he was happy with at all. And it clearly became apparent he was not going to stay.'

Classical compositions used to accompany Callan's first meetings with Joan were Vivaldi's 'Concerto for Four Harpsichords' in D Minor and J. S. Bach's 'Prelude Fugue No 16'. Two modern Reg Tilsley compositions were also included, 'Tracy Baby' and 'Autumn Colours'.[59]

'I think it had a reputation for being a very well-written series, as well as very well-acted,'[60] Clifford Rose said of his first impressions of *Callan*. 'Edward Woodward was certainly a great success in the leading part. I won't say he was a cult figure, but he was a very popular television person and *Callan* was a very popular television character, and it grew from there. It was *very* popular from '69 and I remember watching it from then on.

'I was coming to the end of my time at the RSC. I'd done seven years of rep, ten years with the RSC, and I was thinking of leaving: I thought I'd probably done enough time there and I thought I should do some television, and I hadn't done any for the commercial channels at all. My agent went to see various casting directors, and one of the casting directors was Dodo Watts, who was working for what was then ABC. I think it was through her that I was originally cast in *Callan*... It came out of the blue. I was appearing at the Aldwych [Theatre] when my first episode was made and I didn't know whether I'd be able to fit it in, but it worked out all right. So that was the first one I did and there was never any talk of doing more *Callan*.

'[Snell] was just a character in a TV play as far as I was concerned, and I didn't envisage him having any life beyond that but I did suggest – and this wasn't written – that he should be a kind of smooth, establishment character, and that he should have an old Etonian tie, and we used that [from his second scene], and the other thing I suggested was the glasses. It seemed to me that it would be nice to make him a kind of boffin as well, that he was involved in things in a cerebral kind of way, that he was not a heavy or a thug – although he did terrible things with drugs and that was his kind of area – and I liked the idea of slightly tinted glasses, which they liked too, so we did that.'

'It seemed logical [that] an outfit like this would have a tame scientist or psychologist on contract, not in the office every day, just as and when needed,'[61] James Mitchell said of his new addition to the Section. 'From the beginning, I saw him having a higher security clearance than Hunter himself, as he was the only one who knew what was going on in Hunter's subconscious, apart from anybody else's like Callan's! Clifford Rose was manna from heaven. At that time, he didn't wear glasses. It was only when he put those glasses on that he looked the way he did. The coldness just came with the glasses.'

This story underwent some changes during rehearsal. Peter Duguid explained, 'You're often faced with a script that you thought was pretty good, and a lot of work was done on the scripts, but as soon as you got it on the floor, with the actors, you hit problem after problem after problem. "He can't say that, because..." It was very much an evolving process.'[62] In this case, a description of Joan as 'not very attractive' was the issue; Woodward, the director recalled, amended dialogue in the read-through to be more complimentary to Elizabeth Bell. 'It was a very gallant and complimentary thing so we let it go [in].' During recording, Woodward was slightly hurt by the discharge from a prop gun but was able to carry on working.

The 'Biological Research Centre', where Joan and Dr. Bradford carry out their research, is a fictional version of the Microbiological Research Establishment (MRE), based near Porton Down, Wiltshire. The site has variously been reopened as the Microbiological Research Authority (MRA) and the Centre for Applied Microbiology and Research (CAMR), and it is name-checked in Len Deighton's *Billion Dollar Brain* in a plot involving stolen virus-injected eggs. Its experiments were stepped up during WW2, and when the conflict finished, British scientists began developing the research into organo-phosphorus and other nerve agents previously undertaken by the Nazis. In the 1950s, weapon tests were carried out on volunteers at this highly-classified research site; a serviceman, Ronald Maddison, died after Sarin was dripped onto his arm. This 'incident' was concealed for years before persistent allegations, and a police investigation – 'Antler' – resulted in a new inquest, which returned an unlawful killing verdict in 2004.[63]

The notion of germ warfare had previously been promulgated in *The Satan Bug* (1965); *Danger Man* also featured a conscience-stricken scientist working in the same field, in the episode 'Dangerous Secret' (1966).

For LSD, see 'Goodbye Mary Lee' (see Chapter 5). Chemical interrogation had previously featured in the film version of *The Guns of Navarone* (1961). Much of Joan's recall concerning cytosine (one of the four main bases found in DNA and RNA), hydrolysis and taxonomic separation is plausible technical speech; Mitchell had clearly scoured scientific magazines for authentic sounding microbiological terminology.

The *TV Times* continued to promote the series' second run, with an article by James Mitchell titled 'Are Our Spies Really Licensed to Kill?'[63] about real spies, and more information on the series' star: 'Edward Woodward, who plays reluctant secret service agent Callan, has a hobby which fits the image he projects on the screen. 38-year-old Woodward collects guns and has a fascinating collection from all over the world. With young son Timothy, who promises to be an expert shot, Edward practises in the grounds of his home, stakes being the target of off-duty Callan's aim.'[64]

MISSION ANALYSIS: *'You're not at the pictures now, Joan. This is all very real... There are no bugles, there are no banners, there are no comrades-in-arms. It's very, very real and very, very NASTY!'*
Viewers would be hard pressed to tell that this was the first *Callan* story to be made using the revised format. The only first night nerves evident are Hunter lying to Callan about his interest in Joan, a plot thread left hanging over from the way the first Hunter manipulated his former agent, which just fades away.

Joan says she is interested in 'science, not politics' but, as with the developers of the atom bomb, the story shows that the one can't be divorced from the other. In the world of espionage, no scientist is innocent and every one is a potential security risk. This point is explicitly made in the dialogue, while the suggestion of a surveillance state is underlined by the Section spying on Joan via CCTV and through a louvered window.

Joan Mather is the first woman seen to be physically destroyed by the Section, and this story sets something of a precedent. Callan's relationships with women seem to be cursed, as his own flippantly disguised misgivings about taking this case in particular are proven right. Meres' observation that Joan is 'naive' is also tragically confirmed, and from now on most women who encounter the Section leave it injured, emotionally scarred or dead. Elizabeth Bell's remarkable performance saves Joan from being a stereotypical victim as she delivers a convincing portrayal of an intellectual, cultured, sheltered woman, just beginning to live her life to the full, whose idealism is systematically chipped away by Callan. The key scene is when Joan accuses Callan of loving killing; he angrily disputes her insight and then tells her to abandon any hope of heroic rescue. At the height of his powers, Woodward's portrayal of Callan's conflicted emotions conveys the brutalised humanity, and perhaps brutalised *idealism*, that make his character so fascinating.

With its running theme of detachment, exemplified by the characters of Donner, Snell and Bradford, the story is made particularly distinctive through the use of hallucinogenic effects, as scenes are visualised through distorting lenses and extreme camera angles.

In arguably the definitive innocent-caught-in-the-crossfire *Callan* story, Horst and Donner work for an organisation with virtually the same name as the Section. As with both sides' treatment of Joan and their joint culpability for her death, it's another assertion of the contemporary idea that East and West are becoming identical.

A brilliant modern tragedy.

S2.3 YOU'RE UNDER STARTER'S ORDERS

Writer: Robert Banks Stewart
Director: Mike Vardy
Designer: Terry Gough

FIRST UK TRANSMISSION

Thames/LWT, Tyne Tees, Southern: Wednesday 22 January 1969, 10:30 pm
ATV, Anglia, Border, Channel, Granada, Harlech, Westward, Yorkshire: 9:00 pm,
Scottish: 8:00 pm
Grampian: Saturday 25 January 1969, 8:30 pm

CAST: Michael Hall (File clerk), Harold Innocent (Millett), Warren Stanhope (Mannix), Kathleen Byron (Hannah), Mark Kingston (Watt), Frank Seton (Betting shop clerk), Morris Perry (Nixon), Jane Walker (Receptionist)

EXTRAS/WALK-ONS: (*Uncredited on screen*) Blair Stewart, John Terry (Special Branch Men), Suzanne Fleuret, Kathleen Cattermole, Mary Rennis, John Tucker, Colin West, George Day (Guests in Hotel), Michael Stephens, Terry Lee, Ken Fraser, Arthur Zan, Donald Baker, Daniel Sinclair, Dennis Balcome, Michael Ealey, John Defoe, John James, Mike Richardson, Nina Hubey, Tracey Alexander, Mary Masters (from David Agency, used during filming)

PRODUCTION

Rehearsals: From Friday 2 February 1968
Location Filming: Fulham, London; adventure playground, Holland Park, London; Hampton Court, Richmond upon Thames; Kingsland Hotel, Baker Street, London (Dates unknown)
Camera Rehearsals/Recording: Teddington Studio Two, Tuesday 13 and Wednesday 14 February 1968[66]

TV TIMES: ' "If you want to get a head, get a pipeline." Has the strain proved too much for Secret Service man Callan? It would appear so when it is discovered he has taken files from the Home Office and is planning to escape from the country...'
18-24 January 1969, London edition

MISSING FILE: The master tapes of this story do not exist in the FremantleMedia archive.

MISSION PROFILE: Knocking out a clerk, Callan leaves the Central Registry with files marked 'LIAISON – U.S. CIA REGION EAST BERLIN'. Hunter tells Meres that Callan will be trying to contact a 'pipeline' that he was supposed to be investigating, an organisation that smuggles defectors out of England. It is run by someone code-named 'Theseus', believed to be Strickland, an ex-Section agent. Mannix, a CIA officer, takes the Section to task for its negligence.

Callan contacts Strickland's wife Hannah, as well as two other members of the organisation, Watt and Nixon, while following a trail from a betting shop to Hampton Court Maze where he is offered 'the way out'. The trio agree to smuggle Callan out of Britain for £5,000, but he insists he will only pay the fee to their leader.

Callan secretly reports back to Hunter – their plan to locate and identify 'Theseus' is working. Hunter later confides in Mannix, unaware that he is in fact a Soviet agent and the ringleader that Callan is looking for. Callan is captured, but after a confrontation on a hotel roof, Mannix is shot.

A MAN LIKE ME: Callan convinces the smugglers that he's apolitical – 'freelance' – defecting to sell stolen information to the highest bidder, rather than approaching the Communist embassies in London for asylum. He saves his demand only to pay 'Theseus' in person until the very end of their meeting.

He bonds with Hannah, sharing her disgust at the pittance the Section paid her late husband. She laments Watt hitting Callan and leaves the pipeline soon after Mannix announces his intent to kill him. She escapes arrest, which neither Callan nor Hunter seem too displeased about.

When he's taken hostage by Mannix, Callan needles him about wanting to get his name in the papers, distracting him long enough for Meres to come to the rescue.
Section Kills: 8

LONELY: Seedy by name and nature, Lonely's associate Dennis Millet is a purveyor of pornography who seeks to increase the 'rent' for the back room of his bookshop when he realises that Callan is on the run. Even though Callan calls Lonely a 'disgusting twit', he still entrusts him with phoning Hunter. Meres initially accepts Hunter's lie that Callan would not ask for Lonely's help in his current predicament, but later pays a visit to the thief, twisting his cap around the wrong way to intimidate him.

A TIE AND A CREST: Mannix plans to 'accidentally' kill Callan and photograph his stolen CIA files to pass on to Moscow. This plan only unravels because Hunter orders Meres to shadow him closely, as the Section chief doesn't want the CIA to steal the Section's credit for uncovering the smuggling operation. Mannix sarcastically calls his unwanted colleague 'old chap'.

ALCOHOL, TOBACCO AND FIREARMS: Hannah placates Callan with alcohol. Watt is irritated by Nixon smoking.

SPY-SPEAK: Pre-dating *Fawlty Towers* – 'Walforf Salad' by a decade, Mannix's American dismissal of the 'crumby' British is played for comic effect – initially: 'There's no security risk in this goddam set up at all – there's no security!' Hunter's struggle to perceive Mannix's whereabouts when Meres refers to him as being 'in the John' was sadly cut from the final draft.

'Just book me in at reception,' Callan sarcastically instructs Lonely at the bookshop, foreshadowing the later hotel setting. The shop-front doorway is fitted with a hatch, reminding Lonely of the confessional.

Hannah's reflections about her late husband, who used to ferry people across the Inner German Border, make Callan very uncomfortable.

PAWNS AND PLAYERS: MIKE VARDY reminisced, 'I started life as an actor without any training and went through the usual rep situation. There were a lot of repertory companies in those days. I came into London and did different jobs: understudy work, stage management and theatre lighting, all living on the bread line, of course! I applied to have a "Board", as the BBC called it, for an Assistant Floor Manager's job. It was just holiday relief for three months because they had such an enormous output – if more than three of their staff went on holiday, they had to have them covered. It was the year of the Asian flu and I was extremely ill that night, but I was determined to get to this Board, so I staggered down there and went through these questions and answers, staggered out again and three weeks later I got a letter saying "You're on". I went to the BBC for a year – they kept renewing the contract – then a further job came up at ABC in Teddington. Fortunately the studio manager I worked with said, "I'll write you out all the questions they'll ask you, and I'll give you the answers." I arrived at ABC and they asked me nine questions out of the ten he'd given me! The rest is history, really.'[67]

Amongst Vardy's initial commissions after qualifying as a director were the Northern youth serial *Sat'day While Sunday* (1967), *The Mind of Mr J.G. Reeder* (1969), *Armchair Theatre* (1969-1971), *Man at the Top* (1970 and 1972), *The Rivals of Sherlock Holmes* (1971) and two episodes of the Dutch crime thriller *Van der Valk* (1973).

His other early work included two period dramas, *Mystery and Imagination* – 'The Suicide Club' (1970) – 'a Robert Louis Stephenson short story which was adapted by Robert Muller. That was a wonderful script, it worked out extremely well' – and *The Haggard Falcon* (1974), 'a Bill Craig period piece about Mary Queen of Scots. Very funny, with a wonderful actor, Alex McAvoy, playing off Ian Ogilvy, and a lot of really good Scottish character actors. It was a very difficult piece to do because it was very dense, but we did it.'

In 1973, Vardy was one of the key people involved in getting Euston Films up and running. This involved making a third series of *Special Branch* and shooting it entirely on film rather than in a studio on videotape with film inserts. The Euston project proved sufficiently popular to continue, and Vardy continued to be a staunch supporter, working on its revamp of *Van der Valk* (1977) and various episodes of its phenomenally popular hit series *The Sweeney* and *Minder*. His experience of film drama led to the BBC commissioning him to make several instalments of the BBC's *Sweeney*-clone *Target* and its Bristol based replacement *Shoestring*. He collaborated with *Sweeney* producer Ted Childs again on the surreal drama *The One Game* (1988), and oversaw the last chapter in the life of Machiavellian MP Francis Urquhart, *The Final Cut* (1995). 'Ian Richardson was tremendous to work with,' Vardy said. 'Working for the BBC was always far more relaxed because there were more people, more facilities and more time, and dare I say it, more money – not for the director, but for the budget. There was quite an uneasy relationship, in my experience, between the writer Andrew Davies and [the novelist] Michael Dobbs. Andrew was, I think, sort of left-of-centre, and Michael Dobbs was a friend of Margaret Thatcher's; Andrew, at the beginning of the first episode, wrote Margaret Thatcher's funeral!'[68]

WARREN STANHOPE (1929-2012) was a Canadian actor who often worked in Britain playing Americans, such as CIA agent Johnson in *Man in a Suitcase* – 'Variation on a Million Bucks' (1967) and 'Web with Four Spiders' (1968). He can be seen in *The Saint* – 'The Pearls of Peace' (1962), 'Judith' (1963), 'Where the Money Is' (1968) and 'Invitation to Danger' (1968), *The Champions* – 'The Silent Enemy' (1969) and *Department S* – 'Spencer Bodily is Sixty Years Old '(1970). In America, he starred in *Jake and the Fatman* (1987-88) and *Picket Fences* (1994).

MORRIS PERRY (born in 1925) appeared in three early episodes of *The Avengers* – 'Dragonsfield', 'Tunnel of Fear' (both 1961) and 'Killer Whale' (1963). He had regular parts in *City Beneath the Sea* (1962) and *Diary of a Young Man* (1964) and his prolific credits also include *Sexton Blake* (1968), *The Champions* – 'The Final Countdown' (1969) and regular DI5 'liaison' Charles Moxon in early episodes of *Special Branch* (1969-1970). Well established as a guest actor by the 1970s, Perry appeared as a memorable *Doctor Who* villain, corporate raider Captain Dent, in 'Colony In Space' (1971) and as a professor who pioneers a new treatment for aggressive mental patients in *Doomwatch* – 'Hair Trigger' (1972). Perry went on to play Regan's caustic boss Maynon in *The Sweeney* and a pessimistic academic who becomes infected with rabies in *Survivors* – 'Mad Dog' (1977). He was also in *Secret Army* (1979), *Strangers* – 'Soldiers of Misfortune' (1981), the Tom Baker version of *The Hound of the Baskervilles* (1982) and *The Dark Side of the Sun* (1983).

HAROLD INNOCENT (1935-1993) trained as an office clerk, but moved into acting after studying at the Birmingham School of Speech Training and Dramatic Art. A few years after his war service, he moved to Hollywood, performing in *Alfred Hitchcock Presents* – 'The Schartz-Metterklume Method' (1960), *The Twilight Zone* – 'The Obsolete Man' (1961) and the long running popular western *Gunsmoke* (1955-1975). In Britain, Innocent appeared on stage at the National Theatre and the Bristol Old Vic and was often cast as a floridly obsequious villain or bureaucrats, cropping up in *The Avengers* – 'The Medicine Men' (1963), 'The Rotters' (1968, as an undertaker), *Randall and Hopkirk (Deceased)* – 'My Late Lamented Friend and Partner' (1969), *The Persuaders!* – 'To the Death, Baby' (1972), and *The Professionals* – 'Not a Very Civil Servant' (1978) and 'Operation Susie' (1982). His more comic roles include the camp scientist Gilbert in *Doctor Who* – 'The Happiness Patrol' (1988), and the butler Manners in *Ripping Yarns* – 'Murder at Moorstones Manor' (1977). Innocent appeared in the cult films *Loot* (1970), *Brazil* (1985) and *Without A Clue* (1988).

KATHLEEN BYRON (1921-2009) appeared in two famous Powell and Pressburger films, the black-and-white-into-colour fantasy *A Matter of Life and Death* (1946) and the intense drama *Black Narcissus* (1947). Her other cinema credits include the witchcraft thriller *Night of the Eagle* (1962), *Twins of Evil* (1971) and *Saving Private Ryan* (1998). On television, Byron appeared in *Danger Man* – 'Name, Date and Place' (1961), the prison drama *Within These Walls* (1976), *Blake's 7* – 'Weapon' (1979) and as the semi-regular character Madame Celeste in *Secret Army* (1977). She was one of the stellar cast in *Reilly – Ace of Spies* (1983).

MARK KINGSTON (1934–2011) appeared as a soldier in the science fiction thriller *Invasion* (1966). He was known for his comic roles, such as his part in the sitcom *Time of My Life* (1980) in which he played the redundant, terminally-ill divorcee Ken Archer, *Shine on Harvey Moon* (1984-5), Stephen Fry's investigative journalism spoof *This is David Lander* (1988) and the black comedy *The Wimbledon Poisoner* (1994).

MICHAEL HALL had minor parts in *The Corridor People* (1966), *Mr. Rose* (1967-68), *Spindoe* (1968) and *Thriller* – 'Screamer '(1974). He was asked to reprise his filing clerk role by director Mike Vardy in a later episode. (See 'A Village Called "G"', page 293.)

INFORMATION: Dialogue amendments to the rehearsal script[69] included toughening up Meres's 'shock' about Callan's behaviour and the Section's attitude towards Mannix, trimming Callan's internal monologues, and hardening his internal comment about Mannix from being a 'double-crossing swine' into 'a bastard'. The musical composition 'Mystery Project' was used for the advert breaks.[70]

'I was asked to be involved in the second series, and as I was a relatively junior member of the drama department at that time it was something of an honour for me,'[71] Mike Vardy said. 'I had worked with Edward in 1968 on a live drama called *The Night of Talevera* so I looked forward to *Callan* a great deal, and I was not disappointed. My one and only abiding memory of 'You're Under Starter's Orders' (apart from a hilarious cameo from Harold Innocent) was the dénouement scene, which took place on the roof of a six-storey hotel in Baker Street. It was a very windy night and more than one actor was sporting a wig. As good as the wigs were, I was warned by the make-up supervisor that they would not survive for long in the force six that was blowing. I then had to change all my plans and re-stage the entire scene, making use of chimney stacks on the roof in order to shelter the actors from the worst of the gale. Needless to say, we went over schedule that night!'

Robert Banks Stewart based the bookshop on a premises he'd researched in Paddington. 'It wasn't just a bookshop – it also sold dirty books,' he said. 'If you nodded to the owner, you got into a back room... I went in and the door was bolted and the guy looked through [an eye hole] to see if any policemen might be in the shop. [It was in] Praed Street. We're talking a long time ago. The guy would say "What would you like? Lesbian? Gay?"... The guy in the script unbolts the door and lets Callan in, although he doesn't ask *him* what he wants: you couldn't have put that line in then!'[72]

'I watch far too much news, and I've always been addicted to reading newspapers,' Banks Stewart said of his journalistic observations of the Anglo-American politics of the time. The scriptwriter certainly had plenty of material to work with. In 1949, while drinking with writer Phillip Toynbee, Donald Maclean, the Head of Chancery in Cairo, wrecked the apartment of two female US Embassy staff and tore up their underwear. He was reinstated on intelligence duties in London despite his 'stress' problems; only later did the realisation dawn that his personal issues originated from his double life as a Soviet agent. Fellow 'Cambridge Five' spy Guy Burgess, the second secretary of the British Embassy in Washington DC, was similarly repatriated following belligerent heavy drinking. MI5 planned to question Maclean, but he and Burgess famously fled; their associate Philby was suspected of alerting the pair from Washington and he was also sent home by the CIA. The Americans continued to suspect Philby of being 'the Third Man' afterwards, naming him in the *New York Sunday News*. The prosecutions of Klaus Fuchs and George Blake, a Berlin case officer handing Eastern European MI6 details over to the Soviets, also served, fairly or not, to fuel impressions of ineffective vetting and slipshod security procedures within British intelligence.

MISSION ANALYSIS: '*He began to disintegrate. It was his nerves at first. Then it became more obviously physical. An ulcer, headaches, a gradual slowing down... he was silver-haired at 40.*' Robert Banks Stewart supplies another fast-moving narrative focusing on people on the fringes of espionage, a novel 'deep cover' villain, a cinematic climax and more Section blunders like those seen in 'Goodbye, Nobby Clarke'. Thinking the pipeline leader is someone close to home, Hunter takes a dangerous risk by revealing Callan's plans to Mannix while withholding them from Meres. (Unfortunately, probably due to the overall format changes, this story passes up a golden opportunity to pit the two agents fully against each other: Callan working for Hunter would also have been a shocking twist had this episode been part of the previous series. The Section chief sending the Stricklands 'a fiver for the wheelchair' is totally in-keeping with Ronald Radd's pitiless interpretation.)

Banks Stewart's perceptive journalistic observations include the pipeline's *modus operandi* at Ajax Travel – bribing genuine holidaymakers to cancel their journeys – and Hannah commenting that the authorities at Gatwick are half-asleep at 2 am. Situating the hotel-based finale in Victoria is another shrewd geographic choice, both for railway access to Gatwick Airport and its close proximity to Scotland Yard (and therefore, the Special Branch.)

The hostility with the CIA recalls the same conflict in *The IPCRESS File*, while quirkier touches like the references to Greek mythology and the fight in a children's adventure playground are reminiscent of *The Avengers*. *The Big Sleep* (1946) and *Torn Curtain* (1966) are also possible influences, respectively featuring a bookshop selling pornography and a false defection.

Unfortunately, this familiarity works against the story as well as in favour of it, as the idea of Callan being turned into Public Enemy Number 1 in the newspapers for several days just does not seem covert enough, or *nasty* enough, to be a Section operation;. Arguably, a few minor changes at the story-editing level could have resolved this point and made the story more consistent with those either side of it. Overall, however, this is a solid story – the late Peter Strickland is another mirror image of Callan, while Hannah is a memorably ambiguous character who bonds with the Section agent and exemplifies the story's theme of betrayal.

S2.4 THE LITTLE BITS AND PIECES OF LOVE

Writer: James Mitchell
Director: Peter Sasdy
Designer: Stan Woodward

FIRST UK TRANSMISSION

Thames/LWT, Tyne Tees, Southern: Wednesday 29 January 1969, 10:30 pm
ATV, Anglia, Border, Channel, Granada, Harlech, Westward, Yorkshire: 9:00 pm
Scottish: 8:00 pm
Grampian: Saturday 1 February 1969 8:30 pm

CAST: Pauline Jameson (Mrs Rule), Fabia Drake (Agnes Gregory), David Rose (Meres's assistant), Vivien Sherrard (Waitress), Vladek Sheybal (Dicer), Laurence Hardy (Dr Rule), David Garfield, Joseph O'Connell (KGB Men), Andy Devine (Brezhevski)

EXTRAS/WALK-ONS: (*Uncredited on screen*) Winnie Holman (Washer Up Woman), Mohand Singh (Indian Kitchen Hand), John Preston, Harry Tiernay (Chefs), Maisie Merry (Cockney Kitchen Hand), Betty Golding (Irish Girl), Peter Rory (Oxford Tutor), Louis Collard (Girl Undergraduate), Peta Collins (Matron-type lady), Nancy Adams (Smart wife of Professor), Peggy Lee (Chinese Girl Undergraduate), Pat Halpin (Retired Army Officer)

PRODUCTION

Rehearsals: From Thursday 18 January 1968
Location Filming: Exeter College, Catte Street, Broad Steet, Cornmarket Street, Magdalen Street East, Oxford; Denham Airfield, Hangar Road Denham
(Sunday 21 – Tuesday 23 January 1968)
Camera Rehearsals/Recording: Teddington Studio One, Wednesday 31 January and Thursday 1 February 1968[73]

TV TIMES: '"The worst days of your life may be years behind – but sooner or later you'll live them again." Fishing in dangerous waters, Callan attempts to persuade a wife to act as bait for her ex-husband, a distinguished scientist now working in East Germany. The government wants him to take a holiday in Britain where he can be of use to them...'
25-31 January 1969, Southern edition

MISSION PROFILE: Callan burgles a house in Oxford on Hunter's orders and is then told to pose as an insurance assessor to get to know the house's occupants, Charles and Sophia Rule. Charles is a psychologist who met Sophia treating her for hysteria in a displaced persons camp in Bonn in 1945. Previously, she was married to scientist Andrei Brezhevski, who she thinks is dead, but he's alive and perfecting rocket fuel for the Soviets' 100-megaton bomb project.

Hunter's plan is to compel Sophia to write a letter saying she's terminally ill and unhappy in her current marriage, to lure Brezhevski to Britain while he attends a conference in Stockholm. She objects, but Callan bullies her into completing the false message.

Callan has asked a Polish criminal, Dicer, to find out more about Brezhevski; Dicer warns him the KGB are aware of the Section's plans. Callan rescues Sophia from abduction by two KGB agents, shooting one dead. He makes her accompany him to a Newcastle to meet Brezhevski, but she is left heartbroken when the scientist is run over by a surviving Russian agent.

A MAN LIKE ME: 'David Tucker' is obnoxious towards Sophia, threatening her with bigamy charges and the stress of a court case. Later he softens his attitude, reassuring her that the ordeal will 'soon be over', perhaps feeling the need to justify himself.

When Charles Rule takes a swing at Callan, he gets thumped and is warned 'You're too old for it... I'd take you apart!' This anticipates a very similar scene in the 1971 gangster film *Get Carter* and its source novel, *Jack's Return Home* (1970), by Ted Lewis.

Section Kills: 9

LONELY: Doing the washing up in a cramped and busy kitchen (possibly in an attempt to go straight, although he denies it). On his breaks, he tries to read a dirty magazine but keeps being interrupted. Lonely is brought in to help out on Callan's robbery, keeps an eye on the Rules' house and sets up the meeting with Dicer. The Pole unsuccessfully tries to cosh Callan where Lonely works and, in turn, Callan cuffs Lonely for being too scared to warn him. He doesn't have enough 'tanners' to phone the Rules' house and, as a result, nearly gets shot in the face by Callan.

A TIE AND A CREST: The letter Sophia writes has been pre-dictated by a Section 'boffin' (presumably Snell). The Section's car pool includes a Cortina. A KGB agent quotes E.M. Forster at Charles Rule and appears to detest jazz and pop music.

ALCOHOL, TOBACCO AND FIREARMS: Dismissing Lonely, Dicer and Callan drink from Callan's hip flask together. (Scotch, probably.) Hunter smokes cigars.

SPY-SPEAK: Plenty of bleak interactions with Callan. When Sophia asks who he works for, he says, 'I hope you never know.'

'How can you justify this? 'I don't have to. That isn't my job.'

'You're not trying to blackmail me are you?' 'Yes.'

Gripping Charles Rule somewhere painful, Callan tells him, 'Think! That's how you make your living isn't it, by *thinking*?'

Having shot and killed a KGB man in the psychiatrist's study, Callan searches the body: 'Twenty quid and a pistol. Not much for a life's work, is it?'

On the phone to Hunter, he fears that Sophia will have another mental breakdown: '*That really bothers me!*'

PAWNS AND PLAYERS: WLADYSLAW 'VLADEK' RUDOLF Z. SHEYBAL (1923-1992) was of Armenian, Scottish and Austrian decent, multilingual and born in the Second Polish Republic. He fought in the resistance against the Germans and was interned by them in prison camps, escaping several times. After WW2 ended, Sheybal studied at the Stanislavsky School of Acting, later appearing in *Kanał (*1957), a film about the 1944 Warsaw Uprising. He moved to the United Kingdom in the early 1960s.

Sheybal's exotic East European accent and sharp features soon landed him acting roles. Meeting Ken Russell at the BBC, he worked with the director on *Billion Dollar Brain* (1967) and *Women in Love* (1969). Other films included *Mosquito Squadron* (1969), *Puppet on a Chain* (1971), *The Lady Vanishes* (1979), *The Jigsaw Man* (1984), the James Bond spoof *Casino Royale* (1967) and the second legitimate Bond film, *From Russia With Love* (1963). This last part, SPECTRE Number 3 and chess champion Kronsteen, was reportedly only taken on by Sheybal after encouragement from Sean Connery, and is still arguably the Polish actor's most famous role.

A small role in the sci-fi film *Doppelgänger* (a.k.a *Journey to the Far Side of the Sun*, 1969) led to Sheybal playing the semi-regular part of Doctor Doug Jackson in *UFO* (1970-73). He appeared in *The Sentimental Agent* (1963), *Danger Man* – 'Fish on the Hook' (1964), *The Saint* – 'The Helpful Pirate' (1966), *The Champions* – 'The Dark Island' (1968) and *The New Avengers* – 'Cat Amongst the Pigeons' (1976). Two acclaimed television performances for the actor were as the Holocaust survivor Egon Sobotnik in the mini-series *QB VII* (1974) and the doomed courier Otto Leipzig in *Smiley's People* (1982). Sheybal died soon after his final appearance in an episode of *The Bill* (1992).

PETER SASDY (born in 1935) was another East European who became a very highly-regarded director for Hammer films, overseeing *Taste the Blood of Dracula* (1969), *Hands of the Ripper* and *Countess Dracula* (both 1971), on which he also has a writing credit. Sasdy's other film work includes the big screen version of *Doomwatch* (1972). TV credits cover *Out of the Unknown* – 'The Midas Plague' (1965), 'Time in Advance' (1965) and 'The Eye' (1966), together with Nigel Kneale's menacing play *The Stone Tape* (1972). Sasdy would continue to be attracted to fantasy and horror, working on both *Hammer House of Horror* (1980) and *Hammer House of Mystery and Suspense* (1984); the latter anthology series' 'Last Video and Testament' features Clifford Rose. He worked with Edward Woodward again on the second series of the political thriller *1990* (1978).

PAULINE JAMESON (1920-2007) was an established radio and stage actress who appeared in *Undermind* – 'Flowers of Havoc' (1965), *Public Eye* (1968) and Ray Jenkins' adaptation of *The Woman in White* (1982). Her final television appearance in *Agatha Christie's Poirot* (1996) harked back to her earlier role in the Margaret Rutherford Miss Marple film, *Murder Most Foul* (1964).

FABIA DRAKE (1904-1990, a.k.a. Ethel McGlinchy) was a life-long friend of Lawrence Olivier. Her first professional role was as a child actress in *Masks and Faces* (1917). She often played eccentric spinsters, such as in *The Saint* – 'The Miracle Tea Party' (1964) and 'The Smart Detective' (1965), *The Avengers* – 'The Danger Makers' (1966) and *The Prisoner* – 'Arrival' (1967). Sasdy cast her again in *Imaginary Friends* (1987).

LAURENCE HARDY (1911–1982, born Aylmer Penn) was in the seminal war film *The Cruel Sea* (1953) and on television featured in *The Adventures of Robin Hood* (1956-1960). He starred in the Francis Durbridge thriller *The World of Tim Fraser* (1961) and the Johnny Speight comedy *If There Weren't Any Blacks You'd Have to Invent Them* (1968). Hardy's other credits include *The Avengers* – 'The Master Minds' (1965) and the Roger Moore film *The Man Who Haunted Himself* (1970).

DAVID GARFIELD had small parts in *The Saint* – 'The Abductors' (1965), 'The House on Dragon's Rock' (1968) and *The Prisoner* – 'Arrival' (1967). He played the machine-hating villager Davy Gordon who persecutes the young heroine in the superior children's series *The Changes* (1975) and was in *Doctor Who* twice, firstly as the monocle-wearing alien Von Weich in the epic 'The War Games' (1969), then in 'The Face of Evil' (1977) as the fanatical High Priest Neeva. Garfield also played recurring character Samuel Plimsoll in *The Onedin Line* (1973), based on the real-life figure who campaigned against dangerously overloading ships, and the Cockney gangster Ronnie Lynch in the final series of *Citizen Smith* (1980).

VIVIEN SHERRARD featured in 'rep' in Perth, Leicester, Birmingham, Canterbury and at the Bristol Old Vic. On television, she was best-known for her portrayal of secretary Barbara Mason in *Doomwatch* (1970-72). She retired from acting in 1972.

DAVID ROSE (1931-2004), Clifford's brother, appeared in the hostage drama *Blood Money* (1981), nautical serial *Howard's Way* (1985-86) and *Hammer House of Mystery and Suspense* – 'The Late Nancy Irving' (1984).

INFORMATION: Originally entitled 'He Only Said My Name', this was the second episode to be made by the new production team. 'It was a gloomy episode with a fair share of violence and menace,'[74] James Mitchell remarked. 'There was also the question, why would a fundamentally decent man do these things?' Radio music includes a quick blast of 'Miniskirt Detroit' by Reg Tilsley before the KGB settle on 'Brahms' Symphony No. 3 in F Major'.[74]

Positive press reaction to the series continued building, with Nancy Banks-Smith commenting, '[Woodward] plays Callan like something repulsively attractive out of the bottom drawer.'[75] Mary Malone of the *Daily Mirror* provided another encouraging review, noting that while Callan had rejoined the Section, he 'still has the stinking aura of an animal at bay... In last night's episode he was allowed to show a hint of chivalry... But no more than a hint.'[76]

Many Polish pilots like Dicer fought in the Battle of Britain, and the 'Free Polish' Callan mentions were known as the Polish Underground State. The near simultaneous invasions of Western and Eastern Poland by the respective military forces of Nazi Germany and Soviet Russia arose from a secret pact between the two countries. The Soviets crushed Polish opposition through summary executions and thousands of arrests, with over 20,000 Polish military personnel and civilians perishing in the Katyn massacre. After the pact broke down and WW2 ended, the Soviet Union was left in control of most of the Eastern Polish territories it had captured.

A similar character to Dicer, Count Komorowski, appeared in James Mitchell's second Callan novel *Russian Roulette* (see Chapter 10).

MISSION ANALYSIS: *'Your argument does not interest me any more. I've seen too many people die. One day I think it will not interest you either.'* This story presents us with the Section's most unfortunate victims yet – an ageing love triangle that includes a concentration camp survivor. As the honey trap closes, we learn Charles Rule and Brezhevski are kindred spirits, the latter only pursuing his career path as a means of finding Sophia. There is also a horrible dramatic irony in the Section literally breaking the Rules. The odd shaky Russian accent aside, the performances are outstanding, particularly from Woodward and Sheybal as the roguish, unreliable Dicer. Peter Sasdy handles both the brutal two-handed dialogue scenes and the climactic airfield action sequence effectively, with the camera's final, cinematic ascent away from the carnage being particularly striking.

Lonely provides the only humour in a very grim story, comically attempting to hide behind a branch of a threadbare shrub outside the Rules' house.

This story was conceived before the decision to reinstate Callan in the Section had been made, and this shows slightly. Retained elements after rewriting include Section agents shadowing Callan and Hunter only informing him piecemeal of what his assignment actually is. The operation itself is disjointed too, with minimal protection for

Brezhevski, and the Section making no effort to intercept the surviving KGB agent on his overnight train trip from Oxford to Newcastle. This might be human error, or part of an unstated deniable plan to let the rocket scientist be killed by his own side. Callan himself is at his most harsh and uncompromising, and there is some truth in Sophia's fatalistic prophecy, another reference to the 'sides' of East and West converging.

Overall, the ironically titled 'The Little Bits and Pieces of Love' is a grim, unsentimental drama in which those who hit the hardest win.

S2.5 LET'S KILL EVERYBODY

Writer: Ray Jenkins
Director: Robert Tronson
Designer: David Marshall

FIRST UK TRANSMISSION

Thames/LWT, Tyne Tees, Southern: Wednesday 5 February 1969, 10.30 pm
ATV, Anglia, Border, Channel, Granada, Harlech, Westward, Yorkshire: 9.00 pm
Scottish: 8.00 pm
Grampian: Saturday 8 February 1969, 10.30 pm

CAST: Peter Welch (Bremer), Henry Knowles (Gould), Hilary Dwyer (Jenny), Heather Canning (Paula), Kenneth Gilbert (Walker), Stanley McGeagh (Fergusson)

PRODUCTION

Rehearsals: From Friday 1 March 1968.
Location Filming: Kingston upon Thames (riverside) (Tuesday 5 March 1968);
Orleans Court, Seymour Gardens, Richmond Road and Scion Road, Twickenham;
ABC Studios car park, Teddington (Wednesdasy 6 March 1968)
Camera rehearsals/recording: Tuesday 12 and Wednesday 13 March 1968[77]

TV TIMES: '"However you play the cards someone must lose – it could be you." An unknown enemy is planning to eliminate systematically the members of Callan's department. Although they have no aces in their hand, Callan and his fellow agents must win the tricks if they are to survive the deadly game they are forced to play. When the score is totted-up, will the assassin have achieved his aim of "abundance declared"?'
1-7 February 1969, London edition

MISSION PROFILE: Callan is on sick leave following a minor operation at Dr Walker's clinic. He's also been dating Jenny Lawther, a nurse who worked there. Since meeting him, she's abruptly given up her career and enrolled as a history student.

At HQ, Meres and a new recruit, Gould, interrogate Bremer, from the Fascist Organisation For Freedom (OFF). Bremer kills himself rather than divulge any more about the OFF plan to assassinate all members of the Section. Aware the department's secrecy has been breached, Hunter orders his staff to watch each other, and to disclose who their recent contacts are. Callan interrogates Jenny, much to her distress.

Her tutor, Paula Goodman, is actually one of two OFF assassins. She kills Gould with poison gas pellets in a phone box, then murders Jenny too as she has overheard a compromising phone call. Hunter is informed by Walker that there is an irregularity in Jenny's nursing records. As he and another Section agent, Ferguson, arrive at the clinic to investigate, they are shot dead.

Lured to Paula's flat, Callan pretends not to know the tutor's real identity, but once she has telephoned the second OFF agent he holds her at gunpoint. When the other assassin – Dr. Walker – and Meres both converge on her flat, Paula dives for her gas capsules and Callan shoots her. Walker is left facing two angry Section agents who clearly feel one death is not enough to avenge their losses...

A MAN LIKE ME: Callan's address is now 31, Duke William Street, Bayswater. He had an operation on his neck in Dr Walker's clinic. While there, he started an affair with Jenny Lawther, an attractive, idealistic nurse ten years his junior. The relationship quickly sours, Callan feeling 'sick' when he discovers that Jenny may be a suspect and realising that he'll have to cross-examine her. He's ruthless in doing so, snarling 'Don't make me feel dirty' as he empties her handbag and challenges aspects of her life story.

Jenny is innocent, but there are several circumstantial coincidences – the deaths of her brother and her best friend, and her knowledge that the clinic exists to treat security agents – that delay her name being cleared, so, tragically, Callan ignores her suspicions about her university tutor until it's too late.

He can barely control himself as he interrogates Dr Goodman, yelling 'You bitch!' at her, and slapping her across the face. He very nearly doesn't come out of the situation alive – shot across the scalp by Walker – and, having placed Dr. Gould's lipstick full of gas pellets just out of her reach, brutally shoots her three times as she lunges for it.

Section Kills: 10 (discounting Walker.)

LONELY: Driving a Black Cab (not for the last time – see 'First Refusal', Chapter 7). He's worried that the police will stop him, so he's probably illegitimately filling in for a real cabbie. It's suggested that he's driving the car on Callan's orders, as the taxi conveniently appears in the vicinity of Dr Goodman's flat when she and Jenny need a lift. Lonely helps Callan with an unconscious Gould and is physically abused by Meres.

A TIE AND A CREST: 'Emergency D' is a top Section directive that orders all operatives to drop their current assignments and cover each other.

Callan suggests Meres looks after 'Sir' (Hunter), another reference to the department's 'public school' hierarchy. Meres seems to relish the danger inherent in the Section being targeted, speculating that the assassin is 'making sure' before they attack.

He plays a practical joke on Callan, breaking into his flat, pointing a finger at him and shouting 'Bang!' when the agent enters; in response, Callan nearly shoots him. The mood then shifts dramatically: following Toby's perverse prelude to breaking the news to Callan that Jenny has been murdered, Meres does so surprisingly sympathetically. It's an early indication of a change in the two agents' relationship.

ALCOHOL, TOBACCO AND FIREARMS: Early on, Callan sarcastically suggests that Meres should help himself to the whisky in his flat, aware that Toby's already done so. After delivering the bad news about Jenny, Meres leaves him with the bottle and a flask.

Goodman's preferred method of assassination is lethal gas while Walker uses a Luger, the favoured firearm of ex-Nazis in TV thrillers.

SPY-SPEAK: Lonely says he has not seen Callan sweating before; Callan replies that he smells 'like eau-de-cologne' in comparison to Lonely's secretions.

Hunter describes the OFF as 'bright, ruthless and right round the bend.'

Callan and Meres both use the farewell 'Be seeing you', the catchphrase popularised by Patrick McGoohan's 1967-68 fantasy series *The Prisoner*. Intriguingly, this is the one and only time they both say it.

Lethally doping Jenny with drugs while debating with her about morality, Paula shows more sick humour by advising her that she can 'always try' to telephone her the next day.

Caught out, Paula's veneer breaks down, and she tells Callan she doesn't want to die. 'That's funny – neither did Jenny,' he snaps mercilessly.

PAWNS AND PLAYERS: KENNETH GILBERT (1931–2015) had early roles in *The Three Musketeers* (1954) and *Hamlet* (1961). He took part in RSC productions and later worked at the Clwyd Theatre. Capable of playing slightly older than his years, he was often cast as authority figures, including doctors or policemen, in *Softly Softly* (1968), *Spindoe* (1968), *The Mind of Mr. J.G. Reeder* (1971), *Crown Court* (1972) and *The Sweeney* – 'Bad Apple' (1976). The latter was 'fun to do – I'd known Dennis Waterman for God knows how long, because I used to teach him when he was at drama school.'[78]

'Bad Apple' also renewed Gilbert's collaboration with the director Douglas Camfield. 'He should have done a *Callan*,' Gilbert reflected, recalling working for the same director on *Doctor Who* – 'The Seeds of Doom' (1976), playing a corrupt civil servant who falls victim to a rampaging alien plant. 'Dougie was totally unfazed by anything. He had it all under control… When you're seen to do quite a lot of TV, the directors seem to know when you are free.' 'Seeds' and *Callan* writer Robert Banks Stewart reformed the Camfield-Gilbert team again for the first *Shoestring* episode, 'Private Ear' (1979).

Gilbert also guested in *The New Avengers* – 'The Midas Touch' (1976), *Scorpion Tales* – 'The Great Albert' (1978, co-produced by Shaun O'Riordan), *The Chinese Detective* (1981) and featured as another villainous doctor in *The Gentle Touch* – 'Blade' (1980): 'I was going to play Jill Gascoigne's boss, but I was in one of the [Christopher] Marlowe plays – I had agreed to do it… I couldn't just walk out. So I missed that opportunity, and I think that's why I'm in an episode.'

He memorably portrayed Harold Earle, one of the contenders blackmailed into withdrawing from the Tory leadership contest in *House of Cards* (1990): 'I was on board with that for about three months, playing a minister who was caught with a rent boy in a restaurant and photographed by the paparazzi. Ian Richardson was brilliant. It was a classic piece of television that broke the mould.' Gilbert's last TV appearance was in *Hustle* (2011). 'It was a very brief part, but very nice. Some of those series like *Life on Mars* were excellent.'

HEATHER CANNING (1933-96) played the rough blonde who tries to steal Marker's wallet, providing a fine 'Welcome to Brighton' for the *Public Eye* (1969). She appeared in *Hine* (1971), *Spyder's Web* (1972), *Reilly – Ace of Spies* (1983) and *Lytton's Diary* (1985). Canning memorably portrayed the sympathetic Ellen, who treats Charles (Denis Lill), in *Survivors'* 'rabies' episode 'Mad Dog' (1977).

HILARY DWYER (a.k.a. Heath, born 1945) briefly featured as Number 73 in *The Prisoner* – 'Hammer Into Anvil' (1967), her character's suicide inciting Number 6 to bring down Patrick Cargill's sadistic Number 2. She also had parts in Michael Reeves' horror film *Witchfinder General* (1968), *Special Branch* – 'Care of Her Majesty' (1969) and the third series of *Hadleigh* (1973), as the lawyer/landowner's wife. Dwyer's final TV role was as a scientist in 'The Troubled Spirit', an unusually disturbing episode of *Space: 1999* (1975-77). Afterwards, she retired from acting, becoming an actors' agent and then a producer, working on Gary Oldman's harrowing film about alcoholism, *Nil by Mouth* (1997).

STANLEY MCGEAGH had supporting roles in *Law and Order* (1978), *Blood Money* (1981), *Big Deal* (1986) and *Ghandi* (1982).

PETER WELCH (1922-1984) played Detective Superintendent Clark in *Spy Trap* (1972-75) and had a brief cameo as a sinister pub landlord in *Doctor Who* – 'The Android Invasion' (1975).

HENRY KNOWLES appeared in the northern family drama *Flesh and Blood* (1982).

RAY JENKINS recalled receiving his first career break while studying at Trinity College, Cambridge. 'In my last year I wrote a play; the theatre group put on a competition for new plays. Peggy Ramsey, the agent, saw them, took two of them, and one was mine. I then went to Paris, came back and became a teacher. I worked on *The Third Programme* [1946-70] radio plays for a bit, then became a teacher of teachers, but there was lots of pressure to come down and actually start in television – which was very nice – from old friends in radio like Michael Bakewell. So I gave it all up and came down to London. I got the last commission for the original *Z Cars* and that was that: they said "If you can do it in two weeks, you can have it." I wrote a story about these tramps by the side of the motorway up in Leicester with bags of rubbish – which I turned into pornography – and that's [how my TV career] started. Two things came together: one was friends who worked [at the BBC], and the other one, possibly more important, was that I'd been a teacher. They were doing a programme called *This Man Craig*, [1966] about a teacher in a comprehensive... and that was right up my street, so I did eight episodes of that. Then, gradually, my reputation spread sideways.'[79]

The Welsh writer contributed many edgy stories, usually with psychological themes, to shows such as *Z Cars* (from 1965-67), *Counterstrike* (in 1969), *Hine* (1971), the anthology series *Menace* (1973) and *Special Branch* (1974). The latter led to him writing two disturbing episodes for the second series of *The Sweeney,* 'Trap' and 'I Want the Man' (both 1975). Later commissions included *Armchair Thriller* – 'The Girl Who Walked Quickly' (1978), the *Gentle Touch* stories 'Knife' (1981), 'Joker' (1982) and 'Dany' (1982), and an adaptation of Wilkie Collins' mystery novel *The Woman in White* (1982). In the 1990s, Jenkins wrote various episodes of the police drama *The Chief* (1994) and 'Kalon' for the short-lived Dennis Waterman espionage drama *Circles of Deceit* (1996).

INFORMATION: The script differed from the finished production as Bremer originally uses the distraction of Hunter entering the office to kill himself. Hunter's death scene was also meant to be recorded in the studio; amid some innocuous seeming repartee about the opulent interior of Walker's office, the medic would suddenly shoot the Section chief with a silenced pistol. Callan was to conclude the episode by wearily saying, 'Long live Hunter.'

This was the first episode of the second series not to feature Russian, or Russian-backed, opposition. 'We contributed very seriously towards making the Russians the bad guys.'[80] John Kershaw reflects. 'There wasn't anyone else around at that time. It's all right for James Bond-type things, which nobody I hope takes seriously. But it was bad in a series like ours when we were trying to be serious. There must be a good Russian guy somewhere, they can't all be evil, they can't all be wishing wickedness on the world; you must be able to trust some.' The incorporation of a Fascist organisation was a 'move away from this endless political broken record.'

Not everyone at Thames liked the title for this story. A script found in the Thames archive in the 1980s, with Lloyd Shirley's handwriting on the cover page, queried, 'Do we really have to use this *Avengers* title?'[81]

Ray Jenkins joined the writing team while Terence Feely was still producer, but already knew James Mitchell and (future story editor) George Markstein. He vividly recalled one of the script discussions between himself, Feely and Mitchell: 'There were three reasonably intelligent people sitting there on a very hot afternoon, trying to work out how to kill somebody, and coming up with the most gruesome solution – pushing somebody into a telephone box, gassing them and watching them die inside the box. I remember thinking, "What am I doing?!"'[82]

Hunter survived in Jenkins's first draft, but this was later amended when the decision to write Goodliffe out was made. 'When you sign on for a series, what you contribute is part what you want to publish, and part what you inherit,'[83] Jenkins said, 'and you inherit not just characters and assumptions about how stories are going to be made, but in fact a very highly-developed production unit, who have needs that are sometimes over and above what you want: maybe casting, maybe keeping somebody, maybe getting rid of somebody, and so on. Sometimes the alterations that take place are nothing to do with style or content, they're to do with production needs. My whole life as an active trade unionist in the Writers' Guild has been to try and stop that kind of control. [But] first time round, writing for a new company, there was a chance I was nervous about that: rather than asking questions, I was just taking things on. I'm sure [the need for change] must have been explained to me at one point.'

'It was during the days when casting directors knew when you were free and literally asked your agent,'[84] Kenneth Gilbert recalled. 'I did quite a lot of television during those years, and I knew Ted Woodward very well because we did seasons in 1958 at Stratford. Heather was the bad girl, and Hilary was a kind of girlfriend to Edward's character. I'd worked a couple of times with Bob Tronson, the director.

'I was aware I was working on a key episode that people would remember,' Gilbert continued, referring to Hunter's death. 'I enjoyed it, and I remember the night we filmed the shooting of Michael Goodliffe – we did it in a car park and my identity was covered up; I wasn't revealed as the killer until the end. It was bitterly, freezing cold and I remember Bob [Tronson] looking miserable: he was obviously feeling it more than anybody!' Gilbert watched the finished episode when it was transmitted: 'I do remember that shot of my approach to the car before I shot Michael Goodliffe, because they did it all with just the feet – the walking to the car, and then – *bang!'*

Goodliffe's departure from the series after only five episodes may have been due to the recurring mental illness that haunted the actor and a general aversion to violence. 'He'd been a prisoner of war ever since Dunkirk, until the end of the war, when he came out and made a good career for himself,'[85] Mike Vardy said. 'He was very well-used in movies and the theatre, but he used to get terrible bouts of depression which would floor him. He left *Callan* quite abruptly. We didn't know quite why, although he was a remote figure. In the rehearsal room, he would always sit on his own, staring out of the window, when he wasn't working; it was very difficult to get anywhere near him. As far as I could see, he didn't socialise with the rest of the cast.' 'Michael was a very private person, that didn't help when it came to cementing relationships,'[86] John Kershaw said sadly. 'He was isolated, he cut himself off,'[87] Peter Duguid added, agreeing that Goodliffe didn't take part in the camaraderie the other cast members enjoyed.

Tragically, in 1976 Goodliffe took his own life. 'He was in hospital being treated,'[88] Vardy explained, 'and it was one of those old-fashioned places where the fire escape goes down the outside of the building, there was a door at the end of the ward, and he walked out and just threw himself off. Awful. Just awful. He was a very fine actor.' 'I was so shocked when I heard he'd died, because he'd had these breakdowns,'[89] Clifford Rose said. 'He was such a good actor. I remember Ted mentioning something about him not enjoying [*Callan*] – without naming names, he just mentioned that things weren't going terribly well.'

Foreign media were continuing to pay attention to *Callan*, with one American reviewer noting: 'Small screen violence, video's most hotly-debated topic, doesn't seem to be inhibiting Thames TV, at least not so far as concerns this late-night counter-espionage strip... *Callan* dishes out the murder and mayhem with cold blooded, humourless efficiency, which would surely cause misgivings if slotted in primetime.'[90] *The Daily Telegraph* adopted an even more censorious tone, appending a fulminating byline 'Mass Killing in Sickening Serial' to its review. 'At once the most sickening, artificial and gripping of Independent television serials, [*Callan*] exceeded itself last night... With the cast much more than decimated there will have to be new faces next week.'[91] The reviewer concluded, 'It is original to kill off a leading character after only six [sic] episodes. But apparently Michael Goodliffe could only manage six, so next week there will be a new Hunter.'

This episode references Martin Bormann's 'escape' from Berlin in 1945. The belief that Hitler's private secretary had fled justice was widespread when 'Let's Kill Everybody' was written, and claims by German eye witnesses that he had died in Lehrter station in West Berlin remained unproven. The West German government put up a significant financial reward for his capture and conspiracy theories that Bormann was alive in South America thrived, even after remains matching his records were discovered during building work on the station in 1972. Even the iconic punk band the Sex Pistols got in on the act, alluding to the hunt for Bormann in the studio version of 'Belsen Was a Gas' (1978). DNA tests on the skeleton in the late 1990s are thought to have drawn a line under the case.

In the same week this episode was transmitted in most ITV regions, Sean Connery returned to the small screen, appearing in *Saturday Night Theatre* – 'MacNeil' (1969).

A trailer for this story survives, consisting of a montage of scenes from the episode.[92]

MISSION ANALYSIS: '*What is antisocial must be removed.*' A string of spies and/or scientists and/or industrialists being imaginatively killed off was a standby formula of *The Avengers* by the late 1960s, but there any resemblance to family-friendly escapism ends. Ray Jenkins nails the programme's style immediately, creating an atmosphere of unease and distrust and deploying sharp irony, with the two trustworthy-seeming establishment characters – an overworked, scatty academic and an avuncular surgeon – gradually revealed as ruthless, professional killers. Director Robert Tronson maximises the feeling of impending danger and urgency, with even the Lonely scenes, normally interior two-handers with Callan, taking place out on the street and on the move, firing bursts of information at the viewer. A post-operation Callan is ill at ease – or just plain ill – from the outset, mistakenly attacking Gould as he's unaware he's a Section agent.

The cast is uniformly impressive, from Canning and Gilbert's duplicitous killers to the excellent Hilary Dwyer, who movingly conveys the confused Jenny's dilemma. As well as continuing the convention that Callan's romantic liaisons all end fatally or badly, Jenkins also puts two strong female characters centre stage. Intriguingly, Jenny and Dr. Goodman are the complete opposite of each other: one innocent and exploited, the other ruthlessly professional. In a clever touch, nearly everything Dr. Goodman says has a double meaning.

There is some confusion in the story, as Hunter's 'double cover' orders to the Section's agents imply they'll all end up following each other around in circles, and there's also a question mark over whether Jenny knowing both Dr. Goodman and Walker is coincidental or not. In the end, however, these uncertainties add to the tension.

The closing action sequence is a little chaotic, but this adds to its realism. The sight of Callan's face bleeding after his forehead has been sliced by a stray bullet is another unexpected shock, as is the abrupt, open-ended conclusion. One of the series' most visceral episodes, 'Let's Kill Everybody' is particularly memorable as a poignant exit for Michael Goodliffe's dignified interpretation of Hunter.

S2.6 HEIR APPARENT

Writer: 'Hugh D'Allenger' (John Kershaw)
Director: Peter Duguid
Designer: Peter le Page

FIRST UK TRANSMISSION

Thames/LWT, Tyne Tees, Southern: Wednesday 12 February 1969, 10:45 pm
ATV, Anglia, Border, Channel, Granada, Harlech, Scottish, Westward, Yorkshire: 9:15 pm
Grampian: Saturday 15 February 1969 8:30 pm

CAST: Barbara Grimes (Harvey's secretary), Peter Cellier (Jenkins), Mario Zoppollini (Italian guard), Martin Lyder, Frans van Norde (East German guards)

PRODUCTION

Rehearsals: From Wednesday 15 May 1968
Location Filming: Teddington and Farnham (Forestry Commission)
(Thursday 9 May – Wednesday 15 May)
Camera Rehearsals/Recording: Teddington Studio One, Wednesday 22 and
Thursday 23 May 1968[93]

TV TIMES: 'Between Callan and Hunter – bitterness and a stretch of wasteland. Hunter is dead – long live Hunter! Callan is detailed to bring the new head of his department to England from behind the Iron Curtain in East Germany. Suspense mounts as the agents try to collect their man and bring him across the border in the face of sharp-shooting guards. With such deadly opponents, it seems that the Heir Apparent might not live to wear his crown...'
8-14 February 1969, Southern edition

MISSION PROFILE: Minutes after Hunter's funeral has finished, Callan and Meres are summoned to the Foreign Office. Sir Michael Harvey briefs them to escort a British agent, John Ramsay, safely back to Britain so he can take over as the new head of the Section. As Callan once trained with Ramsay, he is the logical choice for the job. After a hurried briefing, Callan and Meres set off abroad.

Ramsay plans to meet in a bunker on the border between East and West Germany, flanked by fences, forests and a supposedly defunct minefield. While Callan starts traversing it, mapping out a safe route, the border patrols by East German security forces unexpectedly increase. Callan throws a stone out of his path and this triggers a live mine; having arrived early, Ramsay witnesses the explosion and temporarily goes to ground. When he and Callan finally rendezvous in the bunker, they decide to wait until dark to escape, but the manhunt outside is intensifying. The pair are on the verge of being discovered when Meres stages a diversion. After a firefight that detonates more mines, the trio escape safely back to the West.

A MAN LIKE ME: Callan and Liz walk arm-in-arm after the church service, a hint he might have feelings for her. The funeral has clearly affected him: he says he's sick of the job, its dangers and the way it keeps him alone emotionally. He loses his temper with Meres' gallows humour and regrets that Hunter's wife has been made a widow. When Toby points out that Callan has made widows of a few wives himself, he recognises the contradiction but remains angry.

Callan defends Ferguson's memory and is worried about the mission; typically, Meres mocks him and recommends a more relaxed approach. Despite the tensions between the two agents, the operation in East Germany sees a further shift in their professional relationship – they have to rely on each other.

Ramsey trained with Callan – in at least one exercise at the army base in Catterick – but Callan is initially dismissive of his new chief, as the older man followed him 'around everywhere so he could get a feel for the danger', knowing that one day the 'top job' would be his. When Ramsey arrives at the pill box, Callan's relations with his new boss get off to an inauspicious start as he pulls a gun on him. As they talk, Callan reveals a grudging respect for Ramsey's fluency in German and for his skill in maintaining deep cover in Leipzig: 'At least when I go home, I know it's home.'

Callan is afraid of snakes.

Section Kills: 11

A TIE AND A CREST: Meres attempts to build bridges with Callan, and surprisingly even offers to buy him a drink, but is rebuffed. He's more in his element talking to Harvey, but can't help laughing when Callan sarcastically tells the Whitehall official they 'quite enjoyed' the violent struggle with Doctors Walker and Goodman. In a hint of things to come, the pair join forces in sending up the self-important, visiting landmine expert Captain Jenkins.

Callan moans about the public-school educated Ramsey's entitlement to be head of the Section and, predictably, Meres storms off as the other agent vents his inverted class snobbery.

ALCOHOL, TOBACCO AND FIREARMS: Meres raids the Section's whisky supply, pointedly not pouring Callan one, instead just placing a bottle and glass in front of him. ('Charming!' Callan says). Both men drink beer from Steins in a Bavarian bierkeller, Toby insisting on 'just one more' before they leave.

Callan uses the standard issue Magnum revolver while Meres favours a telescopic-sighted rifle. The East German guards use machine guns and rifles.

SPY-SPEAK: 'What is all the fuss about? You thought he was an idiot anyway!' Meres exclaims to Callan regarding the just buried Hunter, delivering one of the series' most blackly funny lines.

Continuing in this comic vein, Toby sarcastically informs the pompous military visitor Jenkins that Callan has popped out to see his mother.

'I don't think much of yours, old son,' he remarks of a hefty lady vacating a seat near to Callan in the Bierkeller, before complaining archly when Callan wants to arrive early at the rendezvous: 'What can we do stuck in a German ditch for eighteen hours?'

Ramsay reflects on his time in Communist East Germany: 'I was enjoying myself in Leipzig. Ran a sports shop amongst other things. Very keen, the Kraut.' 'Bully for him', comments Callan wryly.

The new Section commander shows he can be cool under pressure too, as he realises the East German security men are agitated. 'Aren't they just!' Callan says.

Perhaps subtly acknowledging that Meres is good at his job, Callan advises: 'Just you stay jumpy, mate, it's safer that way.'

Meres to Callan as he sets off into the border wasteland: 'I'll sit here and get on with the knitting.'

PAWNS AND PLAYERS: DEREK WILLIAM DOUGLAS BOND (1920-2006) was born in Glasgow but grew up in London, educated at the Haberdashers' Aske's Hampstead School. His first job was as a cub reporter with the *Golders Green Gazette*, but Bond switched from his initial career path to become an actor instead, firstly with the Finchley Amateur Dramatic Society then the Colchester Repertory Company. Bond's earliest TV role was in the BBC's short translation/adaptation of Karel Čapek's *R.U.R.* – the play that pioneered the word 'robot' – in 1938.

WW2 intervened soon afterwards. Serving with the Grenadier Guards, Bond was wounded in the thigh and consequently awarded a Military Cross during the North African campaign. Following recuperation in Britain, when he was offered work by Ealing Studios, Bond was posted back to his battalion but became incarcerated in a prison camp in Italy, where he put on shows for the other prisoners. After he was demobbed, he made his film debut playing a British POW only a year after he had been one – in *The Captive Heart* (1946). 'I got a telephone call asking me to lunch on the first weekend of leave that I had and to my amazement they offered me a contract,'[94] the actor recalled. 'They paid me a £2 per week retainer to help with my mess bills, which was a lot of money in those days. I went back and joined my battalion and got taken prisoner, and I flew back into England on VE day and was greeted by news from my then wife that Ealing had been on the phone all the time about a POW film... Six weeks later I was back in a prison camp, playing a part! I made a nuisance of myself saying, "We didn't do that!"' Bond went on to make a further impression in Ealing's production of *The Life and Adventures of Nicholas Nickleby* (1947) and as the ill-fated Captain Oates in *Scott of the Antarctic* (1948) with John Mills.

On stage, he performed in *Murder at the Vicarage* and *No Sex Please, We're British* and built a new career presenting documentaries like *Holiday Island* (BBC, 1959). He wrote an instalment of *Armchair Theatre* entitled 'Unscheduled Stop' (1968), and made further appearances on the big screen in the thriller *The Hand* (1960), the Norman Wisdom comedy *Press for Time* (1966) and the spy film *When Eight Bells Toll* (1971), alongside Anthony Hopkins and Corin Redgrave (see 'Amos Green Must Live', Chapter 7). Bond's guest roles on television included *H. G. Wells' Invisible Man*: 'Picnic with Death' (1959), the short-lived soap *199 Park Lane* (1965), Tommy Cooper's *Cooperama* (1966), *The Saint* – 'To Kill a Saint' (1967), *Dad's Army* (1972) and *Thriller* – 'The Next Scream You Hear' (1974).

In his later years, Bond became President of the actor's union Equity and clashed with Corin Redgrave and his sister Vanessa, as he controversially supported British actors who wanted to work in South Africa. Equity later voted to boycott the apartheid country and Bond resigned; his film and TV parts dried up in the 1980s, possibly as a result of the dispute. His comic memoir, *Steady Old Man! Don't You Know There's a War On?* was published in 1990, and Bond continued to take roles until the mid-1990s, when his war wound made him unsteady on his feet. He died on 15 October 2006 and was survived by his third wife Annie, a son from his first marriage and a daughter from his second.

ARTHUR JOHN WENTWORTH POWELL (1908-1989) played another character called Harvey in *No Hiding Place* – 'Victim of the Dark' (1960) and returned to perform several other parts in that series. He guested in *The Avengers* – 'Six Hands Across a Table' (1963), 'The Master Minds' (1965), *The Saint* – 'Sophia' (1964), *Undermind* – 'Song of Death' (1965), and as the father of Number 6's fiancé – another intelligence chief – in *The Prisoner* – 'Do Not Forsake Me, Oh My Darling' (1968). Often cast as Colonels, Doctors and members of the gentry, Wentworth went on to play Prime Minister Lloyd George in

The Edwardians (1973), later returning to the same address as Sir Henry Campbell-Bannerman in Terence Feely's *Number 10* – 'The Asquiths' (1983). He portrayed a church minister in *The Oblong Box* (1969), a school chaplain in the rather more comic *Ripping Yarns* – 'Tomkinson's Schooldays' (1976) and had a regular part as Henry Castleton in the legal drama *The Main Chance* (1969-1975), opposite John Stride's ambitious lawyer.

PETER CELLIER (born 1928) took the regular role of Judge Robinson in *Crown Court* between 1977 and 1982. In a lengthy career, his other performances have included *Keeping Up Appearances* (1990-91, as the Major), *Never The Twain* (1991) and *Brush Strokes* (1986). Cellier played the sinister Colonel Wright in *Thriller* – 'Someone at the Top of the Stairs' (1973) and a scientist who inadvertently bred a giant rat in *The New Avengers* – 'Gnaws' (1976). He also featured regularly as Sir Frank Gordon, the calculating Permanent Secretary of the Treasury in *Yes, Minister* (1981) and *Yes, Prime Minister* (1986-87). More recently, Cellier appeared in *The Crimson Petal and the White* (2011).

INFORMATION: The script was written in ten days, 'to a quite precise recipe that Reggie and I discussed at length,'[95] John Kershaw recalled. He based the character of the new Hunter on one of his wife's uncles, who had been best man at his wedding. 'He was a retired Air Vice Marshall, very nice fellow, Mountbatten's aide in the war. At the back of my mind, I was thinking about Callan and Hunter. I got home and looked through a Parliamentary booklet that had every MP and senior civil servant and his or her function listed in it. I got to "Head of Intelligence" – and it was this man's name!' Concerning the episode being credited to 'Hugh D'Allenger', he explained: 'there was a policy – largely formed by the Writers' Guild – that story editors mustn't commission themselves to write scripts, as it isn't fair. I quite agree with it... [But] because Michael Goodliffe had gone, we had to put someone else in and there wasn't time, with the scripts we had, to get anybody to rewrite a script to fit our requirements.' After seeking advice from his colleague George Markstein, a compromise was reached whereby Kershaw would use his two middle names.

The finalised camera script for this story contained an unprecedented eighteen pages of telecine as part of a deliberate strategy by the production team to introduce more diversity into the series. Reg Collin recalled that the studio-based, contained video approach was 'so boring that on this one we will do more on film and we'll fiddle the budget between the others to make sure it's possible... you have to ensure there's a variety.'[96] 'They wanted mines, they wanted machine guns firing and they wanted a helicopter,'[97] Peter le Page said. 'There was no way we could do that in the studio – although the interior of the bunker was in the studio – it had to be out on location. It was a big shoot. Looking at it now it's not a bad production.'

'It was mooted we'd go to West Germany and film, then they started doing the sums and realised it couldn't be done,'[98] Peter Duguid recollected. 'There was a lot of filming but we got held up, there was rain.. We had to stay three days longer than planned and it was a nightmare mounting the studio stuff. I had four days to rehearse to get the studio in. Because we were together as a unit for such a long time, nearly all the stuff was done in the same area in Farnham, in the Forestry Commission. There were a lot of nice memories from that. Teddy wrote a song, "Callan's Valley", about the location.'

Derek Bond remembered the rain too. 'We spent most of the time in a tent. I smuggled in a half bottle of Scotch which helped to restore morale a little!'[9]

Reg Collin attempted to visit the site to boost morale – 'I thought if the crew had to suffer I would suffer as well'[100] – but got lost. 'The path got narrower and narrower and muddier and the car got bogged down in mud. So I walked to the location... And it wasn't the location at all! It was a research station where they were catching moths. I never found the film unit that night.'

Edward Woodward also had very vivid memories of this shoot. 'At the end we had to run like hell, because we couldn't take these explosions coming up our bums any more!'[101]

'We had this special effects guy who was highly recommended,'[102] Peter Duguid recalled. 'He was mad, very difficult to control, and he set up these explosives and would "go" without being prompted... I never saw the rushes until transmission – and I could see this little bald man's head popping up!'

Peter Duguid's son Mark remembered that 'Heir Apparent" was his father's favourite episode. 'He certainly saw *Callan* and *Public Eye* as high points of his career, even though I don't think in general he was temperamentally all that well-suited to action stuff. I do remember he was particularly proud of "Heir Apparent" – particularly the sequence in which Callan is crawling through a minefield and sees a snake, and there's rapid cross-cutting zooms between Callan, the snake and a circling helicopter.'[103] Duguid Senior improvised this scene on location, clearly paying homage to a similar sequence in *Dr. No* (1962), in which Bond is threatened by a tarantula, and was particularly pleased with the end result.

'[Meres and Callan] started calling each by their first names,'[104] Anthony Valentine said of the change in the agents' relationship in this episode. 'They became very close, and presumably had that kind of a bond that people in extreme circumstances sometimes forge, almost in spite of themselves, because their dependence on each other is so great. They wouldn't necessarily admit that to themselves, and certainly wouldn't admit that to each other.'

The script implies the pillbox/bunker is located at a point a few kilometres east of Hof. At the time, the eastern side of the Inner German Border was one of the world's most heavily-fortified frontiers, patrolled by 50,000 armed East German guards with *Schießbefehl* – orders to fire at fugitives, making Callan's pre-emptive shooting of a guard understandable in context. Generally, trees and brush were cut down along the border, to clear lines of sight for the guards and in addition the *Signalzaun* fence would have been lined with low-voltage electrified barbed wire designed to sound an alarm if cut. The script carefully skirts round this obstacle with the inclusion of dialogue stating that on this stretch of the border, the fence is 'not wired'.

The series continued to get positive press coverage, long-term supporter Mary Malone welcoming Derek Bond to the *Callan* fold: 'Callan is a born boss-hater and Bond as the new Hunter may give him something solid to hate... His reminiscences in a dugout on the East German border over which Callan was ferrying him through landmine, shot and shell revealed a smoothie with a line in uppishness that already begins to be dislikeable.'[105]

Transmission was delayed in some regions due to a party political broadcast by the Conservative and Unionist Party.

MISSION ANALYSIS: *'Hunters come and go, but we go on forever.'* An atypical story right from the start as Liz, Callan and Meres attend their commander's burial; the two agents are then forced to work together on an equal footing as, unusually, their dysfunctional relationship becomes the focus of the episode. With no Section Chief and no Lonely, Meres becomes the person to have heated arguments with about the mission, as well as providing the story's humour. From a fractious exchange about how dangerous life in the Section is becoming

– a running theme in the second series – through several wisecracks and (slightly contrived) rows, this unlikely partnership finally bonds in the face of adversity. Notably, the scenario anticipates the mismatched buddy team-ups in the hit movie *Butch Cassidy and the Sundance Kid* (1969) and, on television, *The Persuaders!* (1971-72). The continued repositioning of Meres can only go so far, however: his murderous side soon resurfaces when he starts swearing at the patrols and aiming his rifle at them. The final scene, featuring an exhausted Callan and Meres preparing to depart with their boss in a car following a shoot-out, predates by several years the conclusion of several instalments of the action series *The Professionals* (1977-1983).

The other regular characters are equally well-served by the script. Liz – clearly shy, nervous and worried about being in the limelight, rather like the actress playing her – becomes an audience identification figure, nervously waiting for news. Also featured in various 'They also serve who stand and wait' scenes are Sir Michael Harvey and his own rather more prim secretary. Initially officious-seeming, Harvey is presented as a sentimental family friend of the previous Hunter, genuinely worried about the safety of Callan and Meres. Later events in the series will compel the audience to re-evaluate many of his scenes here.

The large amount of location filming and emphasis on action also reinforce this episode's unusual feel. It may also have been part of a deliberate plan to attract new viewers in the wake of the previous week's 'shock death' episode, as this is as mainstream and accessible a spy story as *Callan* ever delivers. The use of Cold War motifs like a helicopter, barbed wire border and a minefield, together with the plot of smuggling an agent out of unfriendly territory, brings to mind several episodes of *Danger Man*. The story also draws on the audience's factual memories of WW2 and general collective suspicions of jack-booted authority figures demanding to see papers, familiar from then-recent films such as *The Great Escape* (1963) and *The Spy Who Came in from the Cold* (1965).

Alternatively, the playing safe with spy fiction conventions, as well as the unprecedented amount of location filming, may simply have been because 'Heir Apparent' was written in a hurry to explain the replacement of Michael Goodliffe. It's notable that the only main studio sets used are the Section HQ and Harvey's office, supplemented by minimal set-ups for a bierkeller, train carriage and the bunker. With limited time available and access to studio time restricted, it made sense to base the story around a major film location.

The helicopter crew and border patrols not noticing that a mine has recently been detonated, or that their fence now has a three-foot wide gap in it, are notable plot holes, but excusable given Kershaw didn't have long to write the script. Overall, 'Heir Apparent' succeeds in its main objectives of giving a strong introduction to Derek Bond's Hunter and fleshing out three of the surviving regulars.

An interesting departure from the norm, this is a significant episode in the overall evolution of *Callan* as a long running series, surprising the audience with some unexpected and welcome character development. In particular, it shows that Callan's new double act with Meres could be just as memorable as his emerging one with Lonely.

S2.7 LAND OF LIGHT AND PEACE

Writer: James Mitchell
Director: Piers Haggard
Designer: Mike Hall

FIRST UK TRANSMISSION:

Thames/LWT, Tyne Tees, Southern: Wednesday 19th February 1969, 10:30 pm
ATV, Anglia, Border, Channel, Granada, Harlech, Scottish, Westward, Yorkshire: 9:00 pm
Grampian: Saturday 22nd February 1969 8:30 pm

CAST: Betty Marsden (Miss Hogg), Alan Cullen (Geoffrey Gleeson), Avril Elgar (Jane Ellis), Ian Cooper (Markinch), Wensley Pithey (Detective Inspector Charwood), Bruce Purchase (Detective Sergeant Lynn), John Barrard (Sir Bruce Ingoe), Robin Lloyd (Sir Bruce's secretary)

EXTRAS/WALK-ONS: *(Uncredited on screen)* Lisa Doran, Cathleen Heath, Rex Rashley, Peta Collins, Mary Warden, Iris Fry, Harry Douglas (Séance attendees), June Turner (Waitress), Derek Chafer, John James (Lorry Drivers doubling as policemen), Ali Hassan (Lorry driver), Kelly Grant (Secretary)

PRODUCTION

Camera Rehearsals/Recording: Teddington Studio One, Wednesday 8 and
Thursday 9 May 1968.[106]

TV TIMES: 'Callan sees the light but misses out on the peace. Is the "League of Light" a *bona fide* spiritualist organisation, or do the ectoplasm and unearthly manifestations cover more sinister activities? Callan dabbles in the occult to call up the truth.'
15-21 February 1969, London edition

MISSING FILE: The master tapes of this episode do not exist in the FremantleMedia archive.

MISSION PROFILE: Missile plans have been leaked from a Ministry of Defence (MOD) office and co-workers Geoffrey Gleeson and Jane Ellis are suspected. The couple live separately, but regularly attend the League of Light, a spiritual/religious gathering hosted by Miss Hogg. Callan infiltrates the group. Gleeson owns a safe, which Callan and Meres break into, but the clerk unexpectedly comes home. Meres knocks him out and he dies because of a weak heart. The agents are forced to flee the scene.

Detective Inspector Charwood investigates the break in. Jane deliberately points him in Callan's direction. Charwood takes Callan's fingerprints off a teaspoon in a cafe, matches them with the agent's past criminal record and accuses him of the murder.

Meres finds incriminating microfilm on Miss Hogg. However, six critical frames are missing, as Jane has withheld them to get more money.

Callan confronts her and angrily threatens to shoot her unless she hands over the missing film. She does so, admitting her and Geoffrey's guilt.

Charwood finds fibres from Callan's sweater at the crime scene, but receives orders from the Home Office to drop his case.

A MAN LIKE ME: Callan uses his locksmith training to study the manufacturer's plans for the safe and calculate the best point to drill into it.

Well aware of Meres's tendency towards disproportionate violence, he instinctively knows something is wrong after his colleague has hit Gleeson, stopping to check the unfortunate clerk for a pulse despite a jibe about 'Florence Nightingale'. Having 'form', Callan immediately recognises the amount of trouble he is in with Charwood, and finds Hunter's off-hand reassurances unconvincing.

Clearly driven by not wanting to serve another prison sentence, and viewing Jane as a devious hypocrite who never loved her partner, he threatens to 'belt' her and goes on to hold her at gunpoint and terrify her into a confession. However, after she has handed him the missing piece of microfilm and broken down in tears, his attitude to her softens.

LONELY: Absent for the second episode running. He is 'visiting' her Majesty and won't be out for ten days. Callan wanted to employ him on the robbery, so Lonely is clearly an even better safebreaker than the agent.

A TIE AND A CREST: Thurlow's of Threadneedle Street are not keen on divulging their trade secrets to Callan and Meres, only doing so because the firm have received an introductory letter from Hunter.

The Section chief is reluctant to take any formal action to help Callan until there is no alternative. Meres visits the fake medium posing as a bereaved upper-class man with more money than sense.

ALCOHOL, TOBACCO AND FIREARMS: Charwood finds four bottles of Scotch in Callan's kitchen cupboard.

SPY-SPEAK: Meres's callous reaction to finding out he has killed Gleeson: 'What a bloody nuisance!'

Callan: 'Do you think it's all light and peace on the other side?' Meres: 'Perhaps he'll tell you at the next meeting.'

Jane says she hates Callan. 'A lot of people do,' he replies.

PAWNS AND PLAYERS: WENSLEY PITHEY (1914-1993) played heavyweight authority figures for several decades on stage and screen. Originating from South Africa, he performed Shakespeare plays with his own company before moving to Britain. On television, Pithey was known for his portrayal of the eponymous Detective Superintendent in *Mister Charlesworth*, *Charlesworth at Large*, *Big Guns* (all 1958) and *Charlesworth* (1959). He later portrayed ballistics analyst Robert Churchill in *Call the Gun Expert* (1964), a historical documentary-drama series for the BBC which predated the channel's later forensic series *The Expert* (1968-1976). On the big screen, he was the taciturn 'Pop' in the remarkable spot-the-up-and-coming-A-lister movie *Hell Drivers* (1957). Later guest turns include *The Saint* – 'Starring the Saint' (1963, as Inspector Teal) and *Return of The Saint* – 'Collision Course' (1979). He took the regular roles of Wilfred Perkins in *Coronation Street* (1973-74) and another policeman, Detective Superintendent Tom Eden, in the first series of *Special Branch* (1969), which was made by some of the same production team as *Callan*. He also appeared in *Beasts* – 'Special Offer' (1976), *Poldark* (1975, minus his trademark moustache) and Dennis Potter's 1950s drama *Lipstick on Your Collar* (1993).

BEATRICE 'BETTY' MARSDEN (1919-1998) needs no introduction to comedy fans, having appeared in *Carry on Regardless* (1961) as Mata Hari and *Carry on Camping* (1969). On stage, she starred in *The Importance of Being Earnest* and Joe Orton's risqué farce *What the Butler Saw* (1969), while on radio she supplied all the female voices, including that of Dame Celia Molestrangler, in *Round the Horne* (1965-1968). She later performed in sketches with *French and Saunders* (1987) and can be seen playing Dot – Rita Tushingham's mother – in the cult gay biker flick *The Leather Boys* (1960). A guest role in *Blake's 7* saw her playing a very arch slave-trader trying to out-camp Jacqueline Pearce's Servalan in 'Assassin' (1981). More serious roles included *The Memoirs of Sherlock Holmes* – 'The Red Circle' (1994) and *Inspector Morse* – 'The Sins of the Fathers' (1990).

JOHN BARRARD (1924-2013) had small roles in *Peeping Tom* (1960), *The Saint* – 'The Pearls of Peace' (1962), *The Avengers* – 'Fog' (1969) and as a shopkeeper in *Doctor Who* – 'The Reign of Terror' (1964). He made cameos in various sitcoms including *Blackadder* (1983, as a Morris Dancer), *Whoops Apocalypse* (1982, as a hapless American tourist) and *One Foot In The Grave* (1990).

AVRIL ELGAR (born 1932) appeared in *Dixon of Dock Green* (1964 and 1964), *Public Eye* – 'I Always Wanted a Swimming Pool' (1971), the superior children's serial *Carrie's War* (1974) and, more recently, *Waking The Dead* (2003) and *New Tricks* (2004).

ALAN CULLEN featured in *Public Eye* – 'If This Is Lucky, I'd Rather Be Jonah' (1968) and 'They All Sound Simple at First' (1975). He reappears as a different character in 'Where Else Could I Go?' (see Chapter 7).

INFORMATION: The camera script makes it clear that Miss Hogg is 'cold reading' Meres – analysing his body language and apparel to deduce his character, while he is doing exactly the same to her.

This was the first story to be recorded with Derek Bond as the third Hunter. The transmission order of episodes differing from the order of production was, Reg Collin explained, 'standard procedure. If two people are writing scripts for me and one delivers on 1 October and the other on 1 November, let's say, and then there is a problem, and one is late but the other can be delivered early... [the order would change].'[107] Bond soon settled in, remembering, 'The nice thing about Hunter, no matter who's doing it, is he sets up the scene. It's slightly tedious in that sense to set the story up. They've become much better at [exposition] in television recently. But the way we took the curse off that was the friendly antagonism.'[108] It's evident that only minimal rewriting to accommodate the new character was done, with Callan soon becoming annoyed at his superior's off-handedness.

This is the first story that specifically refers to Callan's past conviction for safe breaking. Peter Mitchell recalled his father 'romanticised'[109] occupations like Callan's: 'Jack Ford [in *When the Boat Comes In*] wasn't just a fitter, he was the best fitter who ever lived, and Callan was a very, very good locksmith. [Dad] had a big respect for people who worked with their hands.'

'It's a bluff and I think he's scaring [Miss Hogg],'[110] Piers Haggard considered of the harrowing climax in the cinema. 'I think we made it look quite scary, because if *she* was scared, the audience would be scared. It's interesting, because it's a typical Callan killer touch: he's prepared to get his hands dirty and push it further than most people would.

Of course, he's our hero; but for a hero, he's near the edge.'

Mediums became popular in the 19th century in the United States and United Kingdom after the rise of Spiritualism as a religious movement. After the many and varied fraud cases brought against mediums concerning so-called materialization séances, involving testimony from sceptical public figures such as Robert Browning and the magician Harry Houdini, the movement fell into disrepute, although it underwent a revival in the 1960s along with other 'spiritual' beliefs such as astrology, Hinduism and Taoism. Krishna is mentioned in the script; Hare Krishna had been popularised previously by The Beatles in their psychedelic hit 'I Am the Walrus' in 1967 and the Broadway Musical *Hair* (in the same year).

Jane Ellis and Geoffrey Gleeson are reminiscent of two people involved in the Portland Spy Ring. Harry Houghton was an employee at the Underwater Detection Establishment (UDE) in Portland, Dorset, who had drink and marriage problems and sympathised politically with Soviet Russia. After getting divorced, be began a relationship with a record keeper at UDE, Ethel 'Bunty' Gee. She regularly let him handle classified documentation far above his security level, and he in turn smuggled it out of the establishment to pass on to his KGB handlers in London. The thefts were financially as well as politically motivated and continued until an MI5 investigation discovered the group (see 'Death of a Hunter' and Chapter 9).

MISSION ANALYSIS: *'Give me the stuff or I'll kill you.'* Once again, James Mitchell delivers a harrowing script, exploring another facet of how far Callan will go to protect himself – in this case he threatens to shoot an unarmed woman in cold blood. Other series generally take pains to make clear such threats are a bluff; in *Callan* there is much less reassurance.

The casting of Wensley Pithey, a familiar actor from various *policiers* of the time, as Charwood (even his character's name is reminiscent of his previous roles) is a clever touch, putting Callan in a position comparable to a villain in one of Pithey's detective series. As in 'The Little Bits and Pieces of Love', naïve people become embroiled in the Section's plans with unpleasant consequences, and as in 'A Magnum for Schneider', Callan faces the threat of jail in a scenario involving the robbery of a safe and the death of its owner.

The conclusion of the story is classic Mitchell: the Home Secretary orders the prosecution to be dropped as it involves a matter of state security, and a furious Charwood has to return the forensic evidence to Callan, enraged that he can't convict him. The Section pressuring the police to derail an investigation is another intriguing idea that would be expanded on in *Callan*'s third series (see 'Summoned To Appear', Chapter 7).[106]

These grim concepts are offset by some very mordant humour, with even the title being ironic: Charwood is kept in the dark and Gleeson is the only person truly at peace. As soon as the police enter the scene, the mystical trappings of the séance plotline are abruptly and knowingly sidelined in favour of the real world. The irony continues as the hunt for a missing piece of film actually concludes in a cinema, and with the revelation that Jane, while being manipulative enough to deceive the experienced Charwood, is still also naive and reclusive enough to be taken in by Miss Hogg's *faux* mysticism, just like the other League members.

Amusingly there are some slight hints of ambiguity around this unlikely Spiritualist KGB agent. Miss Hogg predicts someone who 'lives alone' should worry about their health – which could refer to either Callan, Gleeson or Jane. In a skilful piece of misdirection, in one scene she seems to be psychically learning of problems in the MOD, only for it to be revealed that she is the one actually responsible for conveying microfilm to the Russians. A further irony is that while apparently speaking in tongues she sings 'Georgie Porgie', which may indicate genuine precognition. This nursery rhyme about a boy who, like Callan, makes girls cry, is thought to relate to the Duke of Buckingham, a dubious character absolved from much of his behaviour by his powerful friends in high places. Psychic phenomena had previously been popularised on UK television through the ABC dramas *Mystery and Imagination* (1966-1970) and *Haunted* (1967, starring Patrick Mower).

Overall, 'Land of Light and Peace' is an interesting example of Mitchell mischievously referencing other genres, while delivering a characteristically hard-hitting story that reveals tantalising details about Callan's past.

S2.8 BLACKMAILERS SHOULD BE DISCOURAGED

Writer: James Mitchell
Director: Jim Goddard[107]
Designer: David Marshall

FIRST UK TRANSMISSION

Thames/LWT, Tyne Tees, Southern: Wednesday 26 February 1969, 22:30
ATV, Anglia, Border, Channel, Granada, Harlech, Scottish, Westward, Yorkshire: 21:00
Grampian: Monday 3 March 1969, 23:00

CAST: Bernard Whitehorn (Toastmaster), Nicholas Selby (Sir Gerald Naylor), Karin MacCarthy (Lady Naylor), John Arnatt (High Commissioner), Barry Andrews (Todd), John Franklyn-Robbins (Richie), Denis Thorne (Benson), John Woodnutt (Bishop)

EXTRAS/WALK-ONS: (*Uncredited on screen*) Peter Lund, Max Latimer (Laycock and Turner), Dennis Balcome, Michael Radd (Photographers), Ray Marioni, Louis Raynes (Waiters), Unknown (others in Reception and Restaurant scenes).

PRODUCTION

Rehearsals: From Friday 7 June 1968
Location Filming: Teddington Cemetery
Camera Rehearsals/Recording: Teddington Studio Two, Tuesday 18 and
Wednesday 19 June 1968[108]

TV TIMES: 'For some people the past is all they think of – for others it's more than they can forget. Sir Gerald Naylor is about to take up a senior position with the Canadian Atomic Corporation and must have an impeccable background to satisfy the authorities. When an anonymous letter throws suspicion on Gerald's past, Callan is asked to investigate.'
23-28 February 1969, Southern edition

MISSING FILE: The master tapes of this story do not exist in the FremantleMedia archive.

MISSION PROFILE: The anonymous letter to the High Commission reads: '*Sir Gerald Naylor is a Communist traitor. His sexual activities are disgusting.*' As Naylor is moving to Canada and taking charge of the Nuclear Research Division of the Three Power Atomic Project, the Section are asked to make enquiries. Callan introduces himself to Naylor and his attractive young wife at a formal dinner. He brings up the allegations openly, reasoning that if they're true, the public servant will react. Naylor is angry but also worried, prompting Callan to delve deeper. He searches Naylor's flat and finds a hidden photograph of Naylor with two other men in their Cambridge university days.

Callan tracks down one of them, Ritchie, who reveals Naylor had male lovers in the past, including the third man in the photo, Ian Bishop. Naylor and Bishop visited Spain together in 1936 during the Civil War, but only the latter got involved politically. Before leaving, Callan uses Ritchie's typewriter to check he wrote the incriminating note.

Getting more information from another associate, Benson, Callan and Hunter realise Bishop is a KGB agent. Callan confronts Naylor and tells him the Russians have been cultivating him as a target for three decades, waiting for sufficient leverage – namely,

Naylor marrying and achieving a career post sensitive to blackmail. Naylor admits that Bishop has now got back in touch and, with no other choice, helps the Section capture his former lover.

A MAN LIKE ME: Callan wears what he refers to as a 'monkey [dinner] suit'; Hunter tells him his medal is too blatant. The Section agent is short to the point of unpleasantness on several occasions with Naylor, firstly when telling him he will be 'retired' for overwork if the allegations aren't too serious, and later, when pushing to get Naylor to admit his homosexual past.

Naylor's wife is perceptive enough to realise Callan is trouble and he remains immune to her appeals. He expects her to stand by Naylor, and feels genuinely sorry for the man when he decides he cannot recommend him for the post in Canada.

LONELY: Todd, a villain who knows Lonely recently burgled Big Mike Kennedy's flat, has been extorting money from him. The crook smashes a Dresden China cup that Lonely was fond of. Callan deals with the situation by abducting Todd and giving him a beating.

A TIE AND A CREST: Callan is said to be with the Foreign Office, in a 'shady' sort of way; the Section appears to be known about, as an unpleasant necessity. Callan thinks the nearest the affluent Naylor got to Communism was the Liberal Club.

There is little in the way of friction with the Section in this episode, except when Hunter finds Callan sitting in his a chair and unwisely sneaks up on him – Callan jumps up and pulls a gun on his commander. (While it is easy to read too much into this, in light of later events it could be seen as cleverly foreshadowing the end of the second series.)

ALCOHOL, TOBACCO AND FIREARMS: On edge, Naylor downs three drinks after his first meeting with Callan; later, he throws another one over the Section man.

Benson is a habitual drunk who prioritises Scotch over food. The Section are clearly confident he won't even remember talking to them.

Callan advises Lonely to stop worrying and go to the off licence.

SPY-SPEAK: Callan studies the letter: 'He gets an awful lot out of ten words, this bloke. I bet he sends marvellous telegrams.' Regarding the 'disgusting sexual activities,' he sarcastically wonders if he should ask Naylor's wife about them.

In his smart apparel, Callan ironically reflects, 'You've come a long way since the Scrubs,' just after he's intimidated someone.

Lonely's question, 'That you, Mr. Callan?' earns the retort, 'No, it's Snow White – and I've brought the seven dwarfs round for coffee!'

PAWNS AND PLAYERS: JAMES 'BIG JIM' GODDARD (1936-2013) joined ABC in 1959, initially working as a production designer on *The Avengers* and *Armchair Theatre* before training to become a director. 'I trained as a painter and while I was trying to work up a few relationships with galleries, I met people in Covent Garden who used to paint props for sets,'[109] he explained. 'They asked me to go and work for them, as they needed someone who could draw and paint, as they were working with a whiz kid Italian director. I was a bit reluctant, I'd never been in the theatre, but I did it and it turned out to be [Franco] Zeffirelli doing his first production in England. Through him I met [Luchino] Visconti and got the bug for directing. I went into commercial television in 1958, with the idea of becoming a director but I had to start as an Assistant Draftsman.' Like several *Callan* colleagues he worked on *Tempo* and *Sat'day While Sunday*; Goddard also became close friends with writer Trevor Preston (see 'Jack-on-Top', page 208). 'Jim and I did a simulation of taking acid for *Tempo* with R. D. Laing,'[110] Preston recalled. 'We used all these weird anamorphic lenses. If that film was around now, it would win every award going. It was all done in a little white studio called Studio 3. White spiral staircase, white table, white chair, white packet of fags, and all the people came down and sat in the chairs. We took this montage of images and put it together, and it was bloody good. Then they burnt the negative! They were *terribly* conservative in television – they still are.' 'It was never hard work if you were working with someone like Jim Goddard,'[111] Russell Hunter said in praise of his former colleague.

Having established himself as a practised studio director whose track record included *Public Eye*, *Man at the Top* (1971-72), *Budgie* (1971-72), and early *Special Branch* (1969-1970), Goddard was another obvious candidate to direct *The Sweeney* under Euston Films' radical new system of production. He later collaborated with Trevor Preston on *Out* (1978) and *Fox* (1981) and with Troy Kennedy Martin on the prestigious *Reilly – Ace of Spies* (1983) for the same company, striving to mix a 'high art'[112] style with the populist thriller format.

NICHOLAS SELBY (1925-2010) played an extremist politician in the ironically banned *Doomwatch* episode 'Sex and Violence' (1972) and 'peers of the realm' in *In the Secret State* (1985) and *Our Friends in the North* (1996). As hapless Lord Billsborough in *House of Cards* (1990) he fell foul of Francis Urquhart's machinations, while in *Poldark* he portrayed Nicholas Warleggan (1975).

JOHN WOODNUTT (1924-2006) appeared in *The Tomorrow People* (1973), *Children of the Stones* (1977) and several *Doctor Who* episodes, including a dual role as a Scottish Duke and an alien warlord in Robert Banks Stewart's 'Terror of the Zygons' (1975). The prolific character actor's comic turn as the plastered surgeon 'Doc' Clare in *The Sweeney* – 'Stay Lucky Eh? '(1975) echoes his role in 'Blackmailers Should Be Discouraged'. Other credits include *The Saint* – 'Luella' (1964), *The Avengers* – 'Quick-Quick Slow Death' (1966), *The Corridor People* – 'Victim as Red' (1966) and *Spindoe* (1968).

JOHN EDWIN ARNATT (1917-1999) was born in Petrograd in Russia; his family fled to Britain during the 1917 Revolution. Another wintry 'authority' actor, his roles included regular inquiry agent Sidney Bulmer in legal drama *The Main Chance* (1969-70), *The Saint* – 'The Arrow of God' (1962), *Randall and Hopkirk (Deceased)* – 'Could You Recognise the Man Again?' (1970) and the Terence Feely scripted *Thriller* – 'Sign It Death' (1974).

Both Arnatt and John Franklin Robbins (1924-2009) played Time Lords in *Doctor Who*; Robbins featured as regular Bill Adler in *Softly Softly: Task Force* (1972-73), interpreted MI5's real-life interrogator William Skardon in the factual drama *Atom Spies* (1979) and played another cleric, in Nigel Kneale's chilling adaptation of *The Woman in Black* (1989).

INFORMATION: This story saw Russell Hunter returning to the fold. 'Lonely didn't appear in every episode because I think he was too much competition for the main man!'[113] Russell Hunter joked about his break. 'I remember when I did come back it was greeted with joy! "Hey, the wee feller's back!", which was nice. It was a programme on which I felt my character was wanted.'

Derek Bond enjoyed working with Jim Goddard and was subsequently godfather to the director's daughter. Sporting a 'white tie and tails'[114] in early scenes in the story, he remembered, 'I was always pleased in the script when I could get out of that bloody awful office!' Regarding the story's subject matter, he recalled it being 'slightly daring then – but none of us got self-conscious about it.' James Mitchell said the storyline 'had to be cleared upstairs – there was a certain amount of worry about it. But as [homosexuality] was appearing in the papers at fairly regular intervals anyway, it was logical.'[115] 'In those days people were still prosecuted,'[116] John Kershaw said. 'Lord Montagu was found with a young man and it was a terrible scandal. The whole business of "coming out" did not exist at all. It was something that was unacceptable. If ever homosexuals were presented in those days they were terribly effeminate and camp. Clearly Callan, with his gun and wild temper, couldn't be one.'

Even after the reforms made under the Sexual Offences Act in Britain in 1967, homosexuality was still seen as an absolute bar to receiving the positive vetting required to carry out any classified work, such as in the nuclear industry. This policy remained in place until the 1990s and adds rationale to Naylor's silence. Parliament was also perceived to be a sensitive area; a 'Stop Jeremy' whispering campaign brewed up against the late Jeremy Thorpe (1928-2014) MP among Liberals in the Commons tea room when he ran for the Party leadership in 1967. (As it later turned out, Thorpe *had* actually been a blackmail target, and subsequent events involving the shooting of a dog in Devon belonging to Thorpe's alleged lover by an alleged hitman could almost *be* a *Callan* story.)

This story also indirectly references the 'Cambridge Five' – the spy ring that included Kim Philby, Donald Duart Maclean, Guy Burgess and Anthony Blunt (who later received a knighthood as Surveyor of the Queen's Pictures). The group (like Naylor and Bishop) were educated in 1930s Cambridge, and viewed the Soviet cause as the only alternative to the emergent Fascism in Germany and Spain.

The Spanish Civil War (1936-39) broke out when General Francisco Franco started seizing control of the country with Nazi support. Socialists, Communists and Anarchists all sided against Franco, aided by volunteers from the United States, Britain, France, Belgium, Germany and Italy who made up the anti-Fascist International Brigades. The writer George Orwell (1903-1950) fought in the conflict, a historical detail alluded to when Hunter tells Benson to 'cut out the journalism'.

Remembering his father's fascination with the country, which also featured in *When the Boat Comes In* and his final *Callan* novel *Bonfire Night*, Peter Mitchell said, 'The period when he went to Spain after leaving university was a period he relived and relived and relived, and retold time and again, because it was Spain under Franco, it was Spain before the tourists got there, it was Spain when it was very cheap to live there. That was when he fell in love with Spain. Later he was to buy property there, and learnt a little Spanish. He loved the food, the culture, the music.'[117]

MISSION ANALYSIS: *'You've taken everything I've ever had.'* This story has similarities to Mitchell's 'But He's A Lord, Mr. Callan' but moves the focus onto the blackmail victim rather than the perpetrator. Overall, this is radical for its time – Naylor's sexuality is dealt with in a matter of fact way and Callan is certainly not critical of it; the situation is simply that the peer's secret life has made him vulnerable. As Callan points out to Naylor during the first of their two-handed scenes, it's what the administrator might divulge in future that is the Section's concern, not his past. Ultimately Naylor seems powerless; he cannot even threaten to take

Callan to court for breaking into his flat because this could theoretically lead to his secret being exposed.

Ritchie writing his poison pen letter is a clever twist that subverts the usual TV stereotype of the genteel vicar. He seems to have done this to avenge an old sexual rejection. Callan advises him to stop his 'muck raking', clearly disliking this garrulous meddler.

Naylor's sentimentality proves to be his undoing in the end. He secretly keeps a photograph of Bishop, has married a much younger woman from a poor, God-fearing background, well aware that she really only wants his money. Once Naylor has lost the Canada posting, she walks out on him, and then he has to watch as the male love of his life is arrested. While the story appears to support the establishment view of what was the *status quo* concerning gay men at the time, its conclusion is characteristically challenging.

When Naylor tells Callan that his life is ruined, it's hard not to feel sympathy.

S2.9 DEATH OF A FRIEND

Writer: Ray Jenkins
Director: Peter Duguid
Designer: Vic Symonds

FIRST UK TRANSMISSION

Thames/LWT, Southern: Wednesday 5 March 1969, 10.30 pm
ATV, Anglia, Border, Channel, Granada, Harlech, Scottish, Westward, Yorkshire: 9.00 pm
Grampian: Monday 10 March 1969, 11.00 pm

CAST: Geoff Cheshire (Jean Coquet), John Devaut (Messmer), Barry Stanton (Lambert), Ann Lynn (Francine), Jerome Willis (Flomard), Rex Robinson (Mason), David Leland (Latour), Lawrence Trimble (Wilson), Maryann Turner (Hospital Sister)

EXTRAS/WALK-ONS: (*Uncredited on screen,* from the David Agency) 'as guards, hospital attendants, nurse, hotel manager, assistant manager, hotel porter, hotel guest [and] mortuary assistant': Dennis Balcombe, Peter Durrent, Arthur Zan, John Beardcombe, Pat Travis, Leslie Weekes, Patricia Fleming

PRODUCTION

Rehearsals: From Saturday 30 March 1968
Location Filming: Dover Harbour (Thursday 28 March), Elcom St, Paddington (Friday 29 March 1968)
Camera Rehearsals/Recording: Teddington Studio One, Wednesday 10 and Thursday 11 April 1968.[118]

TV TIMES: 'A Frenchman dies in England and the OAS wipe off an old score. But can the suffering end? When a French intelligence man is killed in a mysterious crash in England, the French authorities send an agent to investigate the "accident". Callan finds that the agent is an old friend, and together they follow a tortuous and dangerous trail to find the truth behind the death.'
Southern edition, 1-7 March 1969

MISSION PROFILE: Jean Coquet, a French counter-intelligence agent working undercover as a financial correspondent, crashes his car and dies on the road between Dover and London – he was drugged. Coquet's widow Francine reveals to Callan that her husband had been living with Marcel Latour, a minor ministry official helping Coquet research the French terrorist organisation the OAS. Francine is kidnapped from her hotel room and Callan is knocked out. Latour visits Callan's flat, but when Meres collects him, the Frenchman is fatally wounded by a bomb thrown from a car – after hiding Coquet's documents on the new OAS in Callan's kitchen. Francine is really working with the OAS and had plotted the deaths of both her husband and Latour, whom she believed to be lovers. When she's intercepted with her OAS accomplices at Dover, Callan relishes telling her that Coquet was still in love with her.

A MAN LIKE ME: Callan can speak French. Jean Coquet was a friend, even though in general the Section man distrusts French intelligence as 'they've double-crossed me before.' He doesn't like Francine as she's 'too dedicated... to everything – except her husband.'

Revealingly, Callan thinks he's 'nothing' in intelligence. Even though he says he might not have feelings 'any more', he's clearly affected by the death of Coquet. Significantly, Callan is again portrayed as non-homophobic. He is sympathetic to Latour and remorseless in venting his anger at Francine: 'No wonder your husband left you, darling!'

LONELY: In debt again: he scrounges 'a fiver' off Callan otherwise he'll be 'cut up in little bits.' Even in this highly excitable state, Lonely has spotted two men staking out Callan's flat and is able to give him accurate descriptions of both. According to Callan, Lonely makes tea that tastes like 'pig swill'. He locks Latour in Callan's flat and tells him he's a prisoner but, comically, it looks like the reverse is true. When the Frenchman holds him at gunpoint, the petty criminal confesses he 'likes living'.

A TIE AND A CREST: Meres is both homophobic and disdainful towards the French, so Latour receives a double dose of contempt.

The Section's hierarchy is again in evidence: ordered by Hunter to leave the clean-up of his flat, that's just been trashed by OAS agents, Callan orders Lonely to tidy it up to earn the £5 he's just been given.

ALCOHOL, TOBACCO AND FIREARMS: In his meeting with Hunter, French intelligence chief Flomard takes wine while the Section commander sips whisky. After he's been knocked out, Meres asks for a brandy and receives the 'very finest Cognac'. Francine orders two 'big' Scotches from room service for her and Callan.

Latour nervously pulls a revolver on Lonely.

SPY-SPEAK: Callan reflects on his dead friend Coquet: '[He] got his medals putting down the OAS. There are lots of rebels alive today that'll be very glad he's dead.'

Flomard is under no illusion about the delicate political situation in France: 'Extremely influential and very rich men are poised on our borders waiting to move back in, and they can afford revenge.'

Meres gives full vent to his homophobia, describing Latour as 'very pretty' with 'abnormalities'. When the Frenchman confesses he's scared, Meres says that he should 'try and be big and brave.' Later, Meres paints a horrible picture of the treatment Francine will face in a French prison: 'electric bars, wine bottles in unfamiliar places, urine baths...'

PAWNS AND PLAYERS: ELIZABETH ANN LYNN (born 1939) was briefly married to the singer Anthony Newley, star of the bizarre, surreal comedy *The Strange World of Gurney Slade* (1960). Lynn's film roles include the gothic tale *The Black Torment* (1964) and the comedies *Doctor in Distress* (1963) and *A Shot in the Dark* (1964). A strong performer in the burgeoning world of television film series, Lynn was a popular choice for the ITC stable, appearing in *Danger Man* (1965), *The Saint* – 'When Spring is Sprung' (1967) and *The Champions* – 'The Body Snatchers' (1969). She featured in the arms-dealer series *Hine* (1971) and three episodes of the social drama *Man at the Top* (1970, 1972). Later in the 1970s, she played the vampish Rose Mellors, bedding Terry McCann, in *Minder* – 'Bury My Half at Waltham Green' (1979) and 'Diamonds Are a Girl's Worst Enemy' (1980).

JEROME BARRY WILLIS (1928-2014) appeared on TV in *The Life and Death of Sir John Falstaff* (1959), *Bleak House* (1959) and in various Shakespearean parts in the anthology

Age of Kings (1960). Best known for his 'establishment' characters he features several times in *Danger Man* – 'The Mirror's New' (1965), 'English Lady Takes Lodgers' (1965) and 'Someone is Liable to Get Hurt' (1966). Willis's cool, smooth villainy can also be seen in *Adam Adamant Lives!* – 'Sing a Song of Murder' (1966), *The Avengers* – 'Intercrime' (1963), 'How to Succeed... at Murder' (1966) and 'The Rotters' (1968). Fantasy television admirers will also recall his performances as Professor Nero in *Freewheelers* (1971) and Stevens, the brainwashed Director of Global Chemicals, in *Doctor Who* – 'The Green Death' (1973). Willis had regular roles as Deputy Governor Charles Radley in *Within These Walls* (1974-78) and as supercilious Deputy Chief Matthew Peele in the spy drama *The Sandbaggers* (1978-1980). He memorably portrayed a journalist murdered by a poisoned umbrella in *Kessler* (1981), a method based on the real-life killing of Georgi Markov. Other appearances include *Wish Me Luck* (1990), plus guest roles in *Midsomer Murders* and *A Touch of Frost* (both 1999). Willis enjoyed sending up his preferred casting as the pompous and vulgar Sir Austin in *The New Statesman* (1989-1990). A prominent stage actor, he performed with the RSC in *Pericles* at the Roundhouse, London, in 2002.

BARRY STANTON (born 1940) had appeared in *Theatre 625* (1966), *No Hiding Place* (1967) and Peter Yates' film *Robbery* (1967); his ITC credits include *The Saint* – 'The Man Who Gambled with Life' (1969). A sought after character actor, he was later cast in *Thriller* – 'Sign It Death' (1974), *Survivors* – 'Gone Away' (1975), the children's horror anthology series *Shadows* – 'Dutch Schlitz's Shoes' (1975, see Chapter 2), *The Sweeney* (1975) and *Armchair Thriller* – 'The Girl Who Walked Quickly' (by Ray Jenkins). Stanton portrayed a ruthless hit man in *The Professionals* – 'Spy Probe' (1982) and a comically inept security guard with an injured foot in *The Old Men at the Zoo* (1983). His cinema work includes *The Madness of King George* (1994) and, as a director, Stanton has overseen a variety of plays for the RSC.

REX ROBINSON (1926–2015) featured in the Arden Winch drama *Cold Warrior* (1984), *The Professionals* – 'Cry Wolf' (1983) and in three *Doctor Who* stories for his friend, the director Lennie Mayne, between 1973 and 1976. He had recurring roles in *Six Days of Justice* (1973-75) and the naval drama *Warship* (1973).

DAVID LELAND (born 1947) worked with Peter Egan on *Big Breadwinner Hog* (1969) and played the memorably argumentative philosopher Majikthise in the BBC1 version of *The Hitchhiker's Guide to the Galaxy* (1981).

GEOFF (GEOFFREY) CHESHIRE (1927-2004) appeared in *The Saint* – 'The Gadic Collection' (1967), as well as the films *The Skull* (1965) and *On Her Majesty's Secret Service* (1969). He was the chief Roboman in *Daleks – Invasion Earth 2150 AD* (1966).

INFORMATION: This story was originally called 'Gangrene', then 'A Question of Loyalties' was suggested before the final title. 'I've been to France, I'm married to a French girl, I've got a house in France,'[119] Ray Jenkins explained, '[and] the publication, at that time, of a book called *Gangrene*, which contained all this savage stuff about atrocities by the OAS, was where I got [the story] from. There was a lot of anti-French feeling at that time. I do tend to write elliptical titles, I must admit.

'I was always present at the read-through's and some of the filming,' the writer recalled. 'The writer's plea here is that he or she should be there, because decisions are made *ad hoc* during location filming that could alter what you've written. I would write something very specific hoping the director would be able to find it. Of course, sometimes you don't find a house with a leaning gable somebody can hang from – of course you don't – but I think it's [the director's] job to find it. If it's totally impossible, and therefore fundamentally interferes with the script, then I think directors ring you up. Peter Duguid would, Jim Goddard would; some other directors think it's their script and it's "Who are you? You've been paid. Get off." So writers then feel very, very anxious about being there! The other problem is, if you're a successful writer you're writing all the time: you cannot spend four days standing around, very bored, up to your knees in mud, guarding your golden lines. So it has to be a compromise.

'I think it's very important for a writer to produce problems for everybody. There's got to be a major problem for the director, there's got to be a [studio] set problem – you know, it gets people working – and get the leading actor to do something he's never done before, that kind of thing.'

'Death of a Friend' was ahead of its time in the mature and sympathetic treatment of homosexuals. 'There are certain kinds of underlying factors in all this,' Jenkins elaborated. 'The essence of *Callan* is that possibly it was out of date by the time it was created. It's essentially a Cold War series... it seemed to me that you had to try and find, all the time, variations on that. The French [angle] really is a deliberate attempt to try and break down that Cold War ethic. That's what was going on at the time: we're talking about 1968 onwards, and before that. I was in Paris at the time of the [demonstrations] so of course I wanted to write about it. You can't ignore it – it's there.'

The Organisation de l'armée secrète (literally 'Organisation of the Secret Army') was a French paramilitary group that tried to prevent the French African colony Algeria becoming independent. After Algeria was granted sovereignty in March 1962, the OAS tried to derail the process through a campaign of bombings, assassinations and horrifically indiscriminate killing sprees, including attempts to kill philosopher Jean-Paul Sartre and president Charles de Gaulle. Famously, the OAS tried to kill de Gaulle using gunmen in an ambush on the Avenue de la Liberation in Paris, in which several of de Gaulle's body-guards died. This event inspired a reporter, Frederick Forsyth, to write his first espionage novel, *The Day of the Jackal* (1971). The group's activities had wound down by the end of the 1960s, as 'Death of a Friend' observes, but the OAS still exists today. In James Mitchell's *The Man Who Sold Death* (1964), John Craig supplies arms to the Algerian rebels and is targeted for assassination by an OAS cell.[120]

It would be over 50 years before the French entertainment industry felt conmfortable enough to relax about France's colonial failures in Africa. In July 2016, the spy series *A Very Secret Service* began on Nertflix, sending up the complacency of the French intelligence services at the beginning of the 1960s. Bureaucrats are more concerned about the correct receipts being supplied to the expenses department, and when national radio makes an important government announcement about the situation in Algeria, in the HQ office the hip spies swich over, hand out alcohol and start dancing to pop music.

Meres refers to a prison on the Rue des Saussaies, a 50-metre-long street in Paris that adjoins the Ministry of the Interior, part of the French government. In WW2, the Rue des Saussaies was the headquarters of the Gestapo, the Nazi secret police, and suspects were tortured there.

Ann Lynn was possibly cast as Francine because she had guest-starred in *Danger Man* as another French woman, the intelligence agent Suzanne, in the story 'Have a Glass of Wine' (1965). Like Suzanne, Francine has two henchmen helping her (in another coincidence, in both productions one of them sports a moustache). There was the same friction between the British and French secret services as in 'Death of a Friend' – 'the British authorities have been a nuisance,' Suzanne says. 'They have no right sending agents over here without informing us' – and there is the same topical reference to Algeria, as Henri, one of her men, mentions a 'big Algerian' who held out under torture for '36 hours.'

Appropriately for an episode featuring French people and tribal fighting, Petula Clark's rendition of 'Donne Moi Des Fleurs' and Bill Martin and Phil Coulter's 'Mods and Rockers' are used on the soundtrack.[121]

MISSION ANALYSIS: *'Jean... he hated to be touched.'* For the second episode in a row, the subject matter covers homosexuality and a love triangle, but this complex story feels very different to its predecessor, the French politics adding another dimension. Seen now, the episode is strikingly radical, as for the second time in his work on the series, Jenkins turns away from the well-known Cold War clichés of the era and looks for inspiration in other areas.

Much of the story's impact depends on it being seen in the context of early 1969. The background of terrorism by French loyalists that dogged Algerian independence has generally faded from newspaper headlines and gay relationships, the main point of the story, are now an accepted part of everyday life. At the time, however, the portrayal of same sex lovers on television was highly controversial. In the wider world, homosexuality was even more contentious, with gay men in particular on the receiving end of the kind of violent bigotry that Meres displays. In this context, the long scene where Coquet's wife reveals her bitter feelings about being abandoned by her husband for a man makes sense, as does Latour's confession that he was the 'wife' of Jean Coquet, a revelation considered dramatic enough to be the cliffhanger to Part One.

In this respect, the episode goes further than the sympathetic but still pro-establishment line taken in 'Blackmailers Should Be Discouraged'. Francine vindictively dismisses her husband as 'a lover of boys', but, despite living with Latour, Coquet was still in love with her and conflicted about intimate contact with men. The same theme is addressed through Meres' homophobia. In the dramatic highlight of the episode, the agent gives full vent to his prejudices, branding the Frenchman a coward because of his sexual orientation. Satisfyingly, Meres is forced to reappraise his attitude after Latour is fatally wounded saving his life.

By now, the regular cast are at the height of their powers. Woodward simmers with contempt for Francine throughout and, commendably, adds a new dimension to Callan by reaffirming the character's non-judgmental view of gay people. Russell Hunter again supplies the humour and the vulnerability, while the detail in Valentine's performance is a joy to watch. He's effortlessly suave and amusing in the scene where he says 'Evening Lonely', at the same time covering his nose with his handkerchief, before the surface charm evaporates to reveal the public school bully beneath as he interrogates Latour.

With the added appeal of a stand-out guest turn by Ann Lynn, the initial, highly-charged impact of 'Death of A Friend' may have faded with the passing of the years, but Jenkins' progressive and unpredictable writing is as impressive as ever.

S2.10 JACK-ON-TOP

Writer: Trevor Preston
Director: Mike Vardy
Designer: Tony Borer

FIRST UK TRANSMISSION

Thames/LWT, Tyne Tees, Southern: Wednesday 12th March 1969, 10.30 pm
ATV, Anglia, Border, Channel, Granada, Harlech, Scottish, Westward, Yorkshire: 9.00 pm
Grampian: Monday 17 March 1969, 11.00 pm

CAST: John Bailey (Trochee), Anthony Blackshaw (Selby), Clifford Cox (Assistant Governor), Conrad Phillips (Wilson), Dave Carter (AA Man), Philip Ryan, Kenneth Hale (Prison officers), Daphne Slater (Stella Paxton), Richard Mathews (Holbrook), Barrie Fletcher (Special Branch Man)

EXTRAS/WALK-ONS: (*Uncredited on screen*) Daphne Palmer (Waitress in cafe), Terence O'Connor, George Wilde, M. J. Matthews, Toba Lawrence (Customers in café), Stan Saunders, Ben Delahunt, Tony Leary, A. Williams, David James (used in photo call)

PRODUCTION

Location Filming: Wormwood Scrubs, Clemence Street, Frognal Road and Sedgely Road Swimming Baths, London.[122]
Camera Rehearsals/Recording: Teddington Studio One, Thursday 25 and Friday 26 April 1968.[123]

TV TIMES: '"Set a thief to catch a thief and end up in the pool." The KGB – Russian Secret Service – network in London has been detected and the authorities are moving in for the kill. The Russians prepare to leave the country and Callan is detailed to catch the head man.' *Edition unknown*

MISSING FILE: The master tapes of this episode do not exist in the FremantleMedia archive.

MISSION PROFILE: A KGB cell has been collating information on British security procedures. MI5 say if the cell's controller – codenamed 'Jack-on-Top' – escapes from Britain, it will set security back ten years. There is a time limit on the value of 'Jack's' information; he has to get out within a week. However, nobody knows who he is...

Trochee, a burglar, is the only lead. He was paid to safe-break for the spy ring and he's just started serving a four-year sentence in Wormwood Scrubs. He claims he was framed and offers to trade information for remission.

Callan questions him. Trochee says the cell owes him money and he discloses some names. The Section decide to spring the criminal from prison and then follow him to find the controller.

Out and on the run, Trochee is shadowed by Lonely. He visits a cell member, Stella Paxton. Shortly afterwards, Callan finds Trochee has strangled her. Realising Trochee and 'Jack-on-Top' are the same man, Callan pursues and shoots him.

A MAN LIKE ME: Callan is assigned Trochee's case due to a common background. He is distrustful, feeling some sort of sting is going on. He keeps mulling things over, despite being taken in by Trochee's deceptions – which include laying a trail to another cell member, Holbrook.

He realises Trochee would have been skilled enough to open up Holbrook's safe and place some wanted security photographs inside. He seems angry that Trochee has betrayed and killed two of his own side, and says it was 'worth it' after shooting him dead and finding hidden microdots on the agent's body.

Section Kills: 12

LONELY: Lonely is Callan's eyes and ears, watching Trochee after he's been sprung. Like old man Steptoe, he pours tea into his saucer before drinking it.

A TIE AND A CREST: Meres offers to re-interrogate Trochee – perhaps trying to undermine Callan's standing in the Section. Callan has to remind Hunter that a few thousand pounds is a lot of money 'for some people'. Snell is mentioned.

The Section chief muses about playing chess games, unaware someone else is in control. He later toys with Holbrook by asking him about his career and his hobbies, before revealing the Section have found a transmitter in his loft.

ALCOHOL, TOBACCO AND FIREARMS: Trochee has a drink at Stella's, complaining about the lack of alcohol in prison.

SPY-SPEAK: Plenty of spiky early Trevor Preston one-liners. The spy cell is 'causing ulcers'. 'Thieves', Meres thinks, are 'like mistresses – suspicious as hell.' Holbrook is as 'sharp as a sewer rat.'

Callan comments on Lonely's digestion. 'You sound like a bath emptying – not that you're familiar with that sound!'

When Lonely wonders if Trochee is settling in for the night with the prim Stella, Callan rejoins, 'Rather him than me!' Trochee is on the run because 'he didn't like the cuisine in the nick.' Meres, visiting Callan's flat at night, is greeted with the line, 'What a time to come courting!'

This banter contrasts with comments acknowledging police corruption and Callan angrily overcoming Holbrook's reticence by telling him of Stella's murder: 'He snapped her neck like a chicken!'

PAWNS AND PLAYERS: TREVOR PRESTON was in a biker gang and studying at the Royal College of Art when he encountered the world of television. 'I was in my final degree year, and Lloyd Shirley came to us with an invitation, which I thought was terrific... to write, direct, and produce a film,'[124] he reminisced. 'It all bubbled around and I wrote a thing called *A Medium Sized Cage*, which was about a day in the life of an art student, for him to consider. I asked him who was going to direct it and he said "You are!" We had a marvellous time and absolutely fantastic weather, and Lloyd was really buzzing. He was very keen on encouraging young people. And from that, he gave me a job.'

A placement learning directing at ABC fell through; however Jeremy Isaacs (later Director of Programmes at Thames and founding Chief Executive of Channel 4) encouraged Preston to stay and take up writing instead. Following an early stint on the religious miniseries *Four People* (1966), working with the director Voytek (see 'Summoned to Appear',

Chapter 7), he began writing short pieces for the arts programme *Tempo*. It was there, despite feeling 'odd, coming from this South London, rather hard background into this very middle-class, rather gentle place,' that Preston became friends with future *Get Carter* director Mike Hodges, director Jim Goddard and director-turning-producer Pamela Lonsdale.

Through Pamela, Trevor transferred from religious broadcasting, 'which was fun – we went up to Liverpool Cathedral with Kenny Everett to interview the Bee Gees!' – to 'children's stuff, which I loved. I didn't overstep the mark – I knew you couldn't drive Rolls Royces over a cliff! Pamela and I got on famously.' His work on children's serials included a adaptations of *The Lion, the Witch and the Wardrobe* (1967) and *The Incredible Adventures of Professor Branestawm* (1969) for Lonsdale plus a serial, *The Tyrant King* (1968), based on a novel by Aylmer Hall for older children. This involved a chase around London in a series directed by Hodges and shot entirely on film.

Enjoying the idea of a crime-fighting adventure for children, he contributed 'The Big Freeze' (1968) to the Southern Television show *Freewheelers*. 'It was about someone who could control the weather, and it was totally stolen for the film of *The Avengers* [1998]. I thought, "You cheeky buggers!"' He subsequently created his own fantasy show, *Ace of Wands* (1970-72), also produced by Lonsdale, which still has a cult following today.

Preston gives credit to Reg Collin and John Kershaw for letting him break into adult drama through his work on *Callan*. 'Reggie, because he realised I did work very hard, just let me go... The production system [on *Callan*] was very good. They didn't cut great chunks of it. The script editor didn't try and rewrite it.'

On script changes generally, he reflected in the 1980s, 'There were funny things that I had to change: there were certain words I used in the cockney vocabulary where people didn't really know what I was talking about, so to clarify the situation they'd ask me to change it. I used to have certain words for sexual intercourse which they didn't understand... Most of it really was censorship – I tend to get a bit strong with the language sometimes, and I do quite tough programmes... but you cannot hold up a programme just because you're having a bish with the script editor.'

By 1974, Preston had built up a strong track record in the TV crime genre, writing for *Public Eye* (1971), *The Mind of J.G. Reeder* (1971), *Six Days of Justice* (1972-75) and *Special Branch* (1970-73). This work was enhanced by his widespread knowledge of how criminals worked, gained via friends, family and other private contacts around London. 'I could spend ten days explaining the culture because it's so complex, and it changes all the time,' he said. 'There is a situation whereby certain people have certain access to certain pubs or clubs or places where other people just wouldn't be [allowed in]. There'd be someone on the door, 7' 3" tall, full of eight pints of bitter! I can still go into these places in London because I know I'm trusted, but I couldn't take [anyone else].'

He was therefore a natural choice as one of the main writers on *The Sweeney* (1975-78). Having previously pioneered the idea of an independent filmmaking 'nucleus' at ABC, Preston would be associated with Euston Films through much of the 1970s. After this intensive period, he briefly contemplated leaving to go into business, but instead was given the green light for *Out* (1978), a six-part serial expanding on some of the territory he had mapped out in *The Sweeney* by focusing on the newly-released, vengeful, unpredictable criminal Frank Ross. A further London-based family drama, *Fox* (1980) followed. Both series were directed by Jim Goddard.

Preston's other career highlights include *Billy the Kid and the Green Baize Vampire* (1985, directed by Alan Clarke) and *I'll Sleep When I'm Dead* (2003, overseen by Mike Hodges). In addition to the *Ace of Wands* prequel for *Dramarama* – 'Mr. Stabs' (1984), he wrote the witty episode 'The Car Lot Baggers' for *Minder* (1984) and adapted several *Ruth Rendell Mysteries*. In recent years, he has made the transition to writing radio plays, including *Flaw in the Motor, Dust in the Blood* (2008) with Rory Kinnear, *Second Body* (2013) and the semi-autobiographical *Small Acts of Kindness* (2011), which was shortlisted for the Richard Imison Award for Best First Radio Play, as well as a Mental Health in the Media Award. He has retired to the south coast to work on more instalments of another radio project, *The Zone* (2014): 'It's not science fiction, it's not horror, it's not a thriller: it's *all* of them.

'All of my work has got bits of autobiography in it,' Preston revealed. 'Obviously as the disclaimer says, you have to change the names! For instance, a guy came to see me one day, he wanted me to write a story about him. He'd been in prison for ten years for two bank robberies, he'd done two armed robberies on the same day, and shot the bank manager – not fatally. He wanted me to do a film about him making alcohol in prison. He had his own still! I said no, I didn't really want to do it, but I said, "I've got an idea for a film you might like to advise me on as it's in your area". That's the way things used to work... I was the only one who was able to get "in", and that was because of my Dad and my brothers and their history. I was known as someone who could keep his mouth shut.' Laughing, he added, 'I had to, some of the things I knew!'

JOHN BAILEY (1912-1989) had prominent parts in the early Dennis Potter *Wednesday Play* 'Vote, Vote, Vote for Nigel Barton' (1965), *Rasputin: The Mad Monk* (1965, directed by Don Sharp) and *Mosquito Squadron* (1969). He gave a moving performance as the doomed scientist father of *Doctor Who* companion Victoria Waterfield in 'The Evil of the Daleks' (1967), and can also be seen in *The Champions* – 'A Case of Lemmings' (1969), *Department S* – 'Handicap Dead' (1969), *Thriller* – 'Kill Two Birds' (1976), *Return of the Saint* – 'The Nightmare Man' (1978), plus numerous episodes of *The Avengers* and *Special Branch*. One of his final roles was in *Mr. Palfrey of Westminster* – 'Music of a Dead Prophet' (1985).

CONRAD PHILLIPS (1925–2016) was one of British TV's first action heroes, appearing as the title character in 39 episodes of *The Adventures of William Tell* (1958-59). Later in his career he played various authority figures, including doctors in *The Prisoner* – 'The General' (1967), *Hammer House of Horror* – 'The Mark of Satan' (1980) and a guest at 'The Wedding Party' in *Fawlty Towers* (1975). Notably, Phillips portrayed the sinister gamekeeper Mellors in *The Avengers* – 'Silent Dust' (1965).

INFORMATION: Trevor Preston derived the episode's title from an old poker term.

Trochee throttling Stella was depicted with a close-up on his face and then a close-up on just her eyes and nose. Director Mike Vardy deliberately avoided more graphic imagery: 'We were very conscious of violence in those days and we did have our own form of censorship.'[125] Terence Feely argued *Callan* was both more real and more dramatic than the Bond franchise and series like *The Avengers*, precisely because of this contained approach. '*Controlled* violence is much more effective... we censored ourselves; we didn't need [Mary Whitehouse] to tell us how to do it.'[126] Preston was similarly scathing about Whitehouse, having clashed with her after she took against *The Sweeney*.

'There was very little on camera violence in *Callan* although it was denounced in pulpits the length and breadth of the country at the time,'[127] James Mitchell said ruefully. 'It wasn't a violent thing, it was that people were frightened – instead of seeing dummies been blown up, they saw people they believed to be people, being threatened with a single bullet and sometimes getting it.'

'I first saw John Bailey, the guy who played Trochee, when I was doing my national service,'[128] Vardy said of the guest star's casting. 'I went to the theatre one night and there he was, in a touring production of something. I thought how good he was then, and years and years later, I got the chance to work with him, which was great.'

While modern TV scripts often map out action in detail, Preston's description for the climax of this story is minimalist, in common with its contemporaries. It simply states 'Trochee at baths. Callan and Meres arrive and search for Trochee. There is a chase in the baths. Trochee is shot and falls in water.' It was the practice of the time to let the director have free creative reign in staging these sequences, especially when filming on location.

'I realised to make the best of this moment I needed an underwater cameraman,' Vardy recalled. 'In those days they were very rare. Our resourceful director of photography, John Keeling, finally ran one to earth after a long search. His name was Slim McDonnell. It was a source of amusement to us that this man put on his gear, checked his camera and seemingly went to sleep on the bottom of the pool until we were ready for him. We had to shout and splash the water to wake him up as we had no sound communication.' He concluded, 'the whole thing was worth the trouble as it made a very effective climax to an exciting sequence.'

The prison break mirrors that of notorious double agent George Blake née Behar (see 'You Should Have Got Here Sooner' and 'You're Under Starter's Orders').

MISSION ANALYSIS: *The clever bastard – using us to spring him.'* Featuring pared-down, moody studio dialogue sequences abruptly interspersed with bursts of swift film action, this story seems to be striving to break free from static TV play conventions and move towards a more cinematic feel. The pacing is evocative of contemporary films such as the American thriller *Point Blank* (1967), a favourite of Preston's that (maybe coincidentally) also features a reticent convict wanting money, a stark final shoot out, and a dual character (Yost). The twist concerning the identity of 'Jack-on-Top' and the Section lagging several steps behind Trochee both serve well in building up the tension.

Preston gives each of the regular cast some entertaining material. The conversation between Callan and Trochee is of one professional criminal to another, while Stella and Bradwell, two artless KGB agents in the Mitchell/Banks Stewart vein, are particularly well characterised.

The sequence where Trochee makes an old wound open up and bleed to hide a microdot demonstrates his fanatical loyalty to the cause. This vicious, controlled character precedes several unforgettable villains that Preston would go on to create in his work on *The Sweeney*, including Vic Labbett in 'Poppy' (1975) and the softly-spoken Ashcroft in 'May' (1976). With its derelict shops, van-based banter, and an increased quota of slang references to specific London areas, the mood of the script feels much like that of the 1970s series in places. While it may lack some of the subtlety and depth Preston would go on to achieve later, 'Jack-on-Top' is an exciting first mature drama from the writer and, as Mike Vardy said, it showed 'a lot of the promise to come.'

S2.11 ONCE A BIG MAN, ALWAYS A BIG MAN

Writer: Lee Dunne
Director: Bill Bain
Designer: Roger Allan

FIRST UK TRANSMISSION

Thames/LWT, Tyne Tees, Southern: Wednesday 19 March 1969, 10.30 pm
ATV, Anglia, Border, Channel, Granada, Harlech, Scottish, Westward, Yorkshire: 9.00pm
Grampian: Monday 24 March 1969, 11.00 pm

CAST: Michael Bient (Captain West), Michael Forrest (Clive), Bernard Archard (Watt), Jacqueline Pearce (Eva), Mark Moss (Barman)

EXTRAS/WALK-ONS: (*Uncredited on screen*) John Caesar, Robert Murphy, Stan Bray, Fred Doran, George Richardson, Ernest Smith, Roland Nunnery, William Sully (unknown), Roberta Gibbs (Stunts). Gary Hillsden, Billy Shane, Jack Sharpe, John De Marco, Arthur Zan, Henry Rayner, Colin Cunningham, Ralph Katterns (Customers in hotel bar). Roberta Gibbs (Double for Jacqueline Pearce)

PRODUCTION

Rehearsals: From Friday 24 May 1968
Location Filming: Sunday 26 May – Tuesday 28 May 1968 (Locations unknown)
Camera Rehearsals/Recording: Teddington Studio Two, Wednesday 5th and
Thursday 6th June 1968[129]

TV TIMES: 'A ship that sank during the war has been discovered off the coast of Devon. Aboard is a safe which contains a list of people who might have played an important part in the war if events had turned out differently. Callan is asked to retrieve the list. But what should be a simple task proves far from easy when he discovers he is in conflict with very influential people.'
15-21 March 1969, Yorkshire edition

MISSING FILE: The master tapes of this story do not exist in the FremantleMedia archive.

MISSION PROFILE: Despite bureaucratic obstructions, a salvage team has boarded the *Miss Ellen*, a WW2 fishing vessel that sank in a storm off the coast of Devon. On board is a safe which Callan is asked to escort securely back to London.

The safe is a concern for the local businessman Watt, formerly an MP and a 'big man' until he was interned during WW2. He knows the safe held a list of British Fascist collaborators, information that was originally intended for Hitler. Watt reminds his daughter Eva that his name is at the top of the list, and once the information is made public they will have to leave home, which she vehemently rejects.

Harry Vernon, another collaborator, plants a bomb in the harbour but gets burnt when it detonates. The damage only disrupts the salvage operation temporarily. Already losing hope after this setback, Watt meets Callan and, realising the agent cannot be bought off, commits suicide. Eva, who has stubbornly remained in denial throughout, launches a demented attack on the convoy driving the safe back to London. She wounds Meres before Callan shoots her dead.

A MAN LIKE ME: This is the second story where Callan shoots a woman in self-defence, but this time she is no trained assassin, just 'bloody stupid'. He was educated in Devon as a war evacuee and, briefly, refers to the loss of his mother.

Section Kills: 13

LONELY: Dislikes the countryside and automatically associates Devon with Dartmoor Prison. After persuading Lonely he needs some fresh air, Callan keeps depriving him of his expenses. He also tells Lonely to catch a coach rather than the train, and advises him to avoid hotels and instead find an understanding landlady. With a bath.

A TIE AND A CREST: Hunter and Callan similarly wrangle over expenses before the agent's departure; Callan sarcastically suggests he should walk back from Devon to save money. The discussion then moves on to what is really on both men's minds: Hunter has not been fully informed about the safe's content by his superiors.

Significantly, the question of Watt's 'friends in high places' is left unresolved; 'new' far right groups are also referred to, possibly foreshadowing the next story.

ALCOHOL, TOBACCO AND FIREARMS: Meres is disappointed to find that as it's 3 pm the hotel bar is shut. Watt has sherry before dinner. Eva is a good aim with a hunting rifle.

SPY-SPEAK: Meres seems to think Callan is out for sexual gratification when he sees him leaving the hotel with Eva. He won't allow Lonely in his car, saying 'it's too draughty to have all the windows wide open this time of night.'

Hunter refutes Callan's insistence that conveying items from Devon is a job for British Rail: 'Beeching axed that bit of the line.'

Callan wonders if Lonely's tendency to bet on 'three-legged horses' is why he is always broke.

PAWNS AND PLAYERS: CHRISTOPHER LEE DUNNE (born 1934) spent time in early 1960s London working as a stage performer, part-time barman and taxi driver. The prolific Irish author successfully sold television scripts while cabbying, including screenplays for *No Hiding Place* – 'Who Killed Cock Robin?' and the Sid James comedy drama *Taxi!* – 'The Villain' (both 1963). Dunne shot to notoriety when his debut novel, *Goodbye to the Hill* – an edgy, bawdy portrait of Dublin life – was published and became a long-running play. The follow-up novel, *Paddy Maguire is Dead* – a semi-autobiographical work which Dunne maintains 'is pretty much the story'[133] about him, including his struggle with alcoholism – was banned by the Irish Government in 1972 for its sexual content; the film version suffered a similar fate. In the mid-1970s, Dunne wrote a string of comic 'Cabbie' novels with titles punning on the names of popular contemporary films, including *Midnight Cabbie*, *The Cabbie who Came in from the Cold*, *Virgin Cabbies* and *The Cabfather*, which were also banned; since then, a reappraisal of his work has taken place. Dunne provided many episodes of the RTÉ radio soap opera *Harbour Hotel* (1975-1990) and continues to write novels.[130]

BERNARD JOSEPH ARCHARD (1916-2008) featured in *Village of the Dammed* (1960), *The Horror of Frankenstein* (1970) and Roman Polanski's *Macbeth* (1970). He joined the stellar cast of ageing British character actors in *The Sea Wolves* (1980), but was arguably best known for playing Colonel Oreste Pinto in the TV thriller *Spycatcher* (1959-1961).[131] Archard appeared in *Danger Man* – 'The Leak' (1961) and 'I Can Only Offer You Sherry' (1966), having previously acted with Patrick McGoohan on stage. He took other notable guest roles in *Z Cars* and *The Avengers*. Archard regularly played the editor overseeing Peter Bowles' columnist on *Lytton's Diary* (1985-1986), and is well-known among *Doctor Who* enthusiasts for his portrayal of the possessed archaeologist Marcus Scarman in 'Pyramids of Mars' (1975). His final television role was in *Emmerdale* (1992-94).

JACQUELINE PEARCE (born 1943) left RADA in 1963 and began a successful acting career on both the large and small screen. Prominent roles in two Hammer films, *The Plague of the Zombies* and *The Reptile* (both 1966), propelled her towards stardom; in the latter she played the unfortunate creature of the title. She made guest appearances in *Danger Man* – 'Don't Nail Him Yet' (1964), *The Avengers* – 'A Sense of History' (1966) and two instalments of *Man In A Suitcase* – 'Sweet Sue' (1967) and 'Somebody Loses, Somebody... Wins?' (1968). Arguably, her most famous role was that of alluring arch villainess Servalan in *Blake's 7* (1978-1981). 'She was the boss and I was her minder'[132] Brian Croucher said affectionately of his co-star.

MICHAEL FORREST (1932-2004) appeared in the controversial pro-SAS film written by George Markstein and Reginald Rose, *Who Dares Wins* (1982). He was also in *Danger Man* – 'The Man with the Foot' (1966), *The Saint* – 'The Man Who Liked Lions' (1966), *The Avengers* – 'Death Dispatch' (1962), 'The Hidden Tiger' (1967) and *Randall and Hopkirk (Deceased)* – 'The Ghost Who Saved the Bank at Monte Carlo' (1969). As DC Glyn Hicks, he was one of the early regulars in *Z Cars* (1963-64).

MICHAEL BEINT (born 1925) had supporting roles in *The Avengers* – 'Propellant 23' (1962), *The Saint* – 'Paper Chase' (1966), *Special Branch* – 'A Date with Leonidas' (1969), *Thriller* – 'One Deadly Owner' (1974) and *The Sweeney* – 'Hard Men' (1978).

INFORMATION: As John Kershaw recalled, the idea for this story originated from the writer Ian Kennedy Martin. 'He said we could use the idea, the barge that sank with this list.'[133] Kershaw asked Dunne to write the script instead, having been impressed with his debut novel. Dunne was not involved further with the recording of the episode but remembered being pleased with ABC's professionalism.[134]

Kershaw had hoped the episode would be filmed in Devon so the *Callan* team could attend his forthcoming wedding there, but the usual policy of not travelling far from Teddington prevailed.

Stuntwoman Roberta Gibbs performed Eva's death scene, tumbling down a bank.

George Watt appears to be based on several well-known British Fascists from the 1930s, but the primary source is Baronet Oswald Ernald Mosley MP (1896-1980), who was originally in the Labour Party before founding a 'New Party' which became the British Union of Fascists. He was interned for three years from 1940. Another Labourite who swung to the right was John Warburton Beckett (1894-1964); he was also interned under Defence Regulation 18b during WW2, before joining another far-right party and making a living advising about the Stock Exchange. *The Avengers* had dealt with British Fascism in the 1962 story 'The Mauritius Penny', while *The Saint* had exposed another Nazi cell in 'The Saint Plays with Fire' (1963, featuring Joseph Fürst as the villainous Kane Luker).

As the prestigious *Mountbatten* documentary series came to its conclusion in the week this story was transmitted, all ITV networks except Grampian subsequently began synchronising their screenings of *Callan* in the 9.00 pm time slot.

In the week that 'Once a Big Man, Always a Big Man' was transmitted, the *TV Times* ran a small feature on Derek Bond, focusing on his wartime POW experiences, which included an unsuccessful attempt to dig his way out of a church with a bent spoon. Photographs of Bond, Woodward with Russell Hunter and Jacqueline Pearce were used to promote the programme listings in some regions. A few issues later, photos of Woodward and Pearce were used in the 'Playback' section (see 'Death of a Hunter').

MISSION ANALYSIS: *'All I see is some squirming little rat in a stupid trap.'* Similar to Len Deighton's second IPCRESS man novel *Horse Under Water* (1963) which also features a list of Fascist collaborators, this story alludes to *King Lear* in its analysis of a fatalistic, irresolute man who has a fractious relationship with his daughter. Watt talks of the 'old dream' but later also reflects that he made 'a mistake'; Eva refuses to listen to him, scathingly dismissing him as a 'weak old man'. This is no moralistic judgement: she may have been named after Hitler's partner but she has no political ideology, her sole motivation being to retain her inheritance and lifestyle. The pair's constant feuding reflects typical 1960s concerns over the 'generation gap' between children and parents over fashion, music and politics.

The story's title is another ironic one: once 'the big man' finds he cannot buy his way out of trouble, he shoots himself. Having been indulged by her father and his subservient butler, Eva is so accustomed to getting her own way that she launches into a badly thought out assault on Callan that gets her killed.

While Eva's constant refrain of 'old man' might start to grate, elsewhere Dunne's adroit dialogue, about 'sensitivity in the money markets' and rousing the local MP from 'whatever bed he's in', are very sharp and could have been written recently rather than in the last century. The comical misunderstandings work well too, particularly when Lonely believes the hotel barman means Watt was 'high up' on a nearby hill rather than a key influence in government.

The seaside location is effective as a contrasting backdrop to the impending violence, cleverly foreshadowed when Callan sees Watt's display of hunting rifles. The suspense break at the end of the first act is also particularly well-constructed, keeping the audience guessing for several minutes about who might have been hurt in the bomb explosion in the harbour. It's typical of the care that the production team put into sustaining dramatic tension across commercial breaks.

The final twist raises more questions than it resolves, but is nonetheless very fulfilling: due to some misunderstanding, it seems the list was actually never in the safe, so all the deaths have been for nothing. The initial Section wrangling with Hunter over expenses at the beginning of the story has a bleak pay-off at the denouement, as Callan angrily invoices his boss for 'eighteen pounds, seven shillings and sixpence – cheap enough for a couple of lives'.

Dunne's return to Ireland precluded him contributing to the series again, but this episode remains a distinctive one-off.

S2.12 THE RUNNING DOG

Writer: William Emms
Director: Jim Goddard
Designer: Peter le Page

FIRST UK TRANSMISSION

Grampian: Monday 31 March 1969, 11.00 pm
All other regions: Wednesday 26 March 1969, 9.00 pm

CAST: Renny Lister (Felice), Terence Rigby (Holder), Jonathan Newth (Henry), Burt Kwouk (Tao Tsung), Nicholas Courtney (Forbes)

EXTRAS/WALK-ONS: (*Uncredited on screen*) Tom Gaw, Jo Ismail, Chien Hsiang Yang, L.K.F. Ryee Tong (Chinese Guards), Darique (Girl in bar), Michael Patten (Hippie), Gordon Craig, Jean Barry (Middle aged couple).

PRODUCTION INFORMATION

Rehearsals: From Thursday 14 March 1968
Location Filming: Speaker's Corner in Hyde Park, London W2; the Chinese Embassy, Portland Place, London W1 (Sunday 17 – Tuesday 19 March 1969)
Camera Rehearsals/Recording: Teddington Studio One, Wednesday 27 and Thursday 28 March 1968[135]

TV TIMES: 'A neo-Fascist group has unpleasant plans for an official of the Chinese Legation. When the man says that he would consider no sacrifice too great to make for Chairman Mao, Callan takes the law into his own hands.'
22-28 March 1969, Midlands edition

MISSING FILE: The master tapes of this story do not exist in the FremantleMedia archive.

MISSION PROFILE: Relations with Communist China are already poor and Holder, a Fascist, is looking to stir up further trouble. Callan poses as a new recruit to Holder's group and learns of a plan to kill Tao Tsung, the Chinese Chargé d'Affaire in London. Callan tries to infiltrate further but realises his cover is blown when Henry, Holder's bodyguard, follows him. Hunter rejects Callan's suggestion that the group should all be arrested for a few days; it would increase their public support. Meres warns Tao Tsung, but the diplomat refuses to take measures to protect himself and will not allow British security into his Embassy.

The Section staff realise Tao Tsung is offering himself up as a target, hoping to create a diplomatic incident. Callan enlists Lonely's help to break into the Embassy but is caught. When Holder, Henry and another member of their group, Holder's girlfriend Felice, burst in to kill Tao Tsung, the two men are shot down by Chinese security guards. As Callan is also holding a gun, Tao Tsung intends to say he killed Holder – offering as evidence bodies riddled with Callan's bullets – because he is defecting to join the Chinese. However, Callan has outmanoeuvred Tao Tsung because the gun he's carrying is empty and, before entering the Embassy, he was photographed being manhandled into a car being driven by Chinese men. Consequently, he walks free.

A MAN LIKE ME: Callan uses his 'Tucker' pseudonym when encountering Holder's group. As scripted, he drops his 'h's, implying a proletarian accent. He adopts an unreconstructed approach to race relations to impress his new acquaintances: 'Look at the blacks, we give 'em their freedom and wham, nothing but insults.' He offers to help 'put the boot in.' He cynically counters Tao Tsung's party line statement with the comment: 'And I'm a Chinaman – beg your pardon.'

LONELY: Callan won't let him sit on his bed, only a kitchen chair. When Lonely breaks into Holder's office, he's frightened by an armed Henry. Callan has to reassure Lonely that he isn't really getting mixed up with politics – the Embassy break-in is a normal burglary; he offers him £275 for his help. Lonely has cold feet and seems racist too, making disparaging references to 'slit eyes' and warning Callan that he'll end up getting stabbed with 'a great big Oriental shiv.'

A TIE AND A CREST: Forbes of the Foreign Office invites Hunter to his club.

The Honourable Ronald Holder was educated at Rugby, Cambridge and Sandhurst. His Fascism seems of a nationalistic rather than a pro-German bent, but his organisation's membership badges have Nazi-style symbols, as does his hi-tech HQ, which also boasts images of Hitler on the walls. He says people are 'sick and tired of cloth-cap government', a disparaging reference to Harold Wilson's Labour administration that had been re-elected in 1966. Holder makes a rabble-rousing speech referring to the 'yellow races'.

Like Watt (see 'Once A Big Man, Always A Big Man', page 213), he has unknown advocates 'in high places'. Hunter admits the Section have not prioritised identifying these people (probably viewing left-wing organisations as a higher priority).

ALCOHOL, TOBACCO AND FIREARMS: Forbes shares a drink with Hunter. Lonely photographs papers in the Fascist HQ's safe and is nearly caught by Henry Thackeray, Holder's Luger-wielding bodyguard. He's so shaken up that Callan gives him a Scotch. Later, Callan plies Lonely with alcohol again in an attempt to get him to break into the Chinese Embassy. Holder carries a gun to execute Tao Tsung.

SPY-SPEAK: Hunter refers to China as 'a nation gone mad if I ever saw one.' Forbes: 'In this world, how do you identify the sane?'

Callan, on Thackeray's house: 'Small enough to make living uncomfortable, big enough for the mortgage to break your back.'

Tao Tsung is arrogant in the face of Western threats: 'Being frightened by large numbers of people is not one of our natural characteristics'. He tries engaging Meres in political debate: 'The Communists are like seeds and people are like the soil.' Meres counters Tao Tsung with a clever Biblical reference: 'Some fell on stony ground.'

Callan's opinion on the whole ideological conflict is expressed following a stand-off and a gunfight that leaves two corpses on the floor. 'It's all a game, innit?'

PAWNS AND PLAYERS: WILLIAM EMMS (1930-1993) was a schoolteacher who wrote for television in his spare time, contributing to *Z Cars* (between 1965-1971), the BBC anthology series *Detective* (1968-69) and *Mr Rose* (1968). He is probably best-remembered for his fantasy work on *Doctor Who* – 'Galaxy 4' (1965) and *Ace of Wands* – 'The Mind Robbers' (1970).

WILLIAM NICHOLAS STONE COURTNEY (1929-2011) is fondly remembered for his portrayal of Brigadier Alistair Gordon Lethbridge Stewart in *Doctor Who* for well over five decades. This courageous, no-nonsense soldier was very much a Watson figure to the Doctor's Sherlock Holmes. Courtney reprised the popular character in audio plays and even an edition of *Harry Hill* (2000). He played the similarly stiff-upper-lipped Lieutenant-Colonel Robert Witherton in Frankie Howard's sitcom *Then Churchill Said To Me,* recorded in 1982 but not broadcast until 1993, reportedly because of the Falklands conflict. Courtney featured in the thriller *Watch The Birdies* (1966), *The Avengers* – 'Propellant 23' (1962), 'Mission... Highly Improable' (1967) and opposite future *Doctor Who* co-star Roger Delgado in the enjoyable comedy-heist *Randall and Hopkirk (Deceased)* – 'The Ghost Who Saved the Bank at Monte Carlo' (1969). His last work was on the supernatural audio comedy-drama *The Scarifiers* (2007-10).

TERENCE CHRISTOPHER RIGBY (1937-2008) played PC Henry Snow, the dog-handling officer in the police series *Softly Softly: Task Force* (1969-1976). A busy guest artist, his early appearances included the children's comedy *The Queen Street Gang* (1968), *The Saint* – 'The Angel's Eye' (1966), 'The Time to Die' (1968) and *Public Eye* – 'Divide and Conquer' (1969), in which he portrayed a violent biker. Rigby co-starred with John Wells in the satirist's comedy *Anyone For Denis?*, Tom Baker in *Hound of the Baskervilles* (both 1982) and Edward Woodward in the northern comedy-drama *Common As Muck* (1997). He played eccentric 'businessman' Big Al in Alan Plater's gentle comedy thriller *The Beiderbecke Affair* (1985) and *The Beiderbecke Connection* (1988). His film parts include cuckolded gangland boss Gerald Fletcher in *Get Carter* (1971), Stalin in *Testimony* (1988, also featuring William Squire) and another Russian, General Bukharov, in *Tomorrow Never Dies* (1997).

JONATHAN NEWTH (born 1939) was Russell Bryant in the sitcom *After Henry* (1988-1992) and played military characters in *The Return of Sherlock Holmes* – 'The Bruce Partington Plans' (1988) and the final series of *Tenko* (1984, as Brigadier Clifford Jefferson). Newth had further memorable parts in *Ace Of Wands* – 'Nightmare Gas' (1971), *The Brothers* (1973-74), *Poldark* (1975), *The Day of the Triffids* (1981) and the horror thriller *The Nightmare Man* (1981). He returned to *Callan* for Series Four's opening story 'That'll Be the Day'.

RENNY LISTER featured in *Don't Forget To Write* (1977-79) and *Bowler* (1973), a spin-off from the popular high school comedy, *The Fenn Street Gang* (1971-73). She played Jean Stark in early episodes of *Coronation Street* and starred in the Hammer film *Curse of the Werewolf* (both 1961); she married the actor Kenneth Cope in the same year. In 1997, Lister announced her retirement from acting.

For Burt Kwouk see 'The Death of Robert E. Lee'.

INFORMATION: 'It dealt with a very rich right-wing guy, an updated Oswald Mosley and the sympathies of the Fascist aristocracy. The police were very cagey because we shot some scenes in Hyde Park and they said you must be out of here by five o'clock,'[136] Jim Goddard said, remembering a location shoot beset by incidents including some extreme-right supporters mistaking Holder's fictional rally for a real one, plus a delegation from another Embassy. 'Six guys in grey mackintoshes and charcoal three-piece suits, who had obviously come down from the Russian Embassy, cornered me, asking, "What is this film?"

'In retrospect the police were very tolerant towards us. We were causing a bit of trouble. They said, "You can't go that side of Park Lane" when we were trying to drive on to the next location – "It is totally out of bounds". It turned out it was the same day as the Grosvenor Square Riots! It was quite extraordinary.' Cast and crew had heard the noise from this infamous anti-Vietnam war protest but were unaware of what was taking place until later.

For the part of Tao Tsung, Goddard recalled actor Burt Kwouk receiving a Beatles-style haircut, reflecting the style favoured by real staff from the (then closed) Chinese Embassy.

Holder and Felice refer to increasing their party's membership 'next year' (anticipating elections). Real far-right parties at that time included the National Front (formerly the British National Party), the British Movement (or National Socialist Movement), the Greater Britain Movement, the National Democratic Party (or Racial Preservation Society) and the National Independence Party.

Britain and China had supported opposing sides in the Korean War and clashed over the sovereignty of Hong Kong. Mao's 'Great Proletarian Cultural Revolution' was instigated in 1966 to purge Western capitalist elements from Chinese society, primarily through groups of young, fanatical Red Guards. In 1968, one group penetrated the British Embassy in Peking (now Beijing) and assaulted the staff. The phrase 'running dog' was a derogatory term for a capitalist 'lapdog'.

By 1969, relations between Britain and China had improved, making this story appear 'dated' to one vituperative *Daily Mail* TV reviewer: 'As the Cultural Revolution has dwindled in China and the Red Guards have been sent back to school, the episode was meaningless. Why show it now? Talk about Thames being out of its tiny Chinese mind...'[137]

More intellectual newspapers continued taking note of the series as well, the *Sunday Times* acknowledging that from this episode onwards, all ITV regions were synchronised into screening the series at 9.00 pm. 'Of its kind, *Callan*... does for secret service fantasy what Alfred Burke's Marker did for the fantasy of the private eye... It is very astute and I gave credit where credit was due as soon as it started.'[138] The critic approved of the time-slot 'promotion', but also felt the TV schedules now had a surfeit of espionage programmes, concluding, 'from tea-time to 10 pm supper... we are given a solid diet of bloody violence made far more nauseating by being cunningly dressed up in terms of fantasy and hokum.'

'Hokum' seemed to be a common, dismissive term amongst broadsheet TV critics, as jazz musician and *bon viveur* George Melly also used it to describe *Callan* in *The Observer*. While giving qualified praise for the direction, the acting and the 'seedy realism, le Carré rather than Fleming'[139], Melly nevertheless felt the instalment was 'irritatingly self-congratulatory' and 'shouldn't preach quite so obtrusively.' He concluded, however, by saying, 'I must give it another look.'

MISSION ANALYSIS: *'The paper tiger is about to bite.'* A story of intellect versus violence, concluding with an inventive piece of brinkmanship: Callan engineers his escape from the Chinese and succeeds in his political-damage-limitation brief partly by carrying a gun that is for once *not loaded*, so he can't be framed in the way Tao Tsung intends.

Emms also tries to instil some international awareness and a sense of a different culture into the series but the results are mixed, an awkward combination of insightful dialogue and unfortunate stereotypical quips about 'inscrutability'. Unfortunately, the relevance of the script's subject matter has faded with time, and the verbose discourses about the benefits of democracy (endorsing philosopher Jean-Pierre Faye's 'Horseshoe Theory', which suggests that totalitarian, far-left and far-right systems are very similar to each other) appear stilted. The credulity of the viewers is also stretched when Holder first risks his partner Felice's life in his attack on the Chinese Embassy, and secondly when he doesn't suspect the building's lax security is a trap. How he expects his political ambitions to be furthered by his assassination scheme, and the impact his death will have on his supporters, are both questions left unanswered.

Tantalisingly, at one point Callan suggests kidnapping Tao Tsung for his own safety and making it appear as if he has defected to the West. While this foreshadows the scheme the Chinese later try on Callan himself, it is still a more diverting idea than the actual dénouement Emms opted for. Had the script gone down this route, 'The Running Dog' would probably have been more in keeping with the general ethos of the series.

The set photographs and location stills from this episode are a poignant reminder that it no longer exists. Fortunately, all episodes from this point on survived the cull in the archives.

S2.13 THE WORST SOLDIER I EVER SAW

Writer: James Mitchell
Director: Robert Tronson
Designer: Terry Gough

FIRST UK TRANSMISSION

Grampian: Monday 7 April 1969, 11.00 pm
All other regions: Wednesday 2 April 1969, 9.00 pm

CAST: Tessa Wyatt (Sarah Pringle), Allan Cuthbertson (Brigadier Pringle), Julia McCarthy (Mrs Carr), Saeed Jeffrey (Dr Megali), Larry Cross (General Klinger)

EXTRAS/WALK-ONS: (*Uncredited on screen,* used in exterior filming at Mobile Canteen) Walter Swash, Ernest Jennings, Mike Richardson, Robert Cude, Dennis Hayward, Paul Phillips, Eden Fox, John Clamp, Rex Rashley, Bill Richards, Thomas Laird, John Franklyn, Maurice Blake, Donald Groves, John Tucker, Bert Lena, Alec Morton, Nelly Griffiths, Winifred Schne, Maisie Merry, Keith Goodman, John Preston, James Walsh, George Day, Bill Lodge

PRODUCTION

Rehearsals: From Thursday 20 June
Location Filming: Danny Quastel Ltd., Lower Road, Rotherhithe; mobile canteen (location unknown; Monday 24 - Tuesday 25 June 1968)
Camera Rehearsals/Recording: Teddington Studio Two, Monday 1 and Tuesday 2 July 1968[140]

TV TIMES: 'A father, a daughter, a foreign call. And loyalty plays for the highest stakes. Callan joins the domestic staff of his ex-Brigadier – a man who is suspected of being chosen to lead a mercenary army in an emergent African nation.'
31 March-4 April 1969, Southern edition

MISSION PROFILE: Hunter meets his superior, Sir Michael Harvey[141] (see 'Heir Apparent') and his predecessor, Colonel Leslie (see Chapter 5), who is now advising the British government about the problematic Middle East state Abu Tafa. The Soviet-leaning Sultan of this oil-rich Arab country has a large army, but it needs an experienced leader. Brigadier Pringle has been offered this job, and eagerly accepted it. He was once Callan's commanding officer...

Pringle's daughter, Sarah, runs a charity for the homeless. Callan approaches her, posing as a vagrant trying to get work from his former CO; Pringle gives him job as a batman (manservant). Callan maintains this role while observing Pringle use alcohol and drugs to obtain information about America military plans in the Middle East from his friend, the US offcer General Klinger.

Warned by his opposition contact, Dr Megali, that the security services are onto him, Pringle prepares to leave Britain. Having drugged Sarah and knocked Megali out, Callan employs Lonely to break into Pringle's safe to obtain incriminating evidence. Pringle confronts Callan, who tells him he is under arrest. As the Brigadier tries to leave, Callan shoots him dead – in the back.

A MAN LIKE ME: In 'A Magnum for Schneider', it was revealed that Callan was twice demoted from the rank of Corporal, due to confrontations with officers; here we meet the most high-ranking one, his former Colonel, who bluntly states Callan was 'too much of an individualist for the army.'

Callan uses his real identity on this assignment. Mrs Carr, the housekeeper, is suspicious but warms to him when he says he doesn't want to talk about his soldiering in Malaya. He insists he knows silver service waiting – ironic, as starting 'from the outside and [working] in' is practically his job description in the Section.

Sarah catches Callan eavesdropping but agrees to forget it after he says he's worried about his job. Pringle is jealous of the way she, and the 'other ranks' Callan, seem to be bonding. At the same time, Callan thinks he'll be sacked (wrecking the Section's operation) after losing his temper and – once again – showing insubordination towards the Brigadier.

He expresses concern that he's 'getting past it' and lets his emotions get the better of him, visibly trying to control himself as he reveals to Pringle that he's a security agent. In the end, his anger at his old CO is overwhelming and instead of wounding him and taking him in, he vindictively shoots to kill.

Not surprisingly, he's very unsettled to find Colonel Leslie back in charge of the Section, with a backlog of Red Files for him to choose from.

Section Kills: 14

LONELY: Is known to Sarah as 'Mr Bellamy'; it appears that he's relied on her charity before, but it's unclear if it's his real name. He can recognise a key from an impression, follows Pringle to his bank and back, and forgoes a night at the (blue?) movies to help Callan rob the Brigadier's safe. Arriving at the house, he's aghast to find the bodies of Megali and Sarah and assumes Callan has 'croaked' them both. This is the first of several similar, almost comic overreactions whenever Lonely is confronted with evidence of Callan's unpleasant profession, filtered through his own conception of him as a hardened criminal.

An experienced safe-cracker, Lonely uses cushions to muffle the sound of explosives.

A TIE AND A CREST: The first Hunter – Leslie – recommended the third Hunter for his job. Hunter III tries to keep Callan and Leslie apart until he's left for Moscow, knowing that the pair have an antagonistic past. Meres is amused, knowing Callan will react badly.

Meres takes a phone bug for Callan to plant at Pringle's house, but rather than being small and innocuous, it's concealed in a shabby looking radio, reinforcing the cover story that 'Dave', on his uppers, is being forced to sell off some of his possessions. Toby ribs his colleague as he cleans the Brigadier's shoes, saying 'you ever thought of making a career of that?', while Mrs Carr seems quite taken with Meres, who's posing as a wide-boy car salesman in a loud checked jacket – she asks Callan how he could possibly have found 'a friend like 'im.'

ALCOHOL, TOBACCO AND FIREARMS: Callan's aggressive, intoxicated down-and-out acting is *very* convincing. Pringle warns him not to get drunk.

To loosen General Klinger's tongue, Pringle orders up a Martini (which he spikes with truth serum) and two jugs of iced hock. Pringle demands a 'hot as hell' curry'.

Callan relieves Pringle of a Webley service revolver. In an impressive piece of continuity, Callan's pistol has 'Noguchi' branded on the grip, suggesting that it's the same one that Lonely bought him in 'The Good Ones Are All Dead'.

SPY-SPEAK: 'Same old Section,' says Colonel Leslie cheerfully. 'No one ever tells any-one anything.'

'Any army is simply a device for killing the enemy. As a killer Callan, was unequalled,' Pringle opines, showing his innate callousness. He hates his daughter 'playing at being a social worker' but she stands up to him, refusing to emigrate: 'I'm not lying on cushions eating Turkish Delight... I don't belong in *The Arabian Knights*.'

'Call me sir!' the Brigadier barks as he pulls rank on Callan, possibly inspiring a future episode title. He refuses to swear on the Koran, saying, 'I'm C of E.'

Meres is taken aback by Hunter's impending trip to Moscow; the Section chief sarcas-tically apologises, saying he should have sent a memorandum.

Callan gives Lonely money in the betting shop, slyly advising him to put it on the horse 'Turkish Bath'.

There's more subtext when Mrs Carr says, 'there's no peace in service.' Callan replies: 'It's better than starving.'

PAWNS AND PLAYERS: ALLAN CUTHBERTSON (1920-1988) is familiar to comedy fans from *The Tommy Cooper Hour* (1973-75), *Ripping Yarns* – 'Roger of the Raj' (1979), *Terry and June* (1981-83) and *Fawlty Towers* – 'Gourmet Night' (1975), in which he played the twitchy Colonel Hall. This latter casting was inspired by Cuthbertson's portrayals of the officer class in war films like *Ice Cold in Alex* (1958), *The Guns of Navarone* (1961) and the *Armchair Theatre* play 'The Criminals' (1958). He was a frequent guest star in *The Avengers*, appearing in four stories – 'The Deadly Air' (1961), 'Death at Bargain Prices' (1965), 'Death's Door' (1967) and 'Super Secret Cypher Snatch' (1968). Cuthbertson was one half of a duo of gentlemen killers in *Danger Man* – 'The Island' (1961) and played the slave-driving Turner in *Man in a Suitcase* – 'No Friend of Mine' (1968). In *UFO* – 'The Square Triangle' (1970), his character was targeted for murder by Patrick Mower's greedy lothario. Before *Callan*, in 1968 Cuthbertson took part in the controversial gangland/rock star film *Performance* (with Anthony Valentine), not released until 1971.

TESSA WYATT (born 1948) played Vicky in the sitcom *Robin's Nest* (1977-1981) and featured in the horror film *The Beast in the Cellar* (1970), the controversial UFO episode 'The Long Sleep' (1973), which showed her character taking hallucinogenic drugs, *Return of the Saint* – 'Vicious Circle' (1979), *Virtual Murder* – 'A Dream of Dracula' (1992), and *Peep Show* (2003-15). She enjoyed working with 'Al' Cuthbertson, (as the cast knew him). 'Saeed [Jaffrey] came into an episode of *Robin's Nest* with us as well,'[142] she recalled, 'and I knew Russell Hunter at the time, too.'

SAEED JAFFREY (1929-2015) studied as a historian before working for All India Radio, founding his own theatre company in Delhi in 1951 and then moving to London to study at RADA; he was also the first Indian actor to tour Shakespeare's plays in America. He appeared alongside Dame Gladys Cooper in a stage production of *A Passage to India* (1962), and, after moving back to Britain, performed the same play for the *BBC Play of the Month* (1965). In the 1970s, Jaffrey became well-known as Aslam Rafiq, the hard-nosed yet oddly likeable crime lord in Philip Martin's increasingly surreal *Gangsters* (1975-78). In addition to his prolific appearances in Indian films, he guested in *Minder* – 'The Bengal Tiger' (1979), *Strangers* – 'A Dear Green Place' (1981), *Mitch* with John Thaw (1984), the comedy *Tandoori Nights* (1985-1987) and the prestigious TV drama *The Jewel in the Crown* (1984). After he appeared with Edward Woodward in *Common as Muck* (1994–97). in 2001, Woodward featured on the *This is Your Life* edition dedicated to Jaffrey.[143]

LARRY CROSS (1913-1976), an Americam working in Britain, had small roles in *The Saint* – 'The Saint Sees It Through' (1963), *The Avengers* – 'Quick-Quick Slow Death' (1966), *Man in a Suitcase* – 'All That Glitters' (1967) and *Thriller* – 'Where the Action Is ' (1975).

JULIA McCARTHY (1927-1991) played Adam Faith's mother Alice in *Budgie* (1971-72).

INFORMATION: There is a tantalising insight into Callan's history: he was court martialed by Pringle – for an undisclosed crime – and served two years in a military prison ('the glasshouse'). This still leaves gaps, but as in most of his television stories, Mitchell only reveals the bare, formative essentials of David Callan's past. 'Neither Callan or [Jack] Ford [in *When the Boat Comes In*] have a back story,'[144] Peter Mitchell commented, speculating that this was because his father was in 'total denial of his [own past].' Considering Callan's court martial is such a turning point in his life, it's never mentioned in the series again, or in any of Mitchell's novels or short stories.

'It was good fun, no jealousy,'[145] Derek Bond said of working with his predecessor as Hunter, and James Mitchell was similarly pleased with Ronald Radd's return. Mitchell chose to make Pringle a Brigadier as the position was 'nice and remote – not many of the lower ranks would see the man who was commanding [their] brigade.'[146]

The originally-transmitted version of this episode is missing, but it was reconstructed for release on DVD from an unedited recording, by technicians working for the Network DVD label. As the magazine *Primetime* noted, this unedited recording came 'complete with unscheduled guest appearances by the boom mike and actors fluffing their lines, but no opening titles or network logo due to complications from the ABC/Thames switchover... weirder still, the version changing hands among collectors [was] a conversion from the American NTSC format.'[147] This recording has now been released by Network[148] and it illustrates both the dedication of the actors and crew – under the concentrated pressure of recording, Woodward can be seen visibly sweating and shaking while he steels himself for a take – and, charmingly, the voice of a studio manager can be heard at the conclusion, asking everyone to stay behind until the 'all clear' (technical clearance).

There are parallels with Mitchell's John Craig novel *Die Rich, Die Happy* (1965), in which the Department K agent is assigned to protect the Greek millionaire Naxos, who has interests in Middle East oil, and *Danger Man* – 'No Marks for Servility' (1964), where a resentful Drake works as butler to Howard Marion Crawford's arrogant tycoon Gregori. The idea of a sinister member of the domestic staff undermining a household may have been inspired by Joseph Losey's unsettling film *The Servant* (1963).

Colonel Leslie fears 'a Vietnam in the Middle East': in the 1960s, the Soviets sided with anti-Israeli regimes, while America similarly cultivated Turkey and Iran under the Shah, who had been installed in an MI6 and CIA coup in 1953 to protect British oil interests. The fictional Sultan in 'The Worst Soldier I Ever Saw' may be based on Gamal Abdel Nasser, the President of Egypt during the Suez Crisis in 1956 and the Six Day War (1967), who accepted financial aid from Russia to build the Aswan Dam. Middle East economics had previously featured in the TV spy genre in *The Avengers* – 'Death a la Carte' (1963) and *Danger Man* – 'I Can Only Offer You Sherry' (1966).

The Malayan colonial war previously alluded to in 'A Magnum For Schneider'.

MISSION ANALYSIS: *'You bloody taught me how to kill, and when I got too rough you didn't like it, mate, did you?'* While it's the biggest coincidence in the whole series that Callan's old commanding officer is the man chosen to lead the armed forces in a Middle East state sympathetic to the USSR, the story does deliver one of *Callan*'s most powerful scenes. Pringle comes to an ignominious end, shot in the back by the monster he created, having misread just how much pent-up resentment Callan is harbouring towards him. It makes for a very disturbing denouement to the story, reminding the viewers just how ruthless and brutal Callan can be.

Pringle is another conflicted Mitchell creation: a trustee of Sarah's charity who thinks her charges are 'layabouts' and 'scum', is altruistic towards Callan, but only because he wants to use him as a killer. He is motivated by money and warmongering, yet finds it hard to sleep at night. The reactionary/liberal clashes between him and his daughter are movingly conveyed by Allan Cuthbertson and Tessa Wyatt, another example of the series reflecting the contemporary 'generation gap'.

Some of the material feels recycled. This is Mitchell's take on the 'rogue mentor' idea, so it inevitably has some parallels with 'Goodbye Nobby Clarke'. The story also includes another robbery of a safe and a conflicted antagonist. There are nice directorial touches from Tronson highlighting the hierarchy between the characters: the telephone rings and even though Pringle is nearest, he lets Callan walk over and answer it; and although Meres teases Callan about being in service, he helps his colleague wash up. When Lonely arrives, he subserviently opens the door for Callan, neatly suggesting that he's the agent's servant.

A dramatic coda of Sarah reacting to her father's death and Callan's part in it is the only – notable – omission here. Overall, while slow and short on tension in places, this episode still contains much to reflect on. In retrospect, Callan shooting a former superior can also be read as a hint of what lies ahead...

S2.14 NICE PEOPLE DIE AT HOME

Writer: Robert Banks Stewart
Director: Peter Duguid
Designers: Peter le Page, Norman Garwood [Remount]

FIRST UK TRANSMISSION

Grampian: Monday 14 April 1969, 11.00 pm
All other regions: Wednesday 9 April 1969, 9.00 pm

CAST: Harry Towb (Marshall), Frederick Jaeger (Belukov), Angela Morant (Nadia), Jonathan Burn (Chelenko), Roger Bizley (Ross), Kenneth Benda (Doctor)

PRODUCTION

Location Filming: South Kensington Underground station, and Cromwell Road, London, (Saturday 1 July 1967)[149]
Rehearsals: Until 10 July 1967, Steadfast Hall
Camera Rehearsals/Recording: Teddington Studios Two and Three, Tuesday 11 and Wednesday 12 July 1967[150]
Rehearsals (Remount): Wednesday 26–Friday 28 June 1968
Camera Rehearsals/Recording (Remount): Teddington Studio Two, Wednesday 3 July 1968[151]

TV TIMES: 'With a pet shop as their cover, two Russian agents run a highly successful spy ring in Britain. Soon, however, they are to retire and it is known that their replacement is arriving in the country shortly.

'Callan, under the orders of Hunter's temporary replacement (played by Ronald Radd while Derek Bond is on holiday), is instructed to take the place of the new agent, gain the confidence of the pet shop owners and aim for a valuable prize – the head of the Russian intelligence organisation in Britain...'
7-11 April 1969, Southern edition

MISSION PROFILE: Eric Marshall, real name Mareschke, runs a pet shop with his daughter, Nadia; the pair are small-time Russian spies, about to retire. Roscovitch is sent to replace them: the Section intercept him, and Callan is substituted instead. Having infiltrated the KGB cell, he prepares to send a coded signal saying the Marshalls are defecting. This will lure the Russians' London controller, Belukov, out of his Embassy. He is Callan's real target.

Suddenly Marshall collapses, and Callan finds the old man is terminally ill. Disgusted, he tells Colonel Leslie the plan is off. However, the Colonel has arranged for Roscovitch to escape... Aware the Russians will now send someone to kill the Marshalls, Callan returns to the shop to protect them. He is caught off-guard when Belukov himself arrives to carry out the executions. Nadia changes sides and shoots her superior. Callan holds the fatally injured Belukov hostage, so the Section will allow Marshall and Nadia safe passage out of the country.

A MAN LIKE ME: Despite finding it difficult to be 'a stranger in Shepherds Bush', Callan maintains his cover, saying he learnt his authentic English accent off a British army corporal (i.e. himself). He hates working with Colonel Leslie again, knowing the job will be 'dirty'. Ironically, however, Callan has no initial objection to the case: he was seeing a girl in

Beirut whom Belukov shot while trying to kill him. Callan defers revenge, however, when he develops sympathy for the Marshalls. He is furious about the Colonel's pitiless scheme to prosecute them should they emerge unscathed. By abducting the injured Belukov, and threatening a diplomatic incident if he delivers him back to his Embassy, Callan blackmails Leslie into helping the Marshalls leave England. He tries to finish Belukov off, but can't bring himself to shoot a wounded man; the Russian dies from his wounds anyway.

LONELY: Told to deliver Callan's messages, Lonely is starting to query his associate's life-style. Nastily, Callan squashes a drawing pin into his hand to deter his questions and hides a microdot kit from him.

Lonely tells the Colonel and Meres that he only works for Callan, although he does convey a message to them. Knowing Callan is in trouble, he offers to call up some hard men to help, although it's difficult to tell how realistic this proposition is. He briefly holds a gun on Nadia and her father, but handles it as if it were 'a hot potato.'[152]

A TIE AND A CREST: The Section needs Belukov's codename. Like James Bond and John Steed, Meres is a golfer and uses Roscovitch for target practice, employing him as a target on his personal indoor course. (Guy Ritchie's overrated 1998 film *Lock, Stock and Two Smoking Barrels* has a very similar sequence.)

The codename turns out to be 'Oliver Cromwell'. The Colonel thinks this is cheeky: Meres reminds him Cromwell chopped off another Charlie's head, so like every other old Etonian he's been well-drilled in the history of the English Kings and Queens.

Hearing from Lonely that Meres has a rifle trained on him, Callan speculates that 'some day' the Section will be aiming a gun to kill him. He says that a good veal and ham pie can be bought 'round the corner' from the Section HQ.

ALCOHOL, TOBACCO AND FIREARMS: Callan, Nadia and her father down Vodka, 'the drink of spies.' Belukov has one in the Embassy too, bored with paperwork. Nadia has arranged for Callan to stay upstairs in the neighbouring pub; Lonely is delighted by this prospect. Marshall's doctor tells Nadia her father might as well keep smoking, so his diagnosis is not very positive.

There is a lot of firepower on display. Meres intimidates Ross by firing a long-barrelled Smith and Wesson revolver at him; Leslie later tries it out on the Section shooting range. Meres trains a rifle with a telescopic sight on the pet shop, and Callan arranges to have a Luger delivered there. Nadia and Belukov both use hand guns fitted with silencers.

SPY-SPEAK: Callan sardonically says to Colonel Leslie, 'Do you play the national anthem every time you leave the office?'

He tells Lonely that he smells like 'rising damp' and, later, to 'get the lift on your own. That shouldn't be difficult with your BO.'

Belukov is fed up with his underling in the Embassy: 'Your face ripples with humour like a frozen lake.'

Meres, while driving golf balls at Roscovitch: 'Sliced a bit there...'

Leslie is unimpressed when an RSPCA van interrupts his stakeout: 'Oh dear. They really do pick their moments, don't they?'

PAWNS AND PLAYERS: HARRY/HARRIS TOWB (1925-2009) grew up in Belfast, of

Irish and Russian-Jewish ancestry. His abundant stage work included stints with the RSC, roles at Dublin's Abbey Theatre and playing Lenin on Broadway in Tom Stoppard's play *Travesties* (1976). Early appearances in the BBC thriller *The Teckman Biography* (1953) and the Ronald Howard version of *Sherlock Holmes* (1954-55, not screened in the UK at that time) were followed by other television work including *The Saint* – 'The Man Who Was Lucky' (1962), 'The High Fence' (1964), *Mr. Rose* – 'The Less-Than-Iron-Duke' (1968), *The Avengers* – 'Killer' (1968, opposite Anthony Valentine), *The Champions* – 'The Mission' and *The Mind of Mr J.G. Reeder* – 'The Green Mamba' (both 1969), as well as 'The Willing Victim' (1971).

Doctor Who viewers will recall Towb's turn as a hapless factory executive smothered by a killer plastic armchair in 'Terror of the Autons' (1971); the actor also appeared briefly in 'The Seeds of Death' (1969) before being killed by an Ice Warrior. He showed his talent for comedy as regular Private Dooley in *The Army Game* (1959), later performing in the BBC Northern Ireland comedy-drama *So You Think You've Got Troubles* (1991). He was also one of Chris Morris's interviewees in *The Day Today* – 'Factgasm' (1994). Towb's film credits include *The Blue Max* (1966) and Stanley Kubrick's *Barry Lyndon* (1974). Towb continued working into his 80s, appearing in *EastEnders* (in 2008) and *The Bill*. A friend of Edward Woodward's, he returned to *Callan* in the third series, playing the semi-regular part of Judd, the Section armourer (see 'Where Else Could I Go?' and 'A Village Called "G"', Chapter 7).

MANFRED FREDERICK JAEGER (1928-2004) was born in Germany; fleeing the Nazi takeover, his family arrived in England in 1939. Following theatre success in the West End in the 1940s he was ironically cast as Germans in several war films, including *Ice Cold In Alex* (1958). Jaeger successfully broke his typecasting and became known for his roles in *The Inside Man* (1969, as criminologist Dr James Austen) and *Special Branch* (1974, as Commander Fletcher). He also made regular appearances in *The Main Chance* (1975). *The Sweeney* – 'Trojan Bus' (1975) features Jaeger portraying a nonchalantly sleazy art dealer, while in *Doctor Who* he played three very different characters between 1966 and 1977, the last being Professor Marius, inventor of the robot dog K9. Jaeger was therapist to Eddie *Shoestring* in the stand-out episode 'Mocking Bird' (1980) and an untrustworthy senior policeman in *Return of the Saint* – 'Signal Stop' (1978). He collaborated with Kenny Everett, and guested hilariously in *Some Mothers Do 'Ave 'Em* as Frank Spencer's flying instructor (1978), while his film credits include a weary pilot couriering secret film in le Carré's *The Looking Glass War* (1969) and the Sherlock Holmes drama *The Seven Per Cent Solution* (1976).

ANGELA MORANT (Born 1943) was the first wife of the actor Sir Ben Kingsley. She played Octavia in *I, Claudius* (1976, also featuring Roger Bizley) and was the romantic foil Ruth Rawlinson to John Thaw's detective in *Inspector Morse* – 'Service of All the Dead' (1987).

HENRY JONAS JONATHAN BURN-FORTI (born 1939) appeared in the Hammer horror film *Blood from the Mummy's Tomb* (1971, as a 'Saturnine Young Man') and the BBC television adaptation of *Smiley's People* (1982).

KENNETH BENDA (1902–1978) was one of the array of eccentrics being murdered in *The Avengers* – 'From Venus with Love' (1967), a stand-in Supervisor in *The Prisoner* – 'Free For All' (1967), an irritable pathologist in the horror film *Scream and Scream Again* (1969) and a sinister minister in *The Private Life of Sherlock Holmes* (1970).

INFORMATION: Following the decision to hold this episode over from the first series, several scenes were rewritten and reshot to integrate the story into the tail end of the Series Two. Terence Feely was credited as 'series developer' on this episode, reflecting its origin. Woodward, Valentine and a recalled Ronald Radd reprised their roles, along with Roger Bizley as Roscovitch; Lisa Langdon also made a brief appearance. Six new scenes were interspersed with the older footage, the first office sequence became a working lunch 'for old time's sake'; the later argument was toughened so Callan calls the Colonel a 'bastard'. Essentially, however, the original plot points were all preserved.[153]

The earliest draft of the story was entitled 'All Spies Are Alike', an opinion Callan expresses to the Colonel. In this version, one handover method for the Russian microdots involved concealing them on abstract paintings. Callan describes himself as 'out of the game' regarding the Section, tells the Colonel to 'shut up about his stomach' when he says the name Belukov sounds like a make of caviar (Beluga), threatens him with violence and refers to him as 'rusting his rear off' behind a desk. The Colonel shows Callan a dog from the pet shop, the implication being that Callan is his poodle. An excised comic exchange saw Lonely trying to treat his halitosis and BO; Callan sarcastically asks him if he's been 'drinking meths', then adds that he smells like an 'old tom' (a prostitute). Intriguingly, Lonely was to reply, 'You just say that 'cos you know it's my name.' This shows that as with Liz, some consideration was going into fleshing out the character by giving him a full name (see 'The Worst Soldier I Ever Saw', page 222). In Lonely's case the idea was dropped.

Working with Robert Banks Stewart again on the first series of *Bergerac*, John Kershaw contributed the episode 'Nice People Die in Bed' (1981), the title of which may well have been an in-joke. Stylistic touches from the Series One, namely Woodward's voiceover for Callan's thoughts and the use of 'Girl in the Dark' as incidental music, are temporarily reinstated for this story.

'When I was a young reporter, halfway down the road from the office where I worked was a pet shop so, again, you use elements of your previous experience,'[154] Robert Banks Stewart said of this story. 'It might be true to say that hiring me to write a couple of episodes... meant that [with my journalistic background] I brought quite a lot to [the series].'

Peter Duguid recalled looking at the original 1967 recording story of the story for reference while shooting the remount a year later, 'to try and make it match.'[155] Originally two studios had been needed for recording. 'We were so overcrowded we went over to Studio Three for a set-up. Studio Two is only a medium-size, and in this story we had a big set with a walkway and a flat, and [as] there were a lot of animals in the studio, it was a bit smelly!' 'Most of the problems with livestock are to do with sound: they won't shut up,'[156] Peter le Page added. 'The sound was relatively directional because we were using boom mikes. When the animals weren't needed they were taken out [of the set].'

There are more parallels with the real case of the Portland spy ring[157]. In 1960, MI5 surveillance teams identified a 'deep cover' Soviet spy, Konon Molody (alias 'Gordon Lonsdale' , see Chapter 8) receiving stolen papers. He was followed and his Albany Street flat was bugged. Investigators were eventually led to a couple in Ruislip who ran an antiquarian bookshop. They turned out to be veteran American KGB agents Peter and Helen Kroeger (alias Morris and Lona Cohen), and their innocuous-seeming emporium concealed a radio transmitter.

Callan mentions *Dr Zhivago*, the eponymous hero of the Russian novel by Boris

Pasternak, which had been made into an epic feature film in 1965 by David Lean. In the London Underground lift, behind Nadia there is a poster advertising 'The Meeting in the Pool' which carries the telling number '007'. The director positions Angela Morant directly in front of it, so its inclusion was obviously intended as an in-joke.

Reviewer Nancy Banks-Smith continued backing the show, describing Callan as: 'an off-the-peg, undernourished, seedy anti-hero. He looks like a man who is good at his job but unhappy in his work. And maybe most of us can identify with that. A character mixed according to Raymond Chandler's recipe: "If I wasn't hard, I wouldn't be alive. If I couldn't ever be gentle, I wouldn't deserve to be alive."'[158]

MISSION ANALYSIS: *'It's not going to be very hard with a bastard like you.'* Callan temporarily bonds with a surrogate father and sister, figures on the fringe of espionage whose plight is easy for the audience to identify with. The Marshalls' motivation is conveyed well, as is the antipathy between Callan and Belukov. (He's another mirror image villain, like Bunin and Nobby Clarke, showing that Mitchell and Banks Stewart were thinking along similar lines. Like Callan, Belukov likes a drink). As with other contemporary spy fiction, here the KGB is an organisation riddled with paranoia: its retirement plan for former agents involves faking their deaths, with a suggestion that there isn't actually much faking involved. As in Banks Stewart's other scripts, the Section are again prone to making mistakes, not even considering Belukov might have adopted a disguise.

Once again, Callan goes undercover and forms a platonic friendship with a strong female character in a story with everyday settings. An edgy Part Three sees Callan having to switch motivation from killer to protector as he and Nadia finally co-operate against their respective controllers. The pet-shop setting, burst of post-gunfire animal noise and the remounted scenes with 'Colonel Leslie' all work very effectively.

Lonely meeting the Colonel, and being entrusted to hold hostages at gunpoint, raises the question of exactly how much he knows about Callan's real occupation as a secret agent. The issue of continuity regarding Lonely and the Section becomes more inconsistent from this point on.

Belukov's death scene is set in Callan's own temporary 'home'. Even as he lies injured and dying, the KGB man tries to antagonise his opponent while Callan boils with hatred but cannot quite bring himself to shoot him dead. With powerful acting from Woodward and Jaeger, this scene forms a shattering and thought-provoking conclusion to the story, making it a strong swansong for Feely, Banks Stewart and – one small cameo aside – the great Ronald Radd.

S2.15 DEATH OF A HUNTER

Writer: Michael Winder
Director: Reg Collin
Designer: Neville Green

FIRST UK TRANSMISSION
Grampian: Mon 21 April 1969, 11:00 pm
All other regions: Wed 16 April 1969, 9:00 pm

CAST: Terry Scully (Kenny), Barbara Leigh-Hunt (Susanne), John Flanagan (Striker), Derek Waring (Haynes), Norman Wooland (Koralin), Michael Meacham (Andrews)

PRODUCTION
Readthrough: Thursday 4 July 1968
Rehearsals: Saturday 6 – Tuesday 9 July 1968, Thursday 11 – Monday 15 July
Location Filming: Teddington and Surbiton (Friday 5 July)
Camera Rehearsals/Recording: Teddington Studio Two, Wednesday 10 July
Outside Broadcast Recording: Maudes furniture warehouse, Teddington High Street
(Tuesday 16 July – Wednesday 17 July)[161]

TV TIMES: 'A man with a drug in his blood could believe anything – if he does, he might as well be dead. In the last programme of the present series, a hunter dies – but which one? Is it the hard-bitten Callan, the laconic Meres, the enigmatic Hunter or someone else...? Death, an ever-present possibility in the life of an agent, waits in the wings as today's story nears its bizarre conclusion.'
12-18 April 1969, Granada edition

MISSION PROFILE: Working covertly for Hunter, Callan searches for KGB radio operator Striker, renting a flat opposite the man's accommodation, unaware that he's under surveillance himself. Hunter instructs him to steal a codebook of Striker's, copy it, and return it unnoticed; Callan calls Lonely in to help.

Burgling Striker's bedsit, Lonely flees after he finds the man's corpse. Callan is then arrested for 'espionage' and drugged. He is accused of being a Russian spy and a murderer, and is told Striker was a British agent. In a warehouse, he's beaten on the orders of one interrogator, 'Haynes', then apparently befriended by another, 'Susanne'.

The abductors collectively lead Callan to believe they are from 'Section 3' in British security, looking for a spy. In reality, they're KGB. Employing hypnosis, more drugs and an agent resembling Hunter (Koralin), they condition Callan to believe his boss is the traitor.

Having apparently had both Lonely and 'Susanne' killed, the fake Hunter gives orders for Callan to be disposed of. Still drugged, Callan breaks free and, just as the KGB cell intended, he arms himself, bursts into the Section HQ and kills the real Hunter. Meres then shoots Callan twice and he crashes to the floor...

A MAN LIKE ME: Callan believes his chief will rapidly put his captors, whom he thinks are British, right about his loyalty. However, his innate distrust of authority, and Hunter in particular – suppressed recently while working for the urbane John Ramsey – soon resurfaces, cleverly drawn back out by his captors.

Clearly the KGB's ersatz Section have researched Callan well, as they exploit his compassion too. Their psychological conditioning takes a firm grip once he thinks he has heard Lonely being shot, and apparently witnessing 'Susanne' being throttled to death on the fake Hunter's orders completes the process. Convincing Callan that he has three hours to stop Hunter killing the Russian President plays on his sense of duty.

Even while bruised and delirious, he still has the ability – and sufficient inside knowledge of Section HQ's security procedures – to break through to Hunter's office during a 'Red Alert'. He watches Liz leave before mounting his assault and then his marksmanship is, sadly, as deadly as ever.

Section Kills: 15 - Hunter III

LONELY: Previously boasted he once burgled a castle bedroom while its female occupant was sleeping with 'the leading man from the local rep'; typically, Callan doesn't believe him.

He positions marbles on Striker's floor in case he wakes up; it's only on retrieving them, after stealing a small strongbox, that Lonely realises the KGB man has had his throat cut. Despite his fear, he's light-fingered enough to take the strongbox home. The fake Section know where Lonely lives and pull him in – luckily, they don't seem to think it's worth killing him. The (rather wobbly) walls in his flat are simply *plastered* with softcore porn.

'Lonely continuity' issues continue to grow: he witnesses part of Callan's interrogation, and Meres takes him to 'HQ' for questioning, but the thief never mentions these events again.

A TIE AND A CREST: The Section HQ is confirmed as being 'housed in a disused Edwardian School.'[162] As hinted before, the Section seems to subsist on a miserly budget and most of the staff are occupied checking 'undesirables' prior to the Russian President's visit. (Hunter may have been fed some KGB disinformation about an assassination attempt.)

Meres is unhappy when Callan is pistol-whipped, and he's angry with Hunter about the arrest too, before shamefacedly realising he's been deceived. The bedside telephone call he receives from the fake Hunter refers to Snell and uses the 'Charlie' code word, and the ersatz Section also have authentic ID cards for the real 'Section 3'. Their inside information has been provided by Sir Michael Harvey who is the actual traitor. He visits both the Section – to berate Hunter and Meres for incompetence – and the fake Section, to check progress and assist in brainwashing Callan.

Meres gets increasingly concerned about the missing Callan, unusually letting his stress show by punching a wall in frustration.

Tragically, Hunter doesn't quite figure out that while he's trying to identify Harvey, the KGB are targeting him. He has a gun within reach on his desk, but when attacked by Callan, he's too surprised to reach for it.

ALCOHOL, TOBACCO AND FIREARMS: Striker is sent to the pub, to lure Callan out of his flat so the KGB can bug it. The fake Section then drink vodka while eavesdropping on Callan's conversations. Striker is a nervous smoker.

Later, waiting for news of Callan's whereabouts, 'Susanne', 'Haynes' and the fake Hunter all puff away in their warehouse base.

Lonely keeps a gun taped under the bed in his flat, most likely an emergency arrangement with Callan.

SPY-SPEAK: Everyone has a 'cracking point'. 'Take it from me,' Susanne says to Callan when he denies it. 'I know.'

Hunter speculates Callan will be 'blabbing' about the job he was on. 'Not Callan, sir!' Meres surprisingly insists. Later, he is genuinely distraught at having to gun down his old adversary, pleading with Callan: 'Why, David? *Why?*' (which was scripted as 'Why, Callan? Why?')

PAWNS AND PLAYERS: DEREK WARING (1927–2007), born Derek Barton-Chapple, was the son of John Logie Baird's colleague Wing Commander H.J. Barton-Chapple. After securing early roles in *The Jack Benny Programme* (1956) and the first ITC film series *The Adventures of Robin Hood* (1957-58), he went became a *Z Cars* regular, Detective Inspector Goss (1969-1973), and starred in the sitcom *Moody and Pegg* (1974-75) as Roland Moody. Waring took guest roles in *The New Avengers* – 'Tale of The Big Why' (1976), *George and Mildred* (1977), *The Professionals* – 'Discovered in a Graveyard' (1982) and ushered Peter Davison into *Doctor Who,* in the fifth Doctor's first story 'Castrovalva' (1982). At the RSC, he appeared in the plays *Wars of the Roses* (1965) and *The Boy Friend* (1984).

JOHN FLANAGAN (born 1947) appeared in *The Naked Civil Servant* (1975) and as DS Matthews in early episodes of *The Sweeney* (1975); his character was renamed Willard for the spin-off feature film *Sweeney 2* (1978). He had parts in the police serial *Parkin's Patch* (1969-1970, as PC Parkin himself), *Crown Court* (1973-1984, as semi-regular counsel John Lloyd), *Thriller* – 'The Double Kill' (1975), 'Kill Two Birds' (1976), *Secret Army* – 'A Matter of Life and Death' (1978), *The Medusa Touch* (1978), *Brazil* (1985), and, recently, *Whitechapel* (2012). He periodically works as a writer in partnership with another actor, Andrew McCulloch. One of the pair's collaborations was the espionage comedy drama *Sleepers* (1991).

TERRY SCULLY (1936 –2001) would have been familiar to viewers from his appearances as Bicket in *The Forsyte Saga* (1967). He had parts in *Dixon of Dock Green* (1966), *Softly, Softly* (1967-68), and *Z Cars* (1965-1972). He delivered a memorable performance as Fewsham, a cowardly hostage of the Ice Warriors, in *Doctor Who* – 'The Seeds of Death' (1969) and portrayed the crippled regular character Vic Thatcher in *Survivors* (1975). Future Hunter Hugh Walters took over the part after Scully became unwell.

BARBARA LEIGH HUNT, Born in 1935 and a cousin of fellow actor Ronald, played one of the victims of Barry Foster's strangler in *Frenzy* (1972). A theatre veteran of over thirty years, she guested in *Public Eye* – 'You Should Hear Me Eat Soup' (1965), *Special Branch* – 'Exit a Diplomat' (1969) and the *Thriller* spin-off 'Who Killed Lamb?' (1974).

NORMAN WOOLAND (1910–1989) featured in Olivier's films of *Hamlet* (1948) and *Richard III* (1955), Roman drama *Quo Vadis* (1951), *The Guns of Navarone* (1961) and horror film *The Projected Man* (1966). His television credits include the P. D. James mystery *Cover Her Face* (1985) and the Peter Cushing version of *Sherlock Holmes* – 'The Musgrave Ritual' (1968).

MICHAEL MEACHAM appeared in *The Saint* – 'The Rough Diamonds' (1963), and as a group captain in *Get Some In!* (1975).

Little information seems to exist regarding MICHAEL WINDER. 'I never met him. I never even spoke to him on the phone; I don't know who he was,'[163] said Mike Vardy, who directed a future Winder script. The writer's other credited work in the espionage genre included screenplays for *The Saint* – 'Escape Route' (1966), 'To Kill a Saint' (1967), 'Legacy for the Saint' (1968), *The Avengers* – 'Dead Man's Treasure' (1967). He also wrote episodes of *The Mask of Janus* (1965) and its spin-off *The Spies* (1966), two BBC thriller series set in a fictional European country featuring the machinations of British, US and Communist agents. Winder's fantasy contributions are equally eclectic, including *Ace of Wands* – 'The Eye of Ra' (1970), featuring a mad chess player, *Space:1999* – 'Devil's Planet' (1977), the fourth-wall breaking werewolf whodunit movie *The Beast Must Die* (1974) and *The Prisoner* 'homage' *Welcome to Blood City* (1977), a feature film directed by Peter Sasdy.

INFORMATION: This episode was the last to be made in Series Two and was shot in two blocks, the second employing Outside Broadcast (OB) cameras for all the warehouse scenes in the Maudes furniture warehouse. 'They were scenery movers who did a lot of work for Thames,'[164] John Kershaw remembered. 'There were very long OB sessions, whole sequences in which Callan was incarcerated.' He believed these were shot 'as live' – 'we had limited time to hire the place.' The final scenes of the story were slotted into this block too, with the set for Hunter's office being re-erected at the warehouse location.[165]

Throughout the camera rehearsal script the real and fake Hunters were lettered 'A' and 'B' to differentiate between them, with the specification, 'Some of the B Hunter will be played by A, on every occasion he is seen from Callan's POV.' Changes from script to screen included Hunter originally confiding in Meres, then saying, 'Let's hope you aren't the leak!' Dialogue suggesting that Callan had been held prisoner for 'a month' was amended to 'a week'; two brief scenes featuring Callan moving unopposed through corridors in the Section HQ were also cut from the finished version, presumably for reasons of credibility. This episode is unusual in that it shows Meres at home in bed (taped on a small cut-away set) being awoken by a phone call. It is unclear if he has company or not. 'I probably thought that he didn't have much of a private life,' Anthony Valentine reflected.[166]

'From a personal point of view that episode is memorable for me because it was the first TV drama I ever did,'[167] John Flanagan said. 'In fact, it was my first professional engagement after leaving the Central School of Speech and Drama in 1968. I met the producer Reginald Collin at an interview and was offered the minor role that I played.' Flanagan is unsure whether 'Death of a Hunter' was really intended to be the final episode of the series. 'I think [the cast] were all aware they had a good show on their hands and were obviously keen to keep it going. I wasn't aware that was supposed to be the last episode, and I'd never seen the programme before I appeared in it – drama students didn't watch telly much in those days!'

Despite their oddly defensive plot précis (possibly couched that way due to the presence of drugs in the story), in most regions *TV Times* promoted the series with a still on the episode's listings page of Meres threatening Lonely, and a photographic montage on their 'Playback' page. This showed Callan shooting Eva in 'Once a Big Man, Always a Big Man' and then posed the question, 'Will Callan himself be bumped off?'[168] Interviewed by the publication, Reg Collin skilfully hyped the grand finale, revealing that two endings to the series had been recorded and adding that he was now in a 'dilemma' over which to use: 'The difference between the endings we have filmed is that one leaves the way open for more; the other tends to close the book.' The feature concluded, 'If you like Callan, now is the time to cheer very loudly.'

After transmission, the *TV Times'* letters page on 17 May reflected the impact of 'Death of a Hunter' on the audience. 'The last episode of *Callan* was a complete betrayal of the popularity which this series has enjoyed,' [169] opined J. Barron, evidently annoyed at the agent's apparent demise. Mrs Patricia Sygrove of Sheffield was more optimistic: 'Congratulations to all responsible for the *Callan* series,' she wrote. '... I'm hoping that Callan (with permission from Mr Woodward) will make a miraculous recovery to ensure a new series in the future.'

In the real world of espionage prior to this episode, 'One time pads' – employing a disposable key for a coded message – had been found in the possession of the Portland spy ring.[170] The Soviet pads were generated by typists and in the 1940s, MI5 were able to crack some of the coded traffic to Moscow as a result of errors made in generating and distributing the key material. This operation was later codenamed VENONA and used in attempts to identify the group that came to be known as the 'Cambridge Five', whose members, including Philby, Maclean, Burgess and Blunt (see 'You're Under Starter's Orders', Chapter 4 and 'Blackmailers Should Be Discouraged') passed information to the Soviet Union through the 1940s and early 1950s.

Publicly accused of being the 'third man' in the group, Philby continued to deny the allegation, leaving MI6 and returning to journalism; he was later mistakenly exonerated and reinstated by his former employers so he could report on events in the Middle East. Defector Anatoliy Golitsyn (see 'Red Knight, White Knight') provided intelligence implying that five agents in total were at work, although it was some time before this information, and fresh thoughts on the abstruse VENONA profiles, were acted upon. Having been questioned by old colleague and friend Nick Elliot, Philby fled to the Soviet Union in 1963. Following this debacle, public speculation continued that there were more senior traitors like the fictional Harvey at large. (Anthony Blunt, the 'fourth man' in the ring, had in fact confessed in exchange for immunity from prosecution, but this information was kept out of the public domain until 1979; like Harvey, he had a knighthood. Even now, theorising about the possible identity of the 'fifth man' continues. He is generally believed to be another Cambridge graduate, John Cairncross (1913-1995) but there are alternative theories.)[171]

The concept of 'brainwashing' – altering a subject's mind to overlay new ideas – appears to have entered popular culture during the 1950s, as the Soviets, Chinese, and North Koreans all allegedly practiced mind control techniques. (Possibly, however, the notion was put around for propaganda purposes.) The Americans conducted their own dubious research under a project named MKUltra; LSD (see 'Goodbye Mary Lee', Chapter 5) was used in this process and (apparently) administered to CIA staff, soldiers, medical personnel and the public in a study to assess its effectiveness.[172]

'Death of a Hunter' joins other spy fiction of the era in putting its central character through some vivid and surreal brainwashing sequences. On the big screen in *The IPCRESS File* and *The Quiller Memorandum*, electronic hypnosis, violence and drugs are used on Harry Palmer and Quiller. *The Manchurian Candidate* (1962), a thriller directed by John Frankenheimer based on a novel by Richard Condon, featured a prisoner of war played by Laurence Harvey transformed into a programmed assassin, and it's interesting to note the actor's surname (although it's probably a coincidence). On television, in *The Avengers'* John Steed was put through 'The Wringer' (1964) when he was suspected of being a traitor. In *Danger Man*, John Drake has to rescue a Prague section chief from sleep deprivation in 'The Man Who Wouldn't Talk' (1965), and *Man in a Suitcase*'s McGill was almost coerced into killing a white South African politician through image and sound conditioning, in a fake country house in 'Brainwash' (1967). *The Prisoner* cornered the market in surreal interrogations, with the Village using drugs, conditioned reflexes, hypnosis, a faked lobotomy and virtual reality on Number 6 in 'Free For All', 'The Schizoid Man', 'Dance of the Dead', 'A Change of Mind', 'Living in Harmony' and 'Once Upon a Time'. The elaborate deception carried out on Callan is similar to schemes designed to trap the eponymous title character in the episode 'It's Your Funeral', in which the Village authorities manipulate an activist into trying to assassinate a retiring authority figure, so they have a rationale for instigating further repression. The architects of the plan comment on and review it as it unfolds, just as Haynes and his colleagues do in 'Death of a Hunter'.

Ending the series with this story was the preferred option at the planning stage; the new Thames management wanted to clear the decks regarding the older ABC programmes they'd inherited[173], and Woodward himself did not seem averse to moving on, provided cinema options remained open and his character's TV exit was appropriately dramatic. He recalled having a discussion with the production team where he suggested 'killing it'.[174] '"Look, why don't we make him die? It's going to be the end, let's put our money where our mouth is and give him a bloody good death scene." So when we actually shot it, in my mind, he was dead, and in Meres's mind he was dead; leaning over the body and all that.'

Russell Hunter certainly believed the series had ended. 'He upped and moved back to Edinburgh and did a tour of his one-man show, *A Soldier's Story*,'[175] David Bickerstaff recalled.

'We were told, "We're not going on with the series". That was the end,'[176] Derek Bond said. 'In those days you didn't necessarily look for an ongoing series. You signed for what you were contracted for and if they considered doing another thirteen you either thought "Hooray" or "Oh Lor'! Another thirteen of those!", depending on your attitude... I thought the episode was quite exciting. We were all rather sorry in a way when we finished recording, we had a great get together afterwards. There was no idea of it coming back – we all thought we'd had it! With respect to Reg Collin, I think he underestimated what he'd got.'

'I'd suggested to Lloyd that all series can go on beyond the end of their useful life,'[177] Reg Collin said. 'I [felt] that we'd got the best out of *Callan* and should draw it to a conclusion and I think Lloyd agreed with me.'

'James Mitchell would never have been asked to write this one, you could never have persuaded him to do it,'[178] John Kershaw revealed, recalling a row with Mitchell in the Teddington canteen when news of Collin's plan to end the show emerged. 'Out of courtesy we had to tell him, and we had been told it was our job to bring the series to an end... We didn't know that there was the [*Sunday Express*] serialisation that he was setting up; all that would have been wrecked if we'd killed Callan. We wouldn't have dreamt of killing Callan if we had known there was going to be a film. It was only at the very end of my stint that those things began to emerge.'

The penultimate page of Lloyd Shirley's copy of the rehearsal script depicts Callan's shooting as follows:

```
Callan spins round but doesn't make it. Two shots ring out
then a third. All hit Callan who crashes into a wall and
then to the floor, his gun hanging useless in his hand.

Meres: Why Callan, why ?
```

> Callan: (In Great Pain) Hunter... going to kill Soviet
> President on arrival.

> Meres: Are you mad? The President went home three weeks ago,
> you've been missing a month.

The script stops at this point, its final page missing – perhaps kept back to safeguard the shock ending.[178] The end result on screen is indeterminate, leaving Callan badly, maybe even mortally, wounded. 'If it comes back, [then it's] up to the writer to say that he's been in hospital or whatever,'[179] Woodward said of this ambiguity. 'It's been done many times now, but it hadn't been done then.' In the final cut of 'Death of a Hunter', the last close-up on Callan was obviously recorded later: Anthony Valentine's recollection is that 'the end was re-shot. In the original ending, he was shot and died. And in the subsequent ending he was shot and went "Aagh, I'm *not* dead!"'[180]

'That was safety first,'[181] Reg Collin recollected. 'I would guess we decided we'd have an each-way bet on the situation. Just in case.' 'At the time I finished with the programme – a year before it was broadcast – the company had not made a final decision, which was why they kept both endings,'[182] John Kershaw said. 'The original ending was a good, strong thing to do if the company had decided not to [do more]. Sometimes heroes have to die. It would have been very dramatic.'

Having seen a complete script, Anthony Goodman wrote in *Action TV* magazine that the camera script had 'two different final pages, although camera scripts only had dialogue and camera positions, so it is not possible to tell how the two endings differed.'[183] Goodman also observed that the videotape clock on the episode was dated 8 April 1969, a long time after the scheduled recording dates. It appears that the team had made their mind up to continue with the programme by February 1969, and Lloyd Shirley wrote to Mitchell to this effect via his agent, reassuring him that Callan's 'death' would merely be a big publicity stunt; a final scene where the agent groans the additional, unscripted line 'Toby, I've been had' was completed shortly before transmission. Research attempting to confirm this fully led to the discovery of *another* version of the camera script, a partial draft, marked for the attention of a staff member handling continuity links. Again, the endings are light on stage directions in this script[184], but this version is clearly different, concluding on a two-shot of Meres and Callan and having one further additional camera shot as follows:

> M.S Meres being hit.

This suggests the intriguing prospect that the production team were considering an ending that anticipated the climactic shoot-out in the Quentin Tarantino thriller *Reservoir Dogs* (1991) by over twenty years, as Meres and Callan shoot each other then expire lying side by side.

MISSION ANALYSIS: *'No man could last a week.'* From the start, things are off-balance: Callan is a marked man and being photographed; foreshadowing the later deaths, Liz throws flowers in a dustbin; Callan jokes that Hunter is a target and his boss is agitated. While Callan plans a burglary, the audience know a trap is coming, but the exact nature of it wrong-foots expectation for several minutes. Finally, we learn the truth – Callan is not in the hands of some rival, misdirected British security department: he's been caught by the KGB. This time the enemy is not a mirror-image antagonist but a mirror-image *organisation:* an anti-Section.

From then on the brutality escalates relentlessly, including a scene in which Callan's head is fired at with an empty gun. Hope is offered and then snatched back; Lonely flees but is soon recaptured, and on finally meeting Meres, he reveals he can't help him in his search, as he was taken to the warehouse in a van with blacked-out windows. Twice Callan seems about to escape, but instead just collapses back into his chair.

The direction cleverly turns the fade-up after breaks in recording from being a technical necessity into a narrative aid, emphasising Callan's disorientation. Overall the performances are excellent, Woodward's confusion, and Russell Hunter's near-incontinent panic on finding Striker's corpse being particularly notable. (Striker's death is another upsetting touch: the anti-Section kill their own agitated colleague off-screen, just after having a drink with him.)

Rather than indoctrinating Callan into changing sides, the KGB unit play-acts as a hard-edged British security group trying to crack a spy ring before an assassination, effectively making the agent watch what seems like one of his own cases. This alienating idea cleverly reworks Fleming's *The Man with the Golden Gun* novel from the outside in, in much the same way as *The Prisoner* – 'The Schizoid Man' inverts and reinvents the doppelgänger story. It is a simple but captivating deception, showing the writer's awareness of other fictional 'brainwashing' stories and his willingness to allude to these other sources in his script. Solutions from these other works (see 'Information') are toyed with and then discarded as the episode approaches its climax: Callan does *not* wear his interrogators down; they wear *him* down, to the extent he begs for water. There is no change of heart by the female antagonist; her subliminally quick, satisfied smirk on finding Callan has succumbed to the treatment more than cancels out her earlier moment of pity when Callan is beaten up.

In the closing scenes, there are no blood-stained nails to help Callan hold onto his sanity, and no protective bullet-proof shutters falling to protect Hunter. Callan does what he's been deceived and programmed into doing, kills his victim without compunction (in itself ironic) and then is shot himself. The episode again breaks TV taboos, by letting the 'baddies' win outright. As John Kershaw himself said, 'What more shattering blow could you deliver to the British Public than shooting the hero of the day?'[185]

Appropriately for a finale – and what may have been the conclusion of the whole series – ideas used throughout the second season recur. The ersatz Section impersonate officialdom ('Red Knight, White Knight', 'Nice People Die at Home'), conduct interrogations ('The Most Promising Girl of Her Year', 'Let's Kill Everybody', 'Blackmailers Should Be Discouraged'), employ hallucinogenic drugs ('The Most Promising Girl of Her Year'), accuse Callan of being KGB ('You're Under Starter's Orders') and killing a friend of the investigator ('Death of a Friend'), employ a femme fatale ('Let's Kill Everybody', 'Death of a Friend', 'Once a Big Man, Always a Big Man') and an undercover antagonist ('Let's Kill Everybody', 'You're Under Starter's Orders', 'Jack-on-Top'); it's as if every dark deed perpetrated by the Section is being revisited upon it. A high-profile assassination is also central to the plot ('The Running Dog'), and by the end of the episode Callan resembles the shambolic, stubbled vagrant he posed as in 'The Worst Soldier I Ever Saw'. The bogus Section's threat to Lonely (albeit fake) and their attempt to rekindle Callan's antagonism towards Meres refer even further back, to narrative threads in the first series.

In the manner of a classical tragedy, Callan is brought low through his character traits

– his dedication to duty as he sees it, his compassion and mistrust of authority. He remains behind to open Striker's strongbox, rather than take his cue from Lonely and flee from Earls Court, and is angry but not that surprised by his rough handling. Lonely's avarice similarly contributes to *his* troubles, Hunter's secrecy brings about *his* downfall, while, in an ironic pay-off considering their chequered history, Meres is genuinely distraught at shooting Callan.

Exit Derek Bond's Hunter and Sir Michael Harvey. Exit Toby Meres (for now). The alternate ending featuring Meres, Callan and Hunter all dying together would have been a fittingly shocking conclusion to the entire series but, fortunately, there was more to come. Shocked back to reality by the pain of his wounds, Callan finally realises he has been deceived and his last expression on screen for twelve months is a bitterly pained grimace. Overall, 'Death of a Hunter' is a bleak, bare knuckle *tour-de-force*, and an excellent ending to the show's black and white era.

7: SERIES THREE
Somebody Got
Murdered

'It has to be you. You see, you owe this Section something. A private debt... for a faint bloodstain on the carpet beside my desk. My predecessor's blood, Callan.'

Cut dialogue, 'The Same Trick Twice' rehearsal script, 6 February 1970

ASKED IF HE DELIBERATELY played on the uncertainty over Callan's survival, Reg Collin's answer was an unequivocal 'Yes. There can't be too many TV series that have been in the headline news, in the newsstands. [We] had "Callan lives!"'[1] he said, in reference to the graffiti campaign that was reported in the national press – inspired by the slogan "Che lives!", which appeared on walls following the death of the Marxist revolutionary Ernesto 'Che' Guevara in October 1967 – and a sure sign of how much *Callan* had seized the public imagination. 'This cry from the people's heart put the gutsy little fellow from the TV series into the same class as... Guevara,'[2] wrote Mark Henry in the *Evening Standard*, 'and rightly so.'

TV Times played along with Collin's stunt throughout 1969, helping to heighten interest in the agent's fate.[3] 'It was that important,' the producer remembered. '[We had infiltrated] the lifestyle of a nation. The intention was to kill him off, but the outcry was such that we brought him back. I'm still not sure we should have done, but that's history.' 'I was in Los Angeles when it happened and I got strange telephone calls saying "Callan's dead" and all that,'[4] James Mitchell recalled. 'I said "ridiculous" and the Great British Public also said "ridiculous". The "Callan lives!" thing started being chalked up all over the place – it was lovely, one of the nicest things I can remember. There was press coverage from the moment he was shot.' Edward Woodward remembered 'going up to London and there was a big billboard with graffiti saying "Callan lives!" Then, of course, the television company actually picked that up later on, because it was appearing all over the country. It was a strange thing.'[5]

The pinnacle of Thames's exploitation of the public interest in *Callan* came in Nov-ember 1969 when Woodward, Russell Hunter and James Mitchell arrived outside the BBC building in Portland Place. 'We had this amazing PR man for Thames Television,'[6] said Woodward, 'who came up and said "I've had a great idea: we've gotta keep this going, this "Callan lives!"... I've got something coming up – you and Russell, outside the BBC. It's gonna hit the headlines, really hit the headlines... I can't talk about it now; we'll get a couple of cars and bring you up there."... So we got there, and he'd set up a piano in the middle of the street – no permission, no police – and Russell and I said, "*What is this?*" We were furious. He made Russell sit down at the piano, and of course Russell can't play the piano, I had to sing, and James Mitchell had been called in... and it was *packed* with people! There were hundreds of people there, blocking the streets. And then we heard "Wa-wa, wa-wa" and as soon as the police came along, it was like a couple of buskers – we shot into our cars, the piano disappeared, and off we'd gone. So by the time the police got there, there was nothing except people looking at where a piano had been.' The story subsequently appeared in the press, together with the announcement that *Callan* would indeed be returning – in colour.

In a press release announcing the third series, Thames Television freely admitted to being 'always conscious of what the public want'[7] in the resurrection of the nation's favourite state executioner and the document was, inevitably, titled 'Callan Lives!' Reinforcing the series' strengths in the document, Collin informed the audience that '*Callan* will continue to be a straightforward series. We are resisting all temptations to become "Bondish" – for example, there will be, as before, absolutely no background music. Callan will still be involved in violent situations, but the violence will not be dwelt on or exploited. The series as a whole will be less violent rather than more so.'

The ITV and the BBC converted to the new colour broadcasting system at the end of the 1960s. Adapting to the new production process wasn't without its teething problems, however, and those included industrial action. 'It meant [large pay rises all round] and the engineers running the show,'[8] Jim Goddard commented wryly. 'The soundmen wouldn't work in colour unless they got a four-percent pay rise. Colour needed more light, and because they needed more light, there were more boom shadows... There can be eight or nine inches in discrepancy in [actors'] heights but when people are seated they average four-foot-six. [The colour camera manufacturers] raised the lens height on the camera four inches without ever considering consulting anybody apart from the engineers, which was a big drawback; you use the composition of the shot to create a psychological effect – the height you photograph someone from can make them look derelict or powerful. It's part of body language and the actors' and directors' tools. Camera height is very important.'

Peter le Page agreed. 'The first colour cameras were six-foot long and the nearest you could get to the artists was three-foot, so you ended up with four cameras at the edge of the set zooming in and out. Prior to that, with the black and white Emmy [cameras], the distance was two-foot and you could go within three inches on a wide-angled lens. Coming from a situation where a director could pan round three heads and pull focus on any of them, we ended up with four cameras sitting outside the set pulling focus. Anyway, we got rid of those, and we got some Emmys which were a better size, and the lenses were internal to the body. But even then, we were up against very high light levels and if you look at a lot of the early Thames productions, they're radically over-lit.'[9] Fortunately, however, the continuity in tone between *Callan*'s black and white era and the 1970 stories shows that the series suffered less than some from the introduction of colour.

Another innovation that colour cameras brought the third series of *Callan* was OB video (initially used in making 'Death of a Hunter'). Although not offering the clarity and depth of film, the episodes which used this technique had a uniform feel for the first time. 'If they shot it on OB, that was us out: they wouldn't mix the two [formats],'[10] said John Keeling. 'That would be the studio guys working the OB unit. I can think of two reasons why they would have used [OB] more: one, they could do multi-camera setups so it would supposedly be quicker, and two, if those units were not being used in studio, "Let's take them on location to make use of the facilities."' 'Some of the directors were moving towards OB: tape-to-tape rather than film-to-tape,'[11] Collin confirmed. 'Some of us believed the technology had moved on sufficiently for that to happen. In television as a whole it was a moderately short-lived experiment. It wasn't that we sat down and said "Hey fellers, let's do tape!" We'd say to a director, "Can you shoot this on tape?" and he'd say, "I'd rather do film but, okay, you have to try these things." The OB cameras were the same ones as they did horse racing with.' One thing that didn't change was camera crews' willingness to experiment. 'In 1971, we were still in the exciting days of television,' Collin said. 'We could say to a cameraman "Can you run across the road and stick that camera up on a brick?" and they'd do it. We didn't know they were big cameras: they were all we had.'

THE RETURN OF THE SERIES on 8 April 1970 was high-profile. In the week of the first episode's transmission, the ITV and BBC listings magazines the *TV Times* and *Radio Times* both featured stars of the series on their covers. The *Radio Times* foregrounded Anthony Valentine's new starring role in the BBC's rival spy drama, *Codename*. On the cover of the *TV Times* in some regions, Ian Vaughan's moody photograph gave equal prominence to both Edward Woodward and Russell Hunter, reflecting how popular the double act of Callan and Lonely had become. Away from television, in the country's record shops, eager *Callan*/Woodward fans could purchase his LP *This Man Alone*. As a bonus, the title track was the recorded version of the song he'd debuted in the publicity stunt in Portland Place. Showing that Woodward had a very good agent indeed, copies of the record were given away at Thames' April press launch for *Callan*'s third series.

As if this positive media coverage wasn't enough, in early February, the *TV Times* announced the results of its 'TV Person of the Year' poll, which readers had been encouraged to vote in. Welsh singer Tom Jones was number one, followed by the suave actor Gerald Harper, the male lead in the hit drama series *Hadleigh* (which ran intermittently between 1969 and 1976). Behind them was the rank outsider – Edward Woodward. The *TV Times* noted: 'Third place went to the actor who is yet to come back from the dead. Edward Woodward's "death scene" in the final episode of the last series of *Callan* last April produced petitions for his immediate resurrection... Except for a Yorkshire TV play before Christmas (and occasional guest appearances on ITV and BBC as a singer, after starring in a short-run West End musical), Woodward had been off-screen for over seven months when the voting began.'[12] In March, there was an even more prestigious accolade for the actor. At the Society of Film and Television Arts' annual ceremony, hosted by David Frost, actress Wendy Craig presented Woodward with the award for Actor of the Year, 1969.

Something had happened that would have been unthinkable when James Mitchell and Anthony Read had first discussed 'A Magnum for Schneider' at the BBC seven years before: *Callan* had become a British institution. 'Back at the beginning it wasn't very thinkable; suddenly it was,'[13] James Mitchell recalled fondly. 'People were asking us to switch the transmission day because it clashed with midweek matches for Manchester United. We were getting thousand-signature petitions! Those were heady days. It was great fun.'

One sign of how influential the series had become was its impact on other TV drama. The most immediate result of this had been the commission of another realistic espionage series by Thames, produced by Collin and shown in the latter half of 1969. *Special*

Branch starred Derren Nesbitt as Detective Inspector Jordan, Wensley Pithey and then Fulton McKay, as his superiors and (from the second series in 1970) Morris Perry as Moxon, a ruthless government official. The series quickly became popular, largely due to Nesbitt's portrayal of 'a new-style police investigator... A fashionable dresser, with floral shirts, wide ties and flared trousers'[14] – in effect, the exact opposite of Callan – as well as the authentic feel for contemporary espionage that story editor George Markstein brought to *SpecialBranch*. The directors included two who had worked on *Callan*, Peter Duguid and Mike Vardy, while Trevor Preston and Robert Banks Stewart both contributed scripts. When *Special Branch* was awarded a second series, Markstein was on hand to inform *TV Times* that Derren Nesbitt had been the guest of honour at a recent dinner hosted by officers from the series' real-life counterpart. 'We were really rather chuffed about that,'[15] he said proudly.

WHEN COLLIN HAD GOT THE GO-AHEAD for a third series of *Callan*, he enlisted Markstein as story editor. 'There was nothing sinister in [John Kershaw leaving],'[16] the producer explained. 'He went on to be the producer of *Armchair Theatre*, so that's why George came in... [He was] a friend of mine, and we were at one about how the series should go... He was not just story editor on *Callan* but a [script supervisor] for the whole department.'

'John Kershaw is a great friend of mine,'[17] Markstein said, 'and he wasn't working in a watertight compartment any more than I was. When one's colleagues are working on [something], one discusses it. I knew what John was doing and he knew what I was doing... [I was] involved very often without being directly involved. If you take over a series, you take over a trust, and one of the things you take over is a responsibility to maintain the characterisation as far as possible, unless there's a sound reason why it's got to be changed. You go to writers, talk to them, know their work and their interests and discuss ideas, something begins to gel and you say, "That might make a good *Callan*." There were scores of scripts but I suggested many storylines for [the series].'

Born a German Jew, Markstein (1929-1987) fled from the Nazis with his mother before the outbreak of WW2. Having entered television via a career in journalism, he later became Thames' script supervisor, forming a successful working partnership with Lloyd Shirley. 'George read all the scripts that came in,'[18] reveals Gill Hewlett-Case, who worked with him at Thames. 'He was a quiet, driving force there while Lloyd was a loud, blustering one. George had a good working relationship with him, though, and knew when and when not to approach him; he was very good at reading people. With Lloyd, you got to watch his eyes and tell when the red mist was about to come down. When George knew Lloyd was in the right frame of mind, he'd disappear with a pile of scripts into his office for hours.' Between them, the quiet German and the brash Canadian would be responsible for developing some of Thames' best-remembered programmes.

Even close friends and colleagues found the balding, bespectacled and unassuming Markstein an enigmatic figure. While Trevor Preston described him as being a 'roly-poly man who always had a laugh like a girl'[19], Patrick Mower felt Markstein also had 'an air of mystery about him, and a little bit of menace, actually!' The writer Troy Kennedy Martin wryly commented, 'I always thought he was a spy – for the other side!'[20] Perhaps Kennedy Martin was only half-joking. Markstein's work as a military correspondent for American forces in Europe in the aftermath of WW2, as a journalist fluent in German and English, would have been the ideal cover for an agent of either side; on the other hand, it may have been a background embroidered by the writer himself. Whatever the truth, Markstein's colleague Moris Farhi asserts that he had 'an immense background in intelligence and spying. He was almost an encyclopaedic man. If you suggested something, he could give you five examples of when it happened.'[21] Hewlett-Case's husband Geoff, one of the many writers Markstein encouraged throughout his career (others included James Follett and R.D. Wingfield) remembered one particular instance: 'He told me about this idea he had for a film, which I did an outline for, about how a nuclear bomb had been hijacked on a US airbase in East Anglia. George wanted it to be a dark, black comedy, and he delighted in telling me that this incident had actually happened but nobody knew about it.'[22] Markstein's knowledge of the real intelligence community may explain why, while others were praising *Callan*'s apparent realism, the series' story editor intriguingly observed, 'There was no intent to be realistic; in that sense, *Callan* was in a world of its own.'[23]

After a taste of television journalism on the ITV documentary series *This Week* (1956-1978), Markstein demonstrated how resourceful he was in progressing his TV career. Robert Banks Stewart, another former newspaperman and friend, remembered, 'He never actually had a job with any of the major newspapers. He worked for a thing called the North London News Agency, which was a little freelance outfit where people who weren't journalists used to work. George was one of the people who ran it. One day somebody called and said "We're going to make a TV series called *Court Martial,* can you give us any advice?" George said, "I'll phone you back, but I think the man you want is George Markstein." And that was his introduction to television [drama], as a legal advisor.'[24]

Made as an Anglo-American film co-production, *Court Martial* (1965-66) was Markstein's opening to Lew Grade's Incorporated Television Company – ITC – and the beginning of a career path that would eventually lead him to the story editor post on *Callan*. Seizing the opportunity that the series about two US army lawyers offered him, Markstein used his knowledge of the American forces to work his way up to being *Court Martial*'s script consultant, and even wrote for *TV Times*, promoting the series' authenticity. Lewis Greifer, another former journalist and a friend of Markstein's, had become a story editor at Associated TeleVision, the parent company of ITC. He knew that the actor Patrick McGoohan, the star of *Danger Man*, was looking to branch out into other areas of TV production: 'Pat was working on *Danger Man*, wanted to start writing himself and needed someone to edit his stuff; a personal story editor, if you like,'[25] he recalled. 'I recommended George and he started working on *Danger Man*. They both got on really well to start with.'

Working on an espionage show was the ideal creative environment for Markstein. Conversations between the writer and the star, drawing on the ex-journalist's wide knowledge of intelligence work, led to the mutual creation of a new film series on which McGoohan would be able to produce, direct and write. This was *The Prisoner*, incorporating a contemporary update of what Markstein (somehow) knew about a secret WW2 holding facility called Inverlair Lodge in Scotland, for agents who had become a security risk. Almost from the start, however, there was creative tension between the two men. 'George's conception of *The Prisoner* was entirely realistic and Patrick's was fantastic, and he questioned the changes Pat made because he thought it was cheapening his idea,' Greifer explained. 'George would come round to dinner and complain about what Pat was up to. They were at loggerheads fairly early on, and I often found myself as a pacifier, trying to smooth things over.' Nearly 50 years on, it's more than a little ironic that the creative tensions between McGoohan and Markstein – the writer left before the final four episodes were made – resulted in what is widely regarded as a television classic, and that both men are principally remembered for it.[26]

As a dedicated president of the Writers' Guild, Markstein ensured the writers he'd commissioned on *The Prisoner* received the royalties they were owed. 'George, due for a bigger share than any of us, hoisted the torch high enough to set a lawyer on ITC,'[27] recalled script writer Roger Parkes. 'And this, finally, did unlock a trickle. That trickle, never more than a few hundred pounds a year, still continues today.'

Markstein would return to film intermittently, with *Robbery* (1967, written with Edward Boyd), based on the Great Train Robbery of 1963, *The Odessa File* (1974, with Kenneth Ross), adapted from Frederick Forsyth's novel about the hunt for a Nazi war criminal, and the siege-thriller *Who Dares Wins* (1982), adapted from the writer's short story *The Tip Toe Boys* about the Special Air Service. He also wrote a series of critically applauded and best-selling original novels (see Chapter 13). However, it was in the collaborative environment of video drama at Thames, from *Frontier* in 1968 to *The London Embassy* in 1987, that Markstein flourished. 'George was a team player,'[28] offered Hewlett-Case. 'He was always in the gallery, making suggestions about things. He liked it that writing was considered much more important in television than film.' With characteristic wit, the writer likened his role at Thames to a lighthouse: 'You know how useful [they are]. There are sea captains who know the ocean blindfold and don't need a lighthouse to find their way, there are others who need the lighthouses to illuminate their route. The story editor is the person who sees the entire picture, not just the person who does one script. He's the person who's supposed to know the spirit and feel of the series.'[29] Markstein was always keen to push TV drama forward, and he never became complacent. 'One is never totally pleased; I hope the day will never come when someone says "I've just done television perfection."'

Markstein stayed with Thames until his untimely death in January 1987. 'He was a man who knew who he was,'[30] Hewlett-Case reflected. 'He'd had a rough start, and that prob-ably explained why he liked the good life. He liked his lunches, liked to treat people properly, and believed passionately in people's rights.' Reflecting his life-long interest in espionage, one of Markstein's last Thames productions was *Mr, Palfrey of Westminster* (1984-85), about a George Smiley-style spy catcher. 'The idea for *Palfrey* was George's and [producer and writer] Michael Chapman ran with it,' said Hewlett-Case. 'Spies and spying were a big obsession for both of them.'

AT THE END OF THE 1960S, having previously had success with *Spycatcher*, *The Mask of Janus* and *The Spies*, the BBC were attempting to develop another of their own spy series that would match (and hopefully overtake) *Callan*'s popularity. Appearing in *Codename*, Anthony Valentine had, it seems, been lured away from his ITV ratings-winner with the promise of the leading man role, Philip West. Premiering on BBC2 on 7 April 1970 at 8 pm – more than coincidentally, the day before the first episode of *Callan*'s third series was transmitted – the series had a similar cast of character types as its ITV rival: an intellectual spymaster, glamorous junior female operative, a working-class colleague and an energetic leading role for Valentine. The series didn't achieve the same level of popularity or critical acclaim (see Chapter 13) as *Callan*, however, and BBC management chose not to renew it.

Did *Callan*'s mainstream popularity and Woodward's entertaining, if lightweight, guest turns on *Crowther's Back in Town* (1970) and the *Morecambe and Wise Show* (1969-1970) blunt the programme's radical edge? Far from it. Amongst the unprecedented level of press interest in the first episode, 'Where Else Could I Go?', there was almost unanimous praise for 'the skinhead hero of the Secret Service.'[31] *The Daily Telegraph* was shrewd in pinpointing the main reason for *Callan*'s continued success and popularity: 'Edward Woodward, named Actor Of The Year last month and one of the most acute and efficient players on television, succeeds in the highly complex task of making a professional killer appear a human being.'[32] Reflecting on the advent of colour television in the series' third year, the paper went on, 'Most drama series gain from the use of colour but this programme, moving in the twilit half-world of espionage and crime, belonged more aptly in the grey shadows of monochrome.' Considering the appeal of the shabby, sympathetic but cold-blooded agent, *The Sun* suggested that *Callan* was appealing because of 'a feeling that a lot of us are being misused, maligned and falsely accused by a world that doesn't care. *Callan* is the most extreme sort of hogwash. But watchable, dammit. And I'm glad it's back.'[33]

It was a mark of the series' confidence by now that it could withstand another major change in the line-up of regular characters and cast, namely the replacement of Anthony Valentine's Toby Meres with Patrick Mower's James Cross. 'Cross was a bit of a hybrid,'[34] believed James Mitchell. 'He came out of discussions [with George Markstein]. We'd lost Tony and we had to have another "nasty". He's a bit cruder, rougher and tougher. He lacked the polish: much more *gauche*. He really was nasty: Gore Vidal would describe the Mayor of Chicago as being "like Hitler without the charm". I think that's the difference between Cross and Meres, really.'

This change caused mixed feelings among the production team. 'Members of the Section provided the abrasive qualities of jealousy and class snobbery directed against Callan that was needed to make his character work,'[35] Mike Vardy considered. 'The series suffered in this respect when Tony Valentine left, but all in all it was a very balanced ensemble.' Ray Jenkins offered another insight into the differences between Meres and his successor: 'Tony Valentine was very suave, the old-fashioned concept of the Fascist, the well-dressed thug, with that English tone to him which he's so brilliant at. When it came to Cross, I think he was more physical. In a way, he's a normal television character, because he liked solutions which were physical rather than verbal. Whereas [Meres] would slide a knife between your ribs, with a smile or a slight apology, Cross would probably throw you over a bridge. In total honesty, I think [Cross] was a bit of a cipher part. I can remember wanting [him] to be more physical; I tended to write scenes where he moved and pulled people around.'[36]

Mower himself, a young actor who had been spotted by Dodo Watts, had played the lead in the paranormal drama *Haunted* for the network and had been on Lloyd Shirley's radar ever since. 'Reg Collin contacted me,'[37] he said. 'In those days, they didn't put golden handcuffs on you, but it was obvious that Lloyd thought I was rather good, which was very flattering. So they invited [me and my agent Philip Peerman] down, and we went out and had a rather nice lunch on a boat in Teddington Lock. It was when Thames had a lot of money, and they told us they were going to do another series of *Callan*, but Tony Valentine wasn't going to do it. We asked why he wasn't, because it was a big success, but they didn't say, and I didn't pry. I said, "Do you want me to play Anthony's character?" and they said, "No, it's an entirely different [part]."

'My brief was, when I went into it, that I was there to be a new chap, James Cross, who was very ambitious. He admired Callan but he didn't respect him, he thought he could do better and he was always trying to get into Callan's shoes, if you like. He thought that he could be the main man when Callan got killed, because it was quite a dangerous job. That was the brief for the character they were planning for me. In a way, it was a compliment – they were sort of writing the character for me [personally] to play, rather than writing a character that was just anybody – and said they would tailor it to the sort of thing I did best. At the time, and it's difficult not to sound conceited, I was being offered quite a lot of other things. I was just starting to break into films, so I seriously thought about not doing it. I thought: "This is a series that's running already, people are going to think I'm just playing Tony Valentine's character." But all in all, it was a very, very well-written programme. George Markstein [was] very strict on the quality.'

Another cast change was the introduction of noted William Squire as the fourth Hunter. The new Hunter initially seems a little more avuncular and headmasterly, but is soon shown to be just as ruthless as his predecessors, making him 'harder to read,'[38] as Dick Fiddy noted. 'The chief pleasure I had out of it was that I liked Teddy Woodward *immensely*: we respected each other's intentions,'[39] Squire himself said, praising the collaborative way the series was made. 'There was a lot of work went on between the first read through and the final production which wasn't [done just] by the director. A lot of rethinking went on between the [actors]. That was one of the reasons I think *Callan* was so successful, because it was always very well cast, with people who knew their way around and could make a contribution other than just performing. I don't want to be indelicate about this and say that we were rewriting all the time, but there were many, many points between all of us, particularly Teddy and myself, when we got an instinct and knew what was a more fitting way of either saying it or doing it.'

Developing the lead established by John Kershaw in Series Two, under Markstein *Callan* continued to grow as an organic whole, with character narratives running through the nine episodes from the beginning t the end of the series. In a reflection of Lonely's popularity, he was given his own year-long story as he dealt with Callan's abuse of his bail conditions and the imminent threat of prison. There was also a successful attempt at giving Liz's character some substance in 'A Village Called "G"'. Callan himself was on probation after his return to the Section; several episodes conclude with the agent sharing a malt with Hunter in scenes reflecting Callan's gradual, uneasy journey back to a position of trust. This series-long thread is resolved, along with the question of Lonely's prison sentence, in the final episode 'Breakout'.

Except this *wasn't* the last episode shown. The production team found themselves at the mercy of what former Prime Minister Harold Macmillan would call 'events'. The original fifth episode, 'Amos Green Must Live', contained what was felt to be controversial political content so a decision was taken to defer its transmission until after the snap 1970 General Election had concluded. This choice was made a mere three days before the episode was due to be shown.[40] As this date was five weeks after 'Breakout' aired, it wrecked Markstein's carefully constructed series continuity. According to the *Transmission Schedule: Callan* issued by Lloyd Shirley in February 1970, the third series was originally intended to have run as follows:

'Where Else Could I Go?'	8 April
'Summoned to Appear'	15 April
'The Same Trick Twice'	22 April
'Act of Kindness'	29 April
'Amos Green Must Live'	6 May
'God Help Your Friends'	13 May
'A Village called "G"'	20 May
'Suddenly – At Home'	27 May
'TBA [Breakout]'	3 June

Following 'The Same Trick Twice', this schedule was twice disrupted because of high profile football matches. On 29 April, 'Act of Kindness' was postponed because the Cup Final between Leeds United and Chelsea went into extra time. The following week, the coverage of the European Championship match between Celtic and Feyenoord Rotterdam again saw that night's *Callan* episode deferred. By 20 May, the concern over the political content of 'Amos Green Must Live' being transmitted during a general election resulted in 'Suddenly – At Home' being moved into the former's transmission slot. The significance of postponing the fifth story wasn't lost on the next morning's issue of *The Times*: 'The story was about a right-wing politician – threatened with assassination because of his views. A different episode was screened.'[41]

Scheduling and censorship frustrations aside, *Callan* was at its most consistently popular in 1970. Averaging over twelve million viewers for all bar two episodes, and peaking at 13.8 million for the opening episode[42], it was generally in the top five most watched programmes of the week, a placing that left Lloyd Shirley feeling 'gratified. 'You are always surprised, really, because you just don't know [if a series will be successful]. You can never be sure what the public reactions are going to be. These things have a dynamic of their own. The reception of any given piece of work tends to be predicated a great deal on what it's playing against, what else is happening in the industry and all those are factors beyond your control.'[43] Explaining the perhaps curious decision to only make nine episodes in the third series, when Thames could easily have capitalised on Series Two's success with more, Shirley said, 'At the top of each of [the ITV] companies is a guy – the Director of Programmes – playing quite a complicated game of chess, usually trying to work out a forward strategy of his or her own based on the whole range of programming that they've got to use... The British industry has never been particularly orientated towards packages of numbers. The American industry has always been orientated towards that.'

As a consequence of the series' popularity, Edward Woodward's public profile in the UK would never be higher. As well as appearing as the April cover star of the gaming journal *Miniature Warfare* – like his character, the actor was a keen war gamer in his leisure time – his own light entertainment show, *The Edward Woodward Hour*, was commissioned for two productions in 1971. On the day the series resumed on ITV, Thames took the unprecedented step of paying for a full-page advert in the American entertainment journal *Variety*. The headline announced 'A year ago they thought he was dead.'[44] The copy went on, 'An agent cracks up and shoots his boss. Gets shot. And leaves fourteen million viewers wondering if he's alive or dead. The agent was *Callan*, in the last episode of a series that topped the program popularity charts and made Edward Woodward TV Actor of the Year. Not since *The Avengers* has a drama series made such an impact in Britain. (We should know: *The Avengers* was ours too.)' The valedictory advert concluded, 'Watch the British charts for a while and see how often the name Thames appears. Next week you should find it pretty near the top with a new series of *Callan*. (You guessed it. He was alive.)'

Behind the scenes on *Callan*, the new partnership of Reg Collin and George Markstein had been successfully proven by continued good ratings during the series' third year. However, a note of caution was sounded by the *Daily Express*, which speculated that real world events, such as the violent sectarian disturbances in Northern Ireland which from 1969 quickly became a staple of TV news reports, might soon overtake *Callan*'s noted realism: 'Now, with the 1970 theology of petrol bombs and bovver boots... Callan, the gentle assassin, looks as quaint and dated as a 10 [shilling] note. Perhaps it would have been kinder to have allowed him to rest in peace.'[45]

SERIES 3 REGULAR CAST

Edward Woodward (David Callan)
Russell Hunter (Lonely)
William Squire (Hunter)
Patrick Mower (James Cross)

SERIES 3 RECURRING CAST

Lisa Langdon (Liz, Hunter's Secretary) 1, 4–7, 9
Harry Towb (Judd) 1, 6
Clifford Rose (Snell) 1

Uncredited on screen: Michael Allen Potter (Stand-in for Callan)

PRODUCTION TEAM

Producer Reg Collin, *Story Editor* George Markstein

Uncredited on screen[46]: *First Assistant Director* Geoffrey O'Brien (1, 3, 6), Barry Millar (2, 7), *Technical Supervisor* John Eveleigh (1, 3, 7, 8, 9), Peter Kew (2), Campbell Keenan (4, 6), Del Randall (5), *Lighting Supervisor* Ken Brown (1, 7), H. Richards (2), Bill Lee (3), Andy Andrews (8), Brian Turner (6), Louis Battome (9), *Lighting (Outside Broadcast/Filming)* Ken Brown (4, 5), *Lighting (Studio)* Louis Bottone (5), *Location Manager* Barry Millar (1, 2, 5), Eric Parritt (8), Geoffrey O'Brien (4, 9), *Crew Chief* Norman Andrews (5), *Lighting Film Cameraman* Mike Rhodes (2, 9), John Keeling (3), Ricky Briggs (6), *Cameraman* Mike Hobbs (1, 5), Roy Easton (2, 3, 6, 7), Peter Howell (1, 4, 5, 8, 9), Peter Lang (8), *Assistant Cameraman* Tony Jacobs (8), *Sound Supervisor* Peter Bond (1), Mike Ponting (1, 2, 4), Ron Ferris (3, 5), Arthur Duff (8), Bruce Englefield (6, 7), John Tasker (5), *Sound Recordist* Chris Kent (3), Vic Minnell (8), Basil Rootes (6, 9), *Film Editor* Roy Hayden (3, 9), *Vision Mixer* Peter Phillips (1, 2, 3, 4, 7), Peter Boffin (5, 6, 8, 9), *Racks* Jim Fergus-Smith (1, 5, 8), John Turner (2, 6), Bert White (3, 9), Bill Marley (4, 7), *Grams* Peter Willcocks (1, 8), Brian Hibbert (2, 3, 4, 7), Steven Brown (6, 9), Tony Morley (5), *Wardrobe Supervisor* Ambren Garland (1, 2, 4, 5, 9), Jill Silverside (3, 6, 8), Margaret Quigley (7), *Make-Up Supervisor* Jeanette Ablette (1, 6, 7, 9), Launa Bradish (1, 2, 5, 6), Barbara Cole (2, 3, 4, 8, 9), Rosemary Ross (3, 4, 7), Carol Bright (8), Penny Steyne (9), Pauline Saunders (5), *Floor Manager* John Cooper (1), Denver Thornton (2, 3, 4, 5, 6, 8), Tony Parker (7), John Wayne (9), *Production Assistant* Paddy Dewey (1, 2, 3, 9), Ruth Parkhill (2, 5), Dottie Rice (4, 6, 7), Marian Lloyd (8), *Stage Manager* Daphne Lucas (1, 2), Myrtle Vincent (3), Mary Lewis (4, 6, 7), Betty Crowe (8, 9) Miles MacMahon (5), *Assistant Floor Manager* Stuart Orme[47] (1, 3, 4, 6, 7, 9), Peter Groom (8), *Call-Boy* Patrick Vance (1), Peter Ellis (3, 4, 8), Peter Errington (7, 9), Paul Craig (6), *Production Assistant Timer* Edna Ewing (1, 3, 4, 7), Paddy Dewey (8), *Graphic Designer* Ian Kestle (2, 4, 8), Keith Paisley (3), *Wardrobe Dressers* Laurie Kenton (1, 2, 4, 5, 6, 7, 8) Linda Pateman (1), Jean Kelly (2, 4, 5, 7, 9) John Neenan (3, 7), Elsa Noad (8), Alistair Courtney (6), *Prop Men* Ian Coward (1, 2), Laurie Mason (1), Frank McLaughlin (2), Reg Stitch (3, 6, 7) Frank Burke (7), Mike Rose (8), Mike Sands (4), Roger Marchant (9), Ron Marshall (5), David Ganger (5), Lou Casey (5), Bob Haines (5), *Scene Men* John Cavo (6), R. New (6), Dick Lane (5), George Darke (5) *Carpenter* Phil Pollard (5)

S3.1 WHERE ELSE COULD I GO?

Writer: James Mitchell
Director: Jim Goddard
Designer: Mike Hall

FIRST UK TRANSMISSION: Wednesday 8 April 1970, 9.15 pm

CAST: Mona Hammond (Nurse), Frederick Schrecker (Blind Man), Dave Prowse (Wellington), Queenie Watts (Lonely's Auntie), John Baldwin (Prison officer), Denis[48] Thorne (Dodds), Alan Cullen (Merry), Gary Watson (Henshaw), Richard McNeff (Detective Sergeant Wheeler)

EXTRAS/WALK-ONS: (*Uncredited on screen*) On OB inserts, from the David Agency: Pat Halpin (Lawyer), Leslie Weeks (Lawyer), Frank Littlewood (Clerk)

PRODUCTION
Rehearsals: From Wednesday 26 November 1969
Outside Broadcast Recording: Shepherds Bush Market, London W12. (Thursday 4 December 1969; some scenes remounted on 11 December). The Law Courts on Carey Street, London WC2. (Friday 5 December 1969)
Camera Rehearsals/Recording: Teddington Studio Two, Wednesday 10 and Thursday 11 December 1969[49]

TV TIMES: 'They say: "When you've got to go, you've got to go" but in Callan's case, having almost been there – can he come back?'
4-10 April 1970, Southern edition

MISSION PROFILE: Callan has been convalescing in hospital. He's examined by Snell and judged to be severely lacking in aggression. Looking for Lonely, Callan learns that he's been arrested for burglary after being placed in one of the Section's White Files. He persuades a QC, Oliver Henshaw, whose life Callan once saved when the former was his captain in Malaya, to act as Lonely's barrister. Henshaw succeeds in getting Lonely bail, but the amount is a staggering £3,000. In a confrontation with Hunter, which completely restores Callan's ruthless character as his boss had intended, the agent secures the money to keep his friend out of prison. He also earns his place back in the Section.

A MAN LIKE ME: Callan is in a bad way, having been in hospital for five months since being shot by Meres. His hair is noticeably greyer (not surprisingly, considering what he's been through). Callan was completely exonerated by the inquiry into the assassination of the third Hunter, but it's of little comfort to him: he appears distracted, exhibits a subservient demeanour in his dealings with the Section, and is so disorientated he goes to 'the old place' before being sent on to the new HQ. He was shot through a lung, experiences painful, recurring headaches and considers his brainwashing and consequent murder of the previous Hunter, the 'worst thing'. Callan seems a broken man – he can't get his gun out of its shoulder holster to fire at photographic cut-outs of gunmen, and he's been evicted from his old flat. He even thinks about giving up making model soldiers, although the first thing he does in his new flat is unpack them. Significantly, Callan reveals to Henshaw that he's changed his surname since their military service together, suggesting he's had trouble with the police. (This name change ties in with 'Land of Light and Peace', but contradicts 'The Worst Soldier I Ever Saw', in which Brigadier Pringle only knew him as 'Callan'.)

Even when it looks like he might be finished with the Section, there are still traces of his old ruthlessness: Callan improvises a weapon by inserting a razor blade in a bar of soap, and threatens to scald Lonely's aunt with hot tea. Illustrating how complex the agent's relationship with Lonely is, a combination of the petty thief's belligerent attitude towards him, and the threat to Lonely by the Section, fully re-establishes his violent streak. Callan has known Judd, the Section's American armourer, for some time.

Section Kills: In 'Get Callan...', the *TV Times* article that accompanied 'Where Else Could I Go?', James Mitchell contradicted the number of executions Callan carried out for the Section prior to 'A Magnum for Schneider'. That story said the amount was 2; 'Get Callan...' gives the number as 12 (see Appendix 1).

LONELY: Detained at Her Majesty's pleasure in Brixton prison during Callan's absence, a lot is revealed about Lonely's background. He has been in and out of prison and 'approved school'[50] since he was nine, and has been incarcerated for a total of fifteen years 'for 134 known offences' which, he despondently feels, only amounts to '4,000 quid'. He knows a foreign blind man (who considers him 'bad news') who frequents the market where his aunt runs a tea stall, suffers from back pain and his latest arrest, for 'money and goods, 30 quid', could see eleven previous convictions taken into account, getting him a sentence of seven to ten years. Adding to his woes, Lonely's head has been brutally shaved while he's been in prison. (Did he have lice?) He thinks he has lost his touch as a cat burglar.

Although it's clear he doesn't know the meaning of Henshaw's phrase 'an ambivalent attitude', in the episode's comic highlight, Lonely effects a non-committal expression that indicates he doesn't care one way or the other.

Lonely is deeply hurt that Callan wasn't there when he needed him, and he's on the verge of tears after his old 'friend' visits him in prison for the first time. Notably, when he's threatened with violence by Callan, the terrified thief starts calling him 'Mr. Callan' again, and his appalling body odour returns with a vengeance.

A TIE AND A CREST: With Meres on assignment in Washington, the mantle of Callan's tormentor is passed on to James Cross, a smartly-dressed younger man. The conflict between them becomes generational instead of class-based: Cross has absolutely no respect for Callan's previous record with the Section (as Meres did) as he's after his job. Cross has the arrogance of youth, delighting in telling his older rival how he set up Lonely.

ALCOHOL, TOBACCO AND FIREARMS: Promisingly, when Callan attends the Section's firing range under the watchful eye of Judd, he can still draw from his shoulder holster in three tenths of a second. Selecting a Magnum .38, he scores two inners and three bulls, then one inner and four bulls when firing at a normal (as opposed to a photographic) target. There are 'six, possibly seven' men in the Section who are good marksmen, but none in Callan's class.

Hunter offers Callan 'an excellent malt', which he declines. (Instead, he later drinks several cups of tea, although he does craftily add whisky from a flask he carries to a mug at the tea stall owned by Lonely's aunt, implying he's concealing the extent of his alcohol habit from the Section.) Lonely has cigarettes – 'snout' – in prison.

SPY-SPEAK: From the moment they meet, Callan is unimpressed with Cross: 'Oh dear. We must be very short of men.'

Snell is clinically critical of Callan's state of mind: 'In my opinion, there is a gross retardation of the aggressive instinct... in your idiom it might be lack of moral fibre. An NCO might describe him as a "gutless wonder."'

Uncharacteristically and memorably, Lonely stands up to Callan's excuses about not being able to pay his bail: 'Oh dear. You'll just have to pop one of your Botticellis, won't you?'

Hunter's explanation of his White Files is chilling: 'They're to put people in prison, divorce courts, bankruptcy, mental homes... A way of immobilising people we don't particularly want to kill!'

Callan erupts. *Don't you bloody threaten me, mate! You really are the bottom, aren't you? I think you must come from a very special kind of cess pit!'*

PAWNS AND PLAYERS: WILLIAM SQUIRE (1916-1989). 'I came from Wales, where I worked in a bell foundry,'[51] the new Hunter recruit recalled. 'I got a scholarship to RADA, but then the war interrupted that. I was in the navy, I went back to RADA and then I walked on – the usual thing, I carried a spear – in the great Olivier/Richardson seasons at the Old Vic. That sort of marked me for a while; I did develop into what is known as a "Shakespearean actor." But that's where the regular work was, I had a young family growing up by this time, and you needed regular employment. I think for the first eight years I never had a night off... Then there was a big turning point in my life when Richard Burton, who was an old friend, [left] a piece called *Camelot* on Broadway – he was only in it for a few months – to do a movie called *Cleopatra* [1963], where he met Elizabeth Taylor. I took over *Camelot* and did it for two years.' In the late 1950s, back in England, regular television roles started coming. 'I did a lot for Wales, and a lot of that was live: [Welsh TV] had a very good reputation and we did a lot of the classics.' By the late 1960s, Squire was an established character actor in feature films, two of which his friend Richard Burton starred in – *A Man for All Seasons* (1966) and *Where Eagles Dare* (1968). After *Callan* finished, Squire featured in *Spy Trap*, another BBC attempt to steal *Callan*'s espionage crown, in the story 'Scale of Work' (1973). The actor observed self-deprecatingly, 'I had two things going against me, they always used to tell me: I looked like Peter Finch and I sounded like Burton!' He also appeared in the film *Testimony* (1998), the family adventure series *The Black Arrow* (1972-5), *Doctor Who* – 'The Armageddon Factor' (1979), the BBC's *The Hound of the Baskervilles* (1982) and as a ruthless Hunter-like administrator in *Blake's 7* – 'Horizon' (1979). 'Bill Squire was, of course, Bill Squire,'[52] Mike Vardy said fondly. 'Full of actorly tricks – eye business and all that. A charming guy, very funny.'

DAVE PROWSE, formerly the British heavyweight weightlifting champion, was busy in the 1970s, appearing in a series of long running public information films for children. As the superhero the Green Cross Code Man, he recommended the road safety drill. 'Dave [Prowse] hadn't done a good deal of acting then,'[53] Jim Goddard recalled. 'At that time, he was running the sports department of Harrods because he was so big. But he was very fit, too.' Moving into films, Prowse featured as Frankenstein's monster in *Casino Royale* (1967), a bodyguard in *A Clockwork Orange* (1971) and later the ill-fated Arthur in the *Callan* movie in 1974. His most famous movie role was one where his face wasn't seen, as he donned the black helmet and cloak of the seminal villain Darth Vader in the films *Star Wars* (1977), *The Empire Strikes Back* (1980) and *Return of the Jedi* (1983).

GARY WATSON (born 1930) had a major role in *The Avengers* episode 'Lobster Quadrille' (1964) and played a Russian spy in *The Saint* story 'When Spring is Sprung' (1967), based on the George Blake escape. In 1975, he played the hitman John Quentin, in constant pursuit of Colin Blakely in the thriller series *The Hanged Man* (1975). He had a regular role in *Z Cars* as Detective Inspector Fred Connor (1972-74).

QUEENIE WATTS (1926-1980) was well-known as Lily Briggs in the ITV sitcom *Romany Jones* (1972-75) and its spin-off *Yus My Dear* (1976). A genuine cockney, she ran pubs with her husband. 'Queenie was always a great character,' Goddard said. 'She gave a great performance, but always in the same accent!'

HARRY TOWB was engaged by the director because he able to 'do an American accent convincingly.' (See 'Nice People Die At Home', Chapter 6).

INFORMATION: Originally titled 'Back with Charlie', this episode achieved the highest ratings of *Callan*'s original run, most probably because viewers were eager to see how the previous series' cliffhanger would be resolved. 'Structurally, it was very difficult,'[54] James Mitchell recalled of continuing the story. 'I was solving someone else's problem and I wasn't set for that, the fact that he was almost dead. I had to piece it together from there. It's a craft, and if you're a craftsman you enjoy it.' Goddard was impressed with the opening script for the third series: 'If [Callan] doesn't come through [the tests] the organisation will just kill him off, it doesn't matter what he does. He is pushed and pushed and pushed until he becomes useful to [them] again, one more time... It was a good episode because it was all about his mental state... Will he make it or won't he?'[55]

Patrick Mower and William Squire appear in the opening titles for the first time and, indicating his increasing importance, Russell Hunter now has a solo credit. The opening shot is of Callan's face, framed in an almost identical way to the closing image of 'Death of a Hunter', less battered but still pale and drawn. Callan's last line of dialogue, which gives the episode its title, paraphrases the closing comment made by Department K chief Loomis in James Mitchell's novel *The Man Who Sold Death*, when the spy chief reflects on new agent John Craig's lack of options. The title sequence, with the dilapidated ceiling, brick wall, swinging light bulb, Edward Woodward's close-up and the exploding bulb, was reshot on colour film, with the addition of a new photograph of Woodward's face fractured by a gun shot. In the camera script, Callan referred to Hunter as 'Sir' in his climactic dialogue, but this detail was dropped on the day of recording. A Party Political Broadcast on behalf of the Labour Party, shown at 9 pm, delayed transmission of 'Where Else Could I Go?'. For the first time, a voiceover on the end titles informed the viewing public: 'Edward Woodward is a National Theatre Player.'

Cross's visit to the injured Callan, in which he gains entry to hospital by pretending to be his brother, was probably inspired by a real life experience of the producer; Collin had once been hospitalised, and a friend had got in to see him using the same ruse.[56]

'The back-story for [Cross] is that he was fresh out of whatever training they did,'[57] Patrick Mower said of the new recruit to the Section. 'There was never anything spoken or written down about what [they] did. There was a boss, but you don't want it to be too specific. I can't remember now if they had a detailed character background worked out.' He said of his decision to join the series, 'It was a quality production. Rather than going off into a new series where you never know whether it was going to work, with *Callan* it was a proven thing, mainly due to Teddy Woodward, and they were going to put it into colour [so] it was going to be like the launch of a new era. All in all, [I] decided basically to go for it. And it worked – my character was very enjoyable to play.'

'I never saw the black-and-white *Callan*s because I was in the theatre all the time,'[58] Squire remembered. 'Then Reg Collin asked me to go and see him. The first time I met him was in the [Thames] restaurant and he said "You don't remember me, do you?" I said, "Of course I do," lying through my teeth. He said, "You bloody well ought to, I understudied you in *Waiting for Godot*!" Anyway, out of the blue he gave me Hunter in *Callan*. It was marvellous for me, because it was something I'd never done, although I'd played detectives once or twice. I'd done something for Thames television and I played a strongish character in that. Reg saw it and decided I'd be a Hunter.'

'*Where Else Could I Go?*' marked a welcome return to Teddington Studios for Clifford Rose. 'It didn't surprise me [I was asked back]'[59] Rose said. 'I thought Snell was quite an interesting character. James Mitchell wrote quite nicely for him, and when I'd done the very first one [the production team] had said afterwards, "He's the sort of character we might want to bring back from time to time." I never thought of it as a regular character who was around every week. I saw him very much as an occasional regular, and that was very nice.' Woodward had his own views about why Callan was so antagonistic towards Snell: 'The agents never thought he was on their side for the simple reason that he was the psychiatrist, constantly peering into our lives, and his word was usually final. If Snell gave you a bad report, medically speaking – you were out.'[60]

On location, Goddard's team adopted guerrilla film-making tactics in recording the OB video scenes outside the Royal Courts of Justice. 'The police can't let you into a law court. So we decided the only way we could get the shots was use very long lenses and radio mikes. We were parked in Carey Street on meters; what we were doing was technically illegal.'[61] The coffee stall scenes mounted in Shepherds Bush Market also posed problems, as they had to be partly shot in the studio as the stall holders 'wouldn't let us take out the back of the coffee stall. In those days they would carry on their vocation while you shot... The human eye is incredibly sensitive, it can see from 1 unit to 16,000 units of brightness, and TV cameras in those days could only cope with 1 to 500. So the problems of matching were immense. When you start cutting from interior to exterior you have to match it. It was very primitive electronic editing, done by guys switching feeds at just the right moment – "Now!" – and starting to record and hoping it would link.'

In James Mitchell's first Callan novel *A Magnum for Schneider*, released in the year before Series Three was transmitted, Callan's company commander in Malaya was first named as Captain Henshaw. Callan saved him from death at the hands of six Malayans, an act of bravery left unspecified in 'Where Else Could I Go?'. In Mitchell's third novel about John Craig, *The Money that Money Can't Buy*, the Department K agent is broken by physical torture. Like Callan, Craig is made operational again by psychological means, although it's through therapy rather than the manipulation of his character. In the following book *The Innocent Bystanders*, Craig is bitter, disillusioned and seen as a liability by his commander Loomis, a similar situation to the one Callan finds himself in. Both the film and book versions of *Dr. No* open with Bond having spent six months in hospital.

In Callan's model soldier collection are troops of the French Empress Dragoons. Napoleon Bonaparte personally appointed officers of this elite group, otherwise known as the Imperial Guard, and one of their main duties was to act as the French Emperor's bodyguard.

An article entitled 'Get Callan' by James Mitchell, the agent's 'Controller since he became a spy', accompanied *Callan*'s latest *TV Times* cover.[62] Updating the biography of Callan from the 'Appointments Officer' to 'Head of Sections' in the series' 1967 ABC press pack, Mitchell deleted the reference to his agent working for 'Vanburgh's section', but made the intriguing addition that the first Hunter considered Callan 'Very possible next Head of Section.' Together with memos from the new Hunter, the enigmatic 'Head of Sections' and the armourer Judd assessing the spy's fitness for a return to duty, Snell's report observed that 'since he has become aware of his responsibility for the death of Hunter [III] he has lost whatever little conception he had of the word "duty"' and that his 'trend to sadism remains, but [is] held in balance.' The article ended with the Head of Sections advising the new Hunter, 'Callan must be very carefully controlled. What do you suggest?'

Although overall press reaction to *Callan*'s return was positive, *The Financial Times* had mixed feelings about the series' revival, even if the reviewer favoured UK popular drama over the 'synthetic'[63] US imports *Hawaii-Five-O* (1968-1980) and *Ironside* (1967-1975): 'On the screen Mr. Woodward gave it a powerful additional dimension and this remains a plus factor even though the series as a whole... has obviously exhausted itself. But [television] is so voracious that it cannot afford to drop any success until the very last pip has been sucked, dry though it may be.'

The review in *The Times*, however, was more typical in its appraisal. 'While we believe that we need our professional killers, surely there must be drab places where cold men train and manipulate them. The conviction comes not only from our depressing belief or Edward Woodward's remarkable acting – so much said by the flicking of a muscle, a narrowing of the eyes, or tightening of the lips, a stance, a frozen immobility – but also from the fine consistency last night of James Goddard's very quiet, coldly witty and moving production in which only Russell Hunter's pathetic Lonely was allowed explicit emotions. Patrick Mower's Cross is a nice foil to Callan, actually malevolent not morally neutral.'[64]

MISSION ANALYSIS: *'All you gotta do now is pull the trigger.'* The move into colour sees the *Callan* universe turned on its head. Callan himself is pale, ill and mumbling apologies, while Lonely is loud, aggressive and rejects Callan's help. There's no espionage in the story; at its heart is the re-establishment of the status quo between this most unlikely pair of kindred spirits, and it builds towards this with electrifying performances from Woodward and Russell Hunter, as Lonely's goading brings out the violent 'Mr. Callan' of his nightmares. With the two actors given different moods and emotions to play, it's arguably the best performance by either of them in the series so far.

The addition of colour is subtly muted, in keeping with the times. The overall tonal scheme is muddy greys, greens and browns, particularly in the new, tatty Section HQ with damp patches on the walls. The best use of the new colour spectrum is in the prison scenes, as the ominous shadow of criss-crossed bars hovers over Callan and Lonely's heads, while pools of shadow black out Callan's eyes and mouth. Tellingly, when his character snaps back into focus in Hunter's office, he's framed in a stark, brightly lit close-up.

Overall, there's the sense that, along with the technical upgrade, the storytelling has sharpened even further. The episode is all about the re-establishment of the two interdependent, broken relationships in Callan's life, both of which he's ambivalent about. Lonely needs him, although Callan abuses and uses him, just as the Section needs Callan – Hunter admits as much – and uses and abuses *him*. Significantly, Callan (and the audience) knows from the outset that he's being manipulated by the Section, but ultimately and ironically, their ploy takes him back to where he needs to be. The only aspect of the story that looks clumsy now is the equating of Callan's condition with that of his broken model soldier, but symbolism like this was an occasional feature in other TV dramas of the time.[65]

To complete the memorable first night of the third series, Patrick Mower and the vulpine-featured William Squire deliver strong, confident debut performances.

S3.2 SUMMONED TO APPEAR

Writer: Trevor Preston
Director: Voytek
Designer: David Marshall

FIRST UK TRANSMISSION: Wednesday 15 April 1970, 9.00 pm

CAST: Sylvester Morand (Palanka), George Pravda (Mr Karas), Hana-Maria Pravda (Mrs. Karas), Norman Henry (Inspector Kyle), Edward Caddick (Mr. Lorrimer), Edward Burnham (Mr. Leach), Rhoda Lewis (Mrs Kent), Henry Manning (Mr. Arlen), Sylvia Burrows (Mrs. Arlen), Cheryl Hall, Lesley Daine (Girls on bus), Donegal (1st Porter), Warren Clarke (2nd Porter), Michael Martin (Sergeant), Charles Pemberton (Constable)

EXTRAS/WALK-ONS: *(Uncredited on screen)* Jules Walter (Bus Conductor), Chris Walsh (Teenage Boy), Jenny Broadbent (Teenage Girl), Woman (Linda Carol), Wally Bowman, Ricky Lansing, David Pike, Mario Zoppolini, Paul Freemont, Fred Davies, Bill Riley, Chris Achilles (Jury), Peter Kodak (Constable)

PRODUCTION

Rehearsals: From Saturday 27 December 1969
Location Filming: Earl's Court Square, London SW5 (Wednesday 17 December 1969); Marsh Farm Road, Twickenham, and Twickenham Green; Spikins bus garage; Lower Richmond Road, London SW15 (Thursday 18 December 1969); Windsor and Eton Railway Station, Thames Street, Windsor (Monday 29 and Tuesday 30 December 1969)
Camera Rehearsals/Recording: Teddington Studio Two, Wednesday 7 and Thursday 8 January 1969[66]

TV TIMES: 'Callan and Cross are chasing an assassin, and in the confusion Cross kills an innocent man. Callan, who is detained as a witness as Cross escapes, claims the man committed suicide – but another witness says it was murder. The department doesn't want to know...'
11-17 April 1970, Southern edition

MISSION PROFILE: Callan and Cross are tailing a Czechoslovakian agent called Palanka. During the chase, Cross accidentally pushes a man, Arlen, onto a railway track and an approaching train kills him. Callan tells Kyle, the investigating officer, that Arlen committed suicide, but he is contradicted by Mrs. Kent, another witness, who saw Cross. Palanka is in England to kill the Czech dissident author Karas, having already crippled him in a previous attempt on his life. Karas agrees to be bait to lure Palanka while Hunter blocks Kyle's inquiries, but the Section chief refuses to go further and interfere in the local Coroner's Court, leaving Callan to testify alone. Callan comes under extra pressure from Arlen's solicitor, as the victim's widow will lose £8,000 life insurance if a verdict of suicide is returned. Palanka enters the writer's flat and overpowers Cross, but Karas shoots him. Meanwhile, much to the annoyance of the Coroner, Callan changes his story in court, resulting in an open verdict.

A MAN LIKE ME: Callan's new address is 27 Granscombe Terrace, Fulham. He typically enjoys a breakfast of tea and cornflakes, uses Vim in the kitchen and says that he never reads the papers as they're 'too depressing'. He prefers working nights.

Callan exhibits a range of emotions and moods throughout the case. Although he lies proficiently to the police, he is typically disgusted by Hunter's emotionless attitude to Arlen's death, sarcastically using his boss's description of the 'incident' whenever the subject arises; at the other extreme, he finds Lonely's fishing hobby hilarious. Hunter tells Callan he's the best man in the Section, 'perhaps the best it's ever had', although this compliment is of little comfort due to the moral dilemma he finds himself in. After successfully lying in the coroner's court, he looks totally exhausted.

LONELY: Considers Callan's 'one-man wake' for Arlen morbid, can apparently single out foreigners by their eyes and, unsurprisingly, believes Poles and Czechs are the 'same thing'. Lonely amusingly misinterprets another word he doesn't understand: when called an atheist, he replies that he can't be as he's 'read a lot of books'. His choice of interior decor still consists of girly pin ups. He has a taste for the 1970s' school kids' snack of bread and condensed milk, and as he's about to eat it off a pin up in his room, Callan sardonically comments that he 'keeps a lovely table'. Lonely proves his worth by tailing Palanka and can sense his presence even when he can't see him.

A TIE AND A CREST: Callan is in trouble entirely due to Cross's blunder, and thinks he's like Palanka – 'young and arrogant'. Equally disdainful of his older colleague, Cross can't resist a dig about Callan's 'middle aged intuition'. Callan's assessment proves correct, as Cross is knocked out and disarmed by Palanka, who unloads the young Section agent's gun. Only Karas' armed intervention prevents Cross from being killed.

ALCOHOL, TOBACCO AND FIREARMS: Alongside their other similarities, Cross and Palanka use the same hand guns, although the Czech favours a silencer. Karas has a revolver. As his conscience starts to bother him, Callan hits the Scotch. He allows Lonely a rare drop too; when Callan's drink goes down the wrong way, the thief obligingly thumps him on the back and then gives them both a (in his case surreptitious) top-up.

SPY-SPEAK: There is a bleakly funny exchange between Kyle and Callan. 'Very few people experience violent death,' the policeman says knowledgably. 'They don't know how lucky they are', Callan dryly replies.

Callan is disgusted with himself for lying to the police to protect the Section's involvement: 'Oh, don't you worry, sir! I was the soul of discretion earlier on, pouring out my perjury!'

Hunter has grim praise for Cross's emotional detachment: 'Sometimes, James, you delight me... So young. So insensible.'

The inhumanity of the Section brings on one of Callan's most memorable tirades: 'We're trained to treat people like numbers, like ciphers. Dispensable, indispensable – White File, Blue File, Red File, Yellow File... We're all numbers, we're all *bloody zombies!*'

PAWNS AND PLAYERS: VOYTEK (full name Wojciech Roman Pawel Jerzy Szendzikowski, 1925-2014) was born in Warsaw, Poland, and was a multi-talented artist, moving between directing, writing, TV producing and television production design. 'I started as a designer in the theatre at the Old Vic School with George Devine who went on to start the Royal

Court and do *Look Back in Anger* [1956],'[67] he recalled. 'I got engaged as a designer at ABC, [then] Lloyd Shirley asked me if I would like to direct, and I was such an opinionated bastard I thought I could do it myself.'

Voytek directed two other *Callan* stories, 'Rules of the Game 'and 'None of Your Business', as well as episodes of *Special Branch* (1969), *Man at the Top* (1971) and *The Mind of Mr J.G. Reeder* (1971). He also designed an amazing 46 *Armchair Theatre* productions, while his last scenic design duties for TV were on the mini-series *Dandelion Dead* in 1994. The émigré also found time to produce *The Pilgrim's Progress* (1967) for ABC, which featured William Squire, Michael Robbins and George Innes. 'Voytek had been in the Polish resistance during the war,'[68] remembered Peter le Page. 'He was really talented but rather difficult to deal with. He had to have an assistant to help him.'

GEORGE PRAVDA (1918-1985) and his wife Hana-Maria (1918-2008) were inspired casting as the Czech refugee couple Karas and his wife; the actors had both escaped from Czechoslovakia using forged papers after WW2. Once in Britain, Pravda cornered the market in Eastern Europeans in film and on TV, particularly for the ITC adventure series set all over the world, among them *The Saint*, *Man of the World* (1962) and *The Prisoner*. In *Ring of Spies* he was a KGB agent, in the 1965 Bond film *Thunderball* he played Kutze, a scientist who specialised in atomic weapons, and later played George Bulman's colleague Inspector Pushkin in the offbeat crime series *Strangers* (1978-1982), and its sequel *Bulman* (1985-87). During the making of 'Summoned to Appear', Trevor Preston remembered he found out just how strongly Pravda felt about his Communist-run homeland: 'I was having lunch with him and Hana-Maria, and I was running down the UK government – as I was wont to do. He turned on me and said, "Don't you ever let me hear you say that about this country! This is the most amazing country in the world, there is no country like it! I'll take you to dinner one night and tell you what happened in ours."'[69]

HANA-MARIA PRAVDA had worked in Czech theatre prior to WW2; her best-known role on British TV was Emma Cohen in the first series of *Survivors* in 1975. She directed a number of theatre productions and continued to perform in BBC radio drama well into her 80s; a survivor of Auschwitz, she recorded her experiences of the Holocaust for the radio.

EDWARD BURNHAM (1916-2015) was a reliable presence in thriller and science fiction series in the 1960s and 1970s. Like George Pravda he appeared in *Doctor Who* several times, respectively playing Professors Watkins and Kettlewell in 'The Invasion' (1968) and 'Robot' (1974). In *The Avengers*, he played two traumatised victims-of-the-week, in 'The Fear Merchants' (1967) and 'Thingumajig' (1969).

WARREN CLARKE (1947-2014). After appearing in *The Wednesday Play* – 'Sling Your Hook' (1969) with Patrick O'Connell and Stanley Kubrick's movie *A Clockwork Orange* (1971), he went on to have a hugely successful and varied career. He starred in his own crime series as one half of the detective duo *Dalziel and Pascoe* (1996-2007) and in 1991 featured as the Russian agent Vladimir Zelenski (cover name: Albert Robinson), a KGB officer living in England in the BBC comedy-drama *Sleepers* (1991).

CHERYL HALL played Wolfie Smith's long-suffering girlfriend Shirley in John Sullivan's BBC sitcom *Citizen Smith* (1977-1980).

(JOHN) DONEGAL played another railway porter in the 1957 *Armchair Theatre* play 'Now Let Him Go'.

INFORMATION: There is a production error in the film sequence of Callan, Cross, Palanka and two gossiping girls on a double-decker bus: as the bus pulls away, a young woman at the bus stop waves at the camera and the bus conductor tries to suppress a smile. British Rail was not prepared to let the production team film until normal services had finished. 'Mr. Arlen' actor Henry Manning was insured against possible injury when falling towards the edge of the platform, and mattresses were laid on the (non-electrified) line in case he fell on to the track. Until late in the production schedule, Arlen was due to be played by Julian Herington. The exteriors for Karas's flat were filmed outside George and Hana-Maria Pravda's real home[70]

'Summoned to Appear' brings the nature of the new conflict between Callan and Cross into focus. 'My character was really there to annoy Callan,'[71] said Patrick Mower. 'That was my purpose; to needle him. His purpose was to try and put Cross down and get annoyed with him. [Cross] was a catalyst, in a way, for the writers to branch off and think, "We can do something with him." Teddy and I got on very well together socially, so it wasn't like it was on screen. I did two other films with him, but people can misread what you're like on TV.'

The script refers to Callan previously being 'deactivated because of over-involve-ment', referring to his history before 'A Magnum for Schneider', and showed that, despite the many changes in the writing team since the mid-1960s, care was being taken to preserve continuity.

New director Voytek was delighted to be working on Thames' top-rated series. 'I know doing "Summoned to Appear" I was kind of high on it, reinventing the shots. I tried to adhere to the format that Reggie Collin had stipulated, very much *The Spy Who Came in from the Cold*. What was nice about Trevor Preston's stories... was there were innocent par-ties involved; that mixed up the reality of normal life with the people going round stalking each other. In those days it was still a novelty that [the characters] quarrelled and undercut each other. [That approach] became very popular later in American movies.'[72]

'There was a showdown between the Czech killer and the exile: Reggie asked me if he could be killed brutally as he was such a nasty man. Exploding charges weren't used very much in those days. Now everybody sprays blood all over the place! Sylvester [Morand] had a series of charges across his chest and I'd tried it on someone before; I knew we only had one good take. When George Pravda pulled the gun out from under the blanket I think they'd put more powder in [the charges] than expected. Sylvester was rather sur-prised and turned pale and slammed down – partly in shock.'

The story grew out of Preston's interest in Coroner's Courts. 'I find an area I like to work in and I put something round it. I love courts: I go to courts all the time, I find it interesting. Coroner's courts are particularly interesting, so I tried to develop a story about that. One of the fascinating things is that a Coroner is one of the two people the police or the Crown can't touch – the other's Customs and Excise. I wanted to find an institution that was outside the status quo that got involved with [the Section], because they wouldn't be able to control [it].'[73]

The Czechoslovakian characters in the script, the exiled Karas – initially named Otabar Stepanek – his wife and the killer Palanka, grew out of Preston's first-hand experience of the Communist state from a visit there in 1960. 'When I was at the Royal College of Art, I won a travelling scholarship [the George Haslam award],' the writer elaborated. 'It was supposed to be to study art in Rome, but in the end I went to Prague. At that moment, there could only have been 20 Europeans in the whole of Czechoslovakia, so it was very hard to get me in, and a man called Palanka, who was the head of the BBC equivalent [broadcasting service], managed to.

'When I was in Prague, there was a curfew. Everybody had to be in by nine o'clock, including the young people, and we came out of a theatre. Ever since I was a kid, if I see someone getting beaten up my instinct is to steam in, and there were these two honking great policemen absolutely giving this kid, who was about fifteen, a pasting. I moved, and Palanka grabbed me and said, "Don't even look at them." After he got me home, he said, "Don't ever do that again!" Another time he said "Come and see my real work" – he was an artist – and he used to go upstairs into a loft where all his [subversive] paintings [were kept]. Palanka later disappeared.'

Eight years after Preston's trip, the political climate in Czechoslovakia changed. On 5 January 1968, Alexander Dubček was elected as the First Secretary of the Communist Party, ushering in a period of liberal reform. This 'Prague Spring' lasted until 21 August, when, at the urging of Soviet Russia, the Warsaw Pact countries invaded the country and, with the aid of Czech hardliners, crushed Dubček's regime. As well as a rash of protest suicides by people setting themselves on fire, the suppression inspired a wave of emigrations, explaining how Karas and his wife came to England, the subject of the writer's book and his hatred of the state assassin Palanka. Czechoslovakia remained under Communist rule until 1989, when a vindicated Dubček finally became leader of a liberalized country.

Real-life models for Karas may have been Ivan Diviš (1924-1999), the Czech poet and essayist, who emigrated to West Germany in 1969, and the Bulgarian dissident writer Georgi Markov (1929-1978) who defected in the same year. Both men went on to work for Radio Free Europe, the US funded radio station that made pro-Western broadcasts to the Eastern Bloc. Markov was later killed by a Bulgarian agent in a London street. It's likely that the most high-profile inspiration for Karas was the Russian writer and political activist Aleksandr Isayevich Solzhenitsyn (1918-2008), who in 1962 published the ground-breaking book *One Day in the Life of Ivan Denisovich*, a damning exposé of the Soviets' harsh prison system.

TV Times continued to promote *Callan*, most regions printing a photograph of the agent and Lonely sharing bread and condensed milk on the programme listings page for 15 April. Onthe same day, the *Daily Sketch* ran an amusing feature in the style of a spoof memo from the 'Surveillance Section'[74] to Hunter: 'Your agent David Callan has been observed buying and anxiously reading pop music journals. He has also visited a number of record shops and met many possible enemy agents. The routine appears to be for the stranger to produce an autograph book, which Callan signs. Challenged by us, Callan insisted that he was an actor called Edward Woodward. His cover-story is that he has a new LP record *This Man Alone* released this week.Far from being a double agent, he says he is promoting the LP and a single with the same title. Suggest close scrutiny of ITV's *Callan*, in which he chases an enemy assassin, sees an innocent bystander killed, and becomes involved with the police.'

MISSION ANALYSIS: *'Every country has its Palankas.'* After the minor reboot of 'Where Else Could I Go?', *Callan* restates its agenda of showing how a ruthless, secret security service can impact on and damage ordinary people's lives. The story is quietly very subversive. In the George Markstein edited, 1970 episodes of *Special Branch*, Moxon, the secretive intelligence official, would often manipulate the officers Jordan, Eden and Inman for his own ends, but he stopped short of interfering with public institutions. In 'Summoned to Appear', an agent of the state specifically lies to the police and perjures himself in court, something that, in terms of television drama at the beginning of the 1970s, was remarkable for showing how flagrant the secret state's breach of the law could be. The shadowy political agenda of the security services has always been a concern for Trevor Preston: 'Something like this happens somewhere every day in this country... and can only be directed by some [covert] department. I don't truthfully believe that three-quarters of the MPs in Parliament know what's going on, I really don't.'[75] A courtroom setting is ideally suited to the theatrical presentation of video recorded drama, and Woodward's performance, as he presents Callan as a hostile witness in front of the Coroner, is one of the series' greatest sequences.

In a cleverly interwoven script, the Palanka plot highlights intelligence work's contradictions. Although the writer Karas detests Palanka, the man who put him in a wheelchair, at the same time he recognises that men like his would-be killer – and Callan – are a necessary evil. The ideas behind the story intertwine when Palanka, a foreign killer, disguises himself as a policeman, a trusted public servant, like the one whom Callan has consistently lied to throughout the story. The themes of the story satisfyingly fuse together as the climaxes of each storyline are intercut in a nail-biting conclusion to an exceptionally strong episode.

Brilliant though the studio scenes are, a different kind of *Callan* can be glimpsed in the sequences at night shot on 16mm colour film at the beginning of the episode. Fluid, atmospheric and full of edgy silences, they show what the series might have looked like if it had been made entirely on film.

S3.3 THE SAME TRICK TWICE

Writer: Bill Craig
Director: Peter Duguid
Designer: David Marshall

FIRST UK TRANSMISSION: Wednesday 22 April 1970, 9.00 pm

CAST: Andrew Sachs (German Captain/TV Interviewer, *uncredited on screen*), Geoffrey Chater (Bishop), Richard Hurndall (Surtees), Patrick O'Connell (Mallory), Harold Innocent (Freddy), Trisha Noble (Jean Price)

EXTRAS/WALK-ONS: *(Uncredited on screen)* Film: Cy Town (East German Sentry), David Joyce (West German Sentry), Trevor Lawrence (Second West German Sentry), Laurie Goode, Peter Kodak (West German Soldiers) Extras unknown (Two Mercedes Drivers and Two Motor Cyclists), Tony Cordell (Coalman), Rosemarie Croom-Johnson (Housewife)

Studio: Baron Omidi (Russian Spy), Bernard Mistovski (Foreign Office man, doubling in Gents' scene), Jay Neil (British Army Captain, doubling in Gents' scene), Christopher Holmes (British Army Lieutenant, doubling in first Corridor scene), Royston Farrell (West German Lieutenant, doubling in second Corridor scene), Scott Andrew (West German sentry)

PRODUCTION

Rehearsals: From Friday 6 February 1970.
Location Filming: Regimental Depot of the Royal Ordnance Corps in Deepcut, near Pirbright, Surrey (Monday 9 February 1970); the Grand Union Canal between Blomfield Road, London W9, and Delamere Terrace, in Maida Vale, London W2; Lauderdale Mansions in London, W9 (Tuesday 10 February 1970)
Camera Rehearsals/Recording: Teddington Studio One, Wednesday 18 and Thursday 19 February 1970[76]

TV TIMES: 'The Russians agree to a swop [sic] of captured agents with the British, but things soon start to backfire on Callan.'
18-24 April 1970, Yorkshire edition

MISSION PROFILE: Two men, Mallory and Surtees, are returned from Russia and, at a press conference, the latter promises to reveal details of how he was blackmailed into spying by British intelligence. The problem is – he wasn't. Mallory is taken on by the Section and believes that Surtees is a Russian agent. Callan bugs his phone, leading him to the photographer Freddy who took compromising photos of a drugged Surtees with the model Jean Price. With publication of Surtees' articles approaching, Callan is unofficially ordered to kill the man and make it look like suicide; later, he discovers that the house where Surtees was photographed was the site of a KGB cell. Surtees is killed and his notes stolen. Callan realises Mallory is the culprit – he's a double agent, whom Callan shoots dead.

A MAN LIKE ME: Callan knows of a nursing home near East Grinstead used by the SIS. He takes some satisfaction from the possibility that one of the Section's 'dirty' operations may have been exposed. In his downtime, he still suffers from insomnia, and is learning to play chess from the Penguin paperback *The Game of Chess* by British chess champion Harry Golombek (first published in 1955). Callan has brown ale in his fridge, but it's flat. He is annoyed to find his recent trauma has been disclosed to Mallory and Bishop, and he's extremely aggressive throughout, physically intimidating Freddy and Jean Price and humiliating Lonely by trashing the public toilet where he works. Perhaps because Mallory is the first person he's killed since he was tricked into gunning down the last Hunter, Callan shoots the double agent four times, visibly sweating as he does so. His knowledge of an old KGB cell in Camden Town is instrumental in resolving the Surtees case.

Section Kills: 16

LONELY: Lonely has been lying low as a 'hygiene operative' (i.e. a toilet cleaner) in Harry's Strip Bar, where he has his own room. He has to be bullied into working for Callan even though he'll be paid, earning £15 (originally £20; he loses £5 for initially refusing to help). Once again demonstrating his burglary skills, he easily scales the drainpipe of Surtees' apartment block to let Callan in through the front door. He has no trouble breaking into Surtees' roll-top desk.

A TIE AND A CREST: First seen apparently working for the Foreign Office, the outwardly affable Mr Bishop was 'up at Oxford' with Surtees. He has an unspecified role in British intelligence, and Callan's repeated demands to know who he is go unanswered. An unobtrusively powerful man, he quietly takes over the Surtees operation as he has authority over Hunter. (As he appears to occupy the same role over the Section as Sir Michael Harvey, his presence suggests that he's his replacement, and that Harvey was eventually unmasked and either fled abroad or was killed by the Section.)

ALCOHOL, TOBACCO AND FIREARMS: At the spy exchange, Callan has a mug of spirit from his own hip flask painfully thrown back into his face and eyes by the querulous Surtees. Later, after killing Mallory, Callan shares a well-earned glass of Hunter's malt.

SPY-SPEAK: Bishop is amusingly unrepentant about his character: 'In addition to swearing and smoking, I also tell lies.'

The Section is subjected to Callan's sardonic sense of humour: 'Let's face it, a little light blackmail is something we do for relief.'

Always the professional, Lonely complains about the physical maintenance of Surtees' building: 'That drainpipe is dead shaky at the top. They ought to have that seen to. A person could get killed comin' up a thing like that.'

Callan is appalled at the lengths he is being asked to go to in committing an unofficially-sanctioned execution: 'You want a chopping done, you write out a chit!.... I'm telling you, sir – you want a killing, you give an order, direct, straight, in front of *witnesses!*' (Even the Section, it appears, keeps some records of its deniable operations.)

PAWNS AND PLAYERS: BILL CRAIG (1930-2002) reacclled, 'I spent five thoroughly miserable years in an industrial laboratory, decided that wasn't what I wanted to do with my life and started writing for radio. I spent five gloriously happy and irresponsible years there, ITV started up and ATV offered me a contract, then I went freelance.'[77] The Glasgow-born writer began his career on television with *The Winifred Atwell Show* in 1956. From there, Craig went on to work on some of the premier TV dramas made between 1960 and 1980, including adaptations of the Dorothy L. Sayers Lord Peter Wimsey books, *Spy Trap* and *Shoestring*. Like George Markstein, Craig was head of the Writers Guild and, in later years, directed his energies more and more towards productions set in his beloved Scotland, with writing credits on the family dramas *Take the High Road* (1980-2003), *Strathblair* (1992-93) and the revived *Doctor Finlay* (1993-96).

GEOFFREY CHATER (born 1921) was ideal casting for establishment figures. One of director Lindsay Anderson's favourite actors, he featured in his films *If...* (1968) and *O Lucky Man!* (1973), as well as Stanley Kubrick's historical epic *Barry Lyndon* (1975). Shortly before appearing in *Callan*, in 1967 Chater played Gilbert Jarvis, the first victim in *The Avengers* episode 'You Have Just Been Murdered' and, a year later, was one of the directors of a company being targeted by a killer in *The Saint* story 'The Scales of Justice'. Equally skilled in drama and comedy, Chater showed off his comic gifts in *Mapp and Lucia* (1985-86) in the role of Algernon Wyse. His last TV role was in *Midsomer Murders* in the story 'Brother Robert' (2005). Ray Jenkins was delighted with Chater's inclusion in the cast: 'He always did that kind of chumpiness which can be lethal as well as intelligent. Smashing actor.'[78]

TRISHA NOBLE, under her real forenames Patsy Anne, was a singer as well as an actress, and played a pirate DJ in the *Danger Man* episode 'Not So Jolly Roger' (1966), a story in which her own single, 'He Who Rides the Tiger', featured on the soundtrack. Topically, the *TV Times* reported that four days after 'The Same Trick Twice' was transmitted, actress/singer/dancer Noble was heading to the USSR: 'Trisha moves right in on the KGB when she and her husband Alan Sharpe leave for a holiday in Russia.'[79] Wearing a fetching soccer outfit, Trisha appeared on the cover of the 30 May-5 June 1970 issue of *TV Times* under the headline 'How to Survive the World Cup'.

RICHARD HURNDALL (1910-1984) played Laertes at the Shakespeare Memorial Theatre in *Hamlet*, a part that Woodward also performed there. In constant demand, one of Hurndall's last roles was his reinterpretation of William Hartnell's Doctor Who in the 1983 anniversary story 'The Five Doctors'. He was the uncredited voice of the Unmutual Committee in 'A Change of Mind', a particularly disturbing episode of *The Prisoner*. A forceful character actor, he was often cast as authority figures, having regular roles in *The Power Game* (1969) and *Oil Strike North* (1975); he also delivered a memorable performance as gangland boss Henry Mackleson in *Spindoe* (1967). By contrast, his comic ability can be seen in *Ripping Yarns* – 'Whinfrey's Last Case' (1979).

PATRICK O'CONNELL played the memorably selfish black marketeer Ashton in *Doctor Who* – 'The Dalek Invasion of Earth' (1964). In 1967, complete with a fashionable Liverpool accent, he featured with Edward Woodward in *The Saint* episode 'The Persistent Patriots'. Two years later, he was in *The Wednesday Play* – 'Sling Your Hook' by Roy Minton. Before *Callan*, O'Connell starred in two series of *Fraud Squad* (1969-1970) as Detective Inspector Gamble. Between 1973 and 1976, he took over from Glyn Owen in the major role of Edward Hammond in the BBC boardroom drama, *The Brothers*.

ANDREW SACHS went on to become one of the most famous TV faces of the 1970s, thanks to his hapless Spanish waiter Manuel being constantly terrorised by John Cleese in the BBC farce *Fawlty Towers* (1975 and 1979).

INFORMATION: 'I had a phone call from George Markstein and I said "yes" because I'd watched the previous two series,'[80] Bill Craig remembered of how he got involved with *Callan*. 'People either know each other or they know somebody that knows somebody that knows somebody... [Ideas come from true stories] – it might be an extrapolation or an inversion or a complication of the idea. It did link onto something that had happened in the previous six months: someone had defected here and there was talk about whether they were genuine or not, and I thought "Let's see where that takes me." The follow-on thought was what would happen if the security service set up a situation with the patsy who was going to destroy that service.'

Reg Collin was immediately impressed by his friend's debut script, and from later in the lifetime of *Callan* recalled, 'George and I desperately wanted Bill to write another episode, and he was too busy. It was winter, so [on location] we sat in the back of the unit car, the three of us, and eventually twisted his arm into writing it. He was a very important writer.'[81] Peter Duguid had worked with Geoffrey Chater before and had specific input into developing his part: 'I certainly recall doing work on the script with George. I persuaded them to build [Bishop] up; you needed characters coming in to jolly things along. We did build it up into a part that could be in [the story] two or three times. [There was] a nice tension between him and Callan.'[82]

Library music tracks used in the episode were 'Soho Stripper', 'Wild Types, Emperor Quartet', as well as the 'Archduke Trio' by Ludwig Van Beethoven (1770-1827).

The black and white surveillance photos were taken by Thames photographer Gerald Sunderland who also supplied an in-joke: on 6 February, Bill Craig modelled for the portrait of Vassily, the KGB agent responsible for framing Surtees, used in a Red File. David Marshall also needed to source three nude photographs for Freddy's studio; these featured glamour models Lisa French, Raine Rehan and Candy Thager. The end titles again carried a voiceover announcing 'Edward Woodward is a National Theatre Player', and that 'Harold Innocent is appearing in *The Magistrate* at the Cambridge Theatre.'

In the rehearsal draft, there were direct references to 'Death of a Hunter' that were dropped, partly because Craig was unaware that the Section HQ had moved. Cut dialogue for Hunter states that he occupies the same office as his predecessor, with a stain of John Ramsey's blood on the carpet, which would have been a continuity mistake. When Hunter later visits Callan in his flat and orders him to execute Surtees, he says that the agent owes the Section 'a private debt', specifically comparing the way Callan was tricked by the KGB to the way Surtees is being deceived; during the conversation, Callan says that he doesn't blame Meres for shooting him. There is a production mistake in the finished episode: after Surtees shuts the door to his flat when Callan visits him, it swings open behind the two men as they talk.

The completed production benefited from ideas the regular cast sometimes came up with rehearsal, as William Squire remembered. 'I was the first Hunter to give Callan a drink. I remember saying to Teddy, "Does Callan drink?" He said "Like a fish," and so I gave him a Scotch. That was the first time. It sounds really trivial, but it established [that my Hunter] was top drawer.'[83] The climatic shooting between Callan and Mallory showed up the limitations of video recording, as Duguid recalled: 'It took us about two hours to get the sound right for the shooting at the end as there's a lag between video and audio of a couple of frames – you couldn't cut the tape till you'd cleared the sound. So you had this problem of trying to remove the reverb. It's still there! It was still physical editing when we did the colour *Callan*s.'[84]

In Channel 4's repeat showing of 'The Same Trick Twice' on 24 June 1984, the end of the scene where Callan meets Lonely in the toilets of Harry's Strip Bar was cut so the pun 'cash in lieu' – improvised by Woodward and praised by a viewer who wrote into *TV Times* in 1970[85] – was omitted. The edited print of the episode was used on subsequent DVD releases.

A potent image associated with the exchange of real spies was the Glienicke Bridge over the River Havel, which linked West Berlin with Potsdam in East Germany. The Bridge saw the high-profile swap of U-2 spy plane pilot Gary Powers for the Soviet agent Colonel Rudolf Abel on 10 February 1962, as well as the exchange of British spy Greville Wynne for the Communist agent Konon Molody (see 'Nice People Die at Home', Chapter 6) on 22 April 1964. Glienicke was christened 'The Bridge of Spies' by the Western media and became so well-known it featured in the novels *Funeral in Berlin* (1964) and *Smiley's People* (1979); the 2015 film of the same name concentrated on the Powers case. Callan's comment about the Russian spy the Section captured refusing to talk could be an oblique reference to Molody, who successfully kept his identity secret from British intelligence until it was revealed as part of the exchange deal with Wynne.

MISSION ANALYSIS: *'Your move, innit?'* After the preceding episode's shattering collision of espionage and British law, new writer Bill Craig also pushes the envelope, with the ingenious tale of a spy scandal-that-isn't being revealed in the press. In a labyrinthine plot worthy of John le Carré, it's revealed that Surtees' blackmail at the hands of 'Hunter' was actually a KGB operation to discover who among Surtees' contacts in Eastern Europe were sympathetic to the West. In an extra twist, the scheme was also designed to discredit British intelligence after Surtees's release from prison. Craig's ingenious script is compulsive viewing from start to finish – particularly in the final, unexpected shoot-out – and clearly benefits from having espionage expert George Markstein in the story editor's chair.

Every one of the one-off characters, from the oily Freddy to the provocative Mrs. Price, have distinct personalities and believable motivations, while the ingenuity of Craig's writing makes Mallory, an SIS man turned double agent, a low-key, genuinely surprising undercover antagonist. (The casting of O'Connell, previously familiar to the audience as a police inspector, is a further clever means of making this character appear trustworthy and plausible as a further regular addition to the Section team.) From his first appearance, too, the misleadingly genial Bishop, played with evident relish by Geoffrey Chater, makes an impression. Although he doesn't get much to do otherwise, Mower is notably convincing in the scene where he poses as a journalist.

Callan's character continues to fascinate, as two sides of this complex, deeply-conflicted man are visible. It's hard not to feel for him as he is given no choice but to execute Surtees unofficially – risking prison if he's caught – and when he arrives at the man's flat he's sweating with stress. At the same time, his violent intimidation of three weaker people is unpleasant, and in Lonely's case, genuinely upsetting.

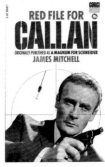

A selection of Callan fiction, including *Callan Uncovered* (2014), the first anthology of short stories published by the *Sunday Express* in the 1970s.

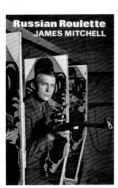

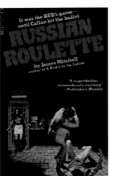

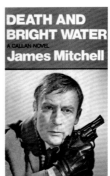

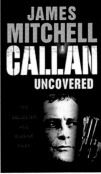

A 1967 publicity shoot on the River Thames for the first series. *Left to right:* Ronald Radd (Colonel Hunter), Anthony Valentine (Toby Meres), Russell Hunter (Lonely) and Edward Woodward (Callan). *Getty Images*

Callan's producers: Terence Feely, 1967-68 (*above*) and Reginald Collin, 1968-1972 (*right*).

Above: Russell Hunter waits for recording to continue in Lonely's flat during the making of 'You Should Have Got Here Sooner'.
Peter le Page collection

Left: In July 1967 *Callan* makes the cover of *TV World*, ATV Midlands' listings magazine.

Below: (Stanley McGeagh) and the second Hunter (Michael Goodliffe) in 'Let's Kill Everybody', shortly before both Section men are shot dead by an assassin. Goodliffe was written out after five episodes because he was unhappy working on the series.
Rex Features

Top: Production designer Peter le Page's set for Holder's Fascist headquarters in the lost episode 'The Running Dog', clearly influenced by the Nazi architect Albert Speer. *Peter le Page Collection*

Left: Third Hunter Derek Bond's signed publicity picture. His character trained with Callan, who knew him as John Ramsey.

Below: Edward Woodward (Callan) and Dicer (Vladek Sheybal) in Stan Woodward's kitchen set from 'The Little Bits and Pieces of Love'. *Peter le Page Collection*

DEREK BOND

Top: Director Peter Duguid (*centre*) and film cameraman John Keeling (*right*) during the location filming at Farnham for 'Heir Apparent'. *Anthony Valentine Collection*

Left: The pill box the production crew built on location for the rendezvous between Callan and John Ramsey. *Peter le Page Collection*

Duguid directs Edward Woodward in Farnham, at the East German border fence. *Anthony Valentine Collection*

The publicity stunt in October 1969 outside BBC Broadcasting House in Portland Place, London, announcing 'Callan Lives!' *Getty Images*

Above: Throughout the series' run, *Callan* and its actors were often cover stars on newspapers, magazines and, once, a boys' comic.

Right: Dr. Snell (Clifford Rose) evaluates the fitness of James Cross (Patrick Mower) in 'If He Can, So Could I'. The episode was the favourite *Callan* story of both actors.

Rex Features

New recruits for Series Three: script editor George Markstein (*left*) and William Squire (*right*), the fourth Hunter. *Far right:* The Spanish poster for the *Callan* film. The title translates as *Agent Callan, Shoot on Sight!*

Right: Voytek was one of the new directors to join during Series Three. He was an Eastern European émigré, who fought in the Polish resistance against the Germans in World War 2.

Below: Lisa Langdon (Liz) and Meres (Anthony Valentine) during a recording break on Hunter's office set in Series Four.

Peter le Page Collection

James Mitchell, his wife Delia and Edward Woodward during filming of the *Callan* feature film in 1973.
Peter Mitchell Collection

'I don't know if I can do it – not any more.' Callan and Lonely come out of retirement in ATV's *Wet Job* (1981).
Rex Features

S3.4 ACT OF KINDNESS

Writer: Michael Winder
Director: Mike Vardy
Designer: Fred Pusey

FIRST UK TRANSMISSION: Wednesday 27 May 1970, 9.00 pm

CAST: Anthony Nicholls (Heathcote Land), Ray Smith (Donovan Prescott), Jacqueline Maude (Janice Land), Peter Beton (Shop assistant), Nicolette McKenzie (Mrs Briggs), Mark Jay (Master Briggs – John)

EXTRAS/WALK-ONS: (*Uncredited on screen*) Film and studio: Eden Fox, Paul Phillips, Crawford Lyall, Richard Atherton, James Haswell, James Brighty, Tom Laird, George Hancock, Ivor Owen
   Studio: Nicholas Kane, Ron Gregory, George Howes, Clive Rodgers, Tony Lang, Victor Croxford, Vernon Preston, William Curran

PRODUCTION

Rehearsals: From Saturday 24 January 1970
Location Filming: The model soldier shop Tradition on 188 Piccadilly, London W1; 28 Chapel Street, W1 (Monday 26 January 1970); Putney Heath, Wildcroft Road, London SW15; Royal Horticultural Hall, Vincent Square, London SW1 (Tuesday 27 January 1970)
Camera Rehearsals/Recording: Teddington Studio One, Wednesday 4 and Thursday 5 February 1970[86]

TV TIMES: 'More than toy soldiers are involved in the war game Callan has to play. Heathcote Land shows fellow director Donovan Prescott compromising photographs taken in Moscow of Prescott and a girl. Callan is instructed to prevent Land exposing Prescott who has been working as a courier to Iron Curtain countries for some years. Callan finds Land at the War Games Convention, a gathering of model soldier enthusiasts...'
April 25- May 1 1970, Anglia edition

MISSION PROFILE: Businessman Heathcote Land confronts Donovan Prescott, the married overseas sales director of Allied Motors, which exports tractors to the Eastern Bloc, with compromising photographs of him and a girl in Moscow taken by the KGB. Prescott refuses to resign. Callan is assigned to stop Prescott, an amateur intelligence courier, being sacked, and gets to know Land at a militaria convention. Both Prescott and Land are rivals and are vying for overall directorship of Allied. Land works out Callan is from state security, while Cross searches for something to use against Callan's new war gaming partner – or a way to kill him. Callan discovers that Land fathered an illegitimate daughter during WW2, but doesn't use the information against him. While Land agrees not to use the photographs, he refuses to inform Prescott of this change of heart, knowing that this will make his rival nervous and that he'll fail the interview for managing director.

A MAN LIKE ME: Callan has two days' leave booked which he intends to spend at a militaria event, and is annoyed when Hunter cancels it so that his attendance becomes part of his assignment to meet Land. More than any other episode, 'Act of Kindness' shows what an enthusiastic aficionado of military history Callan is. He regularly reads the (real) magazine *Miniature Warfare*, and his handmade model of Prince Eugene's Standard Bearer, which Land is searching for, impresses the Allied Motors' director with its detail and craftsmanship. In turn, Callan is complimentary about Land's article on shrapnel in *Miniature Warfare*. The Napoleonic era is Callan's favourite, and he is so skilled at war gaming he gets through to the semi-finals of the convention he's attending. Being allowed to play in Land's personal War Room genuinely excites him.

Callan thinks the Section should stay out of boardroom politics, and has little time for Prescott, the man he's defending, dismissing him as 'a bloody ram' who is a liability both in intelligence work and as the would-be MD of Allied. By contrast, he cultivates a real friendship with Land which, uniquely, survives Callan's 'Tucker' cover being blown and looks like it's going to continue beyond the conclusion of the mission. Callan knows that Land won't use the gun he pulls on him to stop him phoning Prescott, but chooses to pretend Land will, opting to finish their war game instead. The other act of kindness in the episode, it's possibly the noblest thing Callan ever does.

LONELY: Reminisces about 'making coins'. His friendship with Callan has developed to the point where he's now helping him make model soldiers. However, their relationship is soon put under pressure by Lonely's uninvited attendance of the militaria event, during which Callan has to deny knowing him and the anxious little man falls over, demolishing a display of drums. At the same time, Lonely's knowledge of the legal system is so poor that he thinks failing to a report in to a police station for one day will result in him becoming the focus of a nationwide manhunt. It's no wonder that Callan doesn't know why he bothers to help Lonely stay out of trouble.

A TIE AND A CREST: There's class and generational warfare between Land and Prescott. The former is an elderly, educated Englishman, morally upright, apparently anti-union, and he inherited his 25% shares in Allied Motors. Prescott is a young Welshman who worked his way up from the factory floor and is, understandably, a union man. His integrity is suspect though, as he's a philanderer who is only involved in spying for the thrill of it.

The Section can't resist taunting Callan about his hobby, with Hunter ribbing him about 'toy soldiers' and Cross arranging for a dozen toy Hussars to be delivered to 'Master David'. Staking out Land's house, Cross is assigned a VW Beetle rather than his usual white Jaguar. He doesn't look very happy about having to clean it as part of his cover, so perhaps it's not surprising he favours a terminal solution to the Land problem.

ALCOHOL, TOBACCO AND FIREARMS: Callan has a brandy with Prescott, who appears to be fond of a drink.

Guns are confined to the war gaming table, apart from the Beretta pistol Land threatens Callan with. It's one of the few times that the Section agent doesn't carry his Magnum and it prevents him from phoning Prescott – or so he says.

SPY-SPEAK: Unaware of the pun he's making, Callan asks if Prescott was 'on the job' when the KGB photographs were taken. Hunter tells him not to be 'crude'.

Lonely is once again desperate for money: 'I'm a bit low, Mr. Callan.' 'You smell high enough to me, mate,' Callan replies.

Callan can only summon one word when he sees Land's War Room for the first time:

'Blimey!'

Using the terminology of their battle tournament, Land lets the Section's senior man know that he's on to him: 'In this war game, you can never trust a soul. That right, Callan?'

PAWNS AND PLAYERS: ANTHONY NICHOLLS (1902-1977) was a theatre and film veteran by the time he guest starred in *Callan*. He was a contemporary of Peter O'Toole and Laurence Olivier, and featured with them in several highly regarded Shakespearean stage productions. At the same time, Nicholls had impressive cinematic credits to his name such as *Victim* (1961), *A Man for All Seasons* (1966) and *The Omen* (1976). Arguably, Nicholls' most famous role was W.L. Tremayne in the 1968-69 TV adventure series *The Champions*, in which he performed with a wig and false beard. Notably, he played the ill-fated Dr. Warren, opposite the equally ill-fated Hilary Dwyer as Laura, in the terrifying *Space: 1999* episode 'The Troubled Spirit' (1976).

RAY SMITH (1936-1991), who guest starred throughout the 1970s as heavyweight figures in series such as *Thriller* – 'The Next Voice You See' (1975) and *1990* – 'Health Farm' (1977). He played the semi-regular role of Detective Inspector Firbank in *Public Eye* (1971-75) and Dr. Cockcroft in the 1979 TV drama about the *Atom Spies*, based around the traitor Klaus Fuchs. Smith later took on the regular role of the permanently bad-tempered Detective Superintendent George Spikings in the action show *Dempsey and Makepeace* (1985–86). 'I managed to get Ray Smith, which was a great plus, because Ray was always a bit of a naughty boy,'[87] director Mike Vardy said. 'We enjoyed each other's company and he was dead right [for the part]. You could imagine him getting involved with those Russian girls! And he was such an opposite to Anthony Nicholls. In that level of corporate management, you couldn't get anyone more different.'

INFORMATION: There was more library music than usual, which accompanied the various war games: 'Midsummer Scherzo (no.3)' by International Studio on the Impressia label; 'The Great Advance', 'Speedway' and 'Chimes of Victory' by the Irish Guards on Boosey and Hawkes, and 'Military Splendour 'on DeWolfe. In a surprising move for Callan's character, Woodward can be heard whistling 'Toreador's Song' from the opera *Carmen* (1875). On Friday 30 January, there was a photo-call for the photographs of Prescott in bed with a KGB girl. They were strikingly explicit for British television of the time, as the actress and stuntwoman Roberta Gibbs was photographed topless.

The current Hunter mentions his predecessor's fate in 'Death of a Hunter', the previous script by Michael Winder. According to how Callan dates the age of Land's grandson, John, who was born in 1962, the story takes place in 1969. The episode was originally scheduled for 9:20 pm on 29 April 1970, but was deferred to 27 May when the televised Cup Final between Leeds United and Chelsea on the original date ran into extra time.

The episode was a challenging one for Mike Vardy. '[The story] was made complicated by the fact that a great deal of the screenplay was about war games, with explicit moves of famous battles on the board, the discussions of which were also used as dialogue subtext. There are strict rules and protocols attached to these contests of military prowess and Callan becomes very involved. [It] went against the grain with Callan as he grew to like and respect Land... This was long before digital animation had arrived, and so the sequence of moves on the board had to be done in many single shots and fast-edited together to show the audience what was happening. I had to have a technical adviser [Peter Beton, who also played the shop assistant] in terms of the battle moves, both before and after the studio recording. The soldiers had to be moved by hand, stopped, then moved again by hand. It was a bit like doing an old-fashioned cartoon, and then it all had to be edited together very quickly, so it took hours.'[88]

Vardy noted how different the character of Lonely made *Callan* to other series of its type. 'When Lonely walks into the war game and knocks everything over, it takes it into a different realm all of a sudden – and then he calls him "Mr. Callan" when he's pretending to be somebody else! You don't often get that [sort of] humour in spy stories.'

As part of his characterisation, Russell Hunter had rationalised why Lonely was so fascinated by Callan's modelling hobby. 'I think his attitude towards Callan was probably coloured by the fact that Callan's only hobby appeared to be little toys,'[89] he said. 'I don't think Lonely ever had toys in his life! The man he most admired, and the man he was physically most afraid of, was not only playing with these little things, but *making* them. This is wonderful: it's not wrong for a grown-up man to play with little toys! I don't know what Lonely plays with. Probably a wind-up Donald Duck or something, made in bad pink plastic... [Lonely had] great admiration for Callan's ability to cast little lead figures for his model soldiers – *great* admiration for that. He was desperate to take part; he would probably have painted them with a four-inch paint brush, but he would have *loved* to be allowed to join in.'

The shop Callan and Cross visit, Tradition of London, has been trading for over 50 years as a seller of collectable model soldiers. This authentic touch extended to using in the cast Peter Beton, one of the shop assistants who worked there in the 1970s. When he was between acting jobs, military history enthusiast and actor Nicholas Courtney also worked behind Tradition's counter (see 'The Running Dog', Chapter 6).

'Act of Kindness' drew an approving review from the *Daily Mail* the morning after its transmission. 'Against a background of a battle between lead soldiers, the story neatly unfurled itself,'[90] the paper reported, going on to comment favourably on the major cast change that had been made to the programme in its third year: 'You only have to have the villainous Cross flaring his nostrils in a dark alley to get a shiver of horror down your spine... and he certainly didn't spare the flaring yesterday, as he proposed endless plans to bump off [Land] and be done with it.' The next day, *The Sun*, covering Edward Woodward's new theatre role as Cyrano de Bergerac, informed its readers that the 'new *Callan* series is way up in the ratings.'[91]

MISSION ANALYSIS: *'You're asking for trouble, aren't you?'* This is a subtle mould-breaker from the mysterious, talented Michael Winder. Uniquely in the series, there is no violence or gunfighting, nor any use of the Section's trademark nastiness upon innocent people. Exploring similar territory to 'A Magnum for Schneider', Callan's battle with Heathcote Land is conducted through their war gaming, as it becomes the metaphor for the other, psychological battle going on between them. While this symbolism might seem a bit obvious over 40 years on, the script is a smart one as both men acknowledge the parallel, which builds towards the denouement where Land confronts Callan with his 'secret weapon'.

Interestingly, it's one of the few times that Callan – and *Callan* the series – looks on the establishment favourably, in the form of the educated, wealthy Land. The man is clearly decent, providing for his illegitimate daughter and grandson, and worried about what will happen to his company under the unreliable Prescott. By contrast, his opponent is a shady figure, the 'union man' being something of a contemporary bogey man when the story was written. Prescott's unapologetic philandering, and Land's enthusiasm for the military glories of the past, further emphasise the cultural gulf between them.

Mike Vardy's handling of the actors is exceptional. Even though Lonely is only in the story briefly, Russell Hunter still makes an impression, particularly with his slapstick tumble. Woodward again has a chance to show Callan's human side in his affection and respect for Land (one of the few men ever to outwit the Section agent), and in the brief scene where he meets the man's grandson. Anthony Nicholls almost steals the entire episode, so dignified is his portrayal of Land, and, for balance, the colourful Ray Smith is unrepentantly amoral. Add to this some novel stop-motion photography of the war games, together with clever use of military music to add suspense (even more so when it cuts out just as Callan's cover is blown), and 'Act of Kindness' impresses as atypical and surprisingly upbeat. Because of that, it's another of the series' most rewarding stories.

S3.5 AMOS GREEN MUST LIVE

Writer: Ray Jenkins
Director: Jim Goddard
Designer: Peter le Page

FIRST UK TRANSMISSION: Wednesday 24 June 1970, 9.00 pm

CAST: Frank Coda (Taxi driver), Corin Redgrave (Amos Green), Stefan Kalipha (Casey), Annette Crosbie (May Coswood), Lee Donald (Philip Rowland), Elaine Garreau (Shop assistant), Nina Baden-Semper (Anna), Al Garcia (Rutter), Michael Quinto (Gray)

EXTRAS/WALK-ONS: (*Uncredited on screen*) On OB - Quayside: Michael Earl (Inspector), Ronald Gough, Brian Nolan, Walter Henry, Pierce McEvoy (Constables), Keith Ashley (Policeman on Boat), Leonard Kingston (Plain Clothes Policeman), A. Harvey (Arillo). Outside Green's House: Keith Goodman, Terence Denville, Richard Lawrence, Denis Balcombe (Special Branch men), Bill Mathews, John Spradsbury (Thugs), Mark McMahon (Driver)
  Studio: Kathleen Heath, Peggy Scrimshaw (Women in Store Cubicles), Sandy Stein (Man in Evening Dress at Green's Dinner Party)

PRODUCTION

Rehearsals: From Friday 20 February 1970
Outside Broadcast Recording: Hammerton Ferry, Warren Footpath, Marble Hill, Twickenham, Middlesex (Monday 2 March), Twickenham Motor Service Station, 301 Richmond Road, Middlesex (Monday 2 March), Orleans House, Orleans Road, Twickenham, Middlesex (Tuesday 3 March 1970)
Camera Rehearsals/Recording: Teddington Studio Two, Wednesday 4 and Thursday 5 March 1970[92]

TV TIMES: 'Callan is called in to ensure the safety of Amos Green, a prospective Parliamentary candidate with strong anti-immigration views.'
20-26 June 1970, Southern edition

MISSION PROFILE: Joseph Amilcar Arillo, a black fundraiser connected to the subversive political organisation Black Glove, is found dead in the Thames with an Ace of Spades book of matches on him: the $10,000 he brought into the country is missing. Amos Green, a prospective MP who's made an inflammatory speech which is 'very, very strong on immigration', has been sent an identical book of matches, and Hunter suspects he may be the target of an assassination attempt.
  Cross is detailed to be Green's bodyguard while Callan investigates Arillo's death. He discovers that May Coswood, Green's housekeeper, is having an affair with an unemployed black man called Casey (based at a garage in Fetter Street) who killed Arillo for his money, and is planning to use mercenaries to assassinate Green. Callan arrives at Green's home in time to shoot down the hired killers, Gary and Rutter.

A MAN LIKE ME: As soon as the assignment is announced, it's clear that Callan doesn't like Green or his politics, as he looks disgusted. Later, in one of the few times he's seen to watch television, the agent turns off an interview Green is giving. Callan's dislike of racists extends to putting a bigoted cab driver in a choke-hold, a rather reckless move as the man is driving at the time. Conversely, when the Section man visits Black Glove's office, he can barely hide his amusement at their political naiveté.

Callan clumsily loses Mrs Coswood in a clothing store. By contrast, he is so skilled as a burglar that, by torch light alone in Black Power's office, he's able to spot a list of addresses hidden under a map of Central London on a pin board. When Lonely goes missing, Callan is so concerned for him that he investigates every address himself, later angrily sounding-off to Hunter that he's been 'padding all over bloody London!'

Another example of Callan's exemplary eyesight is his ability to see through a gas mask and drifting gas accurately enough to shoot dead two gunmen. He's also adept at employing psychology along with his weapon skills, using the flick-knife wielding Casey's attachment to May to distract him.

Even though he thinks the yellow tartan tie Lonely gives him is horrendous, Callan is considerate enough not to hurt the thief's feelings.

Section Kills: 18

LONELY: Shows how grateful he is to Callan for keeping him out of prison by giving him a tie, even though his assessment of his friend's sartorial taste is wildly misjudged. It's meant to be highly ironic that Lonely thinks 'coloureds' have a different kind of smell.

When he finds the garage on Fetter Street where Casey is hiding, he shows his quick-wittedness by spinning the man a story about his friend 'Big Joe' wanting his car repaired because of a crash. This doesn't save Lonely from being captured and tied up. He's understandably terrified of being knifed to death by Casey. It's the closest – to date – that he's come to being killed.

A TIE AND A CREST: Cross is still needling Callan, calling him 'old man', but gets a taste of his own medicine when he is assigned as Green's bodyguard under the alias 'Mr Lynd'. Green has the arrogance of the wealthy, being rude to his household staff and expecting Cross to 'butle' for him without question at a drinks party.

Hunter's establishment credentials are emphasised when he attends a black-tie dinner at Green's home, as 'Mr Salter' from the Treasury. (This could even be his real name.) The Section commander demonstrates his prowess on the firing range, while deputising for Cross in abusing Callan: '[He] may have a point – you're getting tired.'

ALCOHOL, TOBACCO AND FIREARMS: Casey anxiously smokes cigarettes while Green clearly appreciates alcohol: he enjoys a Scotch, and sherry is handed out by a dutiful Cross at his dinner party.

The assassins Casey hires are technically savvy, using gas grenades and gas masks as well as revolvers.

SPY-SPEAK: Callan is under no illusions about Green's popularity: 'There must be thousands want that one dead.'

Green himself is condescendingly dismissive of the danger he's in: 'Assassination takes place in hot-blooded countries – not Chiswick!' Questioned about Mrs Coswood's background, he sarcastically informs Cross that 'Doctor Hawley Harvey Crippen was her godfather and... she goes to sleep every night with a scimitar between her teeth.'

Hunter has a low opinion of Callan's ability to tail Mrs Coswood: '[Washington] want a report I can't give. Maybe that's because my Section has the grubby habit of getting lost in ladies' underwear.'

At Green's dinner party, Hunter reminds Cross of his priorities: 'If there's any trouble, I'm important. Remember me.' 'How could I ever forget you, sir?' Cross replies, straight-faced.

PAWNS AND PLAYERS: CORIN REDGRAVE (1939-2010) was born into an acting dynasty as the only son of theatre and film star Michael, and brother to the acclaimed actresses Vanessa and Lynn. On the stage, he tackled heavyweight roles like King Lear and Oscar Wilde, and won a prestigious Tony Award for his portrayal of Boss Whalen in Tennessee Williams' *Not About Nightingales* on Broadway in 1999. Williams' 'lost' play was premiered through Corin and Vanessa's Moving Theatre Company, in partnership with the National Theatre, before transferring to America.

On television, Redgrave's choice of parts was impressively eclectic, with roles in *The Avengers*, the sci-fi/horror thriller *Ultraviolet* (1998) and the bawdy drama *Shameless* (in 2004). In complete contrast to Green, he was a lifelong left-winger. 'Jim Goddard thought of using Corin Redgrave,' recalled Ray Jenkins. 'I must admit, [he] was brilliant.'[93] The director explained, 'People who hate things can give a very potent portrayal of the thing they hate; the only thing to watch is they don't go over the top. [Corin] enjoyed doing it because it was a way of getting back at the people he didn't like and didn't agree with.'[94]

STEFAN (a.k.a. STEPHEN) KALIPHA was new to television and 'Amos Green Must Live' was one of his first acting jobs in the UK. From there, among many other productions, he featured in the sitcoms *Mixed Blessings* (1978) and *Desmond's* (1994), which both had a racial theme, the Hollywood epic *Indiana Jones and the Last Crusade* (1989), and the Bond film *For Your Eyes Only* (1981) as the airborne assassin Hector Gonzales. Born in 1940, Kalipha was one of the immigrants the Tory MP Enoch Powell was concerned about, moving from Trinidad to England with various members of his family who became involved in the British arts scene. 'I've never had any trouble with racism – never seen any,'[95] he said, perhaps surprisingly. 'When I did *Callan*, Corin Redgrave, who was very political, said "You must get involved" and he took me along to some Workers Revolutionary Party meetings. I'm an easy-going kind of guy, and I wasn't impressed by their attitude of "We're right and everyone else is wrong," so I stopped going. I like a quiet life.'

ANNETTE ROSS McLEOD CROSBIE is best-known as the frequently exasperated Margaret Meldrew in the BBC comedy *One Foot in the Grave* (1990-2000), and portrayed a memorable Queen Victoria, opposite Timothy West, in the ITV drama *Edward the Seventh* (1975). She also featured in the remake of *Doctor Finlay* (1993-96), the gangland comedy serial *Underworld* (1997), the detective serial *An Unsuitable Job for a Woman* (1997) and the film *Calendar Girls* (2003). At the time of her *Callan* appearance she was known for her portrayal of Catherine of Aragon in the BBC period drama *The Six Wives of Henry VIII* (1970). 'I remember Annette Crosbie being fussed around by everybody: she loved that,'[96] said Ray Jenkins. 'She was *wonderful*.'

NINA BADEN-SEMPER, in an ironic contrast with *Amos Green Must Live*'s controversial politics, is best known as Barbie in the long racial comedy *Love Thy Neighbour* (1972-76).

INFORMATION: Jim Goddard approved of the content of Ray Jenkins' sole contribution to Series Three: 'The nice thing about that one for Teddy's character was that he was defending someone while he hated every damn thing he stood for, and he'd have killed [Green] himself.'[97] The nature of Lonely's present to Callan was changed, much to writer Jenkins' slight disappointment: 'I originally wanted to do a joke about an MCC tie, but [it was vetoed].'[98]

The episode was originally scheduled for 20 May 1970. Two days before it was due to be transmitted, a General Election was announced and both the Independent Television Authority (ITA) and Thames decided to delay the story until after the Election because of its political content. 'The idea is you try to keep contemporary fiction based around contemporary politics off the screen for the immediate few weeks prior to a General Election, on the grounds that in some way you might be accused of altering the outcome,'[99] explained Lloyd Shirley. 'The Representation of the People Act tries to make sure elections are run in the most equitable manner possible. For a given programme, they might decide it's wiser to hold it until the election is over.' 'Suddenly – at Home' was brought forward and shown instead.[100]

However, the story was rather different in the next morning's edition of *The Sun*. *Callan* was so popular in 1970 it made front page news as the paper ran the headline story 'Callan Storm over Election Ban'[101]. Philip Phillips reported that the decision to pull 'Amos Green Must Live' had been made and that, contrary to the united front presented to the media by the ITA and Thames, officials of the latter had 'made it clear that the episode was being forced off the air.' A clearly angry Jenkins was quoted as saying that the story's postponement was 'political censorship. I have simply written a story about two extreme men. We deliberately avoided taking any side in the matter.' Woodward was more conciliatory: 'On the face of it, it seems incomprehensible. When we recorded this play we were most careful. It was read through carefully and alterations were made.' The decision to postpone was apparently taken 'three hours'[102] before transmission.

'Amos Green Must Live' caused such concern because the title character was a fictional version of the former Conservative Shadow Defence Secretary Enoch Powell (1912-1998). On 20 April 1968, without consulting Conservative Central Office, he gave a highly controversial speech about the Labour government's new Race Relations Act. Powell disapproved of the legislation which was designed to curb racial discrimination. He also expressed misgivings about continued immigration, towards the end of his speech quoting from the Roman poet Virgil's verse 'Aeneid' and invoking the provocative image of 'the river Tiber foaming with much blood.' '[The story] was a *deliberate* attempt to bring [Powell] up-to-date,'[103] Jenkins admitted. 'It was my political need to say something about racism. It was a perfect example of using a set-up with inherited characters to tell your own story. Nobody stopped me, within Thames, *at all*. Nobody.' Reg Collin concurred: 'It wasn't a problem that gave us any loss of sleep.'[104] To put the controversy in context, he added, 'I once got chewed over the coals because another series I did showed a man rushing home from work and getting changed to go out, and he took his trousers off. I got really roasted.'

Powell's so-called 'Rivers of Blood' speech was widely covered by the media because Tory leader Edward Heath (1916-2005) immediately sacked Powell on 21 April. Under the headline 'Powell out of Shadow Cabinet: Heath Attacks "Racialist" Speech', *The Times* quoted extensively from the Conservative leader's statement about the incident: 'I have told Mr. Powell that I consider the speech he made in Birmingham yesterday to have been racialist in tone and liable to exacerbate racial tensions. This is unacceptable from one of the leaders of the Conservative Party and incompatible with the responsibility of a member of the Shadow Cabinet.'[105] Questioned about the content of his speech on *ITN News* on the day of his dismissal, Powell didn't help his position by commenting: 'The references to the black man getting the whip hand over the white man [were] made by a perfectly ordinary constituent.'[106]

Nevertheless, there was also wide support for the MP's sentiments. On the 23 April, the day the Race Relations Act was debated in the House of Commons, hundreds of dockers marched on Westminster in protest at Powell's removal, carrying placards reading 'Don't Knock Enoch'; on 24 April, four hundred meat porters from London's Smithfield market handed in a petition in support of the MP. There were other shows of unity in London and Wolverhampton, and an opinion poll organised by the company Gallup at the end of the month indicated that 75% of those canvassed agreed with Powell. With this volatile situation only two years old and the issue of race relations still highly sensitive, it's perhaps not surprising that the ITA and Thames decided to play safe.

'I only knew about [the postponement], I think, the night before it broke in the press,'[107] Jenkins recalled. 'Somebody rang up and said "It's just not gonna happen." I remember contacting the [Writers] Guild as I wanted to know what [my] areas of complaint were, and there were none, of course. Apart from when your script is being written, you cannot complain about [the treatment of it] to the company [you're writing it for]. They will listen if you complain, but there is no guaranteed access, and then you've got the *second* area of access, which is the individual company through to the IBA, and that didn't exist [for me]. So [the postponement was a decision] taken at the top, and we had to take it. In my heart of hearts, I don't really believe I wrote it so it wouldn't be [shown]. I thought there would be some trouble, but I didn't think they'd stop it. Then everybody started ringing up papers and made sure that it was a splash, which it was the next day. It was the front page of [*The Sun* and *The Times*]! We hit the front page with "Amos Green".'

Despite the controversy, Jenkins was happy to be writing for *Callan* in colour, particularly because 'William Squire was an old friend. I loved writing for him.' He did, however, have mixed feelings about the production of his third story. 'Stefan Kalipha did go a bit over the top and he did not allow the thing subtlety, but Jim didn't mind, he thought he was just wonderful, so he let him do it. The whole thing had a kind of over-the-topness, and they couldn't really manage the big scene, the invasion of the house. You could have done the whole thing properly, you could have actually flooded the screen with gas – that's what I wanted, people not seeing what they were doing – and you could have got away with a real phantasmagoria there. When you see things like the initial scene on the river, that was all very nicely done, exactly as I wanted; beautifully done, and it could have been from any film. Then you're into the whole area of "Would *Callan* have been better if it had all been on film?"'

'Amos Green Must Live' was given a publicity boost by the *TV Times* listings page for 24 June in most regions with a picture of Callan and Lonely in the agent's flat. After the episode was finally shown, some critics were at a loss to see what all the fuss had been about. *The Daily Telegraph* thought 'Ray Jenkins' script was a clumsy mixture of caricature and melodrama and the episode could well have been postponed indefinitely.'[108] In the *Guardian*, Nancy Banks-Smith could not believe 'any television programme was likely to send [grown] men and boys rushing into the street, burning and looting... The ban avoided bother. Craven but human.'[109]

On the walls of the Black Glove office there are 'Black Power posters' and a picture of 'Carmichael'. The former phrase was a political slogan of self-improvement and racial pride for people of black African descent, used by the US politician Adam Clayton Powell junior in a 1966 speech when he declared, 'To demand these God-given rights is to see black power'. The Black Panther Party, also founded in 1966, was the revolutionary wing of Black Power and Stokely Carmichael (1941-1998) was its honorary prime minister. He spoke in London in 1967 and later that year, the radical UK Black Power manifesto was published. 'When I was a school teacher, [Black Power] was down in Tulse Hill,'[110] Jenkins said. 'My kids came from Brixton and Stockwell and it was around then; I saw it all coming.' Black Glove is clearly intended to be the UK division of the Black Panther Party and its name also references imagery associated with the black athletes Tommie Smith and Peter Norman, who made black-gloved, Black Power salutes at the 1968 Mexico Olympics.

Hunter fears a UK repeat of the 'Watts riots' – six days of civil disturbance by the black community in Los Angeles over 11-17 August 1965, which ended with a death toll of 34. Casey tells Callan that his hit squad are using CS gas in the assassination, the same chemical agent that American riot police used on the Watts demonstrators.

The Section commander teases Green about an invasion of 'Mekons', referencing the *Dan Dare* cartoon strip in *The Eagle*. He gets the reference slightly wrong, as the Mekon (singular) was the leader of the green-skinned Treens in the 1950s comic.

One of Casey's assassins ironically quotes the title of the musical *Oh! What a Lovely War*, released as a film the year before 'Amos Green Must Live' was shown. Based on the 1963 stage play by Joan Littlewood's Theatre Workshop that incorporated period songs from WW1, the production heralded Richard Attenborough's debut as a film director. Coincidentally, Corin Redgrave featured in *Oh! What a Lovely War* ('the ever popular war game with songs, battles and a few jokes') as Bertie Smith, one of the central characters. (Len Deighton worked on the film's script, although he wasn't credited.)

Lonely is dismissively called 'Worzel Gummidge', a living, mischievous scarecrow created by Barbara Euphan Todd (1890-1976) in a popular series of children's books.

MISSION ANALYSIS: *'Why don't you just get – washed.'* While being Callan's most politically challenging story, this episode also has its flaws, arguably trying to achieve too much within its 50-minute running time. Viewing this story in a modern context, while the lines about 'coloureds' may grate, the anti-racist intent is clear, and the piece can be viewed in a similar vein to John Hopkins' equally controversial *Z Cars* episode, 'A Place of Safety' (1964) and *The Wednesday Play* – 'Fable' (1965). Its themes still have an uncomfortable resonance in 2016, given recent upsurges in British nationalism and hate crime.

With characteristically witty dialogue, Ray Jenkins crafts a sleekly loathsome title character fashioned after Enoch Powell ('Amos' and 'Enoch' are both biblical names), but in contrast the black characters Anna and Casey come across as political manifestos rather than people – perhaps understandable in the context of 1969/1970, owing to the inflammatory subject matter. Casey, unhinged both from being hurt in a car crash where whites didn't help him, and from being unable to find work from white employers, comes across as a hysterical, paranoid figure from the outset. Had a more restrained approach been taken regarding this performance, his final, keynote speech may have had more impact; as it stands, it's uncomfortably melodramatic. Because of this misjudged tone, the message of the piece, and its subtleties – Black Glove being terrified of an activist more extreme than they are, and Casey hiring white American hitmen – are overshadowed.

Casey's affair with Green's housekeeper is clearly to further his plan, but it's still daring as, at the time, mixed race relationships weren't often seen in British television drama. Annette Crosbie's performance, too, as a convincingly plain, sad woman starved of affection, saves the couple's relationship from being a mere device. She's the second character in 'Amos Green' who seems on the verge of a mental breakdown, but this does bring about one of the story's most unsettling scenes, as Cross tries to intimidate her into reacting when he mentions Casey's address. Mower himself has another of his best outings, as Cross has to contend diplomatically with Green's superior, abrasive manner. Green himself is rendered all too plausible by Corin Redgrave's assured mixture of charm, egotism and arrogance.

Putting both Lonely and Hunter in the line of fire, featuring a race-against-time hunt across London and climaxing with the biggest shoot-out in *Callan* to date, this was clearly intended to be a particularly outstanding story, galvanising the audience mid-way through the series in a similar way to Jenkins' previous 'Let's Kill Everybody'. Unfortunately, the re-scheduling problems rather derailed this intent, and additionally the various elements all end up fighting for prominence. Timing cuts to rehearsal script scenes that would have clarified the plot concerning Callan's search, and the budget constraints upon the big climax, also weigh against the story. As a consequence, the end result on screen is in places uncharacteristically rushed, confusing and heavy-handed, despite retaining many worthwhile moments.

S3.6 GOD HELP YOUR FRIENDS

Writer: William Emms
Director: Peter Duguid
Designer: Neville Green

FIRST UK TRANSMISSION: Wednesday 3 June 1970, 9.10 pm

CAST: Stephanie Beacham (Beth Lampton), Michael Jayston (Mark Tedder), Oliver Cotton (Senor Andarez), Rachel Herbert (Jeanette Valden), Edward Harvey (Mr Robinson), Clyde Pollitt (Messenger), John Quarmby (DI5 Man), Clyde Pollitt (Tedder's contact voice)*

EXTRAS/WALK-ONS: *(Uncredited on screen)* On film from the David Agency; Terence Conoley (Army General), Santiago Varella (Air Force Marshal), Vernon Drake (Foreign Office Commissioner), George Day (Security Man), George Howse (First Secretary from the Foreign Office), Dennis Balcombe (Aide), Walter Henry (Security Man), Ned Hood (Distinguished Resident).

Extras on VTR from the David Agency; Alan Vickers, Neville Simons, Yvonne Ball, Edmond Thomas, Diana Veale, Peter Roy, John Beardmore, Harry Tierney, Charles Saynor, Rosemarie Reeves, Derek Sheppard, Rachel Treadgold, Michael Ely, Jo Newman, Joe Santo

PRODUCTION

Rehearsals: From Friday 12 December 1969
Location Filming: 12 Princes Gardens, London W8; Campden Hill Flats and Plane Tree House, Duchess of Bedford Walk, London W8 (Monday 15 December 1969), Campden Hill Flats and Plane Tree House, Duchess of Bedford Walk, London W8 (Tuesday 16 December 1969)
Camera Rehearsals/Recording: Teddington Studio Two, Tuesday 23 and Wednesday 24 December 1969[111]

TV TIMES: 'Beth Lampton is the sort of girl every spy would love. She is a Government interpreter and Daddy is a general. She is secretly engaged to a public relations man whom Hunter suspects of being a spy but, unknown to the couple, their engagement is not as secret as they think. Hunter gets wind of it and decrees that the kissing has to stop. Callan gets the job of killing off the romance but, in this case, he finds a bunch of flowers is more lethal than his gun.'
30 May-5 June 1970, Southern edition

MISSION PROFILE: Callan and Cross are ordered to break up the relationship between Beth Lampton and Mark Tedder, a man suspected of spying for the Eastern Bloc. Lonely and Callan burgle Tedder's flat and discover love letters from, and photographs of, the man's ex-girlfriend Jeanette Valden, which they send on to Beth. The couple survives this attempt to split them up and bring their marriage forward. The Section agents then arrange for Tedder, a jealous man, to see Beth innocently having dinner with a diplomat called Andarez. When the couple meet to discuss what's been going on, Callan arrives with some flowers, apparently from Andarez, which convinces Tedder that Beth has been unfaithful. Unable to cope with the subsequent break-up, she takes a fatal overdose.

A MAN LIKE ME: Predictably, Callan doesn't like this job and, making his feelings known to Hunter, he still risks an international incident by putting a foreign diplomat at the mercy of Tedder's violent temper. The unpleasant nature of the assignment bothers him throughout the story, to the point where he gives Cross a hilariously insincere smile when the latter tells him to 'cheer up'. Callan is also clearly disgusted with himself after he's accepted the tip for delivering the flowers, with a forged note from Andarez, which will conclusively end Beth and Tedder's engagement. Perhaps because of the extra pressure on his conscience, Callan's violent with Lonely, shoving him roughly on to the sofa when he thinks he might have damaged some of his military models.

Always the perfectionist, Callan uses a jeweller's eyeglass when painting his model soldiers. He has a low opinion of DI5.

LONELY: For his mission to burgle Tedder and Beth's home he acquires a dapper suit, trilby, briefcase and businessman's umbrella, proving he can scrub up respectably when necessary. He knows exactly where to look in Tedder's desk for hidden secrets, and gets rather over-excited when he discovers the explicit love letters from Jeanette Valden. Lonely is still moaning about doing break-ins while he's on bail, which is why he's scared stiff by a man delivering flowers after he's just burgled Beth's flat. Oddly, this encounter doesn't make him smell.

A TIE AND A CREST: There's an undercurrent of class war to the Section's attack on Beth and Tedder, as the former is a daughter of a knight of the realm, General Sir George Lampton, while Tedder is the son of 'commoners' from Dulwich.

Demoting Beth to less sensitive work is not considered: she's too valuable, and presumably retains past information that the opposition could still make use of.

There's the customary needling between Callan and Cross, as the young agent says he was brought in because 'some of the big boys are getting soft', sneeringly viewing the Section's senior agent as someone who should be pensioned off. Waiting in his car, Cross listens to a jazz-rock-funk work-out that certainly wouldn't be in Callan's record collection.

ALCOHOL, TOBACCO AND FIREARMS: An affluent young couple, Beth and Tedder drink champagne in the Rococo restaurant, Tedder sips sherry on his birthday and later opts for whisky in a pub. An experienced drinker, Jeanette Valden downs a gin very quickly and buys 'a square one' for the barman.

SPY-SPEAK: Beth is not happy about Tedder's friendship with Jeanette, 'a woman like that.' 'A woman like what?' Tedder asks innocently.

Cross has a jaundiced view of female psychology: 'Take the obvious and turn it upside down.'

The series channels *Steptoe and Son* again, as Lonely very reluctantly parts with risqué pictures of Tedder and Jeanette. 'You are a dirty old man,' Callan tells him.

Callan makes a bitter assessment of his assignment: 'Two people want to get married. But now they don't trust each other any more. That's what I've achieved so far, sir, I thought you'd be pleased.'

Hunter makes a shocking admission about Beth's father after revealing that she's committed suicide: 'As a matter of fact, I know the General quite well. We've been friends for some years.'

PAWNS AND PLAYERS: STEPHANIE BEACHAM played another suicidal woman in the grim *Public Eye* story, 'My Life's My Own' (1969). She went on to appear in the WW2 drama *Tenko* (1981-84) and play the lead role in the ITV rag-trade drama *Connie* (1985), before moving to Hollywood to star in the glossy soap operas *The Colbys* (1985-87) and *Dynasty* (1981-89).

MICHAEL JAYSTON'S first TV role was in *Suspense* (1960, ITV). 'It was one of those times when you couldn't say certain things on television,'[112] he remembered. 'I only had about three lines and I was playing an intense young photographer. I had to say "Eisenstein did this shot through the Admiral's crutch." I was then told I couldn't say that, so I had to say "Eisenstein did this shot past the Admiral's trousers," which was ridiculous!' Having played regular Lincoln Dowling in *The Power Game* (1969), he starred as Tsar Nicholas I in Franklin J. Schaffner's epic 1971 feature film *Nicholas and Alexandra*. In 1975, Jayston moved to the BBC to star as Adam Hall's loner secret agent *Quiller*, revisiting the espionage genre again as one of the cast of the BBC TV adaptation of John le Carré's *Tinker Tailor Soldier Spy* (1979).

'I think it might have been one of Stephanie Beacham's first televisions,' Jayston speculated on their *Callan* appearance together. 'She seemed to be quite nervous, but she was great doing it. This was way before she became well known and started working in America.' The two actors were featured in a photograph that accompanied some *TV Times* programme listings for the series on 3 June.

RACHEL HERBERT was another alumna of *The Prisoner*, playing the East European maid Number 58, later revealed as the Village controller Number 2, in the episode 'Free for All' (1967). During the early 1970s, she featured as Lord Peter Wimsey's sister Mary in the popular BBC TV adaptations of Dorothy L. Sayers' novels.

CLYDE POLLITT (1924-1986) played Time Lords – or the same Time Lord? – twice in *Doctor Who*, in 'The War Games' (1969) and 'The Three Doctors' (1972-73). The Welsh actor also appeared in the dramas *Moll Flanders* (1975) and *The Life and Adventures of Nicholas Nickleby* (1982, directed by Jim Goddard).

INFORMATION: Given the working title of 'End of an Affair', 'God Help Your Friends' was the last *Callan* episode made in the 1960s. Michael Jayston attended a photo call on Monday 15 December 1969 at 1.30 pm for the surveillance stills Hunter looks at in his office; he was also required for a second session on Saturday 20 with Rachel Herbert, for photographs of the lovers in their swimming costumes. Library music tracks consisted of 'Dine and Dance' and 'Ellingtonesque' by the Scottmen and 'Laudation' by the Westway Orchestra, all published by Southern, and 'Chokachooka' by The Studio Group from De Wolfe. Peter Duguid recalled that the flats in 12 Princes Gardens were 'full of MPs'[113] and that the flat at Plane Tree House 'turned out to belong to the actress-turned-agony aunt Katie Boyle,' who at that time wrote a column for the *TV Times*. The episode went out ten minutes later than normal, because of a party political broadcast by the Labour Party concerning the upcoming general election. The story was originally scheduled for transmission on 13 May, as the sixth episode.

Duguid had reservations about this script. 'Those sort of stories don't work in this context: *Callan* is about action, it doesn't work through psychology. The romance stuff was far too top-heavy.' By contrast, William Squire was now really getting into his stride as the Section chief: 'My task, as Hunter, was to goad Callan into efficiency,'[114] the actor reasoned. 'I didn't care how far he went; however angry he got, however violent he got I didn't mind, as that was the way I ran him. It was like running a dangerous animal. You let him have his will, because you knew the only thing he could do was kill himself – there was no way out, no way out at all.' With the agent facing a particularly unpleasant mission in 'God Help Your Friends', Squire disarmingly recalled, 'I'm a very gentle soul, and my sisters used to be horrified at how hard I was on *Callan*.'

'[Getting cast] was one of those run-of-the-mill things,'[115] Michael Jayston said of the audition process. 'I don't think anyone else was up for it as there was so much work going on. I was pleased to get it because *Callan* was well received by the viewers; the [ratings] were amazing. It was a very good script. The scripts were generally very good on *Callan* and of course I'd watched it. It was one of my favourite shows at that time. I always got on well with Edward Woodward, because I'd met him and Patrick Mower several times before. The atmosphere on set was excellent, although the designer was a little upset. He'd done this amazing set [for Mark Tedder's flat] but he didn't know it was going to be mostly used in the dark with close-ups.' Peter Duguid's recollection is that Jayston took the part because he wanted to work with Woodward, which is ironic as the pair never fully share a scene.[116]

MISSION ANALYSIS: *'There are other ways of killing people than with a bullet.'* Comical at first, but ending in tragedy, 'God Help Your Friends' has extra impact following 'Act of Kindness', in which, for once, a guest character got the better of the Section. For a while, it looks as if the dignified, honourable and sensitive Beth (a perfectly cast Stephanie Beacham) and Michael Jayston's subtly ambiguous, though clearly in love, Mark Tedder, will be able to outwit Callan and his colleagues too. Although the couple shrug off the first attempt to break them up and the bond between them becomes stronger, Callan's accurate pinpointing of Tedder's aggressive jealousy as his weak point leads to a conclusion that has the feeling of grand tragedy about it. With hindsight, it's hard not to see Beth as an innocent lamb heading for the inevitable slaughter from the beginning, and her death is made doubly tragic as suspicions about Tedder's spying never harden into fact.

The script constantly cuts between the Section's and the couple's perception of events, the latter significantly never learning what's being done to them, although they do begin to guess. The two views of the situation are brought together in an intelligent, cinematic way by Peter Duguid, as a long tracking shot starting with Beth on the phone pulls back to show Cross eavesdropping on her conversation behind a row of filing cabinets; it's rare to see a heavy studio camera used so fluidly in the series. (On the other hand, the unexpected use of incidental music to accompany a scene of diplomats arriving is rather jarring). Patrick Mower himself has one of his best outings in this episode, particularly when Cross pulls a wonderfully disgusted face after Beth tells him how happy she is.

Containing some amusing, topical griping about expenses and inflation to sweeten the very bitter pill, 'God Helps Your Friends' is one of *Callan*'s bleakest chapters.

S3.7 A VILLAGE CALLED 'G'

Writer: James Mitchell
Director: Mike Vardy
Designer: Stan Woodward

FIRST UK TRANSMISSION: Wednesday 13 May 1970, 9.00 pm

CAST: Billie Hammerberg (Secretary), George Innes (Arnold), Michael Hall (Archivist), Marne Maitland (Berman), Joseph Fürst (Sabovski), Lewis Wilson (Hotel clerk), Graham Crowden (the Groper)

EXTRAS/WALK-ONS: *(Uncredited on screen)* Film: Tony Lane, Gareth Watkins, George Ballantine, Bill Barnsley, Annette Peters, Audrey Kirby, Doris Kitts, (Hotel Guests)
    Studio: Les Shannon, Les Conrad, Keith Goodman (Intelligence Men), Geoffrey Brighty, Clare Rogers, Heidi Lane (People in Pub) Actor unknown (Fred)

PRODUCTION
Rehearsals: From Saturday 7 March 1970
Location Filming: Royal Lancaster Hotel in Bayswater, London W2 (Monday 9 March 1970); St. John's Wood Court, St. John's Wood Road, London NW6; car park on Kilburn Park Road, London NW6 (Tuesday 10 March 1970)
Camera Rehearsals/Recording: Teddington Studio One, Wednesday 18 and Thursday 19 March 1970[117]

TV TIMES: 'Hunter's secretary, Liz, is missing. Callan discovers Liz had a date with Cross the night before she disappeared: she had seemed worried and talked about her childhood...'
9-15 May 1970, Southern edition

MISSION PROFILE: Liz has disappeared. Investigating, Callan learns that she was born in Poland and the only survivor of the massacre of her home village, Gradzisk, at the hands of the Germans. The armourer Judd reveals that Liz had been learning to shoot with a .32 calibre hand gun, which is now missing, while Callan discovers that Cross and Liz are having an affair. She has learned that Kleist, one of the SS men who destroyed Gradzisk, has reinvented himself as the Polish doctor Sabovski and is in London. Liz tries to shoot him, but the Nazi overpowers and drugs her; Callan and Cross just reach her in time before she's gassed by the fire Kleist left on in her flat. While she recovers, Cross kills the SS man. Callan then destroys the romantic attachment between Liz and Cross for good.

A MAN LIKE ME: On his rest day, Callan is seen reading the military history book *Wellington – Years of the Sword*. He questions the use of the 'Charlie' codeword over the phone as he doesn't recognise the voice of Liz's stand-in, later annoying her by persistently calling her 'love'. Helpfully, Callan has a contact called Maurice in Shin Bet, one of the Israeli security services. Working on his military models helps Callan to think and, surprisingly for a tough field agent, he wears hush puppies. He drives a Cortina Mark V Estate, one of the Section's pool cars (presumably because there's enough room for an unconscious, or dead, body in the boot). Callan gives the identifying code 'C4' to the temporary Section secretary. Unsurprisingly, he empathises with Liz's loneliness.

Callan has to handle two particularly unpleasant tasks: firstly, the bribery of Arnold, the porter in Liz's building, a sex pest who spies on the attractive women who live there. Posing as a private detective, Callan gets the information he wants, but afterwards makes no secret of how disgusted he is at having to deal with such a squalid individual. Secondly, he is equally angry at Cross for breaking the Section's rules by becoming emotionally involved with Liz: he has the psychological insight to realise that making the secretary see the truth – that Cross cares more for his job than he does for her – will end their relationship. He clearly finds this task just as unpleasant as having to deal with Arnold.

More is revealed about Callan's relationship with Judd. As he was involved in the agent's training, he's been in the Section at least from the time Callan began working there.

LONELY: Alarmingly, he takes three sugars in his tea; four, if not stopped. He also likes his tea 'interfered with' (i.e. with Scotch added). As he's on bail, Lonely worries about being on remand and has to report regularly to the police, whom he finds 'a sarky lot'. He accepts Callan's offer of £5 to watch Arnold the porter, and becomes rather fragrant when standing in front of Callan's gas fire.

Lonely is strong enough to carry the gassed Liz and suggests taking her to 'the Groper', a struck-off doctor he and Callan knew in prison. Revealing his seedy side, the thief is lecherous over Liz: Callan predictably calls him 'a sex maniac'.

A TIE AND A CREST: Cross drives a white Jaguar Mark II (the ubiquitous car favoured by criminals and filmmakers, due to its fast acceleration and resistance to being smashed up) and is a member of a private club. He thinks Callan should have been dead 'ten years ago' and nearly hits him – from behind – when the latter calls the younger agent 'a bloody liar'. The rivalry that's been brewing between the two men explodes into violence, and Callan easily gets the better of Cross, exposing him as selfish and careerist in front of Liz.

ALCOHOL, TOBACCO AND FIREARMS: Liz has a half-empty bottle of gin and three bottles of tonic in her flat, while Callan adds Scotch to Lonely's tea and has a glass of Hunter's malt. Cross smokes (nervously?) throughout, and spends all morning in the pub drinking when he should be looking for Liz. The Groper also helps himself to Callan's Scotch.

Enterprisingly, Liz steals a .32 Smith and Wesson with a 2-inch barrel from the Section armoury. Callan intimidates Judd by scoring three bullseyes on the Section firing range; Hunter demonstrates his own shooting ability again when he achieves the same score.

SPY-SPEAK: Hunter explains Liz's status to Callan: 'That girl's a walking memory bank. She's been in a Red File since the day she took the job.'

Callan makes it plain to Cross where his dalliance with Liz will take him: 'Mate, you're gonna finish up under a 500 Watt bulb, explaining to the Goon Squad why you've started telling Hunter lies.'

Cross is disgusted with the Section's policy regarding Kleist: 'Marvellous, isn't it? 487 people murdered and we take no action.'

Lonely at first thinks Callan has 'croaked' Liz – another of his comic overreactions – then grumbles as he's asked to carry her. 'I reckon that bloody Nureyev earns his money!' Callan: 'That's all we need, mate. Wit!'

Hunter sardonically sums up the Section after being informed about events by Callan: 'What a lovable little band we are, to be sure.'

PAWNS AND PLAYERS: GRAHAM CROWDEN (1922-2010) was a respected Scottish stage performer and, like Geoffrey Chater, was part of Lindsay Anderson's repertory company of favoured actors. On television, his notable successes were the acerbic pensioner comedy *Waiting for God* (1990-94) and the towering presence of another doctor, Jock McCannon, in Andrew Davies' university satire, *A Very Peculiar Practice* (1986-87). Crowden was another *Callan* actor to feature in the Bond films, as the First Sea Lord in 1981's *For Your Eyes Only*. He also appeared in *Raffles* with Anthony Valentine, and played a memorably over-the-top villain in the *Doctor Who* story 'The Horns of Nimon' (1980-81). 'Graham was outrageous, wasn't he?'[118] director Mike Vardy remarked of Crowden's florid performance as the Groper. 'A very camp doctor!'

In 1987, Crowden played Sir Michael Wallace, a devious character very reminiscent of Bishop in 'Thin Ice', an episode of the private eye series *Bulman* (1985-87).

GEORGE INNES (born 1938) has had a long and varied career on both sides of the Atlantic. With a talent for playing more than slightly shady characters, he has appeared in films and TV as diverse as the sitcom *Open All Hours* (1973-1985) and the naval epic *Master and Commander* (2003); in the early 1970s, he had the regular role of Alfred in *Upstairs, Downstairs* (1971-75). Innes' performance as the seedy Albert was relatively early on in his career.

'I was the guy you went to for small parts like that, someone who could give cameos some life, a bit of substance,'[119] he remembered. 'I wasn't that well-known when I did it. As *Callan* was so popular, it backfired on me a bit as some people thought I was really like Albert! I got a fair bit of leg-pulling from my mates about it.' Innes' role placed him directly opposite the series' star, a performer he remembered well. 'Woodward wasn't really working class, but he certainly had an edge to him, and he used that. He took [his role] very seriously and certainly wasn't complacent about it.' Vardy was as happy with Innes' contribution as he had been with Crowden's: 'George Innes was a really good character [actor]. He had something special is as much as he could look really sleazy, and he had a sort of delivery that made your hair curl a bit... He was certainly great value for money.'[120]

MARNE MAITLAND (1920-1991) had small roles in the films *Camp on Blood Island* (1958), *I'm All Right Jack* (1959), *The Reptile* (1966) and *The Man with the Golden Gun* (1974). Often cast as villainous foreign types, he appeared in *Danger Man* – 'A Date with Doris' (1964, with Ronald Radd), *The Avengers* – 'Death's Door' (1967) and four episodes of *The Saint* (between 1963-69).

For Joseph Fürst, see 'A Magnum for Schneider'.

INFORMATION: 'It was a long-standing idea,'[121] George Markstein said of his script that put Liz centre stage. 'We thought it would be nice that something happened with Liz other than just answering the phone.' Praising the performances, James Mitchell was pleased with the end result. 'It's a thing you can only do once, a love affair between two people in that Section, because it's absolutely forbidden. You can only stretch the credibility of it once. I thought Lisa and Patrick really got it right. One of my own favourite characters appeared in that, and that was the Groper. Graham turned out to be a Scot, and a kind of upmarket Scots queen worked even better: "Oh, we do suffer for love, dear." It was beautiful. I enjoyed that episode very much in the making and the playing, and I know Teddy did as well.'[122]

'I always think when they wrote the storyline about James Cross having an affair with the secretary, that [was] written basically for Callan, for his character to have a reason to dislike Cross,'[123] Patrick Mower reasoned. 'Because Callan probably fancied the secretary without necessarily saying it, and to suddenly find this young upstart has actually been having an affair with her...! It's not written specifically for Cross's character, it's written as something that will annoy the leading man.'

The idea of basing a story around the Section's secretary came from discussion with the series' creator and initially gave Mike Vardy cause for concern. 'James's idea of putting Lisa Langdon into a semi-leading part alarmed me considerably because none of us had any knowledge of whether she could actually act or not!' the director said. 'She had been hired originally as a one-line, two-line extra, although she was on an actor's contract. She had never been given anything to do, and suddenly she got this script where she was given everything to do! She was terribly nervous, but she did it remarkably well, I thought. A lot of it was on film so I could talk her through it.

'Joseph Fürst was a lovely man,' noted Vardy. 'He was actually based in Canada, if I remember rightly. There was a big Canadian connection at ABC because Sydney Newman came from Canada.' In an impressive piece of continuity, Vardy re-cast Michael Hall from 'You're Under Starter's Orders' as the Section archivist. The tune playing on Arnold's radio was 'Even More Electric Banana' from the De Wolfe music library.

The story was originally scheduled for transmission on 20 May, as Series Three's seventh episode. It was brought forward after 'Act of Kindness' was postponed on 29 April, which rather wasted the article 'Callan Crosses Swords with a Lady' in the 25 April-1 May edition of *TV Times*. The feature was a tie-in promoting Edward Woodward's appearance on the adult education programme *Fencing*, shown on Sunday 26.

Callan had previously featured a Nazi war criminal hiding under a false name in 'The Good Ones are All Dead'. By the 1970s, this idea had become a niche within spy fiction: two earlier examples are Orson Welles' 1946 *film noir The Stranger*, and the James Bond novel *Moonraker* (1955), which had the millionaire Sir Hugo Drax (really an ex-Nazi) plotting to destroy London with a missile. In the anthology series *Espionage*, Israeli agents tracked the war criminal Hoffner to Madrid in 'We, the Hunted' (1964). *Danger Man* had explored the moral dilemma of British intelligence protecting a Nazi scientist from an Israeli execution squad in 'Judgement Day' (1965). *The Saint* featured Hans Krolick posing as the gold mine owner 'Henry Coleman' in the unusually serious story 'Locate and Destroy' (1966), while in the *Man in a Suitcase* episode 'Somebody Loses Somebody... Wins?' (1968), East German intelligence hunted the German musician Johann Liebkind, a 'big spoke in a dirty little Nazi wheel that's starting to roll again.' Cinema also drew on the sub-genre in blockbusters such as *The Odessa File* (1974), *Marathon Man* (1976) and *The Boys from Brazil* (1978).

In 1981, Clifford Rose starred in *Kessler*, the sequel to the WW2 drama *Secret Army*. The series followed the former SS officer's life as the rich industrialist Edmund Dorf, his attempts to start a Fourth Reich using money stolen by the Nazis during WW2 and West German and British intelligence's investiagtion into Dorf's identity. (Jerome Willis played an ambitious TV journalist setting out to expose the ex-Gestapo chief.) Strikingly, the series included a similar plot to 'A Village Called "G"': Mical Rak (Nitza Saul), the daughter of parents who were sent to Dachau concentration camp on Kessler's orders, tracks him down and tries to assassinate him; in turn, he attempts to have Mical killed. The British government's policy regarding Nazi war criminals in *Kessler* is the same as in 'A Village Called "G"' – no action unless they constitute a threat to national security.

Rudolf Khametovich Nureyev (1938-1998) was a celebrated Russian ballet dancer who became a star because of his work with the Kirov ballet. In a considerable cultural coup for the West, he defected in Paris in 1961. By 1970, he had been Principal Dancer with the Royal Ballet for nine years, becoming so well known that even Lonely has heard of him.

MISSION ANALYSIS: *'The Section is all she has, David. Her mother, her father... her home.'* In another development from its 1960s roots, the Section is reinterpreted as a dysfunctional family unit, complete with family secrets – Liz and Cross's affair, Liz learning to shoot – that only come to light when one of those family members behaves unusually. For an episode designed to flesh out the character of Hunter's secretary, it's striking how much 'A Village Called "G"' depends for its impact on her absence, in telling visual details like her empty flat, an unopened bottle of milk and the abandoned typewriter on her desk.

It's another of *Callan*'s most affecting episodes due to James Mitchell's melancholy theme of people failing to escape their pasts. The Nazi-with-a-new-identity idea had been explored previously, but it's given a wider resonance here by Liz's quest for revenge. This desire has been with her since she was a Polish three-year-old, simmering away through her adoption by a British family and upbringing as an English subject with a new name. Both Kleist and Liz are unable to outrun their background as it determines who they are, an effective contrast with the hard-headed, pragmatic policy of the Section not arresting or eliminating any Nazi war criminals unless they directly threaten British security. The dramatic highlight of the episode is the harrowing scene where Callan wrecks the relationship between Cross and Liz (Section standing orders forbidding romantic involvement among personnel) which, ironically, ensures that the emotionally sterile Section 'family' can function again.

The regular cast are all on top form, especially Lisa Langdon who, placed centre-stage, rises to the occasion and delivers a troubled and convincingly understated performance. Elsewhere, there's more effective location filming and, to cap it all, a marvellous cameo from Graham Crowden as the Groper, a baroque character made even more memorable by his camp Scottish accent.

S3.8 SUDDENLY – AT HOME

Writer: James Mitchell
Director: Piers Haggard
Designer: Stan Woodward

FIRST UK TRANSMISSION: Wednesday 20 May 1970, 9.00 pm

CAST: Zena Walker (Janet Lewis), Tony Beckley (René Joinville), Douglas Milvain (Host), Dorothy Alison, Frances Tomelty (Housekeepers), Anthony Hall (Police Sergeant), Harry Shacklock (Porter), Stephanie Marrian (Cross's girl)

EXTRAS/WALK-ONS: (*Uncredited on screen*) Film: Allen Keith-Rose, Dennis Moyce (stand-ins for Edward Woodward and Patrick Mower in window cleaning cradle), Michael Allen Potter (Stand-in for Callan)

Studio: Keith Norrish (Photographer), Bill Lodge, Leslie Bryant (Two Waiters), Peter Roy, John Morse (Two Men in Dinner Jackets, doubling as Policemen), James Hamilton, Roger Minnis (Two Young Men in 'Geary' Clothes, doubling as Policemen), Tony Somers (Smart Man), Audrey Mason, Beulah Hughes, Lyn Howard (Three Girls in 'Geary' Clothes), Dolly Brennan (Smart Lady), Mario Zoppelliai (Man in Coffee Bar), Mike Torres, Sandie Duke (Young Couple)

PRODUCTION

Rehearsals: From Friday 9 January 1970
Location Filming: Albany Street Police Station, near Regent's Park, London N1; Albany Street, off the Marylebone Road, London NW7; St George's Hotel, Langham Place, London W1 (Monday 12 January 1970); Flat 61, Northgate, Prince Albert Road, London NW8 (Tuesday 13 January 1970)
Camera Rehearsals/Recording: Teddington Studio One, Thursday 22 and Friday 23 January 1970[124]

TV TIMES: *Due to this episode being rescheduled, a 'TV Times' synopsis never appeared.*

MISSION PROFILE: Documentary-maker René Joinville wants to interview Lady Janet Lewis, the widow of the Foreign Secretary, about her husband's work. Hunter is worried about what she might reveal and puts Callan on the case. He persuades her not to talk to Joinville and, attracted to each other, the pair arrange another meeting, while Cross is detailed to observe Lady Lewis's flat. When she refuses a third approach from Joinville – really a Russian agent – he kills her with a .38 magnum, which will implicate the Section in her death. Failing to stop her murder, Cross flees. After briefly suspecting him, Callan reasons that Joinville must be the killer. Cross is sent to the Frenchman's hotel to capture him, but he is overpowered. Joinville is about to kill Cross when Callan shoots the Frenchman dead.

A MAN LIKE ME: When Callan interviews Lady Lewis, he adopts his regular 'Tucker' alias; intriguingly, he never reveals his real surname to her. Callan is taken with Janet Lewis from the moment he sees her photograph in her file and, when he meets her, is struck by her honesty, good nature and unselfconscious beauty, even though he's professional enough to use her sons as subtle leverage to stop her talking to Joinville. Knowing he's made an impression on her (through military history, no less) Callan wears his 'Tucker' bowler hat at a slightly jaunty angle when he reports back to Hunter. When his and Janet's second meeting moves to a romantic footing, Callan behaves like a gentleman and leaves at her request after their first kiss, as she's not yet ready to go any further. Touchingly, Callan leaves her a gift of his hand-crafted model of Marshal Soult, the First Duke of Dalmatia.

His reaction to her death is far from gentlemanly, as he threatens to 'smash' Lonely's face in and nearly attacks Cross in a rage, before Hunter orders him to stop. Callan deals with the bereavement in the only way he can, through violence: he executes Joinville with two bullets to the heart, despite being instructed to bring the Frenchman in alive.

His anti-authoritarian streak also surfaces when he details Lonely to watch Cross staking out Janet's flat without informing Hunter; disturbingly, Callan threatens the thief with 'the belting of your life' if Cross catches him. Callan has a contact in the 'Gehlen organisation' (West German intelligence) and clearly has a head for heights, judging by the accuracy of his marksmanship from several hundred feet up the side of a tall building.

After Janet's death, he considers making presents of his model soldiers 'bad luck' and he retrieves the one he left in her flat.

Section Kills: 19

LONELY: Typically, he worries that the car Callan picks him up in from outside a police station is 'nicked'. Although he 'can't do no heavy lifting', he poses convincingly as a gardener as he watches Lady Lewis's flat and supplies the crucial car registration number that identifies Joinville as the killer. In his awkward, caring way, Lonely tries to cheer Callan up after Janet's death by complimenting him on one of his model soldiers and clumsily calling Lady Lewis 'a bit of alright'. Always anxious, he hides behind the sofa when Cross visits Callan's flat. By contrast with his terrible tea-making (in 'Death of a Friend'), Lonely makes 'excellent' coffee.

In the best compliment Callan ever pays him, he calls Lonely 'a genius', as no one he's tailing can spot the little man if he doesn't want them to.

A TIE AND A CREST: By now, the evidence is building that Cross is not very good at his job. Callan gets the jump on him in his Jaguar and Joinville later clubs him, taking his gun and nearly killing him before Callan intervenes. This makes Cross's claim that he's 'never fallen down on a job' look decidedly shaky, particularly given the events in 'Summoned to Appear' when, again, he was only saved from being shot dead by someone else's intervention. Cross also doesn't realise Callan is setting him up as a decoy.

Notably, Callan, a working class criminal, intimidates a member of the aristocracy who he then becomes romantically involved with.

ALCOHOL, TOBACCO AND FIREARMS: Callan has a convivial brandy with Lady Lewis at their second meeting, while Lonely helps himself to a bottle of whisky from the glove compartment of Callan's car. Hunter sips his customary malt when Callan goes to see him after Lady Lewis is shot.

Callan slams out of his flat, but not before telling a hysterical Lonely that there is 'beer in the fridge!'

The 'British security section' uses .38 Magnum revolvers. Joinville owns a double-barrelled shotgun.

SPY-SPEAK: Callan dryly points out the consequences of Janet talking about her husband's work: 'Lady Lewis, a year ago we had a formula for attacking Russia first. That's not going to look very good in front of 17,000,000 viewers, is it? And what about the repeats in Moscow?' Hunter enquires (ironically?) after Callan's technique with Janet: 'What did you use? Thumbscrews?'

Joinville's KGB contact 'Barbara' has a pragmatically cynical view of British politics: 'The Section has been a little too active lately. And when Lady Lewis dies, it's possible they will be curbed. Newspaper stories, questions in the House... Well, you know how useful democracy can be.'

PAWNS AND PLAYERS: ZENA WALKER (1934-2003) had played another Janet who was the girlfriend of a fictional secret agent, the fiancée of Patrick McGoohan's eponymous title character in *The Prisoner*. In the same year as her appearance as Lady Lewis, she began playing Susan, the long-suffering wife of Kenneth Haigh's Joe Lampton in the ITV series *Man at the Top* (1970-72). She also starred with Alfred Marks in the historical drama *Albert and Victoria* (1970-71).

An experienced stage actress, Zena won the Tony Award for Featured Actress for her role in the Broadway production of the black comedy *A Day in the Life of Joe Egg*, opposite Albert Finney. She was married to fellow *Callan* guest star Robert Urquhart, although the relationship ended in divorce.

TONY BECKLEY (1927-1980) was often cast as Europeans. He was arguably better known for his villainous roles, particularly Camp Freddy in the heist movie *The Italian Job* (1969), Peter the Dutchman in *Get Carter* (1971) and the insane botanist Harrison Chase in the *Doctor Who* story 'The Seeds of Doom' (1976): 'You know, Doctor, I could play all day in my green cathedral!' As well as his film and TV work, Beckley was the veteran of a remarkable 1,000 stage productions.

FRANCES TOMELTY (born 1948) came to prominence as Detective Constable Linda Doran in the first series of the eccentric crime show *Strangers* (1978). For a while she was married to Sting, lead singer of the reggae-rock group The Police. Other appearances include *A Perfect Spy* (1987), *Inspector Morse* (1988) and the undercover cop drama *99-1* (1994). '*Callan* was my first TV job,' she recalled, 'and I remember that Edward Woodward was very nice to this nervous TV rookie.'[125]

INFORMATION: 'This was one of my favourites,'[126] James Mitchell proudly remembered. 'Zena Walker was lovely in it. I was at a party and someone asked me, "Is [Callan] neutered?" and I remember thinking, "My God, I'd better do something about that." It's always a mistake to fall in love with Callan because you wind up dead, obviously! You can't leave [love interests] hanging around.'

'We did some hand-held camera in the car shots, [without] a low loader,'[127] Piers Haggard revealed of the sequence of Callan collecting Lonely in his car outside Albany Street police station. 'We had a camera and sound man in the back of the car, and a 16mm camera, hand-held. I would have been on the back floor, listening to it. Ideally you want to be there, so you can tell from the voices if it's going to work or not.' The same day, the most ambitious film scene yet staged for *Callan* took place. 'The window cleaners' cradle sequence was shot up near the Langham Church [in Langham Place],' explained Haggard.

'We used St. George's Hotel; later it became BBC offices. It was just outside the new BBC headquarters, the new Broadcasting House, and we were standing on the steps of Langham Church to get some of the shots. We used doubles [experienced window cleaners] in the cradle [for Woodward and Mower] but the actors were in the cradle, too, outside the window – we doubled it for when they were winching themselves up. It wobbled and it was very high. I hate heights: it makes me nervous watching it now!' John Keeling was typically matter of fact about the sequence. 'When you're a cameraman, you just do what they ask, you don't really see danger because the camera's between you and what's there. I never worried about heights.'[128]

Sequences featuring actors Anthony Hall and Stephanie Marrian, respectively playing a police sergeant (who cheekily asks Lonely, 'Come to give yourself up?') and Cross's girlfriend, were trimmed for timing reasons but both the artists remain credited.

Summing up his feelings about *Callan*, Haggard said, 'There were some slightly preposterous elements which don't hold up so well now, but it's interesting that the sympathies, the underlying political attitude, is not right wing. Again, it's part of that alternative view, that slightly anti-establishment view that *Callan* did capture. It really did capture it for a generation.'[129]

The character of Joinville may have been partly inspired by Gillo Pontecorvo (1919 –2006), an internationally famous left-wing Italian filmmaker, screenwriter and composer whose best known work, *The Battle of Algiers* (1966), later received Oscar nominations and won the Venice Film Festival Golden Lion award in 1969. French director Jean-Luc Godard, then well into his Marxist phase, had also recently been in the headlines, visiting London to film *One Plus One* a.k.a *Sympathy for the Devil* (1968) with the Rolling Stones.

Lady Lewis attends a viewing of Joinville's documentary that profiles three of the most significant Communist leaders of the day. Ho Chi Minh (1890-1969) had led the Communist independence movement in North Vietnam, defeating the French colonialists in battle in 1954. He was President of the Democratic Republic of North Vietnam until his death, during which time his People's Army and the Viet Cong successfully resisted the US military. Fidel Castro was another thorn in America's side as he spearheaded a successful socialist revolution in Cuba in 1959, a country only a few hundred kilometres from the American mainland. One of Castro's allies in the Cuban revolution was Ernesto 'Che' Guevara, an Argentinean Marxist who was instrumental in defeating the Bay of Pigs invasion in 1961, and who brokered the deal to import Russian missiles in 1962. Guevara was captured and shot dead in 1967 while attempting to initiate a revolution in Bolivia.

Marshal Soult (1769-1851), the soldier who brings Callan and Janet together, was a French general and statesman known as the 'Hand of Iron'. He distinguished himself in many Napoleonic campaigns, including the Battle of Austerlitz (1805) and the Battle of Jena (1806), and was one of only six French officers to be awarded the title Marshal General of France. The idea of a KGB agent who poses as a housekeeper may have come from *From Russia with Love*, in which Rosa Klebb (Lotte Lenya) infiltrates James Bond's hotel suite in Venice.

On the day that 'The Same Trick Twice' was shown, the publicity for 'Callan's First Kiss', due to take place in the upcoming 'Suddenly – At Home', rather backfired on Thames as *The Sun* ran an amusingly sour write-up. Clearly not a fan of the series, the anonymous journalist reported on 'an event so cataclysmic that it may well cause you to fall asleep'[130] on 'national anaesthetic day.' The story went on: 'the lady [Callan] is kissing is the Foreign Secretary's widow, played by 36 year-old Zena Walker, who can't have seen the show as she leaves her jugular vein totally unprotected.' The writer's ire knew no bounds, as the piece concluded with a dig at Callan's pastime of making model soldiers: 'the fact that there are so few girls about whose brothers indulge in this somewhat exotic hobby may well explain why our hero always looks so miserable.' *TV Times* covered the story in a rather more positive way. Conveniently forgetting the agent's previous relationships, it described Callan and Janet's performance as a 'Moment of History'[131] that would see 'Callan kissing a woman – for the first time in the series.' The writer went on to speculate, 'Could it be love will last? Doubt it. This is *Callan*.'

MISSION ANALYSIS: *'Foreign Secretary Widow to Appear on TV'*. 'Suddenly – At Home' makes an interesting counterpoint to 'A Village Called "G"', as this time Callan's love life is put under the spotlight. As he's rebuked by Hunter for becoming involved with some-one on one of his assignments, the Section's senior man looks rather hypocritical when his previous condemnation of Cross and Liz's romance is taken into account. Thanks to Woodward and Zena Walker's obvious chemistry, the attraction between the elegant and trusting Lady Lewis and the emotionally solitary Callan is entirely believable. However, as the pairing crosses class barriers and involves Callan romantically, it's doomed as, seemingly, are all of his intimate relationships with the opposite sex.

Lady Lewis aside, nearly all the main protagonists in the episode have dual identities, from Callan himself, using the 'Tucker' alias, to the KGB agent posing as a housekeeper, who briefs Joinville while she cleans his hotel room, a scene that adds a quirky realism to the episode. The French assassin himself (despite having an accent that raises a smile), like most opposition agents in Mitchell's writing, is portrayed as a professional doing a job: he's genuinely sorry about executing Lady Lewis after failing for a third time to get her to agree to a filmed interview. In contrast to Callan, however, he follows his orders to the letter, even if he believes them to be wrong.

Straightforward in comparison with some of Series Three's other stories, 'Suddenly – At Home' is significant for the tantalising glimpse of a more fulfilled life for Callan, and for his brand of justice, which he dispenses like some vigilante gunman (at the time, Clint Eastwood's 'Dirty' Harry Callahan was still over a year away from his first feature film). 'She had a lot of admirers you know, Callan,' Hunter tells him. 'Doubt if any would've done what you did. Wonder if she'd be grateful?'

S3.9 BREAKOUT

Writer: James Mitchell
Director: Reg Collin
Designer: Neville Green

FIRST UK TRANSMISSION: Wednesday 10 June 1970, 9.00 pm

CAST: Billy Cornelius (Mellor), Garfield Morgan (Lubin), Frank Mann (Policeman), Robert Cartland (Bonnington), Ernest Hare (Judge), John Corvin (Hughes/Voice out of Vision, *uncredited on screen*), Vernon Joyner (Courroom Policeman), William Fox (Chaplain), Eric McCaine, Derek Cox (Warders)

EXTRAS/WALK-ONS: (*Uncredited on screen*) Frank Eason (Warder) and sixteen men and women: convicts, court officials, jurymen, warder and prisoner's wife, through the J.D. Agency: Peter Kodal, Bob Raymond, Ernest Jennings, Bolly John, Ronnie Laughlin, Jay Nerl, Tom O'Leary, Steve Kelly, Peter Douglas (Remington), Tony Cordell, Brian Gardner, Jerry Alexander, Marke Finbar, Colin Reese, Richard Blake, and one woman.

PRODUCTION

Rehearsals: From Friday 20 March 1970
Location Filming: Bexhill-on-Sea area, Kent; level crossing at Cooden Beach Golf Course; Glyne Gap Gas Works, Bexhill Road, plus nearby roads and beach
(Monday 23, Tuesday 24 and Wednesday 25 March 1970)
Camera Rehearsals/Recording: Teddington Studio Two, Wednesday 1 and Thursday 2 April 1970[132]

TV TIMES: 'The alarm bells ring for an escaped prisoner, but the one they should be ringing for is Callan.'
6-12 June 1970, Southern edition

MISSION PROFILE: KGB agent Nikolai Lubin surrenders to the police and is sent to Castleview prison. Hunter is worried because the agent has memorised the names of all the the West's undercover controllers in Eastern Europe. Callan and Cross are ordered to put a team together, posing as a KGB rescue unit, which will spring Lubin from prison, (using a converted petrol tanker), take him to a secluded coastal location and execute him. By leaving the body there, near the berth of a Russian trawler, they will make it seem as if the Soviets have executed one of their own, deterring other KGB agents. Serving a prison sentence for the offences he was bailed for, Lonely relays the correct code phrase to the Russian agent and the breakout goes ahead successfully. Even though Lubin discovers he has been tricked and tries to escape, Callan kills him as planned.

A MAN LIKE ME: This time, without any crisis of conscience, Callan perjures himself in court when he acts as a character witness for Lonely. (Being a criminal himself, he has his own moral code regarding lying to the judiciary). He tells Lonely's judge that he's a senior partner in 'Callan and Hunter Ltd.'

In his addition to time served in Wormwood Scrubs, Callan was incarcerated in Castleview for six months. (This is likely to have formed another part of his sentence for safe-breaking, rather than for a different offence). Luckily, the court trying Lonely does not seem to know of Callan's own record, possibly due to the change of identity mentioned in 'Where Else Could I Go?'

Callan seems more vulnerable than normal. He's very aware of being the oldest agent in the Section, openly telling Cross that it's the reason he always has to prove he's the best. Twice Callan is forgetful, walking out of Hunter's office without the Nyton security lock he needs to practise on and, even worse, nearly leaving his gloves and balaclava behind when his team sets off for Castleview. Callan shows his usual unease when ordered to attend Snell's interrogation room.

By the end of the Lubin assignment, he's proved himself, shooting the KGB agent with deadly accuracy from a distance, then again at close range. Despite Callan's doubts and moments of weakness, Hunter's unseen masters – including Bishop? – now consider him to be the Section's top man. His probation and ongoing psychological evaluation (which Callan characteristically dismisses as 'claptrap') is over.

Understandably, Callan is amazed that Lonely is a patriot.

Section Kills: 20

LONELY: 'Breakout' is one of Lonely's finest hours. He has a major role throughout, and provides most of the humour, from the moment the judge overseeing his case dryly observes that he was in trouble with the police '25 times' while Callan was away. Lonely's grip on the English language is still shaky; he doesn't understand the word 'concurrent', and mistakenly thinks he will be serving six months for each of his 25 robberies, making his total sentence over twelve years long.

He doesn't like being moved to Castleview, where all 'the hard geezers' are and, with supreme irony, doesn't approve of spying as it's unpatriotic; however, he agrees to communicate with Lubin for £250. In one of *Callan*'s comic highlights, his singing of the KGB code phrase 'You're wanted on the telephone' in the prison chapel during a hymn is hilarious.

He makes an ally of the prison chaplain (even though he tries to steal one of the chapel's candlesticks, and is always apologising for swearing in front of him) and admits that he needs people, which is why he's always ended up in trouble. Even though Lonely nearly lets Callan's name slip during the gaol break, alerting Lubin, his patriotism stands him in good stead: the chaplain decides he was trying to raise the alarm when he was knocked out, announcing that he'll try to get Lonely a free pardon. The little man's reaction? 'Cor, stone the crows!'

A TIE AND A CREST: Cross's jibes have become gentler, as he smilingly chides Callan about being 'the greatest'. He later saves the senior man's life by shouting out his first name – the first time Cross ever uses it – and Callan later thanks him. He admits to Hunter that the younger man was 'damn good' on the Lubin job, an indication that the feud between the two agents is cooling off (for now).

ALCOHOL, TOBACCO AND FIREARMS: Hunter breaks out the malt again, as the Section staff end up on a seaside outing. Callan slips Lonely some cigarettes in prison.

To make Lubin's rescue look like a KGB operation, Callan's team are equipped with Makarov 9mm automatic pistols. This is a rare mistake by the Section, as Lubin knows the guns aren't available in Britain. The Makarov 9mm was the standard issue Russian military sidearm between 1951 and 1991.

SPY-SPEAK: Hunter reprimands Cross severely for his flippancy about Snell's unit: 'You've never been down to the interrogation room, have you... Perhaps you should. Might curb your sense of humour!' (An ad-lib by William Squire that was retained.[133])

The episode has plenty of comic one-liners, such as Callan's descriptions of Cross as a 'long-haired nit' and Lonely as 'the last of the mini spenders'.

Lonely on the dubious profession of espionage: 'I don't hold with spies, sir. They're nearly as bad as sex maniacs.'

The prison chaplain misquotes Shakespeare when appraising Lonely's criminal history: '"Company, vile company, hath been the ruin of me"... It's Falstaff's line. But in his case it was intended as a joke.' 'Oh, yeah, I see,' Lonely replies. 'I bet he wasn't in here when he said it!'

Cross wonders if Lubin is really dead after being shot by Callan. The Russian abruptly revives, taking aim – and Callan slams another bullet into him. 'He is now.' (A near-identical dialogue exchange occurs in the finale of the second series of *Blake's 7*, 'Star One', which occasionally paired the near-psychotic Avon with the cowardly kleptomaniac Vila.)

PAWNS AND PLAYERS: GARFIELD MORGAN (1931-2009) was a veteran villain of TV film series such as *The Baron*, *Randall and Hopkirk (Deceased)*, *Department S* and *The Avengers*, in which he appeared three times, lastly as the florid executioner/chef Sexton in 'Take-Over' (1969). 'There were so many of [those shows],'[134] he recalled fondly. 'Mostly, they were great fun... Typecasting wasn't a problem.' Morgan was often cast as policemen, firstly in the regular part of Detective Chief Inspector Gwyn Lewis in the *Z Cars* spin-off *Softly, Softly* (1966-69), then in his defining role as another DCI, Frank Haskins in *The Sweeney*, starring in 45 episodes between 1974 and 1978. Often cast as criminals or authority figures, in real life Morgan was a very funny man, as outtakes from *The Sweeney* confirm, and was able to show off his comic timing in the ITV sitcom *Shelley* (1982-84). A theatre director as well as an actor, Morgan's favourite role was George in *Who's Afraid of Virginia Woolf?*

BILLY CORNELIUS was a busy bit-part actor and stuntman throughout the 1960s and 1970s. From appearing on television in the police show *No Hiding Place* in 1963, in a long list of productions he featured in no less than eight *Carry On* films and seven episodes of *The Avengers*. His last role was as 'Pete' in the 1980 gangland feature film *The Long Good Friday*.

WILLIAM FOX (1911-2008) was a feted actor on the London stage early in his career, with roles in *Dangerous Cover*, *Rope* and *As You Like It*. On television, he was well-known as Chief Superintendent Maw in the crime series *The Man in Room 17* (1965-66). Fox later took the recurring role of the Duke of Bedlington in James Mitchell's historical TV drama *When the Boat Comes In*.

INFORMATION: The episode also had the working titles 'Breakthrough' and 'Time to Go'. 'Garfield Morgan was excellent,'[135] James Mitchell said in praise of the actor who played Callan's opponent. 'They did a wonderful job on that prison which was just the open studio. This was an easy one for me to write.' The dialogue about Callan being regarded as the 'top man' was deliberately included to set up the next series, as Reg Collin confirmed: 'One is trying all the time to keep the options going. You're putting something in, in the hope that if it doesn't transpire in six months, no one's going to notice. On the other hand, if it does transpire... It's like the cement between the bricks. Far more important than the bricks themselves.'[136] 'You try to finish every single series with an episode that leaves open opportunities: that's common sense,'[137] noted George Markstein.

The South Eastern Gas Board was paid £30 for the use of Glyne Gap Gas Works (used for the exteriors of Castleview prison), the same fee that the production team paid for the use of the beach hut location. During the three-day shoot, the production team and actors stayed at the Queen's Hotel in Hastings.

In another example of what could be George Markstein's detailed approach to continuity, 'The Same Trick Twice' had previously mentioned the 'Lubin network'. However, Markstein himself cautioned, 'All sorts of deliberate intents and significances are read into things, which are very often accidental, and there's no deep reason or subconscious planning: it just happens. One services a series; one has to keep it going and make sure it works.'

'Breakout' was, however, planned as the last episode of *Callan*'s third series and was originally to have been transmitted ninth. For the third time, a voiceover as the end credits rolled reminded viewers that Edward Woodward was a National Theatre player. For some unknown reason, Vernon Joyner, who played the Courtroom Policeman and shared a very funny dialogue scene with Russell Hunter, was not credited in either the end titles or the *TV Times*.

'I don't think Lonely was consciously patriotic,'[138] Russell Hunter considered of the character's unexpected devotion to the Crown in this story. 'The Queen's the Queen and you stand up when someone mentions her name. I do know people like that, particularly of Lonely's kind of age group, who would say "Mr. Churchill was God's Prime Minister," genuinely wept when the late King died, and were very proud when the Queen came to the throne as a very young woman: "No other country could do that. Only happen 'ere." You put up your Union Jacks on the Queen's birthday, you have street parties – you don't think about that. That's *religion*, in a funny way. You don't have to go to church, but you let the vicar say nice things about the Queen: "Gawd bless 'er. And you all have a good drink." You don't argue about the Queen, the Queen is *there*.'

By the end of production on 'Breakout', the relationship between the actor playing the fourth Hunter and *Callan*'s leading man was firmly established. 'Myself and Teddy developed a rapport, both on and off stage, that was tremendous for me,'[139] Squire reflected with evident affection. 'After the first nine [episodes], we had a bit of a shindig and he embarrassed me no end by being very sweet about me in front of the fellers.' 'He was a lovely man, Bill,' Woodward confirmed. 'I think him and Ronnie Radd were two of the best actors in the role of Hunter.'[140]

Almost contemporaneous with 'Breakout' was the 11 August 1970 *Special Branch* episode 'Inside', also script edited by George Markstein. Written by Trevor Preston, the story saw Inspector Jordan (Derren Nesbitt) going undercover in prison to befriend the Soviet agent Gillard, a spy in the George Blake mould, played by none other than Michael Goodliffe.

MISSION ANALYSIS: *'Good luck, Mr C –'.* Mitchell's closing script for *Callan*'s third year is an exemplary illustration of how to write a series finale, as all the running threads of the year – Callan's insecurity in the Section, Lonely's impending prison sentence and the tension between Callan and Cross – are satisfactorily resolved. This is also – relatively speaking – one of *Callan*'s funniest episodes. The series had never shied away from comical scenes as they were essential to lighten up the grim subject matter, and Lonely had always been the focus. Russell Hunter is at his peak here, seizing the opportunity to show his comic talents. There's his faked sneeze when Callan visits, and a classic slapstick moment when Callan knocks him out just before he can say the agent's name in front of Lubin. Equally amusing is his account of attempting to stop the Russian's escape, which reveals an actor with such naturally funny body language you're reminded of comedy giants such as Stan Laurel.

It's testament to how skilled and balanced the writing and direction is that as well as the set-piece raid on Castleview and the shoot-out on a building site, there's time to focus on Callan's introspection and the understated idea that, as he and Lubin are the same age, Callan has an opposite number in the KGB (an idea that would be revisited and developed the following year). In his few scenes, Garfield Morgan gives a controlled, dryly amusing and lethal performance as Lubin.

'Breakout' has it all: sharp one-liners, drama, action *and* comedy. The only aspect to have really dated is the interior set of the petrol tanker, recorded on video, that Callan's team use to transport Lubin. The film sequences either side make up for it as they are, once again, impressively cinematic, with a striking sense of scale. Night filming, in particular, was an expensive luxury for TV series of the early 1970s, and – in a sign of *Callan's* increasing status – the series used it more than ever during its third year.

The upbeat ending has a downbeat punch line, showing the series had not lost its roots. After being told by Hunter that he's the Section's top man again, Callan realises he'll consequently get all the riskiest, dirtiest jobs, and that the KGB will have him on more than one kill list. As we leave him, he stares out to sea and swears inaudibly. All in all, *Callan* had entered British television's new colour era in accomplished, confident and uncompromising style.

8: SERIES FOUR
Last Rat Standing

'Listen! Snell! I'm telling you – you don't end up enjoying it –
you can't... you're too busy not being killed – it's ICE! From
the knees up and brain down – 'til it's frozen, heavy, PACKED!'

Cut dialogue, 'If He Can, So Could I' rehearsal script, 1 January 1972

PUBLISHED IN 1971, the Independent Broadcasting Authority's annual review of
ITV's programming considered 1970 'a good, if perhaps not vintage year'[1] and not-
ed 'the public's interest in police, crime and spy series'. This second point is largely
why *Callan* entered 1972 on a continuing populist high. In the *TV Times*' 'TV Top Ten
for 1971' poll of readers[2], the series had major wins in two categories: Most Compulsive
TV Character (male) and Best Actor on TV for Edward Woodward. Notably, the flawed
Callan won out over the more conventional ITC film heroes, Danny Wilde from *The
Persuaders!* and writer/detective *Jason King* (1971-72); as Best Actor, Woodward triumphed
over *Persuaders!* co-stars Roger Moore (in second place) and Tony Curtis (third). This dou-
ble victory was even more remarkable as, bar repeats, *Callan* had been off the air since
June 1970 while the team pursued other projects.

When the iconic light bulb swings in front of the shadowy brick wall in the opening
moments of 'That'll Be the Day', the first episode of Series Four, it's immediately obvious
that things are going to be different. Adding Geoffrey Chater – returning as Bishop, now
a regular character – to the opening credits immediately signifies an enlarged ensemble
cast. As well as Bishop, the recruitment of the moustachioed Stafford, brought to life in an
enjoyably dry performance by Paul Williamson, together with return appearances by
Clifford Rose's chilly interrogator Snell, swelled the Section's ranks.

Having settled in the story editor's chair, George Markstein began to experiment with
Callan's format, building on and consolidating the idea of running sub-plots that he had
introduced the year before. Making Lonely the driver of the Section's Mobile Communications Facility (in other words, a black London taxi cab) relieved the pressure on the writers,
as Lloyd Shirley pointed out: 'The Lonely character had quite a following, but at the same
time there was a limited use for him, hence the invention of the cab, as it were, putting
him on the strength of the Section. Credibility is important in these things. If you have to
keep inventing reasons why an auxiliary is brought in, it can become dangerously repetitive, and take up screen time.'[3] Perhaps as a reaction against the cavalier way the series
had been treated by ITV schedulers in 1970, the first five episodes – built around Callan's

promotion to Hunter – are densely-plotted and interlinked, with major narrative developments continuing from one episode to the next.

Callan's stablemate series, the low-key and at times downbeat *Public Eye*, had contained long-running narrative threads involving developments in the life of loner detective Frank Marker; the early episodes of *Special Branch*, which Markstein story-edited, had also experimented with this approach. Other ITV dramas would probably have influenced *Callan* at this time: two popular historical series, *A Family at War* (1970-72) and *Upstairs, Downstairs* (1971-75), featured a large company of regular characters having their own individual stories, while series-long plotlines wound to a conclusion in the final episodes.

Through Callan's attainment of the top job in the Section, the team were also alluding to another popular boardroom drama series. For four weeks, *Callan* became a spy version of *The Power Game* (1965-66, 1969), ITV's corporate drama. 'I promoted Callan to become Hunter,'[4] affirmed Reg Collin. 'The idea was that he would fail [as the Section chief]. He would be promoted out of his competence. You would then have this double stress – a man who can't do the job he's in, can't control people, can't go back to what he was, so he's caught, in all those issues. Then you go in close on the actor and find out what the actor can do for you. That's exciting television for me.' Markstein was equally enthusiastic about the idea: 'Callan being Hunter opened many new opportunities for writers; it put him in the position that he was always whining and bitching about! People gave him orders – now let's see how *he* holds up when he has to give those orders.'[5]

Similar character development was also built into the story of Toby Meres, returning to the series as – to his relief – Anthony Valentine had been released from *Codename*. 'It's going to sound like a cop out, but I suppose [Meres had] got older and a little bit more mellow,'[6] the actor suggested. 'I seem to remember he was supposed to have been in Washington, being a diplomat or something like that. And I think it was reflected in the writing in as much as I *don't* think there was quite as much instantaneous violence in the character as there had been... I think he'd got a bit rounder, a bit easier, and I seem to remember that a lot of that series was about his personal ambition to become the Hunter character. So I think that he had become, in a sense, more of a politician and less of an active agent, although he was still running about and firing guns at people.'

At a time when there was growing politicisation of women's roles in British society, another encouraging development under Markstein's editorship of *Callan*'s fourth year was that the female characters are more proactive. In 1970, the roles for actresses had largely been a limited selection: an ex-'glamour model', neurotic middle-aged women, a lubricious journalist, a fragile suicide and Lady Lewis, Callan's passive love interest. Series Four's female contingent are a major step forward. *A Family at War*'s Coral Atkins enjoys herself as Myra Kessler, a devious translator; Jane Lapotaire plays a fanatical terrorist, while Sarah Lawson makes the most of a three-dimensional Soviet agent in Svetlana Souraikin (a.k.a. Flo Mayhew), the stylish opposite of Sheila Fay's severe but conscientious Norah Dowsett: outwardly a plain spinster, Norah is deceiving everyone around her because she's a Russian spy. Significantly, while Callan's lover in the third series was an affluent widow, his new girlfriend Susan Morris – another attractive widow – owns her own retail business.

Despite the integrated nature of the fourth series' stories, the administration of *Callan*'s writers remained as informal as it had been during the first three years. 'There was an office, there were people, you could wander in, and even if you hadn't written the latest episode, you could sit in the gallery while it was being [recorded],'[7] said Trevor Preston. 'You were one of the *Callan* clique and we were all, absolutely, 100% obsessed by it. Writers used to phone each other up and ask, "What have you done with Lonely? I've done this with him." You were given directives: you roughly know the continuity of the area they wanted to move into. Purely practically, you've got to contract the [Hunter] actor to come back, but you didn't get a closely-typed, five-page thing saying, "These are the story areas". It wasn't rigid; everybody by that time knew so much about Callan and Lonely and Hunter and Liz and all those people, so it was quite a loose and flowing series.'

Bill Craig, by now on board as a regular writer, was impressed with the relaxed but focused working atmosphere: 'With the writers I knew – Jimmy and Ray – we met a lot and the same was true of Trevor. We talked about what worked and what didn't work, and [with] directors like Mike Vardy; I'd worked with him before so there was a personal connection. I'd read the previous scripts [and there were] briefing sessions with George Markstein. Archives and biographies had been established so you can't really tamper with them too much. In terms of story development and creating characters, there wasn't much interference at all – none whatsoever, in fact.'[8] Perhaps inevitably during a run of more inter-connected stories than usual written by different writers, there were some minor continuity mistakes (detailed in the episode entries).

'[Series Four] was the only series that was planned, all thirteen, by George Markstein and myself,'[9] confirmed Collin. 'We simply told the writers what we wanted, in the nicest way. They still had the freedom to inject what they wanted, but they were told the shape.' If there's a major criticism to be made of the producer and story editor's plan, it's that after the innovation of the opening five instalments, the stories tread water before the three part conclusion. However, this was not reflected by the ratings from the time, whichsaw the series consistently in the top twenty, with viewing figures as follows (in millions):[10]

'That'll Be The Day'	10
'Call Me Sir!'	8.8
'First Refusal'	10.3
'Rules of the Game'	10.4
'If He Can, So Could I'	13.1
'None Of Your Business'	11.8
'Charlie Says It's Goodbye'	11.2
'I Never Wanted The Job'	12
'The Carrier'	13.2
'The Contract'	12.1
'The Richmond File: Call Me Enemy'	11.3
'The Richmond File: Do You Recognise The Woman?'	12.1
'The Richmond File: A Man Like Me'	12.8

Collin and Markstein's narrative outline[11] for the episodes reveals detailed notes on the first few stories, but the outlines become sketchier and lacking in originality as the document progresses. Episode six was to have been a 'reprise of "Suddenly – At Home"' with 'Callan very much taken with the sister of Zena Walker [Lady Lewis]', while the story that became 'I Never Wanted the Job' is summed up simply as a 'big story revolving around Lonely.' Shirley reflected that this was because the format of the series had been stretched as far as it would go: '*Callan* is a variation-on-a-theme concept. It has a strong basic dramatic premise, which you can't alter beyond a point. We saw it as a balance of fear situation between

Callan and the organisation, and Callan and Lonely. To some extent that means the characters aren't terribly mobile; you can't alter that premise in any fundamental way and still have the same concept.'[12]

Series Four's unusual narrative shape – in any other series, the harrowing fifth episode 'If He Can, So Could I' could have been a finale in its own right – is also explained by compromises behind the scenes. James Mitchell disagreed with the initial direction Markstein and Collin wanted to take *Callan* in during its fourth year: 'I was opposed to the idea,'[13] he stated unequivocally. '[Callan as Hunter] was a new experiment. I don't think it worked but that's only my opinion.' This may explain why Mitchell only contributed three episodes, his lowest ever script count on the series he'd created. Jim Goddard observed, 'I think it was a mistake when [Callan] became Hunter – he was never supposed to be in authority and he actually changed his accent a bit, too. The intrigue was is in this psychopath who is dynamite at physical violence, and when he became an authoritarian figure it de-energised the series. The writers made a mistake, because this guy had absolutely nothing to lose.'[14]

Although he made light of it in later interviews, Edward Woodward wasn't happy keen on Callan's promotion to Hunter: 'I remember being very worried when the idea came up. I said, "It's a good idea for the character, but I'm never sitting behind that bloody desk!" because everyone who'd ever played Hunter, from Ronnie Radd onwards, had said, "You get out and do all these things, and I'm stuck behind this *bloody* desk!" [So] we made [Callan] use that attitude.'[15] In hindsight, Collin accepted that 'frankly, [the idea] didn't really work,'[16] also recalling that Woodward 'wasn't mad' about the change of direction.

The leading man was also unhappy about William Squire's departure from the cast. 'I got the elbow,'[17] Squire remembers. 'Teddy was furious, because in [Series Four] they put him behind the desk. I thought it was quite wrong for Teddy. Quite wrong. I mean, he knew it, he *knew* it instinctively, and they brought me back.' The compromise, of Callan being Hunter for three-and-a-half episodes, was worked out privately. '[Negotiations were] behind closed doors with Reg Collin,'[18] said Mike Vardy. 'Edward came to it perfectly all right as far as I was concerned, but he's not an actor who would have brought that sort of problem onto the studio/rehearsal room floor: he would have thrashed all that out beforehand. That was probably part of the horse-trading that went on.'

Reassuringly, the quality of the series picked up dramatically with another innovation, a closing trilogy revolving around the KGB agents Richmond and Flo Mayhew, introduced in the first two episodes. 'It was the idea to have a long duel and from that we sort of evolved it,'[19] explained Mitchell. 'We went for T.P. McKenna [as Richmond] as he was a very distinguished, very good actor,'[20] said Collin. 'We wanted an opponent of equal calibré to Callan, some opposition right out of the top drawer. Again it's the theme of putting people under stress: Richmond is as good as Callan, and he's a man who Callan identifies with. Richmond also identifies with Callan. They see themselves as equal protagonists who happen to be on different sides. Under different circumstances, they might have ended up working alongside each other.'

Away from the artistic triumphs and shortcomings of Series Four, there was a renewed sensitivity in the Western media about how violence was portrayed on television and the effect (or otherwise) it had on the viewing audience. In England, campaigners against sex and violence on television were becoming more and more vocal. In April 1969, there had been an outcry in the press over an incident in the first episode of the ITV Granada thriller, *Big Breadwinner Hog*, when the title character (played by Peter Egan) threw acid in a man's face. During the transmission of *Callan*'s fourth series, there were an increasing number of concerned comments in the press about the show's level of violence. 'The amount of it in this opening episode was a jolt,'[21] the previously supportive Mary Malone wrote in the *Daily Mirror*. 'For quite two-thirds of the episode, someone, somewhere, was being thumped, kicked, drugged, tortured or threatened.' the *Daily Telegraph* concurred: 'The durability and earthiness of the hero, as played by Edward Woodward, makes the surrounding violence [all] the more distasteful[22]', noting, '*Callan*... is far too good to need it.'[23]

Compared to violent contemporary cinema – 1971 alone offered *A Clockwork Orange*, *Get Carter*, *Straw Dogs* and *Villain* – *Callan* was a model of restraint. The problem with realistic depictions of violence on television is always the same: finding a level of realism acceptable to an audience of varied age ranges. The production team had always treated the issue seriously; James Mitchell was so concerned he did some 'homework'[24] on this subject. 'For every five blows that are struck in *The Saint*, there's only one in *Callan*... for every four or five shots fired in *Danger Man*, there's only one in *Callan*... When Callan is struck, he feels pain, and when someone is shot, he dies... What is important is not so much violence itself, as the fear and inevitability of it.' 'My view is if you sanitise a programme and shoot somebody... so they end up with a little red dot on their head, then kids think that's all there is to it,'[25] Jim Goddard felt. 'Violence should be horrible... It shouldn't be gratuitous, but violence is unacceptable and it should look unacceptable. The IBA [watched] every programme before transmission and sometimes [demanded] changes.' As far back as 'Red Knight, White Knight', Reg Collin remembered receiving complaints, but they were never upheld.[26]

By the end of 1972, however, the media concerns over violence in the series appeared to be academic. After another highly-rated year, with the inclusion of four more episodes than in 1970 – a sure sign of Thames Television's commitment to *Callan* – the future of the show was, surprisingly, far from clear.

Russell Hunter felt that after four years he'd gone as far as he could with Lonely: 'I'd done enough of it and it had become more and more difficult to keep the scripts tidy,'[27] he reflected. 'It had become more and more difficult to keep the production tidy. By that I mean that because it was *Callan*, "Oh, anybody can direct it" seemed to be the kind of attitude at Thames, and anybody *couldn't* direct it. If you see replays now, you realise that good directors, whether it was Peter Duguid, Goddard or Bill Bain, brought a kind of thing to it that, with due respect, Reggie Collin couldn't, although he was producer of the series, and [directed] the last one. He had no idea about the kind of *balls* attached to the production, a kind of *masculinity* that was just masculinity and not necessarily *aggressive* masculinity. It had sex: for want of better words, let's go back to the Victorians – it had "manly wood" about it, it had *muscle*, and the best directors allowed that to come out of the [characters]. Less-good directors failed to even recognise that, and it became a mishmash of playing little games.' Anthony Valentine shared Hunter's feelings about it being time to stop: '[Four years is] quite enough. If you take a series over four years, I think within four years you see a significant change in the viewing public's taste and four years ago, what might have been absolutely right on the money and very fashionable, four years later is probably beginning to look a bit old hat.'[28] Collin himself felt that the team should quit while they were 'on top'.[29]

On 4 November, the *Daily Mail* announced that 'the future of Callan, Britain's most popular secret agent, will be decided soon.'[30] The paper went on to reveal that Teddington Studios were apparently 'booked for months ahead', making a fifth series in 1973 increasingly unlikely. According to the *Mail*, Woodward had 'always been wary about becoming tied to the role' and James Mitchell was now 'far more interested in writing a cinema version.' In June 1973, perhaps buoyed up by the news that a movie adaptation of *Callan* had indeed been green-lit, Woodward told *The Sun*, 'I've been missing Callan. Thames haven't mentioned a new series. But that doesn't mean they're not thinking about it. This is something that could crop up quite suddenly.'[31] Musing on reinvigorating his hit show, the actor suggested 'if Callan does come back, I think we should give him more scope. Callan and Lonely should go on the Continent. Even Australia. The show's very popular there.'[32] Although Mitchell concurred that going abroad might have been good for Series Five, beyond a change of scene, 'I hadn't thought about it because it was a sort of nightmare – what the hell do I do with him now? Because [the series] wasn't plastic: some things you can just go on churning out and it doesn't really matter. But I could think of no way, off the top of my head, of how to move him on. What else could you do to him?'[33]

As 1973 wore on, no positive news was forthcoming from Thames about *Callan*'s future as a TV series. Since 1972, Lloyd Shirley and George Markstein, with another colleague George Taylor, had been busy setting up Thames' new filmmaking subsidiary Euston Films. The first fruits of this new, experimental enterprise had been seen in April with the premiere of a revamped *Special Branch*, co-starring Patrick Mower, shot entirely on 16mm film. It was left to viewers to speculate whether or not Euston had chosen the right cloak-and-dagger series to revive.

There was no reason why *Callan* couldn't have continued to be successful on television. Spy fiction in general remained popular: the James Bond films, by 1973 on to the third actor in the title role in Roger Moore, continued to do profitably at the box office, and in 1974's *Spy Story*, Len Deighton fielded a sardonic character similar to his 'IPCRESS man' of the 1960s. As it is, however, the final scene of 'A Man Like Me', the last episode of the fourth series of *Callan*, has a pleasing finality about it. When Edward Woodward turns to face the camera as his credit appears on the screen beside him, it looks as if the downbeat spy is taking his final curtain call. With no fifth series forthcoming, it was an appropriate place to leave the broken David Callan, British television's most flawed, fascinating and compulsively watchable cold warrior.

SERIES 4 REGULAR CAST
Edward Woodward (David Callan)
Russell Hunter (Lonely)
William Squire (Hunter) 1, 2, 8-13
Patrick Mower (James Cross) 1-5
Anthony Valentine (Toby Meres) 3, 5, 6, 8-13
Lisa Langdon (Liz, Hunter's Secretary) 1-7, 9, 11-13

SERIES 4 RECURRING CAST
Geoffrey Chater (Bishop) 1-6, 11-13
Paul Williamson (Stafford) 2, 6, 11, 13
Clifford Rose (Snell) 1, 5, 13
T.P. McKenna (Richmond) 1, 11-13
Sarah Lawson (Flo Mayhew) 2, 12

Uncredited on screen: Nigel Stevens (Double for Callan)

PRODUCTION TEAM

Producer Reg Collin, *Story Editor* George Markstein

Uncredited on screen[34]: *First Assistant Director* Barry Millar (1), *Technical Supervisor* Del Randall (1), Peter Kew (5, 7, 10), John Eveleigh (13), *Operations Supervisor* Del Randall (3, 12), John Eveleigh (8), Peter Kew (10), *Lighting Supervisor* Bill Lee (3), Ken Brown (10), Brian Turner (5, 8), Andy Andrews (7), Louis Bottone (7), H. Richards (8, 12, 13), *Location Manager* Barry Millar (1), Eamonn Duffy (5), Eric Pavitt (6), Denver Thornton (7, 9, 12), Geoff O'Brien (8), Mike Harvey (11, 13), *Assistant Location Manager* Hilary Steinberg (1), *Lighting Cameraman* John Keeling, Roy Paite (1), Ricky Briggs (5), Michael Rose (9), Roy Pointer (11), *Assistant Lighting Cameraman* David Whittles (1), *Senior Cameraman* Albert Almond (5), Des Tope (8), Roy Easton (8), Peter Howell (12), Mike Hobbs (12), *Cameras* Albert Almond (3, 7), Gerry Whitney (8), Roy Easton (10), John Chapman (12), John White-Jones (13), *Sound Supervisor* Peter Sampson (7), Peter Bond (7, 12), Ivan Agar (8) Mike Pontin (8), Arthur Duff (12), *Sound Recordist* Peter Sampson (3, 13), Ron Ferris (5, 10), Basil Rootes (11), *Film Editor* Roy Hayden (5), *Vision Control* Jim Fergus Smith (10), *Vision Mixer* Peter Phillips (3, 7, 12), Ken Price (5, 8), Martin Perrett (7, 13), Chris Emmins (8), Nigel Evans (10), P. Boffin (12), *Racks* Bill Marley (3, 5, 7, 8 12), Mel Davies (7), Jim Fergus-Smith (13), *Grams* Julian Ford (3, 7, 8, 12, 13), Tony Morley (5, 10), *Wardrobe Supervisor* Dorothy Pope (1), Jill Silverside (2, 7, 10), Ambren Garland (3, 5, 8, 13), Ann Schmidt (4, 9), Gillian Grimes (12), *Make-Up Supervisor* Joan Hills (1, 3, 4, 5, 10, 11, 12, 13), Launa Bradish (2, 7, 8), Pearl Rashbass (5, 6), Rosie Harrison (7), Hazel Young (8), *Make-Up Artist* Meinir Lewis-Jones (11), *Make-Up Assistant* Hilary Steinberg (6), *Costume Supervisor* Jan Ravell (1), Jill Silverside (2, 10, 11, 13), Ambren Garland (3, 8), Ann Schmidt (4, 5 – filming only, 6, 9), *Floor Manager* John Wayne (2, 6, 7, 9, 10, 13), Richard Mervyn (3), Bill Lawford (4), Nigel Cook (7), John Lopes (8), John Cooper (12), *Production Assistant* DottieRice (1, 6, 11) Mary Morgan (2), Christine Rye (3, 10), Mary Ellis (4), Paddy Dewey (5, 7), Edna Ewing (6, 8, 12), Ruth Parkhill (9, 13), *Stage Manager* Shirley Cleghorn (2, 3, 9, 10), Daphne Lucas (4, 11), Gary Brumfitt (5), Aileen Vernon (6), Dorothy Pope (7, 12), May Lewis (8), Betty Crowe (13), *Assistant Floor Manager* Peter Errington (12), Patrick Vance (3, 5, 7, 8), *Call-Boy* Simon Carlton (1, 6, 12), Mike Bridge (5, 6, 7), Peter Errington (12), *Production Assistant Timer* Edna Ewing (5), June Roberts (7), *Graphic Designer* Ruth Bribham (1, 3, 4, 5, 12), Bernard Allum (2), Rob Page (7), *Wardrobe Dressers* Jean Kelly (5), Jenny Matthews (5), David Parsons (5), Frank Van Ray (5, 6, 11), Lynne Pateman (6, 7, 12), Frank Van Raay (7, 8, 12), Jean Kelley (8), *Prop Men* Dave Grange (1), Chris Jeffries (1), Ron Maskell (1), Reg Stitch (1), Peter Gaskin (1, 5) Andy Armstrong (5, 6), Maurice Finn (5, 12), Joe Price (5, 6), Chris Wade (6), Mike Sands (7), Lou Casey (7), A. Armstrong (7), Barry Shack (7), J. Walkham (7), Sid Baker (8), Roger Marchant (8), Frank McLaughlin (8), *Facility Prop Men* Arthur Jones (1), *Scene Men* J. Hooper (1), G. Dawle (1), R. New (6, 7), G. Dowler (6), *Grips* Eric Mundy (5), A. Walker (7) *Carpenter* J. Hayes (7), Dave Young (12), *Painter* J. Keyes (7), *Labourer* W. Marshall

S4.1 THAT'LL BE THE DAY

Writer: James Mitchell
Director: Mike Vardy
Designer: Terry Pritchard

FIRST UK TRANSMISSION: Wednesday 1 March 1972, 9.00 pm

CAST: Jonathan Newth (Parson), Ronald Radd (ex-Hunter), John Joyce (Milkman/ New Scotland Yard Telephone Voice, *uncredited on screen*), Julian Glover (Karsky), Michael Godfrey (Lebidev), Terence Denville (Prison Guard), Queenie Watts (Lonely's Auntie)

EXTRAS/WALK-ONS: *(Uncredited on screen)* Film (From the Cameo Agency): Geoff Clifford (Double for Cross), Howard Kingsley (Double for Stafford), Bernard Barnsley, Reg Turner, Clinton Morris, Lee Conrad (4 KGB Men), Michael Stevens, Stuart Barry (2 Policemen), Bill Barnsley, Les Clarke, Mike Horsburgh, Charles Pickess (4 Pall Bearers), Ian Elliott, Derek Chafer (2 Grave Diggers), Bob Blaine (George) – also used in Studio.

Studio (From Associated Plays and Players): Willie Bowman, Ken Halliwell (2 KGB Bodyguards), Kathleen Heath (Russian Woman), Bob Wilyman, John Cannon, Bill Burridge (3 Workmen), Margaret Pilleau, Jacqueline Blackmore, David J. Graham, Brychan Powell, Stephen Ismay, Jimmy Mac (6 Passers-by).

PRODUCTION

Rehearsals: From Thursday 2 December 1971
Outside Broadcast Recording: Quenington Mansions, Rostrevor Road, London, SW6 (30 November 1971); Twickenham Cemetery and churchyard (6 December 1971); the car park of Heathrow Airport's Terminal One; Exit 10 on St Peter's Road, Twickenham, Middlesex; Staines Road West in Ashford, Middlesex (7 December 1971)
Camera rehearsals/recording: Teddington Studio Two, Tuesday 14 and Wednesday 15 December 1971[35]

TV TIMES: 'The king is dead. He must be – he threw his own ashes on the grave. Intriguing? But then every case is intriguing for Callan. Hunter, his boss, sees to that. In this new series he again moves Callan, pawn-like, into impossible situations.'
26 February - 3 March 1972, Southern edition

MISSION PROFILE: Lonely attends Callan's funeral but, because of a wildly inaccurate eulogy by the parson, doesn't believe his old friend is the man being buried. He's right – Callan is being held for interrogation in the KGB's Lubyanka prison in Russia. Cross and Stafford, the Section's new recruit, pick up Richmond, the KGB's number one agent in England, and then scare Lonely into staying quiet about his suspicions. Although Snell begins interrogating Richmond, he's stopped because Bishop wants to exchange him for Callan and the two agents meet, briefly, as the swap is made in the Saint Christopher Hotel in Helsinki. Back in England, after shaking off some pursuing KGB men, Callan's appearance at his own grave terrifies Lonely into a faint.

A MAN LIKE ME: When the story opens, the shaven-headed Callan has spent eight months in Lubyanka after being captured by East German security. (His mention of dreaming about 'a bird' killed by the KGB is probably a reference to his brief liaison with Janet Lewis.) The psychiatrist, Karsky, informs him that, because of the regular injections of the truth drug Scopolamine, he is three weeks away from revealing all the information the KGB needs, and is also three weeks away from going insane. Despite this, and Karsky's gentle encouragement to co-operate, Callan keeps resisting, going compliantly to his interrogation chair and obediently rolling up his sleeve. He chooses to believe that the KGB has faked his funeral.

As 'therapy', he is modelling soldiers out of wood, among them a 17th Lancer, Grenadier Guard and a Scots Grey. The trio beat the Russians in battle during the Crimean War (1853-1856), and Callan becomes violent when Karsky's assistant Lebidev smashes one of the models. As the Scopolamine affects Callan more and more, he has vivid nightmares about massacring Russian soldiers, clinging on to his sculptures for comfort as he knows he is close to breaking point. Even so, he keeps resisting.

Once he knows he's being exchanged, Callan's spirits and attitude recover quickly. He throws a glass of wine over Lebidev, knowing that the man can't retaliate, and jokes with Karsky and his Helsinki minders. Understandably, Callan's pleased to see Richmond. Back in England, Callan is astute enough to know that the pursuing Russians have been following a tracking device planted on him, which he discovers hidden inside one of his model soldiers. The Section insist that the charge of 'espionage, terrorism and sabotage' against Callan, for which he could serve 25 years in a Russian prison, is dropped. Even after eight months in prison, he is security-conscious enough to demand a gun after the exchange has taken place, and to send his luggage to the Section lab to be searched for bugs.

LONELY: After not knowing where Callan's been for the last eight months, Lonely discovers from his friend's milkman that Callan is being buried that day. Typically, Lonely nicks a floral tribute from another grave. Because of the unlikely eulogy given by the parson, he can't believe it's Callan who's being buried, even though Lonely is upset enough to sob into the grave, 'Where am I gonna go?'

He's so convinced that an injustice has been done, he contemplates talking to a police sergeant who's 'not bad for a rozzer', a breach of underworld etiquette that his aunt says will get them both talked about.

Lonely's 'work' is placing bets on televised horse racing and he's used to being hassled in his flat by the police; he believes they should 'nick a few motorists'. He supports Manchester United football team.

Even when he's being threatened by Cross and Stafford, he refuses to believe that Cross could have killed Callan, defiance that earns him a painful knee to the groin. However, he's terrified into keeping quiet about his suspicions by Cross's game of Russian Roulette with him, fainting when he expects a direct hit by a (blank) round. When Callan appears at his own graveside, Lonely faints again.

A TIE AND A CREST: During Callan's interrogation in Lubyanka, Meres is discussed; Callan reveals that he was posted to Washington and laughs at Karsky's suggestion that the younger man was his superior. A mysterious 'they' think it's time to pick up Richmond, confirming that the Section's chain of command goes higher than Bishop, who relays the order to Hunter. Bishop has a high opinion of Callan, thinking he's 'almost as good as Richmond', and both he and Hunter agree that their top man could be more than just a field agent...

The old tension between Callan and Cross re-emerges when the latter learns the colleague he thought was dead is still alive. Hunter warns Cross to bring Callan back in one piece, even though the young agent thinks that swapping him for Richmond isn't a good deal for the Section. Slyly, Cross says Callan's prison haircut makes him look like 'a plucked chicken'.

The Section laboratory is run by a man called George, who also arrives in a van to collect Richmond.

ALCOHOL, TOBACCO AND FIREARMS: Once the swap is on, the KGB give Callan red wine and steak. Suspicious as ever, he demands Lebidev samples them first.

On the verge of freedom in a hotel room in Helsinki, Callan enjoys a whisky. Cross and Stafford generously give their duty-free allowance to Richmond, and he enjoys a glass of whisky too. Stafford is teetotal. Once he's back in the company of Section men, Callan demands to be given a gun, which Stafford supplies.

Discovering that Richmond has a lethal Tokarev Automatic on him when he was arrested, Hunter tells Cross that it was 'just as well you hit him'. The TT 33 self-loading pistol was the sidearm of the Russian army between 1930 and 1965, after which the Makarov pistol replaced it.

SPY-SPEAK: The parson's rather misleading appraisal of Callan: 'This was a gentle man, always willing to help others, doing good by stealth. A man of peace.' Lonely's reaction? 'Gawd blimey. They're burying the wrong geezer!'

Cross isn't envious of Stafford's assignment to tail Lonely: 'Rather you than me, old man. Like tailing a sewage farm.'

Lonely comments astutely on the racing form of Montezuma: '9-4 favourite?!... That's got no chance, not with that bloody great nana on its back.'

Richmond gives Snell a back-handed compliment: 'You really are extremely talented. I should very much like to kill you.'

Callan on his stoic guards in Helsinki: 'What do you two do when you're happy – burst into tears?'

PAWNS AND PLAYERS: JULIAN GLOVER (born 1935) trained as a classical stage actor and first made an impression on television in the BBC's serialisation of Shakespeare's history plays, *An Age of Kings* (1960). He has been a reliable presence on British TV ever since, appearing in, among many other series, *The Avengers* (three times), *Espionage* (1963-64) and the *Mr. Palfrey of Westminster* episode 'The Defector' (1984). In 1972, he was cast in the regular role of naval officer Commander Anderson in the BBC's *Spy Trap*, 'opposite that wonderful classical actor Paul Daneman'[36]. Glover went on to play big screen villains in *For Your Eyes Only* (1981) and *Indiana Jones and the Last Crusade* (1989), most recently appearing as Grand Master Pycelle in HBO's fantasy drama *Game of Thrones* (2011-).

'I was at the RSC in 1957 at the same time as Edward,' Glover recalled, 'so I knew him well by the time I came to do *Callan*. That made the whole process more pleasant. My scenes were shot all in one day at the studios in Teddington. Some old things I watch now and think "Oh, what was I *doing?*", but *Callan* holds up very well, apart from William Squire's tendency to end all his lines on an upward [inflection], like he's asking a question.'

Glover has had more experience than most actors of Cold War politics. 'One of the most profound experiences of my life came from the TV film *Invasion* [1980],' he said.

'In it, I played Alexander Dubček, the President of Czechoslovakia who initiated the Prague Spring: "Communism with a human face." In 1989, when the Berlin Wall was coming down and the Soviet Union was breaking up, I decided that there would never be a better time to try and meet him. I made some calls, and thanks to a friend in the Foreign Office, I was suddenly heading for Czechoslovakia with a *World in Action* [ITV documentary] film crew. We made it to the Czech government buildings, everything was in chaos and a government official came out and said, "[Dubček] can spare you a quarter of an hour." Four hours later, we were still there. We sat and watched *Invasion* together, we held hands, we cried. It meant so much to me when Dubček said, "On the anniversary of the Russians coming in, we would sit and watch [illegal] tapes of *Invasion* and take heart from knowing that the West knew what was really going on." I don't have the words to describe what that felt like.

'A few years after that, Dubček was killed in a car crash. I believe he was assassinated, because a car crash was the KGB's favourite way of getting rid of people. It was really moving to be one of only three Westerners allowed to attend his funeral.'

PAUL WILLIAMSON (born 1929) had been in repertory theatre with Woodward's first wife, Venetia. He is best remembered for his role as Owen Montagu in *The Bretts* (1987-89), the ITV drama about London's theatreland. Starting his career in 1956, he finally retired in 2013 after 50 years: 'Theatre: 271 parts, TV: 237, film: 26, commercials: 36, corporate and training films: 41, radios: 22, so I got on a bit,'[37] he said wryly. As a policeman – a role he would often play – Williamson had the honour of telling Roger Moore 'It's my job to recognise notorious people like Simon Templar' at the beginning of *The Saint* episode 'Paper Chase' (1966).

For T.P. McKenna, see 'Call Me Enemy'.

INFORMATION: 'Bishop was sort of "on call",'[38] James Mitchell remarked of the first new addition to the regular cast. 'He was always useful if you had to go beyond Hunter.' The second addition, Stafford, was created because 'occasionally you'd need an ad-hoc gentleman.' Callan's creator remembered that his Series Four opener 'was a desperately frightening piece at the time... viewers found the business in the mental hospital [disturbing]. I'd read about putting Russian prisoners into psychiatric hospital, and that's what gave me the idea.' There was a (non-speaking) guest appearance by Ronald Radd at Callan's funeral, as the only other surviving Hunter. 'That was deliberate,'[39] explained Reg Collin. 'Nobody was ever dropped from the series. People came and went because the actors' lifestyle is, if someone offers them another job, they'll take it without waiting for me to make my mind up!' 'I remember Teddy and Reg thanking [Radd] for coming,'[40] recalled Squire, 'because there wasn't much for him to do, just standing about – I think it rained, actually.' Woodward's prison haircut was achieved with a skull-cap and stubbly wig, and the actor felt it was the most uncomfortable performance of his career up to that point. Geoffrey Chater is credited as one of the regular cast in the opening titles from here until episode six; uniquely, T.P. McKenna is billed as a 'Guest Star'. The overall budget for the episode was £35,000.

Originally entitled 'A Funeral Has Been Arranged and Will Shortly Take Place', the outline for this story[41] has some interesting differences to the finished script, and inconsistencies with the forward-planning document[42] for the fourth series. In Mitchell's outline,

Hunter is preparing to move on to 'higher things' and Meres is already back in the Section, having returned from Washington. Liz is in tears over Callan's death and Lonely reads his friend's baffling obituary, about an 'honest, law-abiding... public servant' in a newspaper. 'The surviving Hunters', Lonely, Meres, Cross and Liz all attend Callan's funeral, but Bishop is absent, as he is from the rest of the episode: it's Hunter who arranges the swap with Callan's KGB equivalent, referred to by his Russian name Zhelkov.

The action in Eastern Europe is different. Callan is subjected to beatings rather than truth drugs, and his interrogator is never named. A character who didn't make it into the final draft, Nikich, a prisoner who is also a doctor, nurses Callan back to health and tells him he was betrayed by a KGB man called Karsky (who becomes the Section man's interrogator in the completed episode). During the swap in Helsinki overseen by Cross and Meres, Callan identifies Karsky and breaks exchange etiquette, killing the opposition agent. Intriguingly, the story outline says 'the new Hunter will have a lot to say about that,' so at this very early stage it looked as if Mitchell was unaware of Callan's forthcoming temporary posting as Hunter. The final scene with Lonely remains the same, although the inscription on the gravestone and Callan's closing dialogue is different: "'David Callan. 1934 – 1972. Deeply mourned." "Blimey," says Callan. "You can say that again."' The title of the episode is derived from a cynical remark made by John Wayne's character Ethan Edwards in John Ford's 1956 film *The Searchers*. (The following year, it was co-opted by rock and roller Buddy Holly as the title of his first hit single.)

In the camera script, Lonely was directed to walk up to the chapel saying, 'Blimey – not even any flowers,' a scene that was cut. While under the sunray lamp in Lubyanka, Callan originally poured his wine on the floor instead of throwing it over Lebidev.

Returning to work on *Callan*, Mike Vardy felt it was increasing in stature. 'From Series Three into Series Four it became more and more prestigious,'[43] he said. 'Attracting people like Julian Glover and T.P. McKenna, who were Shakespearean actors, largely speaking, showed that the reputation was building. McKenna was Irish and had got great style and presence and that's what was needed [for Richmond]. He was a joy to work with. He was playing the part with an injury – he fell off a high rostrum during a Royal Shakespeare Company production, and hurt his shoulder very badly – so when he was arrested, violently, we actually had to be quite careful.'

'That'll Be the Day' also saw the return of Queenie Watts as 'Lonely's Auntie.' 'It was only one brief scene, and she obviously had this legendary thing surrounding her', Vardy considered. 'I didn't know her but she was a hand to a glove. She must have played a thousand parts like that.' 'That'll Be the Day' was the only time the director worked with Clifford Rose as Snell, and Vardy remembered being impressed with the Section psychiatrist: 'He's very eloquent and very quietly spoken... Quite a sinister character all together.'

Cross's longer hair and more flamboyant dress sense were an intentional change from his more sober appearance in Series Three, indicating that there were significant changes going on in his character, but as Patrick Mower pointed out, such fashions '[were] also a sign of the times. If you're going out into the world and you're a spy, you shouldn't have a short back and sides and look like a spy, you've got to look like a real person, and that's how people looked at the time.'[44]

Paul Williamson is amusingly self-deprecating about how he became a regular in Series Four. 'The director would have said to an agent, who happened to be mine, "We need someone who can play this anonymous part," and she said "Oh yes, Paul, he's good, he's competent." So I turned up and [did an episode], and then I think whenever they wanted messages brought, or the plot advanced in a fairly anonymous way, they got me along as Stafford. I wasn't contracted; it's a totally casual business. [*Callan*] has brought me a lot of repeat money, even though you don't get much: tuppenece ha'peny from Dubai or something. I'm big in the Gulf!'[45]

Lubyanka, where Callan is held, was the HQ of the KGB and was built on Lubyanka (formerly Dzerzhinsky) Square in Moscow. Opened in 1898, it was originally the head office of the All-Russia Insurance Company. Following the Bolshevik revolution in 1918, it became the control centre of Russia's secret police, initially called the Cheka. Following the dissolution of the KGB after the fall of the Communist system, the building still houses the HQ of Russia's intelligence network, the Federal Security Service of the Russian Federation (FSB). On its ground floor, Lubyanka used to hold a prison, and the testimony of some of its inmates featured in Aleksandr Solzhenitsyn's attack on the repressive Soviet state, *The Gulag Archipelago* (first published in the West in 1973). One of the prison's most famous inmates was the freelance spy Sidney Reilly (1878-1925), prior to his alleged execution on Stalin's orders.

The models Callan fashions were all significant combatants in the Battle of Alma (1854) during the Crimean War. Part of an Anglo-French force, the Grenadier Guards were instrumental in the defeat of an army commanded by General Menshiko, which cost the Russians 6,000 troops. As part of the same battle, the 17th Lancer was a member of the Light Brigade that charged the Russian artillery. Despite heavy losses, the Lancers broke through the opposing guns and pushed back the Russian cavalry. An act of 'folly' as well as grand heroism, the engagement passed into history as 'The Charge of the Light Brigade'. Before this, the Heavy Brigade – consisting of 800 Scots Greys – took on 3,000 Russian cavalry, inflicting 270 casualties and killing the Russian commander, Major-General Khaletski.

The American entertainment journal *Variety* was still watching *Callan*, its reviewer 'Pit' approving of the new series and finding it 'tightly staged (allowing, that is, for the limitations, as per most UK productions, of studio vidtaping [sic]) boasting an appealing anti-hero, crisp dialog and an elliptical style of narrative full of teasing ambiguity.'[46]

By 1972, early electronic video editing was available, resulting in a slightly more polished feel to the Series Four episodes.[47]

On 24 July 1989 at 9 pm on ITV, 'That'll Be the Day' was shown as part of the *Thames Mavericks* season, a series of drama repeats celebrating the company's twenty-first anniversary on the air. Appearing alongside other fondly remembered shows such as *Minder*, *Public Eye* and *The Sweeney*, *Callan* was included 'to remind viewers of one of the most popular and successful secret agents ever seen on television.'[48]

MISSION ANALYSIS: *'Not many people know exactly what they're worth, do they?'* The surprise sighting of Ronald Radd's original Hunter at Callan's 'funeral' in one of James Mitchell's best scripts shows that, four years in, an awareness of the series' rich history is now informing the story. For the first time, the fourth Hunter also has someone he can talk to on an equal footing in the returning Bishop, enabling a subjective appraisal of Callan, the Section's most experienced agent. Most significantly, their joint suggestion that he could be 'more than just a killer' is left hanging, as major plot developments are now part of an overall, ongoing story from episode to episode.

On another level, the scene where T.P. McKenna's Richmond and Callan meet in the middle of a palatial hotel room is the key moment of the episode (and, with the benefit of hindsight, the whole fourth series). One man is the mirror image of the other: everything that happens to Callan in the story happens to Richmond, from interrogation at the hands of a polite psychiatrist working to the limits of safety – as Callan points out, Karsky could have been Snell's 'twin brother' – to a meeting with captors who suddenly become friendly once the spy swap is agreed. McKenna's singular billing as 'Guest Star', despite his brief appearance, hints that the audience could be seeing more of him.

As well as an invigorating change of gear in the way the stories are told, 'That'll Be the Day' has much to commend it as a story in its own right. The blackly comic scenes of Lonely at Callan's funeral, and the disturbing scenes of Callan in Lubyanka, drugged and unfocused, are particular standouts. Mower also has his best moment so far in the series, in a truly terrifying scene where he plays Russian Roulette with Lonely, indicating a shocking, reckless new direction for Cross's character; it's debatable whether even Toby Meres would have gone that far. Packed with intrigue, 'That'll Be the Day' promises much for the stories ahead.

S4.2 CALL ME SIR!

Writer: Bill Craig
Director: Mike Vardy
Designer: Stan Woodward

FIRST UK TRANSMISSION: Wednesday 8 March 1972, 9.00 pm

CAST: Alan Downer (Tramp), Glynn Edwards (Trowbridge) Alan Peters (Barnet, Bishop's driver, *uncredited on screen*)

EXTRAS/WALK-ONS: (*Uncredited on screen*) Cy Town (Receptionist), Terence Convoley, Michael Travers (2 Male Guests), Joyce Windsor, Audrey Searle (2 Female Guests), Michael Buck, Roy Lansford (2 Agents), Leslie Bryant, Mort Hall, Ken Lacey, Roy Kean, Gary Dean, Al Fuller, Colin Thomas, Edward Weston, Francis Batsoni, Ivor Owen (Tramps)

PRODUCTION

Rehearsals: Thursday 21 October 1971
Location Filming: Box Hill, Dorking (Thursday 19 October);
Kingston-upon-Thames (Monday 25 and Tuesday 26 October 1971)
Camera rehearsals/recording: Teddington Studio Two, Tuesday 2 and
Wednesday 3 November 1971[49]

TV TIMES: 'The Section puts Lonely in a Red File – and that means he's totally expendable.'
4-10 March 1972, Southern edition

MISSION PROFILE: Callan is being debriefed at a country house owned by the Section. He wants to leave the organisation, but Bishop says that he can't, and he and Hunter instead urge him to think about promotion – to Hunter. Meanwhile, Lonely is posing for the artist Flo Mayhew, who is very interested in Callan. When the van Lonely's driving blows up, he goes to ground. Callan accepts the job as Head of Section, discovering that Lonely has been placed in a Red File. He also realises that Flo is a KGB agent sent to eliminate him. She's captured, and the freelance assassin she's working with, disguised as a tramp, is killed. Callan tracks down Lonely, but doesn't know what to do about the thief's Red File...

A MAN LIKE ME: A lot of background detail is revealed about Callan. He's classified as a civil servant, would only be entitled to half a pension if he resigned, and his full salary was paid during his imprisonment. His experience in Lubyanka has made him wary of field work. He'll now accept any job, 'as long as it's nine to five and I don't get killed.'

Back in London (he admits to being a city man at heart), he's installed in a luxurious flat in Mayfair fitted with an alarm system. He's very tough: Callan gave nothing damaging away while he was being interrogated, not even on a full dose of the truth drug Scopolamine. Even though he doesn't want promotion, Callan is told that his 50/50 success at war gaming, during which he makes command decisions, is an ideal qualification to moving from playing with soldiers to controlling real agents. Typically, when he's offered the role of Hunter, he responds with what Bishop calls a 'gratuitous and over-emotional outburst.' Told he's ideal material as the Head of Section, in the end Callan is still effectively blackmailed into the position – if he resigned, the merest suspicion of him defecting or turning freelance would be enough to put him in a Red File.

Callan pursues his own agenda in trying to find Lonely, leaving his plush new Mayfair address through the window so he isn't followed. He uses the alias of 'Mr. Grimshaw' from the Ministry of Social Security while searching, lies to the Section, hides Lonely in his Mayfair flat, and uses Section resources to create a set of false papers and a passport for him. After some initial reluctance, Liz helps him, even going so far as to deceive Hunter into thinking she and Callan are sleeping together. She's clearly taken with her new boss, putting fresh flowers on his desk, even though she's more comfortable calling him 'Sir' than 'David'.

Callan feels comfortable enough in his new job to put one of his model soldiers on Hunter's desk. He also treats himself to a new stylish brown suit, matching tie and handkerchief. The new Hunter also knows the proverb 'For Want of a Nail', which chronicles how seemingly unimportant details can have severe consequences.

LONELY: He's 'about 40', born in the East End, and importantly describes his body odour problem as 'excessive glandular activity brought on by excessive nervous tensions'. Lonely hasn't seen Callan since he met him at his graveside and fainted. He's being used by Flo, a KGB agent, to get to his friend. He's completely unaware of this, delighted to be paid 50p an hour as an artist's model, and he is guiltily excited about the prospect of doing it naked: he looks deflated when Flo dismisses this 'gruesome thought'. Flo notes a 'terrible sadness' in Lonely's eyes. He does nothing to correct the scrap metal dealer Trowbridge's belief that he and the artist are having a torrid affair.

The thief is using one of Trowbridge's vans to collect scrap. It's blown up by gelignite Lonely's been looking after for 'a friend', and he was in on the planned robbery the explosive was meant for. Afterwards, Lonely hides out in homeless hostels, surviving on fish and chips. He's clever enough to have worked out that all the strange jobs he's done for Callan over the last few years must mean his friend is a secret agent, although with typical off-key judgment Lonely concludes Callan is 'a Communist spy'.

Callan tries to arrange for Lonely to go to Canada with six months' back pay, working as a steward on the *Cape Hirta* under the alias of John William Cox – which would put him beyond Section scrutiny and save his life – but the criminal doesn't want to go, and hates the idea of posing as a merchant seaman.

To add to his woes, Lonely gets a black eye from Cross.

A TIE AND A CREST: Even though Callan reaches the top job in the Section, he's not in complete control. Bishop is described as 'a senior man', 'senior to Hunter' and, once he takes the job, Callan is told to accept all orders from 'a direct line' via a green phone – which only accepts incoming calls – without question. He's also told that certain files in the archives are 'lead sealed' and that he doesn't have the authority to open them. The previous Hunter, meanwhile, is departing for 'better things' in the 'Scheduled Territories Department'. Unsurprisingly, Hunter and Bishop both belong to the same club.

Callan's promotion brings out more worrying behaviour in Cross. The young agent seethes that calling his former peer 'sir' will 'really stick in my throat' and he storms out of Huntrer's office. Later, having deduced that Lonely is hiding in Callan's new flat, he calls round on the pretext of apologising for his earlier outburst. His contrition is a ruse, as he's vindictively asked the previous Hunter to visit too, aiming to expose Callan as a liar. Tellingly, the departing chief has also noticed that Cross has become increasingly volatile...

ALCOHOL, TOBACCO AND FIREARMS: Hunter pops the cork from a bottle of champagne to welcome Callan back to London and his new flat, although Callan himself later chooses to drink bottled beer. When Lonely's in hiding at his friend's residence, he approves of Callan's taste in brandy, giving it an appreciative sniff. Cross uses a Section gun to dispose of Flo's assassin, while the tramp waits for Callan with a revolver fitted with a silencer.

SPY-SPEAK: Bishop isn't amused by Callan's sardonic view of working for the SIS: 'You must have your work cut out with the Group Insurance Scheme.'

Lonely has fun teasing Trowbridge about his liaison with Flo: 'I think I've ricked my back.' 'Yeah, and I know how you ricked it, you dirty little toerag,' Trowbridge growls. 'It's disgusting what some women will take a fancy to.'

Callan reveals his true feelings about Hunter's command post: 'D'you know what that piece of furniture means to me? That's orders that turn my stomach: lying, cheating, double-dealing, *dying*. That bloody desk has dominated my life!'

Cross's wry comment on Callan's 'funeral': 'That method proved unsatisfactory. Sometimes they come back.'

The old Hunter's reaction on seeing Liz emerge from Callan's bedroom in his dressing gown: 'I am at a loss for words.' Callan's priceless response to Cross's accusation that he's been hiding both Liz *and* Lonely in his bedroom: 'A liar I may be, kinky I am not.'

PAWNS AND PLAYERS: SARAH LAWSON (born 1928) had a prolific career in television and film, beginning with the film adaptation of *The Browning Version* in 1951. She was a stalwart of British adventure shows, featuring in 'Time to Kill' (1960), the pilot for *Danger Man*, *The Saint*'s version of *Goldfinger*, 'The Crime of the Century' (1965), *Department S* (1969-1970) and *The Persuaders!* (1971-72), as well as the science fiction thriller *The Trollenberg Terror* (1956-57). Lawson also starred in the disturbing Hammer film *The Devil Rides Out* (1968, with Patrick Mower) and took the leading role of Prison Governess Sarah Marshall in the fifth series of the ITV prison drama *Within These Walls* (1978). She was married to the distinctively-voiced actor Patrick Allen, and as an aspiring actress had appeared with Edward Woodward in the company of Perth Repertory Theatre when *Callan*'s leading man was seventeen.

GLYNN EDWARDS (born 1931) was once married to *George and Mildred* actress Yootha Joyce. At home playing rough diamond characters in both comedies like *The Fall and Rise of Reginald Perrin* (1977-78) and dramas such as the seminal gangster film *Get Carter* (1971), as well as *The Main Chance* (1972-75) in which he played inquiry agent Walter Clegg, he is now best known as Dave, the philosophical barman of The Winchester Club in ITV's popular *Minder* (1979-1994). Edwards was a police station sergeant in the spy classic *The IPCRESS File* (1965) and in 1969 showed his versatility playing Julie Driscoll's bemused suburban father in *The Wednesday Play* – 'The Season of the Witch'. 'In this country we're actually very fortunate to have this bedrock of wonderful character actors and Glynn Edwards was pitch perfect,'[50] said director Mike Vardy. 'He never brings anything less than full energy and joy, and his comedy timing was tremendous.'

ALAN DOWNER (1930-1995), as well performing as an actor, wrote for the rural soap opera *Emmerdale* (1972-).

INFORMATION: Continuing to build up Liz's part in Series Four, starting with this story, 'was intentional,'[51] Bill Craig asserted. 'There was a thought she was doing very well in the small bits she was being asked to do and more use should be made of her. Some scripts showed she had sympathetic feelings towards Callan – not "hop-into-bed" sympathetic, although she helps him out.' Lonely's accusation that Callan is a Communist spy came to Craig while he was writing the screenplay: 'The ultimate absurdity would be seeing this thick-headed little man not just arrive at the wrong conclusion, but a totally *wrong* conclusion. They both played it beautifully.' This is the last time William Squire is credited in the opening titles until episode six. 'I was worried when I realised they were cutting me out,'[52] Squire remembered, 'but I had the added bonus of knowing that they were bringing me back, and I think that was a lot to do with Teddy, but I shouldn't stress that too much.'

The rehearsal script had Callan discussing his future with Bishop, speculating on '[getting] a new cover, [going] to a new town, [assuming] a different name.' Flo was described as a 'hippie debbie' and Trowbridge as 'big, bowlered, waistcoated, shirt sleeved and aggrieved.' Some of the alcohol intake was amended: Bishop originally drank sherry with Hunter when they discussed making or breaking Callan and, later, Lonely poured himself a brandy in Callan's flat. There's a telling stage direction as the agent finally takes command of the Section: 'Callan stands for a moment, conscious of the emptiness of the office. He stares at the empty chair for a moment then goes round to it. Quite suddenly he sits down in it.' In his first meeting with Liz, the rehearsal script mentions 'the Burroughs dossier' and a 'Foreign Office request.'

When Cross leaves after his first meeting with Hunter-Callan, 'Liz looks after him with some hostility' and later in the Section's Mayfair flat, Lonely was 'scandalised' as the camera was directed to focus on 'Liz's lissom legs as her skirt drops to her ankles.'

Dialogue between Bishop, Hunter and Callan about the agent getting used to his new 'quarters' and the reasons for the agent's 'lenient' treatment by the Russians – 'an easing of international tensions, a thaw in the Cold War, new diplomatic initiatives' and 'Chairman Mao' was dropped during recording, as was a scene of Liz 'buffing her nails' and being told by Hunter to go home. Additional dialogue about Lonely's bogus wife was also cut – 'I mean, whatever he may have thought of her, he was devoted to the nippers... Hasn't seen them for more than a year but he always sent money regularly and a bit extra at Christmas', as well as: 'Youngest boy's only six months.' When Cross called to see Callan, he had some extra dialogue about Lonely: 'Coldly, calmly, efficiently setting up a friend for the chop. I'm not saying you didn't feel anything. I'm just saying that you didn't show it.' Flo's surname was 'Thornton' until just before studio recording. The synopsis gave the Section safe house's location as Sussex.

The draft script gives Lonely's fee for posing for Flo in old money, at 'ten shillings an hour'. The UK's currency came in line with the rest of Europe on 15 February 1971, when the country joined the decimal system – 100 sub-units, or pennies, to one pound. Continuing the series' new awareness of its past, there are references to 'Let's Kill Everybody', 'Death of a Hunter' and 'Breakout'.

'It's a sharp script and has moments of great humour,'[53] Mike Vardy observed. 'I worked with Bill Craig quite a lot after that and his scripts were never less than a joy to do. He was an incisive writer, with wonderful shafts of wit.' The episode involved testing location conditions that only emphasised the professionalism of the *Callan* film crew. 'The house where Callan is sent to recuperate was in Box Hill near Dorking,' Vardy said. 'It was a windy and very wet day when we were shooting the exteriors, so continuity was not up to the usual high standard and the crew spent a very damp day totally exposed to the elements. It's difficult for a director to motivate people in conditions like that, but everyone rose to the occasion.'

With the focus of the series shifting to the internal politics of the Section, Vardy explained where the production team saw Callan's unit fit within the hierarchy of British intelligence: 'In reality, MI5 had and still has to put Special Branch in a position where they can make arrests, and due to intense rivalry the two intelligence services and Special Branch were often bumping into each other in uncoordinated operations. The character of Bishop was the main link with the masters of MI5 and MI6.'

Returning for his second episode, in general Paul Williamson was enjoying working on the series: 'Teddy Woodward was an admirable man to work with. He created a very good atmosphere; a proper old pro in the right way. Mike Vardy was an excellent man. He used me in various other things as well. It was very straightforward and workmanlike and I enjoyed being with nice people, doing interesting things.'[54]

This episode found Williamson on a night shoot with Woodward and Mower: 'I spent a long evening on location standing in a doorway with a pistol in my hand. There was a pub nearby which was a lovely place to get to in between [takes], because I spent an hour or more in this doorway and I remember thinking, "Here I am, trained for Shakespeare and Chekov, and now I earn a living standing in doorways saying nothing." That sort of thing is all part of the business.' Vardy was impressed by Williamson, praising him as 'a very solid performer, very reliable.'[55]

In the 8 March edition of *The Sun*, Patrick Mower was interviewed and reflected on the popularity of Cross. 'He really is a totally unlikeable person,'[56] the actor felt. 'His one complaint about his work is that he doesn't get enough girls to beat up. There are times when I've been attempted to allow him one honest, real smile instead of the sadistic leer. But I repress it.' Mentioning events to come in the fourth series, he referred to Cross assaulting a young girl, commenting 'It all gets very nasty'. The interviewer wryly concluded, 'It almost sounded as if he was looking forward to it.'

Lonely collects scrap metal and Callan jokes about a van being better than a horse, a likely reference to the BBC TV comedy *Steptoe and Son* (running intermittently between 1962 and 1974). By the time 'Call Me Sir!' was made the rag-and-bone men were being superseded by scrap metal dealers or 'totters' (like Trowbridge) and corporation dustmen, and their yards were being bought up by property developers. In another pop culture reference, Lonely is described, with heavy irony, as a 'midnight cowboy.' John Schlesinger's 1969 film of the same name starred Jon Voight in the title role of a male prostitute.

Flo mentions the Gettysburg Address, which ties in with Callan's interest in the American Civil War. It was a speech given by US President Abraham Lincoln at the Soldiers' National Cemetery in Gettysburg, Pennsylvania, on 19 November 1863, four and a half months after the defeat of the Confederate Army. Praising the reunited USA's democratic traditions, Lincoln famously commented that 'government of the people, by the people, for the people, shall not perish from the earth.' That line of the speech was referenced in *The Prisoner*, which George Markstein story edited. Surprisingly, Callan quotes the song title 'Where Have All the Flowers Gone?', a protest folk song written by Peter Seeger in 1953. Perhaps the agent knows the song from the version by Peter, Paul and Mary, from their eponymous debut LP, which in 1962 spent five weeks at Number 1.

In a feature promoting the new Sunday afternoon series *Take a Cine Camera* (1972), the *TV Times* reported that Edward Woodward and Russell Hunter were 'great friends outside the studio.'[57] Both shared an enthusiasm for the Agfa Microflex cassette-loaded camera, and when Russell claimed that 'any idiot can use [it],' the magazine (predictably) couldn't resist commenting that he was the next in line to try.

MISSION ANALYSIS: *'Explanations, like sparks, fly upwards. We are responsible to someone and if you make a decision, you must be prepared to justify it.'* It's easy to see why Bill Craig was brought back. Apart from his talent for intricate (but clear) plotting, in 'Call Me Sir!' he juggles jigsaw pieces that don't look like they're going to fit together – Callan's promotion to Hunter, the artist Flo Mayhew and Lonely's disappearing act – until they knit into a satisfying whole. As Craig created the enigmatic but dryly funny Bishop, he's also natural choice for the script that fully establishes him as a regular, revealing the calculating ruthlessness behind the man's deceptive *bonhomie*. Craig easily fits his story to the production team's aim of making the relationships between the characters more prominent within the stories, while still finding time to display his talent for dramatic irony and wit, particularly when the fourth Hunter uses Callan's catchphrase 'got a job for you'.

When Callan becomes Hunter, it's revealed that nothing has really changed for the Section outsider. Although he's now the top man, he still has a superior – Bishop – and even *more* responsibility, such as Lonely's assignment to a Red File. The corollary of this is the neat metaphorical twist of making the silent tramp that Bishop envies at the beginning for having 'no responsibilities' turn out to be a freelance assassin that 'nobody loves.' If this wasn't enough of a rewarding mix, the humour ranges from sharp one-liners, to the bedroom farce of Liz and Lonely hiding in Callan's flat, to Trowbridge's Steptoe-like grumblings about Lonely's (imagined) sexual couplings with Flo Mayhew. The thief's earthy retort 'Ballcocks!' is worthy of old man Steptoe himself.

Significantly, the issue of how much Lonely knows about Callan's real activities is finally addressed. It's never been entirely consistent, but considering the events of 'Nice People Die at Home', 'Death of a Hunter', 'The Same Trick Twice', 'A Village Called "G"' and 'Breakout', he *really* should have worked out what 'Mr. Callan' was involved in before now; he might be uneducated, but he's not stupid.

'Call Me Sir!' is another episode brimming with ideas, effortlessly manoeuvring Callan into the Head of the Section's chair. It is a bold, sweeping change that revitalises the series at just the right time. The cast all rise to the challenge, in particular Lisa Langdon and Patrick Mower, whose increasingly unstable performance commands the attention in every scene he's in. With the huge, unexpected irony of Callan becoming the new Hunter, with all the dilemmas and responsibilities that entails, Woodward himself is clearly finding new areas of his character to explore.

S4.3 FIRST REFUSAL

Writer: Bill Craig
Director: Jim Goddard
Designer: David Marshall

FIRST UK TRANSMISSION: Wednesday 15 March 1972, 9.00 pm

CAST: Christopher Owen (Anton Bristac), Carl Bohun (Vopo officer), Martin Wyldeck (Kitzlinger), Coral Atkins (Myra Kessler)

EXTRAS/WALK-ONS: *(Uncredited on screen)* Ellen Baumler, Susanne Batrice, Christine Lander, Judith Grimes, Ernest Jennings, Charles Uttley, Bruce Guest, James Muir, Eric Kent, Lionel Taylor

PRODUCTION
Rehearsals: From Friday 19 November
Outside Broadcast Recording: Foxhills estate, Chertsey (Thursday 25); Kingston-upon-Thames (Friday 26) Teddington Studios (Saturday 27 November 1971)
Camera Rehearsals/Recording: Teddington Studio Two, Tuesday 30 November and Wednesday 1 December 1971[58]

TV TIMES: 'A list of [ten] British agents leads Callan into a double, double-cross situation.'
11-17 March 1972, Southern edition

MISSION PROFILE: Lonely is drafted into the Section to drive a London taxi. Kitzlinger, a freelance secrets broker, gives the Section first refusal on buying a list of ten British agents in Eastern Europe. An eleventh, Anton Bristac, is wounded crossing the East/West frontier. Returned from Washington, Meres poses as Kitzlinger's KGB contact. He and Cross are ordered to panic Kitzlinger into revealing his source: Myra Kessler, a translator. Meres and a recovered Bristac capture her, but she outwits them. Callan buys the list, but none of the other ten agents are real. Bristac, working with Myra, prepared the bogus list then betrayed himself to make the con look convincing. Leaving Myra and Kitzlinger to face Callan's wrath, Bristac gets away with most of the money.

A MAN LIKE ME: In his new job, Callan is clearly mastering administrative jargon, as he christens Lonely's taxi a 'Mobile Communications Facility', to be put at the disposal of the whole Section. His attitude to the thief is as contradictory as ever: even though Callan quickly becomes exasperated with Lonely's inability to grasp 'the Knowledge' (cabbys' geography of London's streets) to the point of physically abusing him, he warns Bishop that if he tries to have Lonely killed, he will have to deal with Callan first. Now he's in management, his accent has become slightly more refined, and he's showing a liking for tailored suits (although he rather undoes this suave image by wearing a cardigan.)[59]

Callan's recent time on active duty is invaluable as he settles in as Hunter. He knows that Kitzlinger's list can't have come from field agents because of the security risk. His morality is also intact as Bishop disgusts him when he says that some SIS agents aren't worth the £10,000 apiece Kitzlinger is asking.

Despite Meres having nearly killed him in 'Death of a Hunter', Callan is prag-

324

matic enough to reassure the returned agent that he's prepared to forget the past and thinks Meres is a 'good operator'. Behind the professionalism, though, Callan's angry response to Meres' trigger-happy murder of Kitzlinger – '[You're] a bloody psychopath. You haven't changed, Toby, have you?' – show that his feelings about the upper-class agent are still ambivalent.

In the past, Callan spent time at the Russian Embassy in London, keeping Kitzlinger's KGB contact Eugene Roscoff under surveillance.

LONELY: Coerced by Callan into driving the MCF – licensed cab number 12372, number plate YMM 254H – as a full-time member of the Section. He's not a great reader, haltingly reading the Official Secrets Act (1911-1920), but he suddenly improves when he realises he may be caught up in spying and, having been to prison recently, is terrified that he could get fourteen years. Predictably, he complains about learning 'the Knowledge', and scratches the car on his first day out.

Lonely shows a special talent for getting lost (on Callan's instructions), infuriating Kitzlinger so much by taking him to three wrong destinations in a row that the secrets-broker storms off without paying. Strangely, when Lonely picks Kitzlinger up from his hotel, the European doesn't seem to recognise him, even though the thief puts Kitzlinger's luggage in the taxi's boot.

A TIE AND A CREST: Even though Callan has personally asked for his old colleague Toby Meres to be transferred back from Washington, the public school agent provocatively revives their old rivalry. He discloses that he applied for a transfer when he learned that Callan had been promoted to Hunter, believing that the new chief's 'face doesn't fit' and that some personnel are always destined to be 'other ranks'. Going further, Meres says Callan 'fail[s] to inspire confidence', and sees himself replacing the older man in Hunter's chair. Callan discovers another limit to Hunter's power: his own file has been removed from Records by person or persons unknown. However, he is able to access Bishop's – Section file 491 (it takes two signatures to remove a dossier). Callan's research reveals that 'Bishop' is a real surname, not a codename – of Charles St. John Bishop, age 50, born 23 March 1921. Bishop becomes enraged upon finding that Callan has been investigating his past and treating him as a suspect in the case.

Intriguingly, a 'higher authority' than Bishop approves the payment of the £100,000 that Kitzlinger wants. The Section has its own code-breaking room.

ALCOHOL, TOBACCO AND FIREARMS: Callan takes a conciliatory glass of Bells whisky with the returned Meres.

Toby later offers Myra Kessler vodka, but she declines. At gunpoint, Myra in turn gives Meres and Bristac vodka with added sleeping pills so she can escape.

SPY-SPEAK: Bishop is far from impressed with recruiting Lonely into the Section: 'Fellow appears to have an IQ of 2½!' he protests, and is even more disgusted as he takes a ride in the MCF, as 'it's like sitting behind a smouldering rubbish tip.' Lonely himself comes up with a particularly queasy image to try and excuse learning London's taxi routes by bike, telling an unforgiving Callan that he has 'blisters on me backside like spring onions.'

Callan is quick to put Meres in his place: 'You're a good man – at your job.' Unperturbed, his old rival is on fine sardonic form, dismissing Cross as 'a neurotic boy' and later telling him, 'We live in a changing world, and if things change as they might, you could be a cross I wouldn't bear.' Meres also has a brilliant moment of deadpan humour when he finds a pair of men's boxer shorts in Myra's luggage: 'Good heavens. Minding these for a friend?' Still looking for the list, he orders the woman to strip off, saying, 'I'm afraid I can't offer you a musical accompaniment.' – a line that rebounds on him a few minutes later when she holds him at gunpoint.

PAWNS AND PLAYERS: CHRISTOPHER OWEN has been seen in TV and films as varied as *House of Cards* (1990), *Confessions of a Window Cleaner* (1974) and *Between the Lines* (1992-94). In *Doctor Who*, he was memorable as a talking cactus – 'Meglos' (1980) – and in the movie *The Bank Job* (2008) he played a seasoned Lord Mountbatten. Owen continues to be prolific in his parallel career as a writer, with plays such as *Still Waters, An Evening with Jack and Harry* and *A Parson's Tale*. He remembered that the opening sequences in 'First Refusal' had an unfortunate side-effect. 'I was shot in my first scene and my agent at the time thought that I was dead so switched the TV off, not knowing that I was still alive and had a number of good scenes to go.[60]

'I enjoyed working with Edward Woodward, a real gent,' he continued. 'My part was a man who happened to be working for the "enemy". I played him very low-key. Jim Goddard suggested I played it less low-key, but Edward said no, I played it just right; actually, having seen the episode, I think Jim was correct. After I watched it I decided I must have my teeth straightened, which I did.'

CORAL ATKINS' best-remembered role is Sheila Ashton in the ITV drama *A Family at War* (1970-72). Another alumnus of *Armchair Theatre*, she had starred with Rodney Bewes and Trevor Bannister in Jack Rosenthal's marriage comedy 'The Night Before the Morning After' (1966). Although after *Callan* Atkins would continue to appear in programmes such as *Whodunnit?* (1973), *The Sweeney* – 'Contract Breaker' (1975), *Survivors* – 'Lights of London' (1976) and *Flesh and Blood* (1980-82), from the early 1970s onwards she changed her priorities, financing and running a foster home for neglected children. Atkins' ambitious project was dramatised in the TV film *Seeing Red* (2000), with Sarah Lancashire taking on the role of the actress and campaigner.

For Martyn Wyldeck, see Armchair Theatre: *'A Magnum for Schneider' (Chapter 4).*

INFORMATION: 'There was an element of class consciousness,'[61] Bill Craig said of his favourite script for *Callan*. 'Bishop had terrible blind spots that Callan would never have. Being at Oxbridge might make people automatically "right" for others, but not Callan.' Remarking on the three most notorious members of the 'Cambridge Five' spy ring, the writer continued, 'I never actually thought Hunter knew Burgess, Maclean or Philby or was a member of their "club", but I was absolutely sure Bishop was. It gave Callan the chance to snap "How's Guy Burgess getting on?" [sic]. [Bishop] never for a single second suspected any of them.'

Commenting on the enlarged cast for Series Four, Craig said, 'I personally don't like a large number of characters in a drama series. A continuing series is something else again, because there's an expectation of seeing [the regulars], but it can be inhibiting when constructing a story. I can't say on *Callan* I found it a great problem... One of the principals had to go, and it was Cross who was heading in that direction. I didn't know he was going to be killed off, but I knew he wasn't up to the job.' Craig wrote the 'neurotic boy' line about Cross as he felt the young agent 'did not have the background: he cracked under the strain... All the other spy series about the security services had a mutual trust and liking, to a certain extent. There was mutual loathing in *Callan*. The first thing Meres says to Callan when he's behind the desk is, "Your face doesn't fit" [sic]. There is no love between any of them except perhaps Callan and Lonely. That abrasion is what [made] the series work.'

Anthony Valentine's name is restored to the opening titles in a single credit, rather than the joint one he formerly shared with Russell Hunter. Apart from 'Rules of the Game' and 'Charlie Says it's Goodbye', it would occupy this position until the end of the series. 'One of the episodes that I remember very clearly is when [Meres] and Callan both talked about their ambition to be Hunter,'[62] Valentine recalled. 'If I remember rightly, Meres' attitude to that was that Callan would never be Hunter because he wasn't the right kind of human being to *be* Hunter. I think [Meres] was profoundly shocked when [Callan] became Hunter, because Meres had assumed being public school and a little more controlled and, perhaps, Callan's intellectual superior [he would be given the job]. I think there was a fair bit of that in [the fourth] series and I think that even though Callan was promoted to Hunter, Meres always felt that it wouldn't last very long. In various episodes, Meres was constantly making remarks like "This could be your last job as the guv'nor", or something like that.'

In the rehearsal script, Meres' political ambitions in the Section are much more pronounced. Toby phones Bishop to tell him that Callan has withdrawn his file from Records: 'There's something that's making me unhappy. I think it might make you feel unhappy too.' In his angry confrontation with Bishop, Callan guesses that Meres has been informing on him and when Toby shoots and kills Kitzlinger, the new Hunter accuses him of making a deal with Bishop. A line in the camera script was cut from the completed episode, as, uncharacteristically, Meres defends his shooting of Kitzlinger: 'David, I swear to you – it was a reflex – instinctive –.' Continuity remains strong: there are references to Callan being shot in the back by Meres in 'Death of a Hunter'. In a mischievous touch, Craig based Kitzlinger on George Markstein, a man who also suffered from dyspepsia.

'I think there was a gradual change over the period of years,'[63] Woodward reflected about his character. 'Callan got more and more spiky and suffered fools less and less gladly, and we made him become much more jaded with the work he was doing and the people with whom he was working. [When he became Hunter] that was a very deliberate move, because Jim [Mitchell] worked from an attitude of "What would happen if a person was in this situation and was switched for *another* situation? What happens to a man who's like that and *then* is given [Hunter's job]?" It's like a politician who screams and screams about the leadership of his party and suddenly he's the leader of his party – what happens to him? Nine times out of ten, they nearly always "go establishment" themselves.'

Considering the conflict with Bishop, Jim Goddard, 'I think that Callan, and Edward Woodward himself as the actor, were better at rebelling against authority so they had to bring in authority over Hunter, whereas before Hunter was the ceiling.'[64]

Russell Hunter had previously been given a driving double in 'Let's Kill Everybody', but for the fourth series Reg Collin wanted the actor to learn to handle a car properly. Collin recalled Hunter 'went a bit white and said, "I can't drive". I said, "That's alright... you go and learn to drive and I'll pay for the lessons". For some reason – and I know I flipped my lid at the time – when we came to do [the fourth series] he said, "I still can't drive!"'[65] Possibly infuriating his producer further, Hunter was happy to tell *The Sun* that a low-loader truck was used.[66] Jim Goddard remembered that the shoot involving the loader 'totally jammed the centre of Kingston for four hours!'[67]

The black cab used as the MCF was supplied by a London taxi driver who owned his own vehicle and was known in the trade as a 'Musher'. 'He was a very nice man from the East End,' Goddard said, 'and you could get hold of him through the property department. He was a great guy: the first time anything had to happen to his cab he went crazy, then, when it had all been put right, he had a bloody workshop standing by with spares in case we'd smashed up the cab! He started to enjoy it then: "What are we going to smash up this week, guv?"' As a designer, the director had created a train in the studio for the *Armchair Theatre* play 'Thank You and Goodnight' (1956), a skill he brought to realising a London Underground carriage for the meeting between Meres and Kitzlinger: 'The side of [the train] was... against black drapes and we'd move the platform. I think we [prepared] the set so I could do lots of wide shots with long lenses and make it more "spy life". On the ground plan we had lots of gaps between sets [so] we shot through glass on a long lens, so the glass is blurred but the actors' faces [were] sharp. It really makes the audience look at them.'

Bishop mentions Oleg Penkovsky (1919-1963), who was one of British intelligence's greatest successes. A senior KGB officer, he spied for the UK and America, alerting the West to the deployment of Russian missile bases in Cuba.

Kitzlinger uses the London Reference Library as a 'dead letter box'; this term describes a secret location that agents and their controllers can leave and pick up covert information. Memorably, a Communist agent once discovered a Western intelligence dead letter box and left the sardonic message, 'Better luck next time, Mr. Bond.'

The list of agents is encoded and hidden in a biography of Thomas Cranmer (1489-1556), a leader of the English Reformation who encouraged Henry VIII to annul his marriage to Catherine of Aragon, initiating the English church's break with Rome. The one-time key[68] needed to decode this list of SIS agents is contained within *War and Peace* (1869) by Leo Tolstoy (1828-1910). Considered one of the greatest works of world literature, this novel examines the effect of Napoleon's 1812 invasion of Russia on five families of Russian nobles, breaking literary convention by becoming a philosophical discussion in places, instead of continuing as a character-driven narrative. As it's also one of the longest books ever written, using a few paragraphs within it to contain a one-time code key is ingenious, effectively hiding a needle in a haystack.

MISSION ANALYSIS: *'You really are a very bad Hunter. You'll have to do much better on your first big job.'* Once again, Bill Craig finds ingenious ways to twist a plot in unexpected directions. The story is in progress before the episode starts, with Toby Meres back working for the Section as a bogus KGB contact. As a result, his reintroduction is so underplayed that when he appears, meeting Kitzlinger in a London Underground carriage just before the end of Part One, it's a genuine surprise and for a moment it's hard to believe it's him. (Valentine's name featuring in the opening titles would still have given the game away to longer term followers; modern production teams are rather more conscious of 'spoilers'.) Craig uses the same ploy that he did in 'The Same Trick Twice', hiding the real villain, Bristac, in plain sight as a Section recruit, although as so much around this ruse is different, the similarity goes unnoticed.

In places the episode is lit very imaginatively, in an almost *film noir* style, emphasising that a lot of the action takes place at night. Fittingly, Callan and Meres' first on-screen meeting since the former's promotion takes place in the brooding nocturnal hours, the delicately subdued lighting emphasising the tension between the pair. It's a deftly written scene, as newer viewers don't need to have seen the first two series to understand that there's a complicated, antagonistic relationship between them, and the attention of long term viewers is also rewarded. Considering Craig had never written for Meres before, he captures the character perfectly, and it's as if Valentine's never been away. He's cold-eyed and chilling when Meres threatens to strip-search Myra, and coolly mocking as he's about to drink a drugged Vodka, raising his glass to her with an ironic 'Cheers'.

Apart from the relative novelty of a proactive female villain – Coral Atkins enjoying herself with a just-under-over-the-top German accent – the story is a cerebral one, owing a debt to the notion of fictitious agents in Graham Greene's novel *Our Man In Havana* (1958), and being another variation on the spy fiction convention of the reality of a situation not being what it at first appears to be. Finally, for the first time in quite a while, the Section is outwitted, suggesting that the new Hunter is more human, and therefore more fallible, than his ruthless predecessors.

Add a sprinkling of Craig's peppery humour, and Series Four's unbroken run of quality continues.

S4.4 RULES OF THE GAME

Writer: Ray Jenkins
Director: Voytek
Designer: Bernard Spencer

FIRST UK TRANSMISSION: Wednesday 22 March 1972, 9.00 pm

CAST: Mike Pratt (Medov), Virginia Stride (Alevtina), Verna Harvey (Danera), Philip Brack (Vasyayev), James Cossins (Wingfield), Timothy Carlton (Kane), Joan Ogden (Hard-faced woman) Matron (Shelagh Wilcocks)

EXTRAS/WALK-ONS: (*Uncredited on screen*) Clinton Morris, Barry Kennington (film), Ken Wade (studio).

PRODUCTION
Rehearsals: From Thursday 4 November 1971
Outside Broadcast Recording: Brunswick Boys Club, Clarendon Crescent, Twickenham, Middlesex (Friday 5, Monday 8 and Tuesday 9 November 1971)
Camera Rehearsals/Recording: Teddington Studio One, Wednesday 17 and Thursday 18 November 1971[69]

TV TIMES: 'Callan, now acting as Hunter, is drawn into a grim game of tit-for-tat. But certain information is withheld from him.'
18-24 March 1972, Southern edition

MISSION PROFILE: Bishop orders Callan to intimidate the Russian cultural attaché Adam Artemyevich Medov, together with his wife Alevtina and daughter Danera, into leaving London; ostensibly, this is in retaliation for the expulsion from Russia of a junior British diplomat. After continued harassment by Cross, Medov eventually tells his Embassy security people, planting the belief that he may be an undercover KGB agent they don't know about. Suspicious because some information about the case has been restricted, Callan discovers that the 'journalist' Neville Dennis – real name Dennis Wingfield – is really an SIS agent, skilled in cryptography, deported from the USSR following his unmasking by the KGB. His expulsion is the real reason Medov is being victimised in a belated 'tit-for-tat' exercise. Medov unexpectedly asks Cross for political asylum as by now he'll never be able to shake off the suspicions of his own people. The defection goes badly wrong, Danera recognising Cross for harassing her family and she attacks him. He clubs Danera with his gun butt, accidentally severely injuring her.

A MAN LIKE ME: Callan has been to his tailor again, as he's sporting a new, classically-cut suit in subtle shades of blue. He also wears a suit in exactly the same brown favoured by the previous Hunter and, as befits a man in command, has swapped his hush puppies for polished leather shoes. Asked by Cross why he's been detailed to harass Medov, Callan replies with the Section party line of 'not why, just who', an order he often disobeyed. Not practicing what he officially preaches, he tries to discover who the diplomat is who was expelled from Russia. Despite now being the Section's commander, he's still independently minded enough to work outside the brief he's been given.

Aware of how vulnerable he is as the Section controller, Callan says he cares about Cross as what he does reflects on him. Callan is worried that increased harassment of Medov could have serious political repercussions; he would prefer Bishop took the responsibility, as he ordered the diplomat's intimidation. Callan proves to be an accomplished administrator, overseeing fourteen separate projects in the Section at once.

His instincts as a field man take him out of the office at the mention of the name 'Neville Dennis', whom he discovers is really an upper-class SIS agent called Dennis Wingfield he trained with (along with 'old Peewitt'). Still sharp in interrogation techniques, Callan has no hesitation in using 'the full sweaty treatment' on his former colleague to get him to admit that he was recently expelled from Russia for spying.

Callan gives Wingfield a very un-executive V-sign after he recovers from being knocked out. Disturbingly, it sounds like killing is part of a British agent's training.

LONELY: Appears to suffer a slight memory loss, as Callan has to remind him about learning the taxi routes in London. (Callan did the same thing in 'Call Me Sir!'). Lonely's allowed to keep the money from the fares he picks up, although the thought doesn't cheer him up. He's confused about who his 'guv'nor' really is, Callan or 'poncey bags' Cross. Showing uncharacteristic bravery, Lonely uses the MCF to block a car-load of Russian security agents from chasing Cross and Medov. There's a priceless comment from the little man as he shouts at one of the occupants of the car while they gesture for him to get out of the way: 'What do you mean, "wave, wave"?!' (This line wasn't in the camera script, so Russell Hunter may have improvised it and other dialogue in this scene).

A TIE AND A CREST: Bishop and Callan conduct their meetings in an anonymous, featureless office away from the Section HQ[70]. The chain of command is emphasised as Callan has to call Bishop 'sir', standing up as he does so. In turn, Callan makes Cross address him as 'sir' too. Responsibility in the Section cuts both ways, as Cross later asks for a firm directive from Callan about how far he can go in intimidating Medov's family.

Callan quickly realises that even though he's now at a senior level, he still can't get all the information he wants – particularly his own file.

Uniquely, Callan apologises to Cross – even if he does it with bad grace.

ALCOHOL, TOBACCO AND FIREARMS: Cross fires a rifle to smash a milk bottle in Alevtina's hand and carries a Magnum. This is the first appearance of Callan's own Magnum since he became Hunter, retrieved from the desk drawer where he stored it when he accepted the position. There's a lot of nervous smoking by Medov and Vasyayev.

SPY-SPEAK: Callan clearly has a low opinion of Cross: 'Nice mucky little job. Harassment. Right up your street, should enjoy it.'

Callan lets Bishop into a trade secret: 'I was trained to never take anyone or anything on trust. You start off with one simple premise: everything smells – yourself, the job you're doing and the man who tells you to do it. You're told something, you test the opposite.'

Lonely comes up with a colourful image to describe his conflicting Section duties: 'I'm like a bit of knicker elastic, stretched all ways.'

Wingfield paints a memorably unappetising picture of life in Moscow's British Embassy: 'All those unhealthy pure people... can't go out, chewing each other's toenails for sex.' He cheekily asks Callan, 'Are you too up in the world to load your own chamber?'

PAWNS AND PLAYERS: MIKE PRATT (1931-1976) was something of a renaissance man. As well as acting, he wrote sketches for revues and TV shows, performed with his folk group The Cotton Pickers and composed the hit single 'The Little White Bull' for the singer Tommy Steele. As an actor, Pratt impressed the *Danger Man* production team with a small part in 1965's 'The Ubiquitous Mr Lovegrove' and was promoted to larger roles in three other episodes; notably, he played a Russian intelligence clerk turned blackmailer in 'The Black Book'. Dying tragically early at 45, Pratt is fondly remembered for his starring role as the down-at-heel private detective Jeff Randall in the comedy drama *Randall and Hopkirk (Deceased)* (1969-1970). He appeared in the films *Repulsion* (1965) and *The Vault of Horror* (1973) and had a regular role as Don Stacey in *The Brothers* (1975-76).

JAMES COSSINS (1933-1997) specialised in haughty establishment characters. As the greedy Henry Lasindall, he brainwashed Tara King (Linda Thorson) in 'Pandora' (1969), a superior episode of *The Avengers'* sixth series that also featured Julian Glover. He had a regular part as desk sergeant Michaelson in early *Z Cars* (1962-63), but Cossins' most famous roles all come from the 1970s: the seedy Brown in the gangster movie *Villain* (1971), an exasperated outboard motor salesman in *Fawlty Towers* (1975, 1979) – 'Bordeaux is a claret' – and a pompous dinner guest in *The Sweeney* – 'Lady Luck' (1976).

TIMOTHY CARLTON (born 1939) also made a name for himself in upper class roles, beginning with the 1965-67 BBC series *The World of Wooster*. He played Gerard Mace in the Mediterranean drama *The Lotus Eaters* (1973) and his comic appearances include *Ripping Yarns* (1977), *Executive Stress* (1986) and *The Fall and Rise of Reginald Perrin* (1977-79, as Colin Pillock).Today, he is also well-known as the father of *Sherlock* actor Benedict Cumberbatch. Art imitated life in the third series in 2014, when Carlton and his wife Wanda Ventham played Sherlock's parents.

INFORMATION: There were several script changes, the biggest of which was the loss of the opening scene where Lonely pretends he's waiting for a call from his pregnant wife in a public call box. The comic highlight is when he calls Callan 'darling' on the phone.

Most of the other changes from the rehearsal script concerned Cross. He originally attacked Medov's car in a 'bowler and city gear' (and the camera script had him wearing 'a bowler hat and dark suit' when he shot the milk bottle from Alevtina's hand) and bet Callan £5 that Medov isn't a spy. The script directions make it clear that he allows himself to be seen by Medov's family, and when warned to 'keep clear of little girls' by Callan, the script says 'there is pain in Cross's eyes' and he threatens to make his superior 'apologise for that remark.' Originally, the episode was written to end on a freeze-frame of Cross's face 'showing fright, tears, despair, and self-disgust,' but his trauma in the final shot was considerably played down. Elsewhere, Medov and his family playing the word game *Scrabble*, Wingfield pointing a gun at Callan and the agent taking a call from Lambert House, then contacting Lonely on the radio, were all cut. In strong series continuity, there are references to Callan's exchange for Richmond in 'That'll Be the Day' and his promotion to Hunter in 'Call Me Sir!'

'It just means that he's less and less mobile!'[71] Jenkins laughed, discussing Callan's promotion to Hunter. 'It's rather nice, because what I liked about it was that he still retained the chippiness. He's now at the top, especially in his relationship with Cross, and he can put him down each time with slightly more authority, rather than sarcasm. [Having a sympathetic Russian was] precisely the kind of variation on a theme one was seeking all the time: the assumption would be that he would not be that way, and you turn it round. A writer's only real reason for existence is fighting cliché.'

Jenkins continued his tradition of writing game changing and/or controversial scripts for *Callan*, in the first of two episodes that revolve around Cross. 'You had to have a reason to get through that kind of facade that [he'd] built up,' the scriptwriter said. 'One presumes it's a facade, otherwise Cross is just a thug... One had to find something that would actually get through all the sheet metal reserve that's part of his job.' This led Jenkins into more contentious territory than ever, which was sensitively handled in 'Rules of the Game'. 'The idea of hurting a child came from a friend of mind in Ealing police,' he explained. 'I was researching something else at the time, we were having a pint and I said, "What is it that upsets policemen most of all?" It was the annual toy exhibition at Olympia, and hundreds and thousands kids go there to look at trains going round and all the rest of it, and of course it attracts every bloody child molester – it's their holiday time. [The police's] job there is to try and infiltrate them. There's very little tolerance of child molesters, and my mate said that's what upsets the police the most: somebody who hurts a child.'

Jenkins made his own contribution to the series' continuity with Lambert House, which also appeared in the following episode. 'That was just functional. I didn't want to believe that these guys, who were fit and everything else, just went along to some dusty little office in Whitehall, although I'm sure there are places [like that]... James [Mitchell] invented a place where they shot guns, a firing alley, and Lambert House was a tuning-up area, a gymnasium [and holding area]. I don't think it was regarded as a major contribution in the sense that everybody would have to go there. I just used it as I wanted to use it.'

Returning to direct his second *Callan* story, Voytek included a tribute to one of his favourite film directors, Alfred Hitchcock: '[As] Callan was coming in to search the flat, I thought it would be more menacing to show we know there is somebody there; then we show Callan can't find that person and thinks maybe he's in the shower, a *Psycho* [1960] tribute. Then someone comes out and smashes a mirror in his face! I tried to wait it out as long as possible.'[72] 'Rules of the Game' also included the disturbing interrogation of Wingfield by the new Hunter. 'He was trying to disorientate him,' Voytek explained. 'Cossins was particularly good at this trembling fear, the implicit fear that he could be drowned in the basin. Callan wasn't hitting him hard, just enough to make him scared.' The director recalled that the unpleasant sound of Danera's head being hit by Cross was simulated using a cabbage: 'Sometimes if you hear [something] it's more effective than actually seeing it.'

Wingfield's theft of a coat hanger from an East European hotel room, made from the same alloy as a new jet fighter, was based on a real incident that story editor George Markstein knew about.

It's curious that Wingfield refers to Callan as 'David, my old Dillinger,' as the Depression-era gangster only had one charge of murder against him, which was never proven. However, John Dillinger (1903-1934) and his gang did rob 24 banks and four post offices in their crime spree across America. Perhaps Wingfield is reminded of Dillinger because the criminal bore more than a passing resemblance to Edward Woodward.

Wingfield mentions World Cup Willie, a football playing, cartoon lion, that was the mascot designed for the 1966 World Cup, the first time such an emblem was used. Every World Cup since has had one.

Kim Philby gets another mention. The Medovs have a bust of Karl Marx in their hall.

MISSION ANALYSIS: *'Spy wife...'* Compared to the previous two episodes, Ray Jenkins' screenplay has a much more sombre mood, in a slow-moving character drama that has fatal implications beyond the end of the episode.

With a convincing Russian accent, Mike Pratt's prematurely-aged, chain-smoking Medov suggests a man worn out by paranoid Embassy life – even his bedroom is bugged – and concern for his family. In a subtle performance, he's sharp enough to play on that paranoia and make his colleague Vasyayev think that he *might* be a deep cover KGB agent, a ploy that keeps the audience guessing until the end of the episode. Medov's exact opposite in the tit-for-tat politicking is Dennis Wingfield, an upper-class spy in the Guy Burgess mould, brought to life in an enjoyably mannered performance by James Cossins. Wingfield is a single, *louche* character totally at ease in the amoral world of espionage while Medov, a devoted family man, has that family destroyed by his dealings with the security services. At the end of the episode, it's doubly ironic that the Russian believes the Section's harassment was designed to make him defect, as he really is just a cultural attaché.

And then there's Cross. Callan's statement that his subordinate is a good agent 'providing he keeps away from the little girls' is shocking even by today's standards, and it's significant that Callan makes this remark just after he's been reading Cross's Section file. The revelation adds a worrying slant to Cross's plan to kidnap Danera, Medov's young daughter, particularly after Callan learns that Cross has been following her for some time. Although the implications of Callan's comment are never followed up, young women are clearly a weakness for the younger agent. After he's clubbed Danera into a coma, the last shot of the episode is of Cross, grim-faced and brooding, standing outside her room at Lambert House; he's a man who's been heading for a fall for some time.

Cerebral and disturbing, 'Rules of the Game' is memorable for the very human story at the centre of its Cold War politics that, given the series' track record with innocent bystanders, inevitably ends in tragedy.

S4.5 IF HE CAN, SO COULD I

Writer: Ray Jenkins
Director: Peter Duguid
Designer: Mike Hall

FIRST UK TRANSMISSION: Wednesday 29 March 1972, 9.00 pm

CAST: Morris Perry (Vadim/Burov), John Abineri (Cuthbertson), Andrew Burt (Foster), Alan Chuntz (Sato), Peter Blythe (Trofimchuk), Vicky Williams (Karen), David Hargreaves (Harris)

EXTRAS/WALK-ONS: (*Uncredited on screen*) Film: Reg Cranfield (College Porter), Patrick Gorman (Male Nurse)

Studio: (Through Associated Plays and Players): George Romanov (Rodovic), John Scott-Martin (College Scout), Armourer (Evan Ross), Dennis Plenty (Harris), Patrick Gorman (Male nurse)

PRODUCTION

Rehearsals: From Thursday 30 February 1971
Location Filming: Cloisters and School Yard at Eton College; large gymnasium on Common Lane, Eton (Friday 31 December 1971); Cloisters and School Yard at Eton College; large gymnasium on Common Lane, Eton; Godolphin House, Eton; Old Town Hall, Market Street, Windsor (Monday 3 January 1972)
Camera Rehearsals/Recording: Teddington Studio One, Wednesday and
Thursday 13 January 1971[73]

TV TIMES: 'The instability of Cross becomes a grave problem, to which only he can provide an answer. But Cross's solution precisely concerns Callan's future.'
25-31 March 1972, Southern edition

MISSION PROFILE: Callan orders Cross to be re-evaluated by Snell, as he's worried the younger agent might be physically and mentally unfit for duty. At the same time, Bishop orders Callan to investigate the trade missionary Lev Leonidovitch Vadim, suspected of really being the Ukrainian executioner Illich Burov. Meres is put on the case, and he and Callan realise that near the route Vadim takes across the country, the Ukrainian poet Trofimchuk lives in exile in Cambridge, so he could be a potential target for assassination. Put back on duty, Cross is assigned to protect Trofimchuk, but the young Section agent is shot and killed by Burov. In the Red Alert that follows, against standing orders Callan leaves the Section, pursues Burov and shoots him dead. Callan's belief that Cross just forgot his training is crushed when Snell discovers eighteen books in Cross's flat, all marked with passages about suicide.

A MAN LIKE ME: Ironically, Callan finds himself in the same situation the previous Hunter was in 'Where Else Could I Go?': reassessing a once effective, now potentially unreliable agent. He even points out the parallels between his own past and Cross's current position to Snell. He barely tolerates the doctor, finding his clinical psychological insight unnerving. Callan admits that he's on Cross's side, even though he doesn't like it. Callan is experienced in martial arts, referring to the fist strike '*Atimi*' Cross uses in his fight with the Section martial arts expert Sato.

Typically, once Cross has been killed, Callan takes the law into his own hands. He authorises Meres to use extreme force to get information from a Russian agent and, despite being ordered to stand down by Bishop, kills Burov himself. Although they disliked each other, Callan evidently felt loyal to Cross as a member of the Section for whom he was responsible.

He also clearly empathised with him on a professional level. Drunk and rambling – and, significantly, in a much more down market flat rather than the one in Mayfair – Callan admits to Lonely that he was on a firing squad during the Malayan Emergency, executing ten native prisoners with 'the hardest man I've ever met.' To control and protect himself he learned to be like this soldier. At his most vulnerable, Callan holds on to Lonely for emotional support, clinging to the belief that Cross forgot his training and didn't crack up. The next day, a hung-over Callan is visibly distressed when he learns from Snell that Cross *was* planning to kill himself.

Section Kills: 21

LONELY: He's only in one scene, but more than any other in the series, it's the defining moment of his relationship with Callan: apart from the twisted psychology of needing someone to abuse and dominate, above all Callan needs someone to talk to.

Going from a typically inane Lonely comment about breaking his jaw by yawning, the little man elicits pathos by helping Callan sit up when he's drunk, and even though he doesn't really understand his friend's emotional trauma, he silently weeps in sympathy.

A TIE AND A CREST: Bishop has to authorise Cross's removal from a White File so he can go back on duty. Later, when Callan disobeys standing orders by leaving the Section HQ and klls Burov without authorisation, Bishop has the authority to suspend him from active service. However, during the emergency he helps the team go through address lists to track the hitman down.

Cross uses another alias, 'Lever'. Other Section agents are seen and referred to: Foster, Harris and Patterson respectively. The Section has a forensic department and the power to draft in the civil police to work on their investigations.

ALCOHOL, TOBACCO AND FIREARMS: Meres pulls Cross's own gun on him, which he shouldn't have left behind in his flat. The two men have the same score with electronic guns on the Section's firing range: three bulls and three inners. Switching to real guns – Magnums – aiming for 'one to the head, five to the heart', Meres rates 3.8 seconds while Cross scores 4.1 seconds.

For the first time since becoming Hunter, Callan uses his own Magnum to kill. Agonising over Cross's death, he gets drunk on Scotch.

SPY-SPEAK: Cross isn't fooling Meres: 'There's something rather sad, James, about people who keep saying "There's nothing wrong with me".'

Bishop makes a characteristically sardonic assessment of Snell: 'That quack even smiles like a breast fed Nazi.' 'You mean he smiles?' Callan replies. (Ironically Rose himself felt that Snell was reminiscent of the Auschwitz physician Josef Mengele.[74])

Trofimchuk expresses his melancholy to Cross: 'When did you last... eat a meal that

wasn't always good, or weep, just weep, because the girl in your bed was *so beautiful?* Drink wine – cold wine – in hot summer? Take off your clothes in a hurry? "Shades of the prison house begin to close upon the growing boy." We are grown. We are dead... Prison.'

PAWNS AND PLAYERS: JOHN ABINERI (1928-2000) was another character actor rarely out of work between the 1960s and 1980s. In the second Harry Palmer film *Funeral in Berlin* (1966), he played the German burglar Otto Ruke, who Harry employs to rob a suspect. For the BBC, Abineri was the head of a crime syndicate, as well as a politician even more right-wing than Amos Green, at the end of the first series of *Gangsters* (1977), before taking the regular role of the devious Hubert in *Survivors* (over 1977-78). Abineri also featured in *Spy Trap* (1972) and appeared in seventeen episodes of *Doctor Who* between 1968 and 1978.

ALAN CHUNTZ (1927-2009) was, like Billy Cornelius, a bit-part actor-come-stunt-man, who began his career being knocked down some stairs by Patrick McGoohan in the *Danger Man* story 'I Can Only Offer You Sherry' (1966). He went on to perform stunts, act and advise on action scenes for series that included *The Avengers, Fox* (1980), *Gangsters* (in 1978) and *Hazell* (in 1979). Chuntz was also part of the specialist company HAVOC, who provided most of the stunts for Jon Pertwee's time in *Doctor Who* in the early 1970s. For the big screen, he worked on the 007 epic *You Only Live Twice* (1967) and the Dan Ackroyd comedy *Spies Like Us* (1985). 'He looked good... he looked like a killer,'[75] Peter Duguid recalled. 'There weren't many people around in those days who had the skills. He was very helpful. Indeed, he went on to do all sorts... I used him several times, including on *King and Castle* [1986].'

JOHN SCOTT MaRTIN (1926-2009) was regularly employed as a monster in *Doctor Who*, playing Daleks, Zarbi, a Mire Beast and a Mark 3 Servo Robot ('Charlie') between 1965 and 1988.

INFORMATION: Reg Collin emphasised that the decision to kill Cross wasn't to make room for the returning Meres: 'It wasn't a *Crossroads* situation where you have to kill off a character...It was [more] a deliberate attempt to show members of the department are killed from time to time. Otherwise, you have a department that is absolutely marvellous, that goes round killing everybody else, but never gets any damage itself! There were other reasons as well; Patrick went on to do a film.'[76] 'I'm a great believer if something happens to a regular character then it comes as a shock,'[77] George Markstein felt. 'Fourteen million viewers switch on their sets believing the characters in a regular series are sacrosanct, and nothing will ever happen to them. I think it's marvellous if in episode seventeen there's somebody blown sky high – it unsettles [the audience] for weeks!' *Callan*'s creator James Mitchell had no say in Cross's death: 'They don't ask your permission for anything! You discuss it but I had no veto.'[78] 'There was a bit of worry about [the episode's title], that people wouldn't understand it, although it was ultimately kept,'[79] Ray Jenkins remembered. For obvious reasons, it's the last time Patrick Mower's name appears in the opening titles.

Between the rehearsal script and the completed story, the scene in the shooting gallery had a significant change: Meres and Cross originally used an electronic gun each to shoot at a TV screen showing a picture of a child. Snell had an amusing, if uncharacteristic, line of dialogue that was dropped: 'as Callan would say – dodgy.' Other cuts include a presumptuous Meres sitting at Hunter's desk, and Callan and Liz sitting at Section HQ,

motionless, waiting for a report from Cambridge. After Cross is shot, Liz opens her desk drawer to look at a picture of him, then touches his file. In the script directions, it was made clear that Cross is 'magnetised by the sound' of Karen, but the finished episode is more ambiguous. The young agent was originally shot through the head and when his body falls into the courtyard, 'Karen runs round and round in circles, screaming.'

Some revealing dialogue was cut from Callan's drunken speech to Lonely. In the rehearsal and camera scripts, he rages: 'Have you ever, ever, ever seen a shot skull?! [which was replaced in the camera script with 'Have they ever, ever, ever had to stand in front of a man and shoot him?'] – neat in the front, yeah – but look at the ravage at the back – the security of killing – he must be bloody joking!... Yeah, the micro-second matters – I know that, Cross knows it – so you don't let anything get on your mind, you *don't*. You train so you don't – you can't!' He then reveals to Lonely a microphone hidden behind a picture on the wall: the Section have bugged the flat. 'And if I'm being recorded – listen! Snell! I'm telling you – you don't end up enjoying it – you can't! You're too shit-scared!'

The story grew out of Ray Jenkins' interest in contemporary politics and military history. 'It was related to Rudi Dutschke [1940-1979], a German student activist who got shot in the head and came to Cambridge in 1968,' the writer said. 'What fascinated me was, one minute he's a rabble-rouser on the streets, the next he's being looked after in a setting which is very, very comfortable and highly-charged intellectually. I also remember reading a thing about the First World War and the number of people who were killed by sniper's bullets, on the Western front. [The snipers] only showed themselves for a fraction of a second, and then they were gone. If you showed yourself for longer than a fraction of a second, which was diametrically opposed to what you'd been trained to do, you'd end up dead. One presumes, then, that [Cross] had things on his mind and that was it.' The death of the young Section agent had an amusing postscript. 'I had an extremely funny letter from a lady in Eastbourne,' Jenkins chuckled, 'and she had this immortal line in it: "Why couldn't Callan have given him the kiss of life?"!'

A literate and complex script, in a first for *Callan*, 'If He Can, So Could I' also had a philosophical dimension. 'That was Camus' line, that "suicide is the only genuine philosophical problem",' Jenkins elaborated. 'Very simply, the argument is that in an absurdist world, if you've got rid of God, then you've got rid of the person making decisions for you. If no one's making a decision for you, and you are the sum of your own decisions – straightforward existentialism – then the only way you can act as God is to terminate your own existence. Therefore, you become God by committing suicide.'

For various reasons, the episode was one of Woodward's favourites. 'It was a *very* dark episode. It's not joyous in any way: it's about murder, it's about the *pressure* on people at certain times, in this kind of job, that there must have been and must still be. Callan has been promoted to Hunter and he *hates* it, he *loathes* it.'[80] The actor was particularly impressed by the set-piece fight between Cross and Sato. 'It took a long time, I remember. They did a tremendous amount of work on it, and Patrick was extraordinarily good at it... This, to me, isn't about action, because Snell says at the very beginning of the sequence, "If he loses his temper, he's dead" or "If he loses his temper, he's out", so you are *waiting* for him to lose his temper. And he doesn't and he doesn't and he doesn't... I think it's extraordinarily exciting.' The highlight for Woodward, though, was the emotional scene between Lonely and a drunken Callan in the third act. 'It's one of the best we ever had. It's so unbelievably well written. What's fascinating about it is what Russell does with it. Those are natural tears – nobody came in with stuff to put in [his] eyes. The tears are rolling down his cheeks,

and you suddenly realise what a relationship Callan and Lonely have. It's an inseparable relationship and one depends entirely on the other, for some strange reason. Callan needs Lonely as a sounding board and Lonely requires Callan as a friend and somebody who gives him money. It was hard to learn, because it was all one long take. It gives you a tremendous insight into Callan, as he talks about being in the army in the past and the hard man that he met.' Reviewing the episode nearly 40 years later with his wife, Woodward was impressed that the scene retained its emotional power: 'Michele watched it today and tears were running down her face.'

'It was one of my favourite episodes,'[81] said Patrick Mower unsurprisingly. 'When they said they were going to kill [Cross] off, again this was not for me, it was to the end of making the Teddy Woodward character react: "Did he jump or was he pushed?" That was the implication. It caused a tremendous furore at the time. It was a very big shock, one of the favourite characters in a major TV production suddenly dying, and it was there for a purpose, to put pressure on Callan. If this hard, ruthless, dynamic, anti-heroic character could crack up under stress [Callan could too.]' Mower's dramatic exit only five episodes into what would be the final series of *Callan* was down to the actor's personal philosophy of always leaving the audience wanting more: 'I don't want to be involved in something that gets taken off because it's run its course,' he said. 'It's always best to leave something hanging in the air – quit whilst you're ahead – and I've done that all my career: *Target*, *Special Branch*... you leave and then hopefully they want more of you.' Intriguingly, Mower said he would have replaced Callan as the lead if Edward Woodward had wanted to move on. 'In retrospect, I would have said yes to that... [but] only because of the quality that was around, the quality of the writers like George Markstein, and the directors. It was a quality product, but [taking over] was never my ambition.'

'If He Can, So Could I' saw the fourth appearance of Clifford Rose in a story he nominates as '*easily* my favourite episode. I had a lot to do. It was a jolly good episode for Snell.'[81] Apart from the psychiatrist's central role, the story proved memorable for the actor because of production issues. 'In the cross-questioning of Cross, particularly in the shooting gallery, there were a lot of references to things that had happened before that Cross had done. Snell was trying to expose weaknesses in his character, [but] I didn't understand [the scene] at all: I referred to names and brought out photographs of various people. They gave me the scripts so I could find out [what had happened], but it's not *quite* the same as having seen it.'

However, the story wasn't without its lighter side for Rose: 'Peter Blythe was playing Trofimchuk and he was being kept in a room at Cambridge College. Callan arrived, from London presumably, to see him, or to get him. The room had a big door, and Callan had to beat on it. On the actual recording, when Callan hit it, it fell over flat on the floor into the set! They had to stop the recording for about 20 minutes and get the carpenters in to put the door back on its hinges properly. The door was meant to be locked, which made it even worse.'

Despite the enthusiasm of the cast for 'If He Can, So Could I', Peter Duguid had severe reservations about the story he made such an impact with. 'This was an unhappy script because the story editor insisted Cross would commit suicide, but nobody on my side of the fence could accept there was any motivational reason for doing that. It was nonsense – I would have the argument all over again. Cross was really being put through it, but the script was being cooked to support this fallacy that Cross could crack... It took George [Markstein] and I some years to patch up our falling out over that.'[83] Voytek agreed with his colleague: 'The story about Cross feeling guilty was awkward. Cross was a cold bastard: he would have sold his own mum. If he bashed someone's head in, he'd just write it off as a bad experience. Obviously if the series was written that way, that's the way you have to play it. It was hard for Patrick to find the *raison d'être*, being the character he was in the series, but he arrived at it.'[84] Mower himself also recalled arguing that Cross wouldn't kill himself, but conceded that it was 'nice to play the dual line of thought.'[85]

'The roof stuff [at] Eton was delicate,'[85] Duguid said of the principal filming location. 'It would have taken a film camera but not a whole unit; they were doing restoration work and it was full of scaffolding. We were worried whether we'd be allowed to do it. The wrestling stunt was done in their gym – and fucked up, actually! It took a day and [Patrick Mower] trained for a fortnight beforehand with [Alan Chuntz]. [Next day] I was filming with Morris Perry outside a loo in Windsor High Street and the police came up to me and said "Are you Thames Television – Peter Duguid?" "Yes." "Well, you've got to phone Euston immediately." There was a problem with all the film from the previous day: some lunatic had opened the can of film when it got back to Film Dispatch and it was ruined, so we had to grab the gym and set it up again for another half day's shooting.' The episode also featured the return of Peter Blythe, who Duguid had previously directed in 'The Most Promising Girl of Her Year': 'I used [him] a lot: he was a bloody good actor who wouldn't let you down. I don't cast actors, I cast the parts... you don't often in television have a very wide choice at your disposal.'

'If He Can, So Could I' was the most continuity-heavy episode of *Callan* made, with specific references to 'Where Else Could I Go?', 'Summoned to Appear', 'A Village Called "G"', 'Suddenly – At Home', 'Act of Kindness', 'Breakout' and 'Rules of the Game'. 'I'd read other people's scripts and I'd seen other episodes,'[87] Ray Jenkins confirmed. Despite this, Rose pronounces 'Medov' incorrectly and Kleist's alias Sabovski is incorrectly given as 'Jaborski' in the rehearsal and camera scripts. 'Well, there you go!' Ray Jenkins laughed. 'People are paid bloody salaries to be script editors, that means they edit scripts, right? It's not *my* bloody fault if there's a mega typing error. I'll accept no guilt. None at all!'

Apart from Albert Camus, the episode includes other diverse cultural references. Perhaps subconsciously, Callan quotes The Beatles' 'With a Little Help from My Friends' and mockingly refers to Meres as 'John the Baptist', the saint in the Bible who had the singular ability to baptise Christians and forgive their sins.

Trofimchuk quotes from the sad poem 'Intimations of Mortality from Recollections of Early Childhood' by William Wordsworth (1770-1850), published in 1807. He also mentions the Russian historical figures Alexander Pushkin (1799-1832) and Joseph Stalin (1879-1953). They represent the opposite ends of the Russian cultural spectrum: Pushkin was a nobleman who was a precociously talented writer – his first poem was published when he was fifteen – who was considered politically subversive by the Tsar and kept under surveillance by his secret police. Pushkin's most famous work is *Boris Godunov*, a drama based on the Tsar who ruled between 1598 and 1605. Joseph Stalin (1879-1953) became the dominant force in Soviet politics following the death of Vladimr Lenin (1870-1924), founder of the Russian Communist Party. Stalin's dictatorship enabled him to implement policies of centrally planned agriculture and industrialisation, but the downside to the regime were the purges of the 1930s in which millions were executed and sent to gulag labour camps. After WW2, Stalin's Russia became the second nuclear superpower, but following his death in 1953, his successor Nikita Khruschev (1894-1971) began a programme of de-Stalinisation and (comparatively) liberal reforms.

MISSION ANALYSIS: *'Big men have to snivel sometimes, Hunter.'* In this extraordinary episode, the suspense slowly builds from the first scene until the end, when Callan emotionally collapses with the knowledge that Cross was a suicide waiting to happen. Fittingly, Mower gives his best performance in the series, by turns restrained, angry, urbane, violent, and, crucially, suggesting emotional turmoil under a cool exterior he can barely hold in place any more. In a story where one of the lead characters dies – still something of a rarity[88] in 1970s television and, consequently, a major shared cultural event – every member of the large regular cast gets either a memorable scene or significant dialogue. Despite Duguid's reservations over the script, it is excellently realised and a memorable farewell for Patrick Mower.

What also makes 'If He Can, So Could I' special is the bleakly poetic way Jenkins equates Cross's mental disintegration and the demands of being a security agent with a loss of innocence. The series had touched on symbolism before, usually through Callan's war gaming and chess, but Jenkins and Duguid here take it to another level – using white and *red* chess pieces – with a finesse that perfectly complements the tougher elements of the story, such as the dream-like, slow motion fight between Cross and Sato.

The Ukrainian writer Trofimchuk likens growing up to prison, speaking in a college room that is large, spartan and lit like a cell. While he speaks, Cross is seen in close-up, eyes closed, in a remarkable piece of expressionistic camera work. Innocence being destroyed by the harsh, adult world is alluded to: Cross is taunted by the waxwork of a female child with a bullet hole in its head, designed to remind him of the comatose Danera. Later, the young girl Karen, who spots the assassin Burov on the college roof, witnesses Cross being murdered. The loss of virtue is also there in the amazing scene where Callan recounts to Lonely how his younger self had to grow up fast after being assigned to a firing squad. It's an astonishing piece of acting by Woodward, simultaneously angry, aggressive and vulnerable. At the same time, Russell Hunter's stock rises even higher because of Lonely's achingly sincere reaction.

The best episode of *Callan*? Debatable. However, mixing a finely-crafted spy drama about people under intense pressure with metaphorical direction and dialogue, this story is such a perfect summation of *Callan*'s themes, preoccupations and tensions that, in some ways, it's a shame that Ray Jenkins' best script for the programme wasn't the series' final episode.

S4.6 NONE OF YOUR BUSINESS

Writer: Trevor Preston
Director: Voytek
Designer: Stan Woodward

FIRST UK TRANSMISSION: Wednesday 5 May 1972, 9.00 pm

CAST: Tony Selby (Lucas), Peter Eyre (West), David Black (Whitman), Brian Murphy (Reeves), Wendy Hamilton (Stella), Donald Webster (Dorman), James Walker (Mealing)

EXTRAS/WALK-ONS: (*Uncredited on screen*) Film (From the Blyth Agency): John Laker (Vowden/Body), Terence Sartain (Policeman), Tony Woolley (Ambulance Attendant), Nicole Yerna (Victim), Eileen Day, Pat Dooley (Shoppers), Laurie Goode (in Gallery); from Associated Plays and Players: Archie Wilson, Charles S. Hesketh, Vi Kane, Reg Cranfield, Michael Moore, Willie Bowman, John Tatham, Colin Cunningham, Aubrey Danvers Walker, Brychan Powell, George Hancock, Ernest Blyth, Lewis Alexander, Aileen Lewis, Ursula Granville, Naomi Sandford, Cy Town, Ron Tingley, Diana Chapman (Bridge Players), Steve Tierney, Walter Goodman (Chefs)*, Joyce Freeman, Ann Evans (Ladies on Stairs), Bill Matthews (Man on Stairs). Studio (From Associated Plays and Players: John Cannon (Car Salesman)

* *Only one is seen on screen*

PRODUCTION

Rehearsals: From Thursday 27 February 1972
Location Filming: Down Hall Road, Kingston; Martin Motors, 43-47 Richmond Road, Kingston, Surrey; Riverside Drive, off Upper Ham Road, Richmond, Surrey (Monday 31 January 1972); Lorry Car Park, Richmond Road, Kingston; No. 11, Paved Court, off Richmond Green, Richmond, Surrey (Tuesday 1 February 1972); Asgill House, Old Palace Lane, Richmond, Surrey (Wednesday 2 February 1972)
Camera Rehearsals/Recording: Teddington Studio One, Wednesday 9 and Thursday 10 February 1972[89]

TV TIMES: 'How easy is it to get a false passport? Even Callan has difficulty, but when he solves the problem, he finds he has also broken a ring for getting enemy agents out of the country.'
1-7 April 1972, Southern edition

MISSION PROFILE: Callan wants to go abroad but is denied access to his passport, which is kept at the Section. At the same time, Meres has discovered that a university lecturer named West is involved in the forging of passports and other documents, enabling a KGB executioner named Jonas Vowden, 'responsible for at least three killings, two of whom were women', to enter Britain. Looking for a way out of the country, Callan contacts a forging organisation fronted by the cockney crook Lucas. Working independently, both Callan and Meres realise an art gallery owner named Black has been forging the passports Lucas sells. He's also been charging high prices to make extra money over and above what he agreed with the KGB. Black and West are killed by Reeves, a Soviet agent, who is later captured by Callan and Meres.

A MAN LIKE ME: Perhaps due to the stress of recent months, Callan's hair is now completely iron grey. For the last time, Callan is seen in one of the bespoke tailored suits and overcoats he was able to afford when he was Hunter. He dutifully pays his respects at Cross's funeral, gives vent to his anger when confronted by Bishop's clinical attitude to Cross's death and, by his standards, thinks he did act correctly in the Burov affair. Completely ignoring orders to stay in Britain (he hasn't had a proper holiday for seven years), Callan tries to find an illegal way to leave the country. This shows his anti-establishment attitude is again to the fore; he doesn't stand up in the presence of the fourth Hunter when he returns to the Section, even though Meres and Stafford do.

Callan's ambivalence towards Lonely is re-established when he punches him for giving away his address and allowing one of his WW2 German soldier models to be stolen from his display cabinet. Callan's time behind Hunter's desk clearly hasn't dulled his skills as an agent, as he quickly and aggressively deals with Lucas's heavy, Dorman. He's concerned about how Liz is coping after Cross's death and is astonished that she won't help him with his passport. Clearly, her loyalty to and liking for him only goes so far.

Despite his demotion, Callan is billeted in a considerably less run-down flat than in the past. The number of his new home is '4' (a possible in-joke, as this is the fourth series). Callan uses his Tucker alias again.

LONELY: Found asleep in the MCF under a newspaper and abruptly woken by Callan pressing the horn, he typically complains about a 'dodgy pump' and suggests, unconvincingly, that he was 'checking on the upholstery and the vehicle suspension.' Unsurprisingly considering what happened to him in 'You Should Have Got Here Sooner', he seems more scared of Meres than Callan, going along with Toby's order not allow his friend access to the taxi (at least initially). It seems that Lonely is always destined to be caught in a cycle of violence, as both Dorman and Callan assault him. He's more nervous than usual, dropping his shopping in his flat when Callan surprises him.

Either trying to improve his sex life or being voyeuristic (or both), Lonely reads a magazine article entitled 'The Mouth and Oral Sex'.

A TIE AND A CREST: Even though he doesn't say anything, Meres is clearly unhappy about the former Hunter coming back to run the Section again, as it derails his own designs on the top job. Callan and Meres attend a Bridge Club, with Toby in black tie and dinner jacket, while Callan, notably, wears a conventional suit and tie. 'Do you play Bridge?' Meres enquires. 'No, just Snap and Happy Families,' Callan replies, deadpan.

The laconic Stafford becomes irritated by West scraping cutlery while he eats a meal under house arrest. Later, the pair get on better as West starts teaching the agent Bridge, before unexpectedly dropping dead as his food was poisoned.

Emphasising Callan's demotion, by the end of the episode he's back working for his previous boss. Liz, meanwhile, has become Lonely's agony aunt.

ALCOHOL, TOBACCO AND FIREARMS: The fourth Hunter and Callan share an expensive whisky, and when his former boss leaves before finishing his drink, Callan pours the remainder into his glass. He doesn't approve of the 'ratbag' Scotch Bishop (who usually drinks sherry) brought into the Section. Lucas quaffs from the bottle of another brand, kept on his desk. Later, he nervously smokes a fag while he waits for Callan.

Section-issue guns are frequently on display.

SPY-SPEAK: Callan harangues Bishop over his dispassionate attitude to Cross's murder: 'Mr. Bishop, I would give *anything – dear God, anything!* – to have put you up on that roof with Burov, just for one minute. *Just so you can see what it's really like out there!* Just so we could get one second of total commitment, *from you!*'[90]

Meres delights in telling West how he's been exploited: 'You've been used. Conned. Shafted. Your white charger has turned out to be a three-legged donkey!'

Callan to a post-slumber Lonely: 'You look almost human when you're asleep.'

Lucas has a low opinion of Reeves: 'What a schpunker. I've got his bleeding heart all over my carpet.' The middle man is uncertain of Black's sexual preferences: 'I always thought he was a bit AC/DC, if you know what I mean.' 'Yeah, I know what you mean,' Callan wearily replies.

One cut scene at the Bridge club has Callan and Meres rushing past a bystander who remarks, 'Gracious, they're in a hurry, aren't they?'

PAWNS AND PLAYERS: PETER EYRE (born 1942) is an American-born actor who has made a reputation for himself in Britain through his distinguished stage work for the Royal Shakespeare Company, National Theatre and the Old Vic. In the same year as 'None of Your Business', he starred in Tom Stoppard's *Rosencrantz and Guildenstern are Dead*; two years later, he took the lead role in *Hamlet* for the Greenwich Theatre. Eyre's television work includes James Mitchell's BBC series *Spyship* (1983), in which he played the ruthless intelligence officer Francis Main.

TONY SELBY's (born 1932) portrayal of Lucas is virtually a dummy run for his performance as the rather nastier wide-boy robber Tony Lyon in *The Sweeney* story 'Queen's Pawn' (1975). Selby more or less cornered the market in cockney Jack-the-Lad parts, in films and series such as *Villain* (1971), *Adolf Hitler – My Part in His Downfall* (1972), *Ace of Wands* (1970-71), *Special Branch* (1973) and *Love Hurts* (1992-94). He also became well-known as the drill instructor Corporal Marsh in the RAF sitcom *Get Some In!* (1975-78). One of his first TV roles was in James Mitchell's 'Soldier in the Snow', an ITV *Play of the Week* in 1961.

BRIAN MURPHY (born 1933) is fondly remembered for his comic roles, especially that of the hen-pecked George Roper opposite Yootha Joyce in the sitcom *Man about the House* (1973-6), a part which continued in the spin-off series *George and Mildred* (1976-9). 'Chemistry is one of those things you can't plan,'[91] Murphy said of his partnership with Joyce. 'You get two good actors together and they don't always hit it off. It's lucky. It was unlucky that Yootha died so young, she was only 53... The humour was cheeky, but it wasn't in your face, we didn't spell it out. It was for all the family. I used to get letters from three year-olds saying they hoped George hadn't hurt himself falling off that ladder!' In the film spin-off in 1980, Murphy was paired with Hugh Walters as a camp hotel waiter. Scandalised that Mildred is in the hotel's casino, Walters' character says, 'What do you think they do in there? Play snakes and ladders for Smarties?' For several years, Murphy was in the pensioner comedy *Last of the Summer Wine* and more recently he appeared in the first series of the ITV2 comedy *Plebs* (2013).

DONALD WEBSTER played a biker in *The Avengers*' 'generation gap' episode 'Build a Better Mousetrap' (1964). He was also one of the heavies in Sam Peckinpah's violent thriller *Straw Dogs* (1971), which features T.P. McKenna.

INFORMATION: '*Callan* got more sophisticated,'[92] Preston considered of a series that had by now been on the air for over four years. 'Different writers came in. It got more middle class; it changed quite a bit. It was still a good character to punt around. I actually preferred the *Callan*s at the beginning of the series when I wasn't writing on it, the same as I preferred the early *Avengers* episodes. Things only change when the writers take it along, and the writers are briefed by the producer. What I used *Callan* for, which was marvellous, was to find out if I could write television and make a living at it, which I found I could. Otherwise, I'd have gone back on the scaffolding!'

The inspiration for Lucas and Dorman came from real South London criminals Trevor Preston knew. '[One] was a real hard working printer. He was a very clever man who made a lot of money. The stuff he used to print was quite rare – to forge a passport, say, because you can't get the paper – but he could do anything that passed muster as long as there was nobody really heavy that knew about it. If you'd had your licence taken away three for speeding, he used to do these wonderful Maltese driving licences. He also used to [forge] VAT forms. They were perfect: it was like looking at a Leonardo! I know one guy he knew was caught because he owed £300,000 in VAT; he got this printer to do one of those forms. Now he's skipped the country and he's running a shirt factory.'[93]

'There was this other guy, a real friend, but wherever he went, he couldn't help stealing something. It didn't have to be silver spoons, he just had to always take something. My wife used to say, "Is he coming round?", hide all the valuables and tell me, "You keep your eye on him!" I used to have three rules when [friends] came in the house: No violence, no drugs at all, nobody thieves. And these were my best mates!'

The story mentions the real Whitcombe Street in Finchley. 'I always try and use actual places,'[94] Preston said. 'I usually got them out of the *A-Z*!' The inclusion of Bridge, that West tries to teach Stafford to play and which appears in the story's climax, was borne out of Preston's frustration with the sophisticated card game. 'Jim Goddard was potty about Bridge and he started trying to teach me. I couldn't understand a word of it.'[95] Contract Bridge was thought to have originated from the Russian community in Istanbul in 1886 (perhaps explaining why the KGB agent 'Reeves' is an enthusiast.) 'Bridge' is the English translation of 'Binirche' and the game is also known as Russian Whist. An extremely complex and demanding game, it's played with a 52 card deck by four players in two opposing couples.

Voytek brought some of his wartime experience to bear on the fight scene between Callan and Dorman: 'When I was a kid in the resistance you were told, "You do not go for the high kicks or kung fu, you do not start fisticuffs, you pick up and use anything in reach as a weapon. Don't use your hands because if you cripple your hands, you've had it. Use a box of matches if you have to!"'[96] During the sequence, he directed Woodward to 'just kick over the table and spill [food] on [Dorman's] lap.' The criminal was intended to look 'respectable,' Voytek adds. 'We said, first of all, he should look like the Kray brothers, in a suit. We wanted quiet menace. Donald Webster... put on weight for the part but he had so many clothes on he was quite formidable anyway.'

It was Voytek's first time directing Anthony Valentine: '[He] introduced a different note into the story because he was the ambitious bloke trying to take Callan's place. Peter Eyre was an interesting actor too; he'd present himself as vulnerable to physical onslaught and nervousness [as Meres] walked round him... I tried to make it as tense as possible, visually trying to increase the pressure on him. Brian Murphy was great fun, and Tony Selby was another great friend for a long time.' The backdrop of the Bridge party to the story's climax was another example of the production team grounding the series in realism. 'We were trying to present reality,' Voytek suggested, 'and make a drama where there's a couple living in Surbiton for 45 years, they've got a cat and a dog, they're friends with the vicar, and then you discover they've been carting tons of microprocessors out of the naval establishment or whatever. You could present the two different images [together].'

Initially in the script, Meres and Hunter did not recognise each other when the latter arrived to resume control of the Section and, emphasising Meres' anger at not becoming the next Section chief, he slammed the office door as he left.

William Squire's name reappears in the opening titles and remains there until the end of the series. Returning as Stafford after three episodes, Paul Williamson had mixed feelings about the story's director: 'Voytek was a designer and he went for what things looked like, not necessarily what the actors would go for, which would be the truth of the story. He was all right.'[97] Conversely, guest actor Brian Murphy was pleased to be cast as the KGB agent Reeves. 'I remember [Callan and Meres] picked me up in the [Bridge] rooms when they spotted me,'[98] he said. 'I enjoyed it, and it was nice that they didn't cast me in a comic role, because the director knew what else I'd done, like Z Cars and the early Avengers with Ian Hendry. I'd met Edward Woodward before when we were working in theatre. Those were good days for television, because you rehearsed. They don't rehearse anything now: it's instant, and either it works and you get by, or you stumble and it doesn't.'

In the TV Times for the week 'None of Your Business' was transmitted, an overdue question was finally asked: 'Callan – Fact or Fiction?'[99] The magazine sought answers from Miles Copeland, an ex-CIA agent who had worked in the Middle East with British intelligence, including one Kim Philby[100]. Copeland felt strongly that 'A unit like the Section could not exist in any intelligence service. It would not be tolerated, nor would some of the things that Callan gets up to. Also the situations that he confronts each week would not happen to a real agent over a space of five years... No secret service would draw its men from prison or the criminal world... British intelligence groups do not use British agents for Callan's sort of espionage. They would use foreigners, like Egyptians perhaps.' Conversely, the ex-spy had nothing but praise for the dramatic standards of the TV series: 'the characterisation is excellent, and the programme is easily the best thing on television.'

Reg Collin offered a persuasive defence in the same article. 'The activities of any secret service are, for obvious security reasons, secret,' he replied. 'And, while Callan's role cannot be fully proved, it also cannot be disproved... We are trying to be as authentic as possible about something for whose authenticity nobody can really vouch. It would appear that organisations like [the Section] are used in certain other countries, and therefore it's difficult to think that we British would be loathe to involve ourselves in the same shady business.'

Picking up on Copeland's comment about British intelligence not using British agents for 'dirty tricks', Collin said: 'It seems reasonable to us that they would use a Briton. We've always laughed at the Carruthers type who is told: "Remember, old chap, if you get into trouble, we won't be able to stand by you." Callan always questions his assignments and basically loathes killing – but he's prepared to do it for something he believes in.

'Callan and the others are not sadistic – the Russian Roulette sequence involving Cross and Lonely, in the first episode of the new series, is about as far as that sort of thing goes. Another point to bear in mind is that a foreigner employed by British intelligence is less likely to be loyal to his job and his superiors. However, Mr Copeland's comment on this has already been acknowledged in the new series, with the admission by Soviet security people that the man they used to kill Callan [in 'Call Me Sir!'] was "not one of ours" – in other words, he was not a Russian.'

MISSION ANALYSIS: *'Mr Bishop, you can take your suspension and work it right up your –'* This is an engaging pause between the two main phases of Series Four, Callan's tenure as Hunter and his return to being a field agent. The story is the flipside to the previous year's 'Summoned to Appear', also by Preston, as this time the writer examines what happens when the Section becomes mixed up with criminals rather than the police. With his knowledge of the South London underworld, Preston adds to the believable rogues' gallery of the series with Tony Selby's perpetually smiling Lucas, a man who thinks he can talk his way out of anything, and his minder, Dorman. In stark contrast to the violence Dorman visits on Lonely, the thug reveals an unexpected softer side, singing 'The Grand Old Duke of York' and stealing one of Callan's soldiers for his one of his children. Preston's blue-collar background also offers a memorable scene of class war between Callan and Bishop.

It's a great episode for the regulars, with Valentine clearly enjoying the limelight in his solo scenes where he has to drive the story forward; the moment where Meres realises, silently, that he won't be the next Hunter is equally memorable. Lisa Langdon also shines, carrying on with her Section duties to try and cope with Cross's death. It speaks volumes that if she went on leave, as Callan suggests, she wouldn't know what to do with herself. There's also a well observed moment of realism, as Bishop – temporarily running the Section – gets food poisoning and the previous Hunter has to cover for him. Casting against type also works to the story's benefit. Initially seen portraying the downtrodden archetype that he would perfect later in the 1970s, Brian Murphy makes an unexpectedly effective and literate opposition agent.

The criminal slant gives the story an unusual if less intense feel after the interwoven drama of the previous five episodes, emphasised by the pursuit of a KGB agent through a very upper-class Bridge party in Part Three. With Callan demoted back to a field agent by the end, the revival of the Meres/Callan double act feels almost reassuring, as does the reinstatement of the fourth Hunter. A more subdued restatement of intent is seen in how the Section are once again out-thinking and manipulating their best man: the final scene reveals that Callan's passport was out of date all the time.

S4.7 CHARLIE SAYS IT'S GOODBYE

Writer: James Mitchell
Director: Peter Duguid
Designer: David Marshall

FIRST UK TRANSMISSION: Wednesday 12 April 1972, 9.00 pm

CAST: Dennis Price (James Palliser), Beth Harris (Susan Morris), Richard Morant (Trent), John G. Heller (Komorowski), Alison Hughes (Shop assistant)
   Uncredited on screen: Richard Eden (Carter), Daniel Jones (French voiceover), 'Curly' (Cab Driver – Lonely's Driving Double)

EXTRAS/WALK-ONS: (*Uncredited on screen*) From the Roberta Kanal Agency: Judith Ferency, Clare West (Polish Models/Hotel Guests), Yona Gallit, Lorna Kilner (Visitors to Fair), Douglas Mann (Page Boy/Visitor to Fair), Angela Graham (Visitor to Fair/Shop Customer), Jean Moran, Yvette Ray, Richard Atherton, Roy Lansford, Audrey Searle, David Melbourne, Sandra Hale, Donald Groves (Visitors to Fair/Hotel Guests), Section Guards (Peter Spraggon, Peter Roy)
   From the HAVOC agency: Betty Wheeler, Veronica Griffiths, (Shop Customers), Les Conrad (Police Sergeant), Mike Stevens (PC)

PRODUCTION

Rehearsals: From Friday 11 February 1972.
Outside Broadcast Recording: Empty shop (No. 2), Castle Street, Kingston-on-Thames, Surrey (Monday 14 February 1972); County Hall, The Bittoms, off Penrhyn Road, Kingston-on-Thames, Surrey (Tuesday 15 February 1972)
Camera Rehearsals/Recording: Teddington Studio Two, Tuesday 22 and Wednesday 23 February 1972[102]

TV TIMES: 'Callan is as serious about his work as he is about falling in love. Unfortunately, these two pluses produce a negative result.'
8-14 April 1972, Southern edition

MISSION PROFILE: Callan is detailed to watch MP James Palliser, an economist who is planning to defect. During his assignment, he meets Palliser's friend, a widow called Susan Morris (owner of a sports shop called Sol Y Mar). Callan and Susan become emotionally involved, even though Andrew, her naval officer husband, was suspected of giving secrets to the Russians and driven to suicide by the subsequent security investigation. The Polish opposition agent Komorovski is engineering Palliser's defection and is using Trent, an arrogant and inexperienced gunman, as Palliser's minder. Callan captures the MP, but Trent escapes; later, Susan tells Callan she wants to marry him. She tries to engineer his departure from the Section by sending an anonymous letter about their relationship to the Home Office.
   Komorowski's use of such an unreliable operator as Trent is deliberate, as the Pole has drawn attention to himself in order to defect to the West. Trent follows Callan to Susan's shop where the agent uses a harpoon gun to kill the gunman in self defence. Susan is horrified and disgusted and her brief, intense romance with Callan is over.

A MAN LIKE ME: Symbolically, Callan is back in his workaday brown suit. His brief command of the Section is summed up in his Red File with the conclusion, 'an excess of subjectivity.'

Callan is stoic about going back to normal Section duties, but the speed with which he becomes involved with Mrs Morris may indicate, like his previous desire to leave the country, that he's looking to escape his job. He is openly defiant of Hunter when he is warned to stay away from Susan, and he seems to seriously contemplate leaving the Section. Callan is a bashful suitor, awkwardly delivering a box of chocolates to her shop, and when he learns it was Mrs Morris who wrote the letter revealing their relationship to Hunter, he admonishes her gently, rather than becoming angry.

Callan isn't being ironic when, looking at the harpoon guns in Susan Morris's shop, he says he 'can't understand people who go around killing things for pleasure.' He's not on 'permanent record' in the intelligence files MPs can access. In a sign of how much he cares for Susan, Callan leaves his gun in his car when he goes to see her.

Section Kills: 22

LONELY: In such a grim episode the thief, first seen in a black trilby and raincoat behaving like a character in a John le Carré novel, supplies some much-needed humour. Callan makes a wonderfully apologetic face when Lonely calls into Section HQ from the MCF, surprising Hunter, and later there's an amusing exchange about the smashed milk bottles outside Trent's flat beginning to smell. 'That milk isn't half beginning to pong,' Lonely points out. Callan replies: 'You should know, you're the expert.'

Lonely is also detailed to keep a watch on Mrs. Morris; with typical coarseness, he describes her as 'a lovely bit of stuff' but thinks she might be a 'Mata Hari'. He's instrumental in solving the mystery of the anonymous letter sent to the Home Office about Callan and Mrs. Morris' involvement, breaking into Susan's flat to study her typewriter. Amusingly, he doesn't feel right entering Palliser's flat with a key. By now, Lonely knows Callan well enough to ask him if there's anything wrong when the Section man apologises to him. Intriguingly, he says he can't thieve anymore because his nerve's gone.

A TIE AND A CREST: Meres is absent from this episode. The upper class element is provided by Palliser, 'Winchester and Cambridge', a naïve but arrogant member of the establishment who is being driven to defect because of his love for a young Russian man called Yulac. Nevertheless, his high-powered acquaintances want British intelligence to deal with him leniently. 'He's got friends in high places,' Callan spits bitterly. 'I wish to bloody hell I had!'

There is a new Section agent, 'Mr Carter', on the staff.

ALCOHOL, TOBACCO AND FIREARMS: Mrs Morris smokes at the Polish Trade Exhibition and later, when she tells Callan about her husband committing suicide following an investigation by the security services. In a notable contrast to Callan, Trent doesn't drink, while the Section man takes Scotch with Susan.

Callan is surprised by Palliser, accidentally discharging his Magnum, then firing at and missing Trent. He demonstrates he's as lethally adept with a harpoon gun as a revolver.

SPY-SPEAK: Callan is sardonic about watching someone as well-connected as Palliser: 'I'll have to buy a bowler.'

KGB agent Komorovski delivers one of James Mitchell's best insults: 'I've been in this business since before your mother first wondered who your father was.'

Callan makes a heartfelt admission about the nature of his job to Mrs Morris: 'This is a job and someone's got to do it. Now I know that is the oldest excuse in the world, but it does happen to be true... We do the best we can. And sometimes innocent people get hurt and sometimes they die. I've said before we're not very proud of it, but it happens.'

Palliser is proud of his homosexual philandering: 'I quite often spend the night in the flats of handsome boys. I'm becoming notorious for it.'

Callan's final bitter comment about Susan: 'She doesn't like the work I do. She thinks I might come home – dirty.'

PAWNS AND PLAYERS: DENNIS PRICE (1915-1973) was one of the stalwarts of the golden age of British film comedy, appearing in such landmark films as *Kind Hearts and Coronets* (1960), *Private's Progress* (1956), *I'm Alright Jack* (1959) and *School for Scoundrels* (1960). He was equally adept at straight parts, with strong roles in the Dirk Bogarde film *Victim* (1961) and the BBC's 1960s *Sherlock Holmes* series. The year before 'Charlie Says It's Goodbye', in *Jason King* Price played the avuncular 'Sir Brian', Jason's MI6 boss in 'A Deadly Line in Digits' and 'A Page Before Dying' (both 1971). In the mid-1960s, he was a memorable Jeeves in *The World of Wooster*, opposite Ian Carmichael as his accident-prone employer Bertie. Palliser was one of his last roles.

RICHARD MORANT (1945-2011) had been the sadistic school bully Flashman in the BBC's production of *Tom Brown's Schooldays* (1971). In 1975, he joined Robin Ellis in the first series of BBC Cornish drama *Poldark* as Dr Dwight Enys; by complete contrast, in 1984 Morant took over from Paul Greenwood in the BBC children's series *Captain Zep – Space Detective*. One of his most prestigious roles was as Captain 'Titus' Oates in the Ferdinand Fairfax-directed drama *The Last Place on Earth* (1985).

BETH HARRIS (1935–2012) was married to Kenneth Gilbert. She appeared in shows such as *Dixon of Dock Green* (1972), *Special Branch* and *Van der Valk* (both 1973) and as Goneril in the TV adaptation of *King Lear* (1974). She regularly appeared as welfare officer Miss Clarke in the women's prison drama *Within These Walls* (1974-78).

JOHN G. HELLER fled with his family from Czechoslovakia to Britain when the Nazis invaded. This was slightly ironic, as for a lot of his career Heller was cast as Germans, appearing in war films such as *The Colditz Story* (1955) and *Where Eagles Dare* (1968), as well as more contemporary fare like the Marianne Faithfull mod odyssey *Girl on a Motorcycle* (1968). In the same year, he was seen as the opposition agent Hinnel – an Eastern European, but not a German – in *The Avengers* story 'Split!'

INFORMATION: Originally entitled 'It's Never That Easy', this story was originally planned as a sequel to 'Suddenly – At Home', with Callan attracted to Lady Lewis's sister. Because of his job, she wanted nothing to do with him.[103] The script as made grew out of a discussion between Woodward and James Mitchell. 'I thought it was about time he had another girl,'[104] the writer said. 'Teddy Woodward, his wife and my wife and some of the kids were on holiday in Cyprus and we looked in a window and saw a spear gun and I said, "Wouldn't that be great?" and [Ted] said, "Wouldn't it just, I'd love to kill someone with a spear gun." So that's how it started.' A humorous idea William Squire came up with sadly didn't make it into the final cut of the episode. 'I put in a line as Callan came in to the effect of, "My

God, this place is in a mess since I left it!", knocking the previous Hunter. It went in as a gag in rehearsal [and] Teddy loved it.'[105]

For a second time in the fourth series, Peter Duguid was concerned about the quality of a script. 'I remember at the readthrough, Jimmy was there and Ted was saying "They're not going to believe this, are they?" Two-and-a-half minutes into the play and Callan says, "I think I'm in love with you" [sic]. As soon as you put a protagonist like Callan into a situation like that, you're taking away from him, not adding to him: the more [viewers] know how he reacts to [romantic situations] the less interesting he is. The story was highly implausible.'[106] There were some compensations for the director: 'We managed to pull off a few tricks towards the end, I think, with that awful spear... [and] Dennis Price was a lovely man.' Mitchell was equally impressed with the episode's respected guest star: '[He] was fabulous – he became very good friends with my wife and I. Tragically he died very soon after. He was the most actorly actor I've ever come across in my life. He used to play it up disgracefully; pieces of advice like, "Never play Shakespeare, my boy. By the time you get your tights off all the pubs are shut!"'[107]

Originally the choice of the Hawkwind track which Trent chills out to was to have been the band's 'You Know You're Only Dreaming'. This selection was amended during production to the more dramatic and disorientating 'You Shouldn't Do That'. Both tracks feature on the band's second album, *In Search of Space*, released in October 1971.

Two lines of dialogue were cut from the exchange between Callan and Hunter about Trent: Callan said, 'I'm sure of him. Lonely's spent his whole life with heavies and dips and brasses,' to which Hunter demanded the agent 'talk English!' The scripted kiss between Susan and Callan as he leaves her shop was dropped. Callan's line to Hunter after he's told to stay away from Mrs. Morris – 'Stuff it!' – was probably improvised by Edward Woodward, as it wasn't in the camera script.

The Dutch erotic dancer 'Mata Hari' is still arguably the best-known female spy in history. Originally born Margaretha Geertruida MacLeod (1876-1917), Mata first achieved notoriety with her sensual, half-naked dance act. When her dancing career ended in 1912, she quickly became a sought after courtesan, conducting affairs with businessmen, royalty and military officers across Europe. As the Netherlands were neutral in WW1, Mata was able to travel freely around the continent, an ideal cover for spying. When decoded radio transmissions revealed her as the German agent H-21, she was arrested in France, tried, and shot by firing squad on 15 October 1917. In a sign of Mata's continuing longevity, the 1967 spy spoof *Casino Royale* saw spy fact and fiction collide, with Mata and Sir James Bond the parents of a daughter, the appropriately named Mata Bond (Joanna Pettet).

The *Daily Mirror*, alerted by the relative novelty of Callan becoming emotionally involved with a woman, particularly as he had 'a heart as pliable as granite,'[108], flagged up the episode in its TV highlights of the day. A Thames spokesman was on hand to stimulate interest: 'We can't reveal whether Callan will get the girl, because that would reveal the plot of this episode. But she doesn't wind up dead.' Asked whether Susan Morris would be appearing later in the series, Thames' reply was a tantalising, 'We are not saying.'

MISSION ANALYSIS: *'When you're in as deep as I am, they don't let you go.'* Perhaps because *Callan* creator James Mitchell is back in the writer's chair and Callan is back on the streets, the focus is very much on the Section agent and Lonely double-act. And because Mitchell is back, his anti-hero's private life (what there is of it) is again put through the wringer, just as it was in 'Suddenly – At Home'. Once again, emotional attachments are either shown to be a fatal weakness which can be exploited (Palliser and Yulac, by Komorowski) or to have no place in a Section agent's life (Callan's feelings for Susan). Significantly, Palliser and Susan both do questionable things motivated by their finer feelings, and although Hunter is notably supportive of Callan's tenure in the command chair, he refuses point blank to allow him to become involved in a romantic relationship. The twist that Komorowski has engineered Palliser's defection so he can defect himself is also a clever one.

Trent is an interesting character, listening to space rock as he reads the *Financial Times*. With his arrogant, reckless attitude, he's very similar to Cross (and it's easy to imagine Patrick Mower in the role), but his teetotal, freelance gunman status also points to him being a younger, more arrogant version of Callan. In the end, experience wins out as the veteran kills the young pretender; once again, nobody loves a freelance. Elsewhere, John G. Heller's velvet-voiced Komorovski is a joy to watch.

Apart from the sense of creative *deja vu*, the episode's fault is that the 50-minute running time makes Callan's romance seem less plausible than his tentative involvement with Lady Lewis the year before. When Susan Morris says she wants to marry him, it's at a point where they haven't even kissed (at least on screen). The credibility of their romance is carried entirely by the acting. Woodward is particularly impressive in the initial stages of the courtship with his hesitant body language, as if scared of reaching out emotionally, and later wearing a conflicted expression as he sits in his car, mulling over whether to try and leave the Section.

Satisfyingly, Mitchell drives home just how trapped Callan is by his profession. With no influential friends to support him, he has no protection against people like Trent, and there's a bitterly tragic irony in Callan's experience as a killer saving Susan's life but destroying their relationship. Her horrified reaction to Callan's killing of Trent, and the look on his face as he sees how terrified she is of him, is one of the defining moments of the whole series.

S4.8 I NEVER WANTED THE JOB

Writer: John Kershaw
Director: Jim Goddard
Designer: Peter le Page; *Uncredited on screen:* John Plant

FIRST UK TRANSMISSION: Wednesday 19 April 1972, 9.00 pm

CAST: Paul Angelis (Steve), Michael Deacon (Sunshine), Cleo Sylvestre (Tina), Val Musetti (Dollar), Robert Grange (Fred), John Levene (Harold), Ron Pember (Albert), Frank Coda (Detective Sergeant), Frank Jarvis (Detective Constable), William Marlowe (Abbott), Peter Hutchins (Driver), *Actor unknown (Radio Announcer)*

EXTRAS/WALK-ONS: (*Uncredited on screen*) Alex Hood, Ronald Nunnery (Taxi Drivers), Vera Hill, Eileen Brady (Char Ladies) (all from Associated Plays and Players) Actor unknown (Lonely's Driving Double), Actor unknown (Abbott's Driver)

PRODUCTION

Rehearsals: From Saturday 18 December 1970
Outside Broadcast Recording: Harrowdene Gardens, Teddington; Thames, Hanworth (Tuesday 21 December 1971); Hanworth (Wednesday 22 December and Thursday 23 1972)
Camera Rehearsals/Recording: Teddington Studio Two, Thursday 30 December and Friday 31 December 1971[109]

TV TIMES: 'After he has witnessed a murder, Lonely is wanted by police and killers. Can Callan save him from both sides of the law?'
15-21 April 1972, Southern edition

MISSION PROFILE: Lonely witnesses the murder of criminal Edward George Dollar – 'The Chairman' – a taxi fare he shouldn't have taken on. The killers, Steve and 'Sunshine', work for a rival gangster, Dick Abbot, who orders them to frighten Lonely into staying silent. He tells Callan; the killers smash up the MCF and Callan attempts to keep news of the damage from Hunter. Callan visits Abbot and tries to intimidate him into leaving him and Lonely alone, but this only makes the gangster determined to have the Section man killed. On Hunter's orders, Meres investigates the MCF in the Section garage. In a shoot-out with Callan and Meres in the garage, Abbot is killed and 'Sunshine' and Steve are taken prisoner.

A MAN LIKE ME: In a pleasing touch of realism, Callan suffers from a bad cold and a cough throughout the story. This doesn't stop him from rebuking Lonely with a slap round the face, again reminding the audience of how unpleasant he can be; conversely, he takes on Abbot's gang single-handed to protect the petty thief. Even though he's probably bluffing, Callan threatens to kill Tina, Abbot's girlfriend. He does kill Abbot.

The most striking thing about him in this episode, however, is his sudden adoption of a car coat, leather cap and beige V-neck pullover for the climactic gunfight, an ensemble Callan's never worn before (and never will again) which gives him a more than slightly camp look. Did an assignment for Hunter involve going undercover somewhere risqué?

From somewhere, Callan has acquired a hippy cash-in towel with the branding 'Love!'
Section Kills: 23

LONELY: Takes paying customers when he was explicitly told not to, getting him into a lot of trouble. (This contradicts 'Rules of the Game', in which Callan, who rebukes him about it here, told him he *could* take fares and keep the money). This is the second closest he comes to being killed (so far), as not only does Abbot order his death, but Hunter also contemplates authorising it. Lonely lies to the police and Albert, the owner of the taxi-drivers' caff he frequents, backs him up even though he doesn't approve of Lonely's behaviour.

Desperate for Callan's help throughout, Lonely still finds the strength to stand up to him and tell Callan he's 'fed up' with being threatened: 'You're dangerous, mate! *Dangerous!* I don't want to drive your lousy car!' In a rare relaxed moment, he's seen reading the comic strip 'The Gobblers' in the comic *Beezer* (1956-1993).

Significantly, Lonely alerts Callan that he's in danger by using the agent's first name when the thief is taken to Callan's flat by Abbot's men.

More humour about smells: he hates the decongestant vapour Callan's using on his cold.

A TIE AND A CREST: Meres can't resist sending up Callan's modest flat: 'You know, David, I've always admired your taste.' Despite his contempt for Lonely and a threat to hurt him – as in 'You Should Have Got Here Sooner' – Meres recognises that Callan is in trouble and arrives at the Section garage to back up his colleague in the ensuing gunfight with Abbot's men. Their conspiratorial banter in front of Hunter, after the gang has been dealt with, suggests this is the closest the two men have ever come to being friends; by now, they know each other so well that Meres can drop into Callan's flat for a cup of tea. Toby even compliments Callan on how good his model soldiers are.

The Section are working with Special Branch, foreshadowing the next story.

ALCOHOL, TOBACCO AND FIREARMS: Abbot and Tina are habitual drinkers. They take Scotch as they debrief Steve and Sunshine, and during Callan's *blitzkrieg* on his club, Abbot coolly helps himself to another. The pair hit the Scotch again when Tina informs Abbot about what she's discovered about Callan. A DC smokes when he questions Lonely in the caff.

The shoot-out in the garage is the ambitiously staged, involving Abbot, his driver, Steve, Sunshine, Lonely, Callan and Meres.

SPY-SPEAK: Lonely's BO still penetrates Callan's illness: 'I've got the worst cold I've ever had in my life and I can still smell you, so put some space between us, all right?'

Tina, Abbot's girlfriend, wonders if Callan's concern for Lonely is because they're a gay couple. The agent cattily replies: 'No, darling. But with scrubbers like you around, it's a wonder we're not all bent, innit?' Callan and Abbot's conversation continues in the same vein.

Abbot: 'You've been reading too many paperbacks.' Callan: 'It's a pity some of your boys don't read a few more – if they can read.' (A good follow-up visual joke has Abbot reading one).

Abbot can't resist gangster cliché either: 'Whoever [Callan] *is*, he won't be for much longer, I promise you that.'

Hunter is amused by his senior man's apparently public-spirited attitude: 'Since when has it been your job to clean up the underworld, Callan?'

Callan (truthfully) claims he and Meres were 'held up', and that he and Meres are 'civil servants', adding an obligatory reference to the Queen: 'Gawd bless her.'

PAWNS AND PLAYERS: PAUL ANGELIS (born 1943) was the very convincing voice of Ringo Starr, as well as the screechingly camp Chief Blue Meanie, in The Beatles' psychedelic cartoon odyssey *Yellow Submarine* (1968). He also took over the voice of George Harrison when Peter Batten, the original voice artist, was arrested half way through recording for deserting from the Rhine army. Angelis played the regular PC Bannerman in *Z Cars* (from 1968-69) and went on to appear twice in the caseload of DI Jack Regan and DS George Carter, in the first series of *The Sweeney* (1975) and later in the *Sweeney!* feature film (1977). In the 1981 James Bond film *For Your Eyes Only* he was Karageorge, a silent member of Columbo's smuggling gang.

WILLIAM MARLOWE (1932-2003) was on the right side of the law as a policeman in the 1967 feature film *Robbery,* co-written by George Markstein, and had a leading role in the ITV series *Villains* (1972). Marlowe starred as DCI Russell, DI Maggie Forbes' boss, in 54 episodes of *The Gentle Touch* (1980-84) and also played the Department agent Fairfax, in the 1969 *The Avengers* story 'Who Was That Man I Saw You With?'

He appeared twice in *Doctor Who*, firstly as Mailer, a memorably ruthless convict in 'The Mind of Evil' (1971), which also featured John Levene.

RON PEMBER (born 1934) was a specialist at playing cockney rogues, featuring in *The Sweeney* (in 1976) and *Target* the following year. He was a renowned stage director and dramatist, until a stroke compelled him to take early retirement. He is perhaps best known for his role as the rugged Alain Muny, part of the Lifeline escape route in Geard Glaister's *Secret Army* (1977-79).

JOHN LEVENE (born 1941, with the surname Woods) played a Cyberman and a Yeti in *Doctor Who* (1967-68). He became part of the 'UNIT family' in the series in the early 1970s, appearing as the dependable Corporal, Sergeant then RSM Benton in sixteen stories between 1968 and 1976. Levene also had minor roles in *The Dirty Dozen* (1967) and Don Sharp's cult film *Psychomania* (1973).

CLEO SYLVESTRE featured in the 21st century films *Kidulthood* (2006) and *Paddington* (2014).

INFORMATION: The heavy cold Callan suffers from was an example of art imitating life, as the originally assigned director Voytek recalled: 'The cast all got 'flu and they wrote it in: Callan with a cold! Often you have to incorporate these things or they're unusable. I cast it and got it all organised and got as far as rehearsals. Jim took over at the last minute as I was laid up.'[110] Any consequent rewrites took place very close to production, as there were no references to Callan's illness in the camera script.

The Musher's London taxi received the worst damage of its time on the series when its windscreen was smashed in, as Goddard remembered: 'We didn't retake because Michael Deacon did it with a sledgehammer. But the first time, he didn't break it at all, the hammer flew out of his hand across the garage! Shows how tough these things are. We had several windscreens. The old Musher was really into it by then, and enjoyed the idea of smashing his cab up. He'd drive it home after shooting and probably pick up a couple of fares on the way!'[111] Helming his last script for *Callan*, the director recalled that the atmosphere on the series was getting 'a bit tense towards the end', as Woodward was going through an unhappy period.

There is an unfortunate production mistake in the first OB sequence: Lonely's driving double can be clearly seen as he drops off Abbot and Tina. In the closing gun battle, Woodward unusually wears a leather cap throughout, perhaps indicating that his hairpiece was missing.

The music featured in Abbot's club consisted of three pieces of library music: 'I Still Remember You' and 'Fly By Night' by the Otto Keller Band, published by Aphonic Music Ltd, and 'Red Roses for a Blue Lady' by Bryan Johnson, published by Lawrence Wright.

'The writing changed,'[112] Russell Hunter reflected of *Callan*'s fourth series. 'Maybe I changed my performance too, but I think [the scripts] got a bit glib: "Oh, in a bit of a difficulty, bring in Lonely and make a joke about bathing and washing and all the rest of it, and the smell." I think, originally, Lonely's expertise as a burglar, and particularly his expertise in going to ground and disappearing, so that the people who were following him passed him and didn't even recognise him... I think *that* was terribly important, that Lonely was very good at disappearing when he wanted to disappear... He was just a little animal, and I think that was lost later on. I don't think he should ever have *met* some of the people he met. I think he was used as a kind of social joke, which was probably legitimate, but I would have approved more if he had been more carefully handled. He was probably better when he was a very small-part character in the story.'

The underworld feud Lonely gets involved in is likely to have been inspired by the rivalry between the Kray and Richardson gangs in the 1960s, who controlled East and South London respectively. This dispute came to a head in March 1966 when George Cornell, a member of the Richardson Gang, was shot through the head at close range by Ronnie Kray. Holding court amiably in his fashionably flock-wallpapered club, Abbot may also have been partly based on the pornographer James Humphreys (1930-2003), who controlled all the porn rackets in London's Soho in the 1960s and early 1970s. Infamously, Humphreys was responsible for the corruption of the Metropolitan Police's Flying Squad Commander, Kenneth Drury.

Hunter quotes Izaac Walton (1594-1683), the English writer best known as the author of *The Compleat Angler*, a volume which celebrated fishing through poems and other compositions. The best known edition was published in 1824.

The quote 'We also serve, who only stand and wait' originates from John Milton's 1673 poem 'On His Blindness', in which the 'We' is replaced by 'They'. The wording Meres uses was adapted to accompany the Dickin medal, awarded since 1943 to courageous animals in war and peace time. As he specificaly quotes this latter version, it's likely that Meres is being extremely sarcastic.

MISSION ANALYSIS: *'I never wanted the bloody job! You can keep it!'* In the last major story based around him, Lonely is threatened by Callan, gangsters and the Section, caught in the crossfire between the London underworld and the Cold War. Significantly, the Section and Abbot both threaten their employees with execution if they fail. For the second time this year, there's an examination of what happens when spies and criminals meet (as before, there was only ever going to be one winner) and there's some authentic use of working-class codes of honour, when the café owner Albert automatically covers for Lonely as he's questioned by the police.

The seriousness of Lonely's predicament is tempered by the story being considerably lighter and more straightforward than those around it. The entertainment value comes largely from the performances, with the regulars and guest cast, namely William Marlowe and Paul Angelis, on top form in terms of characterisation and the deployment of sharp one-liners. There are hints that Kershaw may have seen the influential gangster movie *Get Carter*, released the year before and featuring a double act of suited-and-booted hoodlums similar to Steve and Sunshine. Like 'I Never Wanted the Job', the Michael Caine film also shows a gang boss remaining ominously cool in his lair when he's confronted by the anti-hero.

This is the Callan/Meres' double act's finest hour, as they cover up their wiping out of Abbot's gang in front of Hunter like two naughty school boys up before the headmaster. Even Hunter plays along, reprimanding them but then smiling indulgently after they've left. (Evidently, if the British state had wanted to end the reign of the Krays and the Richardsons earlier than it did, all it had to do was give the Section the job). There's also some pleasingly underplayed continuity, as Meres saves Callan's life after nearly killing him in 'Death of a Hunter'.

As enjoyable as 'I Never Wanted the Job' is, it comes dangerously close to feeling cosy at times, and if there's one episode that shows how far *Callan* has moved from the series' original intentions, it's this one. It's also notable that for the second time in three episodes the show is covering old ground, in the same *milieu* it had dealt with only two stories ago. Kershaw's story even repeats one of the situations in 'None of Your Business', as Callan trounces more gangsters in his flat before confronting their boss on his own ground. A sign, perhaps, that Series Four had lost its way slightly after bringing closure to Callan's tenure as Hunter.

S4.9 THE CARRIER

Writer: Peter Hill
Director: Jonathan Alwyn
Designer: Neville Greene

FIRST UK TRANSMISSION: Wednesday 26 April 1972, 9.00 pm

CAST: Peter Copley (Peter Rose), Terry Wright (PC Ballantine), Jeffrey Segal (Sir Charles Braden), Michael Turner (Detective Inspector Vanstone), Windsor Davies (Detective Superintendent Brown), Ralph Nossek (Tamaresh), Brian Vaughn (Immigration officer), Jean Rogers (Mary), Roy Herrick (Allan), Marc Boyle (Chauffeur); *Uncredited on screen -* Derek Ware (Stuntman, film only)

EXTRAS/WALK-ONS:*(Uncredited on screen)* Sarah McDonald (Rent-a-Car Girl), Eddie Sommers (News Stall Salesman), Charles Rayford (Barman), Ian Munro (Police Constable) Alf Coster, Derek Chafer (Customs Officers), Erci French (Merchant Navy Officer), Ricky Logan, Pat Donaghue (Porters), Wendy Johnson, Betty Pevan (Women Passengers), Fred Woolfe (Male Passenger), Bob Blaine (Police Constable), Jill Hope (Secretary doubling Passenger), Steve Emerson, Sylvia de la Mare, Keith Goodman, Betty Morgan, Henry Rayner, Willie Bowman (Passengers doubling Customers in Pub). All artists engaged through the Jeff Shane Agency.

PRODUCTION

Rehearsals: From Thursday 24 February 1972
Location Filming: Claygate Railway Station, Claygate; Woods area, Esher Common, Oxshott; Effingham Common Road, Effingham Junction; The Black Swan Pub, Ockham Lane, Martyrs Green (Monday 28 March 1972); Junction of Fairfax Road and Cromwell Road, Teddington (Tuesday 29 February, Wednesday 1 March 1972)
Camera Rehearsals/Recording: Teddington Studio One, Tuesday 8 March and Wednesday 9 March 1972[113]

TV TIMES: 'When Callan finds himself once again out in the cold, he seeks a warmer climate. But he discovers that going abroad is sometimes easier for the other side – until he works out their secret!'
[Confusingly, this reads like unused blurb for 'None of Your Business']
22-28 April 1972, Southern edition

MISSION PROFILE: Professor Peter Rose is planning to give details of a new radar system to the Russians and the Section must stop him. Special Branch become involved in the case after Callan and Lonely burgle Rose's house in Hampstead to check if he has the plans of the device; unfortunately, Lonely can't resist stealing a trophy. To Hunter's annoyance, after he's lied to Superintendent Brown of the Branch about the Section's interest in Rose, he has to ask the police officer to have Lonely and Callan released from custody as they've been arrested for stealing from the scientist's house.

Joost Amstel, Rose's Dutch contact, arrives in Britain and is tailed by two young Special Branch officers, Allan and Mary. They're unaware that he is really the KGB Colonel Gregori Tamaresh – in the past year, he's killed two Section agents. He shoots both officers dead. Callan follows Tamaresh and his chauffeur (who's also a KGB operative) to Rose's house, gunning them both down before the plans can be handed over. Hunter tells Callan that Rose will never be trusted again and, one day, a KGB executioner will assassinate him.

A MAN LIKE ME: There is a highly authentic feel to the scenes where Callan and Lonely break into Rose's house, showing them both to be masters of their craft. The edges of curtains are taped over so no-one can see the lights have been turned on; they photograph the objects on Rose's desk so they can be put back in exactly the right position; they tune in to the police's radio wavelength so they can be warned of any police interest in Rose's house, and they wait silently for several moments after turning on the living room lights to make sure the house is empty. Unfortunately, Lonely's theft of an award from the Society for the Advancement of Electronic Research undoes all these careful precautions.

Callan knows about the KGB Section Leader, Tamaresh.

Section Kills: 25

LONELY: Is so in tune with Callan's methods that during a burglary he can anticipate his moves and they can work together in total silence. Tellingly, knowing he'll be violently reprimanded by Callan for stealing Rose's award and getting them both arrested, Lonely goes to the Section man's flat anyway; it's implied he's a kleptomaniac and he just can't help himself. After being put out of action in 'None of Your Business', the MCF is back on the road but, astonishingly, after the trouble accepting taxi fares caused in the previous episode, Lonely is *still* doing it.

Using his initiative, he blinks twice at Callan to alert him to say to the police that the pair were together at 2.00 am.

A TIE AND A CREST: When Callan complains about being up all night, Meres delights in telling him, 'It's your age, old boy.'

The hierarchy in 'The Carrier' comes from the ranking of the UK's intelligence services. The Section flouts the laws of the land, Callan and Hunter lie to the police, the Section chief withholds crucial information from Special Branch, and they pay the price with two dead officers. When Hunter disingenuously says he hopes the Branch know what they're doing, Meres sardonically comments, 'It'll be the first time, sir.'

The Section has a monitoring room, with equipment that can eavesdrop on bugged telephones and police radio wavebands.

ALCOHOL, TOBACCO AND FIREARMS: Hunter enjoys a 1961 Burgundy with his evening meal, 'the best... since the war.' The Section chief share a malt after the case is concluded.

Tamaresh stops at a pub on his drive from the coast, and Allan and Mary follow him in and have a drink; later, Allan smokes as he follows Tamaresh through a forest. Tragically, Allan and his colleague Mary aren't carrying guns and are callously and needlessly shot down by the killer. Callan later shoots and kills both Tamaresh and his accomplice, shoving the dying chauffeur into Rose's house to draw the KGB Colonel's gunfire.

SPY-SPEAK: Hunter is rather deflated when he discovers that Liz's culinary skills aren't the source of his gourmet evening meal; instead, as Meres tells him, it's from 'Dial-a-Banquet'. Showing a photograph of the KGB agent Tamaresh to Meres, Hunter wryly says, 'He's the one on the left, appropriately enough.'

When Lonely asks how he's going to stop a copper approaching Rose's house, Callan tells him to 'tie his boot laces together.'

Amstel/Tamaresh delights in black humour. He tells Rose 'I have worked for peace in my own way for many years now' and that he 'got rid of' the people bothering him.

Callan vents his feelings at Hunter: 'Look, mate, I go out in the field and I meet them face-to-face, not you, you sit there in that comfortable chair. You say one bloody word, some bastard dies a thousand miles away. You say *nothing,* and two kids end up on a bloody slab. That chair, *that bloody chair!'* (This tirade has similarities with Callan's 'bloody desk' speech in 'Call Me Sir!')

PAWNS AND PLAYERS: PETER HILL had served in the Metropolitan Police, reaching the rank of Detective Inspector when he was only 31. He left the force because of his ambition to become a writer and a growing disillusionment with where the police service was heading. 'I began to have grave doubts about the ability and suitability of senior officers I encountered,'[114] he told *TV Times.* 'So many of them were utterly ruled by "the book" and seemed to view the job and the law as all important. To me, the law and the force should be for the benefit of the people, not the other way round. I disagreed with popular opinion in the force since I was utterly opposed to hanging, and I could see little value in imprisonment in the vast majority of cases.'

Having already written for children's television, Hill was given the 'help and encouragement' of George Markstein in realising his first adult drama script, the *Special Branch* story 'Error of Judgment' (1970). From there, Hill brought his authentic knowledge of the police to his 1971 *Armchair Theatre* play 'Man Charged', as well as scripts for series such as *Z Cars* (over 1976-67), *New Scotland Yard* (1973-74) and *The Sweeney* story 'Sweet Smell of Succession' (1976), in which a gangster's son outwits both the criminals and the police. Between 1982 and 1986, Hill produced the documentary series *Rough Justice*, which profiled miscarriages of justice in the British legal system. Now based in New Zealand, he writes novels and continues to produce.

JONATHAN ALWYN (born 1940) is a producer and director who worked on some of television's most highly regarded shows between the 1960s and 1980s. Early in his career, he directed two episodes of the Associated Rediffusion spy show *Top Secret* (1961), before helming seven episodes in *The Avengers'* video era. A veteran of *Armchair Theatre*, Alwyn also directed *Public Eye* (1965-1975), the eco-thriller *Doomwatch* (1970-71) and produced the second series of *Enemy at the Door* (1980). His other producer credits include *Juliet Bravo* (1982), *By the Sword Divided* (1985) and *Bergerac* (1983-87).

PETER COPLEY (1915-2008)'s career lasted over sixty years. Alongside an abundant career on stage, he made more than 150 screen performances, appearing in productions as varied as *Maigret* (1960), *Armchair Theatre*, The Beatles' second movie *Help!* (1965), *Frankenstein Must Be Destroyed* (1969) and Steven Spielberg's *Empire of the Sun* (1987). In the *Danger Man* episode 'Yesterday's Enemies' (1964) he played Brett, another traitor passing secrets to the Eastern bloc.

WINDSOR DAVIES (1930-) is better known for his later comic roles, appearing most notably as Sergeant Major 'Shut Up!' Williams in the WW2 concert party comedy *It Ain't*

Half Hot, Mum (1974-1981), and as one of two rival antique dealers with Donald Sinden in *Never the Twain* (1981-1991). He also appeared in a more serious vein in *The Mind of Mr. J.G. Reeder* (1969-1971), *Hawkeye, the Pathfinder* (1973), *Sam* (1975) and various episodes of *Z Cars* and its spin-offs.

RALPH NOSSEK (1923-2011), among many parts, played Roland, the suspicious head of Marseilles airport security, in *The Avengers* story 'Propellant 23' (1962). He also appeared in Robert Banks Stewart's sci-fi thriller *Undermind* (1965) and the 1996 film version of Joseph Conrad's *The Secret Agent*. In 1965, Nossek took the leading role of Professor Ramsay in the sci-fi series *Object Z* and its sequel in 1966.[115]

MICHAEL TURNER played other establishment figures under pressure in *The Avengers* – 'Have Guns, Will Haggle', and the *Doctor Who* story 'The Wheel in Space' (both 1968).

MARC BOYLE, like Alan Chuntz, was a member of the stunt company HAVOC run by Derek Ware.

INFORMATION: Special Branch's tailing of Amstel was another victim of the budget restrictions the team had to cope with. 'They were tracking some spy from the coast,'[116] Neville Greene said, 'and I persuaded Reg to let me have [two] cars rather than the one he'd allocated. One of them was mine!' The amount of screen time given to Callan and Lonely's burglary may have been a result of the script running short. 'You aim for 52 minutes and depending on a number of factors you will come close to that,'[117] Reg Collin explained. 'When you're under or over you talk to the transmission controller to ask "Can you cope with it?" He'd ring around the network and if they were short of advertising it'd be fine. Or they'd say, "You've got to have 52 minutes", so you'd look at it with the director. You can get rid of two minutes mostly by trimming. Under-runs are not that frequent.' In terms of continuity, there's a mention of the Section man George, last seen in 'That'll Be the Day'.

Meres's line 'It's your age, old boy' was added after the camera script was finalised. The last two lines of dialogue in Tamaresh's confrontation with Mary were cut: the Special Branch officer exclaimed, 'You bastard, he didn't have a gun,' to which the KGB agent replied – 'Pity.'

'The Carrier' is particularly cynical about the relationship between the UK's security services. 'The whole history of spydom is based on the need to know,'[118] considered Woodward, 'so there's always going to be somebody above you who needs to know more than you do. This hierarchy goes all the way up to the Home Secretary or the Foreign Secretary in the government. There was always somebody looking over somebody's shoulder, and I imagine it's exactly the same today.'

Special Branch is the division of the police responsible for national security throughout the UK and the British Commonwealth. Its remit is to gather intelligence about political crime and investigate threats to the state, including terrorism, and to arrest suspects. By 1972, the Branch was involved in undercover operations against the IRA in Northern Ireland. Even though the Section doesn't rate its sister service, Special Branch officers were instrumental in arresting all the members of the Portland spy ring in 1961 (See 'Jack-on-Top' and 'Nice People Die at Home', Chapter 6).

In the book stall at Passport Control, a poster for the book *Papillon* can be seen. Written by Henri Charrière (1906-1973) about the continual attempts of the eponymous character to escape from the French penal colony Devil's Island, Charrière's novel became a worldwide bestseller after its publication in 1969. In 1973, it was made into a moving feature film, starring Steve McQueen and Dustin Hoffman.

Tamaresh's Dutch alias of Amstel is likely to be another example of Tamaesh's sense of humour, as it's the name of a well known brewery founded in Holland in 1780. In the 1950s, Amstel was the first Dutch brewer to export beer in cans.

MISSION ANALYSIS: *'Lord save me from meddling policemen.'* Lonely's one act of avarice starts a tragic chain of events that ends in the murder of two Special Branch officers. Their deaths are depressing as Hunter knows the real identity of the suspect they are tailing, but chooses not to inform their superiors. The admission that he never shares information with Special Branch underlines how quietly ruthless the fourth Hunter really is, as he's prepared to let people from allied security organisations die, even when he has the influence to prevent it.

Apart from the dispiriting lack of co-operation between organisations dedicated to the defence of the realm, in Peter Hill's only script for the series, Britain is presented as a country where the secret state can do what it likes: burgle houses with impunity, tap phone lines, eavesdrop on the radio transmissions of the police and overrule them so criminals can be released from arrest. The grim subtext is that, in some ways, the UK and Soviet Russia are disturbingly similar. In this context, Rose's principled espionage is shown up for the naive gesture it is – as Callan bluntly tells him – and the Section's sending of an anonymous wreath to the two dead officers' funeral, even without Callan's disgust, is shown up for the cynical hypocrisy it is. Prominently displaying in the episode a poster for the book *Papillion*, written by a petty criminal convicted for a murder he insisted he never committed, is a sophisticated and subtle piece of symbolism by Hill and Alwyn that reinforces the main themes of the screenplay.

Hill also has an impressive eye for detail and naturalism, with authentic-sounding radio call signs for the Special Branch offices Allan (Central 2-5) and Mary (Central 2-6), and Callan turning a sink plunger into a weapon; in the space of one scene, he goes from unblocking his sink to abusing Lonely with it. Elsewhere, the duo's burglary of Rose's house is performed with no talking and goes on for several minutes (and might have been influenced by the famous half hour sequence of a dialogue-free robbery in the 1954 French film *Rififi*). Because these scenes were written by an ex-police officer, their novelty and authenticity is very striking in an otherwise run-of-the-mill episode by *Callan* standards, but the amount of screen time devoted to the break-in – nearly a quarter of an hour – suggests it was at least partly designed as padding.

Maybe, in hindsight, Collin and Markstein missed a good opportunity to make this episode into an official crossover with their own *Special Branch* series; it's not too hard to envisage that programme's Detective Inspector Jordan (Derren Nesbitt) and Detective Superintendent Inman (Fulton Mackay) being present in the story instead of the similar figures of Vanstone and Brown. The meeting of the two series would certainly have enlivened the drama.

S4.10 THE CONTRACT

Writer: Bill Craig
Director: Reg Collin
Designer: Neville Green

FIRST UK TRANSMISSION: Wednesday 3 May 1972, 9.00 pm

CAST: Robert Urquhart (Major Harcourt), Bernadette Milnes (Vera), Michael Pennington (Lafarge), Hugh Morton (Stepan), Jane Lapotaire (Kristina). *Uncredited on screen:* Roberta Gibbs (Double for Vera), Actors unknown (Barker, Nicholls)*, *uncredited on screen:* 'Curly' (Lonely's Driving Double).

EXTRAS/WALK-ONS: (*Uncredited on screen*) From the Shane Agency: Hugh Elton (Barman), Rodney Cardiff (Young Waiter).

Rosa Gold (Cashier in Restaurant), Richard Egan, Mary Winslow (Couple in Restaurant Scenes – change of clothes), Philip Stewart (Customer in Restaurant), Paul Drake, Michael Reynell, George Ballantyne, Clinton Morris (Four Businessmen in the Daytime Restaurant Scene – suits – and Darts Team in Pub – casual clothes), Glen Hayes, George Howard (Two Workmen in the Pub), Sally Avery, Pip, James Lyon, Michael Torres (Hippy-type Group in Pub – change of clothes for second scene), Cy Wallis, Chalmers Peddie, Brenda Armstrong, Peta Collins (Customers in Pub/Customers in Night Restaurant Scene), Mary Masters, Peggy Bullock (Two Elderly Lady Customers in Pub).

PRODUCTION

Rehearsals: From Friday 14 January 1972
Outside Broadcast Recording: St. James Road, Maple Road, North Road, St Andrews Road, Surbiton (Monday 17 January 1972, Tuesday 18 January 1972)
Camera Rehearsals/Recording: Teddington Studio Two, Wednesday 25 and Thursday 26 1972[119]

TV TIMES: 'To stop an assassination plot, Callan poses as a hired gunman, knowing that the real assassin is close at hand.'
29 April - 5 May 1972, Southern edition

MISSION PROFILE: Freelance assassin Major Warren Harcourt has been contracted by a young French woman called Kristina to kill a visiting foreign Field Marshal from her country. He's captured by Meres and Callan in a bedsit at number 39 Bala-clava Terrace and Callan takes his place. The assignment is complicated by the Major escaping and the Section man learning that Bellini, the partner of Etienne Lafarge – the man sharing the contract with Harcourt – was apparently murdered by the Major in Genoa. Harcourt arrives at the assassination vantage point, the attic of Flat 6 Denby Court, exposing Callan as a fraud. He talks for his life, convincing Lafarge that he has been set up by the Field Marshal's own people. The Frenchman kills Harcourt in revenge and, with Kristina taken in by the Section, abandons the hit.

A MAN LIKE ME: Once again, Callan shows how adept at acting he is, reusing the alias 'Mr. Grimshaw' (from 'Call Me Sir!') and adopting the guise of a prospective client to pick up a local prostitute called Vera. As in 'Red Knight, White Knight', he's fond of cats, liking one he finds enough to take it inside the MCF. Predictably, he's resentful about impersonating a British officer but carries it off with some finesse, right down to the Major's patronising attitude to women, even if his accent lapses slightly. In turn, Major Harcourt pays Callan the compliment of being 'a considerable liar.'

As he waits in the dark of Harcourt's bedsit, Callan demonstrates great control and patience in his ability to remain silent and still for long periods. In disguise as the Major, he explicitly identifies the organisation he works for as the Special Intelligence Service.

LONELY: Has one of his finest seedy moments as he's seen eating crisps in the back seat of his taxi, surrounded by crumbs and empty packets. This is the last time Lonely demonstrates his burglary skills, forcing the window on Harcourt's bedsit and opening the door to let Callan in.

A TIE AND A CREST: The white cat Callan finds bites Meres' hand. 'They can tell, you know,' Callan delights in telling him. Apart from Callan's class-conscious quip that he doesn't know 'what British officers are coming to', Major Harcourt is insulted by the working class agent's impersonation of him, viciously kicking him when he's tied up. As part of his undercover alias, Callan borrows Toby's 'British warm' – an officer's overcoat.

When he's held at gunpoint by Harcourt, Meres is visibly frightened and admits as much. Meres is backed up by two new Section agents, Barton and Nichols.

ALCOHOL, TOBACCO AND FIREARMS: Both 'Mr. Grimshaw' and Harcourt ply Vera with gin. By contrast, the gunman Lefarge enjoys a bottle of Riesling. The assassination weapon is a Safari .303 rifle with a telescopic sight. Lefarge uses a handgun to dispose of Harcourt. Bellini, Lefarge's business partner, was killed by Meres using a Browning revolver 'at 20 yards.'

SPY-SPEAK: On the unfortunate demise of the white cat, which Meres erroneously shot: 'Curiosity...' says Hunter, before Callan interrupts '...epitaph for a dead cat.' 'Oh, very funny!' responds an affronted Meres.

Later, Meres notes with much mirth that Novaks, the restaurant that Callan has chosen for his meeting with Kristina, his contact for the hit, is hardly discreet: 'Special Branch [officers] take their wives there for the chicken pilaf!'

Major Harcourt is not amused by the humiliation he's suffered at the hands of the Section: 'You made me jump out of a window, Mr. Callan. It was most undignified.'

PAWNS AND PLAYERS: JANE LAPOTAIRE (born 1944) was the first choice for the role of Kristina, after Reg Collin saw her playing a black girl opposite Edward Woodward during the 1969 National Theatre production of *The White Devil*; 'The Contract' was her first television part for six years. Five years later, Lapotaire went on to become well-known for her leading roles in the TV series *Marie Curie* (1977) and *The Devil's Crown* (1978). One of the founders of the Young Vic theatre, she played the troubled singer Edith Piaf to great acclaim in an RSC production.

ROBERT URQUHART (1922-1995) was another *Callan* alumnus to also have taken on Patrick McGoohan's John Drake in *Danger Man,* firstly as Charles Grover, a would-be defector in 'It's Up to the Lady', an inept station chief in 'English Lady Takes Lodgers' (both 1965) and the equally clumsy opposition enemy agent Monckton in 'The Man with the Foot' (1966). Staying with the spy genre, Urquhart played the radio expert Johnson in the feature film *The Looking Glass War* (1969), starring Anthony Hopkins. He had a regular role as test pilot Henry Forbes in *The Plane Makers* (1963-65).

BERNADETTE MILNES (1932-2012) began her television career in 1952. She was an usherette in *The Quatermass Experiment* (1953) and in 1970 took the title role in 'Mrs. 22 Khartoum Road', an episode of the ITV sitcom *The Dustbinmen* (1970). Milnes was a villain's wife in *The Sweeney* – 'Cover Story' (1975), and had the regular role of Polly in the comedy *The Upchat Line* (1977) with John Alderton, and the follow-up *The Upchat Connection* (1978, when Robin Nedwell took over the part of the womanising Mike Upchat). Milnes' last TV performance was in the horror series *She Wolf of London* (1990); the entertainment business runs in her family, as she was the mother of the actress and producer Lysette Anthony. Her film appearances include *Cover Girl Killer* (1959) and *The Elephant Man* (1980).

MICHAEL PENNINGTON (born 1943) frequently plays authority figures and academics, appearing in *Between the Lines* (1993), *Waking the Dead* and *State of Play* (both 2003). A busy theatre actor, he has also contributed to various educational programmes including the acting class *Playing Shakespeare* (1982). He appears as a servant of the evil Empire in *Return of the Jedi* (1983).

INFORMATION: 'Years and years before ['The Contract'] I wanted an assassination,'[120] Bill Craig said concerning how the idea for the script originated. 'I wanted to make it different, so I thought of a shot that could only take place over three seconds while somebody crossed a window. So, it requires an expert marksman with prior knowledge. It started from there, but that wasn't the final element: the final element was that Callan knew Meres had been sent to kill this father figure, yet kept up this bluff. [sic]' To begin the episode, Craig added a white cat, which caused difficulties during the location shoot.[121]

There is a production error in the scene where Meres follows Harcourt from a chip shop: a schoolboy stands in the doorway and very obviously watches the camera crew recording Valentine and Urquhart's scene. Cuts from the camera script sadly meant the loss of scenes where Callan talks about turning 'a brain surgeon loose' on Lonely, the thief eats a 'sixth bag of crisps' and two meat pies in the MCF, and Meres threatens to 'hit [Vera] again – this time with equal accuracy, but a little more force.' Meres originally said he shot Bellini at '2.33' while he was sitting at a pavement café in Genoa, 'drinking Lachryma Christi'.

Unusually for *Callan*, the exact nature of Kristina's political loyalty remains obscure. As she and Lafarge are both French, and are planning to assassinate a politically powerful 'Field Marshal', the strong implication is that the character is based on President General Charles De Gaulle, who was the target of an assassnation attempt in 1962.

In a story where allegiances are largely driven by money, Lafarge's reference to Nicolas Chauvin is clearly ironic. Born (apparently) in 1780, the possibly fictitious French patriot enlisted in the First Army of the French Republic aged eighteen and was wounded seventeen times, before being awarded the Sabre of Honour by Napoleon Bonaparte. The description 'Chauvinism' derives from his name; originally it meant a fervent love of one's country.

Showing off his public school education, Meres quotes from the patriotic 'Cry God for Harry, England and St. George' speech in Shakespeare's *Henry V* (Act 3, Scene 1), another example of Bill Craig's taste for irony.

It's tempting to think that the inclusion of the short-lived, long haired white cat is an in-joke about the James Bond films, as 007's nemesis Ernst Stavro Blofeld was particularly fond of the breed. *Diamonds are Forever*, featuring the SPECTRE mastermind and two white felines, premiered in the year 'The Contract' was written.

Interviewing James Mitchell in 1974, *The Guardian*'s Peter Petersen spoke highly of Bill Craig: '[he] can hand turn a cracking 52 minutes even the [series'] creator can't better.'[122]

MISSION ANALYSIS: *'What does it take, darling, to get into your revolution? A degree in domestic science?'* After the feeling that the series has been marking time slightly over the last three episodes, Bill Craig again delivers one of the best stories of *Callan*'s fourth year – indeed, one of the best *Callan* stories ever – packed with wit, detail and complex intrigue. There is a nicely observed contrast between the seedy and the sophisticated, as Lonely pines for a pie in a pub and the gourmand Lafarge dines on rice and asparagus tips. Elsewhere, Meres' shooting of the white cat makes for one the tragi-comic highlights of his and Callan's doubel act.

You can only admire Bill Craig's skill, as he uses these lively moments to enrich a multi-layered tale of deceit in which there appears to be no loyalty anywhere. The amoral tone is set by the 'tatty bird' Vera that Callan picks up, a prostitute who despite being seriously injured by Harcourt, later takes his money. The Major himself once worked for the Section and is now their target. The Field Marshal is being set up to be assassinated by his own people and Callan, posing as Harcourt, finds himself working with the part-ner of Bellini, whom the Major supposedly executed. Even that proves to be a piece of misdirection, as the final, cynical twist reveals that the real killer of Bellini was Meres.

The scenes between Woodward and Pennington simmer with generational tension, emphasised by the cramped attic set they share, while Robert Urquhart's officer class bully is one of the nastiest opponents Callan faces. The Section man's fate is all the more uncertain as, tied up, he has to talk for his life instead of fighting for it. In a story that almost makes your head spin with the level of double-crossing going on, it's fitting that Lefarge's avenging of Bellini's murder is the climactic moment.

A return to form, and a terrific piece of television.

S4.11 THE RICHMOND FILE: CALL ME ENEMY

Writer: George Markstein
Director: Bill Bain
Designer: David Marshall

FIRST UK TRANSMISSION: Wednesday 10 May 1972, 9.00 pm

CAST: Charles Rea (Engineer), Brian Croucher (Jarrow). *Uncredited on screen* - Peter Beton (Radio announcer)

PRODUCTION

Rehearsals: From Friday 10 March 1972
Location Filming: Fox Hills Estate, Longcross, near Chertsey, Surrey; Staines by-pass and nearby roads (Tuesday 14 March 1972)
Camera Rehearsals/Recording: Teddington Studio One, Wednesday 22 and Thursday 23 March 1972[123]

TV TIMES: 'The two top agents of East and West come face to face.'
6-12 May 1972, Southern edition

MISSION PROFILE: The KGB Colonel 'Richmond' has apparently defected to the West and Callan is detailed to debrief him at a safe house deep in the countryside; Hunter listens in. The two men play psychological games with each other until Richmond tries to convince Callan that Meres is a traitor. Having apparently converted Callan to his arguments and persuaded him to join him in going back to Russia, in the end Richmond can't take the chance that the Section agent is deceiving him and knocks him out. The Colonel escapes alone, with Section agents tailing him. Bishop congratulates Callan for drawing out Richmond's real loyalties.

A MAN LIKE ME: Richmond knows a great deal about Callan's background. His father was on the dole and the agent never had a decent education; later, Callan himself was demoted in the army, who took away his medal – awarded for an unspecified act of bravery[124] – and he served a prison sentence in Wormwood Scrubs (as well as in Castleview and possibly Pentonville). When Callan was in Lubyanka, the KGB decided that he held the rank of Major. Richmond also says that on 23 June 1964, Callan killed his lover, meaning the Soviet defector has a goodreason to murder his SIS minder – if his claim is true. A previous opposition agent Callan debriefed died in 'an accident'.

Richmond acquired his Irish identity from a dead man buried in Dublin. He says he works for Section Nine of the First Directorate, commanded by Rodin, the KGB's equivalent of Hunter. Before that, he worked for the Second Chief Directorate under General Bribanov and was an instructor at Pushkino, 'Zyranov's outfit.' Richmond claims that his father was a Russian shoemaker hanged by the Germans and that his mother is dead. In a striking similarity, Callan's parents were killed by a German V2 attack in the Blitz. As well as a seemingly dead girlfriend, Richmond also has a wife called Helena and two children living in the Soviet Union.[125]

Section Kills: 26 (Assuming Richmond is telling the truth, his lover; shot by accident, not on the first Hunter's orders.)

LONELY: Ferries Richmond and Callan to an SIS safe house eleven miles from Oxford and predictably complains about being so far from London and not even getting a cup of tea for his trouble. Callan warns him to forget ever seeing the house. 'You know me,' Lonely says brightly. 'Exactly', replies Callan ominously.

A TIE AND A CREST: Callan's prickly class-consciousness is easily riled by Richmond when the KGB man reveals that he holds a higher rank: 'Oh, I do beg your pardon, Colonel, *sir!* Fancy having to share quarters with an NCO. Perhaps I should stand up when you eat!'

In a calculated attempt to rile Callan, Richmond mentions that Meres was protected from court martial for his involvement in the death of a private soldier, because his father is in the House of Lords. 'I wonder where you'd be now, Callan, if you had a Lord for a father?' Despite his complicated relationship with Meres, Callan refuses to believe that his fellow agent is a traitor.

Regardless of their last acrimonious meeting, Bishop remains supportive of Callan, demanding that he's pulled out of the debriefing in order to protect him. He also congratulates the Section's senior man on the way he handles Richmond's interrogation.

The Section have a country home safe house near Oxford protected by an electronic alarm system. Every room is bugged: the microphones' signals are relayed to Hunter's office and there are hidden CCTV cameras.

ALCOHOL, TOBACCO AND FIREARMS: Once again, the Section lays on a ready supply of Scotch, as well as wine, which Callan bluntly categorises as 'red with meat, white with fish.' Aside from the SIS men's Section-issue handguns, Callan comes face-to-needle with the KGB's latest 'hydrocyanic acid-ejecting pen', which induces heart failure. Back in the real world, the KGB were using very similar assassination weapons.

Richmond steals Callan's Magnum before leaving the safe house.

SPY-SPEAK: The battle of wills and wits between Callan and Richmond produces some wonderfully earthy verbal jousting at each other's expense. 'That the best you can do? Cuisine à la British Rail?' Richmond complains as Callan presents him with an ostentatiously proletarian fry up for breakfast. Throughout, Richmond's eloquence seems to give him the upper hand. 'What has [the job] got you?' he asks the Section man. 'Only their contempt. And believe me, they have contempt for you. Maybe they're a little afraid too, but only a little. They've got you too well trained, you see... You're a good mechanic, Callan. But you'll never be good enough to sit at their table.' 'When I want your advice, mate, I'll send you a wire,' Callan tightly replies.

His counter move to the KGB man's psychological jabs is more direct: 'We've got you now, Richmond. And we don't need anyone your end,' referring back to the spy exchange in 'That'll Be The Day'.

In the end, there's no one more aware of his failings than Callan himself: 'A recidivist, a relapser... a loser.'

PAWNS AND PLAYERS: THOMAS PATRICK MCKENNA (1929-2011) was born in Ireland and over the course of his career became one of his homeland's most respected actors. He starred at the celebrated Abbey Theatre and featured in stage productions by highly regarded writers like Harold Pinter, George Bernard Shaw, James Joyce and Anton

Chekov. McKenna's choice of movie and TV roles was as diverse as Corin Redgrave's, covering titles such as the film version of Brendan Behan's *The Quare Fellow* (1962), *Straw Dogs* (1971), *Espionage* (1963), *The Sweeney* – 'Night Out' (1975), *Beasts* (1976), *Blake's 7* – 'Bounty', and *Doctor Who* – 'The Greatest Show in the Galaxy' (1988). In 1967, six years before his guest appearance in *Callan*, he starred with William Squire in the *Armchair Theatre* production of Jordan Lawrence's 'Quite an Ordinary Knife'. A year later, McKenna was in the tense and bleak 'Day of Execution', an episode of the downbeat *Man in a Suitcase* (1968).

In Ireland, the T.P. McKenna Scholarships and the T.P. McKenna Perpetual Trophy commemorate the nationally cherished actor. There was a deliberate, political dimension to his casting: 'The fact that Richmond is [portrayed as an] Irishman is a comment on England's attitude to the Irish,'[126] noted Edward Woodward, 'which of course was in the news all through this period. The IRA were going great guns, in more ways than one, so it was interesting that he was Irish.'

BRIAN CROUCHER (born 1942) was a genuine 'recidivist'[127] and 'working-class boy from Hackney.' Another early 1970s part that saw him involved with espionage was *The Jensen Code* (1973), a serial for older children. Later in that decade, and into the early 1980s, he made a name for himself playing tough characters in a variety of crime and thriller shows such as *Out* (1980), *The XYY Man* (1977), *Minder* – 'Monday Night Fever' (1980), *The Chinese Detective* (1981), *Edge of Darkness* (1985) as well as Trevor Preston's film *I'll Sleep When I'm Dead* (2003). He appeared regularly in *EastEnders* (1995-97) and spoofed his tendency to be employed by the film-making wing of Thames TV in the anarchic BBC2 comedy *The Young Ones* (1984), when he could be seen holding a bank cashier at gunpoint and telling him to 'keep putting the money in the bag' marked 'Property of Euston Films'.

Croucher also made his mark in the fantasy genre, appearing with Russell Hunter in the *Doctor Who* story 'The Robots of Death' (1977) and as the recurring villain Travis in the second series of *Blake's 7* (1979). Croucher was happy to be cast as villains, "cos it gives you a lot of freedom. You can be who you want and most of the time the directors like it. If you look like Roger Moore you've got to wear the suit and have the quiff; you can't do too much, you've got to do "debonair" acting.'

INFORMATION: 'Richmond was definitely sympathetic and T.P. McKenna played him beautifully,'[128] James Mitchell remarked on the character he'd introduced in 'That'll Be the Day'. 'Callan had by [now] become top man. It was manifest he was not Hunter. But he was, as it were, the executive arm – which is what the KGB call their killers! Hunter's realised by now that he's totally reliant on Callan because no one else can do a job quite as he can.' 'Call Me Enemy' was the only *Callan* story credited to story editor George Markstein; evidently he found a way round the relevant Writers' Guild commissioning restrictions (see 'Heir Apparent'). 'It became a mental duel between him and his counterpart,'[129] Markstein said of the story, modestly elaborating, 'I felt very unsure about people following it. I simply hoped the story would be tense enough, and the setting would be claustrophobic enough, and – with two very fine actors like that getting sparks off each other – that the audience would hold.'

'George was an absolute joy,'[130] Woodward recalled affectionately. 'He was a delightful man and an extremely good writer. He and James [Mitchell] worked so closely together, because George was [story] editor as well and so knew every nuance of the whole thing.

He reintroduced [Richmond] and gave him this marvellous strength matching Callan, as they had the same job on different sides of the fence. This was at the height of the Cold War – it looked many times as if America was going to go to war with Russia – so it was a very dangerous period for us all. Therefore, the Russians were the really bad guys.' Reg Collin recollected that the idea of an episode based around two actors was 'just to change the pace. I seem to recall George had the idea for a trilogy and masterminded all three scripts.'[131]

From here until the end of the series, T.P. McKenna is back in the opening titles as 'Guest Star', together with Geoffrey Chater as part of the regular ensemble cast. Like the rest of Series Four, 'Call Me Enemy' was continuity heavy, with references as far back as 'The Good Ones Are All Dead', as well as 'Death of a Hunter', 'Breakout' and 'That'll Be the Day'. Anthony Valentine's scenes with Woodward and McKenna were the last ones of the episode to be recorded.

'The whole three [episodes] of 'The Richmond File' were my favourite,'[132] Woodward fondly said. 'It was made into a three-parter because T.P. McKenna agreed to do it and he was probably one of the best actors around at that time. I absolutely loved working with him and 'Call Me Enemy', in particular, was incredibly well written and directed. Reginald Collin, the producer, was brilliant and a good director himself, and had one overriding thing of importance, and that was that nothing, in terms of writing, should be rushed; there should be pace when it needs the pace, but nothing should be *rushed*. The time is taken to speak the lines, understand the lines, get the nuance behind the lines. The interesting thing about [the episode] is Callan and Richmond undercutting each other, each trying to outwit the other. Both of them are on exactly the same level in intelligence, so it becomes a *real* chess game.

'It was one of the biggest series sets that we had,' Woodward noted of the Section's country safe house. 'In fact, I think it was *the* biggest set that we had.' By contrast, the Section tape recorder must have been outmoded even in 1972. 'Isn't it wonderful?' Woodward chuckled. 'This was the organisation that our nation depended on, and they didn't have the money to get the up to date equipment! There was an enormous budget for sending operatives here, there and the other way in cars and planes, but *nothing* for the office. Here's this beautiful big house, presumably being run by a caretaker when there's nobody there, with the grounds maintained, but they've got a terrible tape recorder in a tatty office! That was deliberate, too: it wasn't a [production] mistake.'

Rewatching the episode in 2007, one scene in particular highlighted the passing of the years for Woodward. 'I threw myself across this big table, and slid from one side to the other, clearing everything on it as I went, and my wife, lovely Michele, said to me this morning when we watched it, "My God, you couldn't do that today!" I can hardly *sit* at a table, let alone throw myself over it.'

'I first saw Edward Woodward in Shakespeare in Nottingham – I think it was in *Measure for Measure*,'[133] Brian Croucher remembered. 'He was a consummate stage actor and so was Russell [Hunter], up in Scotland. He was a lovely, lovely man.' Croucher remembers that 'Call Me Enemy' was 'one of the first real television jobs I did. I turned up early at the studio, and they said, "You can't go in there," because [Edward and Anthony] were having their spiders [hairpieces] fitted. As a young actor, I thought, "This is weird. It's like people who won't grow old gracefully." I wanted [my character] to have longish hair and a tie-dyed shirt because I wanted him not to be a "company man", as it were. I played him as a hippy and they couldn't believe it: "Is this our technician?"'

In *The Sun*, McKenna intriguingly told Chris Kenworthy 'I based my performance on Gordon Lonsdale. After all, he was a Russian spy who floated around for a long time in this country.'[134] McKenna's choice was important because Gordon Arnold Lonsdale was one of the highest-profile Russian agents caught during the Cold War and 'regarded as the most dangerous Communist agent to operate here since [WW2].'[135]

Konon Trofimovich Molody (1922-1970) adopted the cover identity of the dead Canadian Gordon Arnold Lonsdale (1924-1943) in 1953 when he was posted to the USA. While there, he assisted the atomic secrets spy Rudolph Abel (1903-1971) in his operations and met the KGB agents Peter and Helen Kroger, who worked with him when he was sent to England in 1954. By 1959, Molody was involved in what became known as the Portland spy ring (see 'Jack-on-Top' and 'Nice People Die at Home', Chapter 6). In 1961, Molody was caught being handed top secret information on Waterloo Bridge. He managed to conceal his real identity throughout his Old Bailey trial and subsequent prison term, until his Russian masters revealed it as part of the deal to exchange him for the British spy Greville Wynne in April 1964.

Clearly, like McKenna the writing team were heavily inspired by Molody in creating the character of Richmond, as 'Lonsdale' is even used as a placeholder name for him in early story outlines.[136] Like Richmond, Lonsdale/Molody was outgoing and gregarious, an inventive entrepreneur and had a wife, Galina, at home in Russia, although he also enjoyed other female company, like Richmond again.

Strikingly, Molody's fate after he returned to the Soviet Union reflected his fictional counterpart's comment that 'safety can only be found among our enemies.' After his return, he was given low level intelligence duties and, perhaps feeling let down by his employers, began drinking heavily. During the following six years, Molody was regularly treated by KGB doctors and after the consultations repeatedly complained of feeling worse instead of healthier, until he was found dead at only 48 in 1970. In a final irony, Molody was celebrated as a hero of the Soviet Union, along with Abel, in a set of Russian stamps released in 1990. The Portland affair was so infamous that it became the subject of the feature film *Ring of Spies* (1963) directed by Robert Tronson and starring William Sylvester as Molody. As well as possibly inspiring several *Callan* scripts, the case also formed the basis of the *Danger Man* episode 'Don't Nail Him Yet' (1964).

The plot point of the media announcing the defection of a spy without the security services informing him first – heard as Callan and Richmond listen to the radio news – may have been inspired by the same gambit MI6 use on Alec Leamas in *The Spy Who Came in from the Cold*.

Richmond mentions *Pravda* and the *People's Daily*, the daily Communist newspapers of Russia and China respectively. *Pravda* (English translation: 'Truth'), the official voice of Communism during the Cold War, was started by revolutionaries before WW1, and, at its height, sold in millions. It's still produced today, from the same building on Pravda Street in Moscow. (A vintage edition can be seen on the back cover of the 2012 reissue of Len Deighton's novel *Spy Story*.) The *People's Daily*, which began publishing in June 1946, is the official paper of the Central Committee of the Communist Party of China. It has a worldwide circulation of between three and four million editions in Arabic, English, French, Japanese, Korean, Russian and Spanish.

When Callan asks Lonely if he wants 'green stamps', he's referring to the trading stamps produced by the Green Shield Trading Stamp Company, popular in Britain and Ireland in the 1960s and 1970s. Available from shops and garages, they encouraged spending as a certain collected amount rewarded the consumer with a choice of free gifts. They ceased being issued in 1991.

On 8 July 1995, 'Call Me Enemy' was shown as part of Channel 4's *Vintage Thames* evening, a six-week season celebrating the TV company. Although the *Mail on Sunday*'s TV critic was dismissive of that night's Sid James comedy *Bless this House*, he considered *Callan* 'a more worthwhile repeat'.[137]

MISSION ANALYSIS: *'It's our friends who kill us.'* With this simple closing sentence, George Markstein restates *Callan*'s bleak view of the espionage world. From 'A Magnum for Schn-eider' onwards, people have regularly been seen falsely befriending each other and manipulating or killing them later, while genuine friends have betrayed each other and colleagues have gambled with each others' lives – on both sides.

On close inspection, Richmond's plan doesn't make a great deal of sense: why risk pretending to defect to the SIS if he's really on a mission? Surely arriving in England discreetly would have been easier, even if a watch is being kept for him at ports and airports? However, this conceit allows the series to undertake a virtual two-hander for over 30 minutes of the overall running time, with 'two champions facing each other on equal terms.' It's not surprising this is one of Edward Woodward's favourite episodes. *The Prisoner* – 'Once Upon a Time' (1968) and *Storyboard* – 'The Traitor '(1983), respectively story edited and scripted by Markstein, feature similarly extensive one-on-one interrogations.

Throughout, the real people inside the agents are teasingly revealed – or are they? Part of the story's appeal lies in trying to separate the truth from the lies in what the two men say to each other. In their war of nerves, even Callan repeatedly mentioning the fish pie regularly served up amid the routines of Pentonville prison is a psychological tactic. Additionally, Markstein skilfully sets up and explores the last three episodes' overall theme – that professionals like Richmond and Callan, even though they're on opposite sides, have more in common with each other than the people they work for.

All the way through, the point is made that Callan could one day find himself in the same position as Richmond. In a third layer of intrigue, which anticipates how adept Markstein would become at intertwining multiple plot strands in his later spy novels, he keeps the audience – aware that Meres had previously shot Callan – hooked on the distinct possibility that Meres might be a deep-cover traitor, and Valentine is on excellent, danger-ous form. Amid the drama, there are some enjoyable moments of humour, supplied by Lonely moaning about driving so far outside London, Hunter's surprise at Jarrow's rather relaxed dress code, and the Section commander's affronted eavesdropping on Richmond.

Seeing two acting heavyweights like Woodward and McKenna going head-to-head in such committed performances conclusively affirms *Callan*'s reputation as a mature, intel-ligent appraisal of the ethical contradictions of espionage. Together with 'If He Can, So Could I', 'Call Me Enemy' is arguably why the series is still so highly regarded today.

S4.12 THE RICHMOND FILE: DO YOU RECOGNISE THE WOMAN?

Writer: Bill Craig
Director: Peter Duguid
Designer: Mike Hall

FIRST UK TRANSMISSION: Wednesday 17 May 1972, 9.00 pm

CAST: Sheila Fay (Norah), John Moore (Dowsett), Harry Walker (Technician), Cheryl Hall (Gladys), Bella Emberg (Prison officer)

EXTRAS/WALK-ONS: (*Uncredited on screen*) Dennis Redwood (Down-and-out outside mission), Winifred Sabine, Varely Thomas, Aubrey Danvers Walker, Laurence Archer (Down-and-outs inside mission), Brian Justice (Section man, Hunter's assistant), Gill Godstone, Iris Fry (Prisoners in kitchen)

PRODUCTION

Rehearsals: From Friday 24 March 1972
Outside Broadcast Recording: St. Luke's Social Centre, Elm Road, Kingston, Surrey; the duck pond, Ham Common, Richmond, Surrey (Tuesday 28 March), City Council Central Depot (the old prison), Stanhope Road, St. Albans, Hertfordshire (Wednesday 29 March)
Camera Rehearsals/Recording: Teddington Studio One, Wednesday 5 and Thursday 6 April 1972[138]

TV TIMES: 'Richmond, on the run from the Section, fulfils his grim assignment and once again eludes Callan.'
13-19 May 1972, Southern edition

MISSION PROFILE: The Section discovers that Flo Mayhew (real name: Svetlana Souraikin, codename: Osprey – see 'Call Me Sir!') was on Richmond's team. In an attempt to discover his whereabouts, they involve her in a fake spy exchange. Hunter and Bishop offer Flo her freedom, then take it away in an effort to make her crack and reveal where Richmond (codename: Egret) is hiding. Not realising Richmond has been sent to England specifically to spring her from prison, Flo escapes from Callan's care and meets with Richmond at the spy cell he's taken command of, based in a homeless mission. It's too late: Moscow has learned that Flo has been cooperating with the Section and has sent orders for her to be killed. Richmond reluctantly complies before escaping.

A MAN LIKE ME: There are '4,000 words' in Callan's KGB file. He goes along with the plan to destabilise Flo, but after he learns that Flo is a single mother he's no longer comfortable with the idea, suggesting reducing her prison sentence. He's also visibly upset on seeing her body, pushing past Hunter and ignoring his question as to whether he's caught Richmond.

Unusually, Callan takes some of his model soldiers with him when flat sitting Flo.

LONELY: He's asleep inside the MCF again when Callan wakes him up, and accidentally hits the horn when he turns around. Confronted by Flo, he gives vent to his hatred for spies, particularly 'Mata Hari' until, warned off by Callan, he shuts up and drives.

A TIE AND A CREST: The scene where Meres finds Callan handcuffed under the sink, courtesy of Flo, in the bathroom of the Section's safe house in Mayfair, is a minor comic masterpiece; Toby sits on edge of the bath as he visibly tries to hide his amusement at Callan's predicament. Making it even funnier, Meres has to leave Callan where he is for some time, returning to the Section to send someone back with 'bolt cutters'.

ALCOHOL, TOBACCO AND FIREARMS: Callan and Flo both have a Scotch when she's installed in the Section's Mayfair flat. He pours her another to steady her nerves after she's been given the bad news about having to complete her prison sentence.

Flo later pretends to switch to bleach in a fake suicide attempt. Like Richmond in the previous episode, she steals another of Callan's Magnums, but, significantly, doesn't take the opportunity to kill him.

Meres shoots Dowsett in the hand to stop him from using a coded radio transmitter, and Richmond executes Flo, presumably with the Magnum revolver he took from Callan.

SPY-SPEAK: Meres is not impressed with the Section's tracking operation, which is hidden in a TV detector van, trying to triangulate the Russian cell's radio signals. 'Eight groaning days, orbiting this miserable manor, and what's been achieved? A queue for television licences at the post office!'

'From the general atmosphere of cloying smugness I infer that the code has been broken?' says Bishop, on his usual sardonic form. His quick wit is at its most cruel when he commends Flo on facing going back to prison, knowing that, as anticipated, she's anything but ready: 'Your bearing in the face of this bitter disappointment can only compel admiration.' 'I'll have fourteen years to practice it' is her tremulous response.

Meres sums up Hunter's approach to how he handles his operatives with his usual acid wit: 'Don't applaud, sir. That way your right hand would know what your left hand was doing.'

Richmond describes Flo/Svetlana as 'soft, like a marshmallow – with a ball bearing inside it. Try biting one some time.'

PAWNS AND PLAYERS: SHEILA FAY (1926-2013) was best known as Beryl Hennessy's gobby Mum in *The Liver Birds* (1969-72).

BELLA EMBERG (1937-) is equally adept at comedy and drama, appearing in the relaunched *Doctor Who* (2006), *Pennies from Heaven* (1978) and *Trial and Retribution* (2002), although she is probably best known as a comedy foil to the comedian Russ Abbot. She played another prison officer in *Within These Walls* (1975-76).

JOHN MOORE first appeared on television in 1957 and, among roles in many other dramas, played seven different characters throughout the run of *Z Cars*.

INFORMATION: In his last script for the series, Bill Craig decided to kill off Flo Mayhew. '[Richmond] had been recruited into the Committee for State Security Bureau Four; very early on, there was an affair and her daughter was his daughter.'[139] Reflecting on the story's bleak conclusion after the preceding lighter tone, he added, 'My own thesis here is that when you are dealing with a potentially tragic situation, the salt in that situation is comedy. Comedy and tragedy are very close indeed.' Recalling his last contribution to *Callan*, Peter

Duguid said, 'I thought this was quite a strong piece. [Watching it again] the acting was much stronger than I thought it was at the time. It was a good story, Bill Craig again, and it was getting jolly near to John le Carré. Sheila Fay was rather good I seem to remember, and Sarah Lawson was quite fetching.'[140] The director remembered that the disused prison in St. Albans had another claim to fame: 'The titles to *Porridge* [1974-77] used the same red brick arch.' There are continuity references to 'That'll Be the Day', 'Call Me Sir!' and 'Call Me Enemy', and for *Callan* die-hards, it's tempting to think that Cheryl Hall is playing the same cockney character as she had in 'Summoned to Appear'.

There are some interesting stage directions in the rehearsal script. Dowsett is described as 'a small man in his early 50s, ill-clad in a badly fitting suit and frayed pullover' while his 'sister' was 'a severe woman in her late 40s: uncompromising in dress: unprepossessing in features.' When Flo started a fight in the prison kitchen, there was 'the sound of a well-built prison officer being chucked through a rack of cooking utensils.' Endearingly, Liz was mistakenly called 'Lisa' in the rehearsal draft. Woodward improvised the dialogue as he dragged Flo from the bathroom to the sofa (as it is not in the camera script).

The mission congregation sings the last two verses of 'Soldiers of Christ Arise', hymn 436 in Congregational Hymnary. Radio signals from Russia are relayed to Richmond's cell via a Russian fishing trawler, previously mentioned in 'Call Me Enemy' and a common disguise for spy ships during the Cold War.

In the same week that 'Do You Recognise the Woman?' was transmitted, Woodward was singing on the ITV show *Saturday Variety* (1972).

George Markstein would reuse the storyline of a female criminal released from prison to draw out Communist agents again in his script *Return of the Saint* – 'The Debt Collectors' (1978). The tone is notably darker than usual for that glossy show, with the MI5 chief Sir Charles Medley (Geoffrey Keen) telling Simon Templar 'using people is necessary in my business.' Notably, Simon Templar (Ian Ogilvy), makes an almost identical comment to the one Callan made in 'Summoned to Appear', about not reading 'the papers' because the news is depressing . MI5 is also as impoverished as the Section and its agents use Magnum revolvers.

A likely model for Flo/Svetlana is the Polish allied spy Krystayna Skarbek (1908-1952), well-known after WW2 as she was awarded the OBE, the French Croix de Guerre and in 1952 featured in the international magazine *Picture Post* in a series of illustrated articles about her life. After joining the Polish Special Operations Executive, Krystayna operated throughout the war under her cover name Christine Granville in Cairo, France and between Poland and Hungary, relaying essential information via her expertise as a skier. Known as Churchill's favourite spy, Krystayna was rumoured to have had an affair with Ian Fleming and been the model for Vesper Lynd and Tatiana Romanova in his James Bond novels *Casino Royale* and *From Russia with Love*.

MISSION ANALYSIS: *'Not everything goes in the file, does it, not least the way it really is.'* Previous characterisations of women in the series, and the spy genre generally, had alternated between glamour interest, victims or femme fatales, or a combination of all three. Even the notable exception *The Avengers*, with its independent martial arts heroines, tended to present Cathy Gale and Emma Peel as feminist superheroines rather than real people. Up until now, even *Callan*'s only female regular was someone who did the typing and answered the phone, although honourable attempts had been made to give Liz more depth.

In this context, Flo Mayhew is a major breakthrough. A recurring character previously seen as a cool, sardonic artist in 'Call Me Sir!', here she comes into her own. Bill Craig's thoughtful script and Sarah Lawson's considered performance present a woman who is as wily, flawed and as human as Callan, in a variation on the overall theme in 'The Richmond File' that agents share more common ground with their opposite numbers than their controllers – a point explicitly made in Flo's dialogue. Although the episode betrays its age when Callan says a long prison sentence will break Mayhew because 'she's a woman', and emphasis is placed on providing her with a fashionable new wardrobe and fragrant bath oils, she succeeds as a convincing portrait of a desperate person driven to breaking point. A fourteen-year prison sentence would destroy anyone's spirit, regardless of their gender.

From taking centre stage in the previous episode, Richmond is relegated to the sidelines as controller of a spy cell. Gender politics are present here too: Norah emnity for Flo is visually conveyed through her plainness versus Flo's femininity, while Norah's suspicions of Richmond's real motives present her as a more dedicated agent than Mayhew. It's an interesting inversion of the status quo in the Section, where Callan, a field agent, is the unpredictable character who often has his own agenda.

As the series approaches its close, its penultimate episode is bleakly sophisticated. Aside from Callan and Flo's almost marital banter, being humane is portrayed as a weakness, from the opening scenes where a Soviet cell is seen operating from the cover of a homeless mission, via Flo's delight at being freed being ruthlessly exploited by the Section, to Callan's concern for her during her faked suicide, which allows her to steal his gun and escape. Ironically, this act leads to her death at the hands of Richmond, when duty ultimately wins out over sentiment. The scene where Flo prepares for death, asking her lover/executioner to shoot her in the heart, not the head, and to look after her child, Irena – Richmond promises he will, as 'she's my daughter too' – is all the more chilling for the controlled, matter-of-fact performances of Lawson and McKenna.

Dramatically, the effect is shattering.

S4.13 THE RICHMOND FILE: A MAN LIKE ME

Writer: James Mitchell
Director: Reg Collin
Designer: Bill Palmer

FIRST UK TRANSMISSION: Wednesday 24 May 1972, 9.00 pm

CAST: Robin Ellis (Harris), Belinda Carroll (Caroline), Peter Sallis (Routledge), Gwen Nelson (Mrs Glover), Stephen Whittaker (Deane), Wally Thomas (Security Man). *Uncredited on screen:* Derek Ware (Stuntman for Richmond)

EXTRAS/WALK-ONS: (*Uncredited on screen*) Audrey Searle (Lady), Fred Davis (Passer-by, exterior), Les Shannon (Hunter's agent)

PRODUCTION

Rehearsals: From Wednesday 12 April
Location Filming: Clarence Road, Kingston Hill, Kingston, Surrey; Ladderstile Ride, Kingston-upon-Thames (Friday 7 April 1972); Vine Products Ltd, The Winery, Kingston-upon-Thames, Surrey (Friday 7 April 1972, Monday 10 April and Tuesday 11 April 1972)
Camera Rehearsals/Recording: Teddington Studio One, Thursday 20, Friday 21 April 1972[139]

TV TIMES: 'The last episode in the present series brings a fitting climax to the running battle between Callan and Richmond. But if Richmond loses the ultimate showdown, Callan certainly doesn't win…'
20-26 May 1972, Southern edition

MISSION PROFILE: Trapped in Britain and on the run from the Section, Richmond hides in the home of Peter Harris, a sleeper agent. Hunter authorises the computer EDNA (Electronic Distributed Number Assessor) to compile a list of the people most likely to help Richmond – it produces Harris's name but also suggests Callan himself as a candidate. At the same time, Callan locates the KGB colonel's hiding place, via Harris's one-off purchase of a Russian magazine called *Krocodil* from a left wing bookshop; the foreign journal carries details of Richmond's escape route.

The Section closes in and while Meres interrogates Harris, Callan is ordered to prevent Richmond, hiding out in a Vodka warehouse in Wapping, from leaving England on a Russian ship. In a gun battle between the two agents, Lonely is wounded and Richmond, after being shot by Callan, begs him for a fatal bullet instead of interrogation by Snell. Callan obliges. Hunter is furious, and Callan walks away from the Section, an outcast once again.

A MAN LIKE ME: In the series' last episode, it's ironic that Callan's emotional responses have become so predictable that a computer can dispassionately conclude that he will help Richmond. However, his intuition about the KGB relaying instructions to Richmond through a Russian paper leads him to Peter Harris ahead of EDNA's list of other suspects. Predictably, Callan doesn't like taking orders from a computer.

Both Richmond and Callan are genuinely, realistically afraid of facing each other. The KGB man is sincere in his disappointment when his opposite number turns down the offer of going freelance. In their final confrontation, Callan paradoxically remains loyal to the service that has exploited him for so long.

Disturbingly, Callan appears to enjoy intimidating Harris and Caroline.

Section Kills: 27

LONELY: Lonely has always owed Callan a debt, unspecified in the TV series (but explained in the novels, see Chapter 9) concerning a gangster, Rinty. This is finally repaid as Lonely crashes the MCF into the lorry coming to take Richmond to a waiting ship and then takes a bullet for his friend, saving his life. In one of the series' most affecting scenes, Lonely, swigging Vodka and tearful, pledges his continued friendship: 'I think we're even. I don't owe you anything any more... We're still mates, Mr. Callan. You're the only mate I got.'

A TIE AND A CREST: Tellingly, when Bishop visits Hunter, he sits in the former's command chair. Harris went to a public school, and Meres passes himself off as Arthur Dixon, a fellow alumnus from two years above, who's organising the annual old boys' reunion. Later dropping his alias, it's a final bow for Toby's public school bully: 'Do you know, when I was at school... I was an absolute *stinker*. And I haven't changed a bit.' (The dialogue echoes one of his nastiest moments, hospitalising Lonely in 'You Should Have Got Here Sooner'.) He then does something very unpleasant to Harris off-screen.

A dedicated Section man to the end, Meres is impassive as Callan throws down his gun and walks away after killing Richmond, emphasising the gulf that still exists between them.

ALCOHOL, TOBACCO AND FIREARMS: Once installed in Harris's flat, Richmond helps himself to Scotch, taking another after Meres has called. Routledge, the EDNA technician, has to smoke outside the computer room as his machine is sensitive to tobacco fumes. Appropriately enough for a series that has always been awash with alcohol, the final shoot out is in a vodka warehouse.

The agents use different guns: further emphasising how similar thay are, Callan and Richmond are both armed with Magnums. Meres carries a Walther PPK.

SPY-SPEAK: Like Callan, Hunter is not a fan of new technology: 'The only experience I've had with computers is with my bank statements. They don't inspire confidence.'

Richmond takes great pleasure in the coded 'joke' hidden in *Krocodil*: '"Woman to night watchman: 'I though you said you were a good Communist?' Night watchman: 'I am.' Woman: 'But you keep saying you see nocturnal spirits.' Watchman: 'I do. I'm a watchman in a dockside vodka depot.'"'

Stafford asks Hunter about using force to take Richmond: 'Can I shoot first?' 'Only if he's already dead. I want him alive,' the Section chief replies.

Hunter's ominous last words: 'I'm going to break you this time, Callan.' The agent's bitter rejoinder: 'You are too late. *You are too. Bloody. LATE!*' As originally written, Callan's last line was to have been the equally effective, 'I'm already broken, Hunter.'[142]

PAWNS AND PLAYERS: PETER SALLIS (born 1921) appeared as Norman Clegg in a staggering 295 episodes of the BBC twilight-years comedy *Last of the Summer Wine* between 1973 and 2010. Late in his career, he found fame with a younger audience as the voice of the cheese-loving inventor in the various adventures of Wallace and Gromit, having previously provided the voice of Rat for *The Wind in the Willows* (from 1984-88). Elsewhere in the spy genre, Sallis appeared opposite Honor Blackman's Cathy Gale in *The Avengers* – 'The Wringer' (1964) and played John Drake's boss Henry Gordon in the first series *Danger Man* episode, 'Find and Destroy' (1961). He portrayed Sidney Bliss, Britain's last hangman, in *The New Statesman* (1987) and, like Belinda Carroll, appeared in *Raffles* with Anthony Valentine.

BELINDA CARROLL (born 1945) of Irish ancestry, is the younger sister of the late Kate O'Mara. She taught herself acting, which she said 'wouldn't happen these days. My first role was playing the part of a blind girl in the theatre. The director said "I'll give her a try," and within weeks I was in [the musical] *Salad Days*.'[143] Her first television series appear-ances were in a series of melodramas under the title *Gaslight Theatre* (1965), with Ronnie Barker. 'I recorded them at the BBC Theatre in Wood Lane, and it was quite nerve wracking,' she said, adding, that, at that time, 'being a stage actress I didn't have much television experience.'

Carroll later appeared in *Malice Aforethought* (1979) with Harold Innocent: 'I was very proud of that, Harold was a lovely man. It was a very good series.' Of her *Raffles* appearance, in the pilot episode 'The Amateur Cracksman' (1975), she remembered, 'I was three months pregnant with my daughter and had to fit into those costumes!' More recently, Carroll appeared in the film version of Ray Cooney's long-running farce, *Run for Your Wife* (2012), reflecting her abundant career on stage, particularly in highly successful comedies such as *There's a Girl in My Soup*, *Charley's Aunt* and *No Sex, Please – We're British*.

ROBIN ELLIS (born 1942) became famous for his starring role in the BBC's lusty Cornish drama *Poldark* (1975-77); in the first series of the BBC remake in 2015, he was granted a cameo role as a harsh judge opposite the new Poldark, Aidan Turner. Ellis was also a hotel guest who annoyed John Cleese's repressed hotel manager in the first series of *Fawlty Towers* (1975). In 1982, Ellis memorably starred as Sam Howard, 'catching the humanity in the face of unseen forces,'[144] in the satirical science fiction play 'Bright Eyes', one of the productions in the BBC's *Play for Tomorrow* anthology series.

INFORMATION: 'It was another one of those where it was a nightmare stuffing it all into 50 minutes,'[145] James Mitchell remembered of *Callan*'s final episode. 'Again, you see how clever Reg was to enable the sleight of hand of this without the viewers feeling they were being forcibly fed: it was a beautiful job. It's a very delicate line... Richmond is a sympathetic figure really, but he has the same feeling of doom about him as Callan has. The intriguing part in my own mind – without spelling it out – was that Richmond was better than Callan and Callan killed him by chance. The fact that Lonely erupted out of hiding at the critical moment was the only thing that saved Callan's skin.' 'I suspect we asked James to write the last one as a courtesy, knowing it would be the final one,'[146] Reg Collin said. 'I was always pressing that we should finish. Not because any of us didn't want to go on, but I genuinely felt – have always felt – there is an existence beyond which you go at your peril... It was a sentimental journey for me to [direct] the last one.'

'There was a lot of night shooting,'[147] John Keeling remembered. 'We got through it very quickly; it was on that basis that Euston Films asked me to help set up *Special Branch*.' The sequence where Callan self-referentially shoots out a naked light bulb hanging from the roof was improvised during location filming at Keeling's suggestion: 'We were shooting and Reg Colin was looking for shots and discussing it, and I said "Let's shoot the bulb out because that's what the titles do." It just came off the cuff like that... In the [warehouse] scene where Callan and Lonely sit down, it cuts to studio. Reg Collin reshot that, and I don't know why – from the filming point of view I know it was fine, but there must have been something that didn't work. Maybe the dialogue wasn't right. [It] must been expensive to set up.' 'A problem at the lab,'[148] suggested Collin of the reason for the remount. 'Part of the film went up the creek after we finished shooting, so we had to do it in the studio on tape and match it in. So [the scenes of Callan switching on his torch, then talking to an injured Lonely and Richmond], which had a good continuity in [them were] shot at a totally different time. The last scene [between Callan and Lonely] as I recall... was shot against a tiny piece of scenery about four-foot square. We were unable to [fully] recreate the place that we used, which was a bulk wine store in Kingston.'

In the camera script, Harris was to have been rendered unconscious with knockout drops in his tea. One short location scene, of Meres walking up to Harris's front door, was dropped, while Callan originally used his Tucker alias in the bookshop. Lonely's comment 'You're not scared are you, David?' was not scripted and ad-libbed during filming. At the close of the series continuity remains strong, with references to 'That'll Be the Day', 'Call Me Enemy', 'Do You Recognise the Woman?' and Lonely's personal debt to Callan.

The climactic scenes in the warehouse were written slightly differently. Callan's hand shakes as he draws his gun, Lonely climbs into the warehouse through a window to warn him and Richmond hesitates to shoot the thief, as 'even he can't kill Lonely'. A planned scene of the taxi crashing into the Russian lorry was dropped.

A sleeper agent like Peter Harris is a spy in a country or organisation who may lie dormant for several years, until contacted and reactivated as an asset. In June 2010, US intelligence services suspected there was a network of Russian sleeper agents planted all over America. In June of that year, ten suspects were arrested.

Krocodil (English translation: 'Crocodile') was a satirical magazine founded in Russia in 1922. It attacked capitalist countries and leaders and political, religious and ethnic groups opposed to Communism. Contributors included the Futurist writer Vladimir Mayakovsky (1893-1930) and the graphic artist Yulig Abramovich Ganf (1898-1973), who in 1970 was awarded the Fight for Peace Medal. After the fall of Communism in Eastern Europe *Krocodil* ceased publication, but was revived in 2005.

Richmond's copy of *Krocodil* was particularly 'nasty' about Richard Millhouse Nixon (1913-1994), who at the time was President of the United States. The magazine was most likely attacking him because of his visit to China in February 1972, perhaps fearing a Chinese-American alliance. Nixon's trip ultimately had a positive effect on Soviet-American relations, as Russia entered a new period of détente with the USA.

As the 1970s progressed, advances in electronic and computer engineering became increasingly relevant to the worldwide intelligence community, especially at the UK's GCHQ, the government's information gathering facility. This change was reflected in espionage fiction: in James Mitchell's 1974 Callan novel *Death and Bright Water*, in a similar ploy to the one seen in 'A Man Like Me', the KGB use a computer to analyse who is the most efficient candidate for a mission and, unsurprisingly, it turns out to be David Callan. In the same year's *Spy Story*, Len Deighton's 'IPCRESS man' could (perhaps) be found working for a UK government department[149] that used computers to run war game simulations. In the cinema, Francis Ford Coppola's minimalist masterpiece *The Conversation*, also released in 1974, examined the effect that electronic surveillance methods can have when they are turned against the people who use them. 'Computers changed everything on television,'[150] admitted John Keeling. 'It's very amusing in the episode the way they're using that really antiquated computer.'

Among the regular cast and crew, opinions differ as to whether or not 'A Man Like Me' was designed as the final episode of *Callan*. When he wrote the script, James Mitchell hadn't been told, but on reflection was 'glad it was. I think it peaked there.'[151] Reg Collin always maintained that Mitchell's script was intended to be the series' swansong. 'The last episode has more of what the series was about than many others – all of us involved were very emotional about that last episode. By the end of the last series we knew it was the end. It wasn't going any further.'[152] John Keeling cautiously agreed: 'We knew it was going to be the last episode – there was a lot of chat going on, but you never know... we didn't talk so much about "the next series" in those days – [the process] wasn't quite like that.'[153]

'I certainly don't think *I* was under the impression that it was going to be the end,'[154] said Clifford Rose. 'If I had been, I would have remembered that and I certainly don't remember Edward Woodward saying anything. I got the impression that, like so many series, it was open ended – it might have continued, it might not.' For Russell Hunter, after four years the series had reached a natural conclusion. 'There was not any feeling of regret on my part. It was something that was over. I'd done enough of it,'[155] he reflected. Hunter's co-star Anthony Valentine admitted, 'I honestly don't know if we were aware if [it] was the last series or not.'[156]

Some of the cast might have known. Of the atmosphere on set, Belinda Carroll said, 'I remember coming back [afterwards] thinking, "They're not very jolly"... maybe they were under pressure (for time).'[157] She adds, 'It was a big series, I was very pleased to be in it. It was very gritty and you weren't quite sure if Callan was a villain or not as well. [Woodward] was very lucky having Russell as a sidekick, the most unobvious person you could think of. It's just lovely to see [the episode] again and be reminded of that time and those lovely actors who aren't with us any more. At the time it meant an awful lot to me and it's nice to be reminded of it.'

William Squire (who became friends with Carroll and attended her first wedding) recalled receiving a directive during location filming. 'We were in a warehouse and I remember Reg giving me a note about the very last scene with Callan, saying, "Don't make it look too final." I asked why and he said, "There may be another series after this." Teddy would tell me things privately but I don't know how he had left it; whether they could have persuaded him to do some more or not, I don't know. He had [*The Wicker Man*] in mind... I don't think any of us actually believed it was the last one.'[158]

Perhaps the producer was once again considering hedging his bets, but it seems the leading man felt the series had run its course for the time being. 'By this time I was doing a lot of other work and very much wanted to get back into the theatre,'[159] Woodward said. 'I think Jim was tired and felt he couldn't write anymore *yet*; Thames had other things they wanted to bring on-stream. As far as I remember, we still had good viewing figures.' He added, 'There's no way I would have done [*Callan*] if Jim wasn't going to write the beginning one, the middle one and the end one – at least four in the series – and, of course, look at all the other scripts overall. And, I think, there was a general consensus of opinion that "This is probably the end."'[160]

MISSION ANALYSIS: *'He's like you, Callan, in many ways.'* Callan is amused by the idea of using a new-fangled computer in the search for Richmond, but the machine is proved right in its assessment that, under extreme pressure, he'll help the KGB agent. His comment 'ever get the feeling that human beings are becoming redundant?' is prescient as, appropriately for the series' last episode, technology points the way to the future. For two-thirds of the running time, however, Callan and Meres' more traditional approaches of investigation and intimidation still produce results in a straightforward manhunt. There's a last call, too, for the series' trademark nastiness, in the blackmail of Peter Harris through his girlfriend Caroline, bribed by the Section into demanding money for a (bogus) abortion.

Nearly all the climactic duel between Callan and Richmond is fluidly shot on film in a moodily-lit, vast warehouse, so it grates when scenes recorded on video – Callan taking his torch out of his pocket, the agent sitting with a shot Lonely against the wall – are inserted. This production shortcoming aside, the atmospheric setting is perfect for the sad, understated closure to Lonely and Callan's relationship. Mixing fear, relief, tears and gratitude and lit like the *film noir* luminary he should have been, Russell Hunter has rarely been better.

The ethos of the whole series comes into focus in the gunfight, symbolised by Callan shooting out a light bulb in the warehouse where Richmond is hiding. As each episode has always begun with a close-up of a light bulb being shattered by a bullet in front of a brick wall, the clear implication is that this is where Callan has been heading all along.

The trilogy of 'Richmond' stories, with their running theme that opposing foot soldiers in the Cold War share a professional empathy, comes to an intense climax in the final moments. The computer prediction that Callan would aid Richmond – anticipating an ominous new world, where human reactions can be accurately calculated by technology – is fulfilled, and there's a final, cruel irony as Callan's 'help' is to take his KBG's counter-part's life. As well as being a final statement of defiance against Hunter's authority and of solidarity with Richmond, Callan's last act of humanity in the series is again to kill. After he's pulled the trigger, Callan wears a similar, anguished expression to the one he displayed at the end of 'A Magnum for Schneider'. Five years on, he is an exile again, revolted by the killing of another man he liked.

The series couldn't have ended any other way.

9: File On a Working Writer

'Before you settle down with your deckchair on the beach
or in the garden next weekend, make sure you have handy the
opening instalment of the new Callan casebook.'

Sunday Express advert, August 1971

T HE CHILDREN OF THE 1960S AND 1970S were spoilt for choice when it came
to merchandise from their favourite TV shows and films. Mum or Dad's visit to
a toyshop on any high street in England could bring home treats based on *Doctor Who*
(battery-operated Daleks), *Batman* (dressing-up outfits and plastic Batmobiles), *Thunder-birds*, *The Avengers*, *Captain Scarlet and the Mysterons* (die-cast metal models, usually cars), as
well as the James Bond films (anything from a Corgi Aston Martin DB5 to an Airfix model
kit of 007 and Goldfinger's henchman, Oddjob).

Books were also part of this commercial equation, and were the main spin-off for the
older members of the audience. A series watched by all the family, *The Man from UNCLE*
offered sixteen original novels in the UK between 1965 and 1968; *Danger Man*, *The Avengers*
and, particularly, *The Saint*, with its host of Leslie Charteris's short stories and novels to
draw from, also benefited from tie-in books.

Callan lives as vividly on the printed page as it did on television and, between 1967
and 2002, in one TV listings magazine, one tabloid newspaper and five novels, James
Mitchell achieved what must be something of a record in spy fiction: 46 original stories
– over double the amount of Ian Fleming's James Bond missions – that expanded on
David Callan and his twilight world. They all reached an appreciative international audience, with the short stories, all but two of which were published in the *Sunday Express*,
reprinted in Australia's *Sydney Morning Herald* and Malaysia's *Strait Times* newspapers.

Because Mitchell was already an established novelist, the Callan books were conceived
as stand-alone tales using characters from the television series and all of them were published in hardback, with a paperback edition following a year or so later. This set them
apart from being marketed simply as spin-offs like the paperbacks associated with ITC's
canon of adventure shows, such as *UFO*, *Jason King* and *The Persuaders!*, which were often
adaptations of television scripts (a valid approach in the 1960s and 1970s, with repeats
a rarity and no DVD releases). A measure of how seriously the Callan books were taken by

their publishers was the treatment of the covers. *A Magnum for Schneider* featured the image of Edward Woodward's shattered face from the title sequences of Series One and Two, while the paperback edition (*Red File for Callan*) uses a Thames publicity still and a graphic of the swinging light bulb. Hamish Hamilton Ltd. commissioned a special photographic session from Beverly Lebarrow for the cover of *Russian Roulette*, centred on a serious-looking Woodward posing in a firing range with a rifle (for the hardback) and a revolver (for the paperback). The hardback editions of *Death and Bright Water* and *Smear Job* used stills from a photo session for the *Callan* movie of Woodward with a bleeding mouth and holding a Magnum, while the paperback versions featured film poster style illustrations.

According to James Mitchell the title of his first Callan novel was changed to make it more marketable; he recalled writing the first four books in 1969, 1973, 1974 and 1975 respectively. The later books in the series offer some insight into how he might have continued the television series after 'A Man Like Me'. He decided to restore Callan to a position similar to that in the first television series. As a consequence of events in *Russian Roulette*, both *Death and Bright Water* and *Smear Job* have Callan outside the Section and being coerced into working for it, as much a victim of Hunter's intrigues as anyone else. 'It's the direction I would have gone in [on television],'[1] he admitted. 'I had nowhere else to go.' Other elements that hark back to the first series are the mutual loathing between Meres and Callan, and Hunter threatening the ex-agent with execution if he doesn't work for him. Clearly this seemed to be Mitchell's preferred framework. 'It's a very strong area and a thing that can be explored and explored,' he said.

Whether the Thames production team of Collin, Shirley and Markstein would have gone along with this change is a matter for speculation. Mitchell clearly relished being liberated from the need to adhere to television budgets. 'In the books one went abroad quite a bit which I couldn't do [before], they'd go to the US or wherever,' he remarked. 'Also you can introduce more people... I introduced a black agent into the novels.' Had television production continued, he would have attempted to add this character to the ensemble cast: 'There was an automatic flare between Meres and Fitzmaurice that would have been very good value.' Summing up his feelings about presenting his characters in prose form, he simply concluded, 'writing about Callan was something I enjoyed doing.'

IN 1970, THE YEAR BEFORE the popular *Red File for Callan* paperback appeared, Beaverbrook Newspapers commissioned the author to write five short stories for the *Sunday Express* (following a one-off for the Christmas edition of the *TV Times* in 1967). Premiering in August, the initial run was restricted to one page, the plots were straight-forward but showed promise due to the accurate characterisations of Callan and Lonely. Increased to a full spread, the ten stories that followed in 1971 and 1972 are, as a con-tinuous run, the range's highpoint. Each story has surprising, original plotting, is full of the tough, descriptive style familiar from the novel *A Magnum for Schneider*, and stars a Callan straight out of the TV series – dryly witty, sometimes unpleasant and deadly. The *Express* stories differ from the TV continuity as Callan and Meres are working for the fourth Hunter; on television at the time, Callan was paired with James Cross.

From 1973 onwards, the *Sunday Express* stories settle down to an enjoyable formula. Typically, each begins with Hunter's M-style, exposition-heavy briefing, more back-ground information as Callan reads his target's file, followed by a scene in which Lonely is persuaded to work for the agent over a beer (and the thief's constant trips abroad in the latter part of the run do start to get monotonous). As well as the gimmick of alliterative titles, in general the stories feature locations you would never see Callan in on television, from Spain to America.

Even at their most insubstantial, the latter short stories have a novel, even outlandish idea, or contain a scenario with an ingenious action sequence, like 'File on an Angry Actor'; at their best, such as in 'File on a Weeping Widow' and 'File on a Doomed Defector', they enlarge on and develop the *Callan* mythology. Callan himself is much more of a conventional hero in later parts of the run, and perhaps because of this change has more success with women than he did on television. Mitchell says he added these romantic elements to prevent the stories being simply about 'a psychopath', adding, 'in the 1960s you could assume he had some sex life going somewhere. In the novels he has a humane attitude towards women.'

With the exception of *A Magnum for Schneider* and the 1971-72 *Express* short stories, the big change in both the novels and short fiction is Callan's relationship with Lonely. By contrast with the more ambivalent relationship portrayed in the television series, Callan considers him a genuine friend, and their companionship develops over the books to the point where they start a successful security business together. By the fifth and final novel *Bonfire Night* (2002) they are both millionaires (unlikely though that might seem).

Even though the *Callan* TV series wasn't sold to America or Italy, Mitchell's previous form as an internationally successful thriller writer ensured healthy overseas sales of *A Red File for Callan* and *Smear Job* in both countries. That the books thrived as successes in their own right is a testament to Mitchell's appealingly lean prose style, as well as his ability to tell a thrilling story with immediately engaging and vibrant characters. In 1973, *The Spectator* commented, 'Callan has been justly praised as a television character, and the Callan books, therefore, constantly underrated. The latest *Russian Roulette* is superb... All the action is splendidly economical and convincing... This is one of the best, most gripping, straightforward thrillers I have read in a long time.'[2] When Mitchell died in 2002, the *New York Times* delivered an obituary which revealed just how much Callan had thrived as a literary character in his own right, quoting from Newgate Callendar's contemporary review of *Smear Job*. 'The high-level manoeuvring eclipses anything in Ian Fleming's books,'[3] the critic wrote in 1977. He went on, 'We have had a lot of tough operatives in our day. Callan makes most of them, from James Bond on, look like prep-school classics teachers. Callan, who is a British intelligence agent licensed to kill, is so lethal that a glance from him makes the strongest of men quail.'

It's relatively rare for a fictional protagonist to conquer more than one medium – Sherlock Holmes, The Saint, 007, 'Harry Palmer' and George Smiley are the obvious exceptions – but Callan's popularity worked the opposite way: he was created for television but also subsequently flourished on the page. Callan remains unique as a TV anti-hero who also became a bestseller. That's how good James Mitchell's storytelling is.

THE SHORT STORIES 1: 1967

MERRY CHRISTMAS FROM THE SECTION

Publication: TV *Times*
Date: Issue dated December 23-29 1967 (Christmas supplement).
Featuring: Callan, Lonely, Meres (referred to)
Mission Profile: On Christmas Eve Callan prepares to kill Henderson, a double agent in the

Section who is being protected by KGB agents in a London safe house. As the agent waits for his chance, the minutes tick down to Christmas Day.

A Man Like Me: Callan is in a pensive mood as he waits for the kill. He reflects on his and Henderson's weaknesses, as well as his last Christmas with his parents before a V-2 rocket attack in WW2 killed them. He appears to be spending Christmas Day alone.

Section Kills: 6*

Lonely: Instructed by Callan to watch Henderson's safe house, the thief clearly has a sentimental side, using his breaking and entering skills to open Callan's flat and leave him a Christmas present. Predictably, Lonely uses dirty wrapping paper he finds in the gutter.

A Tie and a Crest: With great foresight, Meres demonstrates his understanding of the media by posing as an executive from a 'Christmas wish' TV show, offering the family in the house Callan needs to use a new car so they can visit relatives in Birmingham. Callan thinks Toby's performance is 'as smooth as a billiard ball.'

Alcohol, Tobacco and Firearms: Lonely's Christmas present to Callan is a bottle of whisky. Callan uses an ArmaLite AR-7 Explorer rifle to execute Henderson.

Mission Analysis: 'Callan wondered how much longer he had to live, and Christmas had never seemed further away.' This chilly tale is extremely bleak for a short story in a festive publication, ending with the image of a Christmas present stinking of Lonely's rank body odour. The scenario is reminiscent of Ian Fleming's James Bond short story *The Living Daylights* (first published in 1962) that has 007 stationed in Berlin on a solitary vigil.

There's nothing better than the nostalgic social gatherings of Christmas to emphasise what a solitary existence Callan leads. Mitchell makes the comparisons skilfully, highlighting the well-meaning greetings in the Christmas cards in the house the agent uses for the hit, as well as the carols played by a brass band as Callan waits for Henderson to show himself. Following in the tradition of the TV series' use of tragic irony, the double agent is killed by his sentimental attachment to Christmas, opening the windows so he can hear the music better and offering Callan a perfect target.

A taut, acerbic tale with a terse prose style recalling Raymond Chandler at his best, on this form it looked like Callan was more than ready to embrace the literary medium.

THE NOVELS: 1

A MAGNUM FOR SCHNEIDER

Publisher: Herbert Jenkins Ltd., hardback
Released: 1969
Price: 21 shillings
Cover design: Ian Kestle

Dedication: 'For Edward Woodward'

REPRINTS

Re-titled *A Red File for Callan*: Simon and Schuster hardback, USA, 1971
Re-titled *Red File for Callan:* Corgi paperback, UK, 1971

---

* 'Section Kills' for the *TV Times* and *Sunday Express* short stories, the novels, *Bonfire Night* and TV episodes have diffeent totals as their continuities are all different.

Re-titled *A Red File for Callan:* Dell paperback, USA, March 1974
Re-titled Callan: Corgi paperback, UK, 1974. Reprinted twice.
A Magnum for Schneider: Ostara Publishing Limited paperback/Ebook, UK, 2013

Featuring: Callan, Lonely, Hunter, Meres, Garstang, Miss Brewis, Hunter's secretary

MISSION PROFILE: Outcast from the Section, executioner David Callan is offered a second chance if he'll agree to assassinate businessman Rudolf Schneider. He is ordered to carry out the hit without any help from the Section and uses Lonely, an underworld contact, to get him a gun.

Becoming acquainted with Schneider he instinctively takes a liking to the extrovert German, especially on finding they share an interest in model soldiers and war gaming. *At the same time, rival agent Toby Meres organises surveillance on Callan.* *

Needing to know why Hunter wants Schneider killed, Callan searches the entrepreneur's office and home, finding he's been selling armaments made by a Japanese firm, Noguchi, to Indonesia, where they are being used to kill British troops. He asks Lonely specifically to get him a Noguchi Magnum .38 revolver for the forthcoming execution.

Hunter rebukes Callan for his curiosity.

The ex-agent's assignment is complicated when he's interrogated by Lonely's arms supplier the Greek; Callan kills the criminal's bodyguard Arthur and the Greek is drugged and brainwashed by Garstang, the Section psychiatrist. Callan is repelled by this and aware the Section could be conditioning the Greek to testify against him in court instead of to forget about him.

Distrusting Hunter, he records a confession, but Meres knocks him out and erases the tape.

The police and Meres both converge on Schneider's home, where Callan and the German play war games. Meres breaks in. Schneider catches him and prepares to kill both him and Callan, but Callan shoots him. He then knocks Meres out and frames him for the killing.

Hunter assigns Callan to a Red File – marking him for death.

A MAN LIKE ME: Before joining the army, Callan was an apprentice with the safe makers Bartrams, winning their award for Apprentice of the Year. Joining the army at 20, he served with a commando unit in Malaya and discovered he was a natural shot. Prone to heavy drinking, Callan lost the rank of corporal after a fight in Kuala Lumpur, but was reinstated after more terrorist kills in the jungle. During one sortie, Callan saved the life of his company commander Captain Henshaw by killing six guerrillas. However, another drunken fight again cost him the rank of corporal, as well as a medal for bravery.

After being demobbed and despite meeting a girl called Shirley, civilian life proved dull for Callan. Going back to Bartrams, he installed a safe in a supermarket and later robbed it, but was surprised by an elderly night watchman. Holding back from attacking him, Callan was caught and at 23 was sentenced to two years in Wormwood Scrubs. When he was released, Callan only saw Shirley once: 'pushing a pram, and another kid on the way.'

While in prison, he met the petty thief Lonely, wh he shared a cell with. Recruited by the Section shortly after leaving the Scrubs, Callan worked for them for seven years and was paid £206, five shillings and seven pence a month plus expenses. After four success-

---

* Major differences between the novel and the *Armchair Theatre* play are shown in italics.

ful kills – Naismith, Bunin, Orthez and Megali – worries about Donner, Callan's fifth target, led to him drinking heavily and he quit. Since then, he has been working in a job the Section commander Hunter found for him, as a book keeper for 'J.G. Waterman, Wholesale Grocer'.

Even though Callan hasn't been on active service for six months, he easily loses two men from the Section who tail him. He still has nightmares about Donner. Callan appears to have a romantic weakness for typists; it was Shirley's job, and he dated another who worked for the company 'Rossiter and Phee' in Waterman's building.

A trained killer, Callan can determine someone's physical condition and potential as a fighter just by glancing at them. As in the TV series he is a skilled locksmith and burglar who studies military history and wargaming and lives in a small, shabby flat while being obsessively clean.

Callan has no compunction about physically punishing Lonely, seeing it as the lesser of two evils as the thief would suffer far more at the hands of the Section.

Section Kills: 7 (including Schneider and Arthur)

LONELY: Shared a prison cell with Callan and a delusional arsonist. After Callan was given a beating by some warders for fighting other inmates, Lonely tended to his injuries. When he was released, Callan visited the gangster Rinty who had been threatening Lonely, successfully warning him off. Lonely has been in Callan's debt ever since.

Helpfully, the little man has 'the most comprehensive system of underworld connections Callan had ever heard of' and is able to purchase guns and ammunition – for a price. Lonely hides out in properties belonging to his Uncle Alfred and Aunty Mildred, just two members of a sprawling clan of relations involved in petty crime.

In a moment of self-awareness, the thief realises he's always hated Callan and is the victim in an abusive relationship: 'But it made no difference. No difference at all. Mr. Callan was still the strong one.'

A TIE AND A CREST: Reinforcing the rigid hierarchy of the Section, it's based in an old school; Hunter has the Headmaster's office. Meres, Callan's rival agent, is described as 'a tall, lean man, with a languid grace of body and a hungry mouth'. Meres uses Eltringham, a contact at the Home Office he was at Eton and in the Brigade of Guards with, to have the police removed from investigating Schneider.

ALCOHOL, TOBACCO AND FIREARMS: Unusually for the late 1960s, neither Callan nor Lonely smoke. Their alcohol consumption, however, is habitual. Lonely's favourite pastime is enjoying a pint of bitter in one of several central London pubs, while drink is Callan's Achilles' heel: drunken fighting twice lost him the rank of corporal, and he drank heavily when his conscience began to interfere with his Section assignments. At one point, five whiskies leave him open to being clubbed unconscious by Meres. When he's in control of himself, he typically enjoys a Scotch and water and accepts a glass of Hunter's prized Chivas Regal. Meres is a connoisseur of alcohol, enjoying a sherry in Hunter's office; later, with Eltringham, he takes white burgundy, Lascombes '59 and Bisquit brandy, but avoids Sauternes as he 'despises' sweet wine. Jenny, Callan and Schneider drink German wine before an afternoon of war gaming.

The Section firing range holds Colt and Smith and Wesson .38 revolvers, 9mm Browning semi-automatics and a Noguchi .38 centre-fire Magnum with a three-inch barrel. Initially, Lonely gets Callan a Smith and Wesson Airweight pistol, but the ex-agent wants it swapped for a Noguchi Magnum once he learns that Schneider has been making illegal armsdeals using Noguchi weapons. Arthur carries a Webley 380 Mark II revolver, a model used in WW2. Schneider owns a modern 9mm Walther semi-automatic.

SPY-SPEAK: Callan has mixed feelings about his opponent, Schneider: 'Callan sensed the first intimation of combat between them, but there was something else too: something that could develop into respect, even affection.'

Garstang is impressed with Callan's proficiency in unarmed combat: 'We did an autopsy on Arthur, you know. Quite amazing what a man's hands can do.'

Not dialogue, but a superb example of Mitchell's prose. 'On the way up the road he thought... of what *he* had done. Arthur, dead: the Greek, Papadopoulos, drugged out of his mind: Lonely scared out of his: Jenny, planning the death of Callan even as she ran. And Meres, good old Toby, about to wake up to a murder charge. He wished Hunter could wake up on one too, and went into the phone booth.'

INFORMATION: An expansion of the original *Armchair Theatre* play, James Mitchell's first Callan novel fills in a lot of biographical detail about him. It also adds new sub plots like the gun dealer the Greek and the Section keeping Callan under surveillance, all of which enlarge and enrich the canvas of what was still a modestly budgeted TV series when the book was commissioned.

Schneider went to college in Potsdam, capital city of the German state of Brandenburg and home of Prussian kings, the German court and the Kaiser. In 1942, the businessman fought in the Caucasus in WW2 as a member of 1942's Operation Edelweiss, Germany's attempt to capture the oil fields of Azerbaijan in the Soviet Union. The Wehrmacht's advance was checked after Russian gains in the area around Stalingrad; in September 1943, German forces retreated.

Published at the height of interest in *Callan*, *A Magnum for Schneider* was enthusiastically received, with *The Yorkshire Post* succinctly naming it 'a superb thriller'[4]. Even though the TV series was never sold to North America, Callan was a success in print there. The *New York Times* pronounced the first book 'tough... realistic... awfully good', while the *Columbus Dispatch* recommended that it 'should be read in one sitting.'[5]

MISSION ANALYSIS: '*But going back to Hunter's section... He didn't fancy that now. Hunter had shown him too much.*' It's easy to see why *A Magnum for Schneider* stood out in written spy fiction at the end of the 1960s. Critics were often comparing the TV series to Len Deighton and John le Carré's anti-heroes, but if anything in print the differences between Callan, the 'IPCRESS man' and Alec Leamas are more apparent. Although promoted from the ranks, the second had no motive for baiting his officer-class superiors other than his own amusement, and the latter's slide into alcoholism and disillusionment was at least partly a deep cover assignment. Callan, on the other hand, is a working class, flawed man full of ethical contradictions who, under his shabby suit and mended shoes, is a gifted executioner, something the IPCRESS man and Leamas never were.

Mitchell emphasises Callan's ordinariness – and his difference from the contemporary spy norm – by placing him in a London instantly recognisable to commuters: one of smoky pubs, public transport and frequent rain where people have to work on Saturday. As far as the characters in this novel are concerned, the 'Swinging Sixties' never happened.

This is significant, because all the way through, Mitchell highlights a power structure in the Section based on social class – in Hunter and Meres – that the cultural changes of the 1960s were supposed to have weakened, if not swept aside. The absence of these changes reinforces the sense of fatalism hovering over Callan.

The most compelling aspect of the novel, though, is being inside the head of a criminal and killer, a development of the insight into Callan's thoughts that his occasional voiceovers allowed in the TV series. Callan might be a man who drinks too much in a dead-end job, but he's a tough, shrewd, inventive, ruthless and – for the reader – a compelling chara-cter. Almost chapter by chapter, Mitchell reveals more information about Callan's background and personality, so you gradually realise why he's found himself in his desperate position in life. You sympathise with Callan, while at the same time being as repelled and ambivalent as he is about his lethal profession. Schneider, who significantly had a parallel career as a soldier, also has nightmares about his service, is interested in military history and war gaming and is the wealthy, successful man Callan could have been under different circumstances.

The plot is relatively simple; it's the detail and authenticity of the gritty metropolitan setting and the memorable gallery of amoral, complex characters that keeps you turning the pages. On this compulsive first showing, it was certain that Callan's first full-length literary outing wouldn't be his last.

THE SHORT STORIES 2: 1970

Publication: Sunday Express
Date: 13 September 1970
The week before they began, the first run of short stories was advertised by the following introduction on the front page. The text was accompanied by an illustration of a hand holding a Magnum revolver.

'CALLAN BLASTS IN...

Three years ago a cold, hard, enigmatic character in a rumpled raincoat
    made his first appearance on British television screens.
He was a special agent. He could if necessary be a killer.
He had no pretty girls to decorate his activities.
He did not go on his assignments in fast, expensive cars.
He had no gimmicks. But he had authority and credibility.
He quickly shot up in the viewing charts – and stayed there.
His fame is now world-wide.
His name is Callan.
Now the cynical, lonely Callan, brilliantly acted on television by Edward
    Woodward, is to appear in a new medium.
His creator, author James Mitchell, has written a series of *Callan* adventures
    for the *Sunday Express*.
Like the Callan stories which have gripped television viewers, they are
packed with action and suspense – and have an unexpected twist at the end.
The *Sunday Express Callan* series is a must for all *Callan*'s TV viewers.
It is a must for all who enjoy a tensely, tersely told story of suspense
    and mystery.
Watch for *Callan* next week in the *Sunday Express*.'

FILE ON A HAPPY HIPPY

Publication: Sunday Express
Date: 20 September 1970
Featuring: Callan, Lonely, the fourth Hunter
Mission Profile: Callan investigates Janet Cruze, the wayward daughter of a US diplomat who may have been targeted by Easter Bloc agents.

A Man Like Me: Callan assumes the identity of a drug dealer operating from a fashionable London mews. He knows what drugs hippies use and that Haight-Ashbury in is a counter cultural haven in San Francisco.

Section Kills: 1

Lonely: Doesn't like doing daylight burglaries. Paid £25 to follow Janet's Rolls Royce on a scooter. With heavy irony, Lonely disapproves of hippies because they don't wash.

A Tie and a Crest: Hunter is acting in the interests of Anglo-American relations.

Alcohol, Tobacco and Firearms: Janet gets stoned on marijuana. Callan and Danny – the KGB agent posing as a hippy drug user – use unidentified hand guns.

Spy-Speak: Referring to the scruffy Danny, Callan is immediately recognisable as his hard-bitten TV self: 'There is where I live. Some kinds of dirt I won't let in here.'

Information: As well as a photograph of Woodward as Callan, the story was accompanied by an uncredited picture of a blonde hippy girl.

Mission Analysis: 'I've always heard you flower children were gentle and sensitive.' After the introspective power of 'Merry Christmas from the Section', with a tighter word count there's the sense that Mitchell is finding his form as a short story writer. The story draws on elements of the unused TV script 'Goodbye Mary Lee', recycling an American politician estranged from his daughter, together with the hippy counter culture (also briefly alluded to in *A Magnum for Schneider*). The plotting is straightforward and 'File on the Happy Hippy' ends dramatically, if rather suddenly. Even so, Mitchell's singular, quick-fire dialogue, knack for detail – Callan assessing a possible opponent's physical condition in one glance, as in his debut novel – and the hysterical prospect of Lonely being invited to a hippy love-in, promise much for *Callan* as a newspaper thriller series.

FILE ON A FAITHFUL HUSBAND

Publication: Sunday Express
Date: 27 September 1970
Featuring: Callan, Lonely, the fourth Hunter
Mission Profile: The double agent Albrecht Dekker once worked for the Section. Callan is ordered to kill him.

A Man Like Me: On expenses, Callan buys a dictionary to find out the meaning of 'uxorious'. Discovering it means 'excessively fond of one's wife', he cold-bloodedly uses this aspect of Dekker's personality to devise a humiliating death for the treacherous agent. Callan also threatens Lonely with a beating. Throughout, he has no reservations about what he's doing.

Section Kills: 2

Lonely: Paid £100 to steal items from one hotel room and place them in the hotel room of Dekker's bodyguards, which he understandably finds confusing.

A Tie and a Crest: In a rare lapse of judgement, Hunter was fooled by Dekker. His death is partly revenge for the betrayal and killing of two Section agents.

Alcohol, Tobacco and Firearms: Callan carries a Magnum .38, although Dekker is killed by having his head smashed into a marble mantelpiece. The double agent carries an unknown hand gun.

Spy-Speak: Mitchell paints a vivid picture of the shabby London hotel where Dekker stays: 'Almost its entire clientele was middle aged, male, sedentary and foreign... [including] salesmen suffering from a lack of faith in their products.'

Mission Analysis: 'You've had seven men killed. It's a bit late to be squeamish.' Another simple story that builds up to a single killing, but it's a particularly grubby one – an executioner devoted to his wife is set up to be found dead in a prostitute's room. It concludes with a particularly disturbing scene, as Dekker weeps and pleads with Callan not to let him die in such a humiliating way. 'File on a Faithful Husband' succeeds because of the clever plotting that includes stolen goods being planted on Dekker's minders so they're arrested, as well as the uncompromisingly downbeat tone. The story is brief, tough and nastily memorable.

FILE ON A LOVING SISTER

Publication: Sunday Express
Date: 4 October 1970
Featuring: Callan, Lonely, the fourth Hunter
Mission Profile: Callan is ordered to become emotionally involved with Enid Matthews, the devoted sister of a Foreign Office official who has sold secret defence files to the Chinese. Enid is Callan's route to finding her brother.

A Man Like Me: Callan left school at 15. Although he's disgusted by the way he's been ordered to behave he follows orders and, tragically, falls in love with Enid.

Lonely: Paid £10 to testify to Callan's good nature. He's ordered to call the agent 'Dave' in Edith's presence but has trouble doing it. Lonely is nevertheless impressed by her, complimenting Callan on 'a real lady.'

A Tie and a Crest: Coldly and correctly, Hunter predicts that love can be a double-edged weapon as Callan develops genuine feelings for Enid. Working with the Section, Special Branch officers arrest Matthews, an authentic detail as arresting political criminals is one of their real-life duties.

Alcohol, Tobacco and Firearms: Lonely is bought 'several' drinks in a pub in order to give Callan a glowing character reference.

Spy-Speak: Callan's observations as he falls for Enid are bitter-sweet: 'This girl *needed* love. She had given for too long.' And later: 'It was strange, he thought, how easily the weak ones could tie the strong ones down.'

Information: The story featured a photograph of Woodward and Zena Marshal kissing from that year's episode 'Suddenly – At Home'. Callan's dialogue 'I think I'm falling in love with you' is used word for word by him in the 1972 episode 'Charlie Says It's Goodbye'.

Mission Analysis: 'Inside, he could feel nothing at all, except disgust at himself.' The first high point of the *Express* stories is a story in which Callan doesn't use his gun and no-one dies, but 'File on a Loving Sister' is *Callan* at its bleakest. Mitchell focuses on the relationship between the agent and the lonely Edith, heart-breakingly conveyed through sensitive, almost lyrical prose. The picture he draws of a woman lacking confidence slowly blossoming as Callan romances then betrays her is one of his finest pieces of writing. In fact, the story had the potential to be a better TV episode than the similar 'Charlie Says It's Goodbye', particularly as the ending is so affecting: '"I don't understand," she said. "You said you loved me." "I meant it," said Callan.'

FILE ON A PAINLESS DENTIST

Publication: Sunday Express

Date: 11 October 1970

Featuring: Callan, Lonely, the fourth Hunter

Mission Profile: A. J. Clarkson, a dentist in Kent, is suspected of being the KGB spy and executioner Piotr Orlov. Callan is ordered to kill him or bring him in for interrogation.

A Man Like Me: In complete contrast to 'File on a Loving Sister', Callan has no qualms about romantically using Clarkson's receptionist to get information. For the first time, Callan goes with Lonely to see a cowboy film; he also buys him an iced lolly at the cinema. Even though he's frightened by Orlov's reputation, Callan goes ahead with the mission anyway. He uses the alias of Peters, a travelling salesman.

Section Kills: 3

Lonely: Unsurprisingly, he's broke again, and terrified of dentists after a painful experience in Wormwood Scrubs. He travels to Kent by bus as Callan knows in that situation he's 'just about invisible.' Lonely is confused by Callan's orders again, as he's paid £100 to break into Clarkson's surgery and pull over a book case.

A Tie and a Crest: Orlov is responsible for the death of three Section agents: Patterson, Chalmers and Gregg.

Alcohol, Tobacco and Firearms: Callan buys Lonely several pints of beer to persuade him to help. Callan and Clarkson both use unidentified guns.

Spy-Speak: A memorably sardonic exchange between Hunter and Callan: 'How are your teeth?' the Section commander enquires. 'The ones I've got left are fine,' Callan replies.

Callan thinks Lonely's tailing ability is 'about as noisy as a leaf in the gutter.'

Information: The story features some striking period detail regarding age, as Clarkson's secretary is described as being 'well past thirty, with the first signs of desperation.'

Mission Analysis: '... the sort of calm strength that belongs only with those who pull teeth.' Clarkson/Orlov is the first stand-out adversary in the *Express* canon, employing gallows humour and ruthless cunning – bugging his receptionist's flat – and it's easy to see why Callan is intimidated by him. Callan's appalling 007-style pun in the last line, 'Who ever heard of a dentist being drilled?', is the first time the James Bond films influence Mitchell's writing.

FILE ON A FANCY LAWYER

Publication: Sunday Express

Date: 18 October 1970

Featuring: Callan, Lonely, the fourth Hunter

Mission Profile: Callan investigates the lawyer Christopher Mainwaring Davenport, under surveillance by the Section because he enjoys a lifestyle that his income can't support.

A Man Like Me: Callan is exhausted by following Davenport for five days on a round of clubs, restaurants, embassies and race courses. He's experienced enough to spot that a 'live drop' – information exchanged between Davenport and a contact in a public place – is being done in a hurry. Callan uses a set of skeleton keys and poses as an estate agent.

Section Kills: 4

Lonely: Paid £50 to drive Callan around in a cab and he's allowed to keep the fares.

A Tie and a Crest: The Section have a man stationed at an unspecified London Embassy.

Alcohol, Tobacco and Firearms: Callan carries a Magnum .38 revolver.

Spy-Speak: Freda Miller, the wife of Davenport's contact Harry, is described as 'a woman approaching middle-age, who had learned to live with the problems of a mortgage, and growing kids, and never enough money.'

Callan is conflicted as ever, 'hating the waste his trade created.'

Information: The story anticipates Lonely's regular job two years later in Series Four, driving a London taxi owned by the Section.

Mission Analysis: 'He didn't do a bloody thing.' Just when you think that Harry Miller will turn out to be an opposition agent, the narrative takes an unexpected twist into a suburban tragedy. Callan's suspect, who works at the Ministry of Technology, was blackmailed by Davenport into stealing secrets and hangs himself at home. Although the master blackmailer himself remains frustratingly opaque, Mitchell conveys the tedium of surveillance well and Davenport's domestic tragic death packs a genuine emotional punch.

A satisfyingly strong end to the first batch of *Express* short stories.

THE SHORT STORIES 3: 1971

WHAT'S CALLAN DOING NOW?

Publication: Sunday Express
Date: 8 August 1971
The second run of short stories was advertised by the following introduction on the front page of the paper the week before they began:

'Of all the "special investigators" who have invaded the living-rooms of Britain via the small screen, which one rivets your attention most closely?

Millions of people would unhesitatingly answer: Callan.

And they ask: when can we expect the next series of Callan adventures?

And the answer is: starting next Sunday – in the *Sunday Express.*

Callan, the sardonic agent in the rumpled raincoat – so brilliantly acted by Edward Woodward on television – is the creation of writer James Mitchell.

Mitchell has written a special series of Callan adventures for the *Sunday Express.*

He brings to these stories the taut, tense style which is the secret of the *Callan* success on TV.

Callan does not have the normal appurtenances of high-level agents – no glamorous [girlfriends], no fast cars.

He does not need them.

Mitchell has given him authority and credibility.

This exciting new series is a MUST for Callan addicts – and for everyone who enjoys a vivid, realistic suspense story.

You can never anticipate the end of a Callan adventure. You have to stay with it to the end.

Before you settle down with your deckchair on the beach or in the garden next weekend, make sure you have handy the opening instalment of the new Callan casebook. It is called: 'File on a Chinese Hostess'.

In next Sunday's *Sunday Express.*'

CALLAN: FILE ON A CHINESE HOSTESS

Publication: Sunday Express

Date: 8 August 1971

Featuring: Callan, Lonely, the fourth Hunter, Meres

Mission Profile: Peter Arnold, Parliamentary Private Secretary to the Minister of State for Foreign Affairs, has a Chinese girlfriend, Rose Li, who works at the oriental restaurant The Middle Kingdom. She's also a Red Chinese spy: Hunter has set her up as a double agent and Callan must intercept the men sent to kill her.

A Man Like Me: Callan appreciates good Chinese food and is experienced enough to know that a large cooked breakfast will see him through a demanding operational day. He practises drawing his .38 Magnum from his holster, but fatalistically knows that one day he'll meet a gunman who's faster. Callan apparently misquotes The Beatles' 'Can't Buy Me Love'.

Section Kills: 6

Lonely: Paid to watch Rose Li's flat and signals with a lit cigarette if he sees anyone, typically using a dog end. Lonely knows a motorcyclist called Danby who Callan sometimes uses to follow suspects.

A Tie and a Crest: Meres makes his debut in the *Express* stories. The Section operation on Rose Li is a typically nasty one: they feed her disinformation so that her controllers think she's turned traitor, to the point where they order her execution.

Alcohol, Tobacco and Firearms: Lonely smokes. (This was implied in the television series – see 'Where Else Could I Go?' and 'Breakout'.) Callan augments his Magnum with a silencer. One of the two Chinese agents he confronts is armed with two throwing knives.

Spy-Speak: Callan decides that Rose Li is so attractive 'she would turn on a stone statue.' Later reflecting on Lonely's taciturn friend Danby, he wonders 'if he could talk at all, except to his motorbike.'

Arriving after Callan has shot one of the Chinese agents, 'Meres looked around with that regret he always showed when he'd missed a shooting.'

Pawns and Players: One of the most distinctive features of the *Sunday Express* stories are the illustrations, introduced with this story, which feature accomplished likenesses of Woodward, Hunter, Valentine and Squire. They were drawn by the artist Andrew Robb (born 1907), who studied at Edinburgh College of Art. He made his reputation as a fashion illustrator for *Vogue* and the *Daily Express* after WW2, before embarking on a career that lasted nearly fifty years with Beaverbrook/Express Newspapers. Robb – who only used his surname as a signature on his drawings – became well known for his serialised comic strip adaptations of the James Bond stories. They ran in the *Daily Express* from April 1956, beginning with *Diamonds Are Forever* and concluding with Kingsley Amis's story *Colonel Sun* in 1968. In 1967, Robb illustrated the *Daily Express* serialisation of Len Deighton's fourth IPCRESS man novel, *Billion Dollar Brain*.

The *Callan* illustrations went through two styles. In the second run of stories, Robb adopted an exciting, pop art approach, running a comic strip across the top of the newspaper spread; from 1972 onwards the layout of the stories was more varied, as Robb drew stand-alone pictures that were dropped in throughout the text.

Mission Analysis: 'I keep my mind clear for more important things – like staying alive.' Allowed a bigger word count, James Mitchell immediately makes an impression with detailed and authentic descriptions of surveillance, house breaking and the many hours of waiting in an agent's life that are followed by a rush of a violent action. The texture of the story is enlivened by Mitchell's enthusiasm for (then highly fashionable) Chinese cuisine and, consistent with the TV series, a typically unpleasant twist: Arnold knew Rose Li was a Communist agent, and was willingly passing on Hunter's disinformation because of the 'compensations' of being with her.

An improved, compulsively readable return for the series, clearly designed to be read after a satisfying Sunday lunch.

CALLAN: FILE ON A WILLING VICTIM

Publication: Sunday Express
Date: 15 August 1971
Featuring: Callan, Lonely, the fourth Hunter
Mission Profile: Callan is detailed to find out why Andrew Hardy, an upper class, left wing writer, is being targeted by the NVA (East German intelligence).

A Man Like Me: Callan says he watches cowboy films and understands German. Going by what he tells Hardy, he's used to taking hangover remedies. His unpleasant side is very evident: Callan threatens the writer with his Magnum to get him to talk and when Hardy calls him 'a Fascist', the agent strikes him across the face. Callan also threatens Lonely with 'a belting.'

Section Kills: 8

Lonely: Bullied by Callan into driving a taxi, for which he'll be paid £50 'tax free'. He's suspicious of why Callan needs him and starts smelling, at which point the agent tells him to get an 'aerosol or something.'

A Tie and a Crest: Unusually, Hunter doesn't know what to do: the fatalistic Hardy has refused the Section's help. Typically, the Section commander doesn't give the full facts regarding the writer: Hardy was working for the Section in Europe and is distraught that his girlfriend was caught and traumatically tortured. She's sent to a nursing home in England to lure Hardy into the sights of two NVA executioners.

Alcohol, Tobacco and Firearms: Hardy has a case of whisky by his sofa and is drunk at 11.30 am in the morning. Callan is armed with his usual Magnum while the NVA agents carry Makarov semi-automatic pistols.

Spy-Speak: There's memorable doorstep exchange between a drunken Hardy and Callan: 'I have no wish to buy encyclopaedias, brushes or subscriptions to magazines.' 'And I have no wish to sell them. I'm from the NVA.'

For Lonely, driving a taxi won't be 'anything undignified, like working.'

Mission Analysis: 'Can't you understand? I want to die. Please go.' Making the most of the new two page format, Mitchell draws in Hardy an unsettling portrait of a once proud, idealistic man having a breakdown, cleverly sketched in through details like Hunter's comment that the writer 'was a brilliant sprinter, but totally unreliable over a distance' and Callan's observation that 'in the window boxes the flowers were half dead.' Hardy is a brilliant Mitchell character, disappointed, bitter, full of class guilt and – a favourite theme – crippled by his past; in fact, his characterisation is so well thought out you're left wondering whether this story started life as a TV script. Concluded by a smart action scene where real violence between Callan and the NVA is counter-pointed by make believe violence on television, 'File on a Willing Victim' is the second high point ,so far, of the *Express* stories.

CALLAN: FILE ON A KINDLY COLONEL

Publication: Sunday Express
Date: 22 August 1971
Featuring: Callan, Lonely, the fourth Hunter, Meres
Mission Profile: Callan is assigned as bodyguard to Colonel Obra, a diplomat for a new West African nation.

A Man Like Me: Callan again threatens Lonely with violence if he doesn't help him. He has to hold back from fatally injuring a dealer in explosives.

Lonely: Acts as a chauffeur (as he did in 'But He's a Lord Mr Callan') for Obra. He's comfortable behind the wheel of a Mercedes 600, using the correct tone of voice and demeanour. Lonely has a contact in the underworld who can supply plastic explosives, and Callan pays the thief £50 to deliver an OHMSS letter to Obra.

A Tie and a Crest: Hunter doesn't like visiting Whitehall. The Section has a blast-proof area for detonating bombs. Meres acts as Callan's back-up, who is 'the best man [Hunter's] got.' Callan tells Meres 'Got a job for you,' the instruction he usually gives Lonely.

Alcohol, Tobacco and Firearms: A poerful bomb is concealed in a government stationery envelope. Callan's Magnum is identified as a Smith and Wesson and Meres, with a silenced gun, shoots an 'automatic' out of the Red China agent Mrs Obra's hand.

Spy-Speak: Sir Robert Dundee can't hide his distaste for the Section, as he 'looked at [Hunter] as if he were a road sweeper with something very nasty indeed in his shovel.'

Callan's is threatened with a letter bomb at dinner: 'I seem to have lost my appetite.'

Meres apologises for marksmanship: 'I'm most awfully sorry. One was brought up never to shoot at ladies.'

Mission Analysis: 'In the end he had to choke him with his Old Etonian tie.' Another high-light. Just as it looks as if a formula is about to emerge – Callan investigating a suspect before a climactic gunfight in the final paragraphs – Mitchell delivers a neat thriller set in Whitehall's corridors of power and London's fashionable restaurants, as Callan has to discover the identity of an assassin in this engaging flipside to 'Amos Green Must Live'. The story is also notable for scenes viewed from Obra's and Hunter's perspectives, in which it's revealed that government ministers 'despised' the latter 'and his trade, and made little effort to conceal the fact.'

With topical references to Chinese interference in African politics and the IRA bombing campaign in the UK, together with the bizarre touch of an explosives dealer who went to Eton, 'File on a Kindly Colonel' is a full of distinctive moments and memorable descriptions. It's also the best outing for Meres so far in the short stories.

CALLAN: FILE ON A CHELSEA SWINGER

Publication: Sunday Express
Date: 29 August 1971
Featuring: Callan, Lonely, the fourth Hunter
Mission Profile: Hunter details Callan to guard Sarah Vane (real name Annie Woods), a Chelsea socialite who has been targeted by the KGB.

A Man Like Me: Stays in Sarah Vane's block of flats, Fuchsia Lodge. Portraying the sexual attitudes of the time, Callan says he'd be 'queer' if he didn't find Sarah attractive, although, when she kisses him, aware that she's still married, he doesn't take advantage of her. Callan owns an Italian suit and is visibly impatient during Hunter's briefing.

Section Kills: 9

Lonely: Callan treats him to fish and chips and a cowboy movie. Uncharacteristical-ly, Lonely seems rather prudish about going to the strip club Nudissima where Sarah performs, and can't believe Callan's paying him £20 to do it. The agent says he'll make it £50 if Lonely can find out what happened near the club the night Sarah left, which he does. The thief has been in prison with Bolger, Nuddisima's doorman.

A Tie and a Crest: Hunter learns of the KGB threat to Sarah from French intelligence, although he doesn't trust them (c.f. 'Death of a Friend'). Callan calls the Records Section for details of the execution of a Czech dissident.

Alcohol, Tobacco and Firearms: Lonely has the second of many beers in the short stories with Callan. The Vanes are awash with alcohol: Alasdair spills gin and tonic over Callan and buys him a large Scotch to apologise, before going back to his own 'two thirds empty bottle of gin'. Sarah starts on gin and moves on to cola.

The KGB use a French gunman (as in 'Suddenly At Home').

Spy-Speak: There's a revealing insight into the Section chief's sense of humour: 'Hunter laughed, an indulgence he allowed himself perhaps three times a year.'

Callan's description of Lonely is equally evocative: 'Soho was for rats, and for rats you needed a terrier. An ageing terrier and more than a little smelly, but the best nose in the business.'

Alasdair is a stylish drunk: 'If nobody minds, I'll pass out.'

Mission Analysis: 'It's a tough world for Cinderellas.' The story has the characteristic Mitch-ell contrast of the seedy and sophisticated mixed with contemporary detail, this time a provincial girl who's come to London to seek her fortune, an idea borrowed from films such as *Darling* (1965) and *Smashing Time* (1967); Sarah marries Alisdair Trenton Vane, 'sixth in line to a barony.' For the first time, the suggestion of an emerging formula inhibits Mitchell's gift for defining his characters: Callan's relationship with Sarah is revealed through reported speech, a particularly noticeable weakness as she's the title char-acter. However, the political angle keeps the story interesting: Vane, an impoverished aris-tocrat, is blackmailing the KGB over Sarah witnessing one of their agents, now 'a rising star in the Politburo', executing a Czech dissident.

CALLAN: FILE ON A MISSING POET

Publication: Sunday Express

Date: 5 September 1971

Featuring: Callan, Lonely, the fourth Hunter

Mission Profile: The Section's Number Two in Moscow has concealed a microdot on the poet R.E. Digby: it carries the names of Soviet government members in favour of an H-Bomb attack on China. Digby has disappeared in Paris and Callan is ordered to retrieve the information.

A Man Like Me: Callan's impersonal restraining hold terrifies Angela Cosgrove, Digby's girlfriend, as the Section man expertly intimidates a strong woman into revealing information about her lover.

Section Kills: 11

Lonely: Abused by his school teachers because of his BO. Lonely proves his worth by helping Callan burgle both Digby's house and Angela's flat, although Callan has to warn him not to steal a snuff box as the thief has a weakness for them. Lonely knows a rude limerick about a 'young feller from Wapping'.

A Tie and a Crest: The Section has a network of contacts and agents spread throughout the British media. The unit has the resources to keep Digby's house under surveillance.

Alcohol, Tobacco and Firearms: For the first time in the short stories, Callan enjoys a whisky in his flat after the mission. He again uses a silenced Magnum while two KGB agents are again equipped with Makarov semi-automatics.

Spy-Speak: Lonely's wry appraisal of Angela: 'School teachers has changed since my day.'

Mitchell's description of how Angela reacts to the way Callan restrains her is terrifying: 'No man had held with such a lack of feeling for as long as she could remember.'

Mission Analysis: 'He's a messenger – and he doesn't even know that himself.' This is the fourth time that a story begins with Callan investigating someone, ends with gunmen storming into a room and the agent shooting one or both. However, the edgy confrontation scene between the agent and Angela (recalling the scene in 'The Most Promising Girl of Her Year' when Callan confronts the Rules), which shows just how unpleasant, threatening and unpredictable Callan can be, is so enthralling you don't notice the formula. The climactic shoot-out is equally novel: there's a welcome touch of *The Avengers*-style oddness, as the KGB men are dressed like bowler-hatted city businessmen. Concealing the microdot above the letter 'i' in the word 'hip' in one of Digby's poems is both smart and sexy, as the poet's eloquent prose about the mole Angela has on her left hip alerts Callan to the microdot's location.

THE SHORT STORIES 4: 1972

CALLAN: FILE ON A FRIENDLY LADY

Publication: Sunday Express
Date: 23 April 1972
Featuring: Callan, Lonely, the fourth Hunter, Meres
Mission Profile: Callan bodyguards Susan Francis and Mary Lou Harper, the wife and sister of a United States senator tipped for the Presidency, who are staying at London's Savoy hotel. One of the women is being blackmailed...

A Man Like Me: Lives in Bayswater. As in the TV series, Callan has a healthy interest in attractive young women, even though he's intimidated and made to feel foolish by Susan and Mary Lou. He injures the blackmailing photographer Peter Grant to the point where 'even Meres... was impressed.' Callan has his first romantic interlude in the short stories.

Section Kills: 12

Lonely: Predictably, he's terrified of beautiful women and uncomfortable in the Savoy. Lonely burgles Grant's flat in Bayswater, steals a cashbox full of blackmail photography and is again confused when Callan tells him to put it back.

A Tie and a Crest: Susan and Mary Lou are in Yellow Files – surveillance only. Callan wouldn't normally carry a gun on a surveillance job, but Senator John Francis insists that he does. Meres is Callan's back up.

Alcohol, Tobacco and Firearms: Presumably, a lot of alcohol is drunk in the various discotheques that Susan, Mary Lou, Callan and Grant visit. Callan is again armed with a Magnum and silencer and a KGB man hides his pistol on a waiter's trolley.

Spy-Speak: Callan's opinion of Susan Francis: 'This was a blonde who could debauch a bishop.'

Callan has met his match in Mary Lou's sardonic comments: 'If we didn't have Mr. Callan to take care of us, we might have to cross the street on our own.'

Mission Analysis: 'Two gorgeous birds over here on their own, and me at the Savoy looking after them. Where's the catch, Hunter?' The third run of *Express* stories gets off to a good start with a comedy of manners which finds Callan adrift in social hell, 'a nightmare of shopping' consisting of clothes shops, furriers, jewellers and antique shops, courtesy of Susan and Mary Lou. The fish-out-of-water humour between the agent and the two girls is very funny and tempered by a very nasty twist: Meres copies Grant's incriminating photograph of Susan on drugs, so Hunter can use it as leverage against the senator in the future. Callan's knowledge of this treachery makes his concluding romantic clinch with Mary Lou satisfyingly bitter-sweet.

CALLAN: FILE ON A JOLLY MILLER

Publication: Sunday Express
Date: 30 April 1972
Featuring: Callan, Lonely, the fourth Hunter, Meres
Mission Profile: Callan is ordered to retrieve the plans of the Hero, a new British tank, stolen by the freelance spy Miller, before he sells them to an East German agent. There's a snag – Lonely can't break into Miller's house...

A Man Like Me: Callan uses the alias of the 'form filling, penny pinching' 'Mr Tucker' (which he's used 'for years') from the Ministry of Housing, helping the authenticity of his cover by distributing form PY38 to other houses along Miller's street. Callan again threatens Lonely with violence.

Section Kills: 13

Lonely: Hides his keys and pick locks under the floorboards of his room. He admits he can't break through the Manton locks on Miller's house and is scared by the size of the man's dog. An expert at tailing people, Lonely quickly spots that Callan's car is being followed and the agent gives him the alias of Mr Tucker's colleague, Mr Renfrew: 'Lonely in the civil service was a thought to conjure with.'

A Tie and a Crest: The Section efficiently tail the East German agent Christina Lund back to Miller's house, keep it under surveillance and eavesdrop on Miller's radio frequency. The Section also has a duty room – where Meres is currently on shift – and a chemist.

Alcohol, Tobacco and Firearms: Callan has to buy Lonely three pints to calm him down. The agent has a whisky in a pub, which Christina deliberately spills on him so she can buy Callan another and question him. She has a Campari.

Meres uses an air rifle to tranquilise Miller's dog.

Spy-Speak: Hunter is a demanding boss: 'I want everything... And when I don't get it I'm extremely disappointed.'

Callan surprises Lonely by pretending to be the police: '[He] seemed to shoot up in his raincoat like toothpaste in a tube.'

Callan dryly concludes that Christina is from Berlin, 'the part with the wall round it.'

Information: First illustration of Russell Hunter as Lonely. Triple-action Manton locks were used in the TV story 'Breakout'. It's the short story debut of Callan's 'Tucker' alias.

Mission Analysis: 'Callan knew that his luck had run out at last.' Mitchell continues to surprise with an original and offbeat story. As well as the unusual set up, there is added unpredictability because the Section are more fallible than usual. Christina clubs Meres unconscious, and Callan is only saved from execution because the Section chemist got the knockout dose for Miller's dog wrong, so the woozy beast takes Miller's bullet instead. Like a lot of Mitchell's spy fiction, there's an effective sense of extraordinary events happening alongside the everyday.

CALLAN: FILE ON A DEADLY DOCTOR

Publication: Sunday Express
Date: 7 May 1972
Featuring: Callan, Lonely, the fourth Hunter, Meres
Mission Profile: Callan is assigned to rescue Pete Merrick, an injured CIA gunman, from KGB agents who want to smuggle him back to Russia by sea for interrogation.

A Man Like Me: Callan is worried about guarding Hunter to the point of paranoia. He's ordered to kill deep cover agent Dr. Ernest Webb (formerly Weber, who's involved in Merrick's abduction) as a separate assignment that 'is no concern of the CIA.'

Section Kills: 14

Lonely: Foder, the CIA agent working with Callan, is sensitive to Lonely's 'fragrance.' Installed at the yacht club in Southbay as an informant, Lonely is on to a good earner, making £15 a week plus a £50 bonus from Callan. The thief supplies crucial information about when Webb's cruiser is sailing. He had to recite a poem about smugglers at school and is impressed that Callan might be tracking a gang of them down.

A Tie and a Crest: Hunter owes the CIA a favour and doesn't like it. He can't leave HQ without a bodyguard as 'it's a rule.' The Section has access to a seagoing diesel cruiser.

Alcohol, Tobacco and Firearms: Callan has a Scotch in a pub with Hunter. Lonely does 'all right' in the yacht club bar. Callan carries his customary .38 Magnum. In the final shoot out, Foder kills Webb, and then a hidden Meres shoots Foder – a fellow allied agent – dead.

Spy-Speak: Callan has a cynical view of Southbay: 'Small, well-off and nosey.'
Foder on Lonely: 'Nothing like sea air for getting rid of a fug.'

Mission Analysis: 'If he goes on like this I'm going to have to kill him before Hunter does.' Another mould-breaking narrative, building towards a confrontation at sea, contains some very dark Cold War politics and a shock ending: Callan's sardonic homicidal thoughts about a boorish CIA contact anticipate the ending where British and American intelligence try to double cross each other and Foder is shot dead. Even more shocking, the implication is that Merrick, an ally, will be interrogated in the Section as mercilessly as any Communist agent. The matter-of-fact approach of Callan and Meres to the situation, as if it's part of their everyday relationship with the CIA, makes for one of the bleakest *Callan* stories in any medium. Even the TV series never went this far.

CALLAN: FILE ON A MAN CALLED... CALLAN

Publication: Sunday Express
Date: 14 May 1972
Featuring: Callan, Lonely, the fourth Hunter, Meres
Mission Profile: Two freelance assassins are paid £10,000 to take out the KGB's Colonel Lubov, the best defector the Section have ever had. Callan poses as the Russian to bring the contract killers into the open – and eliminate them.

A Man Like Me: It's a tense assignment for Callan: he's literally in the firing line, hidden behind bandages as Lubov, and feels guilty about lying to Lonely – on Hunter's orders – about how dangerous the mission is. The only time he 'needs' a drink is after a job and he sometimes gets the shakes. Callan gets his first taste of the high life in the short stories, staying in

Westlake, a luxurious health farm, and travelling there by Rolls Royce. For good measure, he ends the story heading for a romantic interlude with Sister Lynn, a pretty nurse.

Section Kills: 15

Lonely: Doesn't like the countryside, due to memories of more physical abuse he suffered from a farmer he stayed with as an evacuee in WW2. Lonely's not been fully briefed on the situation so he won't panic. He proves to be a remarkably efficient undercover investigator of new arrivals around Westlake, posing as a door to salesman and – very 007 – using a camera hidden in a transistor radio.

A Tie and a Crest: A rare continuity mistake – in this story a White File means surveillance only. The Section has the resources to give defectors plastic surgery and has an interest in the Westlake health farm. Hunter smiles 'five times a year' (as well as laughing three times). Callan's driver once won a Monte Carlo rally. Meres is assigned as Callan's bodyguard.

Alcohol, Tobacco and Firearms: Alcohol is forbidden in Westlake – Hunter says Callan will 'detest it' – but luckily he gets to share a bottle of whisky in Sister Lynn's quarters. Lonely has a pint while Callan briefs him. One of the twin contract killers is an Olympic pistol shot, but is no match for Callan's .38 Magnum.

Spy-Speak: Hunter tries to reassure his top man: 'Don't look so worried, David. [Meres is] is an excellent bodyguard.' 'Yeah... and I'm an excellent target,' Callan replies, sourly.

Meres threatens Lonely with (more) violence: 'Keep very schtum indeed. Otherwise I might just have to pay you a little visit.'

Information: Meres and the fourth Hunter feature in the illustrations, although only the Section commander is recognisably the actor who plays him. There's a possible oblique reference to 'You Should Have Got Here Sooner' when Meres threatens Lonely.

Mission Analysis: 'At least I know I could win a medal.' Mitchell adds another unexpected twist, with Lonely's amusing point of view during his undercover mission as a door-to-door salesman, a very 1970s occupation (and once again he supplies information crucial to the completion of the mission). Elsewhere, there's some effective misdirection, as the reader – and Callan – is led to believe that Sister Lynn is one of the killers. Above all, there's the fascination of seeing Callan stressed, uncomfortable and borderline paranoid as a target, which keeps the atmosphere tense throughout.

CALLAN: FILE ON A GALLIC CHARMER

Publication: Sunday Express
Date: 21 May 1972
Featuring: Callan, Lonely, the fourth Hunter, Meres (mentioned), Liz, George
Mission Profile: A rare 'surveillance only' job for Callan. He has to break off the affair between the chef Marcel Christophe and Jane Everitt, the wife of Professor Harvey Everitt, designer of a new missile tracking system. If Chrisophe is an enemy agent, Callan has orders to kill him.

A Man Like Me: Callan initially doesn't think sex is 'a nuisance' as Hunter does, but concedes the Section controller is always right. His investigation reveals a fourth corner of the square love triangle, Dr. Laura Cobb, who is having an affair with the professor.

Section Kills: 16

Lonely: Predictably doesn't like French cuisine, which he describes as 'foreign muck.' Callan pays Lonely £5 to use his criminal insight to discover whether or not Christophe has been in prison; he concludes the Frenchman has, because of the way he smokes a cigarette. The thief burgles Christophe's cookery school with Callan and, despite Lonely's aversion to Gallic food, he manages to digest a cup of cold consommé, a slice of Ardennes paté and Duck a l'orange. Quite rightly, Callan makes him do the washing up afterwards. In the short story continuity, Lonely taught Callan house-breaking.

A Tie and a Crest: Hunter has access to revealing information from Everitt's security people. As in the contemporary TV story 'That'll Be the Day', the Section lab is run by a man called George. He loans Callan a device to distort Liz's voice on the phone when she poses as Jane Everitt.

Alcohol, Tobacco and Firearms: Callan and Lonely have Scotch and beer respectively in the pub as they discuss Christophe, who confuses Lonely by buying a bottle of wine to cook with. Lonely enjoys a bottle of Clos de Vougeot '61 with his banquet at Christophe's place.

Callan carries his customary Magnum, while the KGB man posing as one of the Frenchman's students is armed with a Makarov semi-automatic.

Spy-Speak: Callan has doubts about joining a cookery school: 'I can't even fry chips. They'd be on to me in a minute.'

Callan's memorably dry comment on seeing Lonely's impromptu banquet: 'Aren't you going to save a bit for me?'

Mission Analysis: 'Tiny bit? You've got a whole bloody duck there.' More originality, built around the *ennui* of the suburban middle class – another very 1970s theme – and around Mitchell's own enthusiasm for good food. The detail of Christophe's cookery school is very authentic and Mitchell cleverly uses cuisine to highlight the social hierarchies in the story: Callan and Lonely dine on fish and chips, the professor and the scruffy Laura tackle pub food while Christophe and the sophisticated Jane Everitt indulge in *cordon bleu* cooking. Although the story finishes with another Callan/KGB showdown, 'File on a Gallic Charmer' succeeds because of inventive touches like clever misdirection, the comic highlight of Lonely's feast during a burglary – which is as funny as anything in 'Breakout' – and notably, the most pro-active use of Liz in the short stories. Hugely enjoyable, very funny and very novel.

THE SHORT STORIES 5: 1973

CALLAN: FILE ON A DEADLY DEADSHOT

Publication: Sunday Express
Date: 11 March 1973
Featuring: Callan, Lonely, the fourth Hunter
Mission Profile: Callan is sent to Whitmore House, Lord Marsden's Northumberland estate, to protect the influential businessman Baumer from being killed by an assassin.

A Man Like Me: Under his own name, Callan poses as a wealthy adventurer to attend Marsden's shooting party, complete with 'a new and ostentatious Bentley' and the fashionably flamboyant evening dress of ruffled shirt, maroon bow tie and corded velvet dinner jacket. He loses at poker for the Section and it won't be the last time. He was taught to track a man through undergrowth by a Gurkha while serving in Malaya.

Lonely: Showing once again how essential to the Callan saga the thief is, all the humour comes from Lonely posing as Callan's valet – or 'valley' in his language – for 'a hundred nicker.' Typically, he takes pride in doing the job well for 'Mr. Callan'.

Section Kills: 17

A Tie and a Crest: Unusually, Hunter reveals details of his personal background to Callan, taking him to his club for dinner. The agent also knows his commander has no children.

Alcohol, Tobacco and Firearms: As well as Callan, the men who attend Marsden's party – Baumer, Lorimer, Endicott and Minns – are all good shots. Callan takes a Magnum .38 revolver with him to Northumberland and enjoys Marsden's brandy the night before the shoot. The assassin uses a sawn-off shotgun. Hunter loans Callan one of a pair of Purdey* shotguns his father owned.

Spy-Speak: Hunter appraises Callan's table manners: 'Not as good as your shooting. But then nothing could be.'

Lonely gets the better of some rival valets: 'I knew they'd be la-di-da. Still – look on the bright side. They can't, none of them, play brag.'

Mission Analysis: 'Who are you supposed to be...? Dick Turpin?' A familiar situation: an unknown killer among several suspects. 'File on a Deadly Deadshot' reuses a scenario Mitchell had created for the first series episode 'But He's a Lord, Mr. Callan', namely, an evening card game at a Lord's country house prior to a shooting party. In the story's favour are Mitchell's typically concise and to-the-point descriptions and dialogue, as well as the opening and closing scenes in which, surprisingly, Hunter gives some insight into his personal life. Once again, Lonely nearly steals the show and the way the assassin is dealt with is satisfyingly nasty.

CALLAN: FILE ON AN ANGRY ARTIST

Publication: Sunday Express
Date: 18 March 1973
Featuring: Callan, Lonely, Meres, the fourth Hunter
Mission Profile: Callan is assigned to find out if the artist Richard Hodge, who is in a Yellow File, has Foreign Office papers his brother stole.

A Man Like Me: Callan poses as art dealer Matt Jackson. Courtesy of the Section, he has 'a new suit, ready-made and expensive and just a little vulgar; a tie that didn't quite belong with the shirt – or the suit. Money, credit cards, cheque-book, a gold fountain pen that was very vulgar indeed.'

He easily bests the aggressive Hodge in a fight and shoots an Arab agent dead. Callan understands Hodge's love of art well enough to get him to talk, threatening to destroy one of his paintings. Gallantly, he resists the drugged charms of a hippy girl offered to him by Hodge at a party. He can get quite drunk on champagne.

Section Kills: 18

Lonely: Paid a generous £100 to tail Hodge and search his flat. Unsurprisingly, he has a dim view of cous-cous and the hippy counter culture (because of his experience in 'File on a Happy Hippy').

A Tie and a Crest: Meres is kept out of the main mission, arriving to collect the corpses of the Arab agent and Hodge, along with the artist's painting which conceals the Foreign Office documents.

Alcohol, Tobacco and Firearms: Callan shares two bottles of Taittinger champagne with Hodge, drinking out of a beer glass. Lonely has a pint in Notting Hill but Callan sticks to tomato juice.

---

* Miss-spelt as 'Purdy' in the story.

Spy-Speak: Lonely rebuffs Callan's dig about him being filthy minded when looking at artist's models: 'Nothing dirty about it. Beauty unadorned. It's art, that is.'

Mission Analysis: 'But I don't even know what I like.' The beginning of the *Express* stories' theme of putting Callan into situations not seen in the television series, here the agent comes face to face with *avant garde* art and, once again, the fag end of 1960s hippy culture. Mitchell's realisation of the *milieu* is very convincing, particularly in the party scene (and there's a similarly credible scene in 'Goodbye Mary Lee'). In a few descriptive phrases and sharp dialogue, Hodge lives and breathes as an aggressive boor, while in his few scenes Lonely is as amusing as ever.

CALLAN: FILE ON A RECKLESS RIDER

Publication: Sunday Express
Date: 25 March 1973
Featuring: Callan, Lonely, Meres, the fourth Hunter
Mission Profile: 'If not the fox, why not the hunter?' Pamphlets with this slogan are sent to the press after the shooting of two riders during a foxhunt and horse race. Hunter guesses this is a KGB plot to disguise the assassination of Enderby, a keen rider and the Foreign Office official who helped the Egyptians '[kick] the Russians out.' Callan is ordered to stop the killer.

A Man Like Me: Callan loses £8 in betting on a horse race. With £50 of his own money, he makes it back on Pretty Lady, which comes in at 100-8 in another race. Callan is able to tell from a considerable distance that a jockey has been shot from 300 yards range, and from which direction.

An expert marksman, from a helicopter he accurately uses a rifle to shoot dead the sniper – the sister of the man he suspects of being the killer. Although shooting dead a woman sickens Callan, he's still professional enough to dump her body at sea.

Section Kills: 19

Lonely: Ordered to become a stable hand. Predictably, he's scared of horses, causing an outbreak of his BO. Amazingly, after being in the stables all day he wants a bath.

A Tie and a Crest: Hunter treats Callan to a picnic at the races; occasionally, he rides with a hunt full of wealthy people. Also an experienced rider, Meres is ordered by Hunter (on Callan's behalf) to keep close to Enderby during the hunt. Unsurprisingly, Callan has no experience of horses.

Alcohol, Tobacco and Firearms: Hunter and Callan drink wine at the races. Beaune wine is served at the hunt dinner. Callan uses a Mannlicher hunting rifle to kill the assassin.

Spy-Speak: Fun is had with Callan's inexperience with the equine fraternity. 'Don't tell me you want me knock off a horse?' he asks at one point and later admits, 'The last thing I rode was a donkey at the seaside.'

Mission Analysis: 'It's not every day I get a chance to shoot a lady.' The story revolves around an effective red herring. The reader is led to believe that Lawson, the jockey who rides Pretty Lady, is the assassin: the twist is that it turns out to be his sister, female villains being relatively rare in Mitchell's Callan fiction at this time. Showing off his descriptive skills, the picture the author draws of the horse riding fraternity is detailed and evocative, but overall the story feels rather lightweight.

CALLAN: FILE ON A WEEPING WIDOW

Publication: Sunday Express

Date: 1 April 1973

Featuring: Callan, the fourth Hunter

Mission Profile: Callan dates Pamela Ramirez to find out if she is carrying on the work of her dead husband Enrique, an international racing driver and KGB courier.

A Man Like Me: When the story begins, Callan has seen Pamela eight times and admits to himself that he's falling in love with her. He destroys their relationships forever by shooting down a KGB agent, Pamela's mechanic Sacha Morel, in front of her. Making the end of their affair tragically ironic, Morel had convinced Pamela that Callan was working for Soviet intelligence.

Section Kills: 20

Lonely: Uniquely in the short stories, the thief doesn't appear.

A Tie and a Crest: Callan once again joins the wealthy classes under the alias Robert Philbin (not Tucker, surprisingly), Managing Director of Philbin Enterprises.

Alcohol, Tobacco and Firearms: Callan's Magnum duels with Morel's unidentified 9mm hand gun. On his way to the finish line of Pamela's race, Callan has a Scotch to steady his nerves while she wins a bottle of champagne. After the assignment, a depressed Callan takes generous measures of Hunter's Chivas Regal.

Spy-Speak: Callan sums up Pamela's appeal eloquently: 'You're never on time, it takes you two hours to decide what dress to wear – yet put you behind the wheel of a car, and you'd think every road was Brands Hatch.'

Hunter's assessment of Callan's handling of the mission: 'Messy, stupid and bungling.'

Mission Analysis: 'She'll never see me again.' James Mitchell saved the best until last in the fifth batch of short stories. Tense and atypical, the story begins with Callan already engaged on his assignment, and with Lonely absent there's room to effectively explore the dilemma the Section man finds himself in. Like the best of the TV episodes and the novels, the conflict between Callan's feelings and his duty to the Section is prominent, making forgivable the similarity of the final gun battle to the one in 'Charlie Says It's Good-bye'. Through good description and dialogue, the strong Pamela Ramirez impresses as a potential soul mate for Callan, making the ending spectacularly bitter.

KILL CALLAN

Publication: Sunday Express

Dates: 2, 9, 16, September 1973

Information: Three-part serialisation of *Russian Roulette*, illustrated by Andrew Robb, ahead of the book's publication in December. The *Express* brand serialised other thriller novels, including high profile titles such as *Billion Dollar Brain* (1966) by Len Deighton and *The Savage Day* (1971) by Jack Higgins.

THE NOVELS: 2

RUSSIAN ROULETTE

Publisher: Hamish Hamilton Ltd. hardback

Released: December 1973

Price: £1.95

Cover Photograph: Beverly Lebarrow

Dedication: 'To George and Anne Greenfield'

REPRINTS
Book Club Associates hardback, UK, 1974
William Morrow hardback, USA, 1974
Corgi paperback, UK, 1975
Dell paperback, USA, December 1975
Retitled *Les javas des truquers*: Gallimard paperback, France, 1976
Retitled *Pistola Circasi*: Arnoldo Mondadori Editoire hardback, Italy, September 1977
Ostara Publishing Limited paperback/Ebook, UK, 2013

Featuring: Callan, Lonely, Hunter, Meres, Liz, Judd, Snell, Miss Brewis, 'The Groper'

MISSION PROFILE: The KGB offers Hunter a deal: they will return a top British double agent, a KGB colonel called Zhilkov, in exchange for three of their executioners being allowed into Britain to kill Callan. Hunter agrees, depriving Callan of guns, Section protection and the means of leaving the country; Lonely can't get him a gun as all his contacts have been warned off, and Callan is even more vulnerable because his eyesight is deteriorating. His illness is held in check by eye-drops administered by Nurse Amanda Somerset, and Callan becomes romantically involved with her. With Lonely's help, Callan kills all three of the Russian agents but discovers that Amanda is also a KGB operative. She commits suicide, and, once again, Callan tells Hunter that he's finished with the Section.

A MAN LIKE ME: Callan lives at Flat 3, Stanmore House, Duke William Street, Bayswater. His back-story is restated: parents killed in the Blitz, the aunt who brought him up dying while he was in the army in Malaya, and his imprisonment for stealing £25,000; since leaving prison, he has hated thieving. Even before Callan was trained, he was considered the best man the Section ever had. Due to his violent job, which has also given him three scars from knife and bullet wounds on his back, the retinas in Callan's eyes have become detached, putting him in danger of permanent blindness. Callan dreams about killing Leb-ichev, one of his early assignments, as well as Karski and Kliegman, none of whom were mentioned in *A Magnum for Schneider*.

He is wanted by the KGB for, among other 'crimes', 'the exposure of Tania Andreyev-na [and] the Bokharian scandal'. As part of Hunter's deal with the Russians, Callan's safety net – his hidden Magnum .38 revolver, passport, money and 54 mm Napoleonic model sol-diers that he could sell for £500 – are all impounded by the Section. However, Callan proves himself highly resourceful in using London's environment against his attackers: a rolled-up copy of the soft-core magazine *Penthouse* becomes a weapon, he buries an vicious dog under a pile of bricks on a building site and uses a rifle range in an office, where he was once sent on an assignment, to kill one of the KGB men.

Callan's ethical values are as contradictory as ever. He is fiercely loyal to Lonely and although he knew the Groper, a homosexual doctor, was in love with him in prison he didn't use this knowledge against him. Offered a job as a bodyguard by the gangster Adam Komorowski, which would save his life, Callan declines; later, he shops Komorowski to the police as the latter has betrayed him to the Russians. Even though Callan discovers

Amanda, the fellow loner and misfit who becomes his lover, is a KGB agent with orders to kill him, he allows her to take her own life rather than be interrogated by the Section.

Section Kills: 13

LONELY: Started his criminal career stealing sweets from Woolworths. He served time with Callan for housebreaking, 'money and goods value fifty pounds, with seventeen other offences taken into consideration.' Much more than during *A Magnum for Schneider*, Lonely acts as the go-between between Callan and London's underworld, trying to get his old cell mate a gun from Harry Head and Manny Mandel. When this fails, he puts Callan in touch with 'the Polisher' – Komorowski – and later suggests using 'The Groper', a struck-off doctor he and Callan served time with, to treat his eyes. ('The Groper' had previously appeared on TV in 'A Village Called "G" 'while Komorowski could almost be Dicer from 'The Little Bits and Pieces of Love'.)

Lonely introduces more of his relations to Callan: Aunty Glad, otherwise known as 'Miss de Courcy Mannering', an ex-prostitute who worked for Komorowski, and Aunty Gertie, who runs a tea stall on a market (and *must* be the same aunt as seen on TV in 'Where Else Could I Go?' and 'That'll Be the Day'). Initially suspicious of Callan because she brought Lonely up, she comes to respect the agent's loyalty to her nephew. This makes Gertie's death, from a KGB bomb planted in Lonely's flat, bitterly ironic: without thinking, Lonely acts bravely to try and save Gertie, forcing his way into the burning flat, and significantly, he doesn't stink while trying to rescue her. Lonely later bravely poses as Callan to draw out one of the Soviet executioners, partly in revenge for Gertie's murder, but he has qualms about Callan looting the dead man's body.

A skilled burglar, Lonely knows how to spot houses that are empty and, after breaking into one, thinks having twin beds when a couple is married is 'ridiculous'. Whisky gives him heartburn.

A TIE AND A CREST: Meres hates Callan more than ever, although his delight in setting him up as a target for the KGB is short-lived. Living dangerously, he is supplying 'one of' his girlfriends, Susan Marsden, with cannabis. Hunter is aware of this and orders him not to see her again. Later, Callan uses Toby as a decoy to draw the last Russian killer's fire, in retaliation for Meres (exceeding orders by) telling the Russians that the older agent was going blind.

With rare self-awareness, Toby believes the Section is all he and Callan are 'fit for.'

ALCOHOL, TOBACCO AND FIREARMS: Before being expelled from the Section, Callan uses a .22 Colt Woodman target pistol on the Section's firing range. He believes the Russians use Makarov semi-automatics, but the second one he kills – with two bullets he kept from the Woodman, in a Long Rifle – carries a Walther semi-automatic. Later, he relieves Komorowski of a Smith and Wesson .38 Magnum, becoming 'Two Gun Callan'. Clearly a believer in German efficiency, Meres uses a Walther P38.

Despite, or more likely because of, the danger Callan is in, alcohol features prominently. He's told that he's been sold out to the Russians as he's pouring a glass of Hunter's Chivas Regal so he can't pull his gun. When Callan is hiding out with Lonely and his Aunty Gertie, the trio share beer and whisky. After helping him kill a Russian agent, Callan decides Lonely needs a drink. In an echo of the situation with Hunter, the ex-agent takes a Scotch with Komorowski as he tells him he's shopping him to the police.

His affair with Amanda is a much needed respite from the extreme danger he's in and, ,unsurprisingly, it's also awash with alcohol.

SPY-SPEAK: 'I never expected to get a pension out of this job – or even a gold watch. But I never thought I'd be fired either,' Callan says, retaining his dry sense of humour even though the Section have betrayed him.

Callan's neat summary of Lonely: 'It was like going mates with a sewage farm.'

Callan's memorable view of office employees as prisoners of their occupations: 'Another great swarm of workers surged past him through the "Out" doors, let off on parole until next morning. The vast foyer was crowded with other potential escapers, and the four commissionaires on duty looked like benevolent gaolers.'

Heartbreakingly, Amanda tells Callan of her dualistic, conflicting feelings for him: 'I'm in love with you – and I hate you.'

Callan matter-of-factly tells a KGB agent he's just shot, 'You're dying. There's nothing we can do about it, even if we could... You can't expect me to say I'm sorry I killed you – and I'm not. But I'm sorry about one thing – this whole stupid bloody mess.'

INFORMATION: George Greenfield was James Mitchell's literary agent in the 1970s and the novel is dedicated to him and his wife. As Lonely has 'never seen anybody killed before', contradicting several TV episodes, *Russian Roulette* reinforces the idea that the books exist in a different continuity, despite the appearance of the Groper.

Mitchell reprises the scene where Callan and Amanda look at Sir Christopher Wren's house in *Spyship* (1983): 'He could wake up every morning, look out of the window and see how his cathedral was doing.'[6]

American studios Bing Crosby Productions and Lorimar both expressed an interest in acquiring the film rights to the book.[7] However, by the time *Russian Roulette* was published in December 1973, a deal was already in place with Derek Horne's UK company Magnum Productions to turn Mitchell's previous Callan novel, *A Magnum for Schneider*, into a movie. Buoyed up by the positive response to screenings of *Callan* at the 1974 Cannes Film Festival, Horne commissioned Mitchell to write a full screenplay of *Russian Roulette*, but sadly the film was never made.

There was some consolation for Mitchell for this cancelled movie adaptation as the book reviews were the most positive of any of the Callan novels. The *Birmingham Post* applauded 'a real winner. Mitchell's beautifully judged prose, his economic dialogue and his enormous inventiveness are a shining example to wordier and less easily digestible thriller writers.' The *Financial Times*, meanwhile, delighted in 'a satisfying amount of wicked blood [being] shed' and recommended the book as 'readable and deftly written.' On Mitchell's home turf, the *Newcastle Journal* was equally impressed by 'a tense and well-told story – excitement mixed with sour wit,'[8] while the *Coventry Evening Telegraph* declared the novel 'quite as good as any of the television stories'[9]: the highest possible praise.

MISSION ANALYSIS: *'You're bad news.'* *Russian Roulette* stands out among British thriller novels because, even more than in *A Magnum for Schneider*, Mitchell's London, with its different daily rhythms and the contrast between the law abiding and the criminal, feels like a character in its own right. There are touches of both the Western *High Noon* (1952), as Callan is disowned by his own people and has to face enemy gunmen alone, and of Hitchcock's *Frenzy* (1972), featuring a man on the run, hunted through a seedy, hostile capital.

Callan is forced to take refuge in packed tube trains, cafes, pubs and parks from dawn until dusk and, significantly, the major confrontations with the KGB all take place at ordinary places of work: a building site, an office block and a factory. This feeds into the novel's other theme – while the ordinary, workaday world is oblivious to the fatal secret one that Callan, Lonely and the Section inhabit, the two exist side by side. After the virtuoso sequence in which Callan kills a Russian agent and a vicious dog in a partially constructed building, he is reprimanded by a policeman who thinks he's drunk and disorderly; after his Auntie Gertie is killed, Lonely mourns her in a busy caff, crying alone at a table. This contrast is at its most effective in the blackly ironic scene where, having dealt with one highly trained KGB executioner, Callan is punched by a stumbling drunk in a homeless hostel.

The characterisation is razor sharp. The dialogue of Callan, Meres, Hunter and Lonely would fit seamlessly into any of Mitchell's TV scripts, and you can almost hear Graham Crowden and Queenie Watts saying the Groper and Aunty Gertie's lines. The relationship between Callan and Amanda is touchingly written as these two loners grow close, but, as was the pattern by now, any romantic attachment Callan has with a woman ends badly. Mitchell also highlights how crossing Callan's path can be lethal for people he becomes involved with, as Gertie, the Groper's boyfriend Terry and Amanda either die or are maimed for life. Perhaps fittingly, the most upbeat aspect of the story is that Lonely and Callan's friendship endures, as the killer comes to admire 'the little man who'd found courage in grief, and dignity too.'

Russian Roulette would have a made a stunning two-part TV series finale or an excellent second Callan feature film. Combining suspense, lyrical prose and sharp characterisation, it's arguably the definitive Callan novel.

THE SHORT STORIES 6: 1974

CALLAN: FILE ON AN ANGRY ACTOR

Publication: Sunday Express
Date: 26 May 1974
Featuring: Callan, Lonely, Meres
Mission Profile: The film star Noel Empson throws parties at which, on behalf of the KGB, prominent British politicians are killed or compromised. One of his protégés is intending to kill Olga Lubova, a Russian émigré who's writing her memoirs near the location of Empson's latest movie. Callan is detailed to stop the assassination.

A Man Like Me: Using his Tucker alias (with the addition of the Christian name 'George'), Callan is completely in his element as technical adviser on a historical epic, which features 'Wellington versus Napoleon's marshals'. It's the perfect cover for him, as he throws himself into checking the authenticity of weapons and uniforms.

Section Kills: 22

Lonely: While watching the film crew on Callan's orders, he proves himself surprisingly good casting as 'Lonely the terrible', a ragged soldier kitted out with a moustache, muskets and daggers. However, after he's done multiple takes of the same scene, the glamour of the film industry quickly evaporates for him.

A Tie and a Crest: At Callan's request, Meres is ordered to pose as Olga, wearing one of her dresses and a wig. Naturally, he's furious.

Alcohol, Tobacco and Firearms: In a break between takes, Callan gives Lonely a bottle of beer. After acting as a decoy for the killer, a shaken Meres drinks Scotch. Callan again uses an Armalite AR-7 rifle, shooting down the assassin – the wardrobe supervisor Dino, who's packing a Colt Woodsman Pistol.

Spy-Speak: Lonely is confused about his part in the film: 'When you said I was going to be a guerrilla, I thought you meant a bleeding monkey.'

Dressed as an old woman, Meres caustically agrees to remove Dino's body, 'Just as soon as I've slipped into something a little less formal.'

Mission Analysis: 'I could break you in two.' Of the second phase of stories this arguably works best, as Callan is thrust into a scenario that's as far from the province of the TV series as it's possible to get. The setting is so far outside *Callan*'s usual remit that it verges on the surreal – Meres in drag – and the reader really doesn't know what to expect. 'File on an Angry Actor' is the beginning of Mitchell putting the Section regulars in increasingly outlandish and often quirky, amusing scenarios.

Although he's only in a few scenes, Empson convinces as an arrogant bully sure of his own talent and importance, and has a wonderfully egocentric line in the style of *The Avengers* as he's about to expire: 'You bastard, I didn't finish the picture.' A satisfying, original story that authentically captures the feel of a movie in production.

CALLAN: FILE ON A LUCKY LADY

Publication: Sunday Express
Date: 2 June 1974
Featuring: Callan, Lonely, Meres, the fourth Hunter
Mission Profile: Callan serves as bodyguard to the wilful Angela Balboa, at risk of kidnap from Corsican gangsters. They want to blackmail her millionaire father into surrendering his shares in super-conductors, which produce cheap electricity.

A Man Like Me: Angela pays Callan £500 day for his services, rather more than he gets as an employee of the Section. Predictably given his attraction to wealthy, cultured women in the past, Callan and Angela are attracted to each other and become lovers. For the first time, it's revealed that Callan broke the gangster Rinty's arm to stop him terrorising Lonely.

Section Kills: 24

Lonely: Paid £250 by Callan to break into a house on the Kent coast and conceal two Magnum revolvers in a toilet cistern. Callan cures him of his reluctance to help by reminding the housebreaker of the debt he owes him over Rinty.

A Tie and a Crest: Meres looks good on the disco dance floor, dressing down convincingly to fit in with the London club set.

Alcohol, Tobacco and Firearms: Callan drinks Scotch in a discotheque. For his protection assignment, he's upgraded to a .357 Magnum – which he'll use from now on – fitted with a silencer (see Chapter 10). Meres fakes being drunk very convincingly. Callan buys Lonely a pie and a pint.

Spy-Speak: Callan uses his working class swagger to good effect when he's invited to Angela's apartment: 'What happens to the dog if you change the colour scheme? Do you dye it?'

Angela gives as good as she gets. In a casino with Callan next to her, she says: 'You don't mind if my mascot sits beside me? He's a bit big to put on the table.'

Mission Analysis: 'People like you forget the one important thing about guns... they go off.' 'File on a Lucky Lady' couldn't be more 1974 if it tried. The plot turns on the energy crisis, and features both the sort of London night club Patrick Mower would have frequented, and a gambling club that Lord Lucan might have belonged to. The story is given an extra *frisson* by the attraction between Callan and Angela: from the moment they start sniping at each other, it's clear they're going to get together and there's the kinky, if underplayed, suggestion that the heiress is aroused by violence. In keeping with the 1974 *mien*, after bedding Angela Callan offers Roger Moore Bond-style innuendo when he says, 'one thing and another I had a busy night'. This *The Taming of the Shrew* dimension – helpfully, Hunter even mentions the Shakespeare play – makes this story another entertaining read.

CALLAN: FILE ON A DANCING DECOY

Publication: Sunday Express
Date: 9 June 1974
Featuring: Callan, Lonely, the fourth Hunter
Mission Profile: Callan investigates the Russian ballerina Varvara Arenskaya, whom the economist and occasional Section agent Routledge is obsessed with. Hunter suspects she may be working for the KGB and that Routledge is her target.

A Man Like Me: Attending a party full of ballet dancers, Callan wears one of his most flamboyant undercover disguises: dark blue 'slacks', powder blue sweater and silver medallion. During the case, he plays the Battle of Samalanca with his soldier models to help him think. Callan enjoys another taste of luxury by staying at the Ilion hotel (which costs Hunter £20 a night!) and makes one of his few uses of a covert gadget – a directional microphone.

Section Kills: 25

Lonely: Employed by Callan to follow Varvara. Unusually, he's tricked by her swapping coats with fellow dancer Valerie Prout and feels terrible that he's let Callan down.

A Tie and a Crest: Hunter treats Callan to a performance of the ballet *Les Sylphides* and dinner. The Section bug Varvara's flat and have the influence to place a story about a fake accident in the press.

Alcohol, Tobacco and Firearms: Lonely has the traditional pint of beer courtesy of Callan, who is again armed with his .357 Magnum. Nastily, the gunman Massenet, working for the KGB, threatens to shoot Varvara in the knee cap. Callan and Routledge share whisky after Massenet is shot dead.

Spy-Speak: Callan's hilarious observation of male ballerinas: 'They'd have a helluva job hiding a .357 Magnum under those outfits.'

His description of the smitten Routledge is also dryly funny: 'A man in love has no time for telephones.'

Mission Analysis: 'People saying "Shh!" seemed as a much a part of ballet as the music.' A straightforward is-she-or-isn't-she-a-traitor narrative, made engaging by Callan's typically sardonic reactions to the ballet world, as well as lively characters like the agent's camp outfitter Hugh Beaumont, and the seven-and-a-half-stone dancer Valerie, who can demolish a three course meal and coffee with four sugars. She and Varvara swapping clothes to shake off a tail – which nearly costs the Russian her life – is typical of Mitchell's clever, dramatically ironic plotting.

CALLAN: FILE ON A FEARSOME FARM

Publication: Sunday Express
Date: 20 October 1974
Featuring: Callan, Lonely, the fourth Hunter, Liz
Mission Profile: Callan is ordered to track down the KGB agent 'K', the receiver of information stolen by the double-agent 'Chuck' Odell. Callan's inquiries take him to a health farm with the unlikely name of 'Mince'.

A Man Like Me: According to Hunter, Callan recently posed as a school janitor where he drank 'a lot of beer' and he's been eating too much rich West Indian food. After the Section chief points out that he's putting on weight, Callan is extremely self-conscious about it and, buying some bathroom scales, is disgusted to see that he's 5lb overweight. Despite this, he enjoys a dalliance with the buxom 'Natasha Biscayne', a glamour model, and by the end of the assignment has shed the offending weight.

Section Kills: 26

Lonely: Even though he enjoys a pie and a pint at Callan's expense for the second time in two stories, he earns his grub by breaking into a penthouse flat owned by the deceased Odell.

Alcohol, Tobacco and Firearms: Callan's Magnum is stolen at Mince and, much to the agent's disgust, alcohol is off limits at the health farm. An opposition agent carries a Makarov pistol fitted with a silencer.

Spy-Speak: Even Lonely joins in having a dig about Callan's weight: 'You look better now you're on your diet, Mr. Callan.'

Hunter has a typically sardonic view of why a Russian agent was using an American accent: 'If anything goes wrong they can blame it on the CIA.'

Mission Analysis: 'Kooky. Slang of or pertaining to a kook.' There's more than a hint of the James Bond novel *Thunderball* (1961) as Callan is involved in intrigue at a health clinic but, despite a rather strained title, 'File on a Fearsome Farm' offers a well thought out plot about who the agent 'K' really is, what the code letter stands for and how Odell's interest in women – his flat is decorated with portraits of nudes, as Callan and Lonely discover – relates to his old girlfriend Natasha and the theft of secret information. Elsewhere, detailed scenes like Callan and Lonely's burgling of Odell's flat, the tense sequences of the weaponless agent being shot at during the night and the running joke about Callan being overweight, suggest this story might have started out as an idea for a television script.

CALLAN: FILE ON A DEADLY DIARY

Publication: Sunday Express
Date: 27 October 1974
Featuring: Callan, Lonely, the fourth Hunter
Mission Profile: Callan has to prevent the vengeful East German von Kleist, and the Romanian agent Eminescu, from securing the incriminating diaries of the Foreign Office diplomat Sir Arthur Black from his widow, Lady Pamela.

A Man Like Me: Utilising the resources of the Section, Callan uses 'two men with a car, two men and two women on foot' to keep watch on Lady Black. The agent again uses the alias 'Tucker' – 'who had been everything from a lorry-driver to a merchant banker' – as a publisher who approaches Lady Black with the offer of a ghost-written biography. Following her to Scotland, Callan poses with a plaster cast on his left arm, which, craftily, conceals a two-inch, barrelled .32 Smith and Wesson.

Most of the men Callan needs to carry out a robbery are in prison. Once again, he works his charm on a well-bred woman and the story ends with him looking forward to a date with another member of the aristocracy.

Section Kills: 27

Lonely: His antipathy towards Germans is explained: in 1945 a V-2 rocket killed the infant Lonely's family, burying him alive in the explosion; intriguingly, it's the same way Callan's parents were killed. Lonely is paid £10 a day plus expenses by Callan to follow Lady Black. Recognising her when shown a picture, he takes his cap off to show his respect and, impressively, puts on a blue serge suit, pork pie hat and I Zingari sporting tie to tail her.

A Tie and a Crest: A stickler for class etiquette, Hunter corrects Callan's assertion that Lady Black is part of the aristocracy: 'I believe one can describe it more properly as the gentry.' In place of Meres, Callan works with the upper-class SAS Captain Lastrange.

Alcohol, Tobacco and Firearms: Going dramatically up-market, Lonely forces himself to have a gin and tonic. In a seemingly never-ending succession of pints that Callan buys him, Lonely's surveillance of Lady Pamela earns him two more. Callan takes Magnum and Smith and Wesson hand guns to the Cairngorms while, for the opposition, von Kleist uses a Mannlicher rifle. At the end of the assignment, Hunter offers Callan his Chivas Regal.

Spy-Speak: Callan's brilliantly sour account of his initial meeting with Lady Black: 'At first she treated me like a cross between an income-tax nark and the man who's failed to clear the drains. But it got better.'

Lady Black comes to terms with Sir Arthur's death: 'I really must stop beginning every third sentence with "My husband". He's dead, and I've been alone too long.'

Mission Analysis: 'Welcome to the over-privileged classes.' The story begins like a rewrite of the TV story 'Suddenly – at Home', with Lonely keeping watch on another Lady whose dead husband has compromising secrets that the Communists want. When the story moves to Scotland, events take an elegant twist because of the conflicting interests of the dispossessed Baron van Kleist and the Romanian security agent Eminescu, who wants Sir Arthur's knowledge kept secret; believably, Eastern Bloc agents as well as Western ones are shown to not always be in accord. It's encouraging to see Callan's opponents given some strong characterisation and, breaking new ground, the agent isn't centre-stage in the denouement. It's also interesting to see that the Section's resources have been seriously upgraded: a RAF plane, the SAS, a Snowcat... in the same year that the *Callan* feature film was released, Mitchell's prose writing has become noticeably cinematic.

CALLAN: FILE ON A CLASSY CLUB

Publication: Sunday Express

Date: 3 November 1974

Featuring: Callan, Lonely, the fourth Hunter; introducing Bulky Berkley

Mission Profile: Callan loses heavily in the prestige gambling club Renfrews, working with the skilled gambler Bulky Berkley to flush out an SSD spy ring.

A Man Like Me: Showing his unpleasant side, Callan uses his Magnum to intimidate Bulky into working for him. Playing the part of the naive gambler to the hilt, he stays at the Hilton hotel under his Tucker alias, wins £3,000 on roulette then loses £18,000 at poker. On foot, he's able to shoot the driver of a Mercedes 600 dead.

Callan knows rush-jobs lead to mistakes: playing poker in Renfrews, he takes cards from the sideboard where they're kept – even though, as Tucker, he's pretending that he's never been to the club before.

Section Kills: 28

Lonely: The thief explains the 'Pullman dodge' swindle and recommends the card player Bulky Berkley as the man the agent needs. Lonely uses his breaking and entering skills to infiltrate Renfrews and, with Callan, places a marked set of cards in a sideboard where the club's packs are kept.

A Tie and a Crest: For once the upper classes are on Callan's side, as an earl and millionaire propose his membership of an up-market gambling club.

Alcohol, Tobacco and Firearms: Callan drinks champagne while attending Renfrews. The SSD agents carry Walther automatics because 'the East Germans still believed in West German technology.'

Spy-Speak: Callan advises Hunter to calm down after he becomes angry over a CIA operation in London he knew nothing about: 'You better watch it, Hunter. The only time I ever saw a colour like yours was on hot-house grapes.'

Mission Analysis: 'Lose money. Lose rather a lot of money.' Although 'File on a Classy Club' has a lot going for it, with the inability of intelligence agencies on both sides of the Iron Curtain to co-operate, it's the weakest in this strong batch of stories. A well written action sequence aside, the story is let down by too much exposition and too many reported events. Without the room to build up the atmosphere and tension, the poker game also falls rather flat. The story is chiefly notable for the first appearance of the jovial gambler Bulky Berkley, later resurrected in the novel *Smear Job*.

THE NOVELS: 3, 4

DEATH AND BRIGHT WATER

A Callan Novel
Publisher: Hamish Hamilton Ltd.
Released: 1974
Price: £2.75
Cover photograph: 'From *Callan*, the Magnum Production by Gloria Films'

Dedication: 'For Derek Horne'

REPRINTS

William Morrow hardback, USA, 1974
G.K. Hall and Company, large print hardback, UK, June 1975 [or 1977]
Corgi paperback, UK, 1976
Ostara Publishing Limited paperback/Ebook, UK, 2014

Featuring: Callan, Lonely, Hunter, Meres, Liz (un-named), Snell, Judd, 'The Groper', Karsky; introducing Spencer Percival Fitzmaurice*

MISSION PROFILE: Elegant Communist Sophie Kollonaki meets Callan in Paris and offers him £10,000 to spring her daughter Helena from a house arrest in Crete. Aware the KGB

---

* In the novels and short stories, Mitchell alternates between two ways of writing the black Section agent's name; the style above and 'FitzMaurice.' For consistency, we have used the style established in his debut novel.

suggested him for this job, Callan turns it down and is convinced it will fail. Returning to London, he is abducted by the Section and told to see the job through – with a few variations of Hunter's own devising – or go into a Red File.

'Nutter' Bradley has been hired to beat up Dr. Blythe, an intermediary working for Sophie. Seeing Bradley off, Callan informs Blythe he will do the job after all. Callan then receives a counter-offer from Michael Vardakis, Sophie's wealthy cousin: the ex-agent's fee will be trebled if he ensures the mission fails and that Dimitri, Sophie's inside man in Crete, is killed. Vardakis intends the debacle to end Sophie's political ambitions.

Callan is shot at in the street and the Parnassos Restaurant where he first encountered Sophie is burnt down. Lonely is wrongly suspected of the firebombing by the police so Callan takes him to Crete, knowing that his cat-burgling skills will be useful.

On the island, Callan meets with Blythe, Dimitri and the resentful Bradley. All of them are to be involved in the forthcoming raid but all are working to their own agenda. Bradley, in the pay of Vardakis, tries to ensure the mission fails, and kills Dimitri. Rescuing Helena, Callan leaves Bradley stranded. Hunter, aware Vardakis is Helena's father, uses this as leverage against the Greek. Bradley returns to London to kill Callan, but Lonely's observational skills pick the assassin out and Callan shoots him dead.

A MAN LIKE ME: Callan is now digging roads for a living and enjoying the freedom, but he still needs danger like 'a special drug'. He passes Blythe's amateurish initiative test with help from the Groper, and later bullies porn photographer Beasley, another prison contact, into forging passports.

When Hunter applies coercion Callan immediately gives in to working for him. His plans for the raid on the Polybios house and the subsequent escape are calculated, manipulative and meticulously prepared. He minimises casualties in the raid to three: two armed policemen whom he unwillingly – but unhesitatingly – shoots in self-defence, and a guard dog he regretfully drugs with sleeping tablets ('poor perisher.') Helena is upset by his innate aggression and by the revelation that he is receiving money rather than acting out of ideology. Despite this, the pair enjoy a brief sexual relationship.

Callan regrets lying to Lonely and envisages Sophie as being 'a magnificent bitch' in her resistance heyday. Predictably, he refuses to show weakness in front of Hunter, but later loses control of himself when he confronts Bradley.

Section Kills: 16

LONELY: Looking after Callan's flat for him whie he works away from London, without being asked: 'Silently Callan cursed himself. This was a mate alright, smell or no smell.' Riding northwards to contact Callan, Lonely borrows a motorbike and leathers from his cousin Alfred, a Hell's Angel excommunicated on age grounds (at 37!).

He keeps tabs on the Parnassos, becoming resentful when the waiters slip him dodgy change. Lonely returns to use the coinage in their cigarette machine, but this coincides with Nutter Bradley's arson and the subsequent police investigation. He is wary of 'foreign grub', Crete and Manchester, and keeps his emergency cash inside a hollowed out book titled *How to Achieve a More Positive Personality*.

In Crete he assists with picking double-action Manton locks in the raid, before 'scarpering' as ordered. At one point, Callan tells him to get a room – 'with an *en suite* bathroom'.

A TIE AND A CREST: Meres arranges for Callan to be given a beating; he wanted to administer it himself but Hunter stops him, reasoning that he 'would have lost.' Instead, the beating is carried out by Spencer Percival Fitzmaurice, the new, gigantic, 'very black' Section operative from Barbados. Fitzmaurice initially poses as a fellow road worker to befriend Callan and the pair cheerfully exchange racial insults and friendly banter. Callan is taken by surprise, and it's the only occasion when a fellow Section agent gets the better of him. He is later assured the attack was not personal but an uneasy stand-off persists between Callan and Fitzmaurice. The black man detests Meres, mocking his Etonian accent, although the pair work together effectively as they pull in a member of Sophie's group, Nicky, for interrogation and, later, intimidate PC Kyle (a stubborn cop in the vein of Charwood from 'Land of Light and Peace') into abandoning his pursuit of Lonely.

In an echo of George Orwell's *Nineteen Eighty-Four* (1949), Snell questions Nicky in a room full of lab rats; the distressed young man later hangs himself in his cell.

ALCOHOL, TOBACCO AND FIREARMS: Brits abroad: Lonely puts away beer in Crete, while Blythe is on medication as part of his own battle with the Ouzo bottle, or so he claims. The Groper's boyfriend Terry (from *Russian Roulette*) committed suicide, so the ex-doctor and Callan have a modest 'drinkette' of Scotch in his honour. At the Section, Hunter offers Callan the usual, ominous glass of Chivas Regal and later the pair drink Beaune and brandy over dinner.

Callan uses a Colt Python .357 Magnum, while Dimitri has a WW2 Webley and Bradley packs a .380 Browning Standard Automatic.

SPY-SPEAK: Callan reflects on Blythe. 'He set to work, deft and efficient and quick, and Callan thought, you may be a terrible spy but you're a bloody marvellous dentist.'

He also ruminates on his time in the Section. 'Callan was sure there'd been enjoyment in his voice. Just like old times, when Hunter had only half-briefed him, just to see if he could figure out the rest of it for himself. And he usually could: but that was when he was set for promotion. Lord High Executioner's Chief Assistant.'

Callan reports Bradley's demise to Hunter, including his disguise, by saying 'There's a traffic warden in my shower.' Hunter complains that it's too early in the morning for Callan to be amusing.

INFORMATION: The novel was an extended rewrite of a film idea discussed with producer Derek Horne, acknowledged by the book being dedicated to him. Planned as a third Callan movie, *Death and Bright Water* reverts to the Series One format of Callan being estranged from the Section. Had it been made, the film would have followed a tendency present in other 1970s British TV spin-off films, such as *Carry on Abroad* (1972), *Are You Being Served* (1977) and *Sweeney 2* (1978), which take familiar characters out of their London habitat and into (in some cases sham) foreign locations. The attraction of filming in convenient proximity to Woodward's holiday home in Cyprus may also have been a factor, at least until the Greek coup and subsequent Turkish invasion in 1974.

Greek politics form the background to the novel, Greece being no stranger to dictatorships. In the 1930s, General Metaxas suppressed the political centre-left and drove most of his opponents into exile. The country attempted to remain neutral during WW2, until Germany overran most of it in 1941 and installed a puppet government. Several resistance groups sprang up in the mountains (numbering Sophie and

Hunter in their ranks), including the Communist run National Liberation Front (EAM), but internecine fighting was rife and civil war broke out after Germany retreated: 'Greek fighting Greek, Right against Left, Monarchist against Communist.' Following an uneasy period of democracy, Brigadier General Stylianos Pattakos seized power in a military coup and his junta was still in control when *Death and Bright Water* was written. It was overthrown in July 1974.

A KGB officer named Karsky appears; he is described as 'young' and 'literal-minded', so although he knows of Callan, he might not be the same coolly relentless interrogator seen in 'That'll Be the Day'. In addition to Gilbert and Sullivan's comic opera *The Mikado* (1885), there is an oblique reference to American writer Gertrude Stein (1874-1946).

MISSION ANALYSIS: *'Callan, Callan... The last thing you should expect of human beings is consistency.'* While many of Mitchell's standard devices – Callan disillusioning another likeable character, taking a rival, arrogant executioner by surprise, and the Section being openly ruthless – remain in place, the presence of a new regular character, hints that Hunter was once a romantic young idealist, together with the KGB's unusual role on the sidelines, express the author's innovative side.

Whether Mitchell was responding to Terence Feely's suggestion that a Callan movie should go overseas or acting on his own initiative, the foreign settings – Moscow, Paris and Crete – make a welcome change and the travelogue aspects are as authentically described as in any in Ian Fleming's James Bond stories. The slower pace and greater page-count allows room for exploration of the characters and the themes of family loyalty and dualism. From the first chapter we know several characters will prove to be more than they seem; this is foreshadowed by the metaphorical presence of the Minotaur and Callan looks at some local figurines of the half-man, half-bull while evaluating the appropriately labyrinthine plot. Vardakis is both Sophie's lover and her political enemy, several characters seem to be working for one person while really working for another, and for a while it's not even certain who Callan will side with.

A *Guardian* book review opined that the story had 'a plot likely to leave you double cross-eyed'[10] and as a result of all the ambiguity, the book occasionally becomes confusing: Callan correctly works out who 'Nutter' Bradley is working for, then appears to forget this information as a major plot twist approaches, while Meres spends several pages speculating on Bradley's whereabouts when the reader is already aware of them. The PC Kyle subplot is also switched off surprisingly abruptly.

Wisely, Mitchell accelerates the pace in the final quarter of the book and the story gels as Callan's dirty third-of-a-dozen go into action. A murder, a suicide, a shoot-out, sex and various escapes back to Britain rapidly ensue before the surviving major characters meet for a final confrontation and several sardonic plot revelations. From a measured start, this story would have made an impressive third entry in the Callan film franchise and, as it stands, remains an impressive and successfully experimental third novel.

SMEAR JOB

A Callan Novel
Writer: James Mitchell
Publisher: Hamish Hamilton Ltd.
Released: 1975
Price: £3.95
Jacket design: 'By Ken Reilly, based on a photograph of Edward Woodward from *Callan*, the Magnum production for Gloria Films'

Dedication: 'For James Mathieson'

REPRINTS

Corgi paperback, UK, 1977
G.P. Putnam and Sons hardback, USA, 1977
Berkeley Publishing Corporation paperback, USA, 1978
Retitled *Uno Sporco Affare:* Arnoldo Mondadori Editoire hardback, Italy, May 1978
Ostara Publishing Limited paperback/Ebook, UK, March 2016

Featuring: Callan, Lonely, Hunter (IV), Bishop, Meres, Snell, Liz, Fitzmaurice, Bulky Berkeley*, Uncle Lennie

MISSION PROFILE: In a copy of Karl Marx's *Das Kapital*, the West German defector Siegfried Lindt has coded the whereabouts of Otrud – or 'Trudi von Nichts' as she's known – the drug addict prostitute daughter of Ludwig Bauer, 'West German Minister to the Common Market'. Lindt was partners in the smuggling of antiques from behind the Iron Curtain with the Earl of Hexham (himself an SSD agent), and the book is hidden in an item of furniture on Hexham's Sicilian estate.

In return for deactivating their Red Files for a year, Hunter orders Callan and Lonely to retrieve the copy of *Das Kapital* so, when the Section chief finds Ortrud, he will have a hold over Bauer; if the politician refuses to co-operate, Hunter will carry out a 'smear job' and destroy his reputation in the media. Hunter also directs Callan and Lonely to make Gunther von Kleist, an exiled East German who now works as an archivist in Bonn, lose heavily at cards. Hunter will then have another man in his debt; he blackmails him into stealing a list of SSD safehouses in Britain from the archives.

The Section operation is complicated by the interference of 'Spanner' and George, London criminals intrigued by why the gambler Bulky Berkeley is working with Lonely, and the ambitious US Senator Edouard Manette, who, helped by his daughter Elisabeth, is searching America for Ortrud so he can blackmail Bauer. Meres and Fitzmaurice successfully deal with 'Loopy' Nichols' gang, who Spanner brings in to watch Berkeley, but, despite violent humiliation by Meres, Spanner persists in his inquires and teams up with Hexham. Callan shot and tortured him and the Earl wants the Section agent dead, while Spanner wants revenge for being frightened by Lonely, who he believes is a professional hitman.

In America and Mexico, Callan and Fitzmaurice's retrieval of Ortrud succeeds, partly because they take Manette and Elisabeth hostage, but in a twist Bishop orders Hunt-

---

* Spelt differently to 'File On a Classy Club'.

er to hand Ortrud over to the Congressman; as a possible future Secretary of State or Presidential candidate, he is British intelligence's 'investment for the 1980s.' Returning to England, Callan deals with Spanner and Hexham, but not before Berkeley's hands have been ruined by a letter bomb. Suborned by Hunter, Kleist commits suicide.

A MAN LIKE ME: Callan is now running a company with Lonely called 'Callan's: Specialists in Security'; the profitable client list includes supermarkets, jewellers, furriers and a merchant bank. As Callan and Lonely's friendship has deepened, Hunter threatens to put Lonely in a Red File to coerce Callan into taking on an assignment for the Section. He will be paid a generous £20,000 for stealing Lindt's copy of *Das Kapital* and an additional £5,000 for making Kleist lose a substantial amount of money at cards. Out of condition after a year, Callan is ordered to undergo refresher training at the Section.

His dependency on alcohol has increased to the point where he openly admits it. He is insensibly drunk on the plane after the initial mission, hating himself for intimidating and hurting people, particularly Lonely and Berkeley. Hunter judges the condition to be so serious that Snell gives Callan some medication to make him stop drinking, and Fitzmaurice is assigned to make sure he doesn't touch alcohol on the assignment to find Bauer's daughter; Callan later admits to being frustrated because he can't drink in Las Vegas. His attention is focused by an additional £5,000 for the retrieval of Ortrud and an affair with the 20 year-old Elisabeth Manette, another young woman attracted to Callan's combination of maturity and ruthlessness. Callan knows the relationship will be short-lived and fatalistically tells her that when she leaves him, he'll 'get drunk'.

Callan is more educated than he lets on, knowing the provenance of the antiques in Berkeley's flat and acquitting himself as a skilled card cheat, as well as alluding to the English Romantic poet John Keats (1795-1821), the Great War poem *In Flanders Field* (1915) by John McCrae and the fantasy novel *Lost Horizon* (1933) by James Hilton; he also recognises that Lonely unknowingly quotes from Shakespeare's play *As You Like It*. In America, as well as being a chauffeur for 'Lord Shekwe' (Fitzmaurice), Callan effortlessly adopts the cover of the fake diplomat's economics consultant. On the downside, he is back to being homophobic, deducing that Hexham isn't 'a queer'.
Section Kills: 19

LONELY: With his financial circumstances improved, he's left Notting Hill and smartened up considerably. His wardrobe now includes a stylish raincoat, a pork-pie hat and a shirt and tie bought in London's West End.

Lonely is 'Callan's' unique selling point: he breaks into prospective clients' offices, disables the alarm systems and leaves a business card behind. As an executive of his and Callan's joint company, he fancies a new, posh alias – Roger de vere Bullivant. Lonely is good in the kitchen, delivering an excellent jugged hare, and is offered £10,000 (plus expenses) for the successful completion of his side of Hunter's mission. While Callan retrains, Lonely goes to stay with another of his relatives, Uncle Lennie, an ex-commando turned black market meat dealer who lives in North London. Thanks to his criminal contacts, Lennie finds Berkeley, the card player Callan needs to ruin Kleist. Once again, Lonely is kept in the dark about working for the Section.

Following on from *Death and Bright Water*, Lonely takes the 'third flight he'd made in his entire lifetime' and is amusingly snobbish and parochial, finding Gatwick airport 'dead common' and moaning that Sicilians drive 'on the wrong side of the road.' (Needless to say, Lonely's delighted to find a café that cooks chips). He's jealous of Callan working with Berkeley, complaining about him flying First Class, but is mollified when Callan supplies him with another set of burglary equipment that the thief pronounces 'tools for a craftsman.'

Staying with Lennie while Callan is in America, Lonely is taught to shoot by his uncle, after convincingly terrifying Spanner and his henchman George with a shotgun. Knowing that his nephew responds to the threat of violence, Lennie threatens Lonely with his belt so he takes the training seriously. In perhaps his finest moment, he bravely draws a shotgun and fires at a pursuing Spanner on Harl Ness mudflats. Lonely's heroism is undone when Lennie points out that his nephew missed the unconscious criminal at point blank range, at which point Lonely faints.

He retains his fondness for snuff boxes and, predictably, needs beer when he's scared. In a touching final scene, Lonely happily declares the business card Callan gives him 'the most wonderful thing I ever got in my whole life' It reads: 'Roger de Vere Bullivant. Technical Director.'

A TIE AND A CREST: Snell, the Section psychiatrist, predicts that a thorough beating from Meres in a bout of unarmed combat will give Callan the incentive he needs to get fit again – it does. The upper class agent has a lot of autonomy, working with Fitzmaurice to discourage the London criminals interested in Berkeley (he enjoys hurting Spanner), investigating Jean Marie Nivelle, Kleist's girlfriend and an SSD agent, and Kleist himself, recruiting the East German as a Section asset. Meres' fatal weakness is that if he's hurt by a woman he loses control: he kills Jean Marie in a rage and is terrified that Hunter will dispose of him for losing a useful contact; fortunately, the woman's address book holds crucial information and wins Meres a reprieve. Toby was a Captain in the Coldstream Guards (and has a middle name beginning with D.) He delights in needling Callan about his drink problem.

Fitzmaurice works well with both Meres and Callan, delighting in more racial banter with both. The Barbadian is quick tempered with the reactivated agent but, after forming an emotional bond with the damaged Ortrud Bauer, becomes as disgusted as Callan is with the Section. Fitzmaurice comes to respect the older man – significantly, he calls him 'David' – and agrees to help Callan deal with Spanner.

The Section bug the phone in 'Loopy' Nichols' Super Cars garage and listen in from a nearby van, from which a messenger on a Honda 250 motorbike takes the recordings back to Hunter. Later, Section operatives with pneumatic drills pose as a road gang to cover the noise of Meres and Fitzmaurice's raid on Super Cars, with a unit of men armed with machine pistols.

In Sicily, Signora Lunari, a Section contact who works in a clothes shop, supplies Callan with a .357 Magnum. Phoning from the island, he contacts Hunter on the phone number 937-7162, answered by 'Mrs. Dinsdale' (Hunter's wife?).

The Section car pool includes a 4.2 Daimler automatic, which Callan uses. Hunter's unit is equally well served abroad: they have a German safehouse in Bad Godesbery, a station in Jamaica, and in Mexico, Callan and Fitzmaurice have access to a hacienda which has clothes, food and a landing strip. British embassies have a communications department who can contact the Section using the codename 'Mr. Evers'. In Britain, the Section has a country safehouse staffed by male nurses with attack guard dogs loose in the grounds. It houses a work room for Snell and every room is bugged.

Hunter is again grumbling about expenses. He makes a rare trip out of Section HQ to meet Kleist in Bonn, which he's worried about as he's known in Germany from doing some 'quiet recruiting' at the 1972 Munich Olympics. Hunter also makes a rare visit to Whitehall to meet his superior Bishop, euphemistically known as 'Information Secretary to the Cabinet'. The meeting between the two men is the most symbolic, and amusing, of the social hierarchies that underpin the Section: they knew each other at (public) school, where Hunter was Bishop's 'fag' and was frequently beaten by him with a squash racket. When Bishop orders a furious Hunter to hand Otrud Bauer over to Manette, the Section chief again feels 'the squash racket... beginning to smart.'

ALCOHOL, TOBACCO AND FIREARMS: The longest Callan novel of the 1970s sees a prodigious amount of alcohol consumed, with nearly every character drinking from a rich selection of cognac, brandy, champagne, bourbon on the rocks, gin and tonic, beer, white wine and port. It's no wonder that Callan gets completely slaughtered on Scotch on the plane out of Sicily, an incident that supports his belief that after drinking four Scotches in one day, he's turning into 'a lush'. That same day, he and Lonely drink more Scotch and light-and-bitter in the pub near a jeweller's shop, while, in the evening, Callan takes wine and light ale to Lonely's flat to accompany dinner. After twice shooting Hexham, he has Scotch and whisky; meeting Lonely in a pub after his work for the Section is finished, he pointedly has a half of bitter so he doesn't get drunk. Predictably, Lonely sticks to beer abroad, while his Uncle Lennie brews a formidable range of beetroot, gooseberry and parsnip wine.

Callan keeps to a .357 Magnum throughout. In America, he relieves two pursuing SSD agents of their Colt .38s and uses one of them, rechristening himself 'Two Gun Callan', the nickname he last used in *Russian Roulette*. In England, Fitzmaurice uses a Colt .45 pistol, transferring to a Section Magnum in the USA. Meres has the same Magnum that Signora Lunari supplies to Callan in Sicily, while in England the upper class agent delights in using a machine pistol on Nichols. Hexham surprises Callan and Lonely with a BSA Monarch rifle. West German security uses Walther automatics and for the opposition, the SSD agent Nivelle has an Armi Calesi .22 automatic. Impressively, Lonely handles Uncle Lennie's shotgun, while Lennie himself favours a Mannlicher rifle and a 1943 Luger.

SPY-SPEAK: Callan explains economics to Lonely: 'You've left the baddies and joined the goodies. Goodies always pay their taxes.'

Bulky Berkeley is described as 'a fat and comfortable man, with a round and innocent face that would have made Mr. Pickwick's look shifty.'

After being humiliatingly tortured, Hexham threatens Callan: 'You'll kill me? It's possible, son. It's possible. But there's a hell of a long queue.'

Jean Marie Nivelle gives a nasty comeback to Callan's rejection of her advances: 'I have never yet achieved satisfaction with a drunk.'

Hunter's pragmatic view of Cold War politics: 'One cannot commute between ideologies, Callan: not unless one pays for the return trip – and the cost is always high.'

Elisabeth Manette gives a chilling description of Callan as 'a quiet, reasonable, empty-eyed man.'

The passage where the compromised Kleist kills himself is particularly unsettling, as he dresses in a clean shirt and tie and burns all his old photographs and papers. It concludes, 'He picked up his grandfather's revolver, leaned back in his chair and blew out his brains.'

INFORMATION: The book was dedicated to a close friend of James and Delia Mitchell's. As with *Death and Bright Water*, *Smear Job* feels like it was written with tailoring into a movie script in mind, as it takes Callan, Lonely and Fitzmaurice from England, to Sicily, to America and back again. Significantly, Mitchell's biography on the cover of the hardback edition optimistically informed his readers that 'the first Callan film has been shown with considerable success.'

Clearly aware of current trends in the thriller genre, Mitchell also taps into the contemporary taste for conspiracy movies such as *The Parallax View* (1974) and *Three Days of the Condor* (1975). The American Watergate scandal that brought down President Nixon in 1974 is reflected in the novel too, as Callan uncovers the dirty secret of a senior politician that a US senator wants to exploit. From his own writing, Mitchell recycles some elements of the unmade script 'Goodbye Mary Lee', as a US senator's daughter has a sexual relationship with Callan, the short story 'File on a Happy Hippy', which features another US politician's daughter on drugs, and the card games of 'But He's a Lord, Mr Callan' and 'File on a Deadly Deadshot'. The scene where Callan encounters Bulky for the first time has similarities to their initial meeting in 'File on a Classy Club'.

There's an implicit reference to 'That'll Be the Day', as Callan is identified by the SSD because of his interrogation in Lubyanka and swap with Richmond, so this time around the Section commander would seem to be TV's fourth Hunter. This and the cameo from Bishop show Mitchell starting to pick and choose elements from the TV continuity, but often still in a contradictory way – Meres does not know who Richmond is – and only when it suits the plot.

Karl Marx (1818-1883) was a German philosopher and radical socialist whose theories on class struggle, organised labour and capital laid the foundations of Communism. The four volumes of *Das Kapital*, written between 1867 and 1894, outlined Marx's philosophy.

The Common Market – or, officially, the European Economic Community (EEC) – was established by the Treaty of Rome in 1957. Although Great Britain applied to join, French President Charles de Gaulle was suspicious of the country's relationship with America and vetoed membership in 1961. Under the succeeding president Georges Pompidou, the veto was lifted in 1967 and the UK joined the Common Market on 1 January 1973. In 1975 a national referendum was held to decide the issue of Britain's continued membership, so it's not surprising that had the UK voted to leave the EEC, Hunter would want a senior Common Market minister as an inside source.

The Baader-Meinhoff gang, who supply the information to Lindt about where Ortrud Bauer is being held, was a left-wing German terrorist group, founded in 1970 under the title the Red Army Faction. Formed by Andreas Baader (1943-1977) and journalist Ulrike Meinhoff (1934-1976), they were the scourge of the West German state in much the same way as the IRA's terror campaign was in Northern Ireland and mainland Britain. Over 1971-72, the Baader-Meinhoff gang were responsible for 34 deaths, bank robberies to raise revolutionary funds and a hundred bomb attacks, on targets such as US military bases and police stations. By the year *Smear Job* was published, key members of the gang had been arrested and incarcerated in Stammheim Prison, built especially to house them.

Fitzmaurice's uses the alias 'Lord Shekwe', a diplomat representing a new African nation that is a member of OPEC. The Organisation of the Petroleum Exporting Countries was formed in 1960 and, by the 1970s, was a major influence on the global economy. In 1973, OPEC's oil embargo on Western Europe, because of the region's support for Israel in the Yom Kippur War, led to a world economic recession. Being a member of OPEC is therefore an ideal cover, as Shekwe is treated with deference – and, crucially, relaxed security – wherever he and Callan go.

MISSION ANALYSIS: '*Why d'you have to resurrect a killer to play cards and thieve a book?*' A year after *Death and Bright Water*, with his biggest word count yet Mitchell perfects his more sophisticated storytelling style, indicated by the division of most chapters into several sub-sections. Each develops a different intrigue, and these grow throughout the book and intertwine, mostly satisfyingly, with several others. The only slight over-indulgence is the intimidation of Nichols' gang by the Section – did they really have to go to so much trouble? – but, as ever when Meres is let loose, the scenes are a highly entertaining read.

Among the involved and involving plotting, the story is given additional weight by some interesting psychology and comparisons. In a world where a young man has 'a hunter's laugh', there is some significant animal imagery. Ortrud is in love with a black panther in her drug trips and sees Fitzmaurice, her protector, as the savage big cat, while Elisabeth sees her father and other men as 'gorillas' and herself as 'a polar bear' (emotionally cold). There are hints, too, that her affair with Callan is partly inspired by vaguely incestuous feelings for her father, as she thinks the agent is the kind of man Manette would like to be. In a book that features two powerful politicians whose daughters have complicated relationships with their fathers, it's striking that both children are the men's Achilles' heels – one as a destructive secret, the other as a hostage.

Considering that the Section regulars have to hold their own amid this large international cast they're as distinctive as ever and, if *Smear Job* was intended to be the last novel, there is a sense of closure for Callan and Lonely: they're finally making decent money in their own security firm and, tellingly, Lonely finishes the book 'almost [smelling] of roses'. Given the assignment of investigating Kleist, Meres really comes into his own, particularly in the blackly funny scene where he overhears the East German and Jean Marie Nivelle having sex; he's disappointed that there's 'only two of them' and sardonically notes that 'Gunther was in charge of the gasp department.' It's equally fascinating to see Meres on the back foot, as he worries about the consequences of rashly killing Nivelle. Tasked with looking after an exploited, damaged woman, Meres' opposite number Fitzmaurice emerges from the book a humane and noble figure (and if *Smear Job* had been made into a film, the actor Rudolph Walker would have been an ideal fit for the character). It's a shame that Bulky Berkeley ends the novel effectively crippled, as the refined card sharp offered a lot more mileage as a regular character.

Mitchell's last Callan novel – for a while – is in some ways the opposite of his first, *A Magnum for Schneider*. That book focused on one metropolitan setting and told largely from Callan's point of view, while in *Smear Job* every character, from the bored salesman Charlie Berman, through the pimp Wino to the corrupt Hexham, has their own perspective within a complex narrative featuring multiple locations.

THE SHORT STORIES 7: 1975

CALLAN: FILE ON A CAREFUL COWBOY

Publication: Sunday Express
Date: 27 July 1975
Featuring: Callan, Lonely, the fourth Hunter, Meres

Mission Profile: On one of his most bizarre assignments, Callan is ordered to kill Mafia drug pusher Nap Martel, a man so obsessed with the Old West he's built his own Western town in Marseilles and stars in his own cowboy movies.

A Man Like Me: Callan and Lonely are still going to the cinema and have moved on to watching Spaghetti Westerns. Lonely's enthusiasm must be rubbing off, as the agent takes a boyish delight in playing the part of a cowboy.

Section Kills: 29

Lonely: Reveals an unexpected – and frankly unbelievable – talent for horse riding and horse whispering (contradicting 'File on A deadly Deadshot'), a skill he acquired at a clearly very progressive reform school. Typically, Lonely didn't fulfil his potential to become a jockey – he stole one of the horses. Hilariously, Callan is stunned at how good the thief is in the saddle.

A Tie and a Crest: Amusingly, Hunter is uncomfortable with the terminology of Westerns. Killing Martel is a favour for the CIA, who's worried that the Mafioso will flood the US with heroin. Meres is as keen on the cowboy role play as Callan, but although he refuses to share an aircraft with Lonely, Meres grudgingly acts as the safe-breaker's minder.

Alcohol, Tobacco and Firearms: Callan and Meres enjoy Chivas Regal and champagne – which they're both aware has been drugged – while Lonely has a light-and-bitter before the mission. In the perfect environment for guns, Callan alternates between his .357 Magnum and the traditional Western revolver, a Colt .45. Meres gets into character with a Winchester rifle.

Spy-Speak: Mitchell deploys Western cliché to entertaining effect, describing Martel 'as dangerous as a rattlesnake, and as vicious.'

There's great comedy value in Lonely dressed as a cowboy: 'Lonely in chaps was unbelievable: the great leather leg-coverings flapped about his lower half like the wings of a giant bat.'

Information: In James Mitchell's third John Craig novel *The Money That Money Can't Buy*, the millionaire working for Red China, Simmons, owns a similar bespoke Western ranch to Nap Martel.

Mission Analysis: '*Well, I guess we cleaned up the town.*' Next to 'File on an Angry Actor', this story is the most outlandish *Callan* ever gets. It's fascinating, though, to see how inter-changeable the archetypes of spy fiction are with the Western genre: Meres (the ruthless gunman who nevertheless does the right thing), Callan (the flawed hero) and Lonely (the cowardly comedy foil who comes good). There's a new element of self-awareness, as Callan's climactic confrontation with his opponent is remodelled as a clichéd Western town 'Main Street' gunfight, complete with treacherous saloon girls, henchmen hiding in the side streets. The self-aware feel extends to the enemy agent Nap Martel, who from his description – 'a Mexican moustache and his hat was black' – is based on Lee Van Cleef, who by the early 1970s was starring in the Sabata series of Spaghetti Westerns.

'File on a Careful Cowboy' is a combonation of the ludicrous and highly predictable, but those elements are what make it so entertaining.

CALLAN: FILE ON A DOOMED DEFECTOR

Publication: Sunday Express
Date: 3 August 1975
Featuring: Callan, Lonely, the fourth Hunter, Meres

Mission Profile: Callan and Meres are dispatched to Spain to collect Ostrava, a Nazi war criminal and KGB torturer who wants to defect.

A Man Like Me: Callan has conflicted loyalties about the assignment. He knows that Ostrava tortured to death the wife of Jan Neruda, a Czech British agent who escaped from Czechoslovakia after the Russian invasion in 1968. Callan debriefed the man and respects and likes him enormously.

Section Kills: 30

Lonely: Unlike the TV series, he takes pride in a 'spotless' and tidy home. Lonely is employed to bug the room of Ostrava's bodyguards and happily flies to Milan on his own. With some foresight, he warns Callan to look after himself; after the agent is shot, Lonely loyally visits him in hospital with grapes.

A Tie and a Crest: Under Callan's command, Meres accompanies the senior Section man to Spain. He has an affinity with cars, expertly tailing Ostrava's car in the Section's men's hired Alfa Romeo, and later bringing it to a stop after the tyres have been shot out.

Alcohol, Tobacco and Firearms: Getting into the holiday spirit, Lonely buys duty free cigarettes (which he doesn't smoke) and a half bottle of Scotch for Callan. Once in Milan, he has an Italian beer, while after the completion of the mission, Callan downs 'two stiff doubles' on the plane back to London. Callan and Meres are equipped with the usual .357 Magnums and a pair are smuggled to them by a flight steward. Ostrava's bodyguards have the Eastern bloc standard Makarov pistols, while Neruda favours a Walther PPK.

Spy-Speak: Callan's wry description of Ostrava's minders: 'The two goons in the kind of dark grey suit... that looks as if it had been cut and sewn by gorillas with hangovers.'

Mission Analysis: 'Oh lord. We're not going to get maudlin, are we?' Despite the wonderful detail in Mitchell's sunny descriptions of Milan, the story is black as pitch as it features a classic *Callan* moral dilemma: he has to protect someone he hates and kill someone he likes. Further marking 'File on a Doomed Defector' out as something special, the assignment is already in progress when the story starts, and, as in the best TV stories, Callan pursues his own agenda; he's also shot and ends up in hospital, indicating just how high the stakes are. An extra plus is that Meres has his best outing in the short stories, accurately characterised as an adrenaline junkie who's easily bored (and only he could find Milan dull). The unexpected, incident-packed plotting, sharp dialogue, and ingenious climax show that if *Callan* had gone to a fifth series and been filmed abroad, 'File on a Doomed Defector' would have been an excellent template to follow.

CALLAN: FILE ON A PINING POET

Publication: Sunday Express
Date: 10 August 1975
Featuring: Callan, Lonely, the fourth Hunter
Mission Profile: In Switzerland Callan investigates the relationship between Arthur Lewis, an economist with the Foreign Office, and Luba Varenskaya, the survivor of a Siberian gulag.

A Man Like Me: After listening to recordings of Lewis quoting poetry to Luba, Callan dispassionately concludes that the government man is obsessed with her. Proving what an accurate marksman he is, he shoots down a female killer on skis. He doesn't like thin women and knows a filthy limerick called 'There Was a Young Man of Calcutta.'

Section Kills: 31

Lonely: This time, he has to be coerced onto a plane to fly to Switzerland. He goes undercover again, improbably posing as an account executive with an advertising agency filming an advert. Again proving his worth, he successfully spots Luba's bodyguards for Callan. Typically, Lonely is worried that a shoulder bag makes him look 'poofy', but it later saves his life as the strap buckle deflects a bullet.

A Tie and a Crest: Hunter admits that he doesn't understand 'this love business'. The Section owns part of an advertising agency and a chamber maid in a Swiss hotel works for them.

Alcohol, Tobacco and Firearms: Plenty of booze on this mission: Callan has the traditional Chivas Regal with Hunter and a whisky and water with Lonely, who has light-and-bitter and the pair go to a rare second round. Once in Switzerland, Callan has more whisky and water and a brandy with Luba, while Lonely samples Lowenbrau, the local brew.

Callan's .357 Magnum is hidden inside a tape recorder and a female assassin wields a machine pistol.

Spy-Speak: Callan makes a particularly dour appraisal of his commander: 'Once Hunter started having intuitions there usually weren't that many survivors.'

The agent's reaction to Lonely's apparent death is memorably emotional: 'Callan screamed and in that scream was rage for what had happened to a smelly, loyal friend.'

Mission Analysis: 'Lonely was dead and it was Callan's turn next.' Take away the shock of Lonely's execution and 'File on a Pining Poet' is rather dull. Not surprisingly in such a high turnover of stories, it sees Mitchell recycling elements he's used before, in this case the plot of 'File on A Dancing Decoy', as Callan investigates whether another important man is being lured into a honey trap – there's even a reference to a 'vulnerable relative' being used as leverage against (another) Russian woman. Arthur Lewis, an interesting character with a tin ear for amorous poetry, disappears early on and after that the story follows a predictable pursuit narrative. It's enlivened by Callan's certain belief that Lonely is dead, as well as action sequences clearly influenced by *On Her Majesty's Secret Service* (1969).

CALLAN: FILE ON A POWERFUL PICADOR

Publication: Sunday Express
Date: 17 August 1975
Featuring: Callan, Lonely, the fourth Hunter
Mission Profile: Callan is ordered to either kill Luis Escobar, a Spanish contract killer and bullfighter, or intimidate him into working for the Section.

A Man Like Me: It's a demanding mission for Callan: he proves his skill with a matador's knife, kills an assailant with his bare hands – callously dumping the body in a laundry basket in an alleyway – and shoots a man off a horse. He doesn't understand Spanish but does enjoy a romantic liaison with Senora Amparo Sanchez, Escobar's employer.

Section Kills: 33

Lonely: Paid £500 for the job in Spain. He's worth every penny, alerting Callan to an intruder in their hotel room, burgling Escobar's suite and stealing Callan's Magnum back from Sanchez. Lonely has rheumatism 'like knives.' His Auntie Gertie makes good roast pork.

A Tie and a Crest: Escobar has killed four agents who work for Hunter, including Litri, a Mexican who was the Section's best man in Central America. Escobar has information about KGB operations in South America that Hunter wants, coded and hidden in the bullfighting novel *Blood and Sand* (which Lonely steals).

Alcohol, Tobacco and Firearms: Callan tempers his usual Chivas Regal in Hunter's briefing with Malvern water (perhaps he's been overdoing it?) Later taking a whisky, Callan uses canned beer to lure Lonely to Spain, and, once on the plane, the thief takes full advantage of the free cigarettes and beer. On the opposition's side, Escobar gets drunk on brandy. In addition to his usual Magnum .357, Callan uses a rifle with dum-dum bullets to – bizarrely – destroy a shrunken head owned by Escobar.

Spy-Speak: Lonely's view of Castile is hilariously insular: '[He] hated it. Not a boozer in sight.'

By contrast, Callan's appraisal of Senora Sanchez verges on the lyrical: 'Her face retained an imperious beauty that was very Spanish, [while] her body was invincibly feminine.'

Mission Analysis: 'He lives dangerously. He's near death all the time.' Mitchell's love for Spain shines through in authentic descriptions, such as 'an old hotel of shabby elegance with big cool rooms' and the genuine detail in the bullfighting scenes. Cleverly, he sells the potentially silly idea of involving Callan in Spain's national blood sport by making Escobar and Sanchez's motivations suitably operatic, as the baroque concluding action sequence boils with pride, revenge and jealousy: Callan faces a horse-mounted Escobar while the assassin and Sanchez finish their vendetta. Despite the unexpected twist that Sanchez was Escobar's KGB controller, the story is let down slightly by her treachery being revealed through closing paragraphs of exposition.

CALLAN: FILE ON A DIFFICULT DON

Publication: Sunday Express
Date: 24 August 1975
Featuring: Callan, Lonely, the fourth Hunter
Mission Profile: Oliver Routledge, Reader in Classics, is also Hunter's cipher expert. He's targeted for extraction by the SSD to East Germany and Callan is ordered to protect him.

A Man Like Me: Hunter considers Callan to be a 'military historian' and Dr Odgers, a military scholar at Oxford, thinks he could have indeed made a historian out of the agent. It's not surprising that Callan's academic alias is so convincing.

Section Kills: 35

Lonely: Thinks it's bad to thieve from a parson. He's paid £50 plus £20 expenses to scale spiked Oxford college walls, which he easily does, and steal from Routledge. He's instructed to leave a case containing £2,000 which, as usual, he finds odd.

A Tie and a Crest: Hunter hates the idea of attacks on Section operatives to the point of 'berserk rage.' Odgers was in the Section during WW2; for security reasons, Routledge's existence has been kept secret from Callan until now.

Santerem House hosts the annual Military Historian Society's conference. Its owner, the Earl of Bruges, is the descendant of Sir Harry Davenant, who fought in the Peninsular War (1807-1815) between France and the coalition of Britain, Spain and Portugal.

Alcohol, Tobacco and Firearms: The story begins and ends with Callan drinking Chivas Regal and Malvern water with Hunter, and he takes a bottle of the same whisky to Oxford. Once there, Callan shares a sherry with Dr. Odgers. At the historians' conference, Bur-gundy and St. Emilion are served. Lonely has a can of beer but, significantly, Routledge doesn't drink. Conchita Davenant, the Earl's daughter, has 'a glass of Chivas Regal about twice the size of Callan's.'

Callan uses his Magnum .357 and an opposition agent carries a Walther automatic, a German gun.

Spy-Speak: As part of his cover, Callan amusingly thinks Routledge is talking about 'Snuffy Hunter,' a boy at his school who had 'terrible adenoids'.

Callan is extremely wary of East German intelligence: 'The SSD plays so rough they even bother the KGB.'

Mission Analysis: 'He's difficult, David. In fact he's a damn prima donna.' Mitchell accurately brings to a life an Oxford of senior common rooms, buffet suppers and academic arrogance, and Callan's cover as a flustered academic is one of his most convincing aliases. There's an amusing piece of misdirection in Conchita, a wealthy, naïve aristocrat who espouses left-wing causes in a 'Power to the People' t-shirt, set up as a potential SSD suspect. (Probably a dig by Mitchell at similar, contemporary, wealthy left-wing figures like Vanessa and Corin Redgrave). The effective double twist at the end is clever and unexpected, revealing that Routledge is a double agent and that Callan has, once again, been manipulated by the establishment: the Earl, secretly working for Hunter, manoeuvres Callan into killing Routledge, who was Conchita's boyfriend.

Additionally, there'spleasingly strong continuity with the TV episode 'That'll Be the Day'.

THE SHORT STORIES 8: 1976

CALLAN: FILE ON A DARLING DAUGHTER

Publication: Sunday Express
Date: 1 February 1976
Featuring: Callan, Lonely, the fourth Hunter, Fitzmaurice
Mission Profile: Through investigations in London and Nice, Callan has to decide whether or not to kill Angela Lawson, the drug-addict daughter of a general who is a senior figure in NATO. Her pusher may be an Eastern Bloc agent who will coerce her father into betraying NATO information...

A Man Like Me: Callan hates heroin. Sir Richard Lawson, Angela's father, thinks the agent is the best shot he's ever seen. For once, Callan has to subdue an agent without a gun, and it's a tough struggle, ending with the Section man burying the dead man in cement. He exceeds his orders by trying to persuade Angela to go into rehab and finally – hating himself – Callan accepts her decision to commit suicide.

Section Kills: 36

Lonely: Despite the amount of international travelling he's done, he still doesn't like going abroad, because foreign travel with Callan inevitably means that he'll 'get physical'. However, £200 plus expenses persuades him to fly to Nice to steal Angela's heroin, dressed in his 'Lonely abroad' ensemble of green suit and shirt, yellow tie and socks and chocolate brown hat and shoes.

A Tie and a Crest: Of all his operatives, Hunter only trusts Callan to know if a killing is necessary. Like Callan, Fitzmaurice and Meres both hate drugs (contradicting *Russian Roulette*, in which Toby supplied his girlfriend with them) and the upper class agent thoroughly enjoys the nasty beating he gives the drug dealer Billy Bone; he's then taken to a Section 'facility' in the country. A Section contact in Nice is 'a large, lethargic lady' who watches over the hotel room next to Lawson's suite.

Alcohol, Tobacco and Firearms: Callan takes a duty free bottle (probably Scotch) to

Nice, where he drinks wine with Lonely who, predictably, doesn't like the local beer. The agent uses an American Sears Auto shotgun to shoot clay pigeons with Lawson and – uniquely – doesn't carry a Magnum, as Lawson's contacts in security prevent Hunter supplying one to Nice.

Spy-Speak: Billy Bone's terrified description of Callan: 'Average height, average build, and yet after one look at him Bone was more afraid of him than the others.'

Meres as he's about to torture the drug dealer: 'Oh dear. Manual labour again.'

Mission Analysis: 'You're destroying me.' The drug dependent daughter of a politically important man, being used as leverage against him by intelligence agents, is borrowed from the previous year's novel *Smear Job.* Beyond that, 'File on a Darling Daughter' impresses by being brutal, varied and emotionally harrowing, with a scale that ranges from a seedy London lifestyle, epitomised by the 'Chelsea layabout' Billy Bone, to the glamour of Nice. Mitchell effectively uses Bone's perception of the regulars to show how terrifying they are to outsiders, and, in an authentic touch, Helmuth, an SSD agent and Angela's drug dealer, pretends to her that he's working for the West German security service. This was a real spycraft tactic used on informants, designed to assure them that their treachery was staying within Western intelligence.

The story has an ending the equal of any of the visceral drama seen in the TV series. Callan tells Angela that he's cut off her drug supply and pleads with her to get treatment; convincing him she's not strong enough, Callan then allows her to go for a night swim and drown. The final scene is desolate and lingers in the memory, largely because of Angela's haunting eulogy to herself: 'Not brave. Just very tired.'

CALLAN: FILE ON AN AWESOME AMATEUR

Publication: Sunday Express
Date: 8 February 1976
Featuring: Callan, Lonely, the fourth Hunter, Meres
Mission Profile: With the aid of part-time spy Cynthia Widgery, Callan arranges the defection of the Russian poet Boris Lubov in Venice.

A Man Like Me: Callan is both alarmed by and uncomfortable with the formidable Ms. Widgery, but even though he usually dislikes amateurs, he comes to respect her. He once more reveals his educated and creative side, reading Sir Edward Creasey's *Fifteen Decisive Battles of the World* (1851), knowing the history of the French Revolution, and cleverly arranging a costumed reception through Cynthia's wealthy sister as the cover for Lubov's defection. Hunter thinks pretty women always distract his top agent, a warning about Ms. Widgery's young and glamorous American friend Barbara Jackson. Callan knows another (probably risqué) limerick, about 'a young man from Penang'. He doesn't like rock music and dresses up as a Corsair at the Venice reception.

Section Kills: 37

Lonely: Paid £50 a day plus expenses to follow Cynthia and 'Babs' Jackson. He thinks old ladies are 'trouble' because they're always going to Harrods, but considers Barbara to be 'a lady'.

A Tie and a Crest: Ms. Widgery is the only amateur Hunter has ever used. He wanted her to join the Section but she wouldn't because of her commitment to the study of ornithology. The Section commander hopes the defection of such a high profile figures as Lubov will provoke a change in Soviet government policy. There are new insights into Meres' character: he loves fancy dress parties – styling himself as a cardinal in Venice –

and claims to get 'stage fright' just before going into action.

Alcohol, Tobacco and Firearms: Lonely enjoys beer and whisky in his briefings with Callan. The agent himself enjoys an alcoholic afternoon with Barbara, knocking back highballs, wine and brandy. Callan is equipped with his customary .357 Magnum and a Mannlicher rifle. Barbara – a CIA agent – uses a Colt Agent revolver and an opposition agent again has a Makarov semi-automatic.

Spy-Speak: Amusingly, Callan thinks Ms. Widgery 'had a grip like a wrestler's.'

Revealing his feelings about modern art, the agent dryly observes at the Biennale exhibition centre in Venice that 'the Russians, it seemed, still went in for pictures that looked like pictures.'

Information: James Mitchell's John Craig novel *Die Rich Die Happy* (1965) also includes a sequence at a costumed ball in Venice, which the author also used as the cover for violence and intrigue.

Mission Analysis: 'I shall not respond to the useless appellations of out worn shibboleths.' This story is further proof that Mitchell could write comedy extremely well. Cynthia Widgery is a great creation, a middle-aged, eccentric intellectual reminiscent of Margaret Rutherford's portrayal of Miss Marple. Wearing 'a pair of brogues that would have terrified a skinhead', she easily intimidates Callan and Hunter.

The story's fault is that it crams in too much – a well written assault on Callan in a Soho street, defecting authors, a costumed ball, enemy agents, switched identities and a speedboat chase. Consequently, as had happened before in the short stories, an interesting character introduced at the beginning all but disappears from the rest of the narrative. There was a lot of mileage in Callan and Ms. Widgery working together, and it's great shame she was never used again.

CALLAN: FILE ON A JOYOUS JULIET

Publication: Sunday Express
Date: 15 February 1976
Featuring: Callan, Lonely, the fourth Hunter, Snell (referred to)
Mission Profile: Callan is detailed to bodyguard the actress Jo Bright, star of a TV production of *Romeo and Juliet* being made in Italy. She is the mistress of Harold Manning, an industrialist who has invented a new nerve gas, and Hunter is worried the KGB may use her as leverage to obtain Manning's formula.

A Man Like Me: Compared to his liberal attitude to gay people elsewhere, here Callan is 1970s-bigoted, internally commenting on the 'poofy' voiceover of a deodorant commercial. Even though he's 'seen and endured everything' he's appalled by Manning's gas, and, significantly, doesn't want to use violence on Lonely 'after all these years.' Callan easily poses as a production accountant on Jo's TV film and, unsurprisingly, doesn't like left-wing theatre.

Section Kills: 39

Lonely: Ordered to Italy by Callan to burgle the rooms of Harold and Julia Manning.

A Tie and a Crest: Unusually, Hunter and Callan dine with Manning, the suspect in a current Section operation. Hunter communicates by letter with Callan in Italy.

Alcohol, Tobacco and Firearms: Chivas Regal and water are again on offer to Callan while Hunter takes sherry; at the end of the mission, the agent is offered a whisky. In a pub theatre watching the experimental production *Circles*, Callan drinks Scotch. The meal with Manning includes Romanée Conti port, which Hunter is fond of. Lonely has two pints of light-and-bitter when Callan briefs him; installed in Verona he orders 'una birra', even though he's convinced it won't be any good.

Callan has two Magnum .357s in Italy, one of which, impressively, Lonely uses to distract two opposition agents.

Spy-Speak: Callan's memorably dismissive view of left-wing theatre: '*Circles* was all about how awful Western society was... The five men and women of good will on the stage... from time to time took their clothes off to prove how uninhibited they were, which accounted for the dirty mackintosh contingent.'

Mission Analysis: 'You want me to act for the telly?' Once again, James Mitchell takes an amusingly jaundiced swipe at the *zeitgeist,* as the story moves from tacky TV adverts and trendy, left-wing theatre to the sophistication of Verona, one of the most beautiful cities in the world, appropriately hosting a TV film of *Romeo and Juliet* (Franco Zeffirelli had made his movie version in the city nine years before). There's an excellent double twist: Manning employs the company Security SA to protect Jo, but they're a KGB front, and the jealous and tough Mrs. Julia Manning unwittingly puts Russian agents on to Callan in an attempt to discredit Jo. The originality of this is let down slightly by the, by now, overdone plot device of an important man put at risk because of a lover. Notably, Snell makes his sole (indirect) appearance in the short story range, as Callan hauntingly reflects 'what he would be doing to the two operatives [he] neither knew nor wanted to know.'

CALLAN: FILE ON A MOURNING MOTHER

Publication: Sunday Express
Date: 22 February 1976
Featuring: Callan, Lonely, the fourth Hunter, Liz, Meres and Fitzmaurice (referred to)
Mission Profile: Roderick Browne, a government scientist working on a new jump-jet fighter, has been killed in a car accident. Callan investigates him as there's been a leak from the project.

A Man Like Me: Callan uses the alias of 'J.G. Tucker', who works in Records at the Ministry of Defence. He's again homophobic, upsetting Browne's friend Miss Townley. As independent as ever, Callan ignores orders to remain 'on stand-by' in the Section, where, it's confirmed, he has his own office (just like 007).

Section Kills: 41

Lonely: Paid £100 to burgle Miss Townley's flat. He doesn't steal anything, instead giving Callan accurate details about the value of her clothes and jewellery. Lonely also supplies Callan with the crucial information that she rides a motorbike.

A Tie and a Crest: Hunter is senior enough in the intelligence hierarchy to attend a Cabinet Security Meeting. Meres (who's of the opinion that blondes 'fade quickly') and Fitzmaurice are in Scotland, investigating the collision of a Russian trawler with an oil rig and can't help Callan. From the Section car pool, the agent uses a red Lamborghini Miura, which has an impressive top speed of 180 mph. The Section includes an operative called Lang.

Alcohol, Tobacco and Firearms: Although she normally drinks sherry, the bereaved Mrs. Browne gets drunk on whisky, while Callan takes whisky and water. During his briefing, Lonely has a pint of light-and-bitter then finishes off Callan's whisky. After a gun battle, the agent is again offered Chivas Regal by Hunter.

Callan uses his Magnum .375 to disable a Jaguar, although a machine-pistol carrying passenger escapes. Mrs Browne uses a shotgun to deadly effect.

Spy-Speak: Callan's detached examination of two agents he's just killed: 'They were just men: one ugly, one handsome, both tough, and anonymous, and dead.'

The Section's top man is being fatalistic again: 'Everyone gives up when they're dead.'

Mission Analysis: 'Callan drove back to London in a mood of savage self-disgust.' Mitchell shakes up the short stories with an adventure structured like a detective thriller: Callan investigates a suspicious death, targeting potential guilty parties before, in the final scenes, explaining to the assembled suspects – in a country house, significantly – who the real criminal is. Combining this approach with a spy narrative, particularly in a rural action sequence and a shocking climactic scene where Mrs Browne takes the law into her own hands, works extremely well; pleasingly, there's no explanatory exposition in the final paragraphs. The story also includes a memorable example of Callan's self-loathing, as it's implied that – in the service of the mission? – he takes sexual advantage of a grieving mother.

CALLAN: FILE ON AN ANGRY AMERICAN

Publication: Sunday Express
Date: 29 February 1976
Featuring: Callan, Lonely, the fourth Hunter, Meres, Fitzmaurice, Liz
Mission Profile: Hunter authorises the execution on British soil, by the CIA, of the apparent double agent Paul Ventris. Callan has to protect the target's wife.

A Man Like Me: Callan has three suits and uses the best of them to pose as a private detective employed by Mrs. Jane Ventris. He has a friend at the auction house Sotheby's who thinks he's a researcher for a national daily newspaper. Callan again uses the Section's Lamborghini.

Section Kills: 43

Lonely: Paid £30 plus expenses to follow Mrs Jane Ventris and burgle her suite at the Savoy hotel. Lonely's intimidated by this as, being patriotic, he knows the Queen sometimes goes to the Savoy. As a mark of respect he wears his 'best suit', which Callan thinks makes him look like an eccentric millionaire. Lonely doesn't know what 'moral obligation' is.

A Tie and a Crest: In Paris, the CIA ask Hunter for a favour – to allow the killing in Britain of Paul Ventris, a Greek freelance working for the CIA as the controller of the Hungarian scientist Arani, who then betrayed him to Eastern security forces. The relationship between the Section and American intelligence is as distrustful as ever, as Liz compiles Yellow Files on the CIA men Mackley and Stone.

Alcohol, Tobacco and Firearms: A lot of alcohol is consumed. During their meal with the CIA in Paris, Hunter and Callan get through four wines and a cognac, Lonely has two beers in his briefing with Callan and later treats him to champagne at the Savoy, where Meres tries to decide between Chambertin and Pomerol.

Callan is again equipped with his Magnum .357, using it to take out an assassin who tries to kill Mrs Ventris with an Armalite rifle. Callan then uses the rifle to eliminate the traitor, Stone. Ventris uses a shotgun to go clay pigeon shooting but he's a terrible shot.

Spy-Speak: Mackley, the CIA controller, describes a murder in technical jargon as 'a health alteration assignment.'

Mrs Ventris likens Callan to a cat – 'precise, elegant and quite pitiless.'

Mission Analysis: 'Mrs Ventris was a very English rose, the expensive kind nurtured by all the right schools.' Well written and intriguing with detailed characterisation, especially with regard to Lonely and, for the second time in two stories, a distinctive female character. The intellectual Mrs. Ventris has a superior air, 'kindly' informing Callan that Palm Springs is in California but, even though she's divorcing her philandering husband, she's prepared to try and save his life. A double twist in the tale is again conveyed through explanations, but the surprises are particularly good ones – Stone is the real double agent and Jane Ventris is Hunter's niece. Mischievously, 'File on an Angry American' marks a highpoint in Callan's love/hate relationship with the Section, as he enjoys a post-mission romantic interlude with Jane that Hunter never finds out about.

THE SHORT STORIES 9: 1976

CALLAN! FILE ON A DIFFICULT DON

Publication: Sunday Express
Date: 15 August 1976
Featuring: Callan, Lonely, the fourth Hunter, Fitzmaurice
Mission Profile: With Lonely and Fitzmaurice, Callan is sent to New York to eliminate the Mafia boss Peter Valence, a drug dealer who betrayed a Section man to Communist China.

A Man Like Me: Callan cleverly exploits Valence's obsession with vintage cars by making the millionaire aware of a Rolls Royce he owns (bought by Hunter), so he'll be invited to the Mafia Don's 1920s party on his Long Island estate.

His relationship with the Barbadian Section agent Fitzmaurice revolves around mutual respect, occasionally enlivened by digs at either Callan's class-consciousness or the black man's sensitivity to racism. Callan reveals his vulnerability when he's outclassed by an assailant who breaks into his hotel room.

More evidence that he reads a lot: Callan refers to a female CIA agent he encounters as 'Lorelei', in German mythology a spirit whose song lured sailors to their deaths.

Section Kills: 45

Lonely: Too proud to go on the dole and typically sees thieving as 'really grafting.' He's scared of flying but steels himself to board a Jumbo jet with Callan and enjoys the in-flight entertainment. In New York, Lonely is paid £500 to infiltrate Valence's domestic staff so he can smuggle two Magnum revolvers hidden in a cake to Callan and Fitzmaurice.

A Tie and a Crest: Once again, Callan enjoys the high life far more than he ever did in the TV series. Posing as a wealthy car owner (under his Tucker alias), he is chauffeur driven by Fitzmaurice and stays at the exclusive Plaza hotel in New York.

Alcohol, Tobacco and Firearms: Chatting about the depressed British economy in Notting Hill, Callan buys Lonely two pints of light-and-bitter while he drinks Scotch. Champagne and malt whisky is offered at Valence's soiree and Callan enjoys the latter. Fitzmaurice and Callan use their customary Magnums (with silencers) while, in keeping with the 1920s fancy dress, the Mafioso carry Tommy Guns.

Spy-Speak: Callan suggests an ingenious new way for Lonely to warn of an outbreak of his body odour: 'Can't you ring a bell or something?'

Fitzmaurice sends up his awareness of racism: 'They've got real good stabling for the niggers. Clean straw, even.'

Mission Analysis: 'You annoy [the CIA] and they fire guns at you... it upsets me.' James Mitchell is really enjoying himself here. 'File on a Deadly Don' is a lively mixture of the vintage gangsterism of 1973's feature film *The Sting*, rewound ten years to the 1920s, and the Mafia of contemporary America shown in *The Godfather* movies which began in 1972. The story is full of sharp dialogue, well described and detailed action, another twist involving the CIA and an effective, topical contrast between the luxury on offer in America and the greyness of broke Britain. Valance is one of the best opposition agents in Mitchell's short fiction, obsessed with classic cars and cake, while pairing Callan with Fitzmaurice adds a fresh dynamic. The conversation between Callan and Lonely in the pub, in which the thief gripes about the deplorable state of the British economy, is vintage *Callan*. Notably, its here that the contradictory worlds of the short stories and novels are bound together when Lonely refers to the events of *Death and Bright Water*.

CALLAN! FILE ON A TIRED TRAITOR

Publication: Sunday Express
Date: 22 August 1976
Featuring: Callan, Lonely, the fourth Hunter, Meres
Mission Profile: Callan is ordered to Spain to bring back Anthony Dawes, the scientist who betrayed H-bomb secrets to the Russians 27 years ago.

A Man Like Me: Aware that Dawes has terminal osteo-arthritis, Callan shows his humane side by allowing him to take his own life.

Lonely: When he and Callan break into the house of the chat show host Sandy Keith, an old friend of Dawes', Lonely again wonders why Callan never steals anything, instead choosing to look through Keith's filing cabinet. Lonely shows his weakness for snuff boxes again – Callan has to warn him off stealing one from Keith's collection.

A Tie and a Crest: From the moment she meets him, Keith's PA Kirsty Lomax treats Callan with disdain. By contrast, on their mission to Spain, there's no friction between Meres and Callan. Characteristically, Toby is upset by his favourite jacket being ruined by an assailant's knife and later, Magnum in hand, suggests a game of Bridge to Kirsty and Keith to pass the time.

Alcohol, Tobacco and Firearms: Hunter and Callan both enjoy a glass of Chivas Regal during the mission briefing. Asking the aggressive Kirsty for a glass of Keith's fifteen year-old single malt, Callan receives 'whisky-flavoured water.' Leaving his Magnum behind when he visits Keith, Callan is at a disadvantage when his car is wrecked by a sniper using a Kalashnikov rifle. Both he and Meres use Magnums on assignment in Spain.

Spy-Speak: Accused of being rude by Kirsty, Callan replies, 'I worry about it. Do you think it could be because of the company I keep?'

'We should not persecute the dying. It would be bad for what Keith would call our image,' says Hunter, mindful of public relations.

Mission Analysis: 'Can you think of a country less likely to harbour a Communist sympathiser?' A straightforward story, the highlight of which is the quiet, powerful scene where Callan confronts the dying Dawes, 'File on a Tired Traitor' is another outing for Mitchell's favourite theme of people unable to escape their personal history. There's more than a touch of creative *deja vu*, as the story reuses plot points from 'The Good Ones are All Dead' and 'Blackmailers Should Be Discouraged'. The unexpected final twist is a good one, but again suffers from condensed paragraphs of exposition, the major weakness of the short stories.

CALLAN! FILE ON A HARASSED HUNTER

Publication: Sunday Express
Date: 29 August 1976
Featuring: Callan, Lonely, the fourth Hunter

Mission Profile: Visiting a Northern town, Callan and Hunter meet the actor Evan Lang, who knows the location of the KGB assassin Lubov.

A Man Like Me: Callan is disorientated by Hunter's breach of Section protocol, leaving his two bodyguards and bullet-proof Bentley behind in London. Impressively, Callan takes on three thugs in crash helmets and floors all of them. He reveals an unexpected liking for Shakespeare's plays, being fond of *Hamlet* and recognising dialogue from *Macbeth*. (He previously referenced *As You Like It* in *Smear Job*).

Alone in his flat, Callan dispassionately reflects that no one will miss him when he dies.

Section Kills: 46

Lonely: Accepts £100 to open Lubov's flat but complains about the late hour.

A Tie and a Crest: Callan is stunned to learn that when Hunter was in Budapest before WW2, he fell in love with a Hungarian girl and fathered a daughter. The Section chief didn't know of her existence until the girl's mother told him several years later. By then, without realising she was his child, Hunter had recruited her into British intelligence and she was killed by Lubov just before the Hungarian uprising in 1956.

Alcohol, Tobacco and Firearms: Not surprisingly considering his emotional investment in the mission, Hunter drinks both sherry and whisky. Callan drinks Scotch on the plane back to London. Devastated by the murder of 'his Ophelia' – Hunter's daughter – Lang is permanently drunk. Callan uses a Magnum to dispatch the 'Plastic Man' and Lubov. Hunter proves himself adept in the field, using a revolver barrel to knock out an assailant.

Spy-Speak: Callan wryly reports to Hunter after a fight outside the theatre where Lang is appearing: 'Three young fellers by the stage door wanted to give me martial arts lessons. It was very educational.'

Mission Analysis: 'Murder most foul.' The penultimate short story breaks the mould completely, sending Hunter out into the field with Callan on a revenge mission, even though the Section chief denies that's his motivation. Unfortunately, this promising scenario isn't as interesting or well-constructed as it could have been. There are unlikely levels of soap opera coincidence in Hunter recruiting his own daughter (who doesn't even get a name) for intelligence work without realising it, as well as Lang transpiring to be her lover. The timescale of Hunter's paternity is also implausible. As a whole, the story is a protracted *longueur* which ends in an anti-climactic execution. It's left to an action scene clearly inspired by the contemporary vogue for kung fu movies, together with the bleak eloquence of Callan's introspection about his own death, to make the story worth reading.

CALLAN! FILE ON A BEAUTIFUL BOXER*

Publication: Sunday Express
Date: 5 September 1976
Featuring: Callan, Lonely, Meres, the fourth Hunter, Fitzmaurice, Liz
Mission Profile: Inventor Rod Mercer is under sentence of death from the Israeli secret service Shin Bet. He's accused of selling a revolutionary motorboat to Israel, with its engines deliberately sabotaged on the orders of Palestine. Callan is ordered to prove him guilty or innocent, but he has to find him first...

A Man Like Me: Callan is in charge of the hunt for Mercer, with Meres and Fitzmaurice reporting to him. He's involved in two unusual combat situations, fighting with

---

* In the 'Next Week' trail at the end of 'File on a Harassed Hunter', the title of this story was given as 'File on a Beautiful Boxer', although it didn't appear in the story itself.

a shotgun-wielding Angela Wain who's dressed in nothing but a towel; later, he exits a shower, naked, to fight an assassin with a knife.

By now used to mixing with the wealthy, Callan has perfected his 'bored millionaire' persona, which he uses to go aboard Mercer's yacht *Joy*. His powers of deduction are as sharp as ever, as he deduces that Shin Bet agents have attached a limpet mine to the boat.

Lonely: After a bad night's thieving, he agrees to watch the flat of Angela, the girl with an effective right hook. Lonely doesn't mind the job Callan gets him to do, as 'following posh birds was his hobby anyway.'

A Tie and a Crest: Without complaint (surprisingly), Meres accepts Callan's command of the Mercer assignment, doing as he's told and handing the older man his tickets to Spain at the airport.

Alcohol, Tobacco and Firearms: Once again, Callan takes a glass of Chivas Regal at his briefing with Hunter. He enjoys a 'cautious whisky' on the plane to Spain and later accepts Dom Perignon champagne from Mercer.

Angela confidently holds Callan at gunpoint with a Purdey* shotgun. The Section man takes his .357 Magnum to Spain, but on this assignment his wits prove to be his best weapon.

Spy-Speak: Angela Wain surprises Callan breaking into Mercer's flat: 'I suppose you're going to tell me you've come about the drains?'

Lonely remains depressed about the state of the British economy: 'Four houses we done, Mr. Callan, and three flats. And we hardly made petrol money. I tell you straight – this old country of ours is in a mess.'

Mission Analysis: *'You're not my friend. I had to slap you with a wet towel.'* It's slightly ironic that 'File on a Beautiful Boxer' is the last *Sunday Express* short story, as it finds Callan firmly on James Bond territory. It's all very *Thunderball*: a glamorous Riviera, a beautiful woman skilled in unarmed combat, frogmen, an assassin breaking into Callan's hotel room... With his talent for plotting back on form, Mitchell cleverly teases the audience that Mercer might be guilty by keeping him out of events for as long as possible. Using Callan's gift for observation as well as gun play, the writer also cleverly avoids a confrontation between British and Israeli intelligence, with the result that the last Callan short story is atypical as it features no deaths. The final *Express* tale again features Mitchell's customary topical references, this time to vandalised phone boxes and feminism, and, appropriately, is set largely in Spain.

MONOLOGUE

MY FRIEND MR CALLAN BY THE FAITHFUL LONELY

Writers: James Mitchell with Ken Roche
Publication: TV Times
Date: Issue dated 23-29 June 1984
Featuring: Lonely
Mission Profile: Lonely reminisces at length about his 'friendship' with the enigmatic ex-con David Callan, whom he first met in Wormwood Scrubs.

Lonely: The thief recounts some intriguing untelevised incidents in his relationship with

---

* Miss-spelt as 'Purdie' in the story

Callan. Breaking into a flat in Kensington to steal some compromising letters, Lonely is instructed to leave the £25,000 he finds: 'I don't argue, not with Mr. Callan I don't.' Later, on one of his solo burglaries, the thief makes the mistake of stealing from a house in Wandsworth owned by South London gangsters. When Lonely is cornered in a park by two of them, Callan arrives and saves his life by killing both men 'with his bare hands.'

However, Lonely considers 'the biggest thing Mr. Callan did for me' took place when he was thieving from a block of flats in Knightsbridge, under observation by the Section because foreign spies were staying there. Discovered by an opposition agent, Lonely accidentally killed him with a screwdriver. Callan framed a drunk enemy operative for the killing and the spy was charged with murder. 'That's the kind of bloke Mr. Callan is, I'm telling you. Wonder why I'd do anything for him...?'

Section Kills: 8

Spy-Speak: Characteristically, Lonely has his own off-beat opinion about the security services: 'The idea of some kind of anti-espionage never came into my mind. When I did find out I felt a bit let down at first. [Mr. Callan] was *working* for the *government* and to me the government is rozzers.'

Mission Analysis: 'Cor, that Mr. Callan! Ooh, you've got to be very careful with a man like him.' The short stories end in the publication where they began with the only Callan fiction written in the 1980s, and it's fitting to see Lonely take centre stage at last, as the character had been so integral to the TV series' success. Tying in with the colour repeats on Channel 4, Lonely is aware that Callan is a spy, while their joint history is pleasingly consistent with the novels and the original *Armchair Theatre* teleplay. Strikingly, though, there's no mention of Callan dealing with Lonely's nemesis Rinty, the single act that made the thief indebted to his old cell mate. Overall, though, this monologue is a delight, bringing Lonely to life with dialogue that Russell Hunter would have relished performing.

THE NOVELS: 5

BONFIRE NIGHT

Publisher: Severn House Publishers Ltd.
Released: 2002
Price: £17.99
Reprint: Ostara Publishing Limited paperback/Ebook, UK, March 2016

Featuring: Callan, Roger Bullevant (Lonely), Hunter VI[?], Bishop (referred to), William Fitzmaurice, John Mars, Melissa, Gerald, Betty (the new Section secretary)

MISSION PROFILE: Callan is now the director, with Lonely (Roger Bullevant*) in a multi-million pound electronic security business. The first female Hunter pleads for Callan's help in training new recruits and stealing blackmail material, which could incriminate prominent young members of the British establishment, from Hermann Voss. The East German was Callan's torturer in Potsdam and is one of three assassins, together with the Spaniard Mendez and the British lawyer Smethwick, who have been contracted by Bishop to kill

---

* Spelt slightly differently to *Smear Job*, so perhaps Lonely has chosen to modify his pseudonym. However, given Callan's heavily revised history, they may not even be the same people.

the ex-agent. A traitor in British intelligence called Bishop betrayed Callan to the Stasi, the East German secret police, and now wants him dead before Callan can find him.

Complicating the situation, Avram, a Mossad agent who helped Callan escape from East Germany, once directed him to the successful theft of KGB funds. Unknown to Avram, the diamonds amounted to a staggering £50,000,000 that Callan invested in his and Bullevant's company BC Electronics PLC. Avram wants reparation and has the Mossad operative Naomi Klein installed as Bullevant's girlfriend. If Avram can't get the money back, Bullevant will work for Israel.

Callan successfully disposes of the three killers and outwits Avram and Klein. At the same time, his romance with Lady Fiona Wilton blossoms; he agrees to adopt her daughter Ellie – who, coincidentally, was married to Voss – and restores all, and more, of her family fortune by auctioning vintage stamps Callan and Bullevant steal from the torturer. Callan and his friends celebrate with the annual burning of a gigantic bonfire on his Spanish estate.

A MAN LIKE ME: Callan used to live near Hoxton in East London but, going dramatically up-market, now has a residence near Eaton Square. He served in the regiment Two Para, attaining the rank of Major. Callan fought in Northern Ireland, Africa, the Falklands War and Iraq before becoming a spy, working for Hunter's Section; like a good secret agent he speaks several foreign languages – French, Spanish and German. Callan was tortured to the point of insanity by Voss, who used a Zippo lighter to burn his skin for two days. When the Berlin Wall fell in 1990, with the assistance of Avram, Callan escaped and was surgically, psychologically and physically rehabilitated by the Israelis in the Negev. Among three other doctors, he was treated by a psychologist called Dr. Rabin. One of his other patients was Fiona, who formed an emotional bond with Callanl.

Callan enjoys a luxurious hacienda in Spain's Andalucia region staffed by servants, among them Carmencita, Bernardo and Angel, who Callan considers family rather than employees. He paid for Angel's physiotherapy when he was injured bullfighting, and has Carmencita on a program of exercises so she's ready to dance at the local fiesta. The property, covering an incredible 25,000 acres, has an expansive War Room, housing Callan's collection of vintage weapons and model displays of the battles of Waterloo and El Alamein. The hacienda also contains a practice room for bullfighting and a firing range, with photographic blow ups of Voss as targets.

He is physically and verbally ruthless with his enemies, threatening the criminal 'Smacker' with heroin addiction, as well as sending the assassin Mendez into heavy traffic on a motorcycle rigged to explode. To his allies Callan is generous with his experience, training the Section agents Mars and Fitzmaurice in unarmed combat to increase their effectiveness, as well as offering the Section the benefit of his company's considerable resources. For the first time, and despite his psychopathic streak, Callan explicitly sees himself as a force for good, as the 'bad guys don't care.' He is devoted to Fiona, adopting her daughter Ellie, and grants each of them a considerable personal fortune. The hardened agent also has a romantic side, as Callan arranges for rose petals to fall on the sunbed at night where he and Fiona consummate their relationship.

Section Kills: 10

ROGER BULLEVANT (LONELY): A former burglar known as 'Lonely' who worked with Callan. He became a genius with computers after taking 'rehabilitation classes' in prison, setting up BC (Bullevant/Callan) Electronics PLC, which specialises in computer-ised security systems for Western intelligence services. Bullevant has retained his criminal skills, helping Callan to burgle Voss's flat in Broughton House.

A film fan, Bullevant owns a 1950s Lincoln Continental like one driven by the actor George Raft. He's also a gifted crooner and dancer, to the extent that Callan calls him a 'right little Fred Astaire.' Since achieving great wealth, his unpleasant BO problem has disappeared. Significantly, indicating that he and Callan are now equals, he calls his friend and business partner 'Dave' (something he hasn't done since 'File on a Loving Sister' in 1970).

Bullevant's good fortune has allowed him to purchase a flat in Grosvenor Place. Despite this prestigious address and a wardrobe containing seven Armani suits, Bullevant has retained his working class cockney attitudes and isn't above cheating at cards. He likes 'big birds' and lives with the barrister Naomi Klein, who, when Callan was imprisoned in East Germany, got the thief off a charge of larceny – '£187.38p, [with] seventeen other offences taken into consideration.' She stayed on as legal adviser to BC Electronics and as Bullevant's lover. He's unaware that she's a Mossad spy.

Despite his attachment to Naomi, when Callan tells Bullevant that she's a liability he accepts his friend's counsel without question (the bond between the two men being stronger than any they may have with women). Bullevant happily moves on to the mail-order bride Tiffany Manners, and is last seen with the buxom blonde on his yacht, happy and relaxed.

A TIE AND A CREST: Still in a scrapyard, but with the addition of a piledriver, the Section is now based in Hoxton. A sign claims 'Hunter the Magician – I Make Wrecks Disappear' and 'What the Heck, It's Just a Wreck.' The unit is nominally headed by the first female Hunter (like her male predecessors, she complains about a lack of money) although she defers to an enigmatic superior known as 'Gerald', a Section Co-ordinator. Liz has been replaced by a new secretary, Betty (also a shortened form of Elizabeth), who likes a drink. The Section is equipped with a gym, uses a Rolls Royce and, in a nod to the 1960s spy craze, in its electronic arsenal has a pair of glasses fitted with a transmitter. Impressively, the department has the power to offer Callan the (temporary) status of a diplomatic courier.

The new generation of Section operatives consists of John Mars, Melissa and William Wilberforce Fitzmaurice, the nephew of the agent Callan used to work with; the racial banter they share is similar to the relationship Callan had with William's uncle Spencer. All three are happy to work under Callan's direction and become part of his extended family.

No one knows what the traitor Bishop looks like as he was on a deep cover assignment for the Foreign Office. After the break-up of the Soviet Union, Bishop became involved with the Russian Mafia and now lives a luxurious life in Saint Petersburg.

ALCOHOL, TOBACCO AND FIREARMS: As Callan and Bullevant are now living the high life, there is more alcohol on offer than ever, mainly in the form of champagne, but also as Larios and Johnny Walker Black Label whisky. Fiona and Ellie get tipsy on gin and tonics and, in a club, Callan buys his female companion Melanie a pint of lager, even though it's not on the menu. Wickedly, he gets the new Section secretary drunk on Scotch and water, while Naomi drinks the same in Bullevant's flat. Uniquely, Callan smokes.

He still favours a .357 Magnum, which are also still in use by the Section. In the shoot-out with Mendez and his men, Callan discovers an arms cache consisting of an Ivor

Johnson PP30, two Hechler and Koch 9mm automatics, a Smith and Wesson .22 target pistol and a sawn-off Remington Speedmaster shotgun. Smethwick, Callan's second opponent, uses shotguns to kill pheasants – and nearly Callan – and Fiona has won prizes for shooting with the same make. Naomi alternates between a Colt Woodsman and a Bernadelli .32 pistol clipped inside her handbag. In the final confrontation between Callan and Voss, the torturer uses a 9mm Makarov, the standard East German secret service weapon. Callan is fianlly able to use a weapon from his favourite historical period, dispatching his nemesis with a double-barrelled musket dating from around 1800. The Guardia Civil on sentry duty at Callan's bonfire carry Llama XV automatics.

SPY-SPEAK: Mitchell again delivers an evocative picture of Spain: 'So much to see. The Sierras for a background, their peaks white, even in the heat, which grew stronger by the minute; and vineyards, olive groves, lemons, oranges, then grass where two young bulls played at combat.'

Bullevant is dismissive of the standard of hospitality in a Section safe house: 'No class this place. No class at all. Worse than the bleeding Hilton.'

Hunter observes Callan and young Fitzmaurice threatening Smacker: 'My God, I've heard of good guy and bad guy, but this is bad guy and worse guy.'

Despite being wealthy and internationally influential, Callan retains his disdain for the British establishment: 'The Foreign Office *will* be pleased. And them – elegant sods. All Lords and Twickers and Ascot. And use us crazies to do their killing and sleep like babies.'

INFORMATION: Talking about his father's decision to write another Callan novel so late in life, Peter Mitchell honestly revealed, 'This is a man who was quite old by now. He's very sick, he's drunk most of the time and he did bloody well to finish it, I think. It kept him alive for a bit longer.'[11] The book was indeed published after Mitchell's death and, in its obituary for the writer, the *Daily Express* touchingly reported that 'Edward Woodward... is eager to learn what happened to Callan [at] the very end.'[12]

Internet reception of the book at the time tended to be negative, but writer Sarah Guiver feels that *Bonfire Night* is now due for reappraisal. 'Yes, it is a bit hard to follow, as it's written more like a script than a book, and has holes in the plot, but it reminds me a lot of James's other writing... [It] has a lot in common with his other, non-Callan books. He loved writing books about toffs, bizarre people and fashionable ladies. It's just so him."[13]

MISSION ANALYSIS: *'We're not spies anymore. We're capitalists.'* It's hard to imagine what the fans who'd waited 32 years for another Callan novel made of *Bonfire Night* when it was published. It's a shock to find the austerity of the earlier books replaced by a millionaire Callan who, like in Woodward's 1980s action series *The Equalizer*, appears to have more extensive assets, weaponry and contacts than the department he once worked for.

One way of looking at this is that Mitchell was writing a wish-fulfilment fantasy for Callan and Lonely. Pointedly, several situations in the TV series are reversed: the author name checks luxury brands – Crockett and Jones, Nina Ricci and Jan Muir, among others – in a similar way to Ian Fleming did in the Bond books, relishing showing off Callan's wealth over the impoverished Section. Romancing a member of the aristocracy didn't work for the agent on television, but it does here – permanently – with Lady Fiona Wilton. Where 'Bullevant' once collected junk he now acquires antiques and, most significantly, Hunter practically begs for Callan's help.

This iconoclastic approach has its good points: there's an excellent opening sequence where rich, well dressed old-man-Callan beats up three young assailants in a subway, and later, another in which he intimidates the criminal Smacker in a night club. Throughout, perhaps in some curious form of homage to Woodward's appearance in *The Wicker Man*, Mitchell adeptly keeps using the symbolism of fire, initially as a source of pain and madness then, in the final scenes, as a cleansing, cathartic force. Pleasingly, too, Callan retains his sardonic and cynical inner voice from the earlier novels, although the narrative style is very different to Mitchell's earlier work.

For all the reformatting to work and really convince, the plotting had to be watertight and the characterisation as sharp as it had been in the past. Unfortunately, this is where *Bonfire Night* falls down. Callan is now so omnipotent it never feels as if he's in any real danger, and the story itself is either frenzied, relayed in slabs of exposition, or confusing. For instance, it's not clear if Naomi Klein (possibly mischievously named after the anti-capitalist author) was a Mossad agent from the moment her involvement with Bullevant began or became one later. Unbelievably Ellie, who was once married to Voss, never once mentions it to Callan. The rewriting of Bishop and Callan's back stories isn't necessary, other characters come and go making little impression and the opposition trio of Smethwick, Mendez and Voss have no personality whatsoever. Most frustratingly, Mitchell puts Callan's relationship with Fiona and her daughter centre-stage. Speaking in a stylised manner, they make parts of the book read like a strangely violent Noel Coward comedy.

Compared with the studied, downbeat naturalism of the rest of Mitchell's Callan and Lonely stories, *Bonfire Night* is a gargantuan ask as a fairy tale conclusion. In mitigation, you can understand (if not endorse) why, in his final days, Mitchell wanted to see his enduring anti-heroes finally beat the system and live happily ever after.

ANTHOLOGIES

CALLAN UNCOVERED

Publisher: Ostara Publishing Limited, hardback/paperback/Ebook, UK, October 2014
Featuring: Callan, Lonely, Meres, the first and fourth Hunters, Liz, Spencer Percival Fitzmaurice, Bulky Berkely
Information: Long overdue reprints of the 1973-76 *Sunday Express* short stories, together with the synopsis for 'A Funeral Has Been Arranged and Will Shortly Take Place' and the unproduced script 'Goodbye Mary Lee'. The book also includes an engaging introduction by Peter Mitchell, featuring memories of his late father and Edward Woodward.

CALLAN UNCOVERED VOLUME II

Publisher: Ostara Publishing Limited, hardback/paperback/Ebook, UK, July 2015
Featuring: Callan, Lonely, Meres, the fourth Hunter, Liz, George
Information: Because of the success of the first volume, and the discovery of a further fifteen stories published by the *Sunday Express* in 1970 and 1972, Ostara published a second omnibus in 2015. This collection also features reprints of Mitchell's screenplays 'Goodness Burns Too Bright' (1967) and 'Blackmailers Should Be Discouraged' (1969), as well as the 1970 *TV Times* feature 'Get Callan...'.

10: 'A Bloody Good Little Film'

'Hotter than Hell... Bolder than Bond!'

Callan film poster strapline (1974)

THE *CALLAN* FILM WAS RELEASED on May 24 1974 in the same month as one of the masterpieces of American cinema, Francis Ford Coppola's paranoid thriller *The Conversation*, and *Can You Keep it Up for a Week?*, a piece of cheap, innuendo-heavy UK comedy fare. It says a lot about the depressed state of the British film industry in the late 1960s and early 1970s that, with honourable exceptions such as Mike Hodges' gangster movie *Get Carter*, the two home-grown genres that British studios saw as safe bets were sex comedies and cinema adaptations of hit TV sitcoms such as *Till Death Do Us Part* (1968), *Dad's Army* (1971) and *Steptoe and Son* (1972 and 1973). Seeing the way the economic wind was blowing, Hammer, chiefly known for their horror features films, had scored a notable success with a run of films based on the LWT series *On the Buses* (1969-1973). With interest in *Callan* at its peak at the beginning of the decade, Hammer were an obvious candidate for a proposed film version. However, by 1972, a terse note in the Hammer directors' minutes for a meeting on the 16 March stated that 'after exhaustive preparation of this subject, rights are now unavailable.'[1]

Callan's first television producer Terence Feely recalled that prior to this he had unsuccessfully tried to promote the idea of moving to film. 'I never got that off the ground. I was pushing like crazy to get a *Callan* film made. It was the logical next step, and if we didn't make it, somebody else would. First of all, I wanted the whole series transferred onto film, because film gives you so much better quality and picture, and so much more pace... I wrote a number of memos about a *Callan* film to Brian Tesler, who was our Programme Controller, and I really made a bloody nuisance of myself.'[2]

Memoranda within Thames indicate that after leaving for Paramount Pictures, Feely continued to ask to produce a *Callan* film, writing to ABC's Managing Director Howard Thomas in April 1969. Internal correspondence from Tesler to Thomas advised against supporting Feely's project, suggesting instead ABC should 'use Mitchell and Woodward in a low budget film, specially written, with an experienced film producer and an associate drawn from those of our people responsible for its current success (Lloyd Shirley, Reginald Collin, John Kershaw).'[3] In closing, Tesler concluded, 'minds must be made up quickly: we want to sign people up for another tape series.'

Nothing emerged from this idea and it would be over four years before a film production went ahead; whether ABC/Thames's stance contributed to the delay is unknown. 'I imagine Thames were invited to invest money but I wouldn't have been the one who would have been asked about that, it would have been the [company] board,'[4] Lloyd Shirley later said of the finalised film. 'We wished it well, but had no vested interest in it.' James Mitchell himself simply recalled 'the idea of the film had been kicked around for long enough... I think Thames weren't too keen on the idea at first – reasonably enough from their point of view, because they didn't want to kill the repeats [of *Callan*].'[5]

LIKE SO MUCH IN JAMES MITCHELL'S LIFE, the *Callan* film's eventual realisation came through a personal friend, the film producer Derek Horne. 'He was a lovely feller, from Dublin,'[6] Peter Mitchell remembered fondly. 'Derek had worked for another producer, an American, who was a friend of the family – a friend of my father's and Delia's – and that's how [Derek and Dad] met, through this American producer called Joe Shaftel. Joe was an old-fashioned movie mogul who veered from being a multi-millionaire to being bankrupt, almost on the strength of one phone call, and he was married to an Italian woman called Beatrice who was a former model who looked like Sophia Loren. They had the most outrageous Hollywood-type lifestyle and treated Derek like shit. Derek and my father got on really, really well. He had been Associate Producer on films produced by Joe and always wanted to dig a way out.' Horne's eventual escape was through his own company Magnum Films Limited (named after the champagne bottle, not Callan's weapon of choice).

'I loved the [*Callan*] series and I loved Jimmy's books,'[7] Horne said, his cultured, very English voice betraying none of his Irish origins. 'Thames wanted to buy the film rights to *Callan* and Jimmy was a bit reluctant about that.' Speculating on why the previous deals might have fallen through, he observed, 'I don't know the details, but there was always a problem, which Jimmy didn't actually help solve. I was floating about a bit for three years then I asked him about *Callan* and he helped me to get the film rights [from] under the noses of Thames. Not unreasonably, as they had made the series which had *huge* prominence, they said "C'mon, give us the film rights", but Jimmy didn't want [to].'

Peter Mitchell elaborated on his father's deal on rights to the series: 'From Dad's original contract, there was no doubt whatsoever that he owned the character rights to David Callan himself and Lonely. That was in the very first contract that [Roger] Hancock negotiated, so [the problem over rights] would have been about something else.'[8] The dispute between Mitchell and Thames was ultimately settled in court.

'Right from the outset, we wanted to do three, maybe four, feature films,' Horne revealed. 'Gloria Films, the German company who financially backed the first film, were very interested. I didn't discuss [a movie series] with [Edward Woodward and Russell Hunter] in any detail, because I didn't know [if there would be any], but during the Cannes Film Festival it became my certainty that there was going to be at least one more, there was going to be a sequel: we were going to do *Russian Roulette*. And I commissioned the script.' Horne remembered that his two stars were a pleasure to work with. 'They were fun and totally professional. They were part of a team and there was none of that "I'm the star" business. They were just great people to be working with. Teddy was unstinting and no nonsense. He was committed to a job, did it to the best of his ability and was good with his workmates. No airs and graces. He was brilliant at playing the trumpet – without a trumpet. He was quite brilliant at it.'

The film began shooting in December 1973, with location filming in and around London and interiors shot at Lee International Studios in Kensington. 'Jimmy wasn't around a huge amount, but he came down as he was a very important ingredient in the

444

film,' Horne said. 'He was very excited about turning Callan into a film character: we had lots and lots of serious chats about that. We wanted to be as true to [the series] as possible, but some of [the actors] weren't available and I thought, tentatively, that some of them we might improve on.' Before a frame was shot, though, Horne had to deal with criticism of his chosen director, who had worked on *The Avengers*, the first two Fu Manchu movies starring Christopher Lee and various Hammer films. 'When it was known in the press that Don Sharp was going to do *Callan*, somebody actually rang me up and said, "Are you out of your mind? What on Earth are you doing getting Don Sharp of all people to direct it?" And I said, "Because he's a bloody good director." His feet were firmly on the floor [and he] had a very good eye. He'd done second unit for the producer Kurt Unger on *Puppet on a Chain* [1971]. It wasn't a very good film, but in it there was a brilliant section that was all Don's work, and that clinched it for me.

'Don was a reasonable man – you could discuss things with him, and if he agreed he would say so, and if he didn't, he'd say, "No, I don't agree with that." He was the director, and one respected that. So I said to Don, very tentatively, because the cameras were set up to film a Range Rover smashing through a greenhouse, "Wouldn't it be better to shoot from the other end, as you'd see the Range Rover moving into it, then cut to it bursting out at the other end?" and he said "Yes". He went over to the crew and explained, and I remember the First Assistant Director saying, "Fucking producers! Why don't they just fuck off and play golf?" but Don said, "No, no, I think he's right" and they switched everything round, and it *did* work better.'

The opinions of his outspoken First Assistant aside, Horne had nothing but praise for his production crew. 'The atmosphere on the film was excellent. The crew all worked extremely hard, as a team, and were committed to the picture. I must tell you this because it nearly brings a tear to my eye all these years later. You have a completion guarantee in order to get the [production] money, which means you have to finish on a certain date. The first day of shooting we were on location on the Thames: thick fog – *thick*. So we went back to the studio and went out again the next day for another go. [The fog] quite clearly wasn't going to lift, so a little after eleven in the morning, I said "Call it a day, we'll go back to the studio". All the gear was out ready for shooting and it all had to be packed up and driven back to London. I got in my car and drove back and I'll remember this as long as I live: sitting in my office, at seven minutes to one, I heard the shooting bell ring – they wanted to get one shot in before lunch. And I was so impressed by that, because normally you think "Oh, we'll start at two." They'd rushed back to the studio, got all the gear out and on to the set, and they got a shot in before lunch: now *that* was dedication. They were a lovely bunch; it really makes me feel quite tearful remembering that.'

The production team's commitment was rewarded when Horne did a crafty deal for some alcohol product placement. 'I've forgotten the name of the whisky[9], but there's a memorable shot in the film in a pub and every bloody thing on the bar was this unknown whisky that I was promoting! I got four hundred quid [off the company], and that paid for a very good Christmas party we had in the studios.'

The *Callan* film was quietly ground-breaking as it was one of the first film productions to use a 'four-wall' studio, namely, a building where lightweight cameras and lights could be hired in. As freelancers predominantly worked on four-wall productions, this method of production was unpopular with the Association of Cinematograph Television and Allied Technicians union (based in traditional film studios), particularly as their membership was in decline in the early 1970s. 'It was just before the boring ACTT lost its stranglehold on the film business,' Horne said. 'They didn't approve because they didn't have their union man in the studio and they tried to block us. Even though the month before, ACTT Films, the union's own production company, had been shooting a feature film *in a barn*, on location in Kent – not even a four-wall studio – they tried to stop *Callan* shooting in Lee International Studios. My crew went and demonstrated in Soho Square [location of the ACTT headquarters'].' Coincidentally, this protest took place in the same year as members of the freelance unit Euston Films – the new TV film making wing of Thames Television, which also used four-wallers' – confronted the ACTT over plans to shut down Euston's production base in Hammersmith.[10] Horne remained proud of his outsider status and the stand his team took against the ACTT: 'At the time, *Callan* was the only feature film shooting in Great Britain, so I *was* the British film industry.'

WITH THE FILM COMPLETED by early 1974, the producer, working with personnel from Gloria Films, took *Callan* to the Cannes Film Festival in the South of France, for promotional screenings in order to secure international sales. The initial signs were positive: 'I actually heard in Cannes, hiding behind one of the potted palms in one of the theatres, two people and one said "That's the best film we've seen in Cannes this year". It might have been the *only* film they'd seen for all I know, but nonetheless it was a nice thing to hear, and Victor Michaelides, who was the sort of senior statesman of Greek distributors, came and put his arm round me and said "Thank God England has started making decent pictures again". I got huge praise... I was talking to two tall South African distributors, when a little Asian chap pulled my sleeve and slipped a piece of paper into my hand. I had it for years, and it said "Whatever offer you receive in writing for the territory of South Africa, we will pay you $1,000 more," and then the name of the company and his signature.

'We sold it to every territory in the world, apart from the US, and I covered the cost of the picture – less $74,000 with America unsold – so we had a [profitable film]. On the basis of that, I commissioned the script for the sequel. I remember Nat Cohen [of EMI] *chasing* the people from Gloria – Barney Bernhard was the boss – because he had two big American pictures, I forget what they were now, and wanted to use *Callan* to make a package of three. Gloria said "Oh, that sounds interesting", but as no one had got a solid commitment from them, [EMI] suddenly cancelled – *cancelled* – all the deals they had from around the world. I had distributors running up to me, *cursing* me, at the end of Cannes as they'd lost the picture and didn't have the time to get anything to replace it. *Cursing!* Now, to be fair, EMI did sell the picture – to Kuwait for £54!'

This disastrous missed opportunity was the beginning of a chain of promotional, financial and marketing blunders that followed *Callan* back to England and beyond. 'In the UK I'd done a deal with EMI, who came begging [for the film]: they wanted to show it right around England, including the coast, during the summer holidays, and they also wanted it for the West End, in the Plaza Cinema on Lower Regent Street. They had a picture which had dropped out so they needed something to go in there. So, *Callan* went into the Plaza without any advertising, because there was no time at all, in May. It turned out there was a heat wave, there was Wimbledon, and some other major sporting event in Europe, so the film did *bugger all*. To add insult to injury, EMI then said "It didn't do very well in the West End, and we only show successful films in the resorts."

'When *Callan* was shot and we were about to release it, Teddy and Russell offered to do personal appearances for free, to promote it. They said, "If they pay our expenses, we'll go anywhere," but EMI said, "Oh no, we don't do promotional things." Now, at that time, those two were getting £500 to go and open a supermarket... [It was] so short-sighted.'

Horne recalled that after the debacle in Cannes, Gloria tried to recoup their costs by having another crack at the American film market. 'They took the picture over to the States, they showed it to either Paramount or Columbia, and the president said it was the best-mounted independent production he'd ever seen, and why wasn't there one single name in the picture that they recognised? So – not interested.'

Unfortunately, and perhaps not surprisingly, as a business Gloria Films subsequently failed. 'Shortly after *Callan* came out they went bankrupt. The American bank behind them had backed them as they thought they had a library of films. Gloria's library was mostly co-productions, so they owned hardly anything. They had a third of a lot of pictures, but they didn't own many. They owned *Callan*, they owned a few more, and I think the people who bought the library sold the UK television rights for *Callan* for more than they paid for all of Gloria Films' library. Incredible.'

His financial backers' dissolution meant that Horne made no money from a film he had enjoyed making and was delighted with. 'It's the big disappointment of my limited and uneventful career,' he reflected good-naturedly. 'I *knew* it was good. It wasn't great – it was never meant to be a *great* film – I saw it as a bit of good entertainment. I thought it was well made and that's a credit to the director and the crew. They were nice people, and they did a bloody good job. It was a very happy experience for me. Afterwards, there was a lot of resentment in the industry, because it was the only picture around. I used to see people [scowling at me].'

Nevertheless, even though EMI had withdrawn their commitment to UK seaside resorts, *Callan* did receive wide distribution throughout the British Isles. After screening 'all over London from Sunday June 23'[11], the ABC cinema chain – coincidentally the parent company of *Callan*'s original TV network – screened it from Dundee to Liverpool to Wolverhampton, and the film was particularly well served by theatres in South East London. Buoyed up by repeats of the TV show's fourth year just before its release, reviews of *Callan* were, with a few exceptions, extremely positive (see 'Information'). 'There was one bad review,'[12] Horne said. 'It actually made me laugh, although I wanted to punch the feller's nose up his face. What did it say...? "The *Callan* spin-off.... If it spins your way, my advice is duck!"' The movie version of a series made by ITV also had a positive response from a member of its rival network. 'I knew a make-up girl at the BBC, and she very excitedly came up and said that she'd been making up the [presenter] of one of the BBC's film review shows and that *Callan* had come up. She'd said, "Oh, I know the pro-ducer of that," and this chap had said, "Then tell him he should be very proud. That's a bloody good little film, that."'

Summing up his feelings on his ambition to launch David Callan on the big screen 40 years after the event, Horne was content and philosophical: 'Although in commercial terms the thing was an absolute bloody disaster, I'm really quite proud of *Callan*. It's the thing that I'm most proud of, of all the things I was involved with. I enjoyed it the most, partially because I had the most free hand in it. I enjoyed the people I was working with and was very pleased with the outcome.'

CALLAN _'A' Certificate

Barney Bernhard presents a Magnum Production

Screenplay (from his novel 'A Red File for Callan'): James Mitchell
Director: Don Sharp
Producer: Derek Horne
GB 1974 101 minutes
UK Premiere: May 1974, Lower Regent Street, London
First UK TV transmission: ITV, Tuesday 12 May 1981, 7.30-9.00 pm

CAST: Edward Woodward (David Callan), Eric Porter (Hunter), Carl Mohner (Rudolf Schneider), Catherine Schell (Jenny), Peter Egan (Toby Meres), Russell Hunter (Lonely), Kenneth Griffith (Waterman), Michael Da Costa (The Greek), Veronica Lang (Hunter's Secretary), Clifford Rose (Snell), Dave Prowse (Arthur), Don Henderson (George), Padilla (Nadim Sawalha), David Graham (Wireless Operator), Yuri Borienko (Security Porter), Peter Symonds (Smart Security Man), Raymond Bowers (Shabby Security Man), Joe Dunlop (Policeman), Mollie Maureen (Old Lady in Strand)

PRODUCTION TEAM: *Associate Producer* Harry Benn, *Composer* Wilfred Josephs, *Conductor* Marcus Dods, *Harmonica* Tommy Reilly, *Director of Photography* Ernest Steward, *Editor* Teddy Darvas, *Art Director* John Clark, *Continuity* Pamela Davis, *Sound Recordist* Derek Ball, *Camera Operator* Freddie Cooper, *Assistant Director* Barry Langley, *Production Manager* Barrie Melrose, *Set Dresser* Simon Holland, *Property Master* George Ball, *Construction Manager* Terry Apsey, *Make-Up* Freddie Williamson, *Hairdresser* Betty Glasow, *Wardrobe* Ray Beck, *Dubbing Mixer* Bill Rowe, *Sound Editors* Charles Grafford, John Poyner, *Lighting Gaffer* Len Crowe, *Casting Director* Lesley de Pettit, *Special Effects* John Richardson, *Fight Arranger* Doug Robinson, *Car Stunting* Joe Wadham and 'Nine Nine Cars', *Colour Processing* Rank Laboratories, *War Games Models* Hinchcliffe Models Limited, *Models Adviser* Peter Gilder

'The original *Callan* television series was produced by Thames Television Limited.'

'Made at Lee International Studios Limited, Kensal Road, London W10 England and on location by Magnum Films Limited, 29 Gloucester Place, London W1, England.'

'CALLAN' CAMPAIGN AIDS, EMI FILM DISTRIBUTORS LTD., *1974 (Press book)*
Accessories: Six different sized newspaper adverts, six black and white stills, 30" x 40" quad poster, eight 10" x 8" full colour stills. The trailer could be ordered 'direct from National Screen Services Ltd.' and 'three free editorial half-tone blocks [were] available.'

MISSION PROFILE: Outcast from the Section, executioner David Callan is offered a second chance if he'll agree to assassinate businessman Rudolf Schneider. He is ordered to carry out the hit without any help from the Section and uses Lonely, an underworld contact, to get him a *Noguchi .357 Magnum revolver.**

Becoming acquainted with Schneider he instinctively takes a liking to the extrovert German, especially after finding out they share an interest in model soldiers and war gaming.

At the same time, rival agent Toby Meres organises surveillance on Callan.

Needing to know why Hunter wants Schneider killed, Callan searches the entrepreneur's office and home, finding he's been selling armaments which are being used to kill British troops.

Hunter rebukes Callan for his curiosity. Meres and Callan fight in the Section gym.

The ex-agent's assignment is complicated when he's interrogated by Lonely's arms supplier the Greek; Callan kills the criminal's bodyguard Arthur.

Callan then has to prevent Schneider from completing an arms deal, and a car chase ensues before the German retreats back to his house.

At the Section the Greek is drugged and brainwashed by Snell, the Section psychiatrist.

Callan is repelled by this and aware the Section could be conditioning the Greek to testify against him in court, instead of to forget about him.

Distrusting Hunter, he records a confession, but Meres knocks him out and erases the tape.

The police and Meres both converge on Schneider's home, where Callan and the German play war games. Meres breaks in. Schneider catches him and prepares to kill both him and Callan, but Callan shoots him. He then knocks Meres out and frames him for the killing.

Hunter assigns Callan to a Red File – marking him for death.

A MAN LIKE ME: Callan is a slightly shabby, cynical, working class man who typically wears a raincoat and battered hush puppies. He's an enthusiast of military history and collects model soldiers – although he usually makes his own – is a keen war gamer and an avid reader of *The Complete History of the Civil War*. He fought in the Malayan Emergency and still suffers from nightmares about his military service there. After leaving the army, Callan spent two years in Wormwood Scrubs (prisoner number 49175228) for 'armed robbery'. Since he left the Section, he's been assigned to a 'Yellow File', which in this version still means surveillance.

Even though Callan's been off active duty for 18 months, he proves naturally accurate with a new Noguchi .357 Magnum and easily loses two of the Section's best men who are following him by stealing a postman's bicycle. He knows how to harden his fists by punching them into bowls of dry, then wet, sand. Callan is able to best the younger Meres in unarmed combat; Meres seems to be gaining the upper hand but Callan is the dirtier fighter, hitting the other man with gym equipment. He is highly skilled at handling a Range Rover. He's a strange mixture of compassion and vindictiveness, giving Schneider's girlfriend Jenny money to get away (a reinstated scene from 'A Magnum for Schneider') but framing Meres. Disturbingly, at one point he contemplates shooting the gregarious Schneider in the back, concealing reaching for his hidden shoulder-holster by pretending to scratch an itch.

Film-Callan still takes pride in his abilities, retains his independent streak by investigating Schneider's arms dealing, and has his own code of honour, turning down the offer of £10,000 a year to bodyguard the criminal Greek. His self-disgust and revulsion with the Section increase throughout his comeback mission for Hunter. He vomits after killing Arthur and is appalled by Snell's treatment of the Greek and his own violent behaviour

* Italics indicate new material that was added to the film script.

towards Lonely. When Callan finally kills Schneider, he's even more visibly sickened than in the TV version. Again, it's no idle threat when he phones Hunter to tell him he won't work for him anymore.

LONELY: Still an old associate of Callan's, still a small, scruffy man in a flat cap and raincoat, retaining his appalling body odour; he can't write but has a good memory. As in the books he's a habitual burglar, and on the big screen his cluttered flat can be seen in detail. It's littered with items he's picked up 'here and there', such as Mickey Mouse and Donald Duck alarm clocks, a Communist flag, china parrots and cockatoos, numerous dolls and a drawer full of knives and forks. (He comically tries to pocket all the cutlery when the police attempt a raid on his flat.)

Even though he's worried about being sentenced to 'ten years' for getting Callan a gun, Lonely agrees to do it, hiding it in a carrier bag of sprouts. He can smarten up when necessary, wearing a trilby hat and clean, dark raincoat to visit the Greek. Having served time with him in prison, Lonely considers Callan his 'mate', turning down the offered commission on the gun deal. However, their relationship is clearly still abusive, as Lonely is terrified of Callan, meekly accepting a painful physical assault from him.

A TIE AND A CREST: Hunter and Meres are both portrayed as upper class, furthering the distance between them and Callan. The rivalry between Meres and Callan, revolving around the former now having the older agent's job, erupts into violence when Meres loses his cool in the Section gym.

Callan frequents run-down, working class areas of London in contrast to his quarry Schneider's lavish country estate, and even though clearly only a few more rungs up the social ladder than Callan, his cantankerous boss Waterman insists on being called 'sir'.

ALCOHOL, TOBACCO AND FIREARMS: Alcohol looms large in Callan's life. He accepts a whisky from Hunter, even though heavy drinking was part of the reason he was sacked. When he and Lonely have a Scotch together, he pours himself a larger one and (in a nice bit of comic business by the actors) stops the thief from taking it. As Callan scrupulously prepares for action, a bottle of whisky is ever-present in his flat and when he starts to feel the pressure he gives it a glance. After killing Arthur, he cracks and drinks another whisky; later, when he goes to see Lonely to apologise for thumping him in the chest on Hunter's orders, he's noticeably drunk. In a clumsy attempt to say sorry, the agent buys Lonely a pint of bitter and a packet of fags. (On the big screen, Lonely smokes.)

At the Section's Firing Range Callan initially scores '2 outers, 3 misses' against wooden figures and says he is getting 'rusty' before switching to the Magnum and showing he still has his old skill. He uses the gun to hit the dashboard on Schneider's motor boat from over forty feet away, while deliberately just missing the German and Jenny. As in previous versions of the story, he conceals the weapon by taping it to his lower leg.

SPY-SPEAK: While reusing many of the best lines from the *Schneider* novel, and therefore the TV play, Mitchell also takes the opportunity to add several new quips, including Callan's unflattering view of his rival in the Section: 'I think he's unconscious, but with Meres it is difficult to tell.' (The same joke, about a different character, was also used in the novel *Smear Job*).

The Greek answers his entry-phone to find Lonely is outside. 'Oh, *God...*'

The villain accurately assesses Lonely's relationship with Callan: 'How interesting. You're even more afraid of him than you are of me.'

Callan needles Meres. 'What's the matter, son? Hasn't Hunter let you kill anybody lately?' Having beaten him in their subsequent fight, Callan yells, 'Now will you *shut up! I am tired!*'

Sarcastically, Meres is impressed with Callan's demolition of Arthur: 'This must be your biggest yet, he'll weigh 250 pounds at least. If I were you I should have him stuffed.'

Hunter bonds with a hippy student: 'Peace, brother.'

PAWNS AND PLAYERS: DEREK HORNE, by his own admission, went into the film business 'by mistake'[13]. He began working in the music division of the BBC and, after being 'sacked', moved on to a company that made film title sequences. From there, he was a founder member of Animation Associates who made adverts and, after the company became a success, wanted to work in the mainstream film industry. This led to him to working with the American producer Josef Shaftel, whom, Horne said, was 'the only man in the history of world cinema to let failure go to his head.' During a short but productive career, the *Callan* producer worked on ten films, including the crime drama *Clegg* (1970), *Alice's Adventures in Wonderland* (1972), with the all-star cast of Michael Jayston, Ralph Richardson, Peter Sellers and Dudley Moore, and another literary adaptation, *Gulliver's Travels* (1977), which starred Richard Harris and Catherine Schell. At home in the bohemian atmosphere of 1960s London, Horne frequented Peter Cook's Establishment club and the celebrity clientele would often decamp to Horne's Soho flat after the venue closed for the night. He was introduced to James Mitchell by John Brason and Norman Hoy, who were both fellow Geordies.

DON SHARP (1921-2011) began his entertainment career as an actor, working in both his native Australia and the UK, where he chose to settle. He switched to directing in the 1950s and by the early 1960s was a regular director on the TV crime series *Ghost Squad* (1962-63). From there, he moved on to big screen thrillers, including the notable Hammer productions *The Kiss of the Vampire* (1963) and *Rasputin: The Mad Monk* (1966). Sharp's style was ideally suited to *The Avengers* and he oversaw three episodes of the Tara King series: 'Invasion of the Earthmen', 'The Curious Case of the Countless Clues' and 'Get-A-Way!' (all 1968). In a similar vein – and just before *Callan* – he helmed the cult horror/biker movie *Psychomania* (1973). In the latter part of his career, Sharp directed mainly for television, including a TV movie of *The Four Feathers* (1978). 'I enjoyed working with him very much,'[14] recalled Peter Egan. 'He was a man who liked actors who could deliver, and obviously he thought Eric [Porter] and I could.'

WILFRED JOSEPHS (1927-1997), also born in Newcastle, was a prolific composer who had previously scored incidental music for *The Prisoner* and its rejected first theme tune. His TVcompositions also include *I, Claudius* (1976), *The Ghosts of Motley Hall* (1976) and *Enemy at the Door* (1978), with film scores for *Fanatic* (1965), *The Deadly Bees* (1966) and, again working with director Don Sharp, *Dark Places* (1973).

TOMMY REILLY (1919-2000) was a highly regarded Canadian harmonica player who began playing the 'mouth organ' aged eleven. Interned for the duration of WW2, he took up residence in the UK in 1945; in 1951, he signed to Parlophone as a solo artist and was produced by George Martin. Film composers who wrote specifically for Reilly included Elmer Bernstein (1922-2004), Jerry Goldsmith (1929-2004) and Bernard Hermann (1911-1975). His distinctive refrain can be heard on the theme for the naval comedy *The Navy Lark* (1959-1977), *Those Magnificent Men in their Flying Machines* (1965), the melancholy score for *Midnight Cowboy* (1969) by John Barry (1932-2011) and Dennis Potter's *film noir* psycho-drama *The Singing Detective* (1986).

ERIC PORTER (1928-1995) was one of Britain's most highly regarded actors. From the Bristol Old Vic to his scene-stealing turn as Professor Moriarty in *The Adventures of Sherlock Holmes* – 'The Red-Headed League' and 'The Final Problem' (both 1985), he was very selective in the roles he took on. His performance as Soames in the BBC's *The Forsyte Saga* (1967) earned him a BAFTA, while, in 1988, he won the *London Evening Standard* Award for Best Actor in the stage version of *Cat on a Hot Tin Roof*. Other stand-outs in Porter's career are *The Belstone Fox* (1972), *The Day of the Jackal* (1973) and the BBC's produc-tion of Arthur Miller's play *The Crucible* (1980). 'He was a great stalwart of the Royal Shakespeare Company and a really terrific guy,' Egan said of his co-star. 'We worked together again on *Hennessy* [1975] with Rod Steiger, which was another Don Sharp film.' Not afraid to drop his serious image, Porter performed a song and dance routine to the song 'If My Friends Could See Me Now' with Eric and Ernie on the *The Morecambe and Wise Christmas Show* (1970). The seasonal special also featured Edward Woodward as a guest.

PETER EGAN's first starring performance on television was only his third TV role (at only 22). Such early fame had its drawbacks, however. '*Big Breadwinner Hog* [1969] caused quite an uproar in its day', he recalled of the crime series that established him. 'Mike Newell and Mike Apted directed it and it was discussed in the Houses of Parliament [and accused of] inciting the youth of Great Britain to treasonable acts, because it was such a violent series. But it put a stamp on my career early on, that I didn't want, of playing villains. I didn't want to be "typed" as an actor. This is why I've done such a cross-section of work throughout my life – either modern, comedy or period. I think I may have done a greater cross-section of work than most actors that I know, from that point of view. So although it was a gift to have *Hog* as a debut series, it was also a problem, because for three years after that I was offered things like *Man of Violence* [1971]... [So] a year-and-a-half later I went to the Royal Shakespeare Company for a season to do some classical work, purely because I didn't want to be locked into a TV career or a career where I was just playing villains.'

Remaining true to his word, Egan's career over the last forty plus years has taken in such diverse fare as the historical dramas *Lillie* (1978, as Oscar Wilde), *Prince Regent* (1979, in the starring role), John Mortimer's *Paradise Postponed* (1986) and the deceptively dark BBC comedy *Ever Decreasing Circles* (1984-1989).[15] Egan also returned to the spy genre, firstly in *Reilly – Ace of Spies* (1983) and then *A Perfect Spy* (1987) for the BBC, based on the author John le Carré's relationship with his father. It was a very special production for Egan. 'It was one of my favourite jobs ever, a great story, and a great character: very, very interesting to portray. I got on with Ray McAnally [who played Rick Pym] like a house on fire, because my father was a Dubliner and Ray was a Dubliner. I'd worked with Ray in 1966, in my first job, in the Chichester Festival Theatre. Just prior to that I'd seen him on stage in *Who's Afraid of Virginia Woolf?* and he was staggeringly good in that. I thought he was a wonderful actor. He reminded me a lot of my Dad. It was interesting playing father and son in *A Perfect Spy*, because in some of the scenes I could look at him and I literally saw my father's face – he had a similar kind of tone to him that my father had – and that sort of resonated right through the relationship I had with him in the filming.' No stranger to the stage, one of Egan's recent productions was Samuel Beckett's one hour monologue *First Love* (written in 1946). For over three decades, he and his actress wife Myra have also been tireless animal rights campaigners.

CARL MOHNER (1921-2005) was originally born Carl Martin Rudolf Möhner, in Vienna, Austria. A well known actor in Europe, he made two memorable films for the French director Jules Dessin. In 1955's *Rififi*, he played Joe Le Suedois, one of a quartet of criminals who carried out a robbery in a sequence that, for all of its 32 minutes, was innovatively shot in silence. Mohner also starred in Dessin's 1920s historical drama *He Who Must Die* (1957) and had major roles in the English speaking films *Sink the Bismarck!* (1960) and Hammer's *The Camp on Blood Island* (1958, with Ronald Radd). Multi-talented as well as multilingual, Mohner wrote and directed the feature films *The Istanbul Adventure* (1958) and *Inshalla Razzia am Bosporous* (1962).

CATHERINE SCHELL (born Katherina Freiin Schell von Bauschlott in 1944) was the daughter of Hungarian refugees. She developed an interest in acting when her family settled in New York. Attending the highly regarded Falconberg School of Performing Arts in the late 1960s, she went on to appear in the well-known genre films *On Her Majesty's Secret Service*, *Moon Zero Two* (both 1969) and *The Return of the Pink Panther* (1975). Schell had regular parts in both the ITC film series *The Adventurer* (1972-73) and, arguably her best remembered role, the shape-changing alien Maya in the second year of the science fiction adventure *Space: 1999* (1977, after guest starring in the first year's story 'Guardian of Piri'). She enjoyed working with Woodward and was impressed by the *Callan* film's ambitious car chase: 'It was one of the first really exciting car chases, I think. They'd done it before in America but this was one of the first times they'd done it in England.'[16]

KENNETH GRIFFITH (1921-2006) was a seasoned Welsh character actor who, early in his varied career, worked for the Boulting Brothers on their satirical films *Private's Progress* (1956), the sequel *I'm All Right Jack* (1959), and won an Emmy for his portrayal of Napoleon in Granada TV's production of *War and Peace* (1963). Like many of the *Callan* franchise's cast he featured in *The Prisoner*, firstly in the madcap 'The Girl Who Was Death' (1968) as a Napoleon-obsessed villain and then the psychedelic final episode, 1968's 'Fall Out', writing much of the dialogue for his character, The President. Griffith was also an accomplished documentary maker who addressed, as he saw it, the injustices of England's colonial past. His film about the Irish Republican leader Michael Collins, *Hang Up Your Brightest Colours* (1973), was banned by the BBC for twenty years.

MICHAEL DA COSTA (1941-1977) had a memorable gallery of grotesques to his credit, including a dodgy hotel manager in the film of *Steptoe and Son* (1973) and a seedy photographer in 'Regan' (1974), the pilot for *The Sweeney*. He had a tragically short life, as Peter Egan remembered: 'I'd been to drama school with Michael in the sixties and he played one of the villains [in *Callan*] – a kind of decadent, flabby, camp character. Very sadly he killed himself a few years afterwards.'[17]

DON HENDERSON (1931-1997) played the small role of George. His most famous role was another George, the glove-wearing Detective Chief Inspector Bulman, who featured in three series on ITV between 1976 and 1987: *The XYY Man*, *Strangers* and, when he retired from the police and became a clock mender/private eye, *Bulman*. Henderson also appeared in James Mitchell's gripping BBC thriller *Spyship* (1983).

INFORMATION: The original draft of Mitchell's screenplay[18] began with Hunter looking through Callan's file. As he did so, there was a flashback to 20 year-old Corporal Callan's National Service in Cyprus. His five man unit searched for terrorists in a farmhouse and Callan shot down a young Cypriot gunman whom the other members of his patrol had failed to notice. The scene then dissolved to a television monitor showing the present day version of Callan approaching Hunter's scrapyard.

'[The film] was a way of looking at what to do next with Callan.'[19] James Mitchell said. 'I know we went back in time, rather than forward in time, as a way of [moving on from the TV series] and making money as well!' Concerning the end result, he recollected being 'happy with it... It certainly had some things which I enjoyed that you never saw before, like the war game which worked much better on film, I thought. The big stunt driving through the glass house added a whole new dimension to it; the sort of thing you can only talk about [doing] on video.'

A list of casting possibilities put together for James Mitchell by the Kilravock Company Limited[20] makes intriguing reading. If Anthony Valentine was 'unavailable' for Meres, the other suggestions were Edward Fox (at the time a hot property because of his performance as the assassin in *The Day of the Jackal*), Michael Jayston, Corin Redgrave and Jeremy Brett. The prospective casting for Hunter and Schneider was no less ambitious: among the names suggested for the Section commander were Laurence Olivier, Ralph Richardson, David Niven and Stanley Baker, while the German arms dealer might have been portrayed by Richard Burton, Anthony Quayle, Robert Shaw, Maximilian Schell or Curt Jurgens.

There was extensive filming in and around London; down the river Thames towards Tower Bridge, outside Conduit House and Charing Cross Underground station (renamed Charing Cross Embankment in August 1974, then Embankment in September 1976), off the Strand on Carting Lane and towards Trafalgar Square. Waterman took delivery of his stock in the now completely redeveloped Docklands, while Derek Horne recalled that 'the scrapyard was in Westbourne Grove, near Notting Hill, and Schneider's place was on the Thames.'[21] The car chase also included him in an uncredited cameo: 'One of the opening shots is a street scene, and a blue Jaguar drives through the shot and turns into a "No Entry" street – starring the producer!'

The Greek's flat was in Eaton Mews North, Belgravia, London SW1. The upmarket location was a favourite with filmmakers and, among other productions, featured in the Terence Rattigan comedy *The Man Who Liked Read Heads* (1955), Alfred Hitchcock's *Stage Fright* (1960), together with ITC series such as *Danger Man*, *Randall and Hopkirk (Deceased)* and *Return of the Saint*.

Snell's interrogation unit was filmed in two locations. The unusual paternoster lifts Hunter and Callan use to enter it were in the GEC Marconi building in Borehamwood. In another connection with *The Prisoner*, the location had also been used as part of the HQ of Patrick McGoohan's character in the episode 'Do Not Forsake Me Oh My Darling'. (By an ironic coincidence, the sequence includes an electronic bleeping sound effect also used in the series.) Clifford Rose remembered the actual ward 'was done in a hospital, somewhere near Twickenham, and it was a real hospital: there were real patients in other wards, and nearby.'[22]

Rose was the only other cast member who made the transition from the TV series. 'I wasn't surprised that they were doing a film because I thought it had been a very, very good series – very successful – and it seemed that a film would very much be the obvious thing to do. They said to me, "We're making this film and Snell appears in it, will you play it?" and they also said that James Mitchell would be very happy if I did so, so I said "Oh, why not?" We ran into trouble, because Peter Egan wore tinted glasses and they said "Oh, you can't have tinted ones as well!" I still wore glasses, but I know they weren't tinted.

'The scene I did was with Callan and Eric Porter, who I thought was extremely good as Hunter. [Having very few of the TV cast in the film] didn't make a great deal of difference to me: Callan was Callan and Eric was a splendid Hunter. I didn't meet Meres. I don't know why the TV actors weren't there, I was just aware that they weren't. One normally assumes if there's a big regular role and that person wasn't there, it's because they weren't available.'

William Squire, though, would happily have taken part if asked: 'I was very disappointed not to get the movie, I must say. I was very upset about that, because – and it's a terrible conceit – I thought I *was* Hunter by that time. I couldn't think of anybody else being better, only because Teddy said so.'[23]

'I knew Don Sharp and he just asked me in to meet the producer,'[24] said Peter Egan. 'There'd been two Toby Meres on television, and one was Tony Valentine who was a mate of mine. I knew him for 40 years, but the two of us playing the same part never came up in conversation. I thought Tony was a terrific Toby Meres. Anyway, for some reason [he and Peter Bowles] weren't free or up for the film so they asked me to go in, and I got it, which was great. I was rather delighted because it was a really interesting character and a slightly smoother kind of villain than the flamboyant Hog. I was thinking he should be a really sharp contrast against the "greyness" of Callan – very much part of that very sharp new world of the '70s that got away a bit from the greyness of the '60s.' Egan himself contributed the distinctive blue glasses his Meres wore: 'I used to wear them myself, and I said, "Should I use these, they're a bit pretentious?" and they thought that was a good idea. I was obviously a very pretentious young actor!'

Egan's most memorable sequence in the film is his fight in the Section gymnasium with Woodward. 'If you're playing those kind of characters you always have a bit of stunt coaching. There was quite a lot of that because it was a difficult fight. They wanted us to do as much of it as possible. It was quite wearing; there was one moment when I had to elbow Edward in the abdomen, then drop down and flip him over my shoulder, which we trained for. We got the stunt director to show us how to do it as we wanted to be as realistic as possible. I remember when we did the take, I elbowed [Edward] and he went over my shoulder but he landed very badly and ricked his neck. We were a bit more careful after that.' It seems this was not the only time Woodward was hurt during the making of the film, as one of Dave Prowse's punches also accidentally landed on him too.[25]

From the outset of production, Horne had championed an innovative noise reduction system for the film's soundtrack, named after its creator Ray Dolby, that the producer felt would make *Callan* distinctive and more commercially appealing. Once more, however, he found himself up against the frustrating short-sightedness of his distribution company:

'If it hadn't been for... EMI the film would have been a success. It was the first film *in the world* to have a Dolby soundtrack and they didn't even want to put it on the poster! I had to fight and fight and shout and scream to get them to mention it. All the hi-fi and audio press came to the press show, and at the reception afterwards, the EMI press people turned them away: "Oh no, this is for the national press," they said, "not for *you*." It was a reel of *Callan* that got Dolby into the Lincoln Centre and into two or three of the major cinema chains across the States. They took a reel over, shared it around and they made an absolute *fortune*. And [EMI] didn't even want to put [Dolby] on the poster! It passes belief.'[26]

Horne elaborated, 'because it was Dolby, you could do [the sound of] an empty room – you didn't get "scratch, scratch, scratch" on the soundtrack. In the cinema, I remember it worked very well: it was very dramatic. There was a very good dubbing mixer out of EMI studios, and I remember discussing it with him. Bill Rowe was his name. Apart from being a genius with sound, he was a very nice man. He had just done the dub on *A Clockwork Orange* [1971]. It was the first film with a Dolby dub, though it hadn't been recorded with Dolby. I said, "That's marvellous, I'll have to look into that," and that got it going. Later, the Dolby laboratories sent a man over to help with the sound equipment. They installed it in the Plaza for the premiere there, and after the premiere Dolby went back in to remove it, and the manager said, "You're not taking that out! Just tell me how much I owe you."' With incredible understatement, Ioan Allen, the marketing manager of Dolby, told *Cinema TV Today* at the time, 'We don't expect it to revolutionise the film industry, but we hope it will bring sound on films up-to-date.'[27] A few years later, the Dolby cinema sound system was a major factor in the ground-breaking success of *Star Wars* and *Close Encounters of the Third Kind* (both 1977).

There are some discrepancies and production mistakes. The tax disc on Schneider's car has the date November 1973 and a placard on a news vendor's stand refers to the wedding of Princess Anne and Captain Mark Phillips, which took place in the same month. Callan goes to dinner with Schneider on Sunday 22 October, making the year 1972 and suggesting this was when the shooting script was finalised. In the alleyway off the Strand where Callan talks to an old lady, in the background an old man wearing glasses begins walking down the steps but suddenly steps back out of the scene. When Callan opens Schneider's safe, the picture on the wall above it shakes slightly, which it wouldn't have done if the wall it was hanging on was solid.

Among many positive press reviews, the *Daily Mail* was the only paper to single out the improved sound: 'The dialogue is a model of clarity thanks to the new Dolby soundtrack system, which makes every whisper needle-sharp and scares you out of your skin whenever the telephone rings.'[28] Of the film itself, an insightful analysis in the media journal *The Listener* noted, 'The essence of this sort of entertainment is to maintain scrupulous authenticity within the larger lunacy, and screenwriter James Mitchell and director Don Sharp manage it with better than polish. Not that you would call the film stylish in any obvious way. But the skills of matching lucidity with mystery, and pace with suspense, and humour with fear are not to be sneered at, for all that they are unobtrusive. There is a scene early on when the unfit and alcoholic Callan is shocked awake by a hostile alarm clock, the kind that finishes you for the day. A long while later in the film his finger snakes out and nips it in the bud one morning and we know he is on his way to Callan's Revenge. It is the small excellences that endear you to *Callan*.'[29]

Films Illustrated was equally complimentary, favourably comparing the film with an earlier movie that had inspired it. 'That *Callan* is the best television spin-off thus far is hardly surprising since Thames Television's long running series was amazingly good. What is surprising is that Don Sharp's film version should turn out to be the freshest and most compelling seedy spy thriller since Sidney Furie's trail blazing *The IPCRESS File* ten years ago.'[30] Among the regional press, the reviewer in the *Manchester Evening News* spoke for many critics, praising 'The best movie of a TV show I have yet seen [which] leaves the way open for an interesting sequel if the movie receives the success it deserves.'[31]

There were mixed opinions among the film's cast about the finished result. 'I went to see it in the cinema and I thought it was a good film,'[32] Egan said. 'They were obviously aiming to do a Len Deighton kind of thing there, make Callan the next character like that, a sort of under-the-stone investigator. I think it could have done very well as a kind of running character like Harry Palmer. I don't know why they didn't do any more; I thought it worked very well as a film. Edward was terrific in the part.' Rose is more equivocal: 'I thought it was alright; I didn't think it was terrible. I wondered why they chose that particular story, actually – why had they gone back to square one? [The film] was very well crafted and technically well done, but the storyline I thought was not all that great. They should have had an original story, a brand new one.'[33]

With the benefit of over a decade's hindsight in 1987, Russell Hunter was even more forthright in his views than Rose: 'These are just opinions of mine on how the movie business spends its money, [but] I didn't think a lot of the film. It glamorised everything about [*Callan*]. It pushed it up, it made it too big, it made it too colourful, it made it too beautiful. [*Callan* had] brought the kind of realism to telly that had been lacking or hadn't been over-marked before that. I think [the film] failed to adapt itself to the new realism of cinema. The big movies had gone ahead: they were now dirty and filthy and *Callan*, which should have been dirty and filthy, was suddenly lovely and *clean*... I mean, all that business with the white Range Rover: that was just too much for *Callan*.'[34]

Speaking around the same time as Hunter, Woodward's reservations also concerned production decisions: 'It's not that you take something from a small screen and put it on a large screen, it's that you take it away from the [production] team – because the actors are only part of it – from the whole ambience of the studio and the people who know it and work on it... I remember all of us saying "It's not the same, is it? It's not the same." [They] took] an hour's television script and elongated it and to my mind it didn't really work. I might have felt it worked better if we had done a new script, but because we'd already done 'A Magnum for Schneider' we were trying to recreate something that I don't think, on the face of it, really could work. I've seen the film quite recently and in many ways it still holds up, but I think it would have held up much more if nobody had ever seen the series or the original teleplay.'[35]

Although no more Callan films materialised, the movie's positive reception at Cannes inspired Horne to '[pay] Jimmy three grand [to write *Russian Roulette*]. He had a way of looking at something and immediately knowing it would make a good film idea. The other films would have been what became *Death and Bright Water* and *Smear Job*.'[36] Sadly, in the wake of Gloria Films going into receivership, this was not to be.

In its 9-15 May 1981 issue, the *TV Times* devoted a quarter of a page to the *Callan* movie's television debut on its listings page for 12 May. Regular film reviewer David Quinlan described the movie as 'perhaps the best television spin-off to date' and noted that 'James Mitchell goes back to his own first novel about Callan... for the storyline, and Don Sharp's tautly-strung direction (especially in a marathon car chase) and

Edward Woodward's tersely convincing performance do the rest.'[37] This was not the only Callan-related article in that particular edition of the magazine: it contained exciting news for *Callan* fans about the making of a brand new 90-minute TV special – *Wet Job*.

MISSION ANALYSIS: *'We weren't all born in the bastions of privilege.'* After the cramped, tense theatrical interiors of the original *Armchair Theatre* version of 'A Magnum for Schneider' and the compelling internalisation of Callan's mind-set in the 1969 novel, the third version of this story emphasises one thing: space. The bustling London Callan inhabits is brought to life through a visual vocabulary of panoramic views, long shots, crowd scenes and – compared with the TV series – enormous, detailed sets like the Section HQ and Schneider's country house. The cinematography has the same authentic lack of glamour as camera-man Dusty Miller's influential work on *Get Carter*, helping immensely in bringing to life the mundane, if slightly less grimy, nine-to-five world of Mitchell's novel.

Carl Mohner is even more avuncular and dangerous than Joseph Fürst's rendition of Schneider. While Valentine, Langdon and Squire are missed, Egan, Veronica Lang and Eric Porter slip effortlessly into their allotted roles. Wilfred Josephs' music is by turns jaunty, military and upbeat, then melancholy, then – during the killings – disturbing, amplifying the mood without being intrusive.

Stripping the novel back down for the cinema, Mitchell cleverly tweaks familiar scenes, adding a long-awaited grudge fight between Callan and Meres, which both subverts the expectation of readers of the book (where there is a stand-off) and magnifies the characters' ongoing conflict. Mitchell also subtly updates the story so Schneider is seen to be financing terrorism generally in addition to anti-British activities, as the press cuttings in his safe include incidents in Cyprus and Northern Ireland, as well as the massacre of civilians at an unspecified airport.

The move to 35mm film also allows for a subtly different interpretation of Callan. Film-Callan is older, greyer and more world-weary than the one originally written in *Armchair Theatre* (seven years having passed since the original television play). He is much more obviously a recovering alcoholic, possibly suffering from post-traumatic stress disorder and the Schneider assignment really feels like his last chance. Woodward buys into all this very effectively, remarking at the time that he was approaching the character as if he'd never played the role before. Sharp's direction also emphasises that Callan is a short man by placing him against the taller Hunter, Meres and Schneider, a neat metaphor for his downtrodden status; it also makes more sense of Snell's line that he thought the man who killed Arthur would 'be bigger'.

The most striking change, though, is in the presentation of violence. The TV series had always relied more on threatening words than actions, and here director Don Sharp seizes on the opportunity to portray cinematic mayhem convincingly on a big budget. Apart from the scene where Callan kills the Greek's minder Arthur, which has a visual flair simi-lar to the trippy gangster film *Performance* (1970), the action sequences, from the witty scene where Callan escapes from Section agents by stealing a postman's bike in the Strand, to his fight with Meres, have a punchy, no-frills style. This approach is at its most effective in the set-piece car chase, reminiscent of the action scenes Mitchell had been writing into the *Callan* short stories. At a time when car chases in the James Bond films had be-come slapstick, cameras fixed to the outside of Carl Mohner and Catherine Schell's car to capture their reactions as they are terrorised, Callan demolishing a greenhouse in a Range Rover and a spectacular collision with a train at a level crossing – none of which use any obvious special effects trickery – makes the sequence every bit as good as the similarly authentic Hollywood car chases in *Bullitt* (1968) and *The French Connection* (1971).

As on television, whenever Russell Hunter and Woodward are on screen together, the ethical and emotional contradictions of Callan's profession are shown through his and Lonely's relationship. The scene where Callan hits Lonely is shocking, and notable for the blank, emotionless face Callan affects straight afterwards. The follow up to this disturbing sequence shows him drunkenly apologising to Lonely in a pub, confessing, 'I shouldn't have got you into this, I don't think you're cut out for it. I don't think *either* of us are cut out for it.' This leaves the way open for the pair to work together again in the future films envisaged by Horne and Mitchell.

Even if some of the regular cast disagreed, revisiting 'A Magnum for Schneider' for a third time was a logical move in attempting to introduce an international audience to Callan and his world. Based on the potential shown in this solid British thriller, it's frustrating that no more Callan films were made. You're left with the lingering feeling that they would have got better and better.

11: NEVER SAY NEVER AGAIN: 'Wet Job'

'I haven't murdered anybody for years.'

Callan, *Wet Job*, 2 September 1981

'CALLAN'S BACK IN BUSINESS,'[1] the *TV Times* unexpectedly announced in its 9-15 May 1981 issue. In the same week that the 1974 *Callan* feature film premiered on ITV, producer and director Shaun O'Riordan excited the followers of 'the defiant anti-hero' by revealing that a new TV play by James Mitchell starring Edward Woodward and Russell Hunter was in production, looking at 'how a middle-aged man can cope with being thrown back into the violent world of spying.' Interest in *Callan* throughout the 1970s had remained strong, with Mitchell's original novels and prolific short stories proving highly popular, so O'Riordan's closing statement was a thrilling one: 'I think the script is so good that somebody may ask if a new series is possible.'

At this time (as discussed further in the next chapter) the portrayal of espionage on British television was continually evolving, from the BBC's prestigious adaptation of le Carré's George Smiley novel *Tinker Tailor Soldier Spy* (1979) to the pessimistic York-shire Television series *The Sandbaggers* (1978-1980) and the slick, hybrid action show *The Professionals*. Reviving popular spies from earlier decades was also fashionable. Patrick Macnee had already brought John Steed's bowler hat and umbrella out of mothballs for two series of *The New Avengers* (1976-77), this time paired with two younger members of 'the Department', Mike Gambit (Gareth Hunt) and Purdey (Joanna Lumley). Robert Vaughn and David McCallum would open Channel D again in the TV movie *The Man from UNCLE: The Fifteen Years After Affair* (in 1983) and incredibly, that same year, Sean Connery would reprise the role that had made him an international star – James Bond. It was amid this curious climate of nostalgia and innovation that moves were being made to bring Callan, the 'prototype sandbagger'[2], out of retirement.

'Quite often on *The Sweeney*, when they were getting towards the end, [Euston Films] were always talking about doing *Callan*,'[3] Trevor Preston recalled, 'so there was always an interest, particularly from Lloyd [Shirley]. It was very much his bag. It was, without a doubt – apart from *The Avengers* – the most popular show.' Possibly as a result of the interest from Euston Films, William Squire recalled the idea for a revival being put to him. 'I don't know if it was Jimmy Mitchell who suggested this, but there was an idea of bringing

Callan back now they're all over the hill. Callan had to go and get old Hunter out of retirement – he was in the South of France in one of those big sun hats, painting – and he turned round and [there was Callan]. I remember talking about it over a drink; maybe [the TV people] didn't think there was enough mileage in it, but I do know that [at the time] Teddy had had enough; he had so many other things going for him.'[4]

By the 1980s any interest from Euston appeared to have waned; Lloyd Shirley said he felt there was 'no particular reason'[5] to revive the series. 'These things tend to have their life, they have a rough relevance when you're doing them, then it's time to move onto something else.' Perhaps mindful of this and of the earlier court case between himself and Thames Television over the film rights to *Callan*, Mitchell opted to revive the Section agent at a different ITV network. 'Jim and I got together as he'd sent me a script about something entirely different,'[6] Edward Woodward recalled. 'We were talking one day and he said, "Look, I've been approached by ATV to do a *Callan* special. Would you be interested?" And I thought, "Hmm, we could see what's happened to the man seven, eight years later." Then I was [formally] asked, and I said, "All things being equal, it might be interesting." It happened to come up at the right time.' Mitchell's recollection was slightly different:'Teddy wanted to do another one. I wasn't sure it was a good idea. We got a big interest from ATV; they very much wanted to do it. Teddy had already planted the idea at ATV and so the three of us [him, Mitchell and O'Riordan] had a talk.'[7]

The Associated TeleVision network – ATV – had begun transmitting in September 1955 as part of the same allocation of regional television franchises from which ABC had been formed. Initially, ATV had the remit to cover the London region at weekends and the Midlands on weekdays; from 1968, in the same shake up of the ITV networks that saw Thames emerge from ABC and Associated Rediffusion, ATV was awarded coverage of the Midlands for a full seven days, an arrangement that lasted until 1 January 1982. The network was chiefly known for its entertainment output, shows marketed through its subsidiary body the Incorporated Television Company (ITC). These film series – *The Saint, Danger Man, Thunderbirds, The Persuaders!* – brought in a great deal of revenue for the British economy, so much so that ITC was awarded the Queen's Award for Industry in 1966. ATV's other global successes included the family series *The Muppet Show* (1976-1981), which alternated between British and American celebrity guests, and the biblical epic *Jesus of Nazareth* (1977), directed by Franco Zeffirelli.

Callan's new home appeared to offer a lot of potential.

'I'M FAIRLY SURE THAT JAMES HAD BEEN TO THAMES and they weren't interested,'[8] Shaun O'Riordan remembered. 'He wanted it totally fresh, and there was no way we would have got [the old title sequence or theme music] out of Thames. James Mitchell approached David Reid [Head of Drama at ATV] with *Wet Job* and there was no question that Edward Woodward and Russell Hunter wouldn't do it. That was fixed: there was no point in making it without them. James was *determined* he wanted it done the way he'd written it – there were no changes.' Events took an ominous turn when Reid departed. 'Because David had gone and there was a new Head of Drama coming in who I didn't get on with at all, either politically or in terms of what I was making, my position was so weak that I didn't feel strongly enough to argue with James about it.

'I have very little doubt that the purpose for which this play was [written] was to reinstitute a *Callan* series, along the lines of the middle-aged Callan,' O'Riordan believed, 'and this was the introduction of how he got back into the business. I think the series would have been done if David Reid had stayed Head of Drama. As it was, what happened was David went to the BBC as the Head of Series and Serials and [his successor] junked it...

'I had no part [in the script] because James said "That's the way I want it." Mind you, I liked James very much indeed. I had a lot of respect and a lot of time for him, but he was determined on this astonishing story where these two idiots pulled this whole building down. He was determined to have that – improbable though it seems – and the reason he did was because he wanted it to be a metaphor for the pulling down of a kind of a society: he wanted to manifest the *pulling down* of capitalism – a big establishment. That's what he had in his mind and that's what I had to do on the screen, and the collapse of the building was one of the most spectacular bits of the show. That was pretty powerful.

'I got [the script], read it, and liked the way it was written. I thought all the scenes with Callan, and Callan and Hunter, were absolutely marvellous. I had just read a book called *The Civil Servants* [by Lord Crowther-Hunt and Peter Kellner], and was *seething* with rage at the effete people who get Firsts from Oxford and Cambridge. They're terrible, smug people who aren't good at anything, but are very, very good at smart-answering, at not giving proper answers, at playing a sort of Delphic, miraculous style of evasion, and I was determined to make my Hunter into the most effete [person] that I could... I had a feeling that [these people] enraged everybody, and... the fact that Hunter wasn't presented as one wants one's leaders to be – he was presented as a cynical, arch, generalist civil servant – [was great].'

For O'Riordan, the production was an unhappy one due to some awful personal news. 'In the second week of rehearsal, my wife discovered she'd got cancer. If you remember, in the play [Haggerty's] daughter had died from lung cancer, and the cause of her getting lung cancer was Callan. I was reading the play, and rehearsing it, and the death of a character from cancer was just another motive until that day. I was in a daze for the whole of the rest of the production. My wife died, and it made me think that you shouldn't be allowed to direct anything unless you *really* know what [the script] means.'

WET JOB

Writer: James Mitchell
Director: Shaun O'Riordan
Designer: David Chandler
First UK transmission: 2 September 1981, 8.30 pm

CAST: Edward Woodward (Callan), Russell Hunter (Lonely), George Sewell (Haggerty), Angela Browne (Margaret), Helen Bourne (Lucy), Hugh Walters (Hunter), Anthony Smee (Thorne), Milos Kerek (Dobrovsky), Donald Hoath (Radlett), Philip Bird (Jebb), Gordon Kane (Pardoe), David Cann (Cawthorne), Josie Kidd (Mrs Radlett), Jeremy Gittins (Robin Miller), Phillip Manikum (Tim), Felicity Harrison (Liz), Mark Draper (Young Man)

PRODUCTION TEAM: *Floor Manager* Guy Frazer-Jones, *Production Assistant* Sue Boyers, *Stage Manager* Sheila Atha, *Make Up Supervisor* Sheila Mann, *Make Up Assisant* Dava Irwin, *Location Administration* Dai Higgon, *Designer* David Chandler , *Programme Administrator* Ron Brown, *Wardrobe Supervisor* Sheila Mann , *Lighting Supervisor* Phil Hawkes, *Senior Cameraman* Bill Brown , *Racks* John Crane, *VTR Editor* Gordon Hunt, *Vision Mixer* Moyra Bird , *Music* Cyril Ornadel, *VTR* A. O'Callaghan

PRODUCTION

Outside Broadcast Recording: Gibson Square, NW1 (Monday 11 May 1981)[9]
'Regimentals', 70 Essex Road, Islington (Monday 11 May 1981);
Northaw House, Northaw Place, Potters Bar (Tuesday 12 - Wednesday 13 May 1981);
Borehamwood Library, Elstree Way, Borehamwood (Thursday 14 May 1981);
Corner of Blenheim Road and Ravenscroft Park Road; Corner of Talvert Road and Puller Road, Barnet (Thursday 14 May 1981)
Camera Rehearsals/Recording: ATV Studio C, Elstree, Wednesday 20-Friday 22 May 1981[10]

TV TIMES: 'Ten years after his last mission secret agent Callan, now a dealer in militaria with his own shop, is prised out of retirement for another assignment.

'To Margaret, Callan's past is part of his charm. But to Callan himself it is a permanent threat – especially when he receives a telephone call from "Charlie". The memoirs of an ex-MP prove very embarrassing.'
29 August – 4 September 1981, Southern edition

MISSION PROFILE: Callan is summoned back to the Section by a new Hunter. Daniel Haggerty, a former left-wing MP, knows about Callan's involvement in the death of Millington, a traitor, and plans to devote a chapter of his autobiography to the incident.

He blames Callan for the death of his daughter, Jenny, who was Millington's lover. Lucy Smith, the niece of Margaret, Callan's landlady, is typing up Haggerty's memoirs; Hunter arranged for her and Callan to become acquainted. The Section chief says he's making Callan aware of the situation, including Haggerty knowing about his identity as 'David Tucker', so he can take 'steps' to protect himself.

Haggerty visits Callan, who now runs a militaria shop, and invites him to Canbury Place, a country house his building firm is demolishing. This is ostensibly to show him some antique guns but Callan realises Haggerty is planning to kill him there. Aware he may be under surveillance, Callan contacts Lonely. The thief brings him his Magnum.

Lucy is emotionally involved with the Czechoslovakian dissident Dubrovsky, a philosopher who has fled his country with the aid of a French gang who have now increased their price. Haggerty supplies her with the extra money needed to bring Dubrovsky to England and hides him at Canbury.

However, the ex-MP is not acting out of altruism: he is a KGB agent. He and his controller, Radlett, arrange to kill Dubrovsky by collapsing a ceiling onto him – the fate Haggerty originally had planned for Callan. Lucy is accidentally killed by the falling debris instead and Radlett and a shaken Haggerty emerge from hiding to murder Dubrovsky. Arriving at Canbury, Callan intervenes, killing Radlett; Haggerty is taken into Section custody. Hunter reveals he had suspected Haggerty of being KGB for some time and by leaking Callan's name to him hoped to provoke the ex-MP into 'an indiscretion'. In a final cynical twist, the Section chief reveals that Lucy was working for him by spying on Callan.

A MAN LIKE ME: Callan is now slightly overweight, wears glasses and is using his old alias permanently. He appears a lot calmer, is charming with women, affects a refined accent and makes a good living from his militaria shop The Old Brigade. He rents a room from the glamorous Margaret Channing and is her on-off lover. He's jealous of her interest in her younger conquest, Robin, and at a house party might be deliberately trying to get him drunk (although this isn't difficult).

When Callan returns to the Section, the first thing he does is ask after the welfare of Toby Meres. He's delighted to see Liz and holds her hand. He was on active service for the Section when he killed Millington. He has heard of Haggerty, but was unaware of his connection with the traitor; the MP's daughter died from cancer contracted from heavy smoking, which she only took up after Millington's death.

Despite moments of his old intimidation, his reunion with Lonely reveals a genuine friendship. Callan went to see him every day in hospital after he was shot by Richmond and, for a wedding present, he gives Lonely two gold Krugerrands. He's both touched by his old colleague's acceptance, as well as hurt by not being invited to the wedding – even though he anticipated that he wouldn't be – showing that he has, perhaps, genuinely mellowed with age after all.

During the reluctant, climactic killing of Radlett, the old killer visibly sweats and keeps his glasses on. There are still traces of Callan's vicious streak, as he deliberately shoots at the new Section man Thorne to frighten him.

Section Kills: 29 (including Millington).

LONELY: Reintroduced singing in Margaret's shower while he mends it. Now a qualified plumber as the proprietor of 'Fresh and Fragrant Bathroom Installations'. The ex-thief learned plumbing on one of his visits to 'the nick'. (There is a continuity error with respect to the original series as that stated he learned to read in prison, but the ability has deserted him here). Lonely really *has* gone straight, running a legitimate business and he's about to be married to his fiancée Mariella – 'she admits to 29' – with a honeymoon planned in Florida. He's terrified of becoming involved with Callan again, initially refusing to help, even though he's offered £50, then £100.

Callan plays on his loyalty and eventually Lonely agrees to help him, retrieving his Magnum .368, some ammunition and gold Krugerrands from Callan's bank deposit box. Even though he's terrified when handing the gun over to Callan, he can still recognise a 'hard geezer' and can elude anyone tailing him. As in the novel *A Magnum for Schneider*, he conceals the smuggled gun in a bag of veg. His self-esteem has improved enough for him to stand up to Callan's intimidation, forcefully reminding the ex-killer that he's not as young as he used to be.

A TIE AND A CREST: The new Hunter served in Washington with Toby Meres – who has met an ignominious end, murdered by an Embassy official he cuckolded.

Thorne is the Section's new upper class man. He says little but clearly considers Callan to be obsolete – 'strictly speaking, you're far too old for this sort of thing' – until the older man scares him by shooting at him.

According to Hunter, people in the Liberal Party 'wouldn't do at all' as spies (perhaps an oblique refernece to ex-leader Jeremy Thorpe, who in 1981 had been involved in a sex scandal).

ALCOHOL, TOBACCO AND FIREARMS: There is an unbelievable amount of alcohol washing around this final TV story. Margaret is fond of Harvey Wallbanger cocktails, as is her toy boy Robin. At her party, Callan serves white wine; Lucy has a gin and tonic. The guests all appear to over indulge, Robin passing out and having to be taken home.

Back in the Section, Callan takes his customary glass of Chivas Regal and again drinks when he gets back to Margaret's flat. When Lonely visits to fix the shower, he and Callan toast the ex-criminal's marriage with Margaret's whisky. The retired agent again has a whisky when he meets Lonely at his shop and *again* when Thorne calls. Feeling rejected after finding Robin with a young woman, Margaret hits the bottle and tells Callan 'It's time this old drunk was in bed.'

Dubrovsky and Lucy share whisky after an unsuccessful attempt at making love.

Even though Callan initially lays off the booze as he prepares for his mission, he has a fortifying slug from his hip flask on site before he goes into action. Debriefed by Hunter, he takes *another* Scotch, before hitting the bottle to confront Margaret about Robin, and his landlady joins him in quaffing the booze. Even while seemingly half-cut, Callan is able to throw the younger man out easily.

Various vintage guns are on display in both The Old Brigade and at Canbury Place, while Haggerty tries to sell Callan two WW2 Luger and Mauser guns, although the ex-agent doesn't have a licence to sell them. Since leaving the Section, Callan has kept a .357 Magnum and ammunition in his bank's safety deposit box.

SPY-SPEAK: The new Hunter is as dispassionate as his predecessors: 'She was on 60 [cigarettes] a day. She didn't smoke at all before you shot Millington,' he tells Callan, amiably.

The ex-agent reflects on what he was told when he left the Section: '"It's over," they said. "Why don't you just go back home and take your pension and start your little business? Because it's all over," they said.' 'You know they lied,' Hunter responds. 'It's never over.'

Margaret is proud of never being unfaithful to her husband when he was alive. 'You have made up for it a bit since,' Callan sardonically reminds her.

Lonely enlightens Callan on the reason for his new found personal freshness: 'I haven't niffed since the last time I worked with you!'

PAWNS AND PLAYERS: SHAUN O'RIORDAN (born 1927) began his entertainment career as a child actor, appearing first in the crime movie *The Wallet* (1952) and then, between 1958 and 1960 in *The Larkins*, one of ITV's first soap operas, as son of the house Eddie.

After playing several parts in ITC's *The Adventures of Robin Hood* (1956-57), O'Riordan switched careers, working behind the camera as a director/producer. He juggled comedy and drama, helming shows like *The Worker* (1969) starring Charlie Drake, as well as seven episodes of the anthology series *Thriller* (1973-75), including 'Nurse Will Make It Better', in which Diana Dors played the Devil, exorcised by Patrick Troughton's alcoholic priest. O'Riordan's bigest success as a producer/director was undoubtedly the disturbing fantasy series *Sapphire and Steel* (1979-1982), starring David McCallum and Joanne Lumley as two mysterious investigators. Originally intended for children, ATV felt the series was strong enough to appeal to adults and it was given an evening time slot. 'Shaun was a one-off,'[11] actor Philip Bird believed. 'Independent, cussed, always right. As the producer as well as the director he could do what he wanted without having to go to a committee or seek permission, although I suspect if he weren't the producer he would have given whoever *was* the producer a hard time. As it was, he could just argue with himself.'

GEORGE SEWELL (1924-2007) was born the son of a Hackney printer and florist. Before going into acting he pursued a variety of careers, including training to be an RAF pilot, serving in the merchant navy as a steward, as well as being a travel courier, photographer and drummer. Age 35, he auditioned for Joan Littlewood's radical Theatre Workshop and won roles in three productions: *Fings Ain't Wot They Used T'Be* (1959) – tailor made for Sewell, as it was a musical about the vibrant cockney culture he'd grown up in – *Sparrers Can't Sing* (1962) and *Oh! What a Lovely War* (1963), in which the East Ender played the WW1 commander Field Marshal Haig.

Breaking into television, Sewell's rough diamond looks brought him roles playing tough characters in the boardroom drama *The Power Game* (from 1965-66) as Hagadan, a rival for the affections of Sir John Wilder's wife, and *Man in a Suitcase*, as a cowardly villain in the memorable story 'The Sitting Pigeon' (1968). His first star part on television was Colonel Alec Freeman in Gerry and Sylvia Anderson's premier live-action film series *UFO* (1970-73). Sewell left after the first production block of episodes, to appear as the London gangster Con in the Michael Caine thriller *Get Carter* (1971).

When Euston Films revamped the Thames series *Special Branch*, Sewell was cast as one of the two leads, Detective Chief Inspector Alan Craven, part of a formidable double act with Patrick Mower's DCI Tom Haggerty, between 1973 and 1974. The two series of *Special Branch* the duo starred in were ratings hits, preparing the British public for Euston's follow-up series *The Sweeney* (1975-78). The two actors both returned as guest stars in that series, Sewell playing the vicious Vic Tolman in the episode 'Bait' (1978). Like a significant percentage of the acting profession between 1963 and 1989, Sewell took part in *Doctor Who*, playing the British Fascist Ratcliffe in 1988's 'Remembrance of the Daleks'. The comedy series *The Detectives* (1993-97) found him sending up his 1970s tough guy image as Superintendent Frank Cottam, the exasperated boss of two inept coppers played by Jasper Carrott and Robert Powell.

ANGELA BROWNE (1938-2001) established her reputation as an actress with a series of well-received stage roles in the 1950s that included *The Marriage Go Round*, *The Bride Comes Back* and *Wolf's Clothing*. She married the actor Francis Matthews in 1963 and, choosing to concentrate on her marriage and two sons, began taking on TV roles as the production schedules were shorter than in theatre and film. With a gift for the American accent, Browne played the regular part of Sergeant Yolanda Perkins in the US co-production *Court Martial* (1965-66) and McGill's old flame Rachel Thyssen in the *Man in a Suitcase* story 'Man from the Dead' (1967). Her children attended the same Catholic school as Patrick McGoohan's family, which may be why she was one of the few actresses to work with the actor more than once, firstly in *Danger Man* – 'The Girl in Pink Pyjamas' (1960) and then *The Prisoner* – 'A Change of Mind' (1967), as the neurosurgeon Number 86.

HUGH WALTERS (1939-2015) was consistently employed in British TV and film as a consummate supporting actor. 'They always say there are three stages in an actor's career,'[12] he recalled. '"Who shall we get to play this part?" "Hugh Walters, he's dead right." The second one is "This is a Hugh Walters part", so I get the part, and the last one is "Who can we get to play the Hugh Walters part?"'

One of his stand-out roles was the crippled Vic Thatcher in the first series of the BBC's eco-apocalypse thriller *Survivors* (1975): 'I took over from Terry Scully at very short notice and [the director] rang me up and asked me to get on the next train. I went to Television Centre, picked up the script and learnt it [on the way there] and we started the next day. I crawled up the stairs, me and Myra [Frances] ended up in bed and got terrible giggles as we couldn't work out how they made love if [Vic's] legs didn't work, because there was no push. It was a very giggly scene.'

From there, Walters became one of the regular cast in the historical saga *Clayhanger* (1976), the soap opera *Gems* (1981-88) and worked with the late David Bowie when he took the lead role in the director Alan Clarke's version of *Baal* (1982) for the BBC. Like George Sewell, Walters appeared in *Doctor Who* (in 1965, 1976 and 1985).[13]

HELEN BOURNE enjoyed only her third TV role with *Wet Job*. In 1971, she'd been in the cast of ATV's *ITV Sunday Night Theatre* production 'Hamlet', featuring Richard Chamberlain and John Gielgud; the production was nominated for a record breaking thirteen Emmy awards and won five. She followed that in 1979 with the part of Mrs Karamanopolis in the ground-breaking children's series *Grange Hill* (1978-2000). Following *Wet Job*, Bourne won her most prestigious TV role, as Martha Bernays in the BBC's production of *Freud* (1984), opposite David Suchet as the famous psychiatrist.

PHILIP BIRD's first role was as a swamp dweller in *Doctor Who* – 'The Power of Kroll' (1978). 'The punk band I was in had broken up and I got a call asking me if I wanted to be an extra on the show,'[14] the musician, actor and writer remembered. 'I had to get up at stupid o'clock and catch the train to Woodbridge where a few of us were picked up and taken to Snape marshes.' Bird was originally only supposed to work on the location filming, but was invited to participate in the studio recording too and during production, make-up artist Kezia Dewinne offered him some useful career advice: 'If I wanted to be an actor, she said, don't take any more roles as a supporting artist. I hadn't realised there was a difference.'

His first full acting role was in another iconic telefantasy series, *Sapphire and Steel* (1980), in a story where he played a malign being without a face. Ironically, under the make-up the actor was almost as unsettled as the viewing audience. 'The fitting of the mask to cover my face was fairly frightening; I just had a little straw to breathe through while they slapped stuff all over my face and I felt very vulnerable and claustrophobic. I remember standing in front of a blue screen so that they could isolate me and slot me into various photographs (the character I played, The Shape, was a kind of Zelig who could hide in photographs) and it was terribly important that I stayed on the mark and all the movements were exact. My eyes were opened to the kinds of things actors are asked to do. It's not just shouting in the evenings.' Bird's other credits include *Reilly – Ace of Spies* (1983), one of John Thaw's final series. *The Glass* (2001), *Fresh Fields* (1984-86), its sequel *French Fields* (1991) and the BBC3 horror thriller *The Fades* (2011), which he describes as 'extraordinary. The atmosphere at the read-through was really special, and we all felt we were hearing something unique and thrilling.'

INFORMATION: By 1981, Outside Broadcast technology had developed to the point where all location scenes could be professionally recorded on video. With exterior and studio sequences both using the same medium, *Wet Job* has a uniform look different to many of the 1960s and 1970s *Callan* productions, even if the quality of the image isn't as high as it would have been if *Wet Job* had been made on film, or even recorded on 1970s-style studio video.

'Yet again [Callan] is jockeyed into doing something,'[15] James Mitchell remarked, 'getting rid of an extreme leftie, one of these firebrand characters who pops up from time to time – but who in actual fact is a sleeper for the KGB.' This part of the story may have its origin in conspiracy theories about the British Labour leader Harold Wilson (1916-1995), who won four general elections during the 1960s and 1970s. The KGB officer Anatoliy Golitsyn (see 'Red Knight, White Knight', Chapter 6) told his interrogators that Wilson was a KGB agent and that the previous Labour leader, Hugh Gaitskell (1906-1963) had been assassinated so Wilson could take over. For several years, MI5 kept an open file on the MP and Prime Minister, before concluding that Wilson had no connection with the KGB. Golitsyn has remained a controversial figure in intelligence circles ever since. The character of Dobrovsky is, again, likely to have been inspired by Aleksandr Solzhenitsyn.

Told that Toby Meres had met his end following an ill-judged dalliance with a diplomat's wife, Anthony Valentine roared with laughter. 'About time, too, I would have thought! Yes, a perfectly good end, very likely. [I'm] surprised it hadn't happened a long time before.'[16]

According to O'Riordan, recalling Lisa Langdon to play Liz was not considered.

'It was a one-off, and as far as I know there was never any intention to carry on and do a series,'[17] Hugh Walters remembered, an opinion curiously at odds with his producer/director's. 'One of my friends, David Reid, had been, the Head of Drama at ATV. When I was in short trousers, I took over Shaun [O'Riordan's] part in *The Larkins*, back in the '60s.

'I'd never watched the original series [of *Callan*]. Obviously one knew its reputation and what it was about, but I'd never seen it. They wanted someone who [could play] upper class, was young, had gone straight into the secret service [from university] and who had got himself, either through work or double dealing, up to the top. [Edward and I] had a big interview, in that scene where [Hunter] comes across as rather superior... It was very much an "establishment" thing.

'The funny thing we all found was that Edward, who was playing Callan – and this is what ten, fifteen years later? – kept saying "How am I going to look older?" And we all bit our lips, because when we were doing rehearsals, it was obvious that he wore a "cap" [toupeé]. And none of us dared tell him, "Take the cap off, dear, 'cos you're bald on top!"

'Everyone seemed to be very happy with [*Wet Job*]. They sent me a tape of it but I wasn't able to play it on my machine – that's how long ago it was. I didn't know Russell Hunter, although we nearly crossed at Bristol [Old Vic], as I was supposed to be in the Shakespeare play *The Two Gentlemen of Verona*. I couldn't do it, because I got the part of Smyke with Martin Jarvis on television, so Russell came along and took over my part. He'd been at [the] Bristol [Old Vic] quite a lot. [Edward] was a nice man. I did *Sword of Honour* with him, which was one of the first BBC things made in colour. He was very easy to work with. He was a proper actor – some are and some aren't. A very good actor and a good singer too.'

'I was aware of the series, and of its being unusually realistic in its portrayal of the world of spies and contract killers,'[18] Philip Bird recalled. 'Callan the character had no particular relish for killing: it was just his unglamorous job. James Bond this wasn't. I had been a huge fan of *Danger Man*, and Patrick McGoohan's *The Prisoner* shared Woodward's refusal to play for sympathy.

'We rehearsed in long rooms at the far end of ATV Elstree. Those rooms have now been transformed into the set for *Holby City* [1999-], which made me feel a bit odd when I went back to do an episode of that show. The interior scenes were recorded in the studio, but the exteriors were outside an old condemned house in Hertfordshire; I had a day wandering about in the nearby fields in the sunshine. To get the sense of scale inside I think the whole studio was given over to the big galleried room where the ceiling fell in.

'Shaun had this thing about shooting people's feet in this production. He would build the tension just by showing shoes walking into a room, while the audience tries to work out whose they are. That, and having to write the figure "£5,000" while talking in French, taught me something early in my career about what an actor is asked to do: tell the story without using one's face. I still think I annoyed Shaun by writing the "£"sign last, and indeed by not writing the number fluently, but with breaks. I thought I was acting rather naturalistically, but I don't think I did that biro close-up very well. It might have helped for me to have seen the first take back, and then I may have realised what was needed, but in those days the control room was miles away, and anyway there was very little of that clustering around the monitor watching playback that there is nowadays.

'The main thing I remember is all the Fuller's Earth everywhere. The set was of course very bare, and the sound bounced off the walls. I didn't have much to say in the scene, so just tried to keep the feeling going between takes and set-ups. The collapse of the ceiling could only really be shot once, so they had to get it right. With big stunts like that the atmosphere on set is always highly charged. There are no second chances, so it feels closer to live theatre than simple dialogue scenes, which are easy to retake if necessary. I wasn't in the studio to see the close-up of Donald [Hoath]'s face as he was shot.

'Hugh Walters was lovely. I worked with him again the following year in *The Agatha Christie Hour* [1982] for Thames, in 'The Mystery of the Blue Jar'. I played a Frenchman in that, and in fact I wouldn't be surprised if Hugh, having seen me speak French on *Wet Job*, put in a word for me to Cyril Coke, the director. He was that kind of generous man. George Sewell was a gentleman. I didn't have any scenes with Russell Hunter, much to my disappointment.'

Russell himself was dissatisfied with *Wet Job* and was typically frank about it. 'I didn't think it was a good idea,'[19] he said. 'I didn't see the actual telly – [but] judging from what went on at the studio, it was not a good idea, from anyone's point of view, to have done it again. I think if you wanted to do it again, it would have been better to have gone back to the beginning and do a series of [one hours] – certainly not a 90-minute "spectacular".

'I did it, I hasten to add, not only to earn some money, [but] because I felt I owed an allegiance to *Callan*. Not just to Teddy, not just to Jimmy Mitchell, I owed something to myself. The programme had been very kind to me, it had given me a lot of good times and if there was one thing I did not want to do, it was to see somebody else play Lonely! After all, I'd already seen at least a couple of other people play it in those cod adverts for beer, where actors had been dressed to look like Russell Hunter as Lonely. Knowing the actors in question, they were *told,* "We want you to look exactly like Russell Hunter as Lonely in *Callan*." One of them I know actually did say, "Why the hell don't you get him?" "Oh no, that would be plagiarism!"

'I did feel I *owed* the character something, and when I agreed to do it I thought it was going to be quite different. It did get very soft, I thought, very soft and complicated. [Lonely becoming a respectable figure] was a mystery to me. I did not know about that when I agreed to play the part. I think that was just a load of rubbish.

'In a funny way, I think it was somebody saying "Look, if this is successful and we go into another series, we'll go in clean with just Callan and nobody else. This'll get rid of Lonely – we'll marry him off: the public like him, we won't kill him off. If necessary, he'll always be in the bank to be dug up, or cashed in one day as a character, if we need him in a future episode." I *do* think a lot of that kind of thinking went on; that that was not a farewell to *Callan*, that was "Hello" to a new series – but it just didn't work. I doubt I would have taken part in the new series. I doubt it even more if it had been scripted that way and "glamorised".'

'I don't think it's always necessarily so that you shouldn't go back, sometimes it works when you go back, but I think we went back in the wrong way,'[20] Edward Woodward agreed. 'I would have liked it to have been written in such a way that [Callan] couldn't cope [with the job] anymore. The powers that be didn't exactly veto that idea – they didn't mind something totally downbeat – but, really, [*Wet Job*] went straight down the middle: it was really neither fish nor fowl.'

He continued, 'To start with, we didn't have the team, we didn't have a director who'd worked on the *Callan* series and there was a whole thing – I don't know where it came from, the hierarchy [of ATV] or wherever – of wanting to change relationships, and I think only to be different because it wasn't Thames doing it; I've got a feeling that's what it was about. But, you know, as an actor you do what you have to do, but you try desperately to keep faith with the characters, and we found it very difficult to do that. The worst thing about it was that the Lonely/Callan relationship was funnied up, and it should never have been funnied up. It was fun – and funny – because of the characters, it wasn't funny because of the dialogue, and they funnied it up with all that business about the plumber and the shower. I don't think it worked at all and I think [ATV] might have thought it was going to go on as a series, but I know that Russ and I didn't. It wasn't good enough to happen. It just was not good enough.'[21]

Woodward and Hunter's misgivings were shared by their former producer. 'I accidentally caught the episode from ATV and it was a joke,'[22] Reg Collin stated bluntly. 'I'm not knocking it, it's not sour grapes, [but] it seemed to me like a batsman might go out and make six runs... then go out again and make two hundred runs – same batsman, same bat – but there is a change that happens that makes it work. That change was *not* in the ATV version.'

Reflecting on *Wet Job*, Mitchell feels there was another reason why a full-scale revival wouldn't have worked: 'It was all right to do it the once, looking back more in sorrow than in anger, but you couldn't make a whole series out of that [idea], because you'd have to bring in somebody else to do the rough stuff. People are thumping people and climbing walls – you've got to be young! And then it would be the other man's series, not Callan's. I think you'd have [had] a different emphasis: less Mossad, less SS men – more [contemporary threats]. Espionage isn't tied to [one] time; it goes on all the time.'[23]

Despite the team's misgivings, *Wet Job* was a ratings success. It made the top ten of eight of the thirteen ITV regions (those where it didn't were Lancashire, North East Scotland, South West, Ulster and Yorkshire) and was sixth nationally for the week of 9-15 May on ITV, opposite *Larry Grayson's Generation Game* in the ratings for BBC1 and *Cricket: Sixth Test* (the Tuesday edition) on BBC2.[24]

Despite the encouraging audience reaction, the press coverage was negative, and this response, coupled with the internal changes at ATV, may have been a deciding factor in there being no further revivals. 'Television chiefs often cannot resist the temptation to repeat a popular formula that has also been a critical success... [and] in itself, [a revival] is not a bad idea,'[25] the *Daily Express* TV critic reasoned. 'The thought of a middle-aged Callan, more or less comfortably settled for ten years, suddenly being called back to his old lifestyle as a secret service agent, has possibilities [but] what little dramatic intensity this plot had was soon decimated. Not least of all by everyone perpetually pouring themselves a Scotch – were they drowning their sorrows?... It was disappointing that such a noble piece of work as the original *Callan* should come to this.'

The Daily Telegraph had little sympathy: 'It was all a long way from the sophistication of John le Carré's *Tinker Tailor*... now starting a repeat on BBC2.'[26] In *The Observer*, Clive James decided that the enterprise was misconceived: 'With Callan still played by Edward Woodward, this was not, alas, a repeat. If it had been, one might have clucked over it with some fondness. Instead there was an emptily up-to-date story climaxed with the most boring line in television: "You set me up, didn't you?"'[27]

Describing the story as 'thin'[28], *The Sunday Times* offered the following insight into what was, and wasn't, successful about Callan's 1981 resurrection: 'There were obviously fine possibilities in Callan's relationship with his smelly minion Lonely... but it didn't seem to have a lot to do with the story in this case.' *The Guardian* possibly summed up the feelings of the audience by saying, 'The crumbling of Callan is a not an untouching aspect of the story... [But] there may be a limit to the decrepitude a faithful fan will take and probably Callan should take it no further than this.'[29]

Although the title wasn't fully explained in the teleplay, 'wet job' is intelligence slang for an execution, particularly one in which blood is spilt. In 1979, the Scottish New Wave band Fingerpintz released their debut LP *The Very Dab*. In a striking coincidence, the album includes the song 'Wet Job', about the assassination of the Bulgarian defector Georgi Markov with a poison-tipped umbrella.

MISSION ANALYSIS: *'I don't want to do it. Christ, I don't know if I can do it – not any more'.* Nearly ten years on from when *Callan* ended in 1972, its revival could have been marketed as an anniversary special and made by Euston Films. An obvious option would have been to use an outline similar to *Russian Roulette*, with Callan in jeopardy from being middle-aged and over the hill and producing a gritty *Sweeney*-style action thriller, working in plenty of screen time with Lonely, together with cameos from the regular and recurring cast.

To its credit, *Callan* has always avoided the obvious; *Wet Job* sees the concept returning to its roots, in another modestly budgeted video production, in effect introducing Callan.2, a man who, like Mitchell and Woodward themselves, had got older and gone up in the world.

It's not fully comparing like with like, but there are some historic parallels with the wittily written, modestly successful maverick James Bond film *Never Say Never Again* (1983). Made by a completely different team to that of the 'official' 007 films, this film was also influenced by a past court case, could not use any of the familiar opening title iconography or theme music, and by necessity recast many of its standard characters, with the exception of the essential male lead, Sean Connery. Sadly, contrasting these two revivals in hindsight, it has to be said the attempt to update *Callan*, as the press reviews of the time – and, crucially, Woodward and Hunter themselves noted – was not as successful.

Wet Job is slow (amazingly, O'Riordan cut an additional 20 minutes) and variably directed (which is understandable, considering what was going on in the director's personal life). There is some atmospheric camerawork and the ceiling collapse of Canbury Place is well staged, but elsewhere the production seems uncertain as to whether it's a thriller, a melodrama or a blottoed black farce. Award winning musician Cyril Ornadel's scores greatly enhanced the atmosphere of *Sapphire and Steel*, but here his compositions seem misjudged, often so intrusive they actively reinforce Reg Collin's view that *Callan* doesn't *need* music. The biggest failing, however, is that Callan himself and Lonely hardly ever engage with the main plot. At times, it seems as if two separate scripts – one about the exposure of a left-wing MP as a Soviet agent and another about a dissident on the run – have been cobbled together, with a few two-hander scenes featuring Lonely bolted on afterwards. Needless to say, Valentine's Toby Meres is badly missed.

Predictably, the best things in *Wet Job* are the two scenes between Woodward and Russell Hunter. The leading man is absolutely spot-on as an older, mellower version of his character, memorably sparring with excellent new recruit Hugh Walters' arch Section chief, as well as awkwardly rebuilding relations with a now more assertive – but still easily terrified – Lonely.

The best scene in the whole production is when Lonely shows Callan a photograph of his fiancée Mariella. Callan says 'very nice', pockets the snap and calmly walks out of the room, leaving Lonely to try and swallow down the fear he's suddenly feeling. If anything sums up the old magic, it's this one moment of subtlety in a production where the mature characters repeatedly say how old (translation: past it) they are.

In a generally strong supporting cast, Philip Bird and Helen Bourne do well, George Sewell gives his usual reliable performance and Angela Brown is convincing as Margaret Channing, an attractive, middle-aged woman worried about losing her looks and drinking too much. As the end titles roll, however, you can't help feeling that Callan deserves better than Margaret and that *Callan* the series certainly deserved a better epitaph than *Wet Job*.

This is by no means *bad* television, but it's the weakest of the TV stories and is a wasted opportunity. Perhaps the obvious option would have been a better approach, after all.

12: MI5 not 9 to 5

'You take a knife and you sharpen it and sharpen
it 'til it'll slit a silk scarf. Then one day you drop
it on a stone floor. After that, it'll still cut bread,
but the silk scarves are safe.'

Innocent Bystanders, 1972

'Cold War – we won. You lost.'

Spooks, 2004

T THE END OF THE 1960S, having lost the opportunity to make 'A Magnum for Schneider', it seems that for its own rival espionage series the BBC attempted to reap some of the benefits of *Callan*'s success, specifically by poaching one of its leading men, Anthony Valentine. BBC2 were clearly expecting great things of *Codename*, their new series. Having achieved a casting coup with one of ITV's stars, the channel also allocated location filming in Portugal to the show and promoted it on the front cover of the *Radio Times* for the week of its premiere episode in April 1970. This programme is one of the various possible legacies from, or *homages* to, *Callan*'s impact and influence.

Codename was a spin-off from an August 1969 pilot play called *Codename: Portcullis*, a 'terribly British tale of improbable espionage'[1]. Devised by Bill Hays and David Sullivan Proudfoot and produced by the experienced Gerard Glaister, the follow-up series was also based around the exploits of an undercover spy unit, called MI17 and based in a Cambridge University college. Valentine joined the ranks to play the department's heroic field agent Philip West, under the command of the intellectual Sir Iain Dalzell (Clifford Evans); West was assisted by Dalzell's daughter, Diana (Alexandra Bastedo) and the working-class handyman Culliford (Brian Peck). While the cover story of a disused school and scrapyard may have been swapped for a university setting, the parallels with some of *Callan*'s line up of characters are obvious. Bastedo had previously played another secret agent in the ITV adventure series *The Champions* (1969-1970), indicating that while *Codename* may have been imitating some of *Callan*'s format, it really had more in common with *Department S* (1969-1970) and *The Man from UNCLE*. Unusually for a BBC production of the time, the pilot was made entirely on film. As Valentine told the *Daily Mirror*, 'It's a Bond-ish sort of series, intended to be humorous and not cerebrally taxing.'[2]

This lighter approach to TV espionage was already dated by 1970 and perhaps this was why the critics were not too impressed. 'There are some programmes so fatuous that you steer well clear of them and hope a foreign power will blow them up. *Codename* is one of them,'[3] wrote a particularly affronted *Daily Sketch* critic, while, after watching the whole series, a *Daily Telegraph* reviewer offered a more considered appraisal: '*Codename* has had an up-and-down run, sometimes suggesting that it had caught the right pattern for a successful parody while at other times failing hopelessly by taking itself too seriously.'[4] As far as Anthony Valentine was concerned one series was enough, and he wasn't too unhappy when *Codename* wasn't re-commissioned.

In March 1972, two weeks after *Callan*'s fourth year began transmission, the BBC tried again. Robert Barr (who had previously written for *Spycatcher* and *Codename*) devised an ambitious new series called *Spy Trap*, which, in a departure for the BBC, was initially shown four nights a week for three weeks, and then twice-weekly. Transmitted at 7 pm complete with a catchy theme tune, the show was a commendable attempt to provide early evening drama that wasn't soap opera, the more typical genre for the time slot. This time the emphasis was on seriousness. Paul Daneman (Commander Ryan), Prentis Hancock (Lieutenant Sanders) and Julian Glover (Commander Anderson) starred as three Naval Intelligence interrogators. (Coincidentally or not, Glover had just played another interrogator – for the opposition – in the first episode of *Callan*'s fourth series on 1 March.)

Glover remembered there being a distinct lack of preparation on the series. 'We had nothing to work with when it came to building up our characters – there were no notes, no biographies, nothing. That made the scripts very hard to do, not least for the writers, so Paul and I sat down and wrote up character histories for ourselves; I decided that Anderson came from Scotland, I remember. Because of all the proactive stuff we did, the producer decided I was a troublemaker, and I was dropped. I've never been a troublemaker in my life!'[5]

Despite the cast's attempt to make their characterisations more three-dimensional, Glover's misgivings about *Spy Trap* were reflected in the press coverage. 'As the characters are not drawn with any great vigour, the only interest is to see who is double-crossing whom,'[6] observed *The Daily Telegraph*. 'It is like watching a rather dull game of poker.' As with *Codename*, which had been shown at 8pm, *Spy Trap*'s transmission time was seen as a hindrance rather than a help. 'Such an early evening slot means a palpably small budget and absence of violence and squalor,' remarked the *Telegraph* again, 'which apparently make for popularity as well as verisimilitude.'[7] Despite not being an outright critical hit as *Callan* had been, the series also ran for four years, with Glover replaced by Tom Adams as Major Sullivan. Notably, after *Callan* ended, Anthony Valentine and William Squire both had guest roles, and as with *Codename*, *Callan* writers contributed some of the scripts.[8]

IN LATE 1972, THE FEATURE FILM VERSION of James Mitchell's last John Craig novel *The Innocent Bystanders* was released, starring a convincingly world-weary Stanley Baker as the Department K agent. Directed by Peter Collinson, who had previously helmed *The Italian Job* (1969) and shot on location in Spain and Turkey, stylistically the movie is caught between OO7 motifs and the brutal realism of Mitchell's original novel. For every cruel scene accurately recreated from the book – such as the merciless reprisals of Russian gulag guards as some prisoners attempt a gaol break, Craig's interrogation by US intelligence agents where just the suggestion of torture makes him scream, and the vicious physical assault on Miriam Loman (Geraldine Chaplin) by the dead-eyed Department K agent Andrew Royce (Derren Nesbitt) – there's an off-key touch. Copying the Bond films' tradition of including a song on the soundtrack by a fashionable singer (in this case 'What Makes the Man' by Hurricane Smith[9]) seems completely out of place, as does the scene where K agent Joanna Benson (Sue Lloyd) does a comic mime for a Turkish police-man who doesn't understand English.

While it was good to see John Craig finally brought to the screen in the wake of *Callan*'s success, the schizophrenic nature of *Innocent Bystanders* suggested creative tension and compromises behind the scenes. Despite this, the film shares common themes with *Callan*. Royce, a young agent, is keen to usurp Craig as Department K's top man – 'We should be ashamed of ourselves, beating old men... Old, and just a little bit past it' – and espionage work is portrayed as a life sentence as much as a career: 'That last job spoiled you. Do you still dream about it?' spy chief Loomis (Donald Pleasence) asks Craig. 'One more job, make or break... [If you fail] you'll be here 'til you die, sharpening pencils.' However, in a month that included the release of the strong movies *Duel*, *The Offence* and *The Candidate*, in a review typical of the press reviews, the film magazine *Sight and Sound* wasn't overly impressed with *Innocent Bystanders*: 'Crisp but formula postscript to the spy thriller cycle, with sundry agents on the trail of a Russian scientist and the familiar [Thomas] Cook's tour of locations. Peter Collinson for once directs without excess, but that's the only novelty.'[10]

AFTER *CALLAN* ENDED, story editor George Markstein put his experience of working on television spy series, as well as his knowledge of real-world espionage, to use in the first of several novels. Published in 1974, *The Cooler* sold a remarkable 200,000 copies, the book's minimalist descriptive prose, screenplay-friendly dialogue and complex plotting telling the story of the secret establishment Inverlair Lodge in Scotland, a WW2 holding facility for Allied agents who have become unreliable. Like all Markstein's subsequent spy novels, it was partly inspired by fact; the real Scottish estate of Inverloch had fulfilled exactly the same function. Fact and fiction were again mixed in *Ultimate Issue* (1981), when the Russian attaché Eugene Ivanov, a central figure in the Profumo scandal, appears in a story revealing that Western intelligence agencies knew about the East's plan to construct the Berlin Wall well in advance. (As in *Callan*, the western spies are frequently just as ruthless as their opponents.)

Other novels explored such Cold War themes as sleeper agents (*Chance Awakening*, 1977), the dangerous possibility of a Fourth Reich (*The Goering Testament*, 1978), the loy-alties of defectors (*Traitor for a Cause*, 1979), spy planes (*Ferret*, 1983) and the fear that a Western army officer would turn rogue and attack the Eastern Bloc (*Soul Hunters*, 1986). Markstein would occasionally drop hints that these stories were inspired by real events, keeping his readers, colleagues and friends guessing to the end of his life about how much or little real involvement he had in the twilight world that he wrote about.[11] De-spite the popularity of these books, none of them were adapted for TV or film, although Robert Banks Stewart recalled, 'George was paid on *enormous* amount of money for those days for the film rights to *The Cooler* – £90,000 – [but] they never made it.'[12]

BACK ON BRITISH TELEVISION, as a critic noted, 'The spy game is catching. Televi-sion on all channels is obsessed with it.'[13] So it continued throughout the 1970s, with spy fiction equally as popular as it had been in the 1960s; not surprisingly, as the Cold War was still headline news. In addition to the last gasp of the escapist ITC adventure shows with a spy slant, *The Persuaders!* (1971-72), *Jason King* (1972-73), *The Adventurer* (1972-73) – by far the most ridiculous of the genre, with an internationally famous film star some-how able to function as a secret agent – *The Protectors* (1972-74) and the decent but slightly dated *Return of the Saint* (1978-79), there was a further BBC attempt at establishing their own spy thriller in *Quiller* (1975), based on the lone operator created by novelist 'Adam Hall', previously seen in the 1966 feature film *The Quiller Memorandum*.

Starring Michael Jayston (who had previously appeared in *Callan* – 'God Help Your Friends', Chapter 7) the programme suffered from a limited budget, which resulted in a series about an international troubleshooter mainly being made in the Home Counties. Despite some limited overseas filming, the constraints on the production were obvious. 'We were meant to be in Guatemala,'[14] Jayston recalled, 'and we were on Littlehampton beach in Sussex because it had some palm trees. But it was raining! It was ludicrous.' The involvement of 'Hall' himself (real name Elleston Trevor) and *The Avengers*' Brian Clemens on the writing side wasn't enough to make the actor commit to a proposed second series and subsequently the BBC shelved *Quiller*.

ONE PECULIAR PART of *Callan*'s legacy was a strip in a boy's comic.[15] *Action*, launched by IPC in 1976, included strips unashamedly plagiarised from either popular films of the time – *Hook Jaw* (*Jaws*, 1975), *Death Game 1999* (*Rollerball*, 1975 again) – and, in the case of *Dredger,* a certain TV series. The source of the strip seems obvious when considering the cockney secret agent uses a Magnum revolver (although also favoured by 'Dirty' Harry Callahan in the popular Clint Eastwood films) and is partnered with Simon Breed, a blazer-wearing, upper-class colleague. Just like its source material, *Action* attracted criticism for its violent content and Mary Whitehouse of the National Viewers' and Listeners Association tried to have the publication banned.[16]

The *Dredger* strip was certainly more extreme than anything seen in *Callan*. A suspect is dissolved by acid sprayed into his shower, and on one occasion Dredger lashes an enemy soldier to the front of a rocket launcher and threatens to fire it. Perhaps worryingly in a comic aimed at youngsters, Dredger didn't show any remorse for the callous actions he practised in the name of state security. The media controversy wouldn't go away and, fearing a boycott of the title by WH Smith and other newsagents, IPC re-launched *Action* with significantly toned-down stories. Sales fell and in 1977 the comic was merged with *Battle Picture Weekly* (1975-1988). *Dredger* survived the reformatting but in a toned down form.

ADAPTED FROM KENNETH ROYCE'S original novels, *The XYY Man* (1976-77), starring Stephen Yardley as Willie 'Spider' Scott, a habitual cat burglar used and abused by the security services, was a successful crime and espionage hybrid for ITV. What's really striking is that when William Squire features as the British intelligence executive Laidlaw in *The XYY Man*'s second series, the characterisation is almost identical to that of his Hunter, a clear indication of where the production team got some of their inspiration. The spin-off *Strangers* (1978-82), built around the supporting characters of Detective Sergeant Bulman (Don Henderson) and Detective Constable Willis (Dennis Blanch), further developed the original series' quirky, *The Avengers*-style template, as well as its theme of the police being compromised by the needs of the secret state.

Opening with a testosterone-fuelled signature tune and a stylish title sequence showing a car smashing through a window, *The Professionals* (1977-1983) demonstrated that what a British spy series needed to compete internationally was to be made entirely on film as a sequence of mini action movies. Anti-terrorist CI5 agents Bodie (Lewis Collins) and Doyle (Martin Shaw) arrived on the scene in fast cars, by hovercraft or helicopter, in an

English take on the American buddy-cop series *Starsky and Hutch* (1975-79). Ethical dilemmas for the duo were relegated to a handful of episodes; in 'Mixed Doubles', pitted against two similar killers, the pair reflect on the nature of their profession, while in 'The Madness of MickeyHamilton', Doyle sympathises with the antagonist, an unbalanced former soldier who is sniping at hospital staff, believing them responsible for the death of his wife. In the moronic 'Klansman', not transmitted during *The Professionals'* original run, Bodie confronts his racial prejudices, while the all together superior 'Discovered in a Graveyard' (1982) features Doyle hovering between life and death and questioning his profession, in a surreal dream sequence. Athough slickly produced, the emphasis in this show was on effect rather than cause.

Any dirty tricks CI5 *did* use – such as threatening to inject someone with heroin to deliberately turn them into a drug addict – were always directed at out-and-out villains, a streamlining of the moral ambiguities central to *Callan*. There were fewer shades of grey in Bodie and Doyle's world, and as a result some critics found *The Professionals* unappealing, although the series was tremendously popular with the public, lasting six years. CI5's new, gung-ho attitude anticipated the outbreak of patriotic fervour in England when the Special Air Service liberated London's Iranian Embassy from terrorists in 1980, in a raid transmitted live on television. Two years later, it wasn't a surprise to see Lewis Collins starring in the feature film *Who Dares Wins* (the SAS motto), about the elite force's operation to stop a fictional terrorist plot. Developed from an initial synopsis by George Markstein, the film also starred Edward Woodward as a police commander, but drew disapproval from some quarters for its jaundiced view of the peace movement.

SIX YEARS AFTER CALLAN walked away from the Section, a series began on Yorkshire Television that is arguably the closest thing the television series has to a sequel. Ian Mackintosh's *The Sandbaggers* focused on the Special Operations Section of MI6 that deploys special agents to the world's trouble spots. It began the year before the BBC's lavish, prestigious (if a little slow) adaptation of John le Carré's novel *Tinker Tailor Soldier Spy*; one critic was quick to note the more proletarian and familiar sounding appeal of the ITV series: 'Whereas... Smiley's kingdom was largely inhabited by unflappable, middle-aged sophisticates, the spy services depicted in *The Sandbaggers* seemed to be staffed by hard-nosed young men with short tempers, and even shorter haircuts.'[17]

As the series' title sequence showing a Home Office briefcase being carried along Whitehall corridors suggested, *The Sandbaggers* introduced internal politics – at the heart of government rather than in an anonymous back street – as a major part of the drama, as MI6 Special Operations Director Neil Burnside (Roy Marsden) was frequently in conflict with his immediate superior, the empire-building Matthew Peele (Jerome Willis). Burnside's 'battles [that were] won and lost in dull, dreary corridors'[18] were mediated by the Special Intelligence Service chief 'C' (Richard Vernon). As in *Callan*, the relationship with the CIA remained ambivalent, demonstrated by Burnside's sometimes awkward friendship with the American Jeff Ross (Bob Sherman), stationed at London's US Embassy. There was also a welcome shift in gender representation, as Laura Dickens (Diane Keen) was recruited as the first female Sandbagger, on equal terms with her male colleague Willie Caine (Ray Lonnen).

In a significant step on from *Callan*, there was little dissension in the ranks; although Caine acted as a voice of conscience, there were few arguments, and Special Ops' callous pragmatism was generally accepted as normal policy. The focus also shifted: overall, stories were told from the commander's perspective rather than that of the foot soldier.

Notably, *The Sandbaggers* and *Callan* shared the same qualities in their leading men, as the *Evening Standard* observed: 'Mr Marsden has the ability, rare in an actor... to imply what is going on in his head. Most actors suggest nothing is. Marsden suggests everything is.'[19] Edward Woodward had the same ability, and like his forerunner, Marsden skilfully revealed the conflicted man behind the intimidating façade, notably in 'Special Relationship', the last episode of the first series. Left with no other option, Burnside deliberately betrays Laura, who by now has become his lover, and she's shot dead in a spy exchange. The production team believed they wouldn't get another series so 'killed off our leading lady'[20], a situation comparable with the end of *Callan* in 1969.

The show's creator was an even more enigmatic figure than George Markstein. Before becoming a TV writer, Ian Mackintosh was a Lieutenant Commander in the Royal Navy – the same rank and service as Ian Fleming – before resigning his commission in 1976 at the age of 34 and, with no public explanation, being awarded an MBE. When *The Sandbaggers* became popular, Mackintosh refused to be interviewed or photographed; even more strangely, he disappeared in a private plane over the Gulf of Alaska in July 1979, two hundred miles from the Russian border. Neither his body, nor those of the pilot and Mackintosh's girlfriend, have ever been found (at least officially). 'Ian never shared the true nature of his relationship with MI6 with me or, as far as I know, with anyone else,'[21] the series' producer-director Michael Ferguson said candidly. 'I chose to believe, and he never denied it, that he had himself been a Sandbagger and still maintained contact with his former colleagues. My job was to produce and direct compelling television drama, not indulge in investigative journalism and perhaps destroy the mystery and authority Ian exuded.

'I don't recall discussing *Callan* with Ian, but I enjoyed the series,' Ferguson reflected. 'The programme followed in the slipstream of *The Spy Who Came in From the Cold*, *The IPCRESS File* and the great wealth of gritty Cold War fiction available in books and on screen at the time. On television, the spy thriller became and remains a strong competitor of the police procedural and medical formats. *Callan* was, perhaps, the first great success of its genre.'

Mackintosh may not have let on, but there are several pointers in his scripts that indicate a *Callan* influence. Familiar character names such as Bunin and Ramsey crop up, and the episode 'Is Your Journey Really Necessary?' appears to pay homage to 'God Help Your Friends'. This story begins with one Sandbagger, Denson (Steven Grives), shooting another, Landy (David Glyder), to prevent him being interrogated. Denson consequently decides to resign, because he wants to get married. Burnside decrees that because he's already lost one of his three 'Sandbaggers', he has to end Denson's relationship with his girlfriend Sally (Brenda Cavendish) so the operative will stay on. Burnside threatens Sally with telling Denson that she's having an affair with an old male friend, but she refuses to be intimidated. Voluntarily, Denson decides to remain a Sandbagger and postpone the marriage but, with tragic irony, the preoccupied agent is then (off screen) run down by a taxi. In the most striking similarity with 'God Help Your Friends', Burnside and Caine then discover that Sally is also dead, having taken an overdose after feeling rejected.

The Mackintosh saga's authentic mixture of bureaucratic intrigue and covert excitement made it essential viewing for three years and, if the writer hadn't inexplicably vanished, *The Sandbaggers* would have continued beyond the cliffhanger at the end of its third year.

1979 OFFERED producer-director Michael Dryhurst's minimalist thriller *The Hard Way*, an Irish variation on 'A Magnum for Schneider' in the context of the sectarian warfare that had been raging in Northern Ireland for eleven years by the time the film was shown on ITV on 20 February 1980. A middle-aged Patrick McGoohan – haggard, greying, his face full of worry lines – is perfect casting as John Connor, another brilliant killer who's sick of killing, a hitman who can't quit a mysterious mercenary organisation. The emptiness of the Western Ireland locations has a distinct Celtic fatalism, emphasising both Connor's spiritual and emotional emptiness and the bleak inevitability of a cycle of violence that none of the male characters can escape (a common theme in other material featuring 'the Troubles' such as the TV mini-series *Harry's Game* (1982) and Mike Hodges' *A Prayer for the Dying* (1987)).

After Connor lets down his boss McNeal (a harsh Lee Van Cleef) on 'one last job', he himself is targeted. Despite a stilted performance by the novelist Edna O'Brien as Connor's estranged wife Kathleen, *The Hard Way* is convincingly desolate. McNeal tells Connor 'men like us don't retire', while his wife says that all her husband 'ever knew was guns' and despite his considerable fortune, Connor lives an almost monastic existence in an isolated cottage. The climax is similar to the 1974 *Callan* film as Connor – armed with a rifle and a Magnum revolver – faces McNeal in a country house, but the fatalism goes one step further. Both men kill each other, the clear implication being that it's the only way out for either of them. At the time, critics found it hard to look at the film objectively and the review in the *Sunday Telegraph* was typical: 'It is difficult to think of a more accurate representation of the sentimental necrophilia which for 60 years has glorified the Irish gunman in his own country.'[22]

DÉTENTE WITH CHINA AND RUSSIA in the 1970s was seen as a failed experiment at the beginning of the 1980s, the temperature of the Cold War increasing when the USSR invaded Afghanistan on 24 December 1979. Newly elected right-wing governments in America and England under Ronald Reagan and Margaret Thatcher subsequently took a hard line against international Communism, an attitude that impacted upon the fiction of the time. This was reflected in the near-identical, reactionary plotlines of the Bond film *Octopussy* (1983) and Frederick Forsyth's novel *The Fourth Protocol* (1984). Both featured Soviet hard-liners planning to detonate nuclear bombs on western soil to foment left-wing revolution.

On television the genre continued to diversify. Further improvements in film technology saw the continuation of lavish productions shot on location, such as the *Tinker Tailor Soldier Spy* sequel *Smiley's People* (1982) and *Reilly – Ace of Spies* (1983), the Euston Films mini-series about the real agent who plotted to bring down the Bolshevik revolution. This approach continued throughout the decade, with Troy Kennedy Martin's ambitious ecological drama *Edge of Darkness* (1985) and *Codename: Kyril* (1988), notable for its casting of Edward Woodward as a Soviet mole in MI6. Although half-studio and half-film, *Bird of Prey* (1982-83) was also innovative, as it was an early TV thriller dealing with computerised espionage. These series all shared the same idea that the world's security services would cheat, betray and kill their own agents, as well as innocent people, showing just how much the jaundiced world view of Mitchell, le Carré, Mackintosh's *et al* had become a standard part of the genre.

Almost a decade on from Alan J. Pakula's conspiracy movie *The Parallax View* (1974), about a journalist's investigation into a killing closely based on the 1963 assassination of

President John F. Kennedy, James Mitchell was instrumental in developing a further strand of British espionage fiction that turned the focus onto crusading members of the press. Based on the book by Tom Keene and Brian Haynes, *Spy Ship* (1983) dealt with the efforts of Martin Taylor (Tom Wilkinson) to expose the true facts behind the sinking of the Newcastle trawler *Caistor*. The Royal Navy had been using it to spy on the Soviet fleet in the Bering Sea, but were ordered to sink the vessel when its operating frequencies came dangerously close to detonating Russian nuclear mines near a NATO fleet.

Post-*Callan*, it's intriguing to see how Mitchell approached spy fiction in the early 1980s. Ordered to bury the *Caistor* affair, the cool, ascetic MI5 officer Francis Main (Peter Eyre) could easily be a more politically astute Meres, simultaneously manoeuvring to replace his immediate boss Hillmore (Michael Aldridge) while ordering 'Evans' (Philip Hyne), an ex-soldier turned hitman, to silence both witnesses and Taylor. There's a grim, characteristic Mitchell twist to this relationship as, to protect himself, Evans has been recording Main's phone calls giving him orders. In overall charge of Hillmore's department is Strang (David Ryall), an intelligence executive with a nice line in Hunter-style cynicism: 'In my business virtue is a commodity. I'm a trader... my reps spend all their time sifting through dirt.'

Spy Ship was transmitted early in a decade where the media often baited an increasingly authoritarian and secretive establishment. In April 1980, the ATV drama-documentary *Death of a Princess* exposed the public execution for adultery of Princess Misha'al and her lover in Saudi Arabia, causing diplomatic repercussions for Britain and America's oil interests in the country. Four years after *Spy Ship*, in January 1987 the offices of the political journal the *New Statesman* and the BBC in Glasgow were raided in an attempt by Special Branch to suppress a six part documentary series called *Secret Society*, one edition of which concerned the UK's spy satellite Zircon; none of the programmes were ever shown. The following year in April, Thames Television drew flack for their *This Week* documentary 'Death on the Rock', which suggested that when three IRA members were shot dead two months earlier on Gibraltar by the previously lionised SAS, no warning was given. The tabloids and the government reacted with fury.

James Mitchell had been ahead of the game in anticipating this topical interest in investigative journalism, to the point where the reporter figure, however outwardly jaded, for a while became UK spy fiction's new anti-hero. Similar characters to Martin Taylor appear in the movie *Defence of the Realm* (1985) and the *Screen Two* production 'Frankie and Johnnie' (1986). The spy/journalism sub-genre has survived into the 21st century, in the BBC's *State of Play* (2003), concerning the investigation of shady deals between government ministers and the oil industry, and notably *The Hour* (2011-12). This historical drama returned to the beginnings of the Cold War and was based around a BBC current affairs programme, reporting on the anti-Communist Hungarian uprising and the Suez crisis in 1956.

DEVISED BY GEORGE MARKSTEIN and with Lloyd Shirley as its executive producer, *Mr. Palfrey of Westminster* (1984-85) combined the le Carré model of the intellectual spymaster[23] – in this case Palfrey (Alec McCowen) – with the Mitchell archetype of the professional executioner, Blair (Clive Wood). Palfrey's small department also included a fashionable Sloane-ranging secretary, Caroline Phelps (Briony McRoberts), while the spy hunter himself reported to the 'Iron Lady' Co-ordinator, a slyly amusing characterisation by Caroline Blakiston clearly modelled on then prime minister Margaret Thatcher.

As the last espionage series overseen by two people instrumental in the production of *Callan*, and bearing in mind Markstein's encyclopaedic knowledge of real and fictional spying, on-screen references suggest that *Mr. Palfrey of Westminster* was subtly paying *homage* to its Thames forerunner and, notably, the first series aired in the same year that Channel 4 repeated the two colour seasons of *Callan*.

In *Palfrey's* pilot episode, shown as part of the anthology series *Storyboard* (1983-89), 'the Section' is name-checked, and in the first instalment of the resulting series, a Foreign Office official is set up as a decoy for disinformation being leaked from the British Embassy in Prague; he is later killed by a dirty tricks department 'that doesn't exist'. The 1985 stories 'Spygame' and 'A Present from Leipzig' respectively feature a spy ring based around war gaming and Palfrey walking past a sign for (the fake) 'Hunter Road' in North London. 'Palfrey is essentially a one-on-one interrogator. That is how his function was formed, patterned off real life counterparts skilled in that type of interrogation,'[24] Lloyd Shirley noted. 'To an extent Callan and his section and what Palfrey does could be acting totally coincidentally with each other, and to some considerable extent not being aware of each other's activities.'

After the concerns expressed by the media in the 1970s over violence on television, the extreme measures Blair took for Palfrey were never seen, apart from the memorable 'Return to Sender' (1985), in which Blair threatens to kill a defector (played by Leslie Phillips) using a bath full of acid unless he returns to the USSR. This more highbrow approach to TV spy fiction found favour with the critics, particularly the viewer of the *Daily Telegraph*: 'Freshness in this well-worn genre is difficult to achieve at the best of times. Yet it was achieved with a nicely light and cynical touch.'[25] The *Daily Mail* was equally approving: 'Mr Markstein believes in writing TV drama that contains no bad language, no shooting, killing, or unnecessary violence – and still [turns] out something that will entertain people in a manner both polished and realistic.'[26]

Played with cold detachment by Wood, Palfrey's right hand man proved popular and by the second series, as in *Callan* before it, the production team couldn't resist getting under their loner's skin. In 'Freedom from Longing' (1985), it's revealed that Blair had been in love with the suspected Eastern Bloc agent Martina Petras (Estelle Kohler), 'the only woman who ever provoked more than an itch in the groin.' Warned off by a security contact and frightened by his loss of emotional control, Blair is later assigned to investigate Martina to test whether or not his involvement with her has made him a traitor. After proving her guilt, Blair warns Martina to leave the country, but the final, bitter twist sees Palfrey have her arrested at the airport. In a sign of the enduring appeal of such shadowy characters, Blair gained his own spin-off TV play for *Storyboard*, 'A Question of Commitment' (1989), but no series featuring him as the central character emerged.

IN THE LATE 1980s citizens behind the Iron Curtain began feeling the benefits of *perestroika* – the liberalising reforms of Russian President Mikhail Gorbachev. On 9 November 1989, East Berlin's Communist Party announced that its populace would once again be free to cross to the west of the city, leading to almost two million people flooding through the checkpoints for a massive street party. People armed with domestic tools then began knocking parts of the Berlin Wall down; cranes and bulldozers soon followed suit. This demolition was a symbolic act, heralding the collapse of Communist regimes across all of Eastern Europe. Spy fiction writers took a while to adjust to the revised ideological and political world map; having released one trilogy of books partly set in Berlin – faithfully adapted for television in *Game, Set and Match* (1988) – Len Deighton revised his follow up book *Spy Sinker* (1990) to take into account contemporary events.

One curious coda to the first generation of fictional espionage on British television was the comedy-drama *Sleepers* (1991), written by John Flanagan and Andrew McCulloch. The KGB discover a disused training facility, built to resemble 1960s London, and realise that two deep cover 'sleeper' agents, played by Warren Clarke and Nigel Havers, are still living in England, to all intents and purposes as naturalised British citizens. The dilemmas that arose from the KGB's mission to track down their two men neatly summed up the complicated legacy of the Cold War.

IN 2001, THE PRODUCTION COMPANY KUDOS announced they would be making a new spy series for BBC1 called *Spooks* (slang for intelligence agents) 'based on extensive interviews with former officers'[27]. Partly inspired by *Open Secret* (2001), the autobiography of Stella Rimmington – the first female Director General of MI5, who subsequently became a spy novelist – the series concerned a Counter Terrorism Department within MI5, overseen by Harry Pearce (Peter Firth), an ex-field agent as ruthlessly practical as any of the Hunters had been. For long term followers of TV spy fiction, there was a familiar ring to executive producer Jane Featherstone's claim that the series would examine the 'moral ambiguity'[28] of spies, focusing on the 'grey world they live in, and it's [that] grey world that we try to show... [Spies] are fallible, like anyone else.' Tantalisingly, *Spooks* was set to feature the 'passion, jeopardy and intrigue of people who have to lie for a living, human dilemmas that [agents] face in their daily lives.' Arguably betraying a lack of research, Featherstone did make something of an espionage fiction *faux pas* with older viewers, when she told *The Guardian* that 'apart from the adaptation of spy novels by John le Carré, the spy services [have] not been treated seriously by television... For me it's new, it hasn't been done before.'

However, Bharat Nalluri, the series' first director, was well aware of where *Spooks* fitted in the history of TV spy drama. 'Going back to *Callan* and *The Sandbaggers,* the Brits do that kind of stuff really, really well – the chess-playing kind of spy... it's very strategic, it's not all car chases. With *Spooks,* we gave it a bit of the car chase element, but if the nation was in trouble and [the characters] didn't understand why, we'd cut to Harry who'd explain the issue.'[29] Featherstone and her production team more than delivered. The series came along at just the right time or, perhaps, the *wrong* time: following the Al-Qaeda terrorist attacks on America on 11 September 2001 and the subsequent 'War on Terror' (the new Cold War by another name) there was wide, renewed interest in the spy community.

Spooks had a remarkable run between 2002 and 2011, with stories about contemporary threats to national security such as Islamic suicide bombers, cybercrime and rogue financial traders, together with spy fiction staples like double agents, Fascist groups and ex-agents threatening to go public and reveal state secrets. Apart from a long overdue equality in the gender balance of intelligence personnel in the regular cast – particularly in the character of the data analyst, Ruth Evershed (Nicola Walker) –*Spooks* also made the cost defending the nation had on relationships and family life an integral part of its format, something even *Callan* and *The Sandbaggers* had also occasionally touched on. When *Spooks* begins, 'Section' D's young field officer Tom Quinn (Matthew Macfadyen) is using a false identity to date a girlfriend, a plot that was apparently based on a true story.

Arguably the most unforgettable aspect of the series, something that *Callan* also utilised, was the shock value and the attendant publicity in killing off main characters. Whereas the deaths of two Hunters and Cross, and nearly Callan himself, had been significant moments in a television culture where the continued survival of a regular cast was the norm, *Spooks* set out its lethal agenda from the start. Introduced in the first episode, new recruit Helen Flynn (Lisa Faulkner) is graphically killed off in the second; her face is shoved into a fryer full of boiling fat and then she's shot in the head. The viewing public immediately sat up and took notice of a series where, to emphasise the dangerous nature of security work and keep the drama unpredictable, death rather than survival was the usual outcome for the protagonists. 'We cast Lisa Faulkner because she was kind of the nation's sweetheart,' explained Nalluri. 'She represents the sort of classic, nine o'clock TV casting you had at the BBC – and we set her up as Tom Quinn's [wife]. Very specifically, we killed her in the second episode *and* had the hero in the room, but he couldn't save the day – all *not* what you did on TV then. Now everyone does it. It's like the Red Wedding in *Game of Thrones* every other weekend.'

Over its ten years, thirteen of Harry's team were killed. Notably, the survial of Ros Myers (Hermione Norris) was left uncertain in an end of series cliffhanger finale, designed to keep the audience guessing for a year. Eventually, this initially gripping, cold-blooded policy towards the cast had diminishing returns. As Harry became a more and more dominant figure in the stories, his agents became less and less well defined, so that when they were killed off it became harder to care. However, the series ended with a fittingly downbeat twist, as Nalluri recalled: 'It was one of the rare instances where I came back to wrap up a show. I did the very first two episodes and the very last two episodes at the end of Series Ten. Tom Quinn had become the silent hitman who Harry uses for wet jobs. I think that was one of the last scenes we shot and I said "We should bring back someone from the beginning." Matthew very kindly had a spare morning so he came in and did it for us.'

Spooks is probably *Callan*'s nearest equivalent in the 21ˢᵗ century. The tough ethical dilemmas – one episode had Adam Carter (Rupert Penry-Jones) having to choose between the execution wife or a friend – plus the fatal turnover of intelligence operatives, the ruthlessness, the cost to agents' humanity and even the cliffhanger endings to series, all have precedents from David Callan's tenure on screen. Some members of the Thames series' cast and crew had diverse views on the BBC's modern take on spying: 'Very few espionage series have been made over the years,'[30] observed Mike Vardy. 'There were hybrid series such as *The Professionals* but not much out-and-out spy stuff, with the honourable exception of *Tinker Tailor Soldier Spy*, but that was, of course, an adaptation from the book. There were others, but not anything that lingers in the memory.

'Then *Spooks* came along and deservedly became very popular. The changes in attitudes, acting styles and the balance of technology both on and off the screen is a perfect comparison of how much drama production has moved on since the late 1960s and early 1970s. *Callan* suffered, as did most drama in those days, from the video/film mix which was always an unhappy marriage. *Spooks*, on the other hand, puts together writing, performance and technology in a masterly manner.'

Patrick Mower was more critical: 'I think *Spooks* was soft and wet and soggy compared to *Callan*,'[31] he felt. '*Callan* was tight and it meant business: it knew where it was going. It was a greyhound, if you like, and *Spooks* was a labrador.' *The Sandbaggers*' producer Ferguson was more approving, with a few caveats: '*Spooks* was glossy, high-powered storytelling and an example of the way in which popular drama has changed during the intervening thirty years,'[32] he considered. 'Compared with *The Sandbaggers*, it's more high-tech, faster, noisier, more violent and less interested in the humanity of its characters.

It's certainly compelling viewing, if not always credible.'

In another similarity with *Callan*, *Spooks* followed the Thames series on to the big screen in an attempt to launch a film franchise, with 2015's *Spooks: The Greater Good*. 'We'd been talking about turning *Spooks* into a movie from around season four/season five,'[33] Nalluri said. 'Everyone felt that it should really finish as a TV show first, otherwise we'd [be] competing with ourselves.'

AT ITS PEAK, *SPOOKS* was the only regular British espionage series which could compete on the same level as slick American counterparts such as *24* (2001-10, 2014). The US and British series shared the same visual conceit of dividing the TV screen into multiple panels showing what various characters were simultaneously doing., although the similarity was coincidental. 'The split screens on *Spooks* weren't influenced by *24*,' Nalluri clarified. 'I hadn't seen *24* then. Rather, [the technique] came about when (unlike any TV then) we shot so much footage with three cameras that I wanted to take advantage of it all. We had such good stuff that was going to be on the cutting room floor that I remembered back to one of my favorite movies, the original *The Thomas Crown Affair* [1968] and its use of split screens, so the split screens were so we could use all our great footage and nothing to do with *24*. Nice coincidence, and as *24* beat us out of the gates, people always say it influenced us. Not true, though: just *zeitgeist*.'

24 preceded *Spooks* by a year, and was based around a counter terrorist agent, Jack Bauer (Kiefer Sutherland), pushed to the limits of his endurance and capable of shocking acts of brutality in the line of duty. The 2014 series *24: Live Another Day* showcases the series at its most exhilarating, despite taking the odd preposterous liberty with plausibility and English geography. It includes furious action sequences in a London being bombed by terrorist controlled drones, and a plot featuring Russian gangsters, American traitors, Wikileaks-style hackers and the rogue Chinese official Cheng Zhi (Tzi Ma). After Cheng Zhi orders Bauer's lover, Audrey, to be killed, the agent brutally decapitates him. Equally graphically, Bauer sends both the English jihadist Margot Al-Harazi (Michelle Fairley) and her son plummeting to their deaths from an office window, but each victory has a price; the harrowing conclusion sees the bereaved Bauer, seemingly with nothing left to live for, captured by the Russians.

Created by Joel Surnow, *24* was part of a line of descent from *The Equalizer* (1984-88), taking in the stylish but cold US spy series *La Femme Nikita* (1997-2001). Surnow co-produced and wrote several episodes to the former and developed the latter for Canadian television.[34] *The Equalizer*'s co-creator Michael Sloan also contributed an episode. The regular staff at 'Section One' in this series consisted of a ruthless supervisor, an armourer, and a psychologist/interrogator, in addition to the titular conscience-stricken assassin. Arguably it was a feminist *Callan* for the MTV generation, featuring hyperactive camerawork, a rock soundtrack, and spies who were outrageously fashion-conscious, favouring designer dark glasses and a lot of black leather. This, together with the inclusion of spy-fi and soap opera elements, rather undercut the drama, although there were several bleak episodes with genuine ethical dilemmas. For the final series, a character played by none other than Edward Woodward joined the team playing Nikita's (secret) father, in what could be seen as a symbolic piece of casting.

SPOOKS AND *24*, together with the visceral, authentic action sequences of the Jason Bourne films, which began in 2002, had a knock-on effect on the elder statesman of the spy genre. In 2006, James Bond was reborn as the blonde haired and cold-eyed Daniel Craig. The opening sequence of *Casino Royale* explicitly deals with how killing slowly erodes an agent's humanity, opening with a vicious fight in a sordid public toilet shot in grimy black and white. The shift away from the 'weaponised lounge lizard'[35] of the past couldn't have been more pronounced, particularly when 'M' (Judi Dench) refers to Bond as 'a blunt instrument,' Ian Fleming's famous description of his character.

Watching 2012's seminal *Skyfall*, it's hard not to believe that 007's writers hadn't been looking through *Callan* episodes for inspiration. (It's worth noting that previously *The Living Daylights*, Timothy Dalton's respectable 1987 debut, had shown Bond killing a war gaming obsessed arms dealer who is restaging the Battle of Gettysburg.) Emphasis is put on Craig's Bond being an orphan (like Callan) and it's stressed that this makes him ideal for security work. In *Skyfall*, Bond is shot and wounded by one of his own team ('Death of a Hunter'), turns to drink then returns to MI6 and resumes active duty even though he's unfit ('Where Else Could I Go?'). The film's villain Silva (Javier Bardem) is a mirror-image of Bond (like Alec Trevelyan (Sean Bean) in *Goldeneye* (1995)) an idea that features in several *Callan* stories, most notably 'The Richmond File' trilogy. At *Skyfall*'s climax, 007's commander M is targeted for assassination and consequently guarded by him at a country house retreat ('Red Knight, White Knight') and then killed ('Let's Kill Everybody', 'Death of a Hunter' again); a colleague of Bond's is subsequently appointed as his new head of department ('Heir Apparent'). Ultimately, any such possible homages are flattering ones, as the James Bond writers returned the franchise to its bedrock characteristics – licensed ruthlessness, pride in a 'filthy business'[36], the psychological cost of being a killer – that Callan and the Bond of Fleming's novels originally shared.

The follow-up *SPECTRE* (2015) more conventional in places – and over-long – but still offers some exceptionally well directed set pieces, as well as a worthy storyline criticising the surveillance state. Other recent small and large screen espionage dramas have included a remake of *Tinker Tailor Soldier Spy* (2011) and period TV thrillers *The Game* (2014) and *Deutschland '83* (2015), set in the 1970s and 1980s respectively. Together with *London Spy* (2015), starring the Craig Bond films' 'Q'-actor Ben Whishaw; and a fresh le Carré adaptation, *The Night Manager* (2016), pitting a deniable agent against an affluent, charismatic arms dealer, it seems that mature, morally complex spy fiction will always have a place in British cinema and on television.

Among the recent spate of spy dramas, to the surprise of many people who'd taken an interest in him over the years, a certain shabby secret agent also turned out to have a few more games of Russian Roulette left to play...

13: Callan Lives!

'At Windsor the other evening, I was killing a bit of
time walking by the river before I had to go into the theatre, and a young woman pushed her head out of
a houseboat and said, "I enjoyed you as Hunter!"
That's extraordinary, isn't it? People did, and do,
[say] that more than anything else.'[1]

William Squire, August 1985

AFTER THE FREEZE FRAME OF CALLAN and Margaret Channing at the end
of *Wet Job* faded from TV screens on 2 September 1981, it seemed that *Callan* was
destined for the television archives and to be no more than a fond memory in the
minds of viewers (showings of the feature film aside). Unlike some of ITC's series such
as *The Saint* and *Danger Man*, which were still being periodically re-run in Britain, *Callan*,
like other studio-video productions, had been made under terms agreed with the Actors'
Union, Equity, which generally restricted repeats to one re-screening within a specified
time frame, usually two years after first transmission: any other 'out of time' repeats were
limited in number and had to be specifically negotiated. Those hoping for more literary
assignments for the agent were also disappointed. After a final run of seven short stories
in the *Sunday Express* in 1976, James Mitchell chose to devote his time to further original
novels and his historical TV drama *When the Boat Comes In*.

An enthusiasm for archive television among the children of the 1960s and 1970s,
by now wanting to discover more about the programmes they had grown up with, resulted
in the founding of the organisation Wider TeleVision Access in 1981. WTVA's promotion
of vintage television through its magazine *Primetime* – which included a *Callan* retrospective article – and the screening of old programmes at special events, helped raise the
profile of television's heritage. When Channel 4 (together with S4C, the Scottish equivalent) was established in 1982, the public service television broadcaster had an initial short-
age of both advertising and programmes, so repeating old TV series became a temporary
part of its official policy.

Only three years after *Wet Job*, between June and December 1984, *Callan* was reintroduced to a welcoming older audience and an appreciative new one, with repeats of Series
Three and Four. Although the two colour seasons were over ten years old, the episodes
stood up remarkably well, as members of the series' cast and crew noted at the time.
'I only saw about two of them,'[2] Russell Hunter admitted, 'but I thought, "That's really not

bad. That stood up very well. In fact it's as good as bloody programmes being made this week!" It really was quite sharp. The only things wrong with it were that the taxi number [plate] and the clothes were a little old-fashioned, and that was it. The story was a good story and it was acted to the best that the actors could do it.'

Anthony Valentine formed an equally positive impression that he shared in a chance meeting with Reg Collin: 'I met [him] on the [London] Underground and he said to me "Have you been watching it?" I said, "I've seen bits of it" and he said, "What did you think?" "Well, it really did seem to stand the passage of time. I wasn't embarrassed. I thought it would be excruciatingly old-fashioned and old hat, but I didn't think it was." I said that I thought it was perfectly acceptable, and he said, "I thought so too."'[3] At the same time, Ray Jenkins was pleased to see that the pace of the writing in his episodes matched contemporary shows: 'They've weathered very well. At the time, people thought I had written too quickly, [they thought] the scenes were a bit pell-melly. Because a lot of time has passed between then and now, [my stories] appear to be of a speed that is acceptable. I enjoyed them.'[4]

The repeats of the series clearly made on impression on TV schedulers and festival planners, as *Callan* became a staple of retrospective seasons both on and off the television. The season *TV Action! Watching the Detectives* at the National Film Theatre over 24 and 25 May 1987 offered 'policemen, private detectives, insurance investigators, Victorian detectives, spies and various groups of heroes all fighting crime to maintain law and order'[5] in a presentation of the best 'crime, action and adventure shows [which] have always been among the most popular themes on British TV.' In the company of other little seen (at the time) TV thrillers like *Adam Adamant Lives!*, *Ghost Squad* and *Zodiac* (1974), 'A Magnum for Schneider' was re-shown for the first time in 20 years, paired with 'The Rhine Maiden', a wryly amusing episode of *The Saint*, on 25 May.

Two years later, in July 1989, 'That'll Be the Day' featured in the ITV 21st Anniversary mini-season *Thames Mavericks* with *Public Eye*, *The Sweeney* and *Van der Valk*, complete with specially recorded introductions by Dennis Waterman. In 1992, 'A Magnum for Schneider' finally had a repeat screening on national television as part of the 1967 programming of Channel 4's *TV Heaven*, an evening of themed programming that concentrated on one specific year; it was introduced by the dryly witty Frank Muir. Three years later in 1995, *Callan* was again a major feature of a nostalgic bill of archive TV on Channel 4, when 'Call Me Enemy' was shown as part of the *Vintage Thames* season.

When satellite networks arrived in the 1990s all the colour episodes had another outing, this time on UK Gold, although they suffered because up to five minutes were edited out of each story to allow for desperately needed revenue-generating advertising. Despite this irritating decision, the channel, accessing both the Thames and BBC archives, UK Gold was still a good way to revisit diverse British dramas such as *The Bill*, *Blake's 7*, *Colditz*, *Doctor Who*, *Doomwatch*, *Survivors*, *The Sweeney* and *Tenko* for several years; sadly, a 1997 merger put an end to the archive screenings when the channel was rebranded .

Curiously, every time *Callan* was repeated from the 1980s onwards it seemed to impact on other contemporary series, including ones outside the spy genre. Screened in 1985, a year after the Channel 4 repeats, *Doctor Who* – 'Revelation of the Daleks' featured a world-weary professional killer Orcini (William Gaunt), accompanied by a malodorous assistant, Bostock (John Ogwen); Hugh Walters was amongst the cast, as one of the pair's clients. A decade later, after the UK gold reruns, the sales pitch for Joe Ahearne's gripping horror thriller *Ultraviolet* (1998) could most have been '*Callan* with vampires'. This rich, complex six-part serial featured a ruthless underground organisation dedicated to hunting down the undead, and its dramatic focus was very much upon the emotional toll placed onthe main characters, through a strong regular cast of Susannah Harker, Idris Elba, Philip Quast and Jack Davenport's conflicted everyman, Michael Colefield. (Corin Redgrave also featured as one of the opposition). 'You're just an old romantic, aren't you?' Elba's battle-hardened Vaughn Rice says to Colefield at the end of the disturbing third episode, 'Sub Judice', after a possibly sympathetic 'Code Five' (vampire) has been destroyed. 'We'll soon fix that.'

ANOTHER OFF-SHOOT of TV's awareness of its own past was the BBC panel game *Telly Addicts* (1985-1998), in which two teams of contestants were quizzed on their knowledge of television history by host Noel Edmonds. Confirming how much *Callan* was becoming known as a seminal example of vintage TV drama, the series featured as a specialist subject. Interestingly, the series' inclusion on *Telly Addicts* highlighted the gap between professional TV researchers and the detailed knowledge of committed fans. It also illustrated how human error can nearly derail a production.

'I was part of a team called "Double Deckers" – I didn't choose the name!'[6] laughed contestant Phil Newman, who took part in 1996. 'When you filled in the application form you had to fill in three possible subjects for what they called the "On the Box" round, the specialist knowledge round. My turn in "On the Box" wasn't until the second [show we were on] and first up was my mate John Heckford, who had chosen as his specialist subjects *Callan* and *M*A*S*H* [1972-1983]. I had never seen an episode of *M*A*S*H* in my life and I remember *Callan* being on but I never watched it, so that was as far as my knowledge of it went.

'We turned up at Pebble Mill [studios, in Birmingham], and at that time *Telly Addicts* had a score keeper. He was an actor who was in *The Archers* [1950-] called Charles Collingwood and when we sat down, he was dressed in green surgical gear, but we didn't know why. John had been told by our team captain that he was going to be doing questions on *Callan*; we'd got halfway through, and we were doing OK. We got to the "On the Box" round and Noel says, "So-and-so from this team is doing so-and-so as his specialist subject, and John Heckford from the Double Deckers is doing as his specialist subject – *M*A*S*H*."　We looked at each other, and John whispered to me, "But I'm doing questions on *Callan*!" We were miked up so they could hear what we were saying, stopped recording and said, "What do you mean?" and John goes, "I was told I was doing questions on *Callan* and that's what I've prepared for. I can do questions on *M*A*S*H* if you want, but I came here expecting to do *Callan*." The crew are hugger-mugger and disappear up to the production gallery; meantime, time's being wasted in the studio, but we were none the wiser – just rather perplexed.

'Eventually they came back and said, "If you say you're answering questions on *Callan*, we'll get you some questions on *Callan*!" and they sent a researcher off and eventually this guy comes down with ten questions for Noel Edmonds. John answers seven or eight questions correctly, then the question is "How many people played Hunter in the series?" John says "five." Noel replies, "No, sorry, it's four." They got to the end of the round and Noel says, "John, you've scored nine out of ten." They had a recording break and John went to Noel, "That question you said I got wrong is actually right, because Edward Woodward played Hunter in a few episodes." So, people disappear up to the gallery again, and you can imagine that by now whoever's up there isn't terribly happy!

Eventually they came down again and said, "You're right" – of course he was, John knew his subject. Bear in mind that in those days there was no internet and no reference books on *Callan*.

'We carried on doing the rest of the show and we won, and then [Noel] got word from their verifier that Woodward *had* played Hunter, so they had to record the end of the "On the Box" round again. John got ten out of ten – full marks, and we'd beaten the other team by three or four points. We were quite jubilant about that, because not many people got ten out of ten! Later, we were in the green room and congratulating ourselves on getting through to the second round, the quarter finals, when the producer comes in with his assistant who had a clipboard. He says, "OK, you won fair and square, but we're not happy." On this clipboard they had [a copy of] the letter they'd sent to the team captain saying that John would, in fact, be doing *M*A*S*H* – which John didn't know about. The producer was clearly not amused by what he saw as our poor conduct and time wasting, because he said, "Fair enough, you got the question right, but you *were* pedantic!"[7] As far as he was concerned, John shouldn't have been doing *Callan* anyway, which is why they'd dressed [Charles Collingwood] up in surgical scrubs at the beginning.

'It got worse then!' Newman remembered, laughing again. 'The producer said, "Who's doing questions on *M*A*S*H*?" It was my turn, and all I knew was that the theme tune was 'Suicide is Painless' and that Alan Alda was in it. I had two weeks to swot up – through John – with his books and videos. Doing *Coronation Street* [1960-] would have been easier, so I was the one who got lumbered in many ways. It shows what a pure memory thing it was, because I got seven out of ten. We still lost and to be quite honest, because of all the stress, I'm glad we didn't get any further.'

IN THE 1980S, THE ARRIVAL OF HOME VIDEO helped meet the demand for nostalgic television. However by contrast with its prominent status in retrospective seasons, *Callan* wasn't given the opportunity to engage with this emergent marketplace in the way the ITC thriller shows or the BBC's *Doctor Who* were. Apart from the one-off VHS releases of the feature film in 1986 and the episodes 'Suddenly at Home' and 'Breakout' in 1987, *Callan* enthusiasts had to wait several years for a complete series of episodes to become available.

Throughout the programme's time in the pop culture wilderness, during the 1980s and 1990s fans continued to 'keep the flame alive' by using their initiative to find out more about the series. Several contacted those involved with the programme, such as Sarah Guiver, whose correspondence with James Mitchell was mainly inspired by her admiration for his novels, and Anthony Goodman and Matthew Morgenstern, who became sufficiently intrigued by the 1984 repeats to interview many members of the cast and crew, visit the Thames archives to read production documents, and view the black and white episodes, at that time unseen in Britain for over a decade. A *Primetime* contributor and a prolific, thorough TV historian since 1979, now also an author and DVD contributor, Andrew Pixley continued to promote and research the series too, his work culminating in a recent book, *Under the Red File* (2015), and the DVD documentary *This Man Alone*. With the growth of the internet, several *Callan* related web pages also appeared (see the Bibliography for further information). Organisations such as the TV archive society Kaleidoscope all played their part, showing rare episodes and hosting interviews with Reg Collin and other ABC staff at their charity events.

Like *Doctor Who* and *The Prisoner* before it, *Callan* also had an organised fan following (albeit one with a smaller membership and lifespan than the clubs based around these other series).

Simply titled the Callan Appreciation Society, it was run by Les Warburton-Marsh and partly inspired by the UK Gold repeats. Subscribers received a membership certificate, as well as newsletters which featured articles, reprints of press articles, news, letters and actor profiles. In the first newsletter published in October 1994, Warburton-Marsh urged members to write to UK Gold requesting repeats of the black and white episodes as well as the already repeated colour seasons, but the campaign proved fruitless. Intriguingly, in November 1994, he issued a news release to members reporting that Thames Video would be releasing *Callan* on sell-through video from March 1995, but ultimately this didn't happen.

By the time the hiatus in availability of commercially available *Callan* recordings finally ended, the medium had moved onto DVD. In 2001 the company Clear Vision released a box set of 3 disks, packaged as 'The Complete First Series' – immediately annoying their target market, as the episodes were actually from Series Three. Some imaginative 'DVD authoring' featuring flickering and exploding light bulbs aside, the set was a disappointment, containing inferior prints, badly abridged advert breaks, and a very minimal set of text-only extra features. Perhaps unsurprisingly, no further releases from Clear Vision were forthcoming.

In 2005 ITV, by now one united network, celebrated its fiftieth anniversary. Between 6 November and 29 December, the National Film Theate led the celebrations with the *ITV 50: 50 Years of Independent Television* retrospective season. Alongside other landmark productions such as *Armchair Theatre, The Avengers, TISWAS, The Naked Civil Servant* and *Made In Britain, Callan*'s first episode 'The Good Ones Are All Dead' was, appropraitely enough, shown with the *Danger Man* story 'Say It with Flowers'; titled 'Sixties Spies', the pairing was open to the public on Saturday 19 and Monday 28 November. In *Broadcast*'s *The Official ITV 50th Anniversary Supplement*, industry insiders voted David Callan 21 in its rundown of the channel's 50 favourite characters[8] (Number 6 was at number 10 and Emma Peel at number 4; the poll was topped by Stan and Hilda Ogden from *Coronation Street*.)

Thankfully, the DVD situation improved considerably in 2007 when the Australian company Umbrella Entertainment staged something of a coup in securing Edward Woodward to record two audio commentaries, for 'If He Can, So Could I' and 'Call Me Enemy'.[9] Umbrella released these in their box set of Series Four in 2007 (also incorporating the feature film previously issued on DVD in 2001 by Stax Entertainment in the UK), having also re-issued Series Three in the same year. 2009 subsequently saw the first DVD release of *Callan* in the USA by Acorn Media, with their Series Four set also including the two Woodward Umbrella commentaries.

In the UK in 2010, the specialist archive label Network Distributing Ltd. finally released the first complete tally of surviving episodes in the series' home market, split over two sets, in the appropriately titled *Callan: The Monochrome Years* and *Callan: The Colour Years*. With their release of *Wet Job* in 2011, all of Callan's surviving television assignments were at last available.

CALLAN'S PUBLIC EXPOSURE in the 40 years since its original transmission may have been sporadic, but the series has always retained its admirers – as the successful DVD releases have indicated – and its reputation for being the peak of well written, quality television drama. Old and new fans of the series, inspired to scour second hand bookshops for copies of Mitchell's Callan novels, became impressed with his exciting and highly readable prose. Fittingly, it was the quality of the author's prose that was the detemining factor in David Callan taking on a recent new lease of life.

In 2012, the BBC's digital radio station Radio 4Extra premiered a spoken word version of *A Magnum for Schneider* under the title *Red File for Callan*, the name of the 1971 paperback edition of the book. Even though she had never seen the original series, the producer Joanna Green was excited by what she read: 'I've got a real love for [spy] writing,'[10] she said. 'I love all the original Fleming Bond books and [*A Magnum for Schneider*] is just *great* storytelling. OK, it might be a bit before my time, but I think there's been a great nostalgia for this kind of thing because it's simple, there's no flabbiness to it – it's to the point, it's lean. I think [Mitchell] is every bit as good as Fleming. Ian's known for his detail and his descriptions, but Mitchell manages to conjure up equally good images, characters and scenes, for me, as the Fleming books.'

Writer Adrian Bean had worked with Green before and, born in 1960, was old enough to remember the original series: 'I'd grown up in the sixties, and remembered watching the TV series as a ten year-old – the amazing title sequence, the toughness, the anti-glamorous look and the performances of Woodward and Hunter, especially, had stuck with me. Of course as the years passed by the memory faded a little, and I hadn't known of the books until I came upon *Red File for Callan* in a second-hand bookshop and loved it.'[11]

'The idea of adapting *A Magnum for Schneider* for radio was mine,' he elaborated, 'and one that I'd been nursing for a few years. I hadn't seen the film at that stage, but the TV series had stayed with me – the atmosphere, the enigmatic relationship between Callan and Lonely, and the appealing idea of an outsider having to do the job he's brilliant at and yet hates at the same time; it was a very strong dramatic brew. But, as with so many ideas, it wasn't a case of simply pitching it straight away – I needed to wait for the right producer, the right broadcaster and it had to be the right time for me.

'All those things fell into place when I was talking to Jo Green... We'd done a very successful adaptation of Ira Levin's *The Boys from Brazil* for Radio 4Extra, and were trying unsuccessfully to adapt the original book that Hitchcock's *The Lady Vanishes* [1938] was based on. The BBC eventually rejected that, and I felt confident enough to float the idea of *Callan*, hoping that it would ring a few bells with the commissioning editor and, if successful, might be the start of a series of *Callan* adaptations. I had originally been thinking of it as a full dramatisation, possibly running for an hour on a Saturday afternoon, but competition for those slots is very high... Jo loved the book as much as I did: she responded to the character, the very strong sense of period as well as the strong story, and luckily the BBC liked it too.'

Bean was particularly impressed with actor Ben Miles' interpretation. '[Jo] chose him for the reading and I think it was an inspired choice. He had enough edge about him to make it intriguing, was close enough to the original Edward Woodward performance to remind those of us old enough to remember what we had loved originally, and to create a new character for those who were new to *Callan*.'

Red File for Callan was well received. *Radio Times* pronounced the new production 'terrific'[12], and the quality of James Mitchell's writing, dialogue and plotting felt as urgent and entertaining as ever. Encouraged by this success, producer and writer suggested *Russian Roulette* as the follow up but, frustratingly, hard economics have to date precluded another Callan audio adaptation appearing. 'The trouble is that 4Extra stopped commissioning novels,'[13] says Green. 'Essentially it's an archive station, and they've got so much that it's sort of pointless commissioning half a dozen books a year, even though we got *Red File for Callan* through. I know the commissioners liked it. It's a shame we couldn't have done *Russian Roulette* as well – it would have worked brilliantly.'

Undeterred and fully aware of the potential in the format, Bean next attempted to put Callan back where he belonged. 'Subsequent to the radio adaptation I discussed the possibility of developing a TV version with my agent, and he put it to Peter Mitchell. It turned out that Peter is a writer himself and had similar ambitions for a revival of *Callan* on TV, but had run into problems with TV executives who couldn't quite see how Callan would translate to the screen. [But] a lot of the things that appealed to me most about Callan – the low-tech spy world, the central dramatic dilemma of being an expert killer and hating yourself for that etc. – simply didn't ring bells with these TV people. I put together a very detailed proposal for an updated version of *Callan* as well as a period version, and we discussed them but neither came to anything. The response tended to be along the lines of "How can we expect the audience to love a killer?" Discuss...!'[14]

This reaction from TV executives is surprising, considering that there have been so many modern series such as *The Sopranos* (1999-2007) and *Breaking Bad* (2008-13) featuring anti-heroic central characters. Given the current movements in espionage drama, vintage or modern, and considering the reception of the audio version of *Red File for Callan*, the conditions for reviving *Callan* on television have probably never been better. That said, the original TV series will always be a very tough act to follow...

RED FILE FOR CALLAN

Adapted by Adrian Bean
Read by Ben Miles
Produced by Joanna Green

A Pier production for Radio 4 Extra

RADIO TIMES: 'Readers of a certain age will see the name David Callan and think of Edward Woodward, who made the part of the professional killer his own between 1967 and '72. But fear not, for this new production for 4 Extra, read by Ben Miles, is terrific.' *'Radio's Five of the Best', 15-21 September 2012*

EPISODE 1: 'CALLAN'S RETURN'[15]
First UK transmission: 17 September 2012, 1.30 pm, repeated 8.30 pm
'Ex-killer David Callan, now a dead-end book keeper, is hired for one last hit on businessman Schneider.'

EPISODE 2: 'DOUBT'
First UK transmission: 18 September 2012, 1.30pm, repeated 8.30 pm
'Hunter has asked Callan to kill German businessman Rudolf Schneider. Now all he needs is a gun from Lonely.'

EPISODE 3: 'PREPARATION'
First UK transmission: 19 September 2012, 1.30 pm, repeated 8.30 pm
'Callan is keen to know why Hunter wants Schneider dead. So he conducts some background research of his own.'

EPISODE 4: 'THE JOB'

First UK transmission: 20 September 2012, 1.30 pm, repeated 8.30 pm

'Schneider invites Callan to dinner on Sunday. Callan has the gun. Sunday is the day he must use it.'

PAWNS AND PLAYERS: JOANNA GREEN is highly experienced in producing spoken word readings, having overseen radio adaptations of Ian Fleming's James Bond short stories, Jonathan Coe's *Expo 58*, and Frederick Forsyth's *The Day of the Jackal*, respectively read by Damian Lewis, Tim McInnery and Sir Derek Jacobi. One of her recent projects was the adaptation of William Boyd's 2013 007 novel *Solo*, voiced by Patterson Joseph.

ADRIAN BEAN is a writer and director. He has written for *Heartbeat* (in 2006) and *Doctors* (from 2000-06) on television. For radio, has scripted adaptations of *Bullitt* (2009) and *Seance on a Wet Afternoon* (2012). Again for TV, he has directed the popular dramas *Grange Hill* (between 1996-2008), *Brookside* (in 1982) and *EastEnders* (over 1996-8).

BEN MILES was born in 1967, the year *Callan* began on television. He studied at the Guildhall School of Music and Drama, becoming a recognisable name in Steven Moffat's relationship comedy *Coupling* (2000-04) as the womanising Patrick Maitland. In other television roles, Miles appeared in *Prime Suspect 6* – 'The Lost Witness' (2003) and *Larkrise to Candleford* (2008, as Sir Timothy Midwinter), and took the male lead in the pilot for the strange medical thriller *Pulse* (2010), opposite Claire Foy. On stage, Miles featured in the Old Vic's production of *Richard II,* and in 2011 starred in Harold Pinter's *Betrayal* (with his best friend Douglas Henshall) and Kristin Scott Thomas. Over 2014-15, Miles starred in the critically acclaimed RSC productions of Hilary Mantel's historical novels *Wolf Hall* and *Bring up the Bodies*. In 2016, he was Somerset in the BBC's Skakespeare drama *The Hollow Crown*.

INFORMATION: Producer Joanna Green explained how the production process on *Red File for Callan* worked: 'Because these were half-hour episodes, we'd sit down and look at the style, first of all, for the narrative and the characters, and once you've got that set up, you can crack on,'[16] she said. 'Ben had a day and a half to record it and we had a day and a half to edit it. Not long. Even then, he did it all in a day. You need good energy as an actor to do something like this, because it's just you. I knew that Ben was a good reader, and not all actors are good readers. He's done quite a few readings on Radio 4. He can do straight, "received pronunciation" voices, and I knew that he was good at characterisations and he's got that slightly London edge.

'When we came to record, we played around with it for a while, and we started off doing the narration in a more RP kind of way then threw in the characterisations, but that just wasn't sounding quite right. And then between us we tweaked it a bit, because it's almost like it's written in Callan's voice or thoughts. So Ben read the narrative with a bit of a London twang and feel, and I thought that worked really well.

'We would go through the episode and check any pronunciations,' Green continued, 'but there weren't any that were a problem in *A Magnum for Schneider*, apart from trying to get the guns right! The BBC has this little office, and I'm surprised it still exists, called the Pronunciation Department [which we went to] and they use it a lot more for news programmes and things – politicians' names, etc. – and the [guns' pronunciation] is the sort of detail I hate getting wrong. If you do, you just know someone will email in saying "I think you'll find..."

'[The theme tune] was library music. I spend a long time picking music because it does make such a difference. On a lot of readings people don't use much music: they'll have a bit at the beginning, a bit in the middle, a bit at the end and that's it. I had a really good Studio Manager working with me called David Thomas, who's been around for quite a while and he's really, really good with music. We weaved it in and out, and whenever there was any action or travelling or something – when "brown overcoat" was following Callan, for instance – it lifts it from being just a reading to something a little bit more. Music shouldn't be intrusive but should enhance the words. I love that music; in fact I've used a tiny bit of it in the Bond reading *Solo* – it's called 'Mr Pink'. It was off an album of kitsch, retro, '60s music, and I think [all the tracks] we used came off that album.'

MISSION ANALYSIS: *'The way things were going, he might need a friend. Even Lonely.'* Nearly 50 years after he was created, 'infamous television character David Callan'[17] makes his radio debut, and Ben Miles' reading makes the character as fresh and vital as his 1967 debut. The adaptation is a triumph because Bean and Green emphasise the almost-first-person narrative of the books. Miles' intimate, confidential reading successfully invites the listener inside the private thoughts of the conflicted hired killer, an atmosphere further enhanced by the galloping, spy-fi theme music. For the second time, *Callan* adopts a piece of library music as its theme and by episode two it's almost as familiar as 'The Girl In The Dark'.

Leaning more towards the East End than Woodward did (and perhaps inspired by Terence Stamp's Willie Garvin in *Modesty Blaise* (1966)), Miles' vocal performance as Callan has the shock of the new, as does his interpretation of an even more cringing, wheedling Lonely than the original. Almost reassuringly, the supporting characters more closely resemble their TV selves. You can hear the upper class sneer in Meres' dialogue, while Hunter is as ruthlessly authoritarian as he always was.

Surprisingly, thrillingly – Callan lives.

FOR A WHILE, CALLAN ENTHUSIASTS had to be content with one new, well-realised spoken word version of a James Mitchell novel, but elsewhere there were positive signs that interest in the state executioner wasn't confined solely to the radio. Just over a year after the Radio 4Extra adaptation, on 17 October 2013, *A Magnum for Schneider* and *Russian Roulette* were reissued in paperback for the first time in over 35 years, courtesy of Top Notch Thrillers, an imprint of Ostara publishing. 'I established the mission statement that our aim would be to "revive great British thrillers which do not deserve to be forgotten",[18] explained imprint editor Mike Ripley, an expert on crime and spy fiction, crime fiction reviewer for the *Daily Telegraph* and a thriller writer himself. Older than Bean, Ripley was a first generation *Callan* viewer and the impact of the series has stayed with him: 'I was a teenager and *Callan* was required viewing in my parents' house, as was (later on) James Mitchell's *When the Boat Comes In*. Both were supreme examples of popular television drama of the highest order, though at the time I can't honestly say I took much notice of the fact that they were both created and written by the same guy.

'I put a Callan novel on my [Top Notch] wish-list straight away but didn't do much about it, for the simple reason I assumed the books would have been republished to coincide with the issue of DVD compilations of the television series. When I discovered the books were out of print – and had been for some time – I got in touch with James Mitchell's son and literary executor, Peter. Initially my idea was to reissue *A Magnum for Schneider* (a.k.a. *Red File for Callan*) alongside one of Mitchell's John Craig thrillers, which hewrote as "James Munro". We have established the practice of publishing Top Notch Thriller titles in pairs and these seemed an ideal match. Things didn't quite work out as I planned – in fact they turned out better.

'Peter Mitchell was immensely helpful,' Ripley said warmly of Callan's literary guardian. 'I'm not sure how surprised he was about my interest, as the issue of DVDs of the television series had shown there was still an interest... The novels were unusual in that they came *after* the show had been a success on television. Callan was born in a screenplay not a novel, and the fact that there were novels at all has come as something of a (pleasant) surprise to people who only saw or had heard of the television series.

'On the phone Peter Mitchell was so enthusiastic about *Russian Roulette* (which I had not read at the time) that I altered our publishing plan and we republished it alongside *A Magnum for Schneider* in 2013 [the latter being popular enough for another audio book version to be released the following year]. In April 2014 we published a new edition of *Death and Bright Water* and alongside it reissued a John Craig novel, *The Innocent Bystanders*, but using the James Mitchell name rather than his Munro pen-name. That was another book on my Top Notch Thriller "wish list" right from the start before it was reissued, as copies of it are now really rather rare. I remember reading it the first time after seeing the film starring Stanley Baker in 1972.

'The next project I worked on with Peter Mitchell was the publication of an unmade *Callan* script along with as many of the short stories I could track down, as I don't think they'd ever been collected and published in book form before.' In October 2014, the handsome volume *Callan Uncovered*, the first new James Mitchell book for twelve years, was published featuring 24 short stories, the unmade script 'Goodbye Mary Lee' and the story outline 'A Funeral Has Been Arranged and Will Shortly Take Place'. A second volume, featuring short stories from 1970-72 and scripts for two lost episodes, followed in 2015. Ostara completed their series of Callan reprints with *Smear Job* and *Bonfire Night* in March 2016.

When asked if he felt Callan could undergo a further literary revival in fresh stories by new writers – a possible next logical and commercial step – Ripley was in two minds: 'I'm just not sure. Clearly, far more fans know Callan from the television than from the novels and the longer the gap, the more difficult it is to revive a series. James Bond books keep being written – there have been about three times as many written by someone other than Ian Fleming than were written by him, and it seems there's a new author every year nowadays. But you can do that with Bond because he's an international brand, backed by big budget films and a whole host of merchandising.

'I have just completed a novel starring Margery Allingham's "Golden Age" amateur detective, Albert Campion, left unfinished in 1969 on the death of Margery's husband. It was only logical to continue to write it set in 1969, so it is classed as something of a historical mystery. But that was only possible because Albert Campion was known through a long series of books from 1929-1968. Would a new Callan novel have to be updated to compete with the Jason Bournes and Jack Reachers of today? Or would he continue in his original '60s/'70s Cold War time frame? Anyone brave enough to take on the Callan mantle would have to think carefully about such things, but if there was somebody who could write a Callan story with as much pace, conviction and shrewd insights into human frailty as James Mitchell did, then yes, I'd be very interested in publishing it.'

At the time of writing, Peter Mitchell has taken up Ripley's challenge and is working on a new novel *Callan: A Death in the Family,* which reboots the Section for the 21st century and the War on Terror. With a continuing undercurrent of interest in James Mitchell's most famous creation coming steadily to the fore over the last few years, it's not surprising that, with quiet confidence, Peter comments, 'I don't think we've seen the last of David Callan.'[19]

CALLAN WAS THAT RARE PHENOMENON – an idea and character exactly right for its time, capturing people's imaginations during the dark days of the Cold War, yet retaining an enduring appeal, as the recent revivals on DVD, radio and in print show. The diverse range of views held by the franchise's production team, actors and publishers on just why *Callan* was so successful illustrate just how enthralling, compelling and ground -breaking the lonely spy's conflicted loyalties and the chilly amorality of the Section remain.

'Putting the real story about espionage on television was all down to James Mitchell,'[20] said Robert Banks Stewart. 'It was his *Armchair Theatre* that started it and he wrote brilliantly. Maybe, just maybe, that second episode "wot I wrote" gave [*Callan*] a certain kind of flavour as I was the earliest new writer. Part of the challenge of it was to create a real life view of spying.' Ray Jenkins agreed: 'Right at the very, very beginning, in the original play that James wrote, there was the idea about it being a *mucky* world: "It's not a place fit for gentlemen. Therefore, Callan, you are ideally suited." There was always this feeling that there is a section somewhere where people have to be killed because the state so demands, [even if] it's now glorified into the SAS and they now have public plaudits for being able to kill in the name of the country. Back then, it was just a dirty little section.'[21]

Jenkins' view was shared by Russell Hunter: 'It was dirty,'[22] the actor said. 'By that I mean *physically* dirty. Callan's place was never the tidiest place in the world – it was a bit of a rat hole he lived in. His business was *dirty,* the way he was treated was *dirty,* the way he treated other people, the way he treated Lonely was *dirty.* Lonely himself was none too clean, shall we say, in all the respects of that word. It was a full department of dirty tricks – nobody liked Callan, except one awful little man, who he didn't like very much... There was nothing beautiful or pretty about [the programme]. I think it might have been the public's reaction to that [which made it successful]. In its own way, *Callan* was a kind of leader on British television of a kind of – not neo-realism – but *realism,* and I think that was terribly important.'

'*Callan* was *extremely* well written,'[23] believed Clifford Rose. 'It came at a time when the idea of that sort of rather low key, un-heroic spy series was just right for that period. That's why it caught on.' Mike Vardy considered that '*Callan* was a monument of its time and will always remain so, and I think it actually drove things forward in terms of TV production. I think it should take its place in the Hall of Fame, if we're talking about the 1960s and 1970s.'[24] The high quality of the finished programmes was a reflection of the creative and professional team that produced them, Vardy noted: 'Although 40 years have gone by, the experience of working on *Callan* was a period I shall always remember with great affection. Age has dimmed my memory for detail but I remember it being a very close band of people. The regular cast members were always generous and welcoming to the guest artists and the effect is very visible in the finished production.' Jim Goddard concurred: 'There was a lot of *esprit de corps* on the whole thing and it was well written. It was strength, the *ensemble* quality of it all,'[25] while Voytek said, 'It was a very good cast and they tried to stay closer to reality than other [spy] series.'[26]

'I thought the second series was a very strong series because it had the best scripts,'[27]

Peter Duguid reflected. 'It had the residue of toughness from the first series. The last series was less happy than the others, I must say. Perhaps we shouldn't have done four: it's a long period of time. Everybody got a bit blasé about it, which won't do. It doesn't work – you've got to be on top all the time. It's a very difficult thing, success, for actors, directors and writers, and *Callan* was a *tremendous* success. It is very difficult to cope with that success; the actors then feel they've got to go onto other things and Hollywood beckons... I suppose [*Callan*] had a veneer of toughness that was quite attractive to people [and] the stories moved well: good stories, which make sense and have a bit of action in them. The BBC always said "We've never made anything as successful as *Callan*" and they never had anything of that calibre going at the time. It was the peak of the spy thing. After that it was time to give it a rest.' Reg Collin had nothing but good memories: 'The crews were marvellous. We were in studio every two weeks for two days for a long period of time. Everybody was a friend. I'm a great believer in team spirit and the spirit was really quite remarkable. Everybody made a contribution to that success. *Everybody*.'[28]

Anthony Valentine's views on why the series was so successful were strikingly detailed and thought provoking. 'First and foremost, it was the credibility. I think Callan's situation was fascinating to the public – and it's one of the things that was so clever about James Mitchell – because you were dealing with an immoral situation, in which you might say "We have to kill this man. This man is actually totally innocent, he doesn't deserve to be killed, but he has to be killed, for political reasons." Therefore to find the man who would do the killing – he would have to be a monster, he would have to be a hired assassin – which Callan was. He would also have to be – probably – fairly unappealing and certainly not a hero. You don't usually cast your hero in those types of roles.[29]

'But by getting a man like Callan, who did not want to do the job, but was *forced* to do it, then the morality becomes [interesting]. He becomes an avenging angel but a reluctant one. He's also admirable, because he has the wherewithal to do it; it is, if you like, the Charles Bronson character of the vigilante. The man is doing something which shouldn't be done, but he's doing it because he is forced to do it. Then you have the other situation where a man is doing something that *should* be done, but we personally as viewers wouldn't have the bottle to do it. We can admire him for what we would like to do, but we would be too frightened to do.

'But if you want to start talking about why [the Callan] character is attractive, that really does take hours, because it's exceedingly complex, it's very subtle, brilliantly drawn, originally, by James Mitchell – an absolute winner. He's an ordinary man, he's not James Bond, he's not a fantasy man, he's the sort of man you could find yourself standing next to in a pub, who told you his job was a salesman: entirely credible. That's extremely attractive, because it's making that world, which hitherto has been a closed, *secret* and possibly fantasy world that didn't really exist... it's put it right there in your lap. It's turning all the pages, it's revealing all the mysteries, and making it not only an open secret, it's making it entirely, mind-bogglingly possible, which to a certain extent is infinitely more telling than saying [it's like 007]. You go "James Bond? Dinner suits, [sports] cars and birds all the time? I don't believe it's like that." But, by God, you believe that *Callan* was possible. You certainly do.'

'It was a very good product, a very high quality show,'[30] Patrick Mower noted. 'I've been an actor for a long time and you get a lot of letters – people asking for autographs. I get letters from *Callan* fans that talk about my character in depth; who respect the art of acting, if you like. It's a different kind of respect and something I'm very proud of. [The series] was a forerunner of many other films showing the dark side of the secret police force. The news today that's just come out [is that] there was a secret police force in Ireland called the "MRF" that wore plain clothes and had a licence to kill and they did. [The government has] admitted there was this secret service.'

Adrian Bean, the dramatist who introduced the character of David Callan to a 21st century audience, agreed: 'The writing is quite hard-boiled in a way that a lot of British spy writing wasn't at the time – too many spies jumping in and out of sports cars and posh parties with beautiful women in tow. There was an undeniable realism about *Callan*. And somehow his very ordinariness fitted in with the sense of Cold War paranoia. He wasn't someone who stood out, or was unusual. He didn't rely on whizz-bang gadgets but on training, brute strength and native wit. The anti-hero element in his character was also very attractive, but I think the fact that most people came to *Callan* as television view-ers mustn't be overlooked, and the reason they did was because of Edward Woodward's performance. He was a superb actor, bringing total belief and commitment to the character, and the series stood out strongly against other more jokey series like *The Man from UNCLE, The Persuaders!* and *The Saint*.'[31]

With an enviable knowledge of 1960s spy literature, Mike Ripley is well qualified to appraise where the character stands in relation to his contemporaries. He summed up why interest in a man in real life you'd cross the street to avoid continues over four decades after he was last on television: 'Callan was a breath of fresh air after the ever-increasingly unreal and fantastic spy fiction heroes of the 1960s, most of which were trying to out-Bond James Bond,'[32] he said, endorsing Bean's opinion. 'On the one hand there were the surreal and slightly camp adventures of *The Avengers* or *The Man from UNCLE*, which certainly had their charm, but on the other side of the spy-fi divide were the downbeat, more believable protagonists: the tragic Leamas in *Spy Who Came in from the Cold*, the insubordinate and rather cool "Harry Palmer" character created by Len Deighton and, of course, David Callan.

'Like Harry Palmer, Callan had come up from the ranks and was not "officer material", but where Deighton's hero was clearly tuned in to the social and cultural changes of Swinging London in the 1960s, Callan was almost deliberately unfashionable, dour and more down-market. Where Deighton's hero often finds things to mock or make fun of, [33] Callan scowls at them, rejects them and sometimes even shoots them! They are very different heroes, but both iconic in their different ways, and very influential on spy-fi writing. Who today remembers the Bond-clones like Dr. Jason Love, Hugo Baron, Charles Hood or Jason Wilde with the same affection they recall Harry Palmer or David Callan?'

In conclusion, the two men who, between them, created such an iconoclastic and well-remembered character have the last word on *Callan*. 'All innovative things have their time and that was the time for that kind of character with an abrasive attitude,'[34] Edward Woodward said. 'I remember at the time a number of the critics said "It's quite interesting, but it's so far-fetched." As we went on – and nowadays it's even more and more apparent – we realised that *nothing* you do in the counter intelligence or spy genre on television, or in fiction, is far-fetched. We were much more naive in those days: the public knew a great deal less than they do now about that kind of work. [The series] hit at just the right time.' James Mitchell concisely and unambiguously summed up all the reasons for Callan's appeal: 'A good man with a wicked skill; a sad man, having that kind of expertise. He hates his job but he can do it better than anyone else. A mess of contradictions.'[35]

Over 40 years later, those contradictions fascinate still.

AFTERWORD
by Bharat Nalluri

THE 1960s AND 1970s CREATED A LEGACY of storytelling so strong that we still see their influence in modern day culture. The through line from shows such as *Danger Man, Callan* and *The Sandbaggers* is obvious to see in modern day renditions such as *Spooks* and US-based television like *Homeland*. I have been in many meetings with American showrunners who talk affectionately about *The Sandbaggers* and its major influence on their writing. Even movies such as the recent and wonderful *Tinker Tailor Soldier Spy* reflect an old school aesthetic, in this case quite literally, with the setting, pace and even acting style being very similar to the original.

With this wonderfully researched book Kenwood and Fairclough have shot an arrow (or, perhaps, fired a service revolver?) from the beginning of early televisual spy fiction and shown it hit its target in the heart of modern day storytelling. These forerunners of the genre paved the way with their grounded characters and verisimilitude, and now, at the centre of all memorable television lie these indispensable traits.

All storytellers, writers, directors, actors and the viewing audience owe a debt of gratitude to these original trail blazers.

Bharat Nalluri
Los Angeles
May 2016

Appendices

Appendix 1

CALLAN D.
From: Appointments Officer
To: Head of Sections (Group)

Callan was born South London 1934. (Age 36). Parents killed by V2 in 1944. Callan found their bodies on way home from school. From then lived with an aunt until he joined the army. Aunt now deceased.

Educated Junior School, Secondary Modern and Technical College. Left school 1946. Worked as apprentice to firm of locksmiths. (Attended Technical courses on day release.)

Army. Could have gone into Royal Engineers. Surprised employers by choosing Infantry (Green Howards).

Highest possible ratings for initiative; unnamed combat; shooting. Very high survival factor. Promoted corporal. Reduced ranks for insolence to superior officer.

Transferred to Commandos. Quickly re-promoted to corporal. Service in Malaya. His unit very successful in catching and killing Communist Chinese. Callan recommended for DSM but involved in drunken brawl with infantry sergeant whom he beat up badly. Reduced to ranks, DSM withheld. Demobbed 1952.

Resumed work at locksmiths. Suddenly and inexplicably attempted to rob jeweller's safe supplied by his firm. Caught by accident. Old night-watchman stumbled on to him, grabbed him and yelled. Callan, who could have killed him, didn't, and was caught.

Sentenced to two years imprisonment. Wormwood Scrubs. Released after 15 months. (Here he first met the burglar known as Lonely.) Hunter's section – then Vanbrugh's section – took him up on basis of (a) Commando record; (b) bugrling skill. Went to 'college' 1953-1954. Developed skills in theft, unarmed combat and shooting. Dead shot with pistol.

First active with Hunter (I), then Vanbrugh's chief execution officer. Involved in blackmail and killing. Very high rating.

Hunter took over section 1955. From then until 1966 Callan carried out 19 missions, including 11 killings. 15 were complete success; 2 failed because of inadequate briefing; 2 because of failure of colleagues. Callan prefers to work alone. (This may influence attitude of colleagues.)

By 1960 Callan was second-in-command to Hunter (I) who rated him very highly. Very possible next Head of Section.

But in 1965 he killed a Russian spy whom he knew well and liked. From that time Callan became too involved with the people who were his targets. He worked with the same skill, but increasing reluctance. Hunter tried hard to change him, but failed.

Callan de-activated from Section 1966. Trained as book-keeper, works for wholesale grocer who believes him to be ex-convict.

Replacement Toby Meres. Age 27. Eton and Coldstream. Resigned commission after 'accident' in which a guardsman died. Hunter knows Meres killed him.

Re-activated 1968. Complete success with Hunter (II) – AA rating in all operations. Complete success with Hunter (III) until brainwashed by KGB into killing him. Shortly after, Callan was shot by Meres. After critical illness Callan is about to be discharged from hospital. Medically A1. No extensive psychiatric tests have yet been carried out.

Callan is a non-smoker, drinks Scotch, cautiously on a job, heavily on other occasions.*

Appendix 2

'HUNTER'
From: Head of Sections (Group)
To: MI5/MI6 liasion (Bishop)

HUNTER I (1955-1967, 1969)

Colonel Leslie ran the Section when Callan became operational after training. He respected Leslie until, in the mid-1960s, he turned against him, questioning orders and drinking heavily. Callan considered Hunter (I) 'dirty' and symptomatic of everything wrong with counter intelligence work. This was mainly because, after Callan's suspension, Leslie considered the ex-agent totally expendable. Unannounced, Hunter (I) left the Section in early 1969, to be the British government's adviser in the Middle East problem state of Abu Tafa. Callan was disgusted to find him standing in for Hunter (III) and actively worked against him during the Belukov affair. Even so, Hunter (I) had enough respect for the man he trained to attend Callan's 'funeral' in 1972.

HUNTER II (1969)

A surprise appointment. According to Meres, Callan initially thought he was 'an idiot', later conceding that Hunter (II) was 'unorthodox,' a view tempered, perhaps, by this him reinstating Callan in the Section. A fastidious man, Hunter (II) rebuked Meres and Gould for allowing violence into his office. Despite his academic and analytical mind, Hunter (II) was careless enough to leave the Section in the middle of an Emergency D alert and was killed. Callan only learned his real name, and that he had a wife and son, at his funeral.

HUNTER III (1969)

The upper class John Ramsey, recommended as Head of the Section by Hunter (I). Callan knew Ramsey during training and he is the only Hunter Callan knew well enough to address by his first name. Hunter (III) proved himself as an undercover man, running a sports shop as a cover behind the Iron Curtain in East Germany. An even tempered man, Ramsey was a major part of the reason why Callan began feeling working for the Section was 'a good job.' Ironically, Callan was brainwashed by the KGB into believing Hunter (III) was a traitor – exploiting his deep-seated distrust of authority – and shot Ramsey dead.

HUNTER IV (1969-1972)

Valuing Callan's skills highly, Hunter (IV) wanted him back in the Section after an enquiry exonerated the agent, telling Callan that he was the best man the Section's 'ever had.' Hunter (IV) is a curious mixture: supportive of Callan as his top agent, to the point where the pair could share a drink out of hours, but also ruthlessly pragmatic: when

Callan was captured in East Germany, Hunter didn't approve of your decision to exchange Callan for a top Russian agent. Hunter (IV) told Callan this when he returned, saying that he tried to be honest with the agent when he could. Hunter (IV) came back to run the Section after Callan's short tenure as Hunter, generously telling him he 'didn't do too badly.' Despite his personal regard for Callan, he has no compunction about telling the agent that he would break him for shooting dead Richmond, a prized Soviet asset.

HUNTER V [1972]

Callan was forced into taking over the Section as he knew too much to leave intelligence work, and because his predecessor had to quickly leave for a promotion in the Scheduled Territories Department. Hunter (V)'s successes were negligible: capturing the Soviet agent Svetlana Souraikin ('Flo Mayhew'), uncovering an intelligence fraud and securing a low-level defection. His misjudgement of the agent James Cross's mental state was catastrophic. Cross was shot dead and Hunter (V) disobeyed standing orders by leaving the Section during an emergency (as Hunter II had done) to – successfully – kill the KGB executioner. Callan was replaced by the recalled Hunter (IV).

HUNTER VI (Restricted)

The youngest Hunter was effete, flamboyantly dressed and Oxbridge educated. In 1981 he expertly manipulated the retired Callan into drawing out the Soviet agent Daniel Haggerty, a retired left-wing MP. The middle-aged agent was easily duped by Hunter (V), forgetting how duplicitous the Section could be. Hunter (V) told Callan, truthfully – 'It's never over.'

Appendix 3: 'CALLAN: A DEATH IN THE FAMILY' novel extract

THIS IS A SHORT, exclusive extract from a new Callan novel by Peter Mitchell, reproduced with his kind permission.

Iraq war veteran David Callan suffers from Post Traumatic Stress Disorder and has been struggling with the condition since leaving the armed forces. Travelling North to attend the funeral of a realtive, he meets Toby Meres from the Ministry of Defence. The man makes Callan an offer of employment...

'Sit still, Callan.'

Callan sat as still as he could – but that wasn't easy. His eyes were wide with panic, sweat was dripping from his nose and his fists were clenched tight. So was his jaw. He couldn't speak.

'Let me tell you how things are going to be.'

Meres's voice had softened again and he predicted the future in calm, measured tones.

'I am going to give you an envelope. In it, you will find £500 in cash and the name and telephone number of the person that wants to meet you. You are going to use that money to travel back to that sad little flat of yours in North London, get yourself a good meal and a couple of sherbets, then tomorrow you are going to phone that number and arrange a meeting.'

Callan was about to try to speak again but Meres stopped him.

'If you don't, you will make me irritated, Mr. Callan. Under those circumstances I will have no choice but to make sure you get done for assaulting those two little boys you duffed up last night. Your friend, the one you stayed with last night, will also get done.'

Callan was bursting with anger and unable to do anything about it.

Meres carried on: 'Possession with intent to supply. I had a little root around while you were on your way here to pay your last respects. Stolen goods too, I shouldn't wonder. Now, do I make myself clear? A nod will do, Callan.'

Callan nodded. He knew he would have no choice but see it through. Deep down he knew it the second he'd sat down in the car.

Meres handed Callan the envelope.

'You twat.' It was all Callan could manage.

Meres was genuinely exasperated.

'You're an ungrateful little sod, aren't you Callan? Look, you get £500 and all you have to do is have a meeting with someone who will see you're a has-been inside 30 seconds. So I've been sent here to get you. So what? You're a busted flush. You talk and go home. Worst case scenario there'll be a two-hour assessment which will reveal what we already know. David Callan is a waste of space.

'Now fuck off out of here before I get cross.'

Callan didn't need to be asked twice. As soon as Meres released the central locking he was out of the car and standing on the pavement. He put the envelope in his pocket and stood watching while Meres drove away. When the white Audi turned right at the 'T' junction and disappeared, Callan stepped across the pavement, walked over the grass verge to the wall and violently threw up. He sat with his head against the bricks and sobbed for a few minutes before he felt strong enough to get to his feet and make his way to the pub.

Appendix 4

CALLAN REPEATS

'THE CALLAN SAGA' - 1971

Transmission details for the ITV Border, Channel, Grampian, HTV, Scottish, Thames, Tyne Tees and Westward regions.

This season consisted of selected episodes from Series Two and most of Series Three, bar 'God Help Your Friends' and the controversial 'Amos Green Must Live', and was transmitted in a late-night slot. This practice of nocturnal reruns was normal in the 1970s, especially regarding ITC series such as *Man in a Suitcase* and *The Prisoner*.

The 1971 repeat season helped fill the eighteenth month gap until Series Four.

8 April	11.00-12.00 pm	'Red Knight, White Knight'
15 April	11.00-12.00 pm	'The Most Promising Girl of Her Year'
22 April	11.00-12.00 pm	'Let's Kill Everybody'
6 May	11.00-12.00 pm	'Heir Apparent'
13 May	11.00-12.00 pm	'Death of a Friend'*
20 May	11.00-12.00 pm	'Death of a Friend'**
27 May	11.00-12.00 pm	'Death of a Hunter'
3 June	11.00-12.00 pm	'Where Else Could I Go?'
17 June	11.00-12.00 pm	'Summoned to Appear'
24 June	11.00-12.00 pm	'The Same Trick Twice'
1 July	11.00-12.00 pm	'A Village Called "G"'
8 July	11.00-12.00 pm	'Suddenly – At Home'
15 July	11.00-12.00 pm	'Act of Kindness'
22 July	11.00-12.00 pm	'Breakout'

* = 'The Callan Saga' was replaced on Thames by a programme covering local results for the 1970 General Election
** = Thames advertised 'Death of a Friend'; the regions advertised 'Death of a Hunter'

AFTERNOON REPEATS - 1974

ITV, subject to regional network variations. Transmission details for Southern television.

It was common practice to repeat drama programmes in the afternoons during the early 1970s. Apart from *Callan*, ITV showed popular series like the Linda Thorson season of *The Avengers*, *A Family at War*, *Love Story* and *The Main Chance*. The *Callan* film opened in UK cinemas in May 1974. Running until early April, the repeats of Series Four helped promote Callan's debut on the big screen.

3 January	3.00-3.55 pm	'That'll Be the Day'
10 January	3.00-3.55 pm	'Call Me Sir!'
17 January	3.00-3.55 pm	'First Refusal'
24 January	3.00-3.55 pm	'Rules of the Game'
31 January	3.00-3.55 pm	'If He Can, So Could I'

7 February	3.00-3.55 pm	'None of Your Business'
14 February	3.00-3.55 pm	'Charlie says it's Goodbye'
21 February	3.00-3.55 pm	'I Never Wanted the Job'
28 February	3.00-3.55 pm	'The Carrier'
7 March	3.00-3.55 pm	'The Contract'
		'The Richmond File:
14 March	3.00-3.55 pm	Call Me Enemy'
		The Richmond File:
28 March	3.00-3.55 pm	Do You Recognise the Woman?'
		The Richmond File:
4 April	3.00-3.55 pm	A Man Like Me'

'Racing from Doncaster' was shown instead of *'Callan'* on 21 March

CHANNEL 4 - 1984

On Saturday 9 June, the *Western Mail* printed an enthusiastic preview by John Barber of the upcoming Channel 4 repeat season: 'Callan is back! The government-hired killer who was television's antidote to James Bond back in the ['60s] and early ['70s] begins a rerun on Channel 4 tonight.[1]

'The new screening begins, sad to say, in the middle rather than at the beginning. The first two series, made by ABC in black and white, are not available. So *Callan* (C4, 9.00) starts with the first episode of the third set, made in colour by Thames – ABC's successor – in 1970.

'The role of the man who sees life on the seamy side made an international star out of Edward Woodward, besides establishing a new and apparently realistic look for spy drama. This agent owes much more to Harry Palmer of *[The IPCRESS] File* fame than to 007. *Callan* also made a star of Russell Hunter, who plays Lonely, unwashed, unloved, unlikeable and spurred on by fear of everyone and everything.'

In this batch of reruns, all the episodes were edited slightly for timing reasons. For instance, in 'The Same Trick Twice' a scene was lost in which Callan agrees to pay Lonely, working as a public toilet attendant, with the Bond-style pun 'cash in lieu.'

When Series Three and Four were repeated, Jeremy Isaacs, the head of Channel 4, admitted that he had forgotten to include a repeat of the *Armchair Theatre* pilot play 'A Magnum for Schneider'. This may be why that when Channel 4 began a nostalgic night of archive TV programming in 1992 called *TV Heaven*, 'A Magnum for Schneider' was finally shown by the network on Saturday 8 February, as part of its presentation of television from 1967. Other vintage programmes screened that night were the comedy *At Last the 1948 Show*, *Coronation Street* (featuring Elsie Tanner's wedding) and the chat show *The Frost Programme*.

The repeat run began on S4C two weeks later.

9 June	9.00-10.00 pm	'Where Else Could I Go?'
16 June	9.00-10.00 pm	'Summoned to Appear'
23 June	9.00-10.00 pm	'The Same Trick Twice'
30 June	9.00-10.00 pm	'A Village Called "G"'
7 July	9.00-10.00 pm	'Suddenly – At Home'
14 July	9.00-10.00 pm	'Act of Kindness'
21 July	9.00-10.00 pm	'God Help Your Friends'

28 July	9.00-10.00 pm	'Breakout'
4 August	9.00-10.00 pm	'Amos Green Must Live'
11 August	9.00-10.00 pm	'That'll be the Day'
18 August	9.00-10.00 pm	'Call Me Sir!'
25 August	9.00-10.00 pm	'First Refusal'
1 September	9.00-10.00 pm	'Rules of the Game'
8 September	9.00-10.00 pm	'If He Can, So Could I'
15 September	9.00-10.00 pm	'None of Your Business'
25 September	9.00-10.00 pm	'Charlie says it's Goodbye'
29 September	9.00-10.00 pm	'I Never Wanted the Job'
6 October	9.00-10.00 pm	'The Carrier'
13 October	9.00-10.00 pm	'The Contract
20 October	9.00-10.00 pm	'The Richmond File: Call Me Enemy'
11 December	9.00-10.00 pm	'The Richmond File: Do You Recognise the Woman?'* *Originally scheduled for 27 October, 9-10 pm*
12 December	9.00-10.00 pm	'The Richmond File: A Man Like Me'* *Originally scheduled for 3 November, 8.30-9.30 pm*

* Both episodes were postponed because of a Channel 4 strike

SC4 - 1984[2]

23 June	9.55-10.55 pm	'Where Else Could I Go?'
30 June	9.45-10.45 pm	'Summoned to Appear'
7 July	9.25-10.25 pm	'The Same Trick Twice'
28 June	9.00-10.00 pm	'A Village Called "G"'
7 July	9.00-10.00 pm	'Suddenly – At Home'
21 July	9.15-10.15 pm	'Act of Kindness'
18 August	9.15-10.15 pm	'God Help Your Friends'
25 August	9.15-10.15 pm	'Breakout'
1 September	9.15-10.15 pm	'Amos Green Must Live'
8 September	10.15-11.15 pm	'That'll be the Day'
15 Septemver	9.15-10.15 pm	'Call Me Sir!'
22 September	10.05-11.05 pm	'First Refusal'
29 September	10.05-11.05 pm	'Rules of the Game'
6 October	10.05-11.05 pm	'If He Can, So Could I'
13 October	10.05-11.05 pm	'None of Your Business'
20 October	10.35-11.35 pm	'Charlie says it's Goodbye'
3 November	10.05-11.05 pm	'I Never Wanted the Job' *Originally scheduled for 27 October, 10.45-11.45pm*

10 November	10.20-11.20 pm	'The Carrier'
		Originally scheduled for 3 November,
		10.05-11.05pm
17 November	10.05-11.05 pm	'The Contract'
		Originally scheduled for 10 November,
		10.20 -11.20 pm
		'The Richmond File:
24 November	10.35-11.35 pm	Call Me Enemy'
		Originally scheduled for 17 November,
		10.05 pm-11.05 pm
1 December	10.30-11.30 pm	'Do You Recognise the Woman?'
		Originally scheduled for 24 November,
		10.35 pm-11.35pm
8 December	10.30-11.30 pm	'A Man Like Me'
		Originally scheduled for 3 November,
		8.30 pm-9.30 pm

'THAMES MAVERICKS' SEASON - 1989

'That'll Be the Day'
Inntroduction by Dennis Waterman

Thames: Monday 24 July 9.00 pm
HTV: Friday 28 July 10.35 pm
Tyne Tees: Monday 7 August 10.35 pm
Granada: Tuesday 22 August 10.35 pm

'VINTAGE THAMES' SEASON - 1995

'Call Me Enemy'

Channel 4: Saturday 22 July 8.30 pm
S4C: Saturday 28 July 9.00 pm

A season of heavily edited repeats was also shown on the satellite channel UK Gold in the early-to-mid 1990s.

Appendix 5: CALLAN FOR SALE

Details of merchandise, most of which can be found reasonably priced online.

RECORDINGS

Eye for An Eye (LP)
Artists: Jack Trombey and Reids, played by the International Studio Group under the direction of Jack Trombey. Featured 'Girl In The Dark'.
Year: 1966
Company: Music DeWolfe
Catalogue No.: DW/LP 2969

This Man Alone (LP)
Artist: Edward Woodward
Year: April 1970
Company: DJM
Catalogue No.: DJLPS 405
Highest chart position: 42
Weeks on chart: 2

Fourteen Great TV Themes (LP)
Artist: Ike Isaacs and His Guitars
Year: 1972
Company: Chapter One Records
Catalogue No.: CMS 102
Re-released: 1974
  Company: Decca Eclipse
  Catalogue No.: ECS 2163
  'Runs the gamut of mood music from Nacini's Western-flavoured *Cade's County* through Jack Trombey's nerve-gripping *Callan* to the very graceful Khachaturian melody of *The Onedin Line*.'[3]

A Magnum for Schneider (Audio Book)
Released: 1 August 2014
Read by: Daniel Coonan
Company: Magna Story Sound
ISBN-10: 0857148435
ISBN-13: 978-0857148438
Audio Download: ASIN B01FGO6TFE
  To date, this is the seventh version (unabridged) of the first Callan novel.

SUPER 8 FILM

Callan: Edward Woodward in 'Counter Chase'
Released: 1974
Company: Walton
Format: Super 8, colour and sound
  Up until the advent of home video in the 1980s, film companies released edited versions of feature films that could be played on domestic Super 8 projectors. *Counter Chase* concentrates on the Schneider/Callan pursuit from the *Callan* movie. The packaging describes the executioner as 'working as an agent for a British undercover section.'

HOME VIDEO

Callan – The Movie
Released: 1985
Company: Cel
Certification: 15
Running time: 1 hour and 41 minutes

This is Callan
Released: 1986
Company: Channel 5
Certification: 15
Catalogue No.: CVF 01502
Running time: 1 hour and 41 minutes
  A re-release of the *Callan* movie with the same cover artwork as the Cel video. The title was incorrectly adapted from the by-line on some of the film's publicity material. It continues: 'He never makes friends, and all his enemies are dead!'

NB: There were also commercial VHS relaeses in other territories. 'Den Aasgeiren Eiskalt Serviert' ['The Secret Agent Service'] was released by Montevideo in West Germany, while Holland's Panorama Video Bio issued 'Death Mission'. In Japan, Vook issued the film under the Japoanese translation of 'Callan'.

**Callan –
Suddenly/At Home, Breakout**
Released: 1988
Company: Thames Video Collection
Catalogue No.: TV 9982
Running time: 104 minutes
Cover Design: Nicky Downes
First commercial release of television episodes (minus original advert breaks). The cover text introduces Callan as 'The spy who is human.'

DVD

Callan – The Movie
Released: 2005
Company: Stax Entertainment Ltd.
Catalogue No.: STX2018
Running time: 101 minutes
Extras: Interview with Edward Woodward. Previously released on 1 September 2001 by Prism Leisure, with a slightly different sleeve.

Callan – The Complete First Series
Released: 2001
Company: Clear Vision
Catalogue No.: CBOXDVD01
Running time: 456 minutes
Extras: Animated menu, scene selection, series overview with pictures, episode info, transmission dates, synopses, cast and credits, 'Secret Service' facts sheet. The packaging is very misleading, as this release is the third, colour series from 1970, minus advert breaks.

Callan – Complete Third Series
Released: 2007
Company: Umbrella British TV
Catalogue No.: DAVID1048
Running time: 486 minutes
Extras: Interview with Edward Woodward filmed in 2000, originally produced for the 2001 UK DVD release of the *Callan* movie by Prism Leisure.

Callan – Complete Fourth Series
Released: 2007
Company: Umbrella British TV
Catalogue No.: DAVID1100
Running time: 670 minutes
Extras: Audio commentaries with Edward Woodward on the episodes 'If He Can, So Could I' and 'Call Me Enemy'. The set also includes the 1974 *Callan* movie, which includes the 2000 Woodward interview from the *Callan – Complete Third Series* box set.

**4 Collection: Drama
Hammers Over the Anvil / The
Intruder / Callan / Marquis de Sade**
Released: 2007
Company: ILC Entertainment Ltd.
Catalogue No.: ILC3654
Running time: 340 minutes (4 films)
A double-sided DVD budget release of the *Callan* film, together with two Roger Corman movies and a Russell Crowe film from 1993.

Callan: Set 1
Released: July 7 2009
Company: Acorn Media
Catalogue No.: 54961828098
Running time: 455 minutes
Extras: Callan trivia and biography of Edward Woodward. The American release of Series 3. The by-line on the packaging reads, 'Secret Agent. Assassin. Antihero'.

Callan: Set 2
Released: July 7 2009
Company: Acorn Media
Catalogue No.: 54961834099
Running time: 663 minutes
Extras: Commentaries with Woodward on 'If He Can, So Could I' and 'Call Me Enemy 'from the 2007 Umbrella British TV release. Biography of Edward Woodward. The American release of Series 4.

Callan – The Monochrome Years
Released: 22 February 2010
Company: Network
Catalogue No.: 7953231
Running time: 600 minutes
All original advert breaks are included.

Callan – The Colour Years
Released: 10 May 2010
Company: Network
Catalogue No.: 7953307
Running time: 1,100 minutes
The Series 3 episodes are included in the originally intended transmission order. All original advert breaks are included.

Callan – Wet Job
Released: 28 March 2011
Company: Network
Catalogue No.: 7953231
Running time: 80 minutes
Extras: Stills gallery.
Original advert breaks are included.

Callan: This Man Alone
Released: 1 February 2016
Company: Network
Catalogue No.: 7953452
Running time: 300 mins
This 3-disc DVD set contains the feature-length documentary *This Man Alone.* Narrated by Peter Woodward, it includes interview contributions from Reg Collin, Jim Goddard, Piers Haggard, Peter Mitchell, Patrick Mower, Trevor Preston, Mike Vardy and Dick Fiddy (supplemented by uncut interview material). The set also includes the complete recording block for the episode 'The Worst Soldier I Ever Saw', *The Edward Woodward Hour,* the documentaries *James Mitchell: A World of My Own/ Flashback,* script PDFs for the whole series and *Wet Job,* as well as merchandise, press cuttings and stills galleries.

The set also features new transfers of *Armchair Theatre:* 'A Magnum for Schneider' – from a film recording which has slightly longer scenes then the version released on *Callan: The Monochrome Years* – and 'The Good Ones are All Dead', as well as the tense trailer for 'Let's Kill Everybody'.

MISSING FILE: *After Network Distributing Ltd. finished releasing their extra-free* Callan *DVD sets in 2011, the company announced* Callan – The Definitive Edition *as a box set. Originally planned for reaease in the autumn of 2011, the set was scheduled to include* Armchair Theatre: *'A Magnum for Schneider', all episodes of the TV series and* Wet Job *(1981), as well as* The Edward Woodward Hour *(1971). Exclusive to the set was a documentary on the making of* Callan (This Man Alone) *and a book of viewing notes by Andrew Pixley* (Callan: Under the Red File). *This box set was subsequently cancelled and* Callan: Under the Red File *and* Callan: This Man Alone *were released separately.*

VIEWING NOTES
Callan: Under the Red File
Author: Andrew Pixley
Released: August 2015
Company: Network
ISBN: 978-0-9929766-1-3
Extensive factual book on the series, thoroughly covering in detail production, script changes and the series' reception in the media.

SHEET MUSIC
This Man Alone
Published: 1970
Company: De Wolfe/Southern Music Publishing Co. Ltd.
Edward Woodward's vocal version of the series' theme.

Appendix 6: THE EDWARD WOODWARD HOURS

EDWARD WOODWARD made two light entertainment specials for Thames Television in 1971. His potential as an all-round entertainer was spotted by Thames' Controller of Light Entertainment Philip Jones in 1969 during the production of Woodward's first *This Is Your Life* when Jones had been impressed by the actor's warm and jovial personality. For Woodward, this chance tied in with his ambition to establish himself as a television personality away from *Callan*.

Transmitted in August 1971 in a primetime slot, the first *Edward Woodward Hour* was overseen by *Callan* producer Reg Collin and saw Woodward demonstrating his singing and comic talents to an appreciative studio audience. Backed by the master of easy listening music Geoff Love (and His Orchestra), Woodward performed MOR standards including 'The Way You Look Tonight'. There were two duets, one with guest actor Patrick Cargill on 'A Couple of Men About Town' and the second with the then-popular Danish singer Nina on 'I Will Wait for You'. In a more serious vein, Woodward also sang the American Civil War ballad 'Today I Killed a Man I Didn't Know' (a track on his LP *This Man Alone*, released the year before).

Apart from Cargill and Nina, his guests for the night were the actress Beryl Reid and 'my old friend Russell Hunter'. As well as the *Callan/Father, Dear Father* crossover sketch, there were two amusing and original skits opposite Reid. The first dealt with a married couple at home who turn out to be burglars, while the second was a witty spoof of the Terence Rattigan and John Osborne styles of theatre. The evening concluded with Woodward joining his guests (except Hunter, oddly) for a celebratory drink on stage.

THE EDWARD WOODWARD HOUR

Executive Producer: Philip Jones
Producer/Director: Reg Collin
Associate Producer: David Clark
Writer: Eric Merriman
Designer: Patrick Downing
Music Associate: Sid Haddon

FIRST UK TRANSMISSION: Wednesday 4 August 1971, 8.00 pm

CAST: Edward Woodward, Beryl Reid, Patrick Cargill, Nina, Russell Hunter, Natasha Pyne, Dany Clare, Ann Holloway, Geoff Love and his Orchestra

TV TIMES: 'For those who are familiar with Edward Woodward mainly as Callan, the next hour or so should come as a surprise.

'Edward sings well-known standards, including "It Had to Be You" and "When I Fall in Love". Musical director Geoff Love and his concert orchestra supply the backing.

'Switching to comedy, Edward joins his guests in sketches.

'The *Father, Dear Father* sketch is written by Johnnie Mortimer and Brian Cooke, and directed by William G. Stewart. Peter Robinson is responsible for the script of the burglar sketch.'
31 July-6 August 1971, Southern edition

'CALLAN' / 'FATHER, DEAR FATHER' SKETCH

CAST: Edward Woodward (Callan), Russell Hunter (Lonely), Patrick Cargill (Patrick Glover), Natasha Pyne (Anna Glover), Ann Holloway (Karen Glover)

MISSION PROFILE: Callan is ordered to retrieve a 'black box' from a suburban house belonging to a double agent and then kill him. Unfortunately, things don't go according to plan. By mistake, Callan goes to the house of the writer Patrick Glover, which he shares with his two grown-up daughters, Anna and Karen. Hilarity ensues.

A MAN LIKE ME: Not performing at his usual operational strength. Callan gets the address of his target wrong and Lonely – of all people – has to correct him. He also thinks UHF is a rival security organization: 'They're not involved, are they?' Everything considered, Callan's lucky to survive being blown up by a bomb.

LONELY: For once, Lonely is the rational side of the partnership, discovering that Callan is mistaken about the location of his assignment.

A TIE AND A CREST: Despite being highly educated, Glover remains completely ignorant of Callan's profession as a spy.

SPY SPEAK: 'Trouble with the KGB?' Callan asks Glover anxiously. Oblivious to the terminology of espionage, the author replies, 'No, the ITV.'

Lonely, perceptive as ever, looks knowingly at Glover's wrecked television and informs him, 'I can tell you what's wrong with that. Somebody's bashed your screen in.'

ALCOHOL, TOBACCO AND FIREARMS: Embarrassingly, Callan gets his gun caught in the lining of his overcoat.

INFORMATION: On the *TV Times* listings page for 4 August, photographs of Woodward and Alfred Burke were headlined 'Double Agents'. The caption read: '8.0: Callan out of character. Singing, dancing. His hour of friendly persuasion. 9.0: Marker in character – and still very much about sleuthing.'

Edward Woodward was upbeat about Callan's detour into situation comedy. 'It seemed a good idea at the time! I remember when we were discussing that, certain producers would have said "We don't want to make fun of [*Callan*]", but when Russell and I did that, we were playing Callan and Lonely, we weren't sending up Lonely or sending up Callan: we played the characters. And anyway, it was like an end of school party, a bit of a release. We were working on the series at that time, still very heavily, and it was just a bit of fun. As far as I can remember, the audience reaction went very well. We did get one or two letters saying: *"Desecration!"*"[4]

He added, 'I can remember at the time us both hating it, saying "God, why are we doing this? This is awful, this is terrible." But in retrospect I don't think it was particularly reprehensible. It worked quite well, I think.' Several years later, while recording *Callan* audio commentaries for Umbrella British TV, Woodward politely stated that he couldn't remember anything about the sketch at all.

Russell Hunter's initial feelings about his foray into light entertainment didn't change. Interviewed in the 1985, the experience was as painful for him then as it had been at the time: 'That was what I call the absolute exploitation of the studio exploiting a studio exploiting a studio... But, you know, if Teddy wanted you to be in it, you said, "Yes! Of course!" but [I thought] "Dear God, is this what we're reduced to *now?*" One was amazed one got paid £5 for doing four minutes one night, which was as much as one got for sweating your heart out for two weeks doing *Callan*. The money that was thrown at you! It was a terrible, terrible temptation to somebody like me who had never had big money. It really was tempting. But, thank God, we only did it a couple of times because it was *truly* embarrassing.'[5]

The reaction to *The Edward Woodward Hour* was overwhelmingly positive. Despite one *TV Times* correspondent dismissing the actor's singing and comedy as 'rubbish'[6], 'a huge postbag' was in favour of Woodward's side-step into variety. K. Hutchins of Eastbourne was particularly impressed: 'How lovely to see someone with "short back and sides" singing songs with feeling, without awful grimaces and wriggles. The best programme for a long time. Congratulations.' 'What a very talented man he is!' declared Doris Catlin of Sussex. 'I am by no means a square and do enjoy some of today's artists. But, compared with some of them – with their weird hair-dos, outlandish clothes and barely audible singing – Edward Woodward's clear, pleasant rendering of songs made the others seem like amateurs... I have always enjoyed his performances in *Callan* but please may we hope for more of his other talents too?' Thames duly obliged by commissioning *Another Edward Woodward Hour* for the Christmas 1971 schedule.

MISSION ANALYSIS: *'Alright, darlin', I want it and I want it quick!'* A sure sign of how popular a TV drama character has become is when he or she starts appearing on variety shows. That's certainly the case here, and there's fun to be had watching a role as subtly con-structed and performed as Callan facing the broad sitcom caricatures of the Glover family. The fun lasts as long as the novelty of the joke, which is roughly the seven-minute duration of the sketch.

Put in a madcap situation like this, it's not surprising Woodward overacts in places. Significantly, Russell Hunter – who has 'funny bones' in the make-up of his personality to start with – stays in character throughout.

The most striking aspect of this bizarre hybrid is watching Woodward prepare to become Callan in front of the studio audience. The first part of the costume he puts on is Callan's scarf and, as he does so, there's an enthusiastic burst of applause. If definitive recognition of *Callan*'s status as a television institution was required, there it was.

ANOTHER EDWARD WOODWARD HOUR

Executive Producer: Philip Jones
Producer: Reg Collin
Director: Peter Frazier-Jones
Writer: Eric Merriman
Music Associate: Sid Lucas
Music Director: Geoff Love

FIRST UK TRANSMISSION: Boxing Day, 26 December 1971, 10.15 pm

CAST: Edward Woodward, Margaret Lockwood, Peter Jones, Julia Lockwood, Russell Hunter, Geoff Love and his Orchestra

MISSING HOUR: A recording of this show no longer exists in the Fremantlemedia archive.

TV TIMES: 'Earlier this year, Edward Woodward left counter-espionage man David Callan at home and starred in his own hour of music and comedy.

'It was so successful that the decision was taken to give Callan Christmas leave and produce another [50] minutes of Edward Woodward and his guests.

'In addition to singing, Edward will be joined by Peter Jones and Russell "Lonely" Hunter in comedy sketches and by star of films and television, Margaret Lockwood, taking a break from her *Justice* series. Margaret's actress daughter, Julia, completes the guest list.'
18-31 December 1971, Southern edition

INFORMATION: Russell Hunter features as Lonely, before changing into evening dress for a song and dance number with Woodward. 'Oh, dear God, it was embarrassing, *truly* embarrassing, *really embarrassing*. I found [it] embarrassing too when Teddy [was] an all singing, all dancing Edward Woodward, and I had to appear as Lonely and then do a lightning quick change into white tie and tails, singing "You've Gotta Have Style". Teddy Woodward, now playing Frank Sinatra, Dean Martin... Dear God, it was enough to make you want to get him as drunk as Dean Martin.'[7]

Woodward appears in a sketch as the strongman who strikes the gong in Rank films' corporate ident, with Margaret Lockwood as the 'Gainsborough lady' – an in-joke as Lockwood starred in movies for Gainsborough films. Publicity photographs of the couple in costume were issued to the press over the 1971 Christmas season.

Footnotes

INTRODUCTION:
'I've got a job for you...'

1 Thanks to Trevor Preston for this description. Interview with authors, 28 August 2013

1: SECTION PERSONNEL
James Mitchell

1 Peter and Charlotte Mitchell interview with authors, 8 October 2013
2 'The Book Page: If Callan met Those Louts on the Train...' By Graham Lord', *Sunday Express*, 8 December 1974
3 'World of People: Real Life is Stranger than Callan. By William Rankine', *News of the World*, 1970
4 *TV Times*, 1972 (edition unknown)
5 Peter and Charlotte Mitchell interview with authors, 8 October 2013
6 'The Book Page: If Callan Met Those Louts on the Train... By Graham Lord', *Sunday Express*, 8 December 1974
7 Peter and Charlotte Mitchell interview with authors, 8 October 2013
8 'No Way Back Now that I'm a Novelist', Dot Butler, *Gazette*, 17 April 1996
9 Peter and Charlotte Mitchell interview with authors, 8 October 2013
10 'No Way Back Now that I'm a Novelist', Dot Butler, *Gazette*, April 1996
11 'Play Bill: Spy-Catcher Hunts a Saboteur', *TV Times*, Southern edition, September 10-16 1961
12 Anthony Read correspondence with authors, 14 October 2013
13 Anonymous, *The Times*, 17 October 1966
14 Peter and Charlotte Mitchell interview with authors, 8 October 2013
15 'The Write Man for the Job', Anonymous, *She*, December 1972
16 Peter and Charlotte Mitchell interview with authors, 8 October 2013
17 Peter and Charlotte Mitchell interview with authors, 8 October 2013
18 'For the Love of My Lost Delia', Shaun Usher, *Daily Mail*, 6 June 1995
19 *Ibid*, 6 June 1995
20 Peter and Charlotte Mitchell interview with authors, 8 October 2013
21 James Mitchell interview with Anthony Goodman and Matthew Morgenstern, 15 August 1985
22 'The Write Man for the Job', Anonymous, *She*, December 1972
23 Edward Woodward commentary on 'Call Me Enemy', *Callan: Complete Fourth Series* DVD box set, Umbrella British TV, 2007
24 Piers Haggard interview with authors, 21 October 2013
25 'James Mitchell by Philip Purser', *Guardian*, 19 September 2002
26 Mike Ripley correspondence with authors, 6 March 2013
27 Peter and Charlotte Mitchell interview with authors, 8 October 2013
28 Discussed within Bill Craig interview with Anthony Goodman and Matthew Morgenstern, 2 September 1985

29 By writing the first, middle and last stories in this series, Mitchell may have believed these episodes were the most the likely to be repeated and earn him re-screening fees. Terry Nation, a fellow client at Roger Hancock Ltd., adopted a similar strategy on *Blake's 7* (1978-1981).
30 Peter and Charlotte Mitchell interview with authors, 8 October 2013
31 'World of People: Real Life is Stranger than Callan by William Rankine', *News of the World*, 13 September 1970
32 Terence Feely interview with Anthony Goodman and Matthew Morgenstern, 22 July 1985
33 Review, Cecil Wilson, *Daily Mail*, 8 March 1970
34 Review, Alexander Walker, *Evening Standard*, 18 March 1970
35 'Make a Nice Living for James by Shaun Usher', *Daily Mail*, 9 October 1972
36 *Ibid*, Shaun Usher, 9 October 1972
37 'Credible Law Scenes of "Justice" by Richard Last', *Daily Telegraph*, 9 October 1971
38 *Ibid*, Richard Last, 9 October 1971
39 Derek Horne interview with authors, 24 January 2014
40 'The Book Page: If Callan met Those Louts on the Train... By Graham Lord', *Sunday Express*, 8 December 1974
41 *Ibid*, 8 December 1974
42 *Ibid*, 8 December 1974
43 Peter and Charlotte Mitchell interview with authors, 8 October 2013
44 'The Lad Who Kept to Land... and Sailed to Success,' Rosalie Horner, *Daily Express*, 28 October 1976
45 *Ibid*, 28 October 1976
46 *Ibid*, 28 October 1976
47 Peter and Charlotte Mitchell interview with authors, 8 October 2013
48 'Fivers Galore,' William Boyd, *New Statesman*, 5 June 1981
49 'Just Good Friends,' Clive James, *Observer*, 7 June 1981
50 'Darling, Your Slip is Showing: TV Review by Herbert Kretzmer', *Daily Mail*, 5 June 1981
51 Shaun O'Riordan interview with Anthony Goodman and Matthew Morgenstern, 5 January 1987
52 'TV Review by Herbert Kretzmer', *Daily Mail*, 10 November 1983
53 'A Trawl in Deep Waters', Nancy Banks-Smith, *Guardian*, 10 November 1983
54 Peter and Charlotte Mitchell interview with authors, 8 October 2013
55 James Mitchell correspondence with Sarah Guiver, 1993
56 Peter and Charlotte Mitchell interview with authors, 8 October 2013
57 *Ibid*, 8 October 2013
58 *Ibid*, 8 October 2013
59 'No Way Back Now that I'm a Novelist', Dot Butler, *Gazette*, 17 April 1996
60 James Mitchell correspondence with Sarah Guiver, 1996
61 James Mitchell correspondence with Sarah Guiver, 1999
62 Peter and Charlotte Mitchell interview with authors, 8 October 2013
63 'TV Greats Tribute to Top Writer: "Mitchell Lifted Us to New Heights", says Callan Star', by David Whetstone', *The Journal*, 18 September 2002
64 'Express Obituaries: James Mitchell, Creator of TV Hit Man Callan: Geordie writer's Thrilling Talent', Kathryn Holloway,' *Daily Express*, 27 September 2002

65 '"Gentleman" James Mitchell dies at 76: Top Author Loses Battle with Cancer, by Sam Wonfor,' *The Journal*, 17 September 2002

66 Peter and Charlotte Mitchell interview with authors, 8 October 2013

Edward Woodward

67 'My Story - Edward Woodward. Part One: The Many Lives of Callan', Ken Roche, *TV Times*, 18-31 December 1972

68 'When a Son Begins to Outshine His Father', Clive Hirschorn, *Sunday Express*, 3 April 1977

69 'My Story - Edward Woodward. Part One: The Many Lives of Callan', Ken Roche, *TV Times*, 18-31 December 1972

70 'My Story - Edward Woodward. Part Two: "Are You Going to Marry Me or Not?"', Ken Roche, *TV Times*, 1-7 January 1972

71 'When a Son Begins to Outshine His Father', Clive Hirschorn, *Sunday Express*, 3 April 1977

72 'My Story - Edward Woodward. Part Two: "Are You Going to Marry Me or Not?"', Ken Roche, *TV Times*, 1-7 January 1972

73 'My Story - Edward Woodward. Part Three: What Callan Has Done for Me', Ken Roche, *TV Times*, 8-14 January 1972

74 He played a disturbed Health & Safety officer in the episode 'Safety Man' (1965); James Mitchell's story 'A Job for Willy' was aired six weeks later.

75 'Crouchback's Mixed Fortunes', Ann Lawrence, *Morning Star*, 4 January 1967

76 'My Story - Edward Woodward. Part Three: What Callan Has Done for Me', Ken Roche, *TV Times*, 8-14 January 1972. Interviewed in 1985, James Mitchell recalled Venetia reading the script first and encouraging Edward to take the part, saying, 'You've got to read this and if you don't play it you're crazy.'

77 Edward Woodward commentary on *If He Can, So Could I, Callan: Complete Fourth Series* DVD box set, Umbrella British TV, 2007

78 Voytek interview with Anthony Goodman and Matthew Morgenstern, 5 November 1986

79 Reg Collin interview with Anthony Goodman and Matthew Morgenstern, 2 August 1985

80 James Mitchell interview with Anthony Goodman and Matthew Morgenstern, 15 August 1985

81 Anthony Valentine interview with Anthony Goodman and Matthew Morgenstern, 10 December 1986

82 Patrick Mower interview with authors, 21 November 2013

83 Piers Haggard interview with authors, 21 October 2013

84 Terence Feely interview with Anthony Goodman and Matthew Morgenstern, 22 July 1985

85 Peter Duguid interview with Anthony Goodman and Matthew Morgenstern, 31 July 1986

86 Trevor Preston interview with authors, 28 August 2013

87 'Showbusiness: After 21 Years, Suddenly He Is a Success. Callan Has Changed Me, says Mr Woodward', Peter Dacre, *Daily Express*, September 1967

88 'All-Round Woodward', Alix Coleman, *TV Times*, 26 April – 2 May 1980, Southern edition

89 'At Last, Callan is Geared Up for Shooting', *The Sun*, 20 May 1972

90 Quoted in 'Back on Top of the Pile', Mick Brown, *You: The Mail on Sunday Magazine*, 1985

91 Jim Goddard interview with Anthony Goodman and Matthew Morgenstern, 23 October 1986

92 'All-Round Woodward', Alix Coleman, *TV Times*, 26 April – 2 May 1980, Southern edition

93 'A Dream That Brought Callan to Life', Peter Dacre, *Sunday Express*, 28 January 1973

94 Quoted from the foreword by Edward Woodward for the book *Inside the Wicker Man: Morbid Ingenuities*, Allan Brown, Sidgwick & Jackson, 2000

95 'A Very Nasty Piece of Work', Mark Kermode, *The Independent Review*, 21 December 2001

96 Preview, Kevin Maker, *The Times T2*, 23 August 2007

97 'Callan's So Glad to Be Back. By Mike Richardson,' *The Sun*, June 1974

98 'Callan in the Stew Queue. The Cyprus War: British Refugees Convoy is Straffed,' *Daily Mail*, 24 June 1974

99 'All-Round Woodward', Alix Coleman, *TV Times*, 26 April – 2 May 1980, Southern edition

100 Promoted by the BBC as "1984 plus 6".

101 'This Frightening Vision', Richard Afton, *Evening News*, 29 September 1977

102 'Television: Electronic Cowboys Ride in 1990', Richard Last, *Daily Telegraph*, 19 September 1977

103 'Uncivil Servants: A Masterly Thrill from the Paper Tyrants', James Murray, *Daily Express*, 19 September 1977

104 Edward Woodward commentary on 'Call Me Enemy', *Callan: Complete Fourth Series* DVD box set, Umbrella British TV, 2007

105 Film review, Felix Barker, *Evening News*, 15 May 1980

106 'The Aussies Storm the Beach', Alexander Walker, *Evening News*, 15 May 1980

107 Film review, Christopher Hudson, *Evening News*, 23 October 1980

108 Edward Woodward commentary on 'Call Me Enemy', *Callan: Complete Fourth Series* DVD box set, Umbrella British TV, 2007

109 Discussed in Robert Banks Stewart interview with authors, 2 and 7 October 2012

110 TV review, Philip Purser, *Sunday Times*, 2 November 1986

111 TV review, writer unknown, *Today*, 15 January 1987

112 TV review, Chris Tookey, *Sunday Telegraph*, 25 January 1987

113 TV review, John Leonard, *New York Times*, 14 October 1985

114 Peter Egan interview with authors, 12 September 2013

115 'The Equalizer! From Terry Willows in Los Angeles', *Daily Star*, 24 March 1985

116 'Cobra versus Callan. By Hilary Bonner, Show Business Editor', *Daily Mirror*, 2 June 1986

117 'The Equalizer! From Terry Willows in Los Angeles', *Daily Star*, 24 March 1985

118 Edward Woodward commentary on 'Call Me Enemy', *Callan: Complete Fourth Series* DVD box set, Umbrella British TV, 2007

119 '"Equalizer" finally learning to take it easy', Susan White, *Herald Journal*, 22 April 1988

120 'The Equalizer! From Terry Willows in Los Angeles', *Daily Star*, 24 March 1985

121 Edward Woodward commentary on *Call Me Enemy*, *Callan: Complete Fourth Series* DVD box set, Umbrella British TV, 2007

122 David Wickes interview with authors, 16 October 2012

123 http://simonpegg.net/2009/11/16/edward-woodward-1930-2009/

124 'Bin There', Caroline Rees, *The Guardian*, 2 December 1996

125 Review, Lynne Touss, *The Times*, 1997

126 Anthony Valentine interview, *ITV News*,
17 November 2009

Russell Hunter

127 Edward Woodward interviewed on *Callan* feature film
DVD, Stax Entertainment, 2000

128 Russell Hunter interview with Anthony Goodman and
Matthew Morgenstern, 8 January 1987

129 Terence Feely interview with Anthony Goodman and
Matthew Morgenstern, 22 July 1985

130 Russell Hunter interview with Anthony Goodman and
Matthew Morgenstern, 8 January 1987

131 Piers Haggard interview with authors,
21 October 2013

132 Terence Feely interview with Anthony Goodman and
Matthew Morgenstern, 22 July 1985

133 Trevor Preston interview with authors,
28 August 2013

134 Russell Hunter interview with Anthony Goodman and
Matthew Morgenstern, 8 January 1987

135 Russell Hunter interview with Alan Stevens,
Magic Bullet Productions, 2000

136 Terence Feely interview with Anthony Goodman and
Matthew Morgenstern, 22 July 1985

137 Ray Jenkins interview with Anthony Goodman and
Matthew Morgenstern, 4 September 1985

138 Trevor Preston interview with Anthony Goodman and
Matthew Morgenstern, 1984-7

139 Peter and Charlotte Mitchell interview with authors,
8 October 2013

140 Mike Vardy interview with authors, 6 February 2013

141 Edward Woodward interview with Anthony
Goodman and Matthew Morgenstern, 24 April 1987

142 Jim Goddard interview with Anthony Goodman and
Matthew Morgenstern, 23 October 1986

143 Dick Fiddy interview, *Callan: This Man Alone*,
Network, 2015

144 Mike Vardy interview, *Ibid.*, 2015

145 Edward Woodward interviewed on *Callan* feature film
DVD, Stax Entertainment, 2000

146 Mrs L. Gray of Worthing wrote: 'Callan and Lonely
remind me of Steptoe and Son. They have the
same bullying manner which hides a genuine feeling
for each other.'
TV Times, Southern edition, 16-22 May 1970

147 Mike Vardy interview with authors, 6 February 2013

148 Trevor Preston interview with authors,
28 August 2013

149 John Flanagan correspondence with authors,
13 November 2012

150 John Keeling interview with authors,
27 September 2013

151 Patrick Mower interview with authors,
21 November 2013

152 David Bickerstaff interview with authors,
16 August 2014

153 Derek Horne interview with authors, 24 January 2014

154 Peter Egan interview with authors,
12 September 2013

155 The title lampoons *Out* (1978), a gangland thriller
made by the same production company and written
by Trevor Preston.

156 Trevor Preston interview with authors,
28 August 2013

157 *Doctor Who Magazine* 413, September 2009

158 Tom Baker interview, 'The Sandmine Murders'
documentary, *Doctor Who – The Robots of Death* Special
Edition DVD, BBC/2 Entertain, 2012

159 Bill Maynard interview with Jonathan Melville on the

website https://adventuresinprimetime.wordpress.
com/2010/10/02/interview-bill-maynard, 2010.

160 Kenneth Gilbert interview with authors,
21 May 2013

161 David Bickerstaff interview with authors,
16 August 2014

162 Trevor Preston interview with authors,
28 August 2013

163 Russell Hunter interview with Anthony Goodman and
Matthew Morgenstern, 8 January 1987

164 'Why Hunter's Always Happy to Be Lonely,' Anon., *The
Sun*, 14 May 1971

165 Clifford Rose interview with Anthony Goodman and
Matthew Morgenstern, 5 September 1985

166 Michael Jayston interview with authors,
22 September 2013

167 Tom Baker interview, 'The Sandmine Murders'
documentary, *Doctor Who – The Robots of Death* Special
Edition DVD, BBC/2 Entertain, 2012

168 *Who Is Michael E. Briant?*, Classic TV Press, May 2012

169 David Bickerstaff interview with authors,
16 August 2014

170 Paul Darrow conversation with authors,
21 September 2013

171 Brian Croucher interview with authors,
2 August 2013

172 David Bickerstaff interview with authors,
16 August 2014

173 Tribute by Alan Stevens, www.kaldorcity.com/people/
rhtribute.html, 2004

174 'Farewell To a Man for All Seasons – Tributes Pour
in for a Legend of the Scottish Theatre,' Billy Briggs,
Scottish Herald, 27 February 2004

175 David Bickerstaff interview with authors,
16 August 2014

176 Russell Hunter interview with Anthony Goodman and
Matthew Morgenstern, 8 January 1987

177 Garron Martin post, *The Callan File* Facebook page,
24 May 2016

Anthony Valentine

177 'The Dancing Years - and How they Led to a Job
with Callan,' interviewer not known, *Evening Standard*,
17 July 1972

178 'Kiss the Villain! How Mr Nasty is Proving He's a Real
Romantic at Heart', by Charles Catchpole, newspaper
not known, 20 December 1979

179 'The Dancing Years - and How they Led to a Job with
Callan,' interviewer not known, *Evening Standard*,
17 July 1972

180 'Sweet Valentine. Out: The Bad Guy from Colditz. In:
The Musical Escapist' by Jack Bell, *Daily Mirror*,
27 January 1979

181 'The Dancing Years - and How they Led to a Job
with Callan,' interviewer not known, *Evening Standard*,
17 July 1972

182 Title not known, interview by Jack Bell,
Daily Mirror, 19 May 1970

183 Title and author not known, interview,
News of the World, 20 April 1975

184 'The Dancing Years - and How they Led to a Job
with Callan,' interviewer not known, *Evening Standard*,
17 July 1972

185 Robert Banks Stewart interview with authors,
2 and 7 October 2012

186 Anthony Valentine interview with Anthony
Goodman and Matthew Morgenstern,
10 December 1986

187 Jim Goddard interview with Anthony Goodman and

Matthew Morgenstern, 23 October 1986

188 Trevor Preston interview with authors,
28 August 2013

189 'Anthony Always Makes a Point of Being Nasty,'
interviewer not known, *The Sun*, 16 June 1970

190 Anthony Valentine interview with Anthony Goodman
and Matthew Morgenstern,
10 December 1986

191 Title not known, interview by Jack Bell,
Daily Mirror, 19 May 1970

192 'The Dancing Years - and How they Led to a Job with
Callan,' interviewer not known,
Evening Standard, 17 July 1972

193 'Well, Blow My Mind,' John Coleman,
New Statesman, 8 January 1971

194 Review, Christopher Hudson, *Spectator*,
9 January 1971

195 'The Dancing Years - and How they Led to a Job with
Callan,' interviewer not known,
Evening Standard, 17 July 1972

196 Reg Collin interview with Anthony Goodman and
Matthew Morgenstern, 2 August 1985

197 'The Dancing Years - and How they Led to a Job with
Callan,' interviewer not known,
Evening Standard, 17 July 1972

198 This was one the BBC's first co-productions,
made with Universal Studios.

199 Review, Shaun Usher, *Daily Mail*, 8 January 1974

200 'Sun TV by Margaret Forwood', *The Sun*,
7 January 1974

201 'Photo News', David Wigg, *Daily Express*,
22 April 1975

202 'Devilment', Shaun Usher, *Daily Express*,
28 February 1977

203 'A Sweet Valentine. Out: The Bad Guy from Colditz. In:
The Great Musical Escapist. By Jack Bell',
Daily Mirror, 27 January 1979

204 'Kiss the Villain! How Mr Nasty is Proving He's a Real
Romantic at Heart. By Charles Catchpole',
The Sun, 27 January 1979

205 'A Sweet Valentine. Out: The Bad Guy from Colditz.
In: The Great Musical Escapist. By Jack Bell',
Daily Mirror, 27 January 1979

206 He also directed Michael Frayn's provincial
newspaper comedy, *Alphabetical Order* in 2007.

207 'Anthony Valentine', obituary, Anon.,
The Daily Telegraph, 4 December 2015

207 Susan Valentine correspondence with authors,
29 July 2016

208 Anthony Valentine interview with Anthony
Goodman and Matthew Morgenstern,
10 December 1986

Patrick Mower

210 p.15, Mower, *Patrick Mower: My Story*,
John Blake, 2007

211 p.30, *ibid*, John Blake, 2007

212 p.31, *ibid*, John Blake, 2007

213 Chris Jones conversation with authors,
November 2013

214 Patrick Mower interview with authors,
21 November 2013

215 Believed to be *Ace of Wands* (1970-72).

216 The *Horse Under Water* audition appears to have been a
front for sounding out actors for the role of the new
James Bond. Michael Gambon recalled in a late-night
TV interview in the 2000s that he also discussed the
part with Broccoli and Saltzman. In his autobiography,
Mower remembered that Anthony Valentine was among
the other actors at the audition.

217 'Films presented by David Quinlan',
TV Times, 20-26 January 1979

218 p.135, Mower, *Patrick Mower: My Story*, John Blake, 2007

219 Patrick Mower interview with authors,
21 November 2013

220 Roger Marshall interview with authors, 2002

221 David Wickes interview with authors, 2002

222 Confirmed in a conversation with *Target* producer
Philip Hinchcliffe, 28 May 2016

223 p.219, Mower, *Patrick Mower: My Story*,
John Blake, 2007

224 p. 218, *Sweeney! The Official Companion*, Robert
Fairclough and Mike Kenwood, Titan Books, 2012

225 p.221, Mower, *Patrick Mower: My Story*,
John Blake, 2007

226 p.221, *ibid*, John Blake, 2007

227 'Mower the Merrier', Linda Hawkins,
*TV Times,1*515-21 September 1984

228 p.285, Mower, *Patrick Mower: My Story*,
John Blake, 2007

229 p.285, *ibid*, John Blake, 2007

230 In what is possibly a *Callan* in-joke, one *Emmerdale*
storyline had Mower's character on-line dating,
using the screen name 'Hunter'

231 Patrick Mower interview with authors,
19 November 2013

2: COLD WARRIORS

1 Quoted in *The Man Who Sold Death*
(Charter, 1980 edition)

2 Conrad's approach was parodied in G.K. Chesterton's
The Man Who Was Thursday (1908), in which the
members of an anarchist cell discover that they are
all police infiltrators.

3 Maugham, quoted by Janet Pate in *The Book of Spies and
Secret Agents* (Webb and Bower, 1978)

4 www.bbc.c.uk/history/ww2peopleswar/stories,
23rd October 2013

5 Quoted in 'The Locations: The USSR',
The Danger Man Collection, DeAgostini, 2005-06

6 Sometimes, but not consistently, typeset as 'OO7'
in Fleming's books.

7 Paul Darrow correspondence with authors,
9 September 2010

8 Quoted on the back cover of *Dr. No*
(Penguin Modern Classics, 2010 edition)

9 Roger Marshall interview with authors, 2002

10 Although location work was still shot within
the British Isles.

11 'Our Man in Argentina goes on the Trail', David Griffiths,
TV Times, August 6-12 1961

12 'The Girl with the Golden Pen', Joanna Harwood
interviewed by Matthew Field, *Cinema Retro Classics
Special Edition* magazine No. 4 – *Dr. No*, published
by Cinema Retro, 2012.

13 Afterword, *The Spy Who Came in from the Cold*,
John le Carré, p257 (Penguin Modern Classics,
2010 edition)

14 *Time*, quoted on the cover of *The Spy Who Came in from
the Cold* (Penguin Modern Classics, 2010 edition)

15 *Billion-Dollar Brain*, Len Deighton, p.11
(Penguin Books edition, 1966)

16 *Ibid* p11

17 *The IPCRESS File*, Len Deighton, p.14 (Triad/Panther
Books edition, 1985)

18 *The Times Literary Supplement*, quoted on the inside
front and back cover of *Funeral in Berlin*
(Penguin Books, 1966 edition)

19 'Callan Series Origins' memorandum, 1966, month unknown
20 *The Money That Money Can't Buy*, James Munro, (Corgi 1967 edition)
21 Quoted on the back cover of *The Man Who Sold Death* (Charter, 1980 edition)
22 Fleming's *Casino Royale* (1953) features Bond being similarly tortured with a carpet-beater.
23 Book review, *Atlanta Journal and Constitution*, 1970
24 Book review, *San Francisco Examiner and Chronicle*, 1970
25 Book review, *Dallas Times-Herald*, 1970
26 'Thriller Plus', Francis Hope, *New Statesman*, 3 January 1964
27 Interview with David McCallum on *The Man from UNCLE: The Complete Series* DVD box set (Time Life, 2007)
28 Curiously, John Drake uses the alias John Craig in (at least) one of the *Danger Man* novels, *The Exterminator* (1966) by W.A. Ballinger (a pseudonym for W. Howard Baker.)
29 'Rat Catchers in a Jam: Nick Haig, Production Manager, Talking to Richard Pollock', *TV Times*, March 19-25 1966
30 'Meet the Rat Catchers', Anthony Davis, *TV Times*, 29 January – 4 February 1966
31 *Ibid*, January 29th – 4 February 1966
32 Quiller was later also adapted as a TV series the BBC. See Chapter 12
33 'Hardboiled Hero with a Grudge', Innes Gray, *TV Times* Southern edition, 30 September – October 4 1967
34 Other contemporary comedies featuring espionage included the reformatted sitcom *Hugh and I Spy* (1968) and the American series *Get Smart* (1965-1970).
35 *The Wrecking Crew* cinema trailer, 1967
36 Review, *Time Out Film Guide* Eighth Edition, p.690 (Penguin, 1999)
37 'The Good Ones are All Dead', *Callan*, 8 July 1967

3: ABC PRESENTS...

1 *Armchair Theatre: The Lost Years*, Leonard White, 2003, p.23
2 *Ibid*, p.30
3 Sydney Newman obituary, Leonard Miall, *The Independent*, 4 November 1997
4 'Newman at the BBC!', Andrew Pixley, *Doctor Who Magazine*, December 2013
5 *Armchair Theatre: The Lost Years*, Leonard White, 2003, p.31
6 'Newman at the BBC!', Andrew Pixley, *Doctor Who Magazine*, December 2013
7 Mike Vardy interview with authors, 6 February 2013
8 *Armchair Theatre: The Lost Years*, Leonard White, 2003, p.32
9 'Television: A Question of Character', Maurice Wiggin, *Sunday Times*, 15 May 1960
10 Robert Banks Stewart interview with authors, 2 and 7 October 2012
11 Trevor Preston interview with authors, 28 August 2013
12 Terence Feely interview with Anthony Goodman and Matthew Morgenstern, 22 July 1985
13 Piers Haggard interview with authors, 21 October 2013
14 Lloyd Shirley and George Markstein interview with Anthony Goodman and Matthew Morgenstern, 1984-87
15 Piers Haggard interview with authors, 21 October 2013
16 Patrick Mower interview with authors, 21 November 2013
17 Peter Bowles interview with authors, 11 October 2013
18 Anthony Valentine interview with Anthony Goodman and Matthew Morgenstern, 10 December 1986
19 Jim Goddard interview with Anthony Goodman and Matthew Morgenstern, 23 October 1986
21 Kenneth Gilbert interview with authors, 21 May 20313

21 Michael Jayston interview with authors, 22 september 2013
22 Peter Duguid interview with Anthony Goodman and Matthew Morgenstern, 31 july 1986
23 Mike Vardy interview with authors, 6 February 2013
24 Piers Haggard interview with authors, 21 October 2013
25 Trevor Preston interview with authors, 28 August 2013
26 Jim Goddard interview with Anthony Goodman and Matthew Morgenstern, 23 October 1986
27 Bill Craig interview with Anthony Goodman and Matthew Morgenstern, 2 September 1985
28 John Keeling interview with authors, 27 September 2013
29 Peter le Page interview with authors, 12 December 2014
30 David Marshall correspondence with the authors, 8 December 2014
31 Terence Feely interview with Anthony Goodman and Matthew Morgenstern, 22 july 1985
32 Clifford Rose interview with Anthony Goodman and Matthew Morgenstern, 5 september 1985
33 Mike Vardy interview with authors, 6 February 2013
34 Trevor Preston interview with authors, 28 August 2013
35 Lloyd Shirley and George Markstein interview with Anthony Goodman and Matthew Morgenstern, 1984-87
36 Michael Jayston interview with authors, 22 September 2013
37 Alfred and Leila Hoffman interview with authors, 22 October 2013
38 Patrick Mower interview with authors, 21 November 2013
39 Piers Haggard interview with authors, 21 October 2013
40 Peter Duguid interview with Anthony Goodman and Matthew Morgenstern, 31 July 1986
41 John Keeling interview with authors, 27 September 2013
42 Peter Duguid interview with Anthony Goodman and Matthew Morgenstern, 31 July 1986
43 Piers Haggard interview with authors, 21 October 2013
44 Alfred and Leila Hoffman interview with authors, 22 October 2013
45 Further information at www.bfi.org.uk, www.kaleidoscope.org.uk
46 Clifford Rose interview with Anthony Goodman and Matthew Morgenstern, 5 September 1985
47 Tessa Wyatt, conversation with authors, 22 March 2014
48 Trevor Preston interview with authors, 28 August 2013
49 Peter Duguid interview with Anthony Goodman and Matthew Morgenstern, 31 July 1986
50 Neville Green interview with authors, 10 December 2014
51 Mike Vardy interview with authors, 6 February 2013
52 John Keeling interview with authors, 27 September 2013
53 Piers Haggard interview with authors, 21 October 2013

4: A MAGNUM FOR SCHNEIDER, A RED FILE FOR CALLAN

1 Anthony Read correspondence with authors, 14 October 2013
2 Terence Feely interview with Anthony Goodman and Matthew Morgenstern, 22 July 1985
3 Lloyd Shirley and George Markstein interview with Anthony Goodman and Matthew Morgenstern, 1984-87
4 James Mitchell interview with Anthony Goodman and Matthew Morgenstern, 15 August 1985
5 '*The Strange Case of the Missing Episodes – The Avengers*' by Alan Hayes, Alys Hayes and Richard McGinlay, publ (Hidden Tiger, 2013)
6 'TV and Radio Topics: Mrs. Gale Will Die on the Throne', *Daily Telegraph*, 9 March 1964
7 Anthony Read correspondence with authors, 14 October 2013

8 Jim Goddard interview with Anthony Goodman and Matthew Morgenstern, 23 October 1986

9 Peter le Page interview with authors, 12 December 2014

10 David Marshall correspondence with authors, 8 December 2014

11 Voytek interview with Anthony Goodman and Matthew Morgenstern, 5 November 1986

12 Anon, *London Evening Standard,* 16 October 1964

13 'A New-Look Spy and Sophia Loren – Isn't That Enough?' Alexander Walker, *London Evening Standard,* 18 March 1965

14 Kenneth Tynan, *The Observer,* 21 August 1965

15 'A Real Actor's Interpretation of a Particular Man in a Particular Situation…' Anon, *The Times,* 18 March 1965

16 'Spying', Isabel Quigley, *The Spectator,* 19 August 1965

17 David Marshall correspondence with authors, 8 December 2014

18 All transmission dates kindly supplied by Simon Coward at Kaleidoscope http://www.kaleidoscopearchive.co.uk/about-kaleidoscope

19 Information from rehearsal script, August 1966, Production No : 2014

20 Piers Haggard interview with authors, 21 October 2013

21 Russell Hunter interview with Anthony Goodman and Matthew Morgenstern, 8 January 1987

22 Terence Feely interview with Anthony Goodman and Matthew Morgenstern, 22 July 1985

23 Anthony Valentine interview with Anthony Goodman and Matthew Morgenstern, 10 December 1986

24 James Mitchell interview with Anthony Goodman and Matthew Morgenstern, 15 August 1985

25 However sensationalist or flawed, the film has its *Callan* connections; along with Radd its strong cast also features Michael Goodliffe (Chapter 7) and Carl Möhner (Chapter 11).

26 Peter Bowles interview with authors, 11 October 2013

27 *Callan: Under the Red File,* Andrew Pixley, (Network, 2015)

28 'I was there, says "Herr Major"', by Derek Meakin and Ray Chapman, *TV Times,* 14-20 February 1960

29 David Marshall correspondence with authors, 8 December 2014

30 Ike Isaacs And His Guitars, *Fourteen Great TV Themes* [Decca Eclipse ECS 2163]]

31 John Peel Session: Tools You Can Trust transmitted 5 December 1984, produced by Mark Radcliffe. (Information from BBC website, with thanks to Alwyn Turner and Darren Giddings; intriguingly, Peel did not seem to realise the tune was a cover version.)

32 Stiff Records, Cat. Number: BUY20, 1977

33 Terence Feely interview with Anthony Goodman and Matthew Morgenstern, 22 July 1985

34 Edward Woodward, interviewed on *Callan* film DVD (Stax Entertainment, 2000)

35 James Mitchell interview with Anthony Goodman and Matthew Morgenstern, 15 August 1985

36 Edward Woodward interview with Anthony Goodman and Matthew Morgenstern, 24 April 1987

37 Mike Vardy interview with authors, 6 February 2013

38 James Mitchell interview with Anthony Goodman and Matthew Morgenstern, 15 August 1985

39 Mike Vardy interview with authors, 6 February 2013

40 Lloyd Shirley and George Markstein interview with Anthony Goodman and Matthew Morgenstern, 1984-87

41 Trevor Preston interview, *Callan: This Man Alone,* (Network, 2015)

42 David Marshall correspondence with authors, 8 December 2014

43 Peter le Page interview with authors, 12 December 2014

44 *TV Times,* London edition, 4 -10 February 1967

45 *Daily Mirror,* 6 February 1967, as noted in *Armchair Theatre: The Lost Years* by Leonard White

46 Reg Collin interview with Anthony Goodman and Matthew Morgenstern, 2 August 1985

47 Peter Egan interview with authors, 12 September 2013

48 Edward Woodward, interviewed on *Callan* film DVD (Stax Entertainment, 2000)

49 Terence Feely interview with Anthony Goodman and Matthew Morgenstern, 22 July 1985

50 James Mitchell interview with Anthony Goodman and Matthew Morgenstern, 15 August 1985

51 Peter Duguid interview with Anthony Goodman and Matthew Morgenstern, 31 July 1986

52 http://www.britishbattles.com/peninsula/peninsula-talavera.htm

53 http://encyclopediavirginia.org/Pickett_s_Charge

5: SERIES ONE:
Nobody Loves a Freelance

1 Edward Woodward interview with Anthony Goodman and Matthew Morgenstern, 24 April 1987

2 Lloyd Shirley and George Markstein interview with Anthony Goodman and Matthew Morgenstern, 1984-87

3 David Wickes interview with authors, 2002

4 David Marshall correspondence with authors, 8 December 2014

5 David Wickes interview with authors, 2002

6 Trevor Preston interview with authors, 28 August 2013

7 Voytek interview with Anthony Goodman and Matthew Morgenstern, 5 November 1986

8 Piers Haggard interview with authors, 21 October 2013

9 Lloyd Shirley and George Markstein interview with Anthony Goodman and Matthew Morgenstern, 1984-87

10 These episodes are missing, believed wiped; the scripts or storylines have been painstakingly reconstructed in 1 *The Strange Case of the Missing Episodes – The Avengers* by Alan Hayes, Alys Hayes and Richard McGinlay, (Hidden Tiger, 2013)

11 Terence Feely interview with Anthony Goodman and Matthew Morgenstern, 22 July 1985

12 'We'd come to the end of the stories that could plausibly be done about a female inspector,' Feely explained. 'There were only so many: after six years we'd come to the end of our tether. So I said, "Look, I want to make her a private eye, or possibly a spy". [The] TVS [network] was looking for something to use their studio space, London Weekend were looking for a new series starring Maggie Forbes, so between the two of them that's how it happened. It all came together at the right time.'

13 'Terence Feely: Writer who Scripted Popular Television Dramas,' Anon, *The Times,* 13 August 2000

14 Terence Feely interview with Anthony Goodman and Matthew Morgenstern, 22 July 1985

15 James Mitchell interview with Anthony Goodman and Matthew Morgenstern, 15 August 1985

16 Terence Feely interview with Anthony Goodman and Matthew Morgenstern, 22 July 1985

17 Edward Woodward interview with Anthony Goodman and Matthew Morgenstern, 24 April 1987

18 *Callan* series format document, November 1966

19 'The Blunt Instrument', *Action TV* Magazine, Issue No. 5, Autumn 2001. Written by Anthony Goodman, based on research by Anthony Goodman and Matthew Morgenstern.

20 Terence Feely interview with Anthony Goodman and Matthew Morgenstern, 22 July 1985

21 Reg Collin interview with Anthony Goodman and Matthew Morgenstern, 2 August 1985

22 Robert Banks Stewart interview with authors, 2 and 7 October 2012

23 James Mitchell interview with Anthony Goodman and Matthew Morgenstern, 15 August 1985

24 Robert Banks Stewart interview with authors, 2 and 7 October 2012

25 Peter Bowles interview with authors, 11 October 2013

26 Lloyd Shirley and George Markstein interview with Anthony Goodman and Matthew Morgenstern, 1984-87

27 Terence Feely interview with Anthony Goodman and Matthew Morgenstern, 22 July 1985

28 Dick Fiddy and Jim Goddard interviews, *Callan: This Man Alone* (Network, 2015)

29 Robert Banks Stewart interview with authors, 2 and 7 October 2012

30 Terence Feely interview with Anthony Goodman and Matthew Morgenstern, 22 July 1985

31 ABC Press Release, May 1967

32 *Ibid.* June 1967

33 'TV Last Night by Mary Malone: A Bitter Day Out for the Five Pub Pals', *Daily Mirror*, 14 August 1967

34 'Showbusiness: After 21 Years, Suddenly He is a Success. Callan Has Changed Me, says Mr Woodward,' Peter Dacre, *Daily Express*, September 1967

35 Audience figures published in *Callan: Under the Red File*, Andrew Pixley (Network, 2015)

36 Lloyd Shirley and George Markstein interview with Anthony Goodman and Matthew Morgenstern, 1984-87

37 Terence Feely interview with Anthony Goodman and Matthew Morgenstern, 22 July 1985

38 Compiled from scripts and call sheets

39 Information taken from camera script, June 1967, Production No 1905, VTR/ABC/6784

40 Lisa Langdon feature, *TV Times*, 18 March 1972

41 Edward Woodward commentary on 'If He Can, So Could I', *Callan: Complete Fourth Series* DVD box set (Umbrella British TV, 2007)

42 Mike Vardy interview with authors, 6 February 2013

43 Edward Woodward commentary on 'If He Can, So Could I', *Callan: Complete Fourth Series* DVD box set (Umbrella British TV, 2007)

44 Information from episode cue sheet: 'Traditional German Marching Song', Telefunken LGX 66064, 20 seconds; 'Hurdy Gurdy Music' (Unknown), 1 minute 20 seconds; 'Die Gotterdammerüng', Richard Wagner, Decca LXT 5205-5211, 50 seconds.

45 Quoted in *Spotts*, 1994

46 James Mitchell interview with Anthony Goodman and Matthew Morgenstern, 15 August 1985

47 'Southern's Summer Look' – 'Callan', Stewart Knowles, *TV Times* Southern edition, 1-7 July 1967

48 'Foreign TV Reviews', 'Otta', *Variety*, 2 August 1967

49 Information from rehearsal script, June 1967, Production No : 1901, VTR 6843

50 *Ibid,* locations supplemented by information in *Callan: Under the Red File*, Andrew Pixley (Network, 2015)

51 Robert Banks Stewart interview with authors, 2 and 7 October 2012

52 http://www.kaleidoscopepublishing.co.uk/books-the-hurricanestail.html

53 *To Put You in the Picture*, Robert Banks Stewart (Miwk Publishing Ltd., October 2015)

54 Peter Duguid interview with Anthony Goodman and Matthew Morgenstern, 31 July 1986

55 Alfred and Leila Hoffman interview with authors, 22 October 2013

56 Information from annotated draft script, date unknown

57 Information from episode cue sheet: 'La Montana', Mozart Educational Publishing, ME/LP 12, 1 minute and 30 seconds; 'Romances at Malarsee', Gaze/Ackerman, 1 minute and 30 seconds.

58 Peter Duguid interview with Anthony Goodman and Matthew Morgenstern, 31 July 1986

59 Alfred and Leila Hoffman interview with authors, 22 October 2013

60 Terence Feely interview with Anthony Goodman and Matthew Morgenstern, 22 July 1985

61 Letters page, *TV Times* Anglia edition, 5-11 August 1967. 'As someone who lived through the emergency in Kenya and knows exactly what the Mau-Mau did, I take exception to this remark,' Mrs C. Bryn-Jones of Eastcote objected. 'It is foolish and ignorant to make flippant remarks of this kind.'

62 Robert Banks Stewart interview with authors, 2 and 7 October 2012

63 This type of storyline later cropped up several times in *The Professionals*

64 These shows also sometimes explored similar subject matter, for example in *Danger Man* – 'The Mercenaries' (1965)

65 Derived from the camera script as this episode is missing; it should be noted the director may have chosen to improvise something slightly different.

66 Information taken from camera script, Production No. 1902, VTR/ABC/6679. Location supplemented by information in *Callan: Under the Red File*, Andrew Pixley (Network, 2015)

67 'The whole series was Patrick McGoohan,' Kwouk reminisced. 'He took over everything he did. It was like when I went to see him in *Brand*: I never noticed any of the other actors; it was just Patrick and he was so powerful in that. The *film noir* look [of *Danger Man*] came from McGoohan – he was tall and had a deep voice and a very *noir* look.' Interview with Robert Fairclough, 2005

68 James Mitchell's original story outline in the *Callan* format document dated November 1966.

69 James Mitchell interview with Anthony Goodman and Matthew Morgenstern, 15 August 1985

70 In his 1983 novel *Ferret* – the nickname for a spy plane of East or West – future *Callan* story editor George Markstein speculated that, after Powers, any pilots shot down were imprisoned for life in the countries they spied upon and no longer officially existed

71 Derived from the camera script, so the previous caveat applies

72 Credited as Gladys Cooper in *TV Times*, North Edition, 29 July - 4 August 1967

73 Information from camera script, April 1967, Production No 1903, VTR ABC 6678

74 Adapted from original story outline written by James Mitchell, contained within *Callan* series format document, November 1966

75 Peter le Page interview with authors, 12 December 2014

76 James Mitchell interview with Anthony Goodman and Matthew Morgenstern, 15 August 1985

77 Peter le Page interview with authors, 12 December 2014

78 Information from camera script, May 1967, Production No 1904, VTR/ABC/6773, supplemented by information in *Callan: Under the Red File*, Andrew Pixley (Network, 2015)

79 Adapted from original story outline written by James Mitchell, contained within *Callan* series format document, November 1966.

80 James Mitchell interview with Anthony Goodman and Matthew Morgenstern, 15 August 1985

81 Peter and Charlotte Mitchell interview with authors, 8 October 2013

82 Derived from the camera script, so the previous caveat applies.

83 Information from camera script, June 1967, Production No 1906, VTR/ABC/6844, supplemented by information in *Callan: Under the Red File*, Andrew Pixley (Network, 2015)

84 Piers Haggard interview with authors, 21 October 2013

85 Information from episode cue sheet: 'The Killer', Jack Trombey, De Wolfe, DW/LP 2969, 51 seconds; 'Darkness', Jack Trombey, De Wolfe DW/LP 2969, 2 minutes 25 seconds.

86 Piers Haggard interview with authors, 21 October 2013

87 Edward Woodward interview with Anthony Goodman and Matthew Morgenstern, 24 April 1987

88 Piers Haggard interview with authors, 21 October 2013

89 Russell Hunter interview with Anthony Goodman and Matthew Morgenstern, 8 January 1987

90 Anthony Valentine interview with Anthony Goodman and Matthew Morgenstern, 10 December 1986

91 James Mitchell interview with Anthony Goodman and Matthew Morgenstern, 15 August 1985

92 Piers Haggard interview with authors, 21 October 2013

93 'A-Way with Women!', Ann Morrow, *TV Times*, 5-11 August 1967, Anglia edition

94 *TV Times*, 2-8 September 1967, Anglia edition

95 'Goodbye Mary Lee' draft script, published in *Callan Uncovered*, James Mitchell, Ostara Publishing, 2014, ISBN 978-1-909619-14-2

6: SERIES TWO:
Hunter/Hunted

1 Edward Woodward, interviewed on *Callan* film DVD, Stax Entertainment, 2000.

2 Mike Vardy interview with authors, 6 February 2013

3 'Research On Callan' Memorandum to Brian Tesler and Programme Policy Committee, dated 1967

4 Terence Feely interview with Anthony Goodman and Matthew Morgenstern, 22 July 1985

5 'Research On Callan' Memorandum to Brian Tesler and Programme Policy Committee, dated 1967

6 Terence Feely interview with Anthony Goodman and Matthew Morgenstern, 22 July 1985

7 Mike Vardy interview with authors, 6 February 2013

8 Lloyd Shirley and George Markstein interview with Anthony Goodman and Matthew Morgenstern, 1984-87

9 Neville Green interview with authors, 10 December 2014

10 John Kershaw interview with Anthony Goodman and Matthew Morgenstern, 1984-7

11 Reg Collin interview with Anthony Goodman and Matthew Morgenstern, 2 August 1985

12 John Kershaw interview with Anthony Goodman and Matthew Morgenstern, 1984-87

13 Robert Banks Stewart interview with authors, 2 and 7 October 2012

14 Edward Woodward interview with Anthony Goodman and Matthew Morgenstern, 24 April 1987

15 This was previously published in an article titled 'The Blunt Instrument' in *Action TV* Magazine Autumn 2001 Issue No 5, written by Anthony Goodman, based on research by Anthony Goodman and Matthew Morgenstern, and in *Callan: Under the Red File*, by Andrew Pixley (Network, 2015). The full wish list reads: '1) More realistic (scripts/sets/direction/action). More feeling for the secret service Section involved. Consistent characterisation and relationships. 2) Where is the series going? How do the relationships develop? 3) Callan should rejoin the section. (a) Need nothing doing to indicate same. (b) At the moment, nothing really indicates he is not in Section.4) If he rejoins, the HOD (Head Of Department)/Callan relationship need not be impaired. 5) Development of Callan inside personal background, i.e. the double life that an agent leads. 6) HUNTER – Now out of series – should be replaced by a different HOD, but one whom Callan can still have an abrasive relationship with. Possibly even more so than with Hunter. 7) NEW head of department. Possibly C. P. Snow / Philby type. Would find Callan unacceptable. 8) MERES Should stop being a foil for Hunter. More credible as agent. Would deal with 'other' types of case. Would dislike Callan and visa-versa - but an expert none-the-less 9) CALLAN/LONELY Lonely should be known to exist to the department, but he must be essentially a Callan man and Callan should shield him from department scrutiny, i.e. he is only of use to the department whilst they pretend he does not exist. Once they know each other, he becomes non-effective as a device for Callan, and also a risk to the Section.'

16 Robert Banks Stewart interview with authors, 2 and 7 October 2012

17 Reg Collin interview with Anthony Goodman and Matthew Morgenstern, 2 August 1985

18 James Mitchell interview with Anthony Goodman and Matthew Morgenstern, 15 August 1985

18 Memorandum 'New Hunter' dated 1967

19 Derek Bond interview with Anthony Goodman and Matthew Morgenstern, 22 August 1985

20 John Kershaw interview with Anthony Goodman and Matthew Morgenstern, 1984-7

21 Mike Vardy interview with authors, 6 February 2013

22 Ray Jenkins interview with Anthony Goodman and Matthew Morgenstern, 4 September 1985

23 John Kershaw interview with Anthony Goodman and Matthew Morgenstern, 1984-87

24 Derek Bond interview with Anthony Goodman and Matthew Morgenstern, 22 August 1985

25 Russell Hunter interview with Anthony Goodman and Matthew Morgenstern, 8 January 1985

26 'The Blunt Instrument', *Action TV* Magazine, Autumn 2001

27 John Kershaw interview with Anthony Goodman and Matthew Morgenstern, 19827 Reg Collin interview with Anthony Goodman and Matthew Morgenstern, 2 August 1985

28 James Mitchell interview with Anthony Goodman and Matthew Morgenstern, 15 August 1985

29 John Kershaw interview with Anthony Goodman and Matthew Morgenstern, 1984-87

30 Reg Collin interview with Anthony Goodman and Matthew Morgenstern, 2 August 1985

31 'The Blunt Instrument', Action TV Magazine, Autumn 2001

32 Lloyd Shirley and George Markstein interview with Anthony Goodman and Matthew Morgenstern, 1984-87

33 Russell Hunter interview with Anthony Goodman and Matthew Morgenstern, 8 January 1987

34 Anthony Valentine interview with Anthony Goodman and Matthew Morgenstern, 10 December 1986

35 Robert Banks Stewart interview with authors, 2, 7 October 1987

36 John Kershaw interview with Anthony Goodman and Matthew Morgenstern, 1984-7

37 Edward Woodward interview with Anthony Goodman and Matthew Morgenstern, 24 April 1987

38 John Kershaw interview with Anthony Goodman and

39 Reg Collin interview with Anthony Goodman and Matthew Morgenstern, 2 August 1985

40 Mike Vardy interview with authors, 6 February 2013

41 Audience figures published in *Callan: Under the Red File*, by Andrew Pixley (Network, 2001)

42 Reg Collin interview with Anthony Goodman and Matthew Morgenstern, 2 August 1985

43 Misspelt in *TV Times* as 'Concharov'.

44 A précis of the news headlines rarely lasting more than a minute was often given at exactly 9 pm as a preview of *News at Ten*. Some, but not all, regional *TV Times* editions attempted to reflect this by showing *Callan* starting at 9.01 pm. We have ignored these minor variations, which were dropped by the end of February 1969, and listed start times on the hour.

45 Compiled from scripts and call sheets, supplemented by information in *Callan: Under the Red File*, Andrew Pixley, (Network, 2015)

46 Subject-based exams, now superseded by GCSEs

47 James Mitchell interview with Anthony Goodman and Matthew Morgenstern, 15 August 1985

48 From www.mgoodliffe.co.uk, maintained by his estate.

49 Garfield Morgan interview with authors, 2002

50 Neville Green interview with authors, 10 December 2014

51 *Ibid.*, 10 December 2014

52 Peter Duguid interview with Anthony Goodman and Matthew Morgenstern, 31 July 1986

53 Listings details, *TV Times* 4-10 January 1969, Southern edition

54 Transmission details for Tyne Tees not known for this week

55 Information from camera script, January 1968, Production No: 1909, VTR/ABC/7358, supplemented by information in *Callan: Under the Red File*, Andrew Pixley, (Network, 2015)

56 A variant spelling of the more correct pentothal. Sodium pentothal or Sodium thiopental, was discovered in the 1930s and used as a sedative

57 Clifford Rose interview with Anthony Goodman and Matthew Morgenstern, 5 September 1985

58 John Kershaw interview with Anthony Goodman and Matthew Morgenstern, 1984-87

59 Information from episode cue sheet: 'Concerto for Four Harpsichords in D Minor', Vivaldi-Dart NC CLP.1120 , 15 seconds. 'Prelude Fugue No 16', J. S. Bach, Keith Prowse, KPM 1003A , 2 minutes 50 seconds. 'Tracy Baby', Reg Tilsley, De Wolfe, DW/LP3032A, 1 minute 17 seconds. 'Autumn Colours', Tilsley/Gray De Wolfe, DW/LP 3032B, 1 minute 7 seconds

60 Clifford Rose interview with Anthony Goodman and Matthew Morgenstern, 5 September 1985

61 James Mitchell interview with Anthony Goodman and Matthew Morgenstern, 15 August 1985

62 Peter Duguid interview with Anthony Goodman and Matthew Morgenstern, 31 July 1986

63 news.bbc.co.uk/1/hi/england/wiltshire/3684503.stm for the BBC report of the inquest

64 'Are Our Spies Really Licensed to Kill?' by James Mitchell', *TV Times*, Southern edition, 11-17 January 1969

65 Listings details, *TV Times*, 11-17 January 1969, Southern edition

66 Information from camera script, production no: 1910 [VTR/ABC/7419], February 1968

67 Mike Vardy interview with authors, 6 February 2013

68 This argument led to Dobbs demanding that his name be removed from the credits

69 'You're Under Starters Orders' draft script, undated

70 Information from episode cue sheet

71 Mike Vardy interview with authors, 6 February 2013

72 Robert Banks Stewart interview with authors, 2 and 7 October 2012

73 Information taken from camera script, January 1969, Production No 1911, VTR/ABC/7394, supplemented by information in *Callan: Under the Red File*, Andrew Pixley, (Network, 2015)

74 James Mitchell interview with Anthony Goodman and Matthew Morgenstern, 15 August 1985

75 TV review, Nancy Banks-Smith, *The Sun*, 30 January 1969

76 'Mary Malone's View – The Brutal Agent with a Hint of Chivalry', *Daily Mirror*, 30 January 1969

77 Information taken from camera script, January 1969, Production No 1911, VTR/ABC/7394, supplemented by information in *Callan: Under the Red File*, Andrew Pixley, (Network, 2015)

78 Kenneth Gilbert interview with authors, 21 May 2013

79 Ray Jenkins interview with Anthony Goodman and Matthew Morgenstern, 4 September 1985

80 John Kershaw interview with Anthony Goodman and Matthew Morgenstern, 1984-87

81 Information taken from camera rehearsal script, marked for the attention of Lloyd Shirley, production no: 1912, February 1968

82 Terence Feely interview with Anthony Goodman and Matthew Morgenstern, 22 July 1985

83 Discussed in Ray Jenkins interview with Anthony Goodman and Matthew Morgenstern, 4 September 1985

84 Kenneth Gilbert interview with authors, 21 May 2013

85 Mike Vardy interview with authors, 6 February 2013

86 John Kershaw interview with Anthony Goodman and Matthew Morgenstern, 1984-87

87 Peter Duguid interview with Anthony Goodman and Matthew Morgenstern, 31 July 1986

88 Mike Vardy interview with authors, 6 February 2013

89 Clifford Rose interview with Anthony Goodman and Matthew Morgenstern, 5 September 1985

90 Review by 'Mull', *Variety*, February 12 1969

91 'Television: Mass Killing in Sickening Serial', Sean Day-Lewis, *Daily Telegraph*, 6 February 1969

92 Available on *Callan: This Man Alone*, Network, 2015

93 Information from rehearsal script, May 1968, production no. 1926, VTR/ABC/7627

94 Derek Bond interview with Anthony Goodman and Matthew Morgenstern, 22 August 1985

95 John Kershaw interview with Anthony Goodman and Matthew Morgenstern, 1984-87

96 Reg Collin interview with Anthony Goodman and Matthew Morgenstern, 2 August 1985

97 Peter le Page interview with authors, 12 December 2014

98 Peter Duguid interview with Anthony Goodman and Matthew Morgenstern, 31 July 1986

99 Derek Bond interview with Anthony Goodman and Matthew Morgenstern, 22 August 1985

100 Reg Collin interview with Anthony Goodman and Matthew Morgenstern, 2 August 1985

101 Edward Woodward interview with Anthony Goodman and Matthew Morgenstern, 24 April 1987

102 Peter Duguid interview with Anthony Goodman and Matthew Morgenstern, 31 July 1986

103 Mark Duguid correspondence with the authors, 22 September 2014

104 Anthony Valentine interview with Anthony Goodman and Matthew Morgenstern, 10 December 1986

105 TV review, Mary Malone, *Daily Mirror*, 13 February 1969

106 Information from camera script, May 1968, Production No: 1914 [VTR/ABC/7589]. This script is entitled 'The Land of Light and Peace' – the *TV Times* dropped the 'The'. Recording is listed as being in Studio "L" which is a typographical error

107 Reg Collin interview with Anthony Goodman and Matthew Morgenstern, 2 August 1985

108 Derek Bond interview with Anthony Goodman and Matthew Morgenstern, 22 August 1985

109 Peter and Charlotte Mitchell interview with authors, 8 October 2013

110 Piers Haggard interview with authors, 21 October 2013

106 It's also an interesting contrast with the first series, where Hunter makes several attempts to get Callan imprisoned

107 Sometimes credited as James Goddard

108 Information from camera script, production no: 1915 [VTR/ABC/7701], June 1968, supplemented by information in *Callan: Under the Red File*, Andrew Pixley (Network, 2015)

109 Jim Goddard interview with Anthony Goodman and Matthew Morgenstern, 23 October 1986

110 Trevor Preston interview with authors, 28 August 2013

111 Russell Hunter interview with Anthony Goodman and Matthew Morgenstern, 8 January 1987

112 For further information see *Made for Television: Euston Films Limited*, Alvarado & Stewart (Methuen Publishing Ltd., 1985), ISBN 978-0423013108

113 Russell Hunter interview with Anthony Goodman and Matthew Morgenstern, 8 January 1987

114 Derek Bond interview with Anthony Goodman and Matthew Morgenstern, 22 August 1985

115 James Mitchell interview with Anthony Goodman and Matthew Morgenstern, 15 August 1985

116 John Kershaw interview with Anthony Goodman and Matthew Morgenstern, 1984-87

117 Peter and Charlotte Mitchell interview with authors, 8 October 2013

118 Information from camera script, February 1968, Production No: 1920, VTR/ABC/7552, supplemented by information in *Callan: Under the Red File*, Andrew Pixley (Network, 2015)

119 Ray Jenkins interview with Anthony Goodman and Matthew Morgenstern, 4 September 1985

120 *The Innocent Bystanders* (Bantam Books, 1971 edition)

121 Information from episode cue sheet. 'Donne Moi Des Fleurs' P Clark / P Delance Welbeck Music VRL 3010, 1 min 18 s, 'Mods and Rockers' B Martin/ P Coulter Keith Prowse KPM 1015A, 8 s

122 *Callan: Under the Red File*, Andrew Pixley (Network, 2015)

123 Information taken from camera script, April 1968, Production No 1925 VTR/ABC/7584

124 Trevor Preston interview with authors, 28 August 2013

125 Mike Vardy interview with authors, 6 February 2013

126 Terence Feely interview with Anthony Goodman and Matthew Morgenstern, 22 July 1985

127 James Mitchell interview with Anthony Goodman and Matthew Morgenstern, 15 August 1985

128 Mike Vardy interview with authors, 6 February 2013

129 Information taken from camera script June 1968, production no 1924, VTR/ABC/7648

130 Lee Dunne correspondence with authors, May 2013

131 Archard was on the brink of giving up acting when the *Spycatcher* offer arrived

132 Brian Croucher interview with authors, 2 August 2013

133 John Kershaw interview with Anthony Goodman and Matthew Morgenstern, 1984-87

134 Lee Dunne correspondence with authors, May 2013 Further information and publications listed on author's own promotional website http://leedunne.com

135 Information from camera script, March 1968, Production No: 1922, VTR/ABC/7528, supplemented by information in *Callan: Under the Red File*, Andrew Pixley (Network, 2015)

136 Jim Goddard interview with Anthony Goodman and Matthew Morgenstern, 23 October 1986

137 TV review, *Daily Mail*, 27 March 1969

138 TV review, Maurice Wiggin, *Sunday Times*, 30 March 1969

139 TV review, George Melly, *The Observer*, 30 March 1969

140 Information taken from camera script, June 1968, Production No 1921 VTR/ABC/7716, supplemented by information in *Callan: Under the Red File*, Andrew Pixley,

(Network, 2015)

141 In this story and in his final appearance in 'Death of a Hunter', Harvey's first name is given as John rather than Michael. As John Kershaw admitted that this was a continuity mistake in his Goodman/Morgenstern interview, the name 'Michael' has been used throughout this book

142 Tessa Wyatt conversation with authors, 22 March 2014

143 Jennifer Jaffrey correspondence with authors, May 2013

144 Peter and Charlotte Mitchell interview with authors, 8 October 2013

145 Derek Bond interview with Anthony Goodman and Matthew Morgenstern, 22 August 1985

146 James Mitchell interview with Anthony Goodman and Matthew Morgenstern, 15 August 1985

147 Deadly Acquaintances – Callan: A Blueprint for Quality', Andrew Pixley, *Primetime*, Spring/Summer 1987

148 *Callan: This Man Alone* (Network, 2015)

149 *Callan: Under the Red File*, Andrew Pixley (Network, 2015)

150 Information from camera script, July 1967, Production No: 1907, VTR 6877

151 Information from 'retakes' script, June 1968, Production No: 1907, VTR/ABC/6877X

152 Direction in rehearsal script, July 1967

153 Information from 'retakes' script, June 1968, Production No: 1907, VTR/ABC/6877X

154 Robert Banks Stewart interview with authors, 2 and 7 October 2012

155 Peter Duguid interview with Anthony Goodman and Matthew Morgenstern, 31 July 1986

156 Peter le Page interview with authors, 12 December 2014

157 Significantly, Marshall says 'two rings were broken some years ago,' a probable reference to the Portland case and the 'Cambridge Five'

158 TV review, Nancy Banks-Smith, *The Sun*, dated 10 April 1969

161 Information taken from camera rehearsal script, June 1968, Production No 1923, VTR/ABC/7725, marked for attention of Lloyd Shirley

162 *Callan* series format document, November 1966

163 Mike Vardy interview with authors, 6 February 2013

164 John Kershaw interview with Anthony Goodman and Matthew Morgenstern, 1984-87

165 Information taken from rehearsal script, June 1968, Production No 1923, VTR/ABC/7725, marked for attention of Lloyd Shirley

166 Anthony Valentine interview with Anthony Goodman and Matthew Morgenstern, 10 December 1986

167 John Flanagan correspondence with authors, 13 November 2012

168 'Callan – Dead or Alive?', *TV Times*, Granada edition, 12-18 April 1969

169 *TV Times* Midlands edition, 17-23 May

170 This encryption involves moving by offsets through the alphabet, with the number of letters moved being the key, which changes with each character – for example applying the key AAAA to the word ABCD would change it into BCDE, etc. The method works unbreakably so long as the key is only known to the sender and the receiver and is thrown away after one use. For more information see http://cryptography.wikia.com/wiki/One-time_pad

171 *Defence of the Realm: The Authorized History of MI5* by Christopher Andrew (Penguin Books, 2010) ISBN-13: 978-0141023304 is a painstaking account. *Their Trade is Treachery* by Chapman Pincher ISBN-13: 978-0283988479, originally published in 1982, advanced a conspiracy theory about the 'fifth man'

172 http://www.washingtonpost.com/wp-dyn/content/article/2005/06/15/AR2005061502685.html

173 *Callan: This Man Alone* (Network, 2015)

174 Edward Woodward interview with Anthony Goodman

and Matthew Morgenstern, 24 April 1987

175 David Bickerstaff interview with authors,
16 August 2014

176 Derek Bond interview with Anthony Goodman and
Matthew Morgenstern, 22 August 1985

177 Reg Collin interview with Anthony Goodman and Matthew Morgenstern, 2 August 1985

178 John Kershaw interview with Anthony Goodman and
Matthew Morgenstern, 1984-87

178 Alternatively, a souvenir collector could have misappro-
priated the last page of Shirley's script, or the producer
could just have lit a fag with it. As Tony Hancock would
say, 'it's enough to send a man round the twist.'

179 Edward Woodward interview with Anthony Goodman
and Matthew Morgenstern, 24 April 1987

180 Anthony Valentine interview with Anthony Goodman
and Matthew Morgenstern, 10 December 1986

181 Reg Collin interview with Anthony Goodman and
Matthew Morgenstern, 2 August 1985

182 John Kershaw interview with Anthony Goodman and
Matthew Morgenstern, 1984-87

183 'The Blunt Instrument', Anthony Goodman, based
on research by Anthony Goodman and Matthew
Morgenstern, *Action TV* Magazine, No 5, Autumn 2001

184 Information taken from partial camera script, same
production, marked for attention of 'John – Link'

185 John Kershaw interview with Anthony Goodman and
Matthew Morgenstern, 1984-87

7: SERIES THREE:
Somebody Got Murdered

1 Reg Collin interview with Anthony Goodman and
Matthew Morgenstern, 2 August 1985

2 'The Day Callan Met Sir Laurence', Mark Henry, Evening
Standard, 3 June 1969

3 The coverage peaked in the 29 November-5 December
1969 issue of *TV Times*, with the story 'For the Record:
Callan is Alive and Well.'

4 James Mitchell interview with Anthony Goodman and
Matthew Morgenstern, 15 August 1985

5 Edward Woodward interview with Anthony Goodman
and Matthew Morgenstern, 24 April 1987

6 Edward Woodward commentary on 'If He Can,
So Could I', *Callan: Complete Fourth Series* DVD box set,
Umbrella British TV, 2007

7 'Callan Lives!', 'Callan from Thames' press release,
10 November 1969

8 Jim Goddard interview with Anthony Goodman and
Matthew Morgenstern, 23 October 1986

9 Peter le Page interview with authors, 6 December 2014

10 John Keeling interview with authors, 27 September 2013

11 Reg Collin interview with Anthony Goodman and
Matthew Morgenstern, 2 August 1985

12 'Tom Leads Your TV Top Ten', *TV Times*,
14-20 February 1970

13 James Mitchell interview with Anthony Goodman and
Matthew Morgenstern, 15 August 1985

14 *25 Years of ITV: 1953-1980*, p.155, ITV Books and
(Michael Joseph, 1980)

15 'Why They Invented the Copper with a Kipper Tie,'
John Deane Potter, *TV Times* 8-14 August 1970

16 Reg Collin interview with Anthony Goodman and
Matthew Morgenstern, 2 August 1985

17 Lloyd Shirley and George Markstein interview with
Anthony Goodman and Matthew Morgenstern, 1984-87

18 Gill Hewlett-Case interview with Robert Fairclough, 2004

19 Trevor Preston, Patrick Mower comments, *Callan: This
Man Alone* (Network, 2015)

20 Troy Kennedy Martin conversation with authors, 2002

21 Moris Farhi interview with Robert Fairclough, 2001

22 Geoff Case interview with Robert Fairclough, 2003

23 Lloyd Shirley and George Markstein interview with
Anthony Goodman and Matthew Morgenstern, 1984-87

24 Robert Banks Stewart interview with authors,
2 and 7 October 2012

25 Lewis Greifer interview with Robert Fairclough, 2001

26 Markstein himself briefly appears behind a desk in
The Prisoner title sequence.

27 Roger Parkes interview with Robert Fairclough, 2003

28 Gill Hewlett-Case interview with Robert Fairclough, 2004

29 Lloyd Shirley and George Markstein interview with
Anthony Goodman and Matthew Morgenstern, 1984-87

30 Gill Hewlett-Case interview with Robert Fairclough, 2004

31 'Last Night by Gerard Garrett', *Daily Sketch*, 9 April 1970

32 'Precise Style of Sombre Spy Series', Sylvia Clayton,
Daily Telegraph, 9 April 1970

33 'What Makes Callan Tick?', 'Point of View by John
Dodd', *The Sun*, 9 April 1970

34 James Mitchell interview with Anthony Goodman and
Matthew Morgenstern, 15 August 1985

35 Mike Vardy interview with authors, 6 February 2013

36 Ray Jenkins interview with Anthony Goodman and Matthew Morgenstern, 4 September 1985

37 Patrick Mower interview with authors, 21 November 2013

38 *Callan: This Man Alone* (Network, 2015)

39 William Squire interview with Anthony Goodman and
Matthew Morgenstern, 28 August 1985

40 *Callan: This Man Alone* (Network, 2015)

41 'Callan Episode is Dropped', The Times, 21 May 1970

42 Audience figures published in *Callan: Under the Red File* by
Andrew Pixley (Network, 2015). Overall, in millions of
viewers, the episodes were rated as follows. 'Where Else
Could I Go?' - 13.8, 'Summoned to Appear '- 13.4, 'The
Same Trick Twice' - 11.8, 'Act of Kindness' - 11.4, 'Amos
Green Must Live' - 12.2, 'God Help Your Friends' - 8.8,
'A Village Called "G"'- 12.3, 'Suddenly – At Home' - 13,
'Breakout '- 7.7.

43 Lloyd Shirley and George Markstein interview with
Anthony Goodman and Matthew Morgenstern, 1984-7

44 'A Year Ago They Thought He Was Dead' advertisement,
Variety, 8 April 1970

45 'Last Night's TV by Martin Jackson', *Daily Express*,
9 April 1970

46 Compiled from scripts and call sheets

47 Stuart Orme went on to become an experienced and
respected TV drama director. His work includes *Foyle's
War, Inspector Morse, Merlin* and the Jack Taylor mysteries.

48 Generally credited as 'Dennis'

49 Information taken from camera script, November 1969,
Production No 32080, VTR/THS/2510 and call sheets

50 Special schools for children who committed crimes or
were otherwise deemed by a court to be out of control

51 William Squire interview with Anthony Goodman and
Matthew Morgenstern, 28 August 1985

52 Mike Vardy interview with authors, 6 February 2013

53 Jim Goddard interview with Anthony Goodman and
Matthew Morgenstern, 23 October 1986

54 James Mitchell interview with Anthony Goodman and
Matthew Morgenstern, 15 August 1985

55 Jim Goddard interview with Anthony Goodman and
Matthew Morgenstern, 23 October 1986

56 Reg Collin interview, *Callan: This Man Alone*,
(Network, 2015)

57 Patrick Mower interview with authors, 21 November 2013

58 William Squire interview with Anthony Goodman and
Matthew Morgenstern, 28 August 1985

59 Clifford Rose interview with Anthony Goodman and
Matthew Morgenstern, 5 September 1985

60 Edward Woodward commentary on 'If He Can, So Could I', *Callan: Complete Fourth Series* DVD box set (Umbrella British TV, 2007)

61 Jim Goddard interview with Anthony Goodman and Matthew Morgenstern, 23 October 1986

62 'Get Callan…', James Mitchell, *TV Times*, 4-10 April 1970, Southern edition

63 'Television: A Slump in Fiction', T.C. Worsley, *The Financial Times*, April 1970

64 'Back to Work', Helen Raynor, *The Times*, 9 April 1970

65 In the *Doctor Who* story 'The War Games' (1969), the Aliens used model soldiers on their war maps to represent brainwashed armies of humans. Among other shows, the business drama *Hine* (1971) and the wartime prison series *Colditz* (1972-74) both use chess to symbolise psychological battles between the leading characters.

66 Information taken from camera script, December 1969, Production No 32082, VTR/THS/2512

67 Voytek interview with Anthony Goodman and Matthew Morgenstern, 5 November 1986

68 Peter le Page interview with authors, 6 December 2014

69 Trevor Preston interview with authors, 28 August 2013

70 *Callan: Under the Red File*, by Andrew Pixley, (Network, 2015)

71 Patrick Mower interview with authors, 21 November 2013

72 Voytek interview with Anthony Goodman and Matthew Morgenstern, 5 November 1986

73 Trevor Preston interview with authors, 28 August 2013

74 'Confidential: Special Security Report', *Daily Sketch*, 15 April 1970

75 Trevor Preston interview with authors, 28 August 2013

76 Information taken from camera script, February 1970, Production No 32085, VTR/THS/2515

77 Bill Craig interview with Anthony Goodman and Matthew Morgenstern, 2 September 1985

78 Ray Jenkins interview with Anthony Goodman and Matthew Morgenstern, 4 September 1985

79 'Trisha's Target: The Bolshoi', *TV Times*, 18-24 April 1970

80 Bill Craig interview with Anthony Goodman and Matthew Morgenstern, 2 September 1985

81 Reg Collin interview with Anthony Goodman and Matthew Morgenstern, 2 August 1985

82 Peter Duguid interview with Anthony Goodman and Matthew Morgenstern, 31 July 1986

83 William Squire interview with Anthony Goodman and Matthew Morgenstern, 28 August 1985

84 Peter Duguid interview with Anthony Goodman and Matthew Morgenstern, 31 July 1986

85 'Penny for 'Em: Lastword', *TV Times*, 30 May-5 June 1970. Mrs Joy Atkinson of Northamptonshire wrote in to say: 'In *Callan*, which is surely the best cloak and dagger series in years, the badinage in the gent's washroom with Lonely as "hygiene attendant" [sic] put many top comedy skits to shame. When Callan promised Lonely "cash in lieu" I was convinced he would add "at your own convenience".'

86 Information taken from camera script, February 1970, Production No 32084, VTR/THS/2514

87 Mike Vardy interview with authors, 6 February 2013

88 *Ibid.*, 6 February 2013

89 Russell Hunter interview with Anthony Goodman and Matthew Morgenstern, 8 January 1987

90 'TV - Virginia Ironside', *Daily Mail*, 28 May 1970

91 'Callan gets Nosey', *The Sun*, 29 May 1970

92 Information taken from camera script, March 1970, Production No 32086, VTR/THS/2632

93 Ray Jenkins interview with Anthony Goodman and Matthew Morgenstern, 4 September 1985

94 Jim Goddard interview with Anthony Goodman and Matthew Morgenstern, 23 October 1986

95 Stefan Kalipha interview with the authors, Primrose Hill, 28 May 2013

96 Ray Jenkins interview with Anthony Goodman and Matthew Morgenstern, 4 September 1985

97 Jim Goddard interview with Anthony Goodman and Matthew Morgenstern, 23 October 1986

98 Ray Jenkins interview with Anthony Goodman and Matthew Morgenstern, 4 September 1985

99 Lloyd Shirley and George Markstein interview with Anthony Goodman and Matthew Morgenstern, 1984-87

100 For context: a few years before, the BBC similarly controversially deferred a broadcast of their popular *Steptoe and Son* sitcom on the night of the 1964 election, after being lobbied by Harold Wilson, who was concerned a number of his supporters might opt to stay in and watch the show rather than go and vote.

101 'Callan Storm over Election Ban', Philip Phillips, *The Sun*, 21 May 1970 (first edition)

102 *Callan: This Man Alone*, interview, (Network, 2015)

103 Ray Jenkins interview with Anthony Goodman and Matthew Morgenstern, 4 September 1985

104 Reg Collin interview with Anthony Goodman and Matthew Morgenstern, 2 August 1985

105 'Dramatic Prelude to Clash on Bill', David Wood, *The Times*, 22 April 1968

106 'Tory MP speaks of "Tragedy"', staff reporters, *The Times*, 22 April 1968

107 Ray Jenkins interview with Anthony Goodman and Matthew Morgenstern, 4 September 1985

108 Sylvia Clayton, *Daily Telegraph*, 25 June 1970

109 Nancy Banks-Smith, *Guardian*, 25 June 1970

110 Ray Jenkins interview with Anthony Goodman and Matthew Morgenstern, 4 September 1985

111 Information taken from camera script, December 1969, Production No 32081, VTR/THS/2511

112 Michael Jayston interview with authors, 22 September 2013

113 Peter Duguid interview with Anthony Goodman and Matthew Morgenstern, 31 July 1986

114 William Squire interview with Anthony Goodman and Matthew Morgenstern, 28 August 1985

115 Michael Jayston interview with authors, 22 September 2013

116 Peter Duguid interview with Anthony Goodman and Matthew Morgenstern, 31 July 1986

117 Information taken from camera script, March 1970, Production No 32087, VTR/THS/2633

118 Mike Vardy interview with authors, 6 February 2013

119 George Innes interview with authors, 16 February 2013

120 Mike Vardy interview with authors, 6 February 2013

121 Lloyd Shirley and George Markstein interview with Anthony Goodman and Matthew Morgenstern, 1984-87

122 James Mitchell interview with Anthony Goodman and Matthew Morgenstern, 15 August 1985

123 Patrick Mower interview with authors, 21 November 2013

124 Information taken from camera script, January 1970, Production No 32083, VTR/THS/2513

125 Frances Tomelty correspondence with authors, 8 May 2013

126 James Mitchell interview with Anthony Goodman and Matthew Morgenstern, 15 August 1985

127 Piers Haggard interview with authors, 21 October 2013

128 John Keeling interview with authors, 27 September 2013

129 Piers Haggard interview with authors, 21 October 2013

130 'Callan's First Kiss', *The Sun*, 22 April 1970

131 'Moment of History – Callan's First Kiss', *TV Times*, 25 April-1 May 1970

132 Information taken from camera script, April 1970,
Production No 32088, VTR/THS/2634

133 William Squire interview with Anthony Goodman
and Matthew Morgenstern, 28 August 1985

134 Garfield Morgan interview with authors, 2002

135 James Mitchell interview with Anthony Goodman
and Matthew Morgenstern, 15 August 1985

136 Reg Collin interview with Anthony Goodman and
Matthew Morgenstern, 2 August 1985

137 Lloyd Shirley and George Markstein interview with
Anthony Goodman and Matthew Morgenstern, 1984-87

138 Russell Hunter interview with Anthony Goodman
and Matthew Morgenstern, 8 January 1987

139 William Squire interview with Anthony Goodman
and Matthew Morgenstern, 28 August 1985

140 Edward Woodward commentary on 'Call Me Enemy',
Callan: Complete Fourth Series DVD box set
(Umbrella British TV, 2007)

8: SERIES FOUR:
Last Rat Standing

1 *IBA Annual Report*, p.12, 1971

2 'Presenting Your Top Ten Personalities', *TV Times*,
11-17 March 1971, Southern edition

3 Lloyd Shirley and George Markstein interview with
Anthony Goodman and Matthew Morgenstern, 1984-87

4 Reg Collin interview with Anthony Goodman and
Matthew Morgenstern, 2 August 1985

5 Lloyd Shirley and George Markstein interview with
Anthony Goodman and Matthew Morgenstern, 1984-87

6 Anthony Valentine interview with Anthony Goodman
and Matthew Morgenstern, 10 December 1986

7 Trevor Preston interview with Anthony Goodman and
Matthew Morgenstern, 1984-87

8 Bill Craig interview with Anthony Goodman and Matthew
Morgenstern, 2 September 1985

9 Reg Collin interview with Anthony Goodman and
Matthew Morgenstern, 2 August 1985

10 Audience figures published in *Callan: Under the Red File*,
Andrew Pixley (Network, 2015)

11 Fourth Series narrative plan, 1971

12 Lloyd Shirley and George Markstein interview with
Anthony Goodman and Matthew Morgenstern, 1984-87

13 James Mitchell interview with Anthony Goodman and
Matthew Morgenstern, 15 August 1985

14 Jim Goddard interview with Anthony Goodman
and Matthew Morgenstern, 23 October 1986

15 Edward Woodward interview with Anthony Goodman
and Matthew Morgenstern, 24 April 1987

16 Reg Collin interview, *Callan: This Man Alone*,
(Network, 2015)

17 William Squire interview with Anthony Goodman
and Matthew Morgenstern, 28 August 1985

18 Mike Vardy interview with authors, 6 February 2013

19 James Mitchell interview with Anthony Goodman and
Matthew Morgenstern, 15 August 1985

20 Reg Collin interview with Anthony Goodman and Matthew Morgenstern, 2 August 1985

21 'Callan Meets a Real Match', Mary Malone,
Daily Mirror, 2 March 1972

22 '50-50 Idea for News-Bulletin Violence', Richard Last,
Daily Telegraph, 9 March 1972

23 'Distasteful Brutality in Callan Plot', *Daily Telegraph*,
2 March 1972

24 'The Book Page. If Callan Had Met Those Louts
on a Train... By Graham Lord', *Sunday Express*,
8 December 1974

25 Jim Goddard interview with Anthony Goodman

and Matthew Morgenstern, 23 October 1986

26 Reg Collin interview with Anthony Goodman and
Matthew Morgenstern, 2 August 1985. 'When [*Callan*]
went out, we would have visiting professors from America
saying "I believe you do the most violent series on
television," Collin says, remembering having to sit with
Brian Tesler to look over the episode. The complaint in
question ultimately came from a scene where a colleague
of Callan's had been [killed], and Callan has the person
who did it in an interrogation situation. [and Meres] gets
so angry with this man he thumps him. That was it. We
watched the programme and [Tesler] said, "Where's the
violence?"... It's kiddiwink stuff.'

27 Russell Hunter interview with Anthony Goodman and
Matthew Morgenstern, 8 January 1987

28 Anthony Valentine interview with Anthony Goodman
and Matthew Morgenstern, 10 December 1986

29 Reg Collin interview, *Callan: This Man Alone*,
(Network, 2015)

30 'How Can Callan Survive this Latest (and Deadliest)
Bid to Kill Him Off?', Shaun Usher, *Daily Mail*,
4 November 1972

31 'Callan's Ready for a Fight!', Chris Greenwood,
The Sun, 25 June 1973

32 *Callan* achieved considerable international reach,
gaining press attention in both Australia and America,
as documented in *Callan: Under the Red File*, Andrew Pixley,
(Network, 2015)

33 James Mitchell interview with Anthony Goodman
and Matthew Morgenstern, 15 August 1985

34 Compiled from scripts and call sheets

35 Information taken from camera script, December 1971,
Production No 35004, VTR/THS/5022 and call sheets

36 Julian Glover interview with authors, 13 November 2012

37 Paul Williamson interview with authors,
28 February 2014

38 James Mitchell interview with Anthony Goodman and
Matthew Morgenstern, 15 August 1985

39 Reg Collin interview with Anthony Goodman and
Matthew Morgenstern, 2 August 1985

40 William Squire interview with Anthony Goodman and
Matthew Morgenstern, 28 August 1985

41 'A Funeral Has Been Arranged and Will Shortly Take
Place' synopsis, 1971, reprinted in *Callan Uncovered*,
(Ostara Publishing, 2014)

42 Series Four narrative plan, 1971

43 Mike Vardy interview with authors, 6 February 2013

44 Patrick Mower interview with authors, 21 November 2013

45 Paul Williamson interview with authors, 28 February 2014

46 'The Spymaker Comes in From the Cold', 'Pit', *Variety*,
15 March 1972

47 *Callan: This Man Alone* (Network, 2015)

48 *Thames Mavericks* press release, July 1989

49 Information taken from camera script, November 1971,
Production No 35001, VTR/THS/5019 and call sheets

50 Mike Vardy interview with authors, 6 February 2013

51 Bill Craig interview with Anthony Goodman and
Matthew Morgenstern, 2 September 1985

52 William Squire interview with Anthony Goodman
and Matthew Morgenstern, 28 August 1985

53 Mike Vardy interview with authors, 6 February 2013

54 Paul Williamson interview with authors, 28 February 2014

55 Mike Vardy interview with authors, 6 February 2013

56 'Girls Can't Stop Writing to the Sadistic Mr. Cross',
Chris Kenworthy, *The Sun*, 8 March 1972

57 'TV Talk', *TV Times*, 4-10 March 1972, Southern edition

58 Information taken from camera script, November 1971,
Production No 35003, VTR/THS/5021 and call sheets

59 This choice not only emulates the fourth Hunter, but also

suggests the stereotypical, 'pipe and slippers' image of retirement, in Callan's case from active duty

60 Christopher Owen correspondence with authors, 6 October 2012

61 Bill Craig interview with Anthony Goodman and Matthew Morgenstern, 2 September 1985

62 Anthony Valentine interview with Anthony Goodman and Matthew Morgenstern, 10 December 1986

63 Edward Woodward interview with Anthony Goodman and Matthew Morgenstern, 24 April 1987

64 Jim Goddard interview, *Callan: This Man Alone*, (Network, 2015)

65 Reg Collin interview with Anthony Goodman and Matthew Morgenstern, 2 August 1985

66 'Taken for a Ride', Anon., *The Sun*, 1 March 1972

67 Jim Goddard interview with Anthony Goodman and Matthew Morgenstern, 23 October 1986

68 See 'Death of a Hunter'

69 Information taken from camera script, November 1971, Production No 35002, VTR/THS/5020 and call sheets

70 Not entirely unlike the one the one used by Security liaison Charles Moxon (Morris Perry) in *Special Branch*

71 Ray Jenkins interview with Anthony Goodman and Matthew Morgenstern, 4 September 1985

72 Voytek interview with Anthony Goodman and Matthew Morgenstern, 5 November 1986

73 Information taken from camera script, January 1972, Production No 35006, VTR/THS/5415 and call sheets

74 Clifford Rose interview, *Callan: This Man Alone*, (Network, 2015)

75 Peter Duguid interview with Anthony Goodman and Matthew Morgenstern, 31 July 1986

76 Reg Collin interview with Anthony Goodman and Matthew Morgenstern, 2 August 1985

77 Lloyd Shirley and George Markstein interview with Anthony Goodman and Matthew Morgenstern, 1984-87

78 James Mitchell interview with Anthony Goodman and Matthew Morgenstern, 15 August 1985

79 Ray Jenkins interview with Anthony Goodman and Matthew Morgenstern, 4 September 1985

80 Edward Woodward commentary on 'If He Can, So Could I', *Callan: Complete Fourth Series* DVD box set (Umbrella British TV, 2007)

81 Patrick Mower interview with authors, 21 November 2013

82 Clifford Rose interview with Anthony Goodman and Matthew Morgenstern, 5 September 1985

83 Peter Duguid interview with Anthony Goodman and Matthew Morgenstern, 31 July 1986

84 Voytek interview with Anthony Goodman and Matthew Morgenstern, 5 November 1986

85 Patrick Mower interview, *Callan: This Man Alone*, (Network, 2015)

86 Peter Duguid interview with Anthony Goodman and Matthew Morgenstern, 31 July 1986

87 Ray Jenkins interview with Anthony Goodman and Matthew Morgenstern, 4 September 1985

88 In 1970, the BBC's series *Doomwatch* (1970-73) caused an outcry when its most popular character Toby Wren was killed off in the episode 'Survival Code'. At the time, this method of removing long-running characters was seen as innovative and unusual

89 Information taken from camera script, February 1972, Production No 35008, VTR/THS/5417 and call sheets

90 A similar rift occurs in Trevor Preston's opening script for *The Sweeney*, 'Ringer', contrasting Regan's street-wise cop with his office-bound superiors

91 Brian Murphy conversation with authors, 22 March 2014

92 Trevor Preston interview with Anthony Goodman and Matthew Morgenstern, 1984-87

93 Trevor Preston interview with authors, 28 August 2013

94 Trevor Preston interview with Anthony Goodman and Matthew Morgenstern, 1984-87

95 Trevor Preston interview with authors, 28 August 2013

96 Voytek interview with Anthony Goodman and Matthew Morgenstern, 5 November 1986

97 Paul Williamson interview with authors, 28 February 2014

98 Brian Murphy conversation with authors, 22 March 2014

99 'Callan – Fact or Fiction?', 'Playback', *TV Times* April 1-7 1972

100 Copeland was also a jazz musician, working with the Glenn Miller Orchestra. One of his children, Stewart Copeland, would go on to achieve fame as both a prolific film and TV music composer – writing the theme for Edward Woodward's 1980s action series, *The Equalizer* – and as the drummer in the New Wave band The Police

102 Information taken from camera script, February 1972, Production No 35009, VTR/THS/5418 and call sheets

103 Series Four narrative plan, 1971

104 James Mitchell interview with Anthony Goodman and Matthew Morgenstern, 15 August 1985

105 William Squire interview with Anthony Goodman and Matthew Morgenstern, 28 August 1985

106 Peter Duguid interview with Anthony Goodman and Matthew Morgenstern, 31 July 1986

107 James Mitchell interview with Anthony Goodman and Matthew Morgenstern, 15 August 1985

108 'Callan has a Secret Love', *Daily Mirror*, 12 April 1972

109 Information taken from camera script, December 1971, Production No 35005, VTR/THS/5023 and call sheets

110 Voytek interview with Anthony Goodman and Matthew Morgenstern, 5 November 1986

111 Jim Goddard interview with Anthony Goodman and Matthew Morgenstern, 23 October 1986

112 Russell Hunter interview with Anthony Goodman and Matthew Morgenstern, 8 January 1987

113 Information taken from camera script, March 1972, Production No 35010, VTR/THS/5419 and call sheets

114 'Murder was My Business', Peter Hill, *TV Times* 17-23 October 1972

115 This show also used 'Girl In The Dark' as part of its incidental music

116 Neville Green interview with authors, 10 December 2014

117 Reg Collin interview with Anthony Goodman and Matthew Morgenstern, 2 August 1985

118 Edward Woodward commentary on 'If He Can, So Could I', *Callan: Complete Fourth Series* DVD box set, (Umbrella British TV, 2007)

119 Information taken from camera script, January 1972, Production No 35007, VTR/THS/5416 and call sheets, supplemented by information in *Callan: Under the Red File*, Andrew Pixley, Network, 2015

120 Bill Craig interview with Anthony Goodman and Matthew Morgenstern, 2 September 1985

121 Craig envisaged the cat as an 'ordinary street moggy' but it turned out to be 'petulant', he recalled. 'The cat had its own agent, a pedigree back to Egypt, and was a magnificent Persian... They were putting the finest chopped liver on the gatepost to make it stay in position; one of the technicians cruelly suggested [gluing] its paws. Eventually it got settled but just as the director said "roll", two genuine moggies came round the corner. We spent the next fortnight racing around Surbiton trying to find the cat!'

122 '...Blood-Stained Roses All the Way, a Couple of Spin-Off Novels, a Clutch of Short Stories, a Callan movie in the Last Stages of Shoot-Up. Pass the Supertax Problems and the Very Dry Sherry. Peter Petersen meets James Mitchell... the inventor of Callan', *The Guardian*, 9 January 1974

123 Information taken from camera script, March 1972, Production No 35011, VTR/THS/5420

124 Possibly this award was related to Callan saving Captain Henshaw's life – see 'Where Else Could I Go?', Chapter 6

125 The next story adds a further lover (Svetlana Souraikin) and a daughter (Irena)

126 Edward Woodward commentary on 'Call Me Enemy', *Callan: Complete Fourth Series* DVD box set (Umbrella British TV, 2007)

127 Brian Croucher interview with authors, 2 August 2013

128 James Mitchell interview with Anthony Goodman and Matthew Morgenstern, 15 August 1985

129 Lloyd Shirley and George Markstein interview with Anthony Goodman and Matthew Morgenstern, 1984-87

130 Edward Woodward commentary on 'Call Me Enemy', *Callan: Complete Fourth Series* DVD box set (Umbrella British TV, 2007)

131 Reg Collin interview with Anthony Goodman and Matthew Morgenstern, 2 August 1985

132 Edward Woodward commentary on 'Call Me Enemy', *Callan: Complete Fourth Series* DVD box set (Umbrella British TV, 2007)

133 Brian Croucher interview with authors, 2 August 2013

134 'A Tough Nut for Tough Guy Callan to Crack', Chris Kenworthy, *The Sun*, 10 May 1972

135 'Film: Stupid Spies but Thrilling Story', Cecil Wilson, *Daily Mail*, 18 August 1964

136 Series Four narrative plan, 1971

137 'Night and Day', Brian Viner, *Mail on Sunday*, 23 July 1995. 'For one thing, it enabled us to see what Edward Woodward looked like 25 chins ago. For another, it reminded us of that long-lost era when a leading character in a popular ITV drama could casually, without subtitles, say, "I'm a recidivist."'

138 Information taken from camera script, April 1972, Production No 35012, VTR/THS/5421

139 Bill Craig interview with Anthony Goodman and Matthew Morgenstern, 2 September 1985

140 Peter Duguid interview with Anthony Goodman and Matthew Morgenstern, 31 July 1986

141 Information taken from camera script, April 1972, Production No 35013, VTR/THS/5422

142 *Ibid.*

143 Belinda Carroll interview with authors, 1 November 2013

144 TV review, Peter Fiddick, *The Guardian*, 28 April 1982

145 James Mitchell interview with Anthony Goodman and Matthew Morgenstern, 15 August 1985

146 Reg Collin interview with Anthony Goodman and Matthew Morgenstern, 2 August 1985

147 John Keeling interview with authors, 27 September 2013

148 Reg Collin interview with Anthony Goodman and Matthew Morgenstern, 2 August 1985

149 After consulting many and various archive interviews with Len Deighton, Rob Mallows, editor of *The Deighton Dossier* website, concluded that 'Patrick Armstrong', the narrator of Deighton's 1970s novels *Spy Story* and *Twinkle, Twinkle, Little Spy*, wasn't the same character the author had written about ten years earlier. However, returning characters like Dawlish and Colonel Stok from the 1960s books suggest that Deighton was deliberately teasing his readers about his 1970s narrator's identity. In the foreword to the Silver Jubilee edition of *Spy Story* he mischievously said, 'One thing is clear. Patrick Armstrong is not the man from *The IPCRESS File*, although he's obviously a close relative.'

150 John Keeling interview with authors, 27 September 2013

151 James Mitchell interview with Anthony Goodman and Matthew Morgenstern, 15 August 1985

152 Reg Collin interview with Anthony Goodman and Matthew Morgenstern, 2 August 1985

153 John Keeling interview with authors, 27 September 2013

154 Clifford Rose interview with Anthony Goodman and Matthew Morgenstern, 5 September 1985

155 Russell Hunter interview with Anthony Goodman and Matthew Morgenstern, 8 January 1987

156 Anthony Valentine interview with Anthony Goodman and Matthew Morgenstern, 10 December 1986

157 Belinda Carroll interview with authors, 1 November 2013

158 William Squire interview with Anthony Goodman and Matthew Morgenstern, 28 August 1985

159 Edward Woodward commentary on 'Call Me Enemy', *Callan: Complete Fourth Series* DVD box set (Umbrella British TV, 2007)

160 Edward Woodward interview with Anthony Goodman and Matthew Morgenstern, 24 April 1987

9: File On A Working Writer

1 James Mitchell interview with Anthony Goodman and Matthew Morgenstern, 15 August 1985

2 Quoted on the back cover of the hardback edition of *Death and Bright Water* (Hamish Hamilton Ltd., 1974)

3 'James Mitchell, Novelist Known for Spy Stories, is Dead', Eric Paice, *The New York Times*, 23 September 2002

4 Quoted on the back cover of the paperback edition of *Red File for Callan* (Corgi, 1971)

5 Quotes from the back cover of the paperback edition of *A Red File for Callan* (Dell, 1974)

6 Thanks to Sarah Guiver for identifying this. This scene was possibly based on a real-life experience of Mitchell's.

7 Correspondence between Frank Rosenberg and Paul Reynolds, Reuben Bercovitch and George Greenfield and Harold Hecht and George Greenfield, 19 October-1 November 1973

8 Quoted on the back cover of the hardback edition of *Death and Bright Water* (Hamish Hamilton Ltd., 1974)

9 Anonymous, *Coventry Evening Telegraph*, December 1973

10 Quoted on the back cover of the hardback edition of *Smear Job* (Hamish Hamilton Ltd., 1975)

11 Peter and Charlotte Mitchell interview with authors, 8 October 2013

12 'James Mitchell, Creator of TV Hit Man Callan', Kathryn Holloway, *Daily Express*, 27 September 2002

13 Sarah Guiver correspondence with authors, 27 May 2016

10: 'A Bloody Good Little Film'

1 Hammer directors' minutes, 16 March 1972

2 Terence Feely interview with Anthony Goodman and Matthew Morgenstern, 22 July 1985

3 Memorandum dated 14 April 1969, transcribed by Anthony Goodman and Matthew Morgenstern

4 Lloyd Shirley and George Markstein interview with Anthony Goodman and Matthew Morgenstern, 1984-87

5 James Mitchell interview with Anthony Goodman and Matthew Morgenstern, 15 August 1985

6 Peter and Charlotte Mitchell interview with authors, 8 October 2013

7 Derek Horne interview with authors, 24 January 2014

8 Peter and Charlotte Mitchell interview with authors, 8 October 2013

9 Thought to be Seagram's 100 Pipers; Callan also has a bottle of this blended whisky in his flat. Richard Allan's *Skinhead* books also frequently name-dropped this product in the 1970s.

10 *Sweeney! The Official Companion*, Chapter 3: 'Euston Films: From Thames to Turkistan'

11 Press advert, *Film Review*, July 1974

12 Derek Horne interview with authors, 24 January 2014

13 *Ibid.*, 17 January 2014

14 Peter Egan interview with authors, 12 September 2013

15 'Five years of sheer bliss, really,' Egan recalled of his work on *Ever Decreasing Circles*. 'Every eighteen months we worked for three months on it. Richard Briers was magical and we became great friends. I miss him desperately.'

16 Catherine Schell conversation with authors, 22 March 2014

17 Peter Egan interview with authors, 12 September 2013. Da Costa married into the aristocracy and adopted the name Edmund Brudenell (though keeping Michael Da Costa for his acting work). His wife was Phillipa Mary Brudenell, descended from the Earls of Cardigan. She died in 1974 and Da Costa died in 1977 – it's likely he killed himself as Egan recalled, although the coroner returned an open verdict due to a lack of evidence. http://www.britmovie.co.uk/forums/actors-actresses/115071-forgotten-actors-michael-da-costa.html

18 *Callan* first draft screenplay, handwritten, dated 1971, courtesy of Peter Mitchell

19 James Mitchell interview with Anthony Goodman and Matthew Morgenstern, 15 August 1985

20 Kilravock Company Limited casting suggestions, 1973

21 Derek Horne interview with authors, 24 January 2014

22 Clifford Rose interview with Anthony Goodman and Matthew Morgenstern, 5 September 1985

23 William Squire interview with Anthony Goodman and Matthew Morgenstern, 28 August 1985

24 Peter Egan interview with authors, 12 September 2013

25 Information from 'The Official Dave Prowse Website', https://www.darthvader-starwars.com

26 Derek Horne interview with authors, 24 January 2014

27 Sound Gets into Line with Picture' by Nicholas Lewin, *Cinema TV Today*, 1 June 1974

28 Film review, Cecil Watson, *Daily Mail*, 24 May 1974

29 'Magnifying Callan' by Gavin Millar, *The Listener*, 6 June 1974

30 Film review, Adrian Turner, *Films Illustrated*, 22 July 1974

31 'Callan Moves Over: Cinema by Keith MacDonald', *Manchester Evening News*, 13 July 1974

32 Peter Egan interview with authors, 12 September 2013

33 Clifford Rose interview with Anthony Goodman and Matthew Morgenstern, 5 September 1985

34 Russell Hunter interview with Anthony Goodman and Matthew Morgenstern, 8 January 1987

35 Edward Woodward interview with Anthony Goodman and Matthew Morgenstern, 24 April 1987

36 Derek Horne interview with authors, 24 January 2014

37 'Films by David Quinlan', *TV Times*, 9-15 May 1981

11: NEVER SAY NEVER AGAIN: 'Wet Job'

1 'Callan's Back in Business', *TV Times*, 9-15 May 1981

2 Review by Clive James, *Observer*, 6 September 1981

3 Trevor Preston interview with Anthony Goodman and Matthew Morgenstern, 1984-87

4 William Squire interview with Anthony Goodman and Matthew Morgenstern, 28 August 1985

5 Lloyd Shirley and George Markstein interview with Anthony Goodman and Matthew Morgenstern, 1984-7

6 Edward Woodward interview with Anthony Goodman and Matthew Morgenstern, 24 April 1987

7 James Mitchell interview with Anthony Goodman and Matthew Morgenstern, 15 August 1985

8 Shaun O'Riordan interview with Anthony Goodman and Matthew Morgenstern, 5 January 1987

9 Production information from *Callan – Under the Red File*, by Andrew Pixley, Network, 2015

10 *Ibid*, supplemented by *Wet Job* Outside Broadcast camera script.

11 Philip Bird interview with the authors, 15 August 2013

12 Hugh Walters interview with authors, 6 March 2013

13 Hugh's second *Doctor Who* role, in 'The Deadly Assassin', was particularly memorable: 'I said "How am I going to be killed?" and they said "You're going to stagger out into the centre of the studio, fall flat on your face, and out of your back will be sticking this space thing that's killed you." I thought "That sounds rather good", but by the time I did it the thing looked like an ordinary chair leg... [The story] was fun to do, the costumes were fabulous and the script was very good indeed, I thought.'

14 Philip Bird interview with the authors, 15 August 2013

15 James Mitchell interview with Anthony Goodman and Matthew Morgenstern, 15 August 1985

16 Anthony Valentine interview with Anthony Goodman and Matthew Morgenstern, 10 December 1986

17 Hugh Walters interview with authors, 6 March 2013

18 Philip Bird interview with the authors, 15 August 2013

19 Russell Hunter interview with Anthony Goodman and Matthew Morgenstern, 8 January 1987

20 Edward Woodward interview with Anthony Goodman and Matthew Morgenstern, 24 April 1987

21 Edward Woodward commentary on 'Call Me Enemy', *Callan: Complete Fourth Series* DVD box set, Umbrella British TV, 2007

22 Reg Collin interview with Anthony Goodman and Matthew Morgenstern, 2 August 1985

23 James Mitchell interview with Anthony Goodman and Matthew Morgenstern, 15 August 1985

24 BARB TV ratings, *Broadcast*, 7 September 1981

25 Review by Rosalie Horner, *Daily Express*, 3 September 1981

26 'Callan, Ten Years Older', by Sylvia Clayton, *Daily Telegraph*, date unknown, 1981

27 Review by Clive James, *Observer*, 6 September 1981

28 Review by Russell Davies, *Sunday Times*, 6 September 1981

29 'Don to Death', by Nancy Banks-Smith, *Guardian*, 3 September 1981

12: MI5 not 9 to 5

1 'No-No Right: Television: Nancy Banks-Smith', *Guardian*, 8 April 1970

2 'The Spy Who Graduates in Non-Violence', Nancy Griffiths, *Daily Mirror*, 7 April 1970

3 'For the Well-Dressed Lady Spy' by Gerard Garrett', *Daily Sketch*, 17 June 1970

4 'The Unbidden Guest', Peter Knight, *Daily Telegraph*, 1 July 1970

5 Julian Glover interview with authors, 13 November 2012

6 Sylvia Clayton, *Daily Telegraph*, 5 May 1972

7 'Suavity and Clichés of Spy Trap', Sean Day-Lewis, *Daily Telegraph*, 14 March 1972

8 Unfortunately, few or no episodes of either *Spy Trap* or *Codename* survive in the BBC archives – of the latter, all that exists is the pilot film. Contributing writers included John Kershaw, Bill Craig and Ray Jenkins.

9 Christened Norman Smith, the gravel-voiced singer began his music career as an engineer for EMI working on records by The Beatles. Graduating to producer, in 1968 he oversaw The Pretty Things' concept album *SF Sorrow*. He embarked on a singing career in 1971, scoring a number 2 UK chart placing with the single 'Don't Let It Die'. Smith was also responsible for the psychedelic rockers The Pink Floyd being signed to EMI, recommending them after he saw them perform in the UFO club in Covent Garden; he recorded several of their early concerts

10 Review, *Sight and Sound*, Winter 1972-73

11 For example his preface to *Chance Awakening* (House of

Stratus, 2001 edition) reads, 'Some of the fiction in this story is fact. Some of the fact is fiction.'

12 Robert Banks Stewart interview with authors, 2 and 7 October 2012

13 'Well, Spy Trap Didn't Capture Me: Last Night's View by James Thomas', *Daily Express*, 14 March 1972

14 Michael Jayston interview with authors, 22 September 2013

15 Comic editors must have assumed their young male readers had some familiarity with *Callan*; the 14 October 1972 edition of *The Valiant* featured an illustration of Edward Woodward on its 'Who Is It?' cover feature, referenced from a 'Heir Apparent' publicity still.

16 *Action': The Story of a Violent Comic*, by Martin Barker, Titan Books Ltd, October 1990 ISBN-10: 1852860235

17 'I Spy a Vain Bid for Realism: Television Review by Herbert Kretzmer', *Daily Mail*, 29 January 1980

18 'Shakespeare and Sandbags. Bill Grundy: Last Night's View', *Evening Standard*, 1 July 1980

19 *Ibid.*

20 Yorkshire Television Head of Drama David Cunliffe, quoted in 'Vanished: The Original Sandbagger', Jane Ennis, *TV Times*, 26 January-1 February 1980, Southern edition

21 Michael Ferguson interview with authors, 30 October 2013

22 TV review, Philip Purser, *Sunday Telegraph*, 24 February 1980

23 The BBC also had its own take on this type of character, casting Michael Denison as the dapper Special Intelligence Service head Captain Percival in a trilogy of espionage series, *Blood Money*, *Skorpion* and *Cold Warrior*, between 1981 and 1984.

24 Lloyd Shirley and George Markstein interview with Anthony Goodman and Matthew Morgenstern, 1984-87

25 TV review, *Daily Telegraph*, April 1984

26 TV review, *Daily Mail*, April 1984

27 'Spy Drama throws Light on MI5', Matt Born, *The Times*, 23 November 2001

28 'Secret Services in TV Drama', Matt Wells, *The Guardian*, 23 November 2001

29 Bharat Nalluri interview with authors, 9 May 2016

30 Mike Vardy interview with authors, 6 February 2013

31 Patrick Mower interview with authors, 21 November 2013

32 Michael Ferguson interview with authors, 30 October 2013

33 Bharat Nalluri interview with authors, 9 May 2016

34 Starring Peta Wilson this series was essentially an Americanised reboot of the French thriller *Nikita* (1990), written and directed by Luc Besson with Anne Parillaud playing the role. In 2010 it was rebooted again, this time featuring Maggie Q as 'Nikita Mears'(!)

35 *The Living Daylights* review, Nick Setchfield, *SFX* website, 2012

36 James Bond, *The World is Not Enough* (1999)

13: Callan Lives!

1 William Squire interview with Anthony Goodman and Matthew Morgenstern, 28 August 1985

2 Russell Hunter interview with Anthony Goodman and Matthew Morgenstern, 8 January 1987

3 Anthony Valentine interview with Anthony Goodman and Matthew Morgenstern, 10 December 1986

4 Ray Jenkins interview with Anthony Goodman and Matthew Morgenstern, 4 September 1985

5 'TV Action! Watching the Detectives' by Tony Mechele, National Film Theatre booklet, May 1987

6 Phil Newman interview with authors, 22 August 2015

7 By the end of *Wet Job* there were technically *six* Hunters – Radd, Goodliffe, Bond, Squire, Woodward and Walters. However as this was a sequel and not part of the original series, everyone clearly, and probably wisely,

avoided the issue

8 'Stars in Our Eyes', Alice de Picarda, *Broadcast: The Official 50th Anniversary Supplement*, p.37, 23 September 2005: 'Secret agent David Callan provided the dark flipside to the decadent lifestyle of the popular James Bond films. The government assassin was a complex character, living on the periphery of society, with only one friend – a petty thief with bad personal hygiene. The solitary, brooding side of Callan was juxtaposed with a rebellious, caring side.'

9 These were executive-produced by Grant Taylor, recorded by André Jacquemin at Redwood Studios, London, facilitated by Henry Holland and produced and moderated by Jaz Wiseman using questions supplied by the authors

10 Joanna Green interview with authors, 3 October 2013

11 Adrian Bean interview with authors, 5 September 2013

12 'Radio's Five of the Best,' *Radio Times*, 15-21 September 2012

13 Joanna Green interview with authors, 3 October 2013

14 Adrian Bean interview with authors, 5 September 2013

15 Programme details from the BBC Radio 4 Extra website

16 Joanna Green interview with authors, 3 October 2013

17 Radio 4 Extra episode introduction, BBC Radio 4 Extra website, 13 September 2012

18 Mike Ripley correspondence with authors, 6 March 2013

19 Peter and Charlotte Mitchell interview with authors, 8 October 2013

20 Robert Banks Stewart interview with authors, 2 and 7 October 2012

21 Ray Jenkins interview with Anthony Goodman and Matthew Morgenstern, 4 September 1985

22 Russell Hunter interview with Anthony Goodman and Matthew Morgenstern, 8 January 1987

23 Clifford Rose interview with Anthony Goodman and Matthew Morgenstern, 5 September 1985

24 Mike Vardy interview with authors, 6 February 2013

25 Jim Goddard interview with Anthony Goodman and Matthew Morgenstern, 23 October 1986

26 Voytek interview with Anthony Goodman and Matthew Morgenstern, 5 November 1986

27 Peter Duguid interview with Anthony Goodman and Matthew Morgenstern, 31 July 1985

28 Reg Collin interview with Anthony Goodman and Matthew Morgenstern, 2 August 1985

29 Anthony Valentine interview with Anthony Goodman and Matthew Morgenstern, 10 December 1986

30 Patrick Mower interview with authors, 21 November 2013

31 Adrian Bean interview with authors, 5 September 2013

32 Mike Ripley correspondence with authors, 6 March 2013

33 In *Funeral in Berlin* (1966), about to enter the East German zone, Palmer sardonically notes, '[I've got] my Luger pistol, my cyanide pills and my inflatable Batman suit.'

33 Edward Woodward interview with Anthony Goodman and Matthew Morgenstern, 24 April 1987

34 James Mitchell interview with Anthony Goodman and Matthew Morgenstern, 15 August 1985

Appendices

1 *The Callan Saga* was replaced on Thames by a programme covering local election results.

2 SC4 repeat information from *Callan: Under the Red File*, Andrew Pixley (Network, 2015)

3 Sleeve notes, Ike Isaacs And His Guitars, *Fourteen Great TV Themes*, 1972

4 Edward Woodward interview with Anthony Goodman and Matthew Morgenstern, 24 April 1987

5 Russell Hunter interview with Anthony Goodman and Matthew Morgenstern, 8 January 1987

6 'Playback: Woodward's Singing Style', *TV Times* Southern edition, August 28-September 3 1971

7 Russell Hunter interview with Anthony Goodman and Matthew Morgenstern, 8 January 1987

Bibliography

'CALLAN' SCRIPTS & PRODUCTION DOCUMENTATION: 1966-1972, 1973, 1981

Armchair Theatre – 'A Magnum for Schneider' (Rehearsal script)

Series One

'The Good Ones Are All Dead'	(Rehearsal script, cue sheet)
'Goodbye, Nobby Clarke'	(Draft and rehearsal script)
'The Death of Robert E. Lee'	(Camera script)
'Goodness Burns Too Bright'	(Camera script, cue sheet)
'But He's a Lord, Mr Callan'	(Camera script, cue sheet)
'You Should Have Got Here Sooner'	(Camera script, cue sheet)
'Goodbye Mary Lee'	(Draft script)

Series Two

'Red Knight, White Knight'	(Camera script)
'The Most Promising Girl of Her Year'	(Camera script, cue sheet)
'You're Under Starter's Orders'	(Draft and camera script)
'The Little Bits and Pieces of Love'	(Camera script, cue sheet)
'Let's Kill Everybody'	(Camera script)
'Heir Apparent'	(Rehearsal script, cue sheet)
'Land of Light and Peace'	(Camera script)
'Blackmailers Should Be Discouraged'	(Camera script, cue sheet)
'Death of a Friend'	(Camera script, cue sheet)
'Jack-on-Top'	(Camera script, cue sheet)
'Once a Big Man, Always a Big Man'	(Camera script)
'The Running Dog'	(Camera script)
'The Worst Soldier I Ever Saw'	(Camera script)
'Nice People Die at Home'	(Draft, rehearsal and camera retake scripts)
'Death of a Hunter'	(Camera and continuity scripts)

Series Three

'Where Else Could I Go?'	(Camera and Outside Broadcast camera scripts, production documentation, synopsis)
'Summoned to Appear'	(Film shooting script, film call sheet, cast list, production documentation)
'The Same Trick Twice'	(Rehearsal and camera script, film shooting script, cast list, production documentation, synopsis)
'Act of Kindness'	(Camera script, film shooting script, shooting order, cast list, production documentation, synopsis)
'Amos Green Must Live'	(Rehearsal script, cast list, synopsis)
'God Help Your Friends'	(Camera script)
'A Village Called "G"'	(Call sheet and schedule for filming, order of shooting, cast list, production documentation, synopsis)
'Suddenly – At Home'	(Production documentation, synopsis)
'Breakout'	(Cast list, production documentation, synopsis)

Series Four

'That'll Be The Day '	(Cast list, production documentation)
'Call Me Sir!'	(Rehearsal script, cast list, synopsis)
'First Refusal'	(Rehearsal script, cast list, production documentation)

'Rules of the Game'	(Cast list, production documentation)
'If He Can, So Could I'	(Rehearsal script, call sheet and schedule for filming, shooting order for filming, cast list, location map, production documentation)
'None of Your Business'	(Call sheet and shooting schedule, film/OB requirements, cast list, location map)
'Charlie Says It's Goodbye'	(Film/OB requirements, cast list, production documentation)
'I Never Wanted the Job'	(Production documentation)
'The Carrier'	(Film location schedule, cast list, location maps, production documentation)
'The Contract'	(Rehearsal script, cast list, production documentation)
'Call Me Enemy'	(synopsis, cast list, production documentation)
'Do You Recognise the Woman?'	(Rehearsal and camera scripts, call sheet and shooting schedule, cast list, production documentation)
'A Man like Me'	(Camera script, production documentation)
Callan (movie)	(Handwritten draft script)
Wet Job	(Outside Broadcast camera scripts)

'Callan Series Format' memorandum, November 1966
'Research on Callan' memorandum, September 1967
'New Hunter' memorandum, November1967
'Fourth Series narrative plan', 1971

ARCHIVES
The British Film Institute Reuben Library, South Bank, London, 2011-13

AUDIO INTERVIEWS CONDUCTED AND RECORDED BY ANTHONY GOODMAN AND MATTHEW MORGENSTERN, 1984-87

Derek Bond, 22 August 1985
Reg Collin, 2 August 1985
Bill Craig, 2 September 1985
Peter Duguid, 31 July 1986
Jim Goddard, 23 October 1985
Terence Feely, 22 July 1985
Russell Hunter, 8 January 1987
Ray Jenkins, 4 September 1985
John Kershaw, date unknown, 1984-7

George Markstein and Lloyd Shirley, date unknown, 1984-87
James Mitchell, 15 August 1985
Shaun O'Riordan, 5 January 1987
Trevor Preston, date unknown, 1984-87
Clifford Rose, 5 September 1985
William Squire, 28 August 1985
Anthony Valentine, 10 December 1986
Edward Woodward, 24 April 1987

CORRRESPONDENCE
Terence Feely letter to David Barrie, 28 July 1997

INTERVIEWS, CONVERSATIONS AND CORRESPONDENCE WITH THE AUTHORS

Robert Banks Stewart, 2, 7 October 2012
Adrian Bean, 5 September 2013
David Bickerstaff, 16 August 2014
Philip Bird, 15, 17 August 2013
Peter Bowles, 11 October 2013
Belinda Carroll, 1 November 2013

Geoff Case, 2003
Brian Croucher, 2 August 2013
Paul Darrow, 9 September 2010; 21 September 2013
Mark Duguid, 22 September 2014
Lee Dunne, 2 May 2013

Peter Egan, 12 September 2013

Moris Farhi, 2001

Michael Ferguson, 30 October 2013

John Flanagan, 13 November 2012

Kenneth Gilbert, 21 May 2013

Julian Glover, 13 November 2012

Kenneth Griffith, 2001

Roger Goodman, 2002, 2005

Joanna Green, 3 October 2013

Neville Green, 10 December 2014

Lewis Greifer, 2001, 2002

Piers Haggard, 21 October 2013

Gill Hewlett-Case, 2004

Philip Hinchcliffe, 28 May 2016

Alfred Hoffman, 22 October 2013

Leila Hoffman, 22 October 2013

Derek Horne, 24 January 2014

George Innes, 16 February 2013

Michael Jayston, 21 September 2013

Stefan Kalipha, 28 May 2013

Troy Kennedy Martin, 2002

John Keeling, 27 September 2013

Burt Kwouk, 2005

David Marshall, 8 December 2014, 1 January 2015

Roger Marshall, 2002

Charlotte Mitchell, 8 October 2013

Peter Mitchell, 8 October 2013

Garfield Morgan, 2002

Patrick Mower, 21 November, 2013

Brian Murphy, 22 March 2014

Bharat Nalluri, Los Angeles, 9 May 2016

Phil Newman, 22 August 2015

Christopher Owen, London, 6 November 2012

Peter le Page, 6 December 2014

Roger Parkes, 2003

Trevor Preston, 28 August 2013

Anthony Read, 14 October 2013

Mike Ripley, 7 March 2014

Catherine Schell, 22 March 2014

Frances Tomelty, 8 May 2013

Susan Valentine, 29 July 2016

Mike Vardy, 6 February 2013

Hugh Walters, 6 March 2013

David Wickes, 2002; London, 16 October 2012

Paul Williamson, 28 February 2014

Tessa Wyatt, 22 March 2014

BIOGRAPHIES

Gant, Richard, *Sean Connery: Gilt-Edged Bond* (Mayflower Dell, 1967)

Mower, Patrick, *My Story* (John Blake Publishing, 2007)

FURTHER/BACKGROUND READING

Action Annual 1978 (IPC Magazines Ltd., 1977)

Alvarado, Manuel; Stewart, John, *Made for Television: Euston Films Limited* (Methuen Publishing Ltd, 1985)

Banks Stewart, Robert, *To Put You in the Picture* (Miwk Publishing, 2015)

Andrew, Christopher, *Defence of the Realm: The Authorised History of MI5* (Penguin Books, 2010)

Barker, Martin, *"Action": The Story of a Violent Comic* (Titan, 1990)

Blundell, Nigel and Boar, Roger, *The World's Greatest Spies and Spymasters* (Octopus Books, 1984)

Briant, Michael E., *Who is Michael E. Briant?* (Classic TV Press, 2012)

Brown, Allan, *Inside The Wicker Man* (Sidgwick & Jackson, 2000)

Callan Campaign Aids (EMI Film Distributors Ltd., 1974)

Caute, David, *'68: The Year of the Barricades* (Paladin, 1988)

Chancellor, Henry, *James Bond: The Man and His World – The Official Companion to Ian Fleming's Creation* (John Murray, 2005)

Cornell, Paul; Day, Martin and Topping, Keith, *The Avengers Programme Guide* (Virgin Publishing Ltd., 1994)

Coward, Simon; Down, Richard; Perry, Christopher, *The Kaleidoscope British Independent Television Drama Research Guide 1955-2005* (Kaleidoscope Publishing, 2005)

Coward, Simon; Down, Richard; Perry, Christopher, *The Kaleidoscope BBC Television Drama Research Guide 1936-2006* (Kaleidoscope Publishing, 2006)

Docherty, Mark J. and McGown, Alistair D., *The Hill and Beyond: Children's Television Drama – An Encyclopaedia* (BFI, 2003)

Downing, Taylor and Isaacs, Jeremy, *Cold War: For 45 Years the World Held its Breath* (Bantam Press, 1998)

Fairclough, Robert, *The Prisoner: The Official Companion to the Classic TV Series* (Carlton Books, 2002)

Fairclough, Robert (Editing and annotation), *The Prisoner – The Original Scripts: Volumes 1* and *Volume 2* (Reynolds and Hearn, 2005, 2006)

Fairclough, Robert; Kenwood, Mike, *Sweeney! The Official Companion* (Reynolds and Hearn, 2002 edition)

Fairclough, Robert; Kenwood, Mike, *Sweeney! The Official Companion* (Titan, 2012 edition)

Fiddy, Dick and Mechele, Tony, *The Saint* (Boxtree, 1989)

Grassner, Dennis (Editor), *James Bond: 50 Years of Movie Posters* (Dorling Kindersley Ltd., 2012)

Goodman, Roger (Editor), *George Markstein and The Prisoner* (Pandqmedia, 2014)

Hastings, Max, *The Secret War* (William Collins, 2015)

Hayes, Alan; Hayes, Alys; McGinlay, Richard, *The Strange Case of the Missing Episodes – The Avengers* (Hidden Tiger, 2013)

Hill, John, *The Man from UNCLE's ABC of Espionage* (Signet Books, 1966)

Joseph, Michael, *25 Years of ITV: 1953-1980* (ITV Books, 1980)

Lewisohn, Mark, *Radio Times Guide to TV Comedy* (BBC Worldwide Limited, 1998)

The Man from UNCLE Magazine (Leo Margulies Corporation, February 1966)

MacCabe, Colin, *BFI Film Classics: Performance* (British Film Institute, 2009 edition)

Macintyre, Ben, *Agent Zigzag: Lover, Traitor, Hero, Spy* (Bloomsbury, 2007 edition)

Meades, Jonathan, *This Is Their Life* (Salamander Books Ltd., 1978)

Melton, H. Keith, *Ultimate Spy* (Dorling Kindersley Ltd., 2002)

Miles, Barry, *The Beatles Diary. Volume 1: The Beatles Years* (Omnibus Press, 2001 edition)

Milward-Oliver, Edward, *The Len Deighton Companion* (Grafton Books, 1987 edition)

Monthly Film Bulletin (May 1974)

Mulley, Clare, *The Spy Who Loved* (Pan Macmillan, 2012)

Orwell, George, *Homage to Catalonia* (Penguin Modern Classics, 2000 edition)

Pate, Janet, *The Book of Spies and Secret Agents* (Webb & Bower Ltd., 1980)

Pincher, Chapman, *Their Trade is Treachery* (Sidgwick & Jackson, 1981)

Pixley, Andrew, *Callan: Under the Red File* (Network, 2015)

Pym, John (editor), *Time Out Film Guide: Eighth Edition* (Penguin Books, 1999)

Richardson, Michael, *Bowler Hats and Kinky Boots: The Unofficial and Unauthorised Guide to The Avengers* (Telos Publishing Ltd., 2014)

Rogers, Dave, *The Avengers* (ITV Books and Michael Joseph, 1983)

Sandbrook, Dominic, *You've Never Had It So Good: A History of Britain from Suez to the Beatles* (Abacus, 2008 edition)

Sandbrook, Dominic, *White Heat: A History of Britain in the Swinging Sixties* (Abacus, 2009 edition)

Seely, Michael, *Prophets of Doom: The Unauthorised History of Doomwatch* (Miwk Publishing, 2012)

Sellers, Robert, *The Battle for Bond* (Tomahawk Press, 2008 edition)

Sisman, Adam, *John le Carré* (Bloomsbury Publishing PLC, 2016 edition)

Various, *National Film Theatre* booklets (BFI Reuben Library, 2014)

Various, *Variety Film Reviews 1964-1967: Volume 11* (R. R. Bowker Performing Arts and Entertainment Publishing Group, 1983)

Various, *Variety Film Reviews 1968-1970: Volume 12* (R. R. Bowker Performing Arts and Entertainment Publishing Group, 1983)

Various, *Variety Film Reviews 1971-1974: Volume 13* (R. R. Bowker Performing Arts and Entertainment Publishing Group, 1983)

Volkman, Ernest, *The History of Espionage* (Carlton Books Limited, 2007)

White, Leonard, *Armchair Theatre: The Lost Years* (Kelly Publications, 2003)

White, J., Patrick, *The Complete Mission: Impossible Dossier* (Boxtree Ltd., 1996 edition)

Wright, Peter, *Spycatcher* (Viking Adult, 1987)

UNPUBLISHED

Collin, Reginald, *BAFTA – Behind the Mask: Personal Recollections*

JAMES MITCHELL FICTION – SELECTED NOVELS AND ANTHOLOGIES

A Way Back (Peter Davies Ltd., 1959)

A Magnum for Schneider (Herbert Jenkins Ltd., 1969)

Russian Roulette (Corgi, 1975 edition)

Death and Bright Water (Corgi, 1976 edition)

Smear Job (Hamish Hamilton Ltd., 1975)

Sometimes You Could Die (Ostara Publishing, 2015 edition)

A Woman To Be Loved (Myriad Books Ltd, 1988)

Bonfire Night (Severn House Ltd, 2002)

Callan Uncovered (Ostara Publishing, October 2014)

Callan Uncovered 2 (Ostara Publishing, June 2015)

JAMES MITCHELL FICTION – 'CALLAN' SHORT STORIES

'Merry Christmas from the Section' (*TV Times* supplement, December 1967)

'File on a Happy Hippy' (Express Newspapers, 20 September 1970)

'File on a Faithful Husband' (Express Newspapers, 27 September 1970)

'File on a Loving Sister' (Express Newspapers, 4 October 1970)

'File on a Painless Dentist' (Express Newspapers, 11 October 1970)

'File on a Fancy Lawyer' (Express Newspapers, 18 October 1970)

'Callan: File on a Chinese Hostess' (Express Newspapers, 8 August 1971)

'Callan: File on a Willing Victim' (Express Newspapers, 15 August 1971)

'Callan: File on a Kindly Colonel' (Express Newspapers, 22 August 1971)

'Callan: File on a Chelsea Swinger' (Express Newspapers, 29 August 1971)

'Callan: File on a Missing Poet' (Express Newspapers, 5 September 1971)

'Callan: File on a Friendly Lady' (Express Newspapers, 23 April 1972)

'Callan: File on a Jolly Miller' (Express Newspapers, 30 April 1972)

'Callan: File on a Deadly Doctor' (Express Newspapers, 7 May 1972)

'Callan: File on a Man Called… Callan' (Express Newspapers, 14 May 1972)

'Callan: File on a Gallic Charmer' (Express Newspapers, 21 May 1972)

'Callan: File on a Deadly Deadshot' (Express Newspapers, 11 March 1973)

'Callan: File on an Angry Artist' (Express Newspapers, 18 March 1973)

'Callan: File on a Reckless Rider' (Express Newspapers, 25 March 1973)

'Callan: File on a Weeping Widow' (Express Newspapers, 1 April 1973)

'Callan: Kill Callan' (Express Newspapers, 2, 9, 16 September 1973)

'Callan: File on an Angry Actor' (Express Newspapers, 26 May 1974)

'Callan: File on a Lucky Lady' (Express Newspapers, 2 June 1974)

'Callan: File on a Dancing Decoy' (Express Newspapers, 9 June 1974)

'Callan: File on a Fearsome Farm' (Express Newspapers, 20 October 1974)

'Callan: File on a Deadly Diary' (Express Newspapers, 27 October 1974)

'Callan: File on a Classy Club' (Express Newspapers, 3 November 1974)

'Callan: File on a Careful Cowboy' (Express Newspapers, 27 June 1975)

'Callan: File on a Doomed Defector' (Express Newspapers, 3 August 1975)

'Callan: File on a Pining Poet' (Express Newspapers, 10 August 1975)

'Callan: File on a Powerful Picador' (Express Newspapers, 17 August 1975)

'Callan: File on a Darling Daughter' (Express Newspapers, 1 February 1976)

'Callan: File on an Awesome Amateur' (Express Newspapers, 8 February 1976)

'Callan: File on a Joyous Juliet' (Express Newspapers, 15 February 1976)

'Callan: File on a Mourning Mother' (Express Newspapers, 22 February 1976)

'Callan: File on an Angry American' (Express Newspapers, 29 February 1976)

'Callan! File on a Difficult Don' (Express Newspapers, 15 August 1976)

'Callan! File on a Tired Traitor' (Express Newspapers, 22 August 1976)

'Callan! File on a Harassed Hunter' (Express Newspapers, 29 August 1976)

'Callan! File on a Beautiful Boxer' (Express Newspapers, 5 September 1976)

With Roche, Ken, 'My Friend Mr Callan by the Faithful Lonely' (*TV Times*, 23-29 June 1984)

JAMES MITCHELL WRITING AS 'JAMES MUNRO'*

The Man Who Sold Death (Charter, June 1980 edition)

The Money That Money Can't Buy (Corgi, 1967 edition)

Die Rich, Die Happy (Corgi, 1967 edition)

The Innocent Bystanders (Bantam Books, 1971 edition)

JAMES MITCHELL FICTION – FURTHER NOVELS*

A Time for Murder (1955, as Patrick O. McGuire)

Here's a Villain (Peter Davies Ltd., 1957) also published under the title: *The Lady is Waiting*
    (William Morrow & Co New York, USA, 1958)

Steady Boys, Steady (Peter Davies Ltd., 1960)

Fiesta for Murder (1962, as Patrick O. McGuire)

Among Arabian Sands (Peter Davies Ltd., 1963)

The Winners (Cassell & Co, 1970)

When the Boat Comes In (Hamish Hamilton Ltd., 1976)

The Hungry Years (When the Boat Comes In Book 2) (Hamish Hamilton Ltd., 1976)

Upwards and Onwards (When the Boat Comes In Book 3) (Hamish Hamilton Ltd., 1977)

The Evil Ones (1980)

Goodbye Darling (Hamish Hamilton Ltd., 1980)

Dead Ernest (Henry Holt & Co, 1987)

KGB Kill ((Hamish Hamilton Ltd., 1988)

Dying Day (Hamish Hamilton Ltd., 1988)

An Impossible Woman (Sinclair-Stevenson, 1992)

Leading Lady (Sinclair-Stevenson, 1993)

So Far from Home (Headline,1995)

Indian Summer (Headline,1996)

Dancing for Joy (Headline,1997)

JAMES MITCHELL – SELECTED FILMS AND TELEVISION

Play of the Week – 'Soldier in the Snow' (ITV, 1961)

Armchair Theatre (ABC) – 'Flight from Treason' (1960), 'The Omega Mystery' (1961)

The Avengers (ABC) – 'Death on the Slipway' (1961), 'Kill the King' (1961), 'Man with Two Shadows' (1963)

* Information from Charlotte Mitchell, Sarah Guiver and www.itssolastcentury.co.uk

Innocent Bystanders (1972)

When the Boat Comes In (BBC, 1976-1982)

Spyship (BBC, 1983)

SPY FICTION

Le Carré, John, *A Small Town in Germany* (Sceptre, 2011 edition)

Le Carré, John, *The Spy Who Came in from the Cold* (Penguin Modern Classics, 2010 edition)

Le Carré, John, *Tinker Tailor Soldier Spy* (Sceptre, 2011 edition)

Le Carré, John, *Smiley's People* (Sceptre, 2011 edition)

Le Carré, John, *Our Kind of Traitor* (Penguin, 2011 edition)

Deighton, Len, *The IPCRESS File* (Triad/Panther, 1985 edition)

Deighton, Len, *Horse under Water* (Penguin Books, 1967 edition)

Deighton, Len, *Funeral in Berlin* (Penguin Books, 1966 edition)

Deighton, Len, *Billion-Dollar Brain* (Penguin Books, 1966 edition)

Deighton, Len, *An Expensive Place to Die* (Triad Paperbacks, 1982 edition)

Deighton, Len, *Spy Story* (Harper, 2012 edition)

Deighton, Len, *Twinkle, Twinkle, Little Spy* (Harper, 2012 edition)

Fleming, Ian, *Casino Royale* (Pan Books, 1964 edition)

Fleming, Ian, *Live and Let Die* (Pan Books, 1963 edition)

Fleming, Ian, *Moonraker* (Pan Books, 1964 edition)

Fleming, Ian, *Diamonds are Forever* (Pan Books, 1964 edition)

Fleming, Ian, *From Russia with Love* (Pan Books, 1965 edition)

Fleming, Ian, *Dr. No* (Pan Books, 1965 edition)

Fleming, Ian, *Goldfinger* (Pan Books, 1963 edition)

Fleming, Ian, *For Your Eyes Only* (Pan Books, 1965 edition)

Fleming, Ian, *The Spy Who Loved Me* (Pan Books, 1969 edition)

Fleming, Ian, *On Her Majesty's Secret Service* (Pan Books, 1965 edition)

Fleming, Ian, *You Only Live Twice* (Pan Books, 1964 edition)

Fleming, Ian, *The Man with the Golden Gun* (Pan Books, 1968 edition)

Fleming, Ian, *Octopussy* (with 'The Property of a Lady' and 'The Living Daylights'), (Pan Books, 1968 edition)

Markstein, George, *The Cooler* (Book Club Associates, 1974 edition)

Markstein, George, *The Man from Yesterday* (House of Stratus, 2001 edition)

Markstein, George, *Chance Awakening* (House of Stratus, 2001 edition)

Markstein, George, *The Goering Testament* (House of Stratus, 2001 edition)

Markstein, George, *Ultimate Issue* (House of Stratus, 2001 edition)

Markstein, George, *Traitor for a Cause* (House of Stratus, 2001 edition)

Markstein, George, *Soul Hunters* (House of Stratus, 2001 edition)

Markstein, George, *Ferret* (Hodder and Stoughton, 1983)

Maugham, W. Somerset, *Ashenden* (Vintage, 2000 edition)

O'Donnell, Peter, and Holdaway, Jim, *Modesty Blaise: The Head Girls/The Black Pearl/The Magnified Man* (American Edition Series, number 4, 1983)

SELECTED ARTICLES

Brown, Mick, 'Back on Top of the Pile', *You: The Mail on Sunday Magazine* (1985)

Coleman, Alix, 'All-round Woodward', *TV Times* (Southern edition, 26 April-2 May 1980)

Cook, Benjamin, 'The Ultimate Interview Part Four: The Irrepressible Tom Baker', *Doctor Who Magazine* 501 (BBC/Panini Magazines, August 2016)

Morrow, Ann, 'Gallant Callan Casts a Line... A-Way with Women!', *TV Times*
(Southern edition, 10-14 August 1967)

Pixley, Andrew, 'Deadly Acquaintances - Callan: A Blueprint for Quality.' *Primetime*
(WTVA, Spring/Summer 1987)

Goodman, Anthony, 'The Blunt Instrument', *Action TV* (Autumn 2001)

Sandbrrok, Dominic, 'Racist Nation?', *BBC History Magazine* (Volume 9, Number 3, March 2008)

Woodward, Edward (with Ken Roche), 'My Story', three parts, *TV Times* (Southern edition, 1971)

BROCHURES, MAGAZINES AND PARTWORK COLLECTIONS

The Avengers: A 50th Anniversary Celebration of the Classic Television Series (University of Chichester, 2011)

Broadcast: The Official ITV 50th Anniversary Supplement (23 September 2005)

Cinema Retro: Movie Classics Special Edition Magazine No. 4 – Dr. No (Cinema Retro Inc., 2012)

The Danger Man Collection (DeAgostini, 2005-06)

Doctor Who – The Complete History: Volume 11, Volume 26
(BBC/Panini Magazines/Hachette Partworks Ltd., 2016)

'My Name is Bond' (Argus Specialist Publications Ltd, 1983)

National Film Theatre – ITV 50: 50 Years of Independent Television (Booklet, November/Decemeber 2005)

The Prisoner: The Official Fact Files (DeAgostini, 2004, 2005-06)

Time Out, June 10-16 1983, Number 668 (Time Out Limited, 1983)

FANZINES

Research Library for Edward Woodward, Edited by Jacquelyn Debes, Volume 2, April 1991

EQ/EW Int'l Bullet, Number 4, May 1990 (EQ/EW Int'l USA, May 1990)

EQ/EW Int'l Bullet, Number 6, September 1990 (EQ/EW Int'l USA, September 1990)

EQ/EW Int'l Bullet, Number 7, November 1990 (EQ/EW Int'l USA, November 1990)

The Callan Appreciation Society Newsletter, Number 1, written by Les Warburton-Marsh, November 1994

The Callan Appreciation Society Newsletter, Number 3, edited by Les Warburton-Marsh, October 1995

The Callan Appreciation Society Newsletter, Number 5, edited by Les Warburton-Marsh, February 1996

EDWARD WOODWARD – SELECTED FILMS AND TELEVISION

1990 (BBC TV, 1977-78)

The Bass Player and the Blonde (Network, 2011)

Breaker Morant (Stax Entertainment, 2001)

CI5: The New Professionals: The Complete Series (Madman Entertainment Ltd., 2012)

Callan: The Colour Years (Network, 2010)

Callan: Complete Fourth Series (with the 1974 movie *Callan*; Umbrella Entertainment Ltd., 2007)

Callan: Complete Third Series (Umbrella Entertainment Ltd., 2007)

Callan: This Man Alone (Network, 2016)

Callan: The Monochrome Years (Network, 2010)

Callan: Wet Job (Network, 2011)

The Equalizer: The Complete Collection (Fabulous Films, 2013)

Euston Films present Armchair Cinema: The Collection (Network, 2009)

Hunted (ATV, 1972)

La Femme Nikita (Warner Brothers Television, 1997-2001)

The Morecambe and Wise Show (BBC TV, 1969-70)

Who Dares Wins (Arrow Films, 2011)

Whodunnit? Series 1 (Network, 2010)

The Wicker Man (StudioCanal, 2013)

OTHER SELECTED FILMS AND TELEVISION

A Touch of Frost: The Complete Collection on DVD – 'Fun Time for Swingers' (DeAgostini UK Ltd., 2005)

Armchair Theatre: Volume Three (DVD, Network, 2012)

Armchair Theatre: Volume Four (DVD, Network, 2013)

The Avengers: The Complete 50th Anniversary Collection (DVD, StudioCanal, 2011)

Bond 50: Celebrating Five Decades of James Bond 007 (Blu-ray, MGM, 2012)

Carry On Spying (DVD, Warner Brothers, 2001)

Casino Royale (DVD, Two-Disc Collector's Edition, Sony, 2008)

Colditz: The Complete Collection (DVD, BBC Worldwide Ltd., 2010)

Danger Man: The Complete 1964-66 Special Edition (DVD, Madman Entertainment, 2008)

Department S: 35ᵗʰ Anniversary Special Edition (DVD, Umbrella Entertainment, 2003)

Edge of Darkness (DVD, BBC, 2003)

Espionage: The Complete Series (DVD, Network, 2009)

The Hard Way (DVD, Network, 2009)

Hunted (BBC, 2012)

Ice Station Zebra (DVD, Warner Brothers, 2005)

If.... (Blu-ray, Eureka! 2014)

The Harry Palmer Collection (DVD, Anchor Bay Entertainment, 2012)

Kessler (DVD, DD, 2004)

The Kremlin Letter (DVD, Eureka, 2011)

The Looking Glass War (DVD, Sony Pictures Home Entertainment, 2005)

Man in a Suitcase: The Complete Series – 8 DVD Special Edition (Umbrella Entertainment, 2004)

The Man from UNCLE: The Complete Series (DVD, Time Life, 2007)

The Man from UNCLE (Blu-ray, Warner Bros. Entertainment, 2015; Guy Ritchie film)

The Manchurian Candidate (DVD, MGM, 2004; 1964 film)

Never Say Never Again (DVD, Twentieth Century Fox, 2013)

Mr. Palfrey of Westminster: The Complete Series (DVD, Network, 2010)

Modesty Blaise (DVD, Second Sight Films, 2010)

The Original Swinger Agent: Matt Helm Lounge (DVD, Sony, 2005)

Our Man Flint / In Like Flint (DVD, Twentieth Century Fox, 2003)

Performance (DVD, Warner Brothers, 2007)

The Prisoner – The Complete Series (Blu-ray, Network, 2009)

The Quiller Memorandum (DVD, Carlton, 2003)

Raffles: The Complete Series (DVD, ITV Studios Home Entertainment, 2010)

Return of The Saint: 25th Anniversary Special Edition DVD Set (Umbrella Entertainment, 2004)

Rififi (DVD, Arrow Films, 2011)

Ring of Spies (DVD, Network, 2014)

The Saint: Set 4 (DVD, Umbrella Entertainment, 2005)

The Saint: Set 5 (DVD, Umbrella Entertainment, 2005)

The Sandbaggers: The Complete Series (DVD, Network, 2008)

Secret Army: The Complete Series 1-3 (DVD, DD Video, 2004)

Skyfall (Blu-ray, MGM, 2013)

SPECTRE (Blu-ray, MGM, 2015)

Spooks – Season One (DVD, Contender, 2003)

Spooks: The Greater Good (Blu-ray, Entertainment One UK Ltd., 2015)

The Third Man (DVD, Warner Brothers, 2002)

Tinker Tailor Soldier Spy / Smiley's People (DBD, BBC, 2003)

Tinker Tailor Soldier Spy (DVD, StudioCanal, 2011; the movie)

Yellow Submarine (DVD, Capitol, 2012)

RADIO

A Magnum for Schneider (4 episodes, Radio 4 Extra, September 2012)

CD/RECORDS

Costello, Elvis, 'Watching The Detectives' (BUY 20, Stiff Records, 1977)

Fingerprintz, *The Very Dab* (Virgin Records Ltd., V12119, 1979)

Various, *Methods of Dance: Electronica & Leftfield '73-'87* (Virgin Records Ltd., CDV 4004, 2013)

Various, *New Gold Dreams: Post Punk & New Romantics '79-'83* (Virgin Records Ltd., CDV 4003, 2013)

Woodward, Edward, *This Man Alone* (DJLPS 405, DJM Records, 1970)

EVENTS

Sci-Fi: Days of Fear and Wonder (BFI Southbank, October-November 2014)

The Wednesday Play (BFI Southbank, September-October 2014)

INTERNET – WEBSITES, ARTICLES AND BLOGS

Action TV (new.startrader.co.uk/acatalog/home.html)

Adventures in Primetime (adventuresinprimetime.wordpress.com)

Aveleyman – Actors' Compendium (www.aveleyman.com)

Avengers TV (theavengers.tv)

BFI Screenonline (www.screenonline.org.uk)

Michael J Bird (www.mjbird.org.uk)

British Battles (www.britishbattles.com)

Coppers and Spies: The Evolution of the Britsish Action Hero: 'Lonely: Callan and Public Eye' by Frank Collins, 27 March 2014 (www.moviemail.com)

The Deighton Dossier (www.deightondossier.net)

Lee Dunne (leedunne.com)

Encyclopedia Virginia (encyclopediavirginia.org)

Michael Goodliffe (www.mgoodliffe.co.uk)

It's So Last Century (www.itssolastcentury.co.uk)

James Bond Memes (jamesbondmemes.blogspot.co.uk)

Kaleidoscope (www.kaleidoscopearchive.co.uk, www.petford.net)

The Mausoleum Club/Timescreen (www.the-mausoleum-club.org.uk /timescreen)

Magic Bullet (www.kaldorcity.com)

Dave Prowse (www.darthvader-starwars.com)

Simon Pegg (simonpegg.net)

The Stage (https://www.thestage.co.uk)

Reel Streets (www.reelstreets.com)

Spotlight (www.spotlight.com)

SFX (www.gamesradar.com/sfx)

Spy Guys and Gals (www.spyguysandgals.com)

Television Heaven (www.televisionheaven.co.uk)

TV Tropes (tvtropes.org)

(Plus assorted others including www.bbc.co.uk, www.imdb.com, www.washingtonpost.com, https://www.wikipedia.org, www.youtube.com.)

Index

Selected related fiction

ROBERT FAIRCLOUGH is the author of *The Prisoner: The Official Companion to the Classic TV Series*, *The Prisoner: The Original Scripts Volumes 1* and *2,* and *Sweeney! The Official Companion*, with Mike Kenwood. 2011's *This Charming Man: The Life of Ian Carmichael* was chosen as one of *The Independent*'s Top Ten Film Books of the Year. As a camera operator, interviewer and producer, he has worked on 20 titles in the BBC's classic *Doctor Who* DVD series. Robert regularly contributes to *SFX* magazine, the *We Are Cult* website and *The Essential Doctor Who* range of special publications. *The Callan File* is his sixth book.

MIKE KENWOOD works in the computer industry. In his spare time he has been a production assistant, interview compiler and associate producer on various DVD extras for the BBC/2 Entertain Ltd., StudioCanal and Umbrella. He has also written features for magazines, CDs and websites. *The Callan File* is his third book; proceeds from his sales are being split equally between two charities: Barnsley Hospice (www.barnsleyhospice.org) and Dorothy House, Bath (www.dorothyhouse.org.uk).

PLAYBOYS
spies
AND
PRIVATE EYES
INSPIRED BY ITC

Edited by
Alan Hayes
& Rick Davy

Foreword by
Annette
André

PLAYBOYS
spies
—AND—
PRIVATE EYES
INSPIRED BY ITC

"Much more personal, intimate and special than any full-colour, bigger-budgeted coffee table book."
Starburst Magazine

ITC Entertainment was a powerhouse of filmed television drama from the 1950s to the 1980s, producing a succession of hit action-adventure series such as *The Saint, Danger Man, The Prisoner, Man in a Suitcase, The Champions, Randall and Hopkirk (Deceased)* and *The Persuaders!*

Edited by Alan Hayes and Rick Davy, *Playboys, Spies, and Private Eyes - Inspired by ITC* celebrates the company's remarkable legacy with 35 chapters by a wide range of writers, who explore how these series have touched their lives.

Published in aid of the Born Free Foundation, this book also boasts a heartfelt foreword by actress Annette Andre, an afterword by Elaine Spooner (daughter of Dennis), and artwork by Shaqui Le Vesconte.

229mm x 152mm   Paperback, 256 pages, illustrated

ISBN: 978-1-911537-03-8

Available from www.quoitmedia.co.uk

the Prisoner
the essential guide

includes officially licensed and previously unpublished photographs

Rick Davy

the Prisoner
the essential guide

"A great vehicle by which those new to The Prisoner can discover all the fun facts about the series and for those who are The Prisoner veterans who hunger for more goodies about the cult classic. Bravo!"

Boyce McClain's Collector's Corner

The Prisoner television series is regarded as one of the finest, yet most bizarre and controversial, programmes ever made. Starring Patrick McGoohan, Britain's highest paid television actor at the time, and filmed at the Italianate village of Portmeirion, it has achieved cult status and has entertained and beguiled viewers since it was screened in 1967/68.

Who was Patrick McGoohan? Why Portmeirion? How was *The Prisoner* made? What car did Number Six drive? Why the giant balloon? And what was it all about?

All these questions, and more, are answered in *The Prisoner – The Essential Guide*, a handy guide to everything that made the series such a cult favourite which is still examined, discussed and loved half a century after it was made. Also included is an easy reference guide to each episode, plus a wealth of behind the scenes photographs, many of which are previously unpublished.

210mm x 148mm   Paperback, 36 pages, illustrated

ISBN: 978-1-911537-05-2

Available from www.quoitmedia.co.uk

WHERE HAVE I BEEN ALL MY LIFE?

A MEMOIR BY ANNETTE ANDRÉ

FOREWORD BY SIR ROGER MOORE   APPRECIATION BY KENNETH COPE

WHERE HAVE I BEEN ALL MY LIFE?

A MEMOIR BY ANNETTE ANDRÉ

> *"Annette Andre's memoir is a vibrant tapestry, woven of eloquent and engaging words that – in equal measure – inspire, intrigue and entice."*
> **Karl Frunz, Glass in Hand Productions, Seattle**

For someone who has professed "terminal shyness," Annette André has written her memoir with arresting honesty and generosity. From a lonely childhood in Sydney, Australia, and overcoming a chronic illness to become a professional ballet dancer, *Where Have I Been All My Life?* reveals the truth behind her storybook romance with a famous bullfighter, how Benny Hill proposed marriage, and why a chance conversation with Prince Charles helped to change the course of her life.

Guest starring with Roger Moore in more episodes of *The Saint* than any other actress, Annette quickly became one of the most popular TV actors of Britain's "Golden Age," in such classic series as *The Avengers, The Prisoner, The Persuaders!* and her most memorable role of all, as Jeannie in *Randall and Hopkirk (Deceased)*. From her fly-on-the-wall view of Burton and Taylor's romance while filming *Cleopatra* to the perils of shooting *A Funny Thing Happened On the Way to the Forum*, and her appearances on the West End stage, Annette found writing the story of her life "excruciatingly hard work, but like a good orgasm, damn well worth the effort."

*240mm x 160mm   Hardback, 272 pages,
with 16 pages of colour and black and white photos*

ISBN: 978-1-911537-10-6

Available from www.quoitmedia.co.uk

CUTTING EDGE

MY LIFE IN FILM AND TELEVISION

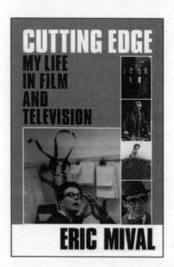

"One of the most wonderful things in life is to get paid for your hobby, and my hobby from the age of sixteen onwards became making movies."
Eric Mival, Author

Eric Mival originally wanted to be an animator, getting his big break working for Halas and Batchelor, the 'UK Disney', in the late 1950s. However, it soon became clear that Eric's talents lay in film making, and an assistant editor's role at World Wide Pictures soon followed. From there, he quickly moved into feature films, working for such greats as Ray Harryhausen, George Harrison and Otto Preminger.

In the 1960s Eric worked as film editor on iconic TV series such as *Doctor Who*, *Top of the Pops* and *Comedy Playhouse*, before he took a job which would change his life forever – assistant editor and then music editor on Patrick McGoohan's thriller series *The Prisoner*. The show's enigmatic co-creator was to remain a life-long friend.

Cutting Edge is not only a fascinating look at life inside the film and television industry, it also includes the inside story of arguably the greatest TV series ever produced. *Cutting Edge* also serves as a fascinating guide to the art of film making, with invaluable inside information for aspiring movie makers.

229mm x 152mm   Paperback, 288 pages, illustrated

ISBN: 978-1-911537-00-7

Available from www.quoitmedia.co.uk

⭐ed Reflections
A cold war journey into Eastern Europe

"A fascinating insight into a pivotal time of the 1960s."

Tom Mayer, theunmutual.co.uk

In 1966 film makers Eric Mival (music editor on *The Prisoner*, film editor on *Doctor Who*) and Richard Owen took a group of international students into the heart of Eastern Europe at the height of the cold war.

What transpired was a fascinating journey into a Europe which looked very different then compared to today.

Meeting other students on their travels, discussing the rights and wrongs of their political systems and circumstances, filming took place in West and East Germany, Hungary, Poland, Czechoslovakia, and into the heart of Russia. Featuring a guest voiceover for one scene by Hollywood star Patrick McGoohan, the film was optioned by Yorkshire TV but never screened.

Red Reflections is presented by Quoit Media for the first time in any format.

Region 2 PAL DVD | Duration 39 minutes plus special features
(Region 1 NTSC version also available)

Special Features: *Red Discussions* – producers Eric Mival and Richard Owen discuss the film 46 years on. *The Retrievers* – Eric Mival's first short film from 1955.

EAN: 0740 781 853487

Available from www.quoitmedia.co.uk

50 years of the prisoner

a special celebration

In January 2018, a special celebration of the 50th anniversary of the iconic The Prisoner TV series tok place at Elstree Studios.

Series crew John S Smith, Ian Rakoff, and Tony Sloman were joined by directors John Hough, Alex Cox, and Chris Rodley, Nicholas Briggs of Big Finish, actor Brian Gorman, studio saviour Paul Welsh MBE, and studio chairman Morris Bright MBE.

The DVD includes highlights from all the on-stage Q&A sessions, with all guests included, and even footage of a derelict MGM studios shot in the early 1970s.

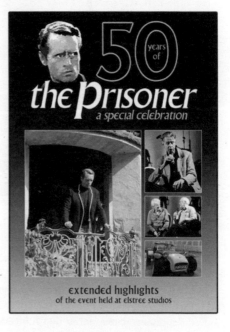

extended highlights
of the event held at elstree studios

As with the event, a proportion of proceeds are donated to Ty Gobaith Children's Hospice.

DVD | Region 2 (UK/Europe) | Duration: 120 minutes

EAN: 0 784862 461604

Available from www.quoitmedia.co.uk

the Prisoner
the essential interviews

PATRICK McGOOHAN

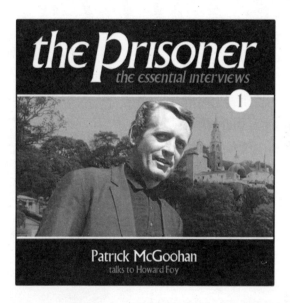

The first in a series of CDs of archive recordings with cast and crew of *The Prisoner* TV series.

In 1990, Patrick McGoohan met with journalist Howard Foy to record an interview for issue one of *The Box* magazine. It would turn out to be McGoohan's last in-depth interview regarding the series.

What inspired the series? How did he find his co-stars? What were his 'essential seven' episodes? How did Rover come to being? What does he think of the series' fans? All this, and more, is discussed in this edited interview.

Audio CD | Duration: 45 minutes

ISBN: 978-1-911537-08-3

Available from www.quoitmedia.co.uk

THE PRISONER DUSTED DOWN

DAVID STIMPSON

"Dusted Down has no padding. It is all meat. It is a fast flowing river from first to last page. You never rest...The depth of analysis is incredible"

Chris Riley, The Tally Ho

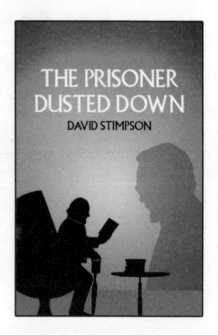

The Prisoner television series, filmed in 1966/67 and starring Patrick McGoohan as Number Six, has inspired much research since it was first broadcast more than 50 years ago. Its universal themes, allegorical content, and on-screen metaphors have stimulated debate, and confusion, amongst its viewers and ardent fans and much that was seen on screen has remained enigmatic. Until now.

The culmination of more than five years of research by series aficionado David Stimpson, *The Prisoner Dusted Down* re-examines the entire series, unearthing new information and offering fresh, personal perspectives on the finished episodes.

Answering questions you always wanted answered, and questioning answers you always believed, *The Prisoner Dusted Down* is a must-read for anyone with an interest in the most thought-provoking TV series of all time.

229mm x 152mm   Paperback, 496 pages,

ISBN: 978-1-911537-09-0

Available from www.quoitmedia.co.uk

DR BRENT'S CASEBOOK

AN UNAUTHORISED GUIDE TO POLICE SURGEON

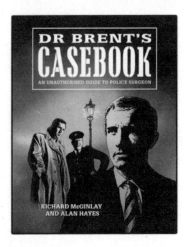

The series that launched a career and inspired a television legend.

Dr Brent's Casebook tells the story of Police Surgeon, a short-lived 1960 television series that gave Ian Hendry (Get Carter) his first regular starring role. It made its mark in TV history not for what it was but for what it led to – the world-beating show The Avengers. Unlike its successor, Police Surgeon has faded from memory.

Richard McGinlay and Alan Hayes now revisit the series, revealing information about the creation of the series, its production, transmission and narratives – including a mysterious episode which never appeared in TV listings – and the circumstances that caused Police Surgeon to be brought to a sudden end after just 13 weeks.

228mm x 152mm   Paperback, 328 pages, illustrated

ISBN: 978-1-326-98277-5

Available from www.hiddentigerbooks.co.uk

TWO AGAINST THE UNDERWORLD

THE COLLECTED UNAUTHORISED GUIDE TO THE AVENGERS SERIES 1

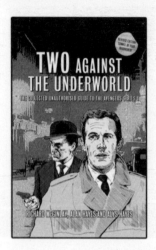

If you think you've read the definitive account of The Avengers' first year... *think again!*

Two Against the Underworld tells the story of the early days
of *The Avengers* from both sides of the camera,
as authors Richard McGinlay, Alan Hayes and Alys Hayes
lift the lid on all 26 Series 1 episodes, most of which are
missing from television archives.

Comprehensive chapters detail the narratives and include a wealth
of behind-the-scenes information. Further chapters explore the
creation of *The Avengers*, the departure of Ian Hendry, the series'
destiny, and the mystery of the missing episodes, and appendices
focus on the unproduced episodes of Series 1, Keel and Steed's
further adventures in comic strips and novels, and more.

228mm x 152mm   Paperback, 592 pages, illustrated

ISBN: 978-1-326-46626-8

Available from www.hiddentigerbooks.co.uk